I0737920

Hittite Etymological Dictionary

Trends in Linguistics
Documentation 1

Editor

Werner Winter

Mouton Publishers
Berlin · New York · Amsterdam

Hittite Etymological Dictionary

by

Jaan Puhvel

Vol. 1   Words beginning with A

Vol. 2   Words beginning with E and I

Mouton Publishers
Berlin · New York · Amsterdam

Professor Jaan Puhvel
Department of Classics
University of California
Los Angeles
California 90024
U.S.A

Library of Congress Cataloging in Publication Data

Puhvel, Jaan.
    Hittite etymological dictionary.

    (Trends in linguistics. Documentation ; 1)
    Contents; v. 1. Words beginning with A — v. 2. Words beginning with E and I.
    1. Hittite language — Etymology — Dictionaries.   I. Title.   II. Series.
P945.Z8   1984   491'.990   83–25085
    ISBN 90–279–3049–X (v. 1)

Phototypeset in Times New Roman by H Charlesworth & Co Ltd, Huddersfield. — Printing: Druckerei Hildebrand, Berlin. — Binding: Lüderitz & Bauer Buchgewerbe GmbH, Berlin. Printed in Germany.

tions of a radical sort as a basis for etymology, e.g. *aku(wa)kuwa-, alalima-, anassa-, arasa-, argatiya-, ass-, asara-, asku-, asma, adda-, auli-, auwawa-*.

In general I have tried to eschew excessive rote uniformity of layout and style in etymological discussions, in order to make as many entries as possible self-contained micro-essays of a format best suited to the item at hand. When no etymology is rated certain, the discussion often proceeds from the less likely possibilities and ends up with the most probable. When a preferred etymology is featured as virtually certain, it is usually stated and discussed first, and discarded alternatives, to the extent that they are deemed historically interesting, are mentioned in a coda. Some past connections which were intrinsically outlandish or wide of the mark from the beginning (e.g. because of incorrect determination of phonetic content or meaning, or untenable phonological assumptions) and have minimal curiosity value, are simply consigned to oblivion. Nor is there any attempt to register and record all the loci where a proposed past etymology — whether accepted or rejected here — has been merely repeated in subsequent literature; in this respect Tischler in his glossary is doing a commendable job of archivist.

The unfolding of Hittite studies since around mid-century has been a rewarding intellectual experience. With no slight to others, two scholars have been in the vanguard of hittitology during this period — Heinrich Otten and Emmanuel Laroche. I close these remarks in mindfulness of what they have achieved and what they have given to the rest of us. Thanks are further due to many other scholars for their helpful attention to these labors. Substantive assistance from the John Simon Guggenheim Memorial Foundation, the American Council of Learned Societies, and the University of California Committee on Research also rates sincere acknowledgement.

J. P.

Preface

Is the time ripe for a Hittite etymological dictionary? Not in the sense that established, finite, well-interpreted corpora — say, Greek or Gothic, are forever 'ready'. But enough has been done with Hittite over the past two thirds of a century to justify a start of a more serious sort than previous preliminaries ranging from A. Juret's pathetic *Vocabulaire étymologique de la langue hittite* (1942) to J. Tischler's compilational *Hethitisches etymologisches Glossar* (1977–). One needs to find a *tertium quid* besides wild hunches off the top of one's head and stolid chronicling of secondary literature.

The only type of potentially viable Hittite etymological dictionary at this point in time is one that is anchored in first-hand philology and in the texts themselves. It has to be in its nature pioneering (and thus 'personal') rather than recapitulative, but its speculative character needs to be supported by visible primary data controlled by the author and laid out for the user's inspection, out of which the etymology rises in such a way as to let any reader test on the spot its degree of probability — and, if the spirit moveth, do better. Before etymologizing any entry I have studied and summarized all its forms and meanings available to me. The work can therefore also render incidental service as a reasonably comprehensive descriptive lexicon of the language, but such is not its primary purpose, and no competition is intended with otherwise oriented descriptive works such as A. Kammenhuber's elaborate new *Hethitisches Wörterbuch* (1975–) or the *Chicago Hittite dictionary* (1980–).

At the same time this undertaking cannot fail to contain new features and suggestions of a purely philological kind. The author of an etymological dictionary of Hittite in our lifetime cannot yet take philological underpinnings for granted. He must weigh the evidence for himself, always critically vis-à-vis previous exegesis, and when necessary strike out on his own to lay the very foundation from which etymological deliberation may proceed. Under the initial A quite a few entries present novel interpreta-

Contents

Notes on transcription

Narrow, hyphenated transliteration is given only sparingly and in instances where the transcription used may obscure or oversimplify the recorded form of a word. The transcription system is a fairly standard one and is meant to be consistent; possible deviations are attributable solely to human frailty. Uniformity in sumerography (where frequency of shifts resembles women's fashions) is also striven for.

Macron indicates repetition of vowel sign after vowel inherent in preceding sign: *ka-a-* = *kā-*.

Vocalism with *e* has precedence over *i* in alphabetization and transcription, e.g. *li-e* = *le*, *si-e-hu-* = *sehu-* (but *se-e-hu-* = *sēhu-*).

Intervocalic *i* is rendered by *y* when its nonsyllabic or glide nature is obvious, e.g. *a-ri-i-e-ir* = *ariyer*. This *y* is counted alphabetically immediately after *i* (and before *k*).

Prevocalic *u* and *ú* are transcribed as *w* before *e* but as *u* before *a* and *i* in order to differentiate the spellings *u-a, ú-a, u-i, ú-i* from *wa* and *wi*. When a distinction between *u* and *ú* may have etymological implications, narrow transliteration is given (see e.g. s.v. *auli-, auri-, au[s]-, awiti-*).

In phonemic transcription /s/ stands for **s* (spelled *s*), but /z/ or /ž/ is used to denote the product of certain clusters (e.g. **dy*), spelled *s*, and the affricate *z* of the script is rendered by /tˢ/.

Notes on symbols and abbreviations

Symbols for Indo-European laryngeals:

H = laryngeal

H_1 = laryngeal surviving as Hittite h (E_2, A_1, A_2^w).

H_2 = laryngeal lost in Hittite, sometimes surviving as intervocalic -y- glide (E_1) or as vocalized reflex (E_1, $A_2 > a$, $A_1^w > u$).

E_1 = voiceless e-coloring laryngeal, lost in Hittite, intervocalically lengthens preceding vowel and yields glide -y-; $E_1 > a$.

E_2 = voiced e-coloring laryngeal, Hittite h-, -h-.

A_1 = voiceless a-coloring laryngeal, Hittite h-, -$h(h)$-.

A_2 = voiced a-coloring laryngeal, lost in Hittite. $A_2 > a$.

A_1^w = voiceless o-coloring laryngeal, lost in Hittite. $A_1^w > u$.

A_2^w = voiced o-coloring laryngeal, Hitt. h-, -h-.

Cf. *Evidence for laryngeals*^{2} 92 (1965). The above symbols are used in this book for etymological discussion only when they are of direct relevance for the Hittite word at hand and not merely for Indo-European phonological theory.

No systematic attempt is made in the citations to classify the textual references into Old (, Middle,) and New Hittite; but "OHitt." is often so marked when the singling out of a truly old attestation (as distinct from a later copy of an older text) may have etymological interest or significance. Sometimes the Old Hittite nature of a citation is evident from an accompanying reference (e.g. "Otten–Souček, *Altheth. Ritual*"). Massive chronologizing of routine attestations into Old and New Hittite is available in Kammenhuber's *HW*^{2} and *MHT*.

Authors whose names figure in the list of abbreviations are normally quoted by last name only. Others are mentioned by initial + last name.

The abbreviations *KUB*, *KBo*, *IBoT*, etc. are spelled out before volume numbers only when first used in an entry or whenever they differ from the immediately preceding locus reference. In case of doubt one should follow the references backwards in the text until reaching one that is spelled out.

Instead of *Bo* 68/000, etc., I write 000/1968, etc., in order to keep parallelism with 000/z, etc.

BoTU references are usually not given, rather the corresponding cuneiform editions. Edition references are to primary scholarly treatments, rather than to didactic versions such as Sturtevant's chrestomathy or Friedrich's primer and reader.

The Hittite laws are referred to as *Code* in Hrozný's numbering; to distinguish the two halves, e.g. paragraph 5 is denoted 1:5, while paragraph 105 is denoted 2:5; paragraphs 100 and 200 are so written.

"dupl." = duplicate text.
"par." = parallel text.
"var." = variant form in duplicate text.

List of abbreviations

../a, etc.: Inventory numbers of Boğazköy excavations since 1931, by year, up to *..*/z in 1967. Since then, *..*/1968, etc.

ABAW: *Abhandlungen der Bayerischen Akademie der Wissenschaften, Philosophisch-historische Abteilung.*

ABoT: *Ankara Arkeoloji Müzesinde bulunan Boğazköy tabletleri* (Istanbul, 1948).

AfK: *Archiv für Keilschriftforschung.*

AfO: *Archiv für Orientforschung.*

AGI: *Archivio Glottologico Italiano.*

AHW: Wolfram von Soden, *Akkadisches Handwörterbuch* (Wiesbaden, 1958–).

AIED: *Ancient Indo-European dialects*, edited by Henrik Birnbaum and Jaan Puhvel (Berkeley and Los Angeles, 1966).

AION(-L): *Istituto Orientale di Napoli, Annali (Sezione linguistica).*

AJPh: *American journal of philology.*

Alalah: Donald J. Wiseman, *The Alalakh tablets* (London, 1953). Continuation in *JCS* 8:1–30 (1954).

Alp, Beamtennamen: Sedat Alp, *Untersuchungen zu den Beamtennamen im hethitischen Festzeremoniell* (Leipzig, 1940).

Anatol. Stud. Güterbock: *Anatolian studies presented to Hans Gustav Güterbock on the occasion of his 65th birthday* (Istanbul, 1974).

ANET: *Ancient Near Eastern texts relating to the Old Testament*, edited by James B. Pritchard, 2nd edition (Princeton, 1955 [1st ed. 1950]).

ANLR: *Atti della Accademia Nazionale dei Lincei. Serie 8. Rendiconti. Classe di Scienze morali, storiche e filologiche* (Roma).

Arch. Or.: *Archiv Orientální.*

ARIV: *Atti del Reale Istituto Veneto.*

Atti La Colombaria: *Atti e Memorie dell'Accademia Toscana di Scienze e Lettere "La Colombaria"* (Firenze).

Bechtel, Hittite Verbs: George Bechtel, *Hittite verbs in -sk-. A study of verbal aspect* (Ann Arbor, 1936).

Benveniste, Hittite: E. Benveniste, *Hittite et indo-européen. Études comparatives* (Paris, 1962).

Benveniste, Origines: E. Benveniste, *Origines de la formation des noms en indo-européen* (Paris, 1935).

Bi. Or.: Bibliotheca Orientalis.

BMitt.: Baghdader Mitteilungen.

Bo: Inventory numbers of Boğazköy excavations 1906–1912.

Bossert, Königssiegel: Helmuth Th. Bossert, *Ein hethitisches Königssiegel* (= *Istanbuler Forschungen* 18) (Berlin, 1944).

BoSt: Boghazköi-Studien, herausgegeben von Otto Weber. 1–10 (Leipzig, 1917–1924).

BoTU: Emil Forrer, *Die Boghazköi-Texte in Umschrift* (Leipzig, 1922–1926).

von Brandenstein, Heth. Götter: C.-G. Freiherr von Brandenstein, *Hethitische Götter nach Bildbeschreibungen in Keilschrifttexten* (= *Mitteilungen der Vorderasiatisch-Aegyptischen Gesellschaft* 46.2 [1943]).

BSL: Bulletin de la Société de Linguistique de Paris.

Burde, Medizinische Texte: Cornelia Burde, *Hethitische medizinische Texte* (= *StBoT* 19) (Wiesbaden, 1974).

BzN: Beiträge zur Namenforschung.

CAD: Chicago Assyrian dictionary (1956–).

Carruba, Beiträge: Onofrio Carruba, *Beiträge zum Palaischen* (= *Uitgaven van het Nederlands Historisch-archaeologisch Instituut te Istanbul* 31) (1972).

Carruba, Beschwörungsritual: Onofrio Carruba, *Das Beschwörungsritual für die Göttin Wišurijanza* (= *StBoT* 2) (Wiesbaden, 1966).

Carruba, Das Palaische: Onofrio Carruba, *Das Palaische. Texte, Grammatik, Lexikon* (= *StBoT* 10) (Wiesbaden, 1970).

Carruba, Partikeln: Onofrio Carruba, *Die satzeinleitenden Partikeln in den indogermanischen Sprachen Anatoliens* (= *Incunabula Graeca* 32) (Roma, 1969).

Chantraine, DELG: Pierre Chantraine, *Dictionnaire étymologique de la langue grecque* (Paris, 1968–).

CHD: Chicago Hittite dictionary (1980–).

Čop, Indogermanica minora: Bojan Čop, *Indogermanica minora, I. K anatolskim jezikom* (= *Slovenska Adademija Znanosti i Umetnosti. Razred za Filološke in Literarne Vede. Razprave* 8) (Ljubljana, 1971).

Couvreur, Hett.: Walter Couvreur, *De hettitische Ḫ* (Louvain, 1937).

CRAI: Académie des Inscriptions & Belles-Lettres. Comptes rendus des séances.

Dict. louv.: E. Laroche, *Dictionnaire de la langue louvite* (= *Bibliothèque*

List of abbreviations

archéologique et historique de l'Institut français d'archéologie d'Istanbul 6) (Paris, 1959).

Dressler, Studien: Wolfgang Dressler, *Studien zur verbalen Pluralität* (= *SbÖAW* 259.1) (Wien, 1968).

EM: Etymologicum Magnum.

Ertem, Coğrafya: Hayri Ertem, *Boğazköy metinlerinde geçen coğrafya adları dizini* (Ankara, 1973).

Ertem, Fauna: Hayri Ertem, *Boğazköy metinlerine göre Hititler devri Anadolu'sunun faunası* (Ankara, 1965).

Ertem, Flora: Hayri Ertem, *Boğazköy metinlerine göre Hititler devri Anadolu'sunun florası* (Ankara, 1974).

Festus: Sexti Pompei Festi *De verborum significatu* quae supersunt cum Pauli *Epitome*, edited by W. M. Lindsay (Leipzig, 1913).

FHG: E. Laroche, "Fragments hittites de Genève", *RA* 45:131–8, 184–94 (1951); 46:42–50 (1952).

Friedrich, HE: Johannes Friedrich, *Hethitisches Elementarbuch. 1. Teil. Kurzgefasste Grammatik*, 2. Auflage (Heidelberg, 1960).

Friedrich, Heth. Ges.: Johannes Friedrich, *Die hethitischen Gesetze, Transkription, Übersetzung, sprachliche Erläuterungen und vollständiges Wörterverzeichnis* (Leiden, 1959).

Friedrich, KS: Johannes Friedrich, *Kleinasiatische Sprachdenkmäler* (Berlin, 1932).

Friedrich, Staatsverträge: Johannes Friedrich, *Staatsverträge des Ḫatti-Reiches in hethitischer Sprache* 1, 2 (= *Mitteilungen der Vorderasiatisch-Aegyptischen Gesellschaft* 31.1 [1926], 34.1 [1930]).

Frisk, GEW: Hjalmar Frisk, *Griechisches etymologisches Wörterbuch* (Heidelberg).

Frisk, Indogerm.: Hjalmar Frisk, *Indogermanica* (= *Göteborgs Högskolas Årsskrift* 44:1 [1938]) [= *Kl. Schr.* 35–62].

Frisk, Kl. Schr.: Hjalmar Frisk, *Kleine Schriften zur Indogermanistik und zur griechischen Wortkunde* (= *Studia Graeca et Latina Gothoburgensia* 21 [1966]).

Furnée, Erscheinungen: Edzard J. Furnée, *Die wichtigsten konsonantischen Erscheinungen des Vorgriechischen* (The Hague, 1972).

Gamkrelidze, Xettskij jazyk: T. V. Gamkrelidze, "Xettskij jazyk i laringal'naja teorija", *Akademija Nauk Gruzinskoj SSR, Trudy Inst. Jazykoznanija* 3:15–91 (Tbilisi, 1960).

Garstang–Gurney, Geography: John Garstang – O. R. Gurney, *The geography of the Hittite empire* (Ankara, 1959).

GGA: Göttingische Gelehrte Anzeigen.

Gött. Nachr.: Nachrichten von der (Kgl.) Gesellschaft der Wissenschaften zu Göttingen, Philosophisch-historische Klasse.

Götze, AM: Albrecht Götze, *Die Annalen des Muršiliš* (= *Mitteilungen der Vorderasiatisch-Aegyptischen Gesellschaft* 38 [1933]).

Götze, Hattusilis: Albrecht Götze, *Ḫattušiliš. Der Bericht über seine Thronbesteigung nebst den Paralleltexten* (= *Mitteilungen der Vorderasiatisch-Aegyptischen Gesellschaft* 29.3 [1925]).

Götze, Madd.: Albrecht Götze, *Madduwattaš* (= *Mitteilungen der Vorderasiatisch-Aegyptischen Gesellschaft* 32.1 [1927]).

Götze, Neue Bruchstücke: Albrecht Götze, *Neue Bruchstücke zum grossen Text des Ḫattušiliš und den Paralleltexten* (= *Mitteilungen der Vorderasiatisch-Aegyptischen Gesellschaft* 34.2 [1930]).

Götze – Pedersen, MS: Albrecht Götze – Holger Pedersen, *Muršilis Sprachlähmung. Ein hethitischer Text mit philologischen und linguistischen Erörterungen* (= *Det Kgl. Danske Videnskabernes Selskab. Historisk-filologiske Meddelelser* 21.1) (København, 1934).

Goetze, Tunnawi: *The Hittite ritual of Tunnawi.* Interpreted by Albrecht Goetze in cooperation with E. H. Sturtevant (= *American Oriental Society Series* 14) (New Haven, 1938).

Güterbock, Kumarbi: Hans Gustav Güterbock, *Kumarbi* (= *Istanbuler Schriften* 16 [1946]).

Güterbock, Siegel: Hans Gustav Güterbock, *Siegel aus Boğazköy* 1, 2 (= *AfO* Beiheft 5, 7) (Berlin, 1940, 1942).

Gurney, Hittite Prayers: O. R. Gurney, *Hittite prayers of Mursili II* (= *Annals of Archaeology and Anthropology* 27) (Liverpool, 1940).

Gusmani, Lessico: Roberto Gusmani, *Il lessico ittito* (= *Introduzione allo studio comparativo delle lingue anatoliche*, vol. I) (Napoli, 1968).

Gusmani, Lyd. Wb.: Roberto Gusmani, *Lydisches Wörterbuch. Mit grammatischer Skizze und Inschriftensammlung* (Heidelberg, 1964).

Haas, Nerik: Volkert Haas, *Der Kult von Nerik. Ein Beitrag zur hethitischen Religionsgeschichte* (= *Studia Pohl* 4) (Roma, 1970).

Haas – Thiel, Rituale: Volkert Haas – Hans Jochen Thiel, *Die Beschwörungsrituale der Allaihturaḫ(ḫ)i und verwandte Texte. Hurritologische Studien II* (= *Alter Orient und Altes Testament*, Sonderreihe, 31) (Kevelaer, 1978).

Haas – Wilhelm, Riten: Volkert Haas – Gernot Wilhelm, *Hurritische und luwische Riten aus Kizzuwatna. Hurritologische Studien I* (*Alter Orient und Altes Testament*, Sonderreihe, 3) (Kevelaer, 1974).

Haase, Fragmente: Richard Haase, *Die Fragmente der hethitischen Gesetze* (Wiesbaden, 1968).

Hawkins – Morpurgo – Neumann, HHL: J. D. Hawkins – Anna Morpurgo-Davies – Günter Neumann, "Hittite hieroglyphs and Luwian: New evidence for the connection", *NAWG* 6: 143–198 (1973).

List of abbreviations

Hendriksen, Untersuchungen: Hans Hendriksen, *Untersuchungen über die Bedeutung des Hethitischen für die Laryngaltheorie* (= *Det Kgl. Danske Videnskabernes Selskab. Historisk-filologiske Meddelelser* 28.2) (København, 1941).

Hes.: Hesychius.

Hethitica: Hethitica. *1.* Travaux édités par Guy Jucquois (*Travaux de la Faculté de Philosophie et Lettres de l'Université Catholique de Louvain – VII. Section de philologie et histoire orientales – I* [1972]).

Hethitica II, III, IV: Hethitica 2, 3, 4. Travaux édités par Guy Jucquois et René Lebrun (= *Bibliothèque des Cahiers de l'Institut de linguistique de Louvain* 7 [1977], 15 [1979], 21 [1981]).

HOAKS: Handbuch der Orientalistik. 1. Abt., 2. Band, 1.–2. Abschnitt. Lieferung 2, *Altkleinasiatische Sprachen* (Leiden, 1969).

Houwink Ten Cate, LPG: Ph. H. J. Houwink Ten Cate, *The Luwian population groups of Lycia and Cilicia Aspera during the Hellenistic period* (Leiden, 1961).

Houwink Ten Cate, Records: Ph. H. J. Houwink Ten Cate, *The Records of the Early Hittite Empire (c. 1450–1380 B.C.)* (= *Uitgaven van het Nederlands Historisch-Archaeologisch Instituut te Istanbul* 26 [1970]).

Hrozný, Heth. KB: Friedrich Hrozný, *Hethitische Keilschrifttexte aus Boghazköi* (= *BoSt* 3) (Leipzig, 1919).

Hrozný, SH: Friedrich Hrozný, *Die Sprache der Hethiter* (= *BoSt* 1–2) (Leipzig, 1917).

HT: Hittite texts in the cuneiform character from tablets in the British Museum (London, 1920).

HW (Erg. 1, 2, 3): Johannes Friedrich, *Hethitisches Wörterbuch* (Heidelberg, 1952–1954), with *Ergänzungsheft* 1 (1957), 2 (1961), 3 (1966).

HW^2: Johannes Friedrich – Annelies Kammenhuber, *Hethitisches Wörterbuch. Zweite, völlig neubearbeitete Auflage* (Heidelberg, 1975–).

IBK: Innsbrucker Beiträge zur Kulturwissenschaft.

IBS: Innsbrucker Beiträge zur Sprachwissenschaft.

IBoT: Istanbul Arkeoloji Müzelerinde bulunan Boğazköy tabletleri.

IEW: Julius Pokorny, *Indogermanisches etymologisches Wörterbuch* (Bern/München, 1959).

IF: Indogermanische Forschungen.

Imparati, Leggi ittite: Fiorella Imparati, *Le leggi ittite* (= *Incunabula Graeca* 7) (Roma, 1964).

Ivanov, Obščeindoevropejskaja: V. V. Ivanov, *Obščeindoevropejskaja praslavjanskaja i anatolijskaja jazykovyje sistemy* (Moskva, 1965).

Jakob-Rost, Ritual der Malli: Liane Jakob-Rost, *Das Ritual der Malli aus Arzawa gegen Behexung* (= *Texte der Hethiter* 2) (Heidelberg, 1972).

JAOS: *Journal of the American Oriental Society.*

JCS: *Journal of cuneiform studies.*

JEOL: *Jaarbericht van het Vooraziatisch-egyptisch Genootschap Ex Oriente Lux.*

JKF: *Jahrbuch für kleinasiatische Forschung.*

JNES: *Journal of Near Eastern studies.*

Josephson, Sentence Particles: Folke Josephson, *The function of the sentence particles in Old and Middle Hittite* (=*Acta Universitatis Upsaliensis. Studia Indoeuropaea Upsaliensia* 2 [1972]).

Juret, Vocabulaire: Abel Juret, *Vocabulaire étymologique de la langue hittite* (=*Publications de la Faculté des Lettres de Strasbourg*, Fascicule 99) (Limoges, 1942) [originally in *RHA* 6:1–66 (1940–1941)].

Kammenhuber, Die Arier: Annelies Kammenhuber, *Die Arier im Vorderen Orient* (Heidelberg, 1968).

Kammenhuber, Hippologia: Annelies Kammenhuber, *Hippologia Hethitica* (Wiesbaden, 1961).

Kammenhuber, MHT: Annelies Kammenhuber, *Materialien zu einem hethitischen Thesaurus* (Heidelberg, 1973–).

Kammenhuber, Orakelpraxis: Annelies Kammenhuber, *Orakelpraxis, Träume und Vorzeichenschau bei den Hethitern* (=*Texte der Hethiter* 7) (Heidelberg, 1976).

KBo: *Keilschrifttexte aus Boghazköi.*

KlF: *Kleinasiatische Forschungen*, Band I (Weimar, 1927–1930).

Kronasser, Etym.: Heinz Kronasser, *Etymologie der hethitischen Sprache. Band 1. I. Zur Schreibung und Lautung des Hethitischen. II. Wortbildung des Hethitischen* (Wiesbaden, 1966).

Kronasser, Umsiedelung: Heinz Kronasser, *Die Umsiedelung der schwarzen Gottheit. Das hethitische Ritual KUB XXIX 4 (des Ulippi)* (=*SbÖAW* 241.3 [1963]).

Kronasser, VLFH: Heinz Kronasser, *Vergleichende Laut- und Formenlehre des Hethitischen* (Heidelberg, 1956).

KUB: *Keilschrifturkunden aus Boghazköi.*

Kühne – Otten, Šaušgamuwa: Cord Kühne – Heinrich Otten, *Der Šaušgamuwa-Vertrag* (=*StBoT* 16) (Wiesbaden, 1971).

Kümmel, Ersatzrituale: Hans Martin Kümmel, *Ersatzrituale für den hethitischen König* (=*StBoT* 3) (Wiesbaden, 1967).

Kuryłowicz, Études: Jerzy Kuryłowicz, *Études indoeuropéennes I* (=*Polska Akademija Umiejętności. Prace Komisji Językowej* 21) (Kraków, 1935).

KZ: *Zeitschrift für vergleichende Sprachforschung*, begründet von A. Kuhn.

List of abbreviations

Laroche, CTH: Emmanuel Laroche, *Catalogue des textes hittites*[2] (Paris, 1971). "Premier supplément", *RHA* 30: 94–133 (1972).

Laroche, HH: Emmanuel Laroche, *Les hiéroglyphes hittites. Première partie. L'écriture* (Paris, 1960).

Laroche, Noms: Emmanuel Laroche, *Les noms des Hittites* (Paris, 1966).

Laroche, Recherches: Emmanuel Laroche, *Recherches sur les noms des dieux hittites* (Paris, 1947). [Also in *RHA* 7:7–77 (1946–1947).]

Lebrun, Samuha: René Lebrun, *Samuha foyer religieux de l'empire hittite* (= *Publications de l'Institut orientaliste de Louvain* 11 [1976]).

Lehmann, PIEP: Winfred P. Lehmann, *Proto-Indo-European phonology* (Austin, 1952).

Lg.:   *Language.*

LHG: *Lraber hasarakakan gitutʻyunneri* (= *Vestnik obščestvennyx nauk*). Akademija Nauk Armjanskoj S.S.R., Erevan.

Ling.:   *Linguistica* (Ljubljana).

LPosn: *Linguistica Posnaniensia.*

Marstrander, Caractère: Carl J. S. Marstrander, *Caractère indo-européen de la langue hittite* (= *Det Norske Videnskaps Akademie, Hist.-fil. Klasse* 1918.2) (Christiania, 1919).

Mayrhofer, KEWA: Manfred Mayrhofer, *Kurzgefasstes etymologisches Wörterbuch des Altindischen* (Heidelberg, 1956–).

MDOG: *Mitteilungen der Deutschen Orient-Gesellschaft.*

Meissner AOS: *Altorientalische Studien Bruno Meissner zum sechzigsten Geburtstag ... gewidmet* (= *Mitteilungen der Altorientalischen Gesellschaft* 4) (Leipzig, 1928–1929).

Meriggi, HHG: Piero Meriggi, *Hieroglyphisch-hethitisches Glossar.* Zweite, völlig umgearbeitete Auflage (Wiesbaden, 1962).

Meriggi, Manuale: Piero Meriggi, *Manuale di eteo geroglifico* (= *Incunabula Graeca*) (Roma, 1966–1975).

MIO: *Mitteilungen des Instituts für Orientforschung* (Berlin).

MSL: *Materialien zum Sumerischen Lexikon* (Chicago).

MSS: *Münchener Studien zur Sprachwissenschaft.*

NAWG: *Nachrichten der Akademie der Wissenschaften in Göttingen, Philosophisch-historische Klasse.*

Neu, Altheth.:   Erich Neu, *Althethitische Ritualtexte in Umschrift* (= *StBoT* 25) (Wiesbaden, 1980).

Neu, Anitta-Text: Erich Neu, *Der Anitta-Text* (= *StBoT* 18) (Wiesbaden, 1974).

Neu, Gewitterritual: Erich Neu, *Ein althethitisches Gewitterritual* (= *StBoT* 12) (Wiesbaden, 1970).

Neu, Interpretation: Erich Neu, *Interpretation der hethitischen mediopassi-...ven Verbalformen* (= *StBoT* 5) (Wiesbaden, 1968).

Neu, Lokativ: Erich Neu, *Studien zum endungslosen "Lokativ" des Hethitischen* (= *IBS, Vorträge und kleinere Schriften* 23 [1980]).

Neu, Mediopassiv: Erich Neu, *Das hethitische Mediopassiv und seine indogermanischen Grundlagen* (= *StBoT* 6) (Wiesbaden, 1968).

Neumann, Untersuch.: Günter Neumann, *Untersuchungen zum Weiterleben hethitischen und luwischen Sprachgutes in hellenistischer und römischer Zeit* (Wiesbaden, 1961).

Oettinger, Eide: Norbert Oettinger, *Die militärischen Eide der Hethiter* (= *StBoT* 22) (Wiesbaden, 1976).

Oettinger, Stammbildung: Norbert Oettinger, *Die Stammbildung des hethitischen Verbums* (= *Erlanger Beiträge zur Sprach- und Kunstwissenschaft* 64) (Nürnberg, 1979).

OLZ: Orientalistische Literaturzeitung.

Ose, Supinum: Fritz Ose, *Supinum und Infinitiv im Hethitischen* (= *Mitteilungen der Vorderasiatisch-Aegyptischen Gesellschaft* 47.1 [1944]).

Otten, Altheth. Erzählung: Heinrich Otten, *Eine althethitische Erzählung um die Stadt Zalpa* (= *StBoT* 17) (Wiesbaden, 1973).

Otten, Bestimmung: Heinrich Otten, *Zur grammatikalischen und lexikalischen Bestimmung des Luvischen* (= *Deutsche Akademie der Wissenschaften zu Berlin. Institut für Orientforschung. Veröffentlichung* 19 [1953]).

Otten, Festritual: Heinrich Otten, *Ein hethitisches Festritual (KBo XIX 128)* (= *StBoT* 13) (Wiesbaden, 1971).

Otten, Kumarbi: Heinrich Otten, *Mythen vom Gotte Kumarbi. Neue Fragmente* (= *Deutsche Akademie der Wissenschaften zu Berlin. Institut für Orientforschung. Veröffentlichung* 3 [1950]).

Otten, LTU: Heinrich Otten, *Luvische Texte in Umschrift* (= *Deutsche Akademie der Wissenschaften zu Berlin. Institut für Orientforschung. Veröffentlichung* 17 [1953]).

Otten, Materialien: Heinrich Otten, *Materialien zum hethitischen Lexikon* (= *StBoT* 15) (Wiesbaden, 1971).

Otten, Sprachliche Stellung: Heinrich Otten, *Sprachliche Stellung und Datierung des Madduwatta-Textes* (= *StBoT* 11) (Wiesbaden, 1969).

Otten, Totenrituale: Heinrich Otten, *Hethitische Totenrituale* (= *Deutsche Akademie der Wissenschaften zu Berlin. Institut für Orientforschung. Veröffentlichung* 37 [1958]).

Otten, Überlieferungen: Heinrich Otten, *Die Überlieferungen des Telipinu-Mythus* (= *Mitteilungen der Vorderasiatisch-Aegyptischen Gesellschaft* 46.1 [1942]).

Otten, Vokabular: Heinrich Otten – Wolfram von Soden, *Das akkadisch-hethitische Vokabular KBo I 44 + KBo XIII 1* (= *StBoT* 7) (Wiesbaden, 1968).

List of abbreviations

Otten – Souček, Altheth. Ritual: Heinrich Otten – Vladimir Souček, *Ein althethitisches Ritual für das Königspaar* (= *StBoT* 8) (Wiesbaden, 1969).

Otten – Souček, Gelübde: Heinrich Otten – Vladimir Souček, *Das Gelübde der Königin Puduhepa an die Göttin Lelwani* (= *StBoT* 1) (Wiesbaden, 1965).

PBH: *Patma-banasirakan handes* (= *Istoriko-filologičeskij žurnal*). Erevan, Armenian S.S.R.

Pedersen, Hitt.: Holger Pedersen, *Hittitisch und die anderen indoeuropäischen Sprachen* (= *Det Kgl. Danske Videnskabernes Selskab. Historisk-filologiske Meddelelser 25. 2*) (København, 1938).

Pedersen, Lyk. u. Hitt.: Holger Pedersen, *Lykisch und Hittitisch* (= *Det Kgl. Danske Videnskabernes Selskab. Historisk-filologiske Meddelelser 30.4*) (København, 1945).

Pokorny BIK: *Beiträge zur Indogermanistik und Keltologie Julius Pokorny zum 80. Geburtstag gewidmet*, herausgegeben von Wolfgang Meid (= *IBK* 13 [1967]).

Puhvel, LIEV: Jaan Puhvel, *Laryngeals and the Indo-European verb* (= *UCPL* 21 [1960]).

RA: *Revue d'assyriologie et d'archéologie orientale.*

RBPhH: *Revue belge de philologie et d'histoire.*

RHA: *Revue hittite et asianique.*

RHR: *Revue de l'histoire des religions.*

RIDA: *Revue internationale des droits de l'antiquité.*

Riemschneider, Geburtsomina: Kaspar Klaus Riemschneider, *Babylonische Geburtsomina in hethitischer Übersetzung* (= *StBoT* 9) (Wiesbaden, 1970).

Robert, Noms indigènes: Louis Robert, *Noms indigènes dans l'Asie Mineure gréco-romaine* (= *Bibliothèque archéologique et historique de l'Institut français d'archéologie d'Istanbul* 13) (Paris, 1963).

Rosenkranz, Beiträge: Bernhard Rosenkranz, *Beiträge zur Erforschung des Luvischen* (Wiesbaden, 1952).

RPh: *Revue de philologie.*

RS: Ras Shamra tablets.

SbÖAW: *Sitzungsberichte der Österreichischen Akademie der Wissenschaften, Philosophisch-historische Klasse.*

Schmitt-Brandt, Entwicklung: Robert Schmitt-Brandt, *Die Entwicklung des indogermanischen Vokalsystems* (Heidelberg, 1967).

von Schuler, Die Kaškäer: Einar von Schuler, *Die Kaškäer. Ein Beitrag zur Ethnographie des alten Kleinasien* (Berlin, 1965).

von Schuler, Dienstanweisungen: Einar von Schuler, *Hethitische Dienstan-*

weisungen für höhere Hof- und Staatsbeamte (= *AfO* Beiheft 10) (Graz, 1957).

Schuster, Bilinguen: Hans-Siegfried Schuster, *Die hattisch-hethitischen Bilinguen. I. Einleitung, Texte und Kommentar.* Teil 1 (Leiden, 1974).

Siegelová, Appu-Hedammu: Jana Siegelová, *Appu-Märchen und Hedammu-Mythus* (= *StBoT* 14) (Wiesbaden, 1971).

SMEA: Studi micenei ed egeo-anatolici (*Incunabula Graeca*) (Roma).

Sommer, AS: Ferdinand Sommer, *Aḫḫijavāfrage und Sprachwissenschaft* (= *ABAW* N.F. 9 [1934]).

Sommer, AU: Ferdinand Sommer, *Die Aḫḫijavā-Urkunden* (= *ABAW* N.F. 6 [1932]).

Sommer, HAB: Ferdinand Sommer – Adam Falkenstein, *Die hethitisch-akkadische Bilingue des Ḫattušili I. (Labarna II.)* (= *ABAW* N.F. 16 [1938]).

Sommer, Heth. I, II: Ferdinand Sommer, *Hethitisches* I, II (= *BoSt* 4, 7) (Leipzig, 1920, 1922).

Sommer Corolla: Corolla Linguistica. Festschrift Ferdinand Sommer zum 80. Geburtstag (Wiesbaden, 1955).

Sommer – Ehelolf, Pāpanikri: Ferdinand Sommer – Hans Ehelolf, *Das hethitische Ritual des Pāpanikri von Komana* (= *BoSt* 10) (Leipzig, 1924).

SPAW: Sitzungsberichte der Preussischen Akademie der Wissenschaften.

Starke, Funktionen: Frank Starke, *Die Funktionen der dimensionalen Kasus und Adverbien im Althethitischen* (= *StBoT* 23) (Wiesbaden, 1977).

StBoT: Studien zu den Boğazköy-Texten (Wiesbaden, 1965–).

Steph. Byz.: Stephanus of Byzantium, *Ethnika.*

Sturtevant, Chrest.: Edgar H. Sturtevant – George Bechtel, *A Hittite chrestomathy* (Philadelphia, 1935).

Sturtevant, Comp. Gr.[1,2]*:* Edgar H. Sturtevant, *A comparative grammar of the Hittite language* (Philadelphia, 1933; 2nd edition New Haven, 1951).

Sturtevant, IHL: Edgar H. Sturtevant, *The Indo-Hittite laryngeals* (Baltimore, 1942).

Szabó, Entsühnungsritual: Gabriella Szabó, *Ein hethitisches Entsühnungsritual* (= *Texte der Hethiter* 1) (Heidelberg, 1971).

TAPA: Transactions of the American Philological Association.

Tischler, Gebet: Johann Tischler, *Das hethitische Gebet der Gassulijawija* (= *IBS* 37 [1981]).

Tischler, Glossar: Johann Tischler, *Hethitisches etymologisches Glossar* (= *IBS* 20 [1977–]).

List of abbreviations

TLy: *Tituli Lyciae* (Wien, 1901).

TPhS: *Transactions of the Philological Society.*

UCPL: *University of California Publications in Linguistics.*

Ünal, Hatt.:   Ahmet Ünal, *Ḫattušili III. Teil I. Ḫattušili bis zu seiner Thronbesteigung* (= *Texte der Hethiter* 3–4) (Heidelberg, 1974).

Ünal, Orakeltext: Ahmet Ünal, *Ein Orakeltext über die Intrigen am hethitischen Hof (KUB XXII 70 = Bo 2011)* (= *Texte der Hethiter* 6) (Heidelberg, 1978).

Van Windekens, Le tokharien: A. J. Van Windekens, *Le tokharien confronté avec les autres langues indo-européennes. Volume I. La phonétique et le vocabulaire* (Louvain, 1976).

VAT: Inventory numbers of tablets in the Vorderasiatisches Museum, Berlin.

VBoT: Albrecht Götze, *Verstreute Boghazköi-Texte* (Marburg, 1930).

Werner, Gerichtsprotokolle: Rudolf Werner, *Hethitische Gerichtsprotokolle* (= *StBoT* 4) (Wiesbaden, 1967).

Witzel, Heth. KU: P. Maurus Witzel, *Hethitische Keilschrift-Urkunden in Transcription und Uebersetzung mit Kommentar* (= *Keilinschriftliche Studien* 4) (Fulda, 1924).

WZKM: *Wiener Zeitschrift für die Kunde des Morgenlandes.*

ZDMG: *Zeitschrift der Deutschen Morgenländischen Gesellschaft.*

Zuntz, Ortsadverbien: Leonie Zuntz, *Die hethitischen Ortsadverbien arḫa, parā, piran* (München, 1936).

Volume 1
Words beginning with A

a-,   sentence-initial particle serving as prop for enclitics, found in
KUB XLVIII 99, 8 *ā-ssi mekki āssu piyaweni* 'we give him much
good' (cf. ibid. 3 *a-ass-a* 'and he'; ibid. 12 *ā-zza*). Cf. Otten,
JKF 2:69 (1951); Laroche, *RHA* 23:174 (1965).

This *a-* is probably a Luwianism, since Luw. (and Hier.) *a-* is
the standard match for Hitt. *nu.* Cf. *Dict. louv.* 21, 144.

a-   'this (one), that (one), the aforementioned (one)', nom. sg. c. *asi*
(plentiful, e.g. *KBo* IV 2 III 46 *asi memias* 'this matter'; cf.
Götze – Pedersen, *MS* 4; *KUB* V 25 III 10 *mān asi memias
asanza* 'if this matter is true'; *VBoT* 58 I 17 *asi hahhimas* 'the
aforementioned [lines 7 and 9] h.'; cf. Laroche, *RHA* 23:83
[1965]; *HT* 25 + *KUB* XXXIII 111, 7–9 *nu asi kuin* ^DKAL-*an
nepis* LUGAL-*un iyawēn nu apās* GIM-*an niwarallis* [with gloss-
wedges] 'that K. whom we made king in heaven, whereas he is
powerless ...'; cf. Laroche, *RHA* 26:37 [1968]), *asis* (vocabulary
fragment *KUB* III 99 II 18), *unis* (*ABoT* 56 I 21), *enis*
(vocabulary *KBo* I 42 III 35 *enis-pat*; cf. Güterbock, *MSL*
13:138 [1971]), acc. sg. c. *asi* (rare, e.g. IV 2 III 44 *asi memiyan*;
KUB XVI 27, 9 *asi marsastarrin*, XVI 34 I 9 *asi marsastarin*
'this fraud'; V 8, 4 *asi* UKÙ-*an* besides ibid. 5 *asi* UKÙ-*as*), *uni*
(e.g. XIV 17 II 10 *uni memian*; *KBo* V 8 III 24 *nu uni kuin* 9 LIM
ERÍN.MEŠ ^I*Pitaggatallis uwatet* 'that 9000-man army which P.
brought'; cf. Götze, *AM* 158), *unin* (e.g. *KUB* VIII 55, 8 *unin
memiyan*; *KBo* X 47a I 9 *unin-wa ku*[*in*; cf. Laroche, *RHA* 26:8
[1968]), nom.-acc. sg. or pl. neut. *eni* (e.g. *KUB* XXIX 4 III 29
eni-pat pedan 'that very place'; cf. Kronasser, *Umsiedelung* 24;
XLIII 75 Vs. 20 *eni annassar* 'the aforementioned [ibid. 12] a.';
XXII 70 Vs. 19 *eni* GILIM [= *harsanalli*] 'that [particular]
wreath'; cf. Ünal, *Orakeltext* 58; ibid. Rs. 18 *eni* UNUTE.MEŠ
'those utensils'; ibid. passim *eni kuit* in alternation with *kī kuit*
'[as regards] this, [namely] that ...'; cf. Ünal, *Orakeltext*
104–5), *ini* (e.g. XXIX 1 I 35 *ini* GIŠ-*ru* 'this wood[en object]'; cf.

B. Schwartz, *Orientalia* N.S. 16:26 [1947]; *KBo* XII 89 III 10 *ini-ma-wa kuit* 'but what [is] that?'), *i-e-ni* (*KUB* I 16 III 40 [OHitt.]; cf. Sommer, *HAB* 12), gen. sg. *uniyas* (XXXIII 113 + I 32 *uniyas halluwain* 'this one's violence'; ibid. 34 *[uni]yas nahsaraddus* 'this one's fearsomeness'; cf. Güterbock, *JCS* 6:12 [1952]), dat. sg. *edani* (e.g. XII 58 I 13 *edani antuhsi* 'for this man'; cf. Goetze, *Tunnawi* 6; *KBo* II 2 II 55 and III 5 *edani memiyani* 'to this matter'; cf. Hrozný, *Heth. KB* 46; IV 4 II 41–42 *man] mān edani* ANA ᴸᵁKÚR [*pāun* 'if I had marched against this enemy'; cf. Götze, *AM* 116), abl. sg. *etez* (*KUB* V 24 I 56 *etez pedaz* 'from this place'; *KBo* V 8 III 18 *nu-za-kan* IGI.HI.A-*wa etez* ANA ¹*Pittapara neyahhat* 'I turned my eyes from there to P.'; cf. Götze, *AM* 156), *ediz* (IV 6 Rs. 22), *edaza* (e.g. IV 14 III 34 'from there'; cf. R. Stefanini, *ANLR* 20:45 [1965]), nom. pl. c. (OHitt.) *e* (XXII 2 Rs. 6 1 *ME* ERÍN.MEŠ-*za-e-a natta* 'and are these not one hundred troops?'; cf. Otten, *Altheth. Erzählung* 10; III 28 II 5, III 38 Vs. 15, *KUB* XXXI 64 II 15 *e-sta*, spelled *es-ta*; cf. Otten, *Altheth. Erzählung* 8; *KBo* XII 3 III 10 *ē-sta*, spelled *e-es-ta*; III 34 II 34 *e+za*, spelled *e-az*), *unius* (e.g. IV 14 II 79–80 *unius* EN.MEŠ *alla[llā]* [with gloss-wedges] *pānzi* 'the above-mentioned [ibid. 74] lords resort to defection'; *KUB* V 1 III 79 *unius* ZAG.HI.A 'those boundaries'; cf. Ünal, *Hatt.* 2:76–8), *enius* (XXXI 71 IV 10–11 *enius-ma-wa-kan* ARÀH.HI.A *karū mān sarā sannapilahhantes* 'but those granaries [are] as if long ago emptied'; cf. Werner, *Festschrift H. Otten* 327 [1973]), acc. pl. c. *uni* (*KBo* III 4 I 26 *nu-wa-mu-kan uni arahzenas* KUR.KUR [= *udneyandus*] ᴸᵁKÚR *piran kuenni* 'smite for me those alien enemy lands!'; cf. Götze, *AM* 22), *unius* (e.g. *KUB* XXXI 71 III 7–8 *nu-mu-kan imma unius* ANŠU.KUR.RA.MEŠ *awan arha pehuter* 'further they have made away with those horses of mine'; cf. Ünal, *Orakeltext* 122; XVIII 57 III 13–14 *mān-ma asi pattarpalhis unius* [MUŠEN.HI.A] *tarahzi* 'if that p. prevails over those birds'; cf. A. Archi, *SMEA* 16:125 [1975]; V 1 III 48–49 *unius-za-kan kuēs* Ù.MEŠ HUL-*lus uskizzi* IZKIM.HI.A-*ya-za arpuwanta kikistari* '[as for] those bad dreams which he keeps seeing, unlucky signs also occur'), dat.-loc. pl. *edas* (e.g. *KUB* XXIX 4 III 27 *nu edass-a* ANA É.HI.A GIBIL.HI.A *ehu* 'come to these new houses'; cf. Kronasser, *Umsiedelung* 24; XXXI 71 IV 13).

Adverbial (locatival) *edi* and ablative *etez*, *ediz* (+ abl.) 'on that side, beyond' ("remote" deixis, like *apa-* 'that'; opp. *kez* from *ka-* 'this'; cf. *KUB* I 1 II 32–33 *apez ... kezz-a-ma* 'on that side ... but on this side'); *Code* 1:22 *kez* íD-*az* 'on this side of the river' vs. *edi* íD-*az* 'beyond the river'; XIX 9 I 12–13 *etez-a ... kezz-a-ma*; XIX 20 Vs. 9–11 *ediz ... kez*; XIX 37 II 28 *edizz-a-ma-ssi* ᵁᴿᵁ*Kazzapaz* 'but on the other side of K.' (cf. ibid. 27, 29, 33; Götze, *AM* 168–70). Cf. Friedrich, *Staatsverträge* 1:160–1; Götze, *AM* 260–1.

enissan 'thus, as stated' (opp. *kissan* 'thus, as follows'), e.g. *KBo* III 4 III 79 ¹*Pihhuniyas-ma-mu* EGIR-*pa kissan hatrāes* 'P. wrote back to me thus:', followed by message, and ibid. 83–84: *nu-mu mahhan* ¹*Pihhuniyas enissan* EGIR-*pa IŠPUR* 'when P. had written back to me thus' (cf. Götze, *AM* 90).

Cf. Friedrich, *ZA* 36:286–9 (1925), *Staatsverträge* 1:155–6, 73–5; Sommer, *HAB* 161.

Of the etymological interpretations since Hrozný (*SH* 184), chronicled by Tischler (*Glossar* 80–1), only those of Pedersen (*Hitt.* 59–63) and Laroche (in *Hethitisch und Indogermanisch* 147–52 [1979]) recognized the systemic unity of the above anaphoric paradigm. The -*i* of *as-i*, *un-i*, *en-i* is deictic (as in Gk. το-ῖ, οὗτοσ-ί); **as* and **un* are the non-enclitic equivalents of nom. sg. c. -*as* and acc. sg. c. -*un* (generally replaced by -*an*) from -*a-* (q.v.), whereas *eni* is an analogical reshaping of nom.-acc. pl. neut. **e* (cf. enclitic -*e*) after *uni*, to allow for parallel deixis. This archaic paradigm was in unequal competition with the regular, uniform, and productive *apa-* (q.v.), tending towards petrifaction and syncretism of numbers and cases: nom. sg. c. *asi* appears sometimes as acc. sg. c., acc. sg. c. *uni* is occasionally found as acc. pl. c., nom.-acc. neut. *eni* and *ini* function as plural or singular (cf. pl. *ke*, sg. *kī* from *ka-*), with no trace of **at* (cf. enclitic -*at*). There is also a trend to incorporate the deictic -*i* into new *i*-stems *asi-*, *uni-*, *eni-* (as in e.g. Latin **is-pse*, *ea-pse* becoming *ipsus*, *ipsa*) and to decline the latter adjectivally (cf. e.g. Latin *ipsum* replacing **id-pse*): nom. sg. c. *asis*, *unis*, *enis*, acc. sg. c. *unin*, gen. sg. c. *uniyas*, nom. and acc. pl. c. *unius*, *enius*. In this fashion the tie to the non-deictic pronominal forms (*edani*, *etez*, *e*, *edas* matching the standard paradigm *kedani, kez, ke, kedas* from *ka-*) has been increasingly broken. Yet the old opposition nom. sg. c. *as-i*: acc. sg. c. *un-i* (like *kās*: *kūn*) is still at the heart of the Hittite and ancient Indo-European pronominal declension (Skt. *ámas*: *amúm*; cf. e.g. Benveniste, *Hittite* 71–2). The root is thus IE **e-/o-* (*IEW* 281), seen in e.g. Skt. gen. sg. m. n. *a-syá*, dat. sg. m. n. *a-smaí* (= Avest. *ahmāi*, Umbr. *esmei*), gen. pl. m. n. *eṣā́m* (= Avest. *aēṣą̄m*, Umbr. *erom* < **e/o-y-sōm*), dat.-abl. pl. m. n. *ebhyás* (= Avest. *aēibyō*, OLat. *ībus* < **e/o-y-bhyos*).

F. Bader's atomistic analysis *a-si, u-ni, e-ni, e-di* (*Essays in historical linguistics in memory of J. A. Kerns* 36–9 [1981]) is a big step backward.

Cf. *anki, apa-, asma*.

-a-   'he, she, it', nom. sg. *-as* (e.g. *KBo* XXII 2 Rs. 14 *s-as sarā* URU-*ya pait* 'he went up to the town'; cf. Otten, *Altheth. Erzählung* 12), acc. sg. c. *-an* (e.g. *KUB* XXIII 1 II 17 *n-an* ᴵNIR.GÁL-*is dās* 'Muwatallis received him'; cf. Kühne – Otten, *Šaušgamuwa* 10), rarely OHitt. *-un* (*KBo* VIII 42 Vs. 7 *ú-ku-un* 'I him'[?]; XII 63 II 5 *nu-un-na-pa*[), nom.-acc. sg. neut. *-at* (e.g. V 3 III 42 *n-at le iyasi* 'do not do it'; cf. Friedrich, *Staatsverträge* 2:126), nom. pl. c. *-e* (e.g. XXII 2 Rs. 13 *s-e akir* 'they died'; cf. Otten, *Altheth. Erzählung* 12), *-i* (e.g. III 1 II 29 *kuw*]*at-war-i akkanzi* 'why are they put to death?'; IV 14 III 52 *n-i-tta* EGIR-*an uwandu* 'they shall come after you'; cf. R. Stefanini, *ANLR* 20:46 [1965]), *-at* (transfer of neuter ending, e.g. XIII 29 III 9 *n-at akkanzi* 'they die'; cf. Riemschneider, *Geburtsomina* 83), acc. pl. c. *-us* (e.g. XXII 2 Vs. 7 *s-us apasila sallanuskat* 'she brought them up herself'; cf. Otten, *Altheth. Erzählung* 6; *KUB* VIII 65, 22 *nahmi-us* 'I fear them'; cf. Siegelová, *Appu-Hedammu* 44), *-as* (e.g. *KBo* III 23 Vs. 4 *namma-as iski* 'then anoint them'; III 4 I 34 *n-as* ᵁᴿᵁKÙ.BABBAR--*si arha udahhun* 'I brought them off to Hattusas'; cf. Götze, *AM* 22), nom.-acc. pl. neut. *-e* (e.g. *KUB* XXIV 8 IV 12 *n-e-ta ūk mema*[*hhi* 'I will tell you these things'; cf. Siegelová, *Appu-Hedammu* 12; *KBo* V 3 III 24 *n-e-tta ŠAPAL NIŠ* DINGIR--*LIM* DÙ-*ru* 'these things shall be put under divine oath for you';

cf. Friedrich, *Staatsverträge* 2:124), *-at* (identical with nom.-acc. sg.).

Pal. *-a-*, nom. sg. c. *-as*, acc. sg. c. *-an*, nom.-acc. sg. neut. *-at*, nom. pl. c. *-as*, nom.-acc. pl. neut. *-e*. Cf. Carruba, *Das Palaische* 44, 48–9.

Lyd. *-a-*, nom. sg. c. *-aś*, acc. sg. c. *-av*, nom.-acc. sg. neut. *-ad*, *-at*. Cf. Gusmani, *Lyd. Wb.* 50–1.

Luw. *-a-*, nom. sg. c. *-as*, acc. sg. c. *-an*, nom.-acc. sg. and pl. neut. *-ata*. Cf. *Dict. louv.* 22.

Hier. *-a-*, nom. sg. c. *-(a)s*, acc. sg. *-(a)n*, nom.-acc. sg. and pl. neut. *-(a)ta*. Cf. Meriggi, *HHG* 13.

The prehistorically significant endings are nom. sg. c. *-as*, acc. sg. c. *-un*, nom.-acc. sg. neut. *-at*, nom. pl. c. *-e*, nom.-acc. pl. neut. *-e*, and acc. pl. c. *-us*. They are enclitic remnants of the independent pronoun *a-* (q.v.) which was supplanted in all these cases by innovational alternatives (except for OHitt. relics of nom. pl. c. *e*).

Cf. Kammenhuber, *HOAKS* 308–9, *MHT* 2–3, Nr. 4 (1973, 18 p.; 1976, 99 p.).

-a (postconsonantal, mostly with gemination of consonant; also after *-e* sometimes, esp. in OHitt.: *ape-a*), *-ya* (generally after vowel or logogram; rarely spelled *-e-a*; cf. Neu, *Interpretation* 35) 'and; also' (different from *-a* 'but' [q.v.] in Old and Middle Hittite), competes with asyndeton in word-copulation (*attas annas* 'father and mother'), common in clause coordination, but mostly as word- rather than sentence-connective, at least in Old Hittite (cf. Rosenkranz, *Symbolae Biblicae et Mesopotamicae F.M.T. deL. Böhl dedicatae* 320–6 [1973]); in iteration 'both … and' (e.g. *KBo* XVII 1 I 12–13 *irm]a-smas-kan dāhhun kardi-smi-ya-at-kan dāhh[un] [harsa]ni-smi-ya-at-kan dāhhun* 'I have taken your ailment from you, both from your heart have I taken it and from your head have I taken it'; cf. Otten – Souček, *Altheth. Ritual* 18), after negation 'either … or' (e.g. *KUB* XIV 1 Vs. 35 *nu-war-an] sannatti-ya le mu[nn]asi-ya-war-an le* 'neither conceal him nor hide him!' (cf. Götze, *Madd.* 8); for 'also', cf. e.g. *KBo* III 4 I 13 *nu-war-an irmaliattat nu-wa-za* *apāss-a* DINGIR-*LIM-is kisat* 'he became ill, and he too became a god' (cf. Götze, *AM* 18); with generalizing function in *kuiss-a* 'everybody' (acc. sg. c. *kuinn-a*, nom.-acc. sg. neut. *kuitt-a*, gen. sg. *kuēll-a*, dat.-loc. sg. *kuēdani-ya*, acc. pl. *kuiuss-a*; q.v.).

Pal. *-(y)a* (e.g. *KBo* XIX 152 I 17 *tabarnai* SAL*tawannannay-a* 'to king and queen'; *kuis-a* 'everybody'; cf. Carruba, *Das Palaische* 22, 49).

Lyd. *qid-a* 'whatever' (cf. Gusmani, *Lyd. Wb.* 49, 185–6).

Luw. *-ha* 'and; also' (at the end of enumerations: *KUB* IX 31 II 30–31 *uraz* ᴰUTU-*az tatinzi* DINGIR.MEŠ-*inzi* ᴰÉ-A-*as-ha* 'great sungod, father-gods, and Ea'; cf. Otten, *LTU* 16; 'also': XXXV 101 Vs. 9 *nanun-ha-wa-s apatin āsd[u* 'now also let it be thus'; cf. Otten, *LTU* 93; *kuis-ha* 'some[body]'; cf. *Dict. louv.* 37, 56, 145).

Hier. *-ha* (Meriggi, *HHG* 46–8; e.g. Karatepe 15–16 WOMAN--natin tati-ha* 'mother and father', vs. Luw. asyndetic XXXV 43 II 5 *ānniyan tātīyan*; cf. Meriggi, *Manuale* 2:72; Karatepe 185 WOMAN-*tī-ha* 'even women'; cf. Meriggi, *Manuale* 2:80; *kwas--ha* 'some[body]'; cf. Meriggi, *Manuale* 1:58, *HHG* 161–2).

Lyc. B (Milyan) *-ke* 'and' (e.g. *TLy* 44d, 66–67 *se-b[e]-ēnesi--ke tedesi-ke* 'both maternal and paternal'; cf. Friedrich, *KS* 69), Lyc. *ti-ke* 'somebody' (beside *ti-se* 'whoever'; cf. *se* 'and'). Cf. Laroche, *BSL* 53.1:172–4, 190 (1957–8), 55–1:177–8 (1960); Carruba, *Partikeln* 103, 105; Neumann, *HOAKS* 387–8.

Attempts to separate *-a* and *-ya* etymologically (e.g. C. Watkins, *Celtica* 6:16–7 [1963]) do not convince. The form *-ya* is presumably more basic and is occasionally found postconsonantally (e.g. *KBo* XV 34 III 8 and XV 36 I 4 and 11 *memal-ya* instead of usual *memall-a*). The *-a* variant may have been generalized after phonetic loss of *-y-* in certain clusters of consonant+*y*, e.g. *-s+ya*; perhaps the gemination of the preceding consonant has the same source (*memal-ya* would thus be an "etymological spelling", as would post-consonantal *-aya* with graphic pleonasm in e.g. *KUB* VI 41 IV 14 *apātt-aya* 'thus too'; cf. Neumann, *IF* 67:200 [1962], *Kratylos* 8:40 [1963]).

Neumann (*IF* 67:200 [1962]) adduced Goth. *jah*, Toch. A *yo* 'and' (but Toch. B *wai!*); Goth. *jah* was compared already by Marstrander, *Caractère* 126. Cf. further IE **yo-* (*IEW* 283), relative pronoun stem in Indo-Iranian, Greek, Phrygian, and Slavic (possibly also interrogative in Arm. *or* 'who'), also found postpositively in Baltic and Slavic definite adjectives (Lith. *naujàs-is*, OCS *novy-jĭ*) and perhaps incrementally in thematic gen. sg. ending **-os-yo* (for further possibilities, such as Mycen. *jo* in *to-so-jo* = *to-so-de*, and Celt. **-yo* in relative forms of the verb, cf. F. Bader, *Minos* 14:96–109 [1975], *BSL* 70.1:27–89 [1975]); cf. the similar relationship of **-kʷe* 'and' (q.v. s.v. *-k[k]u*) to the interrogative-relative stem **kʷo-/kʷi-* 'who' (see e.g. Götze – Pedersen, *MS* 46; Puhvel, *JAOS* 97:597 [1977]). But attempts to bring *-(y)a-* and South Anatolian *-ha* under a common denominator (e.g. **Hyo-*; J. Greppin, *RHA* 30:85–8 [1972]) fail to convince; if IE **yo-* is cognate with **eyo-* (Skt. *ayám*, etc.), the voiceless laryngeal in **Hyo-* (cf. Gk. ὅς) was E_1 which disappeared in Anatolian. Nor is it likely that Hitt. *-a* (unlike Southern *-ha*) lost the *h* (as assumed by Pedersen, *Arch. Or.* 5:184 [1933]), causing gemination of the preceding consonant (thus C. Watkins, in *Flexion und Wortbildung* 375–6 [1975]). More probably *-ha* represents a dialectal development of the particle seen in Hitt. *kuis-ki*, nom. pl. c. *kuēs-qa* 'somebody' (q.v.; cf. Lyc. *ti-ke*); for the trend $k > h$, cf. e.g. Luw. *mannahunna-* vs. Hitt. *maninkuant-* 'short', or Luw. *nahhuwa-* 'consider important' vs. Hitt. *nakkiyahh-*. Cf. *-k(k)u*.

-a 'but', without gemination of preceding consonant in Old and Middle Hittite, as opposed to *-a* 'and; also' (q.v.), e.g. *KBo* VI 2 II 29 (= *Code* 1:42) *takku kussan-a natta piyān* 'but if pay is not given' (vs. VI 2 IV 5 [= *Code* 1:76] *kussassett-a pāi* 'and he gives his pay'); XVII 1 I 7 *u]g-a arhari* 'but I am standing', ibid. 21–22 *wes-a namma anda paiwani* 'but we go in again' (vs. ibid. IV 7 *nu* ᴸᵁAZU *ūgg-a paiwani* 'we go, the medicine man and I'; cf. Otten – Souček, *Altheth. Ritual* 18, 20, 36).

Similarly *kuis-a* 'whoever' vs. *kuiss-a* 'everybody' (e.g. *KBo* III 1 II 46 *namma kuis-a* LUGAL-*us kisari* 'whoever hereafter becomes king'; but ibid. I 17–18 *nu* DUMU.MEŠ-*ŠU kuiss-a kuwatta udnē paizzi* 'and his sons, each goes to one country').

In later texts the preceding consonant tends to be doubled also before *-a* 'but'; alternatively *-a* is either omitted or replaced by *-ma* 'but'. Cf. Houwink Ten Cate, *Acta Orientalia Neerlandica* 39–42 (1971), *Festschrift H. Otten* 119–39 (1973).

Probably an adverbial form of the pronominal stem IE **e-/o-* (Hitt. *a-*, *-a-*, q.v.); cf. e.g. OCS *a*, Lith. õ 'but' (*IEW* 283–4).

ā-, ay-, e-   'be warm, be hot', 3 sg. pres. midd. *āri* (*KUB* XX 88 Rs. 21 *mahhan-ma-ssan* UTÚL.HI.A-*TIM āri* 'but when the dish is hot'; XXV 44 V 12), *ari* (e.g. *KBo* V 1 III 52 *mahhan-ma-ssan* VII ᴰᵁᴳLIŠ.GAL *ari* 'but when the seventh plate is hot'; cf. Sommer – Ehelolf, *Pāpanikri* 10*; XIII 167 II 7–8 IZI-*nit zanuwanzi* [...] UTÚL.HI.A *ari* 'they cook with fire ... [but when] the dish is hot'; ibid. III 6–7 IZI-*it zanuanzi* [...] ᵁᶻᵁ*suppa ari* '... the meat is hot'; *KUB* XVII 28 IV 39 GIM-*an-ma-ssan* UTÚL.HI.A UZU *ari* 'but when the meat dish is hot'; *HT* 1 I 49 *nu-ssan mahhan* ᵁᶻᵁYÀ *ari* 'when the fat is hot'; *KBo* XV 37 III 42), 3 pl. pres. midd. *āanta* (*VBoT* 58 I 24 *k]āsa-wa ammel tueggas-mes āanta* 'lo, my limbs are hot'; cf. Laroche, *RHA* 23:83 [1965]); partic. *ānt-* 'warm, hot', nom. sg. *ānza* (e.g. *KBo* XIII 10 Vs. 6 *āanza* INIM-*as* 'hot matter'; cf. ibid. 7–8; *KUB* XLV 20 I 2 *āanza* NA₄-*as* 'hot stone'), acc. sg. c. *āntan* (ibid. 1 *āantann-a* NA₄-*an*; cf. Neu, *Interpretation* 68; XXXIII 70 II 5 *āantan*; cf. Laroche, *RHA* 23:161 [1965]), nom.-acc. sg. neut. *ān* (e.g. I 11 III 5 *mekki āan* 'very warm'; cf. Kammenhuber, *Hippologia* 114, 323), also in NINDA *āan* 'hotcake' (e.g. *KBo* V 1 I 55; cf. Sommer – Ehelolf, *Pāpanikri* 4*; *KUB* VII 53 I 22, XII 58 IV 29; cf. Goetze, *Tunnawi* 6, 22), gen. sg. *a-a-da-as* (VIII 62 I 13 *ādas* NINDA-*as*; cf. Laroche, *RHA* 26:23 [1968]), instr. sg. *āntet* (passim in Kikkulis-text, e.g. I 11 IV 17–18 *n-as āantet wetenit āandan arha arranzi* 'they wash them off warmly with warm water'; for attestations and incorrect adverbial *āndan* for *ān*, cf. Kammenhuber, *Hippologia* 322–3), abl. sg. *āndaz* (VIII 38 + XLIV 63 III 20–21 *namma-an āandaz* S-*az* ... *arha ānaszi* 'then he wipes him off with warm water'; cf. Burde, *Medizinische Texte* 30), nom. pl. c. *āntes* (e.g. XXXIV 101, 5 *āantes*

NA₄.HI.A; *KBo* XIX 145 III 30 and 32; cf. Haas – Thiel, *Rituale* 302), acc. pl. c. *āndus* (e.g. *KUB* XVII 23 II 16–17 ᴺᴬ⁴*passilus āandus* 'hot pebbles'; cf. ibid. 12–13; same in VII 53 II 22; cf. Goetze, *Tunnawi* 12; XXXIII 49 II 6 *ā]andus* ᴺᴬ⁴*passilus*; cf. Laroche, *RHA* 23:143 [1965]; *KBo* III 5 III 33 *āandus arha arruizzi* 'he washes them off [while they are] warm'; cf. Kammenhuber, *Hippologia* 96), nom.-acc. pl. neut. *ānda* (perhaps XLIII 53 I 18 *āanda-ssan pis[kimi* 'I give hot things'; cf. *KBo* XVII 17 IV 7 and Haas, *Orientalia* N.S. 40:416 [1971]; XVII 65 Rs. 21 NINDA *āanta* 'hotcakes'), *ān*HI.A (e.g. *KUB* X 91 III 11, XXXII 99 V 3 NINDA *āan*HI.A), dat.-loc. pl. *āantas* (*KBo* XV 37 I 58 ANA NINDA *āantas*), *āandas* (ibid. III 61; XV 49 IV 11). Cf. Neu, *Interpretation* 1, *IF* 81:300–3 (1976), *IF* 82:271 (1977); Oettinger, *MSS* 34:136 (1976).

Plausibly unrelated e.g. nom. sg. c. *āanza kuis* (I 30 Vs. 2 and 3), nom.-acc. sg. neut. *āan* (*KUB* V 1 I 66), and XVII 31 I 6 LÚ.MEŠ *āandas iwar* (dupl. *KBo* XV 2 IV 4 LÚ *āandas*); to be read rather A.A-*anza* or A.A-*an(-za)*? Cf. Kümmel, *Ersatzrituale* 60, 90; *MSL* 12:215, 218 (1969); *HW²* 44.

enu-, inu- 'make hot, fry', 3 sg. pres. act. *enuzi* (*KUB* XLIV 61 Rs. 20; cf. Burde, *Medizinische Texte* 20), *inuzzi* (*VAT* 7508 Vs. 9), 3 pl. pres. act. *inuwanzi* (*Bo* 3217 Vs. 7 IŠ]*TU* IZI-*at inuwanzi* 'they fry it with fire'), *inuanzi* (*KBo* XXI 21 III 9; cf. Burde, *Medizinische Texte* 37; Otten, *Materialien* 37), 2 pl. pret. act. *inutten* (XXII 2 Vs. 9; cf. Otten, *Altheth. Erzählung* 6, 28–9); iter. *inuski-*, 3 sg. pres. midd. *inuskittari* (XIII 119 I 7; cf. Neu, *Interpretation* 71), 3 sg. imp. act. *inuskidu* 'let him fry' (VI 34 II 27, paralleling ibid. 22 *zanuanzi* 'they cook'; cf. Oettinger, *Eide* 10).

enumai- 'become hot' (?), 3 pl. pres. midd. *enumandari* (*KUB* I 13 II 37–38 *mahhan-ma enumandari [namm]a* ÍD-*i pehudanzi* 'but when they become hot, one takes them to the river'; cf. Kammenhuber, *Hippologia* 60). Perhaps parallel to *esharnumai-* 'to bloody'; cf. (denom.) *esharnu-* beside (deverb.) *enu-* (see Neu, *Interpretation* 23). On the probably unpertaining Hurrian *enumassi* cf. e.g. Haas – Wilhelm, *Riten* 75–7; Laroche, *RHA* 34:82 (1976).

ayis(s)- 'become hot' (?), 3 pl. pres. act. *ayissanzi* (XXIX 55

II 2; XXIX 44 II 6 and III 5; cf. Kammenhuber, *Hippologia* 154, 158, 162), describing a condition of racehorses followed by washing (cf. *āandus arha arruizzi* and *enumai-* above). Deverb. inchoative like *hates-, lukkes-, kartimmies-, karpies-* (q.v.). Cf. Rosenkranz, *IF* 68:88 (1963); Neu, *Interpretation* 17–8; Puhvel, *JAOS* 97:597 (1977).

Because of the causative *enu-* (< *ai-nu-*) and the inchoative *ayis-* (< *ay-es-*) it is plausible that the spelling *a-a-* of *ā-* points to an etymological **aya-* (cf. Goetze's similar though improbable suggestion s.v. *ara-*, at the end). Cf. in that case IE **ay(-dh)-* 'burn' (*IEW* 11), as suggested by Sturtevant, *Lg.* 14:70 (1938), *Comp. Gr.*² 18, 53; cf. Neu, *Interpretation* 1, *IF* 81:302 (1976); Oettinger, *Eide* 34; H. A. Hoffner, *Alimenta Hethaeorum* 153 (1974); E. P. Hamp, in *Evidence for laryngeals* 126–7 (1965), who adduced Alban. *hī* 'ashes'; O. Szemerényi, *Gnomon* 43:655 (1971), who saw an Asianic loan **a(ya)ntu-rahhi* in Gk. ἄνθραξ 'charcoal'. By the same token Benveniste's adduction (*Hittite* 107) of the isolated Skt. *antī-, antikā* 'hearth, oven' and OIr. *áith* 'stove, oven' (< **āti-*) loses in likelihood, as does the comparison with Arm. *antʻeł* 'fire with ashes' (T. Schultheiss, *KZ* 77:225–6 [1961]).

Carruba (*Das Palaische* 53) equated Hitt. *ā-* with Pal. *hā-* 'be hot', whose true cognate is Hitt. *hantais-* 'heat' (q.v. infra et s.v.).

Cf. *hantais-* 'heat', *wantai-* 'be warm'; at best rhyme words are involved. Kronasser (*Etym.* 1:88–9) improbably assumed etymological unity with initial phoneme variation; H. Wittmann's suggestion of prefix variation (*Die Sprache* 19:42 [1973]) is no improvement.

ahrushi-   (c.), often with determinative [DUG], 'incense vessel, censer, thurible', nom. sg. *ahrushis* (e.g. *KUB* XXX 40 II 1; XXV 49 II 20), acc. sg. *ahrushin* (*KBo* XIX 148, 5), [DUG]*ahrushin* (XXIII 34 I 3 and 16), *āhrushin* (*KUB* XXXII 128 II 5), [DUG]*āhrushin* (*KBo* XXIII 44 I 7), dat.-loc. sg. *ahrushi* (e.g. *KUB* XI 31 I 8; XXV 42 III 12), *āhrushi* (e.g. *KBo* XV 49 I 16), *āhrushiya* (e.g. *KUB* XXVII 19 III 6), [DUG]*ahrushiti* (XXV 42 V 16, with Hurrian ending; cf. Friedrich, *RHA* 8:13 [1947]), abl. sg. *āhrushiyaz* (e.g. *KBo* XXI 33 I 14; cf. Otten, *Materialien* 35), *āhrūshiyaz* (e.g. ibid. III 6), *āhrushiaz* (e.g. *KUB* XII 12 V 2); also undeclined (or sometimes dat.-loc. sg.?) in asyndetic combination with *huprushi-* (*ahrushi huprushi*, e.g. XXVII 1 III 7 [syntactically acc.]; cf. Lebrun, *Samuha* 81; *KBo* XIV 127 IV 8 [syntact. dat.]). Cf. Neu, *IF* 81:303–4 (1976).

Loanword from Hurrian (also in Akk. at Alalah; cf. *CAD* A 1:194–5), derived with suffix *-ushi-* from *ah(a)r-* (*aharri, āhri*) 'incense' (cf. *huprushi-*, s.v.); cf. e.g. *KUB* XXXII 50 Vs. 3 (Hurr.) *āhriya hūbriya*, ibid. 22 *āhrushiya hūbrushiya* (cf. Haas – Wilhelm, *Riten* 245–6); also XLVII 84 Vs. 2 ^{DUG}*ahrushi-ni*, *RS* 24:274, 14–15 *ağrshnd hbrshnd* (i.e. *ahrushi-ni-da hubrushi--ni-da*). Cf. Götze – Pedersen, *MS* 43; Goetze, *JCS* 22:17 (1968); Laroche, *Ugaritica* 5:504–7, 513, *RHA* 28:70 (1970), 34:37–8 (1976); Haas – Wilhelm, *Riten* 103–5. Furnée (*Erscheinungen* 369) compared Gk. κρωσσός 'pitcher, urn' as a "Mediterranean" vessel name.

ayawala- (c.) 'agent, stand-in, deputy'(?), in *KUB* XIV 3 I 11–12 ^{LÚ}*TARTENU-ma ŪL ANA* LUGAL *ayawalas* 'is not the crown prince the deputy of the king?' (cf. Sommer, *AU* 2).

For the suffix, cf. *tarassawala-* 'spokesman, counsel' (s.v.), *karpiwala-* 'furious'. Possibly Luwoid, from *aya-* 'do, make', thus literally 'agent' (cf. *Dict. louv.* 24). Cf. Sommer, *AU* 41–54; N. van Brock, *RHA* 20:95–6 (1962); Kronasser, *Etym.* 1:174. H. C. Melchert *IF* 85:90–5 [1980] suggested 'son' (= DUMU-la-).

a(y)i- (c.) 'pain', basically interjection, acc. sg. in *KBo* XVII 3 IV 26–27 *dā* LUGAL-*as* SAL.LUGAL-*sa ayin (u)wāyin pittulius--(s)muss-a* 'take away the king's and queen's pain, woe, and anxieties' (similarly ibid. 35 = XVII 1 IV 40; XVII 1 IV 14; XVII 7, 9; cf. Otten – Souček, *Altheth. Ritual* 36–40, 93); cf. *uwai-* (n.) 'woe' (s.v.).

Cf. *KBo* XIII 1 + XXVI 21 I 61–63 Akk. *ú-i* = Hitt. *ú-i*, Akk. *a-i* = Hitt. *a-i*, Akk. *ṣarah*[*u*] 'lament' = Hitt. [*pid*]*duliyas* 'anxiety' (Otten, *Vokabular* 11, 18); XIII 119 III 24 *a-i a-i a-i*; XXI 19 Rs. 2 *a-a-i*; *KUB* XXVIII 6 Vs. 16b *a-i* (with gloss-wedge). *KUB* XI 1 IV 7 and 14 *a-a-i pa-ap-pí* resembles Homeric ὦ πόποι (H. Berman, per litt.). For [*a-w*]*a*ₐ*-a-i-ya a-wa*ₐ*-a-i-ya* 'alas, alas' see Neu, *Anitta-Text* 82–3.

Similar rhyming jingles are the Luwoid magical formula *āhras wahras, āhra(n) wahran* (often with *allap*[*p*]*ahh-* 'spit'; perhaps something like "abracadabra"; cf. Rosenkranz, *Beiträge* 49–53; Otten, *Bestimmung* 92–3; *Dict. louv.* 23), *astas wastas* (*KUB* II 1 II 30), ᴰ*Atammira* ᴰ*Watammira* (XLVII 73 II 8).

For other IE attestations of such interjections see *IEW* 10, 1110–1.

aikawartanna- 'one turn', Indo-Aryan technical expression (via Hurrian) in Kikkulis-text, *KBo* III 5 I 17 *namma-as ... aikawartanna parhāi* 'he drives them one turn'; ibid. 21 *aika wartanna* (cf. Kammenhuber, *Hippologia* 80).

Composed of elements comparable with Skt. *éka-* 'one' (< **aika-*, vs. Avest. *aēva-*; not from **aivaka-*) and *vártana-* (n.) 'turn(ing)'; cf. *vartaní-* (f.) 'turning, course, circumference', *eka-vŕt-* 'onefold, simple'. On the Iranian side there are specifically hippological uses of the root *vart-*, e.g. Ossetic (Iron) *äwwärdyn* 'to train horses', Sogdian *wartan* 'chariot'. Cf. Kronasser, *Etym.* 1:144; Kammenhuber, *Die Arier* 201–3; H. W. Bailey, *Rocznik orientalistyczny* 21:64 (1957); V. V. Ivanov, *Mélanges linguistiques offerts à Émile Benveniste* 283–8 (1975), *Etimologija 1979* 132–4 (1981).

(a)impa- (c.) 'weight, burden' (literal and figurative), acc. sg. *aimpan* (*KUB* XXXIII 112+ IV 10; cf. Laroche, *RHA* 26:35 [1968]; XXXIII 120 I 30–31 ɪɴᴀ šà-ᴋᴀ-*ta-kkan anda aimpan tehhun* 'in your innards I have placed a burden'; cf. Güterbock, *Kumarbi *2*; Laroche, *RHA* 26:41 [1968]; XXXVI 74, 2 *aimpan ardumēni* 'let us saw [off] the burden'; cf. Siegelová, *Arch. Or.* 38:136 [1970]), *impan* (*KBo* XVII 54 I 10 ᴢɪ-*nas impan lāu* 'let

14

him loose the soul's burden'; cf. Haas, *Orientalia* N.S. 40:419 [1971]; *KUB* IX 4 III 37 zi-*as impan*; cf. Goetze, *JAOS* 69:181 [1949]), dat.-loc. sg. *aimpi* (*Bo* 2073 IV 9 *nu-wa aimpi piran kā zappeskimi* 'from the burden I keep dripping [sweat] here'), acc. pl. *ayimpus* (*KUB* XXXIII 120 I 33–34 DINGIR.MEŠ-*ya-ta-kkan hatugaus* INA ŠÀ-KA *anda ayimpus tehhun* 'terrible gods have I put as burdens inside your bowels').

anda impai- 'be burdened, be depressed', verbal noun *anda- -kan impauwar* (*KBo* I 42 III 53, glossed by Akk. *ašašum* 'load down'; cf. *MSL* 13:139 [1971]); iter. 2 sg. pres. midd. in *KUB* XXXIII 76, 17 *anda l]e impaiskatta* 'be not depressed'; XXXIII 68 II 6 *nu-za-sa namma anda le impanaitta* 'be depressed no more' (cf. Laroche, *RHA* 23:128 [1965]); caus. *aimpanu-* 'burden, beset', 3 sg. pres. act. in V 1 IV 77–78 *mān-kan* KARAŠ.HI.A ... *hēus* DUGUD-*us* ŪL *anda aimpanuzi* 'if heavy rain does not beset the army' (cf. Laroche, *RA* 45:96 [1951]; Ünal, *Hatt.* 2:88–90).

The *a-* may be somehow incremental, especially in view of the hiatus breaker *r* attested in *KBo* XX 82 II 31 *nu-wa-mu* ANA ZI-YA *arimpan* [...] *dāis* 'and placed a burden upon my soul' (cf. Carruba, *Beschwörungsritual* 28–9); but cf. also ᴳᴵˢ*arimpa-*, s.v.; *a(r)impa-* is reminiscent of *lilai-, lilariski-* (q.v.; cf. Neu, *IF* 82:272 [1977]). *impa-* is plausibly comparable with Gk. ἶπος 'weight, press', fut. ἴψομαι, aor. ἰψάμην (*Iliad+*) 'bear down on, oppress, vex, harm', ἴπτω· βλάπτω (*EM* 481.3), ἰμφθείς· βλαφθείς (Hes.). Origin unknown, presumably noun borrowed from some common source into both Hittite and Greek, with independently developed denominative verbs (*impai-*; *ἴ(μ)π- -ιω > ἴ(μ)πτω*, later also ἰπόω). Cf. Furnée, *Erscheinungen* 271.

a(y)is(s)-, iss-   (n.) 'mouth' (KAxU, e.g. *KUB* XXIX 10 I 10 *is- saz* = XXIX 9 I 14 KAxU-*az*; akkadogram PŪ in *KBo* XVII 105 II 30 PŪ-*i-smi* 'into their mouth', ibid. 33 PŪ-*iya-smi* 'in their mouth', besides ibid. 41 KAxU-*i-smi*, 37 ᵁᶻᵁKAxU-*ŠUNU*), nom.- acc. sg. *ayis* (e.g. XVII 1 I 15 LUGAL-*us* 3-*šu ayis-set ārri* 'the king washes his mouth three times'; cf. Otten – Souček, *Altheth. Ritual* 18; *KUB* XLI 23 III 10 *ayis-(s)mit āratten* 'you [pl.]

wash your mouth!'; XXXVI 91 I 9 and *VBoT* 58 IV 6
ayis-(s?)mit; cf. Laroche, *RHA* 23:85 [1965]; *KUB* VII 1 I 29
n-asta DUMU-*an ayis-sis* [error for -*sit*] *parā arrahhi* 'then I rinse
out the child's mouth'; cf. Kronasser, *Die Sprache* 7:143
[1961]), KAxU-*yis* (*KBo* VIII 56, 6), *ais* (e.g. XII 18 I 8 [OHitt.];
XV 10 I 17 [nom.], ibid. II 8 and III 50 [voc.], followed by EME
'tongue'; cf. Szabó, *Entsühnungsritual* 14, 20, 42; XII 96 I 9–10
ais-za-kan YÀ-*it sūwanza ēs* 'have your mouth filled with fat'; cf.
Rosenkranz, *Orientalia* N.S. 33:239 [1964]; Neu, *IF* 81:304
[1976]; *KUB* XII 63 Rs. 11 *ais-(s)umet*; XIV 4 IV 15 *nu* GIG-*an*
antuhsan ais arha huuittiyat '[he] withdrew [?] the mouth of the
sick man'; XXIX 8 IV 37 *ais suppiyahhuwas* 'mouth-cleansing
[ritual]', Akk. *mēs pī*), KAxU-*is* (e.g. *KBo* III 8 III 35 ᵁᶻᵁKAxU-*is*
hamikta 'he has tied the mouth'; cf. Kronasser, *Die Sprache*
7:158 [1961]; *KUB* XXVI 1 III 64 *apas-ma* KAxU-*is duwarnāi*
'but he breaks his silence [literally: mouth]'; cf. von Schuler,
Dienstanweisungen 14), gen. sg. *issas* (e.g. XXIV 13 II 5 and 25;
cf. Haas–Thiel, *Rituale* 104), dat.-loc. sg. *issi* (VII 1 I 29–30
EGIR-*anda-ma-ssi-kan issi-ssi lahuhhi* 'but afterwards I pour into
his mouth'; cf. Kronasser, *Die Sprache* 7:143 [1961]; VII 5 II
12–13 *n-at-za-kan issi-ssi dāi ekuzi-ya* 3-*ŠU* ᴰ*Uliliyassin* 'he puts
it in his mouth and drinks three times [to] god U.'; XIII 7 I 16),
issī (e.g. *KBo* V 2 IV 60 *nu-kan* … KÙ.BABBAR *issī anda dāi* 'he
puts silver in [so-and-so's] mouth'; XVI 97 Rs. 5 and 9; IX 112
Vs. 5; *KUB* XLIII 53 I 21 *ay]is-set-a issī* GAL-*li* 'his mouth [is]
big [in relation] to the [other's] mouth'; cf. ibid. 4 and Haas,
Orientalia N.S. 40:415–6 [1971]; XV 42 III 32), *ayissi* (*KBo*
VIII 75, 6 *nu-ssi-kan] ayissi anda alla[pahhanzi* 'they spit in his
mouth'), KAxU-*i* (e.g. IV 2 III 42–43 *nu-mu-kan memiyas* KAxU-*i*
anda tepawesta 'word became scant in my mouth'; cf. Götze –
Pedersen, *MS* 4), *issa* (XVII 2 I 6 and 8 *issa-sma* 'into their
mouth'; cf. Otten – Souček, *Altheth. Ritual* 16; III 38 Vs. 4
issa-ssa 'into his mouth'; cf. Otten, *Altheth. Erzählung* 8; XIII
100, 7 *issa-ma-ssi* 'but into his mouth'), instr. sg. *issit* (e.g. *KUB*
XXXI 135 Vs. 11; *KBo* IX 106 III 3 *issit* EME-*it* 'with mouth
[and] tongue'), KAxU-*it* (e.g. ibid. II 57; *KUB* XLV 7 III 7; cf.
Riemschneider, *Geburtsomina* 53), abl. sg. *issaz* (*KBo* XVII 1 I
18–19 *issaz-(s)mit lālan* AN.BAR-*as dāi* '[he] takes from their

mouth the iron tongue'; cf. Otten – Souček, *Altheth. Ritual* 20;
KUB XI 1 IV 8; *KBo* XV 10 I 15; cf. Szabó, *Entsühnungsritual*
14; *KUB* VII 52 Vs. 9; XXXVI 55 II 40), *issāz* (XXXV 148 III
4), dat.-loc. pl. *issas* (XLIII 68 Rs. 9). Cf. Friedrich, *IF* 41:376
(1923); Ehelolf, *OLZ* 36:6 (1933); Sommer, *Festschrift für
Hermann Hirt* 2:291–6 (1936); Kronasser, *Etym.* 1:160, 304.

Exceptional acc. sg. c. (some animate gender synonym?) in
KAxU-*an* (*KBo* V 1 IV 4; cf. Sommer – Ehelolf, *Pāpanikri* 12*;
XVIII 39, 8); acc. pl. c. in *KUB* XIV 4 II 10 *apās-ma*
KAxU.HI.A-*us anda hamanakta* 'that one tied the mouths'. Cf.
Neu, *IF* 81:304–5 (1976).

Luw. *ās(sa)-* 'mouth' (?) perhaps in XXXV 39 II 10 and 26
āssammas (cf. ibid. 7 KAxU-*ŠU*), ibid. 14 *āssati*; but XXXV 88 II
6 *āassanta* (cf. ibid. III 9 *āssatta*) is a verbal form. Cf. Otten,
LTU 39, 86; Bossert, *Orientalia* N.S. 29:426–7 (1960); Meriggi,
Festschrift Johannes Friedrich 337 (1959), *RHA* 18:107 (1960),
OLZ 57:259 (1962); Laroche, *RHA* 23:45 (1965).

Cognate with Skt. *ās-*, Avest. *āh-*, Lat. *ōs* 'mouth' (*IEW*
784–5). Perhaps nom.-acc. sg. $*A_1^w \acute{e}E_1\text{-}es > *\bar{o}yes > *\bar{a}yes > *\bar{a}yis$
(vs. Skt. *ās-*, Lat. $\bar{o}s < *A_1^w \acute{e}E_1\text{-}s$), with ablauting gen. sg.
$*A_1^w E_1 es\text{-}\acute{o}s > *esas$. Luw. *ās(sa)-* may match the Indo-Iranian
and Latin type, or show the typical Luwian *a*-overlay: $*\bar{a}yas\text{-}$
$> *\bar{a}s\text{-}$. Cf. E. Risch, *Sommer Corolla* 196–7; Puhvel, *LIEV* 55;
F. O. Lindeman, *To Honor Roman Jakobson* 1188–80 (1967);
H. Eichner, *MSS* 31:84 (1973), *Die Sprache* 24:162 (1978); J.
Schindler, in *Flexion und Wortbildung* 264 (1975). For different
older reconstructions, see e.g. Pedersen, *Hitt.* 47; Sturtevant,
Lg. 14:292 (1938); for unconvincing more recent attempts,
Kronasser, *Etym.* 1:35, 42; Ch.-J. N. Bailey, *Working Papers in
Linguistics* 2.1, 5 and 136 (Univ. of Hawaii, 1970); A. Bernabé
P., *Revista española de lingüística* 3:425–6 (1973). R. Schmitt-
Brandt's derivation from an **ay-* 'speak' (*Entwicklung* 86) is
implausible. Cf. *issalli-*, *zasgarais* (s.v. *sakkar*).

ak(k)-, ek- 'die; be killed (passive to *kuen-* 'kill', like Gk. ἀποθνή-
σκω to ἀποκτείνω); be put to death by judicial sentence, be
legally executed (like Gk. ἀποθανεῖν ὑπὸ τῆς πόλεως); be

eclipsed' (UG₆), 1 sg. pres. act. *ākmi* (*KUB* XL 33 Vs. 23), *akmi* (XXIV 5+IX 13 Vs. 16=XXXVI 93 Vs. 10; cf. Kümmel, *Ersatzrituale* 8), 2 sg. pres. act. (OHitt.) *ākti* (*KBo* VII 14+*KUB* XXXVI 100 II 6), *akti* (e.g. *KUB* VIII 63 I 3; XXIII 1 II 36; cf. Kühne – Otten, *Šaušgamuwa* 10, 40–1; XXXVI 57 III 8 *nu akti harakti* 'you die [and] perish'; cf. Siegelová, *Appu-Hedammu* 62), 3 sg. pres. act. *aki* (e.g. *Code* 1:6 *takku ... takiya* URU-*ri aki* 'if he is killed in another city'; *KBo* V 3 III 31 *n-as* URU*Hattusi* ŪL *huuissuuizzi aki-pa* 'he does not stay alive at Hattusas; he is put to death'; cf. Friedrich, *Staatsverträge* 2:124; *KUB* VIII 1 passim ᴰ*SIN-as aki* 'the moon is eclipsed'), 1 pl. pres. act. *akkueni* (XVII 1 II 18 *nu* HUR.SAG-*i akkueni* 'will we die in the mountains?'), *ak-ku-u-e-ni* (ibid. 24; cf. Friedrich, *ZA* 49:238 [1950]), 2 pl. pres. act. *ākteni* (*KBo* III 23 Rs. 4; cf. A. Archi, in *Florilegium Anatolicum* 41 [1979]), 3 pl. pres. act. *akkanzi* (e.g. *Code* 1:37, 2:66; IV 14 III 37 ANA LUGAL ÌR.MEŠ ZI *akkanzi* 'intimate servants die for the king'; cf. ibid. II 55; R. Stefanini, *ANLR* 20:46, 69 [1965]), 3 sg. pret. act. (OHitt.) *ākkis* (e.g. VI 2 IV 3 [=*Code* 1:75]; cf. Haase, *Fragmente* 41), *akkis* (III 46 Vs. 48), *akis* (?; III 34 II 12; III 36 Vs. 18; but cf. Otten, *IF* 80:226–7 [1975]), *akta* (e.g. V 9 Vs. 26; XIII 3 III 35), *aggas* (?; *VBoT* 1, 24; cf. L. Rost, *MIO* 4:335, 338 [1956]), often BA.UG₆ (e.g. *KBo* III 38 Vs. 14; cf. Otten, *Altheth. Erzählung* 8), 2 pl. pret. act. *ākten* (*KUB* XIV 1 Vs. 12 *kāstita-man ākten* 'you would have died of hunger'; cf. Götze, *Madd.* 4; Otten, *Sprachliche Stellung* 11), 3 pl. pret. act. *a-ki-ir* (e.g. *KBo* III 38 Rs. 22; cf. Otten, *Altheth. Erzählung* 10; *KUB* XXVI 69 VI 13 *n-at kasti akir* 'they died of hunger'; cf. Werner, *Gerichtspro-tokolle* 44; *VBoT* 58 I 32, 33, 35; *KUB* XXIV 4 Vs. 4), *a-kir* (e.g. *KBo* XXII 2 Rs. 6 and 13; cf. Otten, *Altheth. Erzählung* 10, 12; III 46 Vs. 38; *KUB* XIV 14 Vs. 36; cf. Götze, *KlF* 168), *e-ki-ir* (*KBo* III 38 Rs. 29), *e-kir* (e.g. *KUB* I 8 IV 26 *nu kuyēs* IŠTU GIŠTUKUL *ekir kuyēs-ma* UD.KAM-*za ekir* 'some died by weapon, but others died on the day'; cf. Götze, *Hattusilis* 34; Puhvel, *Studia classica et orientalia Antonino Pagliaro oblata* 3:174 [1969]; XXIV 3 II 7, 10, 13; cf. Gurney, *Hittite Prayers* 26), 1 sg. imp. act. *akkallu* (XIV 1 Rs. 94; cf. Götze, *Madd.* 38), *aggallu* (*KBo* IV 14 II 35; cf. R. Stefanini, *ANLR* 20:41 [1965];

KUB XIX 9 IV 4; XXI 19 + 1193/u III 35 *nu-wa* ANA ^{URU}*Nerik ser aggallu-pat* 'let me die for Nerik!'), 2 sg. imp. act. *āk* (*KBo* IV 14 II 16 *nu* LUGAL-*i* UGU *āk* 'die for the king!'; cf. ibid. 25, 65, 72; R. Stefanini, *ANLR* 20:40, 43 [1965]; *KUB* XXIII 1 + III 25; cf. Kühne – Otten, *Šaušgamuwa* 12), 3 sg. imp. act. *aku* (e.g. *KBo* III 67 II 2; *KUB* XI 1 IV 20 *takku tezzi aku-war-as n-as aku* 'if he says: let him die, then let him die'; XXXI 74 II 11 *n-as aku*, ibid. III 7 *nu apās aku* 'let him die'; *KBo* XVI 25 III 9; *KUB* XIII 3 III 31; XIII 7 I 23; XIV 4 III 20; XXIII 68 Vs. 27 *apāt* É-*ir* LÚ.MEŠ-*it aku* 'this house with the men shall die'; cf. A. Kempinski – S. Košak, *Die Welt des Orients* 5:194 [1970]), *akdu* (VIII 48 I 9; cf. Laroche, *RHA* 26:17 [1968]), 3 pl. imp. act. *akkantu* (XXXVI 113, 5), *akkandu* (e.g. *Code* 2:98 2-*pat akkandu* 'let them both die!'; *KUB* XXIV 5 + IX 13 Vs. 16); partic. *akkant-* 'dead; dead person; soul of a dead person, ghost' (GIDIM), nom. sg. c. *akkanza* (e.g. *KBo* XIII 58 III 10; *KUB* XXXI 66 I 29 *akkanza* TI-*anz-as* 'the dead, he [is] alive'), *agganza* (XLIII 72 III 3 *mān-as agganza mān-as* TI-*anza* 'whether he [is] dead or alive'), *āggānza* (XXIII 72 Rs. 14 *nu antuwahhas kuis āggānza* 'the man who is dead'), acc. sg. c. *akkantan* (e.g. XXX 17 Vs. 7; cf. Otten, *Totenrituale* 52), *akkandan* (XXX 25 + Rs. 20; cf. Otten, *Totenrituale* 28), *aggatan* (*KBo* XIX 120 II 6 *nu-mu aggatan harkanta*[*n* 'the one that died and perished'), gen. sg. *akkantas* (e.g. *akkantas* ZI 'the soul of the dead'; cf. Otten, *Totenrituale*, passim), *akkandas* (e.g. XXXIX 15 I 7; cf. Otten, *Totenrituale* 82), dat.-loc. sg. *akkanti* (e.g. Otten, *Totenrituale*, passim), instr. sg. *akkantit* (XXIX 34 + 37 IV 11 [= *Code* 2:90]), nom. pl. c. *akkantes* (cf. Otten – Souček, *Gelübde* 18), acc. pl. c. *akkanduss-a* 'and the dead' (*KBo* III 3 I 16), gen. pl. in *aggantas hatugatar* 'terror of the dead' (see ref. s.v. *hatuk-*) and *akkantas hūlali*[(see ref. s.v. *hul*[*a*]-), dat.-loc. pl. *aggandas* (*KUB* XII 58 II 7; cf. Goetze, *Tunnawi* 12); verbal noun *aggatar* (n.) 'death', nom.-acc. sg. *aggatar* (e.g. XIII 5 II 16, XIII 6 II 36 SAG.DU-*as aggatar* = XIII 4 II 45 SAG.DU-*as* UG₆-*tar* 'capital penalty'; cf. Sturtevant, *JAOS* 54:372, 376 [1934]; cf. ibid. IV 66 SAG.DU-*as wastul* 'capital sin': Sturtevant, *JAOS* 54:396; Kammenhuber, *ZA* 56:173 [1964]; not 'beheading', despite J. Holt, *Arch. Or.*

17.1:317 [1949]; XV 2 IV 5 ANA LUGAL *aggatar* 'death to the
king'; cf. Kümmel, *Ersatzrituale* 70; XXI 27 I 48 ANA ^{URU}*Neriqqa ser aggatar ē*[*sdu* 'for Nerik let there be death'; cf. A.
Archi, *SMEA* 14:192 [1971]; XXXIII 106 III 34 ^DU-*ni* IGI-*anda
aggatar sanheskizzi* '[Kumarbi] plans death against the storm-
god'; cf. Güterbock, *JCS* 6:26 [1952]), *aqqatar* (XIII 3 I 3
SAG.DU-*as aqqatar*; *KBo* XII 30 II 5–6 *aqqatar irhas ēsdu* 'let
death be the limit'; cf. IV 14 II 29 and 61 *hinkan-ta* ZAG-*as ēsdu*
'let death be your limit'; cf. ibid. 23 and 81; R. Stefanini, *ANLR*
20:40–2, 50 [1965]; *KUB* XXXVI 7a IV 48 *kasza aqqatarr-a*
'hunger and death'; cf. Güterbock, *JCS* 5:158 [1951]), *aqqātar*
(*Bo* 619 III 7 KUR-*eas aqqātar* 'the death of the land'), gen. sg.
aggannas (*KBo* IV 14 III 9 ANA ^DUTU-*ŠI-za aggannas* TI-*annas*
UKÙ-*as ēs* 'to my majesty be a man of death and life', i.e. show
life-and-death devotion; cf. R. Stefanini, *ANLR* 20:44 [1965];
KUB VIII 50 III 9–10 *nu-wa aggannas weten*[*as*] *kuwapi ārti*
'when you come to the waters of death'; cf. Laroche, *RHA*
26:20 [1968]), *akkannas* (*IBoT* I 33, 111 *akkan*[*na*]*s-ma* MU *karū
maninkūwan* 'but is the year of death already close at hand?'; cf.
Laroche, *RA* 52:155 [1958]), dat.-loc. sg. *akkanni* (ibid. 7 *harki
akkanni* 'to destruction-and-death'; cf. Laroche, *RA* 52:152),
abl. sg. *aggannaz* (*KUB* XV 35 + *KBo* II 9 I 39; cf. Sommer, *ZA*
33:100 [1921]; A. Archi, *Oriens Antiquus* 16:299 [1977]), *akkannaza* (*IBoT* I 33, 73 *harkannaza akkannaza* 'from destruction-
and-death'; cf. Laroche, *RA* 52:154); cf. Kümmel, *Ersatzrituale*
109; iter. *akkeski-, akkiski-*, 3 sg. pres. act. *akkiskizzi* (*KUB* IX
31 IV 45), 3 sg. pres. midd. *akkiskittari* (e.g. XIV 13 IV 3–4
kinun-a-mu É-*ir* KUR-*TUM* ... *akkiskittari* 'now my house and
land are dying'; cf. Götze, *KlF* 248; similarly passim in Plague
Prayers; *HT* 1 II 14–15 KUR-*e-kan anda akkiskittari* 'in the land
dying is rife'; cf. ibid. 17–18; *KUB* IX 31 I 2 and II 41, 43, 44;
XLI 17 II 18–19), *akkiskittāri* (XIV 13 I 50 KUR ^{URU}*Hatti
akkiskittāri*; cf. Götze, *KlF* 246), *ak-kis-kat-ta-ri* (e.g. VIII 63 I
9 *dandukis-wa* GIM-*an akkiskatta*[*ri*] 'as mortal man dies'; VII
54 I 2–3 *mān-kan* ŠÀ KARAŠ.HI.A UG$_6$-*an kisari* UKÙ.MEŠ-*tar*
ANŠU.KUR.RA.HI.A GUD.HI.A KAL-*gaza akkiskattari* 'if amid an
army plague occurs and men, horses, and cattle keep dying
terribly'; ibid. IV 10–11 *mān-kan* ŠÀ KARAŠ KAL-*gaza akkiskat-*

20

tari 'if in an army dying is terribly rife'), *akkiskattāri* (ibid. II 8), 3 pl. pres. act. *akkiskanzi* (*KBo* V 3 III 39 *apez-kan uddanaz arha akkiskanzi* 'for this matter men are put to death'; cf Friedrich, *Staatsverträge* 2:126; *KUB* VII 53 I 4 *nasma-kan* SAL-*ni* DUMU.MEŠ-*ŠU akkiskanzi* 'if on a woman her children keep dying'; cf. Goetze, *Tunnawi* 4), 3 pl. pres. midd. *akkiskan-tari* (*IBoT* I 33, 106 ÌR.MEŠ ZI-*KA kuit akkiskantari* 'whereas servants of your soul die [regularly]'), *ak-ki-is-kán-da-ri* (*KUB* XLI 17 II 9–10 *mān-kan* ... *akkiskandari* 'if deaths keep occurring'), 3 sg. pret. act. *akkisket* (*KBo* III 53, 7 *s-as akkiske*[*t* 'he was dying'; cf. Kühne, *ZA* 67:246 [1977]), *akkiskit* (*KUB* XIV 11 II 30), 3 sg. pret. midd. *akkeskittat* (*KBo* XVI 15 Vs. 8 'there was much dying'; cf. Houwink Ten Cate, *JNES* 25:169 [1966]), *akkiskittat* (*KUB* XIV 14 Rs. 2 *nu* KUR ^{URU}*Hatti akkiskittat* 'Hatti was dying'; cf. Götze, *KlF* 172), *akkiskitat* (XIV 10 I 9; Götze, *KlF* 206), 3 pl. imp. act. *akk*[*is*]*kandu* (*KBo* XVI 25 III 12); sup. *akkiskiu(w)an* (*BoTU* 23A I 54 SAL.LUGAL *akkiskiuwan dāis* 'the queen was about to lie'; *KUB* XIV 8 Vs. 28 *nu-kan* ... *hinkan ki*[*sa*]*t n-as akkiskiuan d*[*āis* 'plague broke out and they began dying'; cf. Götze, *KlF* 210). Cf. Kronasser, *Etym.* 1:516; Neu, *Interpretation* 1–3; Kammenhuber, *HOAKS* 232–3, *MHT* 1, Nr. 1 (1973, 45 p.); Dressler, *Studien* 162–3; Otten, *Sprachliche Stellung* 12.

Despite the consistent spellings *aki, akir, ekir, aku* (and the occasional *akis* besides *akkis*), the preponderance of evidence is for *akk-* and thus /ak-/; the irregularity is reminiscent of *has(s)-* 'open' (q.v.): *hāsi, heser, hāsu* beside *hassanzi, hassit, hassant-* (cf. *akkanzi, akkis, akkant-*). Single spelling of *s* seems somehow connected with the paradigmatic *a:e* ablaut (cf. the alternative forms *hesanzi, hesant-*); in the case of *ak(k)-*, however, this ablaut is confined to 3 pl. pret. act. *ekir*, and even there it appears to be a generally younger variant besides *akir* (cf. Otten, *Altheth. Erzählung* 45–6). Initial plene-spelling (*a-ak-* vs. *ak-*) follows certain scribal conventions (it is found sporadically before "*k* + consonant or pause" but not before "*k* or *kk* + vowel") which have nothing to do with vowel quantity or quality in terms of paradigmatic ablaut (pace Kammenhuber, *KZ* 83:270 [1969]; Rosenkranz, *ZA* 54:105–7 [1961]).

ak(k)-, ek-

ak(k)- has no known inner-Anatolian cognates (Luw: *u*[*wa*]*lant-* 'dead'), but IE origin is probable. /ak-/ < IE **ok-* (perfect stem) presupposes a root **ek-* 'die' postulated also in the Venetic funerary vocable *ekupeθaris, ecupetaris, equpetars*, allegedly 'tombstone' (see e.g. V. Pisani, *Le lingue dell'Italia antica oltre il latino*[2] 262 [1964]; G. B. Pellegrini – A. L. Prosdocimi, *La lingua venetica* 2:74–8 [1967]); **ek-*:**nek̂-*(*IEW* 762) have been compared with Lat. *emō*:Goth. *niman*; hence **eku-* 'dead, corpse' besides Avest. *nasu-*, Gk. νέκῡς 'corpse'. Cf. Götze – Pedersen, *MS* 49; Pedersen, *Festschrift für Hermann Hirt* 2:579–83 (1936). Yet *henkan-* 'plague, death' (q.v.) indicates that **nek̂-* is in reality **E₂nek̂-* (cf. *IEW* 45), which leaves an IE **ek-* 'die' a weak reed, propped up on Hittite and an obscure Venetic compound (which latter also occurs as *ekvopetaris* and need not have an inherent mortuary meaning; cf. M. Lejeune, *Manuel de la langue vénète* 85–6 [1974]; E. Pulgram, *Studies ... offered to L. R. Palmer* 299–304 [1976]).

Sturtevant (*Lg.* 3:164–5 [1927], later disowned in *Comp. Gr.*[1] 75) tried to connect Lat. *agō* ([*aevum, aetatem, vitam*] *ēgit* = *vixit* 'he is done with living, he is dead', with 3 pl. perf. *ēgēre* = Hitt. 3 pl. pret. act. *ekir*); cf. W. Petersen, *Lg.* 9:19 (1933); similarly still Carruba, *Scritti in onore di Giuliano Bonfante* 143 (1976). Kronasser (*VLFH* 222) adduced Toch. A *āk*, B *āke* 'end'. H. Eichner (*MSS* 31:81–2 [1973]) explained 3 sg. pres. act. *aki* as **ōke* from a reduplicated **AʷeAʷóke* (i.e. root **A₁ʷek-*), with a putative meaning 'is gone' (vel sim.) and possible relatedness to Ved. *āśú-*, Gk. ὠκύς 'swift'; but the concomitant theory of "lenition" (and single spelling) of intervocalic tenuis after stressed long vowel renders his approach doubly doubtful; similarly Oettinger, *Stammbildung* 403.

The attempts to derive *ak-* from **n̥k̂-* (beginning with Hrozný, *SH* 176) are abortive, since the outcome should be **ank-*; G. Kellermann and V. Ševoroškin (*Linguistics* 107:121 [1973]) loosely assumed *ak-* < **(h)n̥k-* and irrelevantly compared *asiwant-* (q.v.), where **n̥-* yields *a-* in special phonetic conditions.

On *akkatar* vs. *henkan* cf. Puhvel, *Studia classica et orientalia Antonino Pagliaro oblata* 3:174–5 (1969) = *Analecta Indoeuro-*

paea 203-4 (1981); Kammenhuber, *MHT* 1-2, Nr. 1, 40-1 (1973). For other quasi-synonyms, cf. *halliya weh-* (s.v. *hali-*), *hark-, siunis kis-* (s.v. *siu-*).

akkala-   (c. or n.) 'furrow' (AB.SÍN), acc. sg. *akkālan* (*KUB* XXIX 30 III 9 [=*Code* 2:68, OHitt.] 1 *akkālan pedai* '[if anyone violates the boundary of a field and] digs one [additional] furrow'), *aggalan* (later dupl. *KBo* VI 26 I 46-47 *takku* A.ŠÀ-*an* ZAG-*an kuiski parsiya* 1 *aggalan pennāi*, where the redactor has understood *pi-e-da-i* as *pedai-* 'carry off' rather than 'dig' [the latter being consistently spelled *pè-da-i* in Classical Hitt.] and "improved" it to *pennāi* 'drives', i.e. 'rams in, crams in'; *KUB* XXXIX 14 I 5), dat.-loc. sg. *aggali* (ibid. 7; cf. Otten, *Totenrituale* 78), AB.SÍN-*i* (*KBo* XII 73, 5-6 *halkinn-a-kan* AB.SÍN-*i anda waliwalāi* 'he makes grain grow in the furrow'; cf. Laroche, *RA* 58:73, 78 [1964]), instr. sg. in VI 34 IV 16-17 *IŠTU* A.ŠÀ-*ŠU-ma--ssi-kan aggalit welkuwan le uizzi* 'from his field, his furrow may grass not come for him' (cf. Friedrich, *ZA* 35:168 [1924]). Cf. Goetze, *ANET* 195; Ertem, *Fauna* 107-9; Otten, *ZA* 66:93 (1976; skeptical of 'furrow'); Oettinger, *Eide* 14, 50 (who unconvincingly saw in *akkala-* a deep-delving plow, distinct from GIŠAPIN); Puhvel, in *Hethitisch und Indogermanisch* 215-6 (1979) = Analecta Indoeuropaea 362-3 (1981) refuting Oettinger).

Cf. Gk. ὄγμος 'furrow', usually derived from IE *aĝ-*, cf. e.g. ὄγμον ἄγειν ὀρθόν 'draw a straight furrow' (Theocritus 10.2); for similar -*l*- derivatives cf. Gk. ἀγέλη 'herd', Lat. *agolum* 'shepherd's staff' (cf. Kronasser, *Etym.* 1:172; Rosenkranz, *JEOL* 19:502 [1965-6]). But -*kk*- points to IE *k* (cf. N. van Brock, *RHA* 20:101, 166 [1962]), which may, however, be present in ὄγμος < *ὀκ- (as in δεῖγμα from δεικ-, etc.; cf. Benveniste, *Hittite* 107-8, pace O. Szemerényi, *BSOAS* 27:158 [1964]). Čop (*Ling.* 5:26 [1964]) also compared Lat. *occa* (which was kept apart by Benveniste), Gk. ὀξίνη, Lith. *akēčios*, Corn. *ocet* 'harrow' (*IEW* 22). J. Greppin (*PBH* 1972:3 [58], 221-2) adduced Arm. *akaws* 'furrow'.

A tie-in with IE *aĝros* (Kammenhuber in *HW²* 52) is unlikely since it also involves IE *aĝ-* (cf. *IEW* 6).

aganni- (c.) 'cup, bowl', nom. sg. ^{DUG}*agannis* (*KUB* XXXI 71 IV 29). Borrowed from Hurrian (XXVII 13 I 21 *aganni*); cf. (Western) Akk. *agan(n)u*, Ugar. *agn*, Hebr. *aggān*, Egypt. *'ikn*. Cf. Laroche, *RA* 47:40 (1953); Kronasser, *Etym.* 1:245; Kammenhuber, *Die Arier* 154. Furnée (*Erscheinungen* 138) compared Gk. ἀχάνη, name of a Persian and Boeotian hollow measure, also 'box', as an Asianic loanword.

aku- (c.) 'stone', nom. sg. *akus* (*KUB* XXI 19 + 338/v III 14 ^{NA_4}*akus witeni* 'a stone in water'; cf. Haas, *Nerik* 7), acc. sg. *akun* (ibid. 16; XXXVI 12 II 5–6 *nu-za ishamiskizzi* ^{D}*IŠTAR-is nu-za-kan ŠA* A.AB.BA *akun* ^{NA_4}*passilann-a anda zikkizzi* 'Ištar sings, and the stone and pebble of the sea she engages [to attention?]'; cf. Güterbock, *JCS* 6:15 [1952]), acc. pl. *akus* (*VBoT* 134, 2 *ā*]*andus* ^{NA_4}*aku*[*s* 'hot stones'; cf. e.g. *KUB* XXXIII 49 II 6 *ā*]*andus* ^{NA_4}*passilus* 'hot pebbles'; also *KBo* XIX 156 Vs. 17 *a-ku-u-us-(sa)*; cf. Carruba, *Das Palaische* 30; Neu, *Altheth.* 222). Cf. also ^{NA_4}*akur* (*KUB* XLIII 75 Rs. 2)?

akuwant- 'stony', acc. pl. c. in XXXV 84 II 4 ^{NA_4}*akuwandus* KASKAL.HI.A-*us* 'stony roads' (cf. Otten, *LTU* 84). Cf. Kronasser, *Etym.* 1:266.

Laroche's etymology (*RHA* 15:25–6, 29 [1957]) involving IE**ak̂-* 'sharp, edgy' (*IEW* 18–22) is semantically plausible (cf. e.g. Skt. *áśman-*, Lith. *akmuõ* 'stone'); a *u*-stem is seen in Lat. *acus* 'needle', *acūmen* 'sharp point'. Yet the consistent single spelling of *-k-* points rather to /-g-/; hence cf. perhaps instead IE **agh-* in Gk. ἄχυρα, ἄχνη 'chaff' (besides Goth. *ahana* 'chaff', Lat. *agna* 'ear of grain', from **ak̂-*), i.e. **A₂egh-*, with **A₂gh-ádh-* seen in Goth. *gazds* 'sting', Lat. *hasta* 'spear' (**ghadh-tā*). H. Eichner (*MSS* 31:81 [1973]) postulated a proto-paradigm nom.-acc. sg. neut. **A₂ék̂u* : gen. **A₂k̂éws* (or **A₂k̂wés*), yielding Hitt. **heku* : **akkuas* and thence analogically *aku* : **akkuwas* and finally *aku* : **akuwas*; apart from the improbable "lenitional" single spelling of *-k-* after a postulated long vowel, the form **aku* suffers from nonexistence (nom. sg. c. *akus* above).

akkus(s)a- (n.) '(catch-)hole, (trapping-)pit', nom.-acc. pl. *akkus-(s)a*, gloss-wedged (probably Luwoid) hapax legomenon in the Hittite *Gilgameš*: *KBo* X 47c, 22–26 (with dupl. *KUB* VIII 56, 10–14) *nu-wa*] *akkussa* (dupl. *akkusa*) *kue ammu*[*k tarneskimi*] [*ap*]*ās-ma-⟨wa⟩r-at-kan* SAHAR.HI.A-*az* [*sahiskizzi*] *aggatius-ma--wa kuyēs* [*isparnuskimi* (?)] *apās-ma-as sarā d*[*āi nu-war-as-kan* ÍD-*i anda*] *ishūwaiskizzi* 'the pits which I sink, that man stuffs them with earth; but the nets which I (spread), that one takes them up and throws them in the river'; ibid. 14 *akku*[*ssa*. Cf. Otten, *Istanbuler Mitteilungen* 8:100–2 (1958); Laroche, *RHA* 26:9 (1968).

   akkus(s)a- matches *būru* 'pit' in the Akkadian *Gilgameš* (cf. Friedrich, *ZA* 39:40 [1930]; *CAD* B 342). No clear etymology. For the equally gloss-wedged *aggatius* in the above passage see s.v. *ekt-, ikt-*.

akutalla- or **akugalla-** (n.?), name of a container for water, instr. sg. in *KUB* II 13 I 8–9 *akugallit* KÙ.BABBAR *wātar pedai* LUGAL-*us-za* QATI-*ŠU ārri* (dupl. IX 20, 5–6 *akutallit* [... *p*]*edai* LUGAL-*us-za* [... *ā*]*rri*) '(he) brings water in a silver *a.*, and the king washes his hands'.

   One of the forms is a likely misspelling, probably *akugallit*, with omission of the final vertical wedge which distinguishes *ta* from *ga*; the copy looks cramped compared to the generous spacing of IX 20, 5.

   For -*talla*- in vessel names cf. *halwattalla-* (n.) beside *halwani-*. Possibly *akutallan* /ak^wtlan/ or /ag^wdlan/ < IE *ēgh^w-tlom* or *ēgh^w-dhlom*; cf. Hitt. *eku-* 'drink' (s.v.) and Lat. *pōculum* < *pō-tlom* 'drinking tool', or *stabulum* < *stₐ-dhlom* 'standing spot'. Cf. Puhvel, *JAOS* 97:598 (1977); in a similar vein already Ivanov, *Voprosy slavjanskogo jazykoznanija* 2:19 (1957). Thus 'goblet' rather than 'bowl' or 'ewer'? Hence the first part of the etymology by C. H. Carruthers (*Lg.* 9:153–4 [1933]) may be right after all, although there is no tie-in with Lat. *aqua*. Cf. also N. van Brock, *RHA* 20:101 (1962).

   Contrast ^LÚ*akuttara-* (s.v. *eku-*).

aku(wa)kuwa-   (c.) 'spider, tarantula' (?), gen. sg. in *Bo* 2738 I 7–8 *akuwakuwas hattesni* 'to the lair of a tarantula', with duplicate *Bo* 2499 I 7 *akuw*[, dupl. *Bo* 7230, 7]*akukuwa⟨s⟩ ha*[*t-*. There is also the (haplographic?) form *akuwas* in *Bo* 2738 I 17 *akuwas* AMA-*as* GUD-*us*, paralleling a preceding passus preserved in dupl. *Bo* 2499 I 3 *lalawēsnas* ('swarm of ants') AMA-*as* GUD-*us*. Cf. Otten, *ZA* 66:94–5 (1976).

Phonetic variant of *auwawa-* 'spider' (q.v.); thus perhaps some underground variety like tarantula or other large mygalomorph spider. Cf. Puhvel, *Kratylos* 25:137 (1980); *Essays in historical linguistics in memory of J.A. Kerns* 237—42 (1981).

The translation 'frog, toad' (current since E. Forrer apud P. Kretschmer, *KlF* 310; C. H. Carruthers, *Lg.* 6:160 [1930]) was influenced by onomatopoeic terms like Gk. κοάξ (frog-cry), Lat. *coaxō* 'croak' (*IEW* 627). Kammenhuber's 'toad' or 'mole' (*HW²* 54) was no improvement (for 'mole' see rather *asku-*, s.v.). Tischler's argument (*Glossar* 12) that the creature had to make some characteristic sound to rate an onomatopoeic name is contradicted by *lala(k)uesa-* 'ant'.

allayani-   (c.), name of a tree, nom. sg. *allayanis* (950/c IV 1, preceded by [GIŠ]*hasik* 'fig-tree'), *allayani*[*s* (758/u, 10, followed [ibid. 11] by GIŠHASHUR.KUR.RA 'mountain apple'), *allayan*[(*KUB* XXXIII 32 III 9 *nu* ZI-KA GIŠ*allayan*['your spirit [like] a.'), acc. pl. GIŠ*āllayanus* (XXXV 164 III 5; cf. Carruba, *Das Palaische* 32; Neu, *Altheth.* 226). Cf. Ertem, *Flora* 107–8; Otten, *ZA* 66:95 (1976).

Probably a culture tree, possibly olive, usually GIŠ*ZERTUM*, often listed with *hassikka-* 'fig-tree' (q.v.), in which case one may entertain an affinity with Gk. ἐλαίᾱ, Lat. *olea, olīva* 'olive-tree', Arm. *iwł* 'oil'. The suffix *-ani-* resembles Arm. *-eni* forming tree names, e.g. *last* 'boat': *lasteni* 'alder-tree' (for semantics see s.v. *alanza*[*n*]-; cf. J. Greppin, *Classical Armenian nominal suffixes* 83 [1975]). "Oily" nature of the tree in the simile *KUB* XXXIII 32 III 9 would be apposite to the "smooth-flowing", humoral soul-concept of the Hittites (cf. s.v. *war-*[*a*]*s-*).

allallā- (c. or n.?) 'defection', with gloss-wedges, attested almost exclusively in the late text (Suppiluliumas II) *KBo* IV 14 II and IV, acc. sg. *allallān* (IV 62), *allalān* (IV 63), *alla[llān* (II 37 *alla[llān] zilatiya le sanahti* 'in the future do not plan defection'), gen. sg. *allallās* (II 43 INIM *allallās*, II 52 *allallās-ma memiyas* 'an act of defection'), dat.-loc. sg. *allallā* (II 74 *n]asma-mu-kan* EN.MEŠ *kuyēsqa allallā pānzi* 'or if some lords resort to defection from me'; II 43 *allallā le pāsi* 'do not resort to defection'; II 46–47 *allallā pāuwanzi-wa-za* UGU *linqanuwanza* 'regarding the matter of defecting I am bound by oath'; II 59–61 *zik-ma allallā pāuwar* 1-*eda tiyauwar pidi-kan wasdumar le sanahti* 'do not plan defecting, or standing apart, or incurring criminality on your post'; repeated in II 63–65 with *allala pāuwar*, II 69–71 with *allalā pāwar*; IV 74; *KBo* XIII 260 III 37).

allallā pai- resembles *arrusa pai-* 'resort to secession' (q.v.). Gloss-wedges and the Luwoid ritual *KBo* XIII 260 both point to a Luwianism. *allallā-* seems to be a "privileged" term referring to the potential disloyalty of the king's addressee (a vassal or high dignitary) or 'lords', whereas defection in general (II 14 ÌR *kuiski* 'some servant'; II 48 *kuyēsqa* 'some'; II 54 'the king's army and country'; II 2, II 63, III 14, III 28 'country') is expressed by the verb (*kattan*) *niya-* (*neya-*, midd. of *nai-*) 'turn away'. But cf. also II 74 (above) with II 56 *nasma-kan* EN.MEŠ LUGAL-*i* GAM-*an niyantari* 'if lords turn away from the king'. Cf. R. Stefanini, *ANLR* 20:39–50, 52, 60–1 (1965).

Reduplicated? Onomatopoeic? No etymology.

alalamniya- 'cry aloud', iter. 3 sg. pres. act. *alalamniskizzi* (*KUB* XVII 9 I 18; cf. ibid. 21 [2 sg.] *wēskisi* 'lament'), *a-la-la-am-ni-es-ki-iz-zi* (XXX 19+ IV 12; cf. Otten, *Totenrituale* 46). Cf. Friedrich, *ZA* 39:75 (1930).

Perhaps haplological for **alala + lamniya-* 'call out *alala*'; cf. Arm. *alalak* 'cry, scream'; Gk. ἀλαλαί (interjection), ἀλαλή 'outcry', ἀλαλάζω 'cry aloud', ἐλελεῦ 'alas', ὀλολύζω 'cry out'; *RV* 4.18.6 *etá arṣanty alalābhávantīr* 'those (waters) flow, loud-sounding' (cf. *IEW* 29). For *lamniya-*, cf. s.v. *laman-*. Cf. Puhvel, *JAOS* 97:598 (1977).

alalima-, alalam(m)a-   (c.) 'entrenchment, ditch' (*KBo* I 35, 3 íD-*as alalimas* = [Akk.] *hatidu*, i.e. *hattitu* 'entrenchment'), nom. sg. in *KUB* XXXVI 68 I 9 íD-*as alalamma*[*s* 'entrenchment of a river' (cf. ibid. 10 íD-*as wappun* 'river-bank'), XVII 1 II 23 íD-*a*]*s alalamas* (cf. ibid. 21 íD-*as ār*[*aszi* 'river flows'; Friedrich, *ZA* 49:238 [1950]), acc. pl. *alalimu*[*s* (*KBo* XXVI 135, 7; cf. ibid. 6 *a*]*rsarsūra*[*s* 'stream').

Cf. Laroche, *OLZ* 51:423 (1956). Other, incorrect interpretations are based on the ambiguity of the Akk. gloss *hatidu*: 'fright' (Götze, *KlF* 186); standing for *hatītu* 'verminous', misunderstood as *hādidu* 'roar(ing)' (HW^2 55; cf. Laroche, *BSL* 52.1:77–8 [1956]).

Technical term of irrigation like *amiyara-* (q.v.). Cf. perhaps Arm. *olol* 'inundation', *ololanem* 'cover with water'. Cf. Puhvel, *JAOS* 97:598 (1977).

allaniya-   'sweat, perspire', only in hippological context so far, 3 pl. pres. act. *allaniyanzi*, typically *KBo* III 2 Rs. 26–27 *mahhan-ma* ANŠU.KUR.RA.MEŠ *allaniyanzi sīshau arha uizzi nu-smas* KUŠKA. .TAB.ANŠU TÚG.HI.A *arha danzi* 'but when the horses perspire (and) sweat breaks out, they take away the bridle and blankets' (cf. Kammenhuber, *Hippologia* 128–30); following *allaniyanzi*, instead of *sīshau* 'sweat', *KUB* I 11 + XXIX 57 I 22–23 has ZUDU-ŠUNU-*ya* 'and their sweat' (Kammenhuber, *Hippologia* 108), I 11 III 5–6 has (gloss-wedges) ZUDU-ŠUNU-*ya* (ibid. 114), *KBo* III 2 Vs. 36–37 has only gloss-wedges (ibid. 140), and III 2 1.R. 1 has KI.MIN 'ditto, etc.' (ibid. 144); *allaniyanzi* alone in broken context in *KBo* XIV 63a IV 4 (ibid. 220).

There is typical tautological pleonasm (cf. Friedrich, *Orientalia* N.S. 9:208 [1940]) in the sequence *allaniyanzi sīshau* (or: ZUDU-ŠUNU-*ya*) *arha uizzi*, to the point of the copyist merely signalling the quasi-repetition by gloss-wedges or KI.MIN; hence the meaning 'perspire' is likely for *allaniya-* (as opposed to Kammenhuber's guess 'become agitated'; cf. *Hippologia* 322). The true Hitt. noun for 'sweat' is not known (*sīshau* is a possibly Hurroid hapax; cf. ibid. 129); *warsula-* 'moisture, wetness' (q.v. s.v. *wars*[*iya*]-) also denotes 'perspiration'; *zap-*

piya- (q.v.) can mean 'drip (with perspiration)'; but *allaniya-* may well be the normal verb for 'to sweat'.

The comparison with OIr. *allas* (< *aln-?), gen. *allais* (n.) 'sweat' (vs. Welsh *chwys*, IE *sweyd-*), first made by Pedersen (*Féil-Sgribhinn Eóin Mhic Néill* 142 [1940]), is plausible, although formational details of *allaniya-* remain opaque (< *alṇ- -yo-* or *alnon-yo-?*). Cf. J. Vendryes, *Lexique étymologique de l'irlandais ancien* A-62 (1959); Benveniste, *Hittite* 107; Jucquois, *Encyclopaedia Universalis* 8:930 (1968); W. Meid, *Indogermanisch und Keltisch* 11 (1968); J. Puhvel, *JAOS* 97:598 (1977); H. Eichner, *Die Sprache* 24:68 (1978). O. Szemerényi (*Gnomon* 43:653 [1971]) also adduced Gk. ἀλέᾱ 'warmth, body heat' (separating ιι from εἴλη 'sun-heat', IE *swelā*), and Lat. *ad-oleō* 'burn (as sacrifice)'.

allantaru-   (n.) 'oak' (tree and wood), dat.-loc. sg. ᴳᴵˢ*allan*ɢɪˢ*rui* (*KUB* XXXIX 7 II 35), nom.-acc. pl. n. ᴳᴵˢ*allantaru* (XXXIX 8 I 48); ᴳᴵᴵˢ*allan*ɢɪˢ*r[u* (XXXIX 24 Vs. 2). Cf. Otten, *Totenrituale* 38, 134–5.

Compound of Semitic *allan-* (Akk. *allānu*, Hebr. '*allōn* 'oak') and Hitt. *taru-* 'tree, wood' (q.v.). Cf. H. A. Hoffner, *Orientalia* N.S. 35:390–1 (1966); Kümmel, *Orientalia* N.S. 36:366–7 (1967); Goetze, *JCS* 22:17 (1968); Ertem, *Flora* 79; Tischler, *IBK* Sonderheft 50:214 (1982).

Cf. ᴳᴵˢ*taruallinu* at Nuzi (see Haas, *Nerik* 174)?

alanza(n)-   (c.), a tree and its wood, nom. sg. *alanzas* (2064/g Vs. 10 ᴳᴵˢ*tanāu* ᴳᴵˢ*alanzass-a warhuis* 'thick [i.e. shady?] t.- and a.- tree[s]'; cf. Güterbock, *Siegel* 1:77; Riemschneider, *MIO* 6:362 [1958]; XXXIII 81 I 11 ᴳᴵᴵˢ*alanzas*; cf. Laroche, *RHA* 23:80 [1965]; XLII 107 IV 10 and 11 *alanzas*), ᴳᴵˢ*alanza* (VII 53 III 13 *kās* ᴳᴵˢ*alanza mahhan ... parkunuskizzi* 'as this a.-wood cleanses'; cf. Goetze, *Tunnawi* 20; *KBo* XIV 98 II 2 ᴳᴵˢ*alanza[*]), acc. sg. ᴳᴵˢ*alanzanan* (*KUB* XXVIII 102 IV 13; XVII 27 II 17; 574/s, 4, followed by ᴳᴵˢMA 'fig-tree'), gen. sg. ᴳᴵˢ*alanzanas* (XII 58 III 25 ᴳᴵˢ*alanzanas* ᴋᴀ́.ɢᴀʟ-*as* 'gate of a.-wood'; cf. Goetze, *Tunnawi* 18; *KBo* IV 2 III 33 ᴳᴵˢ*alanzanas* ᴳᴵˢ*karsaniyas* 'of a. and soapwort'; cf. Kronasser, *Die Sprache* 8:95 [1962]; *KUB* VII 23, 7; XXXII 123 II 12–13 KĪLILU-*ya* ^{GIŠ}*alanzanas lahhurnuzz[i-...]iyanda* 'wreaths made of a.-branches'; XXXV 142 I 8 and 12; XLV 20 I 9), ^{GIŠ}*alanzas* (VII 53 III 12 ^{GIŠ}*alanzas* KÁ.GAL).

The declension resembles *alkista(n)-, arkamma(n)-, hara(n)-, istanza(n)-, lahanza(n)-, sum(m)anza(n)-, memiya(n)-*; for analogical interactions see s.v. *istanza(n)-*. In the context of 2064/g Vs. 10 *alanza(n)-* grew in pastures. Arboreal identification is difficult and ambiguous. Ertem (*Flora* 77–9) assumed 'laurel' (*Laurus nobilis*), without etymological considerations. M. Poetto (*Istituto Lombardo, Rendiconti, Classe di Lettere* 107:29 [1973]) compared Gk. ἐλάτη 'silver fir' (*Abies cephalonica*) < **elṇtā*, assuming *e > a* before *l* in Hittite and regular **ṇ > an*, but not accounting for *z* in *alanza-*; the coupling with ^{GIŠ}*tanāu* (q.v.) in 2064/g Vs. 10 may strengthen the case for another conifer. Yet etymologically most probable is a comparison with Lat. *alnus* < **al(i)sno-*, Lith. *alksnis*, East Lith. *aliksnis* < **al(i)sni-* 'alder'; while Baltic has treated the -*l(i)sn-* cluster by epenthesis of *k*, Hitt. has metathesized **al(i)sno-* to **alṇso-* > **alansa-* > *alanza-* (with normal /ns/ > /nts/; the same metathesis may be present in *alwanza-*, q.v.). Alternatively, if Lat. *alnus* < **aleno-* (like e.g. *ornus* < **oseno-*), *alanza-* may represent **alṇso-* without metathesis. The alder would grow along stream-banks, and alderwood was as suitable as fir for carpentry (cf. metonymic Lat. *alnus* 'boat', like *abies* 'ship' or Gk. ἐλάτη 'oar; ship'). Cf. Puhvel, *JAOS* 97:598 (1977), and for the extra-Anatolian cognates F. Specht, *Der Ursprung der indogermanischen Deklination* 59 (1943); O. Szemerényi, *Glotta* 38:227–9 (1960); P. Friedrich, *Proto-Indo-European trees* 70–3 (1970).

M. Mayer (*Acme* 27:300 [1974]) tried unsuccessfully to involve Gk. ἐλάτη, Lat. *alnus*, and Hitt. *alanza(n)-* alike in a "Mediterranean" root-etymology meaning 'strong', comparing inter alia also Hebrew *'allōn* 'oak' (cf. s.v. *allantaru-*).

allap(p)ahh-, alpahh-   'spit, spit at', 3 sg. pres. act. *allapahhi* (e.g. *KBo* XXI 6 Rs. 11; *KUB* XXIV 12 II 9; XXV 80 Rs. 11),

30

allappahhi (e.g. *KBo* XVII 1 [=*FHG* 6] I 4–5 LUGAL-*us* ...
GUD-*un* ... *allappahhi* 'the king spits on the cattle'; similarly
ibid. 6, 36; cf. Laroche, *RA* 45:184–5 [1951]; Otten–Souček,
Altheth. Ritual 18–9), *alpahhi* (XXIV 1 I 7), 3 pl. pres. act.
allapahhanzi (e.g. II 3 I 41 *nu-ssi-kan* KAxU-*i anda allapahhanzi*
'they spit in his mouth'; cf. Hrozný, *Heth. KB* 68; L. Rost, *MIO*
1:354 [1953]; XVII 3 IV 32; cf. Otten–Souček, *Altheth. Ritual*
38), *allappahhanzi* (e.g. XVII 1 II 19; cf. Otten – Souček,
Altheth. Ritual 26), 1 sg. pret. act. *allapahhun* (*KUB* XVII 27 III
11), 3 sg. pret. act. *allapahhas* (XXXIII 120 I 38–40; cf.
Güterbock, *Kumarbi* *3; Meriggi, *Athenaeum* N.S. 31:112–4
[1953]; Laroche, *RHA* 26:41 [1968]), *allapahasta* (XXXVI 55
III 24) *arha allapahasta* 'spat out'; cf. Rosenkranz, *RHA* 15:106
[1957]), 2 pl. pret. act. in *idālawēs-wa-kan hūrtāus parā alla-
pahten* 'you have spat out the evil curses' (L. Rost, *MIO* 1:354
[1953], II 31), 2 sg. imp. act. *allapah* (e.g. IX 4 II 41; IX 34 III 22
and 23; XXV 80 Rs. 13), *allappah* (e.g. XLIV 56 Rs. 15); partic.
allappahhant-, nom.-acc. (pl.) neut. *allappahhan* (XVII 27 III
15); iter. *allappahhiski-*, 3 sg. imp. act. ibid. 14–15 *n-us-san ser
[all]appahhiskiddu* 'let him spit on them'. Cf. Kronasser, *Etym.*
1:431; Josephson, *Sentence particles* 49–50.

Etymology uncertain. Perhaps related to the quasi-onomato-
poeic root **lab(h)-, lap(h)-* (*IEW* 651) seen in Gk. λαφύσσω,
λάπτω, OE *lapian* 'lap, slurp, swig, quaff', Arm. *lapʿem*, Alban.
lap, Lat. *lambō*, OHG *laffan* 'lick', etc.

allassi-   'ladyhood, queenship', gen. sg. in *IBoT* II 120 Rs. 3 YÀ
allassias iskiya[uwar 'unction with oil of the queenship', *KBo* X
34 I 3 *allāssiyas* (viz. SISKUR.SISKUR 'rite'; ibid. 2 SISKUR.SISKUR
sarrassiyas 'rite of kingship'; cf. Goetze, *JCS* 23:80 [1970]),
similarly *KUB* XI 31 VI 5 *allassiyanza* (ibid. 3 *sarrassian[za*),
dat.-loc. sg. in e.g. *KBo* XV 43 Vs. 7–8 ANA ᴰU *sarrassiya* [*Ù*
ANA ᴰ*Hepa]t allassiya sipanti* 'he pours to the storm-god for
kingship and to Hebat for queenship' (cf. Goetze, *JCS* 23:78
[1970]). Cf. Laroche, *RA* 54:193 (1960), *RHA* 34:44 (1976);
Kümmel, *Ersatzrituale* 47–9; Haas – Wilhelm, *Riten* 66, 68.

Borrowed Hurr. deriv. from *allai* 'lady' (e.g. *KUB* XXXIV 102 II 12 and III 33 ᴰ*Allai*; XII 11 IV 27 ᴰ*IŠTAR allai*; with article frequent ᴰ*Allan*[*n*]*i-*); cf. e.g. Hurr. *allāssāe* (XXVII 42 Vs. 27), *allassi-ni-pi* 'of the queenship' (e.g. XLV 84 Rs. 4, 7, 9), *allāssi-ni-pi* (ibid. 17); similar abstracts are *sarrassi-* (from Akk. *šarri-* 'king'), *ebrissi-* 'lordship', *damqirasi-* 'merchanthood', with Hurr. *-ssi* = Akk. *-ūtu* (*šarrūtu, bēlūtu, tamqārūtu*).

(a)lattari- (c.), with determinative ᴺᴵᴺᴰᴬ 'bread', a kind of bread or pastry, nom. sg. *lattariyis* (*KBo* XV 37 I 14), acc. sg. *aladdarin* (V 1 III 31), *alattarinn-a* (ibid. 17), *aladdarinn-a* (ibid. 33), *laddarin* (ibid. 12; cf. Sommer – Ehelolf, *Pāpanikri* 10*, 8*), *alāttarin* (*KUB* XXV 48 IV 8), *lattariyen* (XXV 50 II 9), *latarin* (*JRAS* 1909, 977 line 3), nom. pl. in *KBo* XIV 139 II 2 2 [ᴺᴵᴺᴰᴬ*a*]*lattarie*[*s*, acc. pl. in XXI 34 II 17 4 NINDA.KUR₄.RA *allattarius* 'four thick a.-loaves'. Cf. H. A. Hoffner, *Alimenta Hethaeorum* 149–50 (1974).

Hurrian in origin. Unlikely comparison with Arm. *alander* 'dessert' by G. Kapancjan, *Chetto-Armeniaca* 121, 130–1 (1931–3); *Istoriko-lingvističeskie raboty* 81–2, 333–4 (1956); cf. T. Schultheiss, *KZ* 77:225 (1961).

alel- (n.) 'flower, bloom'; *hameshandas alel* corresponds to Akk. *ayar(i)* 'April-May' in the bilingual *KUB* IV 4 Vs. 7–9 *hamishandas-ma-za alel āssiyanni handas ēssa*[*tti* 'but the flower of spring you make for the sake of love' (cf. Laroche, *RA* 58:73 [1964]); nom.-acc. sg. in XXXIX 6 II 15 *nu-ssi alel ud*[*anzi* 'and they bring him a flower' (cf. Otten, *Totenrituale* 48), also *alil* (XXIV 14 I 8 *kuēl imma* GIŠ-*ruwas hahhallas alil* 'the bloom of whatever tree [or] bush'; XXXIII 68 II 1–2; cf. Laroche, *RHA* 23:128 [1965]; *IBoT* II 39 II 22; *KBo* XIV 98 I 14), also *alilas* (c.; unless from *alila-*, q.v.) in *KUB* XII 62 Vs. 13–14 *alilas-za warsuwanzi* ŪL *memmai* 'the flower will not refuse to be picked' (secondary thematization like ibid. Rs. 5 *hariyas* for *hari-*?), dat.-loc. sg. *alili* (ibid. Vs. 11 *alili warsuwanzi paimi* 'I will go to pick the flower'; XI 26 II 8 *alili* TUTITTI 'for the [heraldic?]

flower [or rosette] of the breastplate'; cf. *IBoT* II 62 Vs. 10
Ḏ*alili*, some sacred emblem?), abl. sg. *alilaz* (*KUB* XXVIII 6 Vs.
14b DUMU.MEŠ-*us alilaz uer* 'the offspring [i.e. apples] came
from the bloom'; *KBo* XXII 85 I 8; cf. Haas – Thiel, *Rituale*
132). Cf. Friedrich, *ZA* 49:248 (1950); Kronasser, *Etym.* 1:313,
324, 340.

A possible denom. derivative is *alalessar* (n.), hardly 'flower-
patch, garden' (e.g. Laroche, *RA* 47:40 [1953]; Kammenhuber,
MIO 2:436 [1954]) but a meadow (USALLUM *alalessar*) of
extensive proportions (attestations in Güterbock, *Siegel*
1:76–7; Riemschneider, *MIO* 6:358, 362 [1958]). Cf. Kronasser, *Etym.* 1:290.

International culture word: Cushitic *ilili*, Berber *alili*, Basque
lili, Estonian *lill*, Alban. *l'ul'e* 'flower'; Egypt. *ḫrr-t* (Coptic
hrēri, hlēli), Gk. λείριον, Lat. *līlium* 'lily', etc. Cf. Benveniste,
BSL 50.1:43 (1954); J. Hubschmid, *Mediterrane Substrate* 37–9
(1960); E. Masson, *Recherches sur les plus anciens emprunts
sémitiques en grec* 58–9 (1967); B. Hemmerdinger, *Glotta*
46:240 (1968).

alhuesra-, alhuitra-   (c.), name or title of priestess, nom. sg. SAL*alhu-*
itras (e.g. *KBo* XIV 89 IV 11; *KUB* XXVII 59 IV 14), acc. sg.
SAL*alhuitran* (XXXII 125, 8), dat.-loc. sg. SAL*alhuitri* (e.g. XVII
24 III 18), nom. pl. in *KBo* XXIV 28 IV 12 and 23 SAL.MEŠ*alhui-*
tri[*s*, acc. pl. *alhuesrus* (IX 120 Vs. 7), dat.-loc. pl. in XXI 32 Rs.
8 SAL.MEŠ*alhuesras* (and perhaps XVII 57, 6 *a*]*lhuesras*; cf. Otten,
ZA 66:97 [1976]), *KUB* XX 16 IV 4 3 SAL.MEŠ*alhuyitras*, 122/f, 8
ANA 3 SAL.MEŠ*alhuitra*[*s*, *KBo* XXIV 23, 8 ANA SAL*alhuitras*; also
undeclined, e.g. nom. sg. SAL*alhuitra* (*KUB* XXVII 64 Vs. 6),
dat. sg. ANA SAL*alhuitra* (frequent). Metathetic spelling SAL*hu-al-*
-it-ra- (*KBo* XXIV 24 III 12 and 26).

alhuitra- was the Luwian ministrant in the cult of Huwas-
sanna of Hupesna; *alhuesra-* may be the Hittite phonetic
variant (feminine suffix -*sra-*?); cf. e.g. Luw. *sahuidara-* vs. Hitt.
sakuwassara- (q.v.), or Luw. *huidwali-* vs. Hitt. *huiswant-*. Cf.
Laroche, *OLZ* 54:275 (1959), *Dict. louv.* 176; Kronasser, *Etym.*
1:187.

alhuesra-, alhuitra-   ali-   alila-, ali(li)li-, aliliya-, al(l)iya-, ālli-

Van Windekens (*Annual of Armenian linguistics* 1:40 [1980]) essayed a root-connection with IE **al-* 'grind', tying in nom. sg. c. *al-ha-ri-es* perhaps denoting some kind of stone in *KUB* II 2 II 55 (cf. Schuster, *Bilinguen* 67), and Arm. *ałaxin* 'maid-servant', *alij* 'girl'; for semantics, cf. Gk. ἀλετρίς 'female meal-grinder' (also maiden in ritual role) and Toch. B *kärweñe* 'stone, rock' beside Skt. *grávan-* 'pressing-stone', OIr. *bró* 'millstone'. Such speculation is idle as long as derivation remains opaque.

ali-   (c.), with determinative ˢᴵᴳ 'wool', some kind of wool or wool product in Hurroid rituals, nom. sg. ˢᴵᴳ*alis* (e.g. *KUB* XV 42 II 7–8 *kās* ˢᴵᴳ*alis mahhan parkuis* 'as this a. is clean'; *KBo* XXIII 1 I 30 and III 9), acc. sg. ˢᴵᴳ*alin* (e.g. *KUB* XV 42 II 6, 14, 16, 17, 20; *KBo* XXIII 1 I 26 and 28, III 7; ibid. III 3 ˢᴵᴳ BABBAR *alin* 'white a.'; cf. Lebrun, *Hethitica III* 141–2, 145; wrongly for gen. sg. in e.g. XV 37 III 13–14 1 *kapinan* TUR ŠA ˢᴵᴳ*alin* BABBAR 'one small thread of white a.'), instr. sg. *alit* (e.g. *KUB* XV 42 II 18; *KBo* XV 48 II 12–13 *zuppari* ˢᴵᴳ*alit* SA₅ *anda ishiyanda* 'torches bound with red a.'; cf. Otten, *Materialien* 7, 36; *KUB* VII 56 I 5 *IŠTU* ˢᴵᴳ SA₅ *alit* 'with red a.'; *KUB* XXIX 7 + *KBo* XXI 41 Vs. 39–56 *isnit* ˢᴵᴳ*alitt-a* 'with dough and a.'; cf. Lebrun, *Samuha* 119–20), abl. sg. ˢᴵᴳ*aliyaz* (XXXII 122, 2).

Presumably Hurrian; possibly a "Mediterranean" term for 'wool', from a root meaning 'wind, roll', seen perhaps in Gk. ἀλινδέω (aor. ἤλῑσα), much as Hitt. *hulana-, huliya-* 'wool' (s.v. *hul*[*a*]-) is root-related with *hulaliya-* 'wind, wrap'.

alessar (n.), nom.-acc. sg. in *KUB* IX 31 I 10 *a-li-e-es-sa* ŠA ˢᴵᴳ GE₆ ˢᴵᴳ SA₅ 'a. of black wool (and) red wool' (cf. B. Schwartz, *JAOS* 58:334 [1938]; H. Otten – C. Rüster, *ZA* 68:276 [1978]). For denom. formation cf. *alalessar* s.v. *alel*.

alila-, ali(li)li-, aliliya-, al(l)iya-, ālli-   (c), name of an ornithomantic bird, nom. sg. *alilas* (*IBoT* I 32 Vs. 24; *KBo* XV 28 Vs. 11), *alililis* (*KUB* V 22, 37), *alilis* (e.g. *KBo* II 6 IV 15; XI 68 I 21; *KUB* V 11 I 15), *aliliyas* (e.g. XVIII 12 + XXII 15 I 9, 12, 13; cf.

34

Ünal, *RHA* 31:43 [1973]), *alliyas* (e.g. *IBoT* I 32 Vs. 5 and 9), *ālliyas* (e.g. *KBo* II 6 IV 14; *KUB* XVIII 5 II 1, 4, 7; cf. A. Archi, *SMEA* 16:128 [1975]), *allias* (e.g. V 11 I 52; ibid. 16 *al-li(s)-as*), *āllias* (XVIII 5 III 12), *aliyas* (e.g. XIV 1 Rs. 91; cf. Götze, *Madd.* 38), *āllis* (V 22, 55), acc. sg. *alilin* (e.g. V 17 II 6), *aliliyan* (e.g. XVIII 12 Vs. 28; *Alalah* 454 II 35 *a-li-li(s)-ya-an*), *alliyan* (*KUB* XVI 60 III 7), *ālliyan* (e.g. V 22, 27), *allian* (e.g. *IBoT* I 32 Vs. 9; *Alalah* 454 I 57 *al-li(s)-an*), *aliyan* (*KUB* XIV 1 Rs. 92; *Alalah* 454 II 32), dat.-loc. sg. *alili* (*KUB* XVIII 12 Vs. 34), acc. pl. *alilius* (e.g. ibid. 19). Cf. also possibly *alilas, alili* s.v. *alel.* Cf. Ertem, *Fauna* 204–7; A. Archi, *SMEA* 16:142 (1975); Otten, *ZA* 66:97–8 (1976).

al(l)iya- is patently haplological (or at least haplographic; cf. *a-li-ya-an* or *al-li(s)-an* beside *a-li-li(s)-ya-an*, with *lis = li*) for *aliliya-*, which is itself a thematization of *alili-*. The *alila-* : *alili-* variation may point to Hitt. : Luw. morphologic alternation. The absence of the determinative ᴹᵁˢᴱᴺ 'bird' is typical of augural bird names. Cf. Kronasser, *Etym.* 1:248; for Hitt. augury, see Goetze, *Kleinasien*² 149–50 (1957).

Possible cognates are bird-names of the type Lat. *olor* 'swan' (< **elor*), OIr. *elae* 'swan', OSwed. *alle* 'Fuligula glacialis', Gk. ἐλέᾱ 'reed-warbler' (vel sim.). Cf. *IEW* 304.

allinassi-   (c.), bread-name, nom. sg. ᴺᴵᴺᴰᴬ*allinassis* (*KBo* XIII 167 I 3; 163/x IV 15), acc. sg. in *KUB* XXV 50 II 7 ᴺᴵᴺᴰᴬ*al-l]i-na-as--si-en* (ibid. 2 ᴺᴵᴺᴰᴬ*allina*[).

Probably derived from some proper name with Luw. suffix *-assi-*. Cf. H. A. Hoffner, *Alimenta Hethaeorum* 150 (1974).

alkista(n)-   (c.) 'bough, branch' (Akkadogram *ARTU*, fem. of *aru*[*m*] 'branch[es]', in e.g. *KUB* XXXVIII 1 II 17 *ĀRDU*, XVII 28 III 31 *ARDU*, X 91 II 16 ᴳᴵˢ*ĀRTI*), nom. sg. *alkistas* (*KBo* XVII 1 IV 16 *ta* GIŠ-*ru kattan* 1-*EN* 5 *alkistas-sis* = XVII 3 IV 12]ᴳᴵˢ*tāru kattan* 1-*EN* 5 *alkistās-sis* 'one tree below, five its branch[es]'; cf. Otten – Souček, *Altheth. Ritual* 37; *VBoT* 58 IV 17 ᴳᴵˢ*alkistas ip*[*p*]*ias* 'vine-branch'; cf. Laroche, *RHA* 23:86 [1965]; *KUB* VIII 13, 7 *takku* ᴰ*SIN ANA* SI GÙB-*ŠU alkistas* 'if the moon

alkista(n)-

to[wards] its left horn [is] a branch'; XLV 58 III 7–8 *alkist*[*as
...*] *karsanza* 'a branch [is] cut off'), *alkistanas* (XXXIII 117 IV
10–11 GIŠ-*rui mahhan* [^{GIŠ}*alk*]*istanas arha* ŪL *uizzi* 'as the bough
does not come off the tree'; cf. Laroche, *RHA* 26:80 [1968]),
acc. sg. *alkistān* (*KBo* XVII 1 IV 37 *t-us alkistān tarnahhe* 'I
launch these [birds] onto the branch'; cf. Otten – Souček,
Altheth. Ritual 39, 45), ^{GIŠ}*alkistanann-a* (*KUB* XXX 34 III 1),
instr. sg. *alkistanit* (309/v, 3; cf. Otten, *ZA* 66:99 [1976]), nom.
pl. in VIII 13, 5 *takku* ^{D}SIN SI-ŠU *alkistanes ki*[*sa* 'if the moon's
horn turns to branches', acc. pl. ^{GIŠ}*alkistānus* (X 27 I 15; cf.
ibid. 20 and 24; von Brandenstein, *Orientalia* N.S. 8:70, 75–7
[1939]; M. Vieyra, *RA* 51:85–6 [1957]), ^{GIŠ}*alkistanus* (e.g. XVII
27 II 16 *nu-ta-ma* INBI *hūmandas* ^{GIŠ}*alkistanus d*[*āi* 'he takes
branches of each fruit-tree'; XXVII 29 I 10; cf. Haas – Thiel,
Rituale 134, 206, 208; *KBo* X 47g III 16 ŠA ^{GIŠ}ERIN [...]
^{GIŠ}*alkistanus* 'cedar-branches'; cf. Otten, *Istanbuler Mitteilungen* 8:108 [1958]; Laroche, *RHA* 26:12 [1968]; XXIII 23 Vs.
33 $^{G]IŠ}$*INBI* ^{GIŠ}*alkistanus*; *Bo* 3158 Vs. 8 GIŠ-*ruas* ^{GIŠ}*alkistanus*
'tree-branches'; *Bo* 2967 III 2 ^{GIŠ}*eyas* ^{GIŠ}*alkistanus*), dat.-loc. pl.
alkistanas (see Otten, *ZA* 66:98–9 [1976]).

The element *-ista(n)-* (for declension type cf. *alanza*[*n*]-, s.v.)
is reminiscent of the semantically related *hurpasta(n)-*, *hur-
pusta-* 'leaf, peel' (q.v.); the latter indicates an analysis *alk-
-ista(n)-* besides *hatt-alk-esna-* 'thorn-bush' (q.v.) and perhaps
also the plant-name *tap-alk-usta-na-* (q.v.). Cf. Čop, *Ling.*
3:54–5 (1958); Neumann, *IF* 71:79 (1961); H. A. Hoffner,
Orientalia N.S. 35:381–2 (1966). *alk-* (IE *A_2*é*l-ĝ-*) is related to
OCS *loza* 'vine, tendril, shoot' (*A_2*l-óĝ-*) seen also in Hes.
ὀλόγινον·ὀζῶδες 'branchy' (opp. ἄ(ν)οζος 'branchless'; with
prefix ὀ- as in ὄ-πατρος or ὄζος < *ὄ-σδος; for suffix cf. e.g. λᾶας
'stone' : λάϊνος 'stony'), Hes. κατάλογον · τὴν μύρτον (the
"twiggy" myrtle, Vergil's *densis hastilibus horrida myrtus* [*Aeneid* 3.23], with formation as κατάκομος 'with falling hair'). Cf.
IEW 691; Čop, *Indogermanica minora* 30–1.

A comparison with Skt. **alka-* (in *vyàlkaśa-*) 'root fibril',
alaka- 'curl' (K. Hoffmann apud Mayrhofer, *KEWA* 3:796) is
extremely brittle. The invocation of Hurrian for the suffix *-sta-*
(Kronasser, *Etym.* 1:197–8) is strictly per obscurius.

36

alpa- (c., pl. also n.) 'cloud' (matching the akkadogram *URPU* and Akk. *urpu* in lists of Hitt. and Akk. treaty witnesses, e.g. *KUB* XIX 50 IV 26–27 *sallis arunas* [*nepis tekan*] IM.*TE*.MEŠ *hēwus alpus* 'great sea, heaven, earth, winds, rain, clouds' besides *KBo* V 9 IV 18–19 A.AB.BA GAL AN *Ù* KI [IM.MEŠ] *URPI*.MEŠ 'great sea, heaven and earth, winds, clouds'; cf. Friedrich, *Staatsverträge* 2:16; 1:24), nom. sg. *alpas* (*KUB* XIX 14, 8 *nepisi ŪL alpas* 'not a cloud in the sky'; cf. Güterbock, *JCS* 10:112 [1956]; *FHG* 2, 19 *alpas arais* 'a cloud rose'; cf. Laroche, *RHA* 23:141 [1965]; *KUB* XXXIII 21 IV 17–18]*alpass-a arha paizzi* [...]*alpass-a uizzi* 'and the cloud goes away ... and the cloud comes'; XVII 8 IV 9 *nu alpas* GIG-*an ŪL tarahzi n-an-za ser nepisanza tarahdu* 'the cloud does not overcome illness; heaven above shall overcome it'; cf. Laroche, *RHA* 23:167 [1965]; XX 65, 10; XLIII 62 II 3), *alpās* (*Bo* 3092 Vs. 7 *alpās arāis*), acc. sg. *alpan* (XXXIII 21 IV 15 *idalu alpan uizzi* 'ill comes to the cloud'; cf. Laroche, *RHA* 23:122 [1965]; *KBo* XIII 145 Rs. 11), instr. sg. *alpit* (753/1969, 3 *alpit sūwan*['cloud-filled'), nom. pl. c. *alpas* (*KUB* XL 42 Rs. 9 IM.MEŠ-*as alpass-a* 'winds and clouds'), *alpus* (VI 45 III 10–11 *nepis tekan alpus* IM.HI.A-*us tethimas wantewantemas* 'heaven, earth, clouds, winds, thunder, lightning': *KBo* XIX 109, 3 *nepi*]*si-za-kan alpus* 'clouds in the sky'; cf. Siegelová, *Appu-Hedammu* 58), acc. pl. c. *alpus* (*KUB* X 92 V 23 *alpus tet*[*hessar* 'clouds [and] thunder'; XVII 11, 1 and 3), *alpūs* (XXVIII 5 Rs. 7; cf. Laroche, *RHA* 23:77 [1965]), nom.-acc. pl. neut. *alpa*HI.A (XXXVI 14, 5 *nep*]*isaza arha alpa*HI.A *peda*[*s* 'from the sky he brought clouds'; cf. Güterbock, *JCS* 6:16 [1952]), gen. pl. *alpas* (*KUB* XII 2 III 3 and *KBo* XI 5 I 10 ᴰU *alpas* 'storm-god of the clouds'; XIX 146 Vs. 9 *alpas* ᴰU-*as;* *KUB* XII 2 I 16 DINGIR.MEŠ LÚ.MEŠ *alpas* 'male gods of the clouds'; *KBo* XIII 245 Rs. 6–7 ᴰU.HI.A-*as alpas warsas hēwus* 'to the storm-gods of clouds, precipitation, rain'). Cf. Friedrich, *Staatsverträge* 2:35–6, 166–7; Otten, *ZA* 66:99 (1976).

alparama- 'cloudiness, cloud-deck', hapax in *KBo* III 21 II 20 (hymn to storm-god Adad)]*mit-ma-kan alparamit-tit-a* KUR-*e kariyan* 'with ? and with your cloud-deck the land is covered'. Cf. Laroche, *BSL* 52.1:77 (1956); Kronasser, *Etym.* 1:179.

The variation nom. and acc. pl. c. *alpus* : nom.-acc. pl. neut.

("collective") *alpa*HI.A is matched by e.g. *aniyatt-* (s.v. *an[n]iya-*), *suppala-*, *warsula-* (s.v. *wars[iya]-*), *waspa-*, and corresponds to e.g. Lat. *locī : loca* or Gk. κύκλοι : κύκλα. Cf. Kronasser, *Etym.* 1:254; Neu, *IF* 74:239–40 (1969); C. Watkins, *Lg.* 45:239 (1969), *Flexion und Wortbildung* 365 (1975).

The standard connection, since C. L. Mudge, *Lg.* 7:252 (1931), is with Lat. *albus* 'white' (IE **albho-*; *IEW* 30–1). While **albh-* is found in noun usages (e.g. Gk. ἀλφός 'whitish irruption, leprosy'), the 'cloud' meaning would be unique, and the dominant Hitt. association of clouds with rain and thunder does not advocate "whiteness". Couvreur (*Hett.* 106, 149) adduced instead Goth. *luftus* 'air' (IE **lew-p-*; *IEW* 690–1) and Gk. λαπαδνός 'slack, weak' (cf. IE **lep-* and **leb-*; *IEW* 678, 655–7). An IE **A₂él-p- : *A₂l-ép-* (Skt. *álpa-* 'small'; Lith. *alpùs* 'weak', *al̃pti* 'swoon': Lith. *lepùs* 'coddled, soft', *lẽpti* 'grow slack'; Lat. *lepidus* 'nice, effeminate'; Gk. λαπαρός 'slack') is conceivable (cf. *IEW* 33 and *alpant-*, s.v.); the semantic link to 'air' would be via 'flimsy, insubstantial'; from there to 'cloud' cf. Ionic-Attic ἀήρ 'air', Homeric 'mist, cloudiness', ἠερόεις 'murky, clouded'. A further possible connection for *alpa-* is a group of words suggested by Čop (*Živa antika* 3:183 [1953], 4:147 [1954]) and exemplified by Serbian *lȁp* 'bog-soil' (< **ol-pos*), Gk. λάπη 'scum, murk' (cf. for meaning Lett. *mãkuônis* 'dark cloud': Lith. *makonė* 'puddle', OCS *moča* 'urine', *mokrŭ* 'wet'). Cf. Puhvel, *RHA* 33:61 (1975) = *Analecta Indoeuropaea* 347 (1981), *JAOS* 97:598 (1977).

V. Pisani's comparison (*Paideia* 7:322–3 [1952]) of *alpa-* with Arm. *amb*, Ved. *abhrá-* (n.) 'cloud' (IE **n̥bh-* besides Gk. νέφος, etc.) presupposed Hitt. **amb-* > /alb-/ (cf. *lam-* < IE **nom-* in *laman-*, *lammar*); but the toleration of *-mp-* elsewhere (e.g. *aimpa-*, *ambassi-*) casts doubt on the postulated development.

alpant- 'swooned; weak, mild', nom. sg. c. in *KUB* VII 1 I 1–2 *mān* DUMU-*las alpanza nasma-ssi-kan garāties adantes* 'if a child (is) in a swoon or his innards (are) consumed'; ibid. 39–40 *nu kuis* DUMU-*as alpanza nasma-ssi-kan garātes adantes n-an tuikkus* *isgahhi* 'whatever child (is) in a swoon or his innards (are) consumed, I salve his limbs'; ibid. IV 8 *mān* DUMU-*as alpanza*; XXX 48 Vs. 2–3 *mān* DUMU-*as ālpānza*; XXX 49 IV 16–17 *mān* DUMU-*as* [*ālp*]*anza*; nom.-acc. sg. neut. *alpān* (*KBo* XXIV 40 Vs. 8 and 279/d V 12 'mild', epithet of GA.KIN.AG 'cheese'). Cf. Kronasser, *Die Sprache* 7:142, 144 (1961); Laroche, *CTH* 166; Otten, *ZA* 66:99 (1976).

Götze (*Madd.* 112) assumed a variant of or error for *alwanza-* 'bewitched' (q.v.); so still in *JCS* 23:92 (1970), claiming a confirmatory restoration *ālw*]*anza* in the duplicate XXX 49 IV 17 quoted above (cf. also *HW²* 60–1). Yet the use of *nasma* 'or' points to a symptomatic medical alternative to the internal complaint (both calling for ointment) rather than to any general idea of witchcraft. Cf. rather Lith. *ãlpti* 'to swoon', *álpėti* 'lie in a swoon', *alpìmas* 'a swoon', *alpùs* 'weak', pointing to a productive verbal root of which Hitt. *alpant-* is a participial survival. Cf. Couvreur, *Hett.* 106–7; V. Čihař, *Arch. Or.* 22:483 (1954). For other specific Anatolian-Baltic lexical isoglosses cf. e.g. Hitt. *alpu-* (s.v.), *kutruwa(n)-* (s.v.), and *suwaru-* (s.v. *aru-*). Cf. Puhvel, *RHA* 33:61 (1975) = *Analecta Indoeuropaea* 347 (1981), *JAOS* 97:598 (1977), *Gedenkschrift für H. Kronasser* 181 (1982). Cf. *alpa-*.

alpassi-, adjective in the sequence NINDA.KUR₄.RA BA.BA.ZA *alpassis* 'thick bread (as) porridge' (*KBo* II 4 II 22, with gloss-wedges; ibid. III 26, IV 4; XXIII 95 Vs. 9; cf. Haas, *Nerik* 282, 286, 298).

Laroche (*Gedenkschrift P. Kretschmer* 2:3 [1957]) assumed a Luwian-type adjective in -*assi*-, derived from Hitt. *alpa-* 'cloud', and connected the town name ^{URU}*Alpassiya* (*KUB* XXVI 43 Vs. 42; cf. Imparati, *RHA* 32:28 [1974]). Cf. Kronasser, *Etym.* 1:228; H. A. Hoffner, *Alimenta Hethaeorum* 150 (1974). Hoffner (ibid. 170) also adduced ^{NINDA}*labassis* BA.BA.ZA in 163/x IV 14.

alpu- 'smooth, rounded, dull, blunt' (= Akk. *kepū* 'to bend, blunt' in moon omina, e.g. 1026/u + *KUB* XXIX 11 Vs. 5 [Akk.] SI ZAG-*šu kepi* SI GÙB-*šu ēd* = [Hitt.] *nu* ZAG-*an* SI-*ŠU alpu* SI

GÙB-*la-ma dampu* 'its right horn [is] rounded, but its left horn [is] pointed'); similarly nom.-acc. sg. neut. ibid. 1–2, 3–4, 7–8 and VIII 6 Vs. 1–2, 3–4, 5–6, 7–8; XXVII 67 III 67–68 *nu* ^{GIŠ}*eān dāi ser-at warhuui kattann-at alpu* 'he takes an *eya*-tree; it (is) rough at the top (but) smooth below'.

alpue(s)- 'become blunt, lose one's edge', 3 sg. pres. act. *alpuēszi* (*KBo* XVI 24 + 25 I 47–49 *man-wa ini kūrur arha harakzi ... man-wa ini [kūrur parā a]lpuēszi* '[one who is fed up with a war says:] might that war get lost, ... might that war lose its sting'), *ālpuēszi* (XVI 102, 4); verbal noun *alpuemar* (n.) 'blunting, rounding, smoothness', nom.-acc. sg. in XI 14 I 12–13 *ù ANA* GUD.APIN.LAL-*kan huiswanti ANA SI.HI.A-ŠU alpuemar tepu kuranzi* 'and on a living plow-ox they cut a little blunting onto its horns' (i.e. they trim off some of the point); I 42 III 45 SI-*as alpuimar* 'horn-trimming' = (Akk.) *šabardu* (the latter uncertain and unclear; cf. Goetze, *JCS* 17:62–3 [1963]; Güterbock, *RHA* 22:99 [1964]; Kümmel, *Orientalia* N.S. 36:367 [1967]; *MSL* 13:139 [1971]); *KUB* XVII 26 I 10 *alpuemar* (of a sheep's horn); XXXIII 33, 14 *al]puemar* GUŠKIN-*as* 'sheen of gold' (cf. Laroche, *RHA* 23:125 [1965]); 222/b, 4 *ŠA* GÍR *alpue[* 'blunting (= blunt edge?) of a dagger' (cf. Otten, *ZA* 66:100 [1976]).

alpuemar is from an inchoative-stative stem variant -*e*- of the denom. verbal suffix -*es*- (cf. e.g. *werite*- 'be afraid' beside *werites*- 'become afraid': noun *weritema*- 'fear', and see C. Watkins, *TPhS* 1971:75).

For the correct interpretation of *alpu*- 'rounded' vs. *dampu*- 'pointed' (q.v.) cf. Riemschneider, *Bi. Or.* 18:25–6 (1961); Kümmel, *Orientalia* N.S. 36:367 (1967). Earlier Laroche (*RHR* 148:14 [1955]) posited 'lisse' vs. 'rugueuse', i.e. 'smooth' vs. 'rough' (also *alpu*- 'lisse' rather than 'émoussé' ['blunt'] à propos of *alpuemar* in *OLZ* 58:246 [1963]); J. Holt (*Festschrift J. Friedrich* 213–6 [1959]) assumed 'klar' vs. 'trübe' with IE etymologies (Lat. *albus*, Engl. *damp*; cf. Riemschneider, *Bi. Or.* 18:25–6; Puhvel, *Lg.* 38:302 [1962]); Güterbock (*RHA* 22:98–100 [1964]) reversed the meanings to 'pointed' vs. 'blunt' but was overtaken by the Akk. bilingual 1026/u (cf. ibid. 109; Goetze, *JCS* 22:17 [1968]).

alpu- is the exact formal equivalent of Lith. *alpùs* 'weak' (see s.v. *alpant-*); just as Gk. ἀμβλύς 'blunt, weak' is from *ἀμλύς akin to ἀμαλός 'soft, weak', *alpu-* has developed the meaning 'smooth, rounded', and hence also 'dull, blunt'. Cf. Puhvel, *RHA* 33:59–62 (1975) = *Analecta Indoeuropaea* 345–8 (1981), *JAOS* 97:599 (1977), *Gedenkschrift für H. Kronasser* 181 (1982).

als- 'owe fealty, give allegiance', partic. *alsant-* 'pledged to (forced?) allegiance' (opp. *marsant-* 'false, disloyal'), nom. sg. c. *alsanza* (*KUB* XXVI 85 II 4 *LI*]M ERÍN.MEŠ GÌR *alsanza* 'one thousand allegiant infantry'; doubtful OHitt. reading *KBo* III 22 Vs. 4 URU*Nēsas* LUGAL-*us* URU*Kussaras* LUGAL-*i alsa*[*nza* 'the king of Nesas owed fealty to the king of Kussaras'), acc. sg. c. *alsandan* (*KUB* XXIII 11 II 34 *alsandann-a* 1 SIG₇ ERÍN.MEŠ *Ù* 6 *ME* ANŠU.KUR.RA GIŠGIGIR.MEŠ 'ten thousand [newly] allegiant troops and six hundred horse-and-chariot teams'; cf. R. Ranoszek, *Rocznik orientalistyczny* 9:56 [1934]; Carruba, *SMEA* 18:160 [1977]; *KBo* III 23 Rs. 14 [OHitt.] *alsandann-a*); verbal noun *alsuwar* (n.) 'fealty, allegiance', nom.-acc. sg. in *KUB* XV 34 II 24–25 *nu-ssi* ANŠU.KUR.RA.HI.A-*as* ERÍN.MEŠ-*as alsuwar istamassuwar* EGIR-*an tarnatten* 'restore unto him the allegiance (and) obedience of cavalry (and) infantry' (cf. Zuntz, *ARIV* 96.2:502 [1936–7]; Haas – Wilhelm, *Riten* 192); *Bo* 3234, 10 *a*]*lsuwar* KUR-*ya* DUMU.LÚ.ULÙ.LU-*as* GUD.HI.A-*as*['allegiance, to the land, of men (and) cattle' (similarly dupl. 617/p). Cf. Neu, *Anitta-Text* 16–9.

As a primary verb *als-* is plausibly IE, and root shapes *$A_2él$-s- (if *-mi* conjugation) or *$H_2ól$-s- (if *-hi* conj.) are normal; semantic affinities are best sought in the direction of 'obligate oneself', lit. 'bind, gird' (cf. *ishiya-*, s.v.); cf. perhaps Vedic *ráśnā* 'girdle' (*Hl-és-*), usually explained as a contamination of *raśanấ* 'rope' and *yásnā* = Gk. ζώνη 'girdle', but more plausibly a rhyming parallel formation to a *yásnā. Cf. Puhvel, *JAOS* 97:599 (1977).

altanni- (c.) 'source, spring; pool, basin, tank' (TÚL), with sporadic determinative TÚL, semi-synonymous with (TÚL)*wattaru-* 'well, waterhole, source, spring' (TÚL), *saku(n)i-* 'spring, fountain', *luli-* 'pool, cistern, tank', *harsumna-* 'headwaters, wellspring, watery depths' (q.v.), nom. sg. ^{TÚL}*altannis* (*KBo* II 13 Vs. 23), *altannis* (II 7 Rs. 25 and 26; *KUB* XII 62 Vs. 16–17 *altannis arta andan-asta* GIŠ-*ru arta ... altannis hazzasta* 'there stands a pool, in it stands a tree ... the pool dried up'), *al-da-an-ni-is* (XXXVIII 1 I 10; XXXVIII 6 IV 9, 19, 20; XXXVIII 10 IV 5; cf. von Brandenstein, *Heth. Götter* 10; L. Rost, *MIO* 8:178, 187–8, 196 [1961]), ^{TÚL}*al-dan-ni-es* (XXII 38 I 5, 15, 21; ibid. 18]*al-dan-ni-is*), ^{TÚL}*aldanis* (*KBo* II 13 Vs. 23), dat.-loc. sg. *altanni* (*KUB* XXII 19, 9), *al-da-an-ni* (XL 101 Rs. 4; *KBo* II 8 III 13; ibid. IV 33 and 35; *IBoT* I 33, lines 58, 71, 76, 77, 92, 97, 109), *aldani* (ibid. 9, 33, 36, 37, 40, 44, 47, 51, 54, 112; cf. Laroche, *RA* 52:152–5 [1958]), nom. pl. *altannis* (*KBo* XI 1 Vs. 16 *mān-ma-kan* ^DU HUR.SAG.MEŠ ÍD.MEŠ *altannis* TÚL.HI.A *kuitki* TUKU.TUKU-*nuir* 'but if mountains, rivers, sources, springs have caused the storm-god any anger'; cf. Houwink Ten Cate – Josephson, *RHA* 25:106 [1967]), *altannus* (ibid. 29 HUR.SAG. .MEŠ-*us* ÍD.MEŠ-*us altannus* TÚL.HI.A ^{TÚL}*sayattius* 'mountains, rivers, sources, springs, fountains'), acc. pl. *altannius* (*KUB* XVIII 24 III 9), dat.-loc. pl. *altannias* (*KBo* XI 1 Vs. 30 ^DU-*an* ANA HUR.SAG.MEŠ ÍD.MEŠ *altannias* TÚL.HI.A *menahhanda taksulāndu* 'let [them] reconcile the storm-god with the mountains, rivers, sources, springs'), *al-dan^{an}-na-as* (*KUB* XLI 8 II 21 *n-as-kan hal[lūwas] aldannas paiddu* 'let him go to the deep springs'; cf. Otten, *ZA* 54:126 [1961]).

Town name ^{URU}*Altannan* (acc. in *KBo* V 8 III 11), ^{URU}*Altanna* (dat.-loc. ibid. 39; cf. Götze, *AM* 156–8),]*Altannan* (XVI 8 III 16),]*Aldanna* (*KUB* XXXIII 26, 4). Cf. Laroche, *RHA* 19:79 (1961); Ertem, *Coğrafya* 8.

The sporadic appearance of *a*-stem determinatives with TÚL (nom. sg. TÚL-*as*, abl. sg. TÚL-*az*) is insufficient reason to postulate an alternative *a*-stem *altanna-* (as is done in *HW*^{2} 62); so is ^{URU}*Altanna-* which merely shows the typical toponomastic gravitation to *a*-stems.

Unlike *wattaru-*, *altanni-* is not attested in OHitt. and seems to be an imperial import from Cilicia and Kizzuwatna; it designates also artificial cultic waterworks such as the ophio-

or ichthyomantic tanks used for MUŠ ('snake', i.e. probably eel) divination (cf. Laroche, *RA* 52:150–62 [1958]). Being tied to spring- and river-worship of Luwo-Hurrian provenance, *altanni-* is probably of such origin; cf. *altanni-ma* in the Istanuwa-ritual *KBo* IV 11, 51 (*Dict. louv.* 164) and the river name ᴵᴰ*Alta* (*KUB* XXV 49 III 9 and 13), ᴵᴰ*Alda* (XXV 48 IV 18; *KBo* XVII 102 Rs. 18).

E. Forrer (*Glotta* 26:180–1 [1938]) postulated a root *alt-* 'well up', with an action noun **altatar* in *altannas* (gen.) TÚL 'wellspring', and thence a new noun *altanni-*. Čop (*Živa antika* 4:147 [1954]; *Univerza v Ljubljani, Zbornik Filozofske Fakultete* 2:400 [1955]; *Ling.* 1:28–9 [1955]) posited an IE **el-d(h)-*, **old(h)-* 'moulder', assumed also for Arm. *altiur* or *eltiur* 'moist area, slough, swamp' and allegedly root-related to Lett. *aluôts* 'source, spring'; thus *alt-* < **old(h)-* or **ḷd(h)-*, with suffix *-anni-* as in Skt. *vart-ani-* 'a turning' (cf. also s.v. *alpa-*).

alumpazhi-, alummazhi-, alampazzi-, target or purpose of bird offering in Hurroid rituals, dat.-loc. sg. *alumpazhiya* (*KBo* XIX 137 IV 3; *KUB* XLVII 89 III 8; cf. Otten, *Materialien* 24; Haas – Wilhelm, *Riten* 70), *alummazhiya* (XV 31 IV 34), ANA *alampazzi* (XLI 48 III 7).

Hurrian term, derived with suffix *-bazhi*, comparable to *-bashi* in Nuzi Hurrian; cf. e.g. *KBo* XX 126 II 16 and 19 (Hurr.) *alumpazhi*, *KUB* XXVII 24 IV 3 *alumpazhinihi*, XXVII 34 IV 20 *alupā[zhi]nita*. Boğazköy forms (*alumpazhi, hanumpazhi, kilumpazhi*) show *-um-*, vs. *-am-* at Nuzi (*hulambashi, tehambashi*, etc.); but cf. also *alampazzi-* above. Since *hanumpazhi* is in variation with *hanumasse*, an abstract-forming suffix is probably involved (cf. s.v. *allassi-*). Cf. Haas – Wilhelm, *Riten* 71–3, 136–7; Laroche, *RHA* 34:45 (1976).

alwanza- 'subject to witchcraft, affected by sorcery' (U + KAK = UH₄), attested in derivatives:

alwanzatar (n.) 'witchcraft, sorcery, magic, spell, hex' (UH₄-*tar*; *KBo* I 45 Rs. 8 *alwanzatar*; cf. *MSL* 3:53 [1955]; XXVI 34

I 9 *alwanzatar* = [AH]; cf. Otten, *Vokabular* 40), nom.-acc. sg. *alwanzatar* (e.g. VI 5 IV 20 [= *Code* 1:44] = VI 3 II 56 *alwanza-tar* = VI 2 II 35 *alu*[*wanzatar*; cf. Friedrich, *Heth. Ges.* 30; Haase, *Fragmente* 23; *KUB* XI 1 IV 23 = *KBo* III 67 IV 11; *KUB* XIX 67 I 7–8 *alwanzatar wemir* 'they found witchcraft'; cf. Götze, *Neue Bruchstücke* 16; *KUB* XII 58 II 11 *idalu papratar alwanzatar* 'evil uncleanness [and] witchcraft'; cf. Goetze, *Tunnawi* 12; *KBo* XV 10 II 15 and 27; ibid. III 57; cf. Szabó, *Entsühnungsritual* 22, 24, 44; *KUB* XXIV 13 II passim; cf. Haas – Thiel, *Rituale* 104), *alwazatar* (XII 58 III 4 and 9; VII 53 III 6; cf. Goetze, *Tunnawi* 16–8), *alwāzatar* (ibid. 16), *alwazātar* (XII 58 II 33; cf. Goetze, *Tunnawi* 14), *alwanzata* (*KBo* XIII 157, 2; also Jakob-Rost, *Ritual der Malli*, passim), *alwazata* (*JCS* 24:37 [1971], Rev. 5), gen. sg. *alwanzannas* (*KUB* XI 1 IV 22 = *KBo* III 67 IV 10), dat.-loc. sg. *alwanzanni* (*KUB* XXXVI 83 I 17), UH_4-*anni* (*IBoT* III 97, 6).

alwanzessar (n.) 'witchcraft', nom.-acc. sg. *alw*]*anzessar* (7/t, 4), gen. sg. *alwanzesnas* (*Bo* 3660 II 6), dat.-loc. sg. *alwanzesni* (*VBoT* 111 III 16), UH_4-*esni* (*KUB* IX 34 II 18), abl. sg. *alwanzesnaza* (XIX 67 I 9–10 [URU]*Samuhan alwanzesnaza sunnas* 'he filled Samuha with witchcraft'; *VBoT* 111 III 18), *alwanzes-nanz*[*a* (1410/u, 5). Cf. Otten, *ZA* 66:101 (1976).

alwanzena- 'practising witchcraft, sorcerous; sorcerer', nom. sg. c. *alwanzenas* (e.g. *KUB* XXIV 13 II 28 *alwanzenas kuit* HUL-*lu uttar ēssista* 'what evil thing the sorcerer did'; *KBo* XIX 145 III 14 *alw*]*anzenas* SAL-*za alwanzatar udās* 'the sorceress brought a spell'; *KUB* XVII 27 II 28 UH_4-*nas* UKÙ-*as kue uddār memiskit* 'what words the sorcerer spoke'), *alwanzinas* (XXIV 13 II 9–10 *alwanzinas kuit* HUL-*lu uttar ēssesta arha-ta-kkan ansan ēsdu* 'what evil thing the sorcerer did shall be wiped off you'), acc. sg. c. UH_4-*an* UKÙ-*an* (XVII 27 III 18), gen. sg. *alwanzenas* (e.g. *HT* 6 Reverse 17 *humandas alwanzenas* ['every sorcerer's [tongue]'; similarly *KBo* IX 125 I 5; *KUB* XVII 27 II 33 *nu* UH_4-*nas uddār-set* 'the sorcerer's words'; ibid. III 10 UH_4-*nas* UH_4-*tar* 'the sorcerer's magic'; XXIV 13 II 13–14 *alwanzenas kue uddār ēsta* 'what words of the sorcerer there were'), *alwanzinas* (*KBo* XI 11 I 9 *alwanzinas* EME-*an* 'the sorcerer's tongue'), *alwazenas* (*KUB* VII 53 II 11; cf. Goetze,

Tunnawi 10), dat.-loc. sg. *alwanzeni* (VII 2 I 27; XXIV 14 I
27–28 *n-at-san sarā alwanzeni* UKÙ-*si pessiskimi* 'I throw it
upon the sorcerer'), *alwazeni* (ibid. 21 *alwazeni* UKÙ-*si* SAG.DU-*i*
'on the sorcerer's head'), *alwanzini* UKÙ-*si* (XXIV 9 II 51; cf.
Jakob-Rost, *Ritual der Malli* 38), *alwazini* UKÙ-*si* (ibid. 14; cf.
Jakob-Rost, *Ritual der Malli* 32), abl. sg. *alwanzenaza* (873/u, 7
n-an-kan alwanzenaza arha lā[*wen* 'him we freed from the hex';
cf. Haas – Thiel, *Rituale* 271), *alwazenaz* (XII 57 I 6 *alwazenaz
antuhsaz*), nom. pl. c. *alwanzenes antuhses* (*KBo* XI 12 I 15),
alwanzines antuhsis (XII 126 I 13; cf. Jakob-Rost, *Ritual der
Malli* 22), *alwanzinnes* EME[.HI.A 'sorcerous tongues' (XV 10 I
33; cf. Szabó, *Entsühnungsritual* 18), EME.HI.A *alwanzinas* (*KUB*
XXIV 12 III 12–13), acc. pl. c. *alwazenus* (VII 53 II 16; cf.
Goetze, *Tunnawi* 12), *alwanzinnus* EME.HI.A (*KBo* XV 10 I
30–31). Cf. Güterbock, *RHA* 22:101 (1964).

alwanzahh- 'bewitch, hex', 3 sg. pres. act. *alwanzah*[*hi* (*KUB*
XXXV 145 Rs. 7), 3 sg. pret. act. *alwanzahhiyit* (XXIV 9 I 40;
cf. Jakob-Rost, *Ritual der Malli* 26), 2 pl. pret. act. *alwazahan-
tin* (*VBoT* 132 II 3; cf. Haas – Thiel, *Rituale* 280), 3 pl. pret. act.
UH₄-*ir* (*KUB* XXI 17 I 11; cf. Ünal, *Hatt.* 2:18); partic.
alwanzahhant-, nom. sg. c. *alwanzahhanza* (*KBo* XI 12 I 2; ibid.
11 *nu-za antuwahhas kuis alwanzahhanza* = XII 126 I 9 *nu*
UKÙ-*as kuis* UH₄-*anza* 'the man who is bewitched'; cf. Jakob-
Rost, *Ritual der Malli* 20; *KUB* V 6 III 18–19; XXX 36 III 7),
acc. sg. c. *alwanzahhantan* (e.g. XXIV 14 I 2 *alwanzahhantan*
UKÙ-*an* EGIR-*pa lāmi* 'I set free the bewitched man'), *alwanzah-
handan* (e.g. *KBo* XIX 145 III 41–42 *āski-kan anda alwanzahhandan* SAL-*an lānun* 'in the gate I freed [from the hex] the
bewitched woman'; cf. Laroche, *RHA* 28:60 [1970]; Haas –
Thiel, *Rituale* 304; *KUB* XXIV 13 IV 3–4 *mān alwanzahhandan*
UKÙ-*an* EGIR-*pa* SIG₅-*ahmi* 'when I restore [to normalcy] a
bewitched man'; cf. Haas – Thiel, *Rituale* 110), *alw*]*anzahhadan*
(VII 33 Vs. 2), nom.-acc. sg. neut. *alwanzahhan* (*KBo* V 2 I 6; cf.
Witzel, *Heth. KU* 98; *KUB* XXIV 12 II 22), nom. pl. c.
alwanzahhantes (VII 2 IV 4–5 *mān antuhsi* DINGIR.MEŠ *alwanzahhantes* 'if for a man the gods are affected by magic'; XXIV
12 II 12 EME.HI.A *alwanzahhantes* 'bewitched [i.e. sorcerous]
tongues'; cf. ibid. III 12–13 EME.HI.A *alwanzinas*, quoted

alwanza-

above); inf. *alwanzahhūwanzi* (I 1 II 77; cf. Götze, *Hattusilis* 22), *alwanzahhuuanzi* (dupl. *KBo* III 6 II 56); iter. 3 sg. pres. act. *alwa]nzahhiskizzi* (XII 126 I 34; cf. Jakob-Rost, *Ritual der Malli* 24), 3 sg. pret. act. *alwanzahheskit* (XVIII 145, 5; Jakob-Rost, *Ritual der Malli* 31, I 70), *alwanzahhiskit* (e.g. *KUB* VII 47 Vs. 7; *KBo* XV 10 I 21; cf. Szabó, *Entsühnungsritual* 14; *KUB* XXIV 9 I 49 and II 21; cf. Jakob-Rost, *Ritual der Malli* 28, 34), UH₄-*heskit* (XLI 1 I 8), UH₄-*ahheskit* (ibid. 18; cf. Jakob-Rost, *Ritual der Malli* 30), 3 pl. pret. act. *alwanzahheskir* (XXIV 12 II 5).

alwanzahha- 'witchcraft', instr. sg. in XXX 51 IV 13–14 *alwanzahhi[t] akkiskattari* 'people keep dying from witchcraft', abl. sg. in *VBoT* 120 III 3–4 *āski-ma-kan kuit alwanzahheski[r] n-a[t-kan] alwanzahhaz arha lāwēn* 'what they hexed at the gate, it we freed from the hex' (cf. Haas – Thiel, *Rituale* 144). Cf. Kronasser, *Etym.* 1:166.

The postulated adj. *alwanza-* accounts for denom. abstracts in *-atar* and *-essar* (cf. e.g. *palhatar* and *palhessar* s.v. *palhi-*), denom. adj. in *-ena-* (cf. e.g. *arahzena-* s.v. *arha-*), and factitive verbal stem in *-ahh-* (cf. e.g. *newahh-* s.v. *newa-*). Cf. Götze, *Hattusilis* 88, *Neue Bruchstücke* 14–5; Kammenhuber, *MIO* 2:428 (1954). Laroche's suggestion of a noun *alwant-* 'maléfice' (*BSL* 58.1:72 [1963]) is no improvement and leaves both the *-z-* and the thematization with *-a-* as unexplained as does an adjectival **alw-ant-* (cf. Kammenhuber, *MIO* 3:375 [1955]; Kronasser, *Etym.* 1:265), unless one appeals for the former to an affrication of *t* before *e* starting in and generalized from **alwant-essar* and **alwant-ena-*. Gusmani (*KZ* 86:259 [1972], *Paideia* 32:313 [1977]) interpreted *alwanzahha-* as a graphic representation of **alwan(t)-sha-*, comparing *palzahha-* /paltsha/ (abstract noun suffix as in e.g. *armuwala-sha-* s.v. *arma-*), from which was allegedly abstracted the secondary stem *alwanza-*; but Gusmani himself declared *-sha-* fully deverbative (*KZ* 86:260), yet a verb stem **alwan(t)-* begs credulity, while a participle **alwant-* would be a nominal base.

Extra-Hittite connections are brittle. E. Polomé (*La Nouvelle Clio* 6:45–55 [1954]) compared *alwanza-* with the ON Runic magical term *alu* (of inferential meaning), Gk. ἀλύω 'be beside oneself', and Lett. *aluôt* 'be distraught', under the formal umbrella of an IE *al-w-* and a semantic denominator of 'magical charm'. A more precise comparison might be made with Gk. ἀλύω < *ἀλύσιω (cf. ἀλυσμός 'anguish'): vbl. adj. *alus-no-* 'possessed, distraught' > *alwn̥so-* (metathesis of *-sn-* cluster as in *alanza*[*n*]-, q.v.?) > Hitt. *alwanza-*? But cf. for ἀλύω alternatively s.v. *halluwai-* and *halwammar*. Cf. Puhvel, *JAOS* 97:599 (1977).

am(m)iyant- 'small', nom. sg. c. *ammiyanza* (*KUB* XXX 16 I 3 *hūmanza sallis ammiyanza* 'everyone, large [and] small'; cf. Otten, *Totenrituale* 18; XLV 20 II 14–15 *anzidaz wahnut sallis ammiyanza* 'to us turned great [and] small'; cf. Friedrich, *Arch. Or.* 6:370 [1934]), *ammianza* (XXVIII 6 Vs. r. 15b *ammianza* ... DUMU-*as* 'small son' [vs. ibid. 19b–20b UR.SAG-*is* ... DUMU-*as* 'heroic son']), *amiyanza* (XVII 10 I 38 *partauwa-sset-wa ami-yanta apass-a-uwa amiyanza* 'its wings are small, and it is small itself'; cf. Laroche, *RHA* 23:92 [1965]), acc. sg. c. in XLV 20 II 10 *ammeyantan sallin*, nom.-acc. sg. neut. *ammiyan* (XLIII 59 I 9 *ammiyan pattar* 'small dish' [vs. ibid. 10 GAL-*li paddani* 'in a big dish']), *ammian* (*KBo* XIV 109, 5), gen. sg. c. *amiantas* (*Bo* 2689 III 27), nom. pl. c. *ammiyantes* (*KBo* XX 82 III 15), *amiyantes* (*KUB* XXXIII 66 III 13; cf. Laroche, *RHA* 23:131 [1965]), acc. pl. c. *āmmiyantus* (*KBo* III 34 II 28), *amiyandus* (XII 89 III 12 [vs. ibid. 11 GAL-*lamus*]; cf. Haas – Wilhelm, *Riten* 29), *ammeyandus* (XII 112 Vs. 16), nom.-acc. pl. neut. *amiyanta* (see above), *amiyanda* (*KUB* XXXIII 5 II 13; cf. Laroche, *RHA* 23:100 [1965]), dat.-loc. pl. *āmmiyandas* (*KBo* VIII 107, 7), *amiyantas* (*KUB* XXXII 123 III 24). Cf. Otten, *Überlieferungen* 10–1.

am(m)iyantessar (n.) 'miniature (bread)', nom.-acc. sg. NIN⌐ ᴰᴬ*ammiyantessar* (*KBo* XXII 186 V 8), ᴺᴵᴺᴰᴬ*amiyantessar* (XXII 193 IV 7), ᴺᴵᴺᴰᴬ*amiantessar* (1110/u Vs. 7; 119/s Rs. 9), ᴺᴵᴺᴰᴬ*ammeyant*[*essar* (*KUB* XXX 32 IV 3; cf. V. Haas – M. Wäfler, *Ugarit-Forschungen* 8:98 [1976]). Cf. H. A. Hoffner, *Alimenta Hethaeorum* 150–1 (1974); Otten, *ZA* 66:101–2 (1976).

Petrified privative prefix IE *n̥-* (> *an-*) + *-miya-* (from *mai-* 'grow, ripen') + inner – Hittite-*nt-*, thus literally 'not grown,

stunted' (type of Gk. ἄγαμος; cf. ἀναυξής 'not growing'). Cf.
also Laroche, *JCS* 21:174 (1967); Čop, *Ling.* 8:60 (1966–8).
Carruba (*Istituto Lombardo, Rendiconti, Classe di Lettere*
108:580–1 [1974]) compared Lyc. * am̃mãma* as 'young, small'
(Luwian-type *-mi-* participle); but Neumann (*Die Sprache*
20:110 [1974]) equated this adjective describing cattle with Gk.
ἄμωμος 'unblemished'.

   Cf. for formation *asiwant-, awiti-, newalant-, niwalli-*; for
meaning, *kappi-*; for both, *ummiyant-* 'young' (lit. 'grown up,
adult').

amiyara-   (c.) 'ditch, canal, channel' (PA₅), nom. sg. PA₅-*as* (*KBo*
XXI 4 + *KUB* XXIX 7 Rs. 51; cf. Lebrun, *Samuha* 124; *RS*
25.421 Verso 44; cf. Laroche, *Ugaritica* 5:774 [1968]), acc. sg.
amiyaran (*KUB* XLIII 23 Rs. 8 and 34), PA₅-*an* (*KBo* VI 26 I 18
[= *Code* 1:62]), gen. sg. in A.ŠÀ ŠA PA₅ 'ditch-field' (*KUB* VIII 75
I 61, vs. ibid. 59 A.ŠÀ ŠA ÍD 'river-field' and 64 A.ŠÀ *wappuwas*
'field of the river-bank'; cf. Souček, *Arch. Or.* 27:10 [1959]),
abl. sg. in *KBo* VI 11 I 16 (= *Code* 2:9) *takku amiyaraza*
GIŠ*INBAM kuiski ārgi* 'if anyone cuts fruit-trees off from a(n
irrigation) ditch', with dupl. *KUB* XXIX 23, 12]PA₅-*az* GIŠ*IN-
BAM kui*[*s-* (cf. Friedrich, *Heth. Ges.* 62; Imparati, *Leggi ittite*
122, 260; Haase, *Fragmente* 59; Souček, *OLZ* 56:466–7 [1961]),
nom. pl. in VIII 48 I 18 *nu-ssi-kan ishahru parā* PA₅.HI.A-*us mān*
[*arser* 'his tears flowed like channels' (cf. Laroche, *RHA* 26:18
[1968]; similarly XXXIII 113+ I 29–30; cf. Güterbock, *JCS*
6:12 [1952]). Cf. Otten, *ZA* 66:102–3 (1976).

   Cf. Gk. ἀμάρη 'trench, channel', first in *Iliad* 21:259 χερσὶ
μάκελλαν ἔχων, ἀμάρης ἐξ ἔχματα βάλλων 'with a pick in his
hands, throwing debris out of the channel' (simile of a man
irrigating plants and orchards). Non-IE Anatolian term? For
the phonetic contrast *amiyar-*: ἀμαρ-, cf. e.g. Hitt. *Adaniya-*:
Adana-. Cf. Neumann, *Untersuch.* 91–2; Laroche, *BSL*
51.1.XXXIII (1955). D. Silvestri (*AION* 35:402–5 [1975])
adduced Egypt. *mr* 'canal' and other "Mediterranean" terms.
   Cf. *alalima-, arsi-, artah(h)i-*.

ambassi- (c.), movable cultic gear designed for animal and bread sacrifices, probably a portable fire-altar; sacrificial ritual involving the same; often undeclined (shorthand *am-si-*, e.g. *Bo* 2033a Vs. 9, 14, 18 *am-si* besides parallel *KBo* XI 23 + 24 I 2, 5, 8 *ambassi*; also *am-*, e.g. *IBoT* III 148 II 14 1 UDU *am* 1 UDU *ki-ya* [= *keldiya*] DINGIR.MEŠ LÚ.MEŠ 1 MUŠEN *ambassi* 'one sheep for the a., one sheep for the well-being of the male gods, one bird for the a.'), inflected nom. sg. *ambassis* (e.g. *KUB* XXV 22 Rand 1–2 *n-as-kan ser hilamni anda* [...] *ambassis iyanza* ΄up in the gatehouse an a. has been made'; cf. Haas, *Nerik* 238; *Bo* 4931 + I 7 *ambassis karaptari* 'the a. is raised'; *KUB* XLV 58 III 3), *ampassis* (XXVII 16 III 17 *ampassis karaptari*; cf. M. Vieyra, *RA* 51:91 [1957]), *am-is* (XLIII 53 II 8), acc. sg. *ambassin* (e.g. VIII 62 IV 9; ibid. 18 *ambassien*; cf. Laroche, *RHA* 26:24 [1968]; 1665/u II 4 *ambassin kattan tarna*['lower the a.'; cf. Otten, *Materialien* 45; VI 15 II 16), *amassin* (sic *KBo* VIII 57 I 4; ibid. IV 10 TUKU.TUKU-*as amassin* BIL-*nuanzi* 'they burn an a. against [divine] anger; cf. Lebrun, *Samuha* 196–7), *am-sin* (*Bo* 3481 I 8–10 *nu* INA ᴺᴬ⁴*dahanga am-sin harpanzi suppa arha warnuwanzi am-sin-ma* IŠTU É.GAL-*LIM kuin ueter nu-kan apedani ser warnuskandu* 'on the d.-stone they assemble the a.; they burn off clean meats; but what a. they brought from the palace, upon it let them do their burning'; cf. Haas, *Nerik* 292; *KBo* XV 7 Vs. 10–11 *am-sin tarnanzi*; cf. Kümmel, *Ersatzrituale* 36, 40), gen. sg. *ambassiyas* (e.g. *KUB* XV 34 IV 56 *ambassiyas uttar* 'the a.-procedure'; cf. Haas – Wilhelm, *Riten* 208; *KBo* VII 29 II 18), *ambassias* SISKUR 'rite of a.' (*KUB* XXXII 137 II 21), *āmpāssiyas*[*a* (*KBo* VIII 79 Vs. 6; cf. ibid. 8 *n-us āmpāssi wa*[*rnuzi* 'he burns them at the a.'), dat.-loc. sg. *ambassi* (unless uninflected; e.g. *KUB* XXVII 1 I 12 *nu-kan ambassin annalli ambassi anda sipanti* 'he makes the a.-sacrifice within the former a.'; cf. Lebrun, *Samuha* 75; XXIX 4 III 58 SILÁ *ambassi warāni* 'the lamb is burned at the a.'; ibid. IV 4 SILÁ *ambassi pianzi* 'they give the lamb for the a.'; cf. Kronasser, *Umsiedelung* 26, 28), *ambasi* (ibid. II 12 *kī-ma* ANA SISKUR.SISKUR *ambasi danzi* 'but this they take for the a.-ritual'), *ambassitī* (ibid. II 38 SILÁ *ambassitī warnuwanzi* 'they burn the lamb at the a.'), *ambassiti* (*KBo* IV 6 Rs. 2; cf.

Tischler, *Gebet* 14; XV 59 IV 7=XV 68 IV 14; with gloss-wedges *KUB* XXXVIII 25 I 8–9 *ambassiti* [...] *warnuwanzi*; for the Hurrian ending *-ti* cf. Friedrich, *RHA* 8:14 [1947]), *ampassi* (e.g. XV 32 II 19; cf. Haas – Wilhelm, *Riten* 157), *ambassiya* (XXVII 6 I 33; cf. Lebrun, *Samuha* 83, 95), *am-ya* (XXXII 50 Vs. 4; cf. Haas – Wilhelm, *Riten* 245), nom. pl. *ambassiēs* (597/f II 5), dat.-loc. pl. *ambassiyas* (V 10, 22 ^É*hilamni* UGU *pait nu-war-as ambassiyas kattan āras* '[the dog] went up to the gatehouse, and he came down to the a.').

ambassi- appears in Hurrian texts (e.g. *KBo* XIX 136 I 17 *ambassi-ni*, ibid. IV 15 *ambasse-ni-pi*) and is clearly a Hurrian word, of unknown affinities; cf. Friedrich, *AfO* 10:294 (1935–6), *Kleine Beiträge zur churritischen Grammatik* 49–50 (1939); Sommer, *Hethiter und Hethitisch* 89 (1947). A long history of misinterpretation began earlier with Sommer – Ehelolf, *Pāpanikri* 62–3 (cf. Ehelolf, *KlF* 142–4), who identified *ambassi-* and its frequent concomitant *keldi-* 'weal, well-being' (q.v.) as loanwords from Akk. *ambassu* 'park, game preserve' and *kiltu=kištu* 'wood, forest'. Götze – Pedersen, *MS* 43, assumed instead a Hurrian borrowing of *ambassi-* from Akk. *ambassu*, passed along to Hittite. Akk. *ambassu* itself has been tagged a foreignism (from Hurrian, because of Hurr.-Hitt. *ambassi-*; see e.g. *AHW* 42; *CAD* A 2.44); but the meanings are irreconcilable (cf. Goetze, *Lg.* 36:466 [1960]), and there is probably only a homophony. Friedrich's, Sommer's, and Goetze's intervention has not prevented a Hitt. *ambassi-* 'park' from thriving in the secondary literature, e.g. P. Fronzaroli, *AGI* 41:34 (1956); M. L. Mayer, *Acme* 13:84–5 (1960); Gusmani, *Lessico* 29.

H. Wittmann (*Die Sprache* 19:40 [1973]) rejected both 'park' and 'sacrificial spot' and randomly opted for 'something tangible, possibly liquid'; "without prejudice to the status of Hurr. *ambassi-*", Hitt. *ambassi-* was then connected implausibly with Skt. *ambhas-* 'water', Lat. *imber* 'rain' (as perhaps rainwater on top of a *hilammar*, accessible to a dog; cf. *KUB* V 10, 22, quoted above). Cf. Lebrun, *Samuha* 47–8.

Possible denom. verb 3 pl. pret. act. (Luwoid, with gloss-wedges) in *KUB* XII 26 II 8 *nu-war-an ammassanda* (or *ambassanda*; see Goetze, *Tunnawi* 88) 'they sacrificed (?) it' (viz. a clean young ewe; ibid. 6 *kissir* 'they combed', 7 *arrir* 'they washed'; cf. Laroche, *RHA* 23:168 [1965]; Haas, *Orientalia* N.S. 40:424 [1971]; Haas – Wilhelm, *Riten* 26); also Luw. 3 sg. pret. act. *ammasat*[*a* (513/i, 3; cf. Otten, *LTU* 108). Cf. Puhvel, *JAOS* 97:599 (1977).

ampura- (c.), bread-name, nom. sg. ^NINDA^*ampūras* (*KBo* V 1 II 33; cf. Sommer – Ehelolf, *Pāpanikri* 6*), acc. sg. ^NINDA^*ampūran* (XXI 34 II 17; cf. Lebrun, *Hethitica II* 120).

Cf. the town name ^URU^*Ampuriya* (XIV 77, 2); for a parallel see s.v. *alpassi-*. Cf. H. A. Hoffner, *Alimenta Hethaeorum* 151 (1974).

-an, Old and Middle Hittite sentence particle, similar in fate to *-apa* and *-(a)sta* and in function to *-kan* or *-san* (q.v.), as in *KBo* VI 2 IV 10 (= *Code* 1:78) *nu-sse-an* = VI 3 IV 3 *nu-ssi-kan*, e.g. *KUB* XXX 10 Vs. 24 *nu-mu wasdul-met* [*tēi*]*ddu nu-za-an ganesmi* 'may he tell me my fault, and I shall make acknowledgement'. Cf. Otten – Souček, *Altheth. Ritual* 81–2; Houwink Ten Cate, *Records* 31; Neu, *Gewitterritual* 62; Souček, *Arch. Or.* 38:274–6 (1970); Carruba, *SMEA* 12:68–76 (1970), *Beiträge* 31–2; Josephson, *Sentence Particles* 339–44.

Etymology uncertain. Souček (*Arch. Or.* 38:274–6) tentatively tied in *anda*; Carruba (*SMEA* 12:75, 87) assumed an "enclitic truncation" of *anda(n)* and compared Pal. *-(n)ta*, Luw. *-tta*, Hier. *-ta*, Lyc. *te* (for the latter, see Carruba, *Partikeln* 24–8). Houwink Ten Cate (*Acta Orientalia Neerlandica* 39 [1971]; R. A. Crossland and A. Birchall [eds.], *Bronze Age migrations in the Aegean* 153–5 [1973]) adduced Lyc. *-ẽ* and Gk. ἄν (cf. in the latter case also the interrogative particles Lat. *an*, Goth. *an*).

Cf. *anku*; *man*.

anna-, an(n)i-, demonstrative pronominal stem with remote deixis: *an(n)i-* 'that, yonder', nom. sg. c. *annis* (*KBo* I 42 III 33; cf.

MSL 13:138 [1971]); *anisiwat* '(effective) to-day' (III 45 Vs. 12; *ani-* + suffixless dat.-loc.; cf. *appasiwatt-* [s.v.] and *kedani siwatti*, Akk. *ūma annīta*, Skt. *a-dyá*, OIr. *in-diu* 'to-day'.

annaz 'formerly, once upon a time' (e.g. *KBo* III 3 I 3 and 14; cf. Hrozný, *Heth. KB* 136–8; V 8 IV 5; cf. Götze, *AM* 160; XIV 12 IV 27; cf. Güterbock, *JCS* 10:98 [1956]), also *annaza* (e.g. *KUB* XIII 35 III 1–2 30 ANŠU.HI.A-*wa-mu annaza piyer kinun-*-*ma-wa* 13 ANŠU.HI.A *ēszi* 'once upon a time they gave me 30 asses, but now there are only thirteen'; cf. Werner, *Gerichts-protokolle* 8; XXII 40 II 3 and 34; XXXIV 53 Rs. 3, 4, 5, 14).

annisan 'formerly, before; once; at the time', e.g. *KUB* I 4 III 40–41 *annisan-w*[*ar-an* LUGA]L-*iznanni kuwat tittanut* 'why did you before install him in the kingship?', followed by *kinun-ma* 'but now'; I 1 IV 6 *annisan-pat* 'before', followed ibid. 7 by *apedani mehuni* 'at that time' (cf. Götze, *Hattusilis* 30); XIV 15 IV 23 *annisan-wa-ta-kkan kuwapi* ŠEŠ.MEŠ-*KA* KUR-*eaz arha watkunuir* 'once, when your brothers made you jump the country' (cf. Götze, *AM* 68); VI 41 I 23–24 *annisan-ma kuwapi* [^I]*Mashuluwan* ANA [...] *tittanunun* 'but once I had appointed M. to ...'; *KBo* V 13 I 12 *annisan-ma kuit* ANA [^I]*Mashuluwa* IBILA NU.GÁL *ēsta* 'whereas at the time M. did not have a son and heir' (cf. Friedrich, *Staatsverträge* 1:108, 112).

annal(l)i-, annal(l)a- 'former, earlier, old' (antonym *newa-* [GIBIL] 'new, present'; unlike the partially synonymous *karuuili-* [q.v. s.v. *karū*], not 'ancient, primeval'), nom. sg. c. *annal(l)is* (e.g. *KUB* XXI 27 I 7 *ammuk-ma-za* [^SAL]*Puduhepas annallis* GEME-*KA* 'but I, P., [am] your servant from way back'; XXXVIII 3 I 7–8 É.DINGIR-*LIM* GIBIL-*si* DÙ-[*an* ...] [^LÚ]SANGA-*si annallis* 'a temple has been made new for him, [but] the priest he has [is] a holdover'; cf. XXXVIII 1 IV 7; von Brandenstein, *Heth. Götter* 16, 14); *IBoT* I 33, 11 MUŠ *annalis-kan* 'the earlier snake'; cf. ibid. 81 MUŠ *annalli-ma-kan*; Laroche, *RA* 52:152, 154 [1958]), *annallas* (e.g. *KUB* XL 102 V 5 *kās zammuris annallas*), acc. sg. c. *annallin* (e.g. XV 28 III 12; *KBo* II 7 Vs. 7 1 UDU *annallin* 'one earlier sheep'), DINGIR-*LUM annalien* 'the former (statue of a) god' (*KUB* XVII 32, 2; cf. Haas – Wilhelm, *Riten* 242), *annallan* (e.g. XXXVIII 26 Vs. 13 *annallan* DINGIR--*LUM*; *KBo* XII 56 I 7), nom.-acc. sg. neut. *annalli* (e.g. XI 1 Vs.

25 *nu kuitman* KUR-*TAM annalli* EGIR-*pa tiyazi* 'while the country steps back as of old [= reverts to its former state]'; cf. Houwink Ten Cate – Josephson, *RHA* 25:107 [1967]), *annallan* (e.g. *KUB* I 1 IV 68 *an]nallan kuit ēsta apāt-si parā pihhun* 'the former stuff that was there, that I gave forth to her'; cf. Götze, *Hattusilis* 38; XXXVIII 26 Vs. 22 DUG] KAŠ EZENHI.A TEŠI *annallan pitin harkanzi* 'beer-jar[s] for the spring-summer festivities they have brought in good time'; cf. L. Jakob-Rost, *MIO* 9:182 [1963]; XVII 35 II 6; *KBo* II 1 III 14 and IV 2), *annalan* (ibid. I 34, II 11, 23, 34, 40, III 2 '[as] holdover[s]'; cf. Hrozný, *Heth. KB* 8–22), gen. sg. *annallas* (*KUB* XXXVIII 12 I 5 and 7 *annallas* É-*as* 'of the former house'), *annalas* (XXVII 1 IV 46; cf. Lebrun, *Samuha* 85), dat.-loc. sg. *annalli* (e.g. ibid. I 1–2 [*nu-]kan mān* MU.HI.A *istarna pantes nu-kan* ANA ^DIŠ[*TAR*] *annalli annallan* SISKUR *hapusanzi* 'if years have gone by, one resumes the former sacrifice to the Ištar of old'; cf. Lebrun, *Samuha* 75; *KBo* XXI 37 Rs. 17 *annalli tuppi* 'on an old tablet'), abl. sg. *annalliyaz* (e.g. ibid. 14), *annal(l)az(a)* (e.g. IV 2 IV 44–45 *ambassi keldiya annalaz* IŠTU ^{GIŠ}*LI-U₅* GIM-*an iyan* 'as has been done for a.-sacrifice and well-being based on the old wood-tablet'; dupl. *KUB* XII 27, 13 *annallaz*; cf. Götze – Pedersen, *MS* 10, 12; XLII 103 III 13–14 *annalaz-at-kan* GIŠ.HUR *gulzadanaza arha gulsan* 'it has been erased from the old engraved wooden tablet'), often adverbial 'formerly' (e.g. VII 24 Vs. 1 *annalaza* DINGIR.MEŠ-*tar* ŪL *ēsta* 'formerly there was no godhead [i.e. divine statuary]'; XXXVI 89 Rs. 12 ^{ÍD}*Marassantas-wa annallaza ipattarmayan* [with gloss-wedges] *ārsas* 'the M. river flowed formerly [north]westward'; cf. Haas, *Nerik* 152; XXV 20 IV 10 *annalazza*; XXV 18 III 8 *annallaz*; *ABoT* 14 III 18 *annalaz*), nom. pl. c. *annallies* (e.g. *KUB* XXXVIII 12 I 4–5 *annallies-si* 9 ^{LÚ.MEŠ}*hilammates kinun-a-ssi-kan* 'former gatehouse-keepers she had nine, but now she has …'; ibid. IV 15), *annallis* (e.g. XL 8, 5 LÚ.MEŠ ^{URU}*Isuwa-ma-kan kuyēs annallis e[sir* 'the men of Isuwa who were former [inhabitants]', with dupl. XXXIV 23 I 12–13; cf. H. Klengel, *Oriens Antiquus* 7:67 [1968]; Güterbock, *JCS* 10:83 [1956]; *KBo* II 8 I 16 *annallis* EZEN.HI.A 'former festivals'), *annalas* (*KUB* XXXVIII 23, 8 2 DINGIR.MEŠ *annalas* 'two old gods [i.e. images]', vs. ibid. 11 3

DINGIR.MEŠ GIBIL 'three new gods'; cf. L. Jakob-Rost, *MIO* 9:175 [1963]), *annallius* (XL 2 Rs. 8 *kī-ma* URU.DIDLI.HI.A *annallius* 'these old-time towns'; cf. Goetze, *Kizzuwatna* 64 [1940]), *annalius* (XXI 29 I 16–17 *annalius-ma-kan kuyēs* LÚ.MEŠ [...] EGIR-*an esir* 'but the former people who were left'), acc. pl. c. *annallius* (e.g. XXXVIII 34, 7 *annallius pitin harzi* 'has brought [them] in good time'; *HT* 4, 13 *annallius pitin* [; cf. ibid. 9 *karū* 'earlier'), *annalius* (*KBo* XIII 237 Vs. 11 2 UDU *annalius*), nom.-acc. pl. neut. *annalli* (*KUB* XXXVIII 12 II 16–17 *annalli-ssi* 2 É-*TAM* ... *kinun-a-ssi* 1 É-*TAM* 'former houses she had two, but now she has one house'), *annalla* (XXXIII 106 III 50–51 *annalla attalla hūhadalla* [É.] ᴺᴬ⁴KIŠIB.HI.A 'old fatherly-grandfatherly [Lat. *patrīta et avīta*] storehouses', usage affected by secondary association with *anna-* 'mother', as if 'motherly-fatherly-'; contrast *karuuili-* passim elsewhere in the same passage, e.g. 51 *karuuiliyas addas* ᴺᴬ⁴KIŠIB 'the seal of the ancient fathers'; cf. Güterbock, *JCS* 6:28 [1952]), gen. pl. *annallas* (ibid. II 20 *annallas* INIM.MEŠ-*nas tuppiyas* 'tablets of the former words', vs. III 49 *karuuili ... uddār* 'the ancient words'), dat.-loc. pl. in XL 102 V 5 *annallas* ANA *tuppa*HI.A 'on the old tablets'.

an(n)i- is poorly attested; *annisan* need presuppose an *i*-stem no more than does *kissan* 'thus' vis-à-vis *ka-* 'this' (q.v.); cf. also *enissan, apenissan* (s.v. *a-, apa-*), despite consistent *-s-* in *annisan* (cf. Friedrich, *Staatsverträge* 1:152; Kronasser, *Etym.* 1:357–8). The ablatival adverb *annaz(a)* points to an *a*-stem base. *annal(l)i-* has the same suffix as e.g. *arkammanalli-* 'tributary' or *teshalli-* 'sleepy' (cf. Kronasser, *Etym.* 1:211–3); the variant *a*-stem forms point to intermixture with the suffix seen in e.g. *irmala-* 'ill', *tūwala-* 'distant' (Kronasser, *Etym.* 1: 171–2), or *attalla-* and *huhadalla-* quoted above (vs. Hier. *tatali-* and *huhatali-*); thus this mixed paradigm has nothing to do with any secondary thematization or Hitt.-Luw. *-a-* : *-i-* variation (despite Laroche, *Bi. Or.* 18:255 [1961]).

Pal. *ānnī* (*KUB* XXXV 165 Rs. 23)? Cf. Kammenhuber, *RHA* 17:38 (1959); Carruba, *Das Palaische* 19.

anna- has been connected with IE **ono-* 'that, yonder' (Skt. instr. sg. m. *anéna*, Lith. *anàs*, OCS *onǔ*; *IEW* 319–20) since

Hrozný, *SH* 135; cf. e.g. Couvreur, *Hett.* 91–2; N. van Brock, *RHA* 20:90–1 (1962; esp. on *annalla-*). In view of the constant *-nn-* it may be advisable to posit rather IE **onyo->anna-* (cf. ON *enn*, OHG *ienēr<*y-onyos*), with a variant **oni->an(n)i-*. Cf. *annawali-, an(n)iya-*.

anna-, anni- (c.) 'mother' (AMA; akkadogram *UMMU* in *KBo* XXII 2 Vs. 14 *UMMANI-san wemiyawen* 'we have found our mothers'; cf. Otten, *Altheth. Erzählung* 6), nom. sg. *annas* (e.g. *KUB* I 16 II 20 *annas-sis* MUŠ-*as* 'his mother [is] a snake'; cf. Sommer, *HAB* 5; *RS* 25.421 Recto 32 *annas-mis* 'my mother'; cf. Laroche, *Ugaritica* 5:774 [1968]; *KUB* XVII 10 IV 24 *nu-za annas* DUMU-*ŠU pennista* 'the mother tended her child'; cf. Laroche, *RHA* 23:98 [1965]; XXXIII 117 I 6 *annas-za sallanut* 'mother brought up'; cf. Laroche, *RHA* 26:79 [1968]; VIII 41 II 3 *watruas annas* 'mother of the spring'; cf. Laroche, *JCS* 1:187 [1947]; Neu, *Altheth.* 183; XLIII 60 I 20 *annas-an* UDU-*us* 'mother-sheep', vs. ibid. 19 UDU-*uss-an* '(male) sheep'; XXX 19+ I 9 *annas-ma-kan* GIŠGEŠTIN-*as* 'mother-vine'; cf. Otten, *Totenrituale* 32), acc. sg. *annan* (e.g. *KUB* XLIV 4+ *KBo* XIII 241 Rs. 15; *KUB* XXIII 29, 5; cf. Ünal, *Hatt.* 2:131; *Code* 2:91 *takku* LÚELLUM *arauwannius annanekus anna-smann-a wenzi* 'if a free man rapes free co-uterine sisters and their mother'), gen. sg. *annas* (e.g. I 16 II 10 *annas-sas* MUŠ[-*as* 'his mother's, a snake's'; *KBo* XI 1 Rs. 19 DU-*nas assuli annas* UZUUBUR *mahhan sunnazi* 'the storm-god makes fullness for good like a mother's breast'; cf. Houwink Ten Cate – Josephson, *RHA* 25:110 [1967]), dat.-loc. sg. *anni* (e.g. XII 112 Rs. 12 DUMU-*las-wa-ssan anni-ssi* [*andan* 'the child inside its mother'), *anna* (*KUB* IX 28 II 4 *hassanza* [sic] *anna-ssa dāi* 'he places the newborn with its mother'), abl. sg. *annaz* (e.g. VI 45 III 28–29 DU ...-*ma-mu annaz dās nu-mu sallanut* 'the storm-god took me from my mother and reared me'; XXIV 13 II 15 SALannaza; cf. Haas – Thiel, *Rituale* 104; *annaz kartaz* 'from the mother's womb; since birth'; cf. s.v. *karat*[*t*]-; also Riemschneider, *Geburtsomina* 68), nom. pl. c. in XVII 29 II 6–7 *huhha hannis attes annis* 'grandfather(s)-grandmother(s), father(s) (and) mother(s)' (cf.

Friedrich, *AfO* 4:95 [1927]), acc. pl. *annus* (*KBo* III 22 Vs. 9 *annus attus iet* 'he made them mothers and fathers', i.e. treated them like parents; cf. Neu, *Anitta-Text* 10), *annius* (XXII 5 Vs. 8 *att]us annius iyanun*; cf. Neu, *Anitta-Text* 7–9).

'Mother-father' also in XIX 134, 18 *annas-wa-za attas* and e.g. V 1 I 41 AMA-KA *nasma* ABU-KA 'thy mother or thy father' (cf. Sommer – Ehelolf, *Pāpanikri* 4*), as regularly in South Anatolian (see below). But mostly and often *attas annas*, e.g. *KUB* XXIV 3 I 46 *nu-za* KUR-*eas hūmandas attas annas zik* 'thou art the father (and) mother of every land' (cf. Gurney, *Hittite Prayers* 24); XI 1 IV 9; *Code* 1:28–29 ('parents', dealing with daughter's suitors). Cf. also s.v. *atta-*.

annas (attas) siwatt- or *(attas) annas siwatt-* 'day of death', e.g. ŠA AMA-KA UD-*az ari* 'the day of your death is at hand' (XXI 1 I 64; cf. Friedrich, *Staatsverträge* 2:54), *annas* UD-*za* (V 3 I 45; V 4 II 46), ŠA AMA-ŠU-*wa-ssi* UD.KAM-*za* (XXXIX 49 Vs. 26), Š]A AMA-ŠU ABI-ŠU-*ya* U[D (V 20 + XVIII 56 I 28), UD.KAM ABI-ŠU AMA-ŠU (XXVI 1 III 14–15; cf. von Schuler, *Dienstanweisungen* 13). For origin and implications see Puhvel, *KZ* 83:59–63 (1969) = *Analecta Indoeuropaea* 205–9 (1981).

anniyatar (n.) 'motherhood' in *KUB* XV 35 + *KBo* II 9 I 31–32 ANA SAL.MEŠ-*ma-kan arha anniyatar asiyatar ... dā* 'from women take away motherhood (and) love' (cf. Sommer, *ZA* 33:98 [1921]; A. Archi, *Oriens Antiquus* 16:299 [1977]), dat.-loc. sg. AMA-*anni* (*KUB* XXVI 81 I 6). Cf. Zuntz, *Ortsadverbien* 39; Kronasser, *Etym.* 1:295.

Pal. nom. sg. in *annas pāpas* 'mother (and) father' (*KBo* XIII 265, 4; *KUB* XXXV 163 III 21–22), *pāpaz-kuar tī [ānn]az-kuar tī* (XXXV 165 Vs. 21–22). Cf. Carruba, *Das Palaische* 28, 27, 16.

Lyd. nom. sg. in *ẽna-k taada-k* 'mother and father' (Sardis 10.20), *ẽnaś* (ibid. 18), dat.-loc. sg. *ẽnaλ-t* (ibid. 22). Cf. Gusmani, *Die Sprache* 8:82–3 (1962), *Lyd. Wb.* 106, 254.

Luw. *anni(ya)-* 'mother', nom. sg. *annis* (*KBo* II 1 I 33 and 40; cf. Hrozný, *Heth. KB* 8; *KUB* XXXV 103 II 3 and 15; cf. Otten, *LTU* 95), *ānnis* (*KBo* IX 141 Vs. 16 and 18), AMA-*is tātiyis* 'mother (and) father' (*KUB* XXXV 49 IV 14), AMA-*yis tatiyis* (XXXV 46, 6), acc. sg. *ānnin* (XXXV 103 II 14; *KBo* IX

141 Vs. 17), *ānniyan tātīyan* (XXXV 43 II 5), AMA-*yan tātiyan*
(XXXV 45 II 2), dat.-loc. sg. *ānni* (XXXV 103 III 5), *anni*
(XXXV 102 Rs. 5), instr.-abl. sg. *a]nniyati ta[tiyat]i* (XXXV 92
I 29); genitival adj. *annassi-*, nom. pl. c. *annassinzi-yan* (XXXV
132 II 6).

Hier. SAL-*natin tati-ha* 'mother and father' = Phoen. *l-'b
w-l-'m* 'father and mother' (Karatepe 15–16); thus **anna(n)ti-*,
like *huha(n)ti-* beside *huha-* 'grandfather'? Cf. Meriggi, *Manuale* 2:72.

Lyc. *ẽni* 'mother', e.g. *TLy* 134.4 *ẽni mahanahi* = Luw. *annis
massanassis* 'mother of the god(s)'; *TLy* 56.4 *ẽni* (cf. ibid. 6
Λητώ); *TLy* 86.2 *hrppi atli ehbi sey-ẽni ehbi* 'for himself and for
his mother'. Also *ẽnesi-* (= Luw. *annassi-*) in *TLy* 44d.66-67
ẽnesi-ke tedesi-ke 'both maternal and paternal'. Cf. Friedrich,
KS 85, 71-2, 77, 69; Sturtevant, *TAPA* 59:49–52 (1928);
Laroche, *BSL* 53.1:187–91 (1957–8).

Connected since Hrozný (*SH* 31) and Marstrander (*Caractère* 128) with the group exemplified by Lat. *anna* 'foster-
mother', *anus* 'old woman', Hes. ἀννίς, Arm. *han*, OHG *ana*
'grandmother', OPruss. *ane* 'old mother', Lith. *anýta* 'mother-
in-law' (*IEW* 36–7). This widespread word from infantile
language has in Anatolian supplanted the central IE term
**mā́tēr* (cf. eg. Kronasser, *Etym.* 1:118). Cf. also s.v. *atta-*
'father', *hanna-* 'grandmother'.

Cf. *annaneka-*, *annawanna-*, *anninniyami-*, *annitalwatar*,
siwanzanna-; also *annal(l)i-* s.v. *anna-*, *an(n)i-* (sub nom.-acc.
pl. neut. *annalla*).

anahi(t)-   (n.) 'advance sample, test morsel (of sacrificial offering)',
frequent in "southern type" rituals, nom.-acc. sg. *anahi* and pl.
anahita (e.g. *KBo* V 1 III 17–18 NINDA *alattarinn-a parsiya
n-asta anāhi piran arha dāi* 'and he breaks an a.-bread and then
takes off a morsel'; ibid. 33–34 repeated with *anāhita*; cf.
Sommer – Ehelolf, *Pāpanikri* 10*, 66; *KUB* XXXIX 71 III
25–26 *nu-kan* ANA UDU ANA SAG.DU-ŠU ZAG-*ni-ya* ᵁᶻᵁ*paltani
anahi dāi* 'he takes a trial piece off the sheep's head and right
shoulder'; XII 12 V 2–5 *namma-kan anāhita* ᴰᵁᴳ*āhrushiaz dāi*

n-at-san ^{DUG}*huprushiya hassī parā dāi nu memai ānuis anahuēs kelu* 'then he takes morsels from the censer and places them in the tureen on the hearth and says [Hurrian]'; *IBoT* I 29 Vs. 52 1 NINDA *anahi* 'one bread-sample').

Denom. *anahidai-* 'sample', 3 sg. pres. act. *anahidaizzi* (*Bo* 6730, 10; *Bo* 3288 Rs. 35), 3 pl. pres. act. *anahidanzi* (ibid. 71; *KUB* XLVI 37 Rs. 46 and 52), *anahidazi* (ibid. 51); inf. *anahidauwanzi* (*Bo* 3288 Rs. 74), *anahidauwazi* (*KUB* XLVI 37 Rs. 5; cf. ibid. 7 *anahita*). Cf. Otten, *ZA* 66:103 (1976).

anahitahit- 'sampling, taking of morsels', dat.-loc. sg. (used adverbially) *anahitahiti* (e.g. *KBo* XXI 34 IV 1 *anāhitahiti* 5 NINDA.SIG.MEŠ *parsiya* 'he breaks five flatloaves piecemeal'; ibid. 7 *anāhitahiti-ya kue* NINDA.SIG.MEŠ *parsiya* 'and what flatloaves he breaks piecemeal'; cf. Lebrun, *Hethitica II* 123–4; *VBoT* 89 IV 18 *anahitahiti*).

anahi(t)- may be Hurrian in origin; cf. the Hurr. ergative in *ānuis anahuēs* (i.e. *anu-es anahi-w-es* 'this thy bit') quoted above, or e.g. *KBo* XXI 33 III 8 *anāhitenes tātussines* KI.MIN (i.e. *anahite-ni-s tad-ussi-ni-s* [participle of *tad-* 'love'], ergative ending preceded by def. article; KI.MIN = 'etc.'). On the other hand Luwian provenance (Kizzuwatna) is also possible, involving the denom. abstract suffix *-ahi(t-)* (on possible IE origins of which see C. Watkins, *TPhS* 1971: 55; H. Eichner, *MSS* 31:59–60 [1973]); the latter is probable in *anahit-ahit-*. Cf. Laroche, *RHA* 28:68–70 (1970), 34:48–9 (1976); H. A. Hoffner, *Alimenta Hethaeorum* 151 (1974; cf. ibid. 173–4 on the unpertaining *nah[h]iti-*, q.v. s.v.).

annaneka-   (c.), probably only plural, 'sisters by the same mother, co-uterine sisters', acc. pl. *annanekus* (*Code* 2:91 *takku* ^{LÚ}EL-*LUM arauwannius annanekus anna-smann-a wenzi* 'if a free man rapes free co-uterine sisters and their mother'), *annanikus* (ibid. 2:94; *KBo* XXI 35 I 11 ^{SAL}*annanikus*, ibid. 4 *hurkel* 'capital crime', ibid. 8 *wentas* 'he raped').

This "reciprocal" plural term of relationship, composed of *anna-* 'mother' and *neka-* 'sister (q.v.), was correctly interpreted by Goetze, *Arch. Or.* 17.1:288–90 (1949); cf. Kronasser, *Etym.*

1:126; Imparati, *Leggi ittite* 316; Otten, *Altheth. Erzählung* 36.

Improbable attempt by H. A. Hoffner (*Orientalia* N.S. 35:391–2 [1966]): **annani-* (aphaeretic in Luw. *nani-* 'brother') + "fem." suffix *-ika-* analogous to Luw. *-sri-*, hence *annaneka-* = Luw. *(*an)nanasri-* 'sister' (on the possible presence of the suffix *-ika-* in *neka-* cf. s.v.).

The incorrect sense 'wench, whore', proposed by Friedrich, *Heth. Ges.* 114, still figured in H. Eichner, *Die Sprache* 20:185 (1974), who thought that the base meaning of *annaneka-* was 'aunt' (lit. 'mother's sister').

ananeshi-,   target or purpose of bird and lamb offerings in Hurroid rituals, gen. sg. in *KUB* XV 31 I 17–18 *nu ŠA* YÀDÙG.GA *ananeshiyas memiyanus memai* 'he speaks the words of the good oil of a.' (cf. Haas–Wilhelm, *Riten* 150), dat.-loc. sg. *ananeshiya* (e.g. VII 34, 4 1 MUŠEN *ananeshiya* 'one bird for a.'; XLV 75 III 6 1 MUŠEN *ananeshiya pentihiya* 'one bird for a. and for righteousness'; cf. Otten, *Materialien* 20; XV 31 III 33 1 SILÁ *ananeshiya* 'one lamb for a.'; ibid. 56 and IV 12 *ananeshiya unihiya*; cf. Haas – Wilhelm, *Riten* 164, 168; same in XXXII 50 Vs. 10), *ananishiya* (e.g. XV 34 IV 38–39 1 MUŠEN *enumassiya ananishiya* 'one bird for propitiation and a.'; cf. Haas – Wilhelm, *Riten* 206; XLV 79 Rs. 15 *ananishiya pentih[iya*; cf. Otten, *Materialien* 23); cf. also XV 31 IV 34 1 MUŠEN-*ma alummazhiya* (q.v. s.v. *alumpazhi-*) 1 MUŠEN-*ma neshiya* (cf. Haas – Wilhelm, *Riten* 170); XV 36+ Vs. 28 1 MUŠEN *anishiya pindihiya* (cf. Götze – Pedersen, *MS* 8).

Hurrian term (cf. e.g. *IBoT* II 39 Rs. 16 [Hurr.] *ananeshi-ya--ni unihi-ya-ni keldi-ya-ni*), presumably an abstract concept like the 'righteousness', 'propitiation', 'well-being' (*keldi-*), *alumpazhi-*, and presumably *unihi-* with which it tends to be combined. Cf. Haas – Wilhelm, *Riten* 69–74; Laroche, *RHA* 34:49 (1976).

annanu-   'train, educate', 3 pl. pres. act. *annanuwanzi* (*KUB* XXX 42 I 2; cf. Laroche, *CTH* 161), 3 sg. pret. act. *annanut* (*KBo* III 34 II 29 and 30 [OHitt.] 'he trained', viz. young charioteers; cf.

ibid. 32 *s-us ulkessarahhir* 'they made them experts'; *KUB*
XXIII 108 Rs. 8]^{LÚ}IGI.MUŠEN-*UTTIM annanut* 'he has trained
[him] for birdwatchership'; partic. *annanuwant-* 'trained, cul-
tured' (opp. *dampupi-* 'primitive, unskilled, uncivilized', q.v.
s.v. *dampu-*), nom. sg. c. in *KBo* I 30 Vs. 20 *annanuwa-*
[*nza* = Akk. *gullubu* 'shorn, shaven, barbered' (cf. *MSL* 12:214–5
[1969]; Otten, *ZA* 66:103 [1976]), acc. sg. in VI 26 II 27 (= *Code*
2:77) ^{LÚ}MUŠEN.DÙ-*an annanuwantan* 'a trained auspex' (vs. ibid.
29 *dampūpin*); verbal noun gen. sg. *annanummas* and inf.
annanumanzi in *Code* 200B *takku* DUMU-*an annanumanzi kuiski*
pāi nassu ^{LÚ}NAGAR *nasma* ^{LÚ}E.DÉ.A ^{LÚ}[UŠ.B]AR *nasma* ^{LÚ}AŠGAB
^{LÚ}TÚG *nu annanummas* 6 GÍN KÙ.BABBAR *pāi takku-an ŪL*
walkissarahhi nu-ssi 1 SAG.DU *pāi* 'if someone gives a boy to be
trained, be it as carpenter or smith (or) weaver or tanner or
fuller, he gives six shekels of silver (as fee) of training; if (the
trainer) does not make him expert, he gives him (i.e. the
customer) one person' (cf. Imparati, *Leggi ittite* 182, 325–6);
also *KUB* XXXI 53+ Vs. 9–10 3 MÁŠ.GAL 2 UDU.NITÁ *ANA*
DUG.GA₅.BUR *annanumas* ŠID-*esnaza nāui* EGIR-*pa* (var. XXVI
64 I 4 *annanummas*) 'three he-goats and two rams for training
at the potter's wheel (are) not yet deducted from the count' (cf.
Otten – Souček, *Gelübde* 20–2; Güterbock, *RHA* 25:148
[1967]); also XLIII 29 II 7 *annanumanzi*; iter. *annanuski-*, 3 sg.
pret. act. *annanuskit* (XL 80 Vs. 4).

    annanuhha- 'trained', acc. sg. c. *annanuhhan* in *KBo* VI
2+XIX 1 III 44–46 (= *Code* 1:65) *takku* MÁŠ.GAL *enandan*
takku ŠEG₉.BAR *annanuhhan takku* UDU.KUR.RA *ena*[*ndan*] *ku-*
iski tāyizzi mahhanda ŠA GUD.APIN.LAL *tayazilas kinza*[*n* ...]
QATAMMA 'if anyone steals a tamed he-goat or a trained wild
sheep or a tamed mountain sheep, their (case) is the same as
theft of a plow-ox' (cf. Otten – Souček, *AfO* 21:5–6 [1966]; for
B. Landsberger's alternative reading DÀRA.MAŠ 'deer, stag' for
ŠEG₉.BAR, and the error ŠA MÁŠ.GAL for ŠA GUD.APIN.LAL in the
duplicates VI 3 III 49–50 and VI 8, 3–5, cf. Güterbock, *JCS*
15:77 [1961]), VI 14 I 6–7 (= *Code* 2:18) *takku luliyas* MUŠEN-
-*i*[*n annanuhhan nasma kakkapan*] *annanuhhan kuisk*[*i tāyezzi*
'if anyone steals a trained pool-bird or a trained partridge', VI
10 III 28 (= *Code* 2:49) *ta*]*kku* U[K]Ù *annanuhhan kuiski*

happaraizzi (dupl. *KUB* XXIX 30 II 4 UKÙ]-*an annanuhhan kuiski*[) 'if anyone sells a trained person' (vs. *Code* 2:47 *dampupen* 'unskilled'; cf. Goetze, *ANET* 195; V. Souček, *OLZ* 56:467 [1961]; Imparati, *Leggi ittite* 283–4). Cf. Goetze, *ANET* 192–5; Friedrich, *Heth. Ges.* 101; Imparati, *Leggi ittite* 254–5, 278; Ertem, *Fauna* 58, 70–1; Güterbock, *Die Welt des Orients* 9:90–1 (1980), who plausibly saw in the animals and birds hunting decoys.

annanuzzi- (c.), leather restraining gear for animals, some kind of halter or curb (distinct from *ishima*[*n*]- 'line, rope' and *ismeri-* 'bridle, rein'), acc. sg. in *Code* 2:29 *takku* ANŠU.KUR.RA *nasma* ANŠU.GÌR.NUN.NA ᴷᵁˢ*annanuz*[*zin* 'if (anyone steals) from a horse or mule the halter', acc. pl. ᴷᵁˢ*annanuzzius* (*KBo* XVII 15 Rs. 7; cf. Neu, *Altheth.* 73); denom. verb partic. *annanuzziyant-*, nom. sg. c. in XVII 40 IV 5 AMAR-*us annanu-*[*zziy*]*anza* ANA UDU Ù S[ILÁ *haminkan* 'a haltered calf (is) bound to a sheep and lamb', nom. pl. c. in XVII 15 Rs. 9 1 ANŠU.KUR.RA NITA *kūrkas-siss-a annanuzziyante*[*s* 'one stallion and his foal (are) haltered' (cf. the ᴷᵁˢ*ishimānes* placed on their feet and a cow's feet, ibid. 10–11; cf. H. Eichner, *Die Sprache* 21:161 [1975]; V. Haas – M. Wäfler, *Ugarit-Forschungen* 8:82, 88–9 [1976]; B. Forssman, *KZ* 94:71 [1980]). Cf. Hrozný, *Code hittite* 116–7 (1922); Otten, *OLZ* 50:391 (1955); Alp, *Belleten* 31:538 (1967).

annanu- may be an obscured causative to *an(n)iya-* 'work' (q.v.; cf. Pedersen, *Hitt.* 145). Kronasser (*Etym.* 1:456–7, 312) implausibly suggested haplology for a denominative **annan-unu-* from **annanu-* in *annanuzzi-*, thus a metaphoric meaning 'take by the bit' (vel sim.), but admitted that the reverse derivation (*annanuzzi-* deverbatively from *annanu-*) is also possible. The quasi-participial adjective *annanuhha-* has a suffix reminiscent of some abstract nouns (*alwanzahha-, maninkuwahha-,* unless from factitive stems in *-ahh-*; cf. Kronasser, *Etym.* 1:166); the assumption of adjectivization from an abstract noun **annanuh* 'training' (Sturtevant, *Lg.* 14:242 [1938]; *Comp. Gr.*² 82) is unnecessary; *annanuhha-* is OHitt. (*Code*) only and may well have an otherwise obsolete suffix as a legal archaism. For the deverbative suffix of *annanuzzi-* (lit. 'training gear') cf. e.g. *ishuzzi-* 'band, belt' (*ishiya-* 'bind') and see Carruba, *Beschwörungsritual* 22–3 (*annanu-uzzi-*?).

The comparison of *annanu-* with Toch. AB *en-* 'instruct, enjoin' (W. Krause – W. Thomas, *Tocharisches Elementarbuch* 1:57, 211 [1960]) is implausible, since Toch. *en-* (<*ain-*) is better connectible with Gk. αἰν- (s.v. *enant-*; cf. also Van Windekens, *Le tokharien* 177–8).

annari- (c.) 'strength, force, vigor'; personified as a beneficent daimon or spirit (*KBo* I 44+XIII 1 IV 35 [Akk.] *šedu* = [Hitt.] *tarpis*; ibid. 36 [Akk.] *lamasu* = [Hitt.] *ānnaris*; dupl. XXVI 25, 3 LA.AM.MA = [Akk.] *lamasu* = [Hitt.] ^DKAL-*as*; ibid. 4 A.LA = [Akk.] *šēdu* = [Hitt.] *tarpis*; cf. Otten, *Vokabular* 20), nom. sg. *annaris tarpis* loosely for dat. or acc. sg. (objects of *ekuzi* 'he drinks to') in lists of generally benign entities (*KUB* II 8 I 27, II 13 and 45, V 27; X 81, 8, with gloss-wedges; cf. Bossert, *Königssiegel* 35), acc. sg. *annarin tarpin* (XXXII 87 Rs. 14 and 24; objects of *ekuzi*, next to others in nom. sg.), ^{NA₄}*hegur annarin* ^{NA₄}*h*[*eg*]*ur mūwattinn-a* 'rock (-sanctuaries) a. and m.' (XXVII 13 IV 17; cf. e.g. *Bo* 521 II 2 ^D*Muwatti*), *annarien* (*KUB* XV 35+*KBo* II 9 I 24 *an-na-ri-en-na*, in a list of good things implored of Ištar; cf. Sommer, *ZA* 33:98 [1921]; A. Archi, *Oriens Antiquus* 16:299 [1977]), dat.-loc. sg. (?) XVIII 48 Rs. 2 *annari annari* (with repeated gloss-wedges). Cf. XXX 11 Rs. 18 ^DKAL ^D*Annariss-a* and 453/d Vs. 4 ^D*Innari* ^D*Tarpi* (see Otten, *Festritual* 46–7), showing a twofold associative assimilation to *innar-* (q.v.) and ^D*Inar(a)-* (Hattic female tutelary deity). The asyndetic *annari- tarpi-* is a unitary pair of beneficences much like Akk. *lamassu* and *šēdu*, although the separate *tarpi-* (q.v.), like *šēdu*, tends rather towards malevolence. Cf. Rosenkranz, *Beiträge* 21; Kammenhuber, *MSS* 3:27–44 (1953); W. von Soden, *BMitt.* 3:148–56 (1964); Otten, *Vokabular* 27–32; H. A. Hoffner, *JNES* 27:64–6 (1968).

The ritual material points in a "southern" direction, and the occasional gloss-wedges indicate a foreignism. *annari-* is the Luwoid equivalent of Hitt. **innar(a)-* 'strength, force, vigor', with typical *a : i* phonetic alternation and inversely gravitation

to *i*-stem declension; cf. also the Luwoid *annaru-* in *KUB* XLIV
16 III 12 *annarauwa*[*s labarnas* ^DKAL-*i* 'to the tutelary deity of
the forceful ruler' (vs. pure Luwian *annarummi-* = Hitt. *inna-
rawant-* 'strong, forceful, vigorous', *annarummahit-* 'strength,
forcefulness' = Hitt. *innarawatar*; cf. II 1 III 47 *annarumahitas-
sis* 'of forcefulness', and A. Archi, *SMEA* 16:97, 111 [1975]).
The epanadiplotic *annari annari* may be a Luwoid adverbial
correspondent of Hitt. *innarā* (q.v.).

anassa-,   name of a body-part, gen. sg. or pl. in *KUB* XXXV 148 III
24 *anassas-sas in*[*an* 'illness of his a.('s)', preceded (23–24) by
iskisa[*s* ...] *inan* KI.MIN 'illness of his (lower) back likewise' and
followed (25) by *arras-sas inan* KI.MIN, (26) *genuwas-sas inan*
KI.MIN, (27) *parasnas-sas inan* 'illness of his anus likewise,
illness of his penis likewise, illness of his loins'.
   The strict context seems to place *anassa-* in the rear of the
lower torso, between the (small of the) back (*iskis-*) and the
anal-genital area, thus perhaps 'hips, buttocks'. On the other
hand Hitt. anatomical rosters are not always models of succes-
sive consistency; e.g. *KUB* XLIII 53 I 6–13 lists in order back
(*iskis*), (upper) arm (*paltanas*), breast, heart, liver, lung, the two
shoulders (*BUDĀ*), genitals (*genzu*), stomach, penis (cf. Haas,
Orientalia N.S. 40:415–7 [1971]); therefore a sequence 'back' to
'shoulder' to the anal-genital region is possible here also. In
either case the likely etymon is IE **omso-* 'shoulder' (Skt.
ámsa-, Arm. *us*, Gk. ὦμος, Lat. *umerus*, Umbr. *onse* [loc.],
Goth. *ams*, Toch. A *es*, B *āntse*), with Hitt. *anassa-* showing
anaptyctic resolution of the *-ms-* cluster (cf. Lat. *umerus*)
coupled with assimilation of nasal to *s* as in Lat. *tenebra-
< *temesrā-* (cf. OHG *dinstar*) beside *temere*, Skt. *támisrā-*. In
most IE languages **omso-* seems to have been in complementary distribution with **pletyo-* (cf. OCS *pleště* and MiIr. *leithe*
'shoulder'). Hittite has both *paltana-* and *anassa-*; the former
clearly means 'shoulder' but has also moved "forward" to
'(upper) arm', despite its etymological 'shoulderblade' connotations (cf. Gk. ὠμο-πλάτη); it is thinkable that by semantic
polarization it pushed *anassa-* "backward" to denote either

'rear of shoulders, upper back' (vs. *iskis-* 'lumbar region') or even all the way to 'hips, nates'. Cf. Puhvel, *JAOS* 97:599 (1977).

Ivanov's (*Etimologija 1976* 162 [1978]) and M. Poetto's (in *Hethitisch und Indogermanisch* 205 [1979]) adduction of Lat. *ānus* and interpretation of *anassa-* (with suffix like **genussa-* 'knee-joint') as anal (or possibly vaginal) orifice is unlikely, since *anassa-* is followed by 'anus' (*arra-*) and 'penis' (*genu-*, lit. 'knee'; cf. Akk. *birku* 'knee; penis' and see e.g. Puhvel, *Myth and law among the Indo-Europeans* 95-6 [1970]).

Cf. *gakkartan(n)i-, paltana-*.

annasnant-   (c.), hapax in *KUB* XVII 10 IV 9–10 *parnanz-at tarnau istarniyas-at annasnanza tarnau* ᴳᴵˢ*luttanz-at tarnau* 'may the house let them (viz. Telipinus' wrath, anger, desolation, and rage) go, may the central a. let them go, may the window let them go'.

Derived with suffix *-ant-* from an *r/n*-stem *annassar* (XLIII 75 Vs. 12 and 20) or **annessar* (n.), of inferential meaning ('pillar, column' conjectured by Laroche, *BSL* 57.1:30 [1962]; cf. Otten, *ZA* 66:104 [1976]). Possibly a verbal noun to *an(n)iya-* 'work, carry out' (q.v.), thus literally 'creation' and concretely 'establishment, compound'.

annawali-, annauli- (an-na-ú-li-)   '(of) equal (rank), peer' (akkadogram MEHRU, MIHRU 'equal', e.g. *KBo* IV 10 Vs. 46 MEHIR-ŠU 'his equal'; IV 14 III 68 ŠA KUR URU ᴸᵁMEHRI 'a peer of the realm'; cf. Stefanini, *ANLR* 20:47 [1965]; 842/f, 5 LUGAL.MEŠ MEHRI-YA-mu 'the kings my equals'; with *KUB* XXI 5 III 24–25 ANA ᴰUTU-ŠI *kuēs* LUGAL.MEŠ *annauliēs* cf. par. XXIII 1 IV 1 LUGAL.MEŠ-*ya-mu kuyēs* ᴸᵁMIH[RUT]I 'the kings who are my equals'; cf. Kühne – Otten, *Šaušgamuwa* 14, 44), nom. sg. c. *annawalis* (XIV 3 IV 56), *annaulis* (ibid. II 13–14 *kinun-a-wa-mu* ŠEŠ-YA LUGAL GAL *ammel annaulis* IŠPUR 'but now my brother has written to me as a great king, as my equal'; cf. Sommer, *AU* 6; *KBo* XXII 6 I 25–26 *annaulis-wa-[tta]* ŪL *kuiski* *ēszi* 'there is none equal to you'; cf. dupl. XII 1 I 5 *annauli[s*; Güterbock, *MDOG* 101:19 [1969]; Meriggi, *Gedenkschrift für W. Brandenstein* 263 [*IBK* 14, 1968]), gen. sg. c. *annauliya[s* (*KUB* XIV 3 II 14), nom. pl. c. *annauliēs* (quoted above). Cf. Sommer, *AU* 101–2.

annawali- (for *an-na-ú-li-* cf. Kronasser, *Etym.* 1:78) may contain *wal(l)i-* 'strong' (q.v. s.v. *waliwalai-*); *anna-* is perhaps the largely obsolete demonstrative pronominal stem *anna-*, *an(n)i-* (q.v.), here with the meaning 'self, same' (the suffix *-ila* expresses 'self' in current Hittite, but 'same' seemingly never recovered from the obsolescence of *anna-*, *an[n]i-*); cf. *ani-siwat* 'on the very same day, to-day'. Thus *annawali-* may mean literally 'same-strong', comparable to Lat. *aequi-valē-* 'be of the same strength', where *aequus* could reflect an IE *$\bar{a}i\ k^we$ 'in this very way' (cf. Skt. *ai-ṣámaḥ* 'this year' with Gk. σῆτες < *$ky\bar{a}$-*-wetes* 'this year', and ON *ī-dag* 'to-day' with Hitt. *ani-siwat*). Cf. Puhvel, *JAOS* 100:167 (1980).

Kronasser (*Etym.* 1:212) improbably assumed a "mutter-rechtlich" term, with **annawa-* abstracted from *annawanna-* 'stepmother'.

annawanna-   (c.) 'stepmother', gen. sg. in *KUB* XXIX 34 IV 12 (= *Code* 2:90) *takku* LÚ-*as annawannas-sas katta [wastai* 'if a man sins with his stepmother'; cf. *Code* 2:89 *annas-(s)as katta wastai* 'sins with his mother' (cf. Haase, *Fragmente* 86–7); fragm. 621/f, 10 SAL*annaw[* (cf. Güterbock, *Siegel* 1:79; Riemschneider, *MIO* 6:366 [1958]).

Luw. *annawanni-*, nom. sg. in *KBo* IX 141 Vs. 18 *ānnis ānnawanni[s* 'mother (and) stepmother' (cf. ibid. 19 *t]ātis-pa-ti tātawanni[s* 'father and stepfather'), acc. sg. SAL*annawannin* (477/u, 8), *annauwannin* (XIV 114, 13). Cf. Otten, *ZA* 66:104 (1976).

Native Anatolian formation on *anna-* 'mother' (q.v.); for the tendency to derive such terms by suffixes with phonetic quasi-iteration, cf. e.g. Lat. *mātrāstra*, *patrāster*. For the otherwise rare suffix *-wanna-* see Kronasser, *Etym.* 1:183.

an(n)iya-

an(n)iya- 'work; carry out, perform, execute; make, turn out, produce, procure; officiate, practise; treat, manipulate; record, inscribe; plant, sow, cultivate'; *appa an(n)iya-, arha an(n)iya-* 'discharge, clear, undo, renege on, abrogate, countermand' ; *arha aniya-* also 'copy' (literally 'redo') (KIN), 1 sg. pres. act. *aniyami* (e.g. *KBo* III 4 IV 47–48 *parā-ma-mu ... kuit peskizzi n-at aniyami n-at katta tehhi* 'but what [the goddess] assigns to me I shall carry out and accomplish'; cf. Götze, *AM* 136; *KUB* XXXI 84 III 62–63 NUMUN-*wa-mu pai nu-war-at-za-kan ammel* A.ŠÀ-*ni-mi* [*an*]*da aniyami* 'give me seed, and I shall plant it in my field'; cf. von Schuler, *Dienstanweisungen* 49), *aniyammi* (808/w III 10), *aniemi* (*KBo* XVII 1 II 2 *nu mān* LUGAL-*un* SAL.LUGAL-*ann-a*] *aniemi* 'when I [ritually] treat king and queen'; cf. Otten – Souček, *Altheth. Ritual* 24), 3 sg. pres. act. *aniyazi* (e.g. VI 26 I 13 [= *Code* 2:60] ^{URUDU}PISÀN *aniyazi* '[a smith] turns out a drainpipe'; ibid. 14–15 and 16 [= *Code* 2:60–61] ^{URUDU}*ates ... aniyazi* 'turns out an axe'; *KUB* II 2 II 39 *apiya-kku aniyazi* 'even then [the priest] officiates'; cf. Schuster, *Bilinguen* 1:65; XXVI 1 IV 47–48 *nasma-za-at arha aniyazi* 'or revokes it [viz. the oath]'; cf. von Schuler, *Dienstanweisungen* 16–7; XV 1 II 34 NAM.ERÍM.HI.A *arha aniyazi* 'abrogates the oaths'), *anizzi* (*KBo* XX 10 I 5 and II 1; cf. Neu, *Altheth.* 131–2), *aniezzi* (*KUB* XXIX 30 II 21, 22, 23 [= *Code* 2:60–61]), *aniyazzi* (e.g. VII 1 IV 14 *n-an* SAL ŠU.GI *kissan aniyazzi* 'the old woman treats him as follows'; cf. Kronasser, *Die Sprache* 7:163 [1961]; XVIII 67 Vs. 11 *arha aniyazzi*), *aniyaezzi* (XLI 15 Vs. 13), *anniyazzi* (XLIV 61 IV 6; cf. Burde, *Medizinische Texte* 18), 1 pl. pres. act. *aniyaweni* (*KBo* XIV 111, 16), 2 pl. pres. act. *aniyatteni* (*KUB* XIII 4 IV 12 *halkin aniyatteni* 'you plant grain'; cf. Sturtevant, *JAOS* 54:390 [1934]), *aniyattēni* (XIII 28, 16), 3 pl. pres. act. *aniyanzi* (e.g. *KUB* XXIX 31, 4, 6, 8 [= *Code* 2:60–61]; XXIV 3 II 8 *aniyanzi warassanzi* ŪL *ku*[*iski* 'none sow or reap'; cf. Gurney, *Hittite Prayers* 26; V 6 II 52 *aniūr* GIM-*an n-at* QATAMMA *aniyanzi* 'as the rite [is], so they perform it'; ibid. 47 *nu pānzi* EME.MEŠ EGIR-*pa aniyanzi* 'shall they go and take back what they said [lit. their tongues]?'; cf. Sommer, *AU* 282; *KBo* II 6 I 32 EME ^{ID}*SIN-*^DU ANA DINGIR.MEŠ LUGAL-*UTTI pian arha aniyanzi* 'before the gods of kingship they countermand

66

Armadattas' statement'; cf. Zuntz, *Ortsadverbien* 50–1; ibid. III
44 EGIR-*an arha aniyanzi*; *KUB* IX 15 III 23 *arha aniyanzi* 'they
renege', vs. 20–21 *aniūr-kan* EGIR-*an iyanzi* 'they do the ritual
again'; cf. V. Souček, *MIO* 8:376 [1963]; XVI 32 II 28
MAMETUM arha KIN-*anzi* 'they abrogate the oath'), *anianzi* (e.g.
IBoT I 31 Vs. 14–15 *tuppiaz anianzi* 'they record on a tablet'),
annianzi (III 148 I 70; cf. Haas–Wilhelm, *Riten* 216), 1 sg. pret.
act. *aniyanun* (e.g. *KUB* XXIV 3 IV 2–3 *tuppiyas* AWATE.MEŠ
apiya aniyanun 'the words of the tablet there I recorded'; cf.
Gurney, *Hittite Prayers* 38), *anienun* (*KBo* III 22 Rs. 48
pedi-ssi-ma ZÀ.AH.LI-*an anie*[*nun* 'on its place I planted weeds';
cf. Neu, *Anitta-Text* 12), 3 sg. pret. act. *aniyat* (e.g. *KUB* XXXI
51 + XXVI 5 + *Bo* 8522, 10–11 NUMUN.HI.A ... *aniyat* 'planted
seeds'; cf. Otten – Souček, *Gelübde* 30; *KUB* XV 31 IV 38–40
kī-ma-kan tuppi ... *aniyat* 'inscribed this tablet'; cf. Haas–Wilhelm, *Riten* 170; VIII 79 Vs. 8 INIM.MEŠ *IŠTU ṬUPPI aniyat*
'recorded the words on a tablet'; 767/f, 6–9 *n-asta ke tuppa*HI.A
... *apiya* UD-*at arha aniyat* 'he did on that day copy these
tablets'; cf. Otten, *Bi. Or.* 8:225 [1951]; Carruba, *Orientalia*
N.S. 33:413 [1964]), *aniat* (XXXIII 66 III 4; cf. Laroche, *RHA*
23:131 [1965]), *a-ni-i-e-it* (VII 41 I 16 *nasma-za aniyet* 'or has
practised [viz. sorcery]'; dupl. *KBo* X 45 I 6 *aniyat*; cf. Otten,
ZA 54:116 [1961]), 3 sg. pret. midd. *aniyattat* (III 63 I 13 and
14, perhaps 'underwent ritual treatment'; cf. Neu, *Interpretation* 3), 1 pl. pret. act. *a-ni-ya-u-en* (*KUB* XXIX 8 IV 39 *parā
aniyawen* 'we have inscribed [it]'; cf. Haas, *SMEA* 16:223
[1975]; XXXIV 82, 17), *aniyawēn* (*KBo* XII 126 I 25 *nu-wa
ina*[*n*] *aniyawēn* 'we have treated the illness'; cf. Jakob-Rost,
Ritual der Malli 24; *KUB* XLIII 55 V 3 *arha aniyawēn* 'we
copied [tablets]'), 3 pl. pret. act. *aniyair* (*KBo* XII 3 III 10),
a-ni-i-e-i[*r* (*KUB* XXIII 54 Rs. 6), *a-ni-i-ir* (V 6 III 17 *n-at IŠTU
ṬUPPI aniyir* 'they have recorded them on a tablet'), *anir*
(XXXIII 34 Vs. 8; cf. Laroche, *RHA* 23:127 [1965]), 2 sg. imp.
act. *aniya* (XIII 2 III 40 *nu-ssi* N[UM]UN.HI.A *aniya-pat* 'procure
seed-grain for him'; cf. von Schuler, *Dienstanweisungen* 48), 3
sg. imp. act. *aniyaddu* (*KBo* IX 114, 7 -*w*]*ar-an ammel huitnanza
aniyaddu* 'let my menagerie deal with him'; XVI 54, 13 and 14
[object KIN; cf. Riemschneider, *Arch. Or.* 33:337 [1965]), 2 pl.

imp. act. *a-ni-ya-at-te-en* (IX 126, 2 *a*]*niyattenn-a*; XVI 24 + 25
I 36 *aniyatte*[*n*]); cf. A. M. Rizzi Mellini, *Studia mediterranea P.
Meriggi dicata* 520 [1979]; partic. *ani(y)ant-*, nom. sg. c.
anianza (e.g. XX 95 Rs. 11 EZEN *anianza* 'festival celebrated'),
nom.-acc. sg. neut. *aniyan* (e.g. IV 10 Vs. 39 'recorded'; *KUB*
VIII 78 IV 17, V 12, VI 2 and 6 NUMUN *ŪL aniyan* 'seed not
planted'; cf. Souček, *Arch. Or.* 27:28–32 [1959]), *anian* (e.g.
ibid. V 16 and VI 9), also nominalized (*KBo* I 42 I 18
UD.KAM-*as aniyan kuis ēssai* 'who performs a day's work' =
[Akk.] *iš*^{*ga*}*gar* 'prestation'; cf. E. F. Weidner, *Studien zur
hethitischen Sprachwissenschaft* 60 [1917]; *MSL* 13:133 [1971];
X 45 III 27 *parkunumma*[*s*] *aniyan* = dupl. *KUB* XLI 8 III 18
parkunumas KIN-*TI* 'lustration gear' [= *UNUTI*]; cf. Otten, *ZA*
54:130 [1961]), nom. pl. c. *aniyantes* (e.g. XXXI 84 III 57
GEŠTIN.HI.A SI[G₅-*i*]*n aniyantes* 'vines well cultivated'; cf. von
Schuler, *Dienstanweisungen* 49; V 6 IV 5 *IŠTU ṬUPPI aniyantes*
'recorded on a tablet'; X 63 VI 15–16 *kedani-ma-ssan tuppuya*
UD 2.KAM UD 3.KAM UD 4.KAM *aniyantes* 'on this tablet are
treated the second, third, and fourth days'; cf. M. Vieyra, *RA*
51:89 [1957]), *aniantes* (e.g. XVII 19 Rs. 3), nom.-acc. pl. neut.
aniyanta (VII 53 II 24 and 27; cf. Goetze, *Tunnawi* 12); verbal
noun *aniyauwar* (*KBo* XV 21 I 15 *aniyauwar handaizzi* 'arranges the ritual', with dupl. XV 19 I 18 *aniūr handāizzi*); inf.
aniyawanzi (*KUB* XXIV 7 I 26; XXXII 123 I 19), *aniyauanzi*
(ibid. 30; XIII 4 IV 13 *ANA* NUMUN *aniyauanzi* 'to plant the
seed'), *aniyauwanzi* (e.g. ibid. 14; XXXII 123 III 16; XXIX 4 I 7
and 51 'execute'; cf. Kronasser, *Umsiedelung* 6, 10; XII 26 II 9
'treat'; cf. Haas – Wilhelm, *Riten* 26; XXIV 9 IV 6 'manipulate'; cf. Jakob-Rost, *Ritual der Malli* 52; *KBo* III 57 Vs. 2 and
13, *KUB* XXVI 72, 8 [OHitt.] 'officiate over, govern'; XV 1 II
15 *arha aniyauwanzi* 'discharge [oaths]'); iter. *anneski-*, *an(n)-*
-iski-, 1 sg. pres. act. *an-ni-es-ki-mi* (XII 58 II 31 *paprannas aniūr*
anneskimi 'I am performing the ritual of uncleanness'; cf.
Goetze, *Tunnawi* 14; *KBo* XI 11 II 3; XII 103 Vs. 8), *anniskimi*
(e.g. *KUB* XII 63 Vs. 28 and 34; VII 57 I 1; XXIV 14 I 11),
aniskimi (XII 58 II 9 *n-an kāsa paprannas* SISKUR.SISKUR
aniskimi 'I am performing on him here the ritual of uncleanness'; cf. Goetze, *Tunnawi* 12), 3 sg. pres. act. *an-ni-es-ki-iz-zi*

(e.g. *KBo* VI 3 I 27 [= *Code* 1:10] 'he works'), *anniskizzi* (e.g. VI 2 I 18 [= *Code* 1:10]; XVII 78 I 9; *KUB* IX 4 II 10, III 19 and IV 17; IX 34 I 20 and II 12; V 7 Vs. 36; XII 63 Vs. 8), *anniskizi* (1597/u I 2), 2 pl. pres. act. *an-ni-es-kat-te-e-ni* (XIII 3 III 11), *anniskattēni* (ibid. 4 *nu* LUGAL-*as* ᴷᵁˢE.SIR *kuyēs anniskattēni* 'you who make the king's shoes'; cf. Friedrich, *Meissner AOS* 47), 3 pl. pres. act. *an-ni-es-kán-zi* (e.g. *Code* 1:40 'they work [the land]'; XII 26 II 10 'they treat'; cf. Haas – Wilhelm, *Riten* 26; IX 15 III 22 *arha anneskan*[*zi* 'they keep reneging'; cf. V. Souček, *MIO* 8:376 [1963]), *an-ne-es-kán-zi* (*KBo* XXIII 110 Rs. 13), *a-ni-es-kán-zi* (*KUB* IX 15 III 22 *arha aneskan*[*zi*), *anniskanzi* (e.g. XXXI 84 III 60 NUMUN.HI.A *anniskanzi* 'they plant seed'; cf. von Schuler, *Dienstanweisungen* 49; XXIV 7 I 16, 17, 18, 19; cf. A. Archi, *Oriens Antiquus* 16:305 [1977]), 1 sg. pret. act. *ānniskinun* (*KBo* II 11 Rs. 17; cf. Sommer, *AU* 242), 3 pl. pret. act. *an-ni-es-ki-ir* (e.g. *KUB* XXIV 3 II 7 '[they] used to sow'; cf. Gurney, *Hittite Prayers* 26; *KBo* III 6 II 1; cf. Götze, *Hattusilis* 16), *a-ni-es-ki-ir* (dupl. *KUB* I 6 II 10), *anniskir* (L 6 II 37 and III 2 *arha anniskir* 'they countermanded'; cf. A. Archi, *SMEA* 22:25–6 [1980]), 2 pl. imp. act. *an-ni-es-ki-it-tin* (XL 73 I 6), *anniskittin* (XIII 20 I 8–9 *kuis imma* KIN-*az* ...*n-an sakuwass*[*arit*] ZI-*it anniskittin* 'whatever task ... perform it with loyal heart'), KIN-*eskitin* (ibid. 21; cf. Alp, *Belleten* 11:390, 392 [1947]).

aniyatt- (c. and n.) 'work, task; ritual gear or garments; message' (KIN; *UNUTI*), nom. sg. c. *aniyaz* (ibid. 20 *kuis imma kuis aniyaz*; XIII 8 Vs. 18; cf. Otten, *Totenrituale* 106), acc. sg. c. *aniyattan* (e.g. VII 41 IV 13; cf. Otten, *ZA* 54:138–9 [1961]), nom.-acc. sg. neut. in XXXVI 100 Vs. 13 [OHitt.] *aniat-set*, gen. sg. *aniyattas* (*HT* 1 IV 13 and 16; *KUB* IX 31 IV 7), dat.-loc. sg. KIN-*ti* (XXXVI 74, 2 KIN-*ti handas* 'on account of the task'; cf. Siegelová, *Arch. Or.* 38:136 [1970]), abl. sg. *aniyattaz* (XLIV 61 1.R. 1; cf. Burde, *Medizinische Texte* 20), nom.-acc. pl. neut. *aniyatta*, also 'ceremonial habit, vestments' (e.g. *KBo* XVII 74 I 32 LUGAL-*us-za aniyatta-se*[*t dāi* 'the king dons his vestments'; cf. ibid. II 28; Neu, *Gewitterritual* 14, 20; *KUB* XXV 16 I 5), KIN.HI.A-*ta* (e.g. XI 20 II 13 and 35), KIN-*ta* (e.g. *KBo* IV 9 I 27), *aniyatti* (e.g. *IBoT* II 130 Rs. 4–5 *siunas parnas aniyatti newahhanzi* 'they renovate temple-gear'; cf. Otten, *Totenrituale* 92; *KUB* VII 25 I 3 LUGAL-*us-za aniyatti dāi*; XX 4 I 7; XXV 28 I 5), acc. pl. c. *aniyaddus* 'ritual gear' (X 45 IV 45; cf. Otten, *ZA* 54:138 [1961]), dat.-loc. pl. *aniyattas* (*VBoT* 1, 17; cf. L. Rost, *MIO* 4:334 [1956]). Cf. Goetze, *JCS* 1:176–7 (1947); Kronasser, *Etym.* 1:254. For *aniyaddus* vs. *aniyatta* see s.v. *alpa-*.

aniur- (n.) 'prestation; religious obligation; religious performance, ritual' (KIN-*ur*, SISKUR.SISKUR), nom.-acc. sg. *aniūr* (e.g. *KUB* V 6 II 52, IX 15 III 20, XII 58 II 9 and 31, all quoted above; also e.g. XXIX 4 I 6–7 ANA DINGIR-*LIM-ma aniūr-set mahhan n-an aniyauwanzi* QATAMMA *sarā tittanuwanzi* 'but as their obligation [is] to the goddess, so they endeavor to execute it [viz. an image]'; cf. Kronasser, *Umsiedelung* 6), *aniur* (e.g. XXII 40 III 29 *aniur* KIN-*anzi* 'they perform the ritual'), gen. sg. *a-ni-ur-as* (XXIV 9 II 19 *nu-kan aniuras* KIN.HI.A *anda dāi* 'she deposits ritual gear within'; cf. Jakob-Rost, *Ritual der Malli* 34), *a-ni-u-ra-as* (*KBo* XXI 1 IV 3; *KUB* XXXV 18 I 9; cf. Otten, *LTU* 25), dat.-loc. sg. *a̧-ni-u-ri* (XXXV 54 III 45; IX 4 IV 33), *a-ni-ú-ri* (V 6 III 30). *aniūr* < *aniya(u)war* (see above). Cf. Kronasser, *Etym.* 1:276; Neu, *Anitta-Text* 116.

aniyawarant- (c.) 'ritual', nom. sg. hapax in *KBo* X 45 IV 40 *kās aniyawaranza ... parkunuddu* 'may this ritual purify' (with puzzling var. *apiranza* in par. *KUB* XLI 8 IV 38; cf. Otten, *ZA* 54:138–9, 157 [1961]). Apparently verbal noun *aniya(u)war* + -*ant-*. Cf. Kronasser, *Etym.* 1:268; Laroche, *BSL* 57.1:33 (1962).

Cf. Goetze, *AM* 224–6; Kronasser, *Etym.* 1:483. On the semantic nuances of *aniyatt-* vs. *aniur-* cf. Laroche, *Mélanges linguistiques offerts à Émile Benveniste* 340 (1975), who compared Lat. *opera* vs. *opus* and Gk. πρᾶξις vs. πρᾶγμα.

Pal. *ani(ya)-* 'do, perform', 2 sg. pres. act. *anīyasi* and 3 sg. *anitti*, 2 sg. imp. act. *aniya-* (all *KUB* XXXV 165 Rs. 10), 1 sg. pret. act. *aniehha* (*KBo* XIX 152 I 4). Cf. Carruba, *Das Palaische* 19–20.

Luw. *an(n)i(ya)-* 'work, accomplish', 3 sg. pres. act. *ānniti* (*KUB* XXXV 39 III 26), *ānnīti* (XXXV 14 I 8), *āannī[ti* (XXXV 88 II 11), *annīti* (*HT* 82, 5), 3 pl. pres. act. *aneyant[i* (*KUB*

XXXV 15 II 12; cf. Otten, *LTU* 20), 2 sg. imp. act. (?) *aniya*
(XXXV 133 III 4).

Etymology uncertain. Juret (*Vocabulaire* 30–1) abortively
adduced Gk. ἀνύω 'accomplish' (q.v. s.v. *sanh-*). J. Duchesne-
Guillemin (*TPS* 1946:74) connected Gk. ἀνίᾱ 'distress, grief'
(and Lat. *onus* 'load'), with semantic reference to Lat. *labor*. H.
Eichner (*Die Sprache* 24:161 [1978]) posited *E_1one-yó-, lit.
'move a load'. Oettinger (*Stammbildung* 345) suggested *$A_1^w ŋ$-
-yé- related to Lat. *onus*. More interesting is the attempt by V.
Machek (*Die Sprache* 4:76–9 [1958]; endorsed by Čop, *Ling.*
6:69 [1964]) to find in *an(n)iya-* a multi-purpose "verbum
vicarium" for 'do', of the type of Lith. *anúoti* or Czech *onačiti*;
the latter can be connected with Lith. *anàs*, Slavic *onŭ* 'that'; by
the same token *an(n)iya-* would be a derivative of Hitt. *anna-*,
an(n)i- 'that' (q.v.). Cf. *iya-* (s.v.)

According to O. Szemerényi (*Mélanges de linguistique et de
philologie grecques offerts à Pierre Chantraine* 252–3 [1972]) the
iter. *anisk-* (sic) yielded via syncope and borrowing *ansk-* seen
in Gk. ἀσκέω 'work with materials (metal, wool, horn, etc.),
fashion artfully'.

Cf. *annanu-*, *annasnant-*.

annin(n)iyami-   (c.) 'cousin', nom. sg. in *KUB* XXI 1 III 34–36 ANA
ABI-YA-ma-as [1]MursiDINGIR-*LIM* ... DUMU NIN-*ŠU* ANA ᴰUTU-ši-
-ma-as *ānninniyamis* (dupl. XXI 5 III 51 ᴸᵁ*anninniyamis*) 'to my
father Mursilis he (was) his sister's son, but to my majesty he
(is) a cousin' (cf. Friedrich, *Staatsverträge* 2:72), *KBo* V 3 III
35–36 *nu-tta mān ŠA* DAM-*KA kuwapi* NIN-*ZU nasma* ... ᔆᴬᴸ*āan-
ninniyamis kattan uizzi* 'if ever your wife's sister or ... cousin
comes to you' (cf. Friedrich, *Staatsverträge* 2:126), *KUB* XVIII
9 I 5 ᔆᴬᴸ*anniniyamis* BA.UG₆ 'the cousin died', acc. sg. in *KBo* V
3 III 29 ŠEŠ-[*ŠU*] NIN-*ZU* ᔆᴬᴸ*āanninniyamin ŪL* [*dāi* 'the brother
does not take his sister or (female) cousin' (cf. ibid. 33 and
dupl. XIX 44 Rs. 21; Friedrich, *Staatsverträge* 2:124–6).

Perhaps haplologic for a (probably Luwoid) *$anni$-$nani(ya)$-
'mother's brother' (cf. s.v. *anna-*, *anni-* and *neka-*), with a suffix
-*mi-* indicating filiation, spread by analogy from the originally

participial Luw. *titaimi-* 'nurseling, son', thus 'mother's brother's offspring'. Such designations for 'cousin' tend to be generalized; cf. e.g. Lat. *consobrīnus* 'mother's sister's son', also 'mother's brother's son', subsequently 'cousin' generally, supplanting *patruēlis* 'father's brother's son' and *amitīnus* 'father's sister's son'. In *KUB* XXI 1 III 34–36 (above) Kupanta-^{D}KAL was really Muwatallis' *amitīnus*, and reciprocally M. was K.'s *consobrīnus*; but just as the latter yielded 'cousin' at large, so *annin(n)iyami-* had become a fully reciprocal term. In the case of a Luwoid word, elements of Southern Anatolian avunculate (surviving in Lycian) may have further favored the generalization of 'mother's brother's offspring' as 'cousin' par excellence. Cf. Puhvel, *JAOS* 100:167 (1980).

**anni-nani(ya)-* differs in compound type from the inherently reciprocal *annaneka-* 'sister(s) by the same mother' (q.v.); H. Eichner (*Die Sprache* 20:185 [1974]), who mistranslated *annaneka-* as 'mother's sister, aunt', also misinterpreted a "dialectal" *annin(n)iyami-* as 'mother's sister's offspring'. Kronasser (*Etym.* 1:220–1) assumed a base-stem **annin(n)i-*from Luw. *anni-* 'mother'; before him Alp (*Belleten* 18:458–9 [1954]) had posited *anni-* 'mother' + suffix *-(i)nni-* (thus **anninni-* 'aunt') + suffix of appurtenance *-mi-*.

annit(t)alwatar   (n.) 'motherhood' (vel sim.) in *KUB* XV 34 II 18–19 LÚ-*ni* LÚ-*natar tarhuilatar* SAL-*ni* SAL-*natar annitalwātar* 'to the man virility and potency, to the woman femininity and motherhood' (cf. Zuntz, *ARIV* 96.2:502 [1936–7]; Haas – Wilhelm, *Riten* 190); *KBo* XXI 48 Vs. 5 ANA SAL.MEŠ-*m*]*a-kan arha annit*[*talwatar* 'from women (take away) motherhood' (parallel to II 9 I 31–32 with *anniyatar* 'motherhood', q.v. s.v. *anna-*, *anni-*). Cf. also 617/p II 21 SAL-*n*]*i* SAL-*na-tar tar/has-ni-tal-wa-a-tar*; if read *tar-*, then scribal lapsus following preceding *tarhuilatar*; if *has-*, then perhaps the scribe started writing something like *hassumar* 'child-bearing' but shifted in mid-word to *annitalwātar*.

The denom. suffix *-(a)tar* (Kronasser, *Etym.* 1:296) is common to *anniyatar* and *annit(t)alwatar*. The segment *-t(t)alwa-*

defies analysis; possibly from *anni-p(i)ttalwa-tar* as something like 'mere motherhood' (i.e. plain, straight, physical child-bearing, vs. fosterage and the like; cf. s.v. *pittalwa*[*nt*]-). Cf. *hannitalwa(na)*- (s.v. *hanna*-); Puhvel, *JAOS* 100:167 (1980).

anki   'once' (?), *KUB* IV 2 IV 36 and 38 *a-an-ki* alternating with ibid. 35 1-*šu* and ibid. 37 1-*anki* 'once'. It is not probable that the carefully written tablet would twice repeat an erroneous *a*-sign for the numeral wedge 'one', just before and after the correct 1-*an-ki*.

Perhaps **oyo-nki* or **oy-ŋki* > **ayanki* > *ānki*, with a numeral derivative **oyo*- 'one' from the pronominal root seen in *a*- (q.v.), as in e.g. OPers. *aiva*- 'one' (*IEW* 286); cf. 2-*anki* = **dānki* < **dwoyo-nki* (see s.v. *ta*[*n*])? For -*nki*: Gk. -άκις see Rosenkranz, *KZ* 63:249 (1936); Sommer, *Zum Zahlwort* 21–2 (1951).

ankis-   (n.), name of a green garden-plant, nom.-acc. sg. *ānkis* (*KBo* XXII 135 I 2; *ABoT* 34, 11; ibid. 10 SAR.HI.A *hūman* 'all vegetables'), *āankis* (*Bo* 3367 + 7039 Vs. 7 *āankiss-a* NUMUN-*an* 'a.-seed'; cf. H. Otten – C. Rüster, *ZA* 68:153 [1978]), gen. sg. in *KUB* VII 1 I 20 *ānkisas* NUMUN-*an* 'seed of a.' (near the beginning of a list of 'all' such plants, preceded by *kappāni* 'cumin' and followed [21] by AN.TAH.ŠUM^SAR 'crocus' and *hazzuwanis* 'lettuce'; cf. Kronasser, *Die Sprache* 7:143 [1961]), perhaps nom.-acc. pl. *ankisa*^SAR (*KBo* XIII 248 I 8); XXIII 23 Vs. 33 ^GIŠ*INBI* ^GIŠ*alkistanus ānkis*['fruit-tree branches (and) a.' (cf. Haas – Thiel, *Rituale* 206).

The *s*-stem may point to an IE word, unlike the exotic terms which surround it in VII 1 I 20 ff. Formally identical with Vedic *áñkas*- 'bend, curvature' = Gk. ἄγκος 'bend, hollow, glen'; cf. also Gk. ὄγκος 'barb' = Lat. *uncus* 'hook'. A prickly plant?

anku   'fully, quite, really, absolutely, unconditionally', e.g. *KUB* XLI 23 II 18–20 *marnuwan mān sēssarr-a anku lamtati istanzanas*-[*s*]*mis karaz*-[*s*]*miss-a* 1-*as kisat* 'as m. (a drink) and beer have been fully mixed (and) their mind and heart have become one'; XIV 8 Vs. 20–21 LÚ.MEŠ ᵁᴿᵁ*Mizrī-ma mahhan nahsariyantat n-at uer nu* ANA ABI-YA DUMU-ŠU LUGAL-*uiznanni anku wekir* 'but when the Egyptians became afraid, they came and asked of my father unconditionally one of his sons for kingship' (cf. Götze, *KlF* 210);XXIX 55 I 1–3 *mān lukkatta nu nūwa ispandan appizziyas hāliyas naui anku haruwanāizzi* 'when dawn comes but does not yet quite light up the night of the last watch' (cf. Kammenhuber, *Hippologia* 150); XXXV 132 III 7 *sēhuni anku paizzi* '(so-and-so) must absolutely go to urinate'; *KBo* XXIV 5 Vs. 10 *anku wewiskiuan dāi* '(she) really starts crying out'. Cf. Friedrich, *JCS* 1:275–6 (1947).

No clear etymology. Houwink Ten Cate (in R. A. Crossland and A. Birchall [eds.], *Bronze Age migrations in the Aegean* 155 [1973]) compared the particle *-an + -k(k)u* (q.v.). Cf. Kronasser, *Etym.* 1:349.

Van Windekens (*Festschrift for O. Szemerényi* 912 [1979]) adduced IE **enek̑-* 'attain' (Goth. *ganohs* 'enough', Gk. δι-ηνεκής 'continuous'), presumably **n̥k̑u*.

an(a)s-, an(as)siya-   'wipe', 3 sg. pres. act. *ānsi* (e.g. *KBo* XIX 128 I 19 and VI 9 QATI-ŠU *ānsi* 'wipes his hands'; ibid. I 36 QATAM-ŠU *ānsi* 'wipes his hand'; ibid. I 34 LUGAL-*us-kan ... pūrius ānsi* 'the king wipes [his] lips'; cf. Otten, *Festritual* 2, 4, 16; IV 9 II 25 and 36 ŠU.MEŠ-ŠU *ānsi*; *KUB* XX 59 I 17–18 LUGAL-*us-kan ... pūrius--su[s] ānsi*), *āansi* (XXX 41 I 14 ŠU.MEŠ-ŠU *āansi*), *a-an-as-zi* (VIII 38 + XLIV 63 III 20–21 *namma-an āandaz* A-*az ... arha ānaszi* 'then he wipes him off with warm water'; cf. Burde, *Medizinische Texte* 30), 3 pl. pres. act. *ānsanzi* (e.g. *KBo* IV 9 II 19 and VI 23 ŠU.MEŠ-ŠUNU *ānsanzi*; V 1 IV 4–5 *nu* SILÁ *wetenit katta ānsanzi* KAxU-*an* GÌR-ŠU *arha ārri* 'they wipe down a lamb with water; he washes its mouth and foot'; cf. Sommer – Ehelolf, *Pāpanikri* 12*; XI 73 Rs. 18), *ānsiyanzi* (e.g. *KUB* XXIX 40 II 14 *nu* ANŠU.KUR.RA.HI.A *PANE-ŠUNU ānsiyanzi* 'they wipe off the faces of the horses'; cf. Kammenhuber, *Hippologia* 178), *anassi-yanzi* (*KBo* XIV 63a IV 1 *mahh]an-ma* ANŠU.KUR.RA.HI.A *arha lānzi n-us-kan anassiyan[zi* 'but when they unharness the horses, they wipe them'; cf. Kammenhuber, *Hippologia* 220, who improbably separated this form from this verb; for *-kan* cf. LUGAL-*us-kan* above; alternatively denominative from *anassa-*, q.v.), 1 sg. pret. act. *ansun* (*KUB* XXIV 13 III 19 *n-at-si-kan arha ansun* 'I wiped it off him'), *ānsun* (dupl. XLI 19 Rs. 10, 11, 12, 14; cf. Haas – Thiel, *Rituale* 108, 94–6), 3 sg. pret. midd. (?)]*ānastat* (*KBo* XIX 109, 1; cf. Siegelová, *Appu-Hedammu* 58–9), 2 sg. imp. act. *ānas* (e.g. *KUB* XXXIII 5 II 7 *nu-za* GAB.LÀL *dā n-an arha ānas* 'take wax and wipe him off'; cf. Laroche, *RHA* 23:100 [1965]), 3 sg. imp. act. *ānasdu* (*KBo* III 8 II 33–34 *namma-an* IŠTU LÀL-*it* EME-*ŠU arha ānasdu* 'then let her wipe off his tongue with honey'; cf. ibid. 32 *n-an-kan* EME-*ŠU sartāiddu* 'let her daub his tongue', 33 *iskiddu* 'let her salve'; cf. Kronasser, *Die Sprache* 7:155 [1961]); partic. *ansant-*, nom. sg. c. *ansanza* (VIII 55, 30), *ānsanza* (XVI 97 Vs. 35), nom.-acc. sg. neut. *ansan* (e.g. *KUB* XXIV 13 II 10–21 passim; cf. Haas – Thiel, *Rituale* 104), *ānsan* (V 20 I 11; *KBo* XVI 97 Rs. 14), nom. pl. c. *ānsantes* (XVII 105 II 38); iter. *anaski-, ansiski-, ansaski-, ansiki-* /ans-ski-/, 1 sg. pres. act. *ānaskimi* (XXI 8 II 3; cf. Jakob-Rost, *Ritual der Malli* 29), 3 sg. pres. act. *ānaskizzi* (XIX 163 I 23 and IV 4 *n-apa pūriūs ānaskizzi* 'wipes off the lips'), *ānsiskizzi* (*KUB* XXIV 13 III 16 *n-an arha ānsiskizzi* 'she wipes him off'), *ā*]*nsaskizzi* (*KBo* XXIII 23 Vs. 38; cf. Haas – Thiel, *Rituale* 206), *ānsiki*[*zzi* (ibid. 77). Cf. Sommer – Ehelolf, *Pāpanikri* 71; Kronasser, *Etym.* 1:394; Otten, *Studia mediterranea P. Meriggi dicata* 439–43 (1979).

ans- denotes a "milder" type of action than *wars(iya)-* 'wipe, rub, sweep' (q.v.) and is hence found together with expressions for washing, daubing, and salving. Apart from the alternative 3 pl. pres. act. *ānsiyanzi* or *anassiyanzi* (in hippological texts only), attested forms point to a root-verb *ans-* with *-hi* conjugation 3 sg. pres. act. *ānsi*; but *ans-* can hardly be a primary reflex of an etymological **ons-*, because **ns* yields either *nz* or *ss*. Hence perhaps the internal vowel in *ānaszi, anassiyanzi, ānastat, ānas, ānasdu, anaski-* is historically phonetic rather than merely graphic, and the proto-paradigm an ablauting *anaszi : ansanzi*. Etymology obscure.

Oettinger's (*Stammbildung* 437) reading of *KUB* XLI 8 II 36 as 3 sg. pres. act. *an-si-i-ya-zi* is dubious, in place of DINGIR-*LIM iyazi* (cf. Otten, *ZA* 54:126 [1961]); no more plausible is his postulation of **ns > ss* "immediately after accent", and **ns > nz* elsewhere, hence **assi : *anzanzi* "restored" to uniform *ans-*.

anda,   adverb, postposition, preverb '(with)in, inside, in(to), among; in addition, furthermore'; *andan* '(with)in, inside, in(to)'. In OHitt. *anda* is mainly postpositional and preverbal, rarely adverbial, whereas *andan* is chiefly adverbial, rarely postpositional, and never preverbal. In later Hitt. the distinctions are obscured, with *anda* equally adverbial and *andan* often postpositional and (newly) preverbal; previous sporadic attendant localizing particles (*-kan, -san, -asta, -apa*) become dominant with the adverbial usage but remain spotty with the postpositions and preverbs *anda* and *andan*. E.g. (OHitt.) *KBo* III 23 Rs. 6 *kissari-mi anda* 'in my hand' (postpositional); XVII 2 I 9 *ūk anda paimi* 'I go in' (preverbal; cf. Otten – Souček, *Altheth. Ritual* 16); VI 2 III 57 (= *Code* 1:70) *anda-sse 2-ki pāi* 'in addition he gives him twofold'; *KUB* XXIX 28 I 10 (= *Code* 2:28) *anta-ya-sse* 'and additionally to him'; III 23 Vs. 13 *anda ēsdu* 'let be within' (adverbial, rare); *KBo* VI 2 IV 61 (= *Code* 100) *takku* IN.NU.DA *andan* NU.[GÁL 'if there is no straw inside' (adverbial, vs. later versions *anda*; cf. Haase, *Fragmente* 52); XVII 1 I 9 *tarm]as-san 9-an andan kitta* 'peg(s) nine have been placed inside' (adverbial; cf. Otten – Souček, *Altheth. Ritual* 18); VI 2 IV 54 (= *Code* 1:98 *andan* É-*ri kuit harakzi* 'within, in the house, what perishes' (adverbial); *KUB* XXIX 28 I 8 (= *Code* 2:27) É-*ri andan* 'inside the house' (transition to postpositional); (Later Hitt.) LÚ-*as-kan anda* NU.GÁL 'a man is not among them' (adverbial, lit. 'within'; cf. Otten – Souček, *Gelübde* 30, III 9); XX 76 IV 8 ^É*arkiui antan tiyezzi* 'stands inside the a.' (postpositional); XVII 10 IV 16–17 *kuit andan paizzi* 'what goes in' (preverbal; cf. Laroche, *RHA* 23:97 [1965]); XI 20 I 10 *anda immiyazi* 'mixes in' (preverbal); *anda-kan impauwar* 'depression' (preverbal; q.v. s.v. [*a*]*impa-*); *KBo* XVI 50 Vs. 9 *anda-ma-az-kan* 'but furthermore' (cf. Otten, *RHA* 18:121–3 [1960]; von Schuler, *Die Kaškäer* 126). Cf. Kammenhuber, *Festschrift H. Otten* 141–60 (1973), with previous bibliography 145–7.

Luw. *anta*, adverb, postposition, preverb '(with)in, in(to)', spelled *anta*, *ānta*, *āanta*, *anda*, *ānda*. Hier. *ata* /anda/, preverb, adverb, postposition '(with)in, in(to)', *atatali-* 'inner'. Lyc. *ñte(pi)*, preverb or adverb 'in(to), in(side), at'. Cf. Laroche, *BSL* 53.1:176–7 (1957–8), *Dict. louv.* 28, *HH* 34; Meriggi, *HHG* 40–1; Neumann, *HOAKS* 390.

Hitt. *anda(n)* has been compared with OLat. *endo*, Lat. *indu-* 'in(to)' (*endoitium, endoploro, endo procinctu, induperator, indigena*), Gk. ἔνδον 'within', and Lyc. *ñte* since Hrozný, *MDOG* 56:28 (1915), *SH* 17. OLat. *endo* is mainly prepositional and preverbal like OHitt. *anda*, whereas Gk. ἔνδον is adverbial like OHitt. *andan*. The initial Hittite *a*-vocalism may point to IE *n̥-. Cf. e.g. Kronasser, *Etym.* 1:351–2.

Cf. *antaka-, antiyant-, andurza*.

antaka-, antaki-   'chamber', dat.-loc. sg. in *KUB* XXXVI 44 IV 12 ^DUTU-*us aruni antaga-ssa pait* 'the sun-god went to the sea, to his chamber' (cf. Laroche, *RHA* 23:82 [1965], 28:29 [1970]); XI 20 I 13 *n-an-za-an-kan antaki-ssi dāi* 'places it in his chamber', with dupl. XI 25 III 9 *t-an-za-an-kan antakitti dāi*; XLV 3 IV 17 *antaki-ss[i*; VII 5 I 7–8 *nu-wa-ssi-kan andakitti-ssi kattanta pait* 'he went down to her (bed)chamber'. Cf. Goetze, *ANET* 349; Laroche, *OLZ* 51:421 (1956).

Seemingly derivative of *anda* 'within' (q.v.); since neither *-ka-* nor *-ki-* is productive in Hittite (*antakitti* also shows a Hurroid ending), Kronasser (*Etym.* 1:210–1) assumed a hybrid formation with a "foreign" suffix. Yet inherited origin is possible; perhaps the suffix is *-gh-* as in Gk. στόμαχος, κύμβαχος, οὐραχός, esp. since intervocalic *-k-* is spelled single, unlike e.g. *kurakki-* 'pillar', *tupanzakki-* (a vessel). Laroche (*Fouilles de Xanthos* 5:136 [1974]) compared Lyc. *ñtata* 'chamber', from *ñte* 'in(side)'.

antara-   'blue' (ZA.GÌN), acc. sg. c. *āntaran* (*VBoT* 24 I 23 SÍG *āntaran* SÍG *midann-a* 'blue wool and red wool' (cf. Sturtevant, *TAPA* 58:6 [1927], *Chrest.* 106, 118–9; Goetze, *Tunnawi* 70–1,

JCS 10:34 [1956]), *antaran* (1/a, 7 síg *antaran*; *KUB* XLI 1 I 5 *ant*]*aran* UD.KAM-*an* 'blue day'), *andaran* (ibid. 3; *VBoT* 24 I 4 síg *andaran*), *āndaran* (ibid. 14 and *KBo* V 2 III 19 síg *āndaran*; cf. G. F. Del Monte, *Oriens Antiquus* 12:126 [1973]), *andarān* (*KUB* XLVI 43, 9 sí]G *andarān*).

antarant- 'blue', acc. sg. c. *antarantan* (*KUB* XXIV 9 I 43 síg *antarantan kapinan* QATAMMA *iyazi* 'she makes likewise blue wool into a thread'), *andarandan* (ibid. 45 *and*]*arandan* UD-*an* 'blue day'; cf. Riemschneider, *MIO* 5:142 [1957]; Jakob-Rost, *Ritual der Malli* 26–8).

antariya- 'make blue', iter. 3 sg. pret. act. *antariskit* (XXIV 9 I 44; cf. Riemschneider, *MIO* 5:142 [1957]), *andareskit* (dupl. XLI 1 I 4).

V. Machek (*Arch. Or.* 17.2:131–2 [1949]) convincingly compared *antara-* /andra-/ with Slavic **modrŭ* 'blue' seen in Czech-Slovak *modrý*, Serbo-Croatian *modar*; thus *andra-* < **amdra-* < **ṃd(h)-ró-*, with suffix as in **rudh-ró-* 'red' (Slavic **rŭdrŭ*)? Cf. *asara-* (s.v.). Cf. Puhvel, *JAOS* 100:167 (1980).

Juret's adduction (*Vocabulaire* 31) of Skt. *indīvaram* 'blue lotus-blossom', was abortive. Juret's and W. Belardi's comparison of *antara-* with Ved. *ándhas* 'darkness' (*Rivista degli studi orientali* 25:32–3 [1950]) is improbable, despite Van Windekens, *Festschrift for O. Szemerényi* 910–2 (1979), and G. T. Rikov, *Linguistique balkanique* 24.3:79 (1981).

antiyant- (c.) '(in-house) daughter's husband, (socrilocal) son-in-law', acc. sg. *antiyantan* (*KBo* VI 3 II 27–28 [= *Code* 1:36] *takku* ÌR-*is* ANA DUMU.NITA ELLIM *kūsata pidd*[*aiz*]*zi n-an* LÚ*antiyantan epzi* 'if a slave pays the bride[groom]-price for a free youth and seizes him as an a.'; III 1 II 38–39 *nu kuis* DUMU.SAL *hantezzis nu-ssi-ssan* LÚ*antiyantan* [dupl. XII 4 II 8 LÚ*antiyandan*] *appāndu nu* LUGAL-*us apās kisaru* 'one that is a first-rank daughter, they shall take an a. for her, and he shall become king'), nom. pl. c. in *KUB* XXVI 1a, 10–11 LÚ]*āntiyantes--(s)mas kuy*[*ēs* … ŠA LU]GAL LÚ.MEŠ*HADAN* LUGAL['but those of you who are sons-in-law of the king … brothers-in-law of the king' (cf. von Schuler, *Dienstanweisungen* 10; Laroche, *RHA*

15:126 [1957]); denom. abstract *andaiyandatar* (n.), dat.-loc. sg. in XIII 8 Vs. 14–15 *parā-ma-kan* DUMU.NITA DUMU.SAL AŠŠUM É.GI₄.A-*TIM* ᴸᵁ*andaiyandanni-ya le kuiski pāi* 'but let nobody give forth a youth or a maiden for bridehood or son-in-lawship' (cf. Otten, *Totenrituale* 106; wrongly H. A. Hoffner, *Festschrift H. Otten* 110 [1973]).

Correctly interpreted by K. Balkan (*Ankara Üniversitesi Dil ve Tarih-Coğrafya Fakültesi Dergisi* 6:147–52 [1948]) as **anda--iyant-* 'he who has gone in' (cf. s.v. *anda, i-*), with reference to the expressionally and substantively similar son-in-law institution in Akkadian (*errēbu* 'he that enters') and Turkish (*iç-güvey* 'inside son-in-law', *iç-güveylik* = Hitt. *andaiyandatar*; cf. e.g. Estonian *kodu-väi* 'in-house son-in-law'). V. Machek (*LPosn* 7:81–2 [1959]) adduced Slavic parallels (e.g. Slovak *pristač* 'he who has joined', from *pri-sta-* 'step to') and preferred an analysis **anda tiyant-* 'he who has entered' (with haplology in *antiyant-*, not elision as claimed by H. A. Hoffner, *Orientalia* N.S. 35:393 [1966]); but *andaiyand-* favors Balkan's analysis, with *ant-iyant-* an elisional form. Cf. Güterbock, *Sommer Corolla* 64; Friedrich, *Heth. Ges.* 96; Imparati, *Leggi ittite* 218–9; Kronasser, *Etym.* 1:124, 45, 295.

It is possible that the strict OHitt. usage, seen in the Code and the Edict of Telipinus, was in later Hittite relaxed to 'son-in-law' at large; but Carruba (*Parola del Passato* 24:278 [1969]) was probably wrong in claiming for *antiyant-* the sense of 'brother-in-law' (primarily 'sister's husband') as well, as in Akk. *hadanu* or Gk. γαμβρός; in *KUB* XXVI 1a, 10–11 (quoted above), HADAN is plausibly 'brother-in-law' (=Hitt. *kaena-*, q.v.) in distinction to *antiyant-* 'son-in-law'.

antu(wa)hha-, antuhsa- (c.) 'man, human being, person' (UKÙ, LÚ. .ULÙ.LU), nom. sg. *antuwahhas* (e.g. *KBo* XI 12 I 1; cf. Jakob-Rost, *Ritual der Malli* 20; V 4 Vs. 7 *kuis imma kuis antuwahhas* 'whatever man'; cf. Friedrich, *Staatsverträge* 1:52; *KUB* XIII 20 I 3 *appizzis antuwahhas* 'a person of the lowest rank'; cf. Alp, *Belleten* 11:388 [1947]), *antūwahhas* (e.g. XXIX 4 I 1; cf. Kronasser, *Umsiedelung* 6), *antuhhas* (e.g. *KBo* V 3 II 62; cf.

antu(wa)hha-, antuhsa-

Friedrich, *Staatsverträge* 2:120), *an-uh-tu-has* (*KUB* VII 53 I 1,
with graphic metathesis; cf. Goetze, *Tunnawi* 4, 30–1), *antuhwahhas* (sic XXIV 3 I 41; cf. Gurney, *Hittite Prayers* 24),
antūwahza (sic XII 44 III 7; cf. G. F. Del Monte, *Oriens
Antiquus* 12:122 [1973]), *antuhsas* (e.g. *KBo* V 4 Vs. 5 and Rs.
40; XI 72 II 25 and III 24; *KUB* VII 53 I 7 and 8), acc. sg.
antuwahhan (e.g. *KBo* XI 10 II 20; XI 12 I 13; cf. Jakob-Rost,
Ritual der Malli 22–3), *antuhsan* (e.g. *Code* 1:10, 42, 44,
alternating in dupl. with LÚ.ULÙ.LU-*an*, UKÙ-*an*; cf. Haase,
Fragmente 5, 22–3; III 60 II 3–4 [OHitt.] *mān uwarka[ntan]
antuhsan uwanzi n-an-kan kunanzi* 'if they see a fat man they kill
him'; cf. Güterbock, *ZA* 44:104 [1938]; *KUB* XIV 1 Vs. 38; cf.
Götze, *Madd.* 10; *KBo* V 4 Rs. 39; cf. Friedrich, *Staatsverträge*
1:66), *antūhsan* (*Bo* 3379, 8; cf. Burde, *Medizinische Texte* 50),
anduhsan (e.g. *KUB* XXIII 77 Rs. 51 and 81), gen. sg.
antuwahhas (XXX 10 Vs. 23), gen. sg. or pl. *antuhsas* (e.g. *KBo*
XI 18 V 14 *a]ntuhsas tētanus* 'human hair'), *anduhsas* (XVII 1 I
23 *anduhsas harsārr-a* 'human heads'; cf. Otten – Souček,
Altheth. Ritual 20), *antuhsan* (*KUB* XXXVI 79 II 45 *antuhsan*
TI-*ta[r* 'man's life'), dat.-loc. sg. *antuhsi* (e.g. XII 58 I 13 *edani
antuhsi* 'for this man'; cf. Goetze, *Tunnawi* 6), *antūhsi* (XLIV 64
I 15; cf. Burde, *Medizinische Texte* 48), *antuhse* (XLIV 61 Rs. 7
and 19; cf. Burde, *Medizinische Texte* 18–20), *anduhsi* (e.g. *KBo*
XXIII 23 Rs. 58 *damp]ūpi anduhsi* 'to an uncouth person'), abl.
sg. *antuhsaz* (e.g. *KUB* XII 57 I 6), nom. pl. (OHitt.) *an-tu-wa-
-ah-hi-es* (*KBo* III 60 II 16), *antuwahhis* (ibid. 2), *an-tu-uh-se-es*
(e.g. *KUB* XIX 37 III 25 *kappuwantes-pat-mu-kan antuhses
isparter* 'only a few folk escaped from me'; cf. Götze, *AM* 174;
similarly XIV 1 Vs. 52; cf. Götze, *Madd.* 12), *an-tu-uh-se-is* (e.g.
V 7 Vs. 28), *an-du-uh-se-es* (e.g. *KBo* XII 62 Rs. 13 *anduhses …
sipandandat* 'men were sacrificed'; VIII 35 II 23), *antuhsis* (e.g.
XII 126 I 13; cf. Jakob-Rost, *Ritual der Malli* 22; *KUB* VII 53
II 19; cf. Götze, *Tunnawi* 12), acc. (also syntactically nom.) pl.
antuhsus (e.g. *VBoT* 1, 25 *nu-mu antuhsus Gasgas* KUR-*yas uppi*
'send me men of G.-land'; cf. L. Rost, *MIO* 4:335 [1956]),
anduhsus (*KBo* III 60 III 12), gen. pl. *antuhsas* (e.g. *KUB* XV 34
II 21; cf. Haas – Wilhelm, *Riten* 190), dat.-loc. pl. *antūwahhas*
(*FHG* 1 II 18 *antūwahhas anda* 'among men'), *antuhsas* (e.g.

80

KUB XXX 10 Vs. 7 *āssauas antuhsas anda* 'among good men';
KBo IV 1 Vs. 43 *n-at-kan* DINGIR.MEŠ-*as antuhsass-a āssu* 'it is
dear to gods and men'; V 13 III 28; cf. Friedrich, *Staatsverträge*
1:128), *anduhsas* (*KUB* XV 34 II 30).

antuhsatar (n.) 'mankind; population; body of men, contingent' (*KBo* I 45 Vs. 19 *antuhsatar*=[Akk.] *nīšu* 'men'; cf.
Kammenhuber, *MIO* 2:77 [1954]; *MSL* 3:60 [1955]), sometimes sg. with verb in pl., nom.-acc. sg. *antuhsatar* (e.g. V 4 Vs.
28 *namma antuhsatarr-a kuit marsahhan* 'now because mankind
is corrupted'; cf. Friedrich, *Staatsverträge* 1:56; same in *KUB*
XXI 1 III 16, with dupl. XXI 4 Vs. 40 and XXI 5 III 31
UKÙ.MEŠ-*tarr-a*; cf. Friedrich, *Staatsverträge* 2:68; *KBo* V 8 II
29–30 *antuhsatarr-a-za-kan kuit tēpauwaz anda* [*huu*]*ittiyan
harta* 'and the contingent which he had drawn in there in small
numbers'; cf. Götze, *AM* 154), *antuhsātar* (e.g. V 6 I 19–20
nu-kan antuhsātar kuit INA URU.DIDLI.HI.A-*ŠUNU* EGIR-*pa pān
ēsta* 'the population who had gone back to their towns'; cf.
Güterbock, *JCS* 10:90–1 [1956]; *KUB* VI 41 I 25 *antuhsātar-
-ma-wa-nnas arantallin*[*zi* 'the population is insurgent against
us'; cf. Friedrich, *Staatsverträge* 1:108), gen. sg. *antuhsannas*
(XIX 11 IV 16; cf. Güterbock, *JCS* 10:65 [1956]), UKÙ.MEŠ-
-*annas* (XIII 20 IV 8), dat.-loc. sg. *antuhsanni* (e.g. XIV 4 II 7;
cf. F. Cornelius, *RIDA* 22:30 [1975]), *antuhsani* (*KBo* XIII 2
Rs. 18).

antuhsannant- (c.) 'mankind; population', sg. with verb in pl.,
nom. sg. *antuhsannanza* (*KUB* XIX 10 I 6 *antuhsannanza*
URU.HI.A-*ŠUNU* EGIR-*pa eppir* 'the population reoccupied their
towns'; cf. Güterbock, *JCS* 10:65 [1956]; *KBo* VIII 77 Rs. 14),
UKÙ.MEŠ-*annanza* (III 6 I 26, with dupl. *KUB* I 1 I 30
UKÙ.MEŠ-*annaza*; cf. Götze, *Hattusilis* 8). Cf. Laroche, *BSL*
57.1:33–4 (1962).

The originally paradigmatic (nom.: oblique) stem-alterna-
tion *antu(wa)hha-*: *antuhsa-* (e.g. *KBo* III 60 II 16 nom. pl.
antuwahhes vs. III 12 acc. pl. *anduhsus*) has partly broken down
by spread of *antuhsa-* to nom. and *antuwahha-* to some oblique
cases (e.g. above *KBo* XI 10 II 20 *antuhsas-a-z antuwahhan*; V 4
Vs. 5 nom. sg. *antuhsas* vs. 7 *antuwahhas*; *KUB* VII 53 I 1 nom.
sg. *an-uh-tu-has* vs. 7 and 8 *antuhsas*). No clear etymology.

antu(wa)hha-, antuhsa-

Benveniste (*RHA* 1:203–8 [1932]) posited an original *s*-stem nom. sg. **antu(wa)hs*, gen. sg. *antuhsas*, which Pedersen (*Hitt.* 195, 47–8) modified to *antuhhas*, gen. *antuhsas*, with an ablaut remotely recalling *a(y)is(s)-*, gen. *issas* 'mouth'. Yet the further nom. sg. forms *antuhwahhas*, *antūwahza* make an IE morphological petrifact unlikely. Intimations of non-IE origin in Couvreur, *Hett.* 61. Laroche (*JCS* 1:194–5 [1947]) compared an alleged Hattic *antūh* 'human' (*KUB* XVII 28 II 10 and 20), with its adjective *āntuhhil* (XXVIII 71 Rs. 7), and further adduced Hitt. *danduki-* 'mortal' (q.v.) as another loanword from Hattic (*d-andu-ki-*, with Hattic prefix *ta-/da-*); rejected by Kammenhuber, *MIO* 2:422 (1954), *HOAKS* 193, 432. Kronasser (*Etym.* 1:140, 188) saw in *antu(wa)hha-* a thematization of the Hattic word, and an *s*-derivation in *antuhsa-* (similarly in *antūwahza*?).

The attempts to connect *antu(wa)hha-*, *antuhsa-* with the much-discussed Gk. ἄνθρωπος 'human being' range from P. Kretschmer (*Glotta* 9:231–2 [1918]) to F. Ribezzo (*Rivista indo-greco-italica* 4:127–8 [1920]) to W. Petersen (*AJPh* 56:59–60 [1935]) to A. Braun (*ARIV* 95.2:386–7 [1936]) to V. Pisani (*Studia classica et orientalia Antonino Pagliaro oblata* 3:157–9 [1969]) who posited for ἄνθρωπος (Myc. *a-to-ro-qo*) a "contamination" of an Anatolian **ἄνθυος* with (Hes.) δρώψ · ἄνθρωπος (**nr-ōkʷ-s*).

V. Georgiev (*Linguistique balkanique* 21.4:29 [1978]) postulated 'man' < 'folk' < 'movable goods, chattels' in feudal society (*antu* 'goods' and *weh-* 'turn').

More suggestive is H. Eichner's (*Die Sprache* 25:77 [1979]) postulation of a possessive compound 'having breath within', i.e. *anda* + **dwéA₁os : duA₁s-és* allegedly related to *tuhhai-*'gasp, pant'; but the latter points to a root **dhew-A₁-* cognate with *tuhhui-* 'smoke'; cf. then Gk. ἔνθῡμος 'spirited' vs. Lat. *fūmus* smoke'. Oettinger (*Stammbildung* 373) properly reconstructed **en-dhweA₁o-*.

Toch. A. *oṅk*, B *eṅkwe* 'man, male' is unrelated (cf. Van Windekens, *Le tokharien* 337); hence Čop's construct (*Ling.* 8:48 [1966–8]) **ankwa-* + *has(s)-* 'beget', comparing Goth. *mana-seþs* 'mankind', was abortive.

Gusmani (*Neue epichorische Schriftzeugnisse aus Sardis* 5 [1975]) interpreted Lyd. *antola, anlola* 'funerary stele' as matching Hitt. **antuwahhala-*, with semantic reference to Gk. ἀνδριάς 'human representation, statue'.

Cf. *antu(wa)salli-*.

andurza   '(on the) inside, indoors, in the interior, internally' (*an-dur-za*), e.g. *KBo* V 13 II 30 (rebellion 'in the interior', vs. ibid. 27 attack *arahza* 'from the outside'; cf. Friedrich, *Staatsverträge* 1:124); *KUB* V 4 I 33 BAL *andurza kuiski* DÙ-*yazi* 'someone makes rebellion internally' (vs. ibid. 35 BAL *arahza-ma kuiski* DÙ-*zi*); XIII 4 III 9–10 *arahza ... andurza-ma* 'outside ... but inside' (cf. Sturtevant, *JAOS* 54:380 [1934]); II 6 IV 1–2 *andurza karū arantari* '(they) stand already indoors' (vs. ibid. III 42 INA É ^DUTU *pānzi* '[king and queen] go into the sun-temple'); frequently in rituals *andurza* 'indoors' vs. *āskaz* 'out of the gate, outdoors' (e.g. *KBo* XIX 128 IV–VI passim; cf. Otten, *Festritual* 10–16); *KUB* XXXIV 18 II 11 *andurza* ^{UZU}HAR NU.GÁL 'there is no lung inside' (cf. Riemschneider, *Geburtsomina* 68); *KBo* XXII 101 Rs. 8 *antu]hsan andurza istara[kzi* 'a man falls internally ill' (cf. Burde, *Medizinische Texte* 47); *VBoT* 58 I 14 *andurza ... harzi* 'keeps within' (cf. Laroche, *RHA* 23:83 [1965]).

andurziya (same meaning), e.g. *KUB* XXIX 4 III 8–9 *nu andurziya ... [si]pandanzi* 'they libate indoors' (cf. Kronasser, *Umsiedelung* 22); VII 13 Vs. 5 (cf. ibid. 10 *arahziya*, probably *arahza*+*ya* 'and', q.v. s.v. *arha-*). Cf. Otten, *ZA* 71:140 (1981).

anturiya- 'inner, interior, internal, native, domestic', nom. sg. c. *antūriyas* (e.g. VIII 75 I 16 'inner [field]'; cf. Souček, *Arch. Or.* 27:8 [1959]; XIII 28, 5 *antūriyas* KIN 'inside job'), *andūriyas* (XLIII 38 Rs. 22; cf. Oettinger, *Eide* 20), *anduryas* (e.g. VIII 75 I 12; XLII 16 IV 7; *KBo* IV 14 II 26–27 *nasma-mu* MUD ŠA ÌR.MEŠ *anduryas arahzas* DÙ-*ri* 'or the blood of my subjects turns from native to alien'; cf. R. Stefanini, *ANLR* 20:41 [1965]; *KUB* XVI 19 Vs. 5 MUD *anduryas* 'native blood', vs. ibid. 9 MUD ... *arahziyas* 'alien blood'), *andurriyas* (XXXI 65 Rs. 6 'native [dress]'), nom. pl. c. *antūriēs* (*KBo* V 3 I 7 *hūmantes arahzenies antūriēs* 'all external and internal'; cf. Friedrich, *Staatsverträge* 2:106), *andurriyas* (*KUB* VI 1 Vs. 8, vs. ibid. 10 *arahzenas*), dat.-loc. pl. *anturiyas* (1203/u + *KUB* XXXI 86 II 26 *arahzenass-a-kan anturiyass-a* ANA AN.ZA.KÀR 'to both outer and inner towers'; cf. Otten, *Materialien* 45).

Cf. Friedrich, *Staatsverträge* 1:167–70.

andurza presupposes an **antur* (cf. *anturiya-*), much as *arahza* is akin to *arha* (q.v.; cf. e.g. Laroche, *RPh* 42:246 [1968], *RHA* 28:38 [1970]). Sturtevant (e.g. *Comp. Gr.*[1] 128, *Comp. Gr.*[2] 62) posited **ŋ-dhur-* 'indoors' (Gk. θύρᾱ 'door' etc.) but later (e.g. *Comp. Gr.*[2] 41) also came around to Couvreur's comparison (*Hett.* 92–3) with Lat. *inter*, Skt. *antár*, with vocalism as in Oscan-Umbrian *anter*. Even so the *u* remains unexplained (cf. Benveniste, *Hittite* 70, pace O. Szemerényi, *KZ* 73:73 [1955], who posited *ur* < **r̥*; the *u* of Lith. *kuȓ* 'where?' and similar forms is due to a zero-grade of the stem **kʷo-*, and Lat. *cūr* 'why?' is from OLat. *quōr;* cf. Goth. *hwar* 'where?'). Kronasser (*VLFH* 156, *Etym.* 1:168) still operated with IE **en-dhur-* 'indoors'; so did E. P. Hamp (*BSL* 50.1:44–6 [1954] and in *Evidence for laryngeals* 136 [1965]), Oettinger (*Eide* 56), and Tischler (*IBK* Sonderheft 50:215–6 [1982]); attractive as this construct may be semantically in antonymy with *āskaz* (see above), it remains an Indo-European postulate with little inner-Anatolian probability.

antuwasalli- (c.), high court official, perhaps 'majordomo'. nom. sg. in *KBo* V 7 Rs. 52 [1]*Kar[iyaz]iti antūwasallis* in a list of dignitaries (cf. Riemschneider, *MIO* 6:354 [1958]), *KUB* XL 1 Vs. 33 ID AMAR.UD-DKAL LÚ*āntu*GAL (one of ZAG.MEŠ-*as BELU*.HI. .A 'border-lords', ibid. 32); in Akkadian texts *KBo* I 6 Rs. 22 LÚ[*and*]*uwasalli* (cf. E. F. Weidner, *Politische Dokumente aus Kleinasien* 88 [*BoSt* 8, 1923]), *RS* 17.227.37 ana LÚ*andubsal-limma* (cf. J. Nougayrol in *Mission de Ras Shamra* IX, *Le Palais Royal d'Ugarit* IV, 42, 259 [1956]; M. Dietrich – O. Loretz, *Die Welt des Orients* 3:210 [1966]).

antuwasalli- is most probably a compound, either *antuwa--salli-* or perhaps *antuwas-salli-* (with genitival first part). *salli-*

'great' = GAL 'great; chief' (cf. ᴸᵁ*sapasalli-*, another functionary); *antuwa-* may be the oblique case stem of a neuter noun *antu* meaning approximately 'goods' in *Bo* 2489+4008 II 40–41 *antu-smet parā parā makkiskattaru* 'may their goods keep getting more and more abundant'; thus literally 'inventorial chief, storemaster' (vel sim.; cf. the Old Persian-Greek γαζοφύλαξ 'treasurer'), with ᴸᵁ*andubsalli* at Ugarit matching semantically Akk. LÚ EN É-*ti abusi* (q.v. s.v. *apuzzi-*). Cf. Neu, *Interpretation* 111; Kronasser, *Etym.* 1:214.

Other, implausible interpretations: *-salli-* = GAL is mere phonetic rebus-writing in a foreign title (Kammenhuber, *KZ* 77:198 [1961]); *antu-* is the Hattic word for 'man' (see s.v. *antu*[*wa*]*hha-*), and the whole title may go back to a Hattic **antuwasel*, unless *salli-* = GAL is genuine sumerography after all (and not mere scribal whimsy), in which case *antuwa-salli-* = LÚ GAL 'chief' (N. van Brock, *RHA* 20:115 [1962]); as an unusual type of compound, 'great man' matches e.g. *pittar- -palhi-* 'broad-wing' (q.v. s.v. *pittar*; Rosenkranz, *BzN* N.F. 1:126 [1966]); *antuwasalli-* is not a compound but rather a Hattic or Hurrian **antuws-* or **antubs-* (= Akk. *abūsu?*) + agental suffix *-alli-* (as in e.g. *arkammanalli-* 'tributary'; H. A. Hoffner, *Orientalia* N.S. 35:386–8 [1966]).

-apa, -ap, -pa,   mostly Old Hittite sentence particle, sporadic later, similar in fate to *-an* and *-(a)sta* (q.v.), attached to first word of sentence but last in any string of enclitics. Esp. common in Edict of Telipinus (*n-apa, nu-war-at-apa, mān-as-apa,* etc.); also e.g. *KBo* XII 18, 6 *s-an-za-pa āssu suw*[*a-* 'fill him with good'; III 60 II 5 *s-an-ap atānzi* 'they eat him'; V 3 III 31 *ŪL huuissuuizzi aki-pa* 'he does not stay alive; he is put to death'. Cf. Laroche, *BSL* 53.1:168–9 (1957–8); Carruba, *Orientalia* N.S. 33:418–32 (1964), *Partikeln* 19, 32–5; Josephson, *Sentence Particles* 322–38.

The precise meaning and nuances of *-apa* are uncertain and difficult to render; the attempts by Carruba (localizing sense, movement to a given spot) and Josephson ("telic" action marker of an aspectual sort) suffer from subtle overinterpretation. Carruba's etymology from *appi* or *app(a)*, connectible with *appa, appezzi-* (q.v.) (*Orientalia* N.S. 33:429 [1964], *Partikeln* 19, 33) was in line with his similar adverbial interpretations of *-kan, -san, -(a)sta* (q.v.). More likely is some kind of tie-in with the demonstrative pronoun stem *apa-* (q.v.); Couvreur (*Hett.* 96) postulated a base-form *-pa* related to *apa-*; Kammenhuber (*OLZ* 50:377–8 [1955], *RHA* 17:20, 47 [1959], *HOAKS* 250) compared other Anatolian particles (Pal., Luw., Hier. *-pa*) and Avest. *bā* 'truly', Lith. *bà* 'surely'.

apa- 'that (one); he, she, it; the (very) one in question (frequently with *-pat*); thy, thine, your(s)' (vs. *ka-* 'this; my, mine', like Lat. *iste* vs. *hic*) (BI), nom. sg. c. *apās* (e.g. *KBo* XV 1 I 13–14 *nu tamain uyazi nu* EGIR SISKUR *apās tiyazi* 'he sends another, and that one takes care of the ritual'; cf. Kümmel, *Ersatzrituale* 112), *apas* (e.g. VI 2 III 24 and 28 [= *Code* 1:57–8]), *abas* (VIII 41, 6), BI-*as* (in *KUB* XLIII 8, e.g. III 10 *mā]n* UKÙ-*si* SAG.DU ŠA UR.MAH BI-*as* UKÙ-*as nutaras aki* 'if a man has the head of a lion, that man will die quickly'), acc. sg. c. *a-pu-u-un* (e.g. *Code* 1:2–4; *KBo* VI 3 III 70 [= *Code* 1:74] *apūn-za apās dāi* 'the [person] involved takes the [cattle] in question'; V 4 Rs. 29 *apūn* LÚKÚR 'that enemy'; cf. Friedrich, *Staatsverträge* 1:64), *apun* (e.g. VI 5 IV 15 [= *Code* 1:43] *apun-pat*), *apān* (*KUB* XXVI 12 II 27), nom.-acc. sg. neut. *apāt* (e.g. ibid. 6 *apās-ma apāt memai* 'but that one says thus'; cf. von Schuler, *Dienstanweisungen* 24–5; XIX 49 I 64 *nu-tta apāt* KUR-*e ēsdu* 'let this be your land'; cf. Friedrich, *Staatsverträge* 2:10), *apat* (e.g. XXIX 1 IV 3 *apat-wa-mu āssu* 'this is fine with me'; cf. B. Schwartz, *Orientalia* N.S. 16:36 [1947]), gen. sg. *apel* (e.g. XIV 15 IV 40–41 *nu-wa-tta ... apel* DUMU.SAL-*ZU ... pesta* 'he gave you his own daughter'; cf. Götze, *AM* 72; XIX 50 III 13 *nu-za apel kistati* 'will you become his [i.e. go over to his side]?'; cf. Friedrich, *Staatsverträge* 2:12), *apēl* (e.g. *KBo* VI 3 III 50 [= *Code* 1:65] *sarnikzīl appēll-a* 'its indemnification'), *apil* (II 13 Vs. 12), dat.-loc. sg. *apedani* (e.g. V 3 II 34–35 *apedani lamnī* 'at that very hour'; cf. Friedrich, *Staatsverträge* 2:116; ibid. III 57 *n-as apedani uddanī ser* BA.UG₆ 'he was put to death over that matter'; V 4 Rs. 26 *apedani wekti*

86

'you ask of him'; cf. Friedrich, *Staatsverträge* 1:64; VI 4 IV 19–20 [= *Code* 1:47] *mān apedani udnē mān damēdani* KUR-*e* 'whether in that same country or in another country'), *apidani* (e.g. V 4 Rs. 28), *apetani* (e.g. *KUB* XVI 83 Vs. 28), *apeda* ("directional" 'thither, to your side' in VI 48 II 3; cf. Sommer, *AU* 116; *KBo* III 41 + *KUB* XXXI 4 Vs. 19 'therefore'; cf. ibid. 16 *kuit handa* 'wherefore?', and Otten, *ZA* 55:160 [1962]; cf. the adverbial *apadda*[*n*] below), instr. sg. (or original suffixless loc.?) *apit* (e.g. XXXIII 118, 24 *apit pantalaz-pat* 'from that time on' [cf. s.v. *pantala*-]; cf. 843/v, 5 *apidd-a*, spelled *a-pí-id-da*?), OHitt. instr. sg. *apedanda* (XXVI 71 I 7 *apedanda halissiyanun* 'therewith I overlaid'; cf. Neu, *Anitta-Text* 14, 70–2), *apedanta* (XXXI 110, 4), abl. sg. *a-pí-e-iz* (e.g. *KBo* V 3 III 38 *apez-kan uddanaz arha* 'because of that matter'; ibid. IV 32–33 *apez linkiyaz ... parkuis* 'clear of that oath'; cf. Friedrich, *Staatsver-träge* 2:126, 134; *KUB* XXIV 9 II 26 *n-as-kan apez arha tepu uizzi* 'she goes a little ways away from there'; cf. Jakob-Rost, *Ritual der Malli* 34; I 1 II 32–33 *apez ... kezz-a-ma* 'on that side ... but on this side'; cf. Götze, *Hattusilis* 18), *apezza* (e.g. XIX 49 I 45 'thence' ; cf. Friedrich, *Staatsverträge* 2:8), *apiz* (e.g. XLIV 61 Vs. 10 *mān-ma-as apiz* ŪL SIG$_5$-*ri* 'but if he does not get well from that'; cf. Burde, *Medizinische Texte* 18; XXIV 11 II 7 'from there'), *apizza* (e.g. *KBo* XXI 76, 20 'from that'; cf. Burde, *Medizinische Texte* 26; *KUB* XXI 38 Rs. 4 'from there'; cf. Sommer, *AU* 255), nom. pl. c. *a-pí-e* (e.g. *KBo* XVII 1 II 33; cf. Otten – Souček, *Altheth. Ritual* 28), *a-pí* (e.g. *KUB* XLI 8 IV 26), *a-pu-u-us* (e.g. *KBo* III 38 Vs. 19 *apūss-a*; cf. Otten, *Altheth. Erzählung* 8; III 4 I 9–10 *nu apūss-a* KUR.KUR.MEŠ ^{LÚ}KÚR *kūruriyahhir* 'those enemy countries also made war'; cf. Götze, *AM* 16), acc. pl. c. *apūs* (e.g. XVII 1 I 21 *apūs ... tēhhi* 'I place those'; *KUB* XXIV 5 Rs. 7 *nu-wa-za apūs dā* 'take those!'; cf. Kümmel, *Ersatzrituale* 12), *apus* (e.g. XVII 3 III 3; cf. Laroche, *RHA* 26:19 [1968]), *apāt* (transfer of neuter ending; XIV 1 Vs. 48 *kuyēs tepawes i*[*spar*]*ter apāt-ma-kan hūman a*[*rha h*]*aspir-pat* 'those few who escaped, them all they also destroyed'; cf. Götze, *Madd.* 12), nom.-acc. pl. neut. *a-pí-e* (e.g. 2532/c + 2538/c + 2599/c IV 2–3 *ape-pat uddār* 'those very words'; cf. Otten, *Materialien* 36), gen. pl. *apenzan* (e.g. *KBo* I 42 I 27 *apenzan kussan* 'their wage'; cf. *MSL* 13:133 [1971]; *KUB* IV 1 I 17; cf. von Schuler, *Die Kaškäer* 168), *a-pí-e-en-za-an* (e.g. XLV 49 IV 4 and 6; cf. Otten, *Materialien* 29), *apel* (e.g. *KBo* V 9 II 40 *apel kuiski ŠA* NAM.RA.MEŠ 'one of those captives'; cf. Friedrich, *Staatsverträge* 1:18), dat.-loc. pl. *apedas* (e.g. V 4 Rs. 7; cf. Friedrich, *Staatsverträge* 1:60), *apidas* (e.g. XII 26 I 14; cf. S. Heinhold – Krahmer, *Arzawa* 283 [1977]).

apasila (nom. sg. c.) 'himself, herself, on one's own' (e.g. *KBo* XXII 2 Vs. 7 *s-us apasila sallanuskat* 'she brought them up herself'; cf. Otten, *Altheth. Erzählung* 6; X 2 Vs. 43; cf. F. Imparati and C. Saporetti, *Studi classici e orientali* 14:46 [1965]), *apāsila* (e.g. V 4 Rs. 26 *nasma-an apāsila halziyatti* 'or you call him yourself'; cf. Friedrich, *Staatsverträge* 1:64; *KUB* XIV 1 Rs. 44 *apāsila-pat*; cf. Götze, *Madd.* 30), *apasiel* (XXXVI 89 Vs. 19; cf. Haas, *Nerik* 144), *apāsiel* (KBo XXII 260 Vs. 7), nom. pl. c. *apāsila* (XXXIII 103 II 8 *apāsila mallanzi* '[they] themselves grind'; cf. Laroche, *RHA* 26:49 [1968]; Siegelová, *Appu-Hedammu* 46), acc. pl. c. (with secondary inflection) *apāsilus* (XXV 37 IV 29). Formed like *ukila, ukiel* 'I myself', *zikila* 'thou thyself', *sumāsila* 'you yourselves' (cf. Sommer, *HAB* 141). Cf. Kronasser, *Etym.* 1:236–7.

apatta(n), apadda(n) 'there, thither', (+ *ser*) 'therefore', e.g. KBo XVII 61 Vs. 16 *apatta pidahhi* 'I carry there'; *KUB* XXXI 101 Vs. 10–11 *nu-wa-kan* ÍD *apadda zaiwen* 'at that point we crossed the river' (cf. A. Archi, *SMEA* 16:137 [1975]); *KBo* V 9 I 14 *apaddan* (cf. Friedrich, *Staatsverträge* 1:10); *HT* 91, 10 *apadan*; *KBo* XIV 48 Vs. 2 *apattan ser*; *KUB* XIX 49 I 47 *nu-tta a]paddan ser kariyahhahat* 'therefore I humored you' (cf. Friedrich, *Staatsverträge* 2:8); ibid. 75 *apadda ser*; XXV 37 I 28 *apadda handa* 'therefore'; XXI 5 I 4 *apadda* EGIR-*anda* 'thenceforth' (var. XXI 2, 5 *a-pát-tin*; cf. Friedrich, *Staatsverträge* 2:50; thus also *IBoT* I 33 I 2 *nu-za apattin kuit* EGIR-*an* HUL DÙ-*at* 'because there afterwards evil has occurred'; perhaps Luwoid, cf. Luw. *apat[t]i[n]* below); XIX 2, 9 *apaddan* EGI[R-*anda* (cf. Götze, *KlF* 170). Cf. Kronasser, *Etym.* 1:350.

apiya 'there, then', e.g. *KBo* XXII 2 Rs. 14 Ù LUGAL ŠU.GI *apiya tālis* 'and the old king he left there' (cf. Otten, *Altheth. Erzählung* 12); XV 2 Vs. 5 *apiya-pat* 'right there' (cf. Kümmel,

Ersatzrituale 56); *VBoT* 58 IV 39 *apiya* UD-*ti* 'on that day' (cf. Laroche, *RHA* 23:87 [1965]), *KUB* XXVI 71 I 22 *apiya-pat* MU.KAM-*ti* 'in that very year' (construed like e.g. Skt. *tátra váne* 'in yonder forest', lit. 'there in the forest'). For *apiya-k(ku)* 'even then' cf. s.v. -*k(k)u*.

apenissan 'thus' (*QATAMMA*), e.g. *KUB* VIII 36 II 13 (cf. Burde, *Medizinische Texte* 38), *apinessan* (e.g. *KBo* III 38 Vs. 24; cf. Otten, *Altheth. Erzählung* 8), *apinissan* (e.g. VI 2 III 20 [=*Code* 1:55]). Formed like *enissan* (s.v. *a-*), *ki(ni)ssan* (s.v. *ka-*).

apenissuwant- 'of such kind (or quantity)'; nom.-acc. neut. sg. and pl. also 'thusly, thus much', nom. sg. c. *apenissuwanza*, acc. sg. c. *apenissuwantan, apenessuwantan, apenessūwadan, apinessuwantan, apinessuwandan, apinisuwandan*, nom.-acc. sg. neut. *apenissuwan, apenissūwan, apenisūwan, apenessūwan, apenessuwan, apinessuwan, apinissuwan, apinissūwan, apini-suwan* (*Code* 2:10 *anda-se-ya apenissūwan*, 2:28 *anda-sse-a-sse apenisūwan* or *anta-ya-sse apinissuan* 'and additionally to him thus much [= once again the same amount]'; cf. e.g. Haase, *Fragmente* 59, 66–7; Imparati, *Leggi ittite* 275), dat.-loc. sg. *apenessūwanti, apinessuwanti, apinissuwanti*, nom.-acc. pl. neut. *apenessuwanda, apenisuwanda, apinissuwanda*. For attestations see e.g. Friedrich, *Staatsverträge* 2:180–1; Stefanini, *ANLR* 20:40, 43 (1965); *HW²* 180.

Pal. (-)*apa-* 'that (one)'. Cf. Carruba, *Das Palaische* 51.

Lyd. *bi-* 'he, she', nom. sg. c. *bis*, dat.-loc. sg. *bλ*; possessive adj. *bil(i)-* 'his, her'; *ebad* 'here, there'. Cf. Hrozný, *SH* 191; Gusmani, *Lyd. Wb.* 78, 80–1, 100–1.

Luw. *apa-* 'that (one)', nom. sg. *apas, apās*, acc. sg. *apan, āpan*; gen. adj. *apassa/i-*, acc. pl. *apāssanza; apati, apatī, apatin, apatti* 'thus'. Cf. *Dict. louv.* 28–9.

Hier. *(a)pa-* 'that (same) (one)'; gen. adj. *(a)pasa-* 'his, her'; *(a)pat(i)a, apār* 'there'; *(a)pi(a)* 'then, there'. Cf. Meriggi, *Manuale* 1:54–5, *HHG* 26–30.

Lyc. *ebe-* 'this (one)', gen. sg. *ebehi, ehbi*; possessive adj. *ehbi-* (< **ebesi-*; cf. Luw. *apassi-*); *ebi* 'here'. Cf. Laroche, *BSL* 53.1:174 (1957–8), 55.1:178–85 (1960); Neumann, *HOAKS* 386.

apa-

In older Anatolian *apa-* (corresponding in meaning to Lat. *is*, *iste*, *ille*, vs. *hic*) contrasts with Hitt. *ka-*, Luw. *za-*, Hier. *ī-* 'this (one)'; cf. e.g. *KUB* VII 10 I 4–5 *nu-wa-za kūs sikten apūs-wa-za namma le sekteni* 'take note of these, (but) those do not notice further'. In Lydian *bi-* functions as a stressed personal pronoun (besides enclitic *-a-*), as already in Hittite, e.g. *KBo* V 3 I 9–11 DUMU-YA-*ya kuin … temi kūn-wa hūmanza sākdu … nu-za zikk-a … apūn sak* 'my son whom I proclaim "may everyone acknowledge this one", you too acknowledge him!'. In Lycian there is no deixis opposition, and *ebe-* has moved into an all-purpose slot 'this'.

The origins of PAnat. **aba-* are best sought in the adverb Hitt. *apiya*, Hier. *(a)pi(a)*, Lyc. *ebi*. PAnat. **abi* (pronominal stem *a-* [q.v.], IE **e-/o-*) is comparable with Lat. *ibī*, even as Hitt. *kuwapi* (< **kʷo-bhi*) resembles Lat. *(-c)ubī*. **abi* had the appearance of a dat.-loc. sg. of an **aba-*; the emergence of the latter as a new pronoun stem led to a full paradigm with pronominal declension. From the latter new adverbs could be detached, e.g. Hitt. *apadda(n)*, Lyd. *ebad*, Luw. *apat(t)i(n)*, Hier. *(a)pat(i)a*, which seem to be based on either **abad* (Hitt. nom.-acc. sg. neut. *apāt*) or **abadi* (Hier. dat.-loc. sg. *[a]pati*), with incrementation. Traces of enclitic origin may be seen in the Palaic enclisis of *-apa-* on the one hand, and the Lydian and Hieroglyphic aphaeresis of *bi-* and *(a)pa-* on the other. Cf. Marstrander, *Caractère* 23; Pedersen, *Hitt.* 50–1; Kronasser, *VLFH* 147; Laroche, *BSL* 55.1:180 (1960).

Less probable is the postulation of an IE pronominal stem **ebho-* (Benveniste, *Hittite* 72; Kronasser, *Etym.* 1:184) or **obhó-* (**é/ó-* + suffix **-bho-*; J. H. Jasanoff, *BSL* 71.1:130 [1976]), or of **e/o-* + **bho* (a particle seen also in Hitt. *-[a]pa* and Avest. *bā*, Lith. *bà*; Kammenhuber, *HOAKS* 250). Unnecessary and forced connection with the IE preposition **obhi* 'to(wards)' (Skt. *abhí*) by e.g. Sturtevant, *JAOS* 52:3–4 (1932), *Comp. Gr.*[1] 201; M. Lejeune, *BSL* 46.1:40 (1950); O. Szemerényi, *KZ* 73:67 (1955), who identified PAnat. **abi* with IE **obhi* but followed Benveniste in reconstructing *apa-* as **ebho-* (similarly Jasanoff, *BSL* 71.1:130 [1976], who analyzed **obhi* as **é/ó-* + adverbial **-bhi*).

90

Untenable tie-in with *appa* (q.v.) by e.g. Hrozný, *SH* 137, and W. Petersen, *AJPh* 58:308 (1937); rejected by Couvreur, *Hett.* 96, and Goetze, *Tunnawi* 48.

appa, adverb, postposition (with dat.-loc., gen., abl.), preverb 'behind; afterwards; back, again, further'; *appan* 'behind; after-(wards)' (EGIR, EGIR-*ŠU* or EGIR-*ŠÚ*= Akk. [*w*]*arki-šu*, EGIR-*pa*, EGIR-[*p*]*an*), e.g. *KBo* V 8 III 5 EGIR-*pa-ma* ^HUR.SAG^*Ellurian harta* 'in his rear he had Mt. Elluriya' (cf. Götze, *AM* 156); III 1 I 29 EGIR-*pa-ma-as* ^URU^KÁ.DINGIR.RA *pait* 'afterwards he went to Babylon'; XVII 1 III 16 *āppa sarā petumeni* 'we bring up again'; ibid. 12–13 *t-at āppa sarā le uezzi* 'may it come up no more!'; ibid. IV 3 *āppa le wehzi* 'let it not turn back' (cf. Otten – Souček, *Altheth. Ritual* 30, 34); *IBoT* III 148 III 19 *nu appa tienzi* 'they put back'; *ABoT* 9, 6 *āppa tienzi* 'they stand back'; ibid. 3–4 ^LÚ.MEŠ^*MEŠEDI-an āppan* [*tienzi* 'they stand behind the bodyguard' (cf. Neu, *Gewitterritual* 10); *KUB* XIV 1 Vs. 66 *āppa-ma* ^URU^*Dalauwas kūrur* IṢBAT 'but further D. took to hostilities' (cf. Götze, *Madd.* 16); *KBo* V 4 Rs. 13 *n-as-kan* 1-*as* 1-*edani kunanna* EGIR-*an sarā le kuiski dāi* 'neither shall under-take to kill the other behind his back' (cf. Friedrich, *Staatsver-träge* 1:62) ; III 4 I 5–6 EGIR-*an-ma-as irmaliyattat-pat* 'but afterwards he fell ill' (cf. Götze, *AM* 14); III 22 Rs. 49–50 *kuis ammel āppan* LUGAL-*us kisari nu* ^URU^*Hattusan āppa asāsi* 'who becomes king after me and resettles Hattusas' (cf. Neu, *Anitta-Text* 12). For the frequent combination EGIR-*an arha* (literally 'behind away') see Zuntz, *Ortsadverbien* 41–4.

appa(na)nda 'behind, in the wake (of); back(wards), after-(wards)' (EGIR-[*p*]*anda*), e.g. *KBo* XVII 1 III 3–4 *ta namma* ^MUŠEN^*hāranan nēpisa tarnahhi āppananda-ma-sse ke mēmahhi* 'then I launch the eagle to the sky and in his wake I say this'; ibid. I 33 ERÍN.MEŠ-*nan āppananda petai* 'behind (it) he brings the soldiery' (cf. Otten – Souček, *Altheth. Ritual* 30, 20); *IBoT* II 35 + *KBo* XIX 150 I 4 [*an*]*zas-a āppannanda pehutan*[*zi* 'and in our wake they bring'; *KBo* XII 3 III 12 *appananda-pat* IṢBAT 'afterwards he seized'; XVII 43 I 5 *āppanda*; XVI 68 I 27 *appanda*; V 8 I 24–25 *nu-smas-kan ... * EGIR-*panda ŪL pāun* 'I did

not go after them' (cf. Götze, *AM* 148); *KUB* XIV 15 II 3
n-an-kan EGIR-*anda* KUR ᵁᴿᵁ*Hatti uskit* 'and Hatti looked at
him from behind (as he went away)' (cf. Götze, *AM* 46). Cf.
Kronasser, *Etym.* 1:354–5; Otten – Souček, *Altheth. Ritual*
93–4; Starke, *Funktionen* 194–6, who posited *appan* + instr.
ending -(*an*)*da*; Kammenhuber, *HW²* 152, who separated
appan and *anda* as two words. J. J. S. Weitenberg (*Kratylos*
23:92 [1978]) appositely compared the Homeric ἄναντα κάταντα
πάραντά τε 'uphill, downhill, and along(side)' (*Iliad* 23:116)
which (unlike ἔναντα, ἐσάντα 'facing, opposite'; cf. ἀντί s.v.
hant-) contain a suffix comparable to Hitt. *kattanda* 'down(-
wards)', *parranda* 'along, forth'; the derived adjectives
κατάντης 'downhill, steep', ἀνάντης 'uphill, steep' are matched
by ἐπάντης 'steep' (Thucydides 7:79) which points back to an
adverb *ἔπαντα as well, closest in kind to *appanda*; *appananda* is
an inner-Hittite innovation by rederivation (as if from *appan*
+ *anda*, even seemingly written *appan anda* in the copy of *KBo*
XVII 1 III 4 [= *ABoT* 4, 5], XVII 1 I 33, XII 3 III 12). For
apadda EGIR-*anda* 'thenceforth' see s.v. *apa-*.

   appizzi(ya)-, *appezzi-* (*KBo* XVI 45 Rs. 3 *ap-pí-e-iz-zi*[),
appaizzi- (*Bo* 7777 r. Kol. 6), *appazzi-* 'backmost, hindmost,
last, last-born (= youngest), lowest', adverbial 'in the rear;
later, at last' (EGIR-[*p*]*izzi-*, EGIR-[*z*]*i-*, EGIR-), nom. sg. c.
appizzis (e.g. *KUB* XIII 20 I 3 *appizzis antuwahhas* 'man of
lowest [military] rank, [buck] private'; cf. Götze, *Madd.* 128;
XIV 3 II 60 EGIR-*izzis* UKÙ-*as*; cf. Sommer, *AU* 10), *appizziyas*
(e.g. *KBo* XXII 2 Vs. 18 'the youngest [son]'; cf. Otten, *Altheth.
Erzählung* 6; *KUB* XXIII 68 Vs. 21–22 *nasma* EN *MATKALTI* [...]
nasma-as appizziyas 'whether a garrison-commander or a
private [soldier]'; cf. A. Kempinski – S. Košak, *Die Welt des
Orients* 5:194 [1970]), EGIR-*as* (e.g. XII 63 Vs. 6), acc. sg. c.
appizzin (e.g. *KBo* V 3 I 2 *tuk* ¹*Huqqanān appizzin* UR.SAG-*an*
'you, H., a down-at-the-heels paladin'; cf. Friedrich, *Staatsverträge* 2:106), *appizzian* (e.g. *IBoT* I 36 III 51–52 *mān* ...
zinnantari nu appizzian kuin ... *pihutanzi* 'when [they] come to
an end, and what last [one] they bring'; cf. L. Jakob-Rost, *MIO*
11:194 [1966]), nom.-acc. sg. neut. *appizzi* (ibid. II 67), *āppizzi*
(*KUB* XXXIII 67 I 30), *āppazzi* (XLII 98 I 22 *āppazzi hāli* 'the

last watch'), *appizziyan* (XLIII 55 II 3), adverbial *appizziyan* (e.g. *KBo* III 22 Rs. 46 'later'; cf. Neu, *Anitta-Text* 12; III 38 Vs. 7 'finally'; cf. Otten, *Altheth. Erzählung* 8; *KUB* XIII 3 III 18–19 *appizziyan-ma-at istuwāri* 'but it becomes known at last'; cf. ibid. 7 EGIR-*pizziya-ma-at*; Friedrich, *Meissner AOS* 47), *appizzian* (e.g. *Code* 1:31 'afterwards'), *appizzin* (*Code* 1:29 'subsequently'; analogic for **appizzi*), *apzian* (XIII 4 IV 21 *apzian-ma-as isduwāri*; cf. ibid. III 82 EGIR-*zian-ma-at*; Sturtevant, *JAOS* 54:392, 388 [1934]), gen. sg. or pl. *appizziyas* (e.g. XXIX 55 I 2 *appizziyas hāliyas* 'of the last watch'; cf. Kammenhuber, *Hippologia* 150), dat.-loc. sg. *appizzi* (e.g. *KBo* XIII 31 III 13; cf. Riemschneider, *Geburtsomina* 76), *āppizzi* (*KUB* XXXIII 67 I 10 *āppizzi* UD-*ti* 'on the last day'; cf. Laroche, *RHA* 23:135 [1965]), adverbial abl. sg. *appizziaz* (e.g. *KBo* V 1 I 41 'in the last analysis'; cf. Sommer – Ehelolf, *Pāpanikri* 4*), EGIR-*izziaz* (e.g. VI 26 I 19 [= *Code* 2:62] 'from behind'), EGIR-*az* (V 8 II 10 'in the rear'; cf. Götze, *AM* 152; V 6 III 27 'finally'; cf. Güterbock, *JCS* 10:95 [1956]), nom. pl. c. *appizziēs* (e.g. *KUB* X 53, 2), EGIR-*as* (*KBo* VI 29 II 22–23 *nu-ssi* EN.MEŠ *kuyes* EGIR-*ass-a* UKÙ.MEŠ-*us kattan eser* 'what officers and private soldiers he had along'), acc. pl. c. *appizzius* (e.g. *KBo* VII 14 + *KUB* XXXVI 100 Rs. 11), also in *KUB* XII 66 IV 3 [EGI]R-*izziuss-a hantezzius* 'and last (ones) first' (cf. Laroche, *RHA* 23:70 [1965]), dat.-loc. pl. in *KBo* XXIV 5 II 9 *appizziyas hāl[iyas* 'at the last watch'.

Luw. *appa(n)*, adverb, postposition, preverb 'back, again, after', spelled *āppa(n)*, *appa(n)*; EGIR-*anda* 'afterwards'; **appara-* (see s.v. *appasiwatt-*). Hier. *apa(n)*, postposition, preverb 'after, behind, again'; *apara-* 'later, lower'; *apami-* 'west(ern)'. Lyc. *epñ*, preverb and prefix 'back, after, further'; *epñte* 'afterwards'; *epri* 'later, following'. Cf. Laroche, *BSL* 53.1:184–5 (1957–8), *Dict. louv.* 29, *HH* 24–5, 202, *Studia mediterranea P. Meriggi dicata* 347–52 (1979); Meriggi, *HHG* 28–9, 186–7; Bossert, *Orientalia* N.S. 29:436–8 (1960); Pedersen, *Lyk. u. Hitt.* 23; Neumann, *HOAKS* 391.

appa(n) is cognate with Gk. ἐπί and *ὀπι(ν) in Myc. *o-pi* (e.g. PY Ae 134 *o-pi … qe-to-ro-po-pi o-ro-me-no* 'looking after quadrupeds', besides PY Un 2.1 *e-pi wa-na-ka-te*) and κατόπιν 'behind, after'. *appizziya-* < **opi-tyo-* (or **opey-tyo-*; cf. Neu, *Anitta-Text* 41) closely matches Gk. ὀπίσ(σ)ω 'backwards, hereafter', ὄπι(σ)θεν 'behind, (here)after'; cf. Hes. ἔπισσον · τὸ ὕστερον γενόμενον. The final vowel variation is comparable to that of *katta(n)*, *katti-* (q.v.) beside Gk. κατά, κατι- (> κασι-). Cf. e.g. P. Kretschmer apud Hrozný, *SH* 21; J. F. Lohmann, *IF* 51:324–5 (1933); Couvreur, *Hett.* 94–6; Kronasser, *VLFH* 160, *Etym.* 1:168–9, 352; Gusmani, *AION-L* 3:47–54 (1961); Neu, *Anitta-Text* 67–8; Starke, *Funktionen* 133.

The connection with Gk. ἀπό 'away, from', ἄψ 'again', Lat. *ab(s)* 'away, from', Skt. *ápa* 'away' (e.g. S. Bugge apud J. A. Knudtzon, *Die zwei Arzawa-Briefe* 73 [1902]; Hrozný, *MDOG* 56:27 [1915], *SH* 20–1; Sturtevant passim, e.g. *Lg.* 10:268–9 [1934], *Lg.* 14:70–1 [1938], *Comp. Gr.*[2] 116; Kuryłowicz, *Études* 75; K. Bergsland, *RHA* 4:278–9 [1938]) might be remotely rescuable by root-etymology joining ἀπό with ἐπί and **ὀπι(ν)*, as suggested by Pedersen, *Hitt.* 188; but E_1- is unlikely to have yielded prothetic ἀ- before π in Greek. For the notion that IE **epi* (**opi*) and **apo* have partly coalesced see e.g. *IEW* 53, 324; it may be bolstered by a comparison of Hitt. *appizziya-* with Skt. *ápatyam* 'offspring', of Hier. *apara-* with Skt. *ápara-* 'later, smaller', and of Hier. *apami-* with Skt. *apamá-* 'last', *ápañc-* 'located in the rear, western'.

Cf. *appai-*, *appasiwatt-* (but for the rival reading *ipami-* see s.v. *ipat[t]arma[yan]*).

appai-, appiya- 'be finished, be done' (*QATŪ* 'be finished', 3 sg. stative *QATI*), 3 sg. pres. act. *appāi* (e.g. *KUB* II 8 V 39 *tā appāi* 'it is finished'; cf. ibid. VI 1 *QATI*; II 3 I 50 [OHitt.] *sal]li asessar appāi* 'the great [divine] service is concluded'; XXXIX 4 Vs. 9 *waganna appāi* 'snacking is done'; cf. Otten, *Totenrituale* 24), *āppāi* (e.g. X 18 VI 9 *salli asessar āppāi*; IX 10, 2 and XXX 27 Vs. 6 *ta āppāi*; cf. Otten, *Totenrituale* 98), *āppai* (e.g. XVII 28 IV 41 *nu* LUGAL-*us āppai* 'the king is finished [with the ritual]'; *KBo* V 11 I 25 *mahh]an-ma āppai* 'but when he is done'), *appai* (e.g. IV 13 V 20), *appiyazi* (*KUB* XIII 9 + XL 62 III 7; cf. von Schuler, *Festschrift J. Friedrich* 448 [1959]), 3 pl. pres. act.

appiyanzi (e.g. *KBo* XIX 128 VI 30 LUGAL SAL.LUGAL *appiyanzi* 'king [and] queen are finished'; cf. Otten, *Festritual* 16; *KUB* X 45 III 7 *ta appiyanzi*), *appianzi* (e.g. *KBo* XX 96, 7; XIX 163 IV 19), *āppianzi* (e.g. XVII 100 I 8; XXV 31 II 12 and III 7; cf. Neu, *Altheth.* 79, 81), 3 pl. imp. midd. (?) *appāru* (*KBo* XVII 90 II 15; cf. Neu, *Interpretation* 24). Cf. Friedrich, *ZA* 36:294 (1925); Kronasser, *Etym.* 1:545.

appai- is a verbal derivative from the adverb *appa* (q.v.); cf. e.g. *appizziaz* 'finally, in the last analysis, when all is said and done'. The derivation is comparable to that of *handai-* 'arrange' from *handa(s)* 'according to' (q.v.), or Gk. ἀρτίζω 'prepare, make ready' from ἄρτι 'just now'. Cf. Sturtevant, *JAOS* 52:2–3 (1932), *Comp. Gr.*¹ 213, *Comp. Gr.*² 116 (wrong on compound derivation with **ey-* 'go'); Kronasser, *Etym.* 1:574.

appala- (c.) 'trap, snare, pitfall, ambush', dat.-loc. sg. in *KUB* XXXVI 106 Vs. 8]*āppali datteni* 'you take in a trap' (=entrap, deceive; cf. Otten, *ZA* 52:217, 220 [1957]); *KBo* VI 34 I 16 and 35, II 1 and 12 *n-asta* ANA LUGAL KUR ᵁᴿᵁ*Hatti appāli dāi* 'commits entrapment against the king of Hatti' (cf. Friedrich, *ZA* 35:162–4 [1924]; Oettinger, *Eide* 6–8).

appalai- 'entrap, ensnare, trick, deceive, mislead', 3 sg. pres. act. in *IBoT* I 36 I 54–55 *mān* ᴸᵁ*MEŠEDI-ma* ᴸᵁ*Ì.DU₈ appalāizzi* 'but if the bodyguard tricks the gateman' (cf. L. Jakob-Rost, *MIO* 11:178 [1966]), 1 pl. pres. act. *a-ap-pa-la-a-u-e-ni* (*KBo* XVI 50 Vs. 14; cf. Otten, *RHA* 18:121 [1960]); iter. *appaleski-*, 3 pl. pres. act. *appaleskanzi* (V 6 III 49 and 53 'they are setting a trap [for me]'; cf. Güterbock, *JCS* 10:96 [1956]).

appaliyalla- (c.) 'trapper, ensnarer, ambusher, deceiver', gen. sg. (?) *appaliyallas-a* (*KUB* XXXVI 110 Rs. 17; cf. Neu, *Altheth.* 228). Cf. Friedrich, *JCS* 1:276 (1947).

appala- is probably an abstract or instrument noun from *ep(p)-*, *ap(p)-* 'seize' (q.v.), formed like e.g. *akkala-* 'furrow' (q.v.) or *ardala-* 'saw' (q.v. s.v. *ard-*). *appaliyalla-* is a secondary agent noun from a denominative verb (like e.g. *lahhiyala-* 'warrior' from *lahhiya-* 'make war'). Cf. N. van Brock, *RHA* 20:94–5 (1962); Kronasser, *Etym.* 1:172, 346. The assumption of a neuter stem *appali-* (e.g. Güterbock apud H. A. Hoffner, *Alimenta Hethaeorum* 125 [1974]) is less plausible; *appali da-* matches e.g. *taksuli da-* 'take in friendship', i.e. 'befriend'.

O. Szemerényi (*Gnomon* 49:7 [1977]) saw a loanword from *appala-* in the unexplained Gk. παλεύω 'act as decoy, lure, entrap'.

appala- is also the name of a wooden object on which the stealer of a plow was to be placed as punishment by the wronged owner (*Code* 2:21 ^{GIŠ}*appalas-sas* [dat.-loc. pl.?] *sarā tittanuzzi*), probably identical with *appala-* 'trap, snare' (q.v.), thus something like 'stocks, pillory, gibbet'. For discussion, see e.g. Imparati, *Leggi ittite* 278–9. It was wrongly taken as *appalassa-* 'plow' and compared for formation with *akkala-* 'furrow' (q.v.) by Rosenkranz, *JEOL* 19:505 (1965–6); Rosenkranz connected Lat. *opus* (for the more plausible etymon of which see s.v. *happar-*). The same *appalassa-* was pronounced 'substratal'' (comparing Sum. *apin* 'plow', etc.) by A. Salonen, *Die Fussbekleidungen der alten Mesopotamier* 113 (1969). Cf. also H. A. Hoffner, *Alimenta Hethaeorum* 45 (1974).

appasiwatt-   (c.) 'day(s) after, the future' (EGIR.UD-*MI*; Akk. [*w*]*ar-kat ūmi* 'back of the day'), nom. sg. EGIR.UD-*az* (*KBo* XXVI 23, 2, glossing Akk. *arkā* UD), gen. sg. or pl. (or dat.-loc. pl.) EGIR.UD.KAM-*as* (dupl. I 44 + XIII 1 IV 13, glossing Akk. *arka* UD-*mi*; cf. Otten, *Vokabular* 19), *appasiwattas* (*KUB* XXXI 81 Rs. 8), EGIR-*pa* UD.KAM-*as* (XXIX 9 I 7; cf. Güterbock, *AfO* 18:79 [1957]), dat.-loc. sg. **appasiwatti* in e.g. *KBo* III 3 II 7–9 (with dupl. *KUB* XIX 41 II 11–13) *nu* EGIR-*pa*-UD-*ti kuwapi* ... *aki* LUGAL-*UTTA-ŠU-ma-za-kan* ... *katta tālesdu* 'in the future, when (he) dies, he shall leave behind his kingship' (cf. Laroche, *RA* 52:187 [1958]; H. Klengel, *Orientalia* N.S. 32:35 [1963]), *appasiwatta* (*KBo* VII 28, 43, besides ibid. 41 EGIR.UD-*MI*; cf. Friedrich, *Rivista degli studi orientali* 32:219–20 [1957]). Cf. Otten, *MDOG* 86:64 (1953); Güterbock, *Sommer Corolla* 65; Kronasser, *Etym.* 1:124, 156; H. A. Hoffner, *Orientalia* N.S. 35:384–5 (1966).

Luw. *apparanti-* (c.) 'the future' (EGIR.UD-*MI*), acc. sg. *appar-*

antien (*KUB* XXXV 133 II 29 *apparantien arin* 'long future'; cf. Otten, *LTU* 110), *apparantin* (XXXV 130 Vs. 3, with gloss-wedges), instr. sg. *āpparant*[*ati* (XXXV 44 Rs. 11), *ā*]*prandati* (XXXII 8 IV 15), EGIR-*parantati* (XXXII 9 + XXXV 21 Rs. 13 *ārrayati* MU.HI.A-*ti* EGIR-*parantat*[*i* 'for long years in the future'), EGIR.UD-*MI.HI.A-ti* (XXXV 45 II 8–9 MU.KAM.HI.A GÍD.DA EGIR. .UD-*MI.HI.A-ti* 'long years in the future'; cf. Otten, *LTU* 46). Probably a nominalization of an adjective *appara-nt-* (cf. Hier. *apara-* 'later, posterior'), rather than *appa* + *arant-* 'arrived' (cf. *Dict. louv.* 140 vs. 29; Gusmani, *AION-L* 3:52–3 [1961]; Kammenhuber, *HOAKS* 294). For a possible Hier. *apar(a)ta-* see Meriggi, *Manuale* 1:70; for Arm. *aparni* 'future', J. Greppin, *Drevnij vostok* 3:122 (1978).

Hier. *apasawati* 'in the future' (Bossert, *Die Welt des Orients* 2:355–9 [1957]; Laroche, *HH* 24–5) is doubtful.

appasiwatt- is a hypostatic noun made up of *appa* (q.v.) and *siwatt-* 'day' (q.v. s.v. *siu-*), resulting from the adverbial expression *appa(-)siwatti* (or: *-siwatta*, *-siwattas*) 'on the day after, in the future'; the latter resembles IE **per-ut(i)* 'in the year before, last year' (Gk. πέρυσι, Arm. *heru*, Skt. *parút*, OIr. *ónn-urid*, ON *i fjorð*; cf. Gk. πάρος, Ved. *purā́* 'before'), Ved. *pradívi*, *pradívas*, Gāthic *fraidivā* 'in fore-and-forth day, perennially', Hitt. *parā siwatti* 'on the day forth, next day' (*KUB* XXXVIII 32 Vs. 9 *parā* UD.KAM-*ti warpuanzi* 'in order to bathe the next day'), *parā hameshi* 'next summer' (XXII 56 Rs. 8), *parā hameshanda* (*Code* 100 'until next spring'), *parā witantanni* (e.g. *KBo* XVII 62 + 63 IV 17–18 *parā-ma-*[*wa*] MU-*anni* 'but next year'; XVI 98 II 15 *parā-ma* MU.KAM-*anni*). Of the basic adverbs involved, **per-* refers safely to fore-time (cf. Hitt. *piran* 'before'), **pro* is inherently ambiguous in a time sense (cf. Hitt. *piran parā* 'beforehand', English 'come forth' vs. 'go forth', or 'what went before' vs. 'what lies before us'), while the etymon or etyma of Gk. ἐπί/ὀπι(-), Skt. *ápa*, Hitt. *appa* meant 'behind, back' in a spatial, but uniformly 'after' in a temporal sense (cf. Gk. ὄπισθεν 'behind', ὀπίσ(σ)ω 'backwards' and 'afterwards'; Skt. *ápatyam* 'offspring', *ápara-*'later'; Hitt. *appizziyan* 'afterwards'). The adjectival meaning 'later' (Hier. *apara-*, Skt. *ápara-*; Goth. *afar* 'after[wards], later') > 'future', seen in Luw.

apparanti- (above), is likewise present in Ved. *aparedyús* 'on the following day', *aparíbhyas, aparíṣu, aparám, aparâya* 'hereafter, in the future' (cf. e.g. *RV* 2.28.8 *námas purấ te Varuṇa utá nūnám utá aparám* 'glory before to thee, Varuna, and now, and hereafter', and in Goth. *in þamma afardaga* 'on the day after'. The protean nature of temporal **pro* has resulted in the Greek subordination and polarization of πρόσ(σ)ω to ὀπίσ(σ)ω: πρόσ(σ)ω normally means 'forwards' in space and time, and ὀπίσσω signifies 'backwards' in space, but when contrasted in temporal usage, Homeric πρόσσω καὶ ὀπίσσω amount to 'before and after' (*Iliad* 1:343, 3:109, 18:250; *Odyssey* 24:452; cf. Shelley's 'we look before and after', i.e. to the past and to the future). Rather than such opposition, Hittite shows semantic subdifferentiation, *parā siwatti* 'next day' vs. *appa(-)siwatti* 'in the future'; the special sense and formation of *appasiwatt-* also has areal linguistic overtones, for it matches both Sum. EGIR.UD and Akk. [*w*]*arkat ūmi* 'future', lit. 'back of the day' (*ana warkat ūmim* 'for ever after'; cf. Starke, *Funktionen* 158–9). Cf. also Puhvel, *JAOS* 100:168 (1980), *Kratylos* 25:138 (1980); G. Dunkel, *KZ* 96:66:87 (1982/3).

Cf. *anisiwat* s.v. *anna-, an(n)i-; zilatiya, ziladuwa.*

appat(a)riya-   'seize (as pawn to compel payment of debt), take in pledge, distrain; make seizure, levy distress, exercise distraint', 3 sg. pres. act. in *KBo* VI 3 III 76–77 (= *Code* 1:76) *takku* GUD ANŠU.KUR.RA ANŠU.GÌR.NUN.NA ANŠU *kuiski appatrizzi* (dupl. VI 2 IV 4 *appatarizzi*) 'if anyone seizes as pawn cattle, horse, mule (or) ass', *KUB* XIII 8 Vs. 10–11 GUD.HI.A-*ya-smas* UDU.HI.A *le kuiski appatriyazi n-at-kan hūmantaza arawēs asandu* 'no one shall seize from them cattle (or) sheep, and they shall be free from everything' (spelled *ap-pát-*, vs. usual *ap-pa-at-, ap-pa-ta-*; cf. Otten, *Totenrituale* 106), 3 sg. pret. act. in *KBo* XIV 21 I 32 *appatriyat nu-war-as-kan kuenta-pat* '(he) seized (the two consecrated rams) and even killed them'; inf. in VI 26 I 28–29 (= *Code* 2:64) *takku āppatriwanzi kuiski paizzi ta sullatar iezzi* 'if somebody goes to make a seizure and causes a conflict'.

Correctly interpreted as denom. from *appatar* 'taking, seizure', verbal noun of *ep(p)-* (q.v.), already by Sommer, *Heth. II* 42; similarly Friedrich apud Sommer, *ZA* 46:49 (1940), *Heth. Ges.* 43, 75; Haase, *Arch. Or.* 26:28–30 (1958), *Bi. Or.* 26:311–3 (1969). This legal specialization need not exclude other nuances of 'seizure' in some contexts, e.g. 'requisition, appropriate, induct, draft' (cf. Goetze, *JCS* 18:92–3 [1964], 20:130–1 [1966]). For bibliography regarding improbable alternative suggestions ('lend, lease, hire, borrow') cf. Güterbock, *JCS* 15:69 (1961); Imparati, *Leggi ittite* 261.

For parallel terms in other ancient IE legal contexts (e.g. OIr. *athgabál* 'distraint' from *gab-* 'take', or Lat. *pignoriscapio* 'seizure as a pledge'), cf. D. A. Binchy, *Celtica* 10:22–71 (1973); C. Watkins, *Kratylos* 19:64–5 (1974).

api- (n., rarely c.), necromantic sacrificial pit for summoning up infernal deities or revenants, sometimes personified as ᴰ*Āpi-*, nom.-acc. sg. neut. *āpi* (e.g. *KUB* XXIX 4 IV 34 *āpi pedanzi* 'they dig a pit'; cf. Kronasser, *Umsiedelung* 30; XLVII 59 Vs. 6 *nu āpi hēsanzi* 'they open a pit'; cf. H. Otten – C. Rüster, *ZA* 68:155 [1978]), *api* (XXVII 1 III 9; cf. Lebrun, *Samuha* 81), *a-pí-e* (*KBo* II 9 IV 11 *namma apedani pidi ape kinuwanzi* 'then in that place they open up a pit'), vocatival ᴰ*Āpi* (*KUB* XLI 8 III 17 = *KBo* X 45 III 26; cf. Otten, *ZA* 54:130 [1961]), acc. sg. c. *āpin* (e.g. IX 119A, 16 *āpin iyazi* 'makes a pit'; *KUB* XLI 8 III 13 ᴰ*Āpin* GÍR-*it kinuzi*, with dupl. *KBo* X 45 III 22 ᴰ*Āpi* GÍR-*it ginuzzi* 'he opens up a pit with a knife'; *KUB* XLI 8 III 16–17 1 GAD *ŠA QATI dāi nu-kan* ᴰ*Āpin ser kariyazi*, with dupl. *KBo* X 45 III 24–25 *nu* 1 GAD *ŠA QATI dāi nu-kan āpin kariyazi* 'he takes a hand-cloth and covers [up] the pit'; *KUB* X 63 I 18 ᴰ*Āpin kinuzi*; cf. M. Vieyra, *RA* 51:88 [1957]; ibid. 26 *n-asta* ᴰ*Āpin ser* IŠTU NINDA KUR₄.RA *istāpi* 'then he stops up the pit at the top with thick bread'; cf. XXXII 137 II 27 *nu-kan hattessar istāp[i* 'he plugs the hole'), *apin* (*KBo* XXIII 3 Vs. 10; *KUB* XLVII 62, 11), gen. sg. *apias* (*KBo* II 8 IV 15), dat.-loc. sg. *āpiya* (XIX 145 III 24; cf. Haas – Thiel, *Rituale* 302), *āpi* (e.g. XVII 94 III 25 ANA *āpi kattan lāhuwāi* 'pours down into the pit'; *KUB* X 63 I 20 *n-an-kan* ᴸᵁSANGA ANA ᴰ*Āpi kattanda haddāi* 'the priest slaughters it down into the pit'; cf. XXIX 4 IV 36 *n-a]n-kan hattesni kattanda haddanzi* 'they slaughter it down into the hole'), *api* (XLI 8 III 14–15 ^{D}*Api anda* BAL-*anti*, with dupl. *KBo* X 45 III 23 ^{D}*Āpi anda* BAL-*anti* 'libates into the pit'), dat.-loc. sg. (and sometimes pl.) *āpiti* (with Hurrian ending, e.g. *KUB* XV 31 II 17–18 *namma-kan* ^{GIŠ}KUN₅ KÙ.BABBAR ... *hantezzi āpiti anda dāi* 'then he puts into the first pit a silver ladder'; ibid. 25 *nu kuedaniya* ANA 1 *āpiti* 1 MUŠEN *dāi* 'in each pit he places one bird'; cf. Haas – Wilhelm, *Riten* 156–8; XXXIV 96, 6 ^{D}*Āpiti*), *āpitī* (XXIX 4 II 4–5 1 GÍN KÙ.BABBAR *āpitī* 'one shekel of silver for the pit'; cf. Kronasser, *Umsiedelung* 14), *apiti* (e.g. XV 34 IV 21; cf. Haas – Wilhelm, *Riten* 202), *apitī* (e.g. XV 33a IV 7), *apetī* (IX 19, 7), *āpita* (XVIII 56 II 17), abl. sg. *āpitaz* (XXIX 4 II 19–20 *n-asta* ^{LÚ}SANGA DINGIR-*LAM āpitaz sarā 7-ŠU huittiyazzi* 'the priest draws up the deity seven times from the pit'), *apītaz* (*KUB* XV 34 IV 4), *apetaz* (*Bo* 2738 III 16), *āpidaz* (*KUB* XXXIX 54 Vs. 10), *āpidaza* (XLVI 38 II 23; XLVI 40 Vs. 18), *apidaz* (*KBo* VIII 90 II 8), acc. pl. *apīyas* (XI 19 Vs. 1; cf. Haas – Thiel, *Rituale* 314), nom.-acc. pl. neut. *āpi* (e.g. *KUB* XV 31 II 8–9 7 *āpi kinuwanzi* 'they open seven pits'; ibid. 23 9 *āpi isharnumaizzi* 'he smears with blood nine pits'), gen. pl. *āpiyas* (e.g. ibid. 7 and 10 *āpiyas pedi* 'to the place of the pits'; ibid. 8 *āpiyas-ma uttar* 'but the matter of the pits'), dat.-loc. pl. *āpiyas* (XV 32 II 17 *hūmandās āpiyas* 'to all the pits'; also ibid. 23, vs. dupl. XV 31 II 27 *hūmandas āpiti*, followed in the next line by *āpiyas ser* 'over the pits'), abl. pl. *āpiyaz* (XV 31 II 33), *apiyaz* (XV 32 II 31).

Hitt. *api-* is from Hurrian, cf. e.g. *āpita* in Hurr. context (XXIX 8 IV 26 and 30), or *āpiri* (*KBo* XVII 98 V 10, 11, 17; cf. Haas – Wilhelm, *Riten* 265), or ^{D}*Apinita* (*KUB* XXVII 1 III 8; cf. Lebrun, *Samuha* 81), further the variant ^{D}*Āwa* (XXV 49 III 31). In Hittite, besides *hattessar* (q.v. above and s.v.), such chthonian cavities are also referred to by TÚL 'waterhole, well' (XV 34 III 25 7 TÚL.MEŠ *iyanzi n-at uitenit sunnanzi* 'they make seven wells and fill them with water'; ibid. 36 the gods are 'drawn' out of those wells), AŠRU 'place' (XII 44 III 15 9 AŠRA *pedā[hhi* 'I dig nine spots'; *KBo* XV 25 Vs. 20 3 AŠRA *pedahhi*; cf. Carruba, *Beschwörungsritual* 2), or BURÙ 'hole' (V 1 I 26; cf.

Sommer – Ehelolf, *Pāpanikri* 2*, 18; *KUB* XXX 31 III 52, 54, 56 and IV 1, 3, 4). The functions of the Hittite pit resemble those of the Greek βόθρος of chthonian sacrifices (cf. the necromantic scene in *Odyssey* 11.23–43) and of the Roman subterranean *mundus* which gave access to infernal regions (cf. Varro apud Macrobium 1.16.18: *mundus cum patet deorum tristium et inferum quasi ianua patet*). A similar role of sacrificial pit was played by *apu* or *abu* 'hole', *ēnu* 'spring, waterhole', and *naqbū* (IDÌM) 'spring, fountain' in Assyrian rituals. In Ugaritic there is the problematic *'el 'eb* 'deity of the pit' (possibly referring to spirits of the dead and tying in with the "vents" of Ras Shamra tombs), and Hebrew has *'ôḇ* 'ghost, revenant' (cf. the necromancy of the witch of En-dor in 1 *Sam.* 28, 13–14, where the apparition of Samuel to Saul is described as "a god coming up out of the earth"). In the Sumerian *Gilgameš* (= Akk. Tabl. XII, 83–84) Nergal dug a hole (*ab-làl--kur-ri*) in the earth and (Akk.) raised Enkidu's spirit like a wind-puff from the earth. Cf. Zuntz, *ARIV* 96.2:543 (1936–7); E. Forrer, *Glotta* 26:186–9 (1938); Goetze, *JAOS* 74:187 (1954), *JCS* 22:17 (1968); M. Vieyra, *RA* 51:100–1 (1957), *RHA* 19:47–55 (1961); Ch. Rabin, *Orientalia* N.S. 32:115–6 (1963); H. A. Hoffner, *Journal of Biblical Literature* 86:385–401 (1967), also in D. J. Wiseman (ed.), *Peoples of Old Testament times* 216 (1973); M. Dietrich – O. Loretz – J. Sanmartín, *Ugarit-Forschungen* 6:450–1 (1974); J. Lust, in *Studies on Prophecy* 133–42 (1974); H.-P. Müller, *Die Welt des Orients* 8:68–70 (1975).

The common semantic denominator '(daimon of the) pit' might thus fit Hitt.-Hurr. *(a-)a-pí-*, Assyr. *abu*, Ugar. *'eb*, Hebr. *'ôḇ*, and Sum. *ab(.làl)*. Vieyra (*RHA* 19:52 [1961]) and Rabin awarded primacy to Sumerian *ab* and assumed Hurrian mediation for the rest. Hoffner, basing himself on Goetze, preferred to Hitt.-Hurr. /ābi-/ a "normalization" **ay(a)bi*, postulating Ugar. *'ēb* < **'ayb(i)*, Assyr. *abu* < **ayabum*, and Hebr. *'ôḇ* from (dialectal?) Hurrian, with the ultimate origin obscure ("old substratum word", also in Sumerian *ab*); but the inconsistency of the spelling *(a-)a-pí-* and the uncertainties of Goetze's view (cf. e.g. s.v. *ā-* and *ara-*, at the end) make Hoffner's reconstruction less probable.

G. B. Jahukyan (*Hayerenə ev hndevropakan hin lezunerə* 148 [1970]) adduced also Arm. *opˁ* 'hole'.

apisi- (c.) 'exorcist' (*AŠEPU, AŠIPU*), nom. sg. ^{LÚ}*apisis* (*KBo* XV 9 III 12 and IV 18, 24; cf. Kümmel, *Ersatzrituale* 64, 66), ^{LÚ}*AŠIPU* (ibid. III 15; *KUB* XVIII 62, 6), ^{LÚ}*AŠEPU* (*KBo* XV 5, 4; cf. Kümmel, *Ersatzrituale* 64), nom. pl. ^{LÚ.MEŠ}*apisius* (XV 9 IV 17; XV 11 III 12; cf. Kümmel, *Ersatzrituale* 66), ^{LÚ.MEŠ}*AŠIPI.HI.A* (XV 8 Vs. 6; cf. Kümmel, *Ersatzrituale* 68), ^{LÚ.MEŠ}*AŠIPUTI* (XVI 99 II 10).

Akk. *(w)āšipu(m)* (cf. *CAD* A 2:431–6) is found in Akkadian texts at Boğazköy: ^{LÚ}*ašipu* (e.g. *KUB* XXIX 58 I 30; *KBo* IX 50 Rs. 5; 87/r II 9), ^{LÚ}*ašipi* (*KUB* III 71 Vs. 8), ^{LÚ}*ašipa* (ibid. 9; *KBo* I 10 Rs. 42). Hitt. *apisi-* is a loanword from Akk. *ašipi* (with *i*-stem on the basis of Akk. oblique case, as in e.g. *tuppi-* [q.v.]), with (Hurrian-based?) *s*:*p* metathesis as in Akk. *gurpisu, gursipu* 'hauberk (part of armor)' : Hitt. *kurpisi-* 'id.', *gurzipant-* 'wearing a hauberk' (q.v.). Confusion with Akk. *ēpišu* 'sorcerer' may have been a contributing factor in favor of the Hittite form *apisi-*. Cf. Kümmel, *Ersatzrituale* 95–8; Kammenhuber, *Orakelpraxis* 143–5; Otten, *AfO* 25:175–8 (1974–7).

apuzzi-, only in É *apuzzi* 'storehouse, storeroom', e.g. *KUB* XXIX 4 III 66 *namma* DINGIR-*LAM INA* É *apuzzi asisanzi* 'then they set the (image of the) deity in the storeroom'; ibid. II 22–23 *namma-at-kan* IŠTU É DINGIR-*LIM INA* É *apuzzi parā uwanzi* 'then they come out of the temple into the storeroom' (cf. Kronasser, *Umsiedelung* 28, 16); *KBo* XXIII 93 I 28 and IV 11, *IBoT* I 29 Rs. 6 *INA* É *apuzzi*; *KUB* XVIII 11 Rs. 12 EN É *apuzzi* 'storemaster'.

The last-mentioned functionary (repeatedly attested in lists of Hittite officials, e.g. *KBo* IV 10 Rs. 31; *KUB* XXVI 43 Rs. 32; cf. Imparati, *RHA* 32:38 [1974]; XXVI 50 Rs. 25 EN É *apuzi*) is found also in *RS* 11:732 Recto 8 and Verso 8 *ana* LÚ EN É *abusi* 'to the storemaster' (tribute list in Akkadian from king of Ugarit to Suppiluliumas, his family, and Hittite dignitaries); É ... *u abusi-šu* 'house and its storeroom' already in OAssyr. inscription of Šalim-ahum.

Hurrian origin or mediation of Akk. *abūsu* 'storehouse' (*CAD* A 1:92–3) is possible. The Hittite form shows the typical freezing of the *i*-case variant into an *i*-stem (cf. e.g. s.v. *apisi-*). Cf. Goetze, *RHA* 12:1–3, 5–6 (1952).

Cf. *antuwasalli-*.

appuzzi- (n.) 'animal (sheep) fat, tallow' (UZUYÀ.UDU), nom.-acc. sg. *appuzzi* (e.g. *KBo* XV 49 I 9 ŠA MÁŠ.GAL *ēshar* UZU*appuzzi*[--*ya* 'the he-goat's blood and fat', with dupl. *KUB* XXXII 128 II 22 UZUYÀ.UDU-*ya*; XXXIX 15 IV 7; cf. Otten, *Totenrituale* 82; *appuzzi anda dāi* 'puts in fat', with dupl. UZUYÀ.UDU; cf. L. Rost, *MIO* 1:360 [1953], III 31; XXVII 1 I 43 UZU*appuzzi-ya tepu dāi* 'takes a little fat'; ibid. 39 UZU*wappuzzi-ya tepu dāi*; cf. Lebrun, *Samuha* 76), *appuzi* (dupl. XLVII 64 II 11 UZUYÀ.UDU--*ya*; ibid. 6 UZU*appuzi-ya*), *apuzi* (*Bo* 2839 IV 3 ŠÀ-*as apuzi* 'heart-fat'; cf. Haas, *Nerik* 262; 384/i, 8; cf. Otten, *Materialien* 41), gen. sg. *appuzziyas* (*KBo* IV 2 I 22 [*nu* U]R.TUR.RA *appuzziyas ienzi* 'they make a small dog of tallow'; cf. Kronasser, *Die Sprache* 8:90 [1962]; similarly ibid. II 15 and 25, III 5; *KUB* IX 7 II 9 UZU*appuzziyas-ma* ŠAH.TUR 'a small pig of tallow'; cf. Otten, *LTU* 79), instr. sg. in *n-at* UZUYÀ.UDU-*it hūlaliyazi* 'she wraps it with tallow' (dupl. *n-asta appuzzi anda hūlalizi* 'she wraps tallow within'; cf. L. Rost, *MIO* 1:350 [1953], I 42). Cf. Friedrich, *ZA* 37:191 (1927); Eheloff, *ZA* 43:173 (1936).

appuzziyant- (c.) 'id.', nom. sg. in *VBoT* 58 I 13–14 *takku-as t[innuzi] nu-ma-asta andurza* UZU*ap[p]uzziyanza harzi* 'if he paralyzes (the grains), the fat will keep them within' (cf. Laroche, *BSL* 57.1:26 [1962], *RHA* 23:83 [1965]); also *KBo* XXV 107, 6 (OHitt.) *ap]puzzianza*.

Rather than a phonetically meaningful lectio difficilior, the hapax *wappuzzi-* is perhaps merely a scribal lapsus, with the regular *appuzzi-* occurring four lines later. Hurrian origin (as claimed by e.g. Kronasser, *Etym.* 1:88) is not likely, since most words with a segment -*uzzi*- have either primary (*luzzi*-, *tuzzi*-) or deverbative Indo-European connections (*ishuzzi*-, *ispan-duzzi*-, *kuruzzi*-, *warpuzi*-; cf. Kronasser, *Etym.* 1:240–1). Perhaps (as intimated by Juret, *Revue des études latines* 16:68–9 [1938], *Vocabulaire* 36) related to Lat. *ad-eps* 'suet, lard' (the usual derivation of the latter from Gk. ἄλειφα via Etr. **alipa* and Umbr. **adipa* [>*ařipes*] strains credulity), *opīmus* 'fat' (<**opi-pīmos*, compounded with **pīmos* 'fat[tened]'). Hence an IE **ep*- 'to grease' is conceivable as an Anatolian-Italic isogloss, with a root noun **-ep-*, **op-*; for Lat. **opi-pīmos* cf. e.g. *arti-fex*. Hitt. *appuzzi*- would be a deverbative noun 'greasing stuff', with weak grade of the root (as in the homophone *ep[p]-*, *ap[p]-* 'seize'); cf. e.g. *kuruzzi*- 'cutting tool', from *kuer*- 'cut'.

ar- 'stand (by), be stationed, remain standing; be present, occur'; *anda ar*- 'stand within; be involved, apply oneself'; *appan ar*- 'stand behind, back up, take care of'; *arha ar*- 'stand back, back off'; *sarā ar*- 'stand up(right); stand ready, be provided' (GUB), 1 sg. pres. midd. *arhari* (*KBo* XVII 1 I 7 [*ug*]-*a arhari* 'but I remain standing'; cf. Otten – Souček, *Altheth. Ritual* 18; *KUB* XXXI 147 III 5), *arhahari* (e.g. *KBo* XVI 98 II 15–16 *parā-ma* MU.KAM-*anni* ANA KASKAL ᵁᴿᵁ*Neriqqa* EGIR-*an-pat arhahari* 'but next year I get back on the road to N.'; cf. P. Cornil – R. Lebrun, *Hethitica* 3; *KUB* XXXI 68 Rs. 50; cf. R. Stefanini, *Athenaeum* N.S. 40:28 [1962]; XXXI 47 Vs. 14), 2 sg. pres. midd. *artati* (e.g. *KBo* V 3 II 11 EGIR-*ann-a* ANA ᴰUTU-*ŠI-pat artati* 'and you stand behind my majesty'; cf. Friedrich, *Staatsverträge* 2:114; *KUB* XXXIII 106 IV 10 *le-mu piran* [?] *sarā artati* 'before me do not [?] stand up'; cf. Güterbock, *JCS* 6:28 [1952]), *artari* (XXXII 130 Vs. 28 and 30 *katti-mi assuli artari* 'you will stand loyally by me'), 3 sg. pres. midd. *arta* (e.g. XXXIII 120 I 10 *piran-se[t] arta* 'stands before him'; cf. Güterbock, *Kumarbi* *1; X 78 I 13 EGIR-*an arta* 'stand[s] in the rear' [with pl. subject 'women']; XXX 10 Vs. 22–23 *man-asta mān* [*a*]*ntuwahhas idāluw-a inan arta man-at-si natta kattawatar* 'even if a man's bad illness occurred, it [would be] no challenge for him'; *KBo* III 34 II 36 [OHitt.]), *ārta* (e.g. III 35 Vs. 13; III 46 Vs. 45 [OHitt.]; *KUB* VIII 30 Rs. 11), *artari* (e.g. I 16 III 35 (*nu* ᵁᴿᵁ*Hatt*]*usass-a sarā artari* 'Hattusas shall stand prominent'; cf. Sommer, *HAB* 12; XXX 37, 4 *n-as-kan* ANA UR.MAH GIŠ *artari* 'he stands on a wooden lion'; cf. von Brandenstein, *Heth. Götter* 61; *KBo* IV 8 II 9–10 NINDA-*a-ssi wātar nu hūman sarā artari* ŪL-*a-ssi-ssan kuitki waggāri* 'bread for her and water — everything is provided; nothing is lacking for her'; cf. H. Hoffner, *JAOS* 103:188 [1983]), *ārtari* (*KUB* XXX 43 IV 5 *sarā-ma-at* ŪL *ārtari* 'but it does not stand upright'), GUB-*ri* (e.g. XXXVIII 1 II 6; cf. von Brandenstein, *Heth. Götter* 14), 1 pl. pres. midd. *arwasta* (XVII 21 IV 5–6 *nu* DINGIR-MEŠ-*as ANA* EZEN.HI.A EGIR-*an-pat arwasta* 'we take care of the gods' festivals'; cf. von Schuler, *Die Kaškäer* 160; *KBo* XVI 27 II 3; cf. von Schuler, *Die Kaškäer* 135), 3 pl. pres. midd. *aranta* (e.g. *KUB* VIII 12, 8–9 *takku* ᴰ*SIN-mi* ... 2 MUL.HI.A [*kattan*] *aranta* 'if two stars are stationed by the moon'), *arānta* (II 6 III 37–38 ᴸᚢ.ᴹᴱˢ*MEŠEDI* LUGAL-*i menahhanda arānta* 'the bodyguards are stationed facing the king'), *aranda* (e.g. XXIX 4 II 15 MUL.HI.A *nuwa aranda* 'the stars still stand [in the sky]'; cf. Kronasser, *Umsiedelung* 16; *ABoT* 9 I 6 'they remain standing'; cf. Neu, *Gewitterritual* 10), *arantari* (e.g. *KUB* II 6 IV 2 and *KBo* XIX 128 Vs. 8 *karū arantari* 'they are already standing'; cf. Otten, *Festritual* 2; *KUB* XII 8 II 9 ANA GUNNI *kattan arantari* '[they] stand by the hearth'; *KBo* X 23 V 11–13 EGIR-*ŠU-ma* ᴳᴵˢŠUKUR. .HI.A HUR.SAG.HI.A-*san kuwapi ser arantari* 'but afterwards the spears are stationed somewhere up in the mountains'), *arāntari* (XXVI 105 IV 20), *arantāri* (II 16, 10 *anda arantāri* 'stand within'), *arandari* (e.g. XVII 6 II 15 *a*]*randari*; cf. Otten – Souček, *Altheth. Ritual* 26; *KUB* VII 10 I 3 *karū arandari*; cf. Kümmel, *Ersatzrituale* 129), 1 sg. pret. midd. (OHitt.) *arhati* (*KBo* III 29 I 18 and dupl. VIII 41, 7), *arhahat* (*KUB* XXVI 1 III 30; cf. von Schuler, *Dienstanweisungen* 13; *KBo* VIII 60 Vs. 7), *ārhahat* (*KUB* XII 31 Rs. 16; cf. Götze – Pedersen, *MS* 10), 2 sg. pret. midd. *artati* (*KBo* V 13 II 7–8 IŠTU ŠA ᴰUTU-ŠI *ma*[*hhan*] *artati nu* IŠTU ŠA ᴰUTU-ŠI-*pat* EGIR-*an ārhut* 'as you have stood by my majesty, stand by my majesty hereafter!'; cf.

ar-

Friedrich, *Staatsverträge* 1:122; *KUB* XXXIII 106 IV 10; cf.
Güterbock, *JCS* 6:28 [1952]), *artat* (XXI 1 III 25; cf. Friedrich,
Staatsverträge 2:70; XVII 28 II 59), 3 sg. pret. midd. *artat* (e.g.
RS 17:109 Recto 5 *nu* ¹*Pallariyass-a artat* 'P. stood by [as
witness]'; cf. Laroche, *Ugaritica* 5:769 [1968]; Haase, *Ugarit-
Forschungen* 3:71 [1971]; *KBo* XI 1 Vs. 7 AN-*as* ᴰUTU-*us apiya
kuis* ANA AN-*E ser artat* 'the sun of heaven which stood in the
sky then'; cf. Houwink Ten Cate – Josephson, *RHA* 25:105
[1967]; *KUB* I 1 + 1309/u III 6–7 *nu-nnas-kan* É-*ir kuit ēssuwen
nu-nnas-kan* DINGIR-*LUM anda artat* 'what house we made for
ourselves, the goddess stood within for us'; cf. Götze, *Hattusilis*
22, *Neue Bruchstücke* 12; XIII 33 IV 7; cf. Werner, *Gerichtsprotokolle* 34; XIX 11 I 13 *apiya artat* 'stood there'; cf. Güterbock,
JCS 10:63 [1956]; *IBoT* I 36 II 20 *kuis kattan artat* 'who stood
by'; cf. L. Jakob-Rost, *MIO* 11:184 [1966]), 1 pl. pret. midd.
arwastat (*KBo* XVI 59 Vs. 14 *ammugg-a arwastat* '[so-and-so]
and I, we stood'; cf. Werner, *Gerichtsprotokolle* 54; *KUB* XXIII
115, 11–13 *wēs ... sumās ...* [EGI]R-*an arwastat* 'we have cared
for you'; cf. von Schuler, *Die Kaškäer* 160), 3 pl. pret. midd.
(OHitt.) *arandati* (*KBo* III 35 I 7), *arantat* (e.g. V 8 III 14
ᴸᵁ*auriyalus kuit arantat* 'because guards had been stationed';
cf. Götze, *AM* 156; *KUB* XIII 4 II 37–38 SUM-*ir-wa-at-si
kuwapi nu-wa kās kāss-a arantat* 'when they gave it to him, so-
and-so stood by [as witnesses]'; cf. Sturtevant, *JAOS* 54:376
[1934]; XXI 38 Rs. 8; cf. R. Stefanini, *Atti La Colombaria* 29:15
[1964]), 1 sg. imp. midd. *arhaharu* (*KBo* IV 14 III 6 *nu-wa kedas
ANA MAMIT* GAM-*an arha arhaharu* 'I will stand back from these
oaths'; cf. R. Stefanini, *ANLR* 20:44 [1965]; *VBoT* 120 II 20; cf.
Haas – Thiel, *Rituale* 140), 2 sg. imp. midd. *arhut* (e.g. 552/u, 6
ziqq-a anda arhut 'and you stand inside!'; *KBo* XII 96 IV 27
EGIR-*an zik* ᴰUTU-*us arhut* 'you, sun-god, take care of it!'; cf.
Rosenkranz, *Orientalia* N.S. 33:241 [1964]; V 3 I 31–32
EGIR-*pann-a* ANA ᴰUTU-*ŠI-pat arhut* 'and stand behind my
majesty!'; cf. Friedrich, *Staatsverträge* 2:108–10), *ārhut* (e.g. V
4 Vs. 20 and V 9 II 18 *nu-ssan ... warri lammar ārhut* 'stand by
as an ally right away!'; cf. Friedrich, *Staatsverträge* 1:54, 16), 3
sg. imp. midd. *artaru* (e.g. IV 6 Rs. 15 *nu-tta kās* SAL-*TUM pidi
artaru* 'let this woman be her stand-in for you'; cf. Tischler,

Gebet 16; IV 2 II 35 ANA DINGIR-*LIM* KASKAL-*si arha artaru* 'let him stand out of the god's way'; cf. Kronasser, *Die Sprache* 8:93 [1962]; *KUB* XXIX 1 IV 11–12 *uddār ... artaru* 'may the word[s] stand'; cf. B. Schwartz, *Orientalia* N.S. 16:38 [1947]; XIII 8 Vs. 9 ᴳᴵˢ*eyan artaru* 'let an *eya*-tree stand'; cf. Otten, *Totenrituale* 106; I 16 III 51 [OHitt.] *memal-semet sarā artaru* 'let their meal-dish stand ready'; cf. Sommer, *HAB* 14), GUB-*ru* (XXXVI 89 Rs. 42 *piran* GUB-*ru* 'let [him] stand forth'; cf. Haas, *Nerik* 154), 2 pl. imp. midd. *ardumat* (e.g. XIII 20 I 8 *kuis imma* KIN-*az nu-ssan anda ardumat* 'whatever the task, apply yourselves'; cf. Alp, *Belleten* 11:390 [1947]; XXIII 68 Rs. 11 *linkiya ardumat* 'stand by the oath!'; cf. A. Kempinski – S. Košak, *Die Welt des Orients* 5:196 [1970]; XVII 21 II 3; cf. von Schuler, *Die Kaškäer* 154), *artummat* (XXVI 29 + XXXI 55 Vs. 11 *sumēs-a* ANA ᴰUTU-*ŠI-pat kattan artummat* 'and you, stand by my majesty!'), 3 pl. imp. midd. *arantaru* (e.g. XIII 4 II 41 EN.MEŠ ᵁᴿᵁ*Hatti arantaru* 'let the lords of Hatti stand by'; cf. Sturtevant, *JAOS* 54:376 [1934]; *KBo* IV 12 Rs. 2; cf. Götze, *Hattusilis* 44; *KUB* XXXI 115, 15 [OHitt.]), *arandaru* (XXVI 43 Rs. 21; cf. Imparati, *RHA* 32:36 [1974]; XXXIV 77 I 12; XLIII 40 IV 5; *KBo* XX 82 III 12); partic. *arant-*, nom. sg. c. *aranza* (e.g. XXXIII 93 + 95 + IV 11 'standing'; cf. Güterbock, *JCS* 5:157 [1951]), profusely attested sg. or pl. GUB-*as* '(standing', opp. TUŠ-*as* 'seated'; possibly "genitive absolute"; cf. Carruba, *Beschwörungsritual* 45), instr. sg. *arantet* (*KUB* X 89 I 21; cf. Güterbock, *Oriens* 10:361–2 [1957]; Neu, *Interpretation* 23), nom. pl. c. *arantes* (e.g. *KBo* XVIII 153 Rs. 3–4), nom.-acc. pl. neut. *aranda* (?) in adverbial (*anda*) *aranda* 'all together, collectively' (*KBo* XX 12 I 6; cf. Neu, *Altheth.* 63; IV 4 IV 22; cf. Götze, *AM* 136, 252). Cf. Neu, *Interpretation* 4–11.

Neu (*Interpretation* 6) was wrong in considering *ar-* basically a stative verb like *es-* 'sit' or *ki-* 'lie', with an alleged sense of motion ('step', etc.) and the separate verb *ar-*, *er-* 'come, arrive' as secondary developments. In fact *ar-* shows medial (intransitive) inflection of the IE root **er-* 'move, stir, raise' (*IEW* 326–9), thus e.g. 3 sg. pres. *arta* < **r̥-to*, matching the (augmented) Vedic and Greek 3 sg. (aorist) middles *ārta* (e.g. *RV* 4.1.12 *prá ... ārta* 'came forth'; *RV* 7.34.7 *úd ... ārta* 'went out') and ὦρτο 'stirred, moved, rose'; cf. also Lat. 3 sg. "deponential passive" (= middle) *oritur* 'stands up, rises'. The stative sense of Hitt. *ar-* inheres rather in the mediopassive diathesis which has been fully developed and marked in Hittite.

Cf. *ar-, er-*; *arai-*; *arnu-*; *arriya-*; *aru-*; *aruna-*; *ar(u)wai-*.

ar-, er- 'come (to), light (upon), arrive (at), come around, be at hand'; *arha ar-* 'go away, get away', 1 sg. pres. act. *ārhi* (e.g. *KUB* XV 11 III 21 KUR ^{U]RU}*Kummanni ārhi* 'I shall come to K.'; cf. P. Cornil – R. Lebrun, *Orientalia Lovaniensia Periodica* 3:51 [1972]; XXXI 130 Rs. 6, with parallel XXXVI 75 + 1226/u III 22; cf. H. Otten – C. Rüster, *ZA* 67:56 [1977]; *KBo* IV 14 III 32–33 *arha-man-wa-kan ārhi* 'might I get away!'; cf. R. Stefanini, *ANLR* 20:45, 67, 70 [1965]), 2 sg. pres. act. *ārti* (e.g. V 3 II 30–31 *nu-mu-ssan mān apiya-ya lammar ŪL ārti* 'if not even then do you come to me right away'; cf. Friedrich, *Staatsverträge* 2:116; *KUB* VIII 50 III 9–10 *nu-wa aggannas wetena[s] kuwapi ārti* 'when you come to the waters of death'; cf. Laroche, *RHA* 26:20 [1968]), 3 sg. pres. act. *ari* (e.g. XXI 1 I 64 UD-*az ari* 'the day is at hand'; cf. Friedrich, *Staatsverträge* 2:54; *KBo* VI 26 I 32 [= *Code* 2:65] *kuitman* MU.KAM-*za mēhuni ari* 'until a year comes around in time'; XV 25 Rs. 23 and XIX 128 Vs. 9 KÁ-*as ari* 'arrives at the gate'; cf. Carruba, *Beschwörungs-ritual* 6; Otten, *Festritual* 2; *KUB* XII 58 I 3 *n-as mahhan wappui ari* 'when she arrives at the river-bank'; cf. Goetze, *Tunnawi* 6; XIV 8 Rs. 13 = XIV 11 III 30 *ŠA ABU-ŠU-kan wastul* ANA DUMU-*ŠU ari* 'the father's sin falls upon the son'; cf. Götze, *KlF* 214; *KBo* XII 70 Rs. 9–10 *nu-tta-kkan addas-das [hurd]āis le ari* 'may your father's curse not light upon you!'; cf. Laroche, *Ugaritica* 5:780 [1968]), *āri* (e.g. VIII 112 I 7 KÁ.GAL-*as anda āri* 'arrives at the town gate'; *KUB* XX 88 Rs. 21), *arī* (XIII 3 I 13), 1 pl. pres. act. *e-ru-u-e-ni* (XXXIII 106 II 21 AN]A KÁ É ^D*É-A piran eruweni* 'we arrive before the gate of Ea's house'; cf. Güterbock, *JCS* 6:22 [1952]), *ir-u-e-ni* (XXXVI 15, 10), 2 pl. pres. act. *erteni* (e.g. *KBo* V 3 IV 20–21 *nu-mu-ssan mān hūdāk ŪL erteni* 'if you do not come to me at once'; cf. Friedrich, *Staatsverträge* 2:134; *KUB* XXVI 12 I 9; cf. von Schuler,

Dienstanweisungen 22), *arteni* (XXXI 101 Rs. 31; cf. A. Archi, *SMEA* 16:137 [1975]), *ārteni* (XXIII 68 Vs. 25 and Rs. 25; cf. A. Kempinski – S. Košak, *Die Welt des Orients* 5:194, 198 [1970]), *artēni* (VI 16+XVIII 64 IV 3 and 6), 3 pl. pres. act. *aranzi* (e.g. *RS* 17:109 Recto 11 and 15 *anda aranzi* 'are present', vs. 16 *ŪL apiya* 'not there'; cf. Laroche, *Ugaritica* 5:770 [1968]; Haase, *Ugarit-Forschungen* 3:71 [1971]; *KBo* VI 3 II 16–17 [= *Code* 1:31] *n-at anda aranzi n-an-za* ANA DAM-ŠU *dāi nu-za* É-*ir* Ù DUMU.MEŠ *ienzi* 'they settle down, he takes her for his wife, and they make a household and children'; cf. Imparati, *Leggi ittite* 214–5), *arānzi* (e.g. *KUB* V 1 III 20 *arha-at arānzi* 'they go away'; cf. Ünal, *Hatt.* 2:68), *ārānzi* (e.g. XXV 49 III 29), 1 sg. pret. act. *arhun* (e.g. XIV 3 I 6 *INA* ᵁᴿᵁ*Sallapa arhun* 'I arrived at S.'; cf. Sommer, *AU* 2; *KBo* VI 29 II 22; cf. Götze, *Hattusilis* 48; XII 38 III 11; cf. Otten, *MDOG* 94:20 [1963]; *KUB* XXIII 11 III 1; cf. R. Ranoszek, *Rocznik orientalistyczny* 9:57–8 [1934]; Carruba, *SMEA* 18:160 [1977]), *ārhun* (e.g. ibid. 13; *KBo* III 4 II 15; cf. Götze, *AM* 46; *KUB* XIV 1 Vs. 82; cf. Götze, *Madd.* 20), *arahhun* (e.g. XIX 37 II 8; cf. Götze, *AM* 168), *ārahhun* (e.g. *KBo* II 5 IV 4 *nu m]ahhan* ᵁᴿᵁ*Hattusi ārahhun* 'when I arrived at Hattusas'; cf. Götze, *AM* 190; *KUB* VI 41 I 39; cf. Friedrich, *Staatsverträge* 1:110), 3 sg. pret. act. *ar-as* (e.g. XXIII 93 III 14); *a-ra-as* (VIII 63 I 8); cf. Güterbock, *Kumarbi* *30), OHitt. *ārsa* (*KBo* XXII 2 Rs. 7 'he arrived', with dupl. III 38 Rs. 23 *āras*; cf. Otten, *Altheth. Erzählung* 12), *āras* (e.g. *KUB* XXXI 64 II 44; XXXVI 101 II 2 [OHitt.]; *KBo* IV 4 III 27; cf. Götze, *AM* 126; III 6 II 15 ᴸᵁ́KÚR ... *anda āras* 'the enemy arrived within [=made an incursion]'; cf. Götze, *Hattusilis* 16; IV 2 III 46–47 *nu-mu-kan zazhī anda* ŠU DINGIR-*LIM āras* 'in a dream the god's hand lit upon me'; cf. Götze–Pedersen, *MS* 4; *HT* 21+*KUB* VIII 80, 9–10 ANA ERÍN.MEŠ *kasti āras* 'it came to famine for the troops'; cf. Friedrich, *AfK* 2:120 [1924–5]; *KUB* XIV 8 Rs. 13–14=XIV 11 III 31 *nu-kan ammuqq-a* ŠA ABI-YA *wastul āras* 'upon me too fell the guilt of my father'; cf. Götze, *KlF* 214), 1 pl. pret. act. *e-ru-u-en* (XXI 10, 24 *anda eruwen* 'we arrived'; cf. Güterbock, *JCS* 10:118 [1956]), *e-ir-u-en* (e.g. XXXI 68 Vs. 3 'we arrived'; cf. R. Stefanini, *Althenaeum* N.S. 40:23 [1962]; *Bo* 8417, 12 *e-ru-en*), *ar-ú-en* (*KBo* XVI 61 Vs. 4 *mahhan-ma-wa* ᵁᴿᵁ*Hattusi arwen* 'but when we had arrived at Hattusas'; cf. Werner, *Gerichtsprotokolle* 60), 3 pl. pret. act. *erir* (e.g. *VBoT* 120 II 14 *e-ri-ra-at* 'they arrived'; cf. Haas – Thiel, *Rituale* 140; *KBo* X 47g III 4 and 5 ŠÀ HUR.SAG.MEŠ *erir* 'to the midst of mountains they came'; cf. Otten, *Istanbuler Mitteilungen* 8:108 [1958]; Laroche, *RHA* 26:12 [1968]; *KUB* XXXIII 102 III 17 *nu-kan IT*]*TI* ᴰ*Kumarbi erir* 'to Kumarbi they came'; XXXIII 106 II 30 *MA*]*HAR* ᴰ*A-a erir* 'before Ea they arrived'; cf. Güterbock, *JCS* 5:154 [1951], 6:22 [1952]; *KBo* XIX 108, 9 ᵁᴿᴶᵁ*Ninuwa erir* 'they arrived at Ninive'; cf. Siegelová, *Appu-Hedammu* 16), *e-ri-e--ir* (*KUB* XVI 74, 8), *ierir* (XVI 50, 3 *n-at anda ierir* 'they arrived', vs. e.g. XVI 58 Vs. 5 and XVI 72, 19 *n-at anda erir*), OHitt. *arir* (XXXVI 102, 3; cf. XXXVI 101 II 4]*rir*; *KBo* XXII 2 Vs. 8]*arir* or]*erir*; cf. Otten, *Altheth. Erzählung* 6, 29; *arir* or *erir* also in *KUB* XIX 9 II 17; cf. Ünal, *Hatt.* 2:7), *ariyir* (271/f Vs. 1]É.DINGIR-*LIM-ma-at-kan ariyir* 'but they arrived at the god's house'), *arair* (*KUB* XXIV 8 IV 2 [*n-a*]*t* LÚ-*ni mehuni arair* 'they reached manhood'; cf. ibid. III 18 [*n-at* LÚ-*ni me*]*huni erir*; Siegelová, *Appu-Hedammu* 10), 3 sg. imp. act. *aru* (*KBo* IV 14 III 34 EN-*YA-wa-kan edaza arha aru* 'may my lord get away from there!'; cf. R. Stefanini, *ANLR* 20:45 [1965]; *KUB* XIII 4 III 73 *hūdāk aru* 'let him come promptly'; cf. Sturtevant, *JAOS* 54:388 [1934]; *KBo* XI 68 I 23), 2 pl. imp. act. *artin* (X 37 III 50), *ārtin* (*KUB* XXIII 72 Rs. 28); partic. *arant-*, nom. sg. c. *aranza* (e.g. XII 58 I 18; cf. Goetze, *Tunnawi* 8), nom. pl. c. *arantes* (e.g. *RS* 25:421 Verso 59; cf. Laroche, *Ugaritica* 5:774 [1968]; *Maşat* 75/13 Rs. 15–17 *nu-ssan mān halkiēs arantes n-as-kan arha warastin* 'when grain [has] reached ripeness [lit. arrived], harvest it!'; *Maşat* 75/15 Vs. 5–6 *kasa-wa-ssan halki*ʰᴵ.ᴬ-*as karū arantes* 'behold, grain [has] long since reached ripeness'; cf. Alp, *Belleten* 44:46, 42 [1980]); iter. /*arski-*/, 3 sg. pres. act. *ārsakizzi* (*KUB* XIII 2 I 24–25 ᴸᵁKÚR-*san kuedas* [*hūdā*]*k ārsakizzi* '[towns] where the enemy is apt to arrive quickly'; cf. von Schuler, *Dienstanweisungen* 42), *āraskizzi* (*VBoT* 24 I 32 *nu k*]*uwapi* ᴳᴵˢAPIN-*as ŪL āraskizzi* 'where the plough does not get to'; cf. Sturtevant, *TAPA* 58:8 [1927]), 3 pl. pres. act. *āraskanzi* (*Bo* 6859 I 5), 3 sg. pret. act.

āraskit (e.g. *KUB* I 6 II 7 'made an incursion'; cf. Götze, *Hattusilis* 16; *KBo* III 4 III 70 *n-as parā* INA ^{URU}*Zazzisa āraskit* 'he would arrive at Z.'; cf. Götze, *AM* 88; *KUB* XIX 11 IV 5; cf. Güterbock, *JCS* 10:65 [1956]; XIX 39 II 10 *ār⟨as⟩kit*; cf. Götze, *AM* 164), 3 pl. imp. act. *araskandu* (XIII 2 III 4–5 *nu-ssan* ANA TÚL SISKUR.SISKUR *kittari n-at-si ēssandu araskandu* 'a rite is on the books for the fountain; they shall perform it [and] be on hand for it'; cf. von Schuler, *Dienstanweisungen* 47). Cf. Kronasser, *Etym.* 1:516; Otten, *Altheth. Erzählung* 29.

The initial *a : e* ablaut resembles that of *ak(k)*- but is more widespread (*e* not merely in 3 pl. pret. act. but also in 1 and 2 pl. pres. and pret.); yet it is not as prevalent as in *asas-, has(s)-, karap-, sak(k)*- where it occurs also in 3 pl. pres. and nonfinite forms. The antiquity of the forms with *e* is doubtful, since OHitt. variants favor *a* (*arir, arumen* quoted above), and their expansion seems to show an inner-Hittite trend.

The -*hi* conjugation verb *ar*- probably reflects the *o*-grade of the IE perfect of **er*- 'move, stir, raise' (*IEW* 326–9), with intransitive force. Cf. the Vedic 3 sg. perf. act. *ā́ra* (*RV* 3.30.10 *vy ā̀ra* 'came apart' = 'opened itself up'), 3 pl. perf. act. *ārúr* (*RV* 3.1.4 *śiśum ná jātám ábhy ārur áśvā* 'they came [to him] like mares to a newborn foal'; *RV* 3.7.1 *prá yé ārúḥ* 'who have gone forth'). If old, the iterative /arski-/ < IE **r̥-sk-é-* matches Vedic *r̥ccháti* 'go to, go at, attain', OPers. *rasatiy* 'come to, arrive at' (e.g. Bīsitūn 2.28–29 *yātā adam arasam Mādam* 'until I arrived in Media'; with *KBo* III 4 III 70 *n-as parā* INA ^{URU}*Zazzisa āraskit* cf. e.g. Bīsitūn 2.32 *yaθā Arminam parārasa* 'when he arrived in Armenia', 3.3 *yaθā hauv kāra parārasa abiy Vistāspam* 'when this army came to Hystaspes'). Cf. e.g. Sturtevant, *Lg.* 3:165–7 (1927), *Comp. Gr.*[1] 92, *Comp. Gr.*[2] 42; Gusmani, *Lessico* 51; improbable reduplicative reconstructions in Oettinger, *Stammbildung* 404.

Cf. *ar-; arai-; arnu-; arriya-; aru-; aruna-; ar(u)wai-*.

arr-, ar(r)a-, arriya- (, arrui-) 'wash', 1 sg. pres. act. *arrahhi* (*KUB* VII 1 I 29 *n-asta* DUMU-*an ayis-sis* [error for *-sit*] *parā arrahhi* 'then I wash out the child's mouth'; cf. Kronasser, *Die Sprache*

arr-, ar(r)a-, arriya- (, arrui-)

7:143 [1961]; XXIII 93 III 5–6 GIM-*an-za* [...] *arrahhi* 'as I wash myself'), *ārrahhi* (e.g. *Bo* 2489 I 6), 1 sg. pres. midd. *arrahhari* (*Bo* 5439, 9), 3 sg. pres. act. *ārri* (e.g. *KBo* X 45 IV 37–38 *karizz-a-kan* GIM-*an* URU-*az sēhur* IM-*an ārri* 'as the deluge washes crud [and] mud off the city'; cf. Otten, *ZA* 54:138 [1961]; V 1 IV 4 *nu* SILÁ *wetenit katta ānsanzi* KAxU-*an* GÌR-ŠU *arha ārri* 'they wipe down a lamb with water; he washes its mouth [and] foot'; cf. Sommer – Ehelolf, *Pāpanikri* 12*; XVII 1 I 15 LUGAL-*us* 3-ŠU *ayis-set ārri* 'the king washes his mouth three times'; cf. Otten – Souček, *Altheth. Ritual* 18; *KUB* II 13 I 9 LUGAL-*us-za* QATI-ŠU *ārri* 'the king washes his hands'; VII 53 II 21–22 *nu-za-kan* ŠU.HI.A GEŠTIN-*it ārri* 'she washes her hands with wine'; ibid. 25 EGIR-ŠU-*ma-za-kan wetenit ārri* 'afterwards she washes herself with water'; cf. Goetze, *Tunnawi* 12; IX 22 III 29 *lu*]*kkatta-ma nu-za* SAL *ārri* 'but it dawns, and the woman washes herself'; *KBo* V 2 III 59 *nu-za ... uitenit ārri* 'he washes himself with water'; cf. Witzel, *Heth. KU* 112), *arri* (*KUB* VII 1 I 32–33 *nu-za* DUMU-*as ārri* IŠTU ŠE + NÁG-*ma-za peszi arri-ma--za kuezza wetenaz* ... 'the child washes himself, and lathers himself with soapwort; but the water with which he washes himself ...'; cf. Kronasser, *Die Sprache* 7:143 [1961]; XLV 5 II 21 *n-asta* DINGIR-*LUM* GÌR.MEŠ-ŠU *arri* 'then he washes the deity's feet'), *arrai* (e.g. I 13 IV 44 *n-as āantet arrai* 'he washes them with warm [water]'; cf. Kammenhuber, *Hippologia* 72, 124), *ārrai* (*KBo* III 5 IV 48 *n-as āantet wetenit ārrai*; cf. Kammenhuber, *Hippologia* 102), *arriyazzi* (*KUB* XLIV 63 II 10 *n-at* IŠTU MĒ *arha arriyazzi* 'he washes it off with water'; cf. Burde, *Medizinische Texte* 28), *ārriyezzi* (*KBo* XVII 94 III 23–24 *n-an-kan uitenaz* [...] *sarā ārriyezzi* 'washes it up with water'; cf. Otten, *Vokabular* 13; also XV 9 III 13 *arriya*[, ibid. 14 *ārr*[*i*; cf. Kümmel, *Ersatzrituale* 64), *arrizzi* (*KUB* XLV 47 I 30 and 33), *arruizzi* (*KBo* III 5 III 33 *arha arruizzi* 'washes off'; cf. Kammenhuber, *Hippologia* 96), 3 pl. pres. act. *arranzi* (e.g. *KUB* XVI 16 Vs. 28 *warpanzi-ma-wa-smas* ŪL TÚG.HI.A-*wa--smas-kan* ŪL *arha arranzi* 'but they do not bathe themselves [and] do not wash their clothes'; I 11 IV 17–20 *n-as āantet wetenit āandan arha arranzi namma-as* ÍD-*i katta pehudanzi n-as* 3-ŠU *arranzi namma-as katkattinuanzi* 'they wash them warmly with warm water; then they take them down to the river and wash them three times; then they make them shake [off the water]'; cf. Kammenhuber, *Hippologia* 120; XXIX 50 IV 18–19 *n-us ikunit uit[enit …] [arr]anzi* 'they wash them with cold water'; cf. Kammenhuber, *Hippologia* 212; *KBo* II 3 IV 5–6 *QATITE.*MEŠ*-ŠUNU-ya-za-kan* IGI.HI.A*-ŠUNU arranzi* 'they wash their hands and eyes'; cf. Hrozný, *Heth. KB* 86; L. Rost, *MIO* 1:366 [1953]), *ārranzi* (e.g. V 1 III 25 *nu-za-kan …* ŠU.HI.A*-ŠUNU ārranzi* '[they] wash their hands'; cf. Sommer – Ehelolf, *Pāpani-kri* 10*; III 5 II 53 and III 71 *āantet ārranzi*; cf. Kammenhuber, *Hippologia* 90, 98; *KUB* I 11 III 10–11 *n-as-kan āantet weteni[t] āandan ārranzi*; cf. Kammenhuber, *Hippologia* 114–6; XV 31 II 43; cf. Haas – Wilhelm, *Riten* 158), *arruwanzi* (*KBo* III 5 IV 33 *n-as 5-ŠU arruwanzi* 'they wash them five times'; cf. Kammen-huber, *Hippologia* 100), *arrumanzi* (ibid. I 23 *nu wetenit arru-manzi* 'they wash with water'; ibid. 33, 50, 59, II 8; cf. Kammenhuber, *Hippologia* 80–8), 1 sg. pret. act. *ārrahhun* (*VBoT* 120 III 5–7 *mān-[z]a* EN.SISKUR*-ma ārri nu* SAL ŠU.GI *memai* INA [KASKAL]*-NI-za uitenaz ārrahhun ŠA ZUNNI uetenit warput* 'when the sacrificer washes himself, the old woman says "with water of the road I have washed myself; bathe thou with rain-water!"'; cf. Haas – Thiel, *Rituale* 144), 3 sg. pret. act. *ārasta* (*KUB* XXXIII 88, 9 *anda arrum]anzi pait nu-za ārasta* 'in she went to wash, and she washed herself'; cf. Friedrich, *Arch. Or.* 17.1:238, 251–2 [1949]; Siegelová, *Appu-Hedammu* 54, 75), 3 sg. pret. midd. *arratat* (XXXVI 30, 8 D*Ku]marpis arratat* 'K. washed himself'), *arrattat* (ibid. 9), 3 pl. pret. act. *arrir* (e.g. XII 26 II 7 *nu-war-an-kan arrir* 'they washed it [viz. the ewe]'; cf. Haas – Wilhelm, *Riten* 26; IX 1 III 23–24 *arha arrir*; *KBo* X 24 II 1), 2 sg. imp. midd. *arrahhut* (708/z Vs. 9 UZU ÚR.HI.A *arrahhut* 'wash [your] limbs'), *ārrahhut* (873/u, 9 ŠA KASKAL*-NI-za* A*-az ārrahhut* 'wash yourself with water of the road'; cf. Haas – Thiel, *Rituale* 271), 3 sg. imp. act. *ārru* (*KUB* XLIII 58 I 55), 3 sg. imp. midd. *arrattaru* (*Bo* 3077 II 7–8 and 11–12 *nu-za kedanta u[…] arrattaru* 'with this w[ater] let him wash himself'), 2 pl. imp. act. *āratten* (*KUB* XLI 23 III 10 [OHitt.] *ayis-mit āratten* 'wash my mouth'); partic. *arrant-*, nom. sg. c. *arranza* (e.g. XXX 19+ I 9; cf. Otten, *Totenrituale*

32; I 13 III 14 *arranza halkis* 'washed barley'; cf. Kammenhuber, *Hippologia* 64), *ārranza* (e.g. *KBo* XXI 57 III 7–8 *nu-za--kan* QATE.MEŠ-*KA* ... *ārranza ēs* 'be washed, your hands' [partitive apposition]), nom.-acc. sg. neut. *arran* (*KUB* XXIX 50 I 34 and IV 27 ŠE *arran* 'washed barley'; cf. Kammenhuber, *Hippologia* 210–2; *KBo* XXIII 1 I 46–47 *kinun-a-wa-kan apāt paprā[tar]* ANA DINGIR-*LIM arha arran ēs[du]* 'now let that uncleanness too be washed off the deity'; cf. Lebrun, *Hethitica III* 142), gen. sg. *arrantas* (*KUB* XXXI 57 IV 16; XLII 107 III 6 and 7), nom. pl. c. *ārrantes* (XLIII 58 II 41), acc. pl. c. *arrandus* (I 11 IV 20–21 *n-as arrandus tūriyanzi* '[after they are] washed they harness them'; cf. Kammenhuber, *Hippologia* 120), nom.-acc. pl. neut. *arranda* (XLVI 20 Vs. 6); verbal noun gen. sg. *arrumas* (*KBo* XXII 142 IV 8), *ārrumas* (*KUB* III 94 II 17 *ārrumas lahhus* 'pouring-can for washing' = [Akk.] *lahtanu* 'container'; cf. B. Landsberger, *MSL* 2:117 [1951]), *arrummas* (*KBo* V 1 IV 15–16 *nu* SILÁ *ārranzi namma arrummas wātar* PANI DINGIR-*LIM lāhuui* 'they wash the lamb; then he pours the water of washing before the god'; cf. Sommer – Ehelolf, *Pāpanikri* 12*; *KUB* XLV 5 II 22 *Š]A* DINGIR-*LIM* GÌR.MEŠ-*as arrummas* SÌR-*in* 'the song of washing the deity's feet'; *KBo* II 20, 8; XVIII 181 Rs. 17), *arumas* (XXII 49 III 5 GÌR.MEŠ-*ŠU arumas-ma* A['but the water of washing his feet'), *ārruwas* (*KUB* XV 42 II 4); inf. *arrumanzi* (*IBoT* II 135, 7 *anda arrumanzi pait* 'in she went to wash' [dupl. of *KUB* XXXIII 88, 9 s.v. *ārasta* above]; I 13 II 61–63 *n-as* ÍD-*i arrumanzi pehudanzi n-as* 5-*ŠU arranzi* 'they take them to the river to be washed; they wash them five times'; cf. Kammenhuber, *Hippologia* 62; XXVII 16 I 26–27 *mahhan-ma* DINGIR[.LAM] *arrumanzi zinnanzi* 'when they are through washing the deity'; cf. M. Vieyra, *RA* 51:90 [1957]; XXXIV 59, 3), *arrummanzi* (dupl. XV 34 III 38; cf. Zuntz, *ARIV* 96.2:514 [1936–7]; Haas – Wilhelm, *Riten* 198; XLI 13 II 11–12 ANA DINGIR-*LIM* GÌR.M[EŠ-*ŠU*] *arrummanzi* 'to wash the deity's feet'; also passim Kammenhuber, *Hippologia* 154–62), *arrauwanzi* (XXIV 7 III 57; cf. Friedrich, *ZA* 49:228 [1950]), *arrawanzi* (ibid. 58); iter. *arreski-, ar(r)iski-, arsiki-* (?), 3 sg. pres. act. *ārreskiz[zi* (*KBo* XI 45 IV 19; cf. Haas, *Nerik* 234), *arriskiz[zi* (XVII 70 Vs. 16), *āriskizzi* (*VBoT* 120 II 6), 3

114

pl. pres. act. *arriskanzi* (e.g. *KUB* I 13 II 49; cf, Kammenhuber, *Hippologia* 60; XVII 9 I 19; XLI 13 II 14), 1 sg. pret. act. *arreskinun* (*KBo* IV 2 IV 31–32 *kuez-za arreskinun* '[the wash-basin] out of which I used to wash myself'; cf. Götze – Pedersen, *MS* 10), *arriskinun* (dupl. *KUB* XII 31 Rs. 10, misspelled *ar-is-ri-ki-nu-un*, with metathesis of *ri* and *is*), 3 sg. pret. act. *arreskit* (*KBo* VIII 32 Vs. 5–6 *nu-wa-za* ŠU.MEŠ-*Š*[*U* ...] [*a*]*rha arreskit* 'he washed his hands'; cf. Werner, *Gerichtsprotokolle* 58), 3 sg. pret. midd. *ārsikitta* (*KUB* IX 28 IV 5–8 *n-as-za ārsikitta wātar* DINGIR.MEŠ-*as ēsriya kuit kittati n-at dāi n-at-san tuikki-ssi lāhūwāi* 'he washed himself; the water which had been placed by the image of the gods, that he takes and pours it on his body'). Cf. Kronasser, *Etym.* 1:528; Neu, *Interpretation* 11–2.

Of doubtful appurtenance is nom. sg. c. *arrammis* (*KUB* VIII 75 IV 27, with gloss-wedges; cf. V. Souček, *Arch. Or.* 27:22 [1959]) as a cadastral field-description; possibly Luwian participle in *-mi-*, thus 'washed, watered, irrigated' (cf. *Dict. louv.* 30)?

arr- is the general term for 'wash', whereas *war(a)p-* 'bathe, scrub' (q.v.) takes only animate objects (for further quasi-synonyms denoting wet procedures see s.v. *san[a]h-* 'flush'); cf. e.g. above *KUB* XVI 16 Vs. 28 *warpanzi* 'bathe (themselves)' vs. *arranzi* 'wash (their clothes)', or *VBoT* 120 III 5–7 *ārrahhun* 'I have washed (myself)' besides *warput* 'bathe thou!'; in some hippological passages (*KUB* XXIX 40 II 28; XXIX 41, 6) *warp-* occurs instead of the usual *arr-* describing horse-washing (cf. Kammenhuber, *Hippologia* 168, 182, 307, 350). 'Deities' (icons) can be either 'washed' (XXVII 16 I 27 *arrumanzi* above) or 'bathed' (XXXVIII 32 Vs. 10 *war[panzi*).

The stem *arrui-* is found only on the Kikkulis-tablet *KBo* III 5 and is suspect as a foreigner's nonce distortion (cf. Kammenhuber, *Hippologia* 80, 96, 324); *KBo* III 5 III 4 also has a strange *wahhuzi* besides normal *wehzi* (ibid. IV 18; cf. Kronasser, *Etym.* 1:416–7). *arrumas* besides *ārruwas* is probably due to secondary juncture shift (*arr-uwas* > *arru-was* > *arrumas*); cf. s.v. *ard-*.

arr- has rather consistent *-rr-*; the single spellings (*ārasta, āratten, arumas, āriskizzi*) are stray cases of scriptio facilior.

arr-, ar(r)a-, arriya- (, arrui-)   ara-

The plausible comparison (since Couvreur, *Hett.* 97) is with
Toch. A *yär-* 'bathe' (cf. e.g. Hitt. *eku-* : Toch. AB *yok-* 'drink'),
despite Van Windekens's unlikely attempt (*Le tokharien*
592–3) to find another, indirect source for *yär-* (borrowing
from Toch. B **yär-* < IE **wer-* 'water'); Hitt. *-rr-* may represent
**-rH_2-* (cf. Toch. A inf. *yärnässi*); in the absence of a tertium,
further Indo-European comparison is in abeyance, which does
not lessen the value of the Anatolian-Tocharian isolexeme.

A comparison with Hitt. *ar(a)s-*, *arsiya-* 'flow' (Götze –
Pedersen, *MS* 48; cf. Tischler, *KZ* 86:272 [1972]) is improbable;
equally unlikely is a tie-in with *aruna-* 'sea' with reference to the
nonce stem *arrui-* (A. Bernabé P., *Revista española de lingüística* 3:432 [1973]).

ara- 'belonging (or: proper) to one's own social group, commu-
nally accepted or acceptable, congruent with social order',
found in nominal usages:

ara- (spelled *a-ra-*) (c.) 'member of one's group, peer,
comrade, partner, fellow, friend' (of either sex, often with
determinative ^{LÚ} and sometimes ^{SAL}), nom, sg. *aras* (e.g. *KUB*
VIII 63 I 8 *āssianza kuit aras ēs*[*ta* 'because he was a dear
friend'; cf. Laroche, *RHA* 26:75 [1968]; XXIX 1 I 35 *ŪL-wa*
LUGAL-*was aras-mis zik* '[are] you not a friend of me, the king?';
cf. B. Schwartz, *Orientalia* N.S. 16:26 [1947]), ^{LÚ}*aras* (e.g. *Code*
2:63; XIII 4 III 81), ^{SAL}*aras* (XXXIX 41 I 11), *arās* (e.g. XXIX
1 I 13 [*ar*]*ās-mis arās-mi ēs* 'my friend, be my friend!'), acc. sg.
aran (ibid. 34 *aramman* < *aran-man* 'my friend'; XXVI 1 IV 38;
cf. von Schuler, *Dienstanweisungen* 16), *arān* (XVIII 5 III 19),
dat.-loc. sg. *ari* (e.g. *Code* 2:63), ^{LÚ}*ari* (XIII 4 III 77), *are* (XIII
20 I 33 ^{LÚ}*a-ri-es-si* 'to his friend'; cf. Alp, *Belleten* 11:394
[1947]; XXX 15+ Vs. 29 ^{SAL}*a-ri-es-si* 'to her colleague'; cf.
Otten, *Totenrituale* 68), nom. pl. *a-ri-es* (*KBo* VI 3 III 22
[= *Code* 1:55]; III 60 I 9; *KUB* XXXVI 106 Rs. 8 [OHitt.]; cf.
Otten, *ZA* 52:218 [1957]), *arus* (XXI 19 + 1303/u III 28–29
[*a*]*mmell-a-mu-kan* $^{LÚ.MEŠ}$*arus* $^{LÚ.MEŠ}$*TAPPI-YA*[*-ya*] *sarriskir* 'and
my peers and partners separated from me'; cf. ibid. 31 *ŠA*
$^{LÚ.MEŠ}$*TAPPI-YA-ya*; XL 1 Vs. 24 *ammel* $^{LÚ.MEŠ}$*arus*), *aras* (*KBo*

116

XX 67 IV 33 *aras-tes* 'your friends'), dat.-loc. pl. ^{LÚ.MEŠ}*aras-tes*
(*KUB* I 15 II 8 'to your friends'), ^{LÚ}*aras-tas* (*KBo* XVII 88 III
16), *aras-tas* (XX 67 IV 29). Thus approximately ^{LÚ}*ara-*
= ^{LÚ}*TAPPŪ*= LÚ HA.LA (*Code* 1:53; cf. von Schuler, *Die Kaškäer*
120, 128, 198).

In iteration 'one another', like ŠEŠ 'brother' (ŠEŠ-*as* ŠEŠ-*an*),
the numeral 'one' (1-*as* 1-*an*), and *ka-* 'this', typically *KBo* VI
34 I 20–22 *nu* ^{LÚ}*ar*[*as*] ^{LÚ}*aran le auszi kāss-a le* [*kūn*] *isdammaszi*
'one shall not see the other, nor shall this one hear the other'
(cf. Friedrich, *ZA* 35:162 [1924]; Oettinger, *Eide* 6). ^{LÚ}*aras*
^{LÚ}*aran* (also e.g. *KUB* XX 88 I 1; XXXIV 128 Rs. 2; *KBo* XXII
185 I 9) equals Akk. ^{LÚ}*tappū* ^{LÚ}*tappā(šu)*; cf. OCS *drugŭ druga*
'each other' (*drugŭ* 'friend'); also e.g. ^{LÚ}*aras aran* (XIII 32 Rs.
5), *aras aran* (*KBo* XXI 41 + *KUB* 7 Rs. 38; cf. Lebrun, *Samuha*
123; *KUB* VIII 68 I 9; XX 88 I 3), ^{LÚ}*aras* ^{LÚ}*ari* (e.g. XXXI 44 II
6; cf. von Schuler, *Orientalia* N.S. 25:226 [1956]; XXVI 1 IV 7;
cf. von Schuler, *Dienstanweisungen* 15), ^{LÚ}*arās* ^{LÚ}*ari*[(XLV 49
IV 7; cf. Otten, *Materialien* 29), ^{LÚ.MEŠ}*aras* ^{LÚ.MEŠ}*ari* (*Bo* 1580
Rs. 9; cf. Haas, *Nerik* 304), ^{LÚ}*aras ari* (*KUB* XXI 42 IV 5; cf.
von Schuler, *Dienstanweisungen* 27), *aras ari* (e.g. *IBoT* I 36 I
43; cf. L. Jakob-Rost, *MIO* 11:178 [1966]), *aras arī* (*KBo* XVI
65 I 16), *aran ari* (*IBoT* II 39 Rs. 25). Cf. Sommer, *AU* 174–5;
Kronasser, *Etym.* 1:125. For the literal origin, cf. *KBo* II 5 IV
16–18 *nu-za* ŠEŠ-*as* ŠEŠ-*an kattan peskit* [^{LÚ}*ar*]*as-ma-za* ^{LÚ}*aran*
kattan peskit [*nu-kan* 1]-*as* 1-*an kuwaskit* 'brother would betray
brother, friend would betray friend, and they would kill each
other' (cf. Götze, *AM* 192); also XXII 109 I 2–3 *antuhhas*
^{LÚ}*aran antuhs*[*an* SAG.DU-*an*] GUL-*ahzi* 'a man hits a fellow man
over the head'.

Denom. *aral(l)ai-* 'associate, join', 3 sg. pres. act. *arālaizzi*
(*KUB* XLIII 55 III 10–12 *mān antuhsan* ^DDÌM.NUN.ME-*as ap-*
piskizzi nu-za-kan ^DDÌM.NUN.ME-*an arālaizzi* 'if [the demoness]
D. takes hold of a man, the man hews to [lit. associates to
himself] D.'), 3 pl. pres. act. *arālanzi* (*KBo* XVIII 89 Vs. 10), 2
sg. pret. act. *arallāit* (*KUB* XXI 27 I 10–11 *nu-mu* ANA
^I*Hattusili* ÌR-*KA kuedani arallāit* 'H. your servant, to whom you
joined me [in marriage]'); inf. *aralāuwanzi* (*KBo* XVIII 89 Vs.
9). Cf. Goetze, *Tunnawi* 44; N. van Brock, *RHA* 20:129 (1962);

Kronasser, *Etym.* 1:480, 509; Tischler, *KZ* 86:272 (1972). Of unclear appurtenance is dat.-loc. sg. ^{LÚ}*aralahhi* (*KUB* XL 33 Vs. 16).

āra- (ratio of *a-a-ra* to the spelling *a-ra* better than 10:1) 'right, proper concern, due' (= Akk. *parṣu* in *KBo* I 1 Rs. 11), probably nom.-acc. pl. neut. *āra*, e.g. *KUB* XXIX 1 I 4 ^DUTU-*un* ^D]IM-*ann-a āra ier* 'they did right by the sun-god and the storm-god' (cf. B. Schwartz, *Orientalia* N.S. 16:24 [1947]); XXX 24 I 1 *āra iyan harak* 'have (it) duly made' (cf. Otten, *Totenrituale* 60, 86); *KBo* V 3 III 64 *āra ēskanzi* 'they shall duly treat (her as ...)' (cf. Friedrich, *Staatsverträge* 2:128); *KUB* XXX 27 Rs. 2 *nu-war-a]t-si āra ēsdu* 'let it be his due' (cf. Otten, *Totenrituale* 98); XXXI 106, 4 *n-at-mu ara ēsdu* 'be it my due' (cf. Laroche, *RA* 47:71 [1953]); XXXIX 9 Vs. 12 *ara kīsa* 'it will be right' (cf. Otten, *Totenrituale* 54); *KBo* V 3 II 8 *nu-smas-at le āra ienzi* 'they shall not make it right for you' (cf. Friedrich, *Staatsver-träge* 2:114); *KUB* XIV 3 II 8 *ēshar* INA KUR ^{URU}KÙ.BABBAR-*ti āra* 'is bloodshed in Hatti-land right?' (cf. Sommer, *AU* 6); XIII 7 I 10 *n-as* ANA ^DUTU-*ŠI āra ēsdu* 'he shall be under the jurisdiction of my majesty'; ibid. 24 *natta-at-si āra* 'this (is) no concern for him'.

Most often, however, ŪL *āra* (= *natta āra*) is a set term like Lat. *nefas* ('abomination', = Sum. NÍG.GIG 'tabu' in *KBo* I 42 IV 7; cf. *MSL* 13:140 [1971]), used predicatively without copula to mean 'it is not right, it is forbidden' (e.g. *KUB* XXX 10 Vs. 13 *adanna natta ara* 'is not right to eat'). For a list of the interdictions and their loci see Laroche, *Hommages à Georges Dumézil* 127–8 (1960). Typically, in the Hukkanas treaty (cf. Friedrich, *Staatsverträge* 2:124–8), *KBo* V 3 III 34 (cf. 60) ^{URU}*Hattusi-ma-at* ŪL *āra* 'at Hattusas it is illegal' (as opposed to Hayasa), showing the national, social-group character of the term *āra*.

A ^D*Āras* is attested in *KUB* XVII 20 II 7 (cf. Ehelolf, *KlF* 143; Bossert, *MIO* 4:202–3 [1956]), also ^D*Arās* in *KBo* III 30 Vs. 4, dat. ANA ^D*Āra* in *KUB* XXX 27 Vs. 14, ^D*Āra* in *Bo* 2432, 11 (cf. Otten, *Totenrituale* 98–9). In the god-list *KUB* XVII 20 II ^D*Āras* occurs next to the Hurrian ^D*Hinkallus* 'Abundance' and ^D*Kelti* 'Well-being' and is probably also a deified abstract.

118

arawa- 'free (from)' (*ELLUM*), nom. sg. c. *arawas, arauas, arauwas* (*Code* 1:56), nom.-acc. sg. neut. *arauwan* (*KUB* XXIII 68 + *ABoT* 58 Rs. 9–10 *nepi]s arauwan* ... *[t]ēkan arauwan* 'heaven free ... earth free'), *arāuwan* (*Code* 1:51), nom. pl. c. *arawēs* (*Code* 1:51; also e.g. *KUB* XIII 8 Vs. 6 and 11; cf. Otten, *Totenrituale* 106), *arāwēs* (*Code* 1:51). Construed with infinitive, e.g. *Code* 1:56 GIŠSAR.GEŠTIN *tuhsūwanzi* ... *ŪL kuiski arauwas* 'from harvesting a vineyard none is exempt'; XXXI 57 I 14–15 *terippūwanzi* ... *huganna arauwas* NU.GÁL 'free from plowing ... and sacrificing there is none'. Cf. Ose, *Supinum* 49–50; Kammenhuber, *MIO* 2:55 (1954); Haas, *Nerik* 114.

arawahh- 'make free', 3 sg. pres. act. *arauwahhi* (*KBo* VI 4 IV 13), *arawahhi* (ibid. 30; cf. Friedrich, *Heth. Ges.* 56–8; Imparati, *Leggi ittite* 110–2), 3 pl. pres. act. *a-ra-u-ah-ha-an-zi* (XIII 72 Vs. 9), 1 sg. pret. act. *arawahhun* (e.g. *KUB* XXVI 58 Vs. 12), *arauwahhun* (e.g. *KBo* VI 28 Rs. 22; cf. Imparati, *SMEA* 18:40 [1977]; *KUB* XL 2 Rs. 12; cf. Goetze, *Kizzuwatna* 64 [1940]), 3 pl. pret. act. *arawahhir* (*KBo* IV 2 III 21); partic. *arawahhant-*. Construed with ablative, e.g. VI 28 Rs. 27 *dapiza-kan arauw[ah-]hun n-at arawēs as[and]u* 'from all I freed (them) and they shall be free'; X 2 III 18–19 *n-as-kan sahhanit luzzit arawahhun* 'I freed them from socage (and) corvée' (cf. Imparati, *Studi classici e orientali* 14:52 [1965]); VI 29 III 25 *dapia]ndaza arawa[hh]an ēsdu* '(it) shall be freed from all'; *KUB* XXVI 43 Rs. 13 *n-at-kan dapiza arawahhan* 'it (is) freed from all' (cf. Imparati, *RHA* 32:34 [1974]). Cf. Götze, *Neue Bruchstücke* 50, 54–5.

arawes- 'become free', 3 sg. pret. act. *arawesta* (*KUB* XXIV 3 II 42), 3 pl. pret. act. *arāwēssir* (XXIV 4 Vs. 28). Cf. Gurney, *Hittite Prayers* 30.

arawanni- 'free' (as opposed to unfree), nom. sg. c. *arauwanis* (*KBo* I 45 Vs. 4, matching Akk. *ellum*; cf. *MSL* 3:59 [1955]), *arawannes, arauwanes* (*Code* 2:1), acc. sg. c. (SAL)*arauwannin* (*Code* 2:94, 95), gen. sg. *arawan(n)ias* (*Code* 2:94 varia lectio), acc. pl. c. *arauwannius* (*Code* 2:91 *takku* LÚ*ELLUM arauwannius* ... *wenzi* 'if a free man rapes free women').

Cf. Cappadocian personal names *Arawa, Arawahsu* (Laroche, *Noms* 37, 330). LÚ.MEŠ *Araunna* (*KBo* IX 91 Vs. 3, 8, 13, 17, 20) may refer to inhabitants of a town such as URU*Arawanna* (I 1 Vs.

11 and 20) or ^{URU}*Arauwanna* (*KUB* XXIV 3 II 40; cf. Gurney, *Hittite Prayers* 28) or ^{URU}*Arawunn*[*a* (*KBo* VI 28 Vs. 10; cf. Goetze, *Kizzuwatna* 21 [1940]); cf. LÚ.MEŠ ^{URU}*Arawunna* (*KUB* XXVI 69 VI 6 and 9; cf. Werner, *Gerichtsprotokolle* 44–7, 72). Cf. also ᾿Αρύηνις, daughter of Lydian Alyattes (Herodotus 1.74).

Lycian from Xanthos trilingual: *Lyc.* 27 *arã* 'as a due'; *Lyc.* 12 *seipiyẽtẽ arawã ehbiyẽ esiti* 'and they have given him free what is his' = Gk. 11–12 καὶ ἔδοσαν αὐτῶι ἀτέλειαν τῶν ὄντων 'and they have given him tax-exemption on his possessions'; *Lyc.* 21 *arawa* 'free' matching *Gk.* 19 ἀπελεύθεροι 'freedmen'; *Lyc.* 6 *arus* (from **ara-nt-*?) = Aramaic 6 *b'ly* 'citizens' (cf. Laroche, *CRAI* 1974, 117, 123, *Fouilles de Xanthos* 6:58–9, 62–3, 66, 69, 72, 103, 117–8 [1979]; Heubeck, *Incontri linguistici* 2:85–7 [1975]; Meriggi, ibid. 4:43–4 [1978], cf. 89–98, 235–9; Carruba, *SMEA* 18:276, 285–7, 296 [1977]). Cf. also Steph. Byz. s.v. ᾿Ερευάτης: ἀπὸ ᾿Ερεύας τῆς καὶ ᾿Ελευθέρας, first adduced by Friedrich (*Revue des études indo-européennes* 1:181–3 [1938]; cf. Pedersen, *Lyk. u. Hitt.* 32–3), where ᾿Ελευθέρα is a name of an Anatolian goddess and Ερευα- shows secondary Lycian vocalism (cf. Puhvel, *AIED* 240). There is also a man's name Αραουις (Phrygia; cf. *Monumenta Asiae Minoris Antiqua* 7:11 [1956]).

The most immediate extra-Anatolian cognate (adduced since Hrozný, *MDOG* 56:28 [1915], *SH* 19, 41) is Indo-Iranian **ára-* 'fitting, right, proper', seen in RV *arámati-* 'right thought, devotion', Gathic *ārmati-* (< **aramati-*) 'id.'; RV *evára-* 'truly fitting, just right'; adverbial Vedic *áram*, Avestan *arəm* 'fittingly, enough'. The root is probably **ar-* 'fit, arrange' (*IEW* 55–61), seen also with an ancient socio-religious connotation in Vedic *r̥tá-* 'right, proper', *r̥tám* 'divine order', Avestan *arəta-*, *aša-* 'right, truth, order'; Vedic *ari-* 'righteous, loyal, devout' (distinct from the homophone *ari-* 'stranger, foe'), *aryá-* 'id.', *árya-* 'belonging to the right (one's own) community, Aryan', Avestan *airyō*, OP *ariya-* 'id.'; Vedic neut. *aryamán-* 'propriety, aryanhood' (masc. as deity), also (in partial conflation with the homophone and its possible derivatives?) 'courtesy, hospitality' (masc. 'best friend, best man'), similarly Gathic *airyaman-*

120

'friendship, hospitality', Avestan 'friend, guest' (also deity), Gaulish *Ariomanus*, OIr. *Eremon* besides *aire* 'free, noble' (cf. Puhvel, in *Études mithriaques* 336–41 [1978] = *Analecta Indoeuropaea* 323–8 [1981]).

$^{(1.\acute{c}.)}$*ara-* matches Indo-Iranian **ára-* (IE **áro-*), while the apparent long grade of **āra* is not directly equatable with the derivationally induced *vṛddhi* of Vedic *árya-* (no IE **āri-* can be postulated, even if *āra* should be nom.-acc. pl. neut. of a Hitt. **āri-*). Most probably Hitt. *āra* reflects IE **āró-*, derived from **áro-* in the manner of e.g. **swēḱurós* (OHG *suāgur*) from **swéḱuros* (OHG *suehur*, Skt. *śváśura-*). *arawa-* has a suffix **-wo-* (cf. e.g. Gk. ἴλα[ϝ]ος) and a meaning 'free' < 'properly belonging' analogous to that of IE **lewdh-ero-* 'free' (lit. 'popul-aris'), OCS *svoboda* 'freedom' (cf. RV *svayam-bhū-*), or Goth. *freis* 'free' (cf. RV *priyá-* 'dear', a meaning taken also by *nítya-*, lit. 'insider', Goth. *niþjis* 'kinsman'). Cf. Laroche, *Hommages à Georges Dumézil* 124–8; Benveniste, *Hittite* 108–10; Gusmani, *Lessico* 51–2.

Kronasser's connection of *ara-* with Toch. *ārt-* 'to love' and Gk. ἔρως 'love' (*Studies presented to Joshua Whatmough* 128 [1957]) lacks conviction, despite advocacy by J. Tischler (*KZ* 86:272 [1972]). No better is J. Knobloch's adduction of Gk. ὄμ-ηρος 'hostage' (*Kratylos* 4:33 [1959]). O. Szemerényi (*Acta Iranica* 16:144–8, 115–6 [1977]) connected *ara-* and I.-Ir. **arya-* with Ugar. ʾary 'kinsman', Egypt. ʾiry 'companion', while deriving *arawa-* from IE **n̥-rə-wo* 'not giving' (cf. Myc. *e-re-u-te-ra* : Hitt. **arawatar* 'freedom of impost').

Goetze's argument (*JAOS* 74:187 [1954], *JCS* 22:17–8 [1968]) that *a-a-ra* should be normalized as *ayara-* (suggesting for etymological comparison *iya-* 'do', Luw. *aya-* 'do', and even Gk. ἱερός < **hiyaros* [?]) is based on assyriological convention and hardly binding for Hittite practice.

The comparison of *arawa-* with Lith. *arvas* 'free', proposed by Neumann (*GGA* 209:179 [1955]) and accepted by Kammenhuber (*KZ* 77:52 [1961]), cannot be upheld, since *árvas* belongs with *árdvas* 'wide, roomy' and *ardýti* 'separate, set free' (cf. Laroche, *Hommages à Georges Dumézil* 125; Kronasser, *Die Sprache* 5:60 [1959]; Puhvel, *JAOS* 82:77 [1962]).

arra-, arri-, arru-

arra-, arri-, arru- (c.) 'arse, anus; croup, crupper (of horse)'
(^{UZU}GU.DU; cf. Güterbock, *Festschrift H. Otten* 85 [1973]), nom.
sg. *arris* (*KBo* X 37 II 24–25 *arris-[s?]met*[...] *sēhuganiyauwanza*
sakki['their [?] anus dirty with urine [and] excrement'; X 37 III
48–49 *ais-[s?]mit* ... *arriss-a sēhuganiyauwanza* 'their [?] mouth
... and anus dirty with urine'; cf. Goetze, *JCS* 16:30 [1962]),
arrus (*KUB* XXXI 71 III 33–34 *nu-wa* 1 ANŠU.KUR.RA *arrus-kan*
EGIR-*anda harkis* 'one horse [with] white croup in the rear'), acc.
sg. *arran* (VII 1 III 25 ^{UZU}*arran*; ibid. 7 and 18 ^{UZU}*arrassan*
[< *arran-san*]; cf. Laroche, *RHA* 23:171 [1965]; with duplicates
KBo XXII 145 + 128 III 4 ^{UZU}GU.DU-*an* and *KUB* XLIII 52 III 11
^{UZU}GU.D[U respectively; cf. H. Otten – C. Rüster, *ZA* 67:58–9
[1977]), gen. sg. *arras* (XXXV 148 III 25 *arras-sas inan* 'illness of
his anus'), dat.-loc. sg. in VII 1 I 32 *arri-ssi-ya-ssi-kan anda lāhui*
'and he pours into his anus' (cf. Kronasser, *Die Sprache* 7:158,
143 [1961]), abl. sg. *arraz* (*KBo* XXIV 63 + XXIII 43 II 11), *ārraz*
(dupl. *KUB* XLV 26 II 6–7 *n-asta* EN SISKUR ^{DUG}*palhi ārraz anda*
paizzi parā-ma-as-kan pūriyaz [with gloss-wedge] [*uizzi*] 'the
sacrificer goes inside the cauldron [leading] with his arse, but he
comes forth with his lip'; cf. H. Otten – C. Rüster, *ZA* 68:277
[1978]; Puhvel, *Bi. Or.* 36:58 [1979], *JAOS* 102:178 [1982]), acc.
pl. *arrus* (*KBo* VIII 50 I 11; cf. Kammenhuber, *Hippologia* 154).

Connected since Friedrich (*IF* 41:374–6 [1923], *ZA* 35:21
[1924]) with OHG *ars*, Gk. ὄρρος (< *orsos*) 'arse' (*IEW* 340).
Because -*rs*- persists in Hittite (cf. e.g. *ars-, pappars-, wars-*),
arra- is difficult to derive from *orso-* (unless one assumes
"dialectal phonetics"; cf. e.g. Sturtevant, *Lg.* 11:39–40 [1935];
Kronasser, *VLFH* 221). Perhaps original root noun *ars-*, with
epenthetic nominative *arr(a)s* or *arr(i)s* or *arr(u)s*, and
innovational *a*-stem paradigm *arran, arri, arrus* (cf. Neumann,
KZ 77:79–81 [1961], but also *Untersuch.* 86). Čop (*Ling.*
8:51–2 [1966–8]) suggested that -*rr*- is the regular outcome of
IE *-rs-, vs. (-)ars- < *(-)r̥s-* (cf. *arsana-*).

O. Szemerényi (*Gnomon* 43:657 [1971]) suggested a Hittite
arr(a)ha/i- as the loan source of Gk. ἀρχός 'anus'; for the
latter, see also V. Pisani, *Scritti in onore di G. Bonfante* 713
(1976).

Cf. *arrusa; zasgarais* (s.v. *sakkar*).

122

arai-, ariya- '(a)rise, lift; raise, (a)rouse; pull (horses), rein in, hold in check, inhibit' (cf. Gk. ἀνέχω with the same range of meanings; GUB; Akk. *tebū*), 1 sg. pres. act. *arihhi* (*KBo* XII 103 Vs. 9 *nu-za karū ariwar hūdāk arihhi* 'at daybreak I rise promptly'), 3 sg. pres. act. *arai* (e.g. *KUB* VII 53 II 21 *mahhan-ma zinnai n-as arai* 'when she finishes, she rises'; cf. Goetze, *Tunnawi* 12; VIII 16 + 24 III 12 *asiwanza arai* 'the poor will rise'; cf. M. Leibovici, *Syria* 33:143 [1956]; *IBoT* III 122, 3 and HT 7 Reverse 3 'rouses [anger]'), *arāi* (e.g. *KUB* XXXI 66 IV 4 TUKU.TUKU-*an arāi* 'rouses anger'; cf. Houwink Ten Cate, *Anatol. Stud. Güterbock* 131; *KBo* XIII 13 Rs. 7 LU]GAL-*us* LÚKÚR-*ni arāi* 'the king will rise in hostility'; cf. Riemschneider, *Geburtsomina* 62, 41–2; V 4 II 21–22 *mān tuk-ma kuiski* ... [LÚKÚR] *arāi* 'if some enemy rises against you'; cf. Friedrich, *Staatsverträge* 1:64; *KUB* XXI 1 I 75 *mān-ta* LÚKÚR-*ma kuiski arāi*; cf. Friedrich, op. cit. 2:56; cf. e.g. *KBo* I 4 II 48 [Akk.] LÚ*nakru šanū itabbi* 'another enemy rises'; cf. E. F. Weidner, *Politische Dokumente aus Kleinasien* 62 [*BoSt* 8, 1923]; I 5 II 63 [Akk.] *šumma ana* DUTU-*ši nukurtu tannu itebbi* 'if against my majesty mighty hostility arises'; cf. E. F. Weidner, *Politische Dokumente aus Kleinasien* 100; *KUB* IV 1 IV 31 LÚKÚR *arāi*; cf. ibid. 30 ZI.GA [LÚKÚR] = [Akk.] *itebbi nakru*; VIII 1 III 3 *mān* ... D*SIN-as aki* KUR-*e anda* BURU₆ *arāi* 'if the moon is eclipsed, a locust-swarm will arise in the land'; ibid. II 17 *m]asas parāi* 'a locust-swarm will blow in', perhaps resulting from Akk. *itebbi* being misunderstood as if from *edēpu* 'blow'; cf. Neu, *Anitta-Text* 89; Riemschneider, *KZ* 90:149 [1976]; hardly 'is forthcoming' from *parā*, like *appai-* 'be finished' [q.v.] from *appa* [Oettinger, *Stammbildung* 472]), *araizzi* (e.g. *KBo* VI 26 II 14 [= *Code* 2:73] *takku* ÌR-*as ishi-ssi araizzi* 'if a slave rises up against his master'; *KBo* VI 1 = *KUB* VIII 53, 13–14 *nu* ANA D*Huwawa* IM[.MEŠ-*us*] GAL.MEŠ-*is araizzi* 'against H. [he] raises big winds', besides ibid. 16 8 IM.MEŠ-*as-si arāir* 'eight winds rose against him'; cf. Otten, *Istanbuler Mitteilungen* 8:116 [1958]; Laroche, *RHA* 26:14–5 [1968]), *arayizzi* (*KUB* VIII 81 III 17 *n-]an le arayizzi* 'he shall not restrain him'), *arāizzi* (e.g. *KUB* XXXI 101 Vs. 14 '[the bird] lifts off'; c.f. Ünal, *RHA* 31:49 [1973]; A. Archi, *SMEA* 16:137 [1975]; *KBo* X 27 V 14 'rises';

KUB XVII 10 IV 5 *n-an* LÚ ᴰIM *arāizzi* 'the storm-god's man holds him in check'; cf. Laroche, *RHA* 23:96 [1965]), GUB-*zi* (XI 18 II 17 LUGAL-*us* GUB-*zi* 'the king rises'), 3 sg. pres. midd. *aritta* (XVII 28 II 1–2 *mān-za* SAL-*za h[āsi] nu ēshar-set aritta* 'when a woman gives birth and her blood rises [=hemorrhages?]), 2 pl. pres. act. *aratteni* (VI 15 II 2 'you rise'; cf. Lebrun, *Samuha* 190), 3 pl. pres. act. *ariyanzi* (e.g. II 3 II 28–30 *lūliyaz ariyanzi sawatarr-a 3-šu pariyanzi* '[they] rise from the vat and blow the horn[s] three times'; ibid. I 44), *arānzi* (e.g. XXIX 50 I 22, 25 and IV 11 'they rein in [racehorses]'; cf. Gk. ἀνέχειν ἵππους; Kammenhuber, *Hippologia* 210–2; *KBo* V 6 II 20 *n-an-kan ser arānzi* 'they overpower him'; cf. Güterbock, *Kumarbi* 77, *JCS* 10:93 [1956]), 1 sg. pret. act. *aranun* (*KUB* XXIII 87, 27), 3 sg. pret. act. *arais* (e.g. *KBo* III 22 Vs. 11–12 [OHitt.] *utnē [kuit k]uit-pat arais* 'whatever land made an uprising'; cf. Neu, *Anitta-Text* 10, 63, 89–90; *KUB* XXIV 8 I 38 *arais-apa* ᴵ*Appus* ᴳᴵˢNÁ-*az* 'A. rose from bed'; cf. Siegelová, *Appu-Hedammu* 6; XVIII 5 II 8 *n-as-kan arha arais* '[the bird] lifted off'; cf. Ünal, *RHA* 31:46 [1973]; A. Archi, *SMEA* 16:128, 160 [1975]), *arāis* (e.g. *KBo* III 34 II 18 ᴵ*Askali-ma uddār arāis* 'against A. word[s] arose', vs. dupl. III 36 Vs. 23 *arais*; *KUB* XXVI 71 I 11 *QADU* DUMU.MEŠ-*šu arāi[s* '[he] got up with his sons'; cf. Neu, *Anitta-Text* 14; XII 65 III 10 *n-as-kan sarā hūdak arāis* 'he rose up promptly'; cf. Siegelová, *Appu-Hedammu* 50; Laroche, *RHA* 26:50 [1968]; XXXIII 106 II 2 *n-as sarā hūdāk arāis*; cf. Güterbock, *JCS* 6:20 [1952]), *a-ra-i-is* (*KBo* XVIII 151 Vs. 2, 5, 8, 11, 14, Rs. 4, 13, 18 'rose, stood up'; cf. Ünal – Kammenhuber, *KZ* 88:164 [1974]; XXV 196, 3), *a-ra-a-es* (V 4 Rs. 27 ᴸᔆ]KÚR-*wa-mu kuiski arāes* 'some enemy has risen against me'; cf. Friedrich, *Staatsverträge* 1:64), GUB-*is* (e.g. II 6 I 21 and II 32; *KUB* V 22, 25 and 43), GUB-*es* (e.g. V 5 passim), *arāit* (XVII 10 II 36–III 2 'held in check [anger, rage, etc.]'; cf. Laroche, *RHA* 23:94 [1965]), 3 pl. pret. act. *arāir* (quoted above; also e.g. XXXIV 23 II 5 *kuin arāir* 'whom they held in check' [?]; cf. Güterbock, *JCS* 10:84 [1956]; XXXVI 2c III 8; cf. Laroche, *RHA* 26:34 [1968], 33:67 [1975]), *a-ra-e-ir* (*KBo* II 2 I 49), GUB-*ir* (e.g. II 6 II 40), 2 sg. imp. act. *arāi* (e.g. *KUB* XXXVI 89 Rs. 58 *arāi* ᵁᴿᵁ*Neriqas* ᴰU-*as* 'arise, storm-god of N.!'; cf. Haas, *Nerik* 156; VI 45 III 21 DINGIR.MEŠ *arāi* 'rouse the gods!'), 3 sg. imp. act. *araiddu* (*KBo* XIII 109 III 9–11 LUGAL-*i-ya* ... *papratar* ... *arha araiddu* 'the king's defilement shall lift'; *KUB* XXXIII 65 III 7 *araid*[*du*; cf. Laroche, *RHA* 23:134 [1965]), 3 pl. imp. act. *arandu* (XVII 10 IV 6–7 *uttanāntes* ᴰ*Telipinui karpin kardimiyattan sāwar* QATAMMA *arandu* 'likewise let words check T.'s wrath, anger, and fury'; cf. Laroche, *RHA* 23:96 [1965]); partic. *arant-*, nom. sg. *aranza* (e.g. *KBo* II 2 II 48 *parā* ... *aranza* 'angered', lit. 'risen forth' in the sense 'upset, provoked'; cf. Hrozný, *Heth. KB* 44; Zuntz, *Ortsadverbien* 77, 116), *arānza* (IV 14 II 66; cf. R. Stefanini, *ANLR* 20:43 [1965]), nom.-acc. sg. neut. *arān* (*KUB* XIV 16 I 21 ŪL *arān ēsta* 'had not risen'; cf. Götze, *AM* 28; *KBo* V 8 I 17 *nu-mu* MUŠEN *arān harta* 'a[n augural] bird had risen for me'; cf. Götze, *AM* 148), *aran* (dupl. *KUB* XIX 36 I 12), nom. pl. c. *ārrantes* (sic XXXIII 21 IV 22 'held in check'; cf. Laroche, *RHA* 23:122 [1965]), GUB-*antes* (XII 1 IV 10); verbal noun *arauwar* (III 105 I 6; cf. *MSL* 3:69 [1955]), gen. sg. in II 1 II 42 *arauwas* ᴰLAMA-*i* (cf. A. Archi, *SMEA* 16:95, 109 [1975]), with par. *KBo* II 38, 6 *arawas*; inf. *arauwanzi* (*KUB* XII 62 Rs. 3 HUR.SAG-*i arauwanzi paimi* 'I shall go to raise the mountain'; ibid. 4 HUR.SAG-*as-za arauwanzi memmai* 'the mountain refuses to rise'); iter. *ar(a)iski-*, 3 pl. pres. act. *araiskanzi* in XXIV 7 IV 25 '(birds) take off' (cf. Friedrich, *ZA* 49:230 [1950]), 3 sg. pres. midd. in XXII 7 Vs. 1 *k*]*ūruri*HI.A *araiskattari* 'enemies rise', *ariskattari* (ibid. 4 and 11; cf. Sommer, *HAB* 86). Cf. Kronasser, *Etym.* 1:528; Neu, *Interpretation* 12–13; Houwink Ten Cate, *Symbolae Biblicae et Mesopotamicae F.M.T. deL. Böhl dedicatae* 209–10 (1973).

Denom. (from partic. *arant-*) *arantalliya-* 'make an uprising, be insurgent', 3 pl. pres. act. *arantalliyanzi* (*KUB* XXI 1 I 63 *a*]*ntuhsatarr-a kuit arantalliya*[*nzi* 'because the population is insurgent'; cf. ibid. 64 ŠA AMA-*KA* UD-*az ari* 'the day of your death is at hand'; Friedrich, *Staatsverträge* 2:54), *arantallienzi* (VI 43, 6), *arandallienzi* (dupl. *KBo* IV 7 I 24), *arantallinzi* (dupl. *KUB* VI 41 I 25 *antuhsātar-ma-wa-nnas arantallin*[*zi* 'but the population is insurgent against us'; cf. Friedrich, *Staatsverträge* 1:108). Cf. Götze, *Madd.* 97; N. van Brock, *RHA* 20:129

(1962); Kronasser, *Etym.* 1:509; H. Eichner, *MSS* 27:43 (1970).

Here belongs perhaps *ariyala-* (n.) in *KBo* V 1 II 36, where seven ᴳᴵˢ*ariyala* of wickerwork are filled with fruit, right after fruit has been poured into seven baskets (cf. Sommer–Ehelolf, *Pāpanikri* 8*); possibly something raised, hanging baskets or the like (with deverbative suffix *-ala-* as in *appala-* 'trap', *ardala-* 'saw', thus literally 'raiser, hanger'; cf. Kronasser, *Etym.* 1:172–3); *KUB* XXXVI 104 Rs. 6 [OHitt.] has dat.-loc. sg. *ariyalli* in fragmentary context.

Luw. *ari(ya)-* 'raise' (?), 3 sg. pres. act. *aritt*[*i* (?; *KUB* XXXV 107 II 5; cf. Otten, *LTU* 97), 3 sg. pret. act. *aritta* (*KBo* VII 68 II 19 *issara aritta* 'raised his hands' [?]; cf. Otten, *LTU* 114; Meriggi, *WZKM* 53:210 [1957]), *āritta* (ibid. 20), 3 pl. pret. act. *ārinta* (?; *KUB* XXXV 107 II 8), 2 sg. imp. act. *āriya* (XXXV 89, 18 *ānda āriya*; cf. Otten, *LTU* 87; rather 'arrive'?; cf. *Dict. louv.* 31), 3 sg. imp. act. *ariyaddu* (XXXV 54 II 26; cf. Otten, *LTU* 58). Also perhaps **ariyatt-* 'elevation, mountain', acc. pl. ʜᴜʀ.sᴀɢ.ʜɪ.ᴀ-*tinza* (XXXV 107 III 12; cf. Otten, *LTU* 98), possibly reflected in the mountain name ʜᴜʀ.sᴀɢ*Ariyatti-* (XXVI 43 Vs. 18) and town ᵁᴿᵁ*Ariyattassa-* (ibid. 48; cf. Imparati, *RHA* 32:26, 28 [1974]); cf. Neumann, *Die Sprache* 16:60 (1970); Starke, *KZ* 93:253 (1979).

Forms of *arai-* may coincide with homophones from other verbs (e.g. 3 pl. pres. act. *arānzi* with *ar-*, *er-*; partic. *arant-* with *ar-* and *ar-*, *er-*, and possibly *ariya-*; iter. *ar*[*a*]*iski-* with *ariya-* [q.v.]). Within the verb *arai-* the *-mi* conjugation form 3 sg. pret. act. *arāit* has the meaning 'held in check', the *-hi* conjugation 3 sg. pret. act. *arāis* means 'rose', the 3 sg. pres. act. *arāi* signifies either 'rise' or 'raise, rouse', and the *-mi* conjugation 3 sg. pres. act. *araizzi* covers the range 'rises, raises, holds in check'. Since the meaning 'hold in check' probably originates in a hippological 'pull, rein in', the *-mi* conjugation presupposes a transitive proto-meaning 'raise'. The same transitive meaning may also underlie the sense of 'rise' (for the intransitivization of Hittite verbs of motion see e.g. Houwink Ten Cate, *Symbolae Biblicae et Mesopotamicae F. M. T. deL. Böhl dedicatae* 208 [1973]; cf. e.g. Engl. *drive*, or *lay* which is replacing *lie* in substandard American); but *arāis* 'rose' vs. *arāit* 'held in check' suggest rather that the *-hi* conjugation forms are in origin intransitive (cf. also Pedersen, *Hitt.* 122); secondary developments are exemplified by *araizzi* ('raises' > 'pulls [horses]' > 'holds in check' on the one hand, and 'raises' = 'rises' on the other, based on the identity of forms such as the 2 sg. imp. act. *arāi*).

arihhi, arāi, ariyanzi reflect *$*Ę_1róy(H_2)-A_1ey$*, *$*Ę_1róy(H_2)-e$*, *$*Ę_1ri(H_2)-$*', intransitive perfect from *$*E_1r-éy(-H_2)-$* (*IEW* 330) seen in Gk. *ὀρῑ́νω* 'stir', Arm. imp. *ari* 'stand up!', aor. *y-areay* 'I stood up' (cf. Gusmani, *Lessico* 48; J. H. Jasanoff, *Annual of Armenian linguistics* 2:15–20 [1981]). *araizzi* : *arānzi* may be the corresponding causative *$*Ęroy(H_2)éyeti$* (> *$*aray-eyeti$* > *$*arayiyiti$* > *araizzi*): *$*Ęroy(H_2)éyonti$* (> *$*arayiyanti$* > *$*arayanti$* > *arānzi*). Cf. Puhvel, *JAOS* 102:178 (1982).

Cf. *ar-*; *ar-*, *er-*; *arnu-*; *arriya-*; *aru-*; *aruna-*; *ar(u)wai-*.

aramni-   (c.), metal bird-image, perhaps 'falcon, hawk' (vel sim.), nom. sg. *aramnis* (*KUB* XXXIX 14 III 8 ŠA ZABAR *aramnis* 'bronze falcon'; cf. Otten, *Totenrituale* 80; *Alalah* 454 II 15 ⟨a⟩*ramnis*), nom. pl. *aramnies* (*Bo* 7081, 6]*aramnies* ŠA SI KÙ.B[ABBAR 'falcons of horn, silver'; cf. Otten, *Totenrituale* 81; *KUB* XXXIX 45 Vs. 16 5 *aramnie*[*s*; cf. Otten, *Die Welt des Orients* 2:478 [1959]), acc. pl. *aramnius* (XII 1 III 22 4 *aramnius* GUŠKIN NA$_4$ AN.BAR GE$_6$ 'four falcons of gold, stone, black [= meteoric] iron'), *aramnias* (XXXIX 14 III 6 SI.HI.A ŠA KÙ.BABBAR *aramniyass-a* 'horns of silver and falcons').

aramnant- (c.), the same bird in ornithomantic function, nom. sg. *aramnanza* (e.g. *KUB* V 22 I 42; V 24 II 39; XVIII 12 Vs. 10; XVIII 15 Vs. 10 and 21; XVIII 57 II 71; XXII 65 II 42 and III 23; *KBo* XXIV 134 Vs. 18; also *KUB* V 11 I 63 and probably XXII 45 Vs. 12; cf. Otten, *ZA* 66:100 [1976]), *aramnānza* (XVIII 5 III 8), *aramnaza* (V 25 III 4; XVI 52, 26; XVI 66, 26; XVIII 9 II 9 and III 19; XVIII 12 I 10; cf. Ünal, *RHA* 31:43 [1973]), *arammananza* (XVI 54 Rs. 9), acc. sg. *aramnantan* (XVI 46 IV 6 and 18; XVI 79, 24), *aramnandan* (XLIX 30 Rs. 20), *aramnatan* (V 19, 5), acc. pl. *aramnandus* (XVI 43 Vs. 8 and 14; XVI 46 I 16; XVI 52, 15). Cf. Ertem,

Fauna 207–9. For the tendency of augural bird names to have no ^{MUŠEN} determinative see s.v. *alila-*.

Laroche (*Bi. Or.* 18:83 [1961]) suggested that the Hier. *ar(a)* sign depicting a falcon-type bird of prey (see Laroche, *HH* 79–80) may be acrophonic from *aramni-*.

aramni- may be related to Gk. μέρμνος, μέρμνης 'falcon, hawk', seen also in the ornithonymous name of the Lydian Mermnad dynasty (see Neumann, *Untersuch.* 70). Perhaps *aramni-* reflects a dialectal variant *(m̥)ramn-* (vel sim.) beside *mermn-* (cf. ⟨*a*⟩*ramnis* at Alalah, above).

Tischler's adduction of *ariya-* 'consult an oracle' (*KZ* 86:272 [1972]) is improbable.

arasa-, arasi-, asari- (?) (c.) 'door' (^{GIŠ}IG), nom. sg. ^{GIŠ}*arasas* (*KUB* VII 13 Vs. 21, followed ibid. by ^{GIŠ}*kattaluzi* 'threshold'), dat.-loc. pl. *arasas* or *arasiyas* (*KBo* II 2 IV 20–21 1 [UDU] *A*[*N*]*A* ^{D}EREŠ.KI.GAL ^{GIŠ}*arasass-a hante*[*zzias*] [EGIR-*i*]*zziass-a* 'one sheep to E. and to the doors, the front ones and the rear ones'; cf. Schuster, *Bilinguen* 76; *KUB* XXXVI 15 Rs. 9 ^{GIŠ}*arasas-ma--wa-si* 5-*anki hi*[*nkueni* 'and [again] at his doors let us bow five times'; dupl. XXXIII 106 II 22]^{D}*É-A-as* ^{GIŠ}*arasiyas* 5-*anki hinkueni* '[and again] at Ea's doors let us bow five times'; cf. ibid. 21 ^{D}*É-A-as* ^{GIŠ}IG-*as* 'at Ea's doors'; ibid. 31 EGIR-*izzias* [?] ^{GIŠ}*ara*]*sas-ma-as* 5-*šu hinikta* 'and at the back doors five times he bowed'; cf. ibid. 30 *hantezzi*[*yas* ^{GIŠ}IG-*as* 'at the front doors'; cf. Güterbock, *JCS* 6:40, 59 [1952]).

KBo II 2 IV 20–21 (above), properly emended, makes it likely that *arasa-* means 'door' pure and simple, and analogous emendation of the passages from the Song of Ullikummi confirms the equation ^{GIŠ}*arasa-* = ^{GIŠ}IG; thus *arasa-* alone does not mean 'inner door' (vel sim.), but *hantezzis arasas* and *appizzis arasas* are 'front door' and 'back door' respectively.

Most probably *arasa-, arasi-* is a borrowing from Hurr. *asar* 'gate, door' (vs. Hitt. *aska-* 'gate'), with a metathesis reminiscent of e.g. Hitt. *apisi-* (q.v.) < (Hurroid) Akk. *ašipi-*. It is possible that the dat.-loc. sg. of the non-metathetic form ^{GIŠ}*asari-* is found in *KUB* VII 2 I 8 *andurza* ZAG-*ni* ^{GIŠ}*asari* 'inside at the right of the door' and ibid. 16–17 *n-as* KÁ-*as andurza* [GÙB]-*li* ᴳᴵˢ*asari tianzi* 'they place them inside the gate at the left of the door'; this points up the difference between a (stone) gate (KÁ) and a (wooden) door (ᴳᴵˢIG); similarly XLI 3 Vs. 22, and acc. pl. ᴳᴵˢ*asarius* (XLIII 49, 28). Cf. the similar metathetic fluctuation found once in *asara-, esara-* (s.v.), and Puhvel, *JAOS* 102:178 (1982).

arha-, irha- (c.) 'line, rim, limit, boundary, confine(s)' (ZAG; e.g. *KUB* XVII 29 II 7 *irhass-a* KASKAL-*ass-a* besides ibid. 8 ZAG-*an* KASKAL-*ann-a*), nom. sg. *irhas* (e.g. XIX 37 II 45 *nu-ssan irhas miyanas* NU.GÁL *ē*[*sta* 'there was no limit to the increase'), *irhās* (e.g. ibid. 33 *nu* MULÚ *irhās* 'the elevation [is] the boundary'; cf. Götze, *AM* 170), acc. sg. *arhan* (XXVI 71 IV 14 [OHitt.] LUGAL-*us arunan arhan* IṢBAT 'the king took the sea as his frontier'; cf. Puhvel, *Studies presented to Joshua What-mough* 226 [1957] = *Analecta Indoeuropaea* 28 [1981]; von Schu-ler, *Die Kaškäer* 185; XXIX 30 III 10 [= *Code* 2:68, OHitt.] *arhann-a kuis parsiya* 'he that breaks the boundary', vs. dupl. *KBo* VI 26 I 48 ZAG-*ann-a kuis parsiya*), *irhan* (*KUB* XI 23 VI 8–11 *nu kizza arunas irhan wemiskiddu kizz-iya arunas irhan wemiskiddu* 'on one side let him find the boundary of the sea, and on the other let him find the boundary of the sea'), dat.-loc. sg. *arhi* (*KBo* VI 2 I 7 = VI 3 I 14–15 [= *Code* 1:6] *kuel-as arhi aki* 'within whose confine he dies'; XVI 49 I 9 *lūlias arhi* 'on the edge of the pond'; *KUB* XXXIII 88 Rs. 13 *arunas arh*[*i* 'on the seashore'; cf. Siegelová, *Appu-Hedammu* 54; *KBo* XXV 117 Rs. 9 -]*as arhi*; cf. Neu, *Altheth.* 199), *irhi* (*VBoT* 133 Vs. 9 K]UR-*eas irhi parā arānzi* 'they come to the country's boundary'; *KUB* XV 34 III 32–33 *n-at-san* TÚL.MEŠ-*as irhi zikkizzi* 'he places it on the rim of the fountains'; cf. Zuntz, *ARIV* 96.2:512 [1936–7]; Haas – Wilhelm, *Riten* 198), *irhe* (XLIV 56 Rs. 7 *a-ru-ni ir-hi-es-se* 'on the seashore' [partitive apposition 'on the sea, its shore']), abl. sg. *irhaz* (*KBo* III 21 II 17), acc. pl. *irhus* (e.g. III 1 I 7, 16, 26 *n-us arunas irhus iet* 'he made them boundaries of the sea', dat.-loc. pl. *arhas* (*KUB* XXXVI 49 IV 10 [OHitt.] *arhas-san*), *irhas* (*IBoT* I 30, 7 *irhass-a*).

irḫat(t)- (c.) 'row, series, circuit', dat.-loc. sg. *irḫātti* 'in a row, seriatim, by turns' (*KUB* XXV 32 + XXVII 70 + 1628/u II 16 DINGIR.MEŠ *irḫatti akuwanzi* 'they toast the gods seriatim'), *irḫati* (ibid. II 49 and III 12; cf. A. M. Dinçol – M. Darga, *Anatolica* 3:104–6 [1969–70]), Luwoid acc. pl. (?) *irḫattanza* (XX 74 VI 9), *irḫāt[* (*IBoT* II 19, 5).

arḫai-, irḫai- 'go down the line, circulate, make the rounds; treat in succession, list, enumerate; round out, wind up, conclude, finish', 1 sg. pres. act. *irḫāmi* (*KUB* XXXII 46 Vs. 13), 3 sg. pres. act. *arḫāizzi* (*KBo* XVII 74 II 22 [OHitt.] UGULA LÚ.MEŠMUHALDIM *arḫāizzi* 'the chef de cuisine makes the rounds'; cf. Neu, *Gewitterritual* 20), *irḫaizzi* (e.g. *KUB* IX 4 II 24 *nu* 12 ᵁᶻᵁÚR.HI.A QATAMMA *irḫaizzi* 'she likewise enumerates the twelve body-parts'; cf. *Dict. louv.* 149), *irḫāizzi* (e.g. X 11 VI 9–11 *nu mahhan … ēshar sipanduwanzi irḫāizzi* 'when [he] is done with offering up the blood'; *KBo* XIX 128 III 14–15 EGIR-*anda-ma* GEŠTIN QATAMMA 9-ŠU *irḫāizzi* 'but afterwards he makes the rounds with wine likewise nine times'; cf. Otten, *Festritual* 8), *ir-ha-a-i-iz-zi* (XXI 106 Vs. 9), *ir-ha-a-e-iz-zi* (XXI 49 II 10), *irḫāzi* (*KUB* XV 34 IV 40 *zēāntit-a* QATAMMA *irḫāzi* 'with cooked food he likewise makes the rounds'; cf. Haas – Wilhelm, *Riten* 206), 3 sg. pres. midd. *irḫaitta* (VIII 4, 7), *irḫāitta* (VIII 1 III 4–5 *kuitman* ᴰSIN-*as irḫāitta* 'while the lunar month draws to a close'; cf. ibid. II 11–12 *kuitman* ᴰSIN-*as zinnattari*; XXXIV 7 r.Kol. 11), *irḫaittari* (XXXV 131 IV 2 *akuanna humanza* QATAMMA *irḫaittari* 'everyone is likewise through drinking'; XXV 37 III 16; cf. *Dict. louv.* 173), *irḫāittari* (*KBo* XXV 184 II 2), 3 pl. pres. act. *irḫanzi* (e.g. *KUB* XXIX 40 III 24 *mahhan-ma-at adanna irḫanzi* 'but when they finish eating it'; cf. Kammenhuber, *Hippologia* 182; XXXV 131 IV 6 *akuwanna irḫanzi* 'they finish drinking'), *irḫānzi* (e.g. XXIX 45 I 4 *mahhan-ma-at irḫānzi* 'but when they finish that'; cf. Kammenhuber, *Hippologia* 170; for parallel *zinna-* in other hippological texts cf. ibid. 47–8; XXVII 16 IV 24 *akuwanna-ya apūs-pat* DINGIR.MEŠ *irḫānzi* 'those gods they also finish toasting'), 3 pl. pres. midd. in XXVII 65 I 21 *akuwanna irḫand[a(ri)* 'they are finished drinking', *irḫantari* (318/v, 6), *irḫandari* (ibid. 4), 3 sg. pret. act. *irḫāit* (*KBo* VII 28, 42 [OHitt.]; cf. Friedrich,

Rivista degli studi orientali 32:219 [1957]), 3 sg. pret. midd.
irhāittat (*KUB* XXXIII 84, 16 *arha irhāittat* 'is finished'; cf.
Siegelová, *Appu-Hedammu* 60), 2 pl. imp. act. [*ir*]-*ha-at-te-en*
(*KBo* VII 28, 43); partic. *irhant-*, nom.-acc. sg. neut. *irhān* (e.g.
KUB I 17 III 45 'passed around'; *KBo* VII 28, 41 *uddār irhān*
ēstu 'let the matter be concluded'), acc. pl. c. *irhandus* (*KUB*
XXV 37 IV 15); verbal noun *irhāwar* (*IBoT* II 39 Rs. 7),
irhauwar (e.g. ibid. 9; *KUB* X 88 VI 14–15 *irhauwar ... irhāizzi*
'completes the round'; cf. Haas, *Nerik* 270), gen. sg. *irhauwas*
(e.g. XX 25 I 5); inf. *irhauwanzi* (e.g. II 8 II 21; XXV 19 VI 16),
irhāuwanzi (e.g. XI 18 II 40; XI 30 IV 6; XX 96 III 13); iter.
irh(a)iski-, 3 sg. pres. act. *irhiskizzi* (e.g. II 3 III 29–30 *kuwapit*
kuwapit LUGAL-*us irhiskizzi* 'wherever the king keeps circula-
ting'; X 48 II 6; cf. S. Košak, *Ling.* 16:61 [1976]), *irhāiskizzi*
(*KBo* XXV 84 I 5; cf. Neu, *Altheth.* 164), 3 sg. pres. midd.
irhiskitta (XXV 184 III 8). Cf. Ose, *Supinum* 26–9, 73; Kronasser, *Etym.* 1:477, 302; Neu, *Interpretation* 72–3; Kammenhuber, *SMEA* 14:145–6 (1971), *Orakelpraxis* 47–54.

arha, adverb, postposition (regularly with -*kan*), preverb 'off,
away (from), out of, on account of; off, home', e.g. *KUB* XVII
21 II 10–12 *arha-kan ... iyantat* 'away (they) went' (cf. von
Schuler, *Die Kaškäer* 154); IX 15 II 18–19 *n-as-kan* URU-*riaz*
arha hūdak paiddu 'let him go away from the city at once'; II 13
I 47–48 LUGAL-*us-kan* GIŠAB-*az arha ... sipanti* 'the king libates
out of the window'; XXV 37 I 27–28 *n-at-kan ... apiz arha*
ekuzi '(he) drinks it out of that'; *KBo* V 3 III 38–39 *apez-kan*
uddanaz arha 'on account of that matter' (cf. Friedrich, *Staats-*
verträge 2:126); *KUB* XIV 14 Rs. 18 *karūw-at arha ekir* 'they
died off long ago'; cf. Götze, *KlF* 174; *arha warnu-* 'burn down';
arha wemiya- 'find out'; *arha an(n)iya-* 'discharge, undo,
abrogate; redo, copy' (examples s.v.); *KBo* V 8 IV 2 *nu*
URU*Hattusi arha uwanun* 'I came home to Hattusas' (cf. Götze,
AM 162); *KUB* VII 54 III 27 *n-at arha uwanzi* 'they come home';
V 7 Rs. 21 *arha-ma-war-as* ŪL *uter* 'but they did not bring them
home'. *arha* often strengthens an immediately preceding adverb
or preverb (e.g. *appa*[*n*], *awan*, *katta*[*n*], *pi*[*r*]*an*, *ser*, q.v.). Cf.
Götze, *Arch. Or.* 5:17–8, 21 (1933); Zuntz, *Ortsadverbien* 12–57;
Kammenhuber, *Festschrift H. Otten* 143–4 (1973).

arhaya(n) 'separately, apart, especially, additionally', e.g. *KUB* XXIV 3 IV 7–8 *mūgauwas-ma arhayan hanti tuppi* 'but of the supplication (there is) a tablet separately apart' (cf. Gurney, *Hittite Prayers* 38); XXIX 4 III 33 *n-at arhayan katta tianzi ŪL-at ITTI* DINGIR-*LIM tianzi* 'they put it down separately, they do not place it with the god' (cf. Kronasser, *Umsiedelung* 24); XXIV 8 IV 19 *nu* DINGIR.MEŠ GIM-*an arhayan as[anzi* 'as the gods dwell apart' (cf. Siegelová, *Appu-Hedammu* 12); XXX 24 II 20 *kuinn-a arhayan 1-ŠU ekuzi* 'he toasts each one separately once' (cf. Otten, *Totenrituale* 60); *KBo* III 5 II 47–48 *mahhan--ma-as arha uwadanzi nu-smas memal ... arhaya pianzi* 'but when they bring them home, they give them extra groats' (cf. Kammenhuber, *Hippologia* 90). Cf. Friedrich, *Orientalia* N.S. 9:205–11 (1940); Gurney, *Hittite Prayers* 118–9; W. Belardi, *Ricerche linguistiche* 2:196–8 (1951).

arahza (a-ra-ah-za) 'around; on (or: to, from) the outside, away, absent, abroad' (opp. *andurza* 'inside, in the interior', q.v. for contrastive occurrences), e.g. *KUB* XLI 1 IV 11 *nu arahza kuēs esesir* 'those who sat around' (cf. Jakob-Rost, *Ritual der Malli* 50); XIV 1 Vs. 56 AHITI-ŠU *arahza handāittat* '(he) was secreted by himself' (cf. Götze, *Madd.* 14; Güterbock, *Oriens* 10:362 [1957]); *KBo* XVII 4 III 31 *arahza paiwani* 'we go outside' (cf. Otten – Souček, *Altheth. Ritual* 34); *IBoT* I 36 III 33 *nu-za arahza kuis harzi* 'who keeps to the outside' (cf. L. Jakob-Rost, *MIO* 11:194 [1966]); *KBo* XVII 74 II 48 *arahza udai* 'brings from the outside' (cf. Neu, *Gewitterritual* 22); *KUB* XIII 35 III 38 ¹*K]ukkus-ma ... arahza* 'but K. (is) absent' (cf. Werner, *Gerichtsprotokolle* 10).

arahziya (KUB VII 13 Vs. 10) and *arahzeyaz (IBoT* I 36 III 8; cf. L. Jakob-Rost, *MIO* 11:190 [1966]), *arahziyaz* (ibid. 16) probably represent *arahz(a)+ya* 'and'+*z(a)* (reflexive). Cf. *andurziya* s.v. *andurza.*

arahza(n)da '(all) around', e.g. *KBo* I 42 III 47 *arahzanta wahnumar* 'turnaround' (cf. *MSL* 13:139 [1971]); V 4 Rs. 10 LÚ.MEŠ*ELLUTIM-ya-smas kuyēs arahzanda wehanda[ri* 'the nobles who do an about-face on you' (cf. Friedrich, *Staatsverträge* 1:62); *VBoT* 2, 19–20 *nu-tta* ŠU.HI.A-*us arahzanda assuli har-kandu* 'may they in favor hold their hands around you' (cf. L.

Rost, *MIO* 4:329 [1956]); *KBo* V 3 I 23 šu.ḤI.A-*us-za arahzanda harsi* 'you hold your hands around' (cf. ibid. 25 and Friedrich, *Staatsverträge* 2:108); XXII 2 Rs. 10 ᵁᴿᵁ*Zalpan arahzanda wetet* '(he) built around (= blockaded) Z.' (cf. Otten, *Altheth. Erzählung* 12); *KUB* XXX 15 Vs. 10–11 *apedas ukturiyas arahzanda* 'around that cremation-spot' (cf. Otten, *Totenrituale* 66); *KBo* XI 32 Rs. 45 LUGAL-*un arahzada wahnuzi* 'makes the king turn around'.

arahza- 'alien', nom. sg. c. *arahzas* in *KBo* IV 14 II 26–27 *nasma-mu* MUD ŠA ÌR.MEŠ *anturyas arahzas* DÙ-*ri* 'or the blood of my subjects turns from native to alien' (cf. R. Stefanini, *ANLR* 20:41 [1965]).

arahziya- 'alien', nom. sg. c. *arahziyas* in *KUB* XVI 19 Vs. 9 (vs. ibid. 5 *anduryas* 'native').

arahzena-, *arahzina-* 'bordering, adjoining, surrounding; outer, external, foreign, alien' (opp. *anturiya-* 'inner, internal, domestic', q.v. s.v. *andurza* for contrastive occurrences), nom. sg. c. *arahzenas* (e.g. *KUB* VII 46 Rs. 10 *arahzenas* UKÙ-*as* 'foreigner'), acc. sg. c. *arahzinan* (*IBoT* I 36 III 35 *arahzinan-ma kuinki* ERÍN.MEŠ-*an* 'some foreign legion'; cf. L. Jakob-Rost, *MIO* 11:194 [1966]), *arahzenun* (sic! *KUB* XXI 38 Vs. 49 *nu-za arahzenun* ŠA LUGAL.GAL DUMU.SAL AŠŠUM SAL.É.GI₄.A *dahhun* 'I have taken the foreign daughter of a great king as my daughter-in-law'; cf. R. Stefanini, *Atti La Colombaria* 29:12 [1964]), nom.-acc. sg. neut. *arahzenan* (*Bo* 2489 + 4008 II 6; cf. Ehelolf, *ZA* 43:175 [1936]; Starke, *ZA* 69:81 [1979]; A. Archi, *Studia mediterranea P. Meriggi dicata* 48 [1979]), *arahzinan* (*KBo* VI 26 III 7 [= *Code* 2:83] *takku* A.ŠÀ] *arahzinan-si* 'if [it is] a field adjoining it'), gen. sg. c. *arahzenas* (*KUB* XXVI 1 III 33; cf. von Schuler, *Dienstanweisungen* 13), dat.-loc. sg. *arahzeni* (e.g. XXIX 7 Vs. 44 *arahzeni* KUR-*ya* 'to a foreign land'; cf. Lebrun, *Samuha* 120), *arāhzēni* (XIII 3 III 16 LUGAL-*s-at* ᴸᵁ*arāhzēni-ma uppahhi* 'I, the king, will send it to a foreigner'; cf. Friedrich, *Meissner AOS* 47), *arahzini* (*KBo* IV 10 Vs. 13 *arahzini-ya* KUR-*e* 'also in a foreign land'), *arahzena* (e.g. *KUB* XXI 42 IV 12 ANA ZAG KUR *arahzena* LUGAL-*i* 'to the frontier, to a foreign king'; cf. von Schuler, *Dienstanweisungen* 28), abl. sg. *arahzenaza* (XXIII 68 Vs. 13 *arahzenaza* KUR-*ya-z*[*a* 'from a bordering country'; cf. A. Kempinski – S. Košak, *Die Welt des Orients* 5:194 [1970]; *KBo* IV 10 Vs. 29 'externally'), nom. pl. c. *a-ra-ah-zé-ni(-e)-es* (e.g. *KUB* VIII 83, 3 *arahzenies kunanzi* 'aliens will kill'; cf. Riemschneide , *Geburtsomina* 57; XXIV 4 Rs. 7 *arah]zeniēs udnēantes* 'surrounding lands'; cf. Gurney, *Hittite Prayers* 30), *arahzenus* (e.g. XXVI 1 III 60 LUGAL.MEŠ *arahzenuss-a meqqaus* 'many surrounding kings'), *arahzenas* (e.g. *KBo* III 4 I 3–4 *arahzenas* KUR.KUR.MEŠ; similarly ibid. 9, 19, 23; cf. Götze, *AM* 14–20), acc. pl. c. *arahzenas* (III 4 I 26 *arahzenas* KUR.KUR; similarly ibid. 28–29), nom.-acc. pl. neut. in *KUB* XIV 14 I 28 *damāi arahzena* KUR.KUR.MEŠ 'other foreign lands' (cf. Götze, *KlF* 168), dat.-loc. pl. *arahzenas* (XIII 4 III 28 *arahzenas* BÀD-*as* 'at the outer walls', vs. ibid. 29 *andurza* 'inside'; cf. Sturtevant, *JAOS* 54:382 [1934]; XXIV 3 II 45 *arahzenas* ANA KUR.KUR.HI.A-*TIM*).

arahzenant- 'id.', nom. pl. c. *arahzenantes* (XXIV 3 II 49; cf. Gurney, *Hittite Prayers* 30).

Cf. Hrozný, *SH* 38–41, 182; Friedrich, *Staatsverträge* 1:167–70.

Hier. *arhi-* (questionably revised to *irhi-* by Hawkins – Morpurgo – Neumann, *HHL* 187) 'boundary', pl. 'territory' (cf. Lat. *fīnēs*; e.g. acc. pl. in Karatepe 162–163 *Atanwanai*[CITY] *arhī* 'the territory of Adana' = Phoen. *gbl ʿmq ʾadn* 'the territory of the plain of Adana'; cf. Meriggi, *Manuale* 2:80); *arha*, postposition and preverb 'outside (of), off, away'; *arhat(i)ali-* 'outer, exterior' (opp. *antatali-*); *arhit(i)ana-* 'foreign (country)' (cf. Hitt. *arahzena-*).

Lyc. preverb *eri*; *erizãna*?

Cf. Meriggi, *HHG* 30–2; Laroche, *BSL* 53.1:177–8 (1957–8), *HH* 119–20.

OHitt. has *arha-*, *arhai-*, vs. classical *irha-*, *irhai-*. Accordingly there is nothing Luwoid about the *a*-vocalism; rather the noun *arha-* and its denominative verb have undergone a secondary vowel change (weakening?) $a > i$. This change does encompass the denominative noun *irhat(t)-* (perhaps also spread to Luwian [cf. Luwoid acc. pl. *irhattanza* quoted above]; of the type *kallaratt-*, q.v. s.v. *kallar-*) but not the formations spun off from **arha-* at a PAnat. stage (witness Hier. parallels):

directional dat. *arha*, lit. 'to the limit', adverbial extension *arhaya(n)* (cf. e.g. *parā*:*pariya*[*n*]), adverbialized abl. *arahza* (: *arahzanda* like *appa* : *appanda*, *katta* : *kattanda*, *pariya* : *pariyanda*), lit. '(starting) from the limit' (cf. e.g. *āskaz* 'from the gate, outside'), and adj. *arahza-, arahziya-, arahzen(iy)a-* (cf. e.g. *alwanzena-*), lit. 'pertaining to the limit'. Cf. Laroche, *RHA* 9:21-2 (1948-9), 28:37-8 (1970); Neu, *Gewitterritual* 52; Starke, *Funktionen* 196-200.

The etymon is Lat. *ōra* 'brim, edge, boundary, coast, region; rope, cable', which allows both formal (IE $*orH_1o$- or $*rH_1o$->*arha-*, $*ōrH_1e$-A_2>*ōra*?) and semantic common denomination ('line'='limit', metonymically 'confine[s], region', and 'line'='row, rope'); the standard connection of *ōra* with *ōs* 'mouth' deserves rejection (cf. already Sturtevant, *IHL* 48). Cf. Laroche, *RPh* 42:246-7 (1968); Puhvel, *AJPh* 98:151-2 (1977). Another concomitant cognate may be Lat. *re(d)-* ($<*rE_2e$-), which was connected with *arha* by Pedersen, with reference to meanings like *re-secō* 'cut off', *re-legō* 'send away', *re-linquō* 'leave off' (cf. Hitt. *arha karas-, arha uiya-, arha dala-*), *red-eō* 'come back' (cf. *arha uwa-*), *re-probō* 'disapprove' (cf. *arha an*[*n*]*iya-* 'undo'). Cf. Götze – Pedersen, *MS* 76-7.

Superseded combinations are numerous: Gk. ἀρχή 'beginning' (Hrozný, *SH* 39, hesitantly; E. Forrer, *Die hethitische Bilderschrift* 40 [1932]); Ved. *āré* 'far', *arā́t* 'from far', Lith. *óras* 'open air', IE *ar-* 'plow' (e.g. Sturtevant, *Comp. Gr*[1] 88; A. Vaillant, *Grammaire comparée des langues slaves* 1:241-2 [1950]); Ved. *āré* 'far', *arā́t* 'from far', Lat. *ōra* 'border', separating **ar-* 'plow' (Sturtevant, *IHL* 48, 40-1); Ved. *r̥dhak* 'apart', *árdha-* 'part, region', Arm. *art* 'field', *art(a)-* 'out-' (W. Belardi, *Ricerche linguistiche* 2:187-202 [1951]).

The common source of *arha-/irha-* and *arha* has been generally affirmed since E. Forrer, *Meissner AOS* 33; cf. e.g. Götze, *Arch. Or.* 5:17 (1933). Tischler (*KZ* 86:273-4 [1972]) again separated the two, gratuitously assuming *arha-/irha-* to be non-IE (as Couvreur, *Hett.* 150-1, had done for both *irha-* and *arha*). M. L. Mayer (*Acme* 13:84 [1960]) sought affinity with the Semitic root seen in Akk. [*w*]*arhu, urhu* 'way'.

Cf. *erhui-*.

ariya-, arai- 'consult an oracle; determine by oracle', often with a preverb (*anda, arha, katta, parā, piran*), 1 sg. pres. act. *ariyami* (e.g. *KUB* XXII 25 Vs. 19–20 *parā-ma-za-kan* ᵁᴿᵁ*Nerikkaz arha ariyami* 'but about N. I shall obtain an oracle'; cf. von Schuler, *Die Kaškäer* 176; XIII 20 Vs. 23 *n-an* ... *arha ariyami* 'I will subject it [viz. the army] to oracular determination'; cf. Alp, *Belleten* 11:392 [1947]; XXII 61 I 17–18 ᴸᵁ·ᴹᴱˢAZU-*ya ariyami kuis-mu* ᴸᵁAZU SIxSÁ-*ri* 'the medicine men too I will submit to the oracle; the medicine man who is determined for me ...'; cf. Burde, *Medizinische Texte* 4), 2 sg. pres. act. *ariyasi* (*KBo* XVIII 57a Vs. 15 *arha ariyasi*), 3 sg. pres. act. *ariyazi* (e.g. V 1 I 18 *nu-za arha ariyazi* 'he consults the oracle'; cf. Sommer–Ehelolf, *Pāpanikri* 2*), *ariyezzi* (*KUB* XVII 24 II 9–10 *nu-za BELTI É-TI AŠRI.HI.A ŠA* DINGIR-LIM *IŠTU* DINGIR-*LIM arha ariyezzi* 'the house-mistress determines by oracle from the god the places of the god'), 1 pl. pres. act. *ariyaweni* (e.g. XVI 41+7/v III 9; cf. Ünal, *Hatt.* 2:112; *KBo* II 2 II 32; cf. Hrozný, *Heth. KB* 42; *KUB* XXII 70 Vs. 49; cf. Imparati, *SMEA* 18:30 [1977]; Ünal, *Orakeltext* 70), *a-ri-u-e-[ni* (XVI 40 Vs. 12), 3 pl. pres. act. *ariyanzi* (e.g. V 6 II 64 SISKUR-*ma IŠTU* DINGIR-*LIM ariyanzi* 'but shall they get an oracular fix on the sacrifice from the god?'; cf. Sommer, *AU* 282; XXIII 79 Rs. 11 *IŠTU*] DINGIR-*LIM arha ariyanzi*; cf. Laroche, *RHA* 23:176 [1965]), *arianzi* (e.g. L 92 Rs. 16), *arienzi* (II 3 III 24), 1 sg. pret. act. *ariyanun* (e.g. *KBo* IV 4 II 53–54 *kāsa-wa-tta IŠTU* MUŠEN.HI.A *IŠTU* SU.MEŠ-*ya ammuk piran ariyanun nu-wa-tta* ... *handaittat* 'behold, I gave you the oracle treatment with birds and with flesh, and it was determined for you'; cf. Götze, *AM* 118; IV 2 III 48 *nu ariyanun* 'I consulted an oracle'; ibid. 49 ᴰU ... *katta ariyanun* 'I gave the storm-god an oracular going-over'; cf. Götze–Pedersen, *MS* 4), 3 sg. pret. act. *ariyat* (e.g. XVIII 146, 3 and 11), 1 pl. pret. act. *a-ri-ya-u-en* (e.g. *KUB* XV 31 II 8 *āpiyas-ma uttar* DINGIR.MEŠ-*it kissan ariyawen* 'but the matter of the pits we thus determined by oracle from the gods'; cf. Haas – Wilhelm, *Riten* 156; L 6 III 49 and 56 GAM *ariyawen*; cf. A. Archi, *SMEA* 22:25 [1980]; *KBo* XVI 98 I 2; cf. P. Cornil – R. Lebrun, *Hethitica* 1; II 6 I 30), *ariyawēn* (II 2 II 22; *KUB* V 7 Vs. 49), 2 pl. pret. act. *a-ri-ya-at-ti-en* (XVIII 24 III 10), 3 pl.

pret. act. *ariyair* (*KBo* IV 6 Vs. 26 *nu* DINGIR.MEŠ-*az ariyair*; cf. Tischler, *Gebet* 14), *a-ri-i-e-ir* (e.g. *KUB* V 6 II 42 *n-as* GAM *ariyer* 'they consulted an oracle about them'; cf. Sommer, *AU* 280), *arier* (ibid. IV 17; XV 5 IV 23), *arir* (XXII 70 Rs. 10; cf. Ünal, *Orakeltext* 84), 2 sg. imp. act. *ariya* (*KBo* V 1 I 15–16 *arha-wa-za ariya* 'consult an oracle!'); partic. *ariyant-* (also *arant-*; see below), nom.-acc. sg. neut. *ariyan* (X 17 IV 11; *KUB* V 6 IV 10; XXX 39 Rs. 9); verbal noun *ariyauwar* (XXXIV 19 I 4; cf. Riemschneider, *Geburtsomina* 54), gen. sg. *arha ariyauwas* (XXIV 6 Rs. 10); iter. *areski-, ariski-*, 3 sg. pres. act. *ariskizzi* (e.g. IX 12 II 9 *arha ariskizzi*), 3 sg. pres. midd. *a-ri-es-kat-ta* (XLIII 60 I 25 *nu-ssi le areskatta* 'for her let no oracle be consulted'), *areskattari* (*HT* 10 I 13; *KUB* V 6 II 67), *ariskattari* (ibid. 37 *apāss-a apiya ariskattari* 'he too will there be subject to oracular determination'), 1 pl. pres. act. *a-ri-es-ga-u-e-ni* (XVIII 7 Vs. 5), 3 pl. pres. act. *areskanzi* (V 6 IV 7), *ariskanzi* (XXXI 42 III 20), 3 pl. pres. midd. *areskantari* (V 6 II 44), 1 sg. pret. act. *ariskenun* (XIV 13 I 53; cf. Götze, *KlF* 246), 3 sg. pret. act. *areskit* (XL 80, 6), *ariskit* (XIV 13 I 51; XLIX 97, 11), 3 pl. pret. act. *ariskir* (V 6 III 3 and 17). Cf. Sommer – Ehelolf, *Pāpanikri* 13; Zuntz, *Ortsadverbien* 27; Kronasser, *Etym.* 1:483–4, 301; Neu, *Interpretation* 13.

ari(ya)sessar (n.) 'oracle' (*KBo* I 42 V 15 *ariyasessar* matching MÁŠ, Akk. *bi-e-ru* 'divination'; cf. *MSL* 13:143 [1971]), nom.-acc. sg. *ariessesa* (sic; III 60 I 9 [OHitt.]), *ariyasessar* (e.g. VI 5, 6; *KUB* XXII 26, 14), *ariyasesir* (*KBo* II 6 IV 25), gen. sg. *ariyasesnas* (e.g. *KUB* XVIII 6 I 23 and IV 11; XLIX 2 I 20), dat.-loc. sg. *arisesni* (XVIII 8, 8; cf. Lebrun, *Samuha* 194), abl. sg. *ariyasesnaz* (e.g. XIV 8 Rs. 42; cf. Götze, *KlF* 218; XV 1 II 13), *ariyasesnaza* (e.g. XXXVI 87 III 12; cf. Haas, *Nerik* 190; XIV 11 IV 13; L 89 II 17; *KBo* II 2 II 45), *ariyasessanaza* (*KUB* VI 4 III 9), *ariyassisnaza* (*FHG* 13a IV 5). Rather than obscure variant for **ariyessar*, with unexplained -*s*-, perhaps *ariya-* + *asessar*, literally 'oracle-emplacement, oracular site' (cf. s.v. *asas-*; also URU-*riasessar* 'town settlement' s.v. *happir*[*iy*]*a-*, *tuzziyasessar* 'army camp' s.v. *tuzzi-*); Lat. *ōrāculum* (see below) has the same base-meaning, 'place of soliciting (the gods)'.

ariya-, arai- arriya-

The stem is normally *ariya-*; however, some forms treated under *arai-* (q.v.; e.g. 2 pl. pres. act. *aratteni*, partic. [*parā*] *arant-*; cf. Ünal, *Orakeltext* 101–2; iter. *araiskattari*) may also belong here, as might e.g. *KUB* V 1 IV 80 DINGIR.MEŠ-*za-pat arān* 'determined by oracle from the gods' (cf. Ünal, *Hatt.* 2:90); thus there is evidence of an alternative stem *arai-*. Cf. Houwink Ten Cate, *Symbolae Biblicae et Mesopotamicae F.M.T. deL. Böhl dedicatae* 209–10 (1973), who suggested that, oracles being "elicited" (or impetrated) omina, *ariya-* may be merely a semantic and formal variant of the verb *arai-* in the original sense of 'rouse' (cf. e.g. *ishai-* : *ishiya-*), as in *KBo* VI 45 III 21 DINGIR.MEŠ *arāi* 'arouse the gods!'. But since the *-hi* conjugation verb *arai-* (q.v.) is originally intransitive ('rise'), *ariya-* cannot well be a thematization of its secondary transitive sense only; if it does mean etymologically 'rouse (the gods)', perhaps *ariyazi* < IE **oréyeti* 'raise, stir' (*IEW* 327), seen medially in Gk. ὀρέοντο (e.g. *Iliad* 2:398 ἀνστάντες δ'ὀρέοντο 'they stood up and bestirred themselves').

More probably, however, *ariya-* (and its possible stem variant *arai-*) is related to Lat. *ōrō*<**ōrāyō* 'address, solicit (the gods)', *ōrāculum* (<**ōrā-tlom*) 'oracle' (lit. 'place of soliciting [the gods]'; cf. Benveniste, *RPh* 22:120–2 [1948]); further cognates are uncertain (e.g. Skt. *áryati* 'acknowledge, praise'; Russian *orát'* 'cry out'; Ionic Gk. ἀρή 'prayer'). Cf. Götze – Pedersen, *MS* 47–8; Juret, *Revue des études latines* 16:71 (1938), *Vocabulaire* 43; Čop, *Ling.* 6:72 (1964); Gusmani, *Lessico* 63; Tischler, *KZ* 86:274 (1972): Oettinger, *Stammbildung* 345; Puhvel, *JAOS* 102:179 (1982).

arriya- 'rouse, stir (from sleep), awaken; start (from sleep), be awake', verbal noun *arriyāuwar*=Akk. *talapu* (i.e. *dalāpu*) in *KBo* I 44+ XIII 1 I 41 (cf. Otten, *Vokabular* 10, 13).

One may plausibly seek a connection with the vast group of IE **er-*, **or-* 'stir' (*IEW* 326–32), represented by Hitt. *ar-*; *ar-*, *er-*; *arai-*; *arnu-*; *aru-*; *aruna-*; *ar(u)wai-*; for the meaning cf. e.g. *Iliad* 10:518–9 ὦρσεν δὲ Ἱπποκόωντα ... ὁ δ'ἐξ ὕπνου ἀνορούσας 'he roused H., ... but he, starting from sleep ...'. Since Hitt. *-rr-*

can represent *-rH_2-, a causative *$(E_1)orH_2éye$- may account
for a transitive *arriya*-; cf. the reconstruction of *araizzi* 'raises,
rouses' as *$E_1royéyeti$ (s.v. *arai*-); intransitive sense can inhere
in middle voice or result from secondary intransitivization.

O. Szemerényi (*Studia mediterranea P. Meriggi dicata* 613–6
[1979]) adduced as possible cognates Arm. *artʿown* 'watchful,
alert' and OIr. *ar*- 'be awake', *aire* 'watch, attention', *airech*
'attentive'.

arimpa- (c.), basically wooden (^{GIŠ}*arimpa*-) but sometimes (additionally?) metal stand (vel sim.) in rituals, nom. sg. ^{GIŠ}*arimpas*
(*KBo* XVII 22 III 15 [OHitt.]; cf. S. R. Bin-Nun, *RHA* 30:80
[1972]; *VBoT* 58 IV 28 ^{GIŠ}*arimpas* ZABAR 'a. of [or: with?]
bronze'; cf. Laroche, *RHA* 23:86 [1965]; *KUB* XII 43, 6), acc.
sg. ^{GIŠ}*arimpan* (*KBo* XXI 100 Rs. 13), dat.-loc. sg. ^{GIŠ}*arimpi*
(XX 33 Vs. 9 [OHitt.] LÚ ^{GIŠ}B]ANŠUR ^{NINDA}*zippulasne* ^{GIŠ}*arimpi*
hantāizzi 'the table-man arranges z.-bread on the a.'; cf. Neu,
Altheth. 53), nom. pl. ^{GIŠ}*arimpus* (*IBoT* II 129 Vs. 5), dat.-loc.
pl. (?) ^{GIŠ}*arimpa[s* (*KUB* XV 32 IV 47; cf. Haas – Wilhelm,
Riten 168).

The Old Hittite attestations belong to the Hattic orbit and
make Hattic origin probable, also contraindicating affinity
with the Hurrian-based Mesopotamian loanword ^{GIŠ}*eripi*-,
^{GIŠ}*irimpi*-, ^{GIŠ}*irippi*- 'cedar(wood)' (q.v.). ^{GIŠ}*arimpa*- is also
distinct from *arimpa*- 'burden', where the *r* is a rare hiatic glide
(cf. s.v. [*a*]*impa*-), and from the obscure *arimma*- (*KBo* XVI 65 I
9 *arimmass-a* [nom. sg.]) and *aripa*- (*KUB* XXXVI 55 II 24
aripus [acc. pl.]).

arrir(r)a-, arir(r)a-, ar(r)ara- 'scrape', 3 pl. pres. act. *arrirranzi* (e.g.
KUB VII 13 Vs. 9 *parā purut arrirranzi* 'they scrape off the
clay'), *arriranzi* (e.g. *KBo* XXIV 93 III 28), 3 pl. pres. midd.
arrirrandari (795/c III 10), 2 sg. pret. act. *arirrista* (*KUB* XXX
10 Rs. 5 'you [god] have scraped [off evil]'), 3 sg. pret. act.
arraras (XXXVI 89 Vs. 15 ^{NA₄}*pirunus-wa arraras* 'he scraped
the rocks'; cf. Haas, *Nerik* 144), 1 pl. pret. act. *arrirummen*

arrir(r)a-, arir(r)a-, ar(r)ara-   ark-

(XXXI 76 I 3 *a*]*rha arrirumme*[*n* 'we have scraped off'; cf. ibid.
4 KÙ.BABBAR *arha* ME-*wen* 'silver we have taken away'; Werner,
Gerichtsprotokolle 22), 3 pl. pret. act. *arrir*[*rir* (VII 13 Vs. 11), 3
sg. imp. act. *arrirraiddu* (314/v Rs. 2), 3 pl. imp. act. *arrirrandu*
(XIII 2 II 14–15 *n-at arha arrirrandu n-at dān* EGIR-*pa nēuit
uilanit hanissandu n-at tān* EGIR-*pa newahhandu* 'let them scrape
them clean, let them plaster them once again with new clay, let
them make them new once again'; cf. Goetze, *Tunnawi* 63–4;
von Schuler, *Dienstanweisungen* 44–5), *ārrirandu* (dupl. XXXI
87 II 15 *arha ārriran*[*du*); partic. *arrir(r)ant-, ararant-*, nom. sg.
arrirranza (XVIII 63 Vs. 18 *n-as* IŠTU KÙ.BABBAR *arha arrirranza* 'it [has been] scraped clean of silver'; XVIII 38, 7 *arha
arrirranza*; VI 29 Vs. 3; XVI 9 II 1 *arha arrirr*[*anza*), *araranza*
(*Alalah* 454 II 18–19 ᴰU-*wa araranza ēsta nu-war-an* EGIR-*pa
halissir* 'the storm-god['s image] had been scraped; they refin-
ished it [with silver]'), nom.-acc. sg. neut. *arrirran* (*KUB* V 7 Vs.
10 *nu-kan* ANA HUR.SAG KÙ.BABBAR *arha arrirran* 'from the
mountain the silver [has been] scraped off'; cf. Zuntz, *Ortsadverbien* 28; VII 13 Vs. 3 *arha arrirran*), *arriran* (XLII 39, 9 *arha
arriran*), nom. pl. c. *arrirrantes* (L 95, 3), *arrirante(m)es* (XVIII
66 III 7); inf. *arirauwanzi* (*KBo* XXIV 93 III 21). Cf. Kronasser,
Etym. 1:526.

Phonesthetic reduplicative onomatopoeia of a grating
sound. Etymological connections are largely gratuitous, e.g.
with IE **rey-* seen in Lat. *rīma* 'crack, chink' (Tischler, *KZ*
86:275 [1972]) or **reH-* extracted from Lat. *rādō* 'scrape'
(**ri-rH-o-*; A. Bernabé P., *Revista española de lingüística* 3:432
[1973]); for *rādō* see rather s.v. *ard-*. H. Eichner (*Die Sprache*
27:62–3 [1981]) saw paradigmatic *a : e* ablaut in *ar(r)ar- : arrir*
(cf. *asas- : ases-*) and tied in Lith. *ìrti* 'dissolve' (q.v. rather s.v.
harra-).

ark-   'mark off, (sub)divide, parcel, set apart, sequester', 3 sg. pres.
act. *arki* (1467/u II 4 UDU *arki*), *ārki* (*KBo* VI 3 III 69 [= *Code*
1:73] *takku* GUD *huiswandan kuiski ārki mahhan dayazilas
apāss-a* 'if anyone sequesters a live head of cattle he [is] just like
a thief'; VI 2 II 47 [= *Code* 1:47, OHitt.] A.ŠÀ.HI.A ... *ārki*

140

'divides up the fields'; similarly ibid. 41 [= *Code* 1:46]; *VBoT* 114 III 4), *ārgi* (VI 11 I 16 [= *Code* 2:9] *takku amiyaraza* ᴳᴵˢ*INBAM kuiski ārgi* 'if anyone cuts fruit-trees off from a ditch'; cf. Güterbock, *JCS* 15:70 [1961]), 3 pl. pres. act. *ar-kán-zi* (e.g. XI 45 III 24–25 *nu-kan* UDU.HI.A GUD.MAH.HI.A-*ya arkanzi nu-kan* ᵁᶻᵁNÍG.GIG ᵁᶻᵁŠÀ *sarā danzi* 'they mark off sheep and bulls and take out liver [and] heart'; cf. Haas, *Nerik* 234; *KUB* X 63 I 30 -]*kan hantezzius* GÌR.MEŠ-*us arkanzi* 'they mark off the fore feet'; cf. M. Vieyra, *RA* 51:88 [1957]; VII 1 I 9 *nu-kan* ᵁᴰᵁ*iyantan arkanzi* 'they mark off a sheep'; cf. Kronasser, *Die Sprache* 7:142 [1961]; XVII 28 III 4 UDU-*kan arkanzi*; XX 88 Rs. 8 UDU.HI.A *arkanzi*), *ārkanzi* (VIII 16 + 24 + XLIII 2 III 14; cf. M. Leibovici, *Syria* 33:143 [1956]), *arganzi* (*Bo* 2372 I 5), 3 pl. pret. act. *arkir* (*KUB* XLIII 60 III 20 and 23); partic. *arkant-*, nom. sg. c. *ar-kán-za* (*KBo* XI 45 III 26 *arkanza-ma hūmanza kittari* 'marked off, it is stored in one piece'); inf. *arkuwanzi* (XIX 142 II 20); iter. 3 sg. pres. act. *arkiskanzi* (*IBoT* II 96, 16). Cf. Kronasser, *Etym.* 1:520–1.

In *KBo* XI 17 II 16 *arkanzi* stands between *hattai* 'slits open' (ibid. 14) and *markanzi* 'cut apart' (ibid. 18); it must denote some intermediate step in the performance of animal slaughter, perhaps the tracing or marking of the body in some apportionate sense. Cf. also Goetze, *JCS* 23:89–91 (1970).

Cf. Gk. ἔρχατος · φραγμός 'fence' (Hes.), ὀρχμαί · φραγμοί (Hes.), Ἐρχομενός, Ὀρχομενός (town name), ὀρχάς 'compassing, delimiting', ὄρχατος 'garden, plantation', ὄρχος 'row of fruit-trees', pointing to IE *ergh-*, with *o*-grade in the *-hi* conjugation stem *ark-*. Cf. Puhvel, *JAOS* 95:262–4 (1975) = *Analecta Indoeuropaea* 290–2 (1981).

Alternatively cf. perhaps Lat. *(h)erctum* 'division of inheritance', *(h)ercīscō* 'divide an estate', **dis-erctiō* in *disertiones* 'divisiones patrimoniorum inter consortes' (Festus); with a legal term **erciō* '(sub)divide' cf. *sarciō* beside Hitt. *sarni(n)k-* 'make reparation' (cf. H. Eichner, *Die Sprache* 27:63 [1981], *Gedenkschrift für H. Kronasser* 21–6 [1982])).

Improbable connections with Skt. *ṛte* 'apart from, except for', Lith. *ardýti* 'separate' (J. Duchesne-Guillemin, *TPhS* 1946:88; cf. *IEW* 332–3), and Skt. *ṛkṇá-* 'wounded, chafed',

ark-

Lith. *ràkti* 'poke, rake up' (Tischler, *KZ* 86:275 [1972], *Glossar* 58; cf. *IEW* 335); for the Sanskrit and Lithuanian words see rather s.v. *harra-*. Kronasser's adduction of Gk. ἄρνυμαι 'win' (*Studies presented to Joshua Whatmough* 124 [1957]) was abortive, as was the early tie-in with Lat. *arceō* 'keep away, shut in' (Hrozný, *MDOG* 56:28 [1915], *SH* 78; Sturtevant, *Comp. Gr.*[1] 87), for which latter see s.v. *har(k)-*.

ark- 'mount, cover (in coition), couple, copulate (with)', 3 sg. pres. act. *ārki*, midd. *arga*, and 3 sg. imp. midd. *argaru* in *KBo* X 45 IV 30–32 UDU.A.LUM GIM-*an* UDU.SÍG + SAL *ārki* (var. *KUB* XLI 8 IV 30 *arga*) [*nu-za armah*]*hi kāss-a-za* URU-*as parnas* UDU.A. .LUM [DÙ-*ru nu* LÍL-*ri* GE$_6$]-*in* KI-*an argaru* 'even as the ram covers the ewe and she becomes pregnant, so too let this town (and) settlement become a ram and cover on the steppe the dark earth' (cf. Otten, *ZA* 54:138 [1961]); perhaps also 3 sg. pres. midd. *arkatta* (*KBo* XXII 2 Vs. 9 and 10; cf. e.g. *hinkatta* beside *hinga*; Otten, *Altheth. Erzählung* 6, 30); iter. 3 sg. pret. midd. *arkiskitta* (*KUB* XXIX 1 I 28–30 [address to trees] UR.MAH-*as kattan seskit* UG.TUR-*as-(s)mas kattan seskit hartaggas-ma-smas sarā arkiskitta* 'the lion would pair, the panther would pair by you, but the bear would couple up against you'); partic. acc. sg. c. in *KBo* II 12 V 9–10: 1 UDU *suppistuwaran natta arkantan* 'one (ritually, i.e. sexually) clean sheep that has not been mounted'; ibid. 13 *natta arkantes*; II 12 II 11–12 1 GUD.MAH *suppis*[*tuwaran*] *natta arkanta*[*n* 'one clean bull who has not copulated'; ibid. 13 1 UDU *natta arkan*[*tan*; OHitt. original XX 2 + XXV 15 I 4 *natta arkandan* (cf. Neu, *Altheth.* 47). Cf. Neu, *Interpretation* 14; Kronasser, *Etym.* 1:521, 589. For meaning, compare *iskisa pai-* (s.v. *iskis-*).

arki- (c.) 'testicle', nom. pl. *arkiyēs* (*KBo* XVII 61 Rs. 15) in a list of anatomical parts of a male animal, preceded by *zasgarais* 'anus' (q.v. s.v. *sakkar*) and followed by *ginu* 'penis' (lit. 'knee'; see s.v. *anassa-*), acc. pl. *arkius* (*KUB* X 62 V 7) among body parts cooked at sacrifice. Cf. Haas, *Orientalia* N.S. 40:417–8 (1971); H. Berman, *JAOS* 92:466–8 (1972).

Cognate with Lith. *er̃žilas* 'stallion', *aržùs* 'lustful'; Arm. *orj*

142

'male'; ON *argr* 'passive homosexual' (<*órĝhos*); Gk. ἔνορ-
χος, ἐνόρχης 'testicled', ὄρχις, Arm. *orji-k⁀*, Alban. *herdhë*,
Mi.Ir. *uirgge* (IE *orĝhi-*), Avest. *ərəzi-* (*r̥ĝhi-*) 'testicle(s)'; IE
erĝh-, with *ark-*<*orĝh-*. Cf. J. Greppin, *Glotta* 51:113 (1973);
Puhvel, *JAOS* 95:262–4 (1975)=*Analecta Indoeuropea* 290–2,
416 (1981), *JAOS* 102:179 (1982), *Gedenkschrift für H. Kronasser* 182–3 (1982); C. Watkins, *BSL* 70.1:12–5 (1975).

The attempts by Otten (*ZA* 54:156 [1961]; cf. *ZA* 71:141–3
[1981]) and Friedrich (*HW Erg.* 2:8) to throw a semantic bridge
to *ark-* 'mark off, set apart' (q.v.), postulating a base meaning
'split' in the latter (> an obscene 'penetrate'), do not convince.
Cf. *argatiya-*.

arkamma(n)-, argama(n)-   (c.) 'tribute' (*MANDATTU*; *KBo* I 42 V
17–22 *arkammas*=Akk. *irbu*; cf. Güterbock, *MSL* 13:143
[1971]; also matches Akk. *mandattu*, and in Boğazköy Akkadian specifically *argamannu* [see below]), nom. sg. *ar-kam-ma-
-as* (e.g. XII 38 I 12 *kās arkammas ēsdu* 'let this be the tribute';
cf. Otten, *MDOG* 94:13 [1963]; Güterbock, *JNES* 26:75 [1967];
V 9 I 29–30 *arkammass-a-kan kuis* ANA ABI ABI-KA Ù ANA
ABI-KA *ishiyanza ēsdu* [sic, pro *ēsta*] 'the tribute which had been
imposed on your grandfather and on your father'; cf. III 14 Vs.
9 [Akk.] *mantatta ša abu-ya ana abi a[bi-k]a immidu* 'which my
father had imposed as tribute on your grandfather'; cf. Friedrich, *Staatsverträge* 1:12, 6; VI 29 III 28; cf. Götze, *Neue
Bruchstücke* 50; X 12 I 11; cf. H. Freydank, *MIO* 7:359 [1960];
KUB XL 2 Rs. 19; cf. Goetze, *Kizzuwatna* 66 [1940]), *argamas*
(VII 41 IV 17 [OHitt.]; cf. Otten, *ZA* 54:140 [1961], 71:138–9
[1981]), acc. sg. *arkamman* (e.g. *KBo* XII 38 I 8–9 *arkamman-
-ma-si-kan* [...] *ishiyanun* 'but [this?] tribute I imposed on it';
KUB XXIII 127 III 7; cf. Götze, *Neue Bruchstücke* 48; dupl.
186/v+XXI 15 III 3, with gloss-wedge; cf. H. Otten – C.
Rüster, *ZA* 63:84 [1973]; XVI 32 II 7; cf. Ünal, *Hatt.* 2:104;
VIII 79 Rs. 9; XLII 100 III 18; cf. G. F. Del Monte,
Oriens Antiquus 17:183 [1978]; L 6 III 25; XIV 1 Vs. 74
ar[kamm]an piddānniwan dāir 'they began paying tribute'; cf.
Götze, *Madd.* 18; *KBo* V 9 I 33–34 *tuel addus a[rkamma]n* INA

arkamma(n)-, argama(n)-

KUR ^{URU}*Mizri piddāir* 'your fathers paid tribute to Egypt'; cf. Friedrich, *Staatsverträge* 1:12), *argaman* (XVIII 86, 20 and 24), gen. sg. and pl. *arkammanas* (*KUB* VIII 79 Rs. 20 INIM *arkammanas* 'matter of tribute'; dupl. XXVI 92, 5 INIM *arkammanas*, with gloss-wedge; XIX 37 III 47 *arkammanas iyanun* 'I made [them] of tribute [= tributaries]'; cf. Götze, *AM* 176; *KBo* XVIII 24 IV 8), *argamanas* (*KUB* XVII 21 II 8–9 *sumenzan nepisas* DINGIR.MEŠ-*as kue* KUR.KUR.HI.A ... *argamanass-a ēsta* 'your lands, gods of heaven, which were ... and tributaries'; cf. von Schuler, *Die Kaškäer* 154; XXXIV 37 Vs. 6; XLVIII 110 III 5 *ar-ga-ma-na-sa*), dat.-loc. sg. *arkammani* (*Bo* 5072 I 11; cf. Otten, *ZA* 71:139 [1981]), acc. pl. *arkammus* (*KBo* XVIII 133, 9 and 10), *argamus* (*KUB* XIV 1 Rs. 32 *nu namma* MAHAR ^DUTU-*ŠI argamuss-a* [*u*]*tummanzi* ŪL *tarnai* 'he no longer lets tributes be brought before my majesty'; cf. Götze, *Madd.* 26; XXIV 3 II 42; cf. Gurney, *Hittite Prayers* 30; 1445/u Vs. 4), *arkamannus* (*KUB* XXXV 92 + *KBo* IX 146 IV 14; cf. Otten, *LTU* 89), *argamanus* (*KUB* XVII 21 II 12 DINGIR.MEŠ-*s-a-kan argamanus* 'tributes to the gods').

Denom. abstract *arkammanatar* (n.), dat.-loc. sg. *arkammananni* (*KBo* III 13 Rs. 11 [OHitt.] 'in tribute'; cf. ibid. 12 *piddannis* '[he] paid'; Güterbock,.*ZA* 44:72 [1938]; *KUB* XIX 37 III 48 *nu* ^{URU}*Hattusi* GEŠTIN-*an arkammananni pe harkir* 'to H. they proffered wine as tribute'; cf. Götze, *AM* 176). Cf. e.g. *andaiyandanni* (s.v. *antiyant-*); Kronasser, *Etym.* 1:295.

arkammanahh- 'make tributary', 1 sg. pret. act. in *KBo* XII 38 I 7–8 KUR *Alasiyan-ma-za-kan pide-ssi* [ÌR-*nahhu*]*n arkammanahhun* 'but the land of A. I subjugated and made tributary on the spot' (cf. Otten, *MDOG* 94:13 [1963]; Güterbock, *JNES* 26:75 [1967]).

arkammanalli- 'tributary', acc. pl. c. *arkammanallius* (*KUB* XIX 5 Vs. 15), *arkammanalius* (XIX 8 III 24). Cf. e.g. *annalli-* (s.v. *anna-, an*[*n*]*i-*), *teshalli-* (s.v. *tesha-*); Kronasser, *Etym.* 1:211–2.

arkammanallai- 'make tributary', Luwoid 1 sg. pres. act. *arkammanallāui* (*KUB* XXIII 127 III 6, with gloss-wedge).

arkamma(n)- is common to Hittite and Luwian; the same meaning 'tribute' is found in Akkadian-language treaties at

144

Bogazköy (*KBo* I 4 II 1 *arkammanna-šu* 'his tribute'; I 5 I 48 *argamanna*; cf. E. F. Weidner, *Politische Dokumente aus Kleinasien* 60, 94 [*BoSt* 8, 1923]) and in the Ugaritic version of the Suppiluliuma-Niqmandu treaty, where Akk. *mandat(t)a--ka*= Ugar. *argmn* (cf. M. Dietrich – O. Loretz, *Die Welt des Orients* 3:209 [1966]).

The homophony of Akk. *argamannu*, Ugar. *argmn* (doubtful; cf. Ch. Rabin, *Orientalia* N.S. 32:116–8 [1963]), Hebr. *argaman* 'purple' led Götze (*Madd.* 131) to postulate a metonymic semantic shift 'purple' > 'tribute' in the Hittite(-Luwian) cultural orbit, purple being a conspicuous component of such imposts (cf. *CAD* A 2.253); thus also Friedrich, *ZDMG* 96:483 (1942), and still Goetze, *JCS* 22:18 (1968). But in *HW* Friedrich inclined instead towards Luwian origin of *arkamma(n)-* (cf. P. Fronzaroli, *AGI* 41:34 [1956]; M. L. Mayer, *Acme* 13:87 [1960]), whereas M. Dietrich and O. Loretz (*Die Welt des Orients* 3:218–9 [1966]) tried instead to reverse the semantic development ('tribute' > 'purple'). Ch. Rabin (*Orientalia* N.S. 32:116–8 [1963]) leaned towards separating the Hittite-(-Luwian)-Ugaritic 'tribute' from the Semitic 'red or yellow purple' (cf. Gk. ἀργεμώνη 'wild poppy, agrimony'). Possibly Hitt.-Luw. *arkamma(n)-*, *argama(n)* reflects a borrowed dialectal Akkadian derivative of *ragāmu* 'call for, claim, exact' (cf. Laroche, *RPh* 42:244 [1968]) which also crops up in Ugaritic, perhaps under Hittite influence; the similarity to the cultureword 'purple' in standard Akkadian would thus be originally homophonic only, and the semantic thrust has to do with the exactment rather than the nature or tendering of tribute.

Much less likely is Indo-European origin involving the root *ark-* 'mark off, divide, parcel, set apart', as promoted by Pedersen, *Hitt.* 42; Kronasser, *VLFH* 210, *Studies presented to Joshua Whatmough* 124 (1957), *Etym.* 1:180, 271; Tischler, *KZ* 86:275 (1972); Carruba, *Scritti in onore di Giuliano Bonfante* 139 (1976); Oettinger, *Stammbildung* 414. The alleged semantic parallel of Lat. *tribūtum* from *tribuō* 'impart, allot' is inexact; *ark-* denotes mainly subdivision or sequestering, not parceling for purposes of bestowal. Neu's argument (*Anitta-Text* 123–4) that the mixed declension type of *arkamma(n)-* (cf. e.g.

arkamma(n)-, argama(n)-   arkam(m)i-, argami-

alkista[*n*]-, *alanza*[*n*]-) argues against a loanword is not cogent;
whereas OHitt. *alkista*- predominates and the -*n*- forms are
expansionary, we have OHitt. *arkammananni* and *arkamman*-
in all derivatives, with *arkamma*- probably assimilatory from
**arkamna*- (thus already Götze, *Madd.* 131).

Juret (*Vocabulaire* 43) compared directly Skt. *arghá*- 'value,
price', while Mayrhofer (*KEWA* 1:50) suggested a loanword
from Indo-Aryan.

arkam(m)i-, argami-   (c. and n.) 'harp' or the like (^{GIŠ}BALAG.DI [?]),
nom. sg. c. *arkammis* (*KUB* XXIX 4 I 25 1-*EN* ^{GIŠ}*arkammis* 'one
harp'; cf. Kronasser, *Umsiedelung* 8), acc. sg. c. *argamin* (XLIV
46, 5), nom.-acc. sg. (and pl.) neut. *arkammi* (e.g. *KBo* IV 9 I
39–41 ^{GIŠ}*arkammi* ^{GIŠ}*hūhupal galgaltūri* LUGAL-*i* EGIR-*an piran
hazzikanzi* 'they strike harp, drum [?], and tambourine behind
and in front of the king'), *ārkammi* (e.g. *Bo* 2599 II 5–6
ārkammi walahhanzi 'they strike harp'; cf. Neu, *Altheth.* 86),
arkami (e.g. *KBo* XVII 28, 7–8 *arkami galgaltūri* [*piran
app*]*ann-a walhannianzi* 'they keep striking harp and tambourine in front and behind'; cf. Neu, *Altheth.* 153), *ārkami* (e.g. X
11 I 4 *ārkami galgaltūri*), *argami* (e.g. *KUB* XX 16 I 10–11 *nu*
^{GIŠ}*argami galgaltūri* [...] *hazziyēskiuwan tia*[*nzi* 'they begin
striking harp and tambourine'; cf. *KBo* XXVI 64 II 7 ^{GIŠ}BALAG.
.DI *galgalturi*, ibid. 9 + *KUB* XXVI 12 II 1 ^{GIŠ}[BA]LAG.DI-*ma
galgal*[, XXXVI 12 II 19 ^{GIŠ}BALAG.DI-*ma galgalt*[; *KBo* XX 125
II 4 *argami*; cf. V. Haas – M. Wäfler, *Ugarit-Forschungen* 8:84
[1976]), *ār*[*gā*]*mi* (dupl. XVII 15 Rs. 21; cf. Neu, *Altheth.* 74),
ārgami (e.g. XX 14 + XXV 33 Vs. 14; cf. Neu, *Altheth.* 87),
argāmi (e.g. *KUB* XV 34 IV 43 *piran-ma* GIŠ ^DINANNA.HI.A
argāmi galgaltūri hazziskanzi 'but in front they strike "Ištar-
woods", harps, and tambourines'; cf. Zuntz, *ARIV* 96.2:522
[1936–7]; Haas – Wilhelm, *Riten* 206), instr. sg. *arkammit*
(XXIX 4 III 63 ^{GIŠ}*arkammit galgaltūrit pedanzi* 'to the accompaniment of harp and tambourine they bring'; cf. Kronasser,
Umsiedelung 26), abl. sg. ^{GIŠ}*arkammiaz* (XX 77 III 6), *arkammi-
yaza* (XXXIII 94 I 4; cf. Laroche, *RHA* 26:52 [1968]; Siegelová,
Appu-Hedammu 38).

146

arkam(m)iyala- (c.) 'harpist', nom. sg. ᴸᵁ*arkammiyalas*
(*KUB* XXXVIII 12 I 10), ᴸᵁ*arkammiya⟨la⟩s* (dupl. XXXVIII
15 Vs. 11), gen. sg. ᴸᵁ*arkamiyalas* (*KBo* XXV 13 II 4 ᴍᴇʟꞯᴇᴛ
ᴸᵁ[*arka*]*miyalas* 'wages of the harpist'; cf. Neu, *Altheth.* 40),
nom. pl. ˢᴬᴸ·ᴹᴱˢ*arkammiyales* (X 24 IV 13; X 27 III 16),
ˢᴬᴸ·ᴹᴱˢ*ar*]*kammiyalēs* (ibid. V 32), ˢᴬᴸ·ᴹ]ᴱˢ*arkammiyalē*[*s* (XIX
127, 10), *a*]*rkammiyalis*[(VII 47, 8), ᴸᵁ·ᴹᴱˢ*arkammiyali*[(XXII
238, 6), ᴸᵁ·ᴹᴱˢ*arkammiyalus* (*KUB* XI 23 V 20; cf. A. M. Jasink
Ticchioni, *Studi classici e orientali* 27:159 [1977]). Cf. e.g.
auriyala- (s.v. *auri-*); Kronasser, *Etym.* 1:172.

Unlike the reduplicative and onomatopoeic names for musi-
cal instruments, *arkammi-* makes a sedate phonetic impression.
Ritual attestation since Old Hittite may point to Hattic origin.
If areal culture word origin can be assumed, possibly borrowing from Indo-Aryan (Mitannian); cf. Ved. *árcati* 'sing, praise',
arká- 'hymn, song', harp being the proverbial accompaniment
of songs of praise.

argatiya- 'stoop to rage, come to violence', 3 pl. pret. act. in *KBo*
III 7 I 10 *mān* ᴰɪᴍ-*as* ᴹᵁˢ*illuyankass-a* ɪɴᴀ ᵁᴿᵁ*Kiskilussa*
ar-ga-ti-[*i-*]*e-ir* 'when the storm-god and the dragon fought it
out at K.' (cf. Laroche, *RHA* 23:66 [1965]).

arga-tiya- is a quasi-compound comparable with *kāri tiya-*
(q.v. s.v. *kari*[*ya*]-; lit. 'come to favor', i.e. 'go along with,
humor'; cf. Rosenkranz, *IF* 60:222 [1953]), with a directional
dat.-loc. from **arga-* related to Ved. *ṛghāyáte* 'is impetuous,
rages', *rágha-* 'anger, rage'; the Vedic verb resembles in meaning and usage *vṛṣāyáte* 'behaves like a rutting male' and is
cognate with Gk. ὀρχεῖται 'makes lascivious motions, dances',
Russian *jërzájet, jërgájet* 'fidgets, wriggles, moves in coition'
(cf. C. Watkins, *BSL* 70.1:15–25 [1975]); hence the base-
meaning of Hitt. **arga-* (< IE **órĝho-*; cf. Gk. ὀρχε-, vs. **ṛghā-*
in Vedic and Russian) must be 'coital excitation, sexual frenzy',
as a derivative of *ark-* 'mount, copulate with' (q.v.), and thence
'passionate rage' in general, especially applicable to the battle-
fury of gods (cf. the *ṛghāyámāṇa-, ṛghāvan*[*t*]- Indra of the *Rig-
Veda*). G. T. Rikov (Linguistique balkanique 25.1:82 [1982])

compared the obscure Avest. *arəzah-* 'fight, battle'. Cf. *hulhu-
liya tianzi* 'they engage in wrestling' (*KUB* XVII 35 II 26; cf.
Haas, *Nerik* 58; A. Archi, *Ugarit-Forschungen* 5:26 [1973]),
KITPALU ti[*yanzi* 'id.' (*KBo* XXIII 55 I 21), GEŠPÚ ... *tianzi*
'(they) get into fisticuffs' (ibid. 24), *tarpa ti(y)anzi* 'they indulge
in t.' (ibid. 24, 25, 26; cf. H. A. Hoffner, *Bi. Or.* 35:247 [1978]).
Cf. Puhvel, *Bi. Or.* 36:57–8 (1979), *JAOS* 102:179 (1982),
Gedenkschrift für H. Kronasser 182–3 (1982).

arkiu-, arkiui-, arkaui- (c. or n.?) 'anteroom, foyer, vestibule' (vel
sim.), nom. sg. c. (?) ^É*ar-ki-ú-is*[(*KUB* XXXII 108 Vs. 4), dat.-
loc. sg. ^É*ar-ki-ú-i* (e.g. *KBo* X 26 I 10–11 LUGAL-*us* ^DUTU-*as
parna paizzi ta* ^É*arkiui tiyazi* 'the king goes to the sun-god's
temple and steps into the vestibule'; *IBoT* I 36 I 70; cf. L.
Jakob-Rost, *MIO* 11:180 [1966]; III 1 Vs. 21; cf. V. Haas – M.
Wäfler, *Ugarit-Forschungen* 8:90 [1976]; *KUB* II 3 II 36; XX 27,
2; XX 76 I 11; XXV 18 II 5; XXXIV 130 II 4; *KBo* IX 136 I 4; X
23 II 13, 26, 30; X 24 IV 21 and 32; XXII 189 II 1; cf. Lebrun,
Hethitica II 8), ^É*ar-ki-ú-wi* (*KUB* XLIV 47 II 7), ^É*ar-ki-ú-i-ya*
(XX 87 I 2; cf. V. Haas – M. Wäfler, *Istanbuler Mitteilungen*
23–4:9, 31 [1973–4]; *KBo* X 20 III 44), *ar-ga-u-i* (*KUB* XXX 41
1.Rd. 4), ^É*ar-ga-wi* (*KBo* XXVII 42 II 54), abl. sg. *ar-ki-ú-wa-az*
(XX 8 I 7 [OHitt.]), *ar-ki-i-ú-az* (ibid. 9; cf. Neu, *Altheth.* 69),
^É*ar-ka-u-*[*i-ya-*]*za* (XI 47 I 4), nom.-acc. pl. neut. (?) ^É*ar-ki-ú-i-
-ta* (*KUB* XXXIX 97 Vs. 2; cf. H. Otten – C. Rüster, *ZA* 68:154
[1978]), ^É*ar-ga-i-ú-ta* (*Bo* 6827, 6).

   Hurrian origin is possible (cf. Kronasser, *Etym.* 1:225). I.
Singer (*ZA* 65:86 [1975]) compared Hurroid Akk. *arkabinnu* 'a
kind of door' (*CAD* A 2:272).

   Jakob-Rost (*MIO* 11:210 [1966]) suggested 'chapel' or
'prayer niche', but her hesitant adduction of Hitt. *arkuwai-*
(q.v.) as 'pray' has little merit either formally or semantically.

arkuwai- 'plead, argue, rejoin, riposte, respond, explain oneself,
   make excuses, offer defense', 3 sg. pres. act. *arku*[*wa*]*izzi* (*KUB*
   XLIII 57 IV 7), 3 pl. pres. act. *arku(w)anzi* (e.g. XI 32 II 4–5,

148

14–15, 19–20, 23–24, III 17–18 and 22–23 *ape-ma-ssi kattan* QATAMMA-*pat arkuwanzi* 'those likewise respond to him'; XXVIII 107 passim *ape-ma-ssi kattan* [or: GAM-*an*] *arkuwanzi*; cf. Schuster, *Bilinguen* 19), *ārkuwānzi* (*KBo* XXIII 97 IV 15), 1 sg. pret. act. *arkuwanun* (e.g. *KUB* VI 45 III 35= VI 46 IV 3 *nu* ANA DINGIR.MEŠ *arkuwanun* 'I have pleaded with the gods'; cf. Witzel, *Heth. KU* 94; *KBo* IV 8 III 22), 3 sg. pret. act. *arkuwait* (XI 1 Rs. 4 *nu* ANA ^DLUGAL-*ma arkuwait* 'he has pleaded with Sarrumas'; similarly ibid. Vs. 32; cf. Houwink Ten Cate – Josephson, *RHA* 25:109, 107 [1967]), *arkutta* (*KUB* XXII 70 Vs. 80 ^DUTU-*ma-ssi katta* ŪL *arkutta* 'but his majesty made no excuses to her'; cf. Ünal, *Orakeltext* 78); verbal noun *arkuwessar* (n.), dat.-loc. sg. *ar-ku-(u-)e-es-ni* (VI 45 III 22 *kuedani arkuwēsni*, with dupl. VI 46 III 61 *kuyedani arkuēsni* 'in whatever pleading'); also frequent *arkuwar* (haplologic for **arkuwawar*), nom.-acc. sg. *arkuwar* (e.g. *KBo* III 3 IV 10–11 *nu-za kuis kuit arkuwar* DÙ-*zi* 'what plea each makes'; V 9 III 4–5 *n-an-zan apiya-pat pidi-ssi arkuwar* DÙ-*ya* 'then, in its place, offer an explanation!'; cf. Friedrich, *Staatsverträge* 1:20; *KUB* XIV 1 Rs. 36 *ziga-nnas namma uddanī āppa arkuwar* Ū[L *iyasi* 'thou dost not even make excuses to us in the matter'; cf. Götze, *Madd.* 28; XIV 3 II 65–66 *ehu-wa nu-wa-mu-za arkuw*[*ar*] *iya* 'come, make your plea to me!'; cf. Sommer, *AU* 10; XIV 8 Rs. 23–24 *nasma mān* ANA ÌR-*DI kuedanikki kuitki nakkiyahhan* [...] *nu-za* ANA EN-ŠU *arkuwar iyazzi* 'or if something [is] heavy on some servant['s mind], he makes a clean breast of it to his master'; cf. Götze, *KlF* 216; ibid. 20 *nu-za kāsa* ANA ^DIM EN-*YA hingani ser arkuwar ēssahhi* 'and lo, to the storm-god my lord on account of the plague I make a plea'; XXIV 1 IV 21 UD.KAM-*tili arkuwar ēssai* '[he] daily makes a plea'; cf. Gurney, *Hittite Prayers* 36; VI 45 IV 48 *arkuwar tiyauwar* 'plea-presentation'; cf. *ishunauwar siyauwar* 'bowstring-shooting'; *KBo* XI 1 Rs. 24 DUB.1.KAM ŠA ^DU *arkuwar tiyauwas* 'one [single] tablet of the presentation of the plea to the storm-god'), *arkuar* (e.g. *KUB* V 1 II 109 *arkuar tiyawas* SISKUR 'ceremony of plea-presenting'; cf. Ünal, *Hatt.* 2:65), *ar-ku-u-wa-ar* (e.g. XV 22, 3 *arkūwar tiyauwanzi* 'to present a plea'; *KBo* I 30 Vs. 4–5 *uttani-za kuis arkūwar natta iyazi* 'who does not offer defense in a matter' = [Akk.] *ša tertam irtam lā isū* 'who does not make a turned breast'; cf. *MSL* 12:215 [1969]), *a-ar-ku-u-wa-ar* (*KUB* XIV 10 I 22–24 *nu-za hingani ser* ANA DINGIR.MEŠ *hūmandās ārkūwar ēssahhun* 'on account of the plague I made a plea to all the gods'; cf. Götze, *KlF* 206), nom.-acc. pl. neut. *arkuwarri* (VI 45 I 26–27 *nu-mu ke arkuwarri*HI.A *istamastin* 'hear these my pleadings!', beside dupl. VI 46 I 27 *ar-u-wa-ar-ri-ya* [sic]); iter. *arkueski-, arkuiski-*, 1 sg. pres. act. *arkueskimi* (XIV 8 Rs. 37), *arkuēsk[imi* (XIV 10 IV 2; cf. Götze, *KlF* 216–7), *ar-ku-ú-e-es-ki-mi* (VI 45 III 33), ibid. 19 *nepisas* ᴰUTU-*i arkuiskimi*, with dupl. VI 46 III 59 *nepias* ᴰUTU-*i arkuuīskimi* 'to the sun-god of heaven I am pleading', 2 sg. pres. act. *arkuiskisi* (*KBo* XVIII 24 I 12), 3 sg. pres. act. *ar-ku-ú-e-es-ki-iz-zi* (*KUB* XXI 19a II 4 [= *Bo* 4222]), 3 pl. pres. act. *arkuiskanzi* (XVII 9 I 19; *KBo* XXVI 64 + *KUB* XXXVI 12 II 12).

The correct meaning (Sturtevant, *Comp. Gr.*[1] 222; J. Duchesne-Guillemin, *TPhS* 1946:85) and the etymological connection (IE *arg^w-) with Lat. *arguō* 'assert, prove, accuse', *argumentum* 'representation, proof' (Hendriksen, *Untersuchungen* 45, 74; J. Duchesne-Guillemin, *TPhS* 1946:85), perforce separating the latter from *argentum* 'silver' (q.v. s.v. *harki-*), were re-argued in detail by Laroche, *École Pratique des Hautes Études, Sciences religieuses, Annuaire* 72:13–20 (1964–5), *RPh* 42:242–3 (1968). Cf. Houwink Ten Cate – Josephson, *RHA* 25:121–2 (1967); von Schuler, *JCS* 22:4–5 (1968); Puhvel, *JAOS* 94:293 (1974). Thus *arkuwai-* < *rg^w-āye-?

The superseded rendering 'pray' (since Hrozný, *Heth. KB* 153; still in Hendriksen, *Untersuchungen* 45, 74) and tie-in (via IE *erk^w-) with Skt. *árcati* 'shine, salute, praise', Arm. *erg* 'song', Toch. A *yärk-* 'do honor' (*IEW* 340; Mayrhofer, *KEWA* 1:50) linger on in Neumann, *Untersuchungen* 53, and Kronasser, *Etym.* 1:289, 301, 415, 472. Tischler, *KZ* 86:276–7 (1972), gave the correct meaning ('entschuldigen') but still sided with Kronasser in etymology (whereas Van Windekens, *Le tokharien* 593, separated *arkuwai-* from IE *erk^w-). Juret's adduction of Lat. *rogō* 'ask' (*Revue des études latines* 16:71 [1938], *Vocabulaire* 43) was also a function of the wrong sense 'pray'.

H. Holma's (*Journal de la Société finno-ougrienne* 33.1:60 [1916]), Hrozný's (*SH* 78), and Sturtevant's (*Comp. Gr.*[1] 87) separate interpretation of *arkūwar* as 'warding off, defense', akin to Lat. *arceō* 'keep away' (q.v. s.v. *har[k]-*) has long since fallen by the wayside (cf. Couvreur, *Hett.* 151–2). V. Ševoroškin's connection of *arkuwar* ('Bitte, Gebet') with a purported IE *Herk͏ʷ- 'biegen' (*Orbis* 17:467 [1968]) is antiquated and arbitrary.

For the occasional appearance of *arkuwai-* in place of *ar(u)wai-* 'prostrate oneself' (q.v.) in duplicates of ritual texts see H. Otten – C. Rüster, *ZA* 67:61–2 (1977); presumably 'pleading' before the king entailed proskynesis, and hence some semantic conflation of the two near-homophones was possible in set contexts.

arlip(a), adverb or predicate complement, always in ritual analogies of 'thigh(s)' being positioned in a certain way, and a desirable posture for soul, country, or king ('firm, upright, erect' vel sim.): *KUB* XXXIII 68 III 19–20 *nu* ZI-*KA* ZAG-*as wallas [iwar a]rlip artaru* 'may your soul stand *a.* like the right thigh' (cf. Laroche, *RHA* 23:129 [1965]); XXXIII 45 III 4–5 [*nu* ZAG-*as wallas*] GIM-*am arlipa* [*tiyazi* 'even as the right thigh stands *a.*', picked up in dupl. XXXIII 51, 2–3 [KUR ᵁᴿᵁ*Ha*]*tti--ya* ZAG-*as* [*wallas iwar*] *arlip tiya* 'Hatti, too, stand *a.* like the right thigh!' (cf. Laroche, *RHA* 23:140 [1965]); XXXIII 21 III 16 *arlipa* (cf. ibid. 15 ZAG-*as w*[*allas*; Laroche, *RHA* 23:121); XXIX 1 IV 10–12 *kī-wa waliēs mahhan arlipa artari* LUGAL-*s-a uddār* QATAMMA *arlipa artaru* 'even as these thighs stand *a.*, so, too, may the king's affairs stand *a.*' (cf. ibid. 9 *nu uwallus tianzi* 'they place thighs'; B. Schwartz, *Orientalia* N.S. 16:38 [1947]).

Etymological speculation is idle; very little favors a body part, possibly 'penis' (Laroche, *RA* 47:40 [1953]) or a tie-in with Hattic *alip* 'word' (?; Laroche, *RA* 41:79 [1947]; Kronasser, *Etym.* 1:331).

arma- (c.) 'moon; month; lunula (ornament)' (ᴰ*SIN*, ᴰEN.ZU; ITU[.KAM]), dat.-loc. sg. ᴰ*SIN-mi* (e.g. *KUB* VIII 16+24 III 11

^D*SIN-mi maninkuwan* 'close to the moon'; cf. M. Leibovici, *Syria* 33:143 [1956]), ITU-*mi* (e.g. XVII 15 III 14; epanadiplotic I 16 III 57 ITU-*mi* ITU-*mi* 'every month'; cf. Sommer, *HAB* 14; XIII 3 II 25 ITU-*mi* ITU-*mi*; cf. Friedrich, *Meissner AOS* 47), ITU.KAM-*mi* (e.g. IV 47 Vs. 9 *kuedani imma* ITU.KAM-*mi* 'in the very month when'; XXXV 145 Rs. 3 *kedani* ITU.KAM-*mi* 'in this month'), nom. pl. *a-ar-me-es* (*KBo* XXIII 52 II 10, 12, 15, 17 'lunulae' [of gold], describing blazes or markings of iconographic team oxen, besides golden horns; wrongly 'harness-gear' [H. Eichner, *Die Sprache* 27:207 (1981), comparing Russian *jarmó* 'yoke', Lat. *arma* 'gear']). Common in theophorous anthroponymy of Southern Anatolian origin, e.g. *Arma-*^DU (*KUB* XIX 67 I 6 and 17; cf. Götze, *Neue Bruchstücke* 16–8) besides usual ^D*SIN-*^DU, or (Akk.) *Armaziti* (*RS* 15:77, 13) besides ^{ID}*SIN-ma-*LÚ (*RS* 17:292, 9). Cf. Laroche, *Noms* 39–41, 290.

armatar (n.) in ITU.KAM-*tar* (*KBo* XVIII 88 Rs. 11), perhaps 'month-span' (cf. *uidand-atar* 'year-length').

armanni- (c.) 'moonlet, lunula, crescent' (as metal ornament [= UD.SAR], or with determinative ^{NINDA} 'croissant' bread), nom. sg. or pl. *armannis* (e.g. *KBo* X 23 IV 6 *armannis* GUŠKIN 'lunula of gold'; *KUB* XLII 78 II 15 1-*EN armannis*; cf. ibid. 16 3 *armannis,* ibid. 4 *armannius*; cf. S. Košak, *Ling.* 18:112 [1978]; XXII 37 Rs. 4 *armannis*; II 13 I 15 and 54 ^{NINDA}*armannis*), *ar-ma-an-ni-es* (XLII 43 Vs. 5 1-*EN armannies*), acc. pl. *armannius* (XVII 21 II 14 *sittarius armanniuss-a* 'sun-disks and lunulae'; ibid. III 22 *sittari]ēs armanniuss-a*; cf. von Schuler, *Die Kaškäer* 156–8). Cf. Sommer, *ZA* 46:7–9, 12, 41–45 (1940); H. A. Hoffner, *Alimenta Hethaeorum* 152 (1974); for suffix, see Kronasser, *Etym.* 1:221–2. Cf. also *armannai-ma* (XLII 67, 8) and instr. sg. *armannantit* (XL 56 I 7; cf. Goetze, *JCS* 23:25 [1970]).

arma(n)tal(l)anni- (c.), bread-name, acc. sg. ^{NINDA}*armantalanne[n* (*KUB* XXVII 64 Rs. 8),]*armatalannin* (*Bo* 3162 Vs. 7; cf. Otten, *Materialien* 24), *a]rmatallanninn-a* (*KBo* XXIV 33 IV 6). Apparent suffix agglomeration *arma-*+*-ant-*+*-al(l)a-*+*-anni-*.

armuwalai- 'wax like the moon' (not 'shed moonlight'), 2 sg.

imp. act. in *KUB* VI 45+XXX 14 III 68–70 *nu-mu* [D]U ... *armuwalashas iwar ser armūwalai nepisas-ma-mu* [D]UTU-*as iwar ser wantāi* 'o storm-god, wax over me like the moon, and glow over me like the sun-god of heaven'; *armuwalasha(i)-* (c.) 'waxing of the moon', nom. sg. *armuwalashas* in the figura etymologica above, in *KBo* XIII 20, 6][D]SIN*armuwalashas* [, *KUB* VIII 30 Rs. 3-4 [D]SIN-*an* [... *arm*]*uwa⟨la⟩shas-sis*, and in XXX 55, 14 *arm*]*uwalashas šA* [D]UTU-*as* IZKIM-*as*['waxing of the moon (and) omen(s) of the sun' (cf. ibid. 5 *mān* [D]SIN IZKIM-*ahzi* 'when the moon gives an omen'), *armuwalashais* (VIII 30 Vs. 21 *arm*]*uwalashais tepus* 'waxing [is] scant'), gen. sg. *armuwalashas* (XXXII 41 Rs. 5). Cf. Sommer, *ZA* 46:7 (1940); Friedrich, *JCS* 1:277 (1947); for suffix, see Kronasser, *Etym.* 1:167; Starke, *KZ* 93:257–8 (1979).

That *arma-* 'moon' was a widespread Southern Anatolian lexeme (Hier. MOON-*ma-*) is visible in the survival of Cuneiform and Hieroglyphic Luwian anthroponyms in Lycian and local Greek (esp. in Lycia): e.g. Ερμαδατης (< *Arma-Datta-*), Αρμα-πιας (< *Arma-piya-*), Ερμ]αμοας (< *Arma-muwa-*), Ερμενηνις, *erm̃menēni* (< **Arma-nani-*). Cf. e.g. Laroche, *HH* 102–3, *RHR* 148:24 (1955); Meriggi, *HHG* 32–3; Houwink Ten Cate, *LPG* 131–4; L. Zgusta, *Anatolische Personennamensippen* 1:119–34 (1964). The concomitant meaning 'month' may survive in Lyc. *rm̃mazata* (*TLy* 131:4) if it means 'monthly prestation' (vel sim.; cf. Carruba, *Istituto Lombardo, Rendiconti, Classe di Lettere* 108:579 [1974]; Neumann, *Die Sprache* 20:113 [1974]; Gusmani, *Incontri linguistici* 2:71 [1975]). Lydia is a fringe area: divine and theophorous *arma-* may be sparsely attested at Sardis (*armĩa-*, Αρμαναυδας; cf. A. Heubeck, *Lydiaka* 31–3 [1959]), but 'month' is probably Lyd. *ora-* (cf. Gusmani, *Lyd. Wb.* 61–2, 178).

The stem *arma-* (and **armu-*, judging from *armu-walai-* and Αρμουυανι) is clearly the native Hittite-Luwian term for 'moon', distinct from the Hattic moon-god Kašku and theologically significant mainly by assimilating and conveying the "southern" worship of the lunar deities Sin (of Harran) and the Hurrian Kušuh. Since the common noun *arma-* does not seem to be an indigenous theonym there is no reason to assume non-

IE substratal origin (as supposed by Tischler, *KZ* 86:277 [1972]).

IE 'moon' words usually refer to either brightness (Lat. *lūna*, OIr. *lūan*, OCS *luna*, Arm. *lusin*, Gk. σελήνη) or (time-)measure (Skt. *mā́s-*, Gk. μήνη, Goth. *mēna*, OPr. *menins*, Lith. *mė́nuo*, OCS *měsęcĭ*, Toch. A *mañ*, Toch. B *meñe*), in the latter instance largely coterminously with 'month' (Skt. *mā́s[a]-*, Gk. μήν, Goth. *mēnōþs*, Lith. *mė́nuo, mė̃nesis*, OCS *měsęcĭ*, Toch. A *mañ*, Toch. B *meñe*; but also Lat. *mēnsis*, OIr. *mī*, Arm. *amis*). The first type is clearly supplantive in relation to the 'measure' words (**lowksno-*, cf. Avest. *raoxšna-* 'shiny', OPr. *lauxnos* 'stars'), occasionally competitive (OCS *luna* besides *měsęcĭ*, Gk. σελήνη besides μήνη), and sometimes combinatory (Skt. *candrá-mas-*, lit. 'bright moon'). Anatolian *arma-* also probably reflects a more "poetic" innovation in relation to the IE base type.

In Anatolian the moon was not 'bright' but rather the opposite, viz. 'pale, weak, feeble' (a commonplace, as when Shelley describes death: "pale as yonder waning moon with lips of lurid blue"). It needed "strengthening", as expressed in the compound *armu-walai-* 'wax like the moon' (cf. *waliwalai-* 'make grow'). Hence Laroche (*RHR* 148:18–21 [1955]) was probably on the right track not only in deriving from *arma-* the verb *armahh-* 'make pregnant' (q.v. s.v. *armai-*) but also connecting *arma-* ultimately with *arma(n)-* 'sickness' and Gmc. **arma-*; the latter two have long been mutually compared (see s.v.). Thus Hitt. *arma-* 'moon' is to OE *earm* 'weak(ened), wretched' what OIr. *lūan* 'moon' is to Avest. *raoxšna-* 'bright'. The Anatolian innovation not only involved a unique sense direction but also took over the entire semantic field moon : month, unlike the 'bright' terms in other languages (but cf. Romanian *lună* 'moon, month', vs. e.g. French *lune* : *mois*). Cf. Puhvel, *Bi. Or.* 36:58 (1979).

Goetze's etymology *arma* < **or-mo-* 'moving one' (*JCS* 8:80 [1954]) was abortive. Van Windekens (*Festschrift for O. Szemerényi* 912–3 [1979]) sought in *arma-* a sense of 'measure(ment)' akin to Toch. A. *yärm*, B *yarm* 'measure', tying all in with IE **ar-* 'arrange'. There is little likelihood in Ivanov's reconstruction *arma-* < **yar-meн-* 'year-measurer', with reference to the Old Norse kenning *ār-tali* 'year-counter' = 'month' (*Etimologija 1977* 148 [1979], *1979* 130–2 [1981]); while **ye-* yields Hittite *e-* (see s.v. *e*[*u*]*wa*[*n*]*-*), **ya-* is stable (cf. *iya-* 'go'); besides, IE **yēro-* (Goth. *jēr*, ON *ār* 'year'), **yōro-* (Gk. ὥρᾱ 'season'), **yн̥ro-* (Russian Church Slavic *jara* 'spring') is unattested in Hittite ('year' being *witt-*), and G. T. Rikov (*Linguistique balkanique* 24.3:79–80 [1981] Kammenhuber (*Orakelpraxis* 55–6) pronounced *armuwalasha-* a loanword from Hurrian adduced Hes. ἄρμη · λεική (allegedly pro λεύκη).

armai- 'be pregnant', 3 sg. pres. act. *armaizzi* (*KUB* XLIV 4 + *KBo* XIII 241 Rs. 1 *mān* DUMU-*an armaizzi* 'when [a woman] is pregnant with child' [acc. of respect]; *KBo* XXI 20 I 27 DUMU-*an armaizzi*; cf. Burde, *Medizinische Texte* 44; VIII 130 III 7 *mān* SAL-*za arma*[*izzi* 'if a woman is pregnant'), *armāizzi* (XII 112 Vs. 13); partic. acc. sg. c. *armandan* (VI 3 IV 15 and 17 [= *Code* 1:83–4] ŠAH *armandan* 'pregnant sow'); deverbative adj. *armawant-*, nom. sg. c. *armauwanza* (*KBo* XVII 65 Vs. 47 SA]L-*za armauwanza* 'pregnant woman'; XVII 62 + 63 I 19–20 *mān armauwa*[*nza*] *mān sannapilis* 'whether pregnant or not [lit. empty]'), acc. sg. c. *armauandan* (VI 3 III 78 [= *Code* 1:77] GUD.ÁB *ar-ma-u-an-da-an* 'pregnant cow'; ibid. 79 ANŠU.KUR.RA *armauandan* 'pregnant mare'), nom. pl. c. *armauwantes* (*KUB* XVII 10 I 15, see below); comparable to e.g. *kartimmiyawant-* 'angry' (cf. Kronasser, *Etym.* 1:267); for the variant *arnuandan* for both *armandan* and *armauandan* in *Code* 1:77, 83–4 see s.v. *arnu-*; verbal noun *armawar* (n.), gen. sg. in *KUB* XXXV 103 III 10 *hukmais armauwas* 'conjuration of pregnancy' (cf. Otten, *LTU* 95).

armahh- 'make pregnant, impregnate', *-za armahh-* 'become pregnant, conceive', 3 sg. pres. act. *armahhi* (*KBo* XVII 65 Vs. 1 [= *ABoT* 21 I 1] *m*]*ān-za* SAL-*za armahhi* 'when a woman conceives'; ibid. 44 *armahhi*; ibid. Rs. 1 *ar*]*mahhi*; XXII 102 Vs. 8 *mān-za* SAL-*za ar*[*mahhi*; cf. Burde, *Medizinische Texte* 47; *KUB* XLI 8 IV 29 *nu-za armahhi* '[the ewe] becomes pregnant';

cf. Otten, *ZA* 54:138 [1961]), 3 pl. pres. act. *armahhanzi* (XVII 10 I 14–15 *nu-za namma* GUD.HI.A UDU.HI.A DUMU.LÚ.ULÙ.LU. .MEŠ *ŪL armahhanzi armauwantes-a kuyes nu-za apiya ŪL hassanzi* 'cattle, sheep, and humans no longer conceive, and those [already] pregnant do not then give birth'; cf. Laroche, *RHA* 23:90 [1965]), 1 sg. pret. act. *armahhun* (XXXIII 120 I 31 *āsma-tta armahhun* ᴰIM-*nit nakkit* 'lo, I have impregnated you with the mighty storm-god'; similarly ibid. 32, 33; cf. Güterbock, *Kumarbi* *2), 3 pl. pret. act. *armahhir* (XXXIII 59 IV 9 and 13; cf. Laroche, *RHA* 23:150 [1965]), 3 sg. imp. act. *armahhu* (XXXVI 55 III 22 -*za* ...]*Aranzahin armahhu* 'let [so-and-so] become pregnant with A.!' [acc. of respect]; ibid. 25 -*za* ... -]*sipan armahhu*; ibid. 27 -*za* ...] ZA.BA₄.BA₄-*ma armahhu*; ibid. 29 -*za* ... -]*an armahhu*; rather than 'impregnate A.', etc.; whereas in XXXIII 120 I 31 [above] Kumarbi gets mythically impregnated with the storm-god, the river-goddess Tigris, and Tasmisu, it is very unlikely that someone is ordered to impregnate indiscriminately the Tigris, the war-god, and two other deities), *armahdu* (*KBo* X 45 IV 33), *armahhuddu* (dupl. *KUB* XLI 8 IV 31–32 *nu-za ē[sh]ar papratar wastul* GE₆-*is* KI-*as armahhu[ddu* 'may the dark earth become pregnant with the blood, defilement, [and] sin'; cf. Otten, *ZA* 54:138 [1961]; partic. *armahhant-*, nom. sg. c. *armahhanza* (III 111, 18 *armah-han[za*; XXVI 33 II 8–9 *armah[hanza]* SAL-*as*), dat.-loc. sg. c. *armahhanti* (*KBo* VI 26 II 33 [= *Code* 2:78] GUD.ÁB *armahhanti* 'for a pregnant cow'), nom. pl. c. in *KBo* X 45 IV 34 *armahhantes hassanzi* 'pregnant [they] give birth'; deverbative adj. *armahhuwant-* (cf. *armawant-* besides *armant-* above), nom. sg. c. in dupl. *KUB* XLI 8 IV 32–33 SAL-*za* UDU-*uss-a armah-huwanza hāsi* 'pregnant woman and sheep give(s) birth'; verbal noun *armahhatar* (n.), dat.-loc. sg. in IV 4 Vs. 3–4 *kimmantin armahhanni* 'winter for impregnation' (cf. Laroche, *RA* 58:73 [1964]); *armahhu(wa)r* (n.), gen. sg. *armahhuas* (*KBo* XVII 65 Vs. 6 'of pregnancy'), *armahhuwas* (XXIV 17 Rs. 2 *a]rmah-huwas wassiyaz* 'with the medicament of pregnancy'), abl. sg. *armahhuwazza* (syntactically attractional for gen. sg. in *KUB* XXX 43 III 20–22 *mān hāsauwas* DUMU-*a[n] armahhuwazza wassiyaz* [...] *iskizzi* 'when the midwife daubs the child with the

medicament of pregnancy'; cf. Laroche, *CTH* 177; cf. e.g. VIII
48 I 12 *tuetaza memiyanaz* 'on your command' instead of *tuel
memiyanaz*); iter. *armahhiski-*, 3 sg. pres. act. *armahhiskizzi*
(XXXIII 84+ IV 16; cf. Siegelová, *Appu-Hedammu* 60).

The factitive *armahh-* has been derived directly from *arma-*
'moon' by V. Pisani, *Paideia* 7:323 (1952), Laroche, *RHR*
148:19 (1955), and Kronasser, *Etym.* 1:430; it means literally
'make moon-bound, bring into menstrual orbit', much like e.g.
ishiulahh- 'bind by treaty' or *siuniyahh-* 'imbue with (evil)
divinity, make possessed' (cf. Gk. σεληνιακός, σεληνόπληκτος,
Lat. *lunāticus* 'moon-struck'). Similarly *armai-* signifies verba-
tim 'be in a lunar way' (cf. e.g. *taksulai-* 'be friendly', from
taksul- 'friendship, peace'). For the widespread connection of
the moon with pregnancy cf. e.g. Catullus 34.13–18, where
Diana-Luna as birth-goddess is syncretized with both Juno
Lucina and Hecate: *tu Lucina dolentibus/Iuno dicta puerperis/
tu potens Trivia et notho es/dicta lumine Luna./ Tu cursu dea
menstruo/metiens iter annuum* ...; as another example Gabriel,
otherwise the messenger of the Annunciation, was identified
with the Moon in the planetary interpretation of the seven
archangels in the Cabala. Cf. in general K. Tallqvist, *Månen i
myt och dikt, folktro och kult* (1947), esp. 281–3, 304–8. Cf.
Puhvel, *Bi. Or.* 36:58 (1979).

Tischler (*Glossar* 62–3) wrongly posited an underlying noun
**arma-* 'pregnancy', perhaps (but unexplainedly) related to
arma- 'moon'. The derivational relationships of *arma-* 'moon',
armai- 'be pregnant', and *arma(n)-* 'sickness' have long been
tangled: 'sick' > 'pregnant' (Götze, *AM* 199); 'moon' > 'sick'
and 'pregnant' (Laroche, *RHA* 9:20–1 [1948–9]; Kronasser,
VLFH 39, 242, *Etym.* 1:25, 171, 266, 430); 'moon' > 'pregnant',
but 'sick' in a more remote, "collateral" relationship to 'moon'
(Laroche, *RHR* 148:18–21 [1955]).

arma(n)-, erma(n)-, irma(n)-   (c. or n.) 'sickness, illness' (GIG), nom.
sg. c. GIG-*as* (*KBo* I 42 IV 5, = Akk. [*mu*]*rzu*, Sum. NÍG.GIG; cf.
Güterbock, *MSL* 13:140 [1971]; *KUB* XIV 15 II 6 *n-an idalus*
GIG-*as istarakta* 'a bad illness afflicted him'; cf. Götze, *AM* 48),

arma(n)-, erma(n)-, irma(n)-

acc. sg. neut. (also c.?) *e-ir-ma-an* (*KBo* XVII 1 IV 2 *ha*]*tūgan idālu erman paprātar dāhhun* 'the terror, the evil, illness, uncleanness I have taken'; cf. Otten – Souček, *Altheth. Ritual* 34; ibid. III 11–12 *erma(n)-smet ēsh*[*ar-s*]*amet idālu-smet hatuka(n)-smet hari*[*enu*]*n* 'their illness, their blood[-guilt], their evil, their terror I have buried'), *irman* (XVII 3 I 7 *irma(n)-smas-kan dāhhun* 'I have taken illness from you'; III 4 I 6–7 *mahhan-ma* KUR.KUR.MEŠ ^{LÚ}KÚR ^I*Arnuandan* ŠEŠ-YA *irman istamassir* 'but when the enemy lands heard of my brother's illness', with partitive apposition; cf. Götze, *AM* 14; Frisk, *Indogerm.* 31–2; IV 6 Rs. 16; cf. Tischler, *Gebet* 16; *KUB* VIII 62 I 16; cf. Laroche, *RHA* 26:23 [1968]), *irmān* (XXVI 87, 8 *irmān piyer* '[the gods] gave sickness'), acc. sg. c. GIG-*nan* (XIX 29 I 7; cf. Goetze, *AM* 14), dat.-loc. sg. *irmani* (VIII 62 I 19), abl. sg. GIG-*az* (*KBo* IV 12 Vs. 8 and 10 GIG-*az* TI-*nut* 'saved [me] from the illness'; cf. Witzel, *Heth. KU* 34; Götze, *Hattusilis* 40), GIG-*za* (IV 6 Vs. 16–17 *n-an kez* GIG-*za* TI-*nut* 'restore her from this illness!).

irmanant- (c.) 'illness', nom. sg. *irmananza* (e.g. *KUB* XXXVII 190 Rs. 6, with gloss-wedges), GIG-*anza* (e.g. ibid. 4; *KBo* IV 6 Vs. 24–25 *istarkiat n-an* GIG-*anza tamastat* '[she] has become sick, illness has beset her'; *KUB* XXXIII 121 II 17 [*i*]*dālawanza* GIG-*anza* 'bad illness'; cf. Friedrich, *ZA* 49-234 [1950]). Cf. Luw. IGI.HI.A-*wassanza* GIG-*anza* 'eye-ailment' (XXXV 107 III 16; cf. Otten, *LTU* 98), SAG.DU-*assis* IGI.HI.A- -*wassis* GIG-*antes* 'head- and eye-ailments' (ibid. 17). Cf. Laroche, *BSL* 57.1:33 (1962); Tischler, *Gebet* 36–9, who wrongly assumed an adjective *irmanant-* 'ill' as well.

Denom. *armaniya-, irmaniya-* 'be(come) ill', 3 sg. pres. midd. *armaniyatta* (*KUB* IV 72 Rs. 3 *armaniyatta n-as* SIG₅-*atta* '[a man] will fall ill [but] he will get well'; cf. Ehelolf, *ZA* 43:182 [1936]; Goetze, *JCS* 4:224 [1950]; Neu, *Interpretation* 14); verbal noun *irmaniyauwar* (= Akk. [*maru*]*šdu*, Sum. NÍG.GIG in *KBo* I 42 IV 6). Cf. Kronasser, *Etym.* 1:567.

armala-, irmala- 'sick, ill', with suffix as in e.g. *lissiyala-*'liver-related, hepatic' from *les*[*s*]*i-* 'liver' (cf. Kronasser, *Etym.* 1:171–2), nom. sg. *armalas* (*KUB* XXX 10 Rs. 15–16 and par. XXX 11 Rs. 12 *armalas mahhan* 'like a sick [man]'; cf. Goetze,

JCS 4:224 [1950]; Kammenhuber, *ZA* 56:156 [1964]), *irmalas* (I 1 I 44–45 *mān-mu istarakzi kuwapi nu-za-kan irmalas-pat* [with gloss-wedges] ŠA DINGIR-*LIM handandatar ser uskinun* 'if it ever ail me, even when ill I kept seeing over me the deity's providence'; cf. Götze, *Hattusilis* 10; dupl. *KBo* III 6 I 37 *irmalas-pat*).

irmalant- 'sick, ill', nom. sg. c. *irmalanza* (*KBo* V 9 I 16; cf. Friedrich, *Staatsverträge* 1:10, 32–3; *KUB* V 6 I 47); cf. e.g. *andara(nt)-, arahzena(nt)-*, and Kronasser, *Etym.* 1:265–6.

Deadjectival *armaliya-, irmal(l)iya-* 'be(come) ill; afflict (with illness)' (impersonal subject, or 'illness'; patient in acc.; cf. s.v. *istark-*), 3 sg. pres. midd. GIG-*ri* (*KUB* VIIII 35 Vs. 3), 1 sg. pret. midd. *armaliyahhat* (?; I 16 II 2 *kāsa arm[aliyahhat* 'lo, I am become ill', matching ibid. I 2 [Akk.] *sumruşāku* 'I am suffering', stative of *marāşu*; cf. Sommer, *HAB* 2–3, 31), 3 sg. pret. midd. *irmaliyattat* (e.g. *KBo* III 4 II 20 *n-as irmaliyattat* 'he fell ill'; cf. ibid. 21 and 50 GIG-*at*; Götze, *AM* 48, 60; ibid. I 5–6 EGIR-*an-ma-as irmaliyattat-pat* 'but afterwards he likewise fell ill'; cf. Götze, *AM* 14; XVI 1 I 20 *nu-war-as irmaliyattat* 'he became ill'; cf. Otten, *MIO* 3:162 [1955]), *irmaliattat* (dupl. III 4 I 13 *nu-war-an irmaliattat* 'illness afflicted him'; cf. Götze, *AM* 18), *irmalliyattat* (V 9 I 14–15 *tuk-ma istarakkit nu irmalliyattat* 'it ailed you, illness afflicted you'; cf. Friedrich, *Staatsverträge* 1:10), GIG-*at* (e.g. III 4 II 50 ¹*Uhha*-LÚ-*is kuit* GIG-*at* 'because U. was ill'; cf. Götze, *AM* 60; IV 12 Vs. 5–6 ANA PANI ABU-YA-*mu kappin* DUMU-*an* HUL-*lu* GIG GIG-*at* 'in my father's time illness badly afflicted me as a small child'; cf. Witzel, *Heth. KU* 34; Götze, *Hattusilis* 40); partic. *irmaliant-*, nom. sg. c. ibid. 22 *karū irmalianza ēsta* '(he) was already ill'. Cf. Neu, *Interpretation* 73–4.

The *a>e>i* variation, with *a* most frequent in Old Hittite, matches that of *arha(i)->irha(i)-* and *erhui->irhui-* (q.v.); cf. e.g. Otten–Souček, *Altheth. Ritual* 44, 56; Puhvel, *AJPh* 98:152 (1977). For the declension type *erma(n)-* cf. e.g. *alkista(n)-, arkamma(n)-, alanza(n)-*; in the neuter form *erman* one may possibly postulate analogical interference by *inan-* (cf. Kronasser, *Etym.* 1:270).

The nominal stem *arma(n)-* and its quasi-synonym *inan-*

(q.v.) contrast with the primary verb for 'ail' (*istark-*). The basic meaning of *arma(n)-* is perhaps 'weakness, wretchedness', from an IE **ormo-* seen in OE *earm* 'weak(ened), wretched' and ON *armr* 'wretch(ed), wicked' (antonymous to *heill* 'well, sound'; cf. H. Beck, *Festschrift für Hans Eggers* 21–8 [1972]); cf. C. H. Carruthers, *Lg.* 9:159 (1933). A separate nominalization is Hitt. *arma-* 'moon', literally 'the weak(ened) one' (q.v.). A. Meillet's comparison of Arm. *ołorm* (< **or--orm-*) 'pity, compassion' with Gmc. **arma-* (*Mémoires de la Société de linguistique de Paris* 10:280 [1898]) and Hitt. *erma(-la)-* (*BSL* 37:110 [1936]) seems possible; just as 'compassion' readily enters the semantic sphere of Gmc. **arma-* with the Christian texts (Goth. *arman* 'misereri', *arma-hairts* 'misericors'), it may have evolved in a reduplicated cognate in early Classical Armenian.

T. Burrow's (*Archivum Linguisticum* 7:154 [1955]) and Tischler's (*KZ* 86:283 [1972]) adduction of Skt. *īrma-* 'wound' or Vedic *árma-* 'ruin(-heap)' is less probable, as is K. Strunk's equation of Gmc. **arma-* (original sense allegedly 'desolate, ruinous') with Vedic *árma-* (*Festschrift für Hans Eggers* 35–41 [1972]); for the Indic words see rather s.v. *harra-*.

Luw. *er(hu)wa-, ir(hū)wa-* (noun), *er(hū)walliya-, irwal(-l)iya-* (adjective) are of uncertain meaning and of doubtful relevance to Hitt. *arma(n)-* (cf. e.g. Tischler, *Glossar* 369).

armizzi- (n.) 'bridge', with determinatives GIŠ 'wood' or NA₄ 'stone', nom.- acc. sg. neut. *armizzi* (e.g. *KBo* XVI 36 + *KUB* XXXI 20 + *Bo* 5768 II 14–15 *nu-ssi* ANA ᴵᴰ*Zuliya pir*[*an*] GIŠ*armizzi eppir nu* GIŠ*armi*[*zz*]*i arha pippir* 'they seized the bridge over the river Z. and they wrecked the bridge'; cf. Alp, *Belleten* 41:644 [1977]; *KUB* XIX 9 IV 11 GIŠ*armizzi*[; cf. ibid. 10 *nu-kan* ᴵᴰ *zāiskir* 'they crossed the river', and see K. Riemschneider, *JCS* 16:115 [1962]; XLIII 36, 10 GIŠ*armizzi*; XX 2 IV 19 NA₄*armizzi*; *KBo* XI 72 III 5 *lalas-wa armizzi* 'the tongue [is] a bridge', with dupl. XI 10 III 17 EME-*as-wa* GIŠ*armizzi*), dat.-loc. pl. *armizziyas* (XXII 6 I 18 GIŠ*armizziyas-ma* 2 UDU.ŠIR *huwekta* 'to the bridge he sacrificed two rams'; cf. Güterbock, *MDOG* 101:19 [1969];

XX 123 IV 8 ^{GIŠ}*armizziyas* ANA ^{ÍD}*Zul*[*iya*).

Denom. verb *armizziya-* 'bridge (over)', figuratively 'smooth the way for, abet', 2 sg. pres. act. in *KUB* XXVI 1 III 27–28 *zik-ma-at sakti n-at parā armizziyasi* 'but you know it and abet it' (cf. von Schuler, *Dienstanweisungen* 13, 19), 3 pl. pres. act. *armizziyanzi* (XXXVI 83 I 6 'they bridge over' [viz. pig in sacrificial pit, so that offerant can stand above it]), 3 pl. imp. midd. in XV 34 I 45–46 *nu-smas* HUR.SAG.MEŠ *piran taksatni--yantaru* [ÍD.HI.A]-*smas piran armizziyantaru* 'before you let mountains be levelled, before you let rivers be bridged' (cf. L. Zuntz, *ARIV* 96.2:494 [1936–7]; Haas–Wilhelm, *Riten* 186), *KBo* XV 25 Vs. 14–15 [ÍD.HI.A-*wa piran a*]*rmizziyandaru haries--ma-wa-kan* [*piran taksatniyand*]*aru* 'let rivers be bridged over, let valleys be made level' (cf. Carruba, *Beschwörungsritual* 2). Cf. Neu, *Interpretation* 15.

Etymology uncertain. The adduction of *arma-* 'moon', *ar-manni-* 'crescent' (Sommer, *ZA* 46:8 [1940]; Laroche, *RHA* 9:20 [1948–9]) assumed unproven lunar curvatures of early Anatolian bridges. A possible cognate of *armizzi-* is rather Gk. ὅρμος 'roadstead, anchorage, harbor' (if the latter has secondary aspiration like e.g. ἅρμα and is unconnected with ὁρμή 'rush': Skt. *sárma-* 'flow' or with ὅρμος 'cord, chain', εἴρω 'string together' < εἴρω < *seryō); for the semantics, cf. Avest. *pərətu-* 'bridge' beside Lat. *portus* 'harbor', OE *ford* 'ford', or Lith. *tìltas* 'bridge' beside Vedic *tīrthám* 'watering-place, ford'. Another possible connection is with Gk. ἕρμα(τα) 'ship-prop(s), ballast, reef, cairn, barrow' (if unconnected with Lith. *svarùs* 'heavy'), ἕρμαξ 'stone-barrow', Ἑρμῆς (god of roads and travel), Ἕρμος (Lydian river called πολυψήφιδα 'pebbly', hence fordable, in Herodotus 1:55), and similar onomastic elements of probable Anatolian provenance (separate from Αρμα-, Ερμα- 'Moon-', q.v. s.v. *arma-*). Cf. Kronasser, *Etym.* 1:240.

Tischler (*KZ* 86:277 [1972]) suggested an IE root etymology (**rem-* 'rest upon, support'; *IEW* 864) seen perhaps in OHG *rama* 'prop', Norw. *rande* 'embankment', *rand* 'crossbeam'. Further semantic support might be found in e.g. OCS *mostŭ* 'bridge' besides ON *mastr* 'pole, mast', or ON *brū* 'bridge' besides OCS *brŭvŭno* 'beam'. G. T. Rikov (*Linguistique balkanique* 25.2:22 [1982]) saw a nominal **-ti-* derivative of a denom. verb **armiya-*, comparing Gk. ἁρμός 'joint' and Skt. *sétu-* 'bond; bridge'.

arnam(m)i(ya)-, Luwoid verb describing a ritual action immediately following *sip(p)ant-* 'sacrifice', 3 sg. pres. act. *arnammitti* (*Bo* 4951 Rs. 12 *sipanti nu-za arnammitti* 'he sacrifices, and he *a.*'), *arnamitti* (*KUB* XXIX 7 Rs. 63 *sipanti namma arnamitti* 'he sacrifices, then *a.*'; cf. Lebrun, *Samuha* 125; *KBo* VIII 90 II 21), *arnaminti* (dupl. *KUB* XXIX 4 II 33–34 *sipandanzi nu* EN SISKUR.SISKUR *arnaminti n-as sarā tiyazi* 'they sacrifice, the sacrificer *a.*, and he steps up'; cf. Kronasser, *Umsiedelung* 16).

The Luwoid *arnam(m)itti* is normal; cf. e.g. 3 sg. pres. act. *kalutitti* besides the Hitt. *kalutiyazzi* (s.v. *kaluti-*). The variant *arnaminti* is not a 3 pl. pres. act. (as claimed in e.g. *Dict. louv.* 31)ˉbut rather an erroneous hypercorrection resulting from nasal reduction and consequent neutralization of visible distinction between Luwoid 3 sg. and pl. (cf. 3 pl. *katmarsitti* <*katmarsinti* s.v. *kam[m]ars-*). Kronasser (*Umsiedelung* 49, *Etym.* 1:522) wrongly assumed a stem *arnami(n)t-* (cf. *sip[p]a-[n]t-*), thus regular 3 sg. *arnaminti* and with nasal reduction *arnamitti*.

Perhaps denominative from a Luwian participle **arnam-(m)i-* from a verb akin to Hitt. *arnu-* (q.v.), in the sense of 'make removal, clear away, wind down', which the context seems to favor.

arnu- 'move along, make go; stir, raise; transport, deport, remove; bring, transmit, deliver, produce; further, promote'; *katta arnu-* 'bring down; bring to an end, conclude, terminate', 1 sg. pres. act. *arnumi* (*KBo* XVI 47 Vs. 10 *n-us-kan mān kuemi mān-us arnumi* 'if I kill them [or] if I deport them'; cf. Otten, *Istanbuler Mitteilungen* 17:56 [1967]; *KUB* XIV 1 Rs. 22 KUR] ^{URU}*Hapālla--wa-kan nassu kuemi nasma-war-at* QADU NAM.RA.HI.A GUD.HI.A UDU.HI.A *arnumi* 'I will either smash Hapalla or remove it with deportees, cattle, and sheep'; cf. Götze, *Madd.* 24; V 1 III 29; cf. Ünal, *Hatt.* 2:68; *Maşat* 75/43 Rs. 16; cf. Alp, *Belleten* 44:47 [1980]), *ārnumi* (XXXI 127 III 29), *arnummi* (*KBo* XVIII 127, 6), 2 sg. pres. act. *arnusi* (e.g. V 4 Vs. 22–23 *mān-kan* ERÍN.MEŠ-*ma* ANŠU.KUR.RA.MEŠ *war*[*ri*] *ŪL arnusi* 'but if you do not move up troops [and] cavalry as auxiliaries'; cf. Friedrich, *Staatsverträge* 1:56; *KUB* XXI 27 IV 8–10 *mān … ke* AWATE. .MEŠ [*ist*]*amasti n-at* ANA ᴰIM *tuel huhhi … parā arnusi* 'if you hear these words and pass them along to the storm-god your grandfather'), *arnutti* (*KBo* IV 3 III 11 *ar*]*nutti* = *KUB* VI 41 IV 6 *a*[*rnutti*; cf. Friedrich, *Staatsverträge* 1:132), 3 sg. pres. act. *arnuz(z)i* (e.g. *KBo* V 1 I 9 *n-at-kan mahhan* KÁ-*as parā arnuzi* 'when he brings it forth to the gate'; cf. Sommer – Ehelolf, *Pāpanikri* 2*; *KUB* V 1 I 15 ᴰUTU-*ŠI* ERÍN.MEŠ … *pian arnuzi* 'his majesty moves ahead troops', matching ibid. *pian huinuzi* 'sends ahead'; cf. Ünal, *Hatt.* 2:34; *KBo* VI 2 I 38 [= *Code* 1:19] *nu* É-*ir-set-pat arnuzzi* 'he [viz. the culprit] delivers his very estate [as forfeit]'; VI 3 IV 60–61 [= *Code* 100] GUD.HI..A-*ŠU edreskizzi n-us-san parā hameshanda arnuzi* 'he [viz. the barn-burner] keeps feeding his [viz. the wronged party's] cattle and tides them over till next spring', lit. 'brings them to next spring'; cf. [less probably] Josephson, *Sentence Particles* 318, who considered *parā* preverbal, 'carries forward'; for prenominal *parā* see s.v. *appasiwatt-*; *Code* 1:1–4, 76 *apūn arnuzi* 'he [viz. the responsible party] produces that one [viz. the body of a deceased person or animal]'; VI 2 I 5–6 [= *Code* 1:5] *nasma* INA KUR ᵁᴿᵁ*Hatti nu-zza unattallan-pat arnuzzi* 'or [if it is] in Hattiland, he [viz. the perpetrator] produces the very [body of the] merchant'), 1 pl. pres. act. *arnummeni* (e.g. *KUB* XIX 30 IV 5–6 *nu-war-an*] *anda arnumme*[*ni nu-war-an …*] *parā pīyaweni* 'we shall turn him in and hand him over'; cf. Götze, *AM* 102; XXXIII 106 II 16 *andan arnummeni*; cf. Güterbock, *JCS* 6:22 [1952]; IV 1 II 5–6 *DINAM kuit arnummeni* 'the complaint which we raise'; cf. von Schuler, *Die Kaškäer* 170), 2 pl. pres. act. *arnutteni* (e.g. XIII 4 I 56 *n-at-si parā-pat ŪL arnutteni* 'you do not bring it to him'; ibid. 51 *n-at* DINGIR.MEŠ-*as* ZI-*ni parā ŪL arnutteni*; cf. Sturtevant, *JAOS* 54:368 [1934]), 3 pl. pres. act. *arnuwanzi* (e.g. *KBo* IV 2 IV 41 *mahhan-ma* GUD … *arnuwanzi* 'but when they make the cow move'; cf. Götze – Pedersen, *MS* 10; V 1 II 9 'they bring'; cf. Sommer – Ehelolf, *Pāpanikri* 6*; *IBoT* III 148 III 47 DINGIR.MEŠ ÍD-*i arnuwanzi* 'they bring the deities to the river'; cf. Haas–Wilhelm, *Riten* 226), *ārnuwanzi* (*KBo* VI 26 IV 2–3 [=*Code* 2:96] *t-us ārnuwanz[i k]ūnn-a takiya* URU-*ri kūnn-a takiya* URU-*ri asesanzi* 'they remove them and settle one in one town, the other in another town'), *arnūwanzi* (e.g. *KUB* XXXIX 12, 7 *i*]NA É.NA₄-*ŠU arnūwanzi* 'they move [the body] to its mausoleum'; cf. Otten, *Totenrituale* 70), *arnuanzi* (e.g. XV 31 II 10–11 'they bring'; cf. Haas–Wilhelm, *Riten* 156; V 1 II 48 'they deport'; cf. Ünal, *Hatt.* 2:58; XXX 17 Vs. 2 *parā arnuanzi* 'they move forth [the body]'; cf. Otten, *Totenrituale* 52; [*pennumanzi*] *arnuanzi* 'they make [them] move [in a trot]', passim in Kikkulis-text; cf. Kammenhuber, *Hippologia* 290–2, 324–5), *ārnuanzi* (*KBo* XIII 72 Vs. 8), 1 sg. pret. act. *arnunun* (e.g. V 9 II 38–39 NAM.RA.HI.A ... *kuyēs* ... ABU-YA *arnut ammuqq-at arnunun* 'the captives whom my father deported [and] whom I deported'; cf. Friedrich, *Staatsverträge* 1:18; X 2 II 51–52 *nu-smas* SAHAR.HI.A-*is ser arnunun* 'I stirred up dust for them'; cf. F. Imparati–C. Saporetti, *Studi classici e orientali* 14:50 [1965]; *KUB* XIV 3 II 65 *kī arnunun* 'I dispatched the following'; cf. Sommer, *AU* 10; XXIII 13, 9; cf. Sommer, *AU* 314), 3 sg. pret. act. *arnut* (e.g. *KBo* III 34 II 10 [OHitt.] *s-an arnut s-an* URU*Ankui* IRDI 'he deported him and banished him to A.'; *KUB* XXXIV 23 I 10 *n-as* QADU NAM.RA.MEŠ GUD UDU *arnut* 'he removed them along with deportees, cattle, and sheep'; cf. Güterbock, *JCS* 10:83 [1956]; for the duplicate XL 8, 3 cf. H. Klengel, *Oriens Antiquus* 7:67 [1968]), *ārnut* (XIX 8 I 24). 1 pl. pret. act. *ar-nu-um-me-en* (XX 96 V 10), *ar-nu-um-mi-en* (*KBo* XIII 62 Vs. 18), 3 pl. pret. act. *arnuir* (V 8 III 35 *n-an-kan* INA ID*Dahara kattanta arnuir* 'they made him go down to the D. river', with dupl. XVI 8 III 39; *KUB* XV 36 Vs. 17 *arnu[ir*; cf. Götze – Pedersen, *MS* 6; *KBo* IX 144, 4 *a]rnuir*; cf. S. Heinhold-Krahmer, *Arzawa* 306 [1977]), *arnuer* (*KUB* XIX 14, 20 *anda arnuer* 'they brought in'; cf. Güterbock, *JCS* 10:112 [1956]; XIV 3 I 4–5 *uqq-a* QATAMMA ZI-*ni arnuer nu kedas* KUR-*eas* GAM *uwanun* 'they likewise got through to me [lit. brought to bear on my soul], and I came down to these lands'; cf. Sommer, *AU* 2, 28–33; XIV 8 Vs. 29, with dupl. XIV 11 II 32 *arnuir*; cf. Götze, *KlF* 210), 2 sg. imp. act. *arnut* (e.g. *KBo* III 40a, 14 [OHitt.] *nu-mmu annas-mas katta arnut* 'bring me down my mother's [clothes]'; *KUB* XXXI 68 I 4 *īt-war-as arnut nu-war-as arnunun* 'go, get them moving! And I made them move'; cf. R. Stefanini, *Athenaeum* N.S. 40:23 [1962]; *KBo* IV 4 IV 22 *nu-wa-nnas ... arnut* 'make us march!'; cf. Götze, *AM* 136; *KUB* XIV 1 Rs. 26 *nu-wa-kan īt* KUR ^{URU}*Hapalla-wa-kan kueni nasma-war-at arnut* 'go and smash Hapalla, or deport it!'; cf. Götze, *Madd.* 26; *KBo* V 13 III 1–2 ERÍN.MEŠ-*wa-z* ANŠU.KUR.RA.MEŠ *piran huuinut nu-war--at-mu-kan warri lammar arnut* 'send ahead troops and cavalry and make them move up as my auxiliaries right away!'), *ārnut* (ibid. 3 and 15; cf. Friedrich, *Staatsverträge* 1:124–6), 3 sg. imp. act. *arnuddu* (e.g. *KUB* VII 60 III 13–14 *nu-mu* ^DU EN-YA ZI-*a*[*s*] *iyadu nu-wa-mu-kan* ZI-*as arnud*[*du* 'may the storm-god my lord do my soul's [desire] and further my soul's [desire]'; cf. Haas – Wilhelm, *Riten* 238; for the phraseology, cf. *kardiyas iya-* s.v. *kard*[*i*]-; Sommer, *AU* 31–2; XXXIII 8 II 15 and 16), *aranuddu* (ibid. 17; cf. Laroche, *RHA* 23:101 [1965]), 2 pl. imp. act. *ar-nu-ut-tin* (e.g. XXIII 72 Vs. 41; *Maşat* 75/11, 13; 75/13, 19; cf. Alp, *Belleten* 44:40, 46 [1980]), 3 pl. imp. act. *arnuwandu* (e.g. XXXIII 89 + XXXVI 21 III 14; cf. Laroche, *RHA* 26:69 [1968]), *arnuandu* (e.g. *KBo* V 3 II 9 ^DUTU-*ŠI-ma-ssan* ZI-*as arnuandu* 'but let them further his majesty's soul's [desire]'; cf. Friedrich, *Staatsverträge* 2:114); partic. *arnu(w)ant-*, nom. sg. c. *ārnuwanza* (*KUB* XXIII 92 Rs. 15), acc. sg. c. *arnuandan* (see below), nom.-acc. sg. neut. *arnuwan* (XXI 33 IV 24), *arnuan* (*KBo* XI 1 Vs. 22; cf. *RHA* 25:106, 132–3 [1967]), nom.-acc. pl. neut. *arnuwanda* (*KUB* XXVII 13 IV 14); verbal noun *arnumar* (n.), nom.-acc. sg. *arnumar* (*KBo* I 44 I 13 *katta-ssan arnumar* 'a bringing to an end, termination'; cf. Otten, *Vokabular* 9), *ārnumar* (*KUB* XIV 17 II 7 'a movement [of troops]'; cf. Götze, *AM* 84), *arnummar* (XLIII 55 II 19), gen. sg. *arnumas* (II 1 II 50 *maninkuwan arnumas* 'of bringing near'; cf. A. Archi, *SMEA* 16:95, 109 [1975]; *VAT* 7497 IV 8 ^D*SIN* ZI-*ni arnumas* 'moon-god of soul-influence' [vel sim.]; cf. Sommer, *AU* 30), *arnummas* (*KUB* II 1 II 28 ZI-*as arnummas* 'of furthering the soul's [desire]'; *KBo* V 9 II 34–35 *arnummas uttar* 'a matter of [forcible] removal'; cf. Friedrich, *Staatsverträge* 1:18; *KUB* XVIII 49 Rs. 11); infin. *arnumanzi* (XIV 17 II 15 'to move [troops]'; cf. Götze, *AM* 84; *KBo* XVI 97 Vs. 7), *arnumazi* (XXIII 110 Rs. 10); iter. *arnuski-*, 1 sg. pres. act. *a]rnuskimi* (XVIII 24 I 18), 2 sg. pres. act. *arnuskisi* (*KUB* XXVI 15, 10), 3 sg. pres. act. in IV 1 I 31–32 DINAM *arnuskizzi* 'raises complaint' (cf. von Schuler, *Die Kaškäer* 170), 1 pl. pres. act. in XVII 21 II 6–7 *nu-smas-san* DINAM *arnuskiuwani* 'we shall raise complaint with you' (cf. von Schuler, *Die Kaškäer* 154), 3 pl. pres. act. *arnuskanzi* (XXXII 123 IV 29), 1 sg. pret. act. *arnuskinun* (*KBo* XVI 9, 1), 3 sg. pret. act. *a]rnuskit* (XIII 74, 11), 3 pl. pret. act. *arnuskir* (*KUB* XIX 14, 17 'they kept deporting'; cf. Güterbock, *JCS* 10:112 [1956]; *KBo* IV 12 Vs. 24 and 28 'they had kept promoting'; cf. Götze, *Hattusilis* 42), 2 sg. imp. act. *arnuski* (*KUB* XL 102 VI 5), 3 sg. imp. act. *arnuskiddu* (XXX 40 III 7–8 *nu-war-as-san assuli* ZI-*as arnuskiddu* 'may he in favor keep furthering [their] soul's [desire]'), 2 pl. imp. act. *arnuskitin* (*FHG* 5, 7; cf. Laroche, *RA* 45:138 [1951]), *arnuskittin* (*KUB* XIII 4 IV 5–6 *n-at-kan* DINGIR.MEŠ-*a[s]* ZI-*ni hūdāk arnuskittin* 'bring it at once to the [soul of the] gods'; cf. Sturtevant, *JAOS* 54:390 [1934]). Cf. Kronasser, *Etym.* 1:442, 301.

arnuwala- (c.) 'displaced person (of either sex), deportee (from conquered lands, bound to an assigned residence)' (NAM.RA, lit. 'seized one', from Sum. *ri* 'seize'), nom. sg. *arnuwalas* (*KUB* XXVI 57 I 5–7 LÚ*arnuwalass-a-k[an ...]* KUR.KUR.MEŠ-*as hūmandas [...]* KUR URU*Hatti anda ēszi* 'the DP of all lands is in Hatti'; XIII 2 III 36 *arnuwalas-a-kan kuis* KUR-*ya anda arzananza* 'the DP who is quartered in the country', vs. ibid. 38–39 'who goes out of the country'; cf. von Schuler, *Dienstanweisungen* 48), acc. sg. *arnuwalan* (XIII 14 Rs 1 [= *Code* 200A] *takku arnuwalan kattan kuiski sesk[izzi* 'if anyone sleeps with a DP'), nom. pl. *arnuwalas* (*Bo* 2401 III 1–2 EZEN ... LÚ.MEŠ*arnuwalas ēssanzi* 'the DP's celebrate the festival'; cf. Otten, *ZDMG* 102:342 [1952]), dat.-loc. pl. *arnuwalas* (*KBo* XVI 97 Rs. 1 *mān arahzenas kuitki* ERÍN.MEŠ *arnuwalas idalu iyazzi* 'if an external army does any harm to the DP's'). This term is distinct from *appant-* 'captive'

(ŠU.DIB, Akk. *ṣabtu*), q.v. s.v. *ep(p)-*. Unlike Akk. NAM.
.RA = *šallatu* which encompassed all movable spoils (humans,
animals, goods), Hitt. NAM.RA = *arnuwala-* refers to humans
only (the comprehensive generic term for all manner of booty is
rather *saru-* [q.v.]); for speculations about this Hittite divergence
(traditional asyndetic bipartition of 'moveable possessions' into
'men + beasts[-chattels]', IE **wiro- + peк̂u-*), see C. Watkins in
Hethitisch und Indogermanisch 269–87 (1979). Cf. Goetze, *AM*
217–20; Laroche, *RA* 43:72–3 (1949); Alp, *JKF* 1:113–35
(1950); H. A. Hoffner, *JCS* 22:39 (1968). On the identification
NAM.RA = *arnuwala-* cf. esp. Alp, *JKF* 1:121–4 (1950); on the
suffix *-ala-* see Alp, *JKF* 1:124–6 (1950); N. van Brock, *RHA*
20:95–6 (1962); Kronasser, *Etym.* 1:172–4.

For discussion and bibliography of the many interpretations
of *arnu-* in the *Code*, cf. e.g. Güterbock, *JCS* 15:66–7 (1961);
Imparati, *Parola del Passato* 14:185–8 (1959), *Leggi ittite*
186–7, 204–7, 261, 272; Haase, *Studi in onore di Edoardo
Volterra* 6:471–82 (1971). The meanings posited here are
'deliver, produce' ('deport' once in *Code* 2:96), declining 'bury'
(Sturtevant et al.; cf. Gk. ἐκφέρω) and 'make amends, indem-
nify' (Friedrich – Goetze; cf. Haase, *Bi. Or.* 17:182 [1960], and
G. Klingenschmitt, *Studien zur Indologie und Iranistik*
5–6:143–5 [1980], who assumed a separate verb *arnu-*
'owe reparations' cognate with Skt. *ṛṇám* 'debt'). The acc.
sg. c. participle *arnuandan* (*KBo* VI 2 IV 6–7, 19, 21 [= *Code*
1:77, 83, 84]) is presumably a euphemistic 'brought (viz. to
mating)', hence 'impregnated', besides the corresponding VI 3
III 78–79 *ar-ma-u-an-da-an* and ibid. IV 15 and 17 *ar-ma-an-
-da-an* 'pregnant' (q.v. s.v. *armai-*) in the newer version of the
Code.

arnu- (< **ṛ-new-/ṛ-nu-*) is not only the regular causative
formation from the stem *ar-* but also an ancient match to Gk.
ὄρνυμι 'move, rouse, stir', Skt. *ṛṇóti* 'move, arise', Avest.
ərənaoiti 'set in motion', etc. (*IEW* 326–7). Cf. e.g. Hrozný, *SH*
130; Sturtevant, *Lg.* 3:166 (1927); Couvreur, *Hett.* 96. A
comparison with Gk. ἄρνυμαι 'win', Arm. *aṙnum* 'take' (e.g.
Frisk, *GEW* 1:146) is semantically implausible.

Cf. *ar-*; *ar-, er-*; *arai-*; *arriya-*; *aru-*; *aruna-*; *ar(u)wai-*.

arp-, found in nominal derivatives:

arpa- (c.) 'bad luck, setback, misfortune', nom. and abl. sg. in
KBo XXII 260 Vs. 12–14 *nu arpās-ma* (with gloss-wedges) *kuiski*
DÙ-*ri n-as arpaza* (with gloss-wedges) *ŪL* DÙ-*zi* ... [*nu a*]*rpās kuis*
SIxSÁ-*at* 'some setback occurs and he does not act on account of
the setback ... the setback which was determined ...', acc. sg.
arpan (*KUB* V 1 III 46 ŠA MÈ *arpan* 'setback in battle'; ibid. 49
MÈ-*as arpan*; ibid. 67 ŠA MÈ DUGUD-*un arpan* 'heavy setback in
battle'; cf. Ünal, *Hatt.* 2:72–4; *KBo* XXIII 117 I 8 [with gloss-
wedges]), gen. sg. *arpas* (ibid. 9 [with gloss-wedges]).

Denom. *arpai-* 'be unlucky, turn out badly', 3 sg. pres. midd.
in *KBo* III 21 II 23 -]*anza-mis arpiyattari* 'my ? turns out badly'
(cf. e.g. *aritta* s.v. *arai-*); iter. *arpasa-* (cf. e.g. *halzessa-* from
halzai-), 3 sg. pres. act. *arpasāi* (*KUB* V 1 III 33 KARAŠ.HI.A TA
MÈ *arpasāi* 'the army has reverses in battle'), 3 sg. pret. act.
(Luwoid) *arpasatta* (*KBo* III 6 I 3 *nu-mu arpasatta* [with gloss-
wedges] 'it went badly for me'; cf. Götze, *Hattusilis* 10). Cf.
Kronasser, *Etym.* 1:555, and for the corresponding Luwian
iteratives in *-(s)s(a)-, Dict. louv.* 144.

**arpu-* (n.) 'bad luck, trouble', denom. *arpuwai-* 'be unlucky,
be hazardous, prove troublesome', 3 sg. pres. midd. *arputta*
(< **arpuwatta*; cf. e.g. *sallattari* from *sallai-* [s.v. *salli-*], and
sanhunzi < *sanhuwanzi* (s.v. *sanhuwai-*]; *KBo* VI 26 I 20 [= *Code*
2:62]; cf. Neu, *Interpretation* 15–6; XIX 104, 5; cf. Siegelová,
Appu-Hedammu 14; reservations in H. C. Melchert, *JCS* 31:61
[1979], and Güterbock, *Die Welt des Orients* 9:91–2 [1980],
who read *larputta*); partic. *arpuwant-*, nom. sg. c. *arpuwanza*
(*KBo* XIX 76 + *KUB* XIV 10 I 14 *par*]*kus arpuwanzass-a* 'high
and hazardous' [mountain]; cf. Houwink Ten Cate, in *Florilegium Anatolicum* 161 [1979]), nom.-acc. sg. neut. *arpūwan*
(*KUB* XIV 3 I 24 and XIX 37 II 16 'hazardous' [place]; cf.
Sommer, *AU* 2; Götze, *AM* 168), nom. pl. c. *arpuwantes* (XIX
37 III 50 and 52 'difficult' [roads]; cf. ibid. 51 *warhuis* 'rough';
Götze, *AM* 176–8), nom.-acc. pl. neut. *arpuwanta* (V 1 III 48
IZKIM.HI.A-*ya-za arpuwanta kikistari* 'unlucky signs occur'; cf.
Ünal, *Hatt.* 2:72); verbal noun *arpuwatar* (n.), dat.-loc. sg.
arpuwanni (XX 52 IV 6).

Luw. *arpuwan(n)i-* 'unlucky' (?), instr.-abl. sg. *arpuwanāti*

(*KUB* XXXV 43 II 13; cf. Otten, *LTU* 43).

Hier. ^{MOUNT}*Arputawanas*, epithet of storm-god, perhaps *arpu-(wa)nta-* + ethnic suffix *-wana-*, i.e. 'inhabiting Mt. Arpuwant' (cf. Laroche, *HH* 113; Neumann, *Orbis* 20:484 [1971]).

Laroche (*RHA* 16:98 [1958]) interpreted Lyc. *erbbe* (<**arpa-*; e.g. *TLy* 29.3 *erbbe*; 44a.47 and 44c.13 *erbbedi* [instr.]) as 'defeat', and similarly Lyc. B *erbbesi-* (*TLy* 44d.13) as reflecting a Luw. **arpassi-* (genitival adj.); but he also improbably derived the iterative stem *arpasa-* (see above) from the latter.

For possible survival of *arpa-* in Anatolian onomastics (e.g. Τροκοαρβασις, Αρβασις, esp. in Cilicia and Lycia), see Houwink Ten Cate, *LPG* 147–8; L. Zgusta, *Anatolische Personennamensippen* 1:72–4 (1964).

While *arpuwant-* and *arpuwatar* may alternatively be denominatives from **arpu-* (cf. e.g. *akuwant-* s.v. *aku-*, and *idaluwatar* s.v. *idalu-*), with the disappearance of **arpu-* they would have effectively become part of the paradigm of *arpuwai-*. In view of the wide distribution of both *arpa-* and *arpu-* in both Hittite and Southern Anatolian it is difficult to credit Tischler's postulation (*Glossar* 65–6) of a basic adjective **arpu-* and secondary origin of *arpa-* via a specific inner-Hittite development (cf. e.g. *idālaz* < *idalawaz*); instead *arpa-* and *arpu-* must be parallel formations of at least Proto-Anatolian date.

Couvreur's connection (*Hett.* 105) of *arp-* with *RV* 10.117.2 *raphitá-* 'overcome, wretched', Ved. *rápas-* 'infirmity, (bodily) affliction' is formally and semantically plausible, although the further tie-in with Lat. *rapiō* 'snatch' and an IE **rep-* (*IEW* 865; supported by Tischler, *KZ* 86:278–80 [1972], *Glossar* 65–6) remains doubtful (cf. Mayrhofer, *KEWA* 3:41). PAnat. **arp-* can theoretically reflect either *$A_2 er$-p-, *$H_2 or$-p-, or *$H_2 r̥p$-, with *Hr-$ép$- seen in the Vedic words; possibly *arpa-* < *$H_2 órpo$- (noun), but *arpu-* < *$H_2 r̥pú$- (adjective, neuter used as noun); Hitt. *arpu-* would then be to Ved. *rápas-* what e.g. Ved. *urú-* 'wide' is to *váras-* 'width'.

The tie-in of *arpa-* with Lat. *orbus* 'bereft' (IE **orbho-*; *IEW* 781–2), current since Sturtevant (e.g. *Comp. Gr.*[1] 93; still in Kronasser, *Etym.* 1:184), is implausible (see also s.v. *har[a]p-*).

arp-   arpamar   ar(a)s-, arsiya-

Neumann (*Orbis* 20:482–5 [1971]) adduced Gk. ἀρβύλη
'hiking-shoe' as an Anatolian-based outcome of **arpu(wa)lli-*
(i.e. **arpu-* + *-alli-*) 'suitable for hazardous terrain' (cf. *ar-
puwant-* used of rough places and roads).

Cf. *arpamar*.

arpamar   (n.), bread-name, nom.-acc. sg. or pl. ᴺᴵᴺᴰᴬ*arpamar* (*KUB*
XXX 19 IV 2 and dupl. XXXIX 8 III 38; cf. Otten, *Totenrituale*
44), ᴺᴵᴺᴰᴬ*arpamarr-a* (XXXIX 7 II 64; cf. Otten, *Totenrituale*
40).

This type of bread was deposited together with fruits at the
regal bier. In view of the euphemistic tenor of royal funerary
terminology (e.g. *KUB* XXX 16 I 1–2 *mān* ᵁᴿᵁ*Hattusi sallis
wastāis kisari nassu-za* LUGAL-*us nasma* SAL.LUGAL-*as* DINGIR-
-*LIM-is kisari* 'if great desolation occurs at H., in that either
king or queen becomes a god') it is quite possible to assume a
relationship to *arpa-* 'bad luck, misfortune' (q.v. s.v. *arp-*), with
ᴺᴵᴺᴰᴬ*arpamar* (or NINDA *arpamar?*), denominative like *hila-
-mmar* (Kronasser, *Etym.* 1:282–3), meaning roughly 'mortuary bread' (cf. H. A. Hoffner, *Alimenta Hethaeorum* 152–3
[1974]).

The claims for "foreign" origin (Kronasser, *Etym.* 1:273;
Tischler, *Glossar* 65) are wholly arbitrary.

ar(a)s-, arsiya-   'flow', 1 sg. pres. act. *arasmi* (*KUB* XXXVI
75 + 1226/u III 19 *nu wātar māhhan kuwāpi arasmi* 'I flow like
water somewhere'; cf. H. Otten – C. Rüster, *ZA* 67:56 [1977]),
3 sg. pres. act. *araszi* (e.g. *KBo* XIII 31 I 8 *ēshar araszi* 'blood
flows'; cf. Riemschneider, *Geburtsomina* 74; XXI 22 Rs. 38–9
wātar-sed-a-kan [...] *lūliaz araszi* 'and its water flows from the
pond'; *KUB* IX 3 I 10 ÍD-*as araszi* 'the river flows'; IX 6 I 19,
21, 22, 37 *araszi* '[the liquid] flows'; cf. Otten, *LTU* 38; XV 34
III 23–4 *n-asta wātar kuwapi parā araszi* 'where water flows
forth'; cf. Zuntz, *ARIV* 96.2:510 [1936–7]; Haas – Wilhelm,
Riten 196), *āraszi* (VIII 36 II 11 *ēshar āraszi*; cf. Burde,
Medizinische Texte 38; XVIII 41 II 10 *wātarr-a-wa-kan āraszi*

170

'water flows'; XVII 9 I 20–22 *kuwat-wa wēskisi nu-wa-ta-kkan suppayaza* [IGI.HI.]A-*wa-za ishahru parā āras*[*zi* 'why do you keep wailing and tears flow from your pure eyes?'; cf. Friedrich, *ZA* 39:45 [1930]; XLI 8 II 3–4 *tedanus āraszi*; dupl. *KBo* X 45 II 40 *tēdanas ār*[*aszi* 'hair flows'; cf. Otten, *ZA* 54:124 [1961]; *VBoT* 16 Rs. 6), *ārzi* (X 45 IV 39 *n-at-kan* GAM ^{GIŠ}PISÀN-*az ārzi* 'it flows down the drainpipe'; dupl. *KUB* XLI 8 IV 37 *āraszi*; cf. Otten, *ZA* 54:138 [1961]; XV 42 II 3 *katta ārzi*; dupl. XLIII 58 II 15 *āraszi*), *arsiyazi* (XXXIII 49 II 3; cf. Laroche, *RHA* 23:142 [1965]), *arsiyazzi* (XXIX 9 I 10–11 *nu-ssi-kan issalli parā* ZAG-*ni meni arsiyazzi* 'and spittle flows forth onto his right cheek'; cf. Güterbock, *AfO* 18:79 [1957]), *arsiyezzi* (XXXIII 54, 10–11 ^{GIŠ}PISÀN-*as* GIM-*an āppa parza* ŪL *arsiyezzi* 'as the drainpipe does not flow backwards'; cf. Laroche, *RHA* 23:139 [1965]), *arsiezzi* (XVII 10 III 26; cf. Laroche, ibid. 95; *KBo* XXI 41 + *KUB* XXIX 7 Rs. 59–60 *nu* ÍD-*as māhhan* EGIR-*pa* ŪL *arsiezzi* 'as the river does not flow backwards'; cf. Lebrun, *Samuha* 124–5), *ārassiyazi* (XXIX 9 I 14–15 *nu-ssi-kan* KAxU-*az issalli parā* GÙB-*li meni ārassiyazi* 'and spittle flows forth from his mouth onto his left cheek'), *arsizzi* (XXIX 10 I 6–7 *nu-s*]*si-kan* KAxU-*az issalli parā* ZAG-*ni meni arsizzi*; cf. Güterbock, *AfO* 18:79 [1957]), *ārassizzi* (ibid. 9–11 *nu-ssi-kan issaz issalli parā* GÙB-*li meni ārassizzi*), *ārsiyaizzi* (XXXIX 7 Vs. 28 and 29; cf. Otten, *Totenrituale* 32), 3 sg. pres. midd. *arsari* (?; XXXIV 78, 6), 3 pl. pres. act. *arsanzi* (XXIV 8 IV 10–11 ÍD.MEŠ ... *arsanzi* 'rivers flow'; cf. Friedrich, *ZA* 49:222 [1950]; Siegelová, *Appu-Hedammu* 12; XXXVI 25 IV 4–5 *nu wēskizzi ishahru-ma-ssi-kan* ... *arsanzi* 'he keeps wailing ... and his tears flow'; cf. Laroche, *RHA* 26:73 [1968]; cf. also Güterbock, *JCS* 6:12 [1952]; X 72 V 3), *arsiyanzi* (*IBoT* III 141, 5; cf. Laroche, *RHA* 23:103 [1965]), 3 sg. pret. act. *ārsas* (XXXVI 89 Rs. 12, of the river Marassantas; cf. Haas, *Nerik* 152; XXIV 14 II 3), 3 pl. pret. act. *arser* (e.g. XXXVI 2b II 19; cf. Meriggi, *Athenaeum* N.S. 31:136 [1953]; Laroche, *RHA* 26:33 [1968]), 3 sg. imp. act. *arasdu* (*KBo* XVII 105 II 34), 3 sg. imp. midd. *arsaru* (?; 1190/u Rs. 9); partic. *arsant-*, nom. pl. c. *arsantes* (*KBo* X 47g III 14 '[over]flowing' [with vegetation]; cf. Otten, *Istanbuler Mitteilungen* 8:108 [1958]; Laroche, *RHA* 26:12 [1968]; Puhvel, *Kratylos*

25:138 [1980]), acc. pl. c. *arsantes* (*KUB* XXXIII 41 II 9; cf. Laroche, *RHA* 23:160 [1965]). Cf. Kronasser, *Etym.* 1:394–5; Neu, *Interpretation* 16.

Caus. *ar(as)sanu-*, 3 pl. pres. act. *arassanuwanzi* (*KUB* XXX 32 I 15 *n-asta wātar anda arassanuwanzi* 'they let water flow in'; cf. V. Haas – M. Wäfler, *Ugarit-Forschungen* 8:96 [1976]), 3 sg. pret. act. *arsanut* (XXXVI 89 Rs. 13 and 14, of diverting rivers; cf. Haas, *Nerik* 152; *KUB* IV 5 + *KBo* XII 73, 22 ÍD.MEŠ-*ass-a-*-*kan anda kariddus arsanut* 'into rivers he made floods flow'; cf. Laroche, *RA* 58:73 [1964]). Cf. Kronasser, *Etym.* 1:443.

arsanu- (n.) 'flow, course', nom.-acc. sg. in *KUB* XXXVI 89 Rs. 19 *nu-wa-za-kan ārsanu le wahnusi* 'do not turn the flow!' (cf. Haas, *Nerik* 152) , nom.-acc. pl. *arsanuwa* (ibid. Rs. 41).

arsarsur- 'flowing; stream', nom.-acc. sg. neut. *ar-sa-as-su-u-*-*ur* (*KBo* XXIII 9 I 12), dat.-loc. sg. *ārsa(r)suri* (*KUB* XVII 27 II 21–22 *nassu wappui nasma* ÍD-*as ārsarsuri* 'either to the bank or to the stream of the river'), acc. pl. c. in XXXIII 10 Vs. 10 ÍD.HI.A *arsarsūrus* 'flowing rivers' (cf. Laroche, *RHA* 23:105 [1965]), nom.-acc. pl. neut. *arsarsūra* (XXXIII 13 II 14; cf. Laroche, *RHA* 23:158 [1965]), *arsarsūri-ssit* (XXXVI 55 II 26 'its streams'), *arsāssūri-ssit-ya* (ibid. 20 '[all] its streams'), unclear case *arsasuras* (*KBo* XII 33 III 3).

Luw. 3 pl. imp. act. *ārsiyandu* (*KUB* XXXV 39 I 25; cf. Otten, *LTU* 38). Cf. *Dict. louv.* 31.

Cf. Skt. *árṣati* 'flow', *rása-* 'liquid' (IE **H₂ér-s*, *H₂r-és-*); further possible cognates (e.g. Gk. ἀπ-εράω 'pour out'; *IEW* 336–7) may point to an *e*-colored laryngeal (E_1), in which case Hitt. *ars-* would represent zero grade or conditioned timbre. Cf. e.g. Sturtevant, *Lg.* 8:120 (1932), *Comp. Gr.*[1] 90, *Comp. Gr.*[2] 30; Couvreur, *Hett.* 96–7. On toponymic cognates see Rosenkranz, *BzN* N.F. 1:135–6 (1966).

arsana-   'be angry (at: dat.-loc.), begrudge, envy', verbal -*(a)na*-stem (or adjective?), attested in derivatives:

arsanant-, nom.-acc. pl. neut. in *KUB* XXXIII 9 III 7 *sakuwa arsanand[a* 'envious eyes' (cf. Laroche, *RHA* 23:106 [1965]), original participle (or denominative -*nt*- adjective?); *arsanatal-*

172

(1)a- (c.) 'envier' (equals *ganāu*, i.e. Canaan. *qannā'* 'be jealous'
in *KBo* XIII 1 I 36; cf. Otten, *Vokabular* 10, 12), acc. pl.
arsanatallus (I 1 I 59; cf. Götze, *Hattusilis* 12), *arsanattallus*
(*KBo* III 6 IV 4; cf. Götze, *Hattusilis* 34–5), *arsanattalus* (*KUB*
I 8 IV 25), dat.-loc. pl. *arsanatallas* (I 1 I 54), *arsanattallas* (*KBo*
III 6 I 45; *KUB* XXI 27 III 26); *arsaniya-*, 2 sg. pres. act.
arsanēsi (*KBo* XXV 122 III 2, 4, 6, 8, 10, 12, 14; cf. Starke,
Funktionen 137; Neu, *Altheth.* 205), *arsaniese* (*ABoT* 65 Rs. 6
man zik ŪL arsaniese 'would you not be angry?'; cf. L. Rost,
MIO 4:346 [1956]; possibly graphic error for 2 sg. pret. act.
ar-sa-ni-e-es; cf. C. Watkins, *Indogermanische Grammatik* III/1,
79–80 [1969]), 1 sg. pret. *arsanie[nun* (*ABoT* 65 Rs. 4), 3 sg. pret.
act. *arsaniyat* (*KUB* XIX 65, 14; cf. Götze, *Neue Bruchstücke*
28), 3 pl. pret. act. *arsanier* (cf. Götze, *Hattusilis* 8; with gloss-
wedges in I 1 I 32). Cf. Kronasser, *Etym.* 1:568, 258, 176.

ars- < IE $*E_1\underset{\circ}{r}(E_1)s$- (*IEW* 337), as in Avest. *ərəši-* 'envy' and
perhaps Toch. A *rse* 'hatred'; cf. $*E_1er(E_1)s$- in OE *eorsian*
'wish ill', *yrre* 'angry', $*E_1\underset{\circ}{r}E_1s$- in Skt. *īrṣyā́* 'envy, jealousy',
Avest. *arəšyant-* 'envious', $*E_1rE_1es$- in Skt. *irasyáti* 'be angry',
irasyā́ 'ill-will' (= Hom. ἀρειή 'threats'), Avest. *araska-* 'envy'.
Cf. Benveniste, *BSL* 33:139 (1932); Mayrhofer, *IF* 70:246
(1965); Gusmani, *Lessico* 52; Čop, *Ling.* 8:51–2 (1966–8).

arsi- (c.) 'planting, plantation, cultivation', nom. sg. *arsis* (*KBo* VI
12 I 13 [= *Code* 2:3]), acc. sg. *arsin* (ibid. 20 [= *Code* 2:5];
XVIII 151 Vs. 16; cf. Ünal – Kammenhuber, *KZ* 88:164
[1974]).

arsai-, *arsiya-* 'plant, nurture, cherish, cultivate', (midd.)
'take care of oneself; thrive, succeed', 3 sg. pres. act. *arsāizzi*
(VI 12 I 20 *a]rsin* EGIR-*pa arsāizzi* 'he replants the plantation';
XXIV 4 Vs. 11), *arsaizzi* (*KUB* XXIX 21, 15; cf. Haase,
Fragmente 55), *arsezzi* (*KBo* VI 12 I 12), 2 sg. imp. midd.
arsiyahhut (*KUB* X 72 V 6 and 13), *ārsiyahhut* (I 16 III 30 *nu-za*
UD-*an* 2-ŠU 3-ŠU *et nu-za ārs[iya]hhut* 'eat two or three times a
day, and take care of yourself'; cf. Sommer, *HAB* 12), 3 sg.
imp. midd. *arsiyattaru* (*KBo* VII 28, 16 'may [the libation]
succeed'; cf. Friedrich, *Rivista degli studi orientali* 32:218

[1957]), 3 pl. imp. act. *arsiyandu* (*KUB* XXIX 1 IV 23–25 *ke-wa mahhan arseskanzi nu* LUGAL-*un* SAL.LUGAL-*unn-a hasses hanzasses anda* QATAMMA *arsiyandu* 'as they nurture these [trees], let them likewise cherish the descendants of the king and queen'; cf. Sommer, *HAB* 152; B. Schwartz, *Orientalia* N.S. 16:38 [1947]; Dressler, *Studien* 183); iter. 3 pl. pres. act. *arseskanzi* (XXIX 1 IV 24 above), 3 sg. pret. act. *arsikkit* (*KBo* VI 13 I 8 [= *Code* 2:69] *taknā arsikkit* 'planted in the earth'; dupl. *KUB* XXIX 30 III 13 *tāknā* [*arsik*]*ket*; cf. Friedrich, *Heth. Ges.* 76; Haase, *Fragmente* 78). Cf. Kronasser, *Etym.* 1:501; Neu, *Interpretation* 16.

Cf. Hes. ἄρσεα· λειμῶνες, presumably an Asianic loanword. Possibly *arsi-* is connectible with *ar(a)s-* 'flow' (q.v.). For the remarkable congruence of Hittite and Greek terms denoting (irrigational) cultivation, cf. s.v. *amiyara-*. See also Rosenkranz, *JEOL* 19:502–3 (1965–6); Gusmani, *Studi linguistici in onore di Vittore Pisani* 512 (1969); O. Szemerényi, *Gnomon* 43:657 (1971), *Journal of Hellenic Studies* 94:153 (1974).

M. Mayer (*Acme* 27:303 [1974]) saw in *arsai-* a borrowing from Old Assyrian *arāšu* (standard Akk. *erēšu*, PSem. **hrþ* 'cultivate with a seeder-plow', hence also 'plant'; cf. s.v. *har*[*a*]*s-*); but *arsai-* (like *arsiya-*) is denominatively derived from *arsi-*, not the basis of the latter.

Cf. *arziya-*.

arsi(n)tathi-   (c.), name of an ornithomantic bird, nom. sg. *arsintathis* (e.g. *KUB* V 17 II 27; XVI 54 Rs. 10 and 13; XVIII 12 I 9; cf. Ünal, *RHA* 31:43 [1973]), *ar-si-en-ta-at-hi-es* (V 11 I 17), *ar-si-in-ta-at-hi-es* (XLIX 21 III 12), *ar-si-en-ta-at-hi-is* (V 11 I 54), *arsitathis* (ibid. 19 and 63), *ar-si-in-da-at-hi-es* (*KBo* XXIV 126 Vs. 20), acc. sg. *arsintathin* (e.g. *KUB* V 17 II 24 and 37), *arsitathin* (V 11 IV 35), *arsidathin* (*Alalah* 454 II 4). Cf. Ertem, *Fauna* 209–10. For other augural bird names see e.g. s.v. *alila-*, *aramni-*.

Hurrian origin is patent in the suffix; cf. e.g. *ahrushi-*, *anahi(t)-* (s.v.). Cf. Kronasser, *Etym.* 1:209. But indigenous Anatolian provenance is also possible.

ard- 'saw', 1 pl. pres. act. *ardumēni* (*KUB* XXXVI 74, 2] *aimpan ardumēni* 'let us saw [off] the burden' [gods speaking, perhaps figuratively, in the Atrahasis-epic]; cf. Siegelová, *Arch. Or.* 38:136 [1970]), 3 pl. imp. act. *arduwandu* (XXXIII 106 III 54 ᴰ*Ullukummin* ᴺᴬ⁴ŠU.U-*zin* GÌR.MEŠ GAM-*an arha ardu*[*wandu* 'let them saw off the feet of U. the diorite'; cf. Güterbock, *JCS* 6:28, 41–2 [1952]); verbal noun *ar-du-mar* (KBo XXVI 19,10). For the juncture shift **ard-(u)weni* > **ardu-weni* > *ardumeni* cf. also N. van Brock, *RHA* 20:94 (1972); Kronasser, *Etym.* 1:84; see also s.v. *halluwai-*.

ardala- (n.) 'saw', nom.-acc. pl. *ardāla* (*KUB* XXXIII 106 III 52–53 *nu-kan karuwiliya* ᵁᴿᵁᴰᵁ*ardāla parā tiyandu nepis tekann- -a kuez arha kuerir* 'let them bring forth the ancient saw with which they cut apart heaven and earth'; *KBo* XXVI 65 II 18).

The sense 'saw' is plausible as a specification of the 'cutter' (ᵁᴿᵁᴰᵁ*kuruzzi*) referred to in *KUB* XXXIII 106 III 42, esp. since parallel Greek myth has a 'saw-toothed sickle' (ἄρπην καρχαρόδοντα in Hesiod, *Theogony* 180). The "jagged" root-meaning of *ard-* may hence well be 'gnaw', related to Ved. *rádati* which means not only 'gnaw' but 'cut through, open up (paths, channels, etc.)', also figuratively; other cognates would be Lat. *rōdō* 'gnaw', *rādō* 'tear, strip, scrape, scratch' (cf. *rōstrum* 'bill, snout, sharp point', *rāstrum* 'hoe'). An underlying IE **H₂ér-d-*, **H₂r-éd-* accounts for the Hittite and Vedic forms, while the Latin vocalism is difficult (seeming long-grade *o*-ablaut in *rōd-*, and secondarily differentiated *rād-*?). Hitt. *ard-* is to Ved. *rád-* what e.g. Hitt. *arp-* is to Ved. *rápas-*, or *halzai-* is to Goth. *laþōn*, or *palhi-* is to Lat. *plānus*, or *san(a)h-* 'flush' is to Ved. *snáti* 'bathe'. Cf. Puhvel, *Bi. Or.* 36:58 (1979).

The comparison of *ard-* with Skt. *ṛdhak* 'separately', *ardhá-* 'half', Lith. *ardýti* 'split, separate' (*IEW* 333), advocated by Tischler (*KZ* 86:281 [1972], *Glossar* 69), assumed a special suffixation of the root seen in e.g. *árma-* 'ruins', Lith. *ìrti* 'dissolve' (q.v. rather s.v. *harra-*).

arta- (c.), bird-name, acc. sg. *artan*ᴹᵁŠᴱᴺ (143/r, 3), acc. pl. *ardus* (*KUB* XXX 24a + XXXIV 65 I 155 *arduss-a* MUŠEN.HI.A; cf.

Otten, *Totenrituale* 58, *OLZ* 57:231 [1962]; XXXIX 37 I 5 5
arduss-a[), dat.-loc. pl. ANA *ārtas-ma-kan* (XXXIX 35 I 7).
Derived South Anatolian toponym *Ardussa*[(XXVI 43 Vs. 39;
cf. Imparati, *RHA* 32:28 [1974]; Laroche, *Gedenkschrift P.
Kretschmer* 2:3 [1957]; Garstang – Gurney, *Geography* 124;
Ertem, *Coğrafya* 14), as happens frequently with Anatolian
bird-names (cf. e.g. s.v. *kakkapa-*, *mutamuti-*; Neumann, *Untersuch.* 60).

Cf. perhaps Ἄρδυς, Mermnad king of Lydia in whose family
ornithonymy may have been rife (Μέρμνης, Γύγης, Τουδώ); cf.
Neumann, *Untersuch.* 70; Heubeck, *Praegraeca* 38; Puhvel,
JAOS 82:78 (1962), *Evidence for Laryngeals* 85 (1965); W.
Fauth, *Hermes* 96:257–64 (1968). Differently Carruba, *OLZ*
60:557 (1965), who combined Ἄρδυς with Hitt. *hardu-* 'descendant' (q.v.). V. Georgiev (*Linguistique balkanique* 11.2:7 and 20
[1967]) compared Ἄρδυς : *ardu-* with the Etruscan man's name
Arθ, rendered by *C.* (= *Gaius*) in the Etr.-Lat. bilingual *CIE*
890 = *TLE* 521 (cf. Lat. *gaius* 'jay, magpie').

Cf. Lat. *ardea* 'heron', ON *arta* 'teal', Gk. ἐρωδιός, ἀρωδιός
'heron', Serb. *róda* 'stork', IE *$*A_2er-H_2-d-$, A_2r-oH_2-d- (*IEW* 68).
Perhaps *ardu-* < *$*A_2{r}H_2dú-$, cf. Serb. *róda* < *$*radá$ < *$*A_2rH_2déA_2$.
See also H. Wittmann, *Die Sprache* 10: 144 (1964), 19:39 (1973).

artah(h)i-   (c.) 'sewer' (*KUB* III 94 II 9 [Akk.] *alallu* = GIŠ*a*[*r*]*da*[*hhi-*;
cf. Laroche, *RHA* 24:165 [1966]), dat.-loc. sg. *artahhiya* (XXX
34 IV 14–15 *nu wātar* EGIR-*pa* GIŠPISÀN *lahhutti nu kī-ma*
EGIR-*an artahhiya lahhutti* 'you pour water down the drain; but
afterwards you pour it into the sewer'; cf. V. Haas – M. Wäfler,
Oriens Antiquus 16:230 [1977]), nom. pl. *artahhiēs* (XXXI
87 + 88 II 25), *ārtahius* (par. XIII 2 II 22 *ārtahius wehandaru
n-as uskandu* 'the sewers shall be kept functioning, and let them
inspect them'), *artahhius* (XXXI 89 II 19 *artahhius le sāheskantari* 'let the sewers not be clogged'. Cf. Laroche, *RHA* 9:15–6
(1948–9); von Schuler, *Dienstanweisungen* 44–5, 54–5.

Technical term of canalization like e.g. *alalima-*, *amiyara-*
(q.v.). Possibly of Hurrian origin (cf. Kronasser, *Etym.* 1:210).
V. Georgiev (*Linguistique balkanique* 21.4:30 [1978]) suggested
as cognates Skt. *árdati* 'flow', Gk. ἄρδα 'dirt'.

artarti-, atarti-, artati-   (c.), name of a tree, nom. sg. *a-tar-ti-is* (*Bo*
5176 Vs. 9; cf. Otten, *Materialien* 28), acc. sg. *ar-ta-ar-ti-in*
(*KUB* IX 4 III 30 *n-asta artartin neyari* '[the small pig] turns to
the a.'), *ar-tar-ti-in* (XXIX 1 IV 22 GIŠ*artartin* GIŠ*marsiqqann-a*;
cf. B. Schwartz, *Orientalia* N.S. 16:38 [1947]; *KBo* XIX 142 II
18), *artatin* (*KUB* XXIV 7 II 50; cf. Friedrich, *ZA* 49:224, 247
[1950]), nom. pl. *ar-tar-ti-es* (139/d I 5). Cf. Ertem, *Flora*
108–9.

Not 'truffle, mushroom' (W. Riedel apud Friedrich, *ZA*
49:255 [1950]).

aru-   'high', acc. pl. c. *aramus* restored by Carruba (*Beschwörungs-*
ritual 14) in *KUB* XXXIII 5 II 17 *a-ra-m*[*u-us* HUR.SAG.MEŠ
'high mountains' (cf. Laroche, *RHA* 23:100 [1965]), besides the
usual *pargamus* HUR.SAG.MEŠ.

aru(-)suwaru-, jingle-like (cf. e.g. *ayin* [*u*]*wāyin* s.v. *a*[*y*]*i-*)
adjectival quasi-dvandva made up of *aru-* and *suwaru-*'weighty,
heavy, mighty' (q.v.; cf. Lith. *svarùs* 'heavy', *sveñti* 'heave,
weigh', Lat. *sērius* 'grave', Goth. *swērs* 'respected, honored',
OHG *swār*[*i*] 'heavy'), thus 'high-and-hefty, high-and-mighty'
(vel sim.), nom. sg. c. in *KBo* XIX 155, 5]*arus suwaru*[*s* (cf.
Carruba, *Das Palaische* 25), adverbial nom.-acc. sg. neut. in
KUB XXX 106 III 33–34 *nu* D*Kumarbis arusuwaru-pat kuit*
D*U-ni* IGI-*anda aggatar sanheskizzi* 'that K. high-and-mightily
plans death against the storm-god' (cf. Güterbock, *JCS* 6:26
[1952]). Cf. Puhvel, *Bi. Or.* 36:57 (1979), *JAOS* 101:213–4
(1981).

arum(m)a 'highly, very much', e.g. *KBo* V 3 III 52 *mekki*
aruma usg[*ahhut* 'watch out very greatly' (cf. Friedrich, *Staats-*
verträge 2:128); *KUB* XXIII 21 Vs. 25 *aruma mekki nak*[*ki*]*s*
'very greatly difficult' (said of a mountain; cf. Götze, *Madd.*
156; Carruba, *SMEA* 18:168 [1977]); VIII 13, 14 *takku* D*SIN*
arumma tepawēszi 'if the moon is very much diminished'
(similarly ibid. 13; cf. Götze, *KlF* 220). Cf. Neu, *KZ* 93:70
(1979). The cumulative collocation *mekki aruma* or *aruma*
mekki is reminiscent of *aru(-)suwaru-*; *aruma* (unless *aru-*
+particle *-ma*; cf. H. Eichner, *Die Sprache* 24:69 [1978]) may

be an adverbial nom.-acc. pl. neut. (< *aruwa; cf. aram[us above; Tischler, *Glossar* 71). Cf. perhaps also arummura- (XLIV 64 I 6; cf. Burde, *Medizinische Texte* 48), the god(dess?) [D]Arumura- (e.g. XXXVIII 7, 13; cf. Jakob-Rost, *MIO* 8:193–4 [1961]), and [SAL]Arumuras (XV 5 I 11; XLVIII 126 I 13),]Arummura (XXVI 43 Vs. 51); perhaps arum(m)a + ura- 'great' (q.v.; cf. Neumann, *IF* 81:315 [1976]).

aru-, like suwaru-, is probably an ancient IE u-stem adjective, from the widely attested root *er- 'move, stir, raise' (*IEW* 326–32) which also yields arai- 'rise' and many other Hittite words (see arai-, at end); thus perhaps IE *r̥ú-. There is no need to start from IE *(E₁)r-éw- (seen in Hitt. ar[u]wai-) and assume aru- to be a back-formation from the nom. pl. c. *arawes (as did Tischler, *KZ* 76:281 [1972]), or to toy with an analogical rhyming formation to hallu-, parku- (or, for that matter, suwaru-; thus Tischler, *Glossar* 71). The terms for 'long' in Luwian (ara-, ari-, arrai- 'long', aran[n]u[wa]- 'lengthen'; *Dict. louv.* 30; Kronasser, *Etym.* 1:454), Hieroglyphic (ara- 'long'; Meriggi, *HHG* 30), and Tocharian A (aryu- 'long[-lasting]'; Van Windekens, *Le tokharien* 150–1) are interrelated but have at best a general root-relationship to Hitt. aru-.

Laroche (*RHA* 8:21 [1947–8]) saw in arusuwaru a kind of interjection made up of 3 sg. imp. of ar-, er- 'arrive' and suwa- 'fill' and drawing attention to something preposterous (cf. 'get a load of this!').

aruna- (c.) 'sea' (A.AB.BA), nom. sg. arunas (e.g. *KBo* II 19 Vs. 9 = *KUB* VIII 2 Vs. 8 arunass-a lāhuwai 'and the sea pours'), ārunas (*KBo* V 3 I 59 sallis ārunas 'great sea'; cf. Friedrich, *Staatsverträge* 2:112), arunās (*KUB* XXXVI 25 IV 6; cf. Laroche, *RHA* 26:73 [1968]), acc. sg. arunan (e.g. *KUB* XXXI 4 + *KBo* III 41 Vs. 14 arun]an tarmāmi nu āppa natta [lāhui 'I make fast the sea, and it does not [pour] back'; ibid. 19 arunan-a tarhuen 'and we have overcome the sea'; cf. Otten, *ZA* 55:160 [1962]; *KBo* XII 38 III 3 nu arunan huda[k 'the sea quickly [I reached]'; cf. Otten, *ZA* 55:167 [1962], *MDOG* 94:20 [1963]; Güterbock, *JNES* 26:76 [1967]), gen. sg. arunas (e.g. *KUB* XXXVI 55 II 28 arunas

MUŠ*illuiyankas* 'sea-serpent'; *KBo* XXV 112 II 5–6 [OHitt.] KUR-ZU *edi arunas*[...] *arunas* ZAG-*as* [*ēstu*] 'may his land on this side of the sea [and yonder] be a boundary of the sea'; cf. Otten, *ZA* 55:165–6 [1962]; X 24 III 11 *mān tiyēstes lariyēs arunas tuhhandat* 'when the ? ? of [?] the sea were in agony'), dat.-loc. sg. *aruni* (e.g. III 7 III 22 *n-as namma aruni zahhiya pait* 'then he went to the sea for battle'; cf. Laroche, *RHA* 23:70 [1965]; *KUB* XLI 8 II 18–19 *n-at-kan aruni parranda pedāu* 'may it carry it over the sea'; cf. Otten, *ZA* 54:124–6 [1961]), *arunī* (XXXVI 77, I; cf. Haas, *Nerik* 140), *a-ru-ú-ni* (XXXVI 41 I 13; cf. Laroche, *RHA* 23:173 [1965]), *aruna* (XXIX 1 I 51 *ehu-ta aruna piemi* 'come, I send you to the sea'; XII 60 I 11 ᴰ*Telipinus aruna pait* 'T. went to the sea'; cf. Laroche, *RHA* 23:79 [1965]), abl. sg. *a-ru-na-az* or *a-ru-na-za* (e.g. *KBo* XXIII 1 I 24 and XXIII 2 III 5 *arunaz ehu* 'from the sea, come!'; cf. Lebrun, *Hethitica III* 141, 145; *KUB* XV 31 III 49 *n-as arunaza huuittiyanzi* 'they draw them from the sea'; cf. Haas – Wilhelm, *Riten* 164; 1112/c I 31–32 *kās-wa* KU₆-*us arunas* GUD.MAH-*as nu-wa-kan kās* KU₆ *māhhan arunaz tuhhustat* ... 'this fish [is] the bull of the sea; just as this fish is cut off from the sea ...'; cf. L. Rost, *MIO* 1:350 [1953], I 38–39; *KUB* XXIX 1 I 24 *arunaza udas* 'has brought from the sea'), acc. pl. *arunus* (*KUB* XXXI 4 + *KBo* III 41 Vs. 12), gen. pl. *arunas* (*KUB* XXXVI 89 Rs. 4 *arunass-as* 9-*as wappuui* 'to the shore of the nine seas'; cf. Carruba, *Beschwörungsritual* 12; Haas, *Nerik* 150). For further examples see s.v. *arha-*.

aruni anda can mean literally 'in the sea' (e.g. *KUB* XVII 7 IV 35 *kuis-w*]*a-kan* DINGIR-*LUM nutarriyas aruni anda* [*artari* 'what swift god is standing in the sea?'; = ŠÀ A.AB.BA in e.g. *KBo* XII 38 III 8–9 *n-as-kan* ŠÀ A.AB.BA *lukkun* 'I set them on fire in mid-sea'; cf. Otten, *ZA* 55:167 [1962], *MDOG* 94:20 [1963]) or 'into the sea' (X 45 IV 41 *n-at-kan kariz aruni anda pidāu* 'the deluge shall carry it into the sea'; cf. Otten, *ZA* 54:138 [1961]), like *arunaz arha* 'out of the sea' (*KUB* XXXVI 12 II 7; cf. Güterbock, *JCS* 6:14 [1952]); but elsewhere (e.g. *KBo* III 4 II 51–53) it means 'on an island', and *arunaz arha* (ibid. 54, cf. III 2–3) signifies 'from an island' (cf. Götze, *AM* 60, 66; Sommer, *AU* 310). Cf. the parallel expression Akk. *qabal tāmti* '(in) mid-sea', hence '(on an) island', and further perhaps Lat. *insula* (cf. Gk. ἐνάλιος 'in the sea'), OCS *otokŭ* (*obŭ* 'around' + *tokŭ* 'stream'), *ostrovŭ* (cf. *struja* 'stream'). Cf. P. Kretschmer, *WZKM* 52:249 (1953–5), *Glotta* 33:8–9 (1954); Kronasser, *Festschrift J. Friedrich* 274–5 (1959); Puhvel, *Studies presented to Joshua Whatmough* 231 (1957) = *Analecta Indoeuropaea* 33 (1981); reservations in R. Stefanini, *Atti La Colombaria* 29:54–6 (1964).

arunum(a)na- 'maritime', nom. pl. c. *arunumanes* (*KUB* VIII 14 I 14). Cf. Kronasser, *Etym.* 1:113–4.

aruna- is often listed among treaty witnesses and in ritual enumerations, and is conceived as a male deity in the Hurrian-based Kumarbi and Ullikummi myths. In *KUB* XVII 8 IV 15–20 it is the daughter of the healing goddess ᴰ*Kamrusepa-* (see s.v. *kammara-*), and in XII 60 I 12 has a daughter of its own (cf. von Brandenstein, *Heth. Götter* 72). Yet a formally deified ᴰ*Aruna-* is rare (e.g. XX 1 II 32, ibid. III 5 and 11 ᴰ*Arunan*, ibid. III 16 ᴰ*Aruni*; XXXIII 108 II 17 ᴰU-*as* ᴰ*Arunan tarahzi* 'the storm-god overcomes the sea[-god]'; cf. Friedrich, *JKF* 2:148 [1952]; cf. XXXIII 89, 15 ᴰA.AB.[BA]); it often reflects Hurrian tradition. Cf. Laroche, *Recherches* 72; Puhvel, *Studies presented to Joshua Whatmough* 230 (1957).

Cf. the town ᵁᴿᵁ*A-ru-u-na*ᴷᴵ (*KBo* I 5 IV 43 and 45), ᴰ*Arunitti* (*ABoT* I 14 IV 12), and (the latter's?) festival EZEN ᴰ*Aruni*[(*KUB* XII 27 III 38), EZEN *Arunitas* (XXV 27 I 29), perhaps irregular *i*-stem genitive (cf. *hulugannas*; Friedrich, *HE* 47–8).

Etymology uncertain. Speculations about a contact-based tie-in with the Mitannian (Indo-Aryan) *Uruwana-*, *(V)aruna-* were abortive (cf. Puhvel, *Studies presented to Joshua Whatmough* 231–2 [1957]; Mayrhofer, *KEWA* 3:152–3; Kammenhuber, *Die Arier* 141, 148). Very little argues for Forrer's "Luwian" hypothesis (*Glotta* 26:193–6 [1938]), and Palaic *arūnampi* (*KUB* XXXII 17, 9; cf. Kammenhuber, *BSL* 54:25 [1959], *RHA* 17:22 [1959]; Carruba, *Das Palaische* 17, 52, *Beiträge* 30) remains obscure.

Hattic origin was advocated by Laroche (*Recherches* 72) on the basis of a suffix *-una-* in autochthonous theonyms (e.g.

Zashapuna-; cf. Puhvel, *Studies presented to Joshua What-mough* 232 [1957]), and by Kammenhuber (*ZA* 57:197–8 [1965], *MSS* 24:89, 120 [1968]) on the general grounds that the sea plays a role in Hattic myth (cf. e.g. Halmasuiz and Kamrusepas above; "Telipinus and the Daughter of the Sea" in *KUB* XII 60; cf. Laroche, *RHA* 23:79–80 [1965]; R. Stefanini, *AGI* 54:161–4 [1969]) and that the Hittites had no inherited word for it (having allegedly separated, along with Greek, Armenian, and Indo-Iranian, from an "alteuropäische Sprachgemeinschaft" before the latter reached the sea and partook of a term **mori*). The Hattic word for 'sea' is unknown (the bilingual collocation of *KBo* XXV 112 II 5–6 quoted above, with the lacunous Hattic passage *KUB* XXVIII 75 II 14–16, edited by Laroche, *JCS* 1:197 [1947], is unrewarding). The best linguistic argument for Hattic origin is the possible relationship of *aruna-* with **arinna-* 'fountain' (cf. ^{URU}TÚL-*na* = ^{URU}*Arinna*) and the comparison of *ABoT* I 14 IV 12 *INA* ^{URU}*Arinna ANA* ^{D}*Arunitti* with *IBoT* I 29 Vs. 39 and 47 ^{D}*Ariniddun*, ibid. 42 ^{D}*Ariniti*, ibid. Rs. 22 and 23 ^{D}*Ariniddu*. Thus Hattic would have expanded an "inland" term to the "great sea", much as IE **mori* 'mere, marsh' took this meaning.

By the same token, however, the Indo-European Anatolians may have created the term. It is true that to the historical Hittites their first southern contact with the Mediterranean was a conquistadorial revelation (cf. Otten, *ZA* 55:166 [1962], *Saeculum* 15:117–8 [1964]), and that they were fairly innocent of the northern coast of Anatolia (cf. von Schuler, *Die Kaškäer* 21–2; also Meriggi, *WZKM* 58:80–3 [1962]). But it also strains credulity that they lacked prehistoric contact with salt-water seas such as the Black Sea or the Caspian. Even the name of *Kizzuwatna* in the south is pure Hittite (not necessarily Luwian), a probable hypostasis of **kez wetenaz*, thus 'cisaquinus' (cf. Neumann, *Die Sprache* 4:111–4 [1958]); cf. ^{D}UTU *ú-i-te-e-ni* 'solar deity in water' (*KBo* V 2 II 13), where *watar* means 'sea'. Muwatallis' prayer *KUB* VI 45 III 14 *sarā-kan uwasi nepisas* ^{D}UTU-*us arunaz* 'up you come, sun-god of heaven, from the sea', points to an erstwhile habitat on an eastern litoral (as opposed to the common Egyptian, Mesopotamian, and Hurrian notion of sunrise, e.g. XVII 1 II 14 ᴰUTU-*us-kan kalmaraz uit* 'the sun came from the mountain', in the Hurrian story of the hunter Kessi; cf. Friedrich, *ZA* 49:238 [1950]; Puhvel, *Studies presented to Joshua Whatmough* 228 [1957]). Cf. also the cult-image in XXXVIII 2 III 5–6 ᴰUTU AN-*E* ... SAG.DU-*i* KU$_6$.HI.A-*za* KÙ.BABBAR 'sun-god of heaven ... on his head fishes of silver' (cf. von Brandenstein, *Heth. Götter* 8; L. Rost, *MIO* 8:177 [1961]).

Possible Indo-European origins of *aruna-* were discussed exhaustively by Puhvel, *Studies presented to Joshua Whatmough* 233–7 (1957). **arinna-* is plausibly non-IE; in any event it would not share IE root origin with *aruna-*. For the latter, cf. RV *árvan(t)-*, Avest. *aurva(nt)-* 'swift', *auruna-* 'wild, fierce', Gk. οὖρος 'fair wind' (< **ὄρϝος*), ON *ǫrr* 'swift' (< **arwa-*), and also RV *árṇa-*, *arṇavá-* 'surging; flood', *árṇas-* 'flood, surf', thus IE **er-*, **or-* 'stir' (*IEW* 326–32), with various extensions. Avest. *aurva-* and *auruna-* offer the closest formational analogues to *aruna-*, Ved. *árṇa-* and *arṇavá-* the nearest meaning-parallels ('surging' > 'flood' > 'sea'). Cf. also S. S. Misra, *Bulletin of the Philological Society of Calcutta* 7:37–8 (1966); Tischler, *KZ* 86:282 (1972).

Cf. *ar-*; *ar-, er-*; *arai-*; *arnu-*; *arriya-*; *aru-*; *ar(u)wai-*.

arrusa, in *arrusa pai-* 'resort to secession' (vel sim.), resembling the gloss-wedged Luwoid *allallā* (q.v.) in *allallā pai-* 'resort to defection', *KUB* XIX 23 Rs. 13–16 GIM-*an-ma* ŠA ᴰUTU-ŠI [...] TI-*tar isdammassir n-at-kan namma arrusa* ŪL [*pāir*] *kinun-ma* GIM-*an* ŠA EN-YA *hargan isdammassir n-at namma arrū*[*sa*] *pāir* 'when they heard that his majesty was alive they did not then resort to secession, but now when they heard of my lord's demise they have also resorted to secession' (cf. ibid. 10 and 13 *ārrūsa pāir*; S. Heinhold-Krahmer, *Arzawa* 313 [1977]); XXVI 12 II 16–17 *arrusa pāuwar sanahzi le kuiski* 'let nobody plan secession' (cf. *KBo* IV 14 II 59–61 *zik-ma allallā pāuwar* ... *le sanahti* 'do not plan defection'; cf. von Schuler, *Dienstanweisungen* 24–5); *KUB* VIII 79 Vs. 18 *arrusa pā*[, ibid. 19 *arrusa pāisi* 'you resort to secession'; *KBo* XVIII 69 Vs. 11 *ar-ru-ú-sa.*

Most likely *arrusa* is a directional dat.-loc. sg. of an *s*-stem noun **arrus* (cf. *tapu*[*wa*]*s* 'rib, flank', *tapusa* 'sideways'). The nearest comparison would be with Skt. *áruṣ-* 'wound', ON *err* 'scar' (PGmc. **arwiz*), IE **A₂ér-w-*, **A₂r-éw-* 'tear up, rend, slit' (*IEW* 338, 868); thus the base meaning of **A₂ér-w-us-* was 'rent, split, fissure', whence Skt. 'wound' and (figuratively) Hitt. 'schism'. The literal meaning of *arrusa pai-* would thus be 'head for a split'. Here may belong also *arusan* (acc. sg.?; or adverbial like *appa*[*n*]?) in *KUB* XLIII 60 I 32 *kuwat arusan paimi* 'why am I heading for schism?', and abl. sg. *arusaz* (cf. *tapusza*) in XXXVI 75 + 1226/u III 12–13 *nu-m-asta arusaz sarā huitti* 'draw me up from schism!'.

H. Eichner suggested (*Die Sprache* 24:69 [1978]) that *arrusa* is derived from *arra-* (with ending borrowed from *tapusa*) and thus means 'arseways' or the like; *arrusa* might in fact be tied in with the stem variant *arru-* (q.v. s.v. *arra-*); but such a vulgarism is not likely in the formal style where the word occurs. Cf. Puhvel, *Bi. Or.* 36:58 (1979). G.T. Rikov *Linguistique balkanigue* 25.2:22–3 [1982] implausibly compared Gk. *ἀρνέομαι* 'deny'.

ar(u)wai-   'prostrate oneself, fall down, make obeisance, *προσκυν-εῖν*' (*ŠUKĒNU*, e.g. *KBo* IV 9 III 13–15 LUGAL-*us aruwaizzi* ... besides the identical passage *KUB* X 79, 6–7 LUGAL-*us UŠGEN* ..., and II 6 IV 34–36 LUGAL-*us UŠKEN* ...; X 89 V 10 EGIR-*pa aruwaizzi* besides XI 17 IV 5 EGIR-*pa UŠKEN*), 3 sg. pres. act. *aruwaizzi*, *aruwāizzi* (e.g. II 15 VI 3 LUGAL-*us katta aruwāizzi* 'the king prostrates himself'; *IBoT* I 30, 1 LUGAL-*us* ... DINGIR.MEŠ-*as aruwāizzi* 'the king prostrates himself to the gods'), *arūwāizzi* (e.g. *KUB* II 6 I 9), *aruwāzi* (*KBo* XIII 214 IV 10), *arwaizzi* (XIX 161 I 16; *Bo* 3112 III 10; cf. Haas, *Nerik* 313), *UŠKEN* (e.g. *KUB* XI 26 II 17 LUGAL-*us sarā UŠKEN* 'the king rises from prostration' [lit. 'prostrates himself up']), 3 pl. pres. act. *aruwanzi* (e.g. *KBo* XVII 74 II 47 *asandas tagān aruwa*[*nzi* 'from a sitting position [king and queen] prostrate themselves on the ground'; cf. Neu, *Gewitterritual* 22), *aruwānzi* (e.g. ibid. III 37 *asandas aruwānzi*; ibid. 19 *sarā*] *tienzi ser-pat aruwānzi* '[king and queen] step up and prostrate

ar(u)wai-

themselves above'; VI 3 III 19 [= *Code* 1:55] LÚ.MEŠ *ILKI uer nu*
ABI LUGAL *aruwā*[*nzi* 'liegemen came and make obeisance to the
king's father'), *arūwanzi* (e.g. VIII 117 II 9), *aruwaenzi* (XVII
28, 6; cf. Neu, *Altheth.* 153), *aruwāenzi* (XII 131, 6 LUGAL-*i*
menahhanda aruwāenzi 'they prostrate themselves facing the
king', vs. ibid. 8 *aruwānzi*), *arwanzi* (IV 9 II 39 EGIR-*pa* 1-ŠU
arwanzi 'again they prostrate themselves once'; cf. e.g. *KUB* IX
24, 6 and 11 3-ŠU *UŠKEN* 'prostrates himself three times'),
UŠKENNU (e.g. X 1 I 20–21 ZI *aranta imma UŠKENNU-ma ŪL*
'they just stand but do not prostrate themselves'), 1 sg. pret.
act. *aruwanun* (XXXVI 75+ II 7; cf. *ZA* 64:241 [1975]),
arwānun (XIV 13 I 17–18 *kāsa-smas ... arwānun* 'lo, I have
prostrated myself before you'; cf. Götze, *KlF* 242), 3 sg. pret.
act. *aruwait* (XXIII 36 II 23; XXXVI 101 II 6 and 8; XXXVI
102, 7; XLVIII 106, 18), *aruwāit* (XXXI 127 I 12–13 *kā*[*sa*]-*tta*
... *aruwā*[*it* 'behold, [he] has prostrated himself before thee'), 3
pl. pret. act. *arwair* (*KBo* XII 132 Rs. 1), 3 pl. imp. act.
aruwāiddu (*KUB* XIII 10 Vs. 3, emended; cf. *ZA* 68:151 [1978]);
partic. *aruwant-*, nom.-acc. sg. neut. in *IBoT* III 140, 4 *nu*
aruwan harkanzi 'they have prostrated themselves'; verbal noun
a-ru-u-wa-u-ar (*KBo* III 21 II 10–11 *nu* KUR-*yas arūwauar*
DINGIR.MEŠ *tuk iwārwāir* 'the proskynesis of the lands have the
gods conferred upon thee'); inf. *aruwanzi* (haplologic for
aruwawanzi; XXII 2 Rs. 13 [OHitt.] DINGIR.DIDLI-*as aruwanzi*
uet '[the king] came to make obeisance to the gods', besides
dupl. III 38 Rs. 30 DINGIR.MEŠ-*nas aruwauwanzi uit*; cf. Otten,
Altheth. Erzählung 12; X 11 I 2), *arwān⟨zi⟩* (XIX 161 III 13);
iter. *aru(w)eski-*, *aru(u)iski-*, *aruwaisk*[*i-* (XVII 30 II 9), 3 sg.
pres. act. *aruyiskizzi* (*KUB* IV I 12 and 20; cf. von Schuler, *Die
Kaškäer* 168), *a-ru-ú-is-ki-iz-zi* (XX 46 III 16), *aruyisgazi* (*KBo*
XX 34 Rs. 7), 3 pl. pres. act. *a-ru-ú-e-es-kán-zi* (XXXVI 79 I
34), *aruēskanzi* (e.g. XXXI 134, 8), *a-ru-ú-is-kán-zi* (*Bo*
4696+ *KUB* XXXVI 75 I 12; cf. *ZA* 62:232 [1972]), *aruiskanzi*
(XXXVI 95 II 3), 3 pl. imp. act. *aruēskandu* (XXXIII 22+23 I
26; cf. Laroche, *RHA* 23:112 [1965]); supine *a-ru-ú-e-es-ki-u-*
-wa-an in XIII 9+ XL 62 I 5 *aruwēskiuwan dāis* 'began to make
obeisance' (cf. von Schuler, *Festschrift J. Friedrich* 446 [1959]);
aruēsga[(XXXI 64 II 43), *aruēskat*[(*KBo* XX 93, 6). Cf.

Ehelolf, *OLZ* 27:580–1 (1924); Kronasser, *Etym.* 1:472.

ar(u)wai- is distinct from *haliya-* 'kneel, genuflect' (q.v. s.v. for contrastive co-occurrences of the two verbs). A plausible etymology was proposed by Laroche (*RPh* 42:243–4 [1968]), viz. Lat. *ruō* 'fall down, collapse', *ruīna* 'fall, downfall'; we may also adduce the Homeric aorist ὄρουσα, later Gk. ὀρούω 'rush forth'. *ar(u)wai-* < *ṛw-āye-*, from *(E₁)r-éw-* 'stir, rush' (*IEW* 331–2).

Kronasser (*Etym.* 1:484) wrongly rendered *haliya-* as 'prostrate oneself' and *ar(u)wai-* as 'bow'. An assumed sense 'bow down, do homage, worship' abetted a comparison with Gk. ἀράομαι 'pray, curse' (e.g. Sturtevant, *Lg.* 5:10 [1929], *Lg.* 6:155 [1930], *Comp. Gr.*[1] 87, *Comp. Gr.*[2] 35; so still Tischler, *KZ* 86:282 [1972], *Glossar* 73–4; the same connection for both *aruwai-* and *ariya-* [q.v., is found in *IEW* 781). Neumann (*Untersuchungen* 52–3) assumed *aruwai-* to be a deoccluded variant of *arkuwai-* (q.v.), which latter he still mistranslated as 'pray'.

Cf. *ar-*; *ar-, er-*; *arai-*; *arnu-*; *arriya-*; *aru-*; *aruna-*.

arzana-, arsana- (c.?), in *arzanas* (gen.) *parn-* (= É *arzanas*) 'house of *arzana-*, inn, hostel, brothel', by attraction in oblique cases also dat.-loc. sg. *arzana parna* (= [*INA*] É *arzana*), acc. sg. É *arzanan*, abl. sg. É *arzanaz*, perhaps dat.-loc. pl. É *arzanas* (cf. e.g. *armahhuwazza wassiyaz* from *armahhuwas wassiyaz* s.v. *armai-*), acc. sg. *arzanan* (*KBo* V 6 I 16 *kuyēs* É *arzanan harkir kuyēs-ma-kan hāppiri* EGIR-*pa pantes* 'some were put up in hostel[s] while others [had] gone back to town'; cf. Güterbock, *JCS* 10:90 [1956]), gen. sg. *arzanas* (e.g. XIII 223 III 2 *arzanas parna* 'to the inn'; XVI 84 Vs. 2 and XIX 163 IV 42 *arzanas* É-*ri* 'at the inn'; XXI 79 IV 7 *IŠTU* É *arzanas* 'from the inn'; *KUB* XX 92 VI 14–15 *INA* É *arzanas pānzi ta-z duskanzi* '[the lords] go to the inn and make merry'; ibid. 16–17 SAL.MEŠKI.SIKIL URU ... [...] ŠA É *arzana*[s 'girls of the town ... of the inn'; XXV 51 IV 8–9 *nu-kan* NIN.DINGIR É *arzanas anda paizzi* 'the priestess goes inside the brothel'), dat.-loc. sg. *arzana* (e.g. *IBoT* I 29 Vs. 29 and 50 DUMU.LUGAL *arzana parna paizzi* 'the [young] prince goes to the brothel'; ibid. Rs. 46 *INA* É *arzana paizzi* 'he goes to the brothel' and [ibid. 46–49] eats with twelve prostitutes, as part of the 'feast of begettal' [EZEN *hassumas*]; cf. Güterbock, *AOS Middle West Branch Semi-Centennial Volume* 99–103 [1969]), abl. sg. *arzanaz* (*KBo* VII 42 IV 4 É *arzanaz uizzi* 'comes from the inn'), dat.-loc. pl. (?) *arzanas* (XVII 65 Rs. 25 *nu-za* SAL-*za arha* É *arzanas pai*[*zzi* 'the woman goes out to the inn'; similarly alternatively perhaps É *arzanas anda paizzi* under gen. sg. above). There is also É *arsana-* in unpublished texts (355/t Rs. 10; *Bo* 2965 I 3).

Denom. verb *arzanai-* 'billet, quarter', 3 sg. pret. act. *arzana-*[*it* (?) in *KUB* XXVI 71 IV 8 (cf. von Schuler, *Die Kaskäer* 185); partic. *arzanant-*, nom. sg. c. *arzananza* (XIII 2 III 36 *arnuwalas-a-kan kuis* KUR-*ya anda arzananza* 'the deportee who is quartered in the country'; cf. von Schuler, *Dienstanweisungen* 48; *Bo* 2628 + 7878 I 28–29 *nu kuis kuedani arzananza ēsta* 'if one man has been quartered with another'; cf. ibid. 27 NAM.RA 'deportee'; Otten – Souček, *Gelübde* 30), *arzanānza* (dupl. *KUB* XXXI 51 + XXVI 5 IV 10 and XXXI 58 Rs. 13), nom. pl. c. *arzanāntes* (*KBo* III 39 + *Bo* 7266 I 2; cf. Otten – Souček, *Gelübde* 18); verbal noun *arzanatar* (n.), dat.-loc. sg. *arzananni* (1203/u + *KUB* XXXI 86 II 27–28 BÀD-*ess*[*ar*] *arzananni le kuiski epz*[*i* 'let nobody requisition the fortress for billeting'; cf. von Schuler, *Dienstanweisungen* 44; Otten, *Materialien* 45).

arzanala- (c.) 'innkeeper', nom. sg. LÚ·*arzanala*[*s* (*Bo* 5452 III 5), *arzanālas* (*KBo* XX 16 Vs. 8–10 SAL*siunzannas* [...] [...]*arza-nālas* [...] [...LÚ·]MEŠ*lahhiyales* 'priestess ..., innkeeper ..., warriors'; cf. Neu, *Altheth.* 43), dat.-loc. sg. *a*]*rzanāli* (*Bo* 806, 1), nom. pl. *arzanalas* (174/t IV 3 ILÚ· ISAL· *arzanalas*). Cf. N. van Brock, *RHA* 20:99 (1962).

Arzanahsu (Cappadocian personal name; cf. Laroche, *Noms* 43, 297–302).

Cf. Laroche, *RA* 43:74 (1949); H. A. Hoffner, *Anatol. Stud. Güterbock* 113–21.

arzanas parn- could well have had a wide spectrum, from a commercial inn to an official hostelry, and from a common bawdy house to an establishment akin to temple prostitution (cf. the priestess NIN.DINGIR entering it, the EZEN *hassumas* being held there, and its proprietor [proprietress?] being listed in the same breath with a ^{SAL}*siunzannas*). The basic sense is, however, that of a place dispensing food and lodging, bed and board; Güterbock's suggestion (*JCS* 10:90 [1956]) that *arzana-* represents Sum. AR.ZA.NA, Akk. *ARZAN(N)U* '(barley) groats' is plausible, and the literal meaning would thus be 'porridge-house' (vel sim.); in fact *ARZAN(N)U* is served to the young prince during his formal meal at the EZEN *hassumas* in the *arzana-* house (*IBoT* I 29 Vs. 52 and Rs. 47). Cf. Puhvel, *Bi. Or.* 36:58 (1979).

arziya- (n.) 'cultivated land, agricultural resource, granary (figurative)', nom.-acc. sg. *arziyan* (*ABoT* 60 Vs. 20–22 *pedan mekki nakki* ANA ^{LÚ}KÚR-*ya-as arziyan* '[it is] a very important place; for the enemy it [is] a granary'; cf. Laroche, *RHA* 18:82–4 [1960]), gen. sg. in *KBo* V 7 Vs. 44 A.ŠÀ *arziyas* 'field of cultivation' (cf. Riemschneider, *MIO* 6:347 [1958]), Luwoid genitival adj. in *KUB* VIII 75 II 4 1 A.ŠÀ *arziassis* (cf. V. Souček, *Arch. Or.* 27:12 [1959]; Güterbock, *Orientalia* N.S. 25:127 [1956]), XLII 2, 10 NUMUN-*ŠU arziyassa*.

Probably related to *arsi-* (q.v.). For the *rz* spelling cf. e.g. *hasterza* /hasters/ s.v. *haster-*. G.T. Rikov (*Linguistique balkanique*) 25.2:21–2 [1982] implausibly compared OHG *art* 'plowed land'.

as(s)- 'remain, stay, be left', *katta as(s)-* 'stick' (with *KBo* X 2 I 26 *n-asta* ^{URU}*Hattusas-pat* URU-*rias* 1-*as āsta* cf. X 1 Vs. 12 [Akk.] URU-*lum* ^{URU}KÙ.BABBAR-*ti* 1-*en irteha* 'the town of H. alone remained'; cf. F. Imparati – C. Saporetti, *Studi classici e orientali* 14:46, 77 [1965]), 3 sg. pres. act. *aszi* (IV 14 III 49 -*kan* UL *aszi* 'remains not'; also ibid. 43; cf. R. Stefanini, *ANLR* 20:46 [1965]), *āszi* (e.g. *KUB* XIII 2 III 39 *pidi-ma-ssi-san kuis āszi* 'but he that stays in his place'; cf. von Schuler, *Dienstanweisungen* 48; XIII 4 III 46–47 *n-asta pahhur kuit* ANA GUNNI *āszi* 'the fire that remains on the hearth'; cf. Sturtevant, *JAOS* 54:384 [1934]; XIII 35 IV 45–46 *martari-war-at-kan nu-war-at--kan āszi* 'it is lost, and it is left'; cf. Werner, *Gerichtsprotokolle* 14; VIII 14 Vs. 15] 1-*as* URU-*as āszi* 'one town remains'; XXV

42 II 10 *nu-ssan ... kuit* GEŠTIN *āszi* 'what wine remains'; *KBo* IV 10 Vs. 9 *nu-ssi-kan mān wastul āszi* 'if sin remains for him'; *KUB* XIV 12 Vs. 10 *kuedanikki āszi* 'remains for someone'; cf. Götze, *KlF* 236; *IBoT* I 36 I 14 *nu-kan kue* ^{GIŠ}ŠUKUR.HI.A *āszi* 'what spears remain'; cf. L. Jakob-Rost, *MIO* 11:174 [1966]; V. Haas – M. Wäfler, *Istanbuler Mitteilungen* 23/24:14 [1973–4]; *KBo* XVII 15 Rs. 19 *sīwaz 8 waksur āszi* '[on] the day, eight w. remain'; cf. V. Haas – M. Wäfler, *Ugarit-Forschungen* 8:82 [1976]; Neu, *Altheth.* 74; *KUB* XXX 31 I 41–42 *nu-kan mahhan* ANA UD-*MI* 5 *gipessar 8 waksur āszi* 'when of the day five cubits [and] eight w. remain'; cf. Lebrun, *Hethitica II* 96; for more examples of the latter type see s.v. *gipessar*), 3 pl. pres. act. *āssanzi* (e.g. *IBoT* I 36 III 42 ^{LÚ.]MEŠ}*MEŠEDUTI-ma-kan kuyēs āssanzi* 'those bodyguards who are left'; cf. L. Jakob-Rost, *MIO* 11:194 [1966]; *KBo* XVII 65 Rs. 3 and 27 '[two days] remain'), 3 sg. pret. act. *āsta* (e.g. *KUB* IX 3 IV 8 *āsta-ma-kan* 12 GUD.HI.A 3 *ME* UDU.HI.A 'there remained twelve oxen [and] three hundred sheep'; XXI 38 Vs. 11 *āsta-ma-kan kuit* 'what was left'; cf. R. Stefanini, *Atti La Colombaria* 29:6 [1964]; XXVI 69 VI 19; cf. Werner, *Gerichtsprotokolle* 46; XXX 29 Vs. 14 *pedan* ŪL *āsta* 'did not stay in place'; *KBo* XIV 19 II 19 *nu-smas-kan memiyas katta āsta* 'the [legal] charge against them stuck', i.e. they were found guilty; cf. Houwink Ten Cate, *JNES* 25:174 [1966]; *KUB* I 1 I 62 *nu-mu-kan* HUL-*lu uttar katta* ŪL *kuitki āsta* 'no serious charge stuck against me'), 3 sg. pret. midd. *āstat* (XXII 70 Vs. 18 *takkisra-wa-kan* [with gloss-wedges] *kue* NA₄.HI.A-*ya* EGIR-*pa āstat* 'those t. and stones that were left'; cf. Neu, *Interpretation* 19; Ünal, *Orakeltext* 58), 3 pl. pret. act. *āsser* (*KBo* X 2 I 39 *āsser-ma-kan kuyēs* DINGIR.MEŠ 'those deities who remained'; ibid. 13 *āsser-ma-kan kuyēs*), *āssir* (XIV 42 Vs. 7), 3 pl. imp. act. *āsdu* (*KUB* XXVI 58 Vs. 21–22 and 24–25 *n-asta ... āsdu* 'let [the house] be left', viz. as inheritance; *KBo* IX 137 II 12); partic. *assant-*, nom. sg. c. *āssanza* (IV 10 Vs. 18, 24, 25; XVII 65 Vs. 30), *āssaza* (IV 10 Vs. 28), nom.-acc. sg. neut. *āssan* (e.g. ibid. 17; *KUB* XXII 70 Vs. 49; cf. Ünal, *Orakeltext* 70), *assan* (V 1 III 17 [*k*]*e-kan* HUL-*uwa* IZKIM.HI.A DINGIR-*LIM-ni-pat assan* 'these bad signs [are] left for the god'; cf. Ünal, *Hatt.* 2:142), nom. pl. c. *āssantes* (XIV 8 Rs. 18–19

nu-kan keus kuyēs ... tēpawēs āssantes n-at-mu [le ak]kanzi
'those few who [are] left, let them not die on me'; cf. Götze, *KlF*
214); inf. *-kan ... āssuwanzi* (XXII 70 Vs. 51; cf. Imparati,
SMEA 18:30 [1977]; Ünal, *Orakeltext* 70); iter. *āski-*, 3 sg. pres.
act. *āskizzi* (*KBo* XXIII 55 I 14).

The consistent intervocalic spelling *-ss-* sets *as(s)-* apart
from the verbs *es-* 'be' (3 pl. *asanzi*) or *es-* 'sit' (3 pl. *asanzi* or
asanta) from which it has been implausibly derived (e.g. by
Bechtel, *Hittite Verbs* 92–3) as a "specialized" offshoot ('[con-
tinue] be[ing]', or '[remain] sit[ting]'). *as(s)-* can represent
either /as-/ or /ās-/; but neither *-ss-* nor the dominant spelling
a-as- by themselves point to a long vowel. Further connections
are obscure, but Indo-European origin of such a root-verb is
likely; Čop's adduction (*Ling.* 9:196 [1969]) of Lat. *inānis*
'empty' (lit. 'non-residued, without a remnant') as privative
prefix plus **āsno-* (cf. *in-ermis*) is, however, a weak secundum
comparationis for an IE **ās-* 'remain'.

Any tie-in with Skt. *ása-* 'ashes', Lat. *āridus* 'dry' (Oettinger,
Stammbildung 187) is improbable (see *IEW* 68).

ass-, assiya-   (mostly mediopassive), 'be favored, be dear, be good'
(occasionally, especially in nominal derivatives, SIG$_5$, which
also reflects *lazziya-* [almost always mediopassive] 'be[come]
good, be[come] sound'; cf. Goetze, *JCS* 14:71–3 [1960]; *KUB*
III 111, 17 *āssiyauwa[r]* [verbal noun] 'favor' = Akk. *[rā]mu*; cf.
XXIX 4 III 45 INA URU-*LIM ŠA TARAMMI* 'in[to] the city that
thou [goddess] lovest'; cf. Kronasser, *Umsiedelung* 26; *KBo* X 2
I 27 *Tabarnas* NARAM ^{D}UTU = X 1 Vs. 13 [Akk.] *Tabarna naram*
^{D}UTU 'T. beloved of the solar deity'), 3 sg. pres. midd. *āssāri*
(*Bo* 3182 Rs. 4–6 [emended from lacunous parallel texts *KBo*
XXII 126 Vs. 4–6 and *KUB* XLIII 58 III 4–7] *mahhan*
DINGIR.MEŠ-*as antuhsass-a āssāri* [... DINGIR.MEŠ-*as* ZI-*anza*
and]a QATAMMA SIG$_5$-*anza ēstu* [EN SISKUR.SISKUR-*ya* -]*kan*
QATAMMA *āssiyanza ēstu* 'as [...] is dear to gods and men, let
[the gods' spirit within] likewise be good, let [the sacrificer]
likewise be dear'), *āssiyattari* (*KUB* XXIV 7 IV 37 ^{D}UTU-*i-kan*
kuis āssiyattari 'he that is dear unto the sun-god'; cf. Friedrich,

ZA 49:232 [1950]; ibid. I 14–15 *nu-kan* ^D*IŠTAR-li* É-*ir kuit* [*āssi*]*yattari* 'the house that is dear unto Ištar' [opp. ibid. 25 *pukkan* 'hateful']; ibid . 44 *ās*]*siyattari*; cf. A. Archi, *Oriens Antiquus* 16:305–6 [1977]), 3 pl. pres. midd. *āssantari* (*KBo* XXII 126 Vs. 4 'are dear', parallel to *Bo* 3182 Rs. 4 *āssāri* above), 3 sg. pret. midd. *āssiyattat* (*KUB* XXXIII 121 II 9 DAM-*KA-pat-wa-ta-kkan āssiyattat* 'only your wife has become dear to you'; cf. Friedrich, *ZA* 49:234 [1950]), 3 sg. imp. midd. *āssiyattaru* (254/r Rs. 5 and 7) 3 pl. imp. act. *āssiyandu* (XLI 19 Vs. 6; cf. Haas – Thiel, *Rituale* 94); partic. *assiyant-* 'dear, beloved', nom. sg. c. *āssiyanza* (e.g. VI 45 I 13 *ŠA* ^DU *āssiyanza* DUMU-*as* 'beloved son of the storm-god'; XXI 27 III 44 *āssiyanza hassas* 'beloved granddaughter'; XXVI 88 Vs. 7), *assiyanza* (XXIV 3 I 40–41 *parā handanzas-a-kan antuhwahhas tuk-pat* ANA ^DUTU ^{URU}*Arinna assiyanza* 'the providential man is dear to you, sun-goddess of Arinna'; cf. Gurney, *Hittite Prayers* 24), *āssianza* (VIII 63 I 8 *āssianza kuit aras ēs*[*ta* 'because he was a dear friend'; cf. Laroche, *RHA* 26:75 [1968]; XXI 19 IV 26), nom.-acc. sg. neut. *āssiyan* (e.g. XV 34 II 29 DINGIR.MEŠ-*as āssiyan* 'dear to the gods'; cf. Haas – Wilhelm, *Riten* 192; XX 92 VI 10–11 *nu-tta-kan* TI-*tar Labarnas* LUGAL- -*as āssiyan ēsdu* 'may the life of Labarnas the king be dear to you'; cf. ibid. 1, and Gurney, *Hittite Prayers* 110; Haas, *Nerik* 46), gen. sg. *āssiyantas* (XXI 27 I 14–15 *n-at tuel āssiyantas* DUMU-*as* ... AŠRU 'it is the abode of your dear son'; cf. Haas, *Nerik* 18–9; XIV 7 IV 15), dat.-loc. sg. *āssiyanti* (e.g. *KBo* III 21 III 20, 21, 24; *KUB* XXI 19 III 43; XXI 27 I 12; XXXVI 89 Rs. 56; cf. Haas, *Nerik* 156), *āsseyanti* (XVII 16 I 16), *āssianti* (XIV 7 IV 4), abl. sg. *āssiyantaza* (XXXVI 90 Vs. 20), *āssiyandaz* (ibid. 33; cf. Haas, *Nerik* 178), nom. pl. c. *āssiyantes* (e.g. XV 34 II 31 LUGAL SAL.LUGAL KUR ^{URU}*Hatti-ya* QATAMMA *āssi-yantes asandu* 'may the king [and] queen of Hatti be equally dear'; *KBo* XIV 12 IV 32, 36, 39 *istarni-summi āssiyantes* 'mutually dear'; cf. Güterbock, *JCS* 10:98 [1956]; *KUB* XXIII 102 I 11; XX 92 I 12 [syntact. acc.]; see also Otten, *Istanbuler Mitteilungen* 8:108 [1958]; *KBo* X 47g III 12; cf. Laroche, *RHA* 26:12 [1968]), dat.-loc. pl. *āssiyantas* (*KUB* XXXVI 90 Vs. 16; cf. Haas, *Nerik* 176); verbal noun *āssiyatar* (n.) 'love' (e.g. *KBo*

II 32 IV 3; cf. Haas – Thiel, *Rituale* 284; XII 118 Rs. 22; *KUB* I
1 III 3+XIX 71, 7 *nu-nn*]*as* DINGIR-*LUM ŠA* LÚ*MUDI* D[A]M
āssiyatar pesta 'the goddess granted us the love of man [and]
wife'; cf. Götze, *Neue Bruchstücke* 12; XXIV 7 I 39; cf. A.
Archi, *Oriens Antiquus* 16:306 [1977]; XLV 28+ XLVII 59+
XXXIX 97 Vs. 9; cf. H. Otten – C. Rüster, *ZA* 68:155 [1978];
also XXXIII 84+ IV 6, 7, 26, 27, where it denotes metonymically some fragrant substance; cf. Friedrich, *Arch. Or.* 17.1:234
[1949]; Laroche, *RHA* 26:56 [1968]; Siegelová, *Appu-Hedammu*
58-60, 75-6; Neumann, *IF* 78:241-2 [1973]), *asiyatar* (*KUB*
XV 35+ *KBo* II 9 I 31; cf. *anniyatar* s.v. *anna-, anni-*), gen. sg.
āssiyannas (*KUB* XXIII 1 I 31; cf. Kühne – Otten, *Šaušgamuwa*
6), *asiyanas* (XXIV 7 IV 19; cf. Friedrich, *ZA* 49:230 [1950]),
dat.-loc. sg. *āssiyanni* (IV 4 Vs. 7-9 *hamishandas-ma-za alel*
āssiyanni handas ēssa[*tti* 'but the flower [= acme] of spring you
make for the sake of love'; cf. Götze, *Hattusilis* 92; Friedrich,
ZA 49:248 [1950]; Laroche, *RA* 58:73 [1964]), instr. sg. *ass*]*i-*
yannit (*KUB* XXXIII 64+ *KBo* XXI 60, 8), nom.-acc. pl.
āssiyatar (*IBoT* II 135, 9-10 [with dupl. *KUB* XXXIII 88, 11]
āssiyatar-ma-ssi [UR.TUR.MEŠ GIM-*an* EGIR-*an huway*]*antari* 'but
loves run like puppies behind her'; cf. Laroche, *RHA* 26:57
[1968]; Siegelová, *Appu-Hedammu* 54); *āssiyauar* (n.) 'favor'
(XVII 33 IV 15; XXXIV 53 Rs. 18), *āssiyauwar* (e.g. XV 34 II 9
and 20 DINGIR.MEŠ-*as āssiyauwar* 'favor of [= being dear to] the
gods'; cf. Haas – Wilhelm, *Riten* 190, 240), *asiyauwar* (*Maşat*
75/64, 11 DINGIR.MEŠ-*as asiyauwa*[*r*]; cf. Alp, *Belleten* 44:51
[1980]), instr. sg. *āssiyauwannit* (XXIV 13 II 12; cf. Haas –
Thiel, *Rituale* 104; *KBo* VIII 71, 6), *āssiyaunit* (*KUB* XXXIII
62 II 20), *āssiunit* (ibid. 10 DINGIR.MEŠ-*as āssiunit* 'through
favor of the gods', with Luwian parallel XXXV 45 II 10
wassarahitati; cf. Otten, *LTU* 46; Laroche, *BSL* 55.1:166--7
[1960]); deverb. adj. *āssiyauwant-* 'favorite, lover', nom. sg. c. in
RS 25:421 Verso 62-63 *āssiyauwanzas-ma-as* [...] GIM-*an ilali-*
yauwannit ŪL ha[*ssikanza* 'she (is) like a lover not satiated with
desire' (cf. Laroche, *Ugaritica* 5:774 [1968]); iter. *āssiski*[(XIV
2 Vs. 12; cf. Sommer, *AU* 298). Cf. Bossert, *Asia* 60-6 (1946);
Kammenhuber, *MIO* 2:415-6 (1954); Kronasser, *Etym.* 1:484,
293, 301; Neu, *Interpretation* 19-20.

ass-, assiya-

Caus. *as(sa)nu-*, *assiyanu-* 'favor, keep happy, propitiate
(deities or superiors), set aright (affected parties), treat gently,
massage (racehorses); make good, carry out (well), bring off
(cf. 'he made good his escape'), dispose (properly), get done, be
done with', 1 sg. pres. act. *asnumi* (*KBo* III 5 I 5 *n-as-kan*
asnumi 'I massage them'; ibid. 9 *n-as asnumi;* cf. Kanmenhuber,
Hippologia 78), *assanumi* (*FHG* 13 II 3; cf. Laroche, *RA* 46:44
[1952]; *KUB* XLIII 75 Rs. 8), 2 sg. pres. act. *asnusi* (*KBo* XI 10
III 19–20 and dupl. XI 72 III 6–7 *n-at-kan asnut mān-at-kan*
ŪL-ma asnusi 'make it good; but if you do not make it good'),
assanusi (VIII 63 I 11), 3 sg. pres. act. *asnuzi* (e.g. *KUB* I 13 I
6–7 *n-as arha lāi n-as-kan asnuzi sakruwanzi-ya-as* 'he unharnesses them, massages them, and they water them'; cf. Kammenhuber, *Hippologia* 54; *KBo* III 5 IV 25–26 *mahhan-ma arha*
lāi n-as asnuzi nu-smas wātar ŪL pāi 'but when he unharnesses
[them], he massages them; he does not give them water'; cf.
Kammenhuber, *Hippologia* 100; ibid. I 32 *nu kuitman* 8 MUŠU
asnuzi 'while he gets done in eight nights'; cf. Kammenhuber,
Hippologia 82; *KBo* XXI 41 + *KUB* XXIX 7 Vs. 68 and Rs. 13
n-asta mahhan arahza ANA PANI ÍD *asnuzi* 'when outside he gets
done in front of the river' ; cf. Lebrun, *Samuha* 121–2; *KUB*
XXIX 4 I 5 *nu-kan kuitman wetummanzi humantazz-iya asnuzi*
'meanwhile he is altogether done with building'; cf. Kronasser,
Umsiedelung 6; XVII 23 I 1–2 *mahhan-kan* SAL ŠU.GI *mu-*
gauwanzi asnuzi nu aruwaizzi 'when the old woman is through
praying she prostrates herself'; *KBo* XVII 65 Rs. 8 and 11
SISKUR.SISKUR.MEŠ *asnuzi* 'carries out the rituals'), *āsnuzi* (*KUB*
L 1 IV 11), *asnuzzi* (e.g. *KBo* XVII 65 Rs. 13 SISKUR.SISKUR
asnuzzi), *assanuzi* (e.g. XI 6 Rs. 20), *assanuzzi* (e.g. *KUB* VII 13
Vs. 33 '[he] gets done'), *āssanuzi* (*Bo* 2813 II 10), *assanunuzi*
(*KUB* XLIII 54 V 10), 3 sg. pres. midd. *asnuttari* (XXXII
130, 10–11 *kuwapi-ma-kan* KASKAL ^URU*Ishūpitta* KASKAL
^URU*Tasmaha-ya asnuttari* 'but when the trek to I. and the trek
to T. is over with'; cf. J. Danmanville, *RHA* 14:42 [1956], and
Lebrun, *Samuha* 168, both with wrong translation; 655/u +
KUB XIII 21 II 21 [dupl. to XIII 20 I 10, quoted below]; cf. H.
Otten – C. Rüster, *ZA* 62:104 [1972]), *assanuttari* (*KBo* IX 96 II
3), *assanuddāri* (*KUB* XIII 20 I 10 *mahhan-ma* ^LÚKÚR *aki*

192

nasma-kan KIN *assanuddāri* 'but when the enemy is killed or the task is done'; cf. Alp, *Belleten* 11:390 [1947]), *āssanuddāri* (ibid. 22), 1 pl. pres. act. *asnumeni* (XXXV 18 I 5; cf. Otten, *LTU* 25), *as]sanummeni* (XXII 11 I 11), 2 pl. pres. act. *asnutteni* (*KBo* XX 75 Rs. 11; *KUB* XXIII 68 Vs. 8), *assanutteni* (*KBo* XXIII 113 III 9; *KUB* XXVI 29+XXXI 55 Vs. 22), 3 pl. pres. act. *asnuanzi* (passim in Kikkulis-text, e.g. I 13 IV 9–10 *mahhan-ma-as* EGIR-*pa ūnnianzi n-as-kan asnuanzi wātar-samas pianzi* 'but when they drive them back, they massage them, give them water'; cf. Kammenhuber, *Hippologia* 70; *KBo* III 5 I 18 *mahhan-ma-as arha lānzi n-as asnuanzi wātar-ma* ŪL *akuwanzi* 'but when they unharness them, they massage them; but water they do not drink'; cf. Kammenhuber, *Hippologia* 80; also e.g. *IBoT* III 148 I 51 BIBRI.HI.A-*ya-kan sunnanzi* GAL.HI.A-*kan asnuanzi* 'they fill rhyta and dispose goblets'; cf. Haas – Wilhelm, *Riten* 214; *KUB* XXIX 8 II 12 *n-asta mahhan asnuanzi* 'when they are done'; ibid. 13–14 *mahhan-ma-za-kan warpuanzi asnuanzi* 'when they are done with bathing'; XXIX 4 III 4 *mahhan- -ma-at-kan asnuanzi* 'but when they are done with it'; cf. Kronasser, *Umsiedelung* 20; ibid. 49 *nu-kan mahhan* DINGIR- -LAM *huittiyauwanzi asnuanzi* 'when they are done with drawing the deity'), *asnuwanzi* (e.g. XXIX 51 I 11 and 14 *n-us-kan asnuwanzi* 'they massage them'; cf. Kammenhuber, *Hippologia* 200–2; *IBoT* III 148 III 17–19 GIM-*an-ma-kan kī kisan as- nuwanzi namma-at-za adanna esantari nu-za adanzi akuwanzi* GAL.HI.A-*kan asnuwanzi nu appa tienzi* 'when they are thus done with this, then they sit down to eat, and they eat [and] drink; they dispose goblets and put [them] back'), *assanuanzi* (e.g. *KBo* XIII 13 Rs. 10 LUGA]L *Ù* DUMU.MEŠ-*ŠU* KUR-*nī assanuanzi* 'the king and his sons will set the country aright'; cf. Riem- schneider, *Geburtsomina* 62; *KUB* XVII 35 I 27–28 *nu-smas* KÚ- -*zi* NAG-*zi* [GAL.HI.]A-*kan assanuanzi* 'they eat [and] drink; they dispose goblets'; *IBoT* III 148 II 59–60 BIBRI.HI.A-*ya sunnanzi* [GA]L.HI.A-*kan assanuanzi*; *KUB* XV 31 II 6 *n-asta mahhan* IŠTU 9 KASKAL *assanuanzi* 'when they are done with the nine roads'; cf. Haas – Wilhelm, *Riten* 154; XXVII 49 III 23 *mahhan-kan unumanzi assanuan[zi* 'when they are done with decking him'), *assanuwanzi* (e.g. VII 54 II 3 GIM-*an-ma-kan* SISKUR *assa-*

nuwanzi 'when they carry out the ritual'; VII 24 Vs. 9–10
BIBRI.HI.A-*kan sunnanzi* KÚ-*zi* NAG-*zi* GAL.HI.A *assanuwanzi*;
IBoT III 148 II 50–51 *nu-kan* BIBRI.HI.A *sunnanzi* GAL.HI.A-*kan*
assanuwanzi; *KBo* II 8 IV 20 and 26 GAL.HI.A-*kan assanuwanzi*;
ibid. 15 GAL.HI.A *assanuwanzi*; *KUB* X 91 III 18 *nu halziyari*
nu-kan GAL.HI.A ŠA EZEN GURUN *assanuwa⟨n⟩zi* 'announcement
is made, and they dispose the goblets of the fruit festival'; VII
54 III 10 -]*kan adanna akuwanna assanuwanzi* 'when they are
done with eating [and] drinking'; XVII 18 II 15–16 *memiyanas*
anda memiyauwanzi assanuwanzi 'they are done with speaking
the words'), *āssanuwanzi* (XXXII 103 II 15), *as-sa-nu-u-wa-an-*
-zi (XXV 41 V 12), 3 pl. pres. midd. *asnuwantari* (XXIX 40 II 7
mahha]*n-ma-at-kan asnuwantari n-us* IŠTU YÀ UDU *iskanzi* 'but
when they are massaged they smear them with sheep-fat'; cf.
Kammenhuber, *Hippologia* 178; XXIX 44 III 5 *n-at*] *mahhan*
ayissanzi asnuwantari-ya-at-kan 'when they become hot and
they are massaged'; cf. Kammenhuber, *Hippologia* 162), 1 sg.
pret. act. *assanunun* (e.g. XIII 9 + XL 62 I 4 *nu-kan* DINGIR.MEŠ
assanunun 'I propitiated the gods'; cf. von Schuler, *Festschrift*
J. Friedrich 446 [1959]; *KBo* II 5 III 46–47 GAL-*in* EZEN-*an*
assanunun 'I carried out the great festival'; cf. Götze, *AM* 190;
Ose, *Supinum* 26; IV 4 II 37; cf. Götze, *AM* 116), 3 sg. pret. act.
asnut (XVIII 74, 18), *assanut* (*KUB* VI 45 III 53 *nu-war-an-kan*
assanut '[the god] has favored him'; L 50, 11), 3 sg. pret. midd.
asnuttat (XV 34 IV 41 *n-asta arahza asnuttat* 'it is [all] done on
the outside'; cf. Haas – Wilhelm, *Riten* 206), *asnuttati* (*KBo*
XVII 95 II 11), 1 pl. pret. act. *assanummen* (X 37 IV 35), 3 pl.
pret. act. *assanuir* (II 20, 2 *nu-mu-kan kisan assanuir* 'they thus
favored me'; X 20 II 23), *assanuer* (X 20 III 18), 1 sg. imp. act.
āssanullu (*KUB* XIV 11 III 19–20 *nu* SISKUR ŠA ^{ÍD}[*Māla*] *iyallu*
n-at-kan āss[*an*]*ullu* 'the ritual of the Mala river I will do and
carry out'), *asnullu* (dupl. XIV 8 Rs. 7; cf. Götze, *KlF* 214), 2 sg.
imp. act. *asnut* (e.g. *KBo* XI 72 II 36–37 *kī uttar asnut n-at*
SIG₅-*in iya* 'set this matter aright and make it well'; *KUB* XIII 2
III 30–31 *nu kuedani* DINAM *ēszi n-at-si hanni n-an-kan` asnut*
'who has a legal case, judge it for him and set him aright'; cf.
von Schuler, *Dienstanweisungen* 48; ibid. 32 *nu-smas-at hanni*
n-as-kan asnut 'judge it for them and set them aright'; ibid.

37–38 *namma-an-kan* IŠTU GA.KIN.AG *IMZI* SÍG.HI.A *asnut* 'also keep him happy with cheese, rennet, and wool'), *assanut* (VI 45 III 53; *KBo* XIII 153, 3), 3 sg. imp. act. *assanuddu* (*KUB* XIII 2 III 22–23 *nu auriyas* EN-*as DINAM* SIG₅-*in hannau n-at-kan assanuddu* 'the border-lord shall well judge the case and dispose of it'), 3 sg. imp. midd. *assanuttaru* (XXXVI 30, 5), 2 pl. imp. act. *assanutten* (*KBo* XX 34 Rs. 9), 3 pl. imp. act. *asnuandu* (*KUB* XXXI 86 IV 8–9 [dupl. of XIII 2 III 23] *n-at-kan asnuandu* 'they shall dispose of it'); partic. *asnu(w)ant-, as(s)a-nuwant-* 'favored, dear; well turned out, well disposed', nom. sg. c. *asnuanza* (XXXI 127 I 19), *assanuwanza* (e.g. *KBo* XIII 2 Rs. 18 *antuhsani-kan kuis assanuwanza* 'who is dear to the population'; *KUB* XXIV 3 I 49–50 *karuuiliyas-a-za-kan* DINGIR.MEŠ-*as istarna zik-pat assanuwanza* 'among the ancient gods you are favored'; cf. Gurney, *Hittite Prayers* 24; XXXIII 121 II 5–6 *misriwanza hūmanda[zz-a] assanuwanza* '[she was] beautiful and well turned out in every way'; cf. Friedrich, *ZA* 49:234 [1950]), *asanuwanza* (*KBo* IV 6 Vs. 14 *n-as-kan hūman-daz asanuwanza* 'it [is] in every way well turned out'), SIG₅-*anza* (ibid. 12; cf. Tischler, *Gebet* 12), acc. sg. c. *assanuwandan* (*KUB* XXX 10 Rs. 22–23 *nu-]mu* LUGAL-*an āski* DINGIR-*YA* ŪL *assanuwandan anduhsan le issatti* 'at the king's gate, my god, do not make me a persona non grata'), nom.-acc. sg. neut. *asnuan* (*KBo* III 21 III 3), *assanuwan* (II 13 Rs. 8 GAL.HI.A-*kan assanuwan* 'goblets [are] disposed'), gen. sg. (?) *assanuwandas* (XIII 215 Rs. 3), nom. pl. c. *assanuwantes* (*KUB* XXXVI 30, 4); verbal noun *asnuwauar* (XXIX 50 IV 6 [*s*]*akurūwauar as-nuwauar* 'watering [and] massaging'; cf. Kammenhuber, *Hippo-logia* 212), *asnumar* (L 33 I 3), *assanuwawar* (*KBo* II 8 I 29), *assanumar* (XXVI 18 IV 3), gen. sg. *asnuwas* (*KUB* XLIII 55 V 1), *asnumas* (e.g. *KBo* II 7 Vs. 8, 10, 14, 15, 28; *KUB* XVII 28 IV 42 *asnumas-ma kī danzi* 'for disposal they take the following'), *asnummas* (e.g. *KBo* XXVI 152 Rs. 5), *assanumas* (e.g. *KUB* XVII 35 II 23 and III 7; XXXVIII 25 I 23 *assanuma⟨s⟩*; cf. Haas, *Nerik* 276), *assanumās* (XLVI 22 I 11 and 23, Rs. 5 and 19; XLI 34 Rs. 11), *assanummas* (e.g. *KBo* XIV 142 I 58 ANA ᴰ*Hepat assanummas* 'for propitiation of Hebat'; II 13 Rs. 7; *KUB* VII 24 Vs. 8; XXV 23 I 29; cf. C. Carter, *JAOS* 93:67

[1973]); infin. *as-nu-u-wa-u-wa-an-zi* (XLI 31 Vs. 11), *asnumanzi*
(*ABoT* 14 V 10; *KBo* XIII 237 Vs. 5 and 10), *asnūmanzi* (XXIII
41 Rs. 13), *assanummanzi* (*KUB* XXV 23 I 45); iter. *as(sa)n-*
uski-, assiyanuski-, 2 sg. pres. act. *āssiyanuskisi* (*KBo* XIII 55
Rs. 4 *nu-smas-at-kan anda ŪL āssiyanus[kisi]* 'you do not make
it look good amongst them'), 3 sg. pres. act. *asnuskizzi* (e.g.
KUB XXXI 141 Vs. 2 *h]ūmanda-kan* KUR.KUR.HI.A *kuis asnusk-*
izzi '[Ištar] who sets aright all lands'; cf. Güterbock, *JCS*
21:257 [1967]), 1 pl. pres. act. *āssiyanusgaweni* (XXXI 42 II
22–23 *namma-kan BEL]U*.MEŠ-*NI pangawe QADU* DAM.MEŠ-*ŠU[NU]*
[DUMU.MEŠ-*ŠUNU* DUMU.DUMU.MEŠ-]*ŠUNU āssiyanusgaweni* [*ŪL*]
'and we also do not constantly propitiate our lords collectively
with their wives, their sons, and their grandsons'; cf. von
Schuler, *Orientalia* N.S. 25:227 [1956]; cf. *KBo* XIII 55 Rs. 4
nu-smas-at-kan anda ŪL āssiyanus[), 3 pl. pres. act. *assanus-*
kanzi (e.g. *KUB* XXI 11 Rs. 3 EZEN *nuntaras kuyēs assanus-*
kanzi 'those who speedily carry out the festival'; cf. Ünal, *Hatt.*
2:16; *HT* 1 IV 5 *kuitman-kan* DINGIR-LUM *assa⟨n⟩uskanzi*
'while they are propitiating the deity'), 2 sg. imp. act. *assanuski*
(*KUB* XL 47 Vs. 9). Cf. Ose, *Supinum* 23–6; Kronasser, *Etym.*
1:443–4, 301; Neu, *Interpretation* 17–9.

assu- 'dear, favored (predicatively only; the attributive form
used in this sense is *assiyant-*); favorable, good, auspicious,
propitious, agreeable, valuable' (SIG₅-*u-*; *KBo* I 44 + XIII 1 IV
12 *āssu* = Akk. *busumu* 'pleasant, agreeable', but dupl. XXVI
23, 1 *āssu* = Akk. *bussū* 'goods, possessions'; cf. Otten, *Voka-*
bular 19, 21–2), nom. sg. c. *āssus* (e.g. III 22 Vs. 2 [OHitt.]
ᴰIM-*unni āssus ēsta* 'he was dear to the storm-god'; cf. Neu,
Anitta-Text 10, 99–100; XXII 2 Rs. 4–5 [OHitt.] *ūk-wa a[tti]-*
-m[i] [natt]a āssus 'I [am] not dear to my father'; cf. Otten,
Altheth. Erzählung 10; *KUB* XXXI 127 I 8–9 *handanza-kan*
antuhsas tuk-pat āssus 'the righteous man is dear to thee'; XIX
26 I 17–18 *kuis-a antuwahhas ITTI* LUGAL SAL.LUGAL *āssus ANA*
ᴸᵁSANGA-*ya-as QATAMMA ā[ss]us ēsdu* 'what man is in favor
with king [and] queen, let him likewise be in favor with the
priest'; XXVI 12 II 25 *[s]umēss-as āssus kuedanikki* 'he [is]
favorable to one of you'; cf. von Schuler, *Dienstanweisungen*
25), SIG₅-*us* (XV 5 I 22), acc. sg. c. *āssun* (e.g. XXXVI 49 IV 7

āssun halukan 'good message'; *KBo* XXI 95 I 7 s]AL.LUGAL-*as āssun* UD-*an* QATAMMA *ekuzi* 'the queen likewise drinks to the Good Day'), nom.-acc. sg. (also pl.) neut. *assu* (*KUB* V 7 Vs. 7), *āssu* (e.g. *KBo* III 21 II 9 *āssu* ᵁᶻᵁYÀ *huwappann-a* ᵁᶻᵁYÀ 'good fat and bad fat'; X 37 II 35 *āssu* ᴳᴵˢ*paddur* 'good dish' (opp. ibid. 34 HUL-*lu* 'bad'); V 4 l.R. 4 *āssu lūlu au* 'see good prosperity!'; cf. Friedrich, *Staatsverträge* 1:70; V 3 II 13 *āssu lūlu uski*; cf. Friedrich, *Staatsverträge* 2:114; X 37 III 44 *n-asta* HUL-*lu wahnuttin n-at āssu* DÙ-*attin* 'turn the bad and make it good!'; *KUB* XXXIII 68 II 12 *nu-za āssu uddār dā* 'take good things!'; *KBo* IV 1 Vs. 43 *n-at-kan* DINGIR.MEŠ-*as antuhsass-a āssu* 'it [is] dear to gods and men'; *KUB* X 27 V 10 *nu mān* ANA SAL.LUGAL *āssu* 'if [it is] agreeable to the queen'; cf. M. Vieyra, *RA* 51:87, 99 [1957]; *KBo* XV 1 I 13 *mān* LUGAL-*i-m*[*a* ŪL] *āssu* 'but if [it is] not agreeable to the king'; cf. Kümmel, *Ersatzrituale* 112; VI 5 III 3 [= *Code* 1:28] *takku atti-ma anni* ŪL *āssu* 'if [it is] not agreeable to the father [and] mother'; *KUB* XIV 1 Vs. 83 *mahhan-wa-tta āssu nu-wa* QATAMMA *iya* 'as [is] agreeable to you, thus do!'; cf. Götze, *Madd.* 20; *KBo* XVII 65 Vs. 55 *masiwan* ANA EN SISKUR.SISKUR *āssu* 'as much as [is] agreeable to the sacrificer'; ibid. Rs. 64 *n-an* EN SISKUR.SISKUR *piyanāizzi kuit-si āssu* 'him the sacrificer pays what [is] agreeable to him'; *KUB* XXIX 4 II 27 *nu* ANA EN SISKUR *kuwapi āssu* 'when [it is] favorable to the sacrificer'; cf. Kronasser, *Umsiedelung* 16; ibid. III 34 *mān āssu* 'if favorable'; ibid. III 37 *mān-si* ŪL-*ma āssu* 'but if [it is] not favorable to him'), also used adverbially and nominally (see separate paragraphs below), gen. sg. c. *assauwas* (XLII 69 Rs. 6 3 DUG *assauwas* GUŠKIN NA₄ 'three vessels of good gold [and] stone[s]'; I 8 IV 30 *assauwas-pat memiyanas* 'of favorable disposition'; cf. Götze, *Hattusilis* 36), *āssauwas* (dupl. I 1 IV 51; *KBo* IV 13 I 7, 8, 9 ᴰU-*as āssauwas* 'of the storm-god, the good'), dat.-loc. sg. *a-as-sa-u-i* (ibid. 10 *āssaui* MUL-*i* 'to the good star'; VII 28 + VIII 92, 14 [OHitt.] *āssaui pedi* 'in a good place'; cf. Friedrich, *Rivista degli studi orientali* 32:218 [1957]; X 37 IV 49; XII 30 II 8), SIG₅-*u-i* (ibid. I 51), *a-as-sa-u-e* (*ABoT* 44 IV 1 *āssawe pedi*), instr. sg. or pl. *a-as-sa-u-i-it* (XI 1 Vs. 39 *āssauīt* IGI.HI.A-*it* 'with favorable eyes'; cf. Houwink Ten Cate – Josephson, *RHA* 25:108 [1967]), *a-sa-u-i-it* (ibid. Rs. 18), *a-as-sa-u-e-it* (*KUB* X 92 V 1), *a-as-sa-ú-e-it* (*KBo* VIII 69, 10 *āssawet* IGI.HI.A[-*it*; cf. Laroche, *RHA* 23:124 [1965]), abl. sg. *āssawaz* (*KUB* XLV 20 II 16 *āssawaz ped*[*az* 'from the good place'), *āssuwaz* (XXXIII 120 II 34 *āssuwaz-ma pidaz*), *a-as-su-u-wa-za* (ibid. 84 *ā*]*ssūwaza pedaz*; cf. Laroche, *RHA* 26:43–4 [1968]), nom. pl. c. *a-as-sa-u-e-es* (e.g. IX 6 II 5–6 *n-asta kuyēs* DINGIR.MEŠ *ANA* EN SISKUR [...] *āssawēs* 'the gods who [are] favorable to the sacrificer'; cf. Otten, *LTU* 39; *VBoT* 24 IV 29–30 *kuyēs* DINGIR.MEŠ *āssawēs*; cf. Sturtevant, *TAPA* 58:16 [1927]; *KBo* X 37 II 37 *āssawēs* EME.MEŠ 'good tongues'; *KUB* VII 5 III 22; XXIV 3 II 55–56 *n-asta l*[*e*] *āssawēs idālauwas anda harkanzi* 'let not the good perish among the evil'; cf. Gurney, *Hittite Prayers* 30), *āssāwēs* (dupl. XXIV 4 Rs. 11 *n-apa le āssāwēs*[), acc. pl. *āssamus* (XXXIII 9 III 10 *āssamus* IM.HI.A-*us* 'favorable winds'; cf. Laroche, *RHA* 23:106 [1965]), nom.-acc. pl. neut. *āssawa* (VII 16 Rs. 15; *KBo* XIII 57 Vs. 8), *āssauwa* (e.g. XVII 105 III 7, beside ibid. 6 *idālauwa*; *KUB* XXXVI 89 Rs. 40; cf. ibid. 43 SIG₅.MEŠ; Haas, *Nerik* 154), SIG₅-*uwa* (XXXVI 77, 6), dat.-loc. pl. *āssauas* (e.g. XXX 10 Vs. 7 *āssauas antuhsas anda* 'among good men').

Adverbial nom.-acc. sg. neut. *āssu* and nom.-acc. pl. neut. *āssū* 'in favored fashion, in a good way, well', *āssu har(k)-* 'hold in esteem', e.g. *KBo* V 3 III 18 URU-*a*]*n kuinki āssu parā huu*[*itt*]*iyan harmi* 'I have singled out some town in favored fashion' (cf. below *assuui, assuli* 'for good treatment', also with *parā huittiya-* 'draw forth, single out'; cf. Friedrich, *Staatsverträge* 2:124); *KUB* I 1 I 29–30 ŠEŠ-*YA-ya-mu* ᴵNIR.GÁL *āssu harta* 'my brother Muwatallis held me in esteem' (cf. Götze, *Hattusilis* 8); XXX 10 Rs. 24 *āssu kuyus issah*[*hi* 'whom I treat well'; XXIV 8 II 7–8 *nu-za* DAM-*KA āssu sastan seski* 'sleep well with your wife in bed!' (cf. Siegelová, *Appu-Hedammu* 6); *KBo* VII 28 + VIII 92, 11–13 (OHitt.) *āssū* IGI.HI.A-*KA lāk* ...[LU]GAL-*un anda āssu sakuwaya* GEŠTUG.[HI.]A-*KA lāk nu āssu utta*[*r*] [*i*]*stamas* 'incline your eyes well ..., eye the king well, incline your ears and hear the word well' (cf. Friedrich, *Rivista degli studi orientali* 32:218 [1957]); ibid. 19 *n-asta* ŠUMMI LUGAL *tagnas* ᴰUTU-*i piran āssu taraski* 'and before the solar deity of the earth speak well of the king's name'.

assuwant- 'favorable, good' (SIG₅-[*uw*]*ant-*), nom. sg. c. *āssuwanza* (*KBo* XIV 12 IV 1; cf. Güterbock, *JCS* 10:97 [1956]; XII 30 II 6; XVI 24 + 25 III 22 LUGAL *āssuwanza* 'good king'; *KUB* XlII 4 I 54 *āssuwanza kuiski* ᴸᵁ*UBA*[*RUM*] 'some good foreigner'; cf. Sturtevant, *JAOS* 54:368 [1934]), *āssūwanza* (dupl. 1303/z, 7; cf. H. Otten – C. Rüster, *ZA* 67:55 [1977]; XXVI 1 III 3), acc. sg. c. *assuwandan* (XII 63 Vs. 12 and 21), *āssuwanda-ssan* (XXXIII 81 IV 5; cf. Laroche, *RHA* 23:79 [1965]), dat.-loc. sg. *assuwanti* (*Bo* 2953, 9; cf. Güterbock, *Siegel* 1:5), SIG₅-*uwanti* (*KUB* XXXVI 75 III 11 SIG₅-*uwanti pedi* 'in a good place'), instr. sg. or pl. SIG₅-*antet* (e.g. XXXIV 19 IV 6 SIG₅-*antet memiyanit* 'with a favorable word'; *KBo* VIII 68 IV 6 SIG₅-*antet* IGI.HI.A-*it* 'with favorable eyes'), SIG₅-*tit* (*KUB* XXXVI 89 Rs. 50 SIG₅-*tit* IGI.HI.A-*it*; XX 92 VI 12 SIG₅-*it* IGI.HI.A-*it* may reflect either *āssuwantit* or *āssauit*), nom. pl. c. *āssuwantes* (e.g. *KUB* XXXVI 109, 12; cf. Carruba, *SMEA* 18:190 [1977]; *Bo* 2489 + 4008 II 29; cf. Otten, *Sprachliche Stellung* 21).

assu- (n.) 'favor, good treatment; good(ness), well-being; good stuff, good things, goods, chattels, valuables, wealth, possession(s)' (SIG₅-*u-*; NÍG.GA 'goods, wealth'; cf. e.g. *KUB* XVI 82 IV 14 KUR-*eass-a āssu* ME-*as* 'and he took the wealth of the land' besides VI 26 Vs. 5 NÍG.GA KUR ME-*as*; rarely *MIMMŪ*, cf. Laroche, *Ugaritica* 6:371 [1969]; Akk. *damiqtu, dumqu, damāqu* 'favor, well-being' [see below], *būšu, bušū* 'goods' [see above], *mimmu* 'goods' [*KBo* I 1 Rs. 60], *makkūru* 'goods' [see below], *hišbu* 'yield' [see below]), nom.-acc. sg. *āssu* (e.g. XXX 11 Rs. 19]DINGIR-*YA annaz kartaz āssu ŪL* GU[L-*asta* '[for me] since birth my god has not ordained good'; IX 31 II 38 *idalu-kan parā istapdu āssuw-a-kan anda kurakdu* 'may he shut out the bad and keep in the good'; cf. Otten, *LTU* 16; *KBo* XIII 31 I 3 *āssu kīsa* 'good will come'; cf. Riemschneider, *Geburtsomina* 74, 79; XV 10 II 33–34 *nu idālu harnikten nu* ANA BELI ANA DAM-*ŠU* DUMU.MEŠ-*ŠU āssu namma ēstu* 'destroy evil; to the lord, to his wife [and] children let there again be good'; cf. Szabó, *Entsühnungsritual* 24; ibid. 11 *āssu memiskiten* 'speak good!' [opp. ibid. 10 *idālu*]; cf. Szabó, *Entsühnungsritual* 20; *KUB* XXI 27 III 37 *āssu mematti* 'you speak good'; XVII 28 II

56 ^DUTU-*i āssu* 'hail to the sun!'; cf. E. Tenner, *KlF* 388; V 1 I 42
UGULA-*za* ZAG-*tar parnass-a āssu* ME-*as* 'the boss took' rightness
and wealth of the house'; cf. Ünal, *Hatt.* 2:38; ibid. 49 KUR-*eas*
āssu ME-*as* 'took the wealth of the land'; VIII 1 III 12 *arunas*
āssu harakzi 'the wealth of the sea will perish', matching Akk.
hişib tāmti ihalliq of similar astrological omina; *KBo* X 2 III
8–10 [OHitt.] *āssu-ma-ssi sarā dahhun n-at Hattusi* URU-*ri-mit*
arha udahhun 'but I took up its wealth and brought it off to
Hattusas, my city', matching X 1 Rs. 5 [Akk.] NÍG.GA-*šu ana*
URU-*ya* ^{URU}*Hatti ublam* 'its wealth to my city of Hatti I
brought'; cf. F. Imparati – C. Saporetti, *Studi classici e orientali*
14:52, 79 [1965]; III 22 Vs. 58 KASKAL-*za kuit āssu utahh*[*un*
'what goods I brought back from campaigns'; cf. Neu, *Anitta-*
Text 14; III 1 I 28–29 *nu* ^{URU}*Halpas* NAM.RA.MEŠ *āssu-sset*
[URU]*Hattusi udas* 'he brought deportees of Halpa [and] its
goods to Hattusas'; *KUB* XXIII 11 II 31–32 NAM.RA.MEŠ GUD
UDU KUR-*eas āssu arha* ^{URU}*Hattusi uwatenun* 'deportees, cattle,
sheep, goods of the land I brought off to Hattusas'; XXIV 8 II 2
nu-w]*a-mu āssu pier* 'they have given me goods'; cf. Siegelová,
Appu-Hedammu 6; *KBo* VI 3 I 12 [= *Code* 1:5] *āssu-sett-a*
sarnikzi 'he makes restitution for his [viz. the merchant's]
goods'), *assu* (XVIII 151 Vs. 13 [OHitt.] *t-as assu bayis* 'she
gave the good'; cf. Ünal–Kammenhuber, *KZ* 88:164 [1974];
KUB V 7 Vs. 7), dat.-loc. sg. *as-su-ú-i* (I 16 II 17 [OHitt.] *n-an*
parā assuui hui[*ttiyanneskinun* 'I have constantly singled him
out for good treatment', matching ibid. I 17 [Akk.] *ana*
damāqqim; cf. Sommer, *HAB* 4–5, 46–7), *a-as-su-i* (e.g.
1112/c+ III 26–27 *āssui* TI-*anni* 'for weal [and] life'; cf. L. Rost,
MIO 1:360 [1953]), *a-as-su-ú-i* (e.g. XXXIII 68 II 17; cf.
Laroche, *RHA* 23:128 [1965]), *a-as-sa-u-i* (*KBo* V 8 I 13–14
nu-mu idālaui parā ŪL *tarnai āssaui-ma-mu parā tarnan harzi*
'[he] does not consign me to the evil but has consigned me to
the good'; cf. Götze, *AM* 148; *KUB* XXVI 10 I 5 LUGAL-*was*
āssaui 'for the king's good[s?]'; XVI 50, 6 *anda āssaui* 'in the
good'), SIG₅-*ui* (e.g. V 1 III 59 *anda* SIG₅-*ui*, ibid. 57 ŠÀ SIG₅-*ui*;
cf. Ünal, *Hatt.* 2:74), instr. sg. *āssuitt-a* (XIX 20 Vs. 10), *āssuyit*
(*RS* 25:421 Recto 39–40 *āssuyit sūwanza* 'full of good stuff'; cf.
Laroche, *Ugaritica* 5:774 [1968]), *a-as-sa-u-it* (*HT* 21 + *KUB*

200

VIII 80 II 15 *āssauit sarā sunnes* 'has filled up with good stuff'),
a-as-sa-u-i-it (*KBo* X 2 I 19–20 [OHitt.] *āssu-ma-ssi sarā dahhun
nu* É-*ir-mit āssauīt sarā sunnahhun* 'but I took up its wealth and
filled up my house with the wealth', matching X 1 Vs. 10 [Akk.]
u É SIG₅ *umtalli*; cf. ibid. 36 *u makkur-šu* ᵁᴿᵁKÙ.BABBAR-*ti
umtalli* 'and with its goods I filled the city of Hatti'), abl. sg.
assuwaz (*KUB* XVIII 5 I–II passim *assuwaz uit* [or:*pait*] '[the
oracular bird] came [or: went] favorably'; cf. A. Archi, *SMEA*
16:128 [1975]), *āssuwaz* (e.g. *KBo* III 3 I 21 *nu-war-an* IŠTU
NAM.RA.MEŠ *āssuwazz-aya sarā dahhi* 'I will take it up along
with deportees and chattels'), NÍG.GA-*z* (dupl. XVI 23 I 10
]NAM.RA.MEŠ NÍG.GA-*z-iya sarā dahhi*), *āssauwaz* (*KUB* XIX 18 I
15–16 *n-an āssauwaz* QADU [NAM.RA.MEŠ] GUD.HI.A UDU.HI.A *pe
harta* 'and along with goods he [viz. the ally] proffered it [viz.
the conquered city to Suppiluliumas] together with deportees,
cattle, and sheep'; cf. Güterbock, *JCS* 10:76 [1956]), nom.-acc.
pl. *as-su-u* (II 2 III 13 *assū-ma* 'but good things'; cf. Schuster,
Bilinguen 69), *asū* (*KBo* VIII 47 Vs. 6 'goods'), *āssū* (e.g. *KUB*
XIV 1 Vs. 49, 50, 54, 55 *āssū-ya* 'and chattels' preceded by
'wives, children, deportees'; cf. Götze, *Madd.* 12–4; Otten,
Sprachliche Stellung 19; XVII 21 I 11–13 *nu-za sumenzan* ŠA
[DINGIR.MEŠ] *āssū* KÙ.BABBAR GUŠKIN BIBRI.HI.A TÚG.HI.A *anzel
iwar* EGIR-*an ŪL kuiski kappūwan harta* 'of you gods' valuables,
silver, gold, rhyta, garments, nobody had kept count like we
[did]'; cf. von Schuler, *Die Kaškäer* 152; *KBo* XII 42 Rs. 10
āssū-ya-wa KÙ.BABBAR GUŠKI[N] ᴺᴬ⁴ZA.GÌN 'and valuables, silver, gold, lapis lazuli'; cf. H. A. Hoffner, *JCS* 22:36 [1968];
dupl. *ABoT* 49 + 2007/u Vs. 11 *āssū-ya-w*[*a*; cf. H. Otten – C.
Rüster, *ZA* 62:235 [1972]; *KUB* XXIII 77 Rs. 53 ŠA BELI-ŠU *āssū*
'his master's goods'; XXVI 17 II 12 ŠA BELUM *āssū*; *KBo* XXV
122 II 10–11 [OHitt.] *katta āssū utir* ... GAL.HI.A SIG₅-*anda*
GUŠKIN-*an* SIG₅-*anda*[*n utir* 'they have brought down goods ...
they have brought down good cups [and] good gold'; cf. Neu,
Altheth. 205; XVII 62 + 63 IV 14–15 *kā*[*sa*]-*wa kinun* ŠA
DUMU.NITA *āssū uda*[*hhun*] *parā-ma-wa* M[*U-an*]*ni* ŠA DUMU.SAL
āssū udallu 'lo, now I [viz. the midwife] have delivered the
"blessed event" of a male child, but next year let me deliver the
"blessed event" of a female child' [repeated, mutatis mutandis,

ibid. 16–18, with 'male' and 'female' reversed]; *KUB* XLIII 60 I
22–23 *nu-ssi-ssan kue āssū 9-andas happesnas ser hāssan* 'what
"good things" [i.e. "blessed issue"] [are] born to her on her nine
limbs'; VIII 34 Rs. 17+XLIII 13 III 3 LUGAL-*wa-kan* É.GAL
anda āssū kuekki [in the king's palace some good things ...';
VIII 4, 17), SIG₅-*uwa* (*KBo* XII 38 I 4 SIG₅-*uwa dapida* 'all
goods'; cf. Güterbock, *JNES* 26:75 [1967]), dat.-loc. pl. *āssuwas* (VI 4 I 4 [=*Code* 1:5] *āssuwas kuiski anda kuenzi* '[if]
someone kills [a merchant of Hatti] in the midst of [his] goods',
vs. ibid. 6] *āssu-ma ŪL pe harzi* 'but [if] he has no goods with
him'). On the form *āssū* cf. also C. Watkins, *Gedenkschrift für
H. Kronasser* 250–62 (1982).

assuwant-, assawant- (c.) 'well-being', serving in place of
assu- as animate subject with transitive verbs (cf. e.g. *wetenant-*
beside *watar*; Laroche, *BSL* 57.1:25 [1962]), nom. sg. *āssuwanza* (e.g. *KUB* XVIII 21 II 2), *āssauwaza* (V 3 IV 6),
āssauwasza (sic XXII 64 III 7), SIG₅-*uanza* (e.g. V 1 I 97
SIG₅-*uanza* SILIM-*ul* ME-*as* 'well-being took goodness'; cf. Ünal,
Hatt. 2:48), SIG₅-*uwanza* (XVI 4, 9).

assu(wa)tar (n.) 'favorableness, friendly fashion', nom.-acc.
sg. SIG₅-*utar* (*KUB* XIX 55 Vs. 21; cf. Sommer, *AU* 198),
SIG₅-*tar* (ibid. Rs. 42), dat.-loc. sg. *assuwannī* (XXVI 83 III 9
assuwannī-ya), *āssuwanni* (XXVI 1 III 37–38 *nasma-kan* ANA
ᴰUTU-*ŠI āssuwanni kuiski a*[*nd*]*an neanza* 'or someone [has]
turned in friendly fashion to His Majesty'; cf. von Schuler,
Dienstanweisungen 13; XXVI 13 IV 8 + XXI 43, 15; dupl.
XXVI 12 IV 46 *ās*]*suwanni*; cf. von Schuler, *Dienstanweisungen*
29; XV 18 III 7; XLI 19 Vs. 11; cf. Haas – Thiel, *Rituale* 94),
āssuanni (XXIV 10 III 31; cf. Jakob-Rost, *Ritual der Malli* 48),
SIG₅-*anni* (XIX 55 1.R. 3; cf. Sommer, *AU* 204).

assul- (n.), *assula-* (c.) 'favor, good treatment, friendship,
greeting(s) (>letter); well-being' (SILIM-*ul*), nom.-acc. sg. neut.
assul (e.g. *KUB* XXX 10 Rs. 19 *nu-mu-ssan sēr assul natta
isduwari* 'on my account [divine] favor is not manifest'; *KUB*
XV 35 + *KBo* II 9 I 30 *nu-smas-kan tuēl assul arha dā* 'and take
your favor away from them'; cf. Sommer, *ZA* 33:87, 98 [1921];
A. Archi, *Oriens Antiquus* 16:299 [1977]; III 6 II 55 *assul austa*
'[he] saw [Ištar's and my brother's] favor'; cf. Götze, *Hattusilis*

22; *KUB* XV 34 IV 48 *n-asta anda assul memiyanzi* 'then they say "greetings"'; cf. Haas–Wilhelm, *Riten* 206; *Maşat* 75/43, 23 BELU-*mu assul hatreski* 'my lord, write me ever greetings!'; cf. Alp, *Belleten* 44:48 [1980]), *āssul* (e.g. *KBo* IV 12 Vs. 17–18 *ammell-a-ssi āssul tuqqāt* 'and my favor towards him was patent'; cf. Götze, *Hattusilis* 42), SILIM-*ul(l-a)* (e.g. *KUB* XVIII 11 Vs. 8 SILIM-*ul parnass-a āssu* 'well-being and weal of the house'; V 1 I 9 and passim; cf. Ünal, *Hatt.* 2:32, 195), SILIM-*l-a* (ibid. 67 and passim), nom. sg. c. *assulas* (e.g. XLIX 24 Rs. 11), acc. sg. c. *assulan* (e.g. *KBo* VI 29 I 9–10 GIM-*an-ma-za-kan* ŠA DINGIR-*LIM assulan uskiskiuwan tehhun* 'as I began seeing the deity's favor'; cf. Götze, *Hattusilis* 44; IV 12 Rs. 9–11 *nu-kan* ŠA ᴰUTU-ŠI *assulan anda le daliyanzi nu-smas-kan assulas* AŠAR--ŠUNU-*ya le wehtari* 'let them not forgo my majesty's favor, and may their place of favor not shift'; cf. Götze, *Hattusilis* 44), *āssulan* (III 6 I 27 ŠA ŠEŠ-YA-*ya āssulan auir* 'and my brother's favor [they] saw'; cf. Götze, *Hattusilis* 8), SILIM-*ulan* (e.g. II 32 IV 1; *KUB* X 91 III 9, besides ibid. 10 SILIM-*ul*), gen. sg. *assulas* (*RS* 25:421 Verso 64 *assulas memiyanas-ma-as* 'she [is] a word of well-being'; cf. Laroche, *Ugaritica* 5:775 [1968]; *KBo* XV 10 II 32; cf. Szabó, *Entsühnungsritual* 24), *āssulas* (*KUB* II 1 III 33 ᴰ*Ālas āssulas* 'god A. "della salute"'; cf. A. Archi, *SMEA* 16:98, 110 [1975]), dat.-loc. sg. *assuli* (e.g. XV 31 I 47 ᴰUTU-*i … assuli* 'for the majesty's well-being'; cf. Haas–Wilhelm, *Riten* 152; XXXIII 62 II 9 *assuli* TI-*anni innarauwanni hattulanni* 'for well-being, life, strength, health'; *KBo* V 3 III 21–22 *nu-t[ta mān ap]āt* KUR-*e nasma* URU-*an assu[li] nasm[a* HUL-*anni] parā huittiyan [ha]rmi* 'if I have singled out that land or town for good or bad treatment'; cf. Friedrich, *Staatsverträge* 2:124; dupl. XIX 44 Rs. 10–11 *nasma-za mān apāt […] assuli nasma idālu parā huitt[*; cf. V 3 III 18 URU-*a]n kuinki āssu parā huu[itt]iyan harmi* under adverbial *āssu* above; IV 10 Rs. 11 and V 3 passim 'in favor[able fashion], loyally'; cf. Friedrich, *Staatsverträge* 2:106–36; XVII 105 II 13 *anda assuli nes[h]ut* 'turn in friendship [to the king etc.]'; ibid. 14 *a[nda] assuli nishut*), *as-su-ú-li* (e.g. ibid. 21–22 *anda assūli nēyantes ēstin*; cf. A. Archi, *SMEA* 16:85–6 [1975]; *VBoT* 2, 18 and 20; cf. L. Rost, *MIO* 4:329 [1956]), *assulli* (*KUB* XXI 4 1V 15 *assulli pahsantaru* '[they] shall in favor protect [you]'; cf.

Friedrich, *Staatsverträge* 2:82–3), *āssuli* (e.g. XVII 10 II 11; XXXIII 73+74, 16; cf. Laroche, *RHA* 23:92, 165 [1965]), SILIM-*li* (e.g. *KBo* IV 10 Rs. 10 and 15, besides ibid. 11 *assuli*; *KUB* XV 19 I 6; XXII 40 III 23).

assulatar (n.) 'well-being', dat.-loc. sg. *assulanni* 'in well-being' (*KUB* V 1 IV 40; cf. Ünal, *Hatt.* 2:84), *āssulani* (XLVIII 124 Rs. 12), SILIM-*ulanni* (XL 33 Vs. 17).

On ᴰ*Assiya(n)za* see Laroche, *Recherches* 72. For problematic associations of *assu-* with -*as(s)u-*, a component in Anatolian proper names, see e.g. Tischler, *Glossar* 87–8, with references.

Hier. *asi-* or *aza-* '(be) love(d)'; cf. Laroche, *HH* 15; Meriggi, *HHG* 36–7; Tischler, *Glossar* 81–2; Hawkins – Morpurgo – Neumann, *HHL* 162–3, 186. Doubtful Lyd. *aśaã-* 'favor', *aśfã-*'goods'; cf. Gusmani, *Lyd. Wb.* 66, *Die Sprache* 21:169–70 (1975).

assu- has been traditionally connected (ever since Friedrich, *IF* 41:370–2 [1923], and down to e.g. Gusmani, *Lessico* 50, 92–3) with Gk. ἐΰς 'good, brave, noble', εὐ 'well', gen. pl. (Homeric) ἐάων (< *ἐέων) 'good things' (IE *[e]sú- from *es-'be', like e.g. Skt. *sánt-* 'being; real, true, good', or Gk. τὰ ὄντα 'goods, possessions' with its probable Lycian calque *ahñtãi* on the Xanthos trilingual [*Lyc.* 17]; cf. Laroche, *Fouilles de Xanthos* 6:58, 68 [1979]; already Hrozný, *Heth. KB* 103, adduced the comparison of Akk. *bušū* 'goods' with *bašū* 'be'), besides IE *wesu-* 'good' in other branches of Anatolian (Palaic, Luwian, Hier. *wasu-* 'good; well-being'), somewhat like Skt. *sú* 'well' besides *vásu-* 'good; wealth' (cf. e.g. Mayrhofer, *KEWA* 3: 173–4; Kammenhuber, *KZ* 77:169–70 [1961]). The verbal form *āssāri* has been explained as denominative from *assu-*, analogous to the gloss-wedged Luwoid *wassāri* (q.v. s.v. *was[s]-*) from Luw. *wasu-* (cf. Oettinger, *MSS* 34:136 [1976]), and *assiya-* has been similarly accounted for (cf. e.g. Kronasser, *VLFH* 41; Neu, *Interpretation* 20). Alternatively, *assiya-* has been kept apart from *assu-* and connected (as reflecting *ans-y -or *n̥s-y-) with IE *ans- (*IEW* 47) seen in Goth. *ansts* 'favor, grace', ON *āst* 'favor, love', ON *unna*, OE OS OHG *unnan* 'favor, be ungrudging' (cf. G. Jucquois, *RHA* 22:89–91 [1964]; Gusmani, *Lessico* 72).

Yet the inner-Hittite data cast doubt on the derivation of
assu- from IE **(e)sú-*; a derivational tie to the verb 'to be'
ought to be still palpable in Hittite, and the near universal
geminated spelling *assu-* (vs. constant *asanzi, asant-*) is difficult
to justify (cf. e.g. *KUB* XXXIII 109 I 5 *asanza memias* 'the
matter [is] true' besides *RV* 7.104.12 *sác cásac ca vácasī* 'the
true and the false word'). A chain of semantic developments
'being' > 'real' > 'true' > 'good' > 'dear', while not impossible,
would be unique (Gk. ἐΰς veers off rather in the direction of
'brave, noble'). Furthermore, *assu-* does not basically denote
that which is intrinsically and objectively good (as does
inherently IE **[e]sú-*) but rather that which is found to be
agreeable; hence DÙG.GA 'good' does not cover *assu-* but rather
lazz(a)i- 'good, sound'. It is therefore advisable to start
with the sense 'favored, dear'; for the sequence 'favored,
dear' > 'good' > 'goods' one need but compare Lat. *bonus*
< **duenos,* lit. 'favored'; cf. *beā-* < **dweyā-* 'favor, make
happy', Vedic *dúvas-, duvoyā́* 'favor', *duvasyáti* 'show favor,
honor'). Therefore the root *ass-* can be considered basic, with
assiya- a primary verbal derivative like e.g. *arsiya-* beside *ars-*
or *parkiya-* beside *park-* (cf. also Carruba, *Oriens Antiquus*
13:150 [1974]). *assu-* is a *u*-stem derivative from *ass-* in the
manner of *harpu-* 'hostile' from *harp-* 'separate', or *hatku-*
'tight' from *hatk-* 'squeeze, shut', or *huesu-* 'live, raw' from
hues- 'live', or *sarku-* 'prominent' from *sark-* 'rise'; there are no
"*u*-less" denominative verbs from *u*-stems (e.g. *parku-* 'high' is
derived from *park-* 'rise' [cf. Toch. A *park-*, AB *pärk-* 'rise'],
not *parkiya-* from *parku-*; wrongly Oettinger, *MSS* 34:136
[1976]; correctly J. J. S. Weitenberg, *Kratylos* 23:93 [1978]).
assul- is also well accounted for as a deverbative abstract noun
(cf. e.g. *imiul-* 'mixture', *ishiul-* 'binding, obligation', *wastul-*
'offense, sin'). *as(sa)nu-* is a regular deverbative causative to
ass- (cf. *tepnu-* 'belittle, humiliate' to **tep-* [Skt. *dabh-* 'hurt,
abandon'] besides *tepu-* 'small') rather than to *es-* 'sit' (cf.
Goetze, *JCS* 17:62 [1963]; Neu, *Interpretation* 18; wrongly e.g.
Götze, *Madd.* 103; Sturtevant, *Comp. Gr.*[1] 234; Kronasser,
Etym. 1:443–4). *as(sa)nu-* is thus unrelated to Hier. *as(a)-*
nu(wa)- or *isanuwa-* 'set down, establish, install' (cf. Meriggi,

HHG 37–8; Laroche, *HH* 154; Hawkins – Morpurgo – Neumann, *HHL* 187–8); Hittite did not need to form a causative to *es-* since it had the transitive *asas-* (q.v.) with its own causative *asesanu-* in the sense 'set(tle), establish'.

ass-, *assu-* point to a reconstruction **ans-* or **ņs-*, if we compare e.g. *dassu-* < **donsu-* or **dņsu-*, or *hassu-* < **H₁onsu-*, with **ns* > *ss* rather than *nz* (cf. Kronasser, *VLFH* 73; Oettinger, *Eide* 24). Accordingly *ass-* can be connected immediately with IE **ans-*, **ņs-* 'favor' which Jucquois proposed as the etymon of *assiya-* (see above).

IE **ans-* thus has a rich progeny in Hittite but little in other Anatolian; on the other hand Hittite (unlike most of Anatolian) has little trace of IE **wes-* and does not (unlike Hieroglyphic) form a causative of *es-* 'sit'; of IE **(e)sú-* there are no Anatolian traces at all. Cf. Puhvel, *KZ* 94:65–70 (1980).

O. Szemerényi's derivation of Gk. Ἀσκληπιός from Hitt. **ass(u)lāpiya-* 'health-giver' (*Journal of Hellenic Studies* 94:155 [1974]) richly deserves rejection; for Ἀσκληπιός see rather s.v. *asku-*. Szemerényi (*Kratylos* 11:215–8 [1966]) also questionably interpreted e.g. *ishassara-* 'lady' (q.v. s.v. *isha-*) as **isha-assara-* and isolated an **asar* which he compared either with Gk. ὄαρ 'wife' (as **osŗ) or with *assiya-* 'be dear' (as **ņser* 'loved one' < **'love, affection').

Cf. *assuzeri-*; *nassu, nasma*.

asara-, esara- 'white, bright' (BABBAR), acc. sg. c. *asaran, asāran* (*KUB* XXVII 67 II 15 SÍG *asaran* '[strand of] white wool', which is 'drawn' [ibid. 17 *huittiya-*]; ibid. III 19 SÍG *arasan* [sic]; *KBo* IV 2 I 28 *asaran* and 31 *asāran* 'white [strand of wool]', which is 'tied' [*hamank-*] and then 'cut' [*tuhhus-*]; ibid. II 30 *asaran*; cf. Kronasser, *Die Sprache* 8:90, 93 [1962]; *KUB* XXIV 10 II 10, with dupl. XXIV 11 II 31 and *KBo* X 41, 11 SÍG *asaran*; X 37 I 39 *asaran*), *esaran* (*KUB* XXIV 10 II 4 and dupl. XXIV 11 II 25 SÍG *esaran*; cf. Jakob-Rost, *Ritual der Malli* 38), *asarān* (239/g, 8 SÍG *asarān* SÍG S[IG₇ '[strand of] white wool [and] yellow wool'), nom. pl. c. *asaras* (*KBo* IV 2 I 63–64 *asaras mitiēs paddani-ssan kue kitta* 'white [and] red [strands of wool] which lie in the basket'), nom.-acc. pl. neut. (?) in]síG BABBAR *asara* (XVIII 199 Rs. 2).

asariya- 'make white, whiten', iter. 3 sg. pret. act. *asareskit* (*KUB* XLI 1, 8, with dupl. XXIV 9 I 49 'has made [him] white', following the threading of síG BABBAR 'white wool', even as ibid. 44 *antariskit* 'has made [him] blue' follows síG *antarantan* 'blue wool'; cf. Riemschneider, *MIO* 5:142, 145 [1957]; Jakob-Rost, *Ritual der Malli* 28).

asara-, esara- is a near-synonym of *harki-* (BABBAR) 'white' (q.v.). A shift *a>e*, as before *r* in e.g. *arma(n)->erma(n)-* or *arha->irha-* (q.v.), is unlikely here; more probably *e* is a historically significant lectio difficilior, and *a*-coloration is spreading but secondary (pace Neu, *IF* 82:273 [1977]), whether Luwoid or otherwise. *esara-<*esra-* (with anaptyxis as in e.g. *es[sa]ri-* 'shape') has a suffix matching other Indo-European (esp. Slavic) color adjectives, e.g. Hitt. *antara-* (q.v.)$<$ *$md(h)$- -*ró-* 'blue' or *$rudh$-$ró$- 'red'. A possible *$esra$-$<$ *ays-ro- invites comparison with OCS *jasnŭ* 'clear, bright' $<$ *$(j)ěsnŭ$ $<$ *$ays(k)$-no-, *iskra* 'spark', Lith. *áiškus, iškùs* 'clear, obvious', with Hitt. *e/i*$<$*ai as in e.g. *ekt-, ikt-*$<$*$ayk̂-t-$ or *inan-*$<$*$ayno$- (q.v.). Cf. Puhvel, *JAOS* 100:167 (1980), *Gedenkschrift für H. Kronasser* 182 (1982).

Cf. *iskuna(hh)-*.

asas-, ases- 'make sit, seat, set, place, put, settle, establish, install'; (rarely) 'sit', 1 sg. pres. act. *asashi* (e.g. *KUB* VII 1 I 40 *asashi-ma-ssan* 'I seat [the sick child]'; cf. Kronasser, *Die Sprache* 7:144 [1961]; *KBo* XV 25 Vs. 2–3 *nu-ssan* DINGIR-*LUM ser apiy[a] asashi* 'thereon I place the deity'; cf. Carruba, *Beschwörungsritual* 4; III 64 III 5; *KUB* XXIV 14 I 3), *asashe* (*KBo* III 28 II 24 [OHitt.]), 2 sg. pres. act. *asasti* (e.g. V 13 I 34 *man-za* 1 URU-*LUM-ma kuinki asasti* 'but if you establish one single town'; cf. Friedrich, *Staatsverträge* 1:116), 3 sg. pres. act. *asasi* (e.g. V 2 III 37–38 *n-assan* [$<$*n-an-san] ŠA ^{D}U ^{GIŠ}ŠÚ.A *asasi* 'seats him in the storm-god's chair'; cf. Witzel, *Heth. KU* 110; *KUB* XXIX 4 I 4 and 52–53 *hantī asasi* 'places [the deity] separately'; cf. Kronasser, *Umsiedelung* 6, 12; *KBo* XXI 78 II 5

'seats'; cf. Lebrun, *Hethitica II* 145; X 45 II 20 *nu-ssan kūs*
DINGIR.MEŠ *asasi* 'and he places these deities'; cf. Otten, *ZA*
54:122 [161]; ibid. IV 45 *nu* DINGIR.MEŠ *asasi*), *asāsi* (e.g. dupl.
KUB VII 41 IV 13 *nu* DINGIR.MEŠ *asāsi*; *KBo* III 22 Rs. 49–50
[OHitt.] *kuis ammel āppan* LUGAL-*us kisari nu* ^{URU}*Hattusan
āppa asāsi* 'whoever becomes king after me and resettles
Hattusas'; cf. Neu, *Anitta-Text* 12; ibid. 24 and 28; IV 9 V 20
nu DUMU.MEŠ LUGAL *asāsi* 'he seats the princes'; ibid. 27 and 51
t-us asāsi 'he seats them'; X 41, 13; *VBoT* 58 IV 35 DINGIR-*LUM
asāsi*; cf. Laroche, *RHA* 23:87 [1965]), *asase* (*KBo* VIII 121, 6),
3 pl. pres. act. *asesanzi* (e.g. VI 26 IV 2–3 [= *Code* 2:96] *kūnn-a
takiya* URU-*ri kūnn-a takiya* [UR]U-*ri asesanzi* 'they settle one in
one town, the other in another town'; XXI 34 II 49 and III 8
'they install'; cf. Lebrun, *Hethitica II* 121–2; XV 9 IV 11; cf.
Kümmel, *Ersatzrituale* 66; V 1 II 17 *sarā asesanzi* 'they set up';
cf. Sommer – Ehelolf, *Pāpanikri* 6*; *KUB* XX 1 III 5 *nu-kan*
^D*Arunan ser asesanzi* 'they set up [the image of] the sea-god'),
asisanzi (ibid. 2; XXIX 4 III 66 *namma* DINGIR-*LAM INA* ^É*apuzzi
asisanzi* 'then they place the deity in the storeroom'; cf.
Kronasser, *Umsiedelung* 28; XLIV 52, 11; 238/d I 8; cf. H.
Otten – C. Rüster, *ZA* 64:248 [1975]), *asēsanzi* (*IBoT* I 29 Vs.
5), 1 sg. pret. act. *asashun* (*KUB* XXIII 11 II 36 *n-us* ^{URJU}KÙ.
.BABBAR-*si asashun* 'and I settled them in Hattusas'; cf. R.
Ranoszek, *Rocznik Orientalistyczny* 9:57 [1934]; Carruba,
SMEA 8:160 [1977]; *KBo* IV 8 II 6–7 *n-as katta asanna kuit*
SIxSÁ-*at n-an katta asashun* 'because she was slated for a put-
down, I put her down'; cf. H. Hoffner, *JAOS* 103:188 [1983];
KUB XXI 11 Vs. 10 'I settled'; cf. Ünal, *Hatt.* 2:14; XIX 20 Vs.
13 'I settled'), *assashun* (XXIII 55 IV 7), 3 sg. pret. act. *asasta*
(e.g. *KBo* III 38 Vs. 17 'he settled [them]'; cf. Otten, *Altheth.
Erzählung* 8, 39–40; III 63 I 6 EGIR-*pa* ... ^DU-*an asasta*
'reinstalled the storm-god'; *KUB* XVII 6 I 16–17 *nu* ^I*Hūpasiyan
andan* É-[*ri*] *asasta* 'she installed H. in the house'; cf. Laroche,
RHA 23:67 [1965]), *asesta* (*KBo* III 4 II 20 ^I*Uhha-*LÚ-*n-a
ginus-sus asesta n-as irmaliyattat* 'it [viz. the storm-god's thun-
derbolt] also lodged in Uhhazitis' knees, and he fell ill'; cf.
Götze, *AM* 48), 3 pl. pret. act. *a-se-se-ir* (*KUB* I 16 III 44
[OHitt.] *nu-ss*]*an* ^I*Papahdilmahan aseser* 'they installed P. [as

208

king]'; cf. Sommer, *HAB* 14), *a-se-e-se-ir* (*KBo* III 63 I 11), *a-se-si-ir* (*KUB* XXIII 42 Vs. 1), *a-se-sir* (*KBo* III 34 II 25 and 26 [OHitt.]), *a-sa-se-ir* (XIX 52, 4), *a-sa-sir* (*KUB* XXIII 94, 11), *e-se-sir* (XLI 1 IV 9 *nu arahza kuēs esesir* 'those who sat around'; cf. Jakob-Rost, *Ritual der Malli* 50, 74), 2 sg. imp. midd. *a-se-is-hu-ut* (*KBo* XII 1 IV 6 'be seated!'), *a-se-es-hu-ut* (XXII 6 IV 24; cf. Güterbock, *MDOG* 101:21 [1969]), 2 pl. imp. act. *asesten* (e.g. *KUB* I 16 II 38 [OHitt.] *nu-]ssan apūn aseste*[*n* 'install him [as king]'; cf. Sommer, *HAB* 7), *asestin* (*KBo* XXII 6 IV 3); partic. *asesant-*, nom.-acc. sg. neut. *asēsan* (*KUB* XXXII 121 II 26), nom. pl. c. in XVII 18 II 11 *tapusza asesantes* 'seated sideways'; verbal noun *a-se-su-u-wa-ar* (*HT* 42 Rev. 7, glossed by Akk. [*aš*]*abu* 'sit, inhabit'; cf. *MSL* 3:58 [1955]), gen. *asesuwas* (*KBo* XV 37 I 11), *a-se-su-u-w*[*a-as* (XXIII 85 VI 8), *a-se-es-sar* (n.) 'settlement, emplacement; session, assembly, congregation, (divine) service', nom.-acc. *asessar* (e.g. *KUB* X 18 VI 9 *salli asessar āppāi* 'the great service is concluded'; cf. V. Haas – M. Wäfler, *Istanbuler Mitteilungen* 23–24:22 [1973–4]; XXV 1 VI 41–42 *asessar-ma* [LÚ]*UBARUMTIM arantari-pat* 'but the assembly [and] foreigners remain standing'), *asesar* (*VBoT* 3 V 10), gen. sg. *asesnas* (*KBo* XXIII 60, 14), *asessanas* (ibid., inverted), dat.-loc. sg. *asesni* (e.g. *KUB* I 17 III 42 *asesni-ya hūmanti* 'and to the entire congregation'; II 10 V 26–27 *asesni akuwanna pianzi* 'they give the congregation to drink'; *KBo* IV 9 VI 3 and 4; XXI 78 II 16; cf. Lebrun, *Hethitica II* 145), abl. sg. *asesnaza* (*KUB* XX 90 IV 12), also in the compounds *ari(ya)sessar* 'oracle(-emplacement)', URU- -*riasessar* 'town settlement', *tuzziyasessar* 'army camp', q.v. s.v. *ariya-*, *happir(iya)-*, *tuzzi-*; inf. *asesuwanzi* (XII 5 I 8 DINGIR- -*LUM-ma-z asesuwanzi appanzi* 'they start installing the deity'; cf. J. Danmanville, *RHA* 20:51 [1962]; *KBo* XIX 53 III 8; cf. S. Heinhold-Krahmer, *Arzawa* 288 [1977]), *asesūwanzi* (XVIII 123 Rs. 2); but *asanna* (from the intransitive *es-* 'sit') can occasionally function cross-diathetically as a quasi "mediopassive" infinitive of *asas-* (= 'be seated, be set'; e.g. *KUB* VII 13 Rs. 13 GIM-*an-ma* DINGIR-*LUM asanna zinna*[*nzi* 'but when they are finished installing the deity'; *KBo* IV 8 II 4 and 6 [see under *asashun* above]; cf. Ose, *Supinum* 74–5; Kammenhuber, *MIO*

2:249 [1954]; Kronasser, *Etym.* 1:293, 311); iter. *asaski-, as-eski-, asiski-*, 3 sg. pres. act. *asaskizzi* (XVII 1 I 6 LUGAL-*un* SAL.LUGAL-*ann-a asaskiz*[*zi* 'makes king and queen sit'; cf. Otten – Souček, *Altheth. Ritual* 18; XXIII 23 Vs. 38), 3 sg. pres. midd. *aseskattari* (XV 2 IV 28 AN]*A* AŠRI.HI.A *aseskattari* 'on [what] places [he] is used to seating himself'; cf. Kümmel, *Ersatzrituale* 62; Neu, *Interpretation* 20; XVI 99 VI 10), 3 pl. pres. act. *asiskanzi* (X 45 II 27 'they install [ornaments]'; cf. Otten, *ZA* 54:122 [1961]), 3 sg. pret. midd. *aseskattat* (XIV 19 II 25 -*za-kan* ... EGIR-*pa aseskattat* 'was reestablished').

Causative *asesanu-, asisanu-*, little different in meaning from the transitive *asas-*, 1 sg. pres. act. *asisanumi* (e.g. *KUB* XIV 3 III 68–69 *nu-wa-tta kuedani pid*[*i*] [GAM-*a*]*n asisanumi* 'in the place where I make you settle down'; cf. Sommer, *AU* 14), 3 sg. pres. act. *asesanuzi* (XXII 59 Vs. 5 D*IŠTAR* URU*Samuha asesanuzi* 'installs I. of S.'; cf. Lebrun, *Samuha* 195), 3 pl. pres. act. *asesanuwanzi* (e.g. *KBo* II 6 III 44–45 GIDIM-*ya sarā asesa-nuwanzi* 'and they make the dead person lie in state' [?], besides ibid. 61 GIDIM-*ya sarā asesanzi*), *asesanuanzi* (e.g. *KUB* XXXII 128 II 4), *asisanuanzi* (XLIII 49 Rs. 10), 1 sg. pret. act. *asesanunun* (*KBo* III 6 II 11–12 *n-an hūmandan* EGIR-*pa asesan-unun* 'I resettled them all'; cf. Götze, *Hattusilis* 16; ibid. 47 and 50; *KUB* XXI 19 + 1303/u III 19), 3 sg. pret. act. *asesanut* (e.g. *KUB* VIII 53, 9 *kuit* URU-*ri* EGIR-*pa asesanut* 'what he resettled in the town'; cf. Laroche, *RHA* 26:14 [1968]; XXIII 97 III 3; *KBo* VI 28 Vs. 18 and *KUB* XXI 29 I 13 and 14 'he settled [a town]'), *asisanut* (*KBo* XIII 50, 12); inf. *asesanumanzi* (XXII 246 III 24; XXVI 156 Rs. 5 *asesanuman*[*zi*]); iter. *asesanuski-, asisanuski-*, 1 sg. pres. act. in XI 1 Vs. 26 *kuitman-ma* KUR-*e asesanuskimi* 'but while I am settling the country' (similarly ibid. 24; cf. Houwink Ten Cate – Josephson, *RHA* 25:107 [1967]), 3 sg. pres. act. *asesanuskizzi* (*KUB* XXXI 99, 11), *asesanuskizi* (ibid. 13), 3 pl. pres. act. in *KBo* III 3 III 2–3 URU-*ŠUNU* EGIR-*pa asisanuskanzi* 'they will be resettling their town' (cf. Hrozný, *Heth. KB* 146).

Cf. Sommer – Ehelolf, *Pāpanikri* 50-2; Götze, *Madd.* 103; Kronasser, *Etym.* 1:517, 444-5, 570-2; Oettinger, *Stammbildung* 50-1, 430-2.

asas-, like *karap-* and *sak(k)-*, has thoroughgoing paradigmatic *a*:*e* ablaut, while *ak(k)-*, *ar-*, *han-* and *sarap-* have more limited distribution of forms with *e*, and *has(s)-* teeters between a *-hi* conjugation paradigm 3 sg. pres. act. *hāsi*:3 pl. *hēsanzi* and a *-mi* conjugation one *hēszi*:*hassanzi*. For 'sit' Hittite has mainly a mediopassive paradigm *esa*:*esanta*. Parallel thereto seems to have been a reduplicated *eses-* (with its causative *asesanu-*), still seen in *esesir* 'they sat'; forms like the mediopassive *aseshut* (besides *ēshut* 'sit!') show initial *a*-vocalism as part of the gravitation towards a transitive sense close to that of the causative *asesanu-* itself; the last step was the consolidation of a *-hi* conjugation paradigm on the analogy of e.g. *hāsi*:*hēsanzi*, thus *asasi*:*asesanzi*. In this way the strong-grade form *asas-* can be explained; otherwise it is hard to account for, since IE **ēs-* 'sit' had no paradigmatic ablaut, which rules out an *o*-grade of the Indo-European perfect ($a < *\bar{o}$) and a secondarily generalized zero grade ($a < *H_2$) alike (cf. predominant 3 pl. pres. *esanta*).

asiwant-   'poor', ^LÚ*asiwant-* 'poor man' (^LÚMAŠ.EN.KAK = ^LÚMAŠDÁ; opp. *happinant-* 'rich' in *KUB* XVII 24 II 16–17, XXVII 59 I 26–28, XLIII 4 I 3–5; Akk. *muškēnu*; *lapnu*), nom. sg. c. *asiwanza* (VIII 16 + 24 III 12; cf. M. Leibovici, *Syria* 33:143 [1956]; XLIII 4 I 5; cf. Riemschneider, *Geburtsomina* 18), ^LÚ*asi*KAK (XLIII 8 III 3b), acc. sg. c. *asiwantan* (XXIII 72 Rs. 8), *asiwandan* (*KBo* XXII 1, 29 [OHitt.] ^LÚ*asiwandan-a siet dātti* 'from the poor man you take what is his' [partitive apposition]; cf. A. Archi, in *Florilegium Anatolicum* 46 [1979]), nom.-acc. sg. neut. *āssiwan* (*KUB* XLI 32 Rs. 9), gen. sg. *asiwandas* (*KBo* III 7 III 4–5 *nu-za* DUMU.SAL *ŠA* ^LÚ*asiwandas* ANA DAM-*ŠU dās* 'he took the daughter of a poor man for his wife'; cf. Laroche, *RHA* 23:69 [1965]), *ŠA* ^LÚMAŠDÁ (XXII 1, 24), nom. pl. ^LÚ.MEŠ *asiwantes* (*KUB* XXXIII 120 II 64; cf. Güterbock, *Kumarbi* *4; Meriggi, *Athenaeum* N.S. 31:120 [1953]; Laroche, *RHA* 26:43 [1968]; Goetze, *JAOS* 69:182 [1949], *JCS* 23:92 [1970]).

asiwantatar 'poverty' (XXI 18 Rs. 10 *as[iw]antatar nekmun-tata[r* 'poverty and denudation', matching *muškinutta ù erri-*

šutta in the Akkadian version *KBo* I 1 Rs. 63; cf. Laroche, *Ugaritica* 6:371 [1969]).

asiwante(s)- 'become poor', 3 sg. pres. act. *asiwanteszi* (*KUB* XLIII 4 I 4; cf. ibid. 5 *happineszi* 'becomes rich'), *asiwante[szi* (*KBo* XIII 34 IV 5; cf. Riemschneider, *Geburtsomina* 28), *asiwa[nteszi* (*KUB* XXVI 43 Vs. 57; cf. ibid. 56 *ha]ppineszi*; Imparati, *RHA* 32:30 [1974]), *asiwantezzi* (*KBo* IX 67, 2); iter. 3 pl. pres. midd. in IV 14 II 52–53 LÚ.MEŠ*happinantes-pat* ŪL *asiwanteskantari* 'are not the rich being impoverished?' (cf. R. Stefanini, *ANLR* 20:42 [1965]). For stem formation cf. *alpue(s)*- s.v. *alpu-*.

Cf. Laroche, *RHA* 11:41–3 (1950); Meriggi, *Athenaeum* N.S. 31:105–6 (1953); Kronasser, *Etym.* 1:266, 400; Neu, *Interpretation* 21.

Luw. *āssiwantattanassi-* (*KUB* XXXV 45 III 19, XXXV 46, 4; cf. Otten, *LTU* 47–8), gen. adj. of **āssiwantattana-* 'poverty'. Cf. *Dict. louv.* 33.

Adapting an idea of G. Jucquois (*RHA* 22:87–9 [1964]; cf. Laroche, *JCS* 21:174 [1967], and O. Szemerényi, *Kratylos* 11:218 [1966]), perhaps IE **ņ-dyew-* > **a(n)siu-* (+ *-ant-*) 'not divinely endowed (with riches)', comparable with OCS *ne--bogŭ, u-bogŭ* 'poor' (exocentric possessive compound with privative prefix, with adjectivizing Hitt. *-ant-*; cf. s.v. *am[m]iyant-*). Cf. *siu(ni)-, siwanni-* 'god', *siwatt-* 'day' (Luw. *Tiwat-* 'Sun'); the voiced outcome of **-dy-* ([z] or [ž]?) is denoted by *-s-* rather than *-ss-*, despite the fact that an assimilation of **an-siwant-* is involved (cf. Benveniste, *Hitt.* 8–9; L. Deroy, *Linguistic research in Belgium* 25 [1966]). The Luwian form makes difficulty, but *-s(s)-* might be the Luwian medial outcome of **dy* (vs. initial *t/d-*).

The interpretation *asi-want-* 'having (only) so much' (cf. *masiwant-* 'how much'), proposed by Laroche (*RHA* 11:42–3 [1950]) and retained by Kronasser (*Etym.* 1:266), is improbable.

aska- (c.?) 'gate(way), gate aperture', acc. sg. (?) *āskan* (*KUB* XLIV 57, 12 *a-as-kán*; XV 24 I 6 *a-as-ka-na-kán*; *KBo* XXIV 56

II 8 *a-as-kán-na*), dat.-loc. sg. *āski* (e.g. III 27, 11–12 [OHitt.]
kapru-[*sset*] *hattantaru n-an āski-ssi kankan*[*du* 'they shall cut
his throat and hang him at his gate'; repeated ibid. 9–10 and
20–21; cf. Code of Hammurabi 227: *ina* KÁ-*šu ihallalušu* '[they
kill this man and] hang him at his gate'; *IBoT* II 12, 7 KÁ.GAL-*as*
āski 'in the aperture of the [city] gate'; *KUB* VI 2 II 62 [= *Code*
1:50] *kuel-a* ᴳᴵˢ*eyan āski-ssi sakuwān* 'at whose gate the *eya*-tree
is visible'; *KUB* XXX 32 I 14 *wattaru kuit* É *hestās āski* 'the well
which [is] at the gate of the mausoleum'; XVII 28 I 10–11
NA₄-*ann-a āski tummeni nu* É.ŠÀ-*nas* ᴳᴵˢIG *hinkuwani* 'we take a
stone in the gateway and secure [?] the door of the inner house';
cf. G. F. Del Monte, *Oriens Antiquus* 12:121 [1973]; *KBo* X 24
IV 20 and *IBoT* III 1, 92 ᴰ*Halkias āski* 'at the gate of H.'; *KUB*
XVII 1 II 12–13 *n-as-kan parā āski piddāit āski-ma-za piran*
elliya[*nkus*] ... *wemiyat* 'he ran forth to the gate, but before the
gate he found snakes'; cf. Friedrich, *ZA* 49:238 [1950]; *IBoT* III
1, 17 ᴱ]*hestas āski ari* '[the king] arrives at the gate of the
mausoleum'; cf. V. Haas – M. Wäfler, *Ugarit-Forschungen* 8:90
[1976]; *KBo* IV 9 V 34 *parā āski paizzi* 'goes forth to the gate';
KUB XXX 10 Rs. 22–23 *nu-*]*mu* LUGAL-*an āski* DINGIR-*YA* ŪL
assanuwandan anduhsan le issatti 'at the king's gate, my god, do
not make me a persona non grata'; XIII 9 + XL 62 III 9 *n-an*
LUGAL-*was āski* [*u*]*watettin* 'bring him to the king's gate'; cf.
von Schuler, *Festschrift J. Friedrich* 447 [1959]; *KBo* VI 26 III
20–21 [= *Code* 2:87] *aki-as* LUGAL-*an āski uwa*[*tezz*]*i* 'he is to
die; one brings him to the king's gate'; cf. ibid. IV 16–17
[= *Code* 2:99] *aki-as* ANA KÁ É.GAL-*LIM uwatezzi* 'he is to die;
one brings him to the gate of the palace'), *aski* (e.g. IV 11, 9; cf.
Dict. louv. 163), *askī* (*KUB* XXXIII 4 Rs. 16), *āska* (e.g. *KBo*
XIII 164 IV 16 *parā āska pānzi* 'they go forth to the gate';
XXIII 23 Vs. 62 *n*]*-an-kan parā āska pessizzi* 'throws it out the
gate', with par. *KUB* XXVII 29 I 19 *n-as-kan parā āski*
pessiyazzi; cf. Haas-Thiel, *Rituale* 210, 136; XII 63 Vs. 27 *n-an*
LUGAL-*was āska pehutettin* 'take it to the king's gate!'; *KBo* VI
3 III 63–64 [= *Code* 1:71] *n-an* LUGAL-*an āska ūnnai* 'he drives
it [viz. the animal] to the king's gate'), *aska* (*KUB* XXXIII 61 I
3; cf. Laroche, *RHA* 23:153 [1965]), *āsga* (e.g. *IBoT* I 29 Vs. 26
āsga ANA KÁ 'to the gate-entry' [partitive apposition]), abl. sg.

('out of the gate, outdoors') *āskaz* (e.g. *KBo* XIX 128 IV 47–49
LUGAL SAL.LUGAL TUŠ-*as* ᴰLAMA *āskaz IŠTU BIBRI* ... *akuwanzi*
'king [and] queen sitting toast the tutelary deity outdoors from
a rhyton' [vs. ibid. 45 *andurza* 'inside, indoors']; cf. Otten,
Festritual 12; *IBoT* I 36 I 16 *āskaz-ma kuis kuzza* 'but the wall
which [is] outdoors'; cf. L. Jakob-Rost, *MIO* 11:174 [1966]; V.
Haas – M. Wäfler, *Istanbuler Mitteilungen* 23–24:14 [1973–4];
KUB XI 18 IV 35, vs. ibid. 29 *andurza*; XI 35 IV 9, vs. ibid. 5
andurza), *āskaza* (e.g. ibid. 23, vs. ibid. 18 and 30 *andurza*),
askaza (XI 23 I 4); *āsgaz* (e.g. XX 99 II 27), *āsgaza* (e.g. II 8 V 5
and 13, vs. ibid. 9 and 17 *andurza*; *KBo* IV 13 V 26 and 30, vs.
ibid. 28 and 32 *andurza*), *āsqaza* (ibid. 34), dat.-loc. pl. *āskas*
(*KUB* XXXIII 121 III 13 *parā āskas* 'forth to the gate', dupl. of
XVII 1 II 12 *parā āski* [see above]), *āsgas* (XXX 27 Rs. 8 and
15; cf. Otten, *Totenrituale* 98–100).

KÁ 'gate' is hardly the exact cover of *aska-*, because of
KÁ.GAL-*as āski* or *āsga* ANA KÁ (quoted above) and phonetic
complements (e.g. *KBo* XX 101, 13 KÁ.GAL-*nas*) which point
generally to Hittite pluralia tantum (e.g. *KUB* XII 44 III 2
KÁ.HI.A-*es*, KÁ-*as*; cf. Gurney, *Hittite Prayers* 83). However, no
nom. sg. **āskas* is attested, acc. sg. *āskan* is doubtful, the
adverbialized abl. sg. is ambiguous in number, and dat.-loc. pl.
āskas does occur as a duplicate variant of *āski*; therefore partial
habitual plural usage is not to be ruled out. *aska-* denotes not a
material structure but rather the idea of gate as a built-over
entryway, hence lacking determinatives like ᴳᴵŠ or ᴱ (cf. I.
Singer, *ZA* 65:87 [1975]); it is different from 'door' (ᴳᴵŠ*arasa-*
= ᴳᴵŠIG, q.v.), even as Akk. *bābu* 'gate' is from *daltu* 'door' (cf.
e.g. *KUB* XVII 28 I 10–11 [above] where a ᴳᴵŠIG is inside an
aska-, or *HT* 1 I 17–18 [with dupl. *KUB* IX 31 I 24–25] INA KÁ
[EG]IR ᴳᴵŠIG ᴱ*helas* 'in the gateway behind the courtyard door').
Unlike ᴳᴵŠIG, *aska-* is never attested as 'opened' (*has*[*s*]-),
whereas KÁ (and Akk. *bābu* which it covers) can have a 'wood'
determinative and be opened (e.g. *KBo* X 2 II 7 [OHitt.] *nu*
KÁ.GAL.HI.A EGIR-*pa heser* 'they opened the [city] gates', matching X 1 Vs. 29 [Akk.] ᴳᴵŠKÁ.GAL-*šu ana pani-ya iptate* '[the city]
opened its gate before me').

As a technical term LUGAL-*an* (or LUGAL-*was*) *āski* (or *āska*) meant metonymically 'at (or:to) the king's court' (cf. Gk. ἐπὶ ταῖς βασιλέως θύραις, ἐπὶ τὰς θύρας referring to the Persian court), especially as a place of judgment and possible site of the tribunal termed *hurki-* (q.v.). Such nuances also explain onomastic attestations of *aska-*, e.g. the theonym *Āska-sepa-* (cf. Laroche, *Recherches* 67; Kammenhuber, *KZ* 77:185–6 [1961]) and the Old Hittite ruler's name *Āskaliya-* (Laroche, *Noms* 45, 338; perhaps literally 'gatekeeper, warder'; cf. *VBoT* 9 Vs. 4 LÚ.MEŠ KÁ.GAL), or the Pisidian epithetic theonym Ἀσκαηνός, Ἀσκαῖος (cf. Neumann, *Untersuch.* 44–6).

Like e.g. *parn-* 'house' and *hila-, hela-* 'court(yard)', *aska-* seems to be a native Anatolian term. Its spread, like that of *arasa-* 'door', is into the semantic slots vacated by IE **dhwor-* (*IEW* 278–9; improbably still glimpsed by some in *andurza* 'indoors' [q.v.]); *āskaz(a)* thus matches in meaning Hom. θύρηθι 'outdoors', Gk. θύραζε 'out of doors', Lat. *forīs* 'outdoors', *forās* 'out of doors'. Indo-European 'courtyard' was derived from **dhwor-* (Lat. *forum*, OCS *dvorŭ*), whereas in Hittite 'gate building, portal' (Éhilammar) was inversely derived from 'court(yard)' (*hila-*; cf. Laroche, *RHA* 15:19 [1957]).

asku- (c.), tiny animal of ominous import, nom. sg. *askus* (795/c Rs. 1–2 *askus uizzi* [...] *aki* '[if] an a. comes, [so-and-so] will die'; cf. Otten, *Vokabular* 31), nom. pl. *āskuēs* (*KUB* XXXIV 22 I 5–6 *takkuw-asta āskuēs* GIŠPISÀN-*az* [*watkuanzi*] SAG.GEME .ÌR.MEŠ-*kan mausk*[*anzi* 'if a. jump from a [wooden] drain, servants will fall'; ibid. 7–9 *takkuw-asta āskuēs ŠAPAL* GIŠGU.Z[A *parā*] *watkuwanzi nu apāt* GIŠŠÚ.A [...] *arha pippattari* 'if a. jump forth from under a throne, that seat will be overturned'; ibid. 2–3 *n-asta āsk*[*uēs* ...] *parā hanti watkuanz*[*i* 'a. jump forth separately'), *āskus* (*Bo* 2476 I 10–11 -*k*]*an āskus IŠTU* GIŠÙR *nasma-at-kan ŠA* É-*TI* [*kuez*] *imma kuez pedaz watkuanzi* 'a. jump from a rafter or from whatever place in the house').

Friedrich (*AfO* 15:106 [1945–51], *Bi. Or.* 5:50 [1948], *HW¹* 36) thought of either a noxious insect or some kind of mouse, and H. A. Hoffner (*Alimenta Hethaeorum* 91–2 [1974]) added as creepy-jerky possibilities grasshopper, lizard, frog, toad.

Clearly the uniform portentousness of the creature points to exceptionally sinister characteristics. Some "death beetle" is possible, but most probable is "mole", i.e. the blind, chthonian permutation of the mouse whose daylight emergence would be ominous and whose subterranean burrowings were literally conducive to collapse and downfall (cf. e.g. Pliny, *Natural History* 8.104, telling of a town in Thessaly undermined by moles). If so, the Hittite view of the mole chimes with the Roman one and is at variance with the beneficent, folk-medical traits of the mole found in e.g. Greek and Indic lore (cf. e.g. Puhvel, *Pharos* 39:21 [1976], *Analecta Indoeuropaea* 287–8 [1981]). The word *asku-* may then be related to (the further derived or compounded?) Gk. (ἀ)σκάλοψ > (metathetic) ἀσπά-λαξ 'mole', Ἀσκληπιός (mole-god), ἀσκάλαβος 'gecko'; the *u*-stem *asku-* is also reminiscent of Skt. *ākhú-* 'mole', the explanation of which via *ā+khā-/khan-* 'dig' leaves something to be desired. Cf. Puhvel, *Kratylos* 25:137–8 (1980), *Essays in historical linguistics in memory of J.A. Kerns* 241–2 (1981).

asma '(look) there, lo, behold', *KUB* XXXIII 120 I 30–31 INA ŠÀ.KA-*ta-kkan anda aimpan tehhun āsma-tta armahhun* ᴰIM-*nit nakkit* 'inside your bowel I have placed a burden: lo, I have impregnated you with the weighty storm-god' (cf. Güterbock, *Kumarbi* *2); *KBo* XXVI 65 IV 13–14 *āsma-an hullanun* [...] ... *n-an ittin zahheskittin namma* 'lo, I have smitten him ... go and keep fighting him further' (cf. Güterbock, *Kumarbi* *28, *JCS* 6:30 [1952]); XXIV 8 II 14–15 *āsma-war-a*[*s*] *uizzi* ᴰ[UTU-*u*]*s* 'look, there he comes, the sun-god' (cf. Friedrich, *ZA* 49:218 [1950]; Siegelová, *Appu-Hedammu* 8); *KBo* XXII 86+*KUB* XXXVI 2c III 4–6 *āsma-wa*[*-za*] DINGIR.MEŠ GAL-*TIM* LÚ.MEŠ ŠU.GI *tuēl* [...] *huhhis nu-sma*[*s*] *menahhanda īt* 'lo, the great gods, the old men your grandfathers; go to meet them!'; *KUB* XLIV 4+*KBo* XIII 241 Rs. 25 *āsma-war-at uwanzi* 'look, they are coming'; *KUB* XII 63 Vs. 12 *āsma-uwa-smas-san* and perhaps *KBo* XXII 2 Vs. 12 *ā*[*sm*]*a* at the start of speeches (cf. Otten, *Altheth. Erzählung* 6, 32); *KUB* XXIV 7 II 13 (cf. A. Archi, *Oriens Antiquus* 16:307 [1977]); 1744/u Rs. 11 *nu āsma halza*[.

216

Implausibly rendered as 'first(ly)' (Otten, *KUB* XXXIII.IV; Güterbock, *Kumarbi* 7, 35, 79) or 'for the first time' (Siegelová, *Appu-Hedammu* 9), or as containing a cardinal numeral stem 'one' (Goetze, *Arch. Or.* 17.1:296–7 [1949]), with resulting unlikely etymology *ō-smō (IE *sem- 'one') by Neu (*Anitta-Text* 98).

The meaning 'first' might suit *KUB* XXXIII 106 IV 13–14 ('I smote him first, now you take it from there'), but XXXIII 120 I 30–31 tells first of the main event ('I have placed a burden [*aimpan*] inside you, lo [*āsma*] I have impregnated you with the storm-god'); the secondary (ibid. 32 *dan-ma-tta*) and tertiary (ibid. 33 3-*anna-tta*) happenings (attendant sirings of minor deities) are afterthoughts which necessitate a new adjustment of the ultimate total to 'three burdens' (ibid. 34 *ayimpus*); hence 'first' is redundant where *āsma* occurs, and a listing is embarked on only with *dan-ma* 'but secondly'. In XXIV 8 II 14–15, 'for the first time' is wholly out of place, as if the sun-god had never before come near the storm-god; *āsma* is rather the storm-god's startled 'look, there (he comes)', wondering what bad news (disasters, devastations, defeats, ibid. 16–18) the all-seer might be about to announce on his daily broadcast. E. Forrer (*Mélanges F. Cumont* 694 [1936]) and Friedrich (*ZA* 49:244 [1950]) emended *āsma* to *kāsma* '(look) here, lo, see' in XXXIII 120 I 31 and XXIV 8 II 14 respectively, with Friedrich explicitly rejecting *āsma* 'first' for the latter.

asma may be syncopational for **asa-ma*, much as *kasma* (besides *kasa*) represents **kasa-ma* (cf. *kāsa-tta*) or *nasma* 'or' (besides *nassu*) coexists with non-syncopated *nassu-ma* (see s.v. and Friedrich, *HE* 162). Even as *kasa* (q.v.) is a derivative of the pronominal stem *ka-* 'this' (cf. *kā* 'here, hither'), **asa* may be a parallel formation from the pronominal stem *a-* 'this, that'. Perhaps such an *asa* actually occurs in XXVIII 92 I 5 *asā* URU*Nerikil tezzi* '"hey there, you from Nerik" he says' (cf. Haas, *Nerik* 302); but there is e.g. *a-sa-a a-sa-a Ta-a-ru* also addressing the storm-god in Hattic (XXVIII 60 I 5; cf. Güterbock, in P. Garelli [ed.], *Le palais et la royauté* 309 [1972], who took *asā* as a Hattic 'come!', matching Hitt. *ehu*).

KUB XXXIII 120 II 78 *asmanda* (Güterbock, *Kumarbi* *4, 40,

79) is in fragmentary context and obscure (possibly *asma-an--da* 'ecce eum tibi'?). Cf. Puhvel, *KZ* 92:105–6 (1978) = *Analectra Indoeuropaea* 396–7 (1981).

asrahitassi-,   adjective qualifying a festival, acc. sg. c. EZEN *asrahitassin* (*KUB* V 10, 7 and 9).

The text concerns the cult of Ištar of Nineveh; the element *asra-* may be Hurrian or Hurroid, but the abstract suffix *-ahit-* and the adjectival suffix of appurtenance *-assi-* are Luwian (cf. e.g. *anahit-ahit-* s.v. *anahi*[*t*]*-* and *annarum-ahit-assi-* 'of forcefulness' s.v. *annari-*).

-(a)sta,   mostly Old and Middle Hittite sentence particle, going out of use in the late imperial period, similar in fate to *-apa* and *-an* (q.v.), and in use and function also to *-kan* which survives it (cf. Oettinger, *Eide* 67–70). E.g. *KBo* III 16 Vs. 14 *ta-ssi-sta ēshar siyati* 'his blood shot forth'; *KUB* XXX 10 Vs. 15–16 (OHitt.) GUD-*un-asta hāliaz āppa* ŪL *kussanka karsun* 'an ox from a stable I have never cut off'; XXXI 127 I 39–40 *mān-asta karūwarwar* ᴰUTU-*us* [...] *sarā ūpzi* 'as at daybreak the sun rises'; *KBo* X 2 I 26 (OHitt.) *n-asta* ᵁᴿᵁ*Hattusas-pat* URU-*rias* l-*as āsta* 'the town of H. alone remained' (cf. F. Imparati – C. Saporetti, *Studi classici e orientali* 14:46 [1965]). Cf. Güterbock, *RHA* 22:107–8 (1964); Carruba, *Orientalia* N.S. 33:405–18 (1964); Goetze, *JCS* 22:18 (1968); Josephson, *Sentence particles* 10–14, 114–298, 384–95.

The exact sense and function of *-(a)sta* remain elusive; Carruba thought to detect a nuance of movement in relation to (usually away from) a center, and more vaguely of separation and removal (similarly for Old Hittite Otten – Souček, *Altheth. Ritual* 82–4). Josephson's action-marker hairsplittings of an aspectual kind defy comprehension (e.g. *Sentence particles* 322, 384–5). In line with his adverbial interpretations of *-apa*, *-kan*, *-san* (q.v.), Carruba (*Orientalia* N.S. 33:427–9) saw in *-(a)sta* an enclitic truncation of *istarna* 'midst'; while dubious, such an approach is preferable to attempts at a segmentation *-(a)s* (nom. sg. c. of the enclitic anaphoric pronoun *-a-*) + *-ta* (the

218

latter identified with the Luwian particle *-t*[*t*]*a* by Josephson, *Sentence particles* 419, and with the 2 sg. dat. enclitic personal pronoun *-t*[*t*]*a* ["ethical dative" like Gk. τοι] by H. Wagner, *Arch. Or.* 36:365–70 [1968]; in such analytic vein already Sturtevant, *JAOS* 47:177 [1927]).

-(a)sta is reminiscent of the *-*(a)sma* that lurks in *namma* 'then, also' (<*nu*+*[*a*]*sma*) and resembles the Vedic particle *sma* 'truly, indeed' (cf. Puhvel, *KZ* 92:104 [1978]=*Analecta Indoeuropaea* 395 [1981]). V. I. Georgie (*Linguistique balkanique* 25.3: 13–6 [1982]) compared Lat. *ast* 'but'.

astayarat(t)ar   (n.), nom.-acc. *āstayaratar* (*KUB* VII 53 III 16–18 *idalu papratar alwanzatar āstayaratar* NI⟨Š⟩ DINGIR-*LIM idalamus zashimus* DINGIR.MEŠ-*as karpin aggantas hatugatar* 'evil pollution, sorcery, a., curse [lith. oath], bad dreams, wrath of the gods, terror of the dead'; similarly ibid. 6–7, XII 58 II 11–13 and 33–35, ibid. III 3–5 and 9–10, always with the sequence *idalu papratar alwa*[*n*]*zatar āstayaratar*; also ibid. II 24; cf. Goetze, *Tunnawi* 12–20), *astayaratar* (*KBo* XII 85 II 6; cf. Haas–Thiel, *Rituale* 138), *astayarattar* (2619/c, 8 *astayarattar hurtai*[*n* 'a. [and] curse'; cf. Otten, *Materialien* 37), nom.-acc. pl. *āstayaratar* (XXVII 29 I 27 *nu* 7 *āstayaratar*; cf. Haas–Thiel, *Rituale* 136). Cf. Goetze, *Tunnawi* 87.

astayaratar tends to occur preceded by 'sorcery' and followed by 'curse'; the probably related *astaniyawar* (q.v. s.v. *astaniya-*) also occurs in close connection with 'curses' in the sequel. *KUB* II 1 II 30 *astas wastas* is a rhyming jingle (of the 'mumbo jumbo' type; see s.v. *a*[*y*]*i-*) where *wastas* in a (nonce?) form of *wast(a)-* 'miss the mark, act calamitously, sin', and *asta-* may well contain the proto-stem of *astayara-* and *astaniya-*. By further adducing *marsastarri-* (q.v. s.v. *marsa-*) which denotes religious fraud (cf. Laroche, *RHA* 10:24–5 [1949–50]) and is divisible into *marsa-* 'false' and *asta-*, one may seek in *asta-* a sense of 'deceit, guile, trickery, fraudulence' and tentatively connect (with Neumann apud Tischler, *Glossar* 86) the isolated and unexplained Lat. *astus* 'craftiness, cunning, guile', *astūtus* 'crafty, tricky'.

astayarat(t)ar   astaniya-   asusa-

O. Szemerényi (*Studia meditarranea P. Meriggi dicata* 616–9 [1979]) questionably saw in *āstayaratar* a metathesis for **asta-rayatar*, derived ultimately from an abstract **as-tar-* 'doing evil' (< **ns-tar*) cognate with Avest. *angra-* 'evil' and more closely matching Avest. *āstārayeiti* 'sins' (denom. from a noun **āstāra-*, Pahlavi *āstār* 'sin', a vṛddhi derivative of **as-tar-*). More probably Avest. *āstār-* is from *ā-star-* 'scatter, throw down, lay low, dash', religious sin being equated with devastating debilitation (cf. Avest. *astarəman-* 'illness' and Hitt. *wastul* 'sin' beside *wastais* 'despoliation, calamity').

astaniya-,   3 sg. pres. act. *astaniyai* (*KBo* XXIV 126 Rs. 7 *nu-ssi* ^{LÚ}*patilis ser astaniyai* 'on his behalf the p. ?'; ibid. 2 *ast]aniḫai*[; verbal noun *astaniyawar* (n.), nom.-acc. sg. *astaniyauwar* in *KUB* V 6 V 7–8 *nu* ANA ^DUTU-*ŠI astaniyauwar* ŪL SIxSÁ-*at* ANA DUMU.NITA-*ya* ŪL SIxSÁ[-*at*] *ŠA ABI* ^DUTU-*ŠI-ya-za-kan* Ù *ŠA ABI ABI* ^DUTU-*ŠI MAMETI*.HI.A *ŠA* SISKUR.MEŠ DÙ-*zi* 'for his majesty a. was not established, and for the son it was not established; one makes curses (lit. oaths) of his majesty's father and of his majesty's grandfather in the midst of rituals'. Cf. Goetze, *Tunnawi* 87.

For etymology see s.v. *astayarat(t)ar.*

asusa-   (c.) 'ring', nom. sg. *asusas* (e.g. *KBo* XVIII 172 Vs. 2–3 1 *asusas* GUŠKIN URUDU 'one ring of gold [and] copper'; *KUB* XXXVIII 4 Vs. 6 [*a*]*susas* AN.BAR GE₆ 'ring of black iron'; cf. von Brandenstein, *Heth. Götter* 22), acc. sg. *a-su-ú-sa-an* (*KBo* XI 36 IV 7–9 *asūsan* KÁ.GAL-*as* LÚ.MEŠ ^D*Histā danzi* 'the men of [the deity] Histā take the ring of the gate'; XXV 84 I 3 LUGAL-*us asūsan* KÁ.GAⅠ *m*[*a*; cf. Neu, *Altheth.* 164), gen. sg. or pl. *asusas* (e.g. *Bo* 2505 ⅠII 14 *asusas* KÁ.GAL-*as kattan* 'down to the gate of the ring[s]'; *KBo* X 27 III 4 INA KÁ.GAL *asusas* 'at the gate of the ring[s]'; *KUB* XX 2 IV 24 *katta* KÁ.GAL *asusas*; X 1 I 9 and *Bo* 2393 + 5138 I 25 KÁ.GAL *asusas katta*; cf. Alp, *Beamtennamen* 14; Otten, *Festschrift J. Friedrich* 353, 357 [1959], *Vokabular* 28; I. Singer, *ZA* 65:90 [1975]), nom. pl. *asusus*

220

(*KUB* XII 8 I 9 and *KBo* XVIII 172 Vs. 7 2 *asusus* KÙ.BABBAR 'two rings of silver'), *asusas* (ibid. 6 2 *asusas* KÙ.BABBAR; *Bo* 3826 III 9 2 *asusas* GUŠKIN; cf. Otten, *Totenrituale* 112), acc. pl. *asuses* (*KBo* X 45 II 26–27 *isdammane-ssi-ya-an asuses surassuras* I[*NA* G]ÙB *asiskanzi* 'and at her ear they install rings with s.-birds on the left'; cf. Otten, *ZA* 54:122 [1961]), *asusus* (XVII 9 IV 6 2 SAL.MEŠKAR.KID *asusus danzi* 'two wenches take the rings'; cf. Neu, *Altheth.* 35; *KUB* XII 8 I 9).

Denom. verb *asusai-* 'ring (an animal)', 3 pl. pres. act. *asusanzi* (*KBo* XV 1 I 24 *n-an* GEŠTUG.HI.A-*ŠU asusan*[*zi* 'they ring his [viz. the bull's] ears'; cf. Kümmel, *Ersatzrituale* 112); partic. *asusant-*, acc. sg. c. *asusantan* (ibid. 33 GUD.MAH *a*]*susantan* 'the ringed bull'; ibid. 42 GUD.MAH *asusanta*[*n*).

asusala- (c.), e.g. OHitt. nom. sg. LÚ*asusalas* (*KBo* XVII 36 II 7), LÚ*asusālas* (XX 20 Rs. 4), nom. pl. LÚ.MEŠ*asusales* (XX 17 Rs. 14; XVII 36 III 12), LÚ.MEŠ*asusāles* (ibid. 6), acc. pl. LÚ.MEŠ*asusalus* (XX 17 Vs. 8; XX 22, 4), LÚ.MEŠ*asusālus* (XVII 36 II 14), dat.-loc. pl. LÚ.MEŠ*asusālas* (ibid. III 4). Replaced in the later language by *asusatalla-*, e.g. nom. pl. LÚ.MEŠ*asusatallus* (IV 11 Vs. 22; cf. *Dict. louv.* 163; *KUB* XXXV 133 I 14), dat.-loc. pl. LÚ.MEŠ*asusatallas* (ibid. II 35; cf. Otten, *LTU* 109–10). This denominative agent noun parallels e.g. *auriyala-* : *auriyatalla-* (q.v. s.v. *auri-*). Cf. Otten, *Sprachliche Stellung* 15; Kammenhuber, *MSS* 29:101–2 (1971); Neu, *IF* 82:273–4 (1977), *Altheth.* 118–28.

The meaning 'ring' is made likely by the analogous akkadographic use of *HUPPI* as 'ear-ring'; Akk. *huppu* 'metal ring' is also attested with doors (although *HUPPI* is not used with gates in Hittite), and there is LÚ*HUPPI*= *huppū* 'dancer' reminiscent of LÚ*asusala-* (cf. Otten, *ZA* 54:150 [1961]; Kümmel, *Ersatzrituale* 122–4). A parallel is offered by URUDUZI.KIN.BAR = URUDU*sepik(k)usta-* (q.v.), a copper stick or pin 'planted' (*pask-*) into a bridal head-ornament (*KUB* XXVII 49 III 18–19 URUDUZI.KIN.BAR.HI.A *IŠTU* SAG.DU-*ŠU arha danzi* 'they take the pins away from her head'; ibid. 22 *paskanzi* 'they stick [them in]'; cf. Güterbock, *Oriens* 10:357 [1957]); one may compare *Bo* 5585 III 16 1 *asusas* KÙ.BABBAR 'one silver ring', likewise a part of a trousseau (cf. Otten, *Festschrift J. Friedrich* 357 [1959]). But

furthermore ZI.KIN.BAR URUDU (*KBo* VI 10 II 13) =]*sepikus-
ta*[*n* (dupl. *KUB* XXIX 27, 8) occurs in *Code* 2:26 where its
theft results in a material fine (grain); immediately preceding,
the theft *INA* KÁ É.GAL 'at the palace gate' of a ^{GIŠ}*zahrai-*
(wooden object) draws a fine of six shekels of silver, and that of
a ^{GIŠ}ŠUKUR ZABAR 'bronze spear' from the same spot rates the
death penalty. It is therefore possible that *sepikusta-* is also a
movable object related to a gate ('stick, slat, bar' or the like),
distinct in shape from but parallel to the 'ring(s)' which
apparently distinguished certain gates and could be removed
from them (cf. *KBo* XI 36 IV 7–9, quoted above).

Perhaps /*azuza-*/ < IE **ņĝhwyo-dyo-* 'neck-binder' (referring
originally to a torque-type object), with **ĝhwyo* > **ĝhyu* > /*zu*/
(cf. Aeolic ἄμφην 'neck' < **anĝhw-én* besides Gk. αὐχήν with
metathetic anticipation of labial, and Skt. *ā-dyá-*, Avest. *nī-
-dyā-*, Gk. δέω 'bind'). For /*az-*/ and the palatalization of
**d(h)y* and **ĝ(h)y* see s.v. *asiwant-*, *isiya(hh)-*. Cf. Goth.
hals-agga 'neck', Gk. τραχηλο-δεσμότης 'neck-binder'; 'earring'
is Hitt. *istamahura-* (q.v.), whereas new terms for 'necklace'
include *huwahhuwartalla-*, *kuttanalli-*, and *man(n)inni-*.

assussanni-   (c.) 'horse-trainer' (vel sim.), nom. sg. (uninflected) in
  KUB I 13 I 12 *UMMA* ¹*Kikkuli* ^{LÚ}*ās*[*s*]*ussanni* ŠA KUR ^{URU}*Mit-
  tanni* 'thus [says] K., horse-trainer from Mitanni'; XXIX 48 Rs.
  25 ^{LÚ}*āssussann*[*i* (cf. Kammenhuber, *Hippologia* 54, 166).
    Unlike the (sometimes multiple) UMMEDA ANŠU.KUR.RA.HI.A
  'horse-keeper' (*KUB* XXIX 40 II 13; cf. Kammenhuber, *Hippologia* 178; *KBo* V 7 Vs. 23 and 27, Rs. 3, 13, 42; cf. Riemschneider, *MIO* 6:345–52 [1958]), *assussanni-* is the title of a
  foreign professional hippologist; thus both Indo-Aryan and
  Hurrian linguistic ingredients are conceivable besides Anatolian and Semitic ones. Interpretations have ranged from a
  Sanskritic *aśva-sáni-* 'horse-winner' (Pedersen, *Hitt.* 138–9) to
  a modified Indo-Aryan **aśva-śama-* 'horse-tender' (cf. Gk.
  ἱππο-κόμος), to **aśva-śa(m)-ni* with Hurrian suffix (H. W.
  Bailey, *Rocznik orientalistyczny* 21:64–5 [1957]; Mayrhofer,
  AION-L 1:6–11 [1959], *Die Sprache* 5:87 [1959], *Die Indo-Arier*

im alten Vorderasien 16 [1966], *Die Arier im Vorderen Orient —
ein Mythos?* 33 [1974]), to an Anatolian *assu-sanni-* 'horse-
tender', with *assu-* 'horse' presumably akin to Hier. *aśu(wa)-*
'horse' and *-sanni-* connected to the obscure Luwian hapax
verb *sannaindu* (H. Wittmann, *Die Sprache* 10:147–8 [1964]).
For discussion and criticism of these various constructs see also
e.g. Kronasser, *Etym.* 1:143–4; Kammenhuber, *Die Arier*
208–11; L. A. Gindin, *Etimologija 1970* 310–1 (1972), all
agreeing on Indo-Aryan *aśva-* in *assussanni-*, with doubts
centering on the latter part of the word; but Kammenhuber (p.
210), while rejecting Wittmann, also assumed Hier. *asu(wa)-*
(sic) to be a regular outcome of IE *eḱwo-* (as did Goetze, *JCS*
16:35 [1962]), and I. M. Diakonoff (*Orientalia* N.S. 41:112–3
[1972]), in spite of Kammenhuber, wondered aloud about
Luwian origin of *assussanni-*.

E. Ebeling (*Bruchstücke einer mittelassyrischen Vorschriften-
sammlung für die Akklimatisierung und Trainierung von Wagen-
pferden* 11, 48 [1951]) compared with *assussanni-* the Middle
Assyrian genitive *susani* of a related (borrowed) *susānu* 'horse-
trainer', adducing also Neo-Babylonian *šušānu* 'overseer, tender' (*ša sisī* 'of horses', *ša alpē* 'of oxen') and Syriac *sūsānā*
'servus'. Rather than assuming these forms to be aphaeretic
loans, *āssussanni-* can be taken as a prothetic variant of
**sus(s)anni-* on the analogy of *āssurassura-* besides *suras-
(s)ura-* (q.v.). Such a **susanni-* may then be a (perhaps
Hurroid) derivative from West Semitic **sūsu* 'horse' (cf. Ugaritic *ssw*, Canaanite *sūsu*, vs. Akk. *sīsu*). Neither the Indo-Aryan
element in Mitanni nor the Hurrians monopolized horse-
training in the area; hippiatric text from Ugarit and other data
show West Semitic participation. The term may have spread
eastward to Mesopotamia on the hippological circuit, only to
be reimported westward into Syriac with changed phonetics
and semantics during the Neo-Assyrian expansion.

assuzeri- (n.), a drinking vessel, nom.-acc. sg. *āssuzeri* (*KUB*
XXVII 13 I 13) alternating with ZA.HUM (ibid. 4, 12, 24, 27),
paralleled by *BIBRU* 'rhyton' (*KBo* XIV 142 I 5, 15, etc.); but

ZA.HUM and *BIBRU* also cover Hitt. *hal(u)wani-* (q.v.); instr. sg. *āssuzerit* (XX 67 I 18). Cf. Güterbock, *RHA* 22:110–1 (1964).

Made up of *assu-* 'good' (q.v. s.v. *ass-*) and *zeri-* = (DUG)GAL 'cup' (q.v.), thus a nonce descriptive compound matching the *āssu zēri* GUŠKIN 'good cup of gold' from which the king drinks to divinity in *KUB* I 17 I 5. It is difficult to determine what makes for "goodness" here (cf. H. A. Hoffner, *Orientalia* N.S. 35:378–80 [1966], who opted for "intrinsic", material value); in *RS* 25:421 Recto 20 the female object of exaltation is termed amid other extravagant similes (Akk.) *bibru hussū* 'a red (i.e. gold) rhyton' = (Hitt.) *haliwanis-ma-as* SI[G₅-*anza*] (= *assuw-anza*) 'she (is) a good rhyton'; but even a gold vessel can fail to measure up: *KUB* XV 5 III 8–9 ANA ᴰU-*wa karū* ZA.HUM GUŠKIN DÙ-*nun* UMMA ˢᴬᴸ*Danuhepa ŪL-war-as* SIG₅-*anza* '"I have already made for the storm-god a gold rhyton"; Danuhepa says: "It's no good"'.

In spite of the Hurrian ritual ambiance there is no need to assume that *assuzeri-* is either Hurrian (Goetze, *JCS* 9:23 [1955]) or a folk-etymological product (Kammenhuber, *SMEA* 14:159 [1971]).

atta-   (c.) 'father' (*ABU*; rarely ANA A.A.MU instead of ANA *ABI-YA* 'to my father'; cf. Güterbock, *JCS* 10:118 [1956]), nom. sg. *attas* (e.g. *KUB* XXIII 21 Vs. 26 *attas-mis* ᴵ*Tuthaliyas* 'my father T.'; cf. Carruba, *SMEA* 18:168 [1977]; XII 65 III 6 DINGIR.MEŠ-*as attas* 'father of the gods'; cf. Laroche, *RHA* 26:50 [1968]; Siegelová, *Appu-Hedammu* 50; *Code* 1:28–9 *attas annas* 'father [and] mother'), *addas* (e.g. VI 26 III 31 [= *Code* 2:90] *takku addas-siss-a* TI-*anza* 'if his father is alive'; ibid. 47–48 [= *Code* 2:94] *addas* Ù DUMU-*šu* 'father and son'), voc. sg. *attas* (e.g. XV 34 IV 32 *n-us attas nepisanz[a]* EGIR-*an tarna* 'let them back from heaven, father'; cf. Haas– Wilhelm, *Riten* 204), *addas* (e.g.,*KBo* XXVI, 79 13; cf. Siegelová, *Appu-Hedammu* 68), acc. sg. *attan* (e.g. *KUB* I 16 III 24 *apās-mu-za attan* [*ŪL halzais* 'she has not called me father'; cf. Sommer, *HAB* 12; XXXIV 19 IV 8 *attassin kuna[nzi* '[they] will kill his father'; cf. Riemschnei-der, *Geburtsomina* 56), *addan* (e.g. XI 5 Vs. 10 *addassan* *kuen*[*ta* 'he killed his father'), gen. sg. *attas* (e.g. I 16 III 16 and 28 *attas uttar* 'the father's word'; cf. Sommer, *HAB* 12; *KBo* VI 3 II 3 [= *Code* 1:27] *attas-sas-a* É-*ri* 'in her father's house'; *KUB* XXIX 7 Vs. 45 *attass-a dān attass-a uddani* 'in a matter involving [their] father and second [=father's?] father'; cf. Lebrun, *Samuha* 120), *addas* (e.g. XXIV 13 III 20 É *addas annas* '[of] father's [and] mother's house'), dat.-loc. sg. *atti* (e.g. XXVI 87, 7 *n-at* DINGIR.MEŠ *atti-mi sanhir* 'the gods avenged it upon my father'; *KBo* III 38 Rs. 20 *ūk-wa atti-mi ŪL āssus* 'I am not dear to my father'; cf. Otten, *Altheth. Erzählung* 10; VI 5 III 3 [= *Code* 1:28] *takku atti-ma anni ŪL āss*[*u* 'but if to father [and] mother [it is] not pleasing'; *VBoT* 58 I 17 *atti-ssi anni-ssi* 'to his father [and] his mother'; cf. Laroche, *RHA* 23:83 [1965]), nom. pl. *at-ti-e-es* (*KUB* XVII 29 II 7 *attēs annis* 'father[s] [and] mother[s]'), *attis* (XI 1 IV 16), *addus* (e.g. *KBo* V 9 I 33 *tuel addus* 'your [fore]fathers'; cf. Friedrich, *Staatsverträge* 1:12), *attas* (e.g. *HT* 1 I 55 É-*as attas* DINGIR.MEŠ *azzikandu* 'let the deified fathers of the house eat'), acc. pl. *attus* (*KBo* III 22 Vs. 9 *annus attus* 'mothers [and] fathers'), gen. pl. *addas* (*KUB* XXXIII 106 III 51 *karuuiliyas addas* 'of the ancient fathers'; cf. Güterbock, *JCS* 6:28 [1952]; XVI 39 II 24 É.NA₄ ᴰUTU-*ŠI addas* 'the mausoleum of his majesty's fathers'; ibid. 29 and 30 *ŠA* É.NA₄ DINGIR-*LIM addas* 'of the mausoleum of the deified fathers'; cf. Otten, *Totenrituale* 108), dat.-loc. pl. *addas* (e.g. *KBo* V 1 II 7 and III 3, V 2 III 3 *addas* DINGIR.MEŠ-*as* 'to the deified fathers'; cf. Sommer – Ehelolf, *Pāpanikri* 6*, 8*, 47; Witzel, *Heth. KU* 108).

For collocations with *anna-* 'mother' in the sense of 'parents' see also s.v. *anna-, anni-.* The form *adda* (*KUB* XVI 39 II 20 LÚ.MEŠ É.NA₄ DINGIR-*LIM adda* 'the men of the mausoleum of the deified fathers'; ibid. 22 *a*]*dda peskanzi* '[to?] the fathers [they] give') was amended to *adda⟨s⟩* by G. F. Del Monte (*AION* 35:331 [1975]), which is improbable in view of the proximity to *addas* ibid. 24, 29, 30; *adda* may rather be a residual dual referring elliptically to the king's parents rather than (fore)fathers, as can the intrusive plural *addas* in the sequel. Cf. Puhvel, *KZ* 83:60–3 (1969) = *Analecta Indoeuropaea* 206–9 (1981), *AJPh* 98:399 (1977) = *Analecta Indoeuropaea* 382.

attalla- 'fatherly, dating back to one's father, paternal' (*KUB* XXXIII 106 III 50–51; see context under *annal*[*l*]*i-* s.v. *anna-*, *an*[*n*]*i-*).

Pal. *papa-* (see attestations s.v. *anna-*, *anni-*); voc. sg. in *KBo* XII 135 VII 9 ᴰ*Taru-papa-mi* (cf. Carruba, *SMEA* 5:40 [1968], *Das Palaische* 66)?

Lyd. *taada-* (?); see attestations s.v. *anna-*, *anni-*, and Gusmani, *Lyd. Wb.* 207. Lyd. *ata-* has also been identified as 'father' (e.g. Heubeck, *Die Sprache* 6:208–9 [1960]; Carruba, *Parola del Passato* 24:277 [1969]) but is more probably a man's name (cf. Gusmani, *Lyd. Wb.* 69).

Luw. *tati(ya)-*, nom. sg. *tātis* (*KUB* XXXV 68, 16 *tātis* ᴰ*Tiwaz* 'father sun-god'; cf. Otten, *LTU* 69; XXXV 95, 6; XXXV 103 II 9 and 16; *KBo* IX 141 Vs. 19 *t*]*ātis-pa-ti tātawanni*[*s* 'father [and] stepfather' [cf. s.v. *annawanna-*]), *tātiyis, tatiyis* (see attestations s.v. *anna-*, *anni-*), acc. sg. *tātin* (IX 143 Vs. 10), *tātīyan, tātiyan* (see s.v. *anna-*, *anni-*), dat.-loc. sg. *dātī* (*KUB* XXXV 107 III 10 ᴰUTU-*tī dātī* 'to sun-god the father'; cf. Otten, *LTU* 99), instr.-abl. sg. *tatiyati* (see s.v. *anna-*, *anni-*), nom. (voc.) pl. in IX 31 II 30 (dupl. *HT* 1 II 6) *tatinzi* DINGIR.MEŠ-*inzi* 'father-gods' (cf. Otten, *LTU* 16).

Hier. *tati(a)-* 'father' (see also s.v. *anna-*, *anni-*); *tatali-* 'paternal' (*tatalis huhatalis*, like Hitt. *attalla hūhadalla*, Lat. *patrīta et avīta*). Cf. Meriggi, *HHG* 127–8; Laroche, *HH* 175.

Lyc. *tedi, ddedi-* 'father'; *tedesi* 'paternal' (see also s.v. *anna-*, *anni-*). Cf. Laroche, *BSL* 53.1:191–3 (1957–8).

Hitt. *atta-* has been connected since Hrozný (*SH* 31) and Marstrander (*Caractère* 128) with the group exemplified by Lat. *atta*, Goth. *atta* 'father', Gk. ἄττα 'daddy', OCS *otĭcĭ* 'father' (*IEW* 71). This widespread word from infantile language (like its congeners *papa-* and *tata/i-* in other Anatolian dialects) has supplanted the IE term *pH̥tér* (cf. e.g. Kronasser, *Etym.* 1:118). Cf. also Hurrian *attai* (Laroche, *RHA* 34:63–4 [1976]).

O. Szemerényi (*Journal of Hellenic Studies* 94:154–5 [1974]) implausibly derived Gk. ʾAθηνᾶ from Anatolian as meaning originally 'belonging to the father'.

adda- or **addi-**   (c.), nom. pl. *addes* (*KBo* XV 10 I 16 *ki-nu-na-wa*
ANA ^SAL^*Zi ad-di-es-se-es pal-ha-a-e-es* 'now for Zi[plantawiyas]
her a. [are] wide'; ibid. 17–18 [*tu*]*ekkēs-ses* SIG₅-*antes mis-
riwantes ais apel* [SIG₅-]*in* EME *apel* SIG₅-*anza* 'her limbs [are] well
[and] bright, her mouth [is] well, her tongue [is] well'; cf. Szabó,
Entsühnungsritual 14).

Immediately preceding *tuekka-* (sg. 'body', here pl. 'limbs')
at the outset of a progressively restrictive listing of anatomical
features, the plural of an *adda-* (qualified by 'wide') perhaps
signifies 'compass, frame, build'; in that case one may postulate
**a(n)ta-*, cognate with Skt. (pl.) *átāḥ*, Lat. (pl.) *antae* 'door-
frame', Arm. *dr-and* 'door-post' (*IEW* 42).

ates(sa)-   (n. or c.) 'adze, axe, hatchet', nom.-acc. sg. neut. ^(URUDU)^
ates (ZABAR) '(bronze) adze' (*Code* 2:57, 60, 61; cf. Haase,
Fragmente 72–4; *KUB* XXXVIII 1 IV 3; cf. von Brandenstein,
Heth. Götter 14), acc. sg. c. *atessan* (*HT* 1 I 20 = *KUB* IX 31 I
27; ibid. 21–22 = 28–29 *ser-as-san atessan* ZABAR GÍR ZABAR
^GIŠ^BAN *huittiyan* 1 GI.KAK.Ú.TAG.GA *dāi* 'thereon he places a
bronze adze, a bronze dagger, a strung bow, [and] one arrow';
cf. B. Schwartz, *JAOS* 58:336 [1938]; G. F. Del Monte, *Oriens
Antiquus* 12:111 [1973]), instr. sg. *atessit* (*Bo* 2692, 12–13 LÚ
^D^U-*as tēkan atessit walahzi* 'the man of the storm-god strikes
the earth with an adze'), *atesset* (905/c, 8 EGIR-*an arha* ^URUDU^*a-
tesset* ['with an adze [he cuts?] off'; *KUB* XLI 8 I 3 ^URUDU^*a*]*tesset* [*arha karaszi* 'he cuts off with an adze'; cf. Otten, *ZA* 54:118
[1961]), abl. sg. *atessaz* (*Bo* 2692, 16), nom.-acc. pl. neut. *atissa*
(*HT* 1 I 28 = *KUB* IX 31 I 35), acc. pl. c. *atessus* (97/b r. 7
attessus-ma ZABAR).

The corresponding Akkadogram is PĀŠU or ḪAṢINNU, e.g.
nu-za PĀŠU KÙ.BABBAR … *dāi n-asta* ^GIŠ^GEŠTIN-*an karaszi* 'he
takes a silver adze and cuts off the vine' (Otten, *Totenrituale*
34), ^URUDU^PĀŠU GAL 'big adze' (*KUB* VII 29 Vs. 8, etc.), 2470/c
Vs. 9 1 PAŠU TUR ŠA ZABAR 'one small bronze adze'; *KUB* XII
49 I 15 LÚ ^D^U-*ma* ^URUDU^*HAZZI*[*NNU harzi* 'the man of the storm-
god has an adze' (cf. ibid. 18 ^URUDU^*HAZZINNU-ma kuin harzi*).

Cf. Otten, *ZA* 51:124–6 (1955); Kronasser, *Etym.* 1:328, 341.

The compelling adduction of OE *adesa, adosa* (*n*-stem) 'adze'
(Čop, *Univerza v Ljubljani, Zbornik Filozofske Fakultete*
2:406–7 [1955]; *Ling.* 1:31 [1955]; *Die Sprache* 3:140 [1956];
Ling. 5:43 [1964]) does not clinch an Indo-European etymology. At best Hitt. *-t-* and OE *-d-* would point to a common
**-dh-*. Terms for 'axe' are notoriously international "culture
words", e.g. Akk. *haṣinnu* and Gk. ἀξίνη, Lat. *ascia*, Goth.
aqizi; Lat. *secūris*, OCS *sekyra*: Akk. *šukurru*; Gk. πέλεκυς,
Skt. *paraśú-*, Toch. A *porat*, B *peret* (< Iranian): Akk. *pilaqqu*.
Cf. V. Georgiev, *Lingua Posnaniensis* 4:109–10 (1953). The odd
shape of Hitt. *ates* (normal spelling *e*, rather than accommoda-
tion to normal *s*-stem neuters like *nepis*) may point to its non-
inherited lexical character.

Improbable comparison with Ved. *svádhiti-* 'axe' (H. Eichner
apud Mayrhofer, *KEWA* 3:804) involved IE **E₁sw-é-dhɛ₁-ti-*
'having good fit' vs. IE **o-dhɛ₁-és-* (presumably 'fitted on' vel
sim.) in Hitt. *ates-* (and a Germanic **ađus-on-*). Sturtevant
(*IHL* 47) compared *ates-* as 'metal plate' with OE *e(o)dor*
'fence, roof'.

addu 'further' (vel sim.), *KUB* XXII 70 Vs. 65 *addu mān kī-pat
zankilatarr-a namma-ma* DINGIR-LIM *ŪL kuitki sanhiskisi* 'further, if this (is) the atonement, and you, god, do not seek
anything else' (cf. Ünal, *Orakeltext* 74, 121); XIV 4 III 16 *addu
man-ma-za* DAM-*YA ANA* SAL.LUGAL *isiyahhiskattallas* 'further,
if my wife (were) a spy for the queen'; XXIII 103 Vs. 26 *ŪL-pat
kuitki addu* 'not anything further'; XL 77, 16 *Ū]L-pat kuitki
addu*; XLIII 22 IV 16 *pittuliyas ēszi addu tepu[-* 'there is anxiety;
furthermore, little ...'.

Unlike *namma* of similar meaning (q.v.), which is etymologically *nu+*(a)sma* and may function resumptively for a
conjunction in clause-initial position (see *KUB* XXII 70 Vs. 65
above), *addu* is purely adverbial and can stand by itself
extrasyntactically at the outset of a statement. Etymological
speculation is somewhat idle: perhaps **at-u*; cf. Skt. *áti* 'beyond' and *u* 'also', Lat. *at* 'but' and Gk. πάν-υ 'altogether'?

adupli- (n.), some type of ceremonial raiment or festive garb (perhaps TÚGNÍG.LÁM), nom.-acc. sg. or pl. *adupli* (*KBo* VI 26 II 49 [= *Code* 2:82] TÚG*adupli*; *KUB* XVII 21 II 15 TÚG.HI.A*adupli*; cf. von Schuler, *Die Kaškäer* 156; II 6 IV 3–5 LUGAL-*us-kan* INA É DUTU *anda* TÚG*adupli wassiezzi* 'the king in the temple of the sun-god puts on the a.'), TÚG*atupli* (*IBoT* I 31, 6; cf. Goetze, *JCS* 10:32 [1956]), *aduplita* (*Bo* 2839 III 26; cf. Haas, *Nerik* 260). Cf. Alp, *JCS* 1:175 (1947); Goetze, *Sommer Corolla* 51–2; J. Holt, *Bi. Or.* 15:149 (1958).

The gloss-wedged nom.-acc. sg. neut. *atupalassan* (*KUB* XXII 70 Vs. 18 and 21) denotes a container for precious objects, possibly a chest for expensive garments, with Luwoid suffix *-assi-* (cf. Laroche, *RA* 52:187 [1958], *Dict. louv.* 35; Ünal, *Orakeltext* 58–60, 111).

There is not enough reason for an akkadographic reading TÚG*ADUPLI*, an alleged variant form of Akk. TÚG*uduplu* (doubtful rendering 'waistband' in Friedrich, *Heth. Ges.* 81, 112); if Akk. *uduplu* has a true sense akin to Hitt. *adupli-*, both terms may rather hail from some common culture-word orbit (cf. Goetze, *Sommer Corolla* 52). The form *aduplita* points to Hurrian mediation (cf. e.g. *ispanduzita* beside *ispantuzzi* s.v. *ispant-*).

auli- (c.) 'milt, spleen; (pl. also) inner organs; sacrificial (feast or contingent); some kind of (negative) emotion (cf. Engl. spleen)', nom. sg. *a-ú-li-is* (*KUB* XLVIII 123 + XV 28 + *IBoT* III 125, III 22–23 SAL.LUGAL-*za-kan kui*[*n a*]*ulien* INA URU*Zithar*[*a*] *austa nu* [...] *aulis hantaittari* 'the sacrificial which the queen saw at Z., [that] sacrificial is fixed'; cf. Lebrun, *Samuha* 191; H. Otten – C. Rüster, *ZA* 68:156 [1978]; *KBo* XXIII 56 IV 7 and 23/n, 7 *aulis tarupta* 'the sacrificial is wrapped up [= concluded]'; *VAT* 7497 II 4 *au*]*lis tarupta*; cf. Otten, *Istanbuler Mitteilungen* 19–20:90 [1969–70]; *KUB* XI 18 III 7 *mān aulis taru*[*pta*; *KBo* XII 89 II 9 *aulis arha paiddu* 'may spleen [?] go away'), acc. sg. *a-ú-li-in* (XV 11 III 10 *nu-ssi-kan au*[*lin danzi*; XV 9 IV 15–16 *nu* 1 MÁŠ.GAL *ūnniyanzi* [*nu-ssi-kan aul*]*in danzi n-an* ANA DINGIR.MEŠ *dapiandas* [*wahnuwanzi n-*]*an arha pissi-*

yanzi 'they drive up a he-goat, take the spleen from him, wave it to all the gods, and throw it away'; cf. Kümmel, *Ersatzrituale* 66; *KUB* XI 26 II 10 and *KBo* XI 49 VI 15–16 *aulin karappanzi* 'they remove the spleen', followed ibid. 11 and 18 respectively by reference to blood [*ishanī*]; *KUB* II 8 III 8; *VAT* 7497 II 1; *KUB* XXII 61 Vs. 11 *aulinn-a*), *a-ú-li-en* (quoted above), dat.-loc. sg. *auliya* (*KBo* XV 33 III 11–12 *nu-ssan* LÚEN.É-*TIM ŠA* UDU ŠIR *ŠA* GUD.MAH-*ya auliya* GÍR.ZABAR-*it QATAM dāi* 'the master of the house with a bronze dagger lays hand on the spleen of a ram and of a bull'; *KUB* II 8 III 13), *aulī* (ibid. 15; *VAT* 7497 II 6), *auli* (*KBo* XXI 21 III 11 SIG₅-*in auli-ssi anda* 'well in his[?] spleen'; cf. Otten, *Materialien* 37; Burde, *Medizinische Texte* 37), acc. pl. *a-ú-li-es* (*KUB* VIII 36 III 12–15 [*m*]*ān antuhsi aulies* EGIR-*an pessiyazzi* [*mā*]*n antuhsi* ŠÀ-*i aulies kattan sarā* [...-]*zzi mān-za-kan antuhsan au*[*li*]*es* [... *ku*]*it pedan epzi* 'if [a medicine man] neglects a person's inner organs, if he upsets a person's organs internally, [or] if it [i.e. illness] seizes a person's inner organs some place'; cf. Laroche, *CTH* 189; Burde, *Medizinische Texte* 40), *a-ú-li-is* (ibid. II 6 [*mā*]*n-za-kan antuhsan a*[*u*]*lis epzi*; *KBo* XXI 74 III 6 [*mā*]*n* UKÙ-*an aulis kuitki* AŠRA *epzi* 'if it seizes a person's inner organs some place'; ibid. 9–10 *nu* UKÙ-*an kuit* [AŠRA] *aulis harzi n-an apāt* AŠRA ['the place where it holds a person's inner organs, that place ...'; cf. Burde, *Medizinische Texte* 26–8; XXI 21 III 3–4 *an*]*durza nassu aulis nasm*[*a* ...] [...] *istarakkiyazi nasma a*[*n*- 'internally either spleen or ... ails, or ...'; cf. Otten, *Materialien* 37; Burde, *Medizinische Texte* 36; *KUB* XVII 24 III 3–5 *nu* LÚMUHALDIM UDU *huekzi* [...] UZU*aulis siyezzi* LÚ[...] ANA EN SISKUR *akuwanna pāi* 'the cook slaughters a sheep, squeezes the spleen, the ... gives the sacrificer to drink'), *a-ú-lis* (XXVII 66 III 2 UZU*aulis siyaiz*[*i*; ibid. 8]*siyaizi*; ibid. 13 UZU*aulis s*[*iy*]*aizi*), *a-ú-li-us* (XXIV 1 II 3–6 EZEN.HI.A-*i-tta* EZEN ITU EZEN.HI.A MU-*as mēanas gimmantas hamishandas zenandas aulius mukisnass-a* EZEN.MEŠ *INA* KUR URU*Hatti-pat ēs*⟨*san*⟩*zi* 'for you they perform feasts in the land of Hatti — feast of the month, feasts of Newyear, sacrificials of winter, spring, fall, and feasts of ritual'; cf. Gurney, *Hittite Prayers* 18; *IBoT* III 17, 10; *KBo* XIX 152 I 6 *aulius huittiyanta* 'they drag sacrificial contingents'; cf. Car-

ruba, *Beiträge* 33), *a-ú-li-ú-sa* (*KUB* XVII 21 II 18 *aulius-a-kan*
GUD.MAH.HI.A ŠE ᴳᵁᴰÁB ŠE UDU.HI.A ŠE MÁŠ.GAL.HI.A ŠE 'sacrificial contingents of fatted bulls, fatted cows, fatted sheep, fatted
he-goats'; cf. von Schuler, *Die Kaškäer* 156; in similar context
ibid. III 26 *a-ú-li-us-sa ŠA* ... 'contingents of ...'), *a-ú-li-ú-us*
(*KBo* XXV 178 I 2 UDU.HI.A-*as auliūs* 'sacrificial contingents of
sheep'; *KUB* XXIV 3 II 11 ᵁᴰᵁ*auliūs-kan* GUD.HI.A UDU.HI.A
'sacrificial contingents of cattle [and] sheep'; ibid. 15
ᵁᴰᵁ*auliuss-a* seems to be syntactically nom. pl.; cf. Gurney,
Hittite Prayers 26). Cf. Gurney, *Hittite Prayers* 59–60; Goetze,
JAOS 61:302 (1941); Ertem, *Fauna* 257–9; Kümmel, *Ersatzrituale* 104–5; Burde, *Medizinische Texte* 41.

Luw. *auli-* (?), instr. sg. *aulati* (*KUB* XXXV 79 III 4; cf.
Otten, *LTU* 76).

auli- denotes a fleshy (ᵁᶻᵁ) internal (ŠÀ-*i, andurza*) body part
of animals and humans of both sexes, one that is squeezable
(*siya-*) and yields a liquid. Heart (*kard-*) and liver (*lesi-*) are
eliminated, which leaves as the prime candidate 'spleen', the
body's spongy reservoir for storing excess blood and regulating
its volume in circulation. The spleen has an illustrious history
in early folk belief, religion, and medicine, along with heart and
liver. Gk. σπλήν 'spleen' has beside it a secondary plural
σπλάγχνα as a pars pro toto term for 'internal organs', especially heart, liver, lungs, and kidneys which were eaten initially
and preferentially by sacrificers (e.g. *Iliad* 1:464 and *Odyssey*
3:9 σπλάγχνα πάσαντο); hence σπλάγχνα also means metonymically 'sacrificial feast' (e.g. Aristophanes, *Equites* 410: Διὸς
σπλάγχνοισι 'at the feast of Zeus'). Metaphorically, however,
the word came to denote emotions, especially anxiety, and
σπλήν likewise evolved in the direction of 'bad temper, depression, melancholy' (e.g. Aristophanes, *Thesmophoriazusae* 3: τὸν
σπλῆνα ... ἐκβαλεῖν 'throw out the spleen'). These meanings
match the full semantic range attributed to *auli-* above. There
are even scribal attempts to differentiate the literal, fleshy sense
(ᵁᶻᵁ*auli-*) from the metonymous one (ᵁᴰᵁ*auli-*, since sheep were
the most typical ingredients of animal sacrifice). Cf. Puhvel,
Kratylos 25:137 (1980).

The Indo-European terms for 'spleen' vary, but apart from

auli- auri- (a-ú-ri-), auwari- (a-ú-wa-ri-)

Germanic (OHG *milzi*) they can be reconstructed systemati-
cally: Gk. σπλήν reflects a reshaped **splēĝhen-*, while Gk.
σπλάγχνα and Avest. *sparazan-* jointly mirror **spl̥ĝhn-*; Skt.
plīhán- goes back to **(s)plīĝhen-*, whereas Lat. *liēn* requires
rather a proto-form **s(p)līĝhen-*, and Arm. *pʻaycaln* may be
the outcome of **phaiĝlen* < **(s)plaiĝhen-*; Old Irish *selg* comes
from something like **spelĝhā*, OCS *slězena* points to **s(p)el-
ĝhenā*, and Lith. *blužnìs* and OPruss. *blusne* indicate a reconstruction **bl̥ĝhn-*. Part of the initial cluster variation is due
simply to differing treatments of **spl-*; but the Baltic forms
intimate that the *s-* may be in origin movable and have
unvoiced an erstwhile cluster **bl-*.

   In Hittite the spelling *a-ú-li-* (cf. Kronasser, *Etym.* 1:78) is
etymologically significant as pointing back to a possible **aweli-*
(contrast e.g. *awiti-*, where the "unreduced" variety still predominates and *a-ú-ti-* is the exception). If **aweli-* as a body part
is an old *i*-stem (cf. e.g. *arki-* 'testicle', *lesi-* 'liver', *sakui-* 'eye'),
it might represent **A₂wel-i-*, and IE **bl̥ĝh-* can then possibly be
accounted for as **A₂wl̥-ĝh-*, under the assumption that **A₂w*
could yield IE **b* (for which a primary origin is unlikely due to
rarity). In that case *auli-* may be at the very root of the Indo-
European term for 'spleen', innocent of the manifold developments (such as secondary ablaut and *s* movable) which were
visited upon **bl̥ĝh-* in other branches.

auri- (a-ú-ri-), auwari- (a-ú-wa-ri-)   (c.) 'lookout, watch(tower),
   guard(post), stronghold, fort'; *hantezzis auris* 'first-line guard,
   border post' (alternates in *KUB* XIII 2 and duplicates/parallels
   with MADKALTI, MADGAL[A]TI, MADQALATI, from Akk. *dagālu*
   'look'), nom. sg. *auris* (*KBo* XVI 42 Vs. 20 *auris sannapilis*
   'empty fort'; *KUB* XXVI 79 I 15 [emended from XIV 17 III
   21–22] *nu* ᵁᴿᵁ*Uras kuis* URU-*as ŠA* KUR ᵁᴿᵁ]*Āzzi* IGI-*zis auris
   ēsta* 'U., which town was the border post of A.'; cf. Götze, *AM*
   98), gen. sg. *aurias* (e.g. XIII 2 I 20 *au[r]ias* EN-*as* 'watch
   commander', matching ibid. 18 ᴸᵁ*BEL MADKALTI*; cf. von
   Schuler, *Dienstanweisungen* 42), *auriyas* (e.g. ibid. II 38, III 9
   and 22 *auriyas* EN-*as*; XXXI 87 II 5 *auriyas-a-kan* EN-*as*; cf. von

Schuler, *Dienstanweisungen* 46–8, 44; XXXIII 77a Rs. 15 *han]tezzin-pat auriyas* URU-*an* 'border town'; *KBo* IV 13 I 12, *KUB* XXVII 1 I 61 [cf. Lebrun, *Samuha* 77] *auriyas* ᴰUTU-*i* 'to the solar deity of watch', as a term for ῞Ηλιος πανόπτης), *auwarias* (e.g. XXXI 84 III 60 *auwarias* EN-*as*; cf. von Schuler, *Dienstanweisungen* 49), *auwariyas* (e.g. XIII 2 II 42 and IV 22 *auwariyas* EN-*as*; ibid. II 5 *auwariyass-a-kan* EN-*as*; cf. von Schuler, *Dienstanweisungen* 46, 51, 44; XXVI 17 II 5 *n-an auwariyas ishī parā tittanuddu* 'let him deliver him to the watch commander'; cf. Alp, *Belleten* 11:394 [1947]), dat.-loc. sg. *auriya* (IX 17, 19 *n-as iyannai n-as-kan auriya ser tiyezz[i* 'he goes and he steps up to a watchtower'; *KBo* XVI 24 + 25 III 10 *auriya anda* 'within the fort'; cf. A. M. Rizzi Mellini, *Studia mediterranea P. Meriggi dicata* 532 [1979]; *KUB* XIII 2 I 4 *a]uriya* ERÍN.MEŠ 'troops on guard'; cf. von Schuler, *Dienstanweisungen* 41; XIII 28, 9 *hantezzi auriya* URU-*an*), *auri* (*KBo* XIII 58 III 14 *mahhan* ᴸᵁ.ᴹᴱˢEN.NU.UN *auri halzāi* 'when he summons the watchmen to the guard'; cf. F. Daddi Pecchioli, *Oriens Antiquus* 14:104 [1975]), abl. sg. or pl. *auriyaza* (*KUB* XXXIII 106 II 11 *n-as-kan auriyaza katta iyannes* 'he went down from the watchtower'; cf. Güterbock, *JCS* 6:20 [1952]), nom. pl. *auriēs* (e.g. XXXI 85 I 9 *auriēs* ERÍN.MEŠ 'watch troops'; XXXI 86 I 10 *auriēs kuis* ERÍN[; cf. von Schuler, *Dienstanweisungen* 41), *auwariēs* (XIII 1 I 19 and 33; cf. von Schuler, *Dienstanweisungen* 60), acc. pl. *aurius* (XXVI 12 II 12–13 *namma-smas sumēs kuyēs* BELU.HI.A *hantezi aurius mani-yahheskatteni* 'furthermore you, commanders, who govern the border posts'; cf. von Schuler, *Dienstanweisungen* 24; XIII 20 I 28 *BELU.*MEŠ *kuyēs* ERÍN.MEŠ ANŠU.KUR.RA.HI.A *aurius māniyah-hiskatteni* 'you commanders who are in charge of troops, horses, forts'; cf. Alp, *Belleten* 11:392 [1947]), dat.-loc. pl. *auriyas* (XXXIII 106 II 4 *n-as-kan pargauwas auriyas sarā pai[t* 'he went up to lofty lookouts'; XXVI 9 I 13–14 *a]uriyas* ᴸᵁ.ᴹᴱˢEN.NU.UN [... *i]sgariski* 'post the watchmen on guard'; cf. F. Daddi Pecchioli, *Oriens Antiquus* 14:100 [1975]; XIII 2 I 13 *auriyas-a-ssi kuis* ERÍN.MEŠ 'the troops which he has on guard'; XXXI 85 I 6 *auriyass-a*; cf. von Schuler, *Dienstanweisungen* 41).

pitt(a)uri- (q.v. s.v.) may contain *auri-* (*pitta* + *auri-* 'land-

auri- (a-ú-ri-), auwari- (a-ú-wa-ri-)   au(s)-, u(wa)-

grant inspector'), although other explanation is possible (cf.
Puhvel, in *Hethitisch und Indogermanisch* 214 [1979] = *Ana-
lecta Indoeuropaea* 361 [1981]). There is also a mountain name
HUR.SAG*A-ú-ri-ya-as* (*KUB* VIII 75 II 8, III 61, IV 5 and 55; cf.
V. Souček, *Arch. Or.* 27:12, 18, 20, 24 [1959]), HUR.SAG*A-ú-ri-ya*
(*KBo* XV 46, 6).

auriyala- (c.) 'warder, guard', nom. sg. *auriyalas* (*KBo* IX
114 III 8–9 -]*si auriyalas ūk ispanti-ma-ssi* [*usk*]*imi haliēskimi* 'I
am his warder, and at night I guard him and watch over him';
KUB XIV 1 Vs. 23 LÚ*auriyalas* LÚ*uskisg*[*atallass-a* 'warder and
guard'; cf. Götze, *Madd.* 6; *KBo* XVII 88 III 21 ᴰUTU-*summi*
SAL*tawanannai auriyala*[*s*] 'warder to his majesty [and] to the
queen'), nom. pl. *auriyalus* (V 8 III 14 LÚ*auriyalus kuit arantat*
'because guards had been stationed'; also ibid. III 16; cf. Götze,
AM 156; ibid. I 42 LÚ.MEŠ*auriyalus*).

auriyatalla- (c.), nom. pl. *auriyatallus* (*KBo* XVI 8, III 20,
dupl. of V 8 III 16 LÚ*auriyalus*, quoted above; cf. Otten, *MIO*
3:169 [1955]). Cf. *asusa(tal)la-* s.v. *asusa-*. The terms *haliya-
talla-*, *uskiskat(t)alla-* (s.v. *au*[*s*]-), and *auriya(tal)la-* are
practically synonymous, here rendered by 'watchman', 'guard',
and 'warder' respectively. Cf. Götze, *Madd.* 109–10; Alp,
Belleten 11:409–11 (1947); Otten, *Sprachliche Stellung* 15.

The constant *a-ú-wa-ri-* (never **a-wa-ri-*) indicates that the
spelling *a-ú-ri-* is not "reductional"⁵ but rather the basic variant
(cf. Kronasser, *Etym.* 1:78). Connected since Pedersen (*Hitt.*
173) with *au(s)-* 'see' (q.v.), with suffix as in *es(sa)ri-* 'shape',
edri- 'food', or *kis(sa)ri-* 'skein of carded wool' (cf. e.g.
Neumann, *KZ* 75:88 [1957]; Kronasser, *Etym.* 1:225;
Kammenhuber, *Orientalia* N.S. 41:435 [1972]). Tischler
(*Glossar* 95) suggested a secondary *i*-stem based on an old
action noun in -*war* (**au-war*?), besides the attested *uwatar* and
uskiyauwar.

au(s)-, u(wa)- 'see, look, watch, behold, observe, inspect, read'
(*AMARU*), *katta(n) aus-* 'look into, investigate', *menahhanda
aus-* 'see opposite; look unto, expect; inspect', *parā aus-*
(+ dat.) 'overlook, disregard, pay no attention (to), be neglect-

234

ful (of), condone', 1 sg. pres. act. *u-uh-hi* (e.g. *KBo* III 34 I 23 *ūhhi nāui* 'I do not yet see'; VIII 41, 2; XVI 46 Vs. 9 *n-at ŪL ūhhi* 'I do not see it'; *KUB* XXVI 71 I 23; XXIV 7 IV 22 *pāimi-wa ūhhi* 'I go [and] see'; cf. Friedrich, *ZA* 49:230 [1950]), 2 sg. pres. act. *a-ut-ti* (e.g. *KBo* XXV 122 III 3, 7, 9, 11 *anda le autti* 'do not look in!'; *KUB* XXIX 11 II 14 *takku* ᴰ*SIN autti* 'if you see the moon'; *KBo* V 3 II 18–19 *nu-zan mān* ANA ᴰUTU-*ŠI ser* SAG.DU-*KA-pat ser autti* 'if you look upon my majesty [as] upon your own head'; cf. Friedrich, *Staatsverträge* 2:114; V 13 III 8 *nu-ssan parā le autti* 'do not disregard [it]!'; cf. Friedrich, *Staatsverträge* 1:126), *a-ú-si* (?; *KUB* XI 32 V 1), 3 sg. pres. act. *a-us-zi* (e.g. VII 5 IV 2–3 *nu-za-kan mān* DINGIR-*LUM zashiya ... auszi* 'when he sees the god in his dream'; XXVI 1 IV 1 [*n*]*asma apel kuitki* GÙB-*tar auszi* 'or [if] he sees any sinisterness on that one's part'; cf. von Schuler, *Dienstanweisungen* 15; *KBo* XII 112 Vs. 11 UKÙ-*as* DUMU-*an anda auszi* 'she inspects the human child'; VI 34 I 20–21 *nu* ᴸᵁ*ar*[*as*] ᴸᵁ*aran le auszi* 'one shall not see the other'; cf. Oettinger, *Eide* 6; *KUB* XXI 42 I 12–13 *tamē*[*d*]*a-ma* [*l*]*e kuiski auszi* 'but let no one look elsewhere'; cf. von Schuler, *Dienstanweisungen* 23), 1 pl. pres. act. *ú-me-ni* (*KBo* XVII 1 IV 8 'we inspect'; cf. Otten – Souček, *Altheth. Ritual* 36), *ú-me-e-ni* (III 60 I 11; *KUB* XXVI 62 IV 5; XL 28, 4), *a-ú-me-ni* (XXI 38 Vs. 35 *nu kussan aumeni* 'we shall look at the price'; cf. W. Helck, *JCS* 17:90 [1963]; R. Stefanini, *Atti La Colombaria* 29:10 [1964]), *a-ú-ma-ni* (*VBoT* 1, 12 'let us see'; cf. L. Rost, *MIO* 4:334 [1956]), *a-ú-um-me-ni* (e.g. *KUB* XXI 27 II 4 *katta aummeni* 'we shall observe'), *a-ú-um-mi-e-ni* (XXXIII 88 Rs. 16; cf. Siegelová, *Appu-Hedammu* 54), 1 pl. pres. midd. *u-wa-u-wa-as-ta-ri* (*KBo* XVI 59 Vs. 7 'we are seen'; cf. Werner, *Gerichtsprotokolle* 54), 2 pl. pres. act. *a-ut-te-ni* (e.g. *KUB* XXI 42 I 30 *dammēda-ma le autteni* 'but do not look elsewhere'; cf. von Schuler, *Dienstanweisungen* 24; ibid. IV 3–4 *m*[*ā*]*n-kan ...* GÙB-*an uttar kuitki au*[*tt*]*eni* 'if you see some sinister thing'; XXXI 115, 21), *a-us-te-ni* (XXIII 77, 15 *sumes-as austeni* 'you see them'), *us-te-ni* (*KBo* III 28 II 8–9 LUGAL-*was-a sākuwa-met le usteni* 'do not watch the eyes of me, the king!'; cf. Laroche, *Festschrift H. Otten* 186 [1973]), *us-t*[*e-e*]*-ni* (*KUB* XXXVI 100 Vs. 7 [OHitt.]), 3 pl. pres. act. *ú-wa-an-zi* (e.g. *KBo* III 60 II 3–5

[OHitt.] *mān uwarka[ntan] antuhsan uwanzi n-an-kan kunanzi s-an-ap atānzi* 'if they see a fat person, they kill him and they eat him'; cf. Güterbock, *ZA* 44:104 [1938]; *KUB* XIII 2 I 5–6 *nu mahha[n]* LÚ.MEŠNI.Z[U] ŠA LÚKÚR *ūrkin uwanzi* 'when the spies see the enemy's trail'; cf. von Schuler, *Dienstanweisungen* 41; XIII 4 III 28–29 *n-an arahzenas* BÀD-*as* ŪL *uwanzi nu apūs* LÚ.MEŠ É DINGIR-*LIM andurza uwanzi* 'they do not see him at the outer walls, and they see those temple-men inside'; cf. Sturtevant, *JAOS* 54:382 [1934]; XII 65 III 8–9 *nu-wa-tta ... le uwanzi* '[they] shall not see you'; cf. Laroche, *RHA* 26:50 [1968]; Siegelová, *Appu-Hedammu* 50; *KBo* II 3 II 2 *le uwanzi*), 1 sg. pret. act. *u-uh-hu-un* (e.g. III 28 II 20 *kinun-a* LUGAL-*us idalu mekki ūhhun* 'but now I, the king, have seen great evil'; *KUB* XXXVI 98b Rs. 10; XIV 16 II 15 *m]ahhan-ma-an-za-kan* EGIR-*pa ūhhun* 'but when I caught sight of him'; cf. Götze, *AM* 42; I 1 I 20 *nu-za-kan ... lūlu* (with gloss-wedges) *ūhhun* 'I saw prosperity'; cf. Götze, *Hattusilis* 8; *KUB* XIII 35 + XXIII 80 + *KBo* XVI 62, IV 45 *parā-ya-kan* ŪL *ūhhun* 'nor was I neglectful'; cf. Werner, *Gerichtsprotokolle* 14; *KBo* IV 14 III 35; cf. R. Stefanini, *ANLR* 20:45 [1965]), 1 sg. pret. midd. *a-us-ha-ha-at* (*KUB* XXXI 121a II 20 ŪL *aushahat* 'I was not seen'; cf. Güterbock, *RHA* 18:60 [1960]), *u-wa-ah-ha-at* (XXIV 7 IV 34 *nu-kan* DUTU-*i-ma uwahhat* 'I have made myself visible to the sun-god'; cf. Friedrich, *ZA* 49:230 [1950]; XVII 31 I 18 *nu-kan* ANA DUTU AN EN-*YA uwahha[t* 'I have become visible to you, sun-god of heaven, my lord'; cf. Kümmel, *Ersatzrituale* 62), 2 sg. pret. act. *a-us-ta* (*KBo* V 3 III 56 *zik-wa-kan apūn anda kuwat aus[ta* 'why did you look at that [woman]?'; cf. Friedrich, *Staatsverträge* 2:128), 3 sg. pret. act. *a-us-ta* (e.g. III 34 I 22 *nu ēshar* LUGAL-*us austa* 'the king saw blood'; *KUB* XLIV 4 + *KBo* XIII 241 Rs. 9 *nu-ssan* GAM AN-*za* DU-*as austa eni-ma-wa kuit* 'down from heaven the storm-god looked, [asking] "But what [is] that?"'; *KBo* IV 4 III 35 *nu-mu munnanda harta nu-mu* ŪL *kuiski austa* 'he kept me hidden, and no one saw me'; cf. Götze, *AM* 126; *KUB* I 1 I 61 GIM-*an-ma-kan* ŠEŠ-*YA* ᴵNIR.GÁL-*is uttar katta austa* 'but when my brother Muwatallis had looked into the matter'; cf. Götze, *Hattusilis* 12; XVII 1 II 4, 7, 9, 11 -*za-kan zashain austa* 'he saw a dream'; cf. Friedrich, *ZA*

49:236–8 [1950]), *a-ú-us-ta* (*KBo* III 60 I 8), IMUR (*KUB* XVI 50, 5), 3 sg. pret. midd. *a-us-ta-t(a-an)* (XVII 10 II 35 *austat-an* ᴰ*Kammarusepas* 'K. caught sight of him'; cf. Laroche, *RHA* 23:94 [1965]), 1 pl. pret. act. *a-ú-me-en* (*KBo* XXII 2 Vs. 10 and 11 [OHitt.]; *KUB* XVIII 5 I 33 and 46; IX 34 III 39, 40 [bis], 41), *a-um-me-en* (*Bo* 1850 Rs. 22), *a-ú-um-me-en* (*Bo* 7509, 3; *Bo* 2498 II 6 and III 8; *KUB* XVIII 6 I 17; XVIII 27, 1; cf. Otten, *Altheth. Erzählung* 30), NIMUR (V 22, 8 and 11 *n-as* EGIR-*pa* NIMUR 'we observed them again'; XVIII 55 + V17, II 12, 14, 23, 25, 29, 31, 33), 3 pl. pret. act. *a-ú-ir* (*KBo* X 2 I 31–32 [OHitt.] *nu-mu mahhan … menahhanda auir* 'when [they] saw me opposite'; cf. F. Imparati – C. Saporetti, *Studi classici e orientali* 14:46 [1965]; III 34 II 38 *ape-ma-an natta auir* 'but those did not see him'; III 6 I 27; cf. Götze, *Hattusilis* 8; *KUB* I 5 I 7; cf. Götze, ibid.), *a-ú-e-ir* (*KBo* IV 4 IV 28–29 *mahhan-ma* LÚ.MEŠ ᵁᴿᵁ*Azzi auer* URU.DIDLI.HI.A BÀD-*kan kuit zahhiyaz katta daskiuwan tehhun* 'but when the men of A. saw that I set about to take in battle fortress towns'; cf. Götze, *AM* 138; *KUB* V 8 III 16–17 *man-mu* ᴸᵁ*auriyalus kuit* ŠA ¹*Pitaggatalli auer* 'because P.'s guards would have seen me'; cf. Götze, *AM* 156; I 1 I 32; cf. Götze, *Hattusilis* 8), 3 pl. pret. midd. *ú-wa-an-ta-at* (*HT* 21 + *KUB* VIII 80, 10 L]Ú.MEŠ ᵁᴿᵁ*Āssur-ma namma* ŪL *uwanta[t* 'but the Assyrians were no more to be seen'), 1 sg. imp. act. *ú-wa-al-lu* (*KUB* XIV 8 Rs. 42–43 [*n-at-za-ka*]*n nassu teshit uwallu nasma-at ariyasesnaz* [*handay*]*attaru* 'may I either see it in a dream, or may it be confirmed by an oracle'; cf. Götze, *KlF* 218), *ú-wi-el-lu-ut* (III 110, 15 [vocabulary, Akk. lost]; cf. Friedrich, *ZA* 39:47 [1930]), 1 sg. imp. midd. *u-wa-ah-ha-ru* (XIV 14 Rs. 15 *nu-s[mas]-kan uwahharu* 'may I be visible to you'; cf. Götze, *KlF* 174), *ú-wa-ah-ha-ru* (XIV 14 Rs. 30; cf. Götze, *KlF* 176), 2 sg. imp. act. *a-ú* (e.g. *KBo* III 1 II 47–48 [OHitt.] *kī-wa ēsnas uttar tuppiaz au* 'read from the tablet this story of bloodshed'; III 23 Vs. 5 [OHitt.] LÚ GIG-*an au* 'look after a sick man'; *KUB* XXIII 101 II 3 *n-at au* 'read it!'; *KBo* X 45 III 27 *nu-za-kan menahhanta parkunumma[s] aniyan au* 'inspect the lustration gear!'; cf. Otten, *ZA* 54:130 [1961]; *KUB* XXI 1 IV 45 *nu-kan* ANA ᴰ[UTU-*ŠI*] ŠU-*i anda āss[u lūl]u au* 'in my majesty's hand see good prosperity'; cf. Friedrich, *Staats-*

verträge 2:82; *KBo* V 8 I 12–13 [*nu-z*]*a kāsma au* ᴰU NIR.GÁL-
-*mu* BELI-YA *mahhan piran huuiyanza* 'lo, behold how the strong
storm-god my lord is my ally'; cf. Götze, *AM* 149; *KUB* III 110,
13 and 14 [vocabulary, Akk. lost]), 3 sg. imp. act. *a-us-du* (e.g.
XIV 10 IV 16–17 *n-at-za-kan apiya kuiski teshit ausdu* 'may
someone there see it in a dream'; cf. Götze, *KlF* 218; XIX 28 IV
10–11 *nu-za apās* UKÙ-*as* […] *lulu* [with gloss-wedges] *ausdu*
'may that person see prosperity'; VII 8 III 11 *nu-wa-du-za*
nakkiyatar ausdu 'may he see your [divine] importance'; XXXV
145 Rs. 7–18 passim; *KBo* IX 83 Rs. 4; IV 14 II 18; cf. R.
Stefanini, *ANLR* 20:40 [1965]), 3 sg. imp. midd. *u-wa-ru* (*KUB*
XXXVI 44 IV 4 [OHitt.] *nu warsulas-tes ammel katta uwaru* 'let
your [divine] emanation be seen by me'; cf. Laroche, *RHA*
23:81 [1965]), 2 pl. imp. act. *a-us-te-en* (XXIV 4 + XXX 12 Rs.
14 KUR ᵁᴿᵁ*Hatti-ma-sta an*[*da assaui*]*t* IGI.HI.A-*it austen* 'look
at Hatti with favorable eyes'; cf. Gurney, *Hittite Prayers* 32),
a-us-tin (XXXI 101 Rs. 34 [SIG₅-*a*]*ndus* MUŠEN.HI.A *austin*
'observe auspicious birds!'; cf. A. Archi, *SMEA* 16:137 [1975];
XV 34 II 11–12 *n-asta* LUGAL SAL[.LUGAL] *anda assuli austin*
'look upon king [and] queen in friendship'; cf. Haas – Wilhelm,
Riten 190; *VBoT* 120 II 23; cf. Haas – Thiel, *Rituale* 140), 3 pl.
imp. act. *ú-wa-an-du* (e.g. XXIV 4 + XXX 12 Vs. 11–12 *nasma-
-at*] *zasheaz* DUMU.LÚ.ULÙ.LU *uwandu* 'or let men see it in a
dream'; cf. Gurney, *Hittite Prayers* 26; *KBo* XI 1 Vs. 28 *nu-kan*
DINGIR.MEŠ KUR-*TAM anda taksulit* IGI.HI.A-*it uwandu* 'let the
gods look upon the land with friendly eyes'; cf. Houwink Ten
Cate – Josephson, *RHA* 25:107 [1967]; *KUB* XVII 28 II 44–45
nu-ssi-ssan … idālu IGI.HI.A-*wa uwandu* 'let them give him the
evil eye!'; *KBo* XIII 58 II 24–25 *n-asta* ᴺᴬ⁴KIŠIB *ANA* KÁ.GAL
taksan katta uwandu 'let them jointly check the seal on the town
gate'; cf. F. Daddi Pecchioli, *Oriens Antiquus* 14:102 [1975]), 3
pl. imp. midd. *u-wa-an-da-ru* (*KUB* XXI 19 IV 27–28 ᵁᴿᵁ*Ner-
iqqas* ᵁᴿᵁ*Zippaland*[*ass-a*] ŠA DUMU-*KA* URU.DIDLI.HI.A *uwandaru* 'let N. and Z. be seen as cities of your son'); partic.
ú-wa-an-t- 'seeing; seen', nom. sg. c. *uwanza* (*KUB* XIII 3 III 28
ᴵ*Zuliyas-wa parā uwanza ēsta* 'Z. was neglectful'; cf. Friedrich,
Meissner AOS 47), acc. sg. c. *uwandan* (IX 34 III 34 and 38
uwandan IGI.HI.A-*in* 'the seeing eye'; XIII 35 I 23 *nu-wa-mu* LÚ

parā uwandann-a uier 'they prosecuted [lit. chased; cf. Gk. διώκω] me for negligence [lit. as a neglectful man]'; cf. Güterbock, *Sommer Corolla* 67; Werner, *Gerichtsprotokolle* 4, 16; both with wrong translation), nom.-acc. pl. neut. *uwanda* (*KBo* XII 62 Rs. 14–15 *apinissuwanda* [*Ū*]*L sakkanta ŪL uwanda uddār* 'such things [i.e. human sacrifices] [are] unknown and unheard of [lit. unseen]'), *uwanta* (XIII 13 Rs. 15, unless 3 pl. pres. midd.; cf. Riemschneider, *Geburtsomina* 62); verbal noun *ú-wa-tar* (n.) 'seeing, sight, inspection', nom.-acc. sg. *uwatar* (e.g. *KUB* V 1 II 51 *ŠA* LUGAL IGI-*was uwatar* 'the king's eyesight'; ibid. I 76 IGI.HI.A-*wa uwatar*, with -*wa* haplographic for -*wa-as*; ibid. III 86, IV 37 and 76 IGI-*wa uwatar*; cf. Ünal, *Hatt.* 2:58, 44, 78, 83, 88; XVI 29 Vs. 2 and 22 IGI-*wa uwatarr-a*; ibid. Vs. 3 and XXII 64 II 7 IGI.HI.A-*wa uwatar*), *uwātar* (XXVII 67 II 65 IGI.HI.A-*as-mu uwātar pāi* 'give me eyesight'; *KBo* IV 4 III 28 *nu-za* ANA KARAŠ *uwātar apiya iyanun* 'I made there inspection of the troops'; cf. Götze, *AM* 126; similarly ibid. III 59; II 5 II 2 and III 48; *KUB* XIX 37 III 10), gen. sg. *uwannas* (XXIX 4 I 42 1 QADU ZABAR *uwannas* 'one bronze vessel for inspection'; cf. Kronasser, *Umsiedelung* 10); inf. *ú-wa-an-na* (e.g. XXIV 5 Vs. 14 *tuhhūwain* IGI.HI.A-*it uwanna sanaht*[*a* 'you sought to see the smoke with your eyes'; cf. Kümmel, *Ersatzrituale* 8; XXIV 5 + IX 13 Vs. 35 – Rs. 1 *nu-wa-za-kan tuk* ᴰUTU] ᵁᴿᵁ*Arinna uwanna hassiklu* 'let me satiate myself looking at you, sun-goddess of Arinna'; cf. Kümmel, *Ersatzrituale* 10–12; *KBo* III 21 II 9–10 *āssu* ᵁᶻᵁYÀ *huwappann-a* ᵁᶻᵁYÀ *uwanna* 'to inspect the good fat and the bad fat'; *KUB* XLIII 38 Rs. 24 'to be seen'; cf. Oettinger, *Eide* 20; *KBo* XVII 65 Rs. 17–18 *kuit* ... *uttar teshit uwan*[*na* 'what matter to be seen in a dream').

ú-wa-tal-la- (c.) 'seer, looker', acc. pl. in *KBo* IV 14 III 16–18 *āssaw*[*ēs*] ᴸᵁ·ᴹᴱˢ*haliyatallus asand*[*u*] HUL-*uwas-ma-kan* ᴸᵁ·ᴹᴱˢ *haliyatallus* ᴸᵁ·ᴹᴱˢ*parā uwatalluss-a le* 'good people shall be watchmen, but bad ones and inattentive ones shall not (be) watchmen' (cf. R. Stefanini, *ANLR* 20:45 [1965]). Cf. *uskiskatalla-* (below).

Cf. Kronasser, *Etym.* 1:543; Neu, *Interpretation* 21–2.

Iter. *uski(ya)-* (*KBo* I 39 II 14–15 IGI-*anda uskiz*[*zi*] '[who]

looks unto' = [Akk.] *nattalu ahū*; cf. Güterbock, *MSL* 12:216–7
[1969]), 2 sg. pres. act. *uskisi* (e.g. *KUB* XVII 28 II 56–57
antuhsi ŠÀ-*ta uskisi tuell-a-kan* ŠÀ-*ta* ŪL *kuiski auszi* 'you look
into man's heart, but into your heart no one looks'; cf. Tenner,
KlF 388; *KBo* XX 31 Vs. 18 *nu kuit sākuit uskisi* = dupl. *KUB*
XII 21, 10 *nu kuit* IGI-*it uskisi* 'because you see it with your
eye[s]'; *KBo* V 4 Rs. 45 *nu-ssan idālāui imma parā uskisi* 'you
condone evil'; cf. Friedrich, *Staatsverträge* 1:66; V 13 III 27–28
nu-ssan apedas kuwatqa antuhsas parā uskisi 'you in any way
condone those people'; cf. Friedrich, *Staatsverträge* 1:128; II 2
II 12; cf. Hrozný, *Heth. KB* 40; *KUB* V 1 II 24,, 79, 102, ibid.
III 14, 34, 47, 71; cf. Ünal, *Hatt.* 2:54–76), *usgisi* (XXI 5 III 66
nu-kan HUL-*ue parā usgisi* 'you condone evil'; cf. Friedrich,
Staatsverträge 2:74), *us-kat-ti* (XVIII 56 II 25), 3 sg. pres. act.
uskizzi (e.g. VI 41 I 40 ᴵPÍŠ.TUR-*as-ma-za-kan wasdul kuit
uskizzi* 'since Mashuiluwas sees his fault'; cf. Friedrich, *Staatsverträge* 1:110; *KBo* IV 8 II 11 *nu* ᴰUTU *ŠAMĒ* IGI.HI.A-*it uskizzi*
'the sun-god of heaven she sees with her eyes'; ibid. 19 *nu
nepisas* ᴰUTU-*un* IGI.HI.A-*it uskizzi*; cf. Witzel, *Heth. KU* 174–5;
H. Hoffner, *JAOS* 103:188 [1983]; *KUB* V 1 III 48 *unius-za-kan
kuēs* Ù.MEŠ HUL-*lus uskizzi* '[as for] those bad dreams which he
keeps seeing'; cf. Ünal, *Hatt.* 2:72; XXXIII 113+I 31–32
kuis-war-an [*namm*]*a uskizzi uniyas halluwain* 'who will any
longer face up to it, this one's violence?'; cf. Güterbock, *JCS*
6:12 [1952]; VII 53 I 7 *nu-za-kan apās antuhsas papratar uskizzi*
'that person is faced with uncleanness'; cf. Goetze, *Tunnawi* 4),
ú-us-ki-iz-zi (*KBo* VIII 42 Vs. 2 [OHitt.] ᴳᴵˢ*luttanza ūskizzi*
'looks from the window'; *KUB* XXXIII 59 III 11; cf. Laroche,
RHA 23:150 [1965]), 2 pl. pres. act. *us-ka-te-ni* (*KBo* III 33 I
11), *us-ka-at-te-ni* (*KUB* XXIV 4+XXX 12 Vs. 10 *nu* DINGIR.
.MEŠ *kuit wasdul uskatteni* 'what[ever] sin you gods see'; cf.
Gurney, *Hittite Prayers* 26), *us-kat-te-ni* (e.g. V 1 III 49 MÈ-*as
arpan uskatteni* 'you see setback in battle'; also ibid. 58 and 67;
cf. Ünal, *Hatt.* 2:72, XVI 27, 12; cf. G. F. Del Monte, *AION*
35:334 [1975]), *us-kat-te-e-ni* (XIV 4 II 3–4 *nu sumēs* DINGIR.
.MEŠ ŪL *uskattēni* 'you gods do not see'; cf. F. Cornelius, *RIDA*
22:30 [1975]; *KBo* IV 14 III 11–12 HUL-*ui-ma-kan parā* [*le*]
uskattēni 'do not condone evil!'; cf. R. Stefanini, *ANLR* 20:44

[1965]), 3 pl. pres. act. *us-kán-zi* (e.g. *KUB* XIII 3 II 8–10
suméss-a kissan téteni [LUGAL-*us-wa-*]*nnas ŪL auszi* [LU]GAL-*as-*
-ma-smas DINGIR.MEŠ-[*u*]*s karū uskanzi* 'you speak thus: "the
king does not see us", but the king's gods have long been
watching you'; cf. Friedrich, *Meissner AOS* 46; *KBo* XV 2 Rs.
25–26 [emended from dupl. *KUB* XVII 31 I 25] *nu-ssi* GE₆-*az*
hāli s]er uskanzi 'by night [they] keep watch over him'; cf.
Kümmel, *Ersatzrituale* 62; *IBoT* I 36 I 9 *nu* UD-*az hāli uskanzi*
'by day they keep watch'; cf. L. Jakob-Rost, *MIO* 11:174
[1966]; *KUB* XXXI 105, 7 *ŪL* SIG₅-*in uskanzi* 'do not watch
well'), *u-us-kán-zi* (XXIII 103 Vs. 14), *us-ki-ya-an-zi* (*IBoT* III
148 III 4 *uskiyanzi ŪL-at-kan* 'they do not look at it'; cf. Haas–
Wilhelm, *Riten* 222), 1 sg. pret. act. *uskinun* (e.g. *KUB* I 1 I
44–45 *nu-za-kan irmalas-pat* [with gloss-wedges] *ŠA* DINGIR-*LIM*
handandatar ser uskinun 'even while ill I kept seeing over me the
deity's providence'; cf. Götze, *Hattusilis* 10), 3 sg. pret. act.
us-ki-it (*KUB* XXXIII 109 + 94 + 1549/u, I 15 *nu-kan aruna*[*s*
ᴰ*Kumarbi*]*n* INA UD 7 KAM IGI-*anda uskit* 'the sea was expecting
K. on the seventh day'; cf. Siegelová, *Appu-Hedammu* 38; *KBo*
III 4 II 18 and *KUB* XIV 15 II 3 and 4 'saw'; cf. Götze, *AM* 46),
us-gít (XLII 100 III 37), 1 pl. pret. act. *us-ga-u-en* (e.g. XVIII 5
II 3 *n-an kuitman usgawen* 'while we were observing him'; cf. A.
Archi, *SMEA* 16:128 [1975]; ibid. I 22 and 26; XVI 74, 9), 2 pl.
pret. act. *us-kat-te-en* (XXXI 64a, 7), 3 pl. pret. act. *us-ki-ir*
(XIX 29 IV 10–11 GIM-*an-ma-at* ŠEŠ-*YA* GIG-*an uskir* 'when they
saw my brother ill'; cf. Götze, *AM* 18; *KBo* XIX 76 + *KUB* XIV
20 I 19 *nu-mu tūwaz uskir* 'they saw me from afar'; cf. Götze,
AM 194; Houwink Ten Cate, in *Florilegium Anatolicum* 161
[1979]), 1 sg. imp. act. *us-gal-lu* (*KUB* XXIV 5 Rs. 8 *nu-wa*
ᴰUTU AN-*E* IGI.HI.A-*it usgallu* 'let me see the sun-god of heaven
with my eyes!'; cf. Kümmel, *Ersatzrituale* 12), 2 sg. imp. act.
uski (e.g. XVII 28 II 6 *n-an zik* ᴰUTU-*us uski* 'watch him thou,
sun-god!'; *KBo* V 4 Vs. 26 *n-an-zan kattan* QATAMMA *uski* 'look
upon it likewise'; cf. Friedrich, *Staatsverträge* 1:56; V 3 II 13
āssu lūlu uski 'see good prosperity'; cf. Friedrich, *Staatsverträge*
2:114), 2 sg. imp. midd. *us-ga-ah-hu-ut* (V 3 III 49 *n-an-zan*
mekki usgahhut 'look out for her very much'; similarly ibid. 44,
52, 58; Friedrich, *Staatsverträge* 2:126–8), 3 sg. imp. act. *uskidu*

au(s)-, u(wa)-

(*KUB* XL 56 I 9; cf. von Schuler, *Dienstanweisungen* 50), *uskiddu*
(*VBot* 120 III 14), 3 pl. imp. act. *us-kán-du* (e.g. ibid. 11, 12, 13;
cf. Haas – Thiel, *Rituale* 144–6; *KBo* IV 10 Vs. 51 *nu uskandu
istamaskandu-ya n-at kutruēs asandu* 'let them see and hear, let
them be witnesses'; *KUB* XIII 4 III 9 *nu arahza hāli* LÚ.MEŠ*hali-
yattallis uskandu* 'outside let the watchmen keep watch'; cf.
Sturtevant, *JAOS* 54:380 [1934]; XIII 2 I 2–3 [*nu ŠA* LÚ]KÚR
[*ūrkin*] *uskandu* 'they shall watch the enemy's trail'; cf. von
Schuler, *Dienstanweisungen* 41; XXVI 9 I 4 *h]āli* SIG₅-*in uskandu*
'let them keep watch well'; cf. F. Daddi Pecchioli, *Oriens
Antiquus* 14:100 [1975]; *KBo* XXII 39 III 6; cf. P. Cornil – R.
Lebrun, *Orientalia Lovaniensia Periodica* 6–7:97 [1975–6]);
partic. *uskant-*, acc. sg. c. EGIR-*pa uskantan* (*KUB* VII 38 Vs. 13),
nom. pl. c. EGIR-*pa parza uskantes* 'looking backwards' (cf. S.
Košak, *Ling.* 18:101 [1978]); verbal noun *us-ki-ya-u-wa-ar* (n.),
nom.-acc. sg. in *KBo* XV 25 Vs. 24 IGI.HI.A-*as uskiyauwar*
'eyesight', ibid. 11 IGI.HI.A-*wa us*[...]*ar* (cf. Carruba, *Beschwö-
rungsritual* 2, 19), gen. sg. *uskiyauwas* (*KUB* II 1 II 36–37
NÍ.TE.HI.A-*us uskiyauwas* 'of seeing the persons', with dupl. *KBo*
II 38, 2 NÍ.TE-*as uskiyauwas*; cf. A. Archi, *SMEA* 16:97 [1975]);
inf. *us-ki-ya-u-wa-an-zi* (*RS* 25.241 Verso 55–56 *anda-kan usk-
iyauwanzi kuit sanizzi* 'which [is] excellent to watch'; cf. Laroche,
Ugaritica 5:774, 779 [1968]); iter. *uskiski-* in *KBo* VI 29 I 9–10
GIM-*an-ma-za-kan ŠA* DINGIR-*LIM assulan uskiskiuwan tehhun* 'as
I began seeing the deity's favor' (cf. Götze, *Hattusilis* 44).

uskiskat(t)alla- (c.) 'guard, watchman', nom. sg. *us-ki-is-ga-
-tal-la-as* (*KUB* XIV 1 Rs. 44–45 LÚ*auriyalas*] *uskis*[*g*]*atallass-a*
'warder and guard'; similarly ibid. Vs. 23; cf. Götze, *Madd.* 30,
6; XIV 16 IV 20 [emended from XIV 15 IV 48] [*nu-wa-tta kās* 6]
ME ERÍN.MEŠ SAG.DU-*i uskisgatallas ēsdu* 'let this 600-man troop
be your bodyguard'; cf. Götze, *AM* 74; *KBo* V 3 II 17
LÚ*uskisgatallas*; cf. Friedrich, *Staatsverträge* 2:114), nom. pl.
uskisgatallis (*KUB* XXIII 82 Rs. 11), LÚ.MEŠ*us-ki-is-kat-tal-li-is*
(XLI 8 IV 15; cf. Otten, *ZA* 54:136 [1961], *us-ki*[*s-kat*]*-tal-li-us*
(dupl. *KBo* X 45 IV 16), *us-kis-kat-tal-lu-us* (IV 14 III 10–11
ANA TI LUGAL LÚ.MEŠ*uskiskattallus* [LÚ.MEŠ*h*]*āliyattallus ēsten*
'for the king's life be guards [and] watchmen'; cf. R. Stefanini,
ANLR 20:44 [1965]). Cf. *uwatalla-* (above).

242

uskiskitallatar, uskisgattallatar (n.) 'guard duty', dat.-loc. sg. in *KUB* XIV 16 IV 18 (emended from XIV 15 IV 46) *namma-ssi 6 ME* ERÍN.MEŠ *A]NA* SAG.DU-*ŠU uskiskitallanni pihhun* 'I further gave him a 600-man troop for his bodyguard' (XIV 15 IV 46 reads *uskisgattal[lanni).* Cf. Götze, *Madd.* 106–9.

Cf. Hrozný, *SH* 56; Bechtel, *Hittite Verbs* 72–3.

The basic ablaut is *au-* : *u-*, perhaps reflecting **āu* vs. **au* or **u.* The *-mi* conjugation forms with *-s-* before *-t-* (e.g. *auszi, ausdu*) are secondary and late, patterned on *austa* which is a *-hi* conjugation innovation for original **aus* (like e.g. *naista* for *nais*). The earlier Hittite paradigm may have been: pres. act. *uhhi, autti, *aui, umeni, autteni/austeni/usteni, uwanzi* (cf. e.g. *nehhi, naitti, nāi, piweni, naisteni/pesteni, neanzi*); pret. act. *uhhun, *autta, *aus > austa, auir* (cf. *nehhun, paitta, nais > naista, nāir*); imp. act. *au, *au-u, austen, uwandu* (cf. *pai, nāu, naisten, piandu*). Thus the verb *au-* was basically a diphthongal stem of the *-hi* conjugation like e.g. *nai-* or *pai-*. In the middle voice, too, the exceptional *aushahat* and *austat* are matched by the rare *naista(ri)*, while generally the stem is a secondary *uwa-*, like *ne(y)a-: uwahhat, uwantat, uwaru, uwandaru* (cf. *neyahhat, neyantat, neyaru, neyandaru*). Cf. Kammenhuber, *HOAKS* 241–2, 247; Oettinger, *Stammbildung* 82–3, 405–8.

The correct etymon (Skt. *avati* 'observe, notice') was adduced by Hrozný (*Heth. KB* 73). Pedersen (*Hitt.* 173) added for comparison Skt. *āvís* 'openly, evidently', thus involving the whole group of Avest. *āviš*, OCS *(j)avě* 'openly, clearly', OCS *umŭ* 'intelligence', Gk. *ἀΐω* 'perceive' (*IEW* 78). The specific rapprochement of Hitt. *uhhi* 'I see' with the reinterpreted Vedic hapax *uvé* 'I see, I realize' as reflecting **A₂u-A₁éy* has fueled speculation on the prehistory of Indo-European verb inflection (cf. W. P. Schmid, *IF* 63:144–50 [1958]; Rosenkranz, *IF* 64:68 [1959]; C. Watkins, *Indogermanische Grammatik* III/1, 82–3 [1969]). But the attendant attempts (esp. Schmid 149–50; cf. also Ivanov, *Obščeindoevropejskaja* 153–6) to match the iterative *uski-* with Skt. *ucchǎti* 'shine' (**us-skĕ-*) do not convince; the Indic word reflects IE **Aéw-s-, Aw-és-* 'be bright' (*IEW* 86–7) which has been unsuccessfully foisted on Hitt. *au(s)-* many times (first by Sturtevant, *Lg.* 8:120–1 [1932]; see the chronicle by Tischler, *Glossar* 97); semantic analogues like Vedic *rocaná-* 'brightness': Skt. *locana-* 'eye' or Gk. λευκός 'white': λεύσσω 'see' notwithstanding, the *s* of *au(s)-* is simply not a root suffix but a paradigmatically conditioned morphophonemic accretion. Hitt. *uski-* reflects **u-ske-*.

O. Szemerényi (*Gnomon* 43:665 [1971]) saw in the obscure Gk. δι-οσκέω 'look earnestly' (vel sim.) a loanword from Hitt. *uski-*.

Cf. *auri-*.

auwawa- (c.) 'spider' (?) (*KBo* I 44+XIII 1 I 50 *a-u-wa-wa-as ha-an-za-na-as* matching Akk. *qū ett[uti* 'spider's web, cobweb'; cf. Otten, *Vokabular* 11, 16), nom. sg. (?) in XVI 101, 2 *auw]auwas*, acc. sg. *a-u-wa-u-wa-an* (ibid. 6]GUŠKIN *au-wauwan*), gen. sg. *auwawas* (I 44+XIII 1 I 50, quoted above), *a-u-wa-u-wa-as* (*Bo* 2583 II 8–9 BIBRA GUŠKIN-*ya-smas au-wauwas* KAŠ-*it sūwandan piran pe harkanzi* 'they hand them a gold rhyton of arachnoid [decoration?], filled with beer'), instr. sg. *a-u-wa-u-wa-a-it* (*KBo* XVI 100, 4–7]*n-an* IŠTU BIBRI *auwauwā[it]* [...] EGIR-*ŠU-ma* ^D*Huwassannan* ^DUT[U-*un*] [...] *auwauwāit-pat* TUŠ-*as ekuzi n[-an*] [... *l*]*āhui nu* EGIR-*ŠU ŠA* GUD BIBR[*A* 'her [?] from a rhyton with arachnoid [decoration?] ..., and again [the goddess] H. [and] the solar deity ... from [a rhyton] with arachnoid [decoration?] he toasts [in] sitting [position], ... he pours, and again a rhyton of bovine [design] ...').

Man's name ^I*A-wa-u-wa-a* (*KBo* XV 28 Vs. 2; cf. Laroche, *Noms* 50; Otten, *Vokabular* 16).

auwa(u)wa- is plausibly a (Luwoid?) phonetic variant of *akuwakuwa-* (q.v.), on the lines of *lala(k)uesa-* 'ant' or *tar-(k)uwai-* 'dance' (cf. Neumann, *IF* 76:261 [1971]; Puhvel, *JAOS* 94:294–5 [1974] = *Analecta Indoeuropaea* 265–6 [1981]). Otten (*Vokabular* 16) was unduly reluctant to credit the Akkadian gloss 'spider's web'. Arachnoid decorations are not to be ruled out on rhyta any more than theriomorphic designs. The variant *aku(waku)wa-* points to an insect (associated with ants), and its 'lair' (*hattessar*) agrees with the habitation patterns of certain spectacular spiders such as tarantulas. Neumann's comparison (*Untersuch.* 82) of *akuwakuwa-* with Hes. βάβακοι · ὑπὸ Ἡλείων τέττιγες · ὑπὸ Ποντικῶν δὲ βάτραχοι is phonetically even more apposite for *auwawa-*; but 'cicada' and 'frog' are semantically far enough apart to admit a tertium quid in a term of approximate reduplicative onomatopoeia (nor is any chirping or croaking necessary, any more than an ant had to say *la-lak-*). Cf. Puhvel, *Essays in historical linguistics in memory of J. A. Kerns* 237–42 (1981).

awan   (*a-wa-an*, occasional spelling *a-u-wa-an*), adverb strengthening the notion of motion or direction, found only in *awan arha* 'away, off', *awan katta* 'down', *awan sarā* 'up', e.g. *KUB* XXVII 1 III 21 *awan arha kuirzi namma-kan awan arha wāki* '(he) cuts off (and) then bites off' (cf. Lebrun, *Samuha* 82); for the many attestations see e.g. Götze, *Madd.* 135; Zuntz, *Ortsadverbien* 44–5; Goetze, *Tunnawi* 16, 20, 105; Laroche, *RA* 47:74–5 (1953).

awan is related to Lith. *aurè* 'lo, there', much as *duwan* 'hither' (q.v.) parallels Gk. δεῦρο 'hither' (*IEW* 73–5; cf. OPers. *ava-*, Skt. dual *avóḥ*, OCS *ovŭ* 'that'). For the matching pair *awan : duwan* cf. already Couvreur, *Hett.* 153.

Less probable are much-cited connections of *awan* with the prefix *we-*, *u-* 'to' and/or with Ved. *áva*, *avár* 'down, off', Lat. *au-* 'off', Lith. *au-* 'away' (*IEW* 72–3); cf. e.g. Hrozný, *MDOG* 56:28 (1915), *SH* 35, 70; Sturtevant, *Lg.* 7:1–5 (1931), *Comp. Gr.*[1] 101, 113–4, 212, *Lg.* 14:71–2 (1938); K. Bergsland, *RHA* 4:279–80 (1938); E. Polomé, *RBPhH* 30:1043 (1952), who saw *n : r* alternation in *awan* vs. Ved. *avár*; Laroche, *RHA* 16:101 (1958).

Cf. *pariyawan* s.v. *pariya(n)*.

auisi- (a-ú-i-si-), ausi- (a-ú-si-),   found in *KUB* IX 4 + *Bo* 7125 IV 8 L[Ú.MEŠ]*auisiyalas*, with dupl. *KUB* IX 34 IV 12 LÚ.MEŠ*auisiliyas* and *IBoT* III 102 + *Bo* 3436 I 13 LÚ *ausiyauwas*. Cf. H. Otten– C. Rüster, *ZA* 68:157–8 (1978).

auisiyalas (gen. pl.) may be denominative from an *auisi-* (cf.

e.g. *auriyala-* 'warder' from *auri-* 'guardpost') or deverbative from an *auisiya-* (cf. e.g. *lahhiyala-* 'warrior' from *lahhiya-* 'wage war'), but (LÚ) *ausiyauwas* is rather gen. sg. of a verbal abstract ('[man] of *ausiyauwar*'); *auisiliyas* (gen. pl.) parallels *auisiyalas*, with a denominative adjectival suffix like *karuili-* from *karū* (q.v.) or *tameli-* from *tamai-* (q.v. s.v. *ta*[*n*]). Thus both a noun *auisi-* and its denominative verb *auisiya-* are assured, *ausi-* being a reductional variant (like e.g. *a-ú-ti-* besides *a-ú-i-ti-*, *a-wi-ti-* [q.v.]). Cf. H. Eichner, *Die Sprache* 25:76 (1979).

The 'men of *au(i)si-*' form part of a list of spiritual and temporal individuals and groups (priest[esse]s, soldiers, courtiers, 'multitude', etc.) whose obloquy is to be ritually shunned. Meaning and etymology in abeyance.

awiti-, auti-   (c.), leonine animal in iconographic descriptions, nom. sg. *a-ú-i-ti-is* (*KUB* XXXVIII 2 I 2 *auitis* KÙ.BABBAR GAR.RA GAR-*ri* there lies a silver-covered a.'; XXXVIII 11 Vs. 11 *auitis* KÙ.BABBAR GÌR.MEŠ KAPPI.HI.A NU.GÁL 'a silver a., feet [and] wings are not there'), *a-wi-ti-is* (XII 1 III 15 1-*EN awitis* GUŠKIN 'one gold a.'; ibid. 38 6 UR.MAH GUŠKIN 1-*EN awitis* 'six gold lions [and] one a.' cf. S. Košak, *Ling.* 18:100–1 [1978]), gen. sg. *auitiyas* (XXXVIII 2 I 13 *auitiyas-ma-kan pattanas* ZA[G-*za* GÙB-*za*] ᴰ*Ninattas* ᴰ*Kulittas* 'to the right [and] left of the wings of the a. [are] N. and K.'; ibid. 16 *auitiyas-ma* GA[M-*an pa*]*lzahas* IŠṢI 'but under the a. [is] a wooden base'), *auiteyas* (XVI 83 Vs. 49–50 ANA BIBRI *auiteyas-kan* IGI-ŠU ŠA ᴺᴬ⁴ZA.GÌN EGIR-*an* NU.GÁL 'on the [theriomorphic] rhyton the a.'s eye of lapislazuli is no more there'), dat.-loc. sg. *auitiya* (XXXVIII 2 I 24–25 *auitiya-kan* KUN KÙ.BABBAR GAR.RA GAB-ŠU GUŠKIN GAR.RA GUB-*ri* 'on an a. with silver-covered tail [and] gold-covered breast he stands'), *awiti* (XXXVIII 1 II 8 ANA *awiti* GUŠKIN-*kan ismeriyanti* 'on a bridled golden a.'), *a-ú-ti* (II 10 V 39–40 IŠTU BIBRU *auti* GUŠKIN *akuwanzi* 'they drink from a golden a. rhyton'; cf. Friedrich, *HE* 27), nom. pl. *awitius* (XII 1 IV 17 2 *awitius sasantes* 6 SAG.DU UR.MAH 'two reclining a. [and] six lion's heads').

awiti- is found in contradistinction to UR.MAH 'lion' (e.g. *VAT* 7681 IV 6–7 4 *awiti* KÙ.BABBAR ... 4 UR.MAH KÙ.BABBAR) and probably denotes some type of winged lion or sphinx. Cf. von Brandenstein, *Heth. Götter* 4, 6, 14, 32–3, 64–5, 67–9, 91; Güterbock, *Orientalia* N.S. 15:484 (1946); L. Rost, *MIO* 8:175, 180, 198 (1961); Ertem, *Fauna* 260–5; F. Steinherr, *Die Welt des Orients* 4:320 (1968).

Neumann's explanation of *awiti-* as 'lion' from IE *owi-edi-* 'sheep-eater' (*KZ* 77:76–7 [1961]; cf. e.g. OCS *medvědŭ* 'honey-eater' = 'bear') founders on the uniform Anatolian laryngeal attested in Luw. *hāuĭs* (e.g. *KUB* XXXV 43 II 10; cf. Otten, *LTU* 42; *Dict. louv.* 44–5), Hier. *hawa-* (cf. Meriggi, *HHG* 58–9; Friedrich, *AfO* 21:83–4 [1966]), and Lyc. χαva (cf. Laroche, *BSL* 62.1:59–60 [1967]) 'sheep', pointing to IE *A_2^wewi-* (Neumann's etymology was rejected by Kammenhuber, *KZ* 77:199 [1961], but sustained by Kronasser, *Etym.* 1:162, 239; V. Ševoroškin, *Etimologija 1964* 157 [1965]; R. Eckert, *Baltistica* 6:39–40 [1970]).

Cf. perhaps rather Hom. ἀΐδηλος 'fierce, destructive, hateful', Lat. *invīsus* 'hateful' (*η-wid-* 'not [to be] countenanced', hence 'baleful' as an appellative for a savage animal; for the privative prefix cf. e.g. *ammiyant-*, *asiwant-*, for the suffix *niwalli-* beside *newalant-*, Ved. *anatidṛśyá-*, Skt. *avidya-*, and for the semantics ON *vargr* 'wolf', lit. 'strangler').

Cf. *walwalla-*.

Volume 2

Words beginning with E and I

ehu 'come!', alone or with preverbs *anda, arha, kattan, parā*, e.g.: *KUB* XIV 3 II 65 *ehu-wa* 'come!' (cf. Sommer, *AU* 10); I 6 III 17 *ehu* (cf. Götze, *Hattusilis* 28); I 1 IV 2 *ehu-si* '(when I sent word) "come!" to him' (cf. Götze, ibid. 30); *KBo* III 4 II 13 *kinun-a-wa ehu nu-wa zahhiyauwastati* 'now come, we shall fight!' (cf. Götze, *AM* 46); *KUB* XV 35 + *KBo* II 9 I 18 *nu apiaz* (sic, for *apiz*) *ehu* 'come thence!' (cf. Sommer, *ZA* 33:98 [1921]); *KBo* XXIII 1 I 24 and XXIII 2 III 5 *arunaz ehu* 'come from the sea!' (cf. Lebrun, *Hethitica III* 141, 145); *KUB* XIX 49 I 71 *anda ehu* 'come in!' (cf. Friedrich, *Staatsverträge* 2:10); XIV 3 I 49 *anda-wa-mu-kan ehu* (cf. Sommer, *AU* 4); XXIV 2 Vs. 11 *n-asta* EGIR-*pa* ^É*karimni-tti anda ehu* 'come back again into your temple' (cf. Gurney, *Hittite Prayers* 16); *KBo* XVII 32 Vs. 7 *nu arha ehu* 'come away!'; *KUB* XV 35 + *KBo* II 9 I 16 *nu-smas--kan istarna arha ehu* 'come away from their midst!'; ibid. 19 *n-asta kizza* IŠTU KUR.KUR.HI.A *arha ehu* 'come away from these lands!' (cf. Sommer, *ZA* 33:98 [1921]; A. Archi, *Oriens Antiquus* 16:299 [1977]); *KUB* VII 8 II 2–3 *nu kedani antuhsi kattan ehu* 'come down to this man!'; XIV 1 Vs. 77 *katti-mi-wa ehu* 'come down to me!' (cf. Götze, *Madd.* 18); *KBo* XVI 22 Vs. 5 *parā ehu* 'come forth!' (cf. Güterbock, *ZA* 43:323 [1936]); *KUB* XXXIII 120 II 3 SIG₅-*uazz-a pedaz parā ehu* 'from the good place come forth!' (cf. Güterbock, *Kumarbi* 36); XXIX 1 I 10 *ehu pāiwani* 'come, let us go!' (cf. B. Schwartz, *Orientalia* N.S. 16:24 [1947]); ibid. II 39 *ehu zik* Á^{MUŠEN} *īt* 'come, eagle, go!'.

Much as *īt(tin)* (q.v. s.v. *i-*) serves suppletively as the 2 sg. (pl.) imp. of *pai-* 'go', even so *ehu* is the de facto 2 sg. imp. of *uwa-, ui-* 'come' (cf. e.g. *HT* 1 I 29–30 *ehu ... uwadu* 'come! ... let [them] come'). The opposition is clear in *KUB* XIV 3 III 65 vs. 67–68: *nu-wa* INA KUR *Hatti arha īt* 'go off to H.!'; *mān-ma-wa* ŪL *nu-wa* INA KUR *Ahhiyawā arha ehu* 'but if not, come home to A.!' (cf. Sommer, *AU* 14, 166); for *arha uwa-* 'come home', *arha uda-* 'bring home' see *arha* s.v. *arha-*.

The original verbal (rather than interjectional) character of *ehu* is not in doubt (cf. V. Čihař, *Arch. Or.* 23:349–50 [1955]), but there is little reason to postulate (with e.g. Sturtevant, *Comp. Gr.*[1] 100, *Comp. Gr.*[2] 35) a full-grade active form of IE **ey-* (> Hitt. *e-*; cf. Lat. *ī* 'go!') vs. the weak-grade parallel relic *īt* 'go!'. Already Pedersen (*Hitt.* 110) realized that *ehu* is to be explained rather from the middle voice stem *iya-* 'go'. In fact *ehu* sometimes functions paradigmatically with *iya-* (e.g. *KUB* XXIX 4 III 27–28 *nu edass-a* ANA É.HI.A GIBIL.HI.A *ehu ... nu mahhan iyattari* 'come to these new houses! ... when thou comest'), and *iya-* can have the sense of 'come' in 2 sg. imp. *iyahhut* (e.g. *KUB* XXXIII 8 III 18–19 *nu-ssan iyahhut ... nu-za-kan seski* 'come! ... sleep!'; *KBo* XIII 86 Rs. 3 ᴰUTU-*us iyahhut* 'sun-god, come!'). It is probable that *ehu* is an early, interjectionalized form of this imperative, i.e. **eyehu(t) > ehu* (phonologically regular, unlike the paradigmatically innovated *iyahhut* or *iehut*, q.v. s.v. *iya-, ie-* 'go').

Carruba (*Das Palaische* 58, *Beiträge* 8–9, *Scritti in onore di G. Bonfante* 129 [1976]) inconclusively adduced the obscure Palaic *i-ú* (allegedly 'komm her!') and Luwian *(a-)a-wa*, seeing in Hitt. *ehu* and Pal. *iu* IE **ey* 'go!' + *u* (same as preverbally in *uwa-, uda-*, etc.), and considering *h* a hiatus breaker (as did Kronasser, *VLFH* 209, who, however, took *-u* as an imperatival morpheme and saw in the standard 2 sg. imp. middle ending *-hut* a contamination of the endings of *ehu* and *īt*). Neumann (apud Gusmani, *Lyd. Wb.* 273) even compared with *ehu* the allegedly Lydian Hes. ἰβύ·τινὲς τὸ βοᾶν, thus an interjection **i(w)u*. C. Watkins (*Indogermanische Grammatik* III/1, 69 [1969]) compared *e-hu* with the mid-segment of *pe-hu-te-* 'bring forth', while V. I. Georgiev (*Arch. Or.* 39:430 [1971]) and H. Eichner (*MSS* 31:55, 76 [1973], followed by Oettinger, *Stammbildung* 125, 348, 544) came out for a reconstruct *ehu* 'come!' < **E₁éy-A₁aw* 'go away (from there)!', comparing Lat. *au-ferō*, OCS *u-* (for possible cognates of Lat. *au-* etc. see rather Hitt. *awan* [s.v.] and the preverb *u-* mentioned above in *uwa-, uda-*, pointing to A_2).

The alleged OHitt. *e-hu-ut* (*KUB* XXXVI 99 I 4; Watkins, *Indogermanische Grammatik* III/1, 69 [1969]) is in reality *e-ip-pir* (cf. Starke, *Funktionen* 137).

ehurati-   (c.) '(woollen) plug', acc. pl. in *KUB* XII 58 II 19–20 *IŠTU*
GEŠTUG.HI.A-*šu-ta-si-san* ˢⁱᴳ*ehuratius* GE₆-*TI arha dāi* 'from her
ears she takes away the black wool-plugs' (cf. Goetze, *Tunnawi*
14).

ehuradai- 'plug, stop up', 3 sg. pres. act. in *KUB* VII 53 I 16
SAL-*za-ma-kan* GEŠTUG.HI.A-*šu IŠTU* SÍG GE₆ *ehuradāizzi* 'the
woman plugs her ears with black wool' (similarly ibid. 18
ehuradaizzi; cf. Goetze, *Tunnawi* 4).

Obscure. Various abortive attempts at Indo-European reconstruction have started from 'close, cover' (**wer-*; Goetze,
Tunnawi 51–2), 'wool' (Gk. εἶρος 'wool': A. Cuny, *RHA* 6:86,
91–2 [1942–3]; Gk. ᾦα 'fleece': E. Polomé, *RBPhH* 30:460–1
[1952]), or 'ear' (alleged **ehur* 'ear' cognate with Gk. οὖς +
something akin to OE *e[o]dor* 'fence': Sturtevant, *IHL* 47,
repeated by others along the laryngealist trail; cf. Tischler,
Glossar 102). One may adduce rather the bread name ᴺᴵᴺᴰᴬ*ehū-*
rius (*KUB* XXXVI 83 IV 5) and *istamahura-* 'earring' (q.v.); cf.
H. Eichner, *MSS* 31:55–6, 87–8 (1973).

e(y)a(n)-   (n.), an evergreen tree, nom.-acc. sg. ᴳᴵˢ*eyan* (e.g. *KUB*
XXIX 1 IV 17–20 *nu* ᴳᴵˢ*eyan tiyantiyanzi* KI.MIN ᴳᴵˢ*eyan mahhan*
uktūri iyatniyan nu hurpastanus arha ŪL ishuwai LUGAL-*s-a*
SAL.LUGAL-*s-a QATAMMA iyatniyantes asandu* 'they set up an *eya-*
tree, (saying) likewise: "As the *eya*-tree is ever verdant and does
not shed its leaves, even so may king and queen be thriving"'; cf.
B. Schwartz, *Orientalia* N.S. 16:38 [1947]; XIII 8 Vs. 9
nu-smas-kan piran ᴳᴵˢ*eyan artaru* 'before them shall stand an
eya-tree', as token of their being [ibid. 6, 11] *arawēs* 'free' [ibid. 6]
sahhanaza luziyaza 'from socage [and] from corvée', and [ibid.
11] *hūmantaza* 'from everything'; cf. Otten, *Totenrituale* 106;
KBo VI 2 II 62 [= *Code* 1:50] *kuel-a* ᴳᴵˢ*eyan āski-ssi sakuwān* 'at
whose gate the *eya*-tree is visible [his house is free from imposts]';
KUB XII 20, 9 [with dupl. VII 44 Vs. 13] ᴳᴵˢHAŠHUR.KUR.]RA
ᴳᴵˢŠENNUR ᴳᴵˢ*eyan* 'mountain apple-tree, pear-tree, *eya*-tree';
1142/z + *KUB* XXV 31 Vs. 5–6 ᴳᴵˢ*eyan* ᴳᴵˢZAG.GAR.RA-*as kuit*
harpan ēsta [ᴸᵁSA]NGA ᴰ*Telipinu dāi* 'the *eya*-tree which had been
placed apart on the altars, the priest of T. sets [it] up'; cf. H.

Otten – C. Rüster, *ZA* 62:234 [1972]; ibid. 21 SIG₅-*an* ᴳᴵˢ*eyan* 'a good *eya*-tree'; *KBo* XXIII 49 IV 5–6 *i*]*sdananaz* ...ᴳᴵˢ*eyan* [...-]*anzi* 'from the altar they ... the *eya*-tree'; 245/v Rs. 8 *nu* ANA ᴳᴵˢŠUKUR.HI.A ᴳᴵˢ*eyan* GAM-*an isparr*[*a-* 'fell an *eya*-tree for spears'; *KUB* XII 19 III 20 *kī*ᴳᴵˢ*eyan*; ibid. 24; XII 49 I 13; XXVI 21 III 2; *KBo* VIII 118, 3; XII 86, 14; *IBoT* II 39 Rs. 20; III 37 Vs. 8; II 121 Rs. 10–11 *ta* 8 ᴳᴵˢ*eyan* [...] *n-at lukki*[*zzi* 'eight [pieces of] *eya*-tree ... and he kindles them'; cf. Haas, *Nerik* 136), ᴳᴵˢ*e-a-an* (e.g. *Bo* 5621 IV 11 [dupl. of *KUB* XXIX 1 IV 17 above]; XXVII 67 III 67–68 *nu* ᴳᴵˢ*eān dāi ser-at warhuui kattann-at alpu* 'he takes an *eya*-tree; it [is] rough at the top [but] smooth below'; ibid. IV 9–10 *nu-*]*mu-kan* ᴳᴵˢ*eān dāi nu-mu-kan arauwa*[*h* 'set up the *eya*-tree for me and make me free!' [viz. from *inan* 'disease']; *KBo* XXII 236, 9–11 *hassī lukkizzi* [1 ᴳᴵˢ*e*]*ān* ZAG-*ni* ŠU-*it* 1 ᴳᴵˢ*eān-ma* [GÙB-*i*]*t* ŠU-*it harzi* '[he] kindles on the hearth; one [piece of] *eya*-tree he holds with his right hand and one with his left hand'; *KUB* VII 18, 4 ᴳᴵˢ*eān kittari* 'an *eya*-tree lies'), ᴳᴵˢ*eya* (XVII 10 IV 27–28 ᴰ*Telipinuwas piran* ᴳᴵˢ*eya arta* ᴳᴵˢ*eyaz-kan* UDU-*as* ᴷᵁˢ*kursas kankanza* 'before T. stands an *eya*-tree; from the *eya*-tree is hung a sheepskin'; cf. Laroche, *RHA* 23:98 [1965]; Friedrich, *Staatsverträge* 2:31; Carruba, *Orientalia* N.S. 33:406–7 [1964]; M. Popko, *Altorientalische Forschungen* 2:69 [1975]; *KBo* VI 3 III 2 [= *Code* 1:50, dupl.]; *KUB* VII 23, 2), ᴳᴵˢ*eyanan* (117/r, 4 ᴳᴵˢ*eyanan isparr*[*a-* 'fell an *eya*-tree'), gen. sg. ᴳᴵˢ*eyas* (*Bo* 2967 III 2 ᴳᴵˢ*eyas* ᴳᴵˢ*alkistanus* 'branches of *eya*-tree'; *Bo* 2839 III 14; cf. Haas, *Nerik* 260), ᴳᴵˢ*eyanas* (*KBo* XVII 93 Vs. 3 ᴳᴵˢ*eyanas* ᴳᴵˢ*alkis*[]), dat.-loc. sg. ᴳᴵˢ*eya* (III 8 III 9 ŠEG₉.BAR-*an katta* ᴳᴵˢ*eya hamikta* 'he tied a wild sheep under an *eya*-tree'; ibid. 27 *kattan* ᴳᴵˢ*eya lāttat* 'set [it] free under the *eya*-tree'; cf. Kronasser, *Die Sprache* 7:157 [1961]), ᴳᴵˢ*eyani* (*KUB* XXV 33 I 7–8 *istananni* ᴳᴵˢ*eyani sarā hūkan*[*zi*] 'on the altar above an *eya*-tree they slaughter'; XII 19 III 17), ᴳᴵˢ*e-a-ni* (XXVII 67 III 70), abl. sg. ᴳᴵˢ*eyaz* (XVII 10 IV 28, quoted above; XXXIII 12 IV 14; XXXIII 24 IV 17; XXXIII 38 IV 7; cf. Laroche, *RHA* 23:107, 119, 145 [1965]), nom.-acc. pl. ᴳᴵˢ*eyan* (*IBoT* II 121 Rs. 10 8 ᴳᴵˢ*eyan*), ᴳᴵˢ*e-i-e* (*Bo* 2689 II 30 *ta* ᴳᴵˢ*eye siunas parna petanzi* 'they bring *eya*-trees to the god's house'; cf. Ehelolf, *ZA* 43:173 [1936]).

For the secondary *n*-stem acc. sg. *eyanan*, gen. sg. *eyanas*, dat.-loc. sg. *e(y)ani*, starting from nom.-acc. sg. *e(y)an*, cf. gen. sg. *euwanas* s.v. *e(u)wa(n)-*.

The *eya*-tree was a symbol of verdant lastingness and a planted marker of tax-exemption. It also figures ritually as conducive to freedom from disease and as having hung on it a sheepskin which in the Telipinus myth constitutes a sort of magic cornucopia laden (or implicit) with sheep-fat, cereal, field-fruits, wine, cattle and sheep, long years and progeny (*KUB* XVII 10 IV 28–31). Arboreal identification has proved arduous. Von Brandenstein (*Orientalia* N.S. 8:76 [1939]) suggested some valuable fruit-tree, co-occurring with apple and pear (*KUB* XII 20, 9); this was rightly doubted by Otten (*Überlieferungen* 43). Goetze's (*ANET* 348) and Güterbock's (*RHA* 22:100 [1964]) 'fir' was echoed by H.A. Hoffner (*RHA* 25:41 [1967]) and Ertem (*Flora* 110–6), and underlies V. Pisani's etymological connection with OCS *jela*, Russian *jel'* 'fir, spruce' (*AION-L* 7:47 [1966] = *Lingue e culture* 197 [1969]), but was justly rejected by Szabó (*Bi. Or.* 30:76 [1973]); 'fir' is rather Hitt. *tanau-* (q.v.). Fastening on *KUB* XXIX 1 IV 17–20 (quoted above), Ivanov (*Problemy indoevropejskogo jazykoznanija* 40–4 [1964]) essayed an implausible tie-in with 'eternity' words exemplified by Ved. *áyu-* 'life-force', while H. Eichner (*MSS* 31:77 [1973]) saw a figura etymologica *eyan ... iyatniyan* in the same passage (cf. s.v. *iyatar*).

More cogently, Haas (*Altorientalische Forschungen* 5:269–70 [1977]) tried to make a case for 'oak': *KUB* XXIX 1 IV 18 *hurpastanus* means 'leaves' and can hardly refer to conifer needles; *eya(n)-* is a large tree, judging from *Bo* 2839 III 14–15 ^{GIŠ}*eyas* GAM-*an* [*aruwa*]*izzi* paralleling ibid. 37–38 ANA GIŠ GAL [...] *aruwaizzi*; cf. *Bo* 2710 Vs. 11 GIŠ-*ŠI RABĪ* 'great tree' (Haas, *Nerik* 66–7, 260, 262, 214); it must have been sturdy, being used for spears; evergreen varieties of oak are found in Anatolia; considering parallels between the Greek Golden Fleece and Jason-Medea saga and the Telipinus and Illuyankas (Hupasiyas-Inaras) myths (Haas, *Ugarit-Forschungen* 7:227–33 [1975]), the detail that the Golden Fleece was hung on an oak tree in Kolkhis was to Haas a fine confirmation of *eya(n)-* as 'oak'.

e(y)a(n)-

Since 'oak' is attested as *allantaru* (q.v.), it is better to connect *e(y)a(n)-* rather with a group of Indo-European tree names centering around the etymon and kind of English 'yew', as has been done by Ivanov (*Trudy po znakovym sistemam* 4:66 [Tartu 1969]; *Etimologija 1971* 298–302 [1973]) and P. Friedrich (in *Indo-European and Indo-Europeans* 23–4 [1970], *Proto-Indo-European trees* 121–9 [1970]). These include ON *ȳr*, OE *īw*, OHG *īwa*, Gaulish *ivo-*, OIr. *ēo*, Old Prussian *iuwis* 'yew', and with semantic variation Lith. *ievà* 'buckthorn', Russian *íva* 'willow', Gk. ὄα, οἴη 'rowan', Arm. *aygi* 'grapevine', Lat. *ūva* 'grape' (*IEW* 297). The meaning 'yew' is clearly basic and can be postulated for Hitt. *e(y)a-* as well, with a proto-form **ey-o-* or possibly **ey-yo-*, besides **ey-wo-* or **oy-wo-* in other languages (unnecessary laryngealistic formulations in H. Eichner, *MSS* 31:77 [1973], *Die Sprache* 24:151 [1978]).

The yew is an evergreen with flattened leaves that resemble conifer needles and would probably qualify as *hurpastanus*. It can exceed 15 meters in height, several meters in trunk circumference, and three millennia in age; this would certainly qualify its giant specimens as 'great trees'. The wood is hard, fine-grained, heavy, non-resinous, pliable, and durable, used for making bows (cf. Lat. *taxus*, Russian *tis* 'yew': Gk. τόξον 'bow', τοξικόν [φάρμακον] 'arrow poison') and attested as material for spears both among Hittites (245/v Rs. 8 quoted above) and Romans (Silius Italicus 13:210 *letum triste ferens auras secat Itala taxus*). The poisonous alcaloid in its leaves and berries occasioned the yew's "deadly" reputation in antiquity, and especially in Rome and Germania reinforced its occult, magical, ritual, and talismanic significance (infernal and graveyard associations, warding off witchcraft, judicial staff symbolism, etc.); in Celtic lands it may occur in names of gods and kings (OIr. *Eochu* [= Dagda], *Eochaid* < **Ivo-catus*?). The yew grew and still grows in northern Anatolia and the Caucasus, and among the Hittites seems to have had more "positive" legal and religious connotations. Greek lost the primary meanings of both inherited 'yew' terms (ὄα, τόξον) and had instead an obscure term σμῖλαξ; this dislocation may account for the appearance of the oak rather than the yew in the

256

saga of the Golden Fleece. Cf. Puhvel, *Kratylos* 25:136–7 (1980).

eka- (c. and n.) 'cold, frost, ice', nom. sg. c. (?) *egas* in the fragmentary *KUB* XXI 18 Rs. 19, matched by *erṣetu lū šuripu-ma* 'may the earth freeze over' in the Akkadian version *KBo* I 1 Rs. 67 (cf. Laroche, *Ugaritica* 6:372–3 [1969]), nom. sg. neut. *e-kán* (*KUB* XIII 2 IV 25–26 *ekan dān ēstu* É ŠURIPI *wedan ēstu* 'let ice be taken, let an ice-house be built'; cf. H.A. Hoffner, *JCS* 24:31–6 [1971]), acc. sg. (c. or n.) *e-ka-an* (*KUB* XXXI 4+*KBo* III 41 Vs. 8 *kīdanda pattanit ekan utiskimi* 'I keep bringing ice with this bucket'), *e-kán* (dupl. *KBo* XIII 78 Vs. 8; cf. Otten, *ZA* 55:158 [1962]), gen. sg. *ekas* in *Bo* 6980, 11 *ekas hariulli dāi* 'he takes a container of ice', dat.-loc. sg. *eki* (*KBo* XXII 62 III 24–25 [= *Code* 1:56] *eki* BÀD-[*ni* LUGAL-*as* KASKAL-*s-a taksuanzi* ...] *natta k*[*uiski arawas* 'from ice[-procurement], fortification[-building], and joining royal campaigns ... none is exempt'; cf. H. C. Melchert, *JCS* 31:57–9 [1979]). Carruba (*Festschrift for O. Szemerényi* 197–8, 204 [1979]) improbably saw in the last instance and perhaps in *e-ka-an* (above) the numeral 'one', cognate with Skt. *éka-* (cf. s.v. *aikawartanna-*); similarly Josephson, *Kratylos* 26:99 (1981).

egai-, *igai-* 'cool down, freeze, become paralyzed', 3 sg. pres. midd. *igaetta* (*KUB* VII 58 I 3–5 GIM-*an*] *weteni anda taskupāizzi namma-as igaetta n-as karussiyazi* 'as [it] cries out [= hisses] in water and then cools down and falls silent'; XXXV 79 I 7 *n-at māhhan igaitta* 'when it cools down'; cf. Otten, *LTU* 75), 3 sg. pret. act. *igait* (*VBoT* 1, 27 *nu Haddusass-a* KUR-*e igait* 'the land of H. is paralyzed'; cf. L. Rost, *MIO* 4:335 [1956]), 3 sg. imp. midd. *igattaru* (*KUB* VII 58 I 11–12 *ishunāu-smit* GI-*za* ... *kittaru n-as igattaru* 'may their bowstring [and] arrow be put down and may it be paralyzed'), *egattaru* (ibid. 8), *egaddaru* (dupl. XLV 20 I 23). Cf. Ehelolf, *KlF* 400; Alp, *Anatolia* 2:23–4 (1957); Laroche, *OLZ* 57:30 (1962); Kronasser, *Etym.* 1:473; von Schuler, *Die Kaškäer* 36–7; Neu, *Interpretation* 68–9: all of these except Laroche mistranslated *egai-* as 'burst, crack'; J.

Knobloch (*Kratylos* 4:32 [1959]) and Čop (*Ling.* 5:24 [1964])
consequently compared Lith. *ižti* 'spring open' (said of pods,
buds, etc.); Kronasser (*Studies presented to Joshua Whatmough*
125 [1957]) suggested an equally improbable meaning 'go to
ruin', connecting IE **ey-gh-* (see s.v. *egdu-*).

ekuna-, ikuna- 'cold', figuratively 'unfeeling' (*KUB* I 16 II 7
ekunas = ibid. I 6 [Akk.] *kaṣṣi*; cf. Sommer, *HAB* 2–3), acc. sg.
ikunan (*KBo* IV 9 V 47 *ikunan* ᵁᶻᵁYÀ 'cold fat'), dat.-loc. sg.
ekuni (e.g. *KUB* VIII 35 Rs. 11 and 14 *ekuni* IM-*anti* 'to the cold
wind'), *ikuni* (XXIX 41, 4 *ikuni pidi* 'in a cold place'; ibid. 7
ikuni pedi; ibid. 10 *ikuni wit*[*eni* 'in cold water'; cf. Kammenhuber, *Hippologia* 168), instr. sg. *ikunit* (XXIX 50 IV 18 *ikunit
wit*[*enit* 'with cold water'; cf. Kammenhuber, *Hippologia* 212);
possible Luwianism (dat.-loc.) *ikunta luli* (XXXIII 96 I 16
without, XXXIII 98, 12 with gloss-wedge) 'Cool Pond' (vel
sim.; cf. Güterbock, *JCS* 5:146 [1951], 6:34 [1952]).

ekunima- (c.) 'cold(ness)', nom. sg. *ekunimas* (see below),
dat.-loc. sg. *ekunimi* (*KBo* III 23 Vs. 5–8 [OHitt.] *mān-*[*an*]
*handais walahzi zig-an ekunimi dai takkuw-an ekunimas walahzi
n-an handasi dai* 'if heat strikes him, place him in the cold; if
cold strikes him, place him in the heat' [similarly ibid. IV 9–10
and *KUB* XXXI 115, 9–11]; cf. A. Archi, in *Florilegium
Anatolicum* 41–2 [1979]; VIII 67, 9 ᴳᴵˢHAŠHUR *mān ekunimi
pi*[*ran* 'like an apple-tree from cold'; cf. Friedrich, *Arch. Or.*
17.1:232 [1949]; Laroche, *RHA* 26:169 [1968]; Siegelová, *Appu-
Hedammu* 40; VIII 35 Vs. 4 *apedani* DUMU-*li attas annas
ekunimi kattan* DÙ-*anzi* 'the parents treat that child with
coldness'). Cf. Götze, *KlF* 186; Laroche, *BSL* 52.1:74 (1956).
For derivation cf. *hahlimma-* 'jaundice' from *hahli-*, **hahla-*
'green, yellow' (s.v. *hahhal-*).

ikunes- 'become cold', 3 sg. pres. act. *i-ku-ni-es-zi* (1214/z, 6).
For the possibility that a one-time stative verbal stem **ekunē-*
'be cold' underlies both *ekunima-* and *ikunes-* cf. C. Watkins,
TPS 1971: 76.

ikunahh- 'make cold', *KUB* XXXIX 41 Vs. 6 *ikunahhu*[-.

eka- is from IE **yeg-* (*IEW* 503) seen in MiIr. *aig* 'ice'
(< **yegis*), MiCorn. *yeyn* 'cold', ON *jaki* 'ice-floe', *jökull*
'glacier'; *ekuna-* may be based on **yegu-* (Pedersen's [*Hitt.* 171]

*yeg^w^no- is contradicted by the absence of labiovelarity in ON *jaki*). In view of Hittite, Pokorny's idea (*Celtica* 5:236 [1960], approved by Kammenhuber, *KZ* 77:67 [1961]) of a Germanic-Celtic borrowing from Finno-Ugric (Finnish and Estonian *jää*, Mordvin *jej*, Hungarian *jég* 'ice') is untenable; besides, the Lappish (*jiekŋa*) and Ugric forms (Vogul *jöäŋk*) point rather to Finno-Ugric *jäŋe (cf. e.g. H. Jacobsohn, *Arier und Ugrofinnen* 11–2 [1922]; B. Collinder, *An introduction to the Uralic languages* 137 [1965]; Čop, *KZ* 84:158 [1970]). For Hittite *e-* < *ye-* see s.v. *ewa-*, *is(sa)na-*.

Cf. *ikniyant-*, *iksai-*.

ekt-, ikt- (c.) '(catch-)net', nom. sg. c. *e-ik-za* (*KBo* XVII 61 Vs. 17 *ekza isparranza* 'the net [is] spread'; cf. H. Berman, *JAOS* 92:466 [1972]; *KUB* XXXIX 61 I 11, in a ritual list, immediately preceded by 'dried sheep-thigh', followed ibid. 12 inter alia by 'iron anklet'; 1067/u, 5 KUR ^URU^*Hatt*]*i-ma-kan ekza hu*[*ppan harzi* 'the net holds Hatti ensnared'[?]), *ik-za* (*KBo* III 21 II 15–18 *liliwanza-ma-ssan ikza-tes* KUR-*e katta hūppan harzi iktas-ma-ddu-ssan irhaz* ŪL *nahsariyawanza arha* ŪL *uizzi* 'your swift net holds the land ensnared; from the confine of your net not even the unafraid escapes'), acc. sg. *e-ik-ta-an* (*KUB* XXXI 68 Vs. 27 [*na*]*mma-wa kuin ektan* [with gloss-wedge] *hama*['also what net bind ...'; cf. R. Stefanini, *Athenaeum* N.S. 40:23 [1962]; XLVIII 76 I 2–3 *nu ektan* [*ispar*]*nuzi* 'spreads the net'; cf. Oettinger, *Eide* 6), *e-ik-za-an* (XLV 26 II 2 *ekzan sarā epzi* 'takes up the net'; *KBo* XIII 101 Rs. 6), gen. sg. *iktas* (III 21 II 17; see above), instr. sg. *e-ik-te-it* (473/t Vs. 13–15 GIM-*an ektan ispar*]*nuwanzi nu* ARNABU *ektet* [*appanzi* ...] ... [... *nu* ... QATA]*MMA appandu n-at harninkandu* 'even as they spread the net and catch the hare with the net ..., let them likewise catch ... and destroy it').

Correctly distinguished from *egdu-* 'leg' (q.v.) by Oettinger (*Eide* 22) and interpreted as 'net' by H. A. Hoffner (*Essays on the Ancient Near East in memory of J. J. Finkelstein* 105–7 [1977]). Earlier, superseded renderings as 'leg' by Güterbock, *Kumarbi* 43, *9; Alp, *Anatolia* 2:27–32 (1957).

Luwoid *aggati-* (c.) 'catch-net', acc. pl. *aggatius*, gloss-wedged hapax legomenon in the Hittite *Gilgameš* (*KUB* VIII 56, 12), matching Akk. *nuballu* 'catch-net'; context s.v. *akkus-(s)a-*. Cf. H. A. Hoffner, *Essays on the Ancient Near East in memory of J. J. Finkelstein* 107 (1977).

Hoffner (+ H. Berman apud Hoffner) derived *ekt-* and *aggati-* from IE **yē-k-* seen in Lat. *iaciō, iēcī* 'throw'; but in the latter the guttural suffix is in the nature of a strictly verbal stem formant and unlikely to crop up in an isolated root noun. Cf. perhaps rather Lat. *ictus* 'thrust, stroke', root **ayk̂-* 'aim sharply' (*IEW* 15), with *ekt-* < **ayk̂-t-*; a parallel formation is Gk. δίκτυον 'catch-net', from δικεῖν 'throw' (cf. E. Tichy, *MSS* 38:198–217, 224–7 [1979]). For the Hittite phonetic development *e/i* < **ai* see s.v. *asara-, esara-*. *ekza* /ekt-s/ has preserved the **kt* cluster unassimilated (unlike its regular outcome *tt* in e.g. *lutta[i]-, uttar*), perhaps under the impetus of an anaptyctic tendency (**ekat-*) actually realized in Luw. *aggati-* (which has in addition the typical Luwian marks of *a* coloration and gravitation to *i*-stem declension); *ekzan* is an analogical accusative (spread of affricate from nom. sg., vs. normal *ektan*).

Wholly improbable is E. P. Hamp's comparison of *ekt-* (< **yek-t-*) with OHG *jagōn*, postulating an Indo-European root **yek-* 'hunt' (*IF* 83:119–20 [1978]). H. Berman (ibid. 123) implausibly explained the internal *a* in Luw. *aggati-* as either a thematic vowel or a morphophonemic insert in deverbative noun derivation.

Cf. Puhvel, *Bi. Or.* 37:204 (1980), *Analecta Indoeuropaea* 414 (1981).

egdu-, igdu-   (n.) 'leg', nom.-acc. sg. *egdu* (*KUB* XXVII 1 III 20–21 LUGAL-*us-za* GÍR ZABAR *dāi nu-kan* UZU*walan hastai* UZU*egdu awan arha kuirzi namma-kan awan arha wāki* 'the king takes a bronze knife and cuts off a thigh, a bone, and a leg, and then bites off'; cf. Lebrun, *Samuha* 82), *igdu* (XXXIII 112 IV 15; XXXIII 114 IV 13–15 *nu-ssi-kan* UZU*iskisaza* [...] *markir* UZU*igdu-ma-k[an ...] marke[r* 'from his back ... they cut up, and his leg ... they cut up'; cf. Meriggi, *Athenaeum* N.S. 31:144–6 [1953]; Laroche, *RHA* 26:35–6 [1968]).

This word is unrelated to *ekt-*, *ikt-* '(catch-)net' (q.v.); thus all interpretations of *ekt-*, *ikt-* as 'leg' have been flawed; the alleged nom. pl. *ik*HI.A (*Bo* 2839 III 13–14 GEŠTUG.HI.A-*ŠU ik*HI.A-*ŠU* [*arha k*]*ue kuranta* 'his ears and his "legs" which are cut off') does not even exist (read rather KUN-*ŠU* 'his tail'; cf. Oettinger, *Eide* 22).

A possible etymology is IE **ey-gh-* (*IEW* 296), Lith. *eigà* 'a going', Gk. *οἴχομαι* 'go off, be gone', *ἴχνος* 'footstep, track', also 'foot', Toch. B *yku* 'gone'; thus *egdu-* < **eygh-tu-* 'a going', metonymically 'leg'. For treatment of **g(h) + t*, as opposed to **k + t* in *lutta(i)-*, *uttar*, see also s.v. *ukturi-* and Puhvel, *KZ* 86:111–5 (1972) = *Analecta Indoeuropaea* 220–4 (1981). Cf. Kronasser, *Studies presented to Joshua Whatmough* 125 (1957), *Etym.* 1:252; Frisk, *GEW* 2:372.

J. J. S. Weitenberg (*Mnemosyne* 29:225–32 [1976]) did not distinguish *ekt-* 'net' from *egdu-* 'leg', considered the *i* vocalism primary, and connected *ikt-* (sic) improbably with the rare and dubious Gk. *ἴκταρ* 'female genital' (alleged proto-meaning 'leg'), implausibly deriving the adverb *ἴκταρ* from this noun (for *ἴκταρ* 'close to' see rather s.v. *kitkar*); he also considered *iktu-* (sic) analogical to *genu-* 'knee'.

eku-, aku-   'drink; drink to (+ dat.), toast (+ acc.)' (rarely NAG), 1 sg. pres. act. *e-ku-mi* (*KUB* XXXIII 67 IV 17 *kinun-za edmi ekumi* 'now I eat [and] drink'; cf. Laroche, *RHA* 23:138 [1965]; *IBoT* II 73, 4–5 *nu akuanna wekz*[*i* ...] [...-]*an ekumi* 'asks to drink ... I drink ...'; *ABoT* 32 II 14; cf. Carruba, *Beschwörungsritual* 45), 2 sg. pres. act. *e-ku-uš-ši* (*KUB* I 16 III 29 *wātarr-a ekussi* 'and water you will drink', cf. Sommer, *HAB* 12), *e-uk-ši* (*KBo* XXII 1 Rs. 28 [OHitt.] *parna-ssa paisi ezsi euksi* 'you go to his house, eat [and] drink'; cf. A. Archi, in *Florilegium Anatolicum* 46 [1979]), *ekutti* (XIX 112, 8–10 *kuwat-za ŪL ez*[*atti*] [*kuwat*] *ŪL ekutti ammel ishā-mi* [...] [...] *adātar nu kuit akuwatar ŪL* ...['why do you not eat, why do you not drink, my lord? ... eating, and because drinking not ...'; cf. Siegelová, *Appu-Hedammu* 44), 3 sg. pres. act. *ekuzi* (profuse, e.g. *KUB* XLIII 60 IV 4 [OHitt.] *arha ekuzi* 'drinks up [lit. off]' (like Lat.

ē-pōtat); *KBo* XIX 128 V 50 LUGAL-*us* GUB-*as* ^DLAMA ^{KUŠ}*kursan ekuzi* 'the king toasts standing the tutelary god [of] the fleece'; cf. Otten, *Festritual* 14; *KUB* XXXIX 15 I 7 EGIR-*ŠÚ-ma akkandas* ZI-*ni* 3-*ŠU ekuzi* 'but afterwards one drinks to the deceased's soul three times', besides ibid. 7–8 *mahh*[*an* ...] *apel* ZI-*an ekuzi* 'when one toasts his soul'; cf. Otten, *Totenrituale* 82; *KBo* XV 25 Rs. 15–16 *nu hantezzi* [*pa*]*lsi* ^DUTU *ŠAMĒ ekuzi* EGIR-*ŠU-ma ANA* ^DIM *ekuzi* 'the first time he toasts the sun-god of heaven, but afterwards he drinks to the storm-god'; cf. Carruba, *Beschwörungsritual* 4–6, 40), *ekuzzi* (e.g. *KUB* VIII 65, 3 'drinks'; cf. Siegelová, *Appu-Hedammu* 42; *KBo* XIX 128 V 47 and VI 17 'toasts'; XXI 36, 4 *nu ANA* ^DUTU *ekuzzi*, ibid. 7 *ANA* ^DU *ekuzzi* 'drinks to'), *e-uk-zi* (*KBo* XVII 30 III 4 and 7; cf. Neu, *Altheth.* 149; *KUB* XX 53 V 6 and 10 'toasts'; *Bo* 2923 Vs. 10; *Bo* 3456, 2; cf. Ehelolf, *KlF* 143), *e-ú-uk-zi* (*Bo* 2692 V 23), NAG-*zi* (e.g. *KUB* XVII 35 I 27 *nu-smas* KÚ-*zi* NAG-*zi* '[the priest] eats [and] drinks to them'), 1 pl. pres. act. *akueni* (*KBo* XVII 4 II 8 *adueni akueni* 'we eat [and] drink'; XVII 1 III 15 and IV 6 *atueni akueni*; cf. Otten – Souček, *Altheth. Ritual* 24, 30, 36; *KUB* XXXVI 110 Rs. 5–7 LUGAL-*as* NINDA-*san adue*[*ni*] [GEŠTIN]-*set-a akueni n-asta* GAL GUŠKIN-*as* GEŠTIN-*nan parkuin akkuskiewani* 'the king's bread we eat, and his wine we drink; from a gold goblet pure wine we keep drinking'; cf. Neu, *Altheth.* 227; Starke, *ZA* 69:82 [1979]; A. Archi, *Studia mediterranea P. Meriggi dicata* 50 [1979]; *KBo* III 29 I 19 *atueni mān akueni-zza*), *akuwani* (*Bo* 5709 Vs. 10), *ekueni* (412/b + Vs. 37b NINDA-*an ekueni* [sic]), *ekuwani* (*KBo* XV 26, 7; cf. ibid. 4 *a*]*duwani nu akuwann*[*a* 'we eat, and to drink ...'; Carruba, *Beschwörungsritual* 46), 2 pl. pres. act. *ekuteni* (XIV 41 IV 17 [OHitt.]), *ekutteni* (*KUB* I 16 III 34 and 48 NINDA-*an azzasteni wātarr-a ekutteni* 'bread you will eat and water you will drink'; cf. Sommer, *HAB* 12–4; XIII 4 II 70 *nu* NINDA-*an ezzatteni wātar-ma ekutteni*; ibid. IV 52–53 *n-asta BIBRU* DINGIR-*LIM* ZI-*as arha ekutteni* 'you drink up the rhyton of the soul of the gods'; cf. Sturtevant, *JAOS* 54:378, 394 [1934]), 3 pl. pres. act. *akuanzi* (frequent, e.g. *KBo* XVII 9 IV 4 and 7; cf. Neu, *Altheth.* 35; X 30 III 6 *adanzi akuanzi* 'they eat [and] drink'), *akuwanzi* (profuse, e.g. XIX 128 IV–V passim; cf. Otten, *Festritual*

262

10–4), *akūwanzi* (*KUB* XXX 15 Vs. 19 *nu akūwanna 3-ŠU pianzi nu 3-ŠU-pat apel* ZI-ŠU *akūwanzi* 'they give to drink three times, and three times they toast his soul'; cf. Otten, *Totenrituale* 66; XX 48 VI 8 and 10), *ekuanzi* (*KBo* XV 34 II 3), *ekuwanzi* (*KUB* XX 1 II 20), NAG-*anzi* (e.g. XVII 24 III 16 *n-at-kan arha* NAG-*anzi* 'they drink it up'), NAG-*zi* (e.g. XVII 35 I 33 LÚ.MEŠ ŠU.GI *warsuli* NAG-*zi* 'the old men drink by drops'), 1 sg. pret. act. *ekun* (XXX 10 Vs. 16–17 NINDA-*an-za wemiyanun n-an-za* AHITI-YA *natta kuwapikki edun wātar-ma-z wemiya⟨nun⟩ n-at* AHITI-YA ŪL *kuwapikki ekun* 'bread I found, and never ate it by myself; water I found, and never drank it by myself'), 2 sg. pret. act. *ekutta* (XXXIII 96 IV 21 *nu* ŪL *ekutta* 'you did not drink'; ibid. 20 *nu-za* ŪL *ezatta* 'you did not eat'; cf. Güterbock, *JCS* 5:160 [1951]; *KBo* XIX 104, 12 [probably]; cf. Siegelová, *Appu-Hedammu* 14), 3 sg. pret. act. *ekutta* (*KUB* I 16 III 17 *ēs]har-simit ekutta* 'she has drunk their blood'; cf. Sommer, *HAB* 12; *KBo* XII 3 III 16 [OHitt.] *t-at ekutta* 'he drank it'; *KUB* XXXVI 2 II 4 *e]zzatta ek[ut]ta* 'he ate and drank'; cf. Laroche, *RHA* 26:33 [1968]; XXXVI 12 I 12 *sanizzesta nu e[ku]tta* '[it] turned appetizing, and he drank'; cf. Güterbock, *JCS* 6:10 [1952]), *e-uk-ta* (XXXVI 104 Vs. 6 [OHitt.] MUN-*an suhhair s-an-asta eukta* 'they sprinkled salt, and he drank it'), 1 pl. pret. act. *e-ku-e-en* (*HT* 1 I 44–45 *n-asta* IŠTU ^UZU^NÍG.GIG *huuisawaz wākuēn namma-kan* ^GI^A.DA.GUR-*az ekuēn* 'we have taken a bite from the raw liver, also we have drunk with the straw'), 3 pl. pret. act. *e-ku-ir* (e.g. *KBo* XIII 86 Vs. 15 *ekuirr-a hassikkir-at[-za* ŪL] 'they drank, but they were not satiated'; *KUB* XXXIII 32 III 5; cf. Laroche, *RHA* 23:126 [1965]), *e-ku-i-e-ir* (XVII 10 I 19–20 *eter n-e* ŪL *ispiyer ekuyer-ma n-e-za* ŪL *hassikkir* 'they ate but they were not filled; and they drank but they were not satiated'; cf. Laroche, *RHA* 23:90 [1965]), 2 sg. imp. act. *e-ku* (e.g. *KBo* XIII 114 I 23 *et-za eku* 'eat [and] drink!'; *KUB* XX 92 VI 8–9 *ezza-zza nu-za ispiya eku-ma nu-za nik* 'eat and get full, drink and get your fill!'; *KBo* XXII 178 IV 3 *w]ātar eku* 'drink water!'; *KUB* XXXIII 70 II 6 *eku-ma* GEŠTIN-*an* 'drink wine!'; XXXIII 8 III 15 *nu-za et sanezzi eku-ma sanezzi* 'eat sweet and drink sweet!'; cf. Laroche, *RHA* 23:104 [1965]), inverted spelling *ku-e* (*KBo* IV 6 Rs. 9 *apāt "kue"* *nu-za ninga* 'drink that and get your fill!'), 3 sg. pres. imp. *ekuddu* (*KUB* XLIII 23 Vs. 3]*ezdu ekuddu* 'may he eat [and] drink'; XXXVI 25 I 5 *nu-za ezzaddu eku*[*ddu*), 2 pl. imp. act. *e-ku-ut-te-en* (*KBo* VII 28 Vs. 26 *ezzasten ekutten*; cf. Friedrich, *Rivista degli studi orientali* 32:219 [1957]; *KUB* IV 1 II 4 *nu izzatten ekutten*; cf. von Schuler, *Die Kaškäer* 170; XLIII 23 Rs. 11 and 14–15 [OHitt.] *nu-za ezten ekutten*), *e-ku-te-en* (XXXIII 62 III 10–11 *sumes ezzastin nu-za ispittin ekuten-ma nu-za nikten*), *e-ku-ut-tin* (*KBo* V 3 III 37 *nu-za ezattin ekuttin duskiskittin* 'eat, drink, make merry!'; cf. Friedrich, *Staatsverträge* 2:126; XVII 105 III 30 *nu-za ezzatin ekuttin*; *KUB* XIII 4 II 76 *nu ezzatin ekuttin*; XIII 5 II 7 *n-at ezzatin ekuttin*; cf. Sturtevant, *JAOS* 54:380, 370 [1934]; XVII 30 III 3]*ezzattin ekuttin*; *KBo* X 45 IV 12 *nu-za uwattin izzattin ekuttin* 'come, eat, drink!'; cf. Otten, *ZA* 54:136 [1961]), NAG-*tin* (*KUB* XLI 4 II 14 KÚ-*tin* NAG-*tin*), 3 pl. imp. act. *akuwandu* (XV 34 I 48–49 *ad*[*and*]*u akuwandu n-at-za ispiyandu ninkandu*; cf. Haas – Wilhelm, *Riten* 186); partic. *akuwant-* (active in meaning, like Lat. *pōtus* or Engl. *drunk*; cf. *adant-* s.v. *ed-*), gen. sg. c. in the expression *adandas akuwandas* EME-*an* 'the tongue of him that has eaten and drunk' (e.g. IX 34 IV 15); verbal noun *akuwatar* (n.), nom.-acc. sg. *akuwatar* (*KBo* XIX 112, 10]*adātar nu kuit akuwatar ŪL saqa*[*hhi* '… eating, because drinking I do not know'; cf. Siegelová, *Appu-Hedammu* 44; *KUB* XXXIII 71 III 12 *adatar akuwatar*; cf. Laroche, *RHA* 23:161 [1965]; *KBo* X 20 II 47 *adatar akuwatar*; XXII 178 III 5 *āssu akuwatar-mi*[*t* 'my good drinking'), gen. sg. *akuwannas* (e.g. *KUB* XLIII 58 I 21 GEŠTIN *akuwannas* 'wine for drinking'), NAG-*nas* (XXXIII 120 I 10 NAG-*nas-a-ssi-kan* GAL. .HI.A-*us* ŠU-*i-ssi zikkizzi* 'and drinking goblets he places in his hand'; ibid. 17 NAG-*nas-si-kan*; cf. Güterbock, *Kumarbi* *1–*2), NAG (e.g. *KBo* X 45 III 49 and 56, IV 7 DUG KA.DÙ NAG 'light beer for drinking'; cf. Otten, *ZA* 54:132–4 [1961]); inf. *akuanna* (frequent, e.g. XX 8 Vs. 17 [OHitt.] LUGAL-*us akuanna wekzi* 'the king asks to drink'), *akuwanna* (profuse, e.g. *KUB* XVII 5 I 8 [OHitt.] *nu-wa adanna akuwanna ehu* 'come to eat [and] drink'; cf. Laroche, *RHA* 23:67 [1965]; *KBo* III 34 II 33 [OHitt.] *mān* LUGAL-*was piran sieskanzi kuis hazzizzi nu-sse* GEŠTIN-*an*

akuwanna pianzi 'when they hold a shooting match before the king, who scores a hit, to him they give wine to drink'), *akūwanna* (see e.g. above, sub 3 pl. pres. act. *akūwanzi*), *akuwana* (*KUB* XXXV 4 II 9, vs. ibid. III 9 *akuwanna*; *KBo* XV 58 V 3, vs. ibid. 12 ⟨*a*⟩*kuwanna*), *akuna* (XIX 161 I 8 *akuna pianzi* [cramped spelling on tablet-edge], vs. ibid. 26 *akuwanna piyanzi*), *akuanzi* (XV 36 + XXI 61 III 6 *akuanzi pianzi* 'they give to drink'), NAG-*na* (e.g. *KUB* XVII 24 III 22, vs. ibid. 5 *akuwanna*); iter. *akkuski-*, 2 sg. pres. act. *akkuskisi* (XXVI 25 II 3 KAS-*a kuit akkuskisi* 'and beer that you drink'; XXXI 143 II 9 [OHitt.]; cf. Neu, *Altheth.* 186), *akkuskesi* (ibid. 16), 3 sg. pres. act. *akkuskizzi* (e.g. XIX 28 IV 14 *azzikizzi akkuskizzi* 'keeps eating [and] drinking'), *akkuskizi* (*KBo* XVII 11 IV 7 [OHitt.]; cf. Neu, *Gewitterritual* 34), 1 pl. pres. act. *akkuskiewani* (quoted sub 1 pl. pres. act. *akueni* above), *akkuskiuwani* (XV 25 Rs. 17; cf. Carruba, *Beschwörungsritual* 6), 2 pl. pres. act. *akkuskittani* (*VBoT* 58 I 18 *kī azzikkitani akkuskittani* 'this you keep eating [and] drinking'; cf. Laroche, *RHA* 23:83 [1965]), 3 pl. pres. act. *akkuskanzi* (e.g. *KBo* XVII 74 IV 41–42 [OHitt.] *suwāru kue* GAL.HI.A *akkuskanzi* [*ta*] *apūs-pat akuanzi* 'what cups they are used to drinking heavily, those very ones they drink'; cf. Neu, *Gewitterritual* 34; *KUB* XII 65 III 21 *nu-za azzikkanzi akkuskanzi*; cf. Siegelová, *Appu-Hedammu* 52; *KBo* V 1 III 50–51 *nu-za azzikanzi akkuskanzi*; cf. Sommer – Ehelolf, *Pāpanikri* 10*), *akkuiskanzi* (XV 37 V 31 *nu warsuli akkuiskanzi* 'they keep drinking by drops'), 1 sg. pret. act. *akkuskinun* (IV 2 IV 28–30 IŠTU ^{GIŠ}BANŠUR-*ma-za-kan kuezza azzikkinun* IŠTU GAL-*ya-kan kuezza akkuskinun* 'but from what table I used to eat, and from what cup I used to drink'; cf. Götze – Pedersen, *MS* 10), 3 sg. pret. act. *akkuskit* (XV 30 III 4–5 *wā*[*tar*] *akkuskit* 'he would drink water'; *KUB* XX 2 IV 28), 3 pl. pret. act. *akkuskir* (XXVI 89, 13 *azzikkir wātarr-a-ssi piran akkusk*[*ir* 'they ate, and water before her they drank'; cf. R. Stefanini, *Atti La Colombaria* 29:63 [1964]), 2 sg. imp. act. *akkuski* (VII 1 I 15 *inanas* ^DUTU-*i zik azzikki akkuski* 'to the sun-god of sickness eat [and] drink thou!'; *KBo* X 37 III 10 [*zi*]*qq-a azzikki akkuski*; *KUB* XLI 4 II 14), *akkuskī* (*KBo* VII 28 Vs. 18, 23, 28 *azzikkī akkuskī*), 3 sg. imp. act. *akkuskiddu*

eku-, aku-

(*KUB* I 16 II 33 *nu azzikkiddu akkuskiddu*; cf. Sommer, *HAB* 7;
XLI 17 IV 12 *azzikkiddu akkuskiddu*, with dupl. *HT* 1 IV 26
azziskiddu akkuskiddu, *KUB* IX 31 IV 22 *[az]zikkiddu [ak]-
kuskiddu*, IX 32 Rs. 17 *akkuskiddu*), 2 pl. imp. act. *ak-ku-us-
-kat-te-en* (*KBo* III 28 II 8 [OHitt.] *ītten azzikatten akkuskatten*
'go, eat [and] drink!'; cf. Laroche, *Festschrift H. Otten* 186
[1973]; *KUB* XXXI 64a, 7 [OHitt.] *ak]kuskatten*), *ak-ku-us-ki-
-it-tin* (e.g. *KBo* X 37 III 9 *azzikkittin akkuskittin*), 3 pl. imp.
act. *ak-ku-us-kán-du* (III 1 II 14 [OHitt.] *nu-wa-za azzikkandu
akkuskandu*; XX 73 IV 10 *nu ēshar akkuskandu* UZU YÀ UDU
āzzakuwandu 'let them drink blood, let them eat meat fat of
sheep!'; *KUB* XXV 37 IV 8).

akuttara- (c.) 'drinker, toaster' (priestly title in Hattic-based
rituals), nom. sg. ^{LÚ}*a-ku-ut-tar-ra[-as* (*KBo* V 11 I 14, matching
ibid. Hattic ^{LÚ}*haggazzuēl*; cf. ^{LÚ}*haggazuwasses* in *IBoT* I 36 IV
37), ^{LÚ}*a-ku-ut-tar-as* (*HT* 40 Obv. 3 and 7; 2030/c + 1703/c +
Vs. 2), ^{LÚ}*a-ku-tar-as* (ibid. Rs. 13 and 20), acc. pl. (?) ^{LÚ.MEŠ}*a-
-ku-ut-ta-ru-us* (*Bo* 2257, 11), ^{LÚ.MEŠ}*a-ku-ud-da-ru-us* (ibid. 12),
pl. ^{LÚ.MEŠ}*akudda[-* (*KBo* XX 7, 8 [OHitt.]). Agent noun with
suffix *-tara-* (cf. *wēstara-* s.v. *wesi-*), besides usual *-talla-*,
thematization of IE **-ter/-tor* seen in Lat. *pō-tor* 'drinker'.

Pal. *ahu-* 'drink', 3 pl. pres. act. *ahuwanti* (*KUB* XXXV 168,
6; XXXII 18 I 7 and 18), *ahuwānti* (ibid. 9); infin. *ahūna*
(XXXV 165 Rs. 22). Cf. Carruba, *Das Palaische* 8–9, 19, 49.

Luw. *akuwa-* (?), 3 sg. pret. act. *akuwatta* (*KBo* VII 68 III 13
and 18); *akuwan* (*KUB* XXXV 128 III 10; cf. Otten, *LTU* 107).
But the acc. sg. c. participle (?) *āhhuwāhhuwāmin*, following and
qualifying *[dagan]zipan* 'earth' in XXXV 145 Rs. 10, is a
reduplicated jingle formation of unknown meaning; 'inun-
dated' (Carruba, *Scritti in onore di G. Bonfante* 143 [1976]) is
sheer guesswork.

Except for the second tablet of Kikkulis, where *akuwanzi*
once barbarously occurs in the sense of *sakruwanzi* 'they water'
(viz. racehorses; *KBo* III 5 IV 18–19) and possibly for
akuwanna pianzi (ibid. 60; cf. Kammenhuber, *Hippologia* 100,
102, 308–9, 325–6), *eku-* never has a causative side-meaning
'make (or: let) drink', such as Skt. *pāyáyati*, Goth. *dragkjan*,
German *tränken*, Engl. *drench* (wrongly assumed from Hrozný,

SH 213, to Otten, *Totenrituale* 132); *eku-* + animate or abstract accusative is simply the commoner construction, vs. *eku-* + dat., in the sense of 'drink to, toast', much as conversely *sipand-* 'libate' is mostly construed with a dative of the recipient, but occasionally with the accusative (cf. Puhvel, *MIO* 5:31–3 [1957], *Analecta Indoeuropaea* 411–2 [1981]; C. W. Carter, *Oriens* 15:449 [1962]; H. Eichner, *Die Sprache* 24:66 [1978], 26:81 [1980]; already M. Vieyra, *RA* 51:93, 95, 96 [1957], rendered *ekuzi* in this sense as 'porte un toast'). The syntactic variation 'have a drink (for the god)' : 'toast the god (with a drink)' has parallels in e.g. Lat. *mactāre victimam deō* : *mactāre deum* (*victimā*), or in the two constructions of Gmc. **blōtan* 'sacrifice; worship', or conversely in those of Ved. *saparyáti* and *dāśati* 'honor; offer', or in the meaning shift of OCS *žrŭti* 'sacrifice' (+ acc. of victim) vs. Lith. *gìrti* 'praise' (cf. Skt *yájati* + instr., and H. C. Melchert, *Journal of Indo-European studies* 9:245–54 [1981]).

For Pal. *ahu-* cf. e.g. Luw. *mannahunna-* besides Hitt. *maninkuant-*. The forms *e-ku-zi* and *e-uk-zi* (cf. e.g. *tar-ku-zi* and *tar-uk-zi*, s.v.) point to [ek^{w}t^{s}i] as the phonetic realization (cf. F. O. Lindeman, *RHA* 23:29–32 [1965]), while the constant *-k-* outside of the iterative indicates that [k^w] is a mere conditioned paradigmatic variant of /g^w/ (*akuwanzi* = /ag^{w}ant^{s}i/), whereas in *akkuski-* (= /ak^{w}ski-/) the double spelling *-kk-* is a mark of morphophonemic unvoicing before *-s-* in a new derivative conjugation stem (cf. Puhvel, *JAOS* 94:294 [1974]).

/eg^w-/ : /ag^w-/ has an ablaut pattern like *ed-* : *ad-* 'eat', *es-* : *as-* 'be', or *ep(p)-* : *ap(p)-* 'seize'; there is no reason to assume /ēg^w-/ (wrongly e.g. Oettinger, *Stammbildung* 87–8). Toch. AB *yok-* 'drink', connected with *eku-* since Pedersen, *Le groupement des dialectes indo-européens* 40 (1925), can reflect in its vocalism either **e-* or **ē-* (> **ya-* > *yo-* via "labiovelar umlaut"), and the *k* can go back to any order of labiovelar. The most compelling tertium of this comparison is Lat. *ēbrius* 'drunk' (Juret, *RHA* 2:251–2 [1934], *Revue des études latines* 15:79 [1937]; Friedrich, *Indogermanisches Jahrbuch* 20:321 [1936]; Otten, *AfO* 15:81 [1945–51]; W. Winter, *KZ* 72:173–5

[1955]; Puhvel, *JAOS* 94:294 [1974]), but it needs to be refined and elaborated. *ēbrius* does not mean primarily 'intoxicated' but rather 'having drunk one's fill' (cf. Terence, *Hecyra* 5.2.3: *quom tu satura atque ebria eris* 'when you have had enough to eat and drink', and *ekuten-ma nu-za nikten* [quoted above]); a noun *$egh^w ri$- 'drink(ing)' (cf. Hitt. *edri*- 'food, meal') would yield Lat. **ebri-* (cf. *febris* < *$*dhegh^w ri$-), which appears privatively in the thematized hypostatic compound *sōbrius* 'without drinking, not (having) drunk' (*$*sē + egh^w ris$, like e.g. *sēcūrus* from *$*sē + koysā$; for vocalism cf. *socors* besides *secordis*, or *extorris* besides *exterrāneus*); *ēbrius* is probably abstracted from *$*sēgh^w riyos$, much as the adjectives *decor(is)* and *decōrus* are secondary to *indecor(is)* and *indecōrus* (compounds with samāsānta suffixes from *decus, decor*). Juret's (*Revue des études latines* 15:79 [1937]) and Winter's (*KZ* 72:173–5 [1955]) analysis of Gk. νήφω 'be sober' as *$*ne + egh^w$- 'not drink' may also be strengthened by this interpretation.

The discreditable tie-in of *eku-* with Lat. *aqua* 'water' and some cognates stretches from Hrozný (*MDOG* 56:28 [1915], *SH* 42–3) via Sturtevant (*Lg.* 6:219–20 [1930] et passim) and many others down to e.g. Kronasser (*Acta Baltico-Slavica* 3:77–8 [1966]), H. Eichner (*MSS* 31:82 [1973]), and van Windekens (*Le tokharien* 601–2). It was consistently rejected by Benveniste (*BSL* 33:142 [1932], *Hittite* 96–7) in favor of the binary Hittite-Tocharian isogloss *eku-*:*yok-*, and later by Kammenhuber as well (e.g. *MHT* 3, Nr. 5, 6–11 [1975], in the course of the 371-page treatment of *eku-* by her and A. Archi in *MHT* 3–7 [1975–6]), who, however, joined the chorus in excluding Lat. *ēbrius*.

Equally untenable connections for *eku-* are Skt. *aśnā́ti* 'eat, consume' (Mayrhofer, *KZ* 71:45–8 [1953]) and an alleged Sanskrit verbal root *ac-* 'draw (water)' (V. Pisani, *Pratidānam … presented to F. B. J. Kuiper* 102 [1968]).

Cf. *akutalla-*.

elaniya- 'drive (to extremities), assail, plague', iter. *elaneski-*, *elineski-*, 1 sg. pres. act. *e-la-ni-es-ki-mi* and 3 pl. pret. act.

e-la-ni-es-kir in *KUB* VII 53 II 9–12 *kuyēss-an* ALAM-ŠU *hastai mīluli kiez paprannaz tiyaneskir elaneskir kinun-a paprannas alwanzenas* ALAM-ŠU *hastai mīlūli kāsa* EGIR-*pa tiyaneskimi elaneskimi* 'as for those who have been besetting (and) plaguing his form, bone, and soft tissue with this defilement, now I, behold, once more (viz. as substitute magic) beset (and) plague the form, bone, and soft tissue of (the victim of) sorcerous defilement'; ibid. 17 *nu kāsa kūn tiyaneskimi elaneskimi* (cf. Goetze, *Tunnawi* 10–2, 77), dupl. XXXIX 65, 3 *e-li-ni-es-kir*. Cf. Kronasser, *Etym.* 1:507.

tiyaniya- elaniya- are best interpreted as denominative (**tiyatn-iya-* and **elatn-iya-*) from the *r/n*-stems *tiyatar* and **elatar*, action nouns of verbs *dai-* 'place, set' and **el(a)-*. *tiyaniya-* (q.v. s.v.) thus means 'perform setting', transitively and figuratively 'beset'; **el(a)-* can be tied in etymologically with the isolated Gk. ἐλάω, ἐλαύνω 'drive', also 'harass, persecute, plague' (ἐλαύνεσθαι τὴν γνώμην 'be driven out of one's mind'). Just as *tiyatar* has beside it *tiyauwar* (*kattan tiyannas* and GAM-*an tiyauwas* 'depositional tray', lit. 'of setting down'), **elatar* is matched allomorphically by the heteroclitic **ἔλαϝαρ* which underlies the denominative ἐλαύνω (cf. Benveniste, *Origines* 112).

elzi- (n.) '(pair of) scale(s)' (GIŠ.RÍN, GIŠ.RÍN *ZIBANA*, GIŠ.RÍN *ZIPANITUM* [*KUB* VII 37, 10], GIŠNUNUZ *ZIBANA*; Akk. *gisrinnu, zibānītu*), nom.-acc. sg. or pl. GIŠ*elzi* (*KBo* VI 13 I 6–8 [= *Code* 2:69] *takku* A.ŠÀ-*LAM kuiski wāsi ta* ZAG-*an parsiya* NINDA*harsin dāi t-an* DUTU-*i parsiya* GIŠ*elzi-mit-wa taknā arsikkit* 'if someone buys a field and breaches the boundary, he [viz. the wronged party] takes bread and breaks it to the sun-god [and says]: "He has planted my scale in the earth"'), GIŠ*ēlzi* (dupl. VI 26 I 52 GIŠ*e-el*[-; *KUB* XXX 10 Rs. 12–13 LÚDAM.GAR-*sa* [...] DUTU-*i* GIŠ*ēlzi harzi nu* GIŠ*ēlzi marsanuzzi* 'the merchant holds the scales before the sun-god and [yet] falsifies the scales'); cf. e.g. *KBo* XXI 22 Vs. 18–19 *kāsa* GIŠ.RÍN *karpiyemi nu Labarnas taluqaus* MU.HI.A-*us usneskimi* 'behold, I pick up scales and I put up for weighing the long years of L.'; cf. G. Kellerman, *Tel Aviv*

5:199–200 (1978); XVII 95 III 6–10 ^{LÚ}AZU-*ma-z* GIŠ.RÍN *ZIBANA*
dāi n-as ANA LUGAL *manninkuwan tiyezi nu* ANA LUGAL A.BÁR
pāi nu-ssan LUGAL-*us* A.BÁR *ANA* GIŠ.RÍN *ZIBANA dāi* ^{LÚ}AZU-*ma-*
-kan GIŠ.RÍN *ZIBANA* ^DUTU-*i menahhanda epzi* 'the medicine man
takes the scales, he steps close to the king, and gives lead to the
king; the king places the lead on the scales, and the medicine
man takes the scales before the sun-god'; XV 10 I 9–10
I-*NUTUM* GIŠ.RÍN *ZIBANA ŠA* GIŠ *dāi* 'he takes a set of scales
(made) of wood'; ibid. II 41–42 [*nu-ss*]*an* ANA GIŠ.RÍN KÙ.
.BABBAR GUŠKIN NA₄.HI.A XX.MEŠ ⟨*is*⟩*huwāi nu* [^DUTU-*i*] [*menah-*
h]*anta* 6-*ŠU gankir* 'on scales he scatters silver, gold, (gem)-
stones, and ...; before the sun-god they weighed (them) six
times' (cf. Szabó, *Entsühnungsritual* 12, 26); *KUB* XXX 15+
XXXIX 19 Vs. 26–28 *nu* ^{SAL}ŠU.GI ^{GIŠ}NUN[UZ] *ZIBANA* [*dāi*]
nu-ssan 1-*eaz* KÙ.BABBAR GUŠKIN NA₄.HI.A-*ya hūmandus dāi*
[1-]*edaz-ma-ssan saluinan dāi* 'the old woman takes a pair of
scales; on one (scale) she places silver, gold, and all (manner of
gem)stones, but on the other she places clay-mortar' (cf. Otten,
Totenrituale 68); XXX 19+I 32 *ANA* ^{GIŠ}NUNUZ *ZEPANA-assa*[*n*
'on scales' (cf. Otten, *Totenrituale* 32). Cf. Otten, *ZA* 46:218–9
(1940), *Totenrituale* 131–2.

Formal weighing was apparently performed preferentially in
sight of the all-seeing sun-god. 'Plant someone's scale in the
earth' in the *Code* must mean roughly 'tip the scales against
one, give one a raw deal' (cf. the loser's scale dipping to the
earth [or all the way to Hades] at Zeus's symbolic weighing of
fate-lots in *Iliad* 8:69–74, 22:209–13). Since a twin-scale instrument like the Greek τάλαντα is involved, *elzi* can be interpreted
as originating in an Indo-European neuter dual root-noun
E_1elt-ī matched by the Italic-Celtic isogloss *(E_1)let-* seen in
OIr. *leth*, Welsh *lled* 'half' (< *letom*), OIr. *leth*, Lat. *latus* 'side'
(< *letes-*). *elzi* thus means literally '(instrument with) two
bilateral halves'; cf. Lat. *bilanx* 'having two (scale)plates'
(*lances*) in *bilanx libra* 'pair of scales, balance', Italian *bilancia*
'scales'; for a unit-dual type involving the same etymon, cf. OIr.
leth-sūil '(one) eye' (literally 'half-eye'), singular back-formation from the dual *(dī) sūil* 'eyes'; similarly a neuter singular "*i*-
stem" *elzi-* may have come about. For the frequency of the root

shape *$E_1él-t$- in Hittite, vs. *$E_1l-ét$- in other languages, see e.g.
s.v. *ard-*. Cf. Puhvel, *Bi. Or.* 38:352–3 (1981), *Folklorica:
Festschrift for Felix J. Oinas* 193–6 (1982), *AJPh* 104:221–3
(1983).

Cf. *gangala-* (s.v. *kank-*).

enant-   'tame(d)', nom. sg. c. *enanza* (*KBo* VI 2+XIX 1 III 48
[= *Code* 1:66, OHitt.] MÁŠ.GAL *enanza* 'tamed he-goat'; cf.
Otten – Souček, *AfO* 21:6 [1966]), acc. sg. c. *enandan* (*Code*
1:65; cf. context s.v. *annanu-*; Haase, *Fragmente* 37). Cf. A.
Walther, *The Hittite Code* 258 (*Appendix* IV of J. M. Powis
Smith, *The origin and history of Hebrew law* [1931]); Goetze,
ANET 192; Güterbock, *JCS* 15:77 (1961); Otten – Souček,
Gelübde 22.

Perhaps intransitive participle in *-ant-* ('agreeable, compli-
ant, docile') from a root *en-* < **ain-* 'be agreeable', comparable
with Gk. αἶνος 'agreement, consensus; praise; tale', αἰνέω
'approve, praise; tell', possibly also **αἴνομαι* 'be agreeable' seen
in ἀναίνομαι 'spurn, reject' (similarly transitive ἀνανεύω 'refuse'
vs. νεύω 'nod, assent'; for the secondary aorist ἀνήνατο cf. e.g.
M. Peters, *Untersuchungen zur Vertretung der indogermanischen
Laryngale im Griechischen* 80 [1980]). Toch. AB *en-* (< **ain-*),
allegedly 'instruct, enjoin', is also compared with Gk. αἶνος as
'(edifying) tale' (cf. van Windekens, *Le tokharien* 177–8); but
the Tocharian attestations are all causatival (A *enäs-*, B *enäsk-*;
exceptional A *eñlune* < **enäñ-lune*) and thus do not preclude an
intransitive base-meaning 'be agreeable'.

For the improbable connection of Gk. αἰν- and Toch. *en-*
with Hitt. *hanna-*, and of Toch. *en-* with *annanu-*, see s.v.

enera-, enira-, inira-, innari- (c.), **inniri-** (n.) 'eyebrow' (ŠUR IGI,
ŠU-ÚR E-NI), nom. sg. c. (?) *ene*[*ras* (*KUB* XXXIII 66 II 19; cf.
ibid. 18 IGI.HI.A-*as harki*['the white of eyes', ibid. 20 *laplipass-a*
'and eyelash[es]'; cf. Laroche, *RHA* 23:130 [1965]), *iniras* (*KBo*
XVII 61 Rs. 11 IGI.HI.A-*kan* ANA IGI.HI.A-*ŠU handān iniras-kan
iniri* KI.MIN 'eyes [are] fitted to his eyes, eyebrow to eyebrow

likewise'; cf. Haas, *Orientalia* N.S. 40:417 [1971]; H. Berman, *JAOS* 92:466 [1972]; *KUB* XXXVI 31, 3; cf. Laroche, *RHA* 26:46 [1968]), ŠUR IGI (V 7 Rs. 27 ANA DINGIR-*LIM-wa-kan* 1 ŠUR IGI *arha maussan* 'one of the god's eyebrows has fallen off'), ŠUR ENI (XXII 70 Vs. 20, 25, 71 ŠUR ENI KAPPI ENI ŠA NA₄ 'eyebrow [and] eyelid of [gem]stone'; cf. Ehelolf, *ZA* 43:192 [1936]), acc. sg. c. *e-ni-e-ra-an-na* (XXXII 8 III 6–8 *kuitman--ma-zan* BEL SISKUR.SISKUR *IŠTU* SAG.DU-*ŠU tētan laple*[*pan*] *enerann-a huuittiyannai* 'while the sacrificer pulls from his head a hair, an eyelash, and an eyebrow [hair]'; cf. Otten, *LTU* 21), *eniran* (IX 34 III 40 *eniran aumen laplipanzan aumen* 'we have seen the eyebrow, we have seen the eyelashes' [Luw. acc. pl.; or *-an-san* 'his eyelash'?]), *i-in-na-ri-en* (XXIV 12 II 32 *īnnaren laplappipan* 'eyebrow [and] eyelash'), nom.-acc. sg. or pl. neut. *inniri* (ibid. 20–21 -]*wa-kan* ANA ¹*Tuthaliya* ALAM ᴸᵁKAL [...]*inniri laplapi zamankur* 'for T., his heroic statue, ... eyebrow[s], eyelash[es], beard ...'), *innirī* (ibid. III 6 *innirī laplipi*), dat.-loc. sg. c. *iniri* (*KBo* XVII 61 Rs. 11, quoted above), abl. sg. c. *eniraz* (*HT* 55, 6; cf. ibid. 7 *lapl*]*ipaz*), *eniraza* (*KUB* IX 34 III 46; cf. ibid. *laplapaza*), nom. pl. c. *inirus* (XXXVIII 3 II 10 IGI.HI.A *inirus* NA₄ KÁ.DINGIR.RA 'eyes [and] eyebrows [of] Babylon-stone'; cf. von Brandenstein, *Heth. Götter* 18, 57). Cf. Laroche, *RHA* 9:16–7 (1948–9).

The stem and gender variation *enera-, inira-* (c.) : *innari-* (c) : *inniri-* (n.) resembles that of the semantically contiguous *laplapa-, laplipa-* (c.) : *laplapi-* (n.) : *laplipi-* (n.) 'eyelash' (q.v.). *enera-* stands alone, in contrast to the Indo-European word for 'brow' seen in Skt. *bhrū̆-*, Gk. ὀφρῦς, OIr. *for-bru*, OE *brū*, OCS *brŭvĭ*, Lith. *brùvė*, Toch. B *pärwāne* ("paral" dual); as in the case of *laplapa-*, Luwian-tinged indigenous origin is possible. Hittite clearly distinguishes 'eyebrow', 'eyelid' (*KAPPI ENI*), and 'eyelash', whereas e.g. OE *brū* can denote any of these (and Engl. *brow* can by extension also mean 'forehead').

ep-   'smear, mold' (?), 3 sg. pres. midd. *e-pa-a-ri* (*KBo* VI 11 I 20 [= *Code* 2:11] *takku sēni pur*]*ut kuiski epāri alwanzatar* DIN LUGAL 'if anyone molds clay into a figurine, [it is] sorcery [and

subject to] the king's judgment'; cf. dupl. *KUB* XXIX 23, 15
-]*ni purut k*[*u-*), *e-ip-t*]*a-ri* (dupl. *KBo* VI 10 I 23 [?]). Cf.
Goetze, *Tunnawi* 68; Friedrich, *Heth. Ges.* 62–3, 105; Güterbock, *JCS* 15:70 (1961); Imparati, *Leggi ittite* 124, 275–6;
Kronasser, *Etym.* 1:526.

Hrozný's connection (*Code hittite* 109 [1922]) of *epāri* with
ep(p)- 'seize' was incorrect (it should have been **appattari* [cf.
appattat] or possibly **appari, *eppari* [cf. *hinkatta, hingari* from
hink-]). Neu (*Interpretation* 24) unconvincingly posited a 3 sg.
pres. act. *epār-i* (like *ispāri, isgāri*) from a verb *epar-*. Von
Schuler's 'mold, fashion' (apud Friedrich, *Hethitische Gesetze*
62–3, 105, accepted by Güterbock, Imparati, and Kronasser)
was on the right track semantically, as was Friedrich's postulation of a verb *epa-* (*Heth. Ges.* 119). For the possible variation
epāri : *eptari* cf. e.g. *hingari* : *haiktari* from *hink-*. A primary
verb *ep-* /eb-/ of Indo-European origin can hardly be other
than **(A₁ʷ)eybh-, *(A₁ʷ)oybh-,* or **(A₁ʷ)yebh-* (for *e-* < **ye-* cf.
s.v. *eka-, e*[*u*]*wa*[*n*]*-*), perhaps showing a more general meaning
'smear' > 'mold, fashion' (cf. IE **dheygh-* in Skt. *dih-* 'smear',
Lat. *figūra*) than the sexual sense 'smear' > 'defile, pollute' seen
in Gk. *οἴφω*, Skt. *yábhati*, Russ. *jebú*. The verb *ep-* may be
legalistically archaic and peculiarly suited for use with *purut-*
'clay' (q.v.), which itself is derived from the verbal root seen in
Gk. *φύρω* 'mix (dry with wet), sully, defile'.

ep(p)-, ap(p)- 'take, seize, grab, pick, capture', *-za ep(p)-* 'take to,
resort to, begin' (cf. Lat. *in-cipiō*), *anda ep(p)-* 'take in, hold in,
round up, wrap around, include, inlay, inset', *appa ep(p)-* 'pull
back, withdraw', *appan ep(p)-* 'seize behind, pursue', *arha
ep(p)-* 'take away, dispose of, do away with; receive' (cf. Lat.
re-cipiō), *katta ep(p)-* 'take down; (intrans.) take (root), be
conceived' (cf. Lat. *con-cipiō*), *kattan ep(p)-* 'take down, take
along, come to grips with, undertake', *parā ep(p)-* 'hold forth,
proffer', *piran ep(p)-* 'hold in front, block', *sarā ep(p)-* 'raise,
lift', *ser ep(p)-* lift', *kattan sarā ep(p)-* 'turn upside down',
piran sarā ep(p)- 'take (auspices)', *ser katta ep(p)-* 'grab from
top to bottom' (DIB; ṢABATU; *KUB* I 16 II 8 LUGAL-*s-an*

eppun = ibid. I 8 [Akk.] LUGAL *aṣbat-šu-ma* 'I, the king, seized him'; cf. Sommer, *HAB* 2–3), 1 sg. pres. act. *e-ip-mi* (e.g. *KBo* V 13 II 33–34 *nu apūn antuhsan nasma apāt* ERÍN.MEŠ ANŠU.KUR. .RA.MEŠ *epmi* 'I shall seize that man or those troops [and] horses'; cf. Friedrich, *Staatsverträge* 1:124; *KUB* XIV 1 Rs. 9 *nu-war-an epmi* 'I shall seize him'; cf. Götze, *Madd.* 22; XIX 49 I 72 *epmi-tta* ŪL HUL-*uw*[*anni* 'I shall not seize you in malice'; cf. Friedrich, *Staatsverträge* 2:10; XXIII 127 III 7 *arkamman sarā epmi* 'I raise tribute'; cf. Götze, *Neue Bruchstücke* 48; *KBo* IV 14 IV 56 ŠU-*za epmi* 'I take by the hand'; cf. R. Stefanini, *ANLR* 20:49 [1965]; XVII 1 I 14; cf. Otten – Souček, *Altheth. Ritual* 18), DIB-*mi* (*KUB* XXII 39 III 18 GAM-*an* DIB-*mi* 'I undertake'), 2 sg. pres. act. *e-ip-si* (e.g. XXVI 29 + XXXI 55, 18 ŪL *epsi*; *VBoT* 58 I 41 *le epsi*; cf. Laroche, *RHA* 23:84 [1965]; *KBo* V 13 III 18–19 ŠA MUŠEN-*ya-an-za-kan memian piran sarā le epsi* 'and do not take auspices!'; cf. Friedrich, *Staatsverträge* 1:126; V 3 III 39–40 *n-at zik tuel* ZI-*it le epsi* 'do not [even] conceive it with your mind!'; cf. Friedrich, *Staatsverträge* 2:126), *e-ip-ti* (e.g. X 12 III 32 ŪL *epti*; cf. H. Freydank, *MIO* 7:364 [1960]; *KUB* XIV 4 IV 19–22 *nu-wa* DINGIR-*LUM apūn* ŪL *epti* [ŪL-*wa* DAM-]*ZU* DUMU.MEŠ-*ŠU epti nu-wa ammuk niwallin epti* [...]-*a ep nasma-wa* DAM-*ZU* DUMU.MEŠ-*ŠU ep ammuk-ma-wa le epti* 'you, goddess, do not seize him, his wife [and] children you do not seize, but you seize innocent me; seize [him] or seize his wife [and] children, but me do not seize!'; *KBo* V 13 II 19–20 *epti-ma-an* ŪL *n-an-mu parā* ŪL *pesti* 'but you do not seize him and do not hand him over to me'; cf. Friedrich, *Staatsverträge* 1:124; *KUB* XXI 1 II 73–74 ŠA MUŠEN-*ma-za-kan uttar piran s*[*arā*] [*le kuit*]*ki epti* 'but do not take any auspices!'; cf. Friedrich, *Staatsverträge* 2:64; *KBo* IV 14 III 38–40 *zik-ma-za* [LUGAL-]*i karsis* ÌR-*is ēs* GÚ UGU *le epti karū kuwapi* ¹PU.LUGAL-*as* BA.UG₆ *zik-ma* GÚ UGU *IṢBAT* 'be to the king a true servant, do not raise your neck; once when P. was put to death you did raise your neck'; cf. Stefanini, *ANLR* 20:46 [1965]; *IBoT* III 148 IV 44 *awan parā le epti* 'do not proffer!'; cf. Haas–Wilhelm, *Riten* 230), DIB-*ti* (*KUB* XV 22, 10 *pian* DIB-*ti*), 3 sg. pres. act. *e-ip-zi* (profuse, e.g. VIII 83, 6 LUGAL KUR ᴸᵁKÚR *epzi* 'the king will capture the enemy country'; cf. Riemschneider,

Geburtsomina 57; *KBo* VI 3 III 66 [= *Code* 1:71] ᴸᵁ́Ní.ᴢᴜ-*an natta epzi* 'he does not arrest [him as] a thief'; *KUB* I 1 IV 85 *sahhani-ya-as luzzi le kuiski epzi* 'and nobody shall draft them for socage [or] corvée'; cf. Götze, *Hattusilis* 40; VIII 36 III 6 *nasma-an* ѕᴜʜᴀʟᴜ *epzi* 'or coughing seizes him'; cf. Burde, *Medizinische Texte* 38; XII 58 IV 7 *namma-za-kan* ɢᴜᴅ *usantarin* ѕɪ *epzi* 'she grabs the fertile cow by the horn'; cf. Goetze, *Tunnawi* 20; XIX 18 I 17–18 *nu-za* ᵁᴿᵁ*Tūwa[nuw]an zahhiyauwanzi epzi* 'he takes to fighting Tyana'; similarly ibid. 26; cf. Güterbock, *JCS* 10:76 [1956]; *KBo* XVII 1 I 14 *suppi wātar parā epzi* '[he] proffers clean water'; cf. Otten – Souček, *Altheth. Ritual* 18; *KUB* XII 58 I 36 ᴇɢɪʀ-*anda-ma-ssi-ssan* Šᴀʜ.ᴛᴜʀ *ser epzi* 'but afterwards she lifts a piglet to him'; cf. Goetze, *Tunnawi* 10), ᴅɪʙ-*zi* (e.g. XXIV 5 Vs. 18 *s]ēnann-a* ɢᴀᴍ-*an* ᴅɪʙ-*zi* 'he takes down the figure'; cf. Kümmel, *Ersatzrituale* 10; XI 18 III 12 *parā* ᴅɪʙ-*zi*), 1 pl. pres. act. *e-ip-pu-u-e-ni* (e.g. XXII 57 Vs. 13 *parā eppuweni*), *ip-pu-u-e-ni* (XXXI 44 II 10 *n-an ippuweni* Ū[ʟ] 'we do not arrest him'; cf. von Schuler, *Orientalia* N.S. 25:226 [1956]), *ap-pu-ú-e-ni* (XXXV 18 I 7; cf. Otten, *LTU* 25), 2 pl. pres. act. *e-ip-te-ni* (XIII 5 II 18 *sumas-ma-kan n]assu* ɢᴜᴅ.Šᴇ *nasma* ᴜᴅᴜ.Šᴇ *arha epteni* 'but you take away either a fat ox or a fat sheep'; cf. Sturtevant, *JAOS* 54:372 [1934]; *KBo* IV 7 I 54), *e-ip-te-e-ni* (dupl. V 13 I 6–7 *nu-war-an eptin nu-war-an-mu parā pestin mān-war-an* Ūʟ-*ma eptēni* 'seize him and hand him over to me; but if you do not seize him ...'; cf. Friedrich, *Staatsverträge* 1:112), *ap-te-ni* (*KUB* XII 63 Vs. 15), 3 pl. pres. act. *appanzi* (frequent, e.g. *KBo* XV 1 I 7 1 ᴸᵁ́Šᴜ.ᴅɪʙ 1 ѕᴀʟ-*ᴛᴜᴍ-ya appanzi* 'they seize one captive and one woman'; cf. Kümmel, *Ersatzrituale* 112; *KUB* XXI 29 III 43 and 48 *n-an wastulli appanzi* 'they seize him *in delicto*'; *KBo* XVII 74 + *ABoT* 9 I 12 [OHitt.] *ta-z peda-smet appanzi* 'they take their places'; cf. Neu, *Gewitterritual* 11; *KBo* XXV 31 II 12 *ta* ᴀŠᴀʀ-Šᴜɴᴜ *appanzi* 'they take their places'; cf. Neu, *Altheth.* 79; *KUB* XLIII 38 Rs. 25 ᴇɢɪʀ-*an]-ma-ssan* ɴᴀ₄ Šᴜ-*it katta appanzi* 'but afterwards they take the stone down by hand'; cf. Oettinger, *Eide* 20; *KBo* XVII 74 II 39 [OHitt.] *t-us* ʟᴜɢᴀʟ-*i parā appanzi* 'they hold them forth to the king'; *KUB* XV 31 I 33 *nu-za* ᴅɪɴɢɪʀ.ᴍᴇŠ *huuittiyauanzi appanzi* 'they begin attracting the gods'; cf. Haas – Wilhelm, *Riten* 152), *appānzi* (e.g. *KUB* XIII 27+ Rs. 105), *ap-an-zi* (*KBo* XI 32 Rs. 57), 1 sg. pret. act. *e-ip-pu-un* (e.g. *KUB* XIV 15 IV 36 and 44–45 ERÍN.MEŠ *asandulaz eppun* 'I occupied [towns] with garrison troops'; cf. Götze, *AM* 72; *KBo* XII 38 III 7–9 ^{GIŠ}MÁ.HI.A-*ma eppun n-as-kan* ŠÀ A.AB.BA *lukkun* 'I seized the ships and set fire to them at sea'; cf. Otten, *MDOG* 94:20 [1963]; Güterbock, *JNES* 26:76 [1967]; *KUB* XXXVI 108 Vs. 5 [OHitt.]; cf. Otten, *JCS* 5:129 [1951]; VIII 53 II 11 *nu* KASKAL-*an eppun* 'I took [to] the road'; cf. Friedrich, *ZA* 39:12, 46 [1930]; Laroche, *RHA* 26:14 [1968]; cf. KASKAL-*an iyat* s.v. *iya-*, and *itar ... daskizzi* s.v. *itar*; *KBo* XIV 20 II 22 *anda eppun*; cf. Houwink Ten Cate, *JNES* 25:174 [1966]; VI 29 II 10 *nu* ANA ^D*IŠTAR* ... ŠU-*an sarā eppun* 'to Ištar I lifted up my hand'; cf. Götze, *Hattusilis* 48; III 4 I 22 ŠU-*an sarā eppun*; cf. Götze, *AM* 20), *e-ip-pu-u-un* (e.g. III 13 Rs. 14 ŠU-*mit eppūn* 'I seized with my hand'; cf. Güterbock, *ZA* 44:72 [1938]; III 6 II 7 *nu-za* ERÍN.MEŠ *NARĀRU ŠA* KUR-*TI tepauwaza* GAM-*an eppūn* 'I took along auxiliaries of the land in small numbers'; cf. Götze, *Hattusilis* 16; ibid. 12; *KUB* I 8 IV 18 *n-an eppūn* 'I seized him'; cf. Götze, *Hattusilis* 34), *AṢBAT* (e.g. *KBo* III 4 III 89 ^I*Pihhuniyann-a AṢBAT* 'and I seized P.'; cf. Götze, *AM* 94; ibid. II 28 *namma-an* EGIR-*an-pat AṢBAT* 'then I went in pursuit of him' [lit. 'seized him behind']; cf. Götze, *AM* 50), 2 sg. pret. act. *e-ip-ta* (e.g. *KUB* XIV 1 Rs. 23–24 *namma-ma-kan* KUR ^{URU}*Hapālla kuenta-ya* ŪL *epta-ya-at* ŪL ... *n-at-za* ^I*Madduwattas dās* 'but furthermore you did not smite Hapalla, and you did not seize it ..., and M. took it for himself'; cf. Götze, *Madd.* 26), *IṢBAT* (see above sub 2 sg. pres. act. *epti*), 3 sg. pret. act. *e-ip-ta* (frequent, e.g. *KBo* IV 4 II 15 URU-*an epta* 'he occupied the town'; cf. Götze, *AM* 114; II 5 I 16 *n-an hūmandan epta* 'it all he seized'; cf. Götze, *AM* 180; *KUB* I 1 II 53 *nu* ^{URU D}U-*assan epta* 'he picked Dattassas' [as his residence]; cf. Götze, *Hattusilis* 20; XXXIII 84, 6–7 *nu-kan* [...] *teshas epta* 'sleep overcame [him]'; cf. Siegelová, *Appu-Hedammu* 58; XXVIII 5 Vs. 21b *epta-an nahsaraz epta-an weritemas* 'Fear seized her, Fright seized her', matching ibid. 18a [Hattic] *tūpi tauwa sehkuwat*; similarly ibid. 14b and 15a; cf. Puhvel, *American journal of philology* 98:397 [1977] = *Analecta*

Indoeuropaea 380 [1981]; *KBo* VI 29 II 40 *nu-mu* ...] ... ŠU-*an epta* 'took me by the hand'; cf. Götze, *Hattusilis* 50; *KUB* XXII 70 Vs. 8 ᔆᴬᴸ*Ammat*[*tal*]*lass-a-za-kan kuit* DINGIR-*LIM* IGI.HI.A--*wa epta* 'because A. seized the deity's eyes', i.e. pulled the wool over the deity's eyes; similarly ibid. 78; cf. Ünal, *Orakeltext* 56, 78, 105–6; XXIII 13 Vs. 5 *nu-za-kan* LUGAL KUR *Ahhiyauwa* EGIR-*pa epta* 'the king of Ahhiyawa pulled back'; cf. Sommer, *AU* 314, 317; XXIV 8 I 28–29 and 33–34 *ŪL-wa kussanqa katta epta* [*nu*]-*wa kinun katta epta* 'never was there conception, now has there been conception?', lit. 'it [viz. the insemination] took' [cf. Lat. *con-cipere* 'become pregnant, conceive']; cf. Friedrich, *ZA* 49:216 [1950], and Siegelová, *Appu-Hedammu* 6, both with wrong translation ['it clicked'; 'has embraced']), *a-ip-ta* (*KBo* V 6 I 10–11 *nu-kan ABU-YA* ŠÀ ᴴᵁᴿˑᔆᴬᴳ*Kuntiyan aipta* 'my father seized the middle of Mt. K.'; cf. Güterbock, *JCS* 10:90 [1956]), *IṢBAT* (e.g. II 5 III 52–53 *nu* NAM.RA GUD UDU *tuzziyanza IṢBAT* 'the army seized deportees, cattle and sheep'; cf. Götze, *AM* 190; V 8 IV 19 *IŠTU* NAM.RA-*ma-at* GUD UDU *anda IṢBAT* 'along with deportees, cattle and sheep he rounded it up'; cf. Götze, *AM* 162; V 6 IV 15 *nu ŠA* DUMU-*RI kattan IṢBAT* 'he came to grips with the matter of [dispatching] a son'; cf. Güterbock, *JCS* 10:97 [1956]; ibid. I 9 *nu-za pait* ᵁᴿᵁ*Alminan wetummanzi IṢBAT* 'he went and took to fortifying A.'), 3 sg. pret. midd. *appattat* (II 2 II 42 *ŪL arha appattat* 'there was no reception' [viz. of oracle]), 1 pl. pret. act. *e-ip-pu-en* (III 60 III 5–6 [OHitt.] DUMU.MEŠ *ŠIPRI-ŠU ŠA* LUGAL ᵁᴿᵁ*Hala*[*p* ...] *eppuen* 'the messengers of the king of Halpa we seized'; cf. Güterbock, *ZA* 44:106 [1938]), *ap-pu-en* (*KUB* XXXIV 77 Vs. 2), 2 pl. pret. act. *e-ip-tin* (e.g. XII 63 Vs. 10 and 19), 3 pl. pret. act. *e-ip-pí-ir* (*KBo* III 60 III 7–9 AMA-*ŠU ŠA* ᴵ*Zūppa INA* ᵁᴿᵁ*Tirisipa eppir s-an-kan kuenir s-an-ap eter* 'Z.'s mother they seized at T., they killed her, and they ate her'), *e-ip-pir* (e.g. V 13 I 10 *nu* ᴵᴾᴵᔆˑᵀᵁᴿ-*an eppir n-an-mu parā pier* 'they seized Mashuiluwas and handed him over to me'; cf. Friedrich, *Staatsverträge* 1:112; V 8 III 37–39 *nu sāru kuit* NAM.RA GUD UDU *AKŠUD* ᴸᵁˑᴹᴱᔆₓŠU.DIB-*ya kuin eppir n-an INA* ᵁᴿᵁ*Altanna arha dalahhun* 'the booty in deportees, cattle and sheep which I found, and the prisoners whom they had captured, these I left at A.'; cf. Götze, *AM* 158; II 5 + XVI

ep(p)-, ap(p)-

17 III 36 *nu eppirr-a mekki kuennir*[*r*]*-a mekki* 'and they
captured many and slew many'; cf. Götze, *AM* 188; Otten,
MIO 3:173 [1955]; *KUB* I 16 II 64 *ape-ma-an eppir* 'but they
pounced on him'; cf. Sommer, *HAB* 8; XIX 49 I 36 [*n-an
l*]*inkias* DINGIR.MEŠ *eppir* 'the oath-gods seized him'; cf. Friedrich, *Staatsverträge* 2:6; similarly ibid. 15; *KBo* VI 34 III 16–17
n-an linkiantes eppir n-as-san ŠÀ-ŠU *suttati* 'the oath-gods seized
him, and his innards swelled up' [partitive apposition]; cf.
Oettinger, *Eide* 12; *KUB* XXIV 8 III 15 DINGIR.MEŠ NÍG.SI.SÁ-*an*
KASKAL-*an eppir* 'the gods picked the right path [for him]'; cf.
Siegelová, *Appu-Hedammu* 10; XIV 1 Vs. 71 *nu uer anz*[*el*]
ERÍN.MEŠ KASKAL-*an eppir* 'they came [and] blocked the path of
our troops'; cf. Götze, *Madd.* 18; *KBo* III 4 IV 36 *nu* KUR-*eanza
hūmanza* URU.DIDLI.HI.A BÀD EGIR-*pa eppir* 'the whole country
withdrew to the fortress towns'; cf. Götze, *AM* 132; *KUB* I
1 + 1304/u II 77–78 *nu-mu-za alwanzahhuwanzi ... eppir* 'they
took to hexing me'; cf. Götze, *Hattusilis* 22), 3 pl. pret. midd.
appantat (*KBo* II 2 I 21–22 *kūs* MUŠEN *HURRI kallaranni arha
appantat* 'these bird-oracles were received inauspiciously'; *KUB*
XXXIII 106 II 29 ŠU-*za appantat* '[they] took each other by the
hand'; cf. Güterbock, *JCS* 6:22 [1952]; XXXIII 115 III 13
ŠU-*az-ma-at-kan appanta*[*t*; cf. Laroche, *RHA* 26:65 [1968]),
appandat (XXXVI 12+XXXIII 113 I 15–16 *n*]*u-smas-kan ...*
ŠU-*za appandat*; ibid. 22 *nu-smas-kan* ŠU-*az appandat*; XXXIII
92 IV 4 *a*]*ppandat*; cf. Güterbock, *JCS* 6:10–2 [1952]), 2 sg.
imp. act. *e-ip* (e.g. *KBo* V 9 III 31 *n-an ep* 'seize him!'; cf.
Friedrich, *Staatsverträge* 1:22; *KUB* XIV 1 Vs. 38 *antuhsann-a-
-wa ep* 'seize the man!'; ibid. 40 LÚ *TEMI ep* 'seize the messenger!'; cf. Götze, *Madd.* 10; *KUB* XXIV 9 II 36 + *KBo* XII 127 II
3 *kī idalu zik ep* 'this evil seize thou!'; cf. Jakob-Rost, *Ritual der
Malli* 36; *KUB* XIX 49 I 53–54 *nu* NAM.RA.MEŠ *hūmandan anda
ep n-as-m*[*u par*]*ā pāi* 'arrest all the deportees and hand them
over to me!'; similarly ibid. 57–58; cf. Friedrich, *Staatsverträge*
2:8–10; XXIX 4 III 29 *nu-za eni-pat pedan ep* 'occupy that very
place!'; cf. Kronasser, *Umsiedelung* 24; XXXVI 75 III 12), 3 sg.
imp. act. *e-ip-du* (e.g. XIII 5 II 5 *nu-wa-za-kan apel* É-*ir kattan
sarā epdu* 'may he turn his house upside down!'; cf. Sturtevant,
JAOS 54:370 [1934]; *VBoT* 132 III 11; cf. Haas – Thiel, *Rituale*

278

282; *KUB* XII 22 Vs. 3; *KBo* XI 10 III 21), *e-ip-tu* (*KUB* VIII 81 II 12; cf. Götze, *ZA* 36:11 [1925]), 2 pl. imp. act. *e-ip-tin* (e.g. XIV 15 Vs. 14 *nu-war-as eptin* 'seize them!'; cf. Götze, *AM* 34; XI 1 IV 23–24 [OHitt.] *sumēs-an hassannanza eptin* 'take him out of the family!'; dupl. *KBo* III 67 IV 12 *hassannaz eptin*; III 38 Vs. 28 *nu kurur eptin* 'take to hostilities!'; cf. Otten, *Altheth. Erzählung* 8; *KUB* XIV 1 Vs. 70 *nu-wa-smas* KASKAL-*an piran eptin* 'block their path!'; cf. Götze, *Madd.* 18; XXXIII 88 Rs. 13; cf. Siegelová, *Appu-Hedammu* 54), 3 pl. imp. act. *appandu* (e.g. *KBo* VI 34 III 20–21 *n-an ke* NIŠ DINGIR.MEŠ *appandu n-as-san* ŠÀ-ŠU *suttaru* 'let these oaths seize him, and let his innards swell up!'), *appāndu* (e.g. III 1 II 39 [OHitt.] *nu-ssi-ssan* ^{LÚ}*antiyantan appāndu* 'let them pick an in-house husband for her'), *appantu* (*KUB* XXXVI 106 Vs. 10 NIŠ DINGIR.MEŠ *appantu*; cf. Otten, *ZA* 52:217 [1957]); partic. *appant-*, also nominalized ^{LÚ}*appant-* 'captive, prisoner' (^{LÚ}ŠU.DIB[.BI], ^{LÚ}ZABDU), nom. sg. c. *appanza* (e.g. XXI 1 III 68 'captured'; cf. Friedrich, *Staatsverträge* 2:76; *KBo* IV 4 II 75 *nu-wa kunanzass-a mekki* ^{LÚ}*appanzass-a-wa m[ekki* 'many a one [was] killed, and many a one [was made] prisoner'; cf. Götze, *AM* 122; *KUB* XIX 37 II 22 *sipanduuanzi anda appanza* 'included for sacrificing'; cf. Götze, *AM* 168), *appānza* (e.g. *KBo* XVI 27 IV 9 ^{LÚ}*appānza*, besides ibid. 25 ^{LÚ}*appanza*; cf. von Schuler, *Die Kaškäer* 138; *KUB* XII 1 III 41 *anda appā[nza* 'inclusive, elaborate, outfitted with accessories' [garments], vs. ibid. 40 *pittalwanza* 'plain, basic') acc. sg. c. *appantan* (e.g. XIV 11 II 25–29 *nu* ^{LÚ.MEŠ}*appan[tan] kuin eppir ... nu-kan* INA ŠÀ ^{LÚ.MEŠ} ZABDUTI *hinkan kisat* 'the prisoner[s] whom they captured ..., among the prisoners plague broke out'; dupl. XIV 8 Vs. 28 *nu-kan* INA ŠÀ-*BI* ^{LÚ.MEŠ}ŠU.DIB.BI.HI.A; cf. Götze, *KlF* 210), nom.-acc. sg. neut. *appan* (e.g. XXII 70 Rs. 53 ^{UZU}ŠÀ *appan* = ibid. Vs. 30 ^{UZU}ŠÀ DIB-*an* 'the heart [is] seized, there [is] heart-seizure'; cf. ŠÀ.DIB.BA, Akk. *ṣibit libbi* 'heart-seizure', i.e. offense, outrage; cf. Ünal, *Orakeltext* 94, 62; XIII 33 II 8 *nu-w]ar-at anda* ŪL SIG₅-*in appan ēsta* 'it was not well inlaid'; cf. Werner, *Gerichtsprotokolle* 34), *appān* (e.g. XII 1 III 25 GUŠKIN ^{NA₄}NUNUZ *anda appān* '[of] gold, [with] inset gemstone'; cf. S. Košak, *Ling.* 18:100, 108 [1978]), dat.-loc. sg. *appanti* (*KBo* III 4 IV 20 *appanti kunanti-ya*

'to the captured and killed'; cf. Götze, *AM* 122), nom. pl. c.
appantes (e.g. VI 3 II 31 [= *Code* 1:38] *takku* LÚ.ULÙ.LU.MEŠ
[*h*]*annesni appantes* 'if persons [have been] arrested for trial';
dupl. VI 2 II 13 *appā*[*ntes*; XXVI 82 Vs. 10 *anda appantes asandu*
'let them be included'; cf. Siegelová, *Appu-Hedammu* 70; *KUB*
XV 31 I 8–9 *antuhsas* NÍ.TE.MEŠ-*ass-a anda appantes* 'and human
body parts inclusive'; cf. Haas – Wilhelm, *Riten* 148), nom.-acc.
pl. neut. *appanta* (*KBo* IV 2 IV 39 *ke* TÚG.NÍG.LÁM.MEŠ *anda*
appanta 'these elaborate raiments'; cf. Götze – Pedersen, *MS* 10;
wrongly taken adverbially by e.g. Kronasser, *Etym.* 1:355),
appanda (e.g. VI 14 I 15 [= *Code* 2:22] *takku anda appanda*
GIŠMAR.GÍD.ID *kuiski tāyez*[*zi* 'if anyone steals "inclusive" wag-
ons' [i.e. complete with harnessing]); verbal noun *appatar* (n.),
nom.-acc. sg. *appatar* (I 42 II 35 = Akk. *ṣapādu*, i.e. *ṣabātu*; cf.
Güterbock, *MSL* 13:136 [1971]; I 45 Vs. 11 = Akk. *ṣabadu*; cf.
MSL 3:59 [1955]; I 45 Rs. 4 *kurur appatar* = Akk. *zārum*
'[inception of] hostility'; cf. *MSL* 3:53 [1955]; III 34 II 29 GIŠKU
appatar 'resort[ing] to arms'; *KUB* XXXVII 190 Rs. 6 *irmananza*
appatar-set 'seizure by illness' [hendiadys]; cf. ibid. Vs. 6 [Akk.]
ṣibit 'seizure'; XXIV 5 + IX 13 Vs. 5 *nu-za* UGU *appatar* DÙ-*zi*
'[the king] does lifting' [ritual act]; similarly ibid. 26 and 28; cf.
M. Vieyra, *RHR* 119:126–8 [1939]; Kümmel, *Ersatzrituale*
8–10, 14–5), *appātar* (*KBo* XV 25 Vs. 11 and 24 GÚ-*tar sarā*
appātarr-a 'and neck-lift [i.e. self-assurance; hendiadys]; cf.
Carruba, *Beschwörungsritual* 2, 19; H. C. Melchert, *JCS*
31:58–9 [1979]), gen. sg. *appannas* (e.g. *KUB* XLV 28 Vs. 2
DINGIR.MEŠ UZUGEŠTUG-*as appannas* SISKUR 'ritual of capturing
the ear of deities'; II 1 II 26 ŠU-*an appannas* 'of handclasping';
ibid. IV 12 *sar*]*ā appannas* 'of lift'; cf. A. Archi, *SMEA* 16:109,
111, 95 [1975]; XII 58 I 32–33 *namma* 1 UDU GE₆ *dāi n-an-si-san*
ser epzi nu SALŠU.GI *ser appannas hukmain hukzi* 'then she takes
one black sheep and lifts it to him, and the old woman recites
the spell of lifting'; cf. Goetze, *Tunnawi* 10; *KBo* V 8 II 24
URU.BÀD EGIR-*pa appannas* AŠRU NU.GÁL *kuiski* 'a fortress city,
a place of withdrawal, there was none'; cf. Götze, *AM* 152),
DIB-*annas* (*KUB* XLIV 16 IV 17 EGIR-*pa* DIB-*annas* '[god A.]
"di rifugio"'; wrongly A. Archi, *SMEA* 16:95, 112 [1975]); inf.
e-ip-pu-u-wa-an-zi (*KBo* III 3 III 29–33 *mān* DINU-*ma kuitki*

salleszi n-at arha eppūwanzi ŪL tarahteni ... n-at ^DUTU-*ŠI arha epzi* 'if some legal matter gets big and you are not able to dispose of it ..., my majesty will dispose of it'), *appanna* (e.g. III 21 II 5 *appanna kisri-tti dais* '[he] placed in your hand for taking'; *KUB* XVII 18 III 19; XII 62 Rs. 3), *appānna* (ibid. 5; XXXV 43 II 19; cf. *Dict. louv.* 148); iter. *appeski-, appiski-,* 1 sg. pres. act. *appiskimi* (*KBo* XVII 61 Rs. 10), 3 sg. pres. act. *appeskizzi* (e.g. *KUB* XLI 1 III 15 *n-at-si-pa anda appeskiz*[*zi* 'she holds it within for him'; cf. Jakob-Rost, *Ritual der Malli* 42–3; XXIV 13 II 14–16 *n-an-zan namma ser katta* SAG.DU-*az epzi n-an-si-pa namma* ^{UZU}ÚR ^{UZU}ÚR *anda appeskizzi n-an arha ānsiskizzi* 'then she grabs him from top to bottom, starting with the head, and then she wraps him around limb for limb and wipes him off thoroughly'; cf. Haas – Thiel, *Rituale* 106), *appiskizzi* (e.g. dupl. *KBo* XXIII 23 Vs. 77; cf. Haas – Thiel, *Rituale* 212; XXI 20 I 16 *mān* UKÙ-*an* ^DDÌM.NUN.ME *appiskizzi* 'if [the demoness] D. possesses a man'; cf. Burde, *Medizinische Texte* 42; similarly *KUB* XLIII 55 III 10–11; XXXIII 84 IV 12; cf. Siegelová, *Appu-Hedammu* 60; IX 34 III 27 *anda appiskizzi*; X 11 VI 5–6 *nu* UDU.HI.A-*as ēshani kattan appiskizzi* 'he occupies himself with the blood of the sheep'; XX 90 IV 9 *parā appiskizzi*), 3 pl. pres. act. *appeskanzi* (XIX 37 IV 7; cf. Götze, *AM* 178), *appiskanzi* (*Bo* 3752 II 17; cf. Neu, *Altheth.* 179), 3 sg. pret. act. *appeskit* (e.g. *VBoT* 132 II 7; cf. Haas – Thiel, *Rituale* 280), *appiskit* (*KUB* XXIX 7 Vs. 29 *parā appiskit*; cf. Lebrun, *Samuha* 119; *KBo* IV 14 III 25–26 *ŠA* SAL-*ya-mu-kan kuit* GIG *parā appiskit* 'and whereas woman's sickness afflicted me'; cf. R. Stefanini, *ANLR* 20:45 [1965]), 3 pl. pret. act. *appiskir* (*KUB* XXII 70 Vs. 32 *ANA* IR-*ma-kan anda ŪL appiskir* 'they have not included [it] in the request'; cf. Ünal, *Orakeltext* 62); supine in *KBo* XII 58 + XIII 162 Vs. 3 EZE]N-*an arha appeskiuwan tehhun* 'I began doing away with the festival'.

ep(p)- is semantically akin to *da-* 'take' and *har(k)-* 'have, hold' but has stronger nuances of seizing and grabbing. Hittitology has with touching unanimity ab ovo (H. Holma, *Journal de la Société finno-ougrienne* 33.1:43 [1916]; Hrozný, *SH* 75, 170) connected *ep(p)-* with Skt. *āpnóti,* Avest. *apayeiti* 'attain, obtain', Lat. *apīscor* 'attain', *co-ēpī* 'began' (*IEW*

50–1), and thus an etymological basis of *ēp-: *E_1p- has become standard for ep(p)-: ap(p)- (e.g. Oettinger, *Stammbildung* 88). In reality these connections are a house of cards: even apart from such dubious items as Gk. ἄπτω 'attach, touch', the rest hardly bears scrutiny. Indo-Iranian āp- has a base-meaning 'reach', not 'seize', and is best kept aside. Lat. *apīscor* (perfect *aptus*) is cognate with *apere* 'comprehendere vinculo', *aptus* 'joined, fit(ted)', *cōpula* (< *co-apula*) 'bond', and thus contains an original notion of 'attachment' rather than 'reaching'; *co-ēpī* may also well mean literally 'I have taken hold' and be to *apere* what *ēgī* is to *agere*. The semantic similarity between Skt. *āptá-* 'skilled' and Lat. *aptus* 'fit' is thus fortuitous, due to a convergence of secondary meanings of 'attainment' and 'application' respectively. Now the IE *A_1ep- underlying Lat. *apere* is firmly attested by Hitt. *hap(p)-* 'join, attach' (q.v.; also impersonal and mediopassive 'arrange itself, succeed', e.g. *KBo* XI 34 I 4–5 *takku-smas* ŪL-*ma hapzi* 'but if it does not click for them'); thus -*za ep(p)-* is a semantic match for both Lat. *in-cipiō* and *co-ēpī* but an etymological cognate of neither. All this means that Hitt. *ep(p)-: ap(p)-* is most probably simply from an IE *ep- 'seize, grab' (cf. *es-, *ed-), and so far no credible cognate has been found; curiously there are no visible extra-Hittite Anatolian attestations either.

Cf. *appala-, appat(a)riya-*.

epurai-   'besiege, dam up', 3 sg. pres. act. *epuraizzi* (*KUB* XXXVI 89 Rs. 41 ÍD-*as arsanuwa le epuraizzi* 'let him not dam up the courses of the river'; cf. Haas, *Nerik* 154); inf. *epurawanzi* (*KBo* XVIII 54 Rs. 18–19 *nu mān* BÀD *kuwapi arha* ŪL *pippanzi epurawanzi-ma-kan* ŪL *hapdari* 'if they never overthrow the fortress, and besieging it does not succeed'); verbal noun *epuressar* (ibid. 25); iter. *epureski-*, 1 pl. pres. act. ibid. 13–17 *mahhan epuresgawen nu-nnas-kan epurawanzi* ŪL *hapdat nu-kan* BÀD [GIM]-*an kattan arha haddanneskiwen n-at* ŪL ZAG- -*nahhuwen* 'whenever we besieged, our siege did not succeed; and whenever we tried to demolish the fortress completely, we did not manage it'. Cf. Neu, *Interpretation* 45–6.

Puhvel (*IF* 81:60–6 [1976] = *Analecta Indoeuropaea* 293–9 [1981]) assumed denominative derivation from an **epura*- comparable to Gk. Ἐφύρη (old name of Corinth and other towns; *Odyssey* 1:259 with Scholia) and *ἔφυρια > *ἔφῦρα 'securement, fortification, siege, dam, dyke', seen in the Homeric line-end formula πολέμοιο γέφυραι 'siege-works', originally *γ'ἔφυραι with particle γε, hence commingled with and yielding Ionic gammatic initial of γέφῦρα < *γʷέφυρια (Doric δέφυρα, Aeolic βέφυρα) 'dam, dyke, causeway, bridge' (an international 'culture word' seen also in Armen. *kamurj*, Turkic *köpür* 'bridge'). Similarly *ἐφυράω 'dam up' (= Hitt. *epurai-*) has lost out to the denominative verb γεφῦρόω (*Iliad* 21:245, where a fallen elm dams up the river). The Greek-Hittite accordance *epura(i)-* : *ἐφυρ(ι)α- may point formally to an IE *(E₁)ebh-ur-*, but may also originate in the 'culture word' orbit.

H. Eichner's denominative derivation from an **epur-*, verbal noun of *epp-* 'seize' (*MSS* 31:79 [1973], echoed by Oettinger, *Stammbildung* 88, 367), has a problematic *-p-* and is incorrect semantically.

Cf. *istap(p)-*.

erhui-, irhui- (n.) 'basket' (MA.SÁ.AB), nom.-acc. sg. ᴳᴵˢ*e-ir-hu-u-i* (*KBo* XXI 37 Vs. 4), ᴳᴵˢ*e-ir-hu-i* (XX 4 IV 5), ᴳᴵˢ*irhui* (*KUB* XV 31 I 3–5 and 10; cf. Haas – Wilhelm, *Riten* 148–50), gen. sg. ᴳᴵˢ*irhuiyas* (XXV 42 III 9) ᴳᴵˢ*ir-hu-u-i-ya-as* (XXXII 128 I 3; cf. A. M. Dinçol, *RHA* 27:27 [1969]), dat.-loc. sg. ᴳᴵˢ*irhuiti* (XII 12 I 22, IV 9, V 1; XXXII 128 II 29; *KBo* XXI 34 II 55 and 64, III 38, IV 8), *ir-hu-u-i-ti* (e.g. ibid. II 33 ᴳᴵˢ*INBI.HI.A-ya-kan* ᴳᴵˢ*irhu-uiti kattan ishūwanzi* 'and fruits they pour down into the basket'; cf. Lebrun, *Hethitica II* 120; cf. V 1 II 34–35 *ser-ma--ssan* 7 ᴳᴵˢMA.SÁ.AB *kitta nu-ssan* ᴳᴵˢ*INBI.HI.A ishūwan* 'but seven baskets are placed thereon, and fruits are poured'; cf. Sommer – Ehelolf, *Pāpanikri* 6*-8*; *KUB* XXXII 54, 11), ᴳᴵˢ*ir-⟨hu--⟩u-i-ti* (XXXVIII 25 I 16 and 21; cf. Haas, *Nerik* 276), instr. sg. *erhuit* (*KBo* XVII 15 Rs. 14 *mēmal* ᴳᴵˢ*erhuit* 'groats by basket'; cf. dupl. XVII 40 IV 8 *mema]l* ᴳᴵˢMA.SÁ.AB-*it har[zi* 'he has groats by basket'; cf. V. Haas – M. Wäfler, *Ugarit-*

erhui-, irhui-   eripi-, irimpi-, irippi-

Forschungen 8:82, 88 [1976]; Neu, *Altheth.* 73), abl. sg. *erhuyaz*
(*KUB* XXXIV 69 + 70 I 10 ^{GIŠ}*erhuyaz harkanzi* 'they have by
basket'), ^{GIŠ}*ir-hu-u-i-ya-az* (XXXII 128 II 8 and 13;*KBo* XXIV
13 IV 12), nom.-acc. pl. (?) ^{GIŠ}*irhuit*[*a* (XVII 65 Rs. 63). Cf.
Friedrich, *RHA* 8:14 (1947); Otten, *ZA* 51:126–7 (1955).

   irhu(i)talla- (c.) '(female) basketeer, basket-bearer' (cf. Gk.
καλαθηφόρος), nom. pl. SAL ^{GIŠ}*irhutalles* (*KUB* XXV 49 II 21),
SAL.MEŠ ^{GIŠ}*irhuidallis-a* (ibid. 22). For denom. suffix see
Kronasser, *Etym.* 1:176.

   Hurrian origin has been suggested because of dat.-loc. *-ti*
and occurrence in Hurroid rituals. Yet *erhui-* is the standard
term for 'basket' for fruits and groats (as opposed to ^{GI}*pattar*
or ^{GIŠ}*paddur* [q.v.] which are more of a dish or bucket for bread
and even liquids) and is hence plausibly native (grammatical
foreignism in a special type of text does not automatically
make a Hittite vocable foreign). Cf. *erhui-*, *irhui-* 'basket' with
arha-, *irha(tt)-* 'line, rim, row, circuit' (q.v.), with reference to
the similar relationship of Gk. κάλαθος 'basket' (for fruits,
flowers, wool, etc.) to Hitt. *kaluti-* 'circle', originally 'spun line'
(q.v.). The vocalism of *erhui-* may show an intermediate stage
of the change *a > i*, seen in *arha- > irha-*; the derivation seems
to be that of a secondary *-i-* stem imposed on a *-u-* stem base
(IE *$r̥H_1ú$-?); cf. e.g. *parkui-* 'clean' (IE *$bhr̥E_1k̂ú$- or
*$bhr̥E_1ĝú$-) Cf. Puhvel, *AJPh* 98:150–2 (1977) = *Analecta Indoeuropaea* 353–5 (1981).

eripi- (c.), **irimpi-, irippi-**   (n.) 'cedar(wood)' (^{GIŠ}ERIN[-*pi*]), nom. sg.
c. ^{GIŠ}*eripis* (*KUB* X 92 I 7 and 11 1 ^{GIŠ}*eripis-a* 'and one piece of
cedar'), nom.-acc. sg. or pl. neut. ^{GIŠ}*irimpi* (*KBo* V 1 II 14 2
^{GIŠ}*irimpi*, ibid. 20 and 21 1 ^{GIŠ}*irimpi*; cf. Sommer – Ehelolf,
Pāpanikri 6*), ^{GIŠ}ERIN-*pi* (*KUB* XXXIII 98 II 9 [with dupl.
XXXIII 102 II 11] ^{GIŠ}ERIN-*pi karū duwarnan* 'cedarwood [has]
long been broken'; cf. Güterbock, *JCS* 5:148 [1951]), nom.-acc.
pl. neut. (Hurroid) ^{GIŠ}*irippida* (*ABoT* 17 II 5 and 16, matching
^{GIŠ}ERIN in the almost verbatim parallel *KUB* IX 22 II 22; here,
as in *KUB* X 92 I and *KBo* V 1 II [above], cedarwood is tied
with colored wool; cf. Laroche, *RHA* 9:18–9 [1948–9]).

Borrowed hurrianized derivative with suffix *-pi-* (cf. Kronasser, *Etym.* 1:224–5, 244) of Akk. *erinnu* < Sum. *erin* 'cedar' (cf. Laroche, *Recherches* 94).

es-, as-   'be' (NU.GÁL 'is not, does not exist', pret. NU.GÁL *ēsta*; *KBo* III 67 I 4 [OHitt.] *e-se-ir* = *KUB* III 85, 4 [Akk.] *ip-pa-šu-ú* [*bašū* 'be']; *KBo* I 53, 7 *e-es-zi* = Akk. [*i*]-*šu* [*išū* 'be; have']; cf. *MSL* 3:87 [1955]), *appa(n) es-* 'be behind, back up, support' (cf. *appan tiya-, appan huwai-*), 1 sg. pres. act. *e-es-mi* (*VBoT* 58 IV 3 *ūgg-a* ᔆᴬᴸ*Annannas ēsmi* 'I am A.'; cf. Laroche, *RHA* 23:85 [1965]; *KBo* III 55 Rs. 11 ᵁᴿᵁ*Hattusi ēsmi* 'I am at Hattusas'; *KUB* XXXVI 35 I 12–13 *appan-wa-mu-za-kan ēs* [*namma-wa--ddu-za*] *tuk* EGIR-*pa ēsmi* 'get behind me, and I shall back you all the way'; cf. s.v. *halanza-* and see Laroche, *RHA* 26:26 [1968]), 2 sg. pres. act. *e-es-si* (*VBoT* 124 Vs. 8 and 13; cf. Neu, *Altheth.* 189; *KUB* VIII 41 I 16 *nepisi* [*ē*]*ssi* 'thou art in heaven'; ibid. 9 *nepisi ēs*[*si*; cf. Laroche, *JCS* 1:190–1 [1947]; XXXI 143 II 15 *nepisi ēs*[*si*; cf. Neu, *Altheth.* 184–6), 3 sg. pres. act. *e-es-ti* (XXXVI 98c, 5 [OHitt.] LUGAL-*us ēsti*), *e-es-zi* (profuse, e.g. XXIV 8 I 8–9 ᵁᴿᵁ*Lulluwayas-san* KUR-*e aruni* ZAG-*si ēszi* 'the country L. is on the sea-shore' [partitive apposition, lit. 'at the sea, its shore'; cf. XLIV 56 Rs. 7 *aruni irhe-sse*]; cf. Siegelová, *Appu-Hedammu* 4; *KBo* XVII 74 II 29 [OHitt.] *karū ēszi* 'it is early'; cf. Neu, *Gewitterritual* 20, 40; VI 3 IV 53 [= *Code* 1:98] LÚ.ULÙ.LU-*ku* GUD-*ku* UDU-*ku ēszi* 'whether it is a man or an ox or a sheep'; dupl. VI 2 IV 54 *ēsza* [sic]; cf. Friedrich, *Heth. Ges.* 103; Kronasser, *Etym.* 1:389; *KUB* I 16 II 54 [OHitt.] *takku--wa-at ēszi takku-wa-at* NU.GÁL 'whether it is [so] or it is not'; cf. Sommer, *HAB* 8; V 1 IV 81 *ŪL ēszi* 'does not exist'; cf. Ünal, *Hatt.* 2:90; *KBo* IV 3 IV 42 *nu-ssi mān* DUMU-*ŠU ēszi* 'if she has a son'; cf. Friedrich, *Staatsverträge* 1:146; XII 126 I 27 *nu-ssi* ᴳᴵᔆBAN-*ŠU ēszi* 'he has his bow'; cf. Jakob-Rost, *Ritual der Malli* 24), 1 pl. pres. act. *e-su-wa-ni* (XLIV 60 II 1; cf. *ekuwani, eduwāni* beside *ekueni, edue*[*ni*]), 3 pl. pres. act. *a-sa-an-zi* (frequent, e.g. XXI 1 III 45 *kue* ZAG.HI.A ŠA KUR ᵁᴿᵁ*Hatti asanzi* 'which are the boundaries of Hatti'; cf. Friedrich, *Staatsverträge* 2:72), 1 sg. pret. act. *e-su-un* (e.g. XIV 16 II 11

kuitman-m]a-za INA ^{URU}*Palhuissa esun* 'but as long as I was in
P.'; cf. Götze, *AM* 42; XIX 29 I 10 *amm]uk-ma-za nūwa*
DUMU-*as esun* 'I was still a child'; cf. Götze, *AM* 16; *KBo* IV 4 I
34 *pānza esun* 'I had gone'; cf. Götze, *AM* 110), *e-sú-un* (*KUB*
XXIII 86, 9; XXVI 32 I 10), 2 sg. pret. act. *e-es-ta* (*KBo* V 13 I
19 *kuit* DUMU-*ŠU ēsta* 'because you were his son'; cf. Friedrich,
Staatsverträge 1:114), 3 sg. pret. act. *e-es-ta* (frequent, e.g. III 4
II 32 *n-as-kan apiya anda ēsta* 'he was in there'; cf. Götze, *AM*
50; *KUB* XL 1 Rs. 19 *karū ēsta* 'it was early'; *KBo* V 3 III 53
^I*Mariyas kuis ēsta* 'who was M.?'; cf. Friedrich, *Staatsverträge*
2:128; III 4 I 10 ABU-*ŠU-wa-ssi kuis* LUGAL KUR *Hatti ēsta*
nu-war-as UR.SAG-*is* LUGAL-*us ēsta* 'his father who was king of
Hatti, he was a hero-king'; cf. Götze, *AM* 16; *KUB* I 1 I 51 *ŪL*
ēsta 'was [it] not [so]?', i.e. 'didn't you?'; cf. Götze, *Hattusilis*
10; XXX 10 Vs. 22 *māmman dandukisnas-a* DUMU-*as uktūri*
huiswanza ēsta 'if mortal man were to be living forever', vs.
ibid. 21 *dandukisnas-a* DUMU-*as uktūri natta huiswanza* 'mortal
man [is] not living forever'; *KBo* III 4 III 19–20 *nu-mu* NAM.RA
kuin parā piyer n-as 4 *LIM* NAM.RA *ēsta* 'the deportees whom
they handed over to me, that was four thousand deportees'; cf.
Götze, *AM* 70; V 8 II 24–25 NU.GÁL *kuiski ēsta* 'there was no
one'; cf. Götze, *AM* 152–4; III 4 II 43–44 and III 35 *nu-ssan*
kappūwauwar NU.GÁL *ēsta* 'there was no counting'; ibid. III 54
nu-kan kappūwauwar NU.GÁL *ēsta*; cf. Götze, *AM* 56, 76, 80; IV
4 III 23 *nu-za* MU.KAM-*za ser tēpawessanza ēsta* 'the year had
been getting short'; cf. Götze, *AM* 124; *KUB* XIV 16 I 21 *ŪL*
arān ēsta 'had not risen'; cf. Götze, *AM* 28; XXIII 1 I 14
tarahha[n] ēsta 'had been conquered'; cf. Kühne – Otten,
Šaušgamuwa 6; I 8 IV 34 [emended from *KBo* III 6 IV 15–16]
nahhūwa]s-ma-mu kuis LUGAL-*us ēsta n-as-mu-kan nahta* 'whatever king owed me deference [lit. was of deference to me], he
deferred to me'; cf. Götze, *Hattusilis* 36; VI 29 I 15 *nu-mu* É-*ir*
kuit ēsta 'what house I had'; cf. Götze, *Hattusilis* 46; *KUB* I 1 I
70 *kanissūwar-wa-mu ŠA* ^DIŠTAR-*pat* GAŠAN-*YA ēsta* 'I had my
lady Ištar's favor'; *KBo* IV 12 Vs. 31–32 *ammug* [...] [...] ...
ŠÀ-*ta ēsta* 'I had at heart'; cf. Götze, *Hattusilis* 42), 1 pl. pret.
act. *e-su-en* (*KUB* XXIII 1 I 31–32 *āssiyannas-wa-nnas* ÌR.MEŠ
esuen kinun-ma-wa-tu-za ŪL ÌR.MEŠ 'of our own accord we have

been subjects; but now we [are] your subjects no more'; cf. Kühne – Otten, *Šaušgamuwa* 6), *e-su-u-en* (XIV 3 IV 7–9 LUGAL KUR *Hatti-wa-nnas-kan ūk ... kurur esuwen* 'the king of Hatti [and] I were enemies'; cf. Sommer, *AU* 16; XXXI 47 Vs. 9), 2 pl. pret. act. *e-es-te-en* (e.g. XV 34 IV 12 *hui]ttiyantes ēsten* 'you have been drawn'; cf. Haas – Wilhelm, *Riten* 202), 3 pl. pret. act. *e-se-ir* (e.g. *KBo* V 8 II 16–17 *namma-ya kuyēs* URU.DIDLI.HI.A BÁD *wedantes eser* 'and further what fortress cities had been built'; cf. Götze, *AM* 152; III 6 II 24–25 URU.DIDLI.HI.A-*ma kuyēs ŠA* KUR ^{URU}*Hatti istappantes eser* 'the towns of Hatti which had been blockaded'; cf. Götze, *Hattusilis* 18; III 1 I 19 [OHitt.] *tittiyantes eser* 'had been placed'), *e-sir* (e.g. ibid. 11 *tittiyantes esir*; *KUB* XIX 37 III 45–46 *kuyēs* EGIR-*an esir n-as arha dalahhun n-at esir-pat* 'those who were [left] behind, I left them alone, and they stayed right [there]'; cf. Götze, *AM* 176; *KBo* III 4 II 51 *n-as-kan aruni anda ēsta* DUMU.MEŠ-*ŠUNU-ya-ssi kattan esir* 'he was on the island, and his sons were with him'; cf. Götze, *AM* 60), *e-es-sir* (sic *KUB* XXIV 3 II 39 *n-at* ^{LÚ.MEŠ}SIPAD ŠAH *Ù* ^{LÚ.MEŠ}*E-PIŠ* GAD *ēssir* 'they were swineherds and linen-makers', besides dupl. XXIV 4 Vs. 26]*e-se-ir Ù* ^{LÚ.MEŠ}*E-PÍ-IŠ* GAD.HI.A *e-se-ir*; cf. Gurney, *Hittite Prayers* 28–9), *is-sir* (XXXIV 53 Rs. 11), 1 sg. imp. act. *a-sa-al-lu* (*KBo* IV 14 I 43; cf. R. Stefanini, *ANLR* 20:48 [1965]), *e-es-lu-ut* (e.g. *KUB* VII 2 II 23; VIII 53 II 23 *ammuk-ma-ddu-za* ÌR-*is ēslut* 'let me be your slave!'; cf. Laroche, *RHA* 26:15 [1968]), *e-es-li-it* (e.g. *KBo* V 3 IV 32–33 *nu-za* ^DUTU-*ŠI apez linkiyaz ... parkuis ēslit* 'and I, my majesty, shall be free of that oath'; cf. Friedrich, *Staatsverträge* 2:134; *KUB* XXI 47 + XXIII 82, 16; XXVI 35, 6 *zi]k attas-mis ēs ug-a* DUMU-*as-tis ēslit* 'be thou my father, and let me be thy son'), 2 sg. imp. act. *e-es* (e.g. XXIII 1 III 22 *zik-za* LUGAL ^{URU}KÙ..BABBAR-*ti ēs* 'be thou king of Hatti!'; cf. Kühne – Otten, *Šaušgamuwa* 12; *KBo* V 4 Rs. 7 *zik-ma-mu-za kūrur ēs* 'thou shalt be my enemy'; cf. Friedrich, *Staatsverträge* 1:60; XV 1 I 18–19 *nu-wa-kan ... galangaza ēs* 'be soothed!'; ibid. 37 *galanganza ēs*; cf. Kümmel, *Ersatzrituale* 112–4; *KUB* XXIV 2 I 13 *nu-ssan parā kalānkanza ēs*; cf. Gurney, *Hittite Prayers* 16), 3 sg. imp. act. *e-es-tu* (e.g. *VBoT* 1, 7 *duqq-a katta hūman* SIG₅-*in*

ēstu 'and may all be well with you'; cf. L. Rost, *MIO* 4:334
[1956]; *KBo* III 28 II 14 *n-as* É-*i-ssi-pat ēstu* 'let him stay at
home!'; cf. Laroche, *Festschrift H. Otten* 187 [1973]; XV 10 II 27
n-at arha tuhsan ēstu 'let it be cut off', cf. Szabó, *Entsühnungsritual* 24), *e-es-du* (e.g. VI 34 I 39–40, II 4 and 29–30 *apāt ēsdu* 'let
that be, be it so, amen'; cf. Oettinger, *Eide* 8–10; *KUB* XXIV 8
III 16 NÍG.SI.SÁ-*an* ŠUM-*an ēsdu* 'let [his] name be Righteous!'; cf.
Siegelová, *Appu-Hedammu* 10; XIX 49 I 64 *nu-tta apāt* KUR-*e
ēsdu* 'that shall be your land'; cf. Friedrich, *Staatsverträge* 2:10;
S. Heinhold-Krahmer, *Arzawa* 292 [1977]; *KBo* XII 126 I 29
[ANA A]NŠU.KUR.RA.MEŠ *imiūl ēsdu* 'let horses have a [food] mix';
cf. Jakob-Rost, *Ritual der Malli* 24), 2 pl. imp. act. *e-es-te-en*
(e.g. *KUB* I 16 II 41; cf. Sommer, *HAB* 7; *KBo* XV 10 I 32
galankantes ēste[*n* 'be soothed!'; ibid. II 44 *galankantes* [*ēs*]*ten*;
cf. Szabó, *Entsühnungsritual* 16, 26), *e-es-tin* (e.g. V 4 Rs. 9
1-*NUTUM-ya-smas ēstin* 'be a oneness unto yourselves' [i.e. be
united]; cf. Friedrich, *Staatsverträge* 1:60; *KUB* XIV 1 Rs. 40
ammel-wa-z ēstin 'be mine!'; cf. Götze, *Madd.* 28; I 16 III 50
nahhantes ēstin 'be deferential!'; cf. Sommer, *HAB* 14), 3 pl. imp.
act. *a-sa-an-tu* (e.g. *KBo* XVII 1 III 6–7 ᴰUTU-*us* ᴰIM-*as mān
uktūres* LUGAL-*us* SAL.LUGAL-*ass-a* QATAMMA *uktūres asantu* 'as
the sun-god [and] the storm-god [are] everlasting, may king and
queen likewise be everlasting!'; cf. Otten – Souček, *Altheth.
Ritual* 30; *KUB* XXXVI 106 Rs. 10 [OHitt.]; cf. Otten, *ZA*
52:218 [1957]), *a-sa-an-du* (e.g. *KBo* XV 1 II 6 QATAMMA *uktūres
asandu*; cf. Szabó, *Entsühnungsritual* 20; V 13 I 27–28 ZAG.HI.A-
-*as-ma ... mahhan esir kinun-aya-at tuk* QATAMMA *asandu* 'as the
borders were ..., now too they shall be likewise for you'; cf.
Friedrich, *Staatsverträge* 1:116; *KUB* XIV 1 Vs. 21 *nu-wa-za
am*[*mel*] ÌR-*TUM ēs* ERÍN.MEŠ.HI.A-*KA-ya-wa ammel* ERÍN.MEŠ.HI.A
asandu 'be my servant, and let your troops be my troops'; cf.
Götze, *Madd.* 6; XV 34 II 31 *āssiyantes asandu* 'may [they] be
dear'; cf. Haas – Wilhelm, *Riten* 192; ibid. III 42 *ispiyantes
ninkante*[*s*] *asandu* 'let them be sated [with food] and filled [with
drink]' [Lat. *saturi atque ebrii sunto*]; XXXI 106+XXIII
44+XXVI 32 III 8–9 *nu-kan ammel* MU.HI.A-*u*[*s*] UD.KAM-*us*
ANA ᶦKUG.GA.TÚL-[*ma*] *parā asandu* 'may my years [and] days be
[offered up] to Suppiluliumas' [de facto passive of *parā ep*[*p*]-

'proffer', like Lat. *praestō esse* for *praebēre*]; cf. Laroche, *RA* 47:72–3 [1953]); partic. *asant*-'being, existing, real, true', nom. sg. c. *asanza* (e.g. *KBo* V 4 Vs. 30 and *KUB* VI 41 IV 22 *nu mān memias asanza* 'if the matter [is] true'; cf. Friedrich, *Staatsverträge* 1:56, 134; *KUB* V 25 III 10 *mān asi memias asanza*; XXXIII 109 I 5 *asanza memias* 'the matter [is] true'; cf. Laroche, *RHA* 26:51 [1968]; Siegelová, *Appu-Hedammu* 38; *RS* 17:109 Recto 8 *asanza-war-as memias*; cf. Laroche, *Ugaritica* 5:769 [1968]; Haase, *Ugarit-Forschungen* 3:71 [1971]; *KUB* XXXI 66 IV 4–5 *ŪL-as-za kuit asanza memias* 'because it is not a true word'; cf. Houwink Ten Cate, *Anatol. Stud. Güterbock* 131; XXII 70 Vs. 31 *mān memias asanza mān mahhan* 'whether what she says is true or how [else it might be]'; cf. Ünal, *Orakeltext* 62; *KBo* XII 38 II 12 *asanza* LUGAL-*us* 'true king'; cf. Otten, *MDOG* 94:16 [1963]; Güterbock, *JNES* 26:76 [1967]), *asānza* (e.g. *KUB* XXI 5 III 36 *m]ān memiyas asānza*; cf. Friedrich, *Staatsverträge* 2:70), acc. sg. c. *asantan* (e.g. XV 30 III 6 *kūn* GAB *kissan asantan* 'this bust which is as described'; cf. Lebrun, *Samuha* 193; XV 23, 7 INIM-*an asantan iyaun* 'I made a true speech'; cf. P. Cornil – R. Lebrun, *Orientalia Lovaniensia Periodica* 3:61 [1972]; XIV 3 III 3; cf. Sommer, *AU* 12), nom.-acc. sg. neut. *asan* (XXXIII 108 II 9 *asan iyat* 'truly did' [?]; cf. Laroche, *RHA* 26:72 [1968]), *asān* (XIV 8 Rs. 29 *asān-at iyanun-at* 'it [is] true, I did it'; cf. ibid. 15 *ēsziy-at iyawen-at* 'it is [so], we did it'; cf. Götze, *KlF* 214–6; *KBo* IV 14 II 58; cf. R. Stefanini, *ANLR* 20:42 [1965]), nom.-acc. pl. neut. *asanta* (*KUB* XIV 1 Rs. 29 *ŠA* ᴰUTU-*ŠI namma asanta* KUR.KUR-*TIM dās* 'he also took lands belonging to my majesty' [lit. being my majesty's]; cf. Götze, *Madd.* 26), *asanda* (*KBo* XII 38 II 13–14 *asanda* LÚ-*natar*HI.A '[his] truly manly deeds'); verbal noun *esuwar* (n.), nom.-acc. sg. in *KBo* I 42 I 7 and 8 EGIR-*pa esūwar* matching Akk. *dukuldu* 'strength, support' (cf. Güterbock, *MSL* 13:133 [1971]), literally 'being behind, back-up, (physical) support', gen. sg. *esuwas* (*KUB* XXVI 43 Vs. 11; cf. Imparati, *RHA* 32:24 [1974]).

Pal. *as-*, 2 sg. imp. *ās* (*KUB* XXXV 163 III 10), 3 sg. imp. *āsdu* (XXXV 165 Vs. 28), 3 pl. imp. *asandu* (ibid. Rs. 6, 7, 8), *a-se-en-du* (*KBo* XIX 153 III 13). Cf. Carruba, *Das Palaische* 28, 16, 19, 23.

Lyd. 1 sg. pres. *-im* (?; cf. Gusmani, *Die Sprache* 17:1–7 [1971]), 3 sg. or pl. pret. *el* (?; cf. Gusmani, *Lyd. Wb.* 100).

Luw. *as-*, 1 sg. pret. *asha* (*KUB* XXXV 113, 4 and 5; cf. Otten, *LTU* 102), 3 sg. pret. *āsta* (e.g. XXXV 15 III 3; XXXV 65 III 7; XXXV 101 Rs. 5; *KBo* IX 141 Rs. 4), 3 sg. imp. *āsdu* (e.g. *KUB* XXXV 15 II 5; XXXV 21 II 31; XXXV 54 III 26; XXXV 58 II 6; XXXV 70 II 17; XXXV 85, 4; XXXV 88 III 15 *kisamman āsdu* 'let be combed'; cf. Otten, *LTU* 86; XXXV 103 III 6–7 *pa-as pūwa* [*kuw*]*ati āsta nanun-ha-as apati āsdu* 'but as he formerly was, now also may he be thus'; cf. Otten, *LTU* 95; XXXV 101 Vs. 9 *nanun-ha-wa-as apatin āsd*[*u*]; *KBo* IX 145, 5, 12, 13), 3 pl. imp. *asandu* (e.g. *KUB* XXXV 13, 11; XXXV 78, 15; XXXII 7, 6; XXXII 79, 5; *KBo* VII 66 II 7).

Hier. *as-*, 3 sg. pres. *asti*, 1 sg. pret. act. *(a)sha*, 3 sg. pret. act. *(a)sta*, 3 sg. imp. act. *astu*. Cf. Meriggi, *HHG* 34–5.

Lyc. 3 sg. pres. *esi* (Xanthos trilingual 12 *ehbiyẽ esi-ti* 'what is his'), 3 pl. pres. *hãti* (ibid. 21 *arawa hãti* 'are free'), 3 pl. imp. *esu* (*TLy* 39:5 *nijesu* 'let it not be!'; cf. A. Torp, *Lykische Beiträge* 1:14 [1898]; Pedersen, *Lyk. u. Hitt.* 18); partic. *ahñt-*, gen. pl. neut. *ahñtãi* 'goods, possessions' (Xanthos trilingual 17; cf. Gk. τὰ ὄντα 'goods' or Akk. *bušū* 'goods' [*bašū* 'be'], vs. Hitt. *assū*). Cf. Laroche, *Fouilles de Xanthos* 6:66–9 (1979). *esi, hãti, esu, ahñt-* reflect Luw. **āsti*, **asanti*, *āsdu*, **asant-*.

es- has been identified with IE **es-* 'be' (*IEW* 340–2) since J. A. Knudtzon, *Die zwei Arzawa-Briefe* 45, 61 (1902), who compared *ēstu* with Lat. *estō*; he was followed by H. Holma (*Journal de la société finno-ougrienne* 33.1:18–19 [1916]) and by Hrozný (*MDOG* 56:28, 33 [1915], *SH* 78, 169–70). The ablaut pattern *es-* : *as-* parallels verbs like *ep(p)-* : *ap(p)-* 'seize', *ed-* : *ad-* 'eat', and *eku-* : *aku-* 'drink'.

The sg. pres. *ēsmi, ēssi, ēszi* matches Skt. *ásmi, ási, ásti* and OLith. *esmi, esi, esti,* and 3 sg. imp. *ēstu* equals Skt. *ástu*, while 2 sg. imp. *ēs* agrees with Lat. *es*. The weak grade *as-* appears practically only in 3 pl. pres. *asanzi*, 3 pl. imp. *asantu*, and partic. *asant-*, corresponding to Skt. *sánti, sántu, sánt-*. 3 pl. pret. *eser* has Hittite innovational full grade (cf. *eppir, eter, ekuir, kuenir*). The full grade may on the other hand be basic in the 2 pl. imp. *ēsten* (cf. *eptin, ezten, ekuten*), whence it extends to 2 pl. pret.

ēsten (cf. *eptin*) and 2 pl. pres. **ēsteni* (cf. *eptēni* [beside *apteni*], *ekuteni*); Gk. ἔστε, ἐστέ, Lat. *este, estis,* and OLith. *este* display the same trait (vs. Skt. *st*[*h*]*á*). A spread of full grade to 1 pl. is seen in *esuwani* (cf. *eppuweni, edueni, ekueni*) and *esuwen* (cf. *eppuen, ekuēn*), but is more sporadic (beside *appuweni, adueni, akueni; appuen*) and not matched by either Latin or Sanskrit (*sumus, smás,* vs. OLith. *esme,* Gk. εἰμέν). Cf. C. Watkins, *Indogermanische Grammatik* III/1, 32–4 (1969). Other possible, but hardly compelling paradigmatic parallels can be seen in 2 sg. pret. *ēsta* beside Gk. ἦσθα (vs. 3 sg. pret. *ēsta* /est/ corresponding to Ved. *ās,* Gk. ἦς), and in Luw. 1 sg. pret. *asha* beside Skt. 1 sg. perf. *ása.*

For the "emphatic" meaning 'truly be, be real, be true', seen especially in *asant-* and matching Skt. *sánt-* (and by extension ON *sannr,* Lat. *sōns* 'guilty'), cf. e.g. Sommer, *AU* 69; Ivanov, *Obščeindoevropejskaja* 56, 266–8; C. Watkins, *Studies in historical linguistics in honor of G. S. Lane* 186–94 (1967).

Cf. *es(sa)ri-.*

es-, as- 'sit, remain (seated), reside; (esp. OHitt.) sit down, seat oneself, be seated; (transitive) settle, inhabit, occupy', *-za es-*'sit down, seat oneself, settle down, install oneself', *-za appa(n) es-* 'seat oneself behind, take a back seat, be uncooperative, resist', *katta es-* 'subside, abate' (said of flame, evil, etc.), *-za katta es-* 'sit down' (rarely TUŠ), 1 sg. pres. midd. *ēshahari (KBo* XVI 98 II 12 *nu-za-kan* LUGAL-*iznanni ēshahari* 'I install myself in the kingship'; cf. P. Cornil – R. Lebrun, *Hethitica* 3; *KUB* VIII 48 I 21 *nu-[wa-z]a-kan* ANA GIDIM.[HI.A] *ēshahari* 'among the dead I shall make my abode'; cf. Friedrich, *ZA* 39:18 [1930]; Laroche, *RHA* 26:18 [1968]), 2 sg. pres. midd. *ēstari* (XIV 1 Vs. 44 *nam[ma]-ma-wa-z parā tamāi* KUR-*e [tamāi]nn-a hapā[tin* ZI-*i]t le ēstari* 'but further do not willfully occupy another country and other river-land!'; cf. Götze, *Madd.* 10), 3 sg. pres. act. *ēszi* (e.g. *ABoT* 9 I 5 [OHitt.] LUGA]L-*was piran ēszi* 'sits before the king'; cf. Neu, *Gewitterritual* 10; *KUB* XVII 20 II 1 EGIR-*ŠU-ma* ᴰ*Hūmmunis ēszi* 'behind him sits H.'; similarly passim ibid. 2–16, in a description of iconographic positionings; cf. Bossert, *MIO* 4:201–3 [1956]), 3 sg. pres. midd. *esa* (frequent, e.g. *KBo*

XIX 128 V 38 LUGAL-*us esa* 'the queen [sic!] remains seated', vs.
ibid. 36–37 LUGAL-*us sarā tiya*[*z*]*zi* 'the king stands up'; cf.
Otten, *Festritual* 14; XVII 74 IV 33 [OHitt.] LUGAL-*us esa* 'the
king sits down'; cf. Neu, *Gewitterritual* 34; *KUB* XXX 41 I 20
LUGAL-*us-za esa*; XXX 29 Vs. 6 [*nu*]-*zan* SAL-*za* ^{GIŠ}*kuppisnas ser
esa* 'the woman seats herself on the stool'), *esari* (frequent, e.g.
KBo III 22 Rs. 79 [OHitt.] *perammit kunnaz esari* 'he will sit
down before me on the right'; cf. Neu, *Anitta-Text* 14; XIX 128 I
17 LUGAL-*us esari* 'the king sits down'; cf. Otten, *Festritual* 2; XII
126 I 9–10 *nu-za* ^DUTU-*i menahhanda esari* '[he] seats himself
facing the sun-god'; cf. Jakob-Rost, *Ritual der Malli* 98; XVII 65
Rs. 1 *harnuui-ma-as-za* ŪL *esari* 'she does not seat herself on the
obstetrical stool'; *KUB* XIX 37 II 18–19 *n-an-zan* DUMU *AMILUTI*
[*Ū*]*L kuiski esari* 'no son of mankind will inhabit it'; cf. Götze,
AM 168; XII 66 IV 16 *n-as-san apiya esari* 'he sits down there'; cf.
Laroche, *RHA* 23:71 [1965]), *esāri* (dupl. *KBo* III 7 IV 13), *isari*
(XV 25 Vs. 30 *pah*]*hur katta isari* 'the fire subsides'; cf. Carruba,
Beschwörungsritual 4), 1 pl. pres. midd. *e-su-as-ta* (XVI 25 I 71),
esuwasta (*KUB* XXXI 143 II 36 [OHitt.] *pāiwani esuwasta* 'let us
go sit'; XII 66 IV 9–10 *mān-wa* ANA ^{URU}*Neriqqa paiuwani
nu-wa-ssan kuwapi esuwasta* 'if we go to N., where shall we sit
down?'), *esuwastati* (dupl. *KBo* III 7 IV 5–7 *mān-wa* ANA ^DIM
^{URU}*Nerik pāiwani nu-wa-ssan kuwapit esuwastati*; *KUB* XXIV 8
IV 5–6 *wes*]-*a-wa-za sarraweni nu-wa-nnas a*[*rhayan*] [*e*]*suwas-
tati* 'let us split up and settle apart'; cf. Siegelová, *Appu-
Hedammu* 12; XXXIII 106 II 13 and 14 *INA* ^{HUR.SAG}*Kandurna ser
esuwastati* 'we sit down on Mt. K.', vs. ibid. 15 *ēszi* '[he] sits'; cf.
Güterbock, *JCS* 6:22 [1952]), 2 pl. pres. act. *e-es-tum-ma-at* (XII
66 IV 12 *mān-wa-ssan* ... *ēstummat* 'if you sit down'; dupl. *KBo*
III 7 IV 9), 3 pl. pres. act. *asanzi* (e.g. *KUB* XXIV 8 I 18 *piran-sit
adanna asanzi* '[they] sit before him to eat'; cf. Siegelová,
Appu-Hedammu 4; *KBo* XVII 3 IV 22 LUGAL-*us* SAL.LUGAL-*s-a
asanzi* 'king and queen are seated'; cf. Otten – Souček, *Altheth.
Ritual* 38; Otten, *Altheth. Erzählung* 50; *KUB* XVII 20 II 2, 12,
16; cf. Bossert, *MIO* 4:202–3 [1956]), *esanzi* (XX 76 III 14 LUGAL
SAL.LUGAL *esanzi*), 3 pl. pres. midd. *esanta* (e.g. dupl. *KBo* XI 52
I 20 *es*]*anta*; *KUB* II 5 I 28 *ta* LUGAL SAL.LUGAL *esanta*; X 3 I 22
LUGAL-*us* SAL.LUGAL-*ass-a esanta*), *esanda* (e.g. dupl. *KBo* VIII

119 Vs. 9; XVII 74 I 18 and 19 [OHitt.] *ta esanda* 'and they sit down'; cf. Neu, *Gewitterritual* 12), *asanta* (IV 9 III 26 LUGAL SAL.LUGAL ᴳᴵˢDAG-*ti asanta* 'king [and] queen sit on the throne'), *asanda* (*KUB* X 17 II 9 LUGAL SAL.LUGAL ᴳᴵˢDAG-*ti asanda*), *esantari* (e.g. X 45 III 23–26 *hantezzi-ma-z-kan kuedani* UD-*ti* LUGAL-*us* ANA ᴳᴵˢŠÚ.A LUGAL-*UTTI* SAL.LUGAL-*ma-zza-kan* ANA ᴳᴵˢŠÚ.A SAL[.LUGAL-*UTTI*] *esantari* 'but on the first day when king and queen seat themselves on the thrones of king- and queenship respectively'; cf. Kümmel, *Ersatzrituale* 46; *IBoT* III 148 III 18 *namma-at-za adanna esantari* 'then they sit down to eat'; cf. Haas – Wilhelm, *Riten* 222; *KUB* XXIX 1 III 41 *nu-ssan* DINGIR.MEŠ *esantari* 'the gods are seated'; cf. B. Schwartz, *Orientalia* N.S. 16:36 [1947]; *IBoT* I 29 Vs. 36 [*n*]*u-ssi* 12 LÚ.MEŠAPIN.LAL *piran esantari* 'twelve plowmen are seated before him'; cf. ibid. Rs. 48–49 *nu-ssi* 12 SAL.MEŠKAR.KID [*pir*]*an esanta* 'twelve prostitutes are seated before him'), *esandari* (e.g. ibid. Vs. 53 *nu* ANA DUMU.LUGAL LÚ.MEŠSANGA *hūmantes piran-set esandari* 'all the priests are seated before the prince'; cf. ibid. 18–19 *nu-ssi pir*]*an* 12 LÚSANGA *esanda* 'twelve priests are seated before him'; *KBo* V 1 III 49–50 *nu-za ... adanna esandari*; cf. Sommer – Ehelolf, *Pāpanikri* 10*; VIII 88 Vs. 9–10 *nu mahhan* GUNNI.MEŠ *katta esandari* 'when the hearth[fire]s subside'; cf. Haas – Wilhelm, *Riten* 260), *ēssantari* (dupl. VIII 86 Vs. 6; II 14 IV 10–12 *n-at-za adanna* ANA PANI DINGIR-*LIM ēssantari* 'they sit down to eat before the god'), *esandāri* (*KUB* XXXIV 128 Rs. 9, besides dupl. *IBoT* III 25, 3 *esandari*), 1 sg. pret. midd. *ēshati* (*KBo* III 55 Rs. 6 [OHitt.]]*man* EGIR-*pa ēshati* 'had I resisted'), *ēshahati* (*KUB* XXXVI 98b Rs. 8 [OHitt.] *apiya ēshahati* 'I resided there'), [*e-e*]*s-ha-ha-at-ti* (dupl. XXVI 71 I 21), *ēshat* (e.g. *KBo* III 1 II 16 [OHitt.] *mān-san* ¹*Telipinus* INA ᴳᴵˢGU.ZA ABI-YA *ēshat* 'when I, Telipinus, seated myself on my father's throne'; III 4 I 19 *mahhan-ma-za-kan* ᴰUTU-*ŠI* ANA ᴳᴵˢGU.ZA ABI-YA *ēshat*; cf. Götze, *AM* 20), *ēshahat* (dupl. XVI 1 I 30; cf. Otten, *MIO* 3:162 [1955]; XVI 8 II 14; cf. Otten, *MIO* 3:166; *KUB* XXI 1 I 44; cf. Friedrich, *Staatsverträge* 2:54; *KBo* XIX 78, 7; cf. S. Heinhold-Krahmer, *Arzawa* 308 [1977]), *ishahat* (XVI 8 II 10; *KUB* XXXI 71 III 2–3 *nu-za* SAL.LUGAL *katta ishahat* 'I, the queen, sat down'; cf. Ünal, *Orakeltext* 122), 2 sg. pret. midd. *esat*

(XXXIII 96 IV 56 *nu-za* ŪL *esat* 'thou didst not sit down'; cf. Güterbock, *JCS* 5:160 [1951]), *ēstat* (XIV 1 Rs. 34 URU]*Upnihuwalan-ma-z* URU-*an* ZI-*it* [*ēs*]*tat* 'you willfully occupied U.'; cf. Götze, *Madd.* 28), 3 sg. pret. act. *esati* (*KBo* XII 3 III 4 [OHitt.]; *KUB* XXXI 64 III 12 [OHitt.] *kattan esati*; XII 43, 3; *KBo* XV 34 III 15; *KUB* XVII 10 I 34 *nu-za-kan anda kariyat s-as esati* 'he paused and sat down'; cf. Laroche, *RHA* 23:91 [1965]), *esadi* (XXXIII 59 III 13 *kat*[*t*]*an esadi* 'sat down'; cf. Laroche, *RHA* 23:150 [1965]), *esat* (frequent, e.g. XXXIII 120 I 15–16 GIŠŠÚ.A-*ki-ma-ssan* D*Anus esat* D*Anus-san* GIŠŠÚ.A-*i-ssi ēszi* 'but Anu seated himself on the throne; Anu sits on his throne'; cf. Güterbock, *Kumarbi* *2; *KBo* XIX 112 Rs. 5 GIŠŠÚ.A-*an tiyir* ŪL-*as-za-kan esat* 'they placed a chair, [but] she did not sit down'; cf. Siegelová, *Appu-Hedammu* 44; III 4 I 14 *kinun-ma-wa--za-kan kuis* ANA GIŠGU.ZA ABI-ŠU *esat nu-war-as* DUMU-*las* 'but he who has now seated himself on his father's throne, he [is but] a child'; cf. Götze, *AM* 20; ibid. 57–58 *nu-za* ANA PANI ABI ABI-YA *kuis* URU*Gasgas* HUR.SAG*Tarikarimun* GEŠPÚ-*az esat* 'the Gasga-town which in my grandfather's day had occupied Mt. T. by force'; cf. Götze, *AM* 80; *KUB* XIX 37 III 28 *nu-za* KUR URU*Tapāpanuwa kuit dān* EGIR-*pa esat* 'because the land of T. resisted a second time'; cf. Götze, *AM* 174), *ēssat* (412/b + II 27), *estat* (1490/u, 11 *n-as-mu ishanallis estat* 'he remained me an i.'), *ēstat* (*KBo* V 8 II 14–15 *nu* KUR URU*Tūmmanna kuit* PANI ABI-YA *ēstat* 'because the land of T. remained [loyal] before my father'; cf. Götze, *AM* 152; *KUB* XXX 34 IV 2–4 *n-as-za nassu* É*halinduwas suhhi ēstat nasma-az-zan* INA É DINGIR.MEŠ *suhhi ēstat* 'he sat down either on the roof of the h.-house, or he sat down on the roof in the house of the gods'; cf. V. Haas – M. Wäfler, *Oriens Antiquus* 16:229 [1977]), 1 pl. pret. midd. *ēssuwastati* (1490/u, 14), 3 pl. pret. midd. *esantat* (*KBo* V 8 II 12–14 *nu kuit* KUR-TUM *harninkir kuit-ma-za esantat-pat n-at harkir-pat* 'some land they ravaged, but some they occupied, and they held it'; ibid. 18 and 25; cf. Götze, *AM* 152–4; *KUB* XXVI 43 Rs. 10; cf. Imparati, *RHA* 32:34 [1974]), *esandat* (XIX 29 IV 14–15 *n-at-za-kan apezz-iya* EGIR-*an* [...] *esandat* 'for that reason too they put up resistance'; cf. Götze, *AM* 18; XIX 37 III 5; cf. Götze, *AM* 172), 2 sg. imp. act. *e-es* (e.g. XIV 3 IV 3 *dam*]*edani* *pidi* GAM *ēs* 'settle down in another place'; cf. Sommer, *AU* 16; XIV 1 Vs. 16 *INA* KUR ᴴᵁᴿˑˢᴬᴳ*Zippaslā ēs* 'reside in the mountain-land of Z.!', vs. ibid. 15 *nu-wa-za ŠA ABI* ᴰUTU-*ŠI Ù ŠA* KUR ᵁᴿᵁ*Hatti ēs* 'be of [loyalty to] my majesty's father and the land of Hatti!'), *e-si* (ibid. 19 *nu-wa-za apūn-pat esi* 'inhabit it!'), 2 sg. imp. midd. *ēshut* (e.g. ibid. 17 *ehu-wa-za INA* KUR ᴴᵁᴿˑˢᴬᴳ[*Har*]*i-yati ēshut* 'come, reside in the mountain-land of H.!'; cf. Götze, *Madd.* 4; *KBo* III 21 III 14–15 ᵁᴿᵁ*Zippiri-ma-z* ᴰUTU-*was uktūri* URU-*ri … andan ēshut* 'in Sippar, the eternal city of the sun-god, take up residence!'; ibid. 21 and 25), 3 sg. imp. midd. *esaru* (e.g. *KUB* XIV 3 II 76 *nu-ssi apās pede-ssi esaru* 'let that one sit for him in his place'; ibid. 28, 72; cf. Sommer, *AU* 8–10; XXX 10 Rs. 6 [*n-a*]*t katta namma esaru* 'let it [viz. the ill] subside again'), 2 pl. imp. act. *e-es-te-en* (XV 34 II 15–16 *nu-zan katta sumenzan parkuwai* SIG₅-*anti misri*[*wanti*] ᴳᴵˢŠÚ.A *ēsten* 'sit down on your pure, good, radiant throne!'; cf. Haas – Wilhelm, *Riten* 190; XIV 16 I 17 *nu-wa-kan* KUR-*e piran ēsten* 'occupy the land!'; cf. Götze, *AM* 28), 2 pl. imp. midd. *e*]-*es-du-ma-ti* (XXXI 64 II 3 [OHitt.]), *ēsdumat* (XIV 1 Rs. 40 'occupy!'); partic. *as(s)ant-*, nom.-acc. sg. neut. *a-sa-an* (e.g. XXXVIII 2 II 8 ALAM LÚ GUŠKIN GAR.RA *asan* 'seated likeness of a man, gold-plated'; ibid. III 5 ALAM LÚ KÙ.BABBAR *asan* 'seated likeness of a man, of silver'), *a-sa-a-an* (ibid. I 8; cf. von Brandenstein, *Heth. Götter* 6, 8, 4), *a-as-sa-an* (XXXIX 6 Rs. 18–19 ALAM *āssan … ēszi* 'the seated likeness sits'), TUŠ-*an* (e.g. XXXVIII 1 IV 2 1 ALAM GIŠ SAL-*TI* TUŠ-*an* 'one seated wooden likeness of a woman'; ibid. 9 and I 11 and 16; cf. von Brandenstein, *Heth. Götter* 14, 10, 12), profusely attested sg. or pl. *asandas* '(in a) sitting (position)' (e.g. *KBo* XVII 74 II–III passim [OHitt.], ibid. II 46 *asadas*; cf. Neu, *Gewitterritual* 20–30), TUŠ-*as* (e.g. XIX 128 IV–VI passim; cf. Otten, *Festritual* 10–6, 44; opp. GUB-*as* 'standing'), nom. pl. c. *asandus* (XI 1 Vs. 33 URU.DIDLI.HI.A *asandus kuyēs* 'towns that are inhabited'; cf. *RHA* 25:107 [1967]); also *esant-*, nom. sg. c. *esanza*, nom.-acc. sg. neut. *esan* (e.g. V 8 I 4–5 ERÍN.MEŠ ᵁᴿᵁ*Taggastas-ma parā esanza* KUR ᵁᴿᵁ*Sadduppa … esan harta* 'the enemy from T., positioned forward, had occupied S.'; cf. Götze, *AM* 146; III 4 III 39–40, 43, 60–61 *nu-za … kuis* ᵁᴿᵁ*Gasgas esan harta* 'what Gasga-town had occupied …'; cf. Götze, *AM* 76–80; X 17 IV 5 *esan harta*); verbal noun *asatar* (n.), nom.-acc. *asatar* (e.g. *KUB* XXI 29 II 3 *nu-smas parā asatar* ¹*Hantilis iyat* 'H. established a forward position against them'), *asātar* (e.g. *KBo* I 53, 4, matching Akk. *ašabu* 'seat oneself, settle down'; cf. *MSL* 3:87 [1955]; III 21 III 25 *asātar ēshut* 'set up residence!' [figura etymologica with inner accusative]), gen. sg. *asannas* (*KUB* XXIX 4 I 29–30 1-*NUTIM* ᴳᴵˢ*kishita asannas* 'one set [of] chairs for sitting'; cf. Kronasser, *Umsiedelung* 8; XXX 24 II 8 ᴳᴵˢGIGIR *asannas ser* 'on the sitting-chariot'; ibid. 12 *IŠTU* ᴳᴵˢGIGIR *asannas katta* 'down from the sitting-chariot'; cf. Otten, *Totenrituale* 60, 58; *KBo* XV 10 I 10 4 ᴳᴵˢGIGIR TUR 6 ᴳᴵˢ*āsannas* 1 ᴳᴵˢ*āsnatey-auwas* 'four small chariots, six sitting[-chariots], one sit-stand [chariot]'; cf. *KUB* XIII 3 III 11 ᴳᴵˢGIGIR.HI.A *tiyauwas* 'standing-chariots'; cf. Szabó, *Entsühnungsritual* 12, 61; XVIII 36, 19 and 20 ANA EZEN *asannas* 'for the feast of settlement'; *KBo* II 1 II 44 *ŠA L*[*ab*]*arna* EGIR-*pa asanna⟨s⟩* ᴰLAMA-*i* 'to L.'s tutelary god of resistance'; II 38, 7 EGIR-*pa asannas* KI.MIN; cf. A. Archi, *SMEA* 16:109, 95 [1975]); inf. *asanna* (e.g. *KUB* XII 65 + XXVI 71 III 12–13 *asanna-ssi* ᴳᴵˢŠÚ.A-*an aruni tiyer nu-za-kan sallis* [*arunas*] ᴳᴵˢŠÚ.A-*si esat* 'they placed a chair for the sea to sit on, and the great sea sat down on his chair'; cf. Siegelová, *Appu-Hedammu* 50; XIV 1 Vs. 22 'to inhabit'; cf. Götze, *Madd.* 6), *asānna* (ibid. 18 ¹*Madduwattas-az* KUR ᴴᵁᴿ·ˢᴬᴳ*Hāriyati asānna mimmas* 'M. refused to inhabit the mountain country of H.'; ibid. Rs. 11 and 14); *asanna* occasionally appears cross-diathetically as a quasi "mediopassive" infinitive of *asas-* (= 'be seated, be set'; examples sub *asas-*); iter. *eski-*, 1 sg. pres. midd. *ēskahha* (*KUB* XXXI 4 + *KBo* III 41 Vs. 11 [OHitt.] *nu-sse-ssan ēskahha* 'I shall resist him'; cf. Otten, *ZA* 55:158 [1962]), *ēskahhari* (*KBo* VII 14 + *KUB* XXXVI 100 Vs. 17 [OHitt.] *ē*]*skahhari*), 3 pl. pres. midd. *ēskanta* (*KBo* III 34 III 15 [OHitt.] AHI LUGAL ANA P[ANI ABI] LUGAL *kuyēs ēskanta* 'those who sit as brothers before the father of the king'), 3 pl. pret. midd. *ēskantati* (*KBo* VII 14 + *KUB* XXXVI 100 Vs. 2 [OHitt.] *piran ēskantati*), 2 pl. imp. act. *ēskidumat* (*KUB* XII 63 Vs. 5). Cf. Götze, *Arch. Or.* 5:4–5 (1933); Neu, *Interpretation* 25–31; Oettinger, *MSS* 34:121-2 (1976).

asau(w)ar (n.) '(sheep)fold, pen' (*KUB* III 94 II 14–15

DAG.KISIM₅ x A.MAŠ and MA.AZ.ZA match Akk. *mazzū* and Hitt.
a-sa-a-u-ar; cf. B. Landsberger, *MSL* 2:103 [1951]), dat.-loc. sg.
a-sa-ú-ni (*KBo* VI 2+ XIX 1 III 47–49 [= *Code* 1:66, OHitt.]
takku GUD.APIN.LAL *takku* A[NŠU.KUR.R]A *tūriyauas takku* GUD.
.ÁB *takku* ANŠU.KUR.RA.SAL.AL.LAL *hāleas harapta* [*takk*]*u* MÁŠ.
.GAL *enanza takku* UDU.SÍG + SAL *takku* UDU.NITÁ *asauni harapta*
'if a plowox or a harness horse or a cow or a mare strays to
corrals, or a tamed he-goat or a ewe or a ram strays to a fold …';
cf. Otten – Souček, *AfO* 21:6 [1966]; dupl. VI 3 III 51–53; VI 34
IV 13–15 *nu-ssi-ssan wēllus hāli-ssi asauni-ssi suple-ssi le lu-*
luwaitta 'let meadow not thrive in his corral, in his sheepfold, for
his livestock!'; cf. Oettinger, *Eide* 14), *a-sa-u-ni* (*KUB* XIII 5 II
22 *nasma-za-kan* UDU *asauni anda tarnatteni* 'or you place the
sheep in your fold', vs. ibid. 21 [*nasma-an-zan-kan*] *hāli anda*
tarnatteni 'or you place it [viz. ibid. 20 GUD 'ox'] in your corral';
cf. Sturtevant, *JAOS* 54:372 [1934]), *a-sa-u-na-i* (*Bo* 6002 Vs. 7 1
UDU *asaunai appanzi* 'they seize one sheep in the fold'; cf.
Lebrun, *Samuha* 187), abl. sg. *a-sa-ú-na-az* (*KUB* XXX 10 Vs. 15
GUD-*un-asta hāliaz appa* ŪL *kussanka karsun* UDU-*un-asta asau-*
naz EGIR-*pa* KI.MIN 'an ox from the corral I never cut off; a sheep
off from the fold, likewise'), *a-sa-u-na-az* (XXIV 3 II 11–12
ᵁᴰᵁ*auliūs-kan* GUD.HI.A UDU.HI.A *h*[*āliyaz*] *asaunaz kuezz-as*
karask[*ir* 'from what[ever] corral [or] fold they would sever
sacrificial contingents of cattle [and] sheep'; cf. Gurney, *Hittite*
Prayers 26; XIII 4 IV 59 *n-at-san haliyaz asaunaz mahhan karsan*
'when it [has been] removed from the corral [or] fold'; cf.
Sturtevant, *JAOS* 54:396 [1934]), nom.-acc. pl. *a-sa-u-wa-ar*
(*KBo* X 2 I 7–8 [*nu kue k*]*ue asauwar ēsta* [*n-at-kan* A]NA
ERÍN.MEŠ *asanduli pihhun* 'whatever sheepfolds there were, those
I gave to the garrison troops', corresponding to X 1 Vs. 3 [Akk.]
minam dumqam addin-šunuti 'all goods I gave to them', where
Akk. has either rendered *asauwar* metonymically [cf. Lat. *pecua*
'livestock' > 'possessions, money'] or mistaken it for **āssauwa*
'goods' [normally *āssū*]; for *asauwar* : **āssauwa* cf. ibid. 4
ᵁᴿᵁ*Zalpar* vs. X 2 I 9 ᵁᴿᵁ*Zalpa*, and *a-sa-u-wa* below; cf. F.
Imparati – C. Saporetti, *Studi classici e orientali* 14:44, 77 [1965];
Goetze, *JCS* 16:24 [1962]; H. C. Melchert, *JNES* 37:4 [1978]),
a-sa-u-wa (XVII 92 Vs. 6–7 *nekuz mehur mān* UDU.HI.A-*was*

asauwa anda [...] *n-as-kan* UDU.HI.A-*was menahhanda paizzi* 'at night if sheepfolds ... [...], he goes to meet the sheep'; for lack of *-r* cf. e.g. *-[a]ta[r]* in *iyata, tameta*), *a-sa-a-u-wa-ar* (*KUB* XXX 13 Vs. 7 [dupl. of XXIV 3 II ∣ ˋ -13] [*nu* ^{LÚ.MEŠ}SIPAD.GUD ^{LÚ.MEŠ}SIPAD.UDU *e*]*kir hāliya asāuw*[*ar* 'the neatherds [and] shepherds have died, corrals [and] folds ...'). *asauwar* is an archaic heteroclitic verbal noun from *es-*, entirely parallel to *harsauwar* (dat.-loc. pl. *harsaunas*) from *hars-* (q.v.); unlike the productive *asatar* it has become semantically detached from the verbal paradigm and has therefore not joined the innovational productive type in *-war* (gen. *-was*). Other terms for animal habitat derived from 'sit' are e.g. Engl. *nest* (IE **ni-sdo-*) and Goth. *sitls* 'seat, nest'; cf. also Skt. *ā́sanam* 'encampment'. Wrong connections with *es-* 'be' (Kronasser, *Etym.* 1:298) and *as(s)-* 'remain' (Tischler, *Glossar* 79, thinking of Lat. *mānsiō*; but *ass-* always has intervocalic *-ss-*).

asandul- (n.) 'occupation (force), garrison', gen. sg. *asandulas*, dat.-loc. sg. *asanduli* (*KUB* XIII 20 I 10–11 *nu kuis* ERÍN.MEŠ *asandulas n-an-kan* ^DUT[U-*ŠI*] *asanduli anda talahhi* 'which [is] garrison troops, it I, my majesty, leave in garrison'; cf. Alp, *Belleten* 11:390 [1947]; *KBo* IX 91 Vs. 3–4 ANA LÚ.MEŠ *Araunna* ^{URU}*Nerik asandulas* 'to the men of A. of the garrison at N.'; ibid. 8 and 13–14 ANA LÚ.MEŠ *Araunna asandulas* ^{URU}*Nerik*; ibid. 17–18 and [mutilated] 20–21 LÚ.MEŠ *Araunna asandulas* ^{URU}*Nerik*; *KUB* XIV 16 I 11]*asanduli anda dālista*; cf. Götze, *AM* 26), dat.-loc. sg. *asandula* and pl. *asandulas* (XXVI 17 I 6–7 *nu kuis* ERÍN.MEŠ *asandula n-as-kan anda asandulas dalahhi* 'what troops [are] in garrison those I leave for garrisons'; *KBo* III 46 Vs. 40 *s-us asandulas*; cf. S. Heinhold-Krahmer, *Arzawa* 280 [1977]).

asandula-, asanduli- 'occupation-related, garrison-', adjectivization originating in appositional uses of oblique cases of *asandul-* with ERÍN.MEŠ (= *tuzzi*[*yant*]-), nom. sg. c. *a-sa-an-du--lis* (*KBo* XXVI 20 III 18 *asandulis* ERÍN.MEŠ-*za* 'occupation force', matching ibid. Akk. *birtu* 'fortress', vs. ibid. 17 *warris* ERÍN.MEŠ-*za* = Akk. *nararu* 'auxiliaries'), acc. sg. c. *asandulan* (*KUB* VI 41 IV 10–11 ^DUTU-*ŠI-ya-tta* [*kuin*] ERÍN.MEŠ *asandulan kattan daliyanun* 'what occupation force I, my majesty, have left with you'; dupl. *KBo* IV 3 III 13–14 ^DUTU-*ŠI-ya-tta kuin*

ERÍN.MEŠ LÚ.MEŠ a[sandulan kattan] arha [; dupl. V 13 IV 3
ᴰUTU-ŠI-ya-tta kuin ERÍN.MEŠ LÚ.MEŠ asandulan kattan daliyanun; cf. Friedrich, Staatsverträge 1:132–3; XVI 32 IV 7
ER]ÍN.MEŠ asandulan; cf. P. Cornil – R. Lebrun, Orientalia
Lovaniensia Periodica 6–7:89 [1975–6]), asandulin (V 4 Vs. 25
ᴰUTU-ŠI-ya-tta kuin ERÍN.MEŠ a[sand]ulin katta dāliyanun; cf.
Friedrich, Staatsverträge 1:56), dat.-loc. sg. asanduli (X 2 I 8
[n-at-kan A]NA ERÍN.MEŠ asanduli pihhun 'those I gave to the
garrison troops'), abl. sg. asandulaz (KUB XIV 15 IV 36 n-as
ERÍN.MEŠ asandulaz eppun 'I manned [lit. seized] them with
occupation troops'; similarly ibid. 42 and KBo IV 4 II 62; cf.
Götze, AM 72, 120), asandulaza (KUB XIX 8 III 31 n-an ŠA
ᵁᴿᵁHatti ERÍN.MEŠ asandulaza e[pta 'and he manned it with a
Hittite occupation force'; cf. Riemschneider, JCS 16:117
[1962]).

asandulai- 'serve as occupier, be on garrison duty', 3 pl. pres.
act. asandulanzi (KBo VI 28 Rs. 26 mān LÚ.MEŠ NA⟨RA⟩RI
asandulanzi 'if auxiliaries are on garrison duty'; cf. Imparati,
SMEA 18:40 [1977]; IBoT I 32 Vs. 20 kedani MU-ti KARAŠ.HI.A
asandula[n]zi 'in what year the armies are on garrison duty');
verbal noun asandulatar (n.), dat.-loc. sg. asandulanni (KBo X 2
I 6 [ERÍN.ME]Š 2 AŠRA asandulanni da⟨la⟩hhun 'I left troops in
two places for garrisoning'; KUB XIII 20 I 24 kuiss-a ERÍN.MEŠ
asandulas-ma n-an-kan ᴰUTU-ŠI asandulanni dālahhi 'and which
[is] garrison troops, it I, my majesty, leave in garrisoning'; KBo
V 4 Rs. 33 namma-tta ᴰUTU-ŠI kuyēs ERÍN.MEŠ.HI.A asandulanni
peskimi warri-ya-asta uyiski[mi] 'further what troops I, my
majesty, give you for garrisoning and send you as auxiliaries';
cf. Friedrich, Staatsverträge 1:64); iter. asanduleski-, asandu-
liski-, 3 sg. pret. act. asanduleskit (III 4 I 16–17 ABU-YA-ma-kan
INA KUR ᵁᴿᵁMitanni kuit anda asanduleskit n-as-kan asanduli
anda istandait 'but because my father was garrisoned in the
interior of Mitanni and lingered in garrison'; cf. Götze, AM
20), asanduliskit (IV 4 IV 62 nu-kan anda asanduliskit; cf.
Götze, AM 142).

Unlike most derivatives in -ul (e.g. deverbative imiul-, ishiul-,
wastul-), asand-ul- is a denominative offshoot of the participle
asant- (besides esant- 'occupied'); a parallel may be seen in

kalulupa- (< **kand-ul-*; cf. Puhvel, *IF* 81:27–8 [1976] = *Analecta Indoeuropaea* 351–2 [1981]). Cf. Götze, *AM* 199–201; Kronasser, *Etym.* 1:336. The connection with *es-* 'be', suggested by Hrozný, *Heth. KB* 168 ('be' = 'linger'), was abortively revived by G. Kestemont, *Diplomatique et droit international en Asie occidentale (1600–1200 av. J. C.)* 597–9 (1974).

Hier. *as-* 'sit', *asa-* 'seat'; *as(a)nu(wa)-* or *isanuwa-* 'set down, establish, install'. Cf. Meriggi, *HHG* 35, 37–8; Laroche, *HH* 154; Hawkins – Morpurgo – Neumann, *HHL* 187–8.

es- has been connected with IE *$\acute{e}s$- 'sit' (Ved. $\mathring{a}ste$, Avest. $\bar{a}ste$, Gk. ἧσται; 3 pl. $\acute{a}sate$, $\mathring{a}\eta h\partial nt\bar{e}$, ἧαται; *IEW* 342–3) since Hrozný, *SH* XIII, 14. The etymological vowel length of *$\bar{e}s$- is not in doubt, and not much further is illumined by a reconstruction E_1eE_1s- (Oettinger, *MSS* 34:112 [1976]), let alone a reduplicated $E_1e\text{-}E_1s$- (H. Eichner, *MSS* 31:54 [1973]). The non-gradational medium tantum paradigm of Indo-Iranian and Greek is largely matched by Hittite *ēs-*, while the very defective (and probably secondary) active forms (*ēszi, asanzi, ēs[i], ēsten*) take their cue from verbs of the type *es-* : *as-* 'be'; exceptions are very rare (occasional *asanta, esanzi*). But unlike Indo-Iranian and Greek, Hittite preserves old ablauting nonfinite forms (*asant-* [rarely *esant-*], *asatar, asauwar*) which reflect a genuine extraparadigmatic *$\bar{e}$: $\text{\FE}_1$ alternation. The reduplicated causatival *asas-, ases-* 'make sit' (q.v.) may have secondarily expanded *a-* as part of the consolidation of a causative sense (like that of its own derivative *asesanu-*); cf. *esesir* 'they sat' and OHitt. *aseshut* besides *ēshut* 'sit!'.

essa-, issa-,   iter. of *iya-* 'do, make' (q.v.; *KUB* I 16 II 24–25 [*ēshar*] *īssuwan dāi* = ibid. I 24–25 [Akk.] *dāmi ana epešim* [*išakkan*] 'he will go about shedding blood'; cf. Sommer, *HAB* 4, 56; IV 4 Vs. 9 and 12 *ēssa*[*tti*] 'thou makest' = Akk. *tapanni* [from *banū*] 'thou begettest'; cf. Laroche, *RA* 58:73 [1964]), 1 sg. pres. act. *ēssahhi* (e.g. *KBo* XI 1 Vs. 24 and 27 *n-at ēssahhi-pat* 'I shall carry it out'; cf. *RHA* 25:107 [1967]; *KUB* XXI 27 IV 44–45 *nu-za ke kue* AWATE.MEŠ ANA ᴰIM ABI-KA Ù ANA ᴰUTU ᵁᴿᵁTÚL-*na* AMA-KA *arkuwar ēssahhi* 'these words which I make as a plea to the storm-god thy father and to the sun-goddess of Arinna thy

mother'; XIV 8 Rs. 20 *nu-za ... arkuwar ēssahhi* 'I make a plea';
cf. Götze, *KlF* 216; *KBo* IV 8 III 7 *nu-za* DINGIR.MEŠ *ēssahhi* 'I
celebrate the gods'), *issahhi* (e.g. *KUB* XXVII 38 I 19 *n-us sēnus
issahhi* 'I make them into figures'; VII 5 II 5 *nu* SISKUR.SISKUR
kuedani parni issahhi 'in the house where I perform the ritual'),
ī]ssahhi (I 16 II 43; cf. Sommer, *HAB* 8), 2 sg. pres. act. *ēssatti*
(e.g. II 11 Rs. 6 *kuit-wa ēssatti* 'what are you doing?'; cf.
Sommer, *AU* 245; VI 41 IV 10 and *KBo* V 13 IV 2 *mahhan
ēssatti* 'as you treat'; cf. Friedrich, *Staatsverträge* 1:132), *issatti*
(e.g. V 3 I 35 *nu mān* SIG₅-*in kuwapi issatti* 'if you ever act well';
cf. Friedrich, *Staatsverträge* 2:110; *KUB* XXVI 22 II 5 SIG₅-*in
issatti*; XXX 10 Rs. 22–23 *nu-]mu ... ŪL assanuwandan anduhsan le issatti* 'do not make me a persona non grata!'; XIV 1 Vs.
86 *le issatti*; cf. Götze, *Madd.* 20), 3 sg. pres. act. *ēssai* (e.g. *KBo*
V 13 III 24 *nasma* LÚ ᵁᴿᵁ*Arzawa kuiski* BAL *ēssai* 'or some
Arzawan is making insurrection'; cf. Friedrich, *Staatsverträge*
1:128; *KUB* XXIV 1 IV 21 UD.KAM-*tili arkuwar ēssai* '[he] daily
makes a plea'; cf. Gurney, *Hittite Prayers* 36; XLII 100 IV
22–23 *kinun-ma-ssi* 12 EZEN ITU.KAM 1 EZEN *zeni* EZEN *hameshi*
ᴸᵁSANGA *IŠTU* É-*ŠÚ ēssai* 'but nowadays the priest celebrates for
him out of his house twelve monthly feasts, one feast in fall
[and one] feast in spring'; cf. ibid. 15–17 *nu-wa-za ...*EZEN *...
iyat* 'celebrated the feast'; cf. G. F. Del Monte, *Oriens Antiquus*
17:185 [1978]; *KBo* VI 5 IV 4 [= *Code* 1:41] *sahhann-a ēssai* 'he
does feudal duty'), *ēssāi* (e.g. VI 4 IV 12–13 [= *Code* 1:41] *luzzi
ēssāi* 'does corvée'; cf. ibid. 14 *nu luzzi* ŪL *iyazzi* 'he does not do
corvée'), *īssai* (e.g. VI 2 II 25 [= *Code* 1:41, OHitt.] *sahhann-a
īssai*; XXII 1 Rs. 32 [OHitt.] *kinun kās kissan īssai* 'now this one
will do thus'; cf. A. Archi, in *Florilegium Anatolicum* 46 [1979]),
issai (e.g. VI 3 II 45–46 [= *Code* 1:41] *sahhan issai*; *KUB* I 11 I
42 *QATAMMA-pat issai* 'he does likewise'; cf. Kammenhuber,
Hippologia 110; *KBo* V 2 IV 45–46 SISKUR.SISKUR *mahhan* INA
UD.KAM *MAHRĪ issai n-at* UD.7.KAM *QATAMMA issai* 'as he
performs the ritual on the first day, he likewise performs it for
seven days'; cf. Witzel, *Heth. KU* 116; *KBo* XIX 44 Rs. 1 SIG₅-*in
issai* 'treats well'; ibid. 8 SIG₅-*in-wa issai*), *issāi* (dupl. XIX 43a
III 19 SIG₅-*in-wa issāi*), *ēsseszi* (*KUB* IX 16 IV 9 EZEN.MEŠ
ēsseszi 'celebrates festivals'; analogical from 3 sg. pret. *ēssesta*),

1 pl. pres. act. *e-es-su-u-e-ni* (XXX 27 Rs. 1–2 *[kuit-w]a-ssi kuit* *ēssuweni [nu-war-a]t-si āra ēsdu* 'whatever we do for him, let it be his due!'; cf. Otten, *Totenrituale* 98), *is-su-ú-e-ni* (XXIII 115, 5 *wēs issuwe[ni]*), 2 pl. pres. act. *ēssatteni* (XIII 4 II 53–55 *nu* EZEN *hamesha[ndas]* [*I*]NA *zēni iyatteni* EZEN *zēnandas-ma hameshi ēssatteni* 'you celebrate the spring festival in the fall, and you celebrate the fall festival in the spring'; cf. Sturtevant, *JAOS* 54:378 [1934]), *issatteni* (*KBo* V 3 IV 29–30 *nu mān sumes* SIG₅-*in issatteni* ... ᴰUTU-*us-ya-smas* SIG₅-*in issahhi* 'if you act well ..., I, my majesty, shall also treat you well'; cf. Friedrich, *Staatsverträge* 2:134), *īstēni* (XXII 1 Rs. 27 [OHitt.] *ta* ᴸᵁ*happinandas īstēni* 'you do the rich man's [bidding]'; cf. A. Archi, in *Florilegium Anatolicum* 46 [1979]), *īstenī* (ibid. 33; like 1 pl. pres. *issuweni*, 1 pl. pret. *issuwen*, and 2 pl. imp. *īsten*, analogical from 3 pl. *issanzi*, falsely segmented as **iss-anzi* rather than **issa-anzi*), 3 pl. pres. act. *essanzi* (e.g. *IBoT* III 148 I 69, besides ibid. 70 *annianzi* 'they perform'; cf. Haas – Wilhelm, *Riten* 216), *ēssanzi* (e.g. *KUB* XXIII 92 Vs. 7 -*ma- -smas* DUMU.MEŠ *kuwattin ēssanzi* 'where they make sons for themselves'; cf. Otten, *AfO* 19:40 [1959–60]; *KBo* III 1 II 61 [OHitt.] *kī-ma idālauwa uddār kuyēs ēssanzi* 'who[ever] do these evil things'; *KUB* XII 26 II 12–13 *nu-war-an* EGIR-*pa* AMA-*ni* DUMU-*an ēssanzi* 'they make him again a child to [his] mother'; cf. Laroche, *RHA* 23:169 [1965]; XIII 2 III 17 DINGIR.MEŠ-*ya kuwapi ēssanzi* 'when they celebrate the gods'; cf. von Schuler, *Dienstanweisungen* 47; XXIV 3 I 19 and 20, XXIV 1 II 8 'they celebrate [festivals]'; cf. Gurney, *Hittite Prayers* 18), *issanzi* (e.g. XXIX 1 II 5 *kuit issanzi* 'what are they doing?'; cf. B. Schwartz, *Orientalia* N.S. 16:28 [1947]; XXXI 101 Vs. 11 *nu* ᴸᵁ·ᴹᴱˢMUŠEN.DU-*TIM QATAMMA issanzi* 'the augurs do likewise'; cf. Ünal, *RHA* 31:49 [1973]; A. Archi, *SMEA* 16:137 [1975]), 1 sg. pret. act. *ēssahhun* (XXXI 66 III 17–18 *kūn memian* ANA ZI-*YA ser ēssahhun* 'this remark for my soul's sake I made'; cf. ibid. I 24 *a]pūn memian iyanun* 'I made that speech'; Houwink Ten Cate, *Anatol. Stud. Güterbock* 129–30; XIV 10 Vs. 19 *namma-za* EZEN.HI.A-*ya kuwapi ēssahhun* 'also, when[ever] I celebrated festivals'; ibid. 22–24 *nu-za* ... *ārkūwar ēssahhun* 'I made a plea'; cf. Götze, *KlF* 206), 3 sg. pret. act. *e-es-se-es-ta*

(e.g. *KBo* V 8 II 28 *nu-za-kan* HUR.SAG.MEŠ-*as anda sāsdus ēssesta* 'he made himself lairs in the mountains'; cf. Götze, *AM* 154; *KUB* XXIV 13 II 9 *alwanzinas kuit* HUL-*lu uttar ēssesta* 'what evil thing the sorcerer did'; cf. Haas – Thiel, *Rituale* 104; XXI 40 III 11 *n-an-zan* ᴸᵁ*HADANU ēssesta* 'he made him his son-in-law'; cf. Ünal, *Hatt.* 2:128; *KBo* VI 4 II 29), *e-se-es-ta* (e.g. V 6 II 14 *nu* EZEN.HI.A *esesta* 'he celebrated festivals'; cf. Güterbock, *JCS* 10:92 [1956]; *KUB* XXII 7 Vs. 3), *e-es-se-is-ta* (e.g. XVII 27 II 29 *kue essesta* 'what he has wrought'; XLI 19 Rs. 3; cf. Haas – Thiel, *Rituale* 94), *e-es-si-es-ta* (e.g. XXI 33 IV 18 SISKUR.MEŠ *INA* ᵁᴿᵁ*Perana ēssesta* 'he performed rituals at P.'; cf. R. Stefanini, *JAOS* 84:23 [1964]; XXII 70 Vs. 13, 15, 22; cf. Imparati, *SMEA* 18:27–9 [1977]; Ünal, *Orakeltext* 56–60), *e-es-si-is-ta* (e.g. XXIV 13 II 28 *alwanzenas kuit* HUL-*lu uttar essista*), *issista* (e.g. *KBo* XV 10 I 14 and 31, II 14, III 56; cf. Szabó, *Entsühnungsritual* 14, 16, 18, 22, 44), 1 pl. pret. act. *e-es-su-u-en* (*KUB* XIX 71, 10 [*nu-nnas* É-*ir kuit*] *ēssuwen* 'the house which we made for ourselves'; cf. Götze, *Neue Bruchstücke* 12), *is-su-u-en* (*KBo* XII 126 I 23 *issuwen-wa kue* 'those which we have made'; cf. Jakob-Rost, *Ritual der Malli* 24), 2 pl. pret. act. *e-es-sa-at-te-in* (*KUB* XXI 42 II 5 *namma apāt kuit ēssatten* 'also that which you have done'; cf. von Schuler, *Dienstanweisungen* 25), 3 pl. pret. act. *e-es-se-ir* (e.g. XXXI 66 II 23–24 EGIR-*pa-ya-mu a*[*pāt*] EME *apūs-pat ēsser* 'afterwards those very ones committed that calumny against me'; cf. Houwink Ten Cate, *Anatol. Stud. Güterbock* 130; *KBo* VI 6 I 23 [= *Code* 1:54] *sah*]*han* ŪL *ēsser* 'they did not do feudal duty'), *e-se-ir* (dupl. VI 3 III 18 *sahhan* ŪL *eser*), *e-es-si-ir* (*KUB* XXIV 11 III 3 *alwan*]*zata ēssir* 'have practised sorcery'; cf. Jakob-Rost, *Ritual der Malli* 42), *e-es-sir* (e.g. *KBo* VI 26 I 40 [= *Code* 2:66] *karū kissan ēssir* 'formerly they did thus'), *i-is-se-ir* (VI 2 III 15 [OHitt.] *sahhan natta īsser*), *i-e-es-sir* (XVII 105 II 17–18 *ki-wa kuit iēssir* 'why did they do this?'; cf. A. Archi, *SMEA* 16:86 [1975]), DÙ-*es-se-ir* (*Bo* 5088 Rs. 11–12 EZEN DÙ-*esser kinun-as* ŪL *ier* 'they [usually] observed the feast, but now they have not observed [it]'), 2 sg. imp. act. *e-is-si* (*KUB* I 16 III 63 [OHitt.] *kuit kardi nu-za apāt essi* 'what [has been impressed] upon [your] heart, do that!'; cf. Sommer, *HAB* 17, 187–8), *ēssa*

(*KBo* V 4 Vs. 26 *n-an* SIG₅-*in ēssa* 'treat it well!'; cf. Friedrich, *Staatsverträge* 1:56; VI 41 IV 12 *n-an-zan* SIG₅-*in ēssa*; cf. Friedrich, *Staatsverträge* 1:134), *issa* (*KUB* XXVI 22 II 6 SIG₅-*in issa*; cf. ibid. 5 SIG₅-*in issatti*), *īssa* (XIII 2 III 28 *kuit handan apāt īssa* 'what [is] right, do that!'; cf. von Schuler, *Dienstanweisungen* 48), 3 sg. imp. act. *e-es-sa-ú* (I 1 IV 80; cf. Götze, *Hattusilis* 38), 2 pl. imp. act. *is-sa-at-tin* (XIII 20 I 19 'fulfill [obligation]!'; cf. Alp, *Belleten* 11:390–2 [1947]), *i-is-te--en* (*KBo* XXII 62 + VI 2 III 19–20 [= *Code* 1:55, OHitt.] *ītten māhhanda ar*[*i-* …] *sumes-a apinissan īste*[*n*] 'go, as your peers, even so you shall do'; cf. H. Otten – C. Rüster, *ZA* 62:231 [1972], and see under 2 pl. pres. *īstenī* above), *e-es-te-en* (dupl. VI 3 III 22 *ītten mahhan ares-(s)mes sume*[*s*] *apenissan ēsten*; perhaps misunderstood here, in the later version of the Code, as *ēsten* 'you shall be'; cf. also Starke, *Funktionen* 144), 3 pl. imp. act. *ēssandu* (e.g. IV 4 II 11; cf. Götze, *AM* 112; *KUB* XXVI 43 Vs. 58 *kī-pat sahhan ēssandu* 'let them do this feudal duty'; cf. Imparati, *RHA* 32:30 [1974]; XIII 2 III 4–5 *nu-ssan* ANA TÚL SISKUR.SISKUR *kittari n-at-si ēssandu* 'a rite is on the books for the fountain; they shall perform it for it'; cf. von Schuler, *Dienstanweisungen* 47; ibid. II 44 *kuedaniya* DINGIR--LIM-*ni kuit mehur n-an apedani mehuni ēssandu* 'what time for every god [is proper], at that time they shall celebrate him'), *issandu* (ibid. 43 *namma* DINGIR.MEŠ *mehunas issandu* 'further-more they shall celebrate the gods at the [right] times'; IV 1 I 41 EZEN GAL-*TIM issandu* 'let them celebrate the great festivals'; cf. von Schuler, *Die Kaškäer* 170); partic. *essant-*, nom.-acc. sg. neut. *ēssan* (XVIII 20, 9 *kuit arha ēssan* 'which [has been] carried out [= completed]'; XXXI 66 II 28–29 *man-wa* ANA PAN ABU-YA *k*[*ī*] *ammel* EME *ēssan* 'if this calumny against me [were] committed before my father'; cf. Houwink Ten Cate, *Anatol. Stud. Güterbock* 130); verbal noun *e-es-su-mar* (*KBo* I 35, 14 *kuwapitta* [with gloss-wedges] *parā ēssumar* matching Akk. *masāru* 'let loose', thus literally 'making [someone] move forth somewhere'), **ēssuwar*, **ēssūwar*, **īssuwar* inferrable from the supine (e.g. III 1 I 22 [OHitt.] *nu ēshar-summit ēssuwan tiyer* 'they began to shed their blood'; *KUB* XV 3 I 12 *ēssūwan tehhi* 'I begin to make'; XXIX 24, 2 [= *Code* 2:12] *sahhan*] *ēssūwan* *dāi* 'begins to do feudal duty', vs. ibid. 1 *sahhan*] ŪL *iyaz*[*i*; *KBo* VIII 42 Rs. 2 [OHitt.] *īssuwan dāisten*; *KUB* I 16 II 24–25, quoted at the beginning above); iter. *eseski-*, *essiki-*, 3 pl. pret. act. *e-se-es-ki-ir* (V 22, 21), *e-es-si-kir* (*KBo* III 34 II 6–7 *s-an-asta arha pehuter s-an ēssikir s-as* BA.UG₆ 'then they took him away, and they kept working him over, and he died'); *eseski-*, *essiki-* match e.g. *arseski-*, *arsikki-* from *arsai-*, *arsiya-* (q.v.); *essiki-* should not be confused with *eski-* from *iya-* (q.v.); rather it, like *arsikki-*, is a secondary, awkward spelling variant brought on chiastically by the likes of *ānsiki-*, *ānsiski-* (besides *ānsaski-*, *ānaski-*) as attempts to express /ans-ski-/.

After a false start connecting *es-* 'sit' (Götze, *Madd.* 105; Götze – Pedersen, *MS* 50; Sturtevant, *Comp. Gr.*[1] 85, 246; Bechtel, *Hittite Verbs* 77), Sommer's recognition (*AU* 303–4, *HAB* 56–7) has prevailed that *essa-*, *issa-* is iteratival from *iya-*, *ie-* 'do' (cf. e.g. Sturtevant, *Comp.Gr.*[2] 135; Kammenhuber, *RHA* 17:35 [1959]; Kronasser, *Etym.* 1:553); parallels are *halzessa-* from *halzai-* and *warressa-* from *warrai-*. Here, as with *iya-*, OHitt. forms diverge from the relative regularity of the classical paradigm (e.g. *īssahhi*, *īssai*, *issuweni*, *īstenī*, *issuwen*, *īsten*, *īsser*, *īssuwan*). Unlike Neu (*KZ* 93:71 [1979]) one may hesitate to claim primacy for the nonthematic forms, seeing in them rather an analogical aberration (cf. sub 2 pl. pres. *īstenī* above); but *is-* has claim to relative antiquity (cf. Otten, *Sprachliche Stellung* 24), and *īs-* may be a phonetic outcome of **eye-s-* (>*ēs->īs-*), whereas the standard spelling *ēssa-* is perhaps influenced by the type of *halzessa-* (<**halzai-s-*). Postulating *iesa-* or /yessa-/ as the basic reading (e.g. Sturtevant, *JAOS* 63:2–3 [1943]; Kronasser, *Etym.* 1:554) was a direct, unnecessary consequence of seeing /ye-/ in *ie-*; Rosenkranz's assumption (*ZA* 54:112–3 [1961]) of an "abstracted" *i-* from *iya-* as the basis of *issa-* or *essa-* was simply unnecessary.

eshar, ishar (n.) 'blood', specifically 'dark (venous) blood' (cf. αἷμα κελαινόν; MUD; BAD: *KBo* X 45 IV 10 BAD-*as* DINGIR. .MEŠ = *KUB* XLI 8 IV 9 *ēshanas* DINGIR.MEŠ 'deities of blood'; ADAMMU: *KBo* I 51 Rs. 17 [Akk.] *ad*]*ammu* = Hitt. *ishar*, vs.

ibid. 18 [Akk.] *šarku* = Hitt. *manis* 'bright [arterial] blood' [BAD.UD vs. BAD.GE₆]; ibid. 16 [Akk.] *bubu'du* 'pus' = [Hitt.] *muwas* 'body fluid'; cf. Güterbock, *Arch. Or.* 18.1–2:228–9 [1950]; R. Stefanini, *AGI* 43:18–20 [1958]); 'bloodshed, bloody deed, murder' (*eshar iya-*, iter. *eshar essa-*, pass. *eshar kis-*, lit. 'make blood', i.e. 'shed blood, do bloody deeds, commit murder', copied occasionally in Hittite-influenced Akkadian [Boğazköy, Kültepe, Ugarit] as *dāmi epēšu*; see also s.v. *iya-* and cf. Kronasser, *Festschrift J. Friedrich* 275–6, 286 [1959], *Etym.* 1:125; Gk. εἴργασθαι ... αἷμα, συνδρῶν αἷμα, αἷμ' ἐπράξαμεν [Euripides, *Orestes* 284–5, 406, 1139]); 'lifeblood, vital juices, sap', nom.-acc. sg. *e-es-har* (frequent, e.g. *KBo* III 1 I 22 [OHitt.] *nu ēshar-summit ēssuwan tiyer* 'they began to shed their blood'; ibid. 33 *[nu] ēshar ier* 'they shed blood'; ibid. II 33 URU*Hattusi ēshar pangariyattati* 'at Hattusas bloodshed has multiplied'; VIII 35 II 3 *nu ēshar kisari* 'blood is shed'; XVII 1 I 27 *tarueni-ma-at ēshar* 'but we call it blood'; cf. Otten – Souček, *Altheth. Ritual* 20; XIII 31 I 8 *ēshar araszi* 'blood flows'; cf. Riemschneider, *Geburtsomina* 74; *KUB* XLIII 38 Rs. 14 *[kī-w]a ŪL* G[EŠTIN] *sumenzan-wa ēshar* 'this [is] not wine, [it is] your blood'; cf. Oettinger, *Eide* 20; *KBo* III 23 I 9 *zig-a* SAG.GEME.ÌR. .MEŠ *ēshar-semit sanha* 'but you, exact the blood of servants!'; cf. A. Archi, in *Florilegium Anatolicum* 41 [1979]; XXII 1 Rs. 24–25 [OHitt.] *nu ŠA* LÚMAŠDÁ *ēshar-set natta sanhiskatteni* 'you do not exact the blood [= avenge the death] of the poor man'; cf. A. Archi, ibid. 46; frequent on the "calamity lists" [examples s.v. *ishahru-*]; *KUB* XI 1 III 13 *[n-]asta udnē ēshar akku[skir* 'they quaffed the sap of the land' [partitive apposition]), *is-har* (e.g. *KBo* III 67 II 11–12 *n-apa* DINGIR.MEŠ I*P]iseniyas ishar sanhir* 'then the gods avenged the blood of Pisenis'; *HT* 1 I 37 *nu ishar dāi* 'he takes blood', besides dupl. *KUB* IX 31 I 45 *nu ēshar dāi*; cf. B. Schwartz, *JAOS* 58:338 [1938]; XLIV 63 II 7–8 *nu-ssi-kan ishar arha tarnai* 'lets off blood from him'; cf. Burde, *Medizinische Texte* 28), *e-es-sar* (XLI 8 III 9 *nu-kan kuit* HUL-*lu ēssar anda* 'what evil blood[-shed] [is] therein', besides dupl. *KBo* X 45 III 17–18 *nu-kan kuit* HUL-*lu ēshar anda*; cf. Otten, *ZA* 54:128 [1961]), *i-e-es-sar* (*KUB* XXIV 13 II 23–24 *ansun-ta-kkan* NÍ.TE-*za* HUL-*lu uddār* *alwanzatar iēssarr-a* 'I have wiped from your body evil words, sorcery, and bloodshed'; cf. Haas – Thiel, *Rituale* 104; XLI 21 IV 4 HUL-*lu* U[H₄-*tar papr*]*atar iēssar* 'evil sorcery, defilement, bloodshed'; cf. Haas – Thiel, *Rituale* 278; *KBo* XIX 145 III 7 *alw*]*anzatar iēssar paprātar*; ibid. 15; cf. Haas – Thiel, *Rituale* 300; *KUB* IX 39 II 2; VIII 39, 2, 4, 5), A-DAM-MA (*KUB* XVIII 51 + *KBo* II 6 II 34–35 ᴰDAG-*tis* GUB-*is nu ŠA* LUGAL ADAMMA *muann-a* ME-*as n-an* ᴰMAH-*ni pais* 'Throne rose, took the king's blood and [seminal?] fluid, and gave it to the Mother-goddess'; *VBoT* 121 Vs. 11 ADAMMA-*ya* ME-*as*), A-TAM-MA (*KUB* XVI 29 Rs. 9 *ŠA* LUGAL ATAMMA A.A-*n-a* ME-*as*; VI 7 III 8), gen. sg. *e-es-ha-na-as* (e.g. XLI 8 III 10 *n-at sumes datten n-at ēshanas* DINGIR-*LIM-ni pestin* 'you, take it and give it to the deity of blood!'; XIII 9 + XL 62 II 3–4 *mān ēshanass-a kuiski sarnikzil piyan harzi* 'also if someone has paid wergeld [lit. given restitution for blood]'; cf. von Schuler, *Festschrift J. Friedrich* 446 [1959]), *ishanas* (e.g. dupl. *KBo* X 45 III 19; *KUB* XI 1 IV 19–20 *ishanas-ta uttar kissan kuis ēshar iezzi nu kuit ēshanas--pat ishās tezzi* 'a case of murder is as follows: who commits murder, whatever the one in charge of the murder [i.e. the kinsman entitled to extrajudicial settlement] says ...'; *KUB* XIX 67 + 1513/u I 17–18 *nu-mu* ¹*Arma-*ᴰU-*as* [*ku*]*it ishanas antuhsas ēsta* 'because Armadattas was my blood-relative'; *KBo* XV 10 I 22 *ishanas* ᴰUTU-*un* 'the sun-god of blood'; cf. Szabó, *Entsühnungsritual* 16), *ishānas* (*KUB* XVII 18 II 29), *ishanās* (*KBo* XVII 1 IV 8; cf. Otten – Souček, *Altheth. Ritual* 36; XV 10 I 1 and 32, ibid. II 39 *ishanās* ᴰUTU-*us*), *e-es-na-as* (*KUB* XLI 8 II 36 *ēsnas* DINGIR-*LIM* 'the deity of blood', besides dupl. *KBo* X 45 III 1 *ēshanas* DINGIR-*LUM*; III 1 II 47–48 [OHitt.] *kī-wa ēsnas uttar tuppiaz au* 'read from the tablet this business of blood[shed]!'), *i-e-es-na-as* (*KUB* XVII 18 II 31 [*pap*]*rannas iēsnas*, besides ibid. 29 *ishānas* [see above]), dat.-loc. sg. *ēshanī* (*KBo* XI 1 Vs. 45 [in "calamity list" s.v. *ishahru-*]; XI 45 III 22; cf. Haas, *Nerik* 232), *ēshani* (e.g. *KUB* X 11 VI 5; XLI 8 IV 25 *wastulli ēshani hurtiya* 'sin, bloodshed, curse'), *ishanī* (e.g. dupl. *KBo* X 45 IV 26; XI 49 VI 18; *KUB* XI 26 II 11), instr. sg. *ēshanta* (*HT* 1 I 38 *n-an ēshanta iskiyaizzi* 'he daubs it with the blood'), *ishanda* (*KBo* XVII 4 III 15; cf.

eshar, ishar

Otten – Souček, *Altheth. Ritual* 34), abl. sg. *e-es-ha-na-az* (e.g. *KUB* XVI 77 Rs. 19 *ēshanaz sarnikzel* 'wergeld', lit. 'restitution because of blood[shed]'), *e-es-ha-na-za* (XIX 20 Rs. 9), *e-es-ha--⟨na-⟩az* (XV 42 II 10 [in "calamity list" s.v. *ishahru-*]), *is-ha-na-az* (ibid. 30; XXX 31 + XXXII 114 I 42 [similar lists]), *is-ha-na-za* (XXX 33 I 10 [another such list; see s.v. *ishahru-*]), *e-es-na-za* (*IBoT* I 33, 52 *ēsnaza uit* 'came from the blood'; cf. Laroche, *RA* 52:153 [1958]).

eshanant-, ishanant- (c.) 'blood', nom. sg. *ēshananza* (*KUB* XXX 34 IV 7–8 *nu ēshananza linkiyaza* ^É*halinduwa* É DINGIR. .MEŠ *le epzi* 'may bloodshed and perjury not seize the temples of the palace!'; cf. V. Haas – M. Wäfler, *Oriens Antiquus* 16:230 [1977]; IV 1 II 19–23 *nu* ŠA KUR ^{URU}*Hatti* DINGIR.MEŠ *antuhsuss-a ēshar iyauwanna halzissanzi nu* ŠA KUR ^{URU}*Hatti* DINGIR.MEŠ-*nas iyauwas* [...] *ēshananzass-a antu*[*hs*]*a*[*s* ...] *iyauwass-a* 'they summon the gods and men of Hatti to shed blood; by the gods of Hatti [blood is] to be shed, and also by the men [of Hatti] blood [is] to be shed'; cf. von Schuler, *Die Kaškäer* 172; IX 4 I 38 *ēshananza ē*[*sh*]*anas* [GIG-*an karapzi*] 'blood relieves blood-disease'; cf. Alp, *Anatolia* 2:40 [1957]; Haas, *Orientalia* N.S. 40:414 [1971]), *ishanaza* (dupl. IX 34 II 46–47 *ishanaza* [*ishanas* KI.MIN] 'blood of blood likewise'), *ishananza* (XIV 14 + XIX 2 Rs. 23 *nu* KUR ^{URU}*Hatti-ya apās ishananza arha namma zinne*[*sta*] 'that bloodshed has further-more finished off Hatti as well'; cf. Götze, *KlF* 172; XLIV 63 II 3; cf. Burde, *Medizinische Texte* 28). Cf. Laroche, *BSL* 57.1:26 (1962). On the ablatival origin of such "animate" nominatives to neuter nouns see s.v. *istark(iya)-*.

eshassi-, divine epithet with Luwoid derivation suffix, nom. sg. *ēshassis* (*KUB* XLI 8 III 21 *kuit-san ēshassis tet* 'what the bloody one said'; cf. Otten, *ZA* 54:130, 154 [1961]); probably to be identified with ibid. 10 *ēshanas* DINGIR-*LIM* 'deity of blood'. Derivation makes some difficulty (cf. also Kronasser, *Etym.* 1:228), since **esh(a)n-assi-* might rather have yielded **esnassi-*. On similar divine epithets (e.g. *hilassi-, lalassi-, wasdulassi-*) see Laroche, *Recherches* 68–70.

eshanuwant-, ishanuwant- 'bloody', nom.-acc. pl. neut. *ēshanuwanta* (*HT* 1 I 30 *ēshanuwanta kuyēs wēstata*, with dupl.

KUB IX 31 I 37 *ēsha[nuwan]ta kuēs wēssanta* 'who wear bloody things'; cf. B. Schwartz, *JAOS* 58:336 [1938]), dat.-loc. sg. *ishanuwanti* (XXXVI 89 Vs. 13–14 ANA DUMU.MEŠ-*MELUTTI ishanuwanti isharwa[nti* 'bloody, blood-red mankind'; ibid. Rs. 1 *i]shanuwanti isharwanti*; cf. Haas, *Nerik* 144, 150). **eshn̥--want->eshan-want-* (spelled *eshanuwant-*); cf. e.g. *iyatnuwant-* from *iyatar* (s.v.; analyzable as *iyatn-uwant-*, allophonically regular after light syllable; similarly *saknuwant-* 'shitty' from *sakkar* 'shit'), or *samankurwant-* 'bearded' from *zamangur* 'beard'. Wrongly taken as participle of *esharnu-* 'make bloody' (with loss of *r*) by Haas, *Nerik* 162, even as Laroche (*Dict. louv.* 33) interpreted the matching Luw. *ashanuwant-* as being from *asharnu-* (q.v. infra). For denom. *-want-* cf. Kronasser, *Etym.* 1:266–7.

eshaniya- 'bloody', nom.-acc. pl. neut. *ēshaniya* (*KUB* XLIV 4 + *KBo* XIII 241 Rs. 2 ᴰSIN-*as-ma ēshaniya wassiya* 'the moon-god wears bloody things'. Cf. e.g. *ispant-iya-* 'nocturnal' from *ispant-* 'night'.

**eshaniya-* 'to bloody', iter. **eshaneski-*, syncopational partic. **eshan(i)skant->eshaskant-, ishaskant-*, nom. sg. c. *e-es--ha-as-kán-za* (*KUB* VII 41 Vs. 15 *ēshaskanza linkanza* 'one who has bloodied [and] forsworn himself'; cf. Otten, *ZA* 54:116 [1961]), acc. pl. c. *is-ha-as-kán-tu-us* (*KBo* XVII 4 II 6–7 *hatugaus lālus* [...] *ishaskantus dāhhun* 'I have taken the terrible bloodied tongues'; cf. Otten – Souček, *Altheth. Ritual* 24), nom.-acc. pl. neut. *es-ha-as-kán-ta* (III 34 I 20 TÚG-*ZUNU* ᵀᵁᴳ*ishial-semett-a kuit natta esha[s]kanta* 'how come their garment[s] and their belt[s] are not bloodied?'), *is-ha-as-kán-ta* (XVII 1 I 24 *sākuwa-smet ishaskanta* 'their eyes [are] blood-shot'; cf. Otten – Souček, *Altheth. Ritual* 20). **eshaniya-* parallels *sakniya-* 'to shit' from *sakkar* 'shit'. Cf. H. Eichner, *MSS* 28:12, 18 (1970).

eshariya-, issariya- 'to bloody', 3 sg. pret. act. *issariat* (*KUB* XLI 8 III 24; cf. Otten, *ZA* 54:130 [1961]); iter. *eshar(r)eski-*, 3 sg. imp. act. *es-har-ri-es-ki-id-du* (*KUB* XVII 27 III 12–13 *n-at-kan* ANŠU-*as esharreskiddu [n-at-]kan* GUD-*us kammarsi-eskiddu* 'let the ass bloody them, let the ox defecate on them!'). **eshariya-* parallels *sehuriya-* 'urinate' from *sehur* 'urine'.

esharnu-, isharnu- '(make) bloody, dye blood-red', 1 sg. pres. act. *ēsharnumi* (*KUB* XIV 1 Rs. 47 *nu-wa-za* QAT]E.HI.A-*ya ammuk hūdāk ēsharnu*[*mi* 'and I shall forthwith bloody my hands'; cf. Götze, *Madd.* 30), 3 sg. pres. act. *ēsharnuzi* (XXIII 72 Rs. 29–30 [*k*]*uis-a-za* ITTI LÚ.MEŠ ᵁᴿᵁ*Pahhuwa* [QATI.HI.A-ŠU] ŪL *ēsharnuzi* 'but he that does not bloody his hands with the people of P.'), 3 pl. pres. act. *isharnuwanzi* (*KBo* VI 34+*KUB* XLVIII 76 III 47–IV 1 *kī* KUŠ SA₅ *m*[*a*]*hhan isharnuwanzi nu-ssi-kan i*[*sha*]*rwātar arha* ŪL *paizzi* 'as they dye this skin blood-red, and its blood-coloredness does not go away'; cf. Oettinger, *Eide* 14), 2 sg. imp. act. *ēsharnut* (*KUB* XIV 1 Rs. 18 *nu-wa-za* QATE.MEŠ-*KA zik hūdāk ēsharnut* 'bloody thy hands forthwith!'), 2 pl. imp. act. *e-es-har-nu-ut-tin* (XXIII 72 Rs. 29 ITTI LÚ.MEŠ ᵁᴿᵁ*Pahhuwa-ma-za* QATI.HI.A-*KUNU sumes hūdāk ēsharnuttin*); partic. *isharnuwant-*, nom. sg. *isharnuwanza* (XXXV 145 Vs. 3 *isharnuwanza* ᴰU.GUR 'bloody war-god'; acc. sg. c. *isharnuwandan* (ibid. 15; dupl. XVII 15 II 10 *isharnuwan-da⟨n⟩* ᴰU.GUR; IX 4 III 42–43 *isharnuwanda⟨n⟩* ᴰU.GUR; dupl. IX 34 IV 2 *ishar*]*nuwandan* ᴰU.GUR), gen. sg. *isharnuwandas* (*KBo* XVII 54 I 14 *isharnuwandas* ᴰU.GUR), nom. pl. c. *ishar-nuwantes* (*VBoT* 111 III 15 *isharnuwantes dankunuwantes hahl*[-*iuwantes*] 'reddened, blackened, verdant'; cf. Riemschneider, *MIO* 5:146 [1957]), nom.-acc. pl. neut. *isharnuwanda* (*VBoT* 111 III 9; *KBo* XII 126 I 39 [*isha*]*rnuwanda*; cf. Jakob-Rost, *Ritual der Malli* 26); iter. *esharnuski-, isharnuski-* (ibid. 38 *isharnusk*[*i-*), 1 sg. pres. act. *isharnuskimi* (*KUB* XXX 36 III 1), 3 sg. pres. midd. (?) *ēsharnuskitta* (*Bo* 2709 II 8). *esharnu-* as a denominative verb parallels e.g. *aimpa-nu-* 'to burden'.

esharnumai-, isharnumai- '(make) bloody, smear with blood', 3 sg. pres. act. *isharnumaizzi* (*KBo* V 1 I 25–26 *namma* IŠTU 2 MUŠEN *harnāui* ᴳᴵˢKAK.HI.A-*ya kuiussa arhayan isharnumaizzi* 'then he bloodies also one by one the pegs of the birth stool with [the blood of] two birds'; cf. Sommer – Ehelolf, *Pāpanikri* 2*, 18; *KUB* XV 31 II 23 *nu* 9 *āpi isharnumaizzi* 'he smears with blood nine pits'; cf. Haas – Wilhelm, *Riten* 156), *isharnumāizzi* (dupl. XV 32 II 18), 3 pl. pres. act. *ēsharnumanzi* (XXIX 4 IV 39 ŠA [DINGIR-*LI*]*M* GIBIL *hūman ēsharnumanzi* 'they smear with blood everything of the new deity'; cf. Kronasser, *Umsiedelung*

310

32), *isharnumanzi* (*KBo* V 1 III 41 *n-an* IŠTU MUŠEN *isharnumanzi* 'they bloody it with a bird['s blood]'; *isharnum*[*anzi* in XXI 45 II 2). Denom. from **esharnuma-*, either verbal noun in *-(i)ma-* (cf. Kronasser, *Etym.* 1:178) or a Luwoid participle (cf. Luw. *āsharnumma-* below).

**esharu-*, **isharu-* (n.) 'bloodiness, blood-red color', denom. *isharwai-*, *isharwiya-* 'have bloodiness, bleed, be blood-colored', partic. *isharwant-*, nom. sg. c. *isharwanza* (259/s Rs. 9 *isharwanza* SAL.LUGAL-*as* 'bloody queen'), acc. sg. c. *isharwandan* (*KUB* IX 34 I 26 *isharwandan* ᴰU.GUR; XVII 15 III 2 *isharwand*[*an*?]), dat.-loc. sg. *isharwanti* (XXXVI 89 Vs. 14, Rs. 1, quoted under *eshanuwant-* above), instr. sg. *is*]*harwante*[*t* (*KBo* XVII 25 Rs. 14; cf. Neu, *Altheth.* 225), nom. pl. c. *isharwantes* (*KUB* XXX 93 Vs. 3; cf. Neu, *Altheth.* 222), acc. pl. c. *isharwantus* (*KBo* XVII 1 I 24–25 *wessanda-ma isharwantus* TÚG.HI.A-*us* 'they wear blood-red garments'; cf. Otten – Souček, *Altheth. Ritual* 20), nom.-acc. pl. neut. *isharwanda* (*KUB* XXXIII 54, 13–14 *hameshi-ya-z* BABBAR-*TIM* [*wassasi*] EBUR-*ma-z isharwand*[*a w*]*assasi* 'in the spring you wear white, but at harvest you wear red'; cf. Laroche, *RHA* 23:139 [1965]; similarly XXXIV 76 I 3 *isharwanda wassizzi*, besides ibid. 2 *harki wassizzi*; cf. Otten, *AfO* 16:69 [1952–3]); verbal noun *isharwātar* (n.) 'blood-coloredness' (*KBo* VI 34 + *KUB* XLVIII 76 III 48, quoted under *esharnu-* above); iter. *isharuieski-*, 3 sg. pres. act. *is-har-ú-i-es-ki-iz-zi* (*KUB* XXVIII 6 Vs. 10b–11b ᴳᴵˢHAŠHUR TÚL-*i ser artari n-at isharuieskizzi* 'an apple-tree stands over a well, and it keeps "bleeding"' [cf. Akk. *dam erini* 'cedar-blood', i.e. resin; thus perhaps 'its sap flows']); also factitive *ēsharwahh-*, iter. 3 sg. pres. midd. in *KBo* XV 1 I 27 [LUGAL]-*us-wa kuit ēsharwah*[*heskitta* 'wherewith the king has been made blood-red' (cf. Kümmel, *Ersatzrituale* 112, 124; Neu, *Interpretation* 32). Cf. J. J. S. Weitenberg, *Anatolica* 4:160–3 (1971–2).

e-es-har-ú-i-il, *is-har-ú-i-il* 'of a blood-red kind' (?), attested as qualifier of KUŠ 'skin, hide' (*KUB* IX 4 II 5 *e-es-har-ú-i-il* KUŠ-*an*; VII 13 I 14 KUŠ.UDU-*ya e-es-har-ú-i-il*; ibid. 25 KUŠ.UDU-*ya is-har-ú-i*[*-il* 'blood-red sheepskin'; *Bo* 5969 I 3 KUŠ *is-har-ú-i-il*). The noun underlying KUŠ can hardly be *kursa-*

(c.), because *KUB* IX 4 II 5 kuš-*an* seems to be nominative (4–6: *kāsa-tta ēsharuīl* kuš-*an kāsa-tta suppis* ᵁᴰᵁ*iyanza* 'lo, for you a blood-red skin, lo, for you a pure sheep'); thus *ēsharuīl* is probably nom.-acc. sg. neut., perhaps exceptional for **esharu-*ili*, like e.g. *suwaru-ili-* 'of a weighty sort' from *suwaru-* 'weighty, hefty' (q.v.). *KBo* VI 34 + *KUB* XLVIII 76 III 46 and 47 kuš.sa₅ 'red skin' may stand for kuš *isharuīl* (cf. Oettinger, *Eide* 48–9), with ibid. III 47–IV 1 (quoted under *esharnu-* above) thus a figura etymologica (*isharuīl* ... *isharnuwanzi* 'they dye blood-red', with proleptic predicate complement, followed by *isharwātar* 'blood-coloredness').

Luw. *ashanuwant-* 'bloody', nom. sg. c. *āshanuwantis* (*KUB* XXXV 108, 15 *āshanuwantis* ᴰu.gur-*as* 'bloody war-god'; cf. Hitt. *isharnuwanza* ᴰu.gur, quoted above), nom.-acc. pl. neut. *ashanuwanta* (IX 31 II 23 *ashanuwanta kuinzi wassantari* 'who wear bloody things'; cf. ibid. I 37 [Hitt.] *ēsha[nuwan]ta kuēs wēssanta*, quoted above); *asharnu-* '(make) bloody', partic. nom. pl. c. *āsharnummainzi* (XXXV 18 I 13 gìr.meš-*šunu āsharnummainzi* 'their feet [are] bloodied'; cf. Otten, *LTU* 25). Cf. Otten, *Bestimmung* 36–41.

Hier. *asharmi-* 'bloody' (?). Cf. Meriggi, *HHG* 36; Laroche, *HH* 184.

eshar has been connected with the old heteroclitic IE base word for 'blood' since F. Ribezzo, *Rivista indo-greco-italica* 4:128 (1920). The nearest apparent parallel to *eshar* : gen. *eshanas* is Vedic *ásṛg* : gen. *asnás* 'blood' (post-Vedic *asram*), but a reconstruction $*ésH_r(-g)$: $esH\eta nós$ would have been expected to yield Ved. **asanás* (cf. also F. O. Lindeman, *Einführung in die Laryngaltheorie* 47 [1970]). However, *eshar* : *eshanas* can be interpreted also as reflecting rather $*ésH_1\underset{\circ}{r}$: $ésH_1$-$\underset{\circ}{\eta}$-s ($>$ **eshans* reshaped to regular *eshanas*; cf. Puhvel, in *Hethitisch und Indogermanisch* 212 [1979]), which allows an alternative comparison with Gk. (Hes.) ἔαρ, εἶαρ, ἦαρ, ἶαρ 'blood', also εἰαροπότης, ἠεροπότης, ἰαροπότης 'blood-drinker' (corrupted in Homer into ἠεροφοῖτις ['aerobatic'] Ἐρινύς [*Iliad* 9.571, 19.87]; cf. *Schol. Iliad.* 19.87 εἰαροπῶτις, εἶαρ = αἶμα, and *KUB* I 16 III 17 [OHitt.] *ēs]har-simit ekutta* 'she has drunk their blood'); ἦαρ ($< *ésH\underset{\circ}{r}$) has the long grade like e.g. ἦπαρ 'liver', and gen. *ἔατος (<*ésHṇ-t-; replaced by εἶαρος in Alexandrian poetic usage, on the basis of compositional εἰαρο-; cf. ὑδρο- driving out ὑδατο-) may have alternatively generalized the same grade (cf. ἤπατος). Ved. *ásṛg*, on the contrary, has the same normal grade as *yákṛt* 'liver' (gen. *yaknás*), and *asnás* can be explained as back-formed secondarily on the basis of a suffixless locative *ásan* < *esHṇ (cf. *áhar*, gen. *áhnas*, loc. *áhan*). The Hittite forms without *h* (*ēssar*, *ēsnas*) are also clearly secondary, probably originating in new allomorphic environments such as /eshnas/, with *h* secondarily trapped and lost in nonvocalic surroundings. Thus a combined consideration of the Vedic and Greek cognates affords a fairly full understanding of the Hittite paradigm, whether *ēshar*, *ishar* be interpreted as having long or normal vowel grade in the first syllable. The other cognates (Toch. A *ysār*, B *yasar* [<*esHōr?], Arm. *ariwn* [<*esHṛyon-?], Lettish *asins* [<*esHṇ-?], Lat. *aser*, *assar-*) hardly militate against the assumption of initial *e- or *ē-, granted the amount of secondary sources of *a* in all those languages (cf. e.g. Lat. *magnus*, *salvus*). Cf. also Benveniste, *Origines* 8, 26; R. Stefanini, *AGI* 43:18–41 (1958).

That Gk. ἰχώρ (gen. ἰχῶρος) 'serum' (also denoting what gods have in lieu of normal blood, e.g. *Iliad* 5:340) may be a loanword from Hitt. *ishar* has been sporadically alleged since A. H. Sayce, *Classical review* 36:19 (1922); thus e.g. P. Kretschmer, *KlF* 10–1, *Anzeiger der Österreichischen Akademie der Wissenschaften* 1947, 19–20; cf. Puhvel, in *Evidence for laryngeals* 85 (1965).

es(sa)ri- (n.) 'shape, form, (body-)frame, likeness, image, icon, statue' (ALAM; *KBo* III 94 II 10 ALAM=[Akk.] *ṣalmu*=*ēsri*; I 44+XIII 1 IV 31 [Akk.] *ṣalmu*=*ēssari*; cf. Otten, *Vokabular* 20, 26), ᔆᴵᴳ*es(sa)ri-* (n. and c.) 'fleece' (literally 'woolshape, woolskin', besides UDU-*as* ᴷᵁˢ*kursas* 'sheepskin' [with 'hide' determinative]), nom. sg. c. ᔆᴵᴳ*ēsris* (*KUB* XXXII 133 I 12), acc. sg. c. ᔆᴵᴳ*ēsrin* (*KUB* XLI 1 I 16 ᔆᴵᴳ*ēsrin* GE₆ *dāi* '[she] takes a black fleece'), nom.-acc. sg. neut. *ēsri* (e.g. dupl. *KBo* XXI 8 II 6 *dankui* ᔆᴵᴳ*ēsri dāi*; cf. Jakob-Rost, *Ritual der Malli* 30; *KUB* IX

28 I 11 *nu* DINGIR-*LIM-as ēsri iyazi* 'one is to make a likeness of the deity'; XII 50, 7 UKÙ-*as ēsri-set* 'a likeness of a man'; *KBo* XIII 2 Vs. 2 *ēsri-met* 'my likeness', besides ibid. 3 *sēnas-mes* 'my [substitute] figure'; *KUB* XX 54 + *KBo* XIII 122 Rs. 6 *ēsri-sset--wa nēuwan* 'his [viz. the icon's] frame [is] new' [besides details like breast, head, penis]; cf. Neu – Otten, *IF* 77:182 [1972]; *KBo* XXI 22 Vs. 25 *ēsri-set-wa* GIBIL-*an*; cf. also G. Kellerman, *Tel Aviv* 5:200–1 [1978]; Starke, *ZA* 69:92 [1979]; *KUB* XLIII 63 Vs. 12–13 *nu labarnan* ... *ēsri-sset newāh* 'renovate the ruler's statue!'; XXXIII 54, 16–17 UDU-*us-ma-ta-kkan katti-ti* [*arha paizzi*] [*nu-ss*]*e-sta ēsri* [*huezta* 'the sheep goes off beneath you [viz. the hawthorn], and you pluck[ed] its fleece'; cf. Otten, *AfO* 16:69–70 [1952–3]; Laroche, *RHA* 23:139 [1965]; similarly XVII 10 IV 2, but with ˢᶦᴳ*ēsri*; cf. Laroche, *RHA* 23:96 [1965]; 110/e Vs. 21 ᵁᴰᵁ*iyantas* ˢᶦᴳ*ēsri* 'sheep's fleece'; 110/e Rs. 23 -*k*]*an* ˢᶦᴳ*ēsri anda hūlalianzi* 'they wrap in a fleece'), *ēssari* (e.g. *KUB* XII 63 Vs. 35 *ēssari-sit*; XVII 28 II 43), ˢᶦᴳ*ēssarri* (XXXIV 76 I 5), ALAM-*ri* (*HT* 96 obv. 7), ALAM-*i* (*KUB* XXIX 1 II 52–53 ALAM-*i-ssi* NAGGA-*as ier* SAG.DU-*ZU* AN.BAR-*as ier* 'they have made his frame of lead; they have made his head of iron'; cf. B. Schwartz, *Orientalia* N.S. 16:32 [1947]), dat.-loc. sg. in *e-es-ri-es-si* (*KBo* III 7 III 20–21 *mān ēsre-ssi āppa karuuiliatta* SIG₅-*atta* 'as in his own shape he had been restored to his former state'; cf. Laroche, *RHA* 23:70 [1965]), *ēsri* (*KUB* XXXIII 34 Vs. 12 *ēsri-tti* 'for thy icon'; cf. Laroche, *RHA* 23:127 [1965]), *ēssari* (XLIII 53 I 19 *ēssari-sett-a ēssari* GAL-*li* 'and his frame [is] bigger than the [other's] frame'; cf. Haas, *Orientalia* N.S. 40:416 [1971]; Neu, *Altheth.* 26; XXIV 13 II 7 *ēssari-ta-at-kan dandu* 'for your likeness let them take it'; cf. Haas – Thiel, *Rituale* 340), *ēsriya* (IX 28 IV 5–8 *wātar* DINGIR.MEŠ-*as ēsriya kuit kittati n-at dāi n-at-san tuikki-ssi lāhūwāi* 'the water which had been placed by the image of the gods, that he takes and pours it on his body').

The metonymous variation 'shape, body' : 'skin, hide' is matched by e.g. Hitt. *tuekka-* 'body' besides Skt. *tvác-* 'skin; body' (cf. *RV* 10.171.2 *śiro 'va tvacó bharaḥ* 'you have severed the head from the body'), OPruss. *kērmens* 'body' besides Skt. *cárman-* 'skin', or Gk. χρώς 'skin (complexion), flesh, frame, body', or the sumerogram SU 'flesh' = KUŠ 'skin, hide'. The plausible common denominator is '(physical) being', thence '(concrete) shape, (external) form', and the likeliest interpretation is *es-ri-* from *es-* 'to be' (cf. *esuwar* 'being, existence'; thus already Alp, *Anatolia* 2:32 [1957]), formed like e.g. *edri-* 'eating, food', *auri-* 'looking, lookout', *kis(sa)ri-* 'carding, skein of carded wool'. Neither Kronasser's tie-in with *essa-* 'make' (*Etym.* 1:225; cf. Lat. *fingō* : *figūra*) nor Neumann's posited *es-* 'create' (*KZ* 75:88–90 [1957], comparing *is[sa]na-* 'dough' [the English gloss being cognate with Lat. *figūra*, from IE *dheyĝh-*]), nor H. Eichner's adduction of *es-* 'sit' ('seated image' in *Die Sprache* 21:157–8 [1975]) is plausible (*esri-* being the primary form and *essa-* [q.v.] iterative from *iya-*, and *is[sa]na-* [q.v.] perhaps cognate with Engl. *yeast*); but Neumann was right in insisting on the etymological unity of *esri-* and ^{SÍG}*esri-* and in rejecting Benveniste's (*BSL* 50.1:42–3 [1954]) comparison of the latter with Attic Gk. ἔριον, Homeric εἶρος 'wool' (the latter's proto-form *werwos* being vindicated by Myc. *we-we-e-a* 'woollen', i.e. *werwe[h]ea* = Attic ἐρεᾶ, from *werwes-*).

Kronasser (*Etym.* 1:225) abortively compared *es(sa)ri-* 'fleece' with Hitt. *kis(sa)ri-* ('skein of carded wool') as a Luwianism on the lines of Luw. *issari-* : Hitt. *kessar* 'hand'; the source verb *kis(s)-* 'card' (q.v.) is attested also in Luwian.

Van Windekens (*Annual of Armenian linguistics* 1:41–2 [1980]) explained Arm. *asr* 'sheep's wool, fleece' as borrowed from Hitt. *es(sa)ri*, with "obscure" (Luwoid?) *a*-coloration.

ed-, ad-, ezza- 'eat' (KÚ), 1 sg. pres. act. *e-id-mi* (e.g. *edmi ekumi* 'I eat [and] drink', q.v. sub *eku-*; *KBo* III 34 III 9; XXVI 74 II 3 *nu-tta arha edmi* 'I eat you up'; cf. Siegelová, *Appu-Hedammu* 56; *KUB* XXXIII 120 II 42–43 DUMU-*an-mu pāi* [...] *arha edmi* 'give me the child ... I shall eat up'; cf. Güterbock, *Kumarbi* *3), 2 sg. pres. act. *e-iz-si* ([OHitt.] *ezsi euksi*, q.v. sub *eku-*), *e-iz-za-]as-si* (I 16 III 29 [OHitt.], followed by *ekussi*, q.v. sub *eku-*), *e-z[a-at-ti* (*KBo* XIX 112, 8, followed ibid. 9 by *ekutti*, q.v. sub *eku-*), 3 sg. pres. act. *e-za-az-zi* (e.g. *KUB* VII 1 II 10 *n-us ezazzi* 'he eats them'; cf. Kronasser, *Die Sprache* 7:149 [1961]), *e-iz-za-zi* (e.g. XLIV 61 Vs. 2 *nu* NINDA-*an* ŪL *ezzazi* 'does not eat bread'; cf. Burde, *Medizinische Texte* 18; *KBo* XVII 65 Vs. 19 and 23 SAL-*za* ŪL *ezzazi* 'the woman does not eat'; VIII 88 Vs. 19 ŪL-*as kuiski ezzazi* 'none eats them'; cf. Haas – Wilhelm, *Riten* 262), *e-iz-za-az-zi* (e.g. *KUB* XIII 4 IV 40 *nāui ezzazzi* 'does not yet eat'; cf. Sturtevant, *JAOS* 54:394 [1934]; VIII 16 + 24 II 4; cf. M. Leibovici, *Syria* 33:142, 144 [1956]; XXIX 46 + 53 I 17–18 *nu kuissa* [...] 4 UPNU *ezzazzi* 'each [horse] eats four handfuls'; cf. Kammenhuber, *Hippologia* 192; *VBoT* 15, 5; 97 Vs. 4), *e-iz-za-i* (e.g. *KBo* XIII 130 IV 3 *nu-za ezzai ekuzzi*, with dupl. XIII 93 Rs. 13]*ezzai ekuzzi*; cf. Kümmel, *Ersatzrituale* 41; H. Otten – C. Rüster, *ZA* 68:272 [1978]; *KUB* VIII 65, 6 ŪL *na*]*mma ezzai ekuzz*[*i* 'eats [and] drinks [nothing] more'; cf. Siegelová, *Appu-Hedammu* 42), *e-iz-za-a-i* (e.g. XLIV 64 II 4 NINDA-*an namma ezzāi*; cf. Burde, *Medizinische Texte* 49; XIII 4 IV 5 *nāui ezzāi*; ibid. I 53 *arha ezzāi*; XXXIII 114 I 28 *le ezzāi* 'shall not eat'; cf. Laroche, *RHA* 26:32 [1968]), KÚ-*zi* (e.g. KÚ-*zi* NAG-*zi*, q.v. sub *eku-*), 1 pl. pres. act. *atueni* (e.g. [OHitt.] *atueni akueni*, q.v. sub *eku-*), *adueni* (e.g. [OHitt.] *adueni akueni*, q.v. sub *eku-*), *a*]*duwani* (*KBo* XV 26, 4, followed ibid. 7 by *ekuwani*, q.v. sub *eku-*), *edue*[*ni* (*Bo* 5621 I 6), *eduwāni* (*KUB* XXIX 1 I 15; cf. B. Schwartz, *Orientalia* N.S. 16:24 [1947]), 2 pl. pres. act. *ezzatteni* (e.g. XIII 4 II 70, followed by *ekutteni*, q.v. sub *eku-*), *izzatteni* (ibid. IV 44 *n-at suma*[*s*] *hūdāk izzatteni* 'you promptly eat it'), *azzasteni* (I 16 III 34 and 48 [OHitt.], followed by *ekutteni*, q.v. sub *eku-*), 3 pl. pres. act. *adanzi* (frequent, e.g. *adanzi akuenzi*, q.v. sub *eku-*; *IBoT* III 148 III 18–19 *namma-at-za adanna esantari nu-za adanzi akuwanzi* 'then they sit down to eat, and eat [and] drink'; cf. Haas – Wilhelm, *Riten* 222), *adazi* (*KUB* I 13 I 11; cf. Kammenhuber, *Hippologia* 54), *atānzi* (*KBo* III 60 II 4–5 [OHitt.] *n-an-kan kunanzi s-an-ap atānzi* 'they kill him and they eat him'; cf. Güterbock, *ZA* 44:104 [1938]), 1 sg. pret. act. *edun* (e.g. *KUB* XXX 10 Vs. 16, followed ibid. 17 by *ekun*, q.v. sub *eku-*; XXXIII 36 II 12; cf. Laroche, *RHA* 23:137 [1965]), 2 sg. pret. act. *e-za-at-ta* (XXXIII 96 IV 20, followed ibid. 21 by *ekutta*, q.v. sub *eku-*), 3 sg. pret. act. *e-iz-ta* (*KBo* III

60 II 18 *s-an-ap ezta*), *ezzatta* (*e]zzatta ek[ut]ta*, q.v. sub *eku-*), *ezzas* (*IBoT* I 33, 18; cf. Laroche, *RA* 52:152 [1958]), *ezzasta* (*Maşat* 75/15 Vs. 7–8 *halki*HI.A-*us* BURU₆.HI.A *ezzasta* 'a locust swarm has eaten the grain'; cf. Alp, *Belleten* 44:42 [1980]), 1 pl. pret. act. *eduwen* (477/u, 13), 3 pl. pret. act. *e-te-ir* (e.g. *KBo* III 60 III 3 *s-us-ap eter*; ibid. 9 *s-an-ap eter*; *KUB* XVII 10 I 19, followed ibid. 20 by *ekuyer*, q.v. sub *eku-*; *Bo* 8691, 4 *arha-ma--an eter* 'but they ate him up'; cf. Siegelová, *Appu-Hedammu* 38), 2 sg. imp. act. *e-it* (e.g. *KUB* I 16 III 30; cf. Sommer, *HAB* 12; *KBo* IV 6 Vs. 8–9 and Rs. 7–8 *nu-za* ... ᵁᶻᵁYÀ *et* 'eat fat!'; *et-za eku* 'eat [and] drink!', q.v. sub *eku-*), *e-iz-za* (e.g. *KUB* XXXIII 87, 5 *nu-wa-za ezza* 'now eat!'; cf. Güterbock, *JCS* 6:10 [1952]; XX 92 VI 8 *ezza-zza*, followed ibid. 9 by *eku-ma*, q.v. sub *eku-*), 3 sg. imp. act. *e-iz-du* (XXXI 104 I 8;]*ezdu ekuddu*, q.v. sub *eku-*), *ezzaddu* (*nu-za ezzaddu eku[ddu*, q.v. sub *eku-*), *ezzasdu* (*KBo* VIII 35 II 20), 2 pl. imp. act. *e-iz-te-en* ([OHitt.] *ezten ekutten*, q.v. sub *eku-*; XI 14 III 16), *e-iz-za-te-en* (XVI 24 + 25 I 36; cf. A. M. Rizzi Mellini, *Studia mediterranea P. Meriggi dicata* 520 [1979]), *e-za-at-tin* (*nu-za ezattin ekuttin*, q.v. sub *eku-*; *KUB* XXXVI 97 IV 4), *e-iz-za-tin* (*nu-za ezzatin ekuttin*, q.v. sub *eku-*), *e-iz-za-at-tin* (XXXI 64 III 21 [OHitt.]; XVII 27 II 14 and 20;]*ezzattin ekuttin*, q.v. sub *eku-*), *iz-za-at-te-en* (*izzatten ekutten*, q.v. sub *eku-*), *iz-za-at-tin* (*izzattin ekuttin*, q.v. sub *eku-*), *e-iz-za-as-te-en* (*ezzasten ekutten*, q.v. sub *eku-*), *e-iz-za-as-tin* (XXXIII 62 III 10, followed ibid. 11 by *ekuten*, q.v. sub *eku-*), KÚ-*tin* (KÚ-*tin* NAG-*tin*, q.v. sub *eku-*), 3 pl. imp. act. *adandu* (XXIV 14 IV 25; cf. Laroche, *JKF* 1:175 [1950]; *ad[and]u akuwandu*, q.v. sub *eku-*), *ezzandu* (IX 31 III 2 and dupl. *HT* 1 II 37); partic. *atant-*, *adant-* (partly active in meaning, like Lat. *pransus*; cf. *akuwant-* s.v. *eku-*), nom. sg. c. *adanza* (*KBo* V 2 IV 42 *n-at adanza ekuzi* 'having eaten he drinks it'), gen. sg. c. in *adandas akuwandas* (q.v. sub *eku-*), nom. pl.c. *atantes* (*KUB* VII 1 II 3 *nu-kan* ... *karātis atantes* 'entrails [are] eaten'; cf. Kronasser, *Die Sprache* 7:149 [1961]), *adantes* (e.g. ibid. I 2 *garāties adantes* 'innards [are] consumed'); verbal noun *adatar* (n.), nom.-acc. sg. *adatar* (*adatar akuwatar*, q.v. sub *eku-*), *adātar* (*KBo* XIX 112, 10, followed ibid. by *akuwatar*, q.v. sub *eku-*), gen. sg. *adannas* (e.g.

KUB XXXII 123 II 39 *adannas halkuessar* 'eating supplies'; XIII 4 III 72–73 DINGIR.MEŠ-*as adannas mēhūni* 'at the gods' mealtime'; cf. Sturtevant, *JAOS* 54:388 [1934]), dat.-loc. sg. *adanna* (e.g. dupl. XIII 5 III 42 DINGIR.MEŠ-*as adanna mēhu[ni*; IV 4 Vs. 12 'for eating'=ibid. 11 [Akk.] *ana kurummat*; cf. Laroche, *RA* 58:73 [1964]); inf. *adanna* (profuse, e.g. *adanna akuwanna* 'to eat [and] drink', q.v. sub *eku-*; XLIV 61 Vs. 20 *n-at-si adanna pā[i* 'gives it to him to eat'; cf. Burde, *Medizinische Texte* 18; *KBo* XXVI 71 III 13 ᴳᴵˢBANŠUR-*un-si unuwandan adanna zikkizzi* 'a laid table for eating he sets up for him'; cf. Siegelová, *Appu-Hedammu* 50), *adānna* (*KUB* XIV 1 Rs. 53 *adānna akuanna*; cf. Götze, *Madd.* 32); iter. *azzik(k)i-, azzaki-*, 3 sg. pres. act. *azzikizzi* (e.g. *azzikizzi akkuskizzi*, q.v. s.v. *aku-*; VII 1 II 5), *azzikizi* (ibid. 6), *azzikkizzi* (e.g. VIII 67 IV 18; cf. Siegelová, *Appu-Hedammu* 40), 2 pl. pres. act. *azzikkitani* (*azzikkitani akkuskittani*, q.v. sub *eku-*), 3 pl. pres. act. *azzikanzi* (e.g. *azzikanzi akkuskanzi*, q.v. sub *eku-*), *azzikkanzi* (e.g. *azzikkanzi akkuskanzi*, q.v. sub *eku-*), 1 sg. pret. act. *azzikkinun* (*KBo* IV 2 IV 29, followed ibid. 30 by *akkuskinun*, q.v. sub *eku-*), 3 pl. pret. act. *azzikkir* (*KUB* XXVI 89, 13, followed ibid. by *akkusk[ir*, q.v. sub *eku-*), [*a*]*z-zi-ik-ki-e[-ir* (XXIX 54 I 8), *az-za-ki-[ir* (ibid. IV 2 *nu welku azzakir* 'they ate grass'; cf. Kammenhuber, *Hippologia* 226–8), 2 sg. imp. act. *azziki* (e.g. *HT* 1 I 55; cf. B. Schwartz, *JAOS* 58:338 [1938]), *azzikki* (e.g. *azzikki akkuski*, q.v. sub *eku-*; *KUB* XII 58 IV 26 and 35; cf. Goetze, *Tunnawi* 22–4), *azzikkī* (*azzikkī akkuskī*, q.v. sub *eku-*; *KBo* XXI 60 Rs. 15), 3 sg. imp. act. *azzikidu* (*KUB* XII 58 IV 36), *azzikkiddu* (e.g. *azzikkiddu akkuskiddu*, q.v. sub. *eku-*), *azziskiddu* (*azziskiddu akkuskiddu*, q.v. sub *eku-*), KÚ-*kiddu* (XIII 5 II 14 KÚ-*kiddu akkus[kiddu*; cf. Sturtevant, *JAOS* 54:372 [1934]), 2 pl. imp. act. *az-zi-kat-te-en* ([OHitt.] *azzikatten akkuskatten*, q.v. sub *eku-*), *az-zi-ki-te-en* (*KBo* XV 10 III 50; cf. Szabó, *Entsühnungsritual* 42), *az-zi-ki-it-tin* (*KUB* XV 34 III 51 *sumes azzikittin akkuskit[tin*; cf. Haas – Wilhelm, *Riten* 200), *az-zi-ik-ki-tin* (XXIV 9 IV 16 *sumes azzikkitin akkuskit[t]in*; cf. Jakob-Rost, *Ritual der Malli* 52), *az-zi-ik-ki-it-tin* (*azzikkittin akkuskittin*, q.v. sub *eku-*), 3 pl. imp. act. *az-zi-kán--du* (*VBoT* 132 III 8; *HT* 1 I 55), *az-zi-ik-kán-du* (*KBo* XXII 6

IV 19; cf. Güterbock, *MDOG* 101:21 [1969]; *azzikkandu akkus-kandu*, q.v. sub *eku-*), *a-az-za-ku-wa-an-du* (sic XX 73 IV 10, garbled after preceding ibid. *akkuskandu*, q.v. sub *eku-*).

edri-, *idri-* (n.) 'food, meal, dish', nom.-acc. sg. *e-id-ri* (*KUB* XLI 17 I 22 ANA UR.ZÍR.HI.A-*ma-wa-tta edri udahhun* 'to your dogs I have brought food'; cf. Souček, *MIO* 9:168–71 [1963]; XXXIII 68 III 3 *edri-ti*[*t* 'thy meal'; cf. Laroche, *RHA* 23:129 [1965]), *e-id-ri-es-mi-it* in *KBo* X 37 II 16–17 ANA UR.ZÍR.HI.A ŠAH.HI.A-*ma mūdan-a edre-smit* 'but for dogs (and) pigs refuse (is) their food' (cf. Goetze, *JCS* 16:30, 33–4 [1962]), nom.-acc. pl. *e-id-ri* (*KUB* XXXIII 81 I 7 8 *edri*; cf. Laroche, *RHA* 23:80 [1965]; *KBo* XVIII 193 Vs. 6 9 NINDA*edri*HI.A 'nine bread-dishes'; cf. Werner, *Symbolae Biblicae et Mesopotamicae F.M.T. de L. Böhl dedicatae* 394 [1973]; *VBoT* 24 IV 11–12 9 *edri* KAŠ-*ya sarā danzi n-at arha adanzi akuwanzi* 'they take the nine dishes and the beer, and they eat and drink them up'; ibid. 7 and 15, III 16 9 *edri*; cf. Sturtevant, *TAPA* 58:12–6, 22 [1927]; *KBo* XV 9 I 7 2-*šu* 9 *edri* UD-*ti*[*li* 'twice nine dishes daily'), *id-ri* (*KUB* XVII 14 IV 9 *nu-s*]*si* 2-*šu* 7 *idri*HI.A UD-*tili tiskanzi* 'twice seven dishes they set for him daily'; cf. Kümmel, *Ersatzrituale* 56). Denom. *edriya-* (?), verbal noun gen. sg. in *KBo* XXIII 65, 11 *e-id-ri-wa-as* EZEN 'feast of feeding'; iter. 3 sg. pres. act. *e-id-ri-es-ki-iz-zi* (VI 3 IV 60–61 [=*Code* 100] GUD.HI.A-*ŠU edreskizzi n-us-san parā hameshanda arnuzi* 'he [viz. the barn-burner] keeps feeding his [viz. the victim's] cattle and tides them over till next spring'), *e*]*driskizzi* (dupl. XIX 4 IV 8; cf. Otten – Souček, *AfO* 21:10 [1966]), *edr*]*iskizzi* (dupl. VI 2 IV 59, VI 21 IV 4). Suffix *-ri-* as in e.g. *auri-* 'lookout', *es(sa)ri-* 'shape', *kis(sa)ri-* 'skein of carded wool'.

Pal. *ad-* 'eat', 3 pl. pres. act. *atānti* (*KUB* XXXII 18 I 7 and 8), *adān*[*ti* (*KBo* XIX 159, 7); iter. 2 sg. imp. act. *azzikī* (*KUB* XXXV 165 Vs. 15 and 20, unless Hitt. in Pal. context). Cf. Carruba, *Das Palaische* 8, 37, 14–6, 52.

Luw. *ad-*, *azza-*, 2 pl. pres. midd. *az-tu-u-wa-ri* (*KUB* IX 31 II 28 *nis aztūwari* 'do not eat!'), 2 pl. imp. act. *āzzastan* (ibid. 26; cf. Otten, *LTU* 16), 3 pl. imp. act. *adandu* (*KBo* XIII 260 III 10 and 12); in. *aduna* (VII 68 II 5).

Hier. *ad-*, *ar-*, 3 sg. or pl. imp. act. EAT-*tu*, 3 pl. imp. act.

atatū; infin. *aruna* (EAT *aruna* DRINK-*na-ha*). Cf. Meriggi, *HHG* 41, 34; Laroche, *HH* 4.

An aberrant causative side-meaning 'feed' is found only in the substandard Hittite of Kikkulis (tablets 2–4; cf. the similar case of *eku-* [s.v.] and Kammenhuber, *Hippologia* 82, 88–9, 309–10, 326–7).

Connected since Hrozný (*MDOG* 56:33 [1915], *SH* 61) with IE **ed-* 'eat' (*IEW* 287–9). The basic paradigm (pres. *edmi, ezsi, atueni, adanzi*; pret. *edun, ezta, eter*; imp. *et, ezdu, ezten, adandu*; partic. *adant-*) closely matches the Rig-Vedic (pres. *ádmi, átsi, átti, adanti*; imp. *addhí, attu, attá, adantu*; partic. *adánt-*) and parallels verbs like *es-* : *as-* 'be', *eku* : *aku-* 'drink', *ep(p)-* : *ap(p)-* 'seize'; there is no reason to assume /ēd-/ for Hittite, despite Lat. *ēst*, Lith. *ĕsti*, OCS *jastŭ* < **ĕstŭ* (wrongly e.g. Oettinger, *Stammbildung* 89). Forms like *ezzaz(z)i, ezzatteni, ezatta, ezzaddu, ezzatin* are probably at least partly in origin graphic representations of **ed+t* > /etˢt/, even as *azzik(k)i-* and *azzaki-* reflect /atski-/. But they coexist with *ezzassi, ezzai, azzasteni* (OHitt.!), *ezzas, ezza, ezzasdu, ezzasten, ezzandu* which look rather like "Luwoid" iteratives of the type *essa-, halzessa-* (cf. Luw. *āzzastan*, above), i.e. **ed-sa-, *ad-sa-* beside the normal iterative **ad-ske-*. Thus e.g. *ezzaddu* and *ezzatin* may be interpreted either as graphic for *ezdu* and *ezten* or as morphological variants of *ezzasdu* and *ezzasten* (cf. e.g. *issattin* from *essa-*). A secondary stem *ezz(a)-* might finally also have arisen via false abstraction, /etˢten/ being conceived as *ez-ten* and spawning *ezz-andu* to replace *adandu*. A parallel may be seen in Gk. ἔσθω, ἐσθίω (beside ἔδμεναι) originating in the imperative ἔσθι (= Vedic *addhí*). Cf. Kronasser, *Etym.* 1:392, 552. The suffix of *edri-* has parallels in Hes. ἔδαρ·βρῶμα (besides Gk. εἶδαρ < **edwr̥*, pl. εἴδατα; cf. Luw. *aduna*) and Lith. *ėdrà* 'fodder' (cf. Ivanov, *Studia linguistica in honorem acad. S. Mladenov* 480 [1957]). A stronger semi-synonym is *karap-* 'devour, consume' (q.v.).

Cf. *idalu-*.

e(u)wa(n)-   (n.), name of a cereal, probably 'barley' (ŠE), nom.-acc. sg. *ewan* (*KBo* IV 2 I 10, in a list of grains and seeds; cf.

Kronasser, *Die Sprache* 8:90 [1962]; similarly XI 14 I 6), *e-u-wa-an* (XXI 74 III 8 ŠE *euwan*; cf. Burde, *Medizinische Texte* 26; *KUB* XXX 32 IV 6 ŠE ⟨*e*⟩*uwan*; XXIX 1 III 9 *nu seppit euwann-a suhhair* 'they poured wheat and barley'; cf. B. Schwartz, *Orientalia* N.S. 16:32 [1947]; XXIX 4 II 51 and 63, also IV 17 UTÚL *euwan* 'barley-soup'; cf. Kronasser, *Umsiedelung* 18, 20, 30; XXIV 14 I 7; cf. Gurney, *Hittite Prayers* 91; *KBo* X 34 I 23), gen. sg. *euwas* (*KUB* XXIX 6 + 102/f II 9 UTÚL *euwas*; cf. *ZA* 71:123, 127 [1981]; VII 55 Vs. 6), *euwanas* (*KBo* X 34 I 13; ibid. 21 *euwanas memal* 'barley-meal'). Cf. H. A. Hoffner, *Alimenta Hethaeorum* 78–82 (1974); H. Berman, *JCS* 28: 245–6 (1976).

Cf. *halki-* (s.v.).

The gen. *euwanas* is probably secondary, starting from nom.-acc. *ewan* by analogy with the *n*-stem type *sahhan-*. The etymon is IE **yewo-* 'grain, corn' (*IEW* 512), Ved. *yáva-* 'grain, barley', Avest. *yava-* 'grain', Pers. *jav* 'barley', Lith. *javaĩ* 'grain', Gk. ζειαί, ζεόπυρον 'spelt', ζείδωρος 'grain-giving', φυσίζοος 'grain-growing'. If there was a laryngeal before the **y-*, as indicated by Gk. ζ- and perhaps by Vedic lengthenings like *sū-yávasa-* (cf. Lehmann, *PIEP* 77), Hittite gives no evidence of it; *ewa-* shows rather that **ye-* appears as Hitt. *e-* (cf. s.v. *eka-*). Note also Finnish *jyvä*, Estonian *iva* 'grain'. Cf. Laroche, *RHA* 11:68 (1951); Kammenhuber, *KZ* 77:67 (1961); Mayrhofer, *KEWA* 3:10; Gusmani, *Lessico* 45.

ezzan, izzan (n.) 'chaff'; alone or in asyndetic *ezzan* GIŠ-*ru* 'chaff (and) wood' also symbolic of or idiomatic for '(stored) holdings, (material) goods,' nom.-acc. sg. *e-iz-za-an, iz-za-an* (*KUB* XLI 8 II 15–17 *izzan* GIM-*an* IM-*anza pittenuzzi n-at-kan aruni parranta pedai* 'even as the wind makes chaff fly and carries it over the sea …'; cf. Otten, *ZA* 54:124–6 [1961]; XXXIII 93+ III 21 ᴰU-*an-ma-wa* GUL-*ahdu nu-wa*[*r-an iz*]*zan* GIM-*an arha pussaiddu* 'let him smite the storm-god, let him keep pounding away at him like chaff'; cf. Güterbock, *JCS* 5:152 [1951], 6:36–7 [1952]; XXXIX 4 Vs. 10–11 *nu-kan ezza*[*n*] ᴱ*hi*[...] *anda warnuwa*[*nz*]*i* 'they burn chaff inside the h.-house'; cf. Otten,

Totenrituale 24, 127; XXXIV 68 Rs. 7 1 IM.GÍD.DA *ezzan warnuma* NU.[TÍL] 'one long tablet concerning chaff-burning, incomplete'; cf. Otten, *Totenrituale* 28; XXXIX 6 II 6 *e]zzān warn[uwanzi*; cf. Otten, *Totenrituale* 48; *KBo* XX 64 Rs. 5–6 *ezzan* GIŠ-*ru hahhal* [...]YÀ.NUN LÀL KASKAL-*as* 'chaff, wood, brush ... butter, honey for the journey'; *KUB* I 1 IV 82–83 *ŠA* ^É*garupahiyas-za* [*ez*]*zan* GIŠ-*ru* KISLAH *ŠA* ^DIŠTAR ^{URU}*Samuha ilaliyazi* '[who] covets the chaff [and] wood of the storehouse [and] the threshing floor of Ištar of Samuha'; dupl. I 3 IV 3 *e-iz-za-an*, *KBo* III 6 IV 44 *iz-za-an*; cf. Götze, *Hattusilis* 38–40, 104–5; *KUB* XI 6 II 6–7 [*piyani-ma*] *ŠA* DUMU.LUGAL *izzan* GIŠ-*ru ŪL ā*[*ra* 'to give away the "chaff and wood" of a prince is not right'; VIII 50 II 4–7 INA HUR.SAG *arha piddāit n-as-kan* [...] [*t*]*askupiskizzi izzan-wa-kan ku*[*wapi* ... *arha*] [*pidd*]*anzi* SAL-*-as-ma-wa-kan* É-*irza parā* [...] [*nu-za* ^D]GIŠ.GIM.MAŠ-*us QAT-AMMA* DÙ-*at* 'off he ran to the mountain, and he ... keeps wailing; [as the saying goes:] when they bring off the "chaff", from a woman's house forth [wailing comes?]; Gilgamesh did likewise'; cf. Friedrich, *ZA* 39:22, 54, 78 [1930]; Laroche, *RHA* 26:19 [1968]). Cf. Laroche, *Bi.Or.* 18:83 (1961); H. A. Hoffner, *Alimenta Hethaeorum* 32–3, 37 (1974).

For the use of chaff and wood in the sense of 'material holdings', cf. e.g. the expression IN.NU.DA-*as iwar* 'like straw' = 'amply, profusely' (see Kammenhuber, *Hippologia* 59), or Gk. ὕλη 'wood' > 'stuff, material, matter', or 'scratch' denoting both poultry food and money in American English. The earlier posited meaning 'property, possessions' (Götze, *Hattusilis*; still maintained in *American journal of archaeology* 64:378 [1960]) is thus indirectly vindicated, while Güterbock's 'salt' (*JCS* 6:36–7 [1952], adopted by Otten in *Totenrituale*) is superseded.

ezzan is probably an *a*-stem like e.g. *pedan*, rather than an *n*-stem of the type *henkan, sahhan* (cf. Kronasser, *Etym.* 1:165). Etymology obscure, vs. e.g. Gk. ἄχυρα, ἄχνη, Goth. *ahana*, ON *agnar* 'chaff', Lat. *agna* 'ear of corn'. There may be some hope of connecting *ezza-* with Gk. neut. pl. ἤϊα 'chaff', also 'provisions' (with *KUB* XLI 8 II 15–17 [quoted above] cf. *Odyssey* 5:368–9 ὡς δ'ἄνεμος ζαὴς ἠΐων θημῶνα τινάξῃ καρφαλέων 'as a gale wind scatters a heap of dry chaff ...'), if we reconstruct ἤϊα as *ēsiyo- and explicate the -zz- of ezza- as either a product of *-sy- in *esyo- or as matching IE *s in *eso-, in the manner of e.g. zena- 'autumn' beside Russian osen' or in variants like zama(n)kur 'beard' : samankurwant- 'bearded' (cf. Benveniste, *BSL* 50.1:29–43 [1954]). In view of ancient winnowing practices (see e.g. Puhvel, *California studies in classical antiquity* 9:199–200 [1976] = *Analecta Indoeuropaea* 248–9 [1981]), a root-connection with Skt. *ásyati*, Avest. *aṅhyeiti* 'throw' is possible (chaff being literally what is tossed [into the wind]); but for a possible alternative Hittite cognate of Skt. *ásyati* see s.v. *has(s)-* 'open.' Cf. Puhvel, *AJPh* 104:223–4 (1983).

Von Schuler (*Orientalia* N.S. 52:161–3 [1983]) compared with *ezzan* GIŠ-*ru* Akk. *hāmū u huṣābu* 'straw or splinter' in the sense of 'the least bit, anything at all', but the latter is mainly post-negative ('not a whit'), while *ezzan* (*taru* [*hahhal*]), like Gk. ἤϊα, denotes 'wherewithal, resources, (journey) provisions'.

i-, (i)y- 'go', 3 pl. pres. act. *yanzi* (*KBo* XXII 2 Vs. 7 [OHitt.]
DUMU.NITA.MEŠ *a*[*pp*]*a* ᵁᴿᵁ*Nēsa yanzi* 'the sons go back to
Nesa'; cf. Otten, *Altheth. Erzählung* 6, 25, who translated
'make for Nesa', from *iya-*, perhaps an idiomatic ellipticism for
KASKAL-*an iya-* 'make [their] way, hit the road'; but a literal
'they go' is more plausible and ties in with other relic forms; cf.
Oettinger, *Stammbildung* 349), 2 sg. imp. act. *i-it* (e.g. XVII 3
III 5 *nu īt* ᴰUTU-*i* ᴰIM-*ya mēmiski* 'go, say to the sun-god and
the storm-god'; cf. Otten – Souček, *Altheth. Ritual* 30; IV 4 II
56 *nu-wa īt* 'go ahead!'; cf. Götze, *AM* 118; ibid. I 41–42
*nu-wa-smas īt halki*HI.A-*us arha harnik* 'go and destroy their
grain!'; XVI 17 III 33 *īt-wa-ssi* KUR-*KA piran pahsanuwan harak*
'go and keep your land protected before him!'; cf. Otten, *MIO*
3:173 [1955]; V 4 Rs. 48 *īt-wa walah* 'go [and] strike!'; cf.
Friedrich, *Staatsverträge* 1:68; *KUB* XIV 1 Rs. 26 *nu-wa-kan īt*
KUR ᵁᴿᵁ*Hapālla-wa-kan kueni* 'go and smite H.!'; cf. Götze,
Madd. 26; XVII 10 I 24–25 *īt-war-asta pargamus* HUR.SAG.AS.
.AS.HI.A *sāh* 'go search the high mountains!'; cf. Laroche, *RHA*
23:91 [1965]; *KBo* III 23 I 10 *andan īt* 'go inside!'; cf. A. Archi;
in *Florilegium Anatolicum* 41 [1979]; *KUB* XIV 3 III 65 *nu-wa*
INA KUR *Hatti arha īt* 'go off to Hatti!'; cf. Sommer, *AU* 14;
KBo XV 9 I 25 *parā īt* 'go forth!'; cf. Kümmel, *Ersatzrituale* 58;
KUB XXIX 1 II 39 *ehu zik* Á^MUŠEN *īt* 'come, thou eagle, go!';
KBo XXI 22 Vs. 9 *ehu hāras īt* 'come, eagle, go!'; cf. G.
Kellerman, *Tel Aviv* 5:199 [1978]; V 9 II 43–44 *eh*]*u-wa īt*
kuwapi-wa paisi 'come, go where you are going!'; cf. Friedrich,
Staatsverträge 1:18; *KUB* XXIV 8 II 6 *īt-*[*za*] *eku nu-za ninqa*
'go, drink, get your fill!'; cf. Siegelová, *Appu-Hedammu* 6; *KBo*
V 13 II 22–23 *īt-wa-z* ZI-*an kuwapikki* TI-*nut* 'go, keep yourself
alive somewhere!'; cf. Friedrich, *Staatsverträge* 1:124), 2 pl.
imp. act. *i-it-te-en* (e.g. III 28 II 8 *ītten azzikatten akkuskatten*
'go, eat [and] drink'; cf. Laroche, *Festschrift H. Otten* 186
[1973]; VI 2 III 19 [= *Code* 1:55, OHitt.]), *i-it-tin* (e.g. *KUB*
XXXIII 106 IV 14 *n-an īttin zahheskittin namma* 'go keep

fighting him further'; cf. Güterbock, *JCS* 6:48 [1952]; XV 34 IV
30 *sarā nepisi ittin* 'go up to heaven'; cf. Haas – Wilhelm, *Riten*
204; XIV 1 Vs. 66–67 *ūk-wa walhuuanzi* ^{URU}*Dalauwa paimi*
[*sumes-ma-*]*wa* ^{URU}*Hinduwa ittin* 'I shall go strike at D., but you,
go to H.!'; cf. Götze, *Madd.* 16; *KBo* XIX 145 III 44; cf. Haas –
Thiel, *Rituale* 304), *it-ti-in* (*KUB* XXXI 64 II 22 [OHitt.]), *it-tin*
(e.g. *KBo* IV 2 I 15 *ittin-wa-kan* IŠTU É.GAL-*LIM kallar* INIM-*tar*
parā sūwattin 'go and drive the demon forth from the palace!'; cf.
Kronasser, *Die Sprache* 8:90 [1962]); partic. *iyant-*, nom. sg. c.
iyanza (e.g. X 24 IV 3 '[has] gone inside'; might be equally from
mediopassive *iya-* 'go' [q.v.]), acc. sg. c. *iyandan* (*KUB* IX 34 III
34 *iyandan kinun* 'the walking knee'); iter. *(i)yanna-*, *iyana-*,
(i)yanniya-, *iyaniya-*, 1 sg. pres. act. *i-ya-an-na-ah-hé* (*KBo*
XVII 4 II 8–9 *adueni akueni nu* ^{URU}*Hattusa iyannahh*[*e*] LUGAL-
-*s-a* ^{URU}*Arinna paizzi* 'we eat and drink, and I am on my way to
Hattusas, but the king goes to Arinna'; cf. Otten – Souček,
Altheth. Ritual 24), 3 sg. pres. act. *yannai* (XX 48 Rs. 9 URU-*ya*
yannai n-as INA É SAL.LUGAL *anda pai*[*zzi* 'travels to the town,
and he goes inside the queen's house'), *iyannai* (e.g. *KUB* IX 17,
19 *n-as iyannai n-as-kan auriya ser tiyezz*[*i* 'he goes and he steps
up to a watchtower'; XVII 140 I 23 *katta iyannai* 'goes down';
cf. Kümmel, *Ersatzrituale* 60; 644/b I 18 *t-as* ^{URU}*Arinna iyannai*
'he travels to Arinna', vs. ibid. 19 *mān* LUGAL-*us zēni* ^{URU}*Arinna*
paizzi 'as the king goes to Arinna in the fall'), *iyanniyazi* (VIII
68 I 7), *iyaniazzi* (V 1 I 24 EGIR UGU *iyaniazzi* 'goes back up'; cf.
Ünal, *Hatt.* 2:36), *iyannizi* (*VBoT* 111 III 4), 3 pl. pres. act.
iyanniyanzi (e.g. *KUB* XX 87 I 13–14 *n-as iyannai ape* EGIR-*ŠÚ*
iyanniyanzi nu KASKAL-*an parā* SÌR-*RU* 'he moves along; they go
after him and sing along the way'), 1 sg. pret. act. *iyanniyanun*
(e.g. *KBo* III 4 II 8–9 *namma apedani* MU-*TI* INA KUR *Arzauwa*
iyanniyanun-pat 'also in that same year I marched to Arzawa';
cf. Götze, *AM* 44–6; *KUB* XIV 15 I 8 *zahhiya anda iyanniyanun*
'I marched into battle'; cf. Götze, *AM* 34; *KBo* IV 4 IV 17
lukkatta-ma INA ^{URU}*Dukkamma andan zahhiya iyanniyanun* 'but
at daylight I marched into D. for battle'; cf. Götze, *AM* 134; V
8 III 23–24 *mahhan-ma-kan* ^DUTU-*us ūpta nu-ssi-kan zahhiya*
anda iyanniyanun 'but when the sun rose I marched into battle
against him'; cf. Götze, *AM* 158; ibid. I 14–15 *nu-kan mahhan*

ANA KASKAL ^{URU}*Taggasta tiyanun man iyanniyanun* 'when I set out on the road to T., I would have marched along, [but ...]'; cf. Götze, *AM* 148; XXIII 13, 6 LUGAL GAL-*ma iyanniyanun* 'I, the great king, marched along'; cf. Sommer, *AU* 314), 3 sg. pret. act. *yannis* (*KBo* XXII 2 Rs. 7 [OHitt.] *s-as yannis* 'he marched along'; cf. Otten, *Altheth. Erzählung* 12, 25; dupl. III 38 Rs. 22 *i-ya-an-ni-es*), *iyannis* (e.g. III 46 Vs. 42 ^{URU}*Arzauiya-as utniya iyannis* 'he marched to the land of Arzawa'; *KUB* XLIV 4 + *KBo* XIII 241 Rs. 5 [*n*]-*as-kan andan* ... *iyannis* 'he went inside'; *KUB* XXIV 8 I 24–25 *n-as-za parna-ssa* [*iy*]*annis* 'and he went to his house'; cf. Siegelová, *Appu-Hedammu* 4; ibid. 40 *n-as* ^DUTU-*i kattan iyannis* 'he went along to the sun-god'; ibid. 43 *n-as-si-pa anda iyann*[*is*] 'he went in to him'; ibid. II 10–12 *n-as-za* EGIR-*pa parna-ssa iyannis* ^DUTU-*us-ma-ssan sar*[*ā nep*]*isi iyannis* 'he went back to his house, but the sun-god went up to heaven'; XII 63 Rs. 16 EGIR-*anda iyannis* 'went after'; Teddy Kollek's tablet, line 5; cf. A. Kempinski, *Tel Aviv* 2:92 [1975]), *i-ya-an-ni-es* (e.g. ibid. 11 É.ŠÀ-*na iyannes* 'went to the inner chamber'; XXXIII 106 II 11 *n-as-kan auriyaza katta iyannes* 'he went down from the watchtower'; cf. Güterbock, *JCS* 6:20 [1952]; XXVI 71 I 15 [OHitt.] *s-as iyannes* 'and he was gone'; cf. Neu, *Anitta-Text* 14; *KBo* XXVI 79, 8–9 *nu-kan* ^D*Kumarb*[*is* ... [.] *sarā iyannes* 'K. went up'; cf. Siegelová, *Appu-Hedammu* 68; *KUB* XIV 14 I 30 *nu-ssi* KUR ^{URU}*Hatti hūman piran* SIG₅-*in iyannes* 'and before him all the land of Hatti fared well'; cf. Götze, *KlF* 168), *iyanis* (XXXIII 67 I 32 *n-as-kan iyanis* IŠTU É.ŠÀ 'she went from the inner chamber'), *iyanniyat* (XXXIII 102 I 20 *n-as iyanniya*[*t* 'he went'; cf. Güterbock, *JCS* 5:150 [1951]), *iyanniat* (*KBo* XII 26 IV 10 *n-as* ^{URU}KÙ.BABBAR-*si iyannia*[*t* 'he went to Hattusas'; cf. S. Heinhold-Krahmer, *Arzawa* 284 [1977]), 3 pl. pret. act. *i-ya-an-ni-ir* (e.g. *KUB* XIX 9 II 28 EGIR-*pa iyannir*; cf. Ünal, *Hatt.* 2:7), 2 sg. imp. act. *iyanni* (XXXVI 59 I 5 *nu-za parna-*]*tta iyanni* 'go to your house!', besides dupl. XXIV 8 II 7 *nu-za parna-ssa iyannis*, erroneously copied from ibid. 10 [q.v. supra]; cf. Siegelová, *Appu-Hedammu* 6–7; XVII 10 II 30 KASKAL-*s-a iyanni* 'and go the ways!'; cf. Laroche, *RHA* 23:93 [1965]), 2 pl. imp. act. *i-ya-an-ni-ya-at-tin* (VIII 51 II 16; cf. Laroche, *RHA* 26:13

[1968]) *i-ya-an-ni-ya-tin* (VII 60 II 29 *nu-kan kedas ser arha iyanniyatin* 'over those [roads] go off!'; cf. Haas – Wilhelm, *Riten* 236); partic. *iyanniyant-*, nom.-acc. sg. neut. *iyanniyan* (IX 34 III 37 *iyanniyan ginun* 'the walking knee', with wrong gender [cf. ibid. 34 *iyandan kinun*]); inf. *i-ya-an-ni-ya-u-wa-an-zi* (VIII 53 II 18 *nu-ssi ŪL parā iyanniyauwa*[*nzi*] [eraded *ŪL*] *kisari* 'it is not possible for him to go forward'; cf. Laroche, *RHA* 26:15 [1968]); supine in XIV 1 Vs. 73–74 *n-at ... kattan apedani iyanniwan* [*dāi*]*r* 'they took to marching along with him' (cf. Götze, *Madd.* 18).

iyan(n)a-, iyan(n)iya- supplied an original iterative-"durative" for *i-, (i)y-*, in the manner of *piyan(n)a-* from *pai-* 'give' or *hewaniya-* from **heu-* 'to rain' (cf. Puhvel, *Bi. Or.* 37:203–4 [1980]); the functional similarity of such verbs to the iteratives in *-ski-* is patent from their use in supines (beside the near-exclusivity in the latter of *-ski-* verbs and their functional peers such as *essa-*), e.g. *iyanniwan, piyanniwan, piddānniwan, walhanniuwan* (cf. Otten, *Sprachliche Stellung* 23). Being a residual category, verbs in *-anna-* tended to lose their distinctive sense and to blend in meaning with their underlying simplicia, whether the latter survived (e.g. *walh-*; cf. Otten – Souček, *Altheth. Ritual* 74) or were lost (**hew-*), being consequently potentially subject to iteratival rederivation (*piyaniski-, walhanniski-, hewaneski-*). With *iyan(n)a-* the situation was even more complicated: the near-loss of *i-* neutralized any contrastive "durative" sense, the medial *iya-* (q.v.) had a competing statival nuance built into its voice, while the compounds *pai-, ui-* (q.v.) preempted "goal-direction"; *iyan(n)a-* was thus adrift, staying rather in the vague slot largely vacated by *i-* itself (cf. also Neu, *Mediopassiv* 87, who followed Bechtel, *Hittite verbs* 84, in unnecessarily plumping for a "punctual" sense).

Luw. *i-* 'go', 3 sg. pres. act. *i-ti* (*KUB* XXXII 9 + XXXV 21 Vs. 5, 6, 24, Rs. 19; cf. Otten, *LTU* 28–30; XXXV 54 III 20; cf. Otten, *LTU* 60; XXXV 117, 6; cf. Otten, *LTU* 103; XXXII 8 + 5 IV 24; cf. Otten, *LTU* 22), 3 sg. pret. act. (?) *i-i-ta* (XXXV 109 III 1; cf. Otten, *LTU* 100), 2 sg. imp. act. (?) *i-ya-a* (XXV 39 I 27), 3 sg. imp. act. *i-du* (*KBo* VII 66, 6; cf. Otten, *LTU* 115), 3 pl. imp. act. *iyandu* (*KUB* XXXII 15, 4; cf. Otten, *LTU* 96; XXXV 103 II 13; ibid. III 1 [*p*]*a-wa iyandu* ᴰEN.ᶻᵁ-*inzi* 'let the months pass!'; cf. Otten, *LTU* 95; *VBoT* 60 I 5; cf. Otten, *LTU* 108); partic. *iyant-* (?), perhaps 'going, convenient, passable' in Hittite gloss-words (*KBo* V 13 III 8 = *KUB* VI 41 III 27 *mān-ta iyanta-ya* [with gloss-wedge] 'if [it is] convenient for you'; vs. negated ibid. 10 = 29 *mān-ta* ŪL-*ma iyanta* [with gloss-wedge]; cf. Friedrich, *Staatsverträge* 1:126, 171; *KUB* VI 5 Vs. 15 and XXII 42 Vs. 13 *iyandas*, each with gloss-wedges). Cf. Laroche, *RHA* 16:99–101 (1958).

Hier. readings depend on the new values proposed by Hawkins – Morpurgo – Neumann, *HHL* 189: 1 sg. pres. *iwi*, 1 sg. pret. *iha*, 3 pl. imp. *yatu* (Hawkins, *Anatolian studies* 25:130 [1975]); inf. FOOT₂ *iuna*; with the last-mentioned can be compared Luw. *i-ú-na-(a-)hi-sa* (*Dict. louv.* 53), i.e. an abstract *iunahi(t)-* 'ability to go', and perhaps the military commander's name ¹*Pa-ra-a-i-ú-na-as* (*KBo* III 46 Vs. 37) or ¹*Pa-ra-i-ú--na-as* (dupl. III 53 + XIX 90, 8; cf. S. Heinhold-Krahmer, *Arzawa* 279), fit for a go-go general (cf. Laroche, *Noms* 136; Neumann, *KZ* 90:143 [1976]).

Luw. 3 sg. pres. *iti*, OHitt. 3 pl. pres. *yanzi*, Luw. 3 sg. imp. *idu*, 3 pl. imp. *iyandu*, Hitt. partic. *iyant-* closely mirror the IE paradigm of **ey-* 'go' (*IEW* 293–4) and are matched by e.g. Skt. *éti*, *yánti*, *étu*, *yántu*, *yánt-*. Other forms, notably the Hittite 2 sg. and pl. imp. *īt* and *ītten*, have long (since Hrozný, *SH* 4, 173) been compared with Skt. *ihí*, *itá* or Gk. ἴϑι, ἴτε, but must above all be appraised on inner-Hittite terms; thus it is idle to speculate why the postulated incremental IE **-dhi* in *īt* and similar imperatives (e.g. *arnut*) "has lost the IE -*ī*" and to find various secondary and incidental causes (those of Pedersen, Sommer, Kronasser, and Kammenhuber were listed by Tischler, *Glossar* 335–6, 441); either Indo-European variation, or inner-Hittite allomorphism (cf. -*t*[*i*] appended to mediopassive endings), or mere apocopation (cf. e.g. -[*k*]*ku* < IE **kʷe*) is reason enough.

In Luwian the active paradigm of *i-* is quite alive, whereas in Hittite it has been largely supplanted by the medial *iya-* (q.v.). Luwian also attests a marked compound *a-ú-i-*, *a-wi-* 'come',

while Hittite has the antonymical pair of compounds *ui-* (*uwa-*)
'come' : *pai-* 'go' (q.v.) which still mirror in some forms the
paradigm of *i-* (e.g. 3 sg. pres. *uizzi, paizzi* : cf. Luw. *iti*; 3 sg.
imp. *uiddu, paiddu* : cf. Luw. *idu*). *īt* and *ītten* function as 2 sg.
and pl. imp. of *pai-*, much as *ehu* (q.v.) does for the 2 sg. imp. of
ui- (but in the 2 pl. imp. there is OHitt. *ú-it-te-en* [*KBo* III
41 + *KUB* XXXI 4 Vs. 23] and reshaped *uwatten*). The Hittite
pair *ui-* : *pai-* has a parallel in Slavic (e.g. Russian *ujtí, pojtí*
besides simple *ittí* 'go'; cf. also V. Georgiev, *Arch. Or.*
39:425–31 [1971]; R. L. Fisher, *KZ* 91:223 [1977]).
   Cf. *antiyant-*; *iyant-*; *itar*; *iwar*.

iya-, ie- (deponential) 'go, come, walk, proceed, stride, march;
grow (of vegetation)' (DU = GIN, occasionally wrongly DÙ; cf.
Kümmel, *Ersatzrituale* 106–7), 1 sg. pres. midd. *iyahhari* (e.g.
KUB XIV 11 III 16 [ANA ^{ÍD}*Mā*]*la kuit iyahhari* 'because I am
on my way to the Māla river'; cf. Götze, *KlF* 214; XXI 10, 8 'I
shall march'; cf. Güterbock, *JCS* 10:117 [1956]), 2 sg. pres.
midd. *iyattati* (*KBo* XVIII 28 IV 15–16 *wetumman*[*zi*] *iyattati*
'are you proceeding to build?'; V 3 III 61 [*mā*]*n-ma-kan* INA
É.GAL-LIM-*ya sarā iy*[*atta*]*ti* 'but even if you go up to the
palace'; cf. Friedrich, *Staatsverträge* 2:128), *iyattari* (dupl.
KUB XIX 24 + XIV 6 Rs. 41; *KUB* XXXI 127 + I 58–59 4
halhaltūmari ukturi istarna arha iyattari 'you traverse the four
firm corners'; XXIX 4 III 28 *nu mahhan iyattari* 'when thou
comest'; cf. ibid. 27 *ehu* 'come!'; cf. Kronasser, *Umsiedelung*
24), 3 sg. pres. midd. *iyatta* (frequent, e.g. IX 31 II 11–12 *nu
piran apās iyatta nu* UR.BAR.RA-*ili halzissai* 'that one strides
forth and howls like a wolf'; cf. B. Schwartz, *JAOS* 58:340
[1938]; II 7 I 13 *ta* LUGAL-*us iyatta* 'the king proceeds'; cf. S.
Košak, *Ling.* 16:62 [1976]; XIII 20 I 6 *nu mān* ^DUTU-ŠI *lahhi
apasila iyatta* 'if my majesty goes himself on the campaign'; cf.
Alp, *Belleten* 11:388 [1947]; XXXI 127 + I 66 *kunnaz-tit iyatta*
'[he] strides on your right'; cf. Güterbock, *JAOS* 78:241 [1958];
XXXVI 75 + 1226/u II 4–5 *kunnaz-tet iyatta*; cf. H. Otten – C.
Rüster, *ZA* 67:56 [1977]), *yatta* (XXXVI 106 Vs. 2 [OHitt.]
ER]ÍN.MEŠ ^{URU}*Hatti yatta* 'the army of Hatti is on the march'; cf.

Otten, *ZA* 52:217 [1957]), *iyadda* (XXXIX 54 Vs. 13 *pian iyadda* 'strides forth'), *iyata* (*KBo* II 8 I 34 *parni anda iyata* 'goes inside the house'), *iyattari* (frequent, e.g. *KBo* V 4 Rs. 47 *nasma-kan* ᴸᵁKÚR-*ma tuel* KUR-KA *istarna arha iyattari* 'or an enemy marches right through your country'; cf. Friedrich, *Staatsverträge* 1:68; *KUB* XXIX 4 III 48 EN SISKUR.SISKUR EGIR-*an iyattari* 'the sacrificer walks behind'; *VBoT* 120 III 15 *kutti-kan k*[*ui*]*s* UKÙ-*as anda iyattari* 'what man goes inside the wall'; cf. Haas – Thiel, *Rituale* 146; *KUB* XXVII 29 II 17–18 *uddar-ma-kan kue* KAxU-*az parā iyattari* 'the words which come[s] forth from the mouth'; cf. Haas – Thiel, *Rituale* 142; XIV 3 IV 37–38 *apenisuuanza-kan me*[*mias* ...] KAxU-*za iyattari* 'such a word comes from the mouth'; cf. Sommer, *AU* 18; XXXVI 67 II 20–22 *siyaiskizzi* ᴵ*Gurpāranzaha*[*s n*]*u-ssi-kan* GI-*as* IŠTU ᴳᴵˢBAN *pariyan* MUŠEN-*is mān iyattari* 'G. keeps shooting, and the arrow goes forth from his bow like a bird'; XLIV 61 Vs. 6 UD.KAM-*ma-kan istarna iyattari* 'the day goes by'; cf. Burde, *Medizinische Texte* 18), *iattari* (XLIII 38 Rs. 24 [*le* ...] ... *uwanna iattari* 'he shall [not] come to be seen'; cf. Oettinger, *Eide* 20), *iyattāri* (II 5 V 4–5 *iskisaz* EGIR-*pa iyattāri* '[he] retreats backwards'), *iyaddari* (XIX 23 Rs. 8–9 *nu-kan kuit* AŠRU *paizzi-ya kuit-ma-kan* AŠRU *nūwa ser ar*[*ha*] *iyaddari* 'what place he goes to, and what place he does not yet march up to'; cf. S. Heinhold-Krahmer, *Arzawa* 313 [1977]; *KBo* V 9 II 31–33 *n-at-kan* ANA URU.DIDLI.HI.A *kuit sarā iyaddari nu-smas* ᴵ*Duppi--*ᴰU-*upas adanna akuwanna piskizzi* 'whereas they are on the march up to the cities, Duppi-Tesupas keeps them provided with food [and] drink'; cf. Friedrich, *Staatsverträge* 1:16–8; *KUB* XVII 12 II 12), *iyaddāri* (*KBo* V 1 IV 22 EGIR-*an iyaddāri*; cf. Sommer – Ehelolf, *Pāpanikri* 12*), *iyatari* (*KUB* XXI 1 III 52–53, besides dupl. XXI 5 III 70 *iyattari*; cf. Friedrich, *Staatsverträge* 2:74; *KBo* II 8 III 11 *piran iyatari*; ibid. 12 EGIR *iyatari*; ibid. IV 3 *pirān iyatari*; ibid. 4 EGIR-*pan iyatari*; *KUB* X 17 II 24; XVII 35 I 25; XX 10 IV 14 LUGAL-*us* EGIR *sarā iyatari* 'the king walks back up'; *KBo* XVIII 62 1.Rd. 1), DU-*ri* (IX 82 Rs. 2 GAM-*an* DU-*ri* 'goes down'), DÙ-*attari* (XV 9 IV 28; cf. Kümmel, *Ersatzrituale* 66, 106–7), 1 pl. pres. midd. *i-ya-u-wa--as-ta* (XVII 48 Vs. 6), 2 pl. pres. midd. *iyadduma* (*KUB* XXIII

72 Vs. 55 'you march'; *KBo* XIX 145 III 43–44 [*m*]*ān iyadduma
n-asta hiye*[*ll*]*i ītten* 'when you go, then go to the courtyard'; cf.
Haas – Thiel, *Rituale* 304), 3 pl. pres. midd. *iyanta* (frequent,
e.g. *KUB* X 91 II 8 *piran iyanta* '[they] go before'; *KBo* IV 9 IV
38 ZAG-*naz iyanta* '[they] walk to the right'; *IBoT* I 36 II 51–52
katta iyanta '[they] go down'; cf. Jakob-Rost, *MIO* 11:186
[1966]; *KUB* IX 1 I 17; *KBo* X 27 III 14, IV 10, V 30), *ienta*
(*IBoT* II 12 I 6), *iēnta* (*KBo* XXII 1 Vs. 14 [OHitt.] 1 LÚ 1 SAL
katti-ssi iēnta 'one man [and] one woman go along with him';
cf. A. Archi, in *Florilegium Anatolicum* 46 [1979]), *iyanda* (*KUB*
XXV 17 I 13–14 ZAG-*az iyanda*), *iyantari* (frequent, e.g. *KBo* IV
9 IV 28–29 and *KUB* X 3 II 27 ZAG-*naz iyantari*; *KUB* II 6 III
39–41 LUGAL-*us paizzi nu-ssi* DUMU.MEŠ É.GAL LÚ.MEŠ *MEŠEDI*
EGIR-*an iyantari* ('the king goes; the palace sons [and] the
bodyguards walk behind him'), *ientari* (*KBo* XIV 129 Rs. 11),
iyandari (*KUB* I 13 III 36 *te*]*pu iyandari* 'they walk little'; cf.
Kammenhuber, *Hippologia* 66; XXXVI 5 I 5 KAS]KAL-*an-ma
kuin iyandari* 'but the way which they go'; cf. Laroche, *RHA*
26:36 [1968]; cf. also under *iyahhat* below, and KASKAL-*an iyat*
'made [his] way', s.v. *iya-* 'do, make'), *iyandāri* (*Maşat* 75/43
1.R. 2; cf. Alp, Belleten 44:48 [1980]), DÙ-*tari* (*KUB* XXVII 70
II 24 LÚ.MEŠNAR *pian* DÙ-*tari* 'the singers go before'), 1 sg. pret.
midd. *iyahhat* (frequent, e.g. *KBo* III 4 II 15 *mahhan-ma
iyahhat* 'but when I was on the march'; cf. Götze, *AM* 46; IV 4
III 33 *munnanda iyahhat* 'I marched in secret'; ibid. 43 *parā
iyahhat* 'I marched forth'; cf. Götze, *AM* 126–8; V 8 I 25 *nu
GE₆-az iyahhat* 'I marched at night'; cf. Götze, *AM* 148; ibid. III
21 *nu ispandan hūmandan iyahhat* 'I marched the whole night';
cf. Götze, *AM* 158; *KUB* XIV 20 + *KBo* XIX 76 I 29 *nu-kan
kuitma⟨n⟩* INA [KUR URU*Mal*]*azziya kattanda iyahhat* 'while I
was marching down to M.'; cf. Houwink Ten Cate, in *Florilegium Anatolicum* 162; *KUB* XVII 28 II 59–60 *ūk-za ammel
SIG₅-andan* KASKAL-*an iyahhat* 'I went on my good way'; cf. also
under *iyandari* above; XIV 10 I 20–21 *nu* ANA DINGIR.MEŠ
hūmandās piran EGIR-*pa iyahhat* 'to all gods I walked forth
[and] back' [i.e. I made an ambitus of all cult sites]; cf. Götze,
KlF 206; *KBo* III 6 + *ABoT* 62 I 40), *iyahhahat* (dupl. *KUB* I 1 I
48 ANA PANI DINGIR.MEŠ *kuit parā handandanni iyahhahat*

'because I walked in providentiality before the gods'; cf. Götze, *Hattusilis* 10; ibid. II 80 EGIR-*pa iyahhahat* 'I came back'), *iyahat* (XIV 19, 11 'I marched'; cf. Houwink Ten Cate, *JNES* 25:173 [1966]), 2 sg. pret. midd. *iyattati* (VIII 48 I 15–16 *zik-wa-smas kuit iwar* ^{LÚ}*TAPPI-ŠU* UD.KAM-*tili kattan iyattati* 'because you did go along with them daily like their comrade'; cf. Laroche, *RHA* 26:18 [1968]), 3 sg. pret. midd. *iyattat* (frequent, e.g. *KBo* III 4 III 68 '[he] had come'; cf. Götze, *AM* 88; V 3 III 54 *ŪL* SAL.SUHUR.LAL *iyattat* 'did not a hierodule come?'; cf. Friedrich, *Staatsverträge* 2:128; *KUB* XXII 70 Vs. 77 and Rs. 36 *sarā iyattat* 'has gone up'; ibid. Vs. 8–9 and 78–79 *n-as* ANA DINGIR-*LIM piran* EGIR-*pa ŪL iyattat* 'she did not walk forth and back to all the gods'; cf. Ünal, *Orakeltext* 78, 90, 56; XXXIII 120 II 39 *n-as mahhan iyattat n-as* PANI ^DA.A *tiyat* 'as he went and stepped before Ea'; cf. Güterbock, *Kumarbi* *3; XIX 10 I 11 *apedas walahhūwanzi iyattat* '[he] went to attack them'; cf. Güterbock, *JCS* 10:65 [1956]; *KBo* IV 2 III 43–44 *nu-mu-kan memias tepu kuitki sarā iyattat* 'my speech emerged somehow faltering'; cf. Götze – Pedersen, *MS* 4; *KBo* XVI 14 II 11; cf. Houwink Ten Cate, *JNES* 25:170 [1966]; *KUB* V 6 II 29; cf. Sommer, *AU* 278), 3 pl. pret. midd. *iyantat* (e.g. *ABoT* 60 Rs. 5–6 LÚ.MEŠ ^{URU}*Qasga-ya-mu-ssan kuyēs anda iyantat* '[as for] the Gasgas who had come in to me'; cf. Laroche, *RHA* 18:82 [1960]; *KUB* XVII 21 II 10–12 *arha-kan … iyantat* 'have come away'; cf. von Schuler, *Die Kaškäer* 154; *KBo* V 8 IV 8 *ammug-at kattan lahhi iyantat-pat* 'for me they likewise went to war'; cf. Götze, *AM* 160), *iyandat* (dupl. XVI 8 IV 5 *i]yandat*), 2 sg. imp. midd. *iyahhut* (e.g. *KUB* XXII 70 Vs. 37 *nu-war-at-za* DINGIR-*LIM sāk* ^I*Pallānn-a-wa-kan* EGIR-*an iyahhut* 'know it, god, and go easy on P.' [lit. 'go behind', like EGIR-*pa tiya-*, vs. *hanti tiya-* 'confront, accuse'; cf. Sommer, *AU* 186; Kronasser, *Etym.* 1:463; wrongly Ünal, *Orakeltext* 65, 115; XXXIII 8 III 18 *nu-ssan iyahhut* 'come!'; cf. Laroche, *RHA* 23:104 [1965]; *KBo* XIII 86 Rs. 3; VIII 42 Vs. 16 [OHitt.]), *iehut* (VIII 66 Vs. 8), 3 sg. imp. midd. *iyattaru* (e.g. XIX 145 III 19 *i]yattaru n-an parhiskiddu* 'he shall go and chase him'; cf. Haas – Thiel, *Rituale* 300; IX 82 Vs. 11–12 *nu-wa-mu* UKÙ-*as INA* ^{URU}*Taparuqa* GAM-*an iyattaru* 'let a man come down to me at T.'; *KUB* XXI 29 II 14 DI-*esni-ma-as-kan* GAM *iyattaru* 'but he shall go down for a trial'; XXIII 68 Rs. 2 *iyattaru-ma* DUMU.MEŠ *ELLUTIM kuy*[*ēs* 'but [only those] who [are] freeborn shall march'; cf. A. Kempinski – S. Košak, *Die Welt des Orients* 5:196 [1970]; XXIII 72 Rs. 19 'shall march'; *KBo* XIII 161 Vs. 16; IV 10 Vs. 44), *iyaddaru* (dupl. *ABoT* 57 Vs. 18), *iyataru* (*KBo* VI 34+ *KUB* XLVIII 76 III 43–45 *n-asta apell-a* IŠTU A.ŠÀ-ŠU ZÍZ-*tar* ŠE-AM *sarā le uizzi n-asta* UGU *zahheli iyataru* 'thus shall in his field wheat [and] barley not come up, but let cress [i.e. weed] grow up!'; cf. Oettinger, *Eide* 14), 2 pl. imp. midd. *iyaddumat* (*KUB* XV 34 I 42 *nu-ssan apiya iyaddumat* 'go there!'; cf. Haas –Wilhelm, *Riten* 186), 3 pl. imp. midd. *iyantaru* (e.g. XIII 4 IV 58 'let [them] go'; cf. Sturtevant, *JAOS* 54:396 [1934]; *KBo* X 12 III 10 ŠEŠ.MEŠ-*as iwar piran iyantaru* 'like brothers they shall go before [you]' [= help you; cf. *piran huwai-* 'run before' = 'help']; cf. H. Freydank, *MIO* 7:363 [1960]; *KUB* XXIV 2 Rs. 17 *hūwadus iyantaru* 'may the winds come!'), *iyandaru* (XXIV 3 III 40 IM-*antes iyandaru* 'may the winds come!'; cf. Gurney, *Hittite Prayers* 34–6); partic. *iyant-* (indistinguishable from *i-* [q.v.]). Cf. Neu, *Interpretation* 62–7.

The spelling *yatta* (3 sg. pres., quoted above) is an early unregulated "converse" way of rendering *iyatta*, due to the ambiguity of such as the participle *iyant-* which is derivable from either *iya-* or *i-* and can therefore reflect either /iyant-/ or /yant-/ (cf. 3 sg. pres. act. *yanzi*, iter. 3 sg. pres. *yannai*, 3 sg. pret. *yannis* [beside usual *iyann-*], s.v. *i-*). 3 pl. pres. *iēnta*, *ienta(ri)*, 2 sg. imp. *iehut* resemble comparable forms of *iya-* 'do' (q.v.) and are similarly explainable (**eye- > *ē-* [*> *ī*], but **eyo- > iya-*, with *ie-* as a phonetic variant, perhaps [iä], especially in Old Hittite; contrast the isolated *ehu < *eyehu*[*t*], s.v.).

There is no probability that *iya-* reflects IE **yā-* (*IEW* 296) as an extension of **ey-* 'go', and hence the much-repeated comparison with Skt. *yáti* 'go', Toch. A *yā-* 'go, travel', Lith. *jóti* 'ride', repeated from Hrozný (*SH* 39) to van Windekens (*Le tokharien* 589; cf. Tischler, *Glossar* 343–4) is not plausible. In case of /yā-/ at least an occasional spelling *i-ya-a-* would have been expected; positing /ya-/ from **yA₂-* (i.e. weak grade of stem vowel in middle voice; e.g. Hendriksen, *Untersuchungen* 46, 75) raises the very issue that a medium tantum from IE *$y\bar{a}$- is unparalleled and implausible; a reduplicated *yi-$y\mathit{A}_2$- (suggested in passing by H. Eichner, in *Flexion und Wortbildung* 77 [1975]) suffers the same stricture.

Couvreur (*Hett.* 101) first opposed the connection with *$y\bar{a}$- and advocated a thematic *eyo- > *iya*-. Neu (*Mediopassiv* 86–7) started from the weak-grade stem *i*- and arrived at a secondary *iya*- via false division (*iya-nta* for *i(y)-anta*). Oettinger (*Stammbildung* 348–9) also saw a late, inner-Hittite origin for *$i(a)tari$ and preemptively disassociated Ved. *áyate* 'goes' as equally "einzelsprachlich". Yet unlike such dubious comparisons as that between *iyatta* and Ved. *íyate* 'speeds' (< *E_1i- -E_1y-e-to, mentioned by H. Eichner, in *Flexion und Wortbildung* 77 [1975]), or mismatches of the type *iyahha* : Skt. *iyé*, and *iyatta* : Lat. *ītur* (V. Georgiev, *Arch. Or.* 39:431–3 [1971], postulating *iya* < *ay, *oy, *ey alike), the combination of *iyatta* with Rig-Vedic 3 sg. pres. *ayate* (3 pl. *ayante*, 3 sg. impf. *āyata*, partic. *áyamānas*) is plausible (IE *$eyeto$) in view of the Indo-Iranian antiquity of the opposition RV 3 sg. act. *éti* : midd. *ayate* (like e.g. RV 2 sg. *stoṣi* : *stávase*; cf. e.g. C. Watkins, *Indogermanische Grammatik* III/1, 65 [1969]). A corresponding Anatolian pair, Luw. *iti* (< *$eiti$) : Hitt. *iyatta* (replacing *$\bar{e}ta$ < *$eyeto$) is suggestive of the same kind of voice-opposition, realized as nonthematic active(-intransitive) and thematic medial-deponential respectively, in this instance reminiscent of other, suppletive active-middle combinations such as Gk. εἶσι : ἔρχεται, οἴχεται or Lat. *it* : *graditur*; but there is little need to turn it into a glottogonic pawn in rarefied theoretical discussions on the origins of IE verb inflection, in the manner of C. Watkins (*TPhS* 1971: 80–1) and W. Cowgill (*Proceedings of the Eleventh Int. Congr. of Linguists* 2:564 [1975]).

Cf. *iyatar*.

iya-, ie-, i-   'do, make, treat, beget, perform (duty, ritual), celebrate (deity, feast); (intrans.) do, act, signal (with eyes or spear)';

eshar iya- 'shed blood' (q.v. sub *eshar*), *ishahru iya-* 'shed tears'
(q.v. sub *ishahru-*), *kuelqa* ZI-*ni iya-* 'humor someone' (lit. 'do
[something] for someone's soul'), *appa iya-* 'do over, repeat; do
back, requite', *appan iya-* 'sign' (one's name), *sarā iya-* 'make
high, exalt, extol', *ser iya-* 'erect; exalt' (DÙ; *KBo* I 31 Rs. 13
and 14 *iyauwa*[*r*] = Akk. *ibišu*, i.e. *epēšu* 'make'; cf. Güterbock,
MSL 13:145 [1971]; X 2 III 34 *ŪL kuitki iya*[*zi* matching X 1
Rs. 21 [Akk.] *mimma ūl ipuš* 'did nothing'; cf. F. Imparati – C.
Saporetti, *Studi classici e orientali* 14:52, 79 [1965]), 1 sg. pres.
act. *iyami* (e.g. XI 19 Vs. 5 *sēnus iyami* 'I make icons'; cf.
Haas – Thiel, *Rituale* 314; V 12 III 11–12 *nu-war-an*] ᴰUTU-*ŠI-ya*
SIG₅-*in iyami* 'I, my majesty, shall also treat him well'; cf. Gk. εὖ
ποιεῖν τινα; Friedrich, *Staatsverträge* 2:122; III 7 I 25–26 *nu-wa
uwami kardias-tas iyami* 'I will come [and] do your heart's
[desire]'; cf. Laroche, *RHA* 23:67 [1965]; *KUB* XXIII 103 Rs.
14 *man-wa-za* ŠUM-*an kuitki iyami* 'I would make a certain
name for myself'; cf. Otten, *AfO* 19:42 [1959–60]; XIII 35 I 29
kūnn-a-wa memian ŪL iyami 'I do not make this [kind of]
speech'; cf. ibid. 27 *nu-wa apāt ŪL memahhun* 'I did not say
that'; cf. Werner, *Gerichtsprotokolle* 4; XIII 4 II 63 *nu-wa* EZEN
QATAMMA iyami 'I shall celebrate the festival just so'; cf.
Sturtevant, *JAOS* 54:378 [1934]; XLVIII 119 Vs. 5, 6, 8 'I shall
celebrate [festival]'; cf. G. F. Del Monte, *Oriens Antiquus*
17:179 [1978]), *iyammi* (I 16 III 24 [OHitt.] *ŪL iyammi* 'I shall
not do [evil]'; cf. Sommer, *HAB* 12), *iemi* (e.g. *KBo* XVII 1 III
21 and 23; cf. Otten – Souček, *Altheth. Ritual* 32; *KUB* XXXII
130, 19 *namma-an-za* ᴰUTU-*ŠI iemi* 'furthermore I, my majesty,
shall celebrate her'; cf. J. Danmanville, *RHA* 14:42 [1956];
Lebrun, *Samuha* 168), DÙ-*mi* (e.g. V 1 III 87 *nu ŪL* DÙ-*mi iwar*
ᴵ*Temeti* 'I shall not do like T.'; cf. Ünal, *Hatt.* 2:78), 2 sg. pres.
act. *iyasi* (e.g. XXIII 1 II 15 *Š*[*A* ᴵ*M*]*asturi iwar le iyasi* 'do not
do like M.!'; cf. Kühne – Otten, *Šaušgamuwa* 10; XXXI 68 II 21
nu-war-at le iyasi 'do not do it!'; cf. Houwink Ten Cate, *Anatol.
Stud. Güterbock* 130; XIV 1 Vs. 33 ZI-*it menahhanta le kuedan-
iki iyasi* 'do not act willfully towards anyone!'; cf. Götze,
Madd. 8; *KBo* V 3 III 65 DAM-*an-ma-an-zan le iyasi* 'but do not
make her your wife!'; cf. Friedrich, *Staatsverträge* 2:128; V 9 I
24–25 *mahhann-a* DAM-*KA tatti nu-za mān* DUMU.NITA *iyasi* 'and

when you take yourself a wife, if you beget a son ...'; cf. Friedrich, *Staatsverträge* 1:12; *KUB* XIX 49 I 58–59 *nu mān kī* INIM.MEŠ *hūmanda iyasi* 'if you do all these things'; cf. Friedrich, *Staatsverträge* 2:10; *KBo* V 4 Vs. 32 *nu ITTI* ᴰUTU-*ŠI idālu iyasi* 'you do ill against my majesty'; cf. Friedrich, *Staatsverträge* 1:56), *yasi* (*Bo* 6109, 4 *tamēuman yasi* 'you make alien'), *iesi* (e.g. *KBo* V 3 II 48–49 *apini]suwann-a uttar iesi* 'you do such a thing'; cf. Friedrich, *Staatsverträge* 2:118), DÙ-*si* (e.g. *KUB* XXI 5 III 39 *l]e* DÙ-*si* 'do not do!'; cf. Friedrich, *Staatsverträge* 2:70), 3 sg. pres. act. *iyazi* (frequent, e.g. *KBo* V 13 II 32 *ITTI* ᴰUTU-*ŠI* BAL *iyazi* 'makes insurrection against my majesty'; cf. Friedrich, *Staatsverträge* 1:124; *KUB* XI 13 VI 12 *ser iyazi* 'extols [deities]'; *KBo* VI 4 IV 29 and 35 *luzzi iyazi* 'performs corvée'), *iyazzi* (e.g. ibid. 14 *nu luzzi* ŪL *iyazzi*; V 4 Rs. 14 [*kuis*] *kūn-ma memian iyazzi* 'but he who does this thing'; cf. Friedrich, *Staatsverträge* 1:62; *KUB* XIV 8 Rs. 24 *nu-za* ANA EN-*ŠU arkuwar iyazzi* 'he makes a plea to his master'; cf. Götze, *KlF* 216), *yazzi* (XXXVI 108 Vs. 12 [OHitt.]; cf. Otten, *JCS* 5:129 [1951]; XXXVI 106 Vs. 9 [OHitt.]; cf. Otten, *ZA* 52:217 [1957]), *iyaizzi* (*KBo* II 3 II 7; cf. L. Rost, *MIO* 1:356 [1953]), *iezi* (e.g. VI 2 I 60 [= *Code* 1:26, OHitt.]]*idalus iezi*; III 27 Vs. 5; V 3 III 30 *kuis-ma-at iezi* 'but he who does it'; cf. Friedrich, *Staatsverträge* 2:124), *iezzi* (e.g. VI 26 I 29 [= *Code* 2:64] *ta sullatar iezzi* 'makes a quarrel'; VI 3 III 20 [= *Code* 1:55] *kūsanna* ŪL *kuiski iezzi* 'nobody makes a payroll'; VI 26 II 8 [= *Code* 2:11] *nu-za* DUMU.NITA-*ŠU* EGIR-*pa* DUMU.NITA *iezzi* 'she makes her son her son again' [i.e. rescinds disowning him], with dupl. VI 13 I 18 DUMU-*ŠU* EGIR-*pa* DUMU-*ŠU iyazi*; XXI 8 II 1 *k]āpinan* QATAMMA *iezzi*, with dupl. *KUB* XXIV 9 I 48 SÍG BABBAR *kāpinan* QATAMMA *iyazi* 'she likewise makes white wool into thread'; cf. Jakob-Rost, *Ritual der Malli* 28; XXXII 130, 8 *namma-ssi* EZEN-*an iezzi* 'also he will celebrate a feast for her'; cf. Lebrun, *Samuha* 168; X 3 II 19 *namma* IGI.HI.A-*it iezzi* 'he also signals with the eyes', besides XXV 16 I 52 *namma* IGI.HI.A-*it iyazzi*; XXV 3 II 11–12 *IŠTU* ᴳᴵˢŠUKUR *iezzi* 'signals with a spear', besides *KBo* IV 9 IV 21 ᴳᴵˢŠUKUR-*it iyazi*), *īzzi* (VI 2 II 49–50 [= *Code* 1:48, OHitt.] *hāppar le* [*ku*]*iski īzzi* 'let no one do business'; ibid. 51 [*kuis*]-*za* ... *hāppar īzzi*; par. VI 4 IV 36–37

-*za happar le kuiski iyazi*), DÙ-*yazi* (e.g. *KUB* V 4 I 33
BAL ... DÚ-*yazi* 'makes rebellion'), DÙ-*zi* (e.g. ibid. 35; *KBo* III 3
IV 10–11 *nu-za kuis kuit arkuwar* DÙ-*zi* 'what plea each makes';
KUB V 1 IV 47–48 LÚKÚR-*kan* ANA KARAS.HI.A MÈ-*za wastul* ŪL
DÙ-*zi* 'the enemy in battle does no grievous harm to the army';
cf. Ünal, *Hatt.* 2:84; XVIII 12 + XXII 15 I 1 *nu-za* DINGIR.MEŠ
DÙ-*zi* 'he celebrates the gods'; cf. Ünal, *RHA* 31:43 [1973]; XX
26 VI 4–5 *mān-za* LUGAL-*us zeni* DIŠTAR URU*Samuha* DÙ-*zi* 'when
the king celebrates Ištar of Samuha in the fall'; cf. Lebrun,
Samuha 158), 1 pl. pres. act. *i-ya-u-e-ni* (e.g. *KBo* III 7 II 18–19
ha[*nt*]*ezziyan purull*[*i*] *kuit iyaweni* 'since we celebrate the first
p.-festival'; cf. Laroche, *RHA* 23:68 [1965]; *VBoT* 2, 2–3
man-wa-nnas ishanittarātar iyaweni 'let us make a marital
alliance!'; cf. L. Rost, *MIO* 4:328 [1956]; *ABoT* 60 Vs. 19 *nu-wa
mahhan iyaweni* 'how shall we do?'; cf. Laroche, *RHA* 18:82
[1960]; *KUB* XIX 20 Rs. 18), *i-ya-u-wa-ni* (*KBo* III 8 II 24; cf.
Kronasser, *Die Sprache* 7:155 [1961]), *i-ya-e-ni* (*KUB* XXIV 4
Vs. 9 *nu kunnan kuit iyaeni n-at* NU.GÁL 'there is nothing that
we do right'), DÙ-*u-e-ni* (VII 1 III 9–10 GIM-*an-wa* DÙ-*weni
mān-wa iyaweni* 'how shall we act, if we do act?'; cf. Kronasser,
Die Sprache 7:158 [1961]; *ZA* 67:58 [1977]; V 1 II 86; cf. Ünal,
Hatt. 2:64), 2 pl. pres. act. *iyatteni* (e.g. *KBo* V 3 IV 31 *mān
sumes-ma kuwatqa idālu iyatteni* 'but if you in any way do evil';
cf. Friedrich, *Staatsverträge* 2:134; *KUB* XIII 4 II 71 É-*irr-a-za
iyatteni* 'you shall make a house[hold]'; cf. Sturtevant, *JAOS*
54:378 [1934]; I 16 III 23 *l*]*e iyatteni* 'don't do!'; cf. Sommer,
HAB 12; *KBo* V 4 Rs. 16 *le iyatteni*; cf. Friedrich, *Staatsverträge* 1:62; *KUB* XIII 4 II 63–64 *n-asta* UKÙ-*as* ZI-*ni le-pat
iyatteni* 'do not humor the man!' [Lat. *homini morem ne
gesseritis*]; ibid. 71 UKÙ-*as-ma-at-kan* ZI-*ni le-*[*pat iy*]*atteni* 'do
not humor the man in this!'), 3 pl. pres. act. *iyanzi* (frequent,
e.g. XV 34 III 25 7 TÚL.MEŠ *iyanzi n-at uitenit sunnanzi* 'they
make seven wells and fill them with water'; cf. Haas – Wilhelm,
Riten 196; *KBo* VI 11 I 22 [= *Code* 2:12] *sahhan*] ŪL *iyanzi* 'they
do not do feudal duty'), *ianzi* (e.g. *KUB* XXXII 130, 24 *nu-ssi
apiya-ya* EZEN *ianzi* 'there too, they celebrate a feast for her'; cf.
J. Danmanville, *RHA* 14:42 [1956]; Lebrun, *Samuha* 168),
yanzi (XXXVI 106 Vs. 1 [OHitt.]; cf. Otten, *ZA* 52:217 [1957];

but for *KBo* XXII 2 Vs. 7 see rather under *i-* 'go'), *iyaenzi* (*IBoT* II 115+ *KBo* XV 22+ *KUB* XLI 3 I 9), *ienzi* (frequent, e.g. ibid. 11; *KBo* VI 3 II 17 [= *Code* 1:31] *nu-za* É-*ir* Ù DUMU.MEŠ *ienzi* 'they make for themselves a house[hold] and children'; VI 34 II 33 *ŪL-ma-an* NINDA-*an ienzi* 'they do not make it into bread'; cf. Oettinger, *Eide* 10; *KUB* XV 31 I 11–12 *nu-kan kī handāuwar karuuiliaz tuppiaz ienzi* 'they make this arrangement from an ancient tablet'; cf. Haas – Wilhelm, *Riten* 150; *KBo* V 3 II 8 *nu-smas-at le āra ienzi* 'they shall not make it right for you'; cf. Friedrich, *Staatsverträge* 2:114; *KUB* XXIV 4 Vs. 18 *nu-zan* DINGIR.MEŠ *sarā ŪL ienzi* 'they do not extol the gods'; cf. Gurney, *Hittite Prayers* 28), *iēnzi* (e.g. XI 1 IV 11 *kuit-za iēnzi-ma* 'but what they do'; *KBo* III 40a, 18), DÙ-*anzi* (e.g. *KUB* V 1 III 4 *kī kisan* DÙ-*anzi* 'this they do thus'; ibid. 90 *iwar* ¹*Temetti-pat* DÙ-*anzi* 'they will do exactly like T.'; cf. Ünal, *Hatt.* 2:66, 78), 1 sg. pret. act. *iyanun* (e.g. *KBo* XV 2 IV 14 *kuit iyanu[n* 'what have I done?'; cf. Kümmel, *Ersatzrituale* 62; *KUB* XXXI 66 III 20–1 *iyanun-ma-at-kan damēdaz* IŠTU EME 'I did it on the instigation of another' [lit. 'because of another tongue']; ibid. II 9 *kī-wa-smas ishiūl iyanun* 'I have made you this injunction'; cf. Houwink Ten Cate, *Anatol. Stud. Güter-bock* 130; XXI 17 II 7–8 *nu-ssi* É.MEŠ DINGIR.MEŠ *INA* ᵁᴿᵁ*Urikina iyanun* 'I have made temples for her at U.'; cf. Ünal, *Hatt.* 2:22; Lebrun, *Samuha* 145; *KBo* IV 4 III 28 *nu-za* ANA KARAŠ *uwātar apiya iyanun* 'I made there inspection of the troops'; ibid. 31 *nu-za* UD.KAM.HI.A *ispantius iyanun* 'I made days nights' [i.e. marched around the clock]; cf. Götze, *AM* 126; III 4 III 92 *n-at* EGIR-*pa ŠA* KUR ᵁᴿᵁ*Hatti* KUR-*e iyanun* 'I made it again a land of Hatti'; cf. Götze, *AM* 94; V 3 I 3 *nu-tta* SIG₅-*in iyanun* 'I have treated you well'; cf. Friedrich, *Staatsverträge* 2:106; *KUB* I 1 II 82 *nu-za* DINGIR-*LUM iyanun* 'I celebrated the deity'; cf. Götze, *Hattusilis* 22; *KBo* III 4 II 48–49 *nu-za* EZEN MU-*TI apiya iyanun nu kī INA* MU.1.KAM *iyanun* 'I celebrated there the year-festival; this I did in one year'; cf. Götze, *AM* 60; *KUB* I 8 IV 14 *ŪL manqa iyanun* 'I did not act in any way'; cf. Götze, *Hattusilis* 34), *i-ya-un* (XV 23, 7 INIM-*an asantan iyaun* 'I made a true speech'; cf. P. Cornil – R. Lebrun, *Orientalia Lovaniensia Periodica* 3:61 [1972]), *i-ya-u-un* (*KBo* IV 10 Vs. 50 *nu-tta kī kuit* DUB-*PU* *ishiulas iyawun* 'whereas I have made you this tablet of the treaty'), DÙ-*nun* (*KUB* XXI 5 II 15 *ishi]ullas* DUB-*PA* DÙ-*nun* 'I have made [this] tablet of the treaty'; cf. Friedrich, *Staatsverträge* 2:58; XXIII 1 II 3 *nu-tta* INA KUR ^URU*Amurri* LUGAL-*un* DÙ-*nun* 'in Amurru I have made you king'; cf. Kühne – Otten, *Šaušgamuwa* 8), 2 sg. pret. act. *iyas* (XXX 10 Rs. 12 *zik-]mu iyas zik-mu samnāes* 'you made me, you created me'), *iēs* (XXIII 117, 2 [OHitt.]; XXXI 110, 12 [OHitt.]; XXXVI 103, 6 [OHitt.]), *iyat* (VII 54 III 15–16 *zik-wa* ^D*Iyarris kedani* KUR-*e* KARAŠ.HI.A-*ya idalu iyat* 'you, Iyarris, have done ill to this land and army'), 3 sg. pret. act. *iyat* (e.g. *KBo* III 38 Vs. 8 *taksul iyat* 'made peace'; cf. Otten, *Altheth. Erzählung* 8; *KUB* XII 65+XXVI 71 III 3 KASKAL-*an iyat* 'made [his] way'; cf. Laroche, *RHA* 26:50 [1968]; Siegelová, *Appu-Hedammu* 50; cf. KASKAL-*an eppun* s.v. *ep*[*p*]-, *itar ... daskizzi* s.v. *itar*, KASKAL--*an ... iyandari* (*iyahhat*) s.v. *iya-* 'go'; XXII 70 Vs. 68 *nu mān* SAL.LUGAL *kuitki* EME-*an* EGIR-*anda iyat* 'if the queen in any way afterwards has spoken out [lit. made a tongue]'; ibid. 83 *UNUTE.*MEŠ-*wa kueqa tepauwa* DUMU.SAL GAL *ANA UNUTE.*MEŠ *menahhanda iyat* 'some implements, few in number, the great daughter has substituted for [lit. done vis-à-vis] the [original] implements'; cf. Ünal, *Orakeltext* 76, 80), *i-e-it* (e.g. I 16 III 23 *apās idālu iet* 'she has done evil'; cf. Sommer, *HAB* 12; *KBo* III 22 Vs. 9 [OHitt.] *annus attus iet* 'he made [them] mothers [and] fathers'; cf. Neu, *Anitta-Text* 10; III 1 I 7, 16, 26 [OHitt.] *n-us arunas irhus iet* 'he made them boundaries of the sea'; *KUB* XIV 1 Vs. 13 *tuk ... linkiyas-sas iet* '[he] made you oath-bound [lit. of his oath]'; cf. Götze, *Madd.* 4; ibid. Rs. 50 ^I*Madduwattas-ma-at* EGIR-*an* [HUL-*uw*]*anni iet* 'but M. afterwards treated it with malice'; XXIV 9 II 11–12 *nassu-wa-an ...* [...] *kuiski idalu iet* 'whether ... someone has treated him badly'; cf. Jakob-Rost, *Ritual der Malli* 32), *e-it* (XXXVI 41 I 5 EZEN-*an e-it* 'celebrated the festival'), DÙ-*at* (e.g. VI 45 III 28 *nu-mu-za* ABU-*YA* DÙ-*at* 'my father begot me', besides dupl. VI 46 III 68 *nu-mu-za* ABU-*YA iyat*; XXIII 1 I 39 *nu* INA KUR ^URU*Amurri* ^I*Sapilin* LUGAL-*un* DÙ-*at* 'he made S. king in A.' [cf. Kühne – Otten, *Šaušgamuwa* 8], besides XXI 33 IV 15 [*nu* ^I*Sapi*-DINGIR-*LIM-in*] INA KUR ^URU*Amurri* LUGAL-*un iyat*; cf. R.

Stefanini, *JAOS* 84:23 [1964]; *KUB* XLIV 4 + *KBo* XIII 241 Rs. 8 *n-an-zan* SAG.DU DÙ-*at* 'she treated her head' [partitive apposition]), 1 pl. pret. act. *i-ya-u-en* (e.g. *KUB* XIV 8 Rs. 15 *ēsziy-at iyawen-at* 'it is [so], we did it'; cf. Götze, *KlF* 214; I 1 III 4 [*nu-n*]*nas* DUMU.NITA.MEŠ DUMU.SAL.MEŠ *iyawe*[*n* 'we made ourselves sons [and] daughters'; cf. Götze, *Hattusilis* 22, *Neue Bruchstücke* 12; VII 7, 4–5 [*k*]*āsa-wa tuēl taknas* ᴰ[UTU-*as*] [*mem*]*iyan iyawen* 'lo, to thee, sun of the earth, we have made a speech'; cf. Kümmel, *Ersatzrituale* 131; *KBo* VIII 35 II 8 *nu kāsa lingain iyawen* 'behold, we have made an oath'), *i-ya-u-e--en* (e.g. *KUB* XIV 8 Vs. 12 *ŪL kuwapikki iyawēn* 'we never performed [the rite]'; cf. Götze, *KlF* 208), 2 pl. pret. act. *i-ya-at-te-en* (e.g. *KBo* III 41 + *KUB* XXXI 4 Vs. 7 *kissan iyatten* 'you have done thus'; cf. Otten, *ZA* 55:158 [1962]), *i-ya-at-tin* (e.g. dupl. *KBo* XIII 78 Vs. 7; *KUB* XIV 10 I 5 *kī-wa kuit iyattin* 'this [is] what you have done'; cf. Götze, *KlF* 206), 3 pl. pret. act. *i-e-ir* (e.g. XXXVI 108 Vs. 2 [OHitt.] *taksul ier* '[they] have made peace'; cf. Otten, *JCS* 5:129 [1951]; *KBo* III 1 I 33 [OHitt.] [*nu*] *ēshar ier* 'they shed blood'; *KUB* XLII 100 III 34 *kuit-ma-wa ammuk* ᴸᵁSANGA *ier* 'but because they have made me priest'; cf. G. F. Del Monte, *Oriens Antiquus* 17:184 [1978]; XXIV 9 III 13 *kinun-at ier* 'now they have treated them'; cf. Jakob-Rost, *Ritual der Malli* 44), *i-ya-ir* (XXXIV 90, 7), 1 sg. imp. act. *iyallu* (XIV 11 III 19–20 *nu* SISKUR ŠA ᴵᴰ[*Māla*] *iyallu n-at-kan āss*[*an*]*ullu* 'the ritual of the Mala river I will do and carry out'; cf. Götze, *KlF* 214), 2 sg. imp. act. *iya* (e.g. XIV 1 Vs. 83 *mahhan-wa-tta āssu nu-wa* QATAMMA *iya* 'as [is] agreeable to you, thus do!'; cf. Götze, *Madd.* 20; *KBo* V 9 III 1–2 *kūs-wa memiyas nasma-wa kūn memiyan iya* 'do these things or this thing!'; cf. Friedrich, *Staatsverträge* 1:18; IV 4 III 49 *nu-wa-nnas-za* ERÍN.MEŠ ANŠU.KUR.RA.HI.A *iya* 'make us your troops and horse[men]!'; cf. Götze, *AM* 130; *VBoT* 2, 22–23 *namma-za* ŠUM-*an* EGIR-*an iya* 'also sign your name!'; cf. L. Rost, *MIO* 4:329 [1956]; *KUB* XIV 3 II 65–66 *ehu-wa nu-wa--mu-za arkuw*[*ar*] *iya* 'come, make your plea to me!'; cf. Sommer, *AU* 10), DÙ-*ya* (e.g. *KBo* V 9 III 4–5 *n-an-zan apiya-pat pidi-ssi arkuwar* DÙ-*ya* 'then, in its place, offer an explanation!'), 3 sg. imp. act. *iyadu* (*KUB* VII 60 III 13–14 *nu-mu* ᴰU EN-*YA* ZI-*a*[*s*] *iyadu* 'may the storm-god my lord do my soul's [desire]'; cf. Haas – Wilhelm, *Riten* 238), *iyaddu* (e.g. VII 8 II 9 and III 9; *KBo* IV 10 Vs. 10), *iaddu* (*KUB* XLIII 38 Rs. 23; cf. Oettinger, *Eide* 20), *i-e-id-du* (*KBo* XVII 61 Rs. 5 *taknas-at-za* ᴰUTU-*us* ᴺᴬ⁴*passilus ieddu* 'may the solar deity of the earth make them into pebbles!'; V 3 II 38; cf. Friedrich, *Staatsverträge* 2:118), 2 pl. imp. act. *i-ya-at-tin* (e.g. *KUB* XIII 4 II 69–70 *n-asta* DINGIR.MEŠ-*as-pat* ZI-*ni iyattin* 'humor the gods!'; cf. Sturtevant, *JAOS* 54:378 [1934]), DÙ-*attin* (*KBo* X 37 III 44), 3 pl. imp. act. *iyandu* (e.g. VI 34 III 29 *da*]*nnatta* URU-*yasessar iyandu* 'let them make empty [=lay waste] the town settlements'; cf. Oettinger, *Eide* 12; *KUB* VII 7, 7 SISKUR *iyandu* 'let them perform a rite'; cf. Kümmel, *Ersatzrituale* 132; *KUB* XLIV 4+*KBo* XIII 241 Rs. 15 *nu-kan* ANA DUMU.NITA *dumantiyalas* [with gloss-wedges] *anda iyandu* 'let them treat [viz. with the salve mixed ibid. 14] the insides of the ears [see s.v. *istamas-*] of the male child'), *iendu* (*KBo* VI 34 II 48–49 *n-an ke* NIŠ DINGIR.MEŠ LÚ-*an* SAL-*an iendu tuz*⟨*zi*⟩*us-sus* SAL. .MEŠ-*us iendu* 'let these oaths make him from a man into a woman, and let them make his armies into women'; cf. Oettinger, *Eide* 10); partic. *iyant-*, nom. sg. c. *iyanza* (e.g. *KUB* XII 58 I 18 *nu* ᴳᴵˢZA.LAM.GAR *apiya iyanza* 'there the tent [is] made'; cf. Goetze, *Tunnawi* 8; XLII 100 IV 34 ŠUM-*an iyanza* 'the name [is] celebrated'; cf. G. F. Del Monte, *Oriens Antiquus* 17:185 [1978]; IX 28 I 19 *n-as* ᴰIŠTAR-*is iyanza* 'it [viz. the figurine] [is] made into [a likeness of] Ištar'), *ianza* (e.g. *KBo* XVII 65 Rs. 45 *nu* EZEN *mahha*[*n ien*]*zi n-as* ᴳᴵˢ*kurtas ianza* 'when they celebrate the festival, it [is] done according to a [wooden] tablet'), DÙ-*anza* (e.g. *KUB* XLII 100 III 23 EZEN *hameshandas-ma* ŪL DÙ-*anza* 'the spring festival [was] not celebrated'; ibid. 33 *nu-war-as* ... ᴸᵁSANGA DÙ-*anza* 'he [was] made priest'), nom.-acc. sg. neut. *iyan* (e.g. VII 41 I 17 *nasma-kan* É-*ri anda ēshar iyan* 'or inside the house blood [is] shed'; cf. Otten, *ZA* 54:116 [1961]; VII 53 II 6–7 *n-at duppiza karū iyan* 'this [has] already [been] treated in a tablet'; cf. Goetze, *Tunnawi* 10; *KBo* XII 126 I 13 *nu kūn* UKÙ-*an mān* LÚ-*is iyan h*[*arzi* 'if a man has treated this person'; cf. Jakob-Rost, *Ritual der Malli* 22), nom. pl. c. *iyantes* (e.g. *KUB* IX 22 III

9–10 ᴰ*SIN* ᴰUTU Ù MUL *iyantes* '[images of] the moon, the sun, and a star [are] made'; XLII 100 IV 6), nom.-acc. pl. neut. *iyanta* (e.g. XII 58 I 15–17 EGIR-*an-ma-ssan* ÍD-*i piran* ᴳᴵˢZA. .LAM.GAR.HI.A ŠA GI *karū iyanta iyanzi-ma kuwapi* 'but in her wake by the river tents of reed [have] already [been] made; but where do they make [them]?'), *iyanda* (XXXII 123 II 12–13 6 *KĪLILU-ya ... iyanda* 'six wreaths [are] made'); verbal noun *i-ya-u-wa-ar* (n.), nom.-acc. *iyauwar* (*KBo* I 31 Rs. 13 and 14, quoted at the beginning above; *FHG* 1, 11; cf. Laroche, *RA* 45:132 [1951]), *iyauwa* (*KUB* XXX 10 Vs. 8 *iyauwa zik-pat* DINGIR-*YA maniyahta* 'you alone, my god, directed my doings'; for lack of -*r* cf. e.g. Kronasser, *Etym.* 1:68–9; Neu, *Festschrift für G. Neumann* 219 [1982]), *i-ya-wa-ar* (*FHG* 1, 20 *iyawar zik-pat* DINGIR-*YA maniya*[*hta*]), gen. sg. *iyauwas* 'of doing, to be done' (e.g. *KBo* V 9 III 7–8 *mān memiyas-ma kuis iyauwas zig-*[*an*] ŪL *iyasi* 'but if you do not do a thing which [is] to be done'; ibid. 3 *kuis* ŪL *iyauwas* 'which [is] not to be done'; cf. Friedrich, *Staatsverträge* 1:20; *KUB* IV 1 II 21 and 23 '[is] to be shed' [viz. blood; context sub *eshanant-* s.v. *eshar*]); inf. *i-ya-u-*-*wa-an-zi* (XXIV 3 I 24–25 SISKUR.SISKUR.HI.A EZEN.HI.A *iyauwanzi sarā tittanuskanzi* 'they keep undertaking to perform rites and feasts'; *IBoT* III 148 IV 26–27 *namma mān piran parā* SISKUR ... *iyauwanzi hantaittari* 'further if it has been determined beforehand that the ritual be performed'; cf. Haas– Wilhelm, *Riten* 230), *i-ya-u-an-zi* (*KUB* XIII 4 II 55 EZEN *iyauanzi me*[*h*]*una*[*s*] 'at the time of celebrating the festival'; cf. Sturtevant, *JAOS* 54:378 [1934]; XIX 20 Rs. 9]*iyauanzi* ŪL *āra* 'to do [is] not right'), DÙ-*u-an-zi* (XLVIII 119 Vs. 7 'to celebrate [festival]'; cf. G. F. Del Monte, *Oriens Antiquus* 17:179 [1978]), *i-ya-u-wa-an-na* (IV 1 II 20 *ēshar iyauwanna* 'to shed blood'; cross between *iyauwanzi* and **iyanna*?), *iyauwan* (supine form used as infinitive, in *ishahru iyauwan* 'to shed tears' [examples s.v. *ishahru-*]?); iter. *essa-, issa-* (q.v. separately, with its own iter. *eseski-, essiki-*), but also rarely normal *eski-, iski-* (cf. *teski-, tiski-* from *tiya-, ueski-, uiski-* from *uiya-, peski-* from *piya-*), 3 pl. pres. act. *e-es-kán-zi* (*KBo* V 3 III 64 *āra ēskanzi* 'they shall duly treat [her as ...]'; cf. Friedrich, *Staatsverträge* 2:128), 3 pl. pret. act. *is-ki-ir* (*KUB* IV 1 I 14–15 EZEN.HI.A

GAL-*TIM*-*si kuwapi iskir* 'where they used to celebrate great festivals for him'; cf. von Schuler, *Die Kaškäer* 168), 3 sg. imp. act. *ēskidu* (XII 63 Vs. 5).

No finite passive is formed from *iya-*, but suppletively *kis-* 'become' (q.v.) steps in; cf. e.g. *KBo* VIII 35 II 3 *nu ēshar kisari* 'blood is shed' with *KUB* VII 41 I 17 *nasma-kan ... ēshar iyan* 'or blood [is] shed', or XVI 43 Vs. 10 ZI-*as kisat* 'soul's (desire) was done' with VII 60 III 13–14 *nu-mu ...* ZI-*a*[*s*] *iyadu* 'may (he) do my soul's (desire)'. The probable etymon of *kis-* is Lat. *gerō* (cf. ZI-*ni iya-*, ZI-*as iya-* with Lat. *morem gerere alicui*, or *bellum gerere* 'make war').

Lyd. *i-* 'make', 3 sg. or pl. pret. *il*? Cf. Gusmani, *Lyd. Wb.* 128–9.

Luw. *a(y)a-* 'make', midd. -*ti aya-* 'be made, become' (Hitt. -*za kis-*), 2 sg. pres. act. *āyasi* (*KBo* IX 141 Vs. 16), 3 sg. pres. act. *ati* (*KUB* XXXII 8+5 IV 25 KIN-*an nāwa ati* 'does not perform the rite'; cf. Otten, *LTU* 22), 3 sg. pres. midd. *āyari* (XXXV 54 II 42–44 *pā-ti kuwātin* [*tappi*]*ssa tiyammis nāwa āyari* [*tiy*]*ammis-pa-ti tappissa nāwa āyari zā-ha* SISKUR.SISKUR--*assa* [...] *ap*[*at*]*ī nis āyari* 'but even as heaven does not become earth and earth does not become heaven, even so this ritual shall not come to pass'; cf. Otten, *LTU* 59), 1 sg. pret. act. *aha* (*KBo* XXIX 49 Vs. 6), 2 sg. pret. act. *āyas* (*KUB* XXXV 65 III 5), 3 sg. pret. act. *ayata* (*KBo* XIII 260 II 2, 3, 4), *āta* (*KUB* XXXV 107 III 11 EZEN-*in āta* 'celebrated the festival'; cf. Otten *LTU* 98), *ata* (*KBo* XIII 260 II 10, 12, 14), *ada* (ibid. 16, 18, 20, 22), 3 pl. pret. act. *āyanta* (IX 141 Vs. 20), *aiyanda* (*KUB* XXXV 132 II 8), 3 sg. imp. act. *ādu* (XXXV 125, 5), 3 sg. imp. midd. *āyaru* (XXXII 8 III 26 and 27; cf. Otten, *LTU* 22), *ayaru* (*KBo* VIII 130 III 5), *aiyaru* (*KUB* XXXV 39 II 12, 15, 16, 28, 29; cf. Otten, *LTU* 39); partic. *aiyammi-*, nom. pl. c. *aiyamminzi* (*KBo* IX 145, 6).

Hier. *a(i)a-* 'make', 1 sg. pres. act. *aiawi*, 3 sg. pres. act. *aiati*, 1 sg. pret. act. *aiaha, aiha*, 3 sg. pret. act. *aiata, aita, ata*, 3 pl. pret. act. *aiāta*, 2 sg. imp. act. *aiā*, 3 sg. imp. act. *aiātu*, 3 sg. imp. midd. *aiāru*; partic. (?) *aiāmin*. Cf. Meriggi, *HHG* 15–6; Laroche, *HH* 227. The need to "demolish" these readings (*a-i*[-*ā*]-) in Hawkins – Morpurgo – Neumann, *HHL* 158,

186–7, in favor of *i-zi(-ya)-* allegedly comparable with Hitt. *essa-* (with a possible concession for *ata*; cf. Hawkins – Morpurgo, *Journal of the Royal Asiatic Society* 1975:128; Hawkins, *Anatolian studies* 25:141 [1975]) is mainly an indication of the residual brittleness of the proposed new readings. This dubious *izi-* has been compared by H. Eichner (*Die Sprache* 25:205 [1979]) rather with ON *ið* 'deed', *iðja* 'do', OE *īdig* 'assiduous'.

Lyc. *a-* 'make', 3 sg. pres. *adi* (< **ayati*), 3 pl. pres. *aiti* (< **ayanti*), 1 sg. pret. *aχã*, *agã* (< **ayaha*), 3 sg. pret. *adẽ, ade* (< **ayata*), 3 pl. pret. *aitẽ* (< **ayanta*; Xanthos trilingual: Lyc. 9; cf. Laroche, *Fouilles de Xanthos* 6:64–5 [1979]).

iya- has been connected with Toch. AB *yām-* 'make' (also *ya-* and suppletively *yp-* in A) from H. Holma (*Journal de la Société finno-ougrienne* 33.1:23–4 [1916]) to van Windekens (*Le tokharien* 586). This binary comparison might still have some merit, if it were kept free of further entanglements such as Skt. *yam-* 'hold' (from Holma onward) and especially IE **yē-* 'throw' (Gk. ἵημι, Lat. *iēcī*; first compared with Hitt. *iya-* by Marstrander, *Caractère* 120, assuming 'throw' > 'do' parallel to **dhē-* 'place' > 'do' in Italic, Germanic, and Slavic). Pokorny (*IEW* 502) tied the postulated Hitt.-Toch. isogloss firmly in with **yē-*, and C. Watkins (*Indogermanische Grammatik* III/1, 71 [1969]) tried to quadrangulate Skt. *yam-* as well (IE **yem-* : *yē-* like **gʷem-* : *gʷā-* 'come'); this much-repeated derivation of Hitt. *iya-* from IE **yē-* (see e.g. Tischler, *Glossar* 341–2) lives on in e.g. Čop, *Indogermanica minora* 87, 107, and V. Georgiev, *KZ* 85:38–42 (1971), who equated Hitt. *iezzi* with Gk. ἵησι as **yiyēti*; it is semantically wretched and formally implausible (cf. already Couvreur, *Hett.* 331, and see below).

OHitt. spellings such as *iemi, īzzi, iēnzi, iēs, iet* on the one hand, and *yasi, yazzi, yanzi* on the other (besides the regular *iyami, iyasi, iyazi, iyanzi, iyas, iyat*) have fueled much philological and chronological speculation and abetted either the postulation of /ye-/ as the primary variant (< IE **yē-*; e.g. Kronasser, *Etym.* 1:74), with /ye/ > /ya/ due to some combinatory sound change (see e.g. C. Watkins, *Indogermanische Grammatik* III/1, 71 [1969]), or alternatively the intermingled coexistence of a basic *ya-/ye- and a reduplicated *yiya- (cf. Rosen-kranz, *ZA* 54:111 [1961]). Neither approach is satisfactory. *iya-* is not a nonthematic root verb *yē- (which should have yielded *e-; cf. *eka-, e[u]wa[n]-* s.v.) but a thematic *eye- (> *ē- [> ī- in OHitt. *īzzi* < *eyeti]), *eyo- (> *iya-*; *ie-* being a phonetic variant, perhaps [iyä-]); this is clear from Luw. *aya-* (cf. already Kronasser, *VLFH* 181) and from the general parallelism of verbs in *-iya-* (e.g. OHitt. *tizzi* < *tiyeti beside *tiyazzi, tiezzi*; OHitt. *aniemi, hariemi* like *iemi*; cf. Otten – Souček, *Altheth. Ritual* 75–6). The forms in *ya-* are early unregulated ways of rendering /iya-/ after the manner of e.g. *yatta* for *iyatta* (3 sg. pres. midd. of *iya-* 'go' [q.v.]). *eyo- cannot be segmented *ey-o-, since Hittite has no thematic forms of active root verbs, and hence Oettinger's attempted *ey- 'do' (*Eide* 34–5, drawing in Skt. *énas-* as 'evil deed' [q.v. s.v. *inan-*]) was abortive. An *e-yo-, on the other hand, cannot be a primary verb, since *e- is not a verbal root. What we have here is perhaps a "verbum vicarium" derived from the pronominal stem *e-/o- (q.v. s.v. *a-*) in the same manner as the quasi-synonymous *an(n)iya-* (q.v.) may be denominative from *anna-, an(n)i-* 'that'. This idea of V. Machek (*Die Sprache* 4:79 [1958]) is not so strange if we reflect on the equivalents in modern languages such as the all-purpose English *do (it)*, only it is realized by a grammatical device of denominative verbalization. Just as Hittite could make a synthetic *eshaniya- 'to bloody' besides the expression *eshar iya-* 'to shed blood', Anatolian was apparently capable of an *eya- 'to do it' besides Hitt. *-at iya-*.

No credence accrues to attempts to find root-identity with *iya-* 'go' (Hrozný, *SH* 153; W. Petersen, *Lg.* 9:32 [1933]; N. Holmer, *Årsbok 1955/56 utgiven av Seminarierna i slaviska språk* 5–8 (Lund 1960); P. Hollifield, *Journal of Indo-European studies* 6:177–8 [1978]). A related meaning is found only secondarily in compounds like *parā iya-* (iter. verbal noun *parā ēssumar*, q.v. sub *essa-*; cf. Lat. *proficisco[r]* 'set out, go'), *u-iya-, p-iya-* (q.v.), which have a sense of 'make someone move', hence 'send', sometimes with shadings of 'chase, pursue'; with KASKAL-*an iyat* above ('made [his] way') cf. e.g. *IBoT* I 36 I 12 KASKAL-*an pí-e-ya-an-za* 'sent on (his) way'. Alternatively, IE *yē- 'throw' may lurk in *uiya-, piya-* (cf. Gusmani, *Parola del passato* 16:107–12 [1961]).

Cf. *essa-, iwar.*

iyant-   (c.) 'sheep' (UDU), nom. sg. UDU*iyanza* (*KUB* IX 4 II 5–6 *kāsa-tta suppis* UDU*iyanza* 'lo, for you a pure sheep!'; *VBoT* 24 III 11–13 *namma* ANA UDU.HI.A *istarna paimi nu-kan kuis* UDU*iyanza* IGI.[HI.]A-*wa* D*UTU-i neanza nu-ssi-kan* SÍG*huttulli huuittiyami* 'I also go among the sheep; what sheep [is] turned [with] its eyes [partitive apposition] to the sun, from it I pluck a wool-tuft'; cf. Sturtevant, *TAPA* 58:12 [1927], *Chrest.* 112), *iyanza* (*KUB* XXXV 148 III 38 *iyanza iyanza*; cf. ibid. 40 GUD-*us* 'ox'; unless participle from *iya-* 'do, make' [cf. ibid. 39 *iyanzi*]), acc. sg. UDU*iyantan* (*KBo* VII 1 I 4 *hantezzi-kan* UD-*ti* UDU*iyantan inanas* D*UTU-i sipantahhi* 'on the first day I offer a sheep to the sun-god of sickness'; cf. Kronasser, *Die Sprache* 7:142 [1961]; ibid. 9 *nu-kan* UDU*iyantan arkanzi n-asta* UZU*huisu suppa danzi* 'they trace off a sheep['s carcass] and take clean fresh meat'), gen. sg. UDU*iyantas* (110/e Vs. 21 UDU*iyantas* SÍG*ēsri* 'sheep's fleece'; *KUB* XV 34 I 12 UDU*iyantas* S[ÍG*h*]*uddulli* 'wool-tuft of a sheep'; cf. Haas – Wilhelm, *Riten* 184), UDU*iyandas* (e.g. XXX 15 Vs. 24 UDU*iyandas* SÍG*huttuli*; cf. Otten, *Totenrituale* 66; VII 60 II 14 UDU*iyandas* SÍG*hu*[*ttul*]*li*; cf. Haas – Wilhelm, *Riten* 234; *VBoT* 24 IV 20 UDU*iyandas* SÍG*huddulli*; ibid. III 32–33 UDU*iyandas* SÍG*huddullit anda ishāi* 'wraps it up in the wool-tuft of a sheep'), *iyandas* (*KUB* XV 32 I 35 IŠTU SÍG SA₅ *iyandas* [*huttu*]*llit* 'with a tuft of red sheep's wool'; *KBo* XVIII 193 Vs. 9 Á^MUŠEN-*as pardāuar iyandas* SÍG*huttuli* [spelled -*lis*] 'an eagle's wing, a wool-tuft of a sheep'; cf. Werner, *Symbolae Biblicae et Mesopotamicae F.M.T. de L. Böhl dedicatae* 394 [1973]; *KUB* IX 27 Vs. 10 [.]*iyandas* SÍG*huttulli* [no room in lacuna for UDU]).

iyant- was certainly not the only Hittite word for 'sheep', and perhaps not the principal one (in view of countless UDU.HI.A it is strange not to find any plural forms); cf. UDU-*is* (see s.v. *haui-*), UDU-*us*. The reading UDU*iyant-* (rather than UDU-*iyant-*) has been secure since Ehelolf, *ZA* 43:179 (1936), so that H.

iyant-

Wittmann's (*RHA* 22:117–8 [1964]) and O. Szemerényi's (*Bulletin of the School of Oriental and African Studies* 27:158 [1964], *Kratylos* 11:218 [1966]) UDU-*iyant-* = *hauiyant-* was merely an aberration (cf. e.g. Carruba, *Beschwörungsritual* 52; H. A. Hoffner, *JAOS* 87:354 [1967]; Neu, *Mediopassiv* 118; Kronasser, *WZKM* 62:312 [1969]). Pedersen's (*Hitt.* 148) identification of *iyant-* as in origin the participle of *i-* or *iya-* 'go', and his comparisons with Gk. πρόβατον 'sheep' and ON *ganganda fé* 'walking wealth, livestock (on the hoof)' (vs. *liggjanda fé* 'inert goods'), have been strengthened by the investigations of Benveniste (*BSL* 45:91–100 [1949]; cf. *Hitt.* 12–3) on πρόβατα, dat. pl. πρόβασι 'livestock' and the Homeric collective abstract πρόβασις as 'animate chattels' (vs. κειμήλια 'depositional goods' in *Odyssey* 2:75 κειμήλιά τε πρόβασίν τε): the semantics start not with 'walking cattle' (or 'flocks going in front [of herds]') but rather as 'possessions that go forwards', vs. holdings that just 'lie there', even as the Roman legal house search for stolen goods was conducted *lance et licio* 'with platter and tether' for symbolic removal of the two main categories of larcenous items (cf. C. Watkins, in *Indo-European and Indo-Europeans* 336 [1970]). Either term could metonymically shade over into a comprehensive word for wealth, and hence e.g. Oscan *eítiuvam* 'pecuniam' is in origin a collective abstract **ey-tu-* etymologically cognate with Lat. *itus* 'a going' but semantically (as 'that which goes') akin to Hom. πρόβασις, whereas Toch. A *śemäl* '(small) cattle', rather than derived from *käm-* 'come', may conversely be related to Gk. κειμήλια (cf. van Windekens, *Le tokharien* 477–8), with neutralization of the live : inert opposition, thus the reverse semantic development from that seen in e.g. **peku* > Goth. *faíhu* 'κτήματα, χρήματα, ἀργύριον' (cf. e.g. Gk. κτήνεα 'flocks' < 'possessions', or OCS *skotŭ* 'cattle' < 'money' [Goth. *skatts*]).

C. Watkins (in *Hethitisch und Indogermanisch* 282–3 [1979]) also compared *iyant-* with Hitt. *iyatar* in the sense of 'moveable wealth' (*iyant-* : *iyatar* as πρόβατα : πρόβασις), and further saw in the second member of the asyndetic *iyata tameta* a term for 'inert wealth', matching κειμήλια. But *tameta* (q.v.) means rather 'fat of the land, abundance', and *iyatar* is better interpreted as '(vegetal) growth', thence 'plenty, prosperity' (see s.v.); despite such Vedic analogues as *gávām póṣam* 'prosperity of cattle', or *rayím gómantam* 'wealth in cattle', or *gómat* 'cattle-laden(ness)', *iyatar* is not likely to have meant 'that which goes' > 'mobile chattels' > 'plenty, prosperity'. Organic (animate and vegetal) possessions are rather listed under the binomial heading *iyata tameta* (*KBo* XII 42 Rs. 4–9, quoted s.v. *iyatar*), whereas metal and mineral wealth (ibid. 10–12) is introduced as 'goods' (*āssū-ya*). Thus the live : inert opposition is not lost in Hittite but has been reformulated in a way which sidetracks the isolated *iyant-* into the specific sense of 'sheep', somewhat as Classical Greek has the secondary singular πρόβατον 'sheep' besides oppositions such as χρήματα καὶ κτήματα 'goods and (live) chattels'. Cf. Puhvel, *AJPh* 104:226–7 (1983).

(i)yasha-, 2 sg. pret. act. in *KBo* V 6 IV 3 *nu-wa-mu-kan parā ŪL iyashatta nu-wa-mu enessan imma* TAQBI 'you did not trust (?) me, nay even spoke to me thus' (cf. Güterbock, *JCS* 10:96 [1956]). This inferred meaning rests on the context (widow of Tutankhamen writing to Suppiluliumas, after the latter had expressed skepticism about her previous request for S's son as her new husband).

The form *iyashatta* is "Luwian" (cf. Güterbock, *Orientalia* N.S. 25:121 [1956]), as are the grammatically opaque *(kuin) yashantin* (*KUB* XIX 23 Vs. 11; acc. sg. of pres. partic.?), (ANA GAŠAN-YA) *yashanduwati* (ibid. 13, with gloss-wedges; cf. S. Heinhold-Krahmer, *Arzawa* 312 [1977]), *yashanduwanti* ŠÀ-*ta sāi* 'impress upon your ? heart' (XIV 7 IV 8, with gloss-wedge; dat. of adj. in *-(u)want-*?; or abl.-instr. *-ati*?).

Sturtevant (*IHL* 51, *Comp. Gr.*² 51) connected *iyasha-* with *ishiya-* 'bind' (his inexact translation 'you are bound to' was colored thereby), and both (wrongly) with Avest. *yāsta-* 'girt', etc. (cf. s.v. *ishiya-*). Since *ishiya-* (Luw. redupl. *hishiya-*) reflects IE *sE_2y-, *iyasha-* does not belong, nor is the meaning close. Etymology unknown.

iyatar

iyatar (n.) '(vegetal) growth, fertility, fecundity; plenty, prosperity', ^{SÍG}*iyatar* 'wool-growth, thick wool', nom.-acc. sg. *iyatar* (*KBo* XI 1 Vs. 15 *nu-kan* ŠÀ KUR-*TI āssu taksul assu*[*l miya*]*tar iyatar* 'in the land concord, well-being, growth, prosperity'; cf. *RHA* 25:106 [1967]; *KUB* XLIII 60 I 11–13 *n-apa iyatar-mit udandu takku arunaz-ma n-at lahanza udau n-at-san pedi-ssi dāu* 'let them bring my plenty; but if from the sea, let the 1.-bird bring it and put it in its place'; XXIII 40 Vs. 3), *iyata* (*Bo* 2727 I 4 *LIM* UDU.HI.A *iyata LI*[*M* 'prosperity [of] a thousand sheep, a thousand …'; *KUB* II 2 III 28–29 *nu piyer iyata tamēta* '[the gods] gave fecundity [and] abundance' [followed by prayer for progeny down through generations for the royal couple]; dupl. XLVIII 6, 6 [OHitt.] *iyatada*[-, binomial rendering of Hattic ^D*Wa_a-su-ú-ul* = ^D*Hingallu* 'Abundance'; cf. Schuster, *Bilinguen* 72–3, 122–3; *KBo* XII 42 Rs. 4–5 *nu-wa iyata tamēta pe harweni* 'we purvey growth [and] abundance [=what grows and is abundant]', detailed [ibid. 6–9] as deliveries aplenty [ibid. 6, 8, 9 *mekki*] of human chattels, livestock, and agri- and viticultural products, as opposed to metal and mineral goods [*āssū-ya*, ibid. 10–12]; cf. H. A. Hoffner, *JCS* 22:35 [1968]; *KUB* VIII 22 III 3 *i*]*yata tameta kīsa* 'growth and abundance will be'; IV 5, 13–14 *nu nepisaza iy*[*ata*] *hūman heyauwani*[*sk-izzi*] 'from heaven growth rains down all over', matching ibid. [Sum.] *hingal* and *KBo* XII 72, 13–14 [Akk.] *ištu šamē higalla ušazna*[*n*]; cf. *KUB* IV 5, 15–17 + *KBo* XII 73, 2 *n-asta* KUR-*e iy*[*ata*] *dammēda hū*[*man*] *heyauwaneskiz*[*zi*] 'in the land growth and abundance rains down all over', matching *KBo* XII 72, 15 [Akk.] *higalli*; cf. Laroche, *RA* 58:72–3 [1964]), *iyada* (*KUB* IV 4 Vs. 13–14 *iyada dammeda harti* 'you have growth [and] abundance', matching ibid. [Akk.] *enbu hengalli* 'fruit in abundance'; cf. Laroche, *RA* 58:73 [1964]; XII 63 Rs. 16), *iyāta* (ibid. 29), *iyāda* (*KBo* III 7 I 17–18 [*nu* DU]G *palhas an*[*d*]*an iyāda i*[*et*] 'inside the cauldrons he made plenty' [i.e. filled them to the brim]; cf. Laroche, *RHA* 23:66 [1965]), gen. sg. *iyatnas* (*KUB* XIII 33 II 5–6 *iyatnas-wa-ssi* [*huhu*]*pal* SUM-*an ēsta* 'a vessel of plenty had been given to him'; cf. Werner, *Gerichtsprotokolle* 34; *huhupal* may denote a container for liquids [cf. XXV 37 I 34 *mahhan-ma-kan* ^{GIŠ}*huhupal IŠTU* GEŠTIN

350

sunnanzi 'but when they fill a h. with wine'], in addition to a wooden percussion-instrument [cf. ibid. 10 ^{GIŠ}*huhupal harzi ūl-at* GUL-*ahhiskizzi* 'he has a h. but does not strike it']; XXXIX 7 II 10–11 ^{SÍG}*iyatnass-a* 10 *lahanza*^{MUŠEN} *iyanza* 'and of thick wool ten l.-birds [are] made' [in addition to birds of wood and dough, on top of live specimens, ibid. 7–14]; cf. Otten, *Totenrituale* 36; ibid. 20 ^{SÍG}*iyatna⟨s⟩ lappinan i*[*yanzi* 'of thick wool they make a l.-plant'; XXX 19 I 5–6+XXXIX 7 I 11–12 *namma-an* IŠTU ^{GIŠ}GEŠTIN ^{GIŠ}*INBI mūrinit* ^{SÍG}*iyatnas mūrinit unūwanzi* 'then they deck [the vine] with natural grapes [and] with grapes of thick wool'; XXXIX 7 I 22+XXX 19 I 17 ^{SÍG}*i*]*yatnass*[*-a*] *mūriyanus*; cf. Otten, *Totenrituale* 32, 130), abl. sg. ^{SÍG}*iyatnaza* (XXXI 71 IV 29–30 *nu-wa-kan* ANA 1 ARÀH ^{DUG}*agannis mān anda nu-war-as* ^{SÍG}*iyatnaza sūwanza* 'in one storehouse [there is something] like a bowl, and it [is] filled with thick wool'; cf. Werner, *Festschrift H. Otten* 328 [1973]). For frequent lack of *-r* in *iyata(r)* (as consistently in *tameta*, *dammeda* vs. *dammetarwant-*), cf. e.g. Kammenhuber, *MIO* 3:356 (1955); Kronasser, *Etym.* 1:68–9; Schuster, *Bilinguen* 123; Neu, *Festschrift für G. Neumann* 212–3, 216–7 (1982).

iyatnuwant- 'growing, luxuriant', nom.-acc. sg. neut. *iyatnuwan* (*KUB* XXIX 7+*KBo* XXI 41 Rs. 29–30 ^{LÚ}ŠE.KIN.KUD- -*as māhhan miyān iyatnuwan hāsuwāi*^{SAR} [...] *warasta* 'as the harvester mows [gnomic preterite] the growing, luxuriant soapwort'; ibid. 27–28 *iyatnuwan hāsuwāi*^{SAR}; cf. Lebrun, *Samuha* 123). For denominative formation, cf. e.g. *saknuwant-* 'shitty' from *sakkar* 'shit' (**iyatn-[u]want-*).

iyatniya- 'be in growth', partic. *iyatniyant-*, nom.-acc. sg. neut. *iyatniyan* (*KUB* XXIX 1 IV 18 *uktūri iyatniyan* 'evergreen' (tree; see s.v. *e*[*y*]*a*[*n*]-), dat.-loc. pl. *iyatniyandas* (*KBo* VI 11 I 8 [=*Code* 2:7] *takku* LÚ.ULÙ.LU-*as iyatniyandas* ^{GIŠ}ŠAR.GEŠTIN UDU.HI.A *tarnai* 'if a person lets sheep into growing vineyards').

^{SÍG}*iyatar* resembles ^{SÍG}*es(sa)ri-* 'fleece' (lit. 'woolshape, woolskin'; cf. 132/x, 3 TÚG *iyatnas* 'garment of thick wool' [for lack of ^{SÍG} cf. occasional *ēsri* 'fleece' rather than ^{SÍG}*ēsri*]); the basic sense of *iyatar* shines through in the symbolism of ^{SÍG}*iyatar*: the latter is used to fashion imitation grapes (cf. *iyatniyant-*

referring to vineyards, *KBo* VI 11 I 8 above); from it are also fabricated fake *lahanza*-birds, the same kind as is conjured to bring *iyatar* from the sea (*KUB* XLIII 60 I 11–13, above); the third item made from ᔆᴵᴳ*iyatar* is *lappina*-plant(s) which are notorious for their thick growth (the mountains are '[over]flowing' [*arsantes*] with them when the ogre Huwawa throws up vegetal roadblocks to human passage [*KBo* X 47g III 14]).

Thus *iyatar* is in origin literally 'growth', a petrified verbal noun from *iya-* 'go, walk' in the special sense of 'grow, sprout', used particularly of the spread of vegetation (cf. 3 sg. imp. midd. *iyataru* s.v. *iya-*), in a manner similar to *huwai-* 'run' (*KBo* VI 34 II 40–41 *welluwas anda welkuwan le huwāi* 'in the meadows grass shall not grow'). Its detachment from the living paradigm of *iya-* (**iya-tar*, not **iya-atar*) is marked by the nonassimilation of *-tn-* (cf. e.g. *haratar*, *huitar*, s.v.), thus gen. sg. *iyatnas*, not **iyannas*.

The irreversible asyndetic binomial *iyata(-)tameta* 'growth (and) abundance' is clearly a set expression reminiscent of a verbal biblical turn in *Genesis* 1.28 (LXX αὐξάνεσθε καὶ πληθύνεσθε, Vulgate *crescite et multiplicamini*); it idiomatically and pleonastically renders in tandem what is expressed by Hattic *wasūl* 'abundance', Akk. *enbu hengalli* 'fruit in abundance', even as its parts can occur singly (*iyatar* = Sum. *hingal*, Akk. *higalla*; *dammetarwant-* matching Akkadian terms for 'abundance' [*nuhšu, kuzbu*]).

C. Watkins's attempt to see in *iyatar* a collective abstract 'moveable wealth' (lit. 'that which goes') is criticized and rejected s.v. *iyant-*; Rosenkranz's connection of *iyatar* with *iya-* 'do, make' (*JEOL* 19:501 [1965–6]) has no merit, nor does H. Eichner's attempt (*MSS* 31:77 [1973]) to see a figura etymologica in ᴳᴵˢ*eyan ... ukturi iyatniyan* (see s.v. *e[y]a[n]-*). Cf. Puhvel, *AJPh* 104:226–7 (1983).

iyatti- (c.), a type of bread or cake, acc. sg. ᴺᴵᴺᴰᴬ*i-ya-at-ti-in* (*KBo* XXII 173, 8), acc. pl. *iyattius* (*KUB* X 91 III 15–16 *nu-kan* 3 ᴺᴵᴺᴰᴬ*iyattius* IŠTU INBI GA.KIN.AG *teyantes* ... ME-*i* 'he takes three *i*. decorated [lit. placed] with fruit [and] cheese').

iyatti- makes no sense in terms of Hittite historical phonology, since *-tti-* stands for /ti/ which, if inherited, should have yielded *-zzi-*. Otherwise opaque. *i*-stem may indicate Luwian or Hurrian origin.

iyawa- 'be healed, recover', 3 sg. pres. midd. *i-ya-u-wa-at-ta(-u-wa--ar)* (*Bo* 1391 Vs. 8 *iyauwatta-uwar āssu* 'is well healed' [?]), 3 sg. pret. midd. *i-ya-u-wa-at-ta-at* (ibid. 4–5 *iyauwatta[t] āssu*; ibid. 7 *[iy]auwattat āssu*; cf. Otten, *JKF* 2:65 [1951]); iterative (-"durative") *iyawan(n)a-*, *iyawan(n)iya-*, deverbative adj. *i-ya--u-wa-ni-ya-u-an-za* (*KUB* XXXIII 120 I 42–43 [ᴰ*Kuma*]*rbis-a--kan iyauwaniyauanza* ᵁᴿᵁ*Nipp*[*ur* ...] [...] *pait* 'and K., recovering [viz. from his oral abortion], went to Nippur'; cf. Güterbock, *Kumarbi* *3, 36; Dressler, *Studien* 235; for formation, cf. e.g. *āssiyauwant-* 'favorite, lover', *kartimmiyawant* 'angry', *nahsariyawant-* 'fearful'); double iter. *iyawaneski-*, *iyawaniski-*, 2 sg. pres. act. *i-[ya-w]a-ni-es-ki-si* (XVII 8 IV 15), 3 sg. pres. act. *i-ya-wa-ni-is-ki-iz-zi* (ibid. 14 *nu-ssi lappiyas merta nu iyawaniskizzi* 'his fever has disappeared and he is recovering'), *i-ya-u-wa-ni-is-ki-iz-zi* (ibid. 31; cf. Laroche, *RHA* 23:167–8 [1965]).

iyauwatta relates to the active *iyauwaniya-* much as e.g. the medial *iyatta* (q.v. s.v. *iya-* 'go') stands vis-à-vis *iyaniazzi* (q.v. s.v. *i-* 'go'). The root is IE **A₂éw-A₂-* (*IEW* 77) seen in Skt. *ávati* 'helps, expedites', *avitár-* 'helper', *ūtí-*, *ávas-* 'help', Avest. *avaiti* 'helps', *avah-* 'help', Gk. ἐνηής 'helpful, kind', Lat. *avārus* 'greedy', *avidus* 'eager', *avē-* 'be eager', *audē-* 'be eager, dare'. A reduplicated verbal stem from this root explains Hitt. *iyawa-* as **A₂i-A₂ewA̯₂-*. A Latin cognate may be *iuvā-* 'help, gratify' (<**A₂i-A₂uweA₂-*; cf. F. Specht, *KZ* 65:207–8 [1938], 68:52–7 [1944], who compared *iuvā-* with Skt. *ávati*), and from Greek one might adduce the epic-lyric verb ἰαίνω 'soothe, warm, heal' (<**ἰαϝα-νι̯ω* <**A₂i-A₂ewA̯-*; for loss of digamma between two alphas cf. Hom. ἄτη <**ἀϝάτᾱ*, early enough for the the contractional ᾱ to appear in formulaic metrical arsis [*Iliad* 6:356, 24:28 Ἀλεξάνδρου ἕνεκ' ἄτης]; the old connection with Ved. *iṣaṇyáti* 'drive, impel' has semantically little in its favor). An additional comparison with Gk. $\overset{\text{\tiny 2}}{\iota}\bar{\alpha}$- (Hom. $\overset{\text{\tiny 2}}{\iota}\eta$-), $\iota\bar{\alpha}$- 'heal' is, however, ruled out (*$\iota\alpha\digamma\alpha$- should have yielded Hom. $\bar{\iota}\bar{\alpha}$-; the digamma is contradicted by Myc. *i-ja-te* and Cypr. $\iota\jmath\alpha\sigma\vartheta\alpha\iota$; $\overset{\text{\tiny 2}}{\iota}$- must be attributed to unmotivated metrical lengthening); besides, $\iota\alpha\acute{\iota}\nu\omega$ and $\overset{\text{\tiny 2}}{\iota}\bar{\alpha}$- are very disparate in their range of usages and plausibly not root-related (cf. N. van Brock, *Recherches sur le vocabulaire médical du grec ancien* 255–8 [1961]; for $\overset{\text{\tiny 2}}{\iota}\bar{\alpha}$- see further s.v. *iski[ya]-*).

ikniyant- 'lame, paralytic, crippled', *KUB* XII 62 Rs. 9 *ikniyanza piddai le* 'a lame (person) shall not run'. Cf. Ehelolf, *KlF* 393–4; H. A. Hoffner, *JCS* 29:151 (1977).

Benveniste (*BSL* 35:102–3 [1934]) compared the isolated Gk. $\ddot{o}\kappa\nu o\varsigma$ (*Iliad+*) 'shrinking, hesitation' ($\ddot{\alpha}o\kappa\nu o\varsigma$ 'unhesitating, resolute'), thus seeing in **ikn(i)-* or **ikna-* a corresponding *e*-grade *ekn-*. Cf. e.g. Neumann, *Untersuch.* 20; Frisk, *GEW* 2:374.

More probably *ikniyant-* is related to *eka-* 'cold, ice' (q.v.), thus a participle of a denominative verb formed from **yeg-no-* or **ig-no-* 'frozen, paralyzed'. Carruba (apud Neu, *Interpretation* 68) also collated *egai-* with *ikniyant-*, but postulated the wrong meaning 'burst, crack' for *egai-* (adducing as semantic parallel *duwarnai-* 'break' : *dudduwarant-* 'lame') and assigned it to IE **ayg-* 'move, vibrate' (*IEW* 13–14).

Alp's adduction (*Anatolia* 2:29–30 [1957]) of *ekt-*, *ikt-* (q.v.) was abortive, due to the incorrect meaning 'leg'; nor is it clear how in the absence of privativity 'legless' could be derived from 'leg'; hence Oettinger's (*Eide* 22) connection with *egdu-*, *igdu-* 'leg' also fails to save the day.

iksai-, hapax iter. 3 sg. pres. midd. *ik-sa-a-i-is-ki-it-ta* in *KUB* XXXVI 44 IV 8–10 *nu kuwapi* ^DUTU-*us mumiezzi* [...-]*i-ku happeni-kku* GIŠ-*i-kku hahhali-kku mumiezzi* [...] *iksāyiskitta* 'where(ver) the sun falls, whether into ? or flame or a tree or a bush' (cf. Laroche, *RHA* 23:82 [1965]).

H. Eichner (*MSS* 29:30, 39 [1971]) suggested a meaning

'burst, crack' akin to *igai-* (q.v. s.v. *eka-*); but the latter means rather 'cool down, freeze, become paralyzed', a sense not necessarily inappropriate either for a fallen sun; thus a relationship of *ig-ai-* and *ig-s-ai-* remains possible.

ila- 'weakness' (vel. sim.), nom. sg. *i-la-as* (*KUB* XXIX 1 I 46–48 [*t*]*akku ilas kardi-smi nassu-ma* ᴰUTU-*was istarningais kardi-smi n-at sarā sāhten* 'if weakness [is] in your heart, or the ailment of the sun [is] in your heart, flush it out!'; cf. B. Schwartz, *Orientalia* N.S. 16:28 [1947]), acc. sg. *i-la-a-an* (*KBo* XXI 20 I 15; cf. Burde, *Medizinische Texte* 42).
  No etymology.

ilaliya- 'desire,want', 1 sg. pres. act. *ilāliyami* (e.g. *KUB* XIII 3 II 18 *n-an-zan* LUGAL-*us* ŪL *ilāliyami* 'I the king do not want him'; cf. Friedrich, *Meissner AOS* 46), 2 sg. pres. act. *ilaliyasi* (e.g. *KBo* V 3 III 38 *danna-ma-za le ilaliyasi* 'but do not desire to take [sexually]'; cf. Friedrich, *Staatsverträge* 2:126; V 13 II 16–17 *nu damētani* AŠŠUM BELLUTIM *ilaliyasi* 'you desire for another for lordship'; cf. Friedrich, *Staatsverträge* 1:122; *KUB* XXIII 1 II 13–14 *nu-za apiya* AŠŠUM EN-UTTI *le kuinki ilaliyasi* 'there [i.e. from those] do not desire anyone for lordship!'; cf. Kühne – Otten, *Šaušgamuwa* 8–10), 3 sg. pres. act. *ilaliyazi* (e.g. XXI 42 I 32 [*ku*]*is-ma-za ilaliyazi* 'but he who desires' [viz. another lordship]), 2 pl. pres. act. *ilaliyatteni* (ibid. 30–31 *dammēda-ma le autteni tamāi-ma-*⟨*sm*⟩*as* EN-*UTTA le ilaliyatteni* 'but do not look elsewhere and do not wish for another lordship'; cf. von Schuler, *Dienstanweisungen* 24); partic. *ilaliyant-*, nom. sg. c. *ilaliyanza* (*RS* 25:421 Ro. 36 GIŠ.ŠAR-*as-ma-as* GIM-*an ilaliyan*[*za*] 'she [is] like a desired garden'); verbal noun *ilaliyawatar* (cross between **ilaliyawar* and **ilaliyatar*?; cf. inf. *iyauwanna* s.v. *iya-* 'do'), instr. sg. *ilaliyauwannit* (ibid. Vo. 62–63 *āssiyauwanzas-ma-as* [...] GIM-*an ilaliyauwannit* ŪL *ha*[*s-sikanza* 'she [is] like a lover not satiated with desire', matching ibid. [Akk.] *rām murtamim ša lālū-šu lā išabū* 'love of a lover whose desire is not satiated'; cf. Laroche, *Ugaritica* 5:774,

ilaliya-

444–5, 314 [1968]); iter. *ilaliski-*, 2 sg. pres. act. *i-la-li-is-ki-si*
(*KBo* IV 10 Rs. 9), 3 sg. pres. act. *i-la-li-is-ki-iz-zi* (*KUB* XIX 28
IV 7), *i-la-lis-ki-iz-zi* (*KBo* II 11 Rs. 8; cf. Sommer, *AU* 245–7),
i-la-a-li-is-ki-iz-zi (XXI 22 Vs. 14–15 *nu-za kuit Labarnas*
LUGAL-*us istanzanas-sas* [ŠÀ-*as-s*]*as ilāliskizzi n-at-si anda arān*
ēstu 'what L. the king desires in his soul and heart, let it come
to him'), *i-la-li-is-ki-zi* (ibid. 16, repeated for the queen; cf. G.
Kellerman, *Tel Aviv* 5:199 [1978]), 1 pl. pres. act. *i-la-li-is-qa-u-*
-e-[*ni* (*KUB* XXXI 44 II 27; cf. von Schuler, *Orientalia* N.S.
25:227 [1956]), *i-la-a-li-is-ga-u-e-ni* (XL 15 + XXVI 24 + 583/u
II 7; cf. H. Otten – C. Rüster, *ZA* 68:270 [1978]), 3 pl. pres. act.
i-la-li-is-kán-zi (XXIV 1 III 21–22 *kuedas-ma-z* [sic] *sumenzan*
É.HI.A DINGIR.MEŠ-*KUNU arha warnummanzi ilaliskanzi* 'and
who desire to burn up your temples'; dupl. XXIV 2 Rs. 5–6
kuyēs-ma-z [...] *ilaliskanzi*), 2 sg. imp. act. *i-la-li-is-ki* (*KBo* IV
14 II 20–21 *ziqq-a-za* [QATAMMA] *ishassarwatar* [...] *ilaliski*
'you, too, likewise desire lordship!'; ibid. III 65–66 *nu-za-kan*
ANA ZI LUGAL *āssu ilaliski harnamniyasi-ma-at-kan le* 'desire
good for the king's soul and do not cause ferment against
him!'; cf. R. Stefanini, *ANLR* 20:40, 47 [1965]), 2 pl. imp. act.
i-la-li-is-ki-it-te-en (XVI 24 + 25 I 64; cf. A. M. Rizzi Mellini,
Studia mediterranea P. Meriggi dicata 524 [1979]).

Attested in Anatolian anthroponymy (*Ilalia(hsu)*; cf. Laroche, *Noms* 77–8) and theonymy (*KUB* II 4 IV 27 ᴰ*Ilaliyantas*;
IX 34 III 35 ᴰ*Ilaliyandus*; Pal. ᴰ*Ilaliyant(ik)es*; cf. Carruba, *Das*
Palaische 57); perhaps also in Lyc. *Eliyãna* (dat. pl. on Xanthos
trilingual [Lyc. 40], matching Gk. Νυμφῶν; cf. Carruba, *SMEA*
18:315 [1977], who compared such seeming "Attic reduplica-
tions" as Luw. *elelha-*, *ililha-* beside *elha-*, *ilha-*).

Hier. *alana-* 'covet' (Karatepe 351) has been adduced by F.
Steinherr, *MSS* 32:108 (1974); cf. Hawkins – Morpurgo, *Jour-*
nal of the Royal Asiatic Society 1975:125–8. Perhaps dissimila-
tory for **alala-*.

The comparison of *ilaliya-* with Gk. λιλαίομαι 'desire' (Juret,
Vocabulaire 22; J. Duchesne-Guillemin, *TPhS* 1946:74–5) must
be confined to a general phonesthetic level, since **λιλασ-ιο-* is
matched etymologically by Hes. λάσται·πόρναι, Skt. *lālasa-*
'desirous', and Lat. *lascīvus*. The origins of *ilaliya-* are better

356

sought in home-grown Anatolian expressive (perhaps onomatopoeic) reduplicates, possibly denominatively based on interjectional material like Gk. ἐλελίζω, ἀλαλάζω, ὀλολύζω.

ila(n)- 'stair(case), step(ladder)' (^{GIŠ}KUN$_4$, ^{GIŠ}KUN$_5$), nom. sg. ^{GIŠ}i-
-*la-as* (*KBo* XXII 194, 9; 347/z, 3), gen. sg. *i-la-na-as* (e.g. *KUB*
XX 46 III 4–16 [*ilanas* in 6, 9, 15] LUGAL-*us* INA É ^{D}*Mezzulla*
paizzi nu GAL DUMU.MEŠ É.GAL *ilanas piran happurriyan ispāri nu*
LUGAL-*us ilanas piran tiyezzi nu* ANA DINGIR-*LIM aruwāizzi t-as*
hāliya ta namma aruwāizzi n-aṡ-kan kuitman ilanas sarā ari ta
aruuiskizzi-pat 'the king goes into the temple of M.; the chief of
palace sons spreads h. before the staircase; the king steps
before the staircase and prostrates himself to the deity; he
kneels; he prostrates himself further; and while he makes his
way up the staircase he keeps prostrating himself'; XXXI 89 II
3–4 *namma* KÁ.GAL-*TIM lustaniēs* ^{GIŠ}*ilana*[*s* SAG.DU.MEŠ] BÀD.HI.
.A-*as* ^{GIŠ}AB.HI.A-*us* ^{GIŠ}IG-*antes hattalwant*[*es* 'also [let] gates,
posterns, heads of staircases, and windows of fortifications [be]
shuttered [and] bolted'; dupl. XXXI 86 II 13 *lustaniyas ilanas*
SAG.DU.MEŠ-*us*; cf. von Schuler, *Dienstanweisungen* 43; *KBo*
XXV 187 II 8 *ilanas*; unclear XVIII 181 Vs. 21 5 TÚG GÚ *hurri*
ilanas; cf. TÚG GÚ.È.A ['shirt'] *hurri* [e.g. V 2 I 32, *KUB* XV 23,
10]?), dat.-loc. sg. *i-la-ni* (XL 53 IV 7–8 *n-at … sarā* ^{GIŠ}*ilani dāi*
'places it up on the staircase', vs. ibid. 9–10 *n-at …* EGIR-*an*
katta dāi 'puts it back down'; *KBo* III 6 III 69–70 ^{D}*IŠTAR-ma-*
-*mu-kan* GAŠAN-*YA ilani ilani namma teskit* 'but Ištar my lady
also kept placing me [if from *dai-*; or: attending on me, if from
tiya-] at every step' [viz. of my career ladder]; cf. Götze,
Hattusilis 34; *VBoT* 44, 8 *il*]*ani ilani*?).

For epanadiplotic *ilani ilani* cf. e.g. ITU-*mi* ITU-*mi* 'every
month' (s.v. *arma-*). Gender and stem class remain in doubt.
Like other architectural vocables (e.g. *parn-* 'house', *aska-*
'gate', *hila-* 'court[yard]'), *ila(n)-* may well be a native Anatolian term.

ilessar, ilissar, ilassar, elassar   (n.) 'sign' (IZKIM), dat.-loc. sg. *i-li-es-*
-*ni* (*KUB* VI 3, 6–8 DINGIR-*LUM* TI-*tar kuedani ilesni uskisi*

karū-ssi kuēs MU.HI.A *ariyasesnaza memantes apedass-a* MU.HI.
.A-*as parā* TI-*anza* 'in what sign you watch the deity's life
[partitive apposition], what years have been spoken for him of
old by oracle, in those years [he shall be] living'), *i-li-is-ni* (XXI
38 I 55–56 *mān tesi* LUGAL KUR ^{URU}*Karanduniyas-wa* ŪL LUGAL
GAL *nu-za* ŠEŠ-*YA* KUR ^{URU}*Karanduniyas* ŪL IDI *kuedaniy-at ilisni*
'if you say that the king of Babylonia [is] not a great king, then
my brother [= you] does not know how significant Babylonia
[is]' [Lat. *quantum id insigne*, lit. "*in quo id signo*"]; cf. W.
Helck, *JCS* 17:91 [1963]; R. Stefanini, *Atti La Colombaria*
29:12–3 [1964]), *i-la-as-ni* (*KBo* III 1 III 46–48 [OHitt.] *marsa-
tar ēssanzi nu-ssan ilasni parā n*[*assu* 1 *gipessar*] *nasma* 2
gipessar haminkiskir n-asta u[*dnē ēshar akkusk*]*ir* 'they practise
fraud; glaringly [Lat. *insigniter*, lit. "*in signo*"] they would tie
up either one or two cubits and then quaff the sap of the land'),
e-la-as-ni (*KUB* X 17 II 2–4 *n-at karū i*[-...] ŪL *elasni* [...] *n-at*
IŠTU DINGIR-*LIM* [...] 'it of old ... not signally ... it from the
deity ...'), nom.-acc. pl. *i-li-es-sar* (XXXVI 89 Rs. 40 *āssauwa*
*ilessar*HI.A *pestin* 'give good signs!'; ibid. 43 *ilessar*HI.A SIG$_5$.MEŠ
pāi 'give good signs!', vs. ibid. 46 HUL-*lauwa* IZKIM.HI.A 'bad
signs'; XXXVI 77, 6 SIG$_5$-*uwa ilessa*[*r*HI.A; cf. Haas, *Nerik* 154,
140).

The usual equivalent of IZKIM is *sagai-* (c.) 'sign, omen,
portent' (q.v.), but there is also the heteroclitic *sakiassar* (*KUB*
XVII 28 I 1–2 [*mā*]*n* ^{D}*SIN-as sakiyazzi nu-kan sakiasni* [...
U]KÙ-*an* GUL-*ahzi* 'if the moon gives a sign and in the signaling
strikes a man' (i.e. renders him σεληνόπληκτον 'moon-struck').
ilessar, elassar seems to resemble *sakiassar* in formation and
meaning, down to partial -*assar* rather than normal -*essar* (cf.
Kronasser, *Etym.* 1:288); the nature of an underlying **ela(i)-*
or **eli(ya)-* remains to be discovered.

illuyanka-, elliyanku-   'snake, serpent', nom. sg. ^{MUŠ}*illuyankas* (e.g.
KBo III 7 I 11; *KUB* XVII 5 I 9), also ^{MUŠ}*illuiy*[*ankas* (XVII 6 I
4), *arunas* ^{MUŠ}*illuiyankas* 'sea-serpent' (*KUB* XXXVI 5 II 28; cf.
Laroche, *OLZ* 51:422 [1956]), ^{MUŠ}*ill*]*iunk*[*is?* (*KBo* XII 83 I 7),
acc. sg. ^{MUŠ}*illuyankan* (*KUB* XVII 5 I 15), ^{MUŠ}*illiya*[*nkan* (*KBo*

III 7 III 31), *elliyankun* (XXVI 79, 17; cf. Siegelová, *Appu-Hedammu* 68), gen. sg. ᴹᵁˢ*illuyankas* (III 7 III 7), acc. pl. *elliyankus* (*KUB* XXIV 7 III 70; cf. ibid. IV 28 ᴹᵁˢŠÀ.TÙR-*us* 'venomous snakes'; Friedrich, *ZA* 49:230, 238 [1950]).

Autochthonous term, used especially of the serpent or dragon fought by the storm-god in the etiological myths of the Hattic-origin EZEN *purulliyas* (q.v.). Cf. Laroche, *RHA* 23: 65–72 (1965).

imma, rarely **immakku**   (q.v. s.v. -*k*[*k*]*u*), adverb in several distinctive uses:

'Moreover': e.g. *KBo* V 3 III 55 ABI ᴰUTU-*ŠI-ma-kan imma* ᴳᴵˢAB-*za arha ausz*[*i* 'but moreover my majesty's father looked out of the window' (cf. Friedrich, *Staatsverträge* 2:128); *KUB* XIX 29 I 9 ŠEŠ-*YA* BA.UG₆ *imma* 'moreover (i.e. to top off antecedent calamities) my brother died' (cf. Götze, *AM* 14); *KBo* V 6 III 7–8 *nu-smas-kan* EN-*ŠUNU kuit* ᴵ*Piphururiyas immakku* BA.UG₆ 'because on top of everything their lord Tutankhamon had died on them' (cf. Güterbock, *JCS* 10:94 [1956]).

'Indeed': e.g. *KUB* XIII 4 III 50–51 *nu* É.DINGIR-*LIM-ma imma* 1-*an harakzi* ᵁᴿᵁ*Hattusas-ma* LUGAL-*was āssu* ŪL *harakzi* 'the temple alone will indeed perish, but Hattusas, the king's possession, will not perish' (cf. Sturtevant, *JAOS* 54:386 [1934]); ibid. IV 21–22 *n-an-kan* UKÙ-*si imma taitteni* ŪL-*an-kan* DINGIR-*LIM-ni tayatteni* 'you (may) indeed steal it from a man, but you cannot steal it from a god'; *KBo* IV 14 III 23–24 *tuk-ma karū kuit ke* INIM.MEŠ *piran* GAM *tiyan* DÙ-*nun zikila-ya--at memiskit imma* 'because I have long since had these words laid down before you, and indeed you yourself have kept saying them'; *KUB* XIV 1 Rs. 88–89 *mān* ᴰUTU-*ŠI* NAM.RA.HI.A ᵁᴿᵁ*Alasiya imma āppa wewakki*[*zi*] *nu-war-an-si āppa pi*[*hh*]*i* 'if his majesty does indeed demand back the deportees of A., I shall give them back' (cf. Götze, *Madd.* 38); X 1 I 20–21 *aranta imma* UŠKENNU-*ma* ŪL '(they) do just stand but do not prostrate themselves'.

'(Nay) even': e.g. *KBo* III 1 II 44 (OHitt.) *parkunusi-ma-za*

ŪL kuit nu-za anda imma hatkisnusi 'you pardon nothing, nay even cause confinement' (i.e. far from pardoning you actually order arrest); V 3 I 29–30 apūnn-a-mu antuhsan ŪL tekkussanusi n-an anda imma munnāsi 'you do not point out that person to me, nay you even conceal him' (cf. Friedrich, *Staatsverträge* 2:108).

'Nevertheless': e.g. *KUB* XIII 2 III 6–7 kuedani-ma ANA TÚL SISKUR.SISKUR NU.GÁL n-at-kan sarā imma araskandu 'but the fountain for which there is no rite, let them nevertheless visit it!' (cf. von Schuler, *Dienstanweisungen* 47).

'Really', or merely emphatic, in negative rhetorical questions: e.g. *VBoT* 2, 7–9 nu mān handān ammel DUMU.SAL-ya sanhiskisi nu-tta ŪL imma pihhi pihhi-tta 'if you truly woo my daughter, won't I really give her to you? (Of course) I will give (her) to you' (cf. L. Rost, *MIO* 4:329, 332–3 [1956]); *KUB* XIV 3 II 75 n-as-mu ŪL imma ᴸᵁHA⟨DA⟩NU '(is) he not my in-law?' (cf. Sommer, *AU* 10, 138–9); XIV 7 IV 11–13 mān UKÙ-as-pat atti anni DUMU-an sallanuzi nu-ssi attas annas ŠA ˢᴬᴸUMMEDA ŪL imma pāi 'if a person rears a child for the parents, don't the parents give him what is due a nurse?'; XXI 38 Vs. 48 n-at-mu ANA LÚ.MEŠ KUR ᵁᴿᵁHatti piran ŪL imma walliyatar ŪL kuit ēsta 'were they not a discredit (lit. not any renown) to me before the men of Hatti?' (cf. Sommer, *AU* 106, 253, and R. Stefanini, *Atti La Colombaria* 29:11–2 [1964], who failed to grasp the rhetorical question; L. Rost, *MIO* 4:333 [1956], and W. Helck, *JCS* 17:91 [1963], who mistranslated as 'were they not a [source of] renown for me?'); ibid. 15 ANA ŠEŠ-YA-ma NÚ.GAL imma kuitki 'does my brother really have nothing?'.

As generalizer of relative pronouns and adverbs (following, rarely preceding, or intercalated into iteration): e.g. *KUB* XXVI 8 I 12–13 kui]n-wa-nnas imma sarā tummēni [nu-w]a--nnas apās Ū[L] imma DUMU EN-NI 'whomever (viz. of numerous brothers of the king) we elevate over ourselves, is not that one (equally) a son of our (previous) lord?' (cf. von Schuler, *Dienstanweisungen* 9); *KBo* XXII 101 Rs. 6 ku]it imma AŠRA 'whatever place' (cf. Burde, *Medizinische Texte* 47); *KUB* XV 3 I 15–16 mān ᵁᴿᵁUrikina mān imma kuwapi 'whether at U. or wherever'; V 1 I 79 and 88 nu-kan masiēs imma UD.HI.A UGU *pedai* 'however many days he spends (in the) up(lands)' (cf. Ünal, *Hatt.* 2:46); ibid. III 55 *kuwatin imma kuwatin neyahhari* 'wherever I turn'; *KBo* V 4 Vs. 39 *kuis-as imma kuis* EN *QATI* '(or) whatever manual worker he (is)' (cf. Friedrich, *Staatsverträge* 1:58); *KUB* XV 34 II 33–34 *nu-za kuwapi imma kuwapi nu u[wat]tin* 'wherever you (may be), come!' (cf. Haas – Wilhelm, *Riten* 192).

imma was first connected with Lat. *immo* by Götze – Pedersen, *MS* 77–9, and remarkably resembles it in some usages, e.g. Cicero, *Letters to Atticus* 9.7.4 *causa igitur non bona est? immo optima* 'so the case is not good? not only that, (it is) excellent'; Cicero, *Catilina* 1.1.2 *vivit? immo vero etiam in senatum venit* 'he is alive? not just (alive), he even comes to the senate'; Horace, *Sermones* 1.3.20 *nullane habes vitia? immo alia* 'have you no faults? yes indeed, (but) different ones'. By itself Lat. *immo* is obscure, and reconstruction remains uncertain. Hitt. *imma* has been connected with *namma* 'further' (q.v.) by Marstrander (*Caractère* 27) and Neumann (*MSS* 16:48 [1964]), whereas *namma* was analyzed as *nu* + **(a)sma* by Puhvel (*KZ* 92:104 [1978] = *Analecta Indoeuropaea* 395 [1981]); thus a cluster origin of *-mm-* is possible for *imma* also. Marstrander (*Caractère* 27) and E. A. Hahn (*Lg.* 18:101–3 [1942]) tried to see *-ma* 'but' in Hitt. *imma* (assuming for the first part "the IE pronominal stem **i/e*" and *i* 'go!' respectively), and Hahn unconvincingly extended similar reasoning to Lat. *immo* as well (*-mo* related to Gk. μέν). Until the erstwhile shapes of Hitt. *imma* and Lat. *immo* are independently established, their etymological confrontation is best left in abeyance.

im(m)iya-, imme(y)a-   'mix, mingle', *anda immiya-* 'mix in, mingle together; (intrans. and midd.) mingle (with), get involved (with)', *menahhanda immiya-* 'mix in, mingle together', 1 sg. pres. act. *immiyami* (*KUB* XXIV 14 I 9–10 *nu kī hūman* ANA ZÍD.DA ŠE *isni menahhanda immiyami* 'all this I mix together with barley meal into dough'), *īmmiyami* (dupl. XXIV 15 Vs. 10), *imiyami* (XXIV 14 I 3–4 *nu ŠA* ZÍD.DA ŠE *isnan dahhi nu* UR.ZÍR-*as salpan menahhanda imiyami* 'I take dough of barley

im(m)iya-, imme(y)a-

meal and mix in[to it] dog shit'), 2 sg. pres. act. *im-me-ya-si*
(*KBo* XXI 20 Rs. 17; cf. Burde, *Medizinische Texte* 44),
im-me-at-ti (*KUB* XXI 5 III 15 *nu-kan apeda]ni* UKÙ-*si anda*
immeatti 'you get involved with that person'; cf. Friedrich,
Staatsverträge 2:66), 3 sg. pres. act. *immiyazi* (e.g. XI 20 I 9–10
GAL ^{LÚ.MEŠ}UŠ.BAR SÍG BABBAR SÍG SA₅ *anda immiyazi* 'the chief of
the weavers mingles together white wool [and] red wool'),
immiyazzi (e.g. VII 1 I 25–27 ŠAR.HI.A-*ma hūman kuaskuaszi*
serr-a-ssan harnamma BAPPIR *IŠTU* KAŠ *harnān lāhūwāi n-at*
anda immiyazzi 'he squashes all vegetables, pours over [it] the
yeast [and] barm [that has been] fermented from the beer, and
mixes it up'; cf. Kronasser, *Die Sprache* 7:143 [1961]; *VBoT* 120
II 2–3 *nu* ^{SAL}ŠU.GI SAHAR.HI.A-*us ANA* ŠE + NÁG ZÍD.DA BA[.BA.
.ZA] *anda immiyazzi* 'the old woman mixes powder into
soapwort [and] meal [to make] a paste'; cf. Haas – Thiel,
Rituale 138), 3 sg. pres. midd. *immiyaddari* (*KUB* XXIX 8 II 21
*ANA UNUTE.*MEŠ *anda immiyaddari* 'is mixed in with the implements'), *imiyattari* (XXXII 135 IV 7–8 DUB 1 KAM EZEN ^DEN.ZU
EZEN *tethuwas-a kuwapi anda imiyattari* ŪL *QATI* 'tablet one,
where the feast of the moon and the feast of thunder are
mingled, is not finished'; ibid. I 8–9 [*nu*] EZEN ^D*SIN* EZEN
tēthuwas-a anda [*imi*]*yattari n-at taksan kisantari* 'the feast of
the moon and the feast of thunder are mingled, and they take
place jointly'), *im-me-ya-ta-r*[*i* (*KBo* XVIII 62 Rs. 10), 3 pl.
pres. act. *immiyanzi* (e.g. VI 34 I 31–32 *nu kī harnammar*
mahhan tepu danzi n-at isnūri immiyanzi 'as they take a little of
this yeast and mix it into the dough-bowl'; cf. Oettinger, *Eide* 8;
KUB I 11 IV 11–12 *nu-smas* 3 *UPNU kanza* [2 *UP*]*NU* ŠE 5 *UPNU*
uzuhrinn-a anda immiyanzi 'they mix together for them three
handfuls of wheat, two handfuls of barley, and five handfuls of
hay'; cf. Kammenhuber, *Hippologia* 120), *immianzi* (e.g. *KBo*
III 5 + *IBoT* II 136 IV 65 *namma* 1/2 *UPNA kanza* 1 *UPNA uzuhrin*
anda immianzi 'they also mix together one-half handful of
wheat [and] one handful of hay'; cf. Kammenhuber, *Hippologia*
102), *īmmianzi* (*KUB* XXIX 48 Rs. 16 [*a*]*nda īmmianzi*; cf.
Kammenhuber, *Hippologia* 164), *imiyanzi* (XXIX 4 IV IV
24–26 [É DINGI]R-*LIM kuttan kuez uitenaza arranzi* [*nu-ss*]*i apāt*
karuuili ^{GIŠ}*tallayas* YÀ DUG.GA [*and*]*a imiyanzi* 'with what water

362

they wash the temple wall, into it they mix that old-time quality
oil of the t.-flask'; cf. Kronasser, *Umsiedelung* 30; *KBo* VI 34 II
21–22 *kī-wa* BAPPIR GIM-*an* IŠTU ^{NA₄}ARÀ *mallanzi n-at wetenit
imiyanzi* 'as they crush this barm with the grindstone and mix it
with water'; cf. Oettinger, *Eide* 10; XIV 63 IV 14 [*and*]*a
imiyan*[*zi*; cf. Kammenhuber, *Hippologia* 222), 3 pl. pres. midd.
i-[*im-mi-y*]*a-an-ta-ri* (XX 63 I 7 *anda ī*[*mmiy*]*antari*), 1 sg. pret.
act. *i-mi-e-nu-un* (III 46 Vs. 13 [OHitt.]*man warkan ulinī anda
imienun* 'had I mixed fat into clay'), 1 pl. pret. act. *i-mi-ya-u-en*
(*KUB* XLIII 74 Vs. 13; cf. Riemschneider, *Anatol. Stud.
Güterbock* 269), 3 pl. pret. midd. *immiyandat* (*KBo* XIV 50 Vs.
5–6 LÚ.MEŠ [...] *anda namma immiyandat* 'the men ... then
mingled'), 3 pl. imp. act. *immiyandu* (*KUB* XXXVI 12 III 3), 3
pl. imp. midd. *immeattaru* (XLIII 38 Rs. 18–20 *kī-wa wātar*
GEŠTIN-*ya mahhan* [*immeattati*] [EGIR-*and*]*a-wa kī* NIŠ DINGIR-
-*LIM ina*[*nn-a*] *RAMANI.*MEŠ-[*KU*]*NU* [*QATAMM*]*A immeattaru* 'as
this water and wine were mixed, hereafter let this oath and
disease of your bodies be likewise mixed'; cf. Oettinger, *Eide*
20); partic. *im(m)iyant-, immiant-, immeyant-*, nom. sg. c.
im-me-ya-an-za (XXVIII 102 IV 12 *anda immeyanza* 'mixed
in'), acc. sg. c. *immiyandan* (e.g. I 13 IV 38–39 *anda immiyandan*; ibid. II 58 *menahhanda immiyandan*), *immiandan* (ibid. I 10
anda immiandan; cf. Kammenhuber, *Hippologia* 72, 62, 54,
331), nom.-acc. sg. neut. *immiyan* (e.g. XXXIII 120 I 40; cf.
Güterbock, *Kumarbi* *3; XXIV 14 I 14–15 *ŠA* ZÍD.DA ŠE-*ma isni
kuedani menahhanda wassi*HI.A *immiyan* 'but into what dough
of barley meal the medicaments are mixed'; dupl. XXIV 15 Vs.
15 *im-me-ya-*[*an*), *imiyan* (e.g. *KBo* XI 19 Vs. 12; cf. Haas –
Thiel, *Rituale* 316; XXI 34 II 19 *nu ANA* NINDA.KUR₄.RA.HI.A ŠE
menahhanda ^{GIŠ}*hassikkan imian* 'h. [a fruit] [is] mixed into
heavy cornbread'; ibid. 53–54 *ANA* ^D*Hebat* 4 GA.KIN.AG *parsān*
^{GIŠ}*INBI.HI.A-ya menahhanda imian* 'four cheeses [are] divided up
for Hebat, and fruits are mingled with them'; ibid. 55–56
GEŠTIN YÀ DÙG.GA-*ya anda imian* 'wine and good oil, mixed';
ibid. III 34 and 51 ^{GIŠ}GEŠTIN HÁD.DU.A *anda imian* 'raisins [are]
mixed in'; cf. Lebrun, *Hethitica II* 120–3), instr. sg. *īmmiyantit*
(*KUB* XV 34 I 14–15 IŠTU GEŠTIN LÀL YÀ DUG.GA *anda
īmmiyantit suuan* 'filled with wine mixed with honey and good

oil'; cf. Haas – Wilhelm, *Riten* 184), *im-mi-an-te-it* (1897/u, 8 ŠA GEŠTIN YÀ *anda immiantet* 'of wine mixed with oil'; cf. Haas – Wilhelm, *Riten* 196–7), *īmmiyanzi* (sic dupl. XV 34 III 30), *īmmiyanda* (ibid. I 24–25 ŠA GEŠTIN YÀ DÙG.GA *anda īmmiyanda* 'of wine mixed with good oil'), nom.-acc. pl. neut. *immiyanta* (ibid. II 42 *anda immiyanta-ya lāhuwanzi* 'and they pour what is mixed together'), *immiyanda* (e.g. I 11 I 35, II 30, III 37 *anda immiyanda*; cf. Kammenhuber, *Hippologia* 108, 112, 118), *imiyanda* (e.g. XV 31 III 53, with dupl. XV 32 IV 11 *anda immiya[nda*; cf. Haas – Wilhelm, *Riten* 164); iter. *immiski-*, 3 sg. pres. midd. *immiskittari* (*KBo* XXIII 27 II 28–30 *nu* ÍD SA₅ ANA ᶦᴰ*Marassanda kuedani pedi anda imm[i]skittari nu wātar apedani pidi* ÚL *hānanzi* 'at what spot the Red River mingles with the Halys, on that spot they do not draw water').

im(m)iul- (n.) 'mix(ture)', always in the technical sense 'grain mix, horse feed', nom.-acc. sg. *im-mi-ú-ul* (*KBo* IV 2 II 33 ANA ANŠU.KUR.RA.HI.A *immiūl* '[as] mix for horses'; cf. Kronasser, *Die Sprache* 8:93 [1962]), *im-mi-i-ú-ul* (X 37 II 15 ANA ANŠU. .KUR.RA *halkis immiyūl* 'for horses grain mix' [hendiadys]), *im-mi-ú* (*KUB* VII 54 II 16–17 *nu-wa ke immiu* ANA ANŠU.KUR. .RA *piyandu* 'let them give this mix to the horse'; either *im-mi-ú⟨-ul⟩* shooting over line end, or stray dropping of *-l* comparable to e.g. *iyata* [q.v. s.v. *iyatar*]), *i-mi-ú-ul* (*KBo* XII 126 I 29 [ANA A]NŠU.KUR.RA.MEŠ *imiūl ēsdu* 'for horses let there be mix'; cf. Jakob-Rost, *Ritual der Malli* 24, 63), *i-mi-ú-l(a-as--ma-as)* (*KUB* XXIX 41, 8]*imiul-a-smas wēlku-ya* ÚL *pi[skanzi* 'but mix and grass they do not give to them'; cf. Kammenhuber, *Hippologia* 168), [*i-mi*]-*ú-ul-l(a-as-ma-as)* (XXIX 50 IV 5 [*imi*]*ūll-a-smas*; cf. Kammenhuber, *Hippologia* 212).

immiya- covers roughly the same semantic ground, both active and mediopassive, as Gk. μείγνῡμι and Lat. *misceō*, with the notable discrepancy that the sense 'to have carnal intercourse' is not attested in Hittite. *immiya-* is accompanied by the preverb *anda* (sometimes *menahhanda*), which makes for even more precise comparison with Gk. ἐμμείγνῡμι and Lat. *immisceō*; here the Hittite intransitive meaning 'to mingle, have encounters' is paralleled in Greek: ἔνθ᾽ οἶμαι Θησέα καὶ τὰς ... ἀδμῆτας ἀδελφὰς ... τάχ᾽ ἐμμείξειν 'there I think Theseus and

364

the unwed sisters will soon get together' (Sophocles, *Oedipus at Colonus* 1054–7). The technical sense 'grain mix' appears in Lat. *mixtus* and *mixtīle* (>French *méteil* 'maslin, wheat-rye mix').

Forms spelled *im-me-(y)a-* may point to etymological **e* (cf. Oettinger, *Eide* 56) and hence strengthen Sturtevant's old proposal **en-mey-* (cf. Skt. *máyate* 'exchange', IE **mey-ĝ-* 'mix'; *Comp. Gr.*[1] 133, 224); but the fossilized survival of **en-* as **i(m)-*, vs. the living cognate *anda* (with **n̥-?*), would be isolated and remains doubtful (cf., however, s.v. *istarna*). Another possible origin of *i-* might be a kind of incomplete or irregular reduplication of **mey-* (cf. J. Duchesne-Guillemin, *TPS* 1946:74–5). In any event a Hittite primary thematic 3 sg. pres. act. *immiyazi* must be secondary for **immezzi* < **-mey-ti*, analogic after 3 pl. pres. act. *immiyanzi* (< **-miy-n̥ti?*) and thematic mediopassive forms (*immeyatari, īmmiyantari*).

Unenlightening connection with Skt. *yamá-* 'twin' by H. Eichner apud Oettinger, *Stammbildung* 345.

inan-   (n.) 'sickness, illness, disease, ailment' (GIG), nom. sg. *inan* (e.g. *KUB* XLIII 38 Rs. 27–28 NIŠ DINGIR-*LIM inann-a* ... *dassisdu* 'may the oath and the sickness become heavy'; cf. Oettinger, *Eide* 20; XXX 10 Vs. 23 *inan arta* 'illness came about'), acc. sg. *inan* (e.g. XXX 34 IV 5, 17, 28 *inan ēshar* NIŠ DINGIR-*LIM* 'illness, blood[shed], [false] oath'; VII 1 I 8 and 16 DUMU-*li inan* EGIR-*an arha karas* 'from the child remove the illness!'; cf. Kronasser, *Die Sprache* 7:142–3 [1961]); IX 4 I 20–21 *happisnas inan* 'ailment[s] of the body parts'; cf. ibid. 22–36 passim GIG-*an* with the individual parts; Alp, *Anatolia* 2:38 [1957]; XXXV 148 III 17–35 with many body parts, e.g. 25 *arras-sas inan* 'ailment of his anus'), GIG-*an* (e.g. XXIX 1 II 20 *harassanas* GIG-*an* 'head-ailment'; ibid. 35 *kardiyas* GIG-*an* 'heart-disease'; cf. B. Schwartz, *Orientalia* N.S. 16:30 [1947]), gen. sg. *inanas* (e.g. VII 1 I 3 *inanas* ᴰUTU-*un* 'solar deity of sickness', ibid. 4, 6, 7–8, 12, 15 *inanas* ᴰUTU-*i*; cf. Laroche, *Recherches* 107; XLIV 61 Vs. 1; cf. Burde, *Medizinische Texte* 18), dat.-loc. sg. *inani* (e.g. XXX 10 Rs. 14 *inani piran* 'from illness'), dat.-loc. pl. *inanas* (*KBo* VI 34 I 38 *inanas ser* 'on account of ailments'; cf. Oettinger, *Eide* 8). Cf. Alp, *Anatolia* 2:39 (1957); Oettinger, *Eide* 29.

inan- seems to be largely in complementary distribution with *erma(n)-* (q.v. s.v. *arma*[*n*]-) and thus quasi-synonymous with it, both being listed along with *ēshar* 'blood(shed)' and other assorted afflictions and enormities; but it also has a more focussed sense of 'disease, ailment' of a specific body part.

With *inan-* may be compared a set of Indo-Iranian terms, Ved. *énas-* 'sin, guilt', Skt. *īti-* 'plague, disease', Avest. *aēnah-* 'violence, damage', *iti-* 'injury, offense'; Indo-Iranian derivation is very doubtful (see Mayrhofer, *KEWA* 3:645, 656, 784), which raises the possibility of Indo-European nominal cognates from a root meaning 'assail, afflict' (cf. *IEW* 10), perhaps seen also in Ved. *yātár-* 'avenger', Hes. ζητρός 'executioner' (cf. Puhvel, *LIEV* 71). Thus IE *$A_2éy$-(*A*-), *A_2y-*éA*-, with Hitt. *inan-* and Indo-Iranian *$aynos$- < *$A_2éy$-*no*-, literally 'affliction'; Gk. αἰνός 'dread, terrible' may be a further cognate (lit. 'afflicting'). For Hitt. *e/i* < *ai see s.v. *asara-, esara-.* Cf. Puhvel, *Bi. Or.* 37:204–5 (1980).

innar-, found in derivatives:

innarā 'explicitly, willfully, purposely, on one's own (account), of one's own accord', e.g.: *KUB* XIII 7 I 17–18 *nu-za apās kattawatar sanahzi nu apūn* UKÙ-*an* ANA LUGAL *innarā kunanna pāi* 'he seeks revenge and hands that person over to the king explicitly to be killed'; XXXI 68 Rs. 44 *zik-ma-wa-kan innarā lūri anda tiyasi* 'but you willfully step into disgrace'; ibid. 32 *innara-wa-kan lūrin*[(cf. R. Stefanini, *Athenaeum* N.S. 40:28 [1962]); XXVI 32 I 14–16 *mān-ma-ssi* LÚ.MEŠ ^{URU}*Hatti innarā-ma uwāi uter* UL-*man-ta anda tāliyanun auwan* UGU-*man-si tiyanun* 'if the men of Hatti had purposely aggrieved him, I would not have forsaken thee (sic), I would have stood up for him' (cf. Laroche, *RA* 47:74 [1953]); *Bo* 2073 I 36 *punusdu innarā-wa-mu-kan kuyēs harganuir* 'let him ask: "Who have purposely ruined me?"'; ibid. II 48–50 *nu-wa ammuk* GIM-*an innarā harakmi zik-ma-wa* DINGIR-*LUM* EN-*YA ammel hanni*[*s-*

sar] *punuski* 'when I am purposely ruined, do thou, god my lord, inquire into my case!'; *IBoT* I 36 I 48–50 ^{LÚ}*MEŠEDI-ma* ^É*hilamni anda innar*[*ā*] *ŪL tiyezzi mān-as innara-ma tiyezzi nu-ssi-kan* ^{LÚ}NI.DUH *ka*[*rtimmi*]*yaitta nassu-wa-kan sarā īt nasma-wa-kan katta-ma īt* 'a bodyguard does not on his own step into the gatehouse; but if he does step on his own, the gateman is angry at him: "Either go up, or else go down!"' (cf. Jakob-Rost, *MIO* 11:178 [1966]); *KUB* I 8 IV 8–9 *innara-uwa--smas dariyantes* [KUR.KUR.MEŠ ^{URU}KÙ.BABBA]R-*ti-ma-wa dapianta* ^D*IŠTAR IŠTU* ^{I GIŠ}PA-*si*-DINGIR-*LIM ne*[*hhun* 'on your own you (have) labored (viz. to little avail); but I, Ištar, have turned all the Hittite lands to Hattusilis' (cf. Götze, *Hattusilis* 32); *KBo* X 45 I 45–47 DUMU.LÚ.ULÙ.LU *ŪL innarā uwanun ŪL-ma sullanni uwanun* 'I, mortal man, have not come on my own account, nor have I come for strife' (cf. Otten, *ZA* 54:120 [1961]); *KUB* XXVI 1 III 41–43 *nasma tuk kuiski* HUL-*lus PANI* ^DUTU-*ŠI-ma-as* SIxSÁ-[*a*]*nza zik-ma-an-kan innarā laknusi nu-ssi--kan huwapti kuitki* 'or (if) somebody is bad as far as you are concerned, but righteous in the eyes of my majesty, and you of your own accord (viz. as opposed to another's instigation, ibid. 38–41) trip him and do him ill in any manner ...' (cf. von Schuler, *Dienstanweisungen* 13–4); XXI 33 IV 20]*innarā-as memian IŠTU* EME ['of his own accord word from the tongue he ...' (cf. R. Stefanini, *JAOS* 84:23 [1964]).

in(n)arah(h)- 'make strong, strengthen', 3 sg. pres. act. *inarahhi* (*KUB* XXXVI 110 Rs. 11–12 *labarnas* LUGAL-*us inarauanza nu-sse-pa utniyanza hūmanza anda inarahhi* 'L. the king [is] strong, and him the whole land makes additionally strong'; cf. Neu, *Altheth.* 228; Starke, *ZA* 69:82 [1979]; A. Archi, *Studia mediterranea P. Meriggi dicata* 50 [1979]), 1 sg. pret. midd. *innarahhat* (XXX 10 Vs. 18–19 *māmman innarahhat-ma nu tuēl siunas udanta ŪL innarahhat* 'if I had gained strength, would I not have gained it at thy word, o god?'; cf. Neu, *Interpretation* 70); verbal noun *in-na-ra-ah-hu-ar* (*KBo* XVII 60 Rs. 10 ANA DUMU-*ma* TI-*tar innarahhuar* MU.HI.A GÍD.DA *piski* 'to the child grant life, strength, long years!').

innarai- (?) or *innarawai-* (?) 'be strong', verbal noun *in-na--ra-w*[*a*]*-a-ar* or *in-na-ra-w*[*a-u*]*-a-ar* in *KUB* XXX 10 Rs.

19–20 *kinun-a-ma-pa* [DINGIR-*Y*]*A innarawa(u)ār ù* ^DLAMA *anda tūriya* 'but now, my god, harness together (your) strength and (that of) the tutelary deity' (par. XXXI 127 III 8 *innarawatar--ma-mu* and XXX 11 Rs. 18]^DLAMA ^D*Ānnariss-a* [cf. s.v. *annari-*]).

in(n)arawant- 'strong, forceful, vigorous', nom. sg. c. *i-na--ra-u-an-za* (*KUB* XXXVI 110 Rs. 11 [OHitt.], quoted above), *innarauwanza* (XVII 20 II 3 EGIR-*ŠU-ma in-na-ra-u-wa-an-za* DINGIR-*LIM ēszi* 'but behind him sits the strong god'; cf. Bossert, *MIO* 4:202 [1956]; *Bo* 6044, 4 ^D*Innarauwanza*; *Bo* 2372 III 30 ^D*Innarauwanza*, besides ibid. 26 ^D*Innara-smis*, ibid. 32 ^D*Inara-smis*; cf. Otten, *JCS* 4:125 [1950]; concerning the secondary associative tie-ins between *innar-* and the Hattic tutelary deity ^D*Inar*[*a*]-, ^DLAMA, see also s.v. *annari-*; *VBoT* 24 I 28–29 *parā-wa-kan ehu* ^DLAMA *lulimes anda-wa-kan* ^DLAMA *innarauwanza uizzi* 'go forth, effeminate [vel sim.] L.; potent L. will come in'; cf. Sturtevant, *TAPA* 58:8 [1927]), acc. sg. c. *in-na-ra-u-wa-an-da-an* (ibid. II 30), *in-ra-u-wa-an-da-an* (sic; ibid. IV 35–36 *mān* ^DLAMA *lulimin* ^DLAMA *inrauwandann-a sipanti* 'when one sacrifices to effeminate [vel sim.] L. and potent L.'), dat.-loc. sg. *innarawanti* (*FHG* 1, 19–20 [*i*]*nnarawanti-mu-kan haharrannis*[...] [*i*]*yawar zik-pat* DINGIR--*YA maniya*[*hta*] 'to a strong ? you alone, my god, directed my doings'; cf. Laroche, *RA* 45:133 [1951]), *in-na-ra-u-wa-an-ti* (*VBoT* 24 II 34), *in-na-ra-a-u-wa-an-ti* (*KUB* XXX 10 Vs. 8 *innarāuwanti-ma-mu pedi iyauwa zik-pat* DINGIR-*YA maniyahta* 'to a position of strength you alone, my god, directed my doings'), nom. pl. c. *innarauwantes* (*KBo* XVII 88 III 22 *paiddu-wa innarauwantes inna*[-; *KUB* XV 34 I 48 DINGIR.MEŠ LÚ.MEŠ ^{GIŠ}ERIN-*as innarauwantes* 'the strong male cedar-gods'; cf. Haas – Wilhelm, *Riten* 186; *HT* 1 I 43 and 46 ^DAMAR.UD ^D*Innarauwantess-a*), ^D*Innarawantas* (ibid. 29), ^D*In-na-ra-u-wa--an-ta-as* (dupl. *KUB* IX 31 I 36), ^D*In-na-ra-u-wa-an-da-as* (*HT* 1 I 59), ^D*In-na-ra-ú-wa-an-da-as* (*KUB* IX 31 II 6); cf. ibid. II 22 [Luw.] ^D*An-na-ru-um-mi-en-zi*; B. Schwartz, *JAOS* 58:336–40 [1938]).

innarawatar (n.) 'strength, force, vigor', nom.-acc. sg. *innarawatar* (e.g. *KUB* XXIV 2 Rs. 12–13 ANA LUGAL-*ma* SAL.

.LUGAL DUMU.MEŠ LUGAL *Ù ANA* KUR ^{URU}*Hatti* TI-*tar hattulatar innarawatar* MU.KAM GÍD.DA EGIR.UD-*MI dusgarattann-a peski* 'but to king, queen, their children, and to Hatti grant life, health, strength, long years in the future, and joy!'; cf. Gurney, *Hittite Prayers* 32; XXVII 67 II 23 [T]I-*tar innarawatar* MU.HI.A GÍD.DA *piski*; V 1 I 28 MU.HI.A GÍD.DA *innarawatar*; cf. Ünal, *Hatt.* 2:36; ibid. 83 ZAG-*tar innarawatar* 'rightness [and] strength'; ibid. II 70–71 and III 73 GÙB-*tar innarawatar* 'leftness [and] force'), *innarāwatar* (*KBo* X 37 II 28–29 *nu-ssi innarāwatar* [...] *hastaliyatar peski*[*ttin* 'give him strength [and] heroism'; cf. Oettinger, *MSS* 35:93 [1976]), *innarawātar* (*KUB* XVII 33 IV 14), *innarāwātar* (XV 31 I 54), *in-na-ra-u-wa-a-tar* (dupl. XV 32 I 55–56 *nu-ssi pist*[*in* TI-*tar*] *haddulātar innarauwātar* MU.HI.A GÍD.DA; cf. Haas – Wilhelm, *Riten* 154), *in-na-a-ra-u-wa-tar* (*KBo* XVII 105 II 22 *nu-wa-smas* TI-*tar innārauwatar piskitin*; cf. A. Archi, *SMEA* 16:86 [1975]), *in-na-ra-u-wa-tar* (e.g. XV 25 Vs. 10–11 *ANA* EN SISKUR.S[ISKUR E]GIR-*pa* TI-*tar haddulātar in*[*na*]*rauwatar* MU.HI.A GÍD.DA [IG]I. .HI.A-*wa us*[*kiu*]*ar* GÚ-*tar sarā appātarr-a piski* 'to the sacrificer give back life, health, strength, long years, eyesight, muscle, lift!'; similarly ibid. 23–25; cf. Carruba, *Beschwörungsritual* 2; *KUB* XXXIV 53 Rs. 17 *innarauwatar* MU.HI.A GÍD.DA; VI 3, 19–20 MU.HI.A GÍD.DA *innarauwatar*; XVI 82 Vs. 4 *dapian* ZI-*an innarauwatar* 'entire soul [and] strength'; XXII 26 Vs. 4 *inn*]*arauwatar muann-a* 'strength and [seminal] fluid'; V 4 I 43 *innarauwatar salli-ya wastul* 'force and great transgression'; *KBo* II 9 I 20–21 ŠA LUGAL SAL.LUGAL DUMU.MEŠ LUGAL TI-*tar haddulatar innarauwata*[*r*] MU.HI.A GÍD.DA; cf. ibid. 21 *tarhuilatar* 'potency'; cf. Sommer, *ZA* 33:98 [1921]; Bossert, *MIO* 4:206 [1956]; A. Archi, *Oriens Antiquus* 16:299 [1977]), dat.-loc. sg. *innarauwanni* (e.g. ibid. 33–34 *nu-za* LUGAL SAL.LUGAL DUMU.MEŠ LUGAL DUMU.DUMU.MEŠ LUGAL EGIR-*an assuli* TI-*anni haddulanni innarauwanni* MU.HI.A GÍD.DA EGIR.UD-*MI kappūwai* 'provide king, queen, their sons and grandsons for [their] weal, life, health, strength, long years in the future'; *KUB* XXXIII 62 II 8–10 *ANA* ^{LÚ}*BEL* É-*TIM* ^{SAL}*BELDI* É-*TIM* DUMU.NITA.MEŠ DUMU. .SAL.MEŠ-*as assuli* TI-*anni innarauwanni hattulanni* MU.HI.A GÍD. .DA EGIR.UD-*MI* DINGIR.MEŠ-*as āssiunit* DINGIR.MEŠ-*nas miūmnit kardimiyattan-ma arha tarna* 'for the well-being, life, strength, health, long years in the future of the lord and lady of the house and their children remove wrath, through the favor and kindness of the gods!'; *KBo* IV 1 Vs. 18 TI-*anni hattulanni i[nnar]auwanni*; cf. Witzel, *Heth. KU* 78; dupl. *KUB* II 2 I 19 TI-*anni haddulanni innarauwanni*; XXXIV 77 Vs. 7 TI-*ni innarauwanni*), *innarauwani* (XVII 10 IV 25–26 *n-us-za huiswanni innarauwani* EGIR.UD-*MI kappuwet* 'he [i.e. Telipinus] provided them [viz. the royal couple] for their life [and] strength in the future'; cf. Laroche, *RHA* 23:98 [1965]), instr. sg. *innarauwannit* (XVII 14 I 18–20 [*nu-z*]*an* IŠTU MU.HI.A GÍD.DA EGIR.UD-*MI* TI-*annit* [*h*]*attulannit innarauwannit* [*ass*]*uli kappūwandu* 'may they provide for [my] weal with long years in the future, life, health, strength!'; cf. Kümmel, *Ersatzrituale* 60). Note also nom.-acc. sg. *in-nir-tar* (XXII 62, 17 and 20) and *in-tar* (*IBoT* I 32, 14, 21, 22) as abbreviated spellings (cf. Laroche, *RA* 46:161 [1952]).

innarauwah(h)- 'make strong, strengthen', verbal noun gen. sg. *in-na-ra-u-wa-ah-hu-u-wa-as* in *KUB* II 1 II 17 ŠA *Labarna inn*]*arauwahhūwas* ᴰLAMA-*as* 'tutelary deity of strengthening the ruler', with par. *KBo* XI 40 II 7 *in-na-ra-u-wa*[- (cf. A. Archi, *SMEA* 16:96, 108 [1975]).

innarawes- 'become strong', 3 sg. pres. act. *in-na-ra-u-e-es-zi* (*KUB* VIII 35 Vs. 9 *apās* DUMU-*as innarawēszi* 'that child will become strong').

KAL-*tar* (ᴰKAL = ᴰLAMA!) may occasionally reflect *innarawatar*, e.g. in ᴸᵁKAL-*tar* = ᴸᵁGURUŠ-*tar* 'manly strength, vigor' (*KBo* VI 34 IV 9–11 *apell-a* TI-*tar-set* ᴸᵁKAL-*tar-set lulu-sset* INA EGIR.UD-*MI QADU* DAM.MEŠ-*ŠÚ* DUMU.MEŠ-*ŠÚ* 'his life, his vigor, his prosperity for the future, along with his wives [and] children'); but *KBo* XII 109, 7 KAL-*tar-nu-us-kán-zi*, which Dressler (*Studien* 235) read **innara(wa)tarnuski-* 'make strong' (iter. of denom. -*nu*- verb from *innarawatar*), can represent instead **hatugatarnuski-* 'make formidable' (cf. *hatugatar* s.v. *hatuk-*, e.g. III 21 II 14 *tarhuilātar-tet hatugātar-tet* 'your formidable potency' [hendiadys]).

In addition to the Luwoid *annari-* 'strength, force, vigor', ᴰ*Annari-*, *annari annari* (epanadiplosis matching Hitt. *innarā*, both with original sense 'a fortiori, downright'?), *annaru-* 'strong, forceful', and the divine epithet *annarumahitassi-* 'of forcefulness' (q.v. s.v. *annari-*), there is Luwian proper: *annarummi-* 'strong, forceful', nom. pl. c. *annarumminzi* (*VBoT* 60 I 8; cf. Otten, *LTU* 108), *an-na-ru-um-me-en-zi* (*KBo* XIII 260 III 9), ᴰ*An-na-ru-um-mi-en-zi* (*KUB* IX 31 II 22; cf. Otten, *LTU* 16, and see sub *innarawant-* above); *annarum(m)ahit-* 'strength, forcefulness', acc. sg. *annarumāhi* (XXXV 133 II 29–30 ᵁᴿᵁ *Hattusaya apparantien arin annarumāhi huuitwalāhisa-ha* 'for Hattusas long future, strength, and life!', cf. Otten, *LTU* 110), dat. sg. *ānnarummahiti* (e.g. XXXV 45 II 8–10 *huyitwalahiti ānnarummahiti* MU.KAM.HI.A GÍD.DA EGIR.UD-*MI*.HI.A-*ti* DINGIR. .MEŠ-*assazati wassarahitati huitummanahitati* 'for life, strength, long years for the future, through the favor and kindness of the gods'; cf. Otten, *LTU* 46), instr.-abl. *annarummahitati* (XXXV 43 II 38 *huuiduwalāhitati annarummahitati* 'through life [and] strength'; cf. Otten, *LTU* 43).

Luwoid *annaru-* (adjective) and *annari-* (noun) point to corresponding Hitt. **innaru-* and **innar(a)-* respectively; **innaru-* may in fact underlie *innarawant-*, *innarawatar*, *innarawah(h)-*, *innarawes-* (cf. e.g. *idalawant-*, *idalawatar*, *idalawah[h]-*, *idalawes-*, from *idalu-*), and *innarā*, *in(n)arah(h)-*, *innarai-* can possibly be explained via loss of *-w-* from **innarawa* (nom.-acc. pl. neut.), *innarawah(h)-*, *innarawai-* (cf. occasional *idālaz* < *idalawaz*); yet it is strange that no trace of e.g. **innaru* or **innaruwatar* is found (cf. *idalawa, idaluwatar*). An **innara-* beside **innaru-* is well conceivable (cf. *arpa-* 'bad luck' beside *arpuwai-* 'be unlucky'), and an adjectival **innarawa-* (cf. *arawa-* from *ara-*) would also be a plausible base for *innarawant-* (cf. e.g. *andara-nt-*, *irmala-nt-*, *pittalwa-nt-*) and most other derivatives with *-w-* (*innarawai-* would in fact be better explained from **innarawa-* than from **innaru-*). *innarā* can be an adverbialization starting from **innara-* or an underlying **innar-*, *in(n)arah(h)-* as a denominative factitive from either would match e.g. *kutruwah(h)-* 'summon as witness' or *siuniyah(h)-* 'imbue with evil divinity, make possessed', and *innarai-* would be a regular denominative verb. It is not advisable to derive *innarawant-* as participle from *innarawai-* (the latter being itself dubious), nor to segment *innara-want-*, because such derivatives from *-a-* stems are hard to match (cf., on the contrary, *samankur-want-*, *tametar-want-*). Cf. for earlier discussions Kammenhuber, *MSS* 3:27–44 (1953); J. J. S. Weitenberg, *Anatolica* 4:173–6 (1971–2).

Although *innarawant-* seems to mean 'sexually potent' in the Ritual of Anniwiyanis (*VBoT* 24, quoted above), and *innarawatar* is occasionally coupled with a term like *mu(w)a-* '(seminal) fluid' (e.g. *KUB* XXII 26 Vs. 4, quoted above; *IBoT* I 32, 21 ZAG *in-tar mu-u-wa-an-na*), they are distinct in usage from such starkly male terms as LÚ-*(na)tar* 'manhood, penis, sperm' (= *pisnatar*) and *tarhuilatar* 'potency'. The last-mentioned occurs occasionally in close succession to the typical list of which *innarawatar* forms part (e.g. *KBo* II 9 I 21 quoted above; *KUB* XV 34 II 19 [cf. Haas – Wilhelm, *Riten* 190]) but is never present on such lists detailing 'life, health, *innarawatar*, long years'. Thus *innarawatar* is basically sexually neutral, being craved for royalty and land at large without reference to gender (thus already Kammenhuber, *MSS* 3:30, 32, 38–9 [1953]). Although it sometimes occurs coupled with *hastaliyatar* 'heroism' (*KBo* X 37 II 28–29, quoted above), 'heroic strength' is not the central nuance either. Squeezed in between 'life', health', and 'long years', the basic sense must be 'vital strength, life-force, vigor, élan'.

Hrozný's connection of *innarawatar* with Gk. ἀνήρ 'man', ἠνορέη 'manliness, prowess' (*SH* 74, *Heth. KB* VIII), frequently ignored (e.g. by Sturtevant) or doubted (e.g. by F. Lindeman, *Einführung in die Laryngaltheorie* 70 [1970]), but occasionally upheld (e.g. by Laroche, *RHA* 9:23 [1948–9]; Kammenhuber, *MSS* 3:38–9 [1953]; A. Bernabé P., *Revista española de lingüística* 3:440 [1973]), deserves a new and more enlightened hearing, with special attention to Indo-Iranian cognates. The meaning 'man' in Gk. ἀνήρ, Ved. *nar-*, Arm. *ayr*, Oscan *ner-* is clearly a dialectal IE phenomenon, related to complementary distribution vis-à-vis *wĭro-*; in Vedic, where the two co-exist, *vīrá-* tends to preempt the sexual nuance (*vīrá-karman-* 'penis') and the 'maleness' notion in general (including the 'heroic' aspects), whereas *nar-* denotes 'man, male' almost secondarily and has beside it a feminine *nā́rī* 'woman, wife' (similarly Avest. *nar-*, *nāirī-*). The still palpable base-meaning of *nṛ-* is in the area of 'keen(ness), force(ful)' (Ved. *nṛ́tama-* 'keenest, most forceful', *nṛmnám* 'keenness, forcefulness', *nṛvát* 'keenly, forcefully', *nṛcákṣas-* 'keen-eyed', *nṛmánas-* 'keen-spirited'), and the same base can be extracted from RV *sūnára-* 'rich in vital strength', *sūnṛ́tā-* 'vitality' (applied most to the youthful dawn-goddess Uṣas; cf. Avest. *hunara-*, *hunarətāt-* 'vigor'), *viśvánara-* 'having total vitality' (= *viśvā́yu-*; cf. Mayrhofer, *KEWA* 3:493, 227). In other branches of Indo-European, e.g. Gk. εὐήνωρ 'rich in vital strength' (cf. *IEW* 765) and the Germanic gender-ambivalent theonym *Nerthus-Njörðr* underscore the same basic sexual neutrality of **Hner-* as was observed in Hitt. *innar-*, Luw. *annar-*.

Mutatis mutandis, Hitt. *innarā* and *innarawatar* resemble in their semantic aspects Ved. *nṛvát* and *sūnṛ́tā*. Postulating PAnat. **enar-* 'strength' (cf. Laroche, *RHA* 23:42 [1965]), and matching it with F. B. J. Kuiper's Greek reconstruct **ἄνερ* or **ἄναρ* 'vital strength' (*Mededelingen der Koninklijke Nederlandse Akademie van Wetenschappen, Afd. Letterkunde*, N.R. 14:210–27 [1951]), PAnat. **enar* can be taken back to IE **E_1énṛ̥*, and **ἄναρ* to **E_1ŋ́nṛ̥*; the 'man' words are accentually polarized animate nominative counterparts to those neuters, thus *E_1nér* > Gk. ἀνήρ, or **E_1nér* > Ved. *nā́*, literally 'vitality personified'; the quality of the Greek and Armenian prothetic vowel vouchsafes no clue to the color of the laryngeal, *a* being the "neutral" outcome of *Ḫ*.

Van Windekens (*Essays in historical linguistics in memory of J.A. Kerns* 343 [1981]) adduced Gk. ἔναρα 'armor stripped from a slain foe', comparing German *rüstung : rüstig*.

intaluz(z)i-   (c. or n.) 'shovel' or the like (of wood, metal, etc.), nom. sg. c. ^{GIŠ}*intaluzis* (*KUB* VII 14, 13; cf. ibid. 15 ^{GIŠ}MAR URUDU 'spade'; Otten, *LTU* 57), nom.-acc. sg. neut. ^{GIŠ}*intaluzi* (e.g. XXXV 54 II 28; *KBo* XII 126 I 5; XXV 184 III 58), *intaluzi* (VII 22, 5), ^{GIŠ}*intaluzzi* (e.g. XI 12 I 6; *KUB* IX 4 II 2; XLI 2 I 2), acc. sg. c. ^{GIŠ}*intaluzin* (XLI 43, 5), *intaluzin* (*KBo* XII 111,

5), *indaluzzin* (*KUB* XXXIX 35 IV 11), instr. sg. *intaluzzit* (*KBo* III 38 Rs. 16–17 GIŠ*intaluzzit sunnahhi* 'I fill with a shovel'; cf. Otten, *Altheth. Erzählung* 10; *KUB* XXIV 10 III 12 *intaluzzit* EGIR-*anda suwāi*[*ddu* '[he] shall thereupon fill with a shovel'). Cf. Jakob-Rost, *Ritual der Malli* 20, 44, 59–60.

For the suffix, cf. e.g. *ishuz(z)i-* 'band' (*ishiya-* 'bind'), *warpuzi-* (a bathing utensil; *warp-* 'bathe'), *kataluzzi-* 'threshold', etc. (cf. Kronasser, *Etym.* 1:241; Carruba, *Beschwörungsritual* 22–3). Otherwise obscure. Cf. possibly Gk. ἔντεα 'implements'. "Substratal" origin is assumed, per obscurius, by Rosenkranz, *JEOL* 19:505 (1965–6), and A. Salonen, *Die Fussbekleidung der alten Mesopotamier* 114 (1969). Of the same order is H. A. Hoffner's adduction of a possibly Hurrian *in-te-la-am* on a list of implements from Mari (*JAOS* 88:533 [1968]).

ipa(r)wassi-,   ornithomantic adjective describing a direction or reference point, possibly 'northwest(erly)', because when the augur steps (and presumably faces) *iparwassi*, the bird in its turn (EGIR) comes (*uit*) up (UGU) auspiciously (SIG$_5$) towards the sun (ᴰUTU-*un*) and implicitly towards the observer, thus from a direction away from the sun; nom. sg. *i-pár-wa-as-si-is* (frequent, e.g. *KUB* V 17 II 26–28 *iparwassis-ma-kan* [*arsi*]*ntathis* ᴰUTU-*un* EGIR UGU SIG$_5$-*za uit* [*n-as-kan*] *arha pait* 'a northwesterly [?] a.-bird in its turn came up auspiciously towards the sun, and it went on its way'), *i-pár-wa-as-si-es* (e.g. V 11 III 20), acc. sg. *i-pa-wa-as-si-i*[*n* (XVI 73, 10), nom.-acc. pl. neut. or dat.-loc. sg. (adverbial) *i-pár-wa-as-si* (e.g. V 22, 18 *iparwassi tīyawen* 'we stepped northwest' [?]; cf. ibid. 21 *iparwassiss-a* IZKIM-*aht*[*a* 'and the northwesterly [?] [bird] gave a sign'; ibid. 28 *iparwassi tīyawen nu-kan harraniyis* ᴰUTU-*un* EGIR UGU SIG$_5$ *u*[*it*; XVIII 12 Vs. 21 *iparwassi-ma-kan pittarpalhis* 'in the northwest[?] a "broad-wing"'), *i-pár-wa-as-sa* (*KBo* XI 68 I 21 *iparwassa ālilis-kan*[). For more attestation references see Ertem, *Fauna* 215–6; A. Archi, *SMEA* 16:163–5 (1975), who showed that *iparwassi-* cannot be a bird-name.

iparwasha- (c.), with gloss-wedges in *KUB* XV 26, 8 *i-pár-wa-*

-*as*[-, ibid. 10]*i-pár-wa-as-ha-as* 1 KÙ.BABBAR 1 GUŠKIN 'i., one (of) gold, one (of) silver', seems to point to objects in precious metal, possibly bird-images (cf. *aramni-* KÙ.BABBAR or GUŠKIN, beside *aramnant-* as an oracular bird (s.v.]); not impossible to reconcile with 'northwest(ern)' as a metonymous bird-designation (cf. Engl. 'southwester' for a type of nautical headgear).

For etymology, cf. *ipa-* extracted from *ipat(t)arma(yan)* '(north)westward' (s.v.) and connected with Gk. ζόφος 'dusk, (north)west', ζέφυρος '(north)west wind'. Perhaps an adverb **ipar* 'at dusk' can be postulated (cf. *kariwariwar* 'at daybreak'), whence a derivative **ipar-wa-* (cf. e.g. *pittal-wa-*) outfitted with either the Luwoid appurtenance suffix -*assi-* or the abstract noun suffix -*(a)sha-*. Cf. *mar(r)uwasha-* '(dark) redness' formed on a Luwoid and Luwian *mar(r)uwa-* 'redden', besides [ID]*Marassanta-* = ÍD SA₅ 'Red River, Kızıl Irmak', i.e. the Halys.

ipat(t)arma(yan)   '(north)west(ward)', *i-pa-at-tar-ma-ya-an* in *KUB* XXXVI 89 Rs. 12–14 [ID]*Marassantas-wa annallaza ipattarma-yan ārsas* [D]U-*as-ma-war-an wahnut nu-war-an* [D]UTU-*i* DINGIR--LIM-*an arsanut* [URU]*Ner[ikki-war-an] manninkuwan arsanut* 'the Halys river *in illo tempore* flowed westward (or: northwest), but the storm-god turned it and made it flow eastward (lit. toward the sun of the gods), and made it flow close to Nerik' (cf. Haas, *Nerik* 152, who wrongly transcribed gloss-wedges); other attestations, with gloss-wedges, describe ornithomantic directions: XVI 57 Vs. 6 *p*]*i-an* GAM *i-pa-tar-ma-ya-an*; ibid. 4 *i-pa-tar-ma*; XXII 17 I 3]*i-pa-tar-ma* TUŠ-*at* (cf. A. Archi, *SMEA* 16:166 [1975]). ˙*KUB* XXXVI 89 Rs. 12–14 (quoted above) contains an aetiological mythologem of direction reversal by the Halys river near Nerik, probably relating to the 140° turn from northwest to east that the lower course of the Kızıl Irmak still makes at its confluence with the Devrek near the town of Kargi, thus placing Nerik squarely in Gasga-land (Paphlagonia; cf. Güterbock, *JNES* 20:92–3 [1961]; Haas, *Nerik* 5).

ipatarma(yan) 'westward' and *istanui siunan* 'eastward' (cf. e.g. *KUB* XLI 23 II 18 *siunan* [D]UTU-*ui* 'o gods' sun!'; Laroche,

ipat(t)arma(yan)

RHA 23:34 [1965]) are matched by šú.A ^DUTU-*as* 'west' (lit.
'seat [=setting] of the sun') and ṢĒT ^DUTU-*as* 'east' (lit.
'start[ing point] of the sun'; perhaps Hitt. *marri-* [see s.v.]) in
XXXVI 90 Vs. 9–10 *ehu-wa* ^DU ^{URU}*Nerik* ṢĒT ^DUTU-*as* šú.A
^DUTU-*as* 'come, storm-god of Nerik, from east [and] west!'
(similarly ibid. Rs. 35 *ehu* IŠTU ṢĒT ^DUTU-*as ehu* šú.A [^DUTU-*as*];
cf. Haas, *Nerik* 176–8).

In addition to such solar east-west designations there are
wind-related terms for cardinal points: IM KUR.RA (Akk. IM
šadū) 'east wind', IM MAR.TU (Akk. IM *amurrū*) 'west wind', IM
SI(.SÁ) (IM *ELTANU*) 'north wind', IM GAL or IM GÀL(.LU) (Akk. IM
šūtu) 'south wind'; cf. XXXVI 90 Rs. 39–40 *ehu* IM MAR.TU [I]M
SI IM GÀ[L.LU IM KUR.R]A IŠTU 4 *halhaltuma[rr]as* 'come from
west, north, south, east, from the four corners (i.e. cardinal
points)'. To two of these logograms may correspond Hitt. IM
tarasmeni '(the horn [of the moon] is turned to the)?' (XXIX
11 II 16; cf. ibid. 14 *takku* ^D*SIN autti nu* SI-ŠÚ ANA IM GAL *neiyan*
'if you see the moon and its horn is turned south'; thus
tarasmeni- not 'south') and *ŠĀRU udumeni* 'the ? wind (will
come)' (VIII 34 Rs. 12; cf. Laroche, *RHA* 12:21–2 [1952]).

ipatarma(yan) (cf. e.g. *arha*[*yan*] 'apart'?) can be analyzed as
a compound *ipa-tarma-*, where the second part is *tarma-* 'nail,
peg, stake' (q.v.), often in ritual and magical uses and here
apparently metaphorically for cardinal 'point' (cf. the usual
halhaltumari-, lit. 'corner'); Luwian has *tarmi-* with the same
meaning. *ipa-* may then be the 'west' word proper; in view of
the partial gloss-wedges one might apply the new reading *i* to
Hier. *a* (cf. e.g. J. D. Hawkins, *Anatolian studies* 25:151 [1975])
and compare Hier. *ipami-* 'west' (formerly *apami-*; cf. Meriggi,
HHG 28, and see s.v. *appa*). As /iba-/, an Anatolian *ipa-* may go
back to **A₂ibho-* in apophonic relationship with Gk. ζόφος
'dusk, gloom, (north)west' (**A₂yobho-*; antonymic to ἠώς
'dawn' and/or ἠέλιος 'sun' in e.g. *Iliad* 12:239–40 εἴτ᾽ ἐπὶ δεξί᾽
ἴωσι πρὸς ἠῶ τ᾽ ἠέλιόν τε, εἴτ᾽ ἐπ᾽ ἀριστερὰ τοί γε ποτὶ ζόφον
ἠερόεντα 'whether [the ornithomantic birds] go to the right
eastward, or to the left westward', or *Odyssey* 10:190 οὐ γὰρ
ἴδμεν ὅπη ζόφος οὐδ᾽ ὅπη ἠώς 'we don't know in which
direction either west or east is'). Another cognate would be

376

Zέφυρος (ἄνεμος) 'west wind', sometimes 'northwest (wind)' (blowing from Thrace along with Bορέης in *Iliad* 9:5; cf. Aristotle, *Politics* 1290a, 19), just as indicated by the direction of the Halys for Hitt. *ipattarmayan*. Cf. Puhvel, *AJPh* 104:224–6 (1983).

Güterbock (*JNES* 20:93 [1961]) suggested something like 'astray' for *ipat(t)armayan*, with reference to the Luwian iter. 3 sg. pret. *ip-pa-tar-ri-sa-at-ta* (*KUB* XXXV 45 II 21–22 *kuis-an sahhanissatta kuis-an ippatarrisatta*) or *i-ip-pa-tar-ri-es-sa-ta* (XXXV 48 II 14–15 *kuis-an sahaniessata* [*kuis-a*]*n īppatarries-sata*; *LTU* 46, 49), rendering the whole as 'whoever contaminated him, whoever led him astray (?)' and concluding that Laroche's suggestion of a cardinal point (*OLZ* 51:423 [1956]) "seems not to fit the Luwian verb, unless one would assume that to lead a person west(?)ward had a symbolic implication like 'to the grave' or the like, or that the basic meaning of **ipatar* was 'down', from which 'sundown' and, for the verb, a meaning like that of Hittite *katterahh-* could be derived." Any semantic connection between *ipat(t)arma(yan)* and the Luwian verb *⁽⁻⁾ī̆ppatarri-* (of whatever precise meaning) is suspect, both on account of spelling differences and because Luwian lacks suffixal derivatives in *-(a)tar* (which have been replaced by *-ahit-* or survive as relics in *-atna-*). Even the exclusive Luwian or Luwoid nature of *ipat(t)arma(yan)* is not secure, since gloss-wedges occur only in *KUB* XVI 57 Vs. 4 and 6.

Neumann (*KZ* 85:300 [1971]) also implausibly postulated **ipatar* 'bend, curvature' + Luw. *may(a)-* 'big'; the Nerik reference is not to the great bend of the Halys but to a directional oddity much farther downstream.

Cf. *iparwassi-*.

ippi(y)a-, eppiya-   (c.) '(grape)vine', sometimes with alternating or combined determinatives GIŠ 'tree' and Ú 'plant', nom. sg. GIŠ*ippiyas* (*KUB* II 13 II 21), GIŠ*īppias* (XXXIII 59 III 6–9 D*Hannahannas*-[*a*] 3 *wattaru iet kedani* GIŠ*īpp*[*i*]*as ser arta kedani-ma* GIŠ*hupparas katta kitta kedani-ma pahhur urāni* 'H. made three wells: above one stands a vine; down by another lies an earthen jar; at the third a fire burns'; cf. Laroche, *RHA* 23:150 [1965]), acc. sg. *ippiyan* (XVII 35 I 8 and II 21 *ippiyan marhan tianzi* 'they place a vine-dish'), *ippian* (ibid. IV 28 *ippian marhan tianzi*), ^Ú*ippiyan* 'vine-plant' (XXV 32 I 29; cf. A. M. Dinçol – M. Darga, *Anatolica* 3:102 [1969–70]), GIŠ ^Ú*e-ip-pi--ya*[*-an* (*IBoT* II 131 I 22), GIŠ ^Ú*e-ip-pí*[*-ya-an* (ibid. 25), *ippiya* (*KBo* II 13 Vs. 15 ^{UTÚ}*marhan* ?*ippiya tiyanzi*, with unclear traces of sumerogram or gloss wedges), gen. sg. *ippiyas* (*KUB* XII 2 IV 4 *nu-ssi* EZEN *ippiyas iyanzi* 'they celebrate the vine-festival for him'), ^{GIŠ}*ippiyas* (*KBo* X 24 III 6–7 ^{GIŠ}*ippiyas kapnuēsni āssawēs pūriēs* 'on a *kapnuessar* of vine [are] good lips [= rims]'), *ippias* (*VBoT* 58 IV 17 1 ^{GIŠ}*alkistas ip*[*p*]*ias* 'one vine-branch'; cf. Laroche, *RHA* 23:86 [1965]), ^{GIŠ}*ippias* (*KBo* XI 32 Vs. 21 ^{GIŠ}*ippias murin* 'grape of the vine'), ^{GIŠ}*īppias* (*KUB* XXXIII 59 III 12–13 *uet* ^D*Miyadan*[*zipas*] ^{GIŠ}*īppias kat*[*t*]*an esadi* 'M. came and sat down beneath the vine'; cf. Laroche, *RHA* 23:150 [1965]), *e-ip-pí-ya-as* (*Bo* 884 II 8 *eppiyas mūris*), unclear *īppiya*[- (*KUB* XXXIII 13 II 6; cf. Laroche, *RHA* 23:158 [1965]), *īppian*[- (*KBo* XIII 137, 3).

ippi(y)anza(n)- (c.), nom. sg. *ippiyanza* (*Bo* 2372 I 16), *ippianzas* (*KBo* XIII 77 Rs. 6, with gloss-wedge), nom. or gen. sg. *ippiyanzanas* (*KUB* VII 1 I 22, in a long jumble of obscure terms, preceded ibid. 19–21 by a list of 'all' garden plants; cf. Kronasser, *Die Sprache* 7:143 [1961]; Ertem, *Flora* 38), *īppianza*[(*KBo* XXV 54 IV 11; XXV 56 IV 19; cf. Neu, *Altheth.* 124, 128), nom. pl. *īppiyantes* (*IBoT* III 88, 5). Cf. Ertem, *Flora* 129–30.

While 'wine' is *wiyana-* (GEŠTIN), *ippi(y)a-*, like ^{GIŠ}*mahla-* (q.v.), may well cover ^(GIŠ)GEŠTIN 'grapevine'; with *KBo* XI 32 Vs. 21 ^{GIŠ}*ippias murin* cf. e.g. *KUB* XXXVI 89 Rs. 58 GEŠTIN-*as mu-ri-es* 'grape of the vine'. The hesitation between the determinatives 'tree' and 'plant' fits the vine well. ^{GIŠ}*īppias* figures in native Anatolian myth in the company of the maieutic goddess Hannahannas and the vegetation spirit Miyadanzipas (*KUB* XXXIII 59 III 6–9 and 12–13, quoted above); chances are that it is a native Anatolian term for 'grapevine' (cf. the likewise isolated, "native" Gk. ἄμπελος 'grapevine').

ippi(y)a- /ipya-/ or *eppiya-* /epya-/ would have yielded Gk.

*ιπτα or *επτα and may be seen as the divine name Ιπτα or Ειπτα in inscriptions from Maeonia (Μητρι Ιπτα και Διει Σα[βαζιω], Διει Σαβαζιω και Μητρει Ειπτα, Μελτινη Μητρα Μητρι Ιπτα ευχην), comparable to the Ἴπτα or Ἴππα who appears in Orphic Hymns 48 and 49 as the divine nurse of Dionysus (with Sabazios as father), at home on Phrygian Mt. Ida and Lydian Mt. Tmolus, with epithets like εὐάς κούρη, χθονίη μήτηρ, βασίλεια. P. Kretschmer's attempt (*Glotta* 15:76–8 [1926]) to connect Ἴπτα and Ἴππα with Hurrian-Hittite *Hepit, Hipit, Hepa, Hipa* (i.e. Hebat as the hurrianized Hittite consort of the storm-god) founders both on geographic polarity (NW vs. SE) and on the fact that *H-* yields *K-* in Anatolian Greek (*Hasammilis* : Κασμῖλος, *Harran* : Καρραι, etc.). Whatever the source of the spiritus asper in the Orphic manuscripts, Μητηρ Ιπτα is part of the Bacchic folk-cults of Western Anatolia and may well represent the deified grapevine as nurse of the wine-god (lit. 'Mother Vine'; cf. the botanical expression *annas* GIŠGEŠTIN-*as* [s.v. *anna-*]); she may be close in kind to the maieutic Hannahannas who plants the vine over her sacred well, or to the daimon Miyadanzipas who sits beneath it.

ipul(li)-   (c.) 'wrap, encasement, chasuble, surplice' (vel sim.), nom.-acc. sg. *i-pu-ul* (*KBo* X 23 IV 2 *ipul-set*), nom.-acc. sg. (or pl.?) *i-pu-ul-li* (*KUB* IX 28 I 16–18 SÍG ZA.GÌN *ishuzziyanza* SÍG SA₅ *ipulli-set* INA UZUGAB-ŠU SÍG SA₅ *kitta* '[she is] girt [with] blue wool, red wool [is] her wrap, red wool is placed on her breast'; XVI 83 Vs. 51 ŠA GIŠTUKUL GUŠKIN-*ya-wa-kan ipulli* IŠTU N[A₄ ZA.GÌN?] *arha pippa*[*n*] 'the gold weapon's encasement of lapis lazuli [?] [has been] knocked off'; cf. von Brandenstein, *Heth. Götter* 65; *Bo* 2923 IV 1–2 ᴰ*Halmasuittas* LÚSANGA-*as ipulli-set harzi* 'he holds the chasuble [?] of the priest of H.'; cf. Neu, *Altheth.* 88), instr. sg. *ipullit* (*KBo* X 24 II 4–6 ANA LÚSANGA ᴰU GÙ[B]-*la-*[*za*] *iyatta n-an* SÍG*ipull*[*it harzi*] '[he] walks to the left of the priest of the storm-god and holds him by the [woollen] surplice [?]'), dat.-loc. pl. (or gen. sg.?) *ipulliyas* (*KUB* IX 22 II 22–25 *nu* GIŠERIN GIŠ*paini* GIŠ*ZERTUM* IŠTU SÍG SA₅ *anda ishiyan n-at* LÚ*patilis dāi n-at-kan* ANA SAL *ipulliyas anda dāi* 'cedar, tamarisk, and olive-wood [are] bound up with red wool; the priest takes them, and in [their] wrapping[s] sets them to the woman'; ibid. III 11–14 *kuit* ... ANA SAL *ipulliyas anda dais n-at-si-kan arha dāi* 'what he set in the wrapping[s] to the woman, those he takes away from her'; XLII 11 I 5; cf. P. Cornil – R. Lebrun, *Orientalia Lovaniensia Periodica* 6–7:101 [1975–6]).

Parsing remains partly uncertain, since *ipulli* can also be neut. pl. of *ipul-* (cf. e.g. *ishiuli*HI.A from *ishiul-*). Alp's suggestion 'handle, hilt' (*Belleten* 12:322–3 [1948]) was based solely on *KUB* XVI 83 Vs. 51 and squares ill with the now available dossier, although it has led to such abortive etymologies as the connection with *ep(p)-* 'take, seize' (J. Knobloch, *Kratylos* 4:33 [1959]; Kronasser, *Etym.* 1:213; H. Eichner, *MSS* 31:80 [1973]; Oettinger, *Stammbildung* 540), which founders on vocalism and consonantism alike (*i-* never appears in the paradigm of *ep*[*p*]-, *ap*[*p*]-; cf. N. van Brock, *RHA* 20:114 [1962]; *ep*[*p*]- has constant intervocalic -*pp*-). Even more premature was the attempt by C. H. Carruthers (*Lg.* 9:160–1 [1933], based solely on *KUB* IX 22 II 22–25) to read into ANA SAL *ipulliyas anda* the sense 'into the woman's vagina', connecting *ipulli-* with Gk. οἴφω 'fuck'.

-*ul-* and -*ulli-* can be abstract noun suffixes, either deverbative (e.g. *im*[*m*]*iul-*, *ishiul-*, *sesarul*[*i*]-, *istapul*[*l*]*i-*, *kariulli-*) or denominative (e.g. *assul-*, *asandul-*), but are also found in words of obscure derivation and probable non-IE origin (e.g. *kazzarnul-*, *huppulli-*, *namulli-*, *parnulli-*). In the absence of a wholly unequivocal base-meaning and obvious derivation it is best to assign *ipul*[*li*]- as a technical term to the last-mentioned category (including textiles, utensils, furnishings, trees, and the like); the generic sense of 'cover(ing)' may serve as a common denominator for the attested usages (all indicating something found or placed on ritual persons or objects, which are then 'inside' the *ipul*[*li*]- [*KUB* IX 22 II 24–25 *ipulliyas anda*]).

issalli- (n.) 'spittle' (*KBo* I 45 Rs. 9 *issalli*, I 49, 2–5 [Akk.] *rūtum*; cf. *MSL* 3:53 [1955]), nom.-acc. sg. neut. *is-sa-al-li* (e.g. *KUB*

XXIX 10 I 9–11 *takku-kan* UKÙ-*as* ᴳᴵˢNÁ-*as seszi nu-ssi-kan issaz issalli parā* GÙB-*li meni ārassizzi* 'if a man sleeps in bed and from his mouth spittle flows forth on his left cheek ...'; cf. Güterbock, *AfO* 18:79 [1957], with the 'right cheek' pendant ibid. 5–7, and the duplicate text XXIX 9 I 9–11 and 13–15; XLI 21 I 9 KAxU-*as* ... *issalli* 'spittle of the mouth'; cf. Haas – Thiel, *Rituale* 276; XXXVI 55 III 16).

issallant- (c.), nom. sg. *issallanza* (*KBo* I 44 + XIII 1 IV 3; cf. Otten, *Vokabular* 18, 21; I 45 Rs. 11 *is]sallanza*; cf. *MSL* 3:53 [1955]). Perhaps participle of denom. *issallai-* 'salivate, drool, drivel, slaver', thus 'epileptic' vel sim. (cf. Riemschneider, *Orientalia* N.S. 40:476 [1971]). Neumann (apud Tischler, *Glossar* 404) also adduced ˢᴬᴸ*īsli-* (acc. sg. in *KUB* XXX 15 Vs. 34 ˢᴬᴸ*īslin*; cf. Otten, *Totenrituale* 68), possibly referring to some Pythia-type ecstatic priestess, foaming at the mouth.

issalli- is usually derived from *a(y)is(s)-*, *iss-* 'mouth' (q.v.), with the denom. suffix *-alli-* (Kronasser, *Etym.* 1:211–3). Cf. Ehelolf, *OLZ* 36:6 (1933); Sturtevant, *Comp. Gr.*[1] 159; Laroche, *BSL* 57.1:28–9 (1962); N. van Brock, *RHA* 20:110 (1962). Despite the jingle *issaz issalli* the semantics of this derivation are not compelling. Cf. perhaps rather Lat. *salīva* 'spittle' (*issalli-* < *sH̥li-*?), although further root-connections (*IEW* 879) are doubtful. Cf. V. Pisani, *Paideia* 13:322 (1958); Schmitt-Brandt, *Entwicklung* 102–3; A. Bernabé P., *Revista española de lingüística* 3:424 (1973).

is(sa)na-, essana-   (c.) 'dough', nom. sg. *isnas* (1112/c + III 5–6 *isnas-ma-wa-kan kās* DINGIR.MEŠ-*as* NINDA[A *harsi Ū*]L [*p*]*aizzi* 'this dough does not end up as a breadloaf for the gods'; cf. L. Rost, *MIO* 1:358 [1953]), *issanas* (dupl. *KUB* XV 39 + XII 59 II 18–19 *issanas-ma-wa-kan kās* DINGIR.MEŠ-*as* NINDA *harsi ŪL paizzi*), acc. sg. *isnan*, *issanan* (e.g. XXIV 14 I 3–4 *nu ŠA* ZÍD.DA ŠE *isnan dahhi nu* UR.ZÍR-*as salpan menahhanda immiyami* 'I take dough of barley meal and mix in dog shit'; *KBo* XXIII 1 I 32 EGIR-*pa-ma-za ŠA* BA.BA.ZA *isnan dāi* 'but afterwards she takes paste-dough'; cf. Lebrun, *Hethitica III* 142; dupl. *KUB* XXX 38a, 1 *issana[n*; 1112/c + II 21 *nu* ˢᴬᴸŠU.GI *wātar* [*i*]*snann-*

-*a dāi* 'the old woman takes water and dough'; ibid. 22–23 *na[mma-smas-kan] isnan ser arha wahnuzi* 'then she also waves the dough over them'; ibid. 25 *nu-kan isnan hassī dāi* 'she puts the dough in the fireplace'; dupl. *KBo* II 3 I 35–36 *namma--smas-kan issanann-a ser arha wahnu[zi;* ibid. 37 *nu-kan issanan hassī dāi;* cf. Hrozný, *Heth. KB* 66; 1112/c+ III 21 *i]snan-a--smas-kan ser arha wahnuzi;* dupl. *KBo* II 3 II 29 *issanann-a--smas-kan [s]er a[rha; KUB* VII 53 II 3–5 *issanan … dāi* 'takes the dough'; cf. Goetze, *Tunnawi* 10), gen. sg. *isnas, isnās, issanas, ēssanas* (e.g. XV 31 III 39 *isnas;* cf. Haas – Wilhelm, *Riten* 164; XXXIX 7 II 11 *isnass-a* 10 *lahanza*^MUŠEN *iyanza* 'and of dough ten l.-birds [are] made'; cf. Otten, *Totenrituale* 36; XVII 23 I 12 *nu* PANI ŠAH *isnas kuis* ^GIŠMÁ *kittari* 'the boat which is located facing the pig of dough'; similarly ibid. II 39–40 *nu isnas kuis* ŠAH *nu-ssi* ^GIŠMÁ *kuis isnas piran kittari;* 1112/c+ II 6–8 *isnass-a-sm[as k]uyēs* 2 ALAM *piran katta kianta* ŠU.HI.A *isnas-a-smas-san* EME.HI.A *isnas kue* INA SAG.DU.HI.A--ŠUNU *kianda* 'the two figures of dough which are set down in front of them, and the hands of dough [and] tongues of dough which are placed on their heads'; dupl. XII 34 + XV 39 I 20–22 *isnas-ma-smas kue* 2 ALAM *piran katta kitta [is]nas-ma-smas* QADU EME.HI.A-*ya kue* INA SAG.DU-*ZUNU kianta; KBo* IV 2 I 56 *nu isnas pūrpuran iyanzi* 'they make a lump of dough'; ibid. 63 *pūrpurēs isnas* 'lumps of dough'; cf. Kronasser, *Die Sprache* 8:91–2 [1962]; *KUB* XXVII 67 II 11 *isnas pūrpūrēs;* ibid. III 14 *[p]ūrpūriyas hūrtalliss-a isnās* 'lumps and blobs of dough'; ibid. II 9 *isnās pūrpūrēs hūrtallenzi* 'lumps [and] blobs of dough'; *KBo* XV 10 I 2 2 *kurdāli isnas* 'two containers of dough'; ibid. 3 and 4 7 EME *isnas* 'seven tongues of dough'; ibid. 6 7 *qalulupus isnas* 7 *ishahru isnas* 'seven fingers of dough [and] seven tears of dough'; cf. Szabó, *Entsühnungsritual* 12; ibid. II 2 *nu isnas kurtāli* YÀ LÀL *kuwapi lāhuwan* 'when into the container of dough oil [and] honey [is] poured'; ibid. I 12 1 *kurdāli isnās;* 1112/c+ II 10 *i[s]nas-a* ŠU.HI.A EME.HI.A 'hands [and] tongues of dough'; dupl. *KBo* II 3 I 24 *issanas-a;* XI 19 Vs. 2 *isnās patalhan* TUR INA ^UZUGÚ-*ŠU* 'a small gyve of dough around his neck'; cf. Haas – Thiel, *Rituale* 314; XXIV 8, 4 *isnās patalhan; KUB* XII 47 I 6 *i]ssanas pata[lhan;* cf. Haas – Thiel, *Rituale*

329; *VBoT* 24 I 27 *nu* ŠU-*it issanas* MUŠEN *harzi* 'she holds a bird of dough in her hand'; ibid. 33 *issanas* MUŠEN; cf. Sturtevant, *Chrest.* 108; *KUB* XII 58 I 24 *issanas* ŠAH.TUR 'a small pig of dough'; cf. Goetze, *Tunnawi* 8; IX 34 III 24 *issanas* ŠAH.TUR TI-*andann-a* 'a small pig of dough and a live one'; ibid. 26–27 *ēssanas-ma* ... ŠAH.TUR), dat.-loc. sg. *isni* (XXIV 14 I 9–10 *nu kī hūman* ANA ZÍD.DA ŠE *isni menahhanda immiyami* 'all this I mix together with barley meal into dough'; ibid. 14), instr. sg. *isnit* (*KUB* XXIX 7 + *KBo* XXI 41 Vs. 39, 40, 42, 45, 49, 52, 54, 56 ŠA BA.BA.ZA *isnit* 'with paste-dough'; cf. Lebrun, *Samuha* 119–20), acc. pl. *istanas* (sic, with -*ta*- for -*sa*-, *KUB* XXIV 9 III 6 EGIR-*anda istanas dāi* 'thereafter she takes kinds of dough'), *ēssanas* (dupl. XLI 1 III 21 [EGIR]-*anda-ma ēssanas* [...; cf. Jakob-Rost, *Ritual der Malli* 42–3).

issanauwant- 'doughy, pasty', nom.-acc. pl. neut. *is-sa-na-u--wa-an-ta* (*KBo* XV 33 II 19–20 LÚ.MEŠ NINDA.DÙ.DÙ-*ma kuedani uiteni* QATE.MEŠ-*ŠUNU issanauwanta anda salikianta n-at-kan parā ŪL-pat pidanzi* 'in what water the bakers immerse their doughy hands, that they do not carry forth').

isnura-, isnuri- (c.) 'dough-bowl', nom. sg. *isnuras* (*KBo* II 3 II 34–35]ŠA ᴰ*IŠTAR isnuras*; cf. Hrozný, *Heth. KB* 76), *is-nu-u--ri-is* (dupl. 1112/c + III 26 *kāsa-wa* ŠA ᴰ*IŠTAR isnūris* 'lo, [this is] Ištar's dough-bowl'; cf. L. Rost, *MIO* 1:360 [1953]), acc. sg. *isnūrin* (ibid. 22 EGIR-*anda-ma* I[M]-*as isnūrin iyazzi* 'but afterwards she makes a dough-bowl of clay'), *isnuran* (dupl. II 3 II 30 EGIR-*anda* IM-[*as*] ᴰᵁᴳ*isnuran i*[*ya*]*zi*), *isnūran* (e.g. dupl. 2486/c, 11 *isnūran iezzi*; II 3 II 7–8 *nu* ˢᴬᴸŠU.GI [IM-*as*] ᴰᵁᴳ*isnū-ran iyaizzi nu-kan issanan tepu anda dāi* 'the old woman makes a dough-bowl of clay and puts in a little dough'), *isnurān* (dupl. *KUB* XV 39 + XII 59 II 10–11 *nu* ˢᴬᴸŠU.GI IM-*as* ᴰᵁᴳ*isnurān iezzi nu-kan issan*[*a*]*n tepu anda dāi*; cf. also dupl. 1112/c + II 55–56 *nu* ˢᴬᴸŠU.GI IM-[*as* ᴰᵁᴳ]*hupuwāi iyazzi nu-kan isnan te*[*pu*] *anda dāi* 'the old woman takes a clay pot and puts in a little dough'), dat.-loc. sg. *isnūri* (*KBo* VI 34 I 31–33 *nu kī harnam-mar mahhan tepu danzi n-at isnūri immiyanzi nu isnūran* UD.1.KAM *tianzi n-as putkiyetta* 'as they take a little of this yeast and mix it into the dough-bowl, and let the bowl stand for one day, and it rises ...'; cf. Oettinger, *Eide* 8), nom. pl. *is-nu-u-ri-es*

(XVI 71+ I 28 2 ^{DUG}*isnūres*; cf. Neu, *Altheth.* 40), acc. pl.
isnurus (XV 33 II 32–34 *n-asta* ^{DUG}*isnūr[es] kueaz* [sic] *IŠTU* GAD
DINGIR-*LIM kariyantes n-at* PANI ^{LÚ}EN.É-*TIM sarā appanzi nu*
^{DUG}*isnurus auszi mān-kan* TUM.DUBBIN [?] *sarā uwan* 'the dough-
bowls which [are] covered with the deity's cloth, before the
housemaster they lift them up, and he inspects the dough-
bowls, whether the ?? [has] come up'), *isnūrus* (ibid. 13–14 *nu*
^{DUG}*isnūrus* PANI D[INGI]R-*LIM istanāni piran* [...] *nu-smas-san ser
arha* GAD-*an huittianzi* 'they [set] the dough-bowls facing the
deity in front of the altar, and over them they draw a cloth'),
is-nu-ra-s(a-kan) (*VBoT* 24 III 7 ^{DUG}*isnuras-a-kan sūniyanzi*
'and they fill dough-bowls'; cf. Sturtevant, *Chrest.* 112), dat.-
loc. pl. *isnūras* (*KBo* XV 33 II 30 *is]nūras piran*; ibid. 5 *isn]ūras
anda*).

That *isnura-* or *isnuri-* is derived from *is(sa)na-* is not in
doubt (unnecessary hesitation in Neumann, *Untersuchungen*
30). Nor is "foreign" origin of the suffix plausible (despite
Kronasser, *Etym.* 1:187–8, 226–7), as there are enough inner-
Hittite and other IE parallels (cf. e.g. Carruba, *Beschwörungsritual* 53, and such denominative Sanskrit parallels as *danturá-*
'buck-toothed' from *dánt-* 'tooth' or *aṅgúri-* 'finger' from *áṅga-*
'limb'); it is quite unnecessary to assume (with Čop, *Indogermanica minora* 51) a compound of *isna-* and ^{DUG}*urā-* (poorly
attested name of a receptacle, q.v.).

is(sa)na-, ēssana- reflects IE **yes(o)no-* 'ferment(ation)',
metonymically '(rising) dough', even as the newer term *harnammar* means literally 'ferment(ation)' and thence 'fermenta-
tion-substance, yeast'; the nearest cognate is the Germanic
infinitive from IE **yes-* (*IEW* 506), seen in OHG *jesan* 'ferment'. For **ye->e-, i-* see s.v. *eka-*.

Unconvincing connections with *essa-* 'make' (Sturtevant,
Chrest. 120, 122–3), *es(sa)ri-* 'shape' (Neumann, *KZ* 75:89
[1957]; Gusmani, *IF* 68:293 [1963]), and Gk. ἰαίνω 'soothe,
warm', Skt. *iṣaṇyáti* 'drive, impel' (Goetze, *Mélanges ... Pedersen* 492 [1937], comparing German *heben* 'lift', *hefe* 'yeast'; for
ἰαίνω see s.v. *iyawa-*, whereas *iṣaṇyáti* is secondary to *iṣyati*).
Čop (*Živa Antika* 6:42, 49 [1956], *Ling.* 6:55 [1964]) was briefly
on the right track of IE **yes-* but soon (*Indogermanica minora*

40–1, 51) recanted in favor of a tie-in with Skt. *iṣṭakā-* 'brick', Toch. B. *iścem* 'clay(-brick)', allegedly from an IE **is-* 'knead, mold', synonymous with **dheyĝh-* (as in Lat. *figūra* : English *dough*). A. Bernabé P. (*Revista española de lingüística* 3:424 [1973]) reconstructed *is(sa)na-* as **sHn-*, cognate with **sHl-* in *issalli-* 'spittle'.

isha-, esha-   (c.) 'master, lord, owner, person in charge; mistress, lady' (EN; *BELU, BELTU.* e.g. *KBo* VI 3 IV 20 *ishās ... ishi-ssi* matching dupl. VI 7, 2–3 EN-*as ...* EN-*si* [*Code* 1:86]; *KUB* XXXIII 62 II 18 *parnas ishī parnas ishassari* besides ibid. 8 ANA H^LÚ*BEL É-TIM* ^SAL*BELDI É-TIM* 'for the lord of the house, for the lady of the house'), nom. sg. *ishas* (e.g. XXXVI 51 Vs. 6 *ishas-sis-wa*; cf. Laroche, *RHA* 23:154 [1965]; frequent in the Code, e.g. *KBo* VI 3 III 65 [= *Code* 1:71] *mān-an ishas-sis-a wemiyazi* 'but if its owner finds it'; ibid. IV 55 [= *Code* 1:99] *ishas-ses-a*), *ishās* (e.g. dupl. VI 2 IV 56 *ishās-sis-a*, besides dupl. XIX 4 IV 2 EN-*s[es-a]*; cf. Otten – Souček, *AfO* 21:10 [1966]; V 4 Rs. 1 *zik-pat-ma-za ishās* 'you alone [shall be] lord'; cf. Friedrich, *Staatsverträge* 1:60; VIII 35 II 10 ^D*Isharas linkias ishās* 'I., mistress of the oath'; cf. von Schuler, *Die Kaškäer* 110, 115; Kronasser, *Etym.* 1:106–7), acc. sg. *ishān* (e.g. XIII 31 III 9 *uttanās ishān* 'the owner of the thing'; cf. Riemschneider, *Geburtsomina* 76), voc. sg. *isha* (*KUB* XXXI 127 I 1–2 ^D*UTU-e isha-mi handanza hannesnas ishas* 'sun-god, my lord, righteous lord of judgment!'), *ishā* (XXX 10 Rs. 10 ^D*UTU-i ishā-mi*; likewise XXXI 128 I 1; XXXI 147 II 17 and 34; *KBo* XIX 112, 9 [*kuwat*] *ŪL ekutti ammel ishā-mi* 'why do you not drink, my lady?'; cf. Siegelová, *Appu-Hedammu* 44; H. Berman, *JNES* 33:422 [1974]), gen. sg. *ishās* (VI 2 II 41 [= *Code* 1:46] *iwaruas ishās* A.ŠÀ 'the field of the grantor'; cf. par. VI 4 IV 25 *iwaruwas* EN-*as* A.ŠÀ), dat.-loc. sg. *es-hé* (III 34 I 25 [OHitt.] 'to the lord'), *ishe* (e.g. *KUB* XLI 1 I 6, 10, 14 *is-hi-es-si* 'to its master'), *isha* (dupl. XXIV 9 I 51 *isha-ssi*), *ishi* (e.g. ibid. 46 *ishi-ssi*; cf. dupl. *KBo* XII 126 I 21 BELI-ŠU, and Jakob-Rost, *Ritual der Malli* 28–30, 22; VI 26 II 14 [= *Code* 2:73] *takku* ÌR-*as ishi-ssi araizzi* 'if a slave rises up against his master'), *ishī* (e.g. *KUB* XXVI 17

II 5 *auwariyas ishī* 'to the watch commander'; cf. Alp, *Belleten* 11:394 [1947]), EN-*i-ssi* (*KBo* VI 4 IV 5 [= *Code* 1:45]; cf. ibid. 6 [acc. sg.] EN-*issin-ma* [sic]), nom. pl. *is-hi-e-es* (e.g. *KUB* XXX 68 Vs. 6; cf. Laroche, *CTH* 173), *is-hé-es* (e.g. *KBo* III 46 Vs. 38 *t*]*uzziyas ishes akir* 'the lords of the host were killed'; cf. S. Heinhold-Krahmer, *Arzawa* 279 [1977]), dat.-loc. pl. *ishas* (e.g. III 1 I 21 [OHitt.]).

^D*Ishashuriyas* (*KUB* XXXVIII 3 I 9) who has (or is) a fountain (*aldannis*) in XXXVIII 1 I 10 (cf. von Brandenstein, *Heth. Götter* 16, 10), may well mean 'lord of spray' (vel sim.); cf. ^D*Hūriyanzipas* and see s.v. *hurai-*, at end.

For *ēshanas ishās* 'person in charge of (settling a) murder (case)' see s.v. *eshar*. For EN *DINI* or *BEL DINI* 'legal adversary' see sub *hannessar* s.v. *hanna-*.

ishassara- 'lady, mistress' (GAŠAN; *BELTU*) is a feminine derivative from *isha-* (which latter is basically nonspecific as to sex; when a Šamaš-hymn has been adapted to the Sun-goddess of Arinna, she is still referred to as *hannesnas* EN-*as* in *KUB* XXIV 3 I 35 and 47; cf. Gurney, *Hittite Prayers* 10, 22–4); -*(a)s(s)ar(a)-* thus creates the "marked" member of a male : female pair, somewhat in the manner of **sems* 'one' (Gk. εἷς) : **smteros* 'the other' (Myc. *a₂-te-ro*, Doric ἅτερος, Ionic ἕτερος); for other examples (^{DUMU.SAL}*suppessara-* 'pure girl, virgin', **hassussara-* [SAL.LUGAL-*ra-*] 'queen', **GEME-nassara-* 'female slave', Luw. *nanasri*[*ya*]- 'sister' beside *nani*[*ya*]- 'brother') see e.g. Kronasser, *Etym.* 1:109–12 (who wrongly connected *isha-* with ^D*Ishara-*); implausible speculations on the origin of the suffix in e.g. O. Szemerényi, *Kratylos* 11:206–21 (1966), who assumed compounds with an **asar-* (cf. Hom. ὄαρ 'wife'); either indigenous suffixal origin or IE **-sro-* (as in Skt. fem. *tisrás* 'three', *catasrás* 'four') remains more plausible. Attested in dat.-loc. sg. *ishassari* (*KUB* XXXIII 62 II 18, quoted above) and theonymically as ^D*Ishassara-* 'Lady' (cf. Laroche, *Recherches* 67).

**ishassar* (n.) 'lordship' (cf. e.g. *ilassar* beside *ilessar*; Kronasser, *Etym.* 1:288) underlies **ishassaru-* (n.) 'lordly quality, lordliness' (cf. **esharu-* 'bloodiness' from *eshar* 'blood'), whence a denom. verb *ishassarwai-, ishassarwiya-* 'practise lordliness' (cf. *isharwai-, isharwiya-* 'be bloody'), partic. *ishassarwant-* (cf. *isharwant-*), nom. sg. c. *ishassarwanza* (*VBoT* 120 II 18 *sargauwas-ma-za piran ishassarwanza ēsdu* 'before the exalted let him be lordly'; cf. Haas – Thiel, *Rituale* 140), dat.-loc. sg. *ishassarwanti* (*KUB* XXXIII 120 I 42–44 [ᴰ*Kuma*]*rbis--a-kan iyauwaniyauanza* ᵁᴿᵁ*Nipp*[*ur...*] [...] *pait ishassarwanti--ya-an-zan* [...] [...] *esat* 'and K., recovering, went to Nippur and installed himself in a lordly [station?]'; cf. Güterbock, *Kumarbi* *3); verbal noun *ishassarwatar* (n.) (cf. *isharwātar*), nom.-acc. sg. *is-ha-as-sar-wa-tar* (XXI 38 Vs. 16 ŠEŠ-ʸᴬ-*ma ammēdaza* NÍG.TUKU-*ti kuitki* ŪL-*at* ŠUM-*an ishassarwatarr-a* '[that] you, my brother, in any way enrich yourself on my account, this [is] not [conducive to] lordly repute', lit. '[good] name and lordliness' [hendiadys]; cf. W. Helck, *JCS* 17:88 [1963]; R. Stefanini, *Atti La Colombaria* 29:7, 25 [1964]; ibid. 46; *KBo* IV 14 II 21 *ishassarwatar* [...] *ilaliski* 'desire lordship!'; ibid. 20 *i*]*shassarwatar*; cf. R. Stefanini, *ANLR* 20:40 [1965]), *ishassarwātar* (*KUB* XXIX 1 III 31–34 *mā-wa-za* É-*ir andurza hanesteni nu-wa* MU.KAM.ḪI.A GÍD.DA *hanesteni āssu hanisteni mānn-at arahza-ma hanesteni nu nahsaraddan hani⟨s⟩ten nu ishassarwātar hanesten* 'if you plaster the house within, you plaster long years, you plaster wealth; but if you plaster it outside, plaster fearsomeness, plaster lordliness!'; cf. B. Schwartz, *Orientalia* N.S. 16:34 [1947]; Starke, *ZA* 69:99 [1979]), *ishasarwatar* (*KBo* II 32 Rs. 1–3 SILIM-*ulan* TI-*tar hattulat*[*ar ...*] MU.ḪI.A GÍD.DA *ishasarwatar* [...] ᴳᴵˢ(TUKUL.ḪI.A) NIR.GÁL *āssiyatarr-a* [...] 'well-being, life, health, long years, lordship, strong weapons, and love'; cf. Haas – Thiel, *Rituale* 284), gen. sg. *ishasarwannas* (*KUB* II 1 II 46 ŠA *Laba*[*r*]*na is*[*ha*]*sarwan*[*na*]*s* ᴰLAMA-*i* 'to the tutelary deity of the ruler's lordliness'), *ishasarwanas* (dupl. *KBo* II 38, 11 *ishasarwanas* KI.M[IN; cf. A. Archi, *SMEA* 16:98, 109 [1975]), instr. sg. *is-ha-as-sar-wa-an-ni-t(a-at-kán)* (*KUB* XXIV 13 II 11–13 *ishassarwannit-at-kan āssiyauwannit alwanzatar arha ansan ēsdu* 'through lordliness and love let the hex be wiped off!'; cf. Haas – Thiel, *Rituale* 104); iter. *is-ha-as-sar-u-e-e*[*s-ki-* (XV 12 I 12; cf. *isharuieski-*; unless denom. inchoative *ishassaruēs-* from **ishassaru-*); also factitive *ishassarwahh-* (cf. *ēsharwahh-*), iter. 3 sg. imp. act. in *KBo* X 12 III 9–10 *pa]hsi n-as ishassarwahheski* [...] ŠEŠ.MEŠ-*as iwar piran iyantaru* 'protect [them] and make them lordly; like brothers they shall go before [you]'; cf. H. Freydank, *MIO* 7:363 [1960]). It is preferable to posit a denominative verbal intermediary for *ishassarwant-* and *ishassarwatar*, rather than assume (with e.g. Kammenhuber, *HOAKS* 190) direct deadjectival derivatives like e.g. *dassuwant-* or *idaluwatar*; the latter are parallel forms (besides *dassu-* and *idalawatar*), whereas *ishassarwant-* and *ishassarwatar* stand alone; it is easier to postulate the interim obsoleteness of the intermediate finite denominative verb than to explain the absence of side-by-side **ishassaru-* and **ishassarawatar*.

ishizzi-* 'lordly' (cf. **hassuizzi-* 'kingly' s.v. *hassu-*), denom. verb *ishizziya-* 'be lordly, dominate, prevail', 3 sg. pres. act. *ishizziyazi* (*KUB* XIII 3 II 14 *kuwapi* UD-*at* LUGAL-*was* ZI-*za ishizziyazi* 'on a day when the king's animus gets the upper hand'), 3 sg. pret. act. (Luwoid?) or midd. (?) *ishizzita* (ibid. III 26–27 *nu* LUGAL-*as* ZI-*anza ishizzita nu-kan ... kartimmiyanun* 'the king's [=my] animus took over, and I was angry'; cf. Friedrich, *Meissner AOS* 46–7; for possible act. : midd. fluctuation cf. LUGAL-*izziat* : LUGAL-*izziyatta* 'ruled as king' sub **hassuizzi-* s.v. *hassu-*); wrongly derived by H. Eichner (*Die Sprache* 24:160 [1978], *Hethitisch und Indogermanisch* 61 [1979]) from an **ishizzi-* 'rage' ($<$sA_1ityo-*, comparing Lat. *saevus*, q.v. s.v. *sai-*), which would yield improbable anticlimactic semantics in *KUB* XIII 3 III 26–27 (ZI-*anza ishizzita nu-kan ... kartimmiyanun* '[my] mind flew into a rage ... and I got angry'); denom. factitive **ishizna-* 'make lordly', verbal noun **ishiznatar* (n.), dat.-loc. sg. EN-*iznanni* (e.g. XIV 15 IV 37 *namma* [IN]A URU*Mirā* ¹*Mashuiluwan* EN-*iznanni tittanunun* 'I installed M. in lordship at M.'; cf. Götze, AM 72; *KBo* V 13 I 26 *nu* ANA KUR-*TI* EN-*iznanni tuk-pat tittanunun* 'I have installed you in lordship over the land', with dupl. IV 3 I 14 and *KUB* VI 41 II 1), [EN-*i*]*znani* (dupl. *KBo* IV 7 II 4; cf. Friedrich, *Staatsverträge* 1:114), EN-*izni* (sic *KUB* XIV 24, 11; cf. Götze, *AM* 144), EN-*manni* (sic XXVI 1 IV 4–5 [*nu-z*]*a* ŠA ᴰUTU-*ŠI* EN-*manni* EGIR-*an arha tamel* UKÙ-*as* EN-*UTTA ilaliyazi* 'instead of my majesty's lordship it desires for itself the lordship of

another person'; cf. von Schuler, *Dienstanweisungen* 15), EN-
-*anni* (e.g. XIV 15 IV 45; cf. Götze, *AM* 72); the frequent
EN-*anni*, EN-*UTTI(M)*, EN-*UTTA* (cf. e.g. Kühne – Otten, *Šaušgamuwa* 30–1) may also hide a denom. abstract **ishatar*.

The etymology of *isha-*, *esha-* has been endlessly and inconclusively debated. After Hrozný's preemptive "wohl nicht"
comparison with Gk. ἰσχυρός 'strong' (*SH* 34), Indo-European
origin and connection with Lat. *erus* 'master' ($*esH_1o$-) was
first suggested by F. Ribezzo, *Rivista indo-greco-italica* 4:128
(1920); this much-repeated isogloss (e.g. C. H. Carruthers, *Lg.*
6:161 [1930]; Sturtevant passim; W. Petersen, *Lg.* 10:317
[1934]; Pedersen, *Hitt.* 184; Goetze, *Lg.* 30:355 [1954]; Lehmann, *PIEP* 26) still commanded the adherence of e.g. Čop
(*Indogermanica minora* 62) but has ultimately little in its favor,
because an irreducible thematic root-noun would be odd and
an underlying common verbal root is not visible as a basis for
derivation; T. Milewski's **es-Ho-* 'he that is' (*L'indo-hittite et
l'indo-européen* 18 [1936]) does not make much sense, and Lat.
erus can be and has been otherwise, albeit inconclusively,
explicated (cf. e.g. *IEW* 342). Assuming an independent inner-
Hittite derivation for *isha-* and tying it in with *ishiya-* 'bind',
sahhan- 'feudal duty', or *sesha-* 'ordain' (e.g. E. Forrer, *ZDMG*
76:217 [1922]; Juret, *Vocabulaire* 50, 52; Neumann, *OLZ*
52:425 [1957]; H. Eichner, *Untersuchungen zur hethitischen
Deklination* 57–60 [1974] [$*sH_1oyó$-]; Oettinger, *Stammbildung*
499 [$*sH_1óH_2s$]) is equally implausible.

Arm. *išxan* 'ruler, prince', *išxel* 'to rule' have been compared
with Hitt. *isha-* since P. Jensen, *ZA* 36:82 (1925); cf. e.g. N.
Martirosyan, *Handes Amsorya* 43:537 (1929); J. J. S. Weitenberg, *Kratylos* 24:73 (1979). Either a borrowing from Hittite
into Armenian or into both from some common "culture
word" source is theoretically conceivable. Borrowed Indo-
Aryan origin (via Hurrian; cf. Skt. *īśvará-* 'master, lord') was
suggested for both by V. Bănăţeanu, *Studii şi cercetări lingvis-
tice* 14:405 (1963), *Die Sprache* 10:201 (1964), while regular
derivation from an underlying IE **(e)ik̂(w)-* was preposter-
ously proposed for Hittite (and Armenian) by H. Wittmann,
Glossa 3:24 (1969). Čop (*Indogermanica minora* 79–80) recon-

structed Arm. *išxan* alone as **išu-x-* from IE **ēiḱ-* 'own, possess', comparing Skt. *īśvará-*, Avest. *isvan-* 'capable, in charge'. Most probably Arm. *išxan* is a loanword from Iranian **xšān-* (vel sim.; cf. Benveniste, *RPh* 59:195 [1933]), with a metathesis paralleled by *bde(a)šx* 'great prince' (cf. Pahlavi *pātaxšāh*; J. A. C. Greppin, *Annual of Armenian linguistics* 3:57–9 [1982]); it has thus no truck whatever with Hitt. *isha-*.

There remains an inner-Anatolian approach to *isha-*. Apart from a very doubtful Lyd. *iśa-* (Gusmani, *Lyd. Wb.* 138, *Die Sprache* 17:6 [1971], *Journal of the Royal Asiatic Society* 1975:138), the extra-Hittite equivalents are Luw. *washai-*, *washa(n)t-* 'master' (*Dict. louv.* 109), Hier. *washa-* 'master' (Meriggi, *HHG* 151), and perhaps Pal. *pashullasas* (epithet or attribute of the sun-god Tiyaz), *washullatiyas* (perhaps containing *-Tiyas*; cf. Carruba, *Das Palaische* 67, 78). The Palaic forms especially reek of Hattic (cf. *KUB* XXVIII 67, 7 *waₐ-as-hu-ú-li*[and see Kammenhuber, *RHA* 17:89 [1959]), and there is Hatt. *(a)shap/w-* 'god', "collective" *washap/w-* (= DINGIR.MEŠ) which may have yielded the Hittite(-Lydian) and Palaic-Luwian-Hieroglyphic variants respectively (cf. Laroche, *RA* 41:77–8 [1947]; Kammenhuber, *HOAKS* 441, 473; Tischler, *Glossar* 374). The absence of initial plene-spellings (*i-is-*) on the one hand, and conversely the frequent length-marking of the stem vowel (*ishā-*) may indicate that the source of *isha-* or *esha-* had less than full-grade vocalism in the initial syllable. Such assumption of substratal origin would imply that the term originated in religious language rather than as a secular title (cf. voc. sg. *isha-mi* addressed to deities of both sexes).

ishahru-, eshahru- (n.) 'tear(s), weeping', nom.-acc. sg. or pl. *ishahru* (e.g. *KUB* XVII 9 I 20–22 *kuwat-wa wēskisi nu-wa-ta--kkan suppayaza* [IGI.HI.]*A-wa-za ishahru parā āras*[*zi*] 'why do you keep wailing and tears flow from your pure eyes?'; XXXVI 25 IV 4–5 *nu wēskizzi ishahru-ma-ssi-kan* P[Aₛ.HI.A-*us*] *mān arsanzi* 'he keeps wailing, and his tears flow like channels'; cf. Laroche, *RHA* 26:73 [1968]; XXXIII 113 + I 29–30 *nu-ssi-kan ishahru* [*par*]*ā* PAₛ.HI.A-*us mān arsanzi*; cf. Güterbock, *JCS*

6:12 [1952]; similarly VIII 48 I 18; cf. Friedrich, *ZA* 39:18, 45–6, 77 [1930]; Laroche, *RHA* 26:18 [1968]; *KBo* XV 10 I 6 7 *ishahru isnas* 'seven tears of dough'; cf. Szabó, *Entsühnungsritual* 12; *KUB* VIII 38+XLIV 63 III 20–21 *namma-an āandaz* A-*az ishahru ... arha ānaszi* 'he wipes off his tears with warm water'; cf. Burde, *Medizinische Texte* 30; XL 65+I 16 III 7 [OHitt.] *ishahru-smi*[*t ... sa*]*nhun* 'I sought your tears'; cf. Kühne, *ZA* 62:257 [1972]; XXXIII 66 II 13 *ishahru dais* 'tears he put' [into submarine copper cauldrons with leaden lids, besides ibid. 12 *ēshar dais* 'bloodshed he put', and a number of other bad things ibid. 10–15]; cf. H. A. Hoffner, *JNES* 27:65 [1968]; XXX 31+ XXXII 114 I 49–50 ANA DINGIR.MEŠ-*ma-kan mahhan ishahru danzi n-at hanti* DUB.2.KAM 'how they take tears from the gods, that [is written] separately [on] a second tablet'; cf. ibid. 12–13, 20–21, 28–29; Lebrun, *Hethitica II* 95–6; *KBo* XII 8 IV 32 *i*]*shar ishahru* 'blood [and] tears'; cf. Carruba, *Anatol. Stud. Güterbock* 78), *ēshahru* (*KUB* VII 41 Vs. 18–19 *idālu papratar* NIŠ DINGIR-*LIM ēshar hurtain* [*kurkurain*] *ēshahru wastain* 'evil defilement, perjury, blood[shed], curse, mutilation [?], tears, [and] despoliation'; cf. Otten, *ZA* 54:116 [1961]), gen. sg. *ishahruwas* (XXXI 77 I 7 SISKUR *ishahruwas* 'ritual of weeping'; cf. Otten, *Puduhepa* 14 [1975]), *ēshahruwas* (254/d, 11; cf. Lebrun, *Samuha* 189), dat.-loc. sg. *is-ha-ah-ru-ú-i* (*KBo* XI 1 Vs. 45 *idala*]*ui hurtāi ēshanī ishahruui*; cf. Houwink Ten Cate – Josephson, *RHA* 25:108 [1967]), instr. sg. *ishahruit* (*KUB* XLIII 60 I 21–22 *n-as ishahruit walhanza* 'she [was] hit by [a fit of] weeping'), abl. sg. *ishahruwaz* (XV 42 II 9–11 *sumes-a* DINGIR.MEŠ-*as idāla⟨wa⟩z uddānaz linkiyaz hurdiyaz ēsha⟨na⟩z ishahruwaz* QATAMMA *parkuwaēs ēstin* 'you gods, too, be likewise clean of evil business, perjury, curse, blood [-shed], [and] tears'; similarly XXX 31+XXXII 114 I 15–17; cf. Lebrun, *Hethitica II* 95), *ishahruwaza* (XXX 33 I 10 EME-*za ishanaza ishahruwaza linkiy*[*aza* 'from obloquy, blood[shed], tears, [and] perjury').

ishahruwant- (c.), nom. sg. in 2083/g, 8–9 *nu kūn* EN.SISKUR *namma* [*ish*]*ahruwanza haratnanza le* [*epdu* 'may weeping (and) scandal no further seize this sacrificer' (cf. Laroche, *BSL* 57.1:29 [1962]).

ishahru-, eshahru-

ishahru(w)ai- 'weep', (denom. like Gk. δακρύω or Lat. *lacrimā-*), 3 sg. pret. midd. in *KUB* I 16 II 6 ŪL *ishahruwattat* 'he did not weep', matching ibid. I 6 (Akk.) [*dim*]*āti-šu ūl išpuk* 'his tears he did not shed' (cf. Sommer, *HAB* 2–3, 36–7; Neu, *Interpretation* 74); partic. *ishahruwant-*, nom. sg. c. *ishahruwanza* (XXXIII 87+ I 30–31 *nu* ᴰU-*as* IGI.HI.A-*wa ishahruwanza* 'the storm-god, weeping his eyes [out]'), *ishahruanza* (XLIII 60 I 21 *annas* DINGIR-*LIM-as ishahruanza* 'the mother of the god [was] weeping'). Formed like e.g. *genzuwai-* from *genzu-* or *saruwai-* from *saru-* (cf. Alp, *Anatolia* 2:22–3 [1957]).

There is uncertainty about *KUB* XXX 33 I 9 *apās-ma* LUGAL-*i iyauwan* (with gloss-wedges) *ishahru halz*[*āi* 'that one calls on the king to shed tears' (?); cf. VIII 38+XLIV 63 III 10 *nasma-as ishahru iya*[*uw*]*an marruwasha*[*n dāi*?] 'or he (applies?) "red" to induce lacrimation' (?; cf. Burde, *Medizinische Texte* 30); possibly supine of *iya-* 'do, make' (cf. verbal noun *iyauwar*, inf. *iyauwanzi*), thus *ishahru iya-* 'shed tears', like *ēshar iya-* 'shed blood'? Here may be another supine not formed from an iterative (cf. *karīpuwan, tarahhūwan, parhuwan, hannuan, wassūwan, ninkuwan*; Kammenhuber, *MIO* 3:40 [1955]), and at last one not used in inchoative periphrasis with *dai-* or *tiya-*.

Indo-European 'tear' words are mostly (except Slavic [Russian *slezá*] and Albanian [*lot*]) traceable to **daḱru-* (< **draḱru-*; Gk. δάκρυ, Lat. *lacruma,* OIr. *dēr*, Goth. *tagr*, OHG *zahar*), **draḱur* (Arm. *artawsr*), **draḱnu-* (OHG *trahan*), **aḱru* (Ved. *áśru*, Avest. *asrū-*, Toch. A *ākär* [pl. A *ākrunt*, B *akrūna*], Lith. *ašarà*). E. P. Hamp, who in a series of studies examined these words (cf. *Glotta* 50:291–9 [1972], with back references), explained **aḱru* via false sandhi division from **tod dáḱru* (*Studies in historical linguistics in honor of G. S. Lane* 152–3 [1967]; in reality this is an old idea, among other abortive explanations [cf. Walde – Hofmann, *Lat. etym. Wb.* 746]).

ishahru is clearly the basic spelling, with the occasional *ēshahru* influenced by the proximity of *ēshar* on the "calamity lists" (e.g. *KUB* VII 41 Vs. 18–19, quoted above); hence the *i-* may be phonetically and/or orthographically prothetic (cf. e.g. *ishiya-*), and a possible reconstruction is **sH₁aH₁ru-* (cf. E. P.

Hamp, *Glotta* 50:298–9 [1972]). Oettinger (*Stammbildung* 367) posited *ishahru* < *$sA_1ak̑ru$ (*s*-mobile + [A_1]*ak̑ru*, with *h* < *k* as in occasional *hazhara-* < *hazgara-*), where the attestation of *s*-mobile before laryngeal would be chiastically proportionate to Hitt. *he(w)u-* : Toch. A *swase*, OPruss. *suge* 'rain' (*[*s*]E_2*ew*-*H_2*-*). In that case *$A_1ak̑ru$ can hardly be a secondary aberration from *$dak̑ru$ (the *a*- vocalism of the latter being also unexplained); there is rather *(s-)$A_1ak̑ru$- besides *(d-)$A_1ak̑$-*ru* > *$dak̑ru$-, but with occasional *A_1 > *r in some forms of Indo-European (Arm. *artawsr* < *$drak̑ur$, OHG *trahan* < *$drak̑$-*nu*-), comparable to the Hittite alternation *wahnu-* : *warnu-*; another trace of such "*d*-mobile" may be seen in Lith. *ìlgas* 'long' besides the more usual *d*- forms (Skt. *dīrghá-*, etc.), or in Ved. *áhar* 'day' beside OE *dōgor*. *$A_1ak̑ru$- conceivably has basic truck with *$ak̑ri$-, *ak̑ro* (Skt. *áśri-* 'edge', Gk. ἄκρις 'point, peak', Lat. *ācer*, Lith. *ašrùs*, OCS *ostrŭ* 'sharp'), in the sense of 'bitter, acrid (fluid)' (cf. the universal cliché 'bitter tears').

Implausibly Sturtevant, *Comp. Gr.*[1] 143: *$esHru$-, perhaps reflected in Hitt. *ishahru*, "contaminated" with *$dak̑ru$, yielded *$ak̑ru$-; W. Petersen, *Lg.* 10:319 (1934): *eshahru* < *$esharhu$, comparing Lith. *ašarà*; E. Sapir, *Lg.* 15:181 (1939): *$ěsxn̥$-*$xk̑ru$ 'blood' + 'acrid', with *$xák̑ru$ 'tear' < 'acrid', *^wdr-*$xák̑ru$ 'water-acrid' > IE *$d(r)ak̑ru$ (rejected by E. P. Hamp, *Beiträge zur Geschichte der deutschen Sprache und Literatur* [= *PBB*] 81:265 [Tübingen 1959]); V. Georgiev, *Acta Antiqua* 16:13–4 (1968): *$esHr̥$ *akru* 'bitter blood', besides *$udr̥$ *akru* 'bitter water' in *$d(r)akru$-, with loss of *u*- due to association with *$dr̥k̑$- seen in e.g. Gk. δράκος 'eye' (rejected by E. P. Hamp, *Glotta* 50:298 [1972]); Ivanov, *Studia linguistica in honorem acad. S. Mladenov* 477–83 (1957), adduced alleged Skt. *asram* 'tear' beside *áśru* (cf. *asram* 'blood' beside *ásr̥g-*; but *asram* means rather 'pain, suffering', cognate with Avest. *angra-* 'evil'; cf. Mayrhofer, *KEWA* 3:638), while trying to justify *ishahru-* = /eshru-/ (cf. *túh-uh-s-* besides *túh-s-*, *e-es-ha-ha-at* besides *e-es-ha-at*, and the like) and Sapir's tie-in with 'blood'.

G. A. Kapancjan (*Chetto-Armeniaca* 84 [1931–3], *Khettskie bogi u armjan* 15 [1940], *Istoriko-lingvističeskie raboty* 1:348

[1956]) and G. B. Jahukyan (*Hayerenə ev hndevropakan hin lezownerə* 152 [1970]) compared *ishahru* with Arm. *ašxar* (Luwian-tinged loanword from Anatolian, besides inherited *artawsr?*); but the meaning of *ašxar* is 'grief, mourning' rather than 'tear'.

ishamai- (c.) 'song, melody' (sìR), acc. sg. *ishamain* (*KUB* XII 11 III 30–31 LÚsìR-*ma artari nu ŠA* DINGIR-*LIM ishamain* sìR-*RU* 'the singer stands and they sing the song of the god'), acc. pl. in X 7, 14–15 *mān ishama[us z]innanzi* 'when they finish the songs'.

ishamiya-, ishamai- 'sing; sing of' (sìR-*RU*, *ZAMARU*), 1 sg. pres. act. *ishamihhi* (XXXIII 96 I 4 ᴰ*Kum[arb]in ishamihhi* 'of Kumarbi I sing'; cf. Güterbock, *JCS* 5:146 [1951]), 3 sg. pres. act. *ishamai* (*Bo* 2819 II 6 *ishamai hatili* 'sings in Hattic'), 3 pl. pres. act. *ishamiyanzi* (e.g. *KUB* XX 28 IV 11, V 14 and 25; cf. ibid. III 5 sìR-*RU*= *IZAMMARU* 'they sing'; X 7, 13 sìR-*RU ishami[yanzi-ya* '[they] play and sing'), *ishamianzi* (e.g. XXV 37 II 30; cf. Bossert, *Asia* 109 [1946]; also passim in *KBo* XVII 74; cf. Neu, *Gewitterritual* 85); inf. *ishamiyauanzi* (*KUB* XXV 37 I 40; cf. *Dict. louv.* 172), *ishamiyauwanzi* (XXVII 1 IV 12; cf. Lebrun, *Samuha* 84); iter. *ishameski-, ishamiski-, ishamaiski-*, 1 sg. pres. act. *ishamiskimi* (XXVII 38 I 18), 2 sg. pres. act. *ishamiskisi* (XXXVI 12 II 9; cf. Güterbock, *JCS* 6:14 [1952]), 3 sg. pres. act. *ishamiskizzi* (ibid. 5), *ishamaiskizzi* (*KBo* III 40 I 13), 3 pl. pres. act. *ishameskanzi* (*Bo* 3143, 5), *ishamiskanzi* (e.g. *KUB* XII 5 I 10; cf. J. Danmanville, *RHA* 20:51 [1962]; XI 32 IV 14; XXV 37 II 19 and 27; *KBo* XXI 34 II 27; cf. Lebrun, *Hethitica II* 120), *ishamisganzi* (*Bo* 3316 VI 2), *ishamaiskanzi* (*KBo* XXIII 103 IV 16, vs. ibid. 19 *ishamiskanzi*; cf. Haas, *Nerik* 44); partic. *ishamiskant-*, nom.-acc. sg. neut. *is-ha-mi-is--kán* (*KUB* XXV 37 I 39).

Cf. Götze, *Madd.* 98; Ose, *Supinum* 34; Kammenhuber, *MIO* 2:54 (1954); Kronasser, *Etym.* 1:541, 314; Kümmel, *Festschrift H. Otten* 172–6 (1973).

ishamatalla- (c.) 'singer' (LÚsìR, Akk. *zammaru*), nom. pl. LÚ.MEŠ*is-ha-ma-tal-li-es* (*KUB* XVII 21 II 11 and III 19; cf. von Schuler, *Die Kaškäer* 154), acc. pl. LÚ.MEŠ*ishamātallus* (XXXI

394

124 II 17; cf. von Schuler, *Die Kaškäer* 156), *is-ha-ma-tal-li-lu-us* (sic XVII 21 III 5). Cf. Kronasser, *Etym.* 1:176.

ishamai- goes back to **ishama-* (Kronasser, *Etym.* 1:178, 206; cf. e.g. *hukmai-* vs. *hukma-talla-*). *ishamiya-* has intrusive stem variant *ishamai-* based on the noun, leading to contamination by *-hi* conjugation (3 pl. *ishamiyanzi* > 3 sg. *ishamai* > 1 sg. *ishamihhi* like *tiyanzi, dāi, tehhi*).

**ishama-* is connectible with the root of *ishiya-* 'tie, bind', *ishima(n)-* 'line, cord' (q.v.; c.f. e.g. Kronasser, *VLFH* 87, *Etym.* 1:178; Čop, *Die Sprache* 6:4–6 [1960]; R. Lazzeroni, *Studi e saggi linguistici* 7:53–55 [1967]). The semantic tie-in would be "rhapsodic" in the literal sense (cf. for the meaning Gk. ὕμνος in Hesiod, *Fragm.* 265 [Rzach] = 357 [Merkelbach-West] ὕμνοις ῥάψαντες ἀοιδήν; Skt. *sūtra-* 'thread' > 'canon', etc.). It must be of IE date, since it presupposes the root $*seE_2$- 'bind' (Vedic *sā-*) in a suffixed form $*séE_2$-*m-* (Ved. *sám-an-* 'song'), $*sE_2$-*ém-*, $*sE_2$-*om-*, $*sE_2$-*ṃm-* (> Hitt. *isham-*). From the same root is derivable Gk. οἴμη 'song, lay', °οἶμος 'id.' (*Hom. Hymn* 4.451 °οἶμος ἀοιδῆς), also 'stripe, strip, path', psilotic for °οἶμος (cf. φροίμιον = προ-οίμιον), if we posit $*sE_2$*om-y-* (cf. Benveniste, *BSL* 50.1:39–40 [1954], *Hittite* 10, 88; invalid objections in H. Wittmann, *Die Sprache* 19:41 [1973]; more cogent is the observation by R. S. P. Beekes, *Die Sprache* 18:127 [1972], that the outcome would be °οἶνος, like βαίνω < $*g^w$*ṃ-y-*). Yet οἶμος may also be from the same root in its other suffixed form ($*séE_2$-*y-*, $*sE_2$-*éy-*, $*sE_2$-*y-*, seen in Ved. *syáti* ' bind', Hitt. *ishiya-*, etc.), in which case we should posit $*sE_2$*oy-mo-* and compare ON *seiðr* 'line, rope; magic' ($*sE_2$*oy-to-*). Cf. also Ivanov, *Obščeindoevropejskaja* 16; Gusmani, *Lessico* 49; Oettinger, *Stammbildung* 465.

ishanittarātar (n.), (nom.)-acc. sg. in *VBoT* 2, 2–3 *man-wa-nnas ishanittarātar iyaweni* 'let us make i.!' (quoting a marriage proposal made to the writer concerning the writer's daughter; cf. L. Rost, *MIO* 4:328 [1956]).

Perhaps erroneous diplography for *ishani(ya)t(t)ar* (cf. Hrozný, *SH* 74), verbal noun from **ishanai-* or **ishaniya-*, related to *ishiya-, ishai-* 'bind' (q.v.) as an iterative (cf. e.g.

piddannai- from *pittai-*, s.v. *pi[y]ett-*), thus 'binding, bond, (marital) alliance' (cf. *ishiul* 'binding; treaty'; Skt. *bándhu-* 'relative, kinsman'; Gk. πενθερός 'wife's father'). Cf. Tischler, *Glossar* 382. Cf. perhaps *is-ha-ni-tar* (*KUB* XLIV 15 I 14), SAL *is-ha-ni-it-ta-ra-as* (*Bo* 4952 I 19), *ishanittari-mi[* (*Bo* 2850, 11).

Misrendered as 'blood-tie' since Hrozný, *Journal asiatique* 218:314 (1931), especially by Benveniste (*Hittite* 101–2) who saw a denom. abstract (type of *uskiskitallatar*) from an **eshanittara-* 'blood relative' containing *eshar* 'blood' and IE **-ter-* of terms or relationship (cf. rare Hitt. *-tara-* in agent nouns, besides *-talla-*). Not only is *ishani-* unexplained as to form; there is simply no question of blood ties to the writer, merely of in-law relations extraneous to the writer's family (the bridegroom would be the writer's ᴸᵁ*kaena-* 'in-law', not even his LÚ *hassannas-sas* 'clansman').

ishanattalla- (c.), nom. sg. *is-ha-na-at-tal-la-as* (*KUB* XXI 19 III 8) may be the productive agent noun from the same verb **ishanai-* (cf. e.g. *ishamatalla-* 'singer' from *ishamai-* 'sing'). Literally 'binder', possibly 'the one who marries off a daughter' (vel sim.; cf. ibid. 7 DAM-*YA* 'my wife'). *ishanalli-* (c.), nom. sg. *is-ha-na-al-lis* (1490/u, 11 *n-as-mu ishanallis estat*; cf. ibid. 12 *ishanattallas*) must have similar yet distinct meaning.

isharisk(i)-, isharesk(i)-,   3 sg. pres. midd. *is-ha-ri-is-kat-ta-ri, is-ha--ri-es-kat-ta-ri* (*KBo* XXII 114, 5–6 U]KÙ-*an* ᴰ*Ishara[z...]* [...-]*as ishariskattar[i*; ibid. 8–9]ᴰ*Ishara mān* UKÙ[-...] [...] *ishariskat[tari*; ibid. 11–12]UKÙ-*an* ᴰ*Ishar[az ...]* [... *is*]*hareskattari*).

Interpretation hinges on *KUB* XXX 26 I 1–2 *mān* UKÙ-*an* ᴰ*Isharaz* GIG-*zi n-as isharishari namma-as aki* 'if it ails a man from the goddess Isharas, and he ?, (but) then he dies ...' (cf. Otten, *Totenrituale* 100; Neu, *Interpretation* 75; Burde, *Medizinische Texte* 15), where *isharishari* is preceded by what looks like an erasure for the determinative D(INGIR). Such a 3 sg. pres. midd. from a stem *isharish-* is strange, whether based on a denominal abstract noun **isharesha-* from *Ishara-* (Laroche, *JCS* 21:177 [1967]), or a deverbative **isharisha-* from a denominal verb *ishariy(a)- (Oettinger, *MSS* 34:135, 148 [1976]), or an *isharesha- from an inchoative *ishares-(ski-) (Tischler, *Glossar* 383–4), or haplologically on an iterational *ishar-ishar--ari (Kronasser, *Etym.* 1:548). More probably isharishari is a product of scribal absent-mindedness, i.e. rote repetition of signs is-ha-ri-is-ha-ri in lieu of the intended is-ha-ri-is-kat-ta-ri.

But a denominative mediopassive verb ishariya- (iter. ishar-iski-) 'be Ishara-ized' is itself odd and pleonastic; it has to mean something more and other than 'be zapped by Isharas' (which is already expressed by UKÙ-an ᴰIsharaz GIG-zi). Possibly ishariskattari, ishareskattari, rather than being denominative, is a compound of ⁽ᴰ⁾Ishara- and 3 sg. pres. midd. iskattari of iski(ya)- 'smear, daub' (as in *IBoT* III 148 I 67 and 68), meaning thus 'is administered the (antidotal) Ishara-salving', on the ethnomedical principle ὁ τρώσας ἰάσεται; the ministrant of such (apparently often futile) countermeasures may have been the is-ha-ra-al-li-is of *KUB* XXX 28 + XXXIX 23 Vs. 13 and 16 (cf. Otten, *Totenrituale* 94, 144, and e.g. parnalli- 'houseboy' from parn- 'house'). On Isharas see Laroche, *Recherches* 51, and Burde, *Medizinische Texte* 12–6; she was a destroyer-healer of Sumerian-Hurrian provenance, ambivalent in the manner of the Greek Apollo or the Vedic Rudra-Śiva, neither 'goddess of medicine' (Laroche) nor necessarily exclusively baleful (Burde).

ishawar, ishaur (n.), nom.-acc. sg. ᴳᴵˢis-ha-a-u-wa-ar (fragmentary *KUB* XXXIII 81 I 3, followed ibid. 4 by 1 ᴳᴵˢŠUDUN 1 ᴳᴵˢAPIN 'one yoke [and] one plow'; cf. Laroche, *RHA* 23:80 [1965]), ᴳᴵˢis-ha-u-wa-ar (XLIII 34,5, and in 702/z, 3 ishauwar--samit), nom.-acc. pl. ᴳᴵˢis-ha-a-ur-ra or ᴳᴵˢishāurr-a with 'and' (*KBo* XXIII 52 III 3–6 nu kuissa ᴸᵁALAM K[AxUD ishā]ur harzi ᴳᴵˢishāurra[... K]Ù.BABBAR-it halissian 1 GÍN.GÍN [KI.LAL Á]ᴹᵁˢᴱᴺ-ŠUNU laksenis-(s)mis-a Z[ABA]R 'each actor holds an i.; the i.'s [are] plated with silver; their eagle-weight is one shekel, and their l. [is] of bronze').

Judging from the contexts, the object may have been a mythically conceived or ritually displayed and manipulated (miniature) yoke-plow set, intrinsically wooden but ornamentally encased or elaborated with metals, thus perhaps literally 'tie-in, combination', detailed as '1 yoke + 1 plow'. Such a dual contraption is reminiscent of the talismanic golden plough-yoke combination (ἄροτρόν τε καὶ ζυγόν) which fell from the heavens in the Scythian legend of origins (Herodotus 4:5).

Conceivably isolated verbal noun from *isha- 'bind' beside ishiya-, ishai-; just as the latter two stems match Ved. present syáti and perfect (si)ṣāya respectively, *isha- represents a thematization of the non-suffixed root *seE₂- 'bind', thus *sE₂-é/ó-, besides the nonthematic Vedic aorist stem sā- (see s.v. ishiya-). A parallel verbal noun *ishatar may underlie the possible infinitive ishanna in KUB XXI 38 Vs. 14 apedas-an-kan kuwapi UL GAM-an isha[nn]a tarahmi 'whereas I cannot join him to those [in marriage]' (cf. W. Helck, JCS 17:88 [1963]; R. Stefanini, Atti ... La Colombaria 29:6–7 [1964]).

ishiya-, ishai- 'bind, wrap; obligate with, impose upon' (Akk. rukkusu [rakāsu] in KBo I 38 Rs. 5 and 7; also Akk. emēdu, KUB III 119 Vs. 10 ishiyan harta = III 14 Vs. 9 immidu 'had imposed'; cf. Friedrich, Staatsverträge 1:6), 1 sg. pres. act. ishihhi (KBo XVIII 74, 2), 3 sg. pres. act. ishāi (e.g. KUB XIII 15 Rs. 4 [= Code 2:58] sēpan ishāi 'he binds sheaves'; XII 58 III 26 ser anda] ... ishāi 'she wraps up'; cf. Goetze, Tunnawi 18; KBo X 45 II 12 anda ishāi; cf. Otten, ZA 54:122, 148 [1961]), ishiyazi (XXI 34 I 58; cf. Lebrun, Hethitica II 119), ishiyazzi (KUB XXXIV 26, 16), ishiyezzi (XXXIII 67 I 5; cf. Laroche, RHA 23:135 [1965]), 3 pl. pres. act. ishiyanzi (e.g. XVII 12 III 18 ŠU.HI.A ishiyanzi 'they tie the hands'), ishianzi (e.g. KBo VI 2 IV 43 [= Code 1:94] tepu-ssi ishianzi 'they impose little on him'), ishanzi (e.g. VI 2 IV 42 [= Code 1:94]), also misspelled ishianza (VI 26 II 6 [= Code 2:58]), 1 sg. pret. act. ishiyanun (e.g. III 3 I 18 nu-ssi ... ishiul ... ishiyanun 'I placed an obligation on him'; cf. H. Klengel, Orientalia N.S. 32:34 [1963]), ishihhun (III 4 III 26 and 31 nu-smas-kan ERÍN.MEŠ ishihhun 'I imposed troop-levy on them'; cf. V 8 II 3; Götze, AM 74, 76, 152), ishihun (KUB XXI 48 Rs. 7), 3 sg. pret. act. ishiyat (e.g. KBo VI 29 II 35 n-an ishiyat n-an-mu parā pesta 'she bound him and handed him over to me'; cf. Götze, *Hattusilis* 50), 2 pl. pret. act. *is-ha-is-te-en* (XII 22, 11 *nu-mu*]*-ssan kī iukan ishaiste*[*n* 'you have bound this yoke on me'; cf. Otten, *ZA* 55:158, 163 [1962]), 3 pl. pret. act. *ishiyer* (VI 34 I 26), 2 pl. imp. act. *is-hi-ya-at-tin* (X 45 II 8 GÌR.M]EŠ-*ŠÚ* ŠU.MEŠ-*ŠÚ ishiyattin* 'bind [its] feet and hands'; cf. Otten, *ZA* 54:122 [1961]), 3 pl. imp. act. *ishiandu* (VI 34 I 24 ŠU.MEŠ-*ŠUNU ishiandu* 'they shall bind their hands'; cf. Friedrich, *ZA* 35:162 [1924]; Oettinger, *Eide* 6), *ishiyandu* (ibid. 28); partic. *ishiyant-*, nom. sg. c. in V 9 I 29–30 *arkammass-a-kan kuis* ... *ishiyanza ēsdu* 'the tribute which shall be imposed' (cf. Friedrich, *Staatsverträge* 1:12, 35), acc. sg. c. *ishiyantan* (e.g. XIX 145 III 39; cf. Haas – Thiel, *Rituale* 302), *ishiyandan* (e.g. ibid. 45; cf. Laroche, *RHA* 28:59–60 [1970]), nom.-acc. sg. neut. in e.g. V 1 II 30 *IŠTU* SÍG *anda ishiyan* 'wrapped in wool' (cf. ibid. 15 and Sommer – Ehelolf, *Pāpanikri* 6*), nom. pl. c. *ishiyantis* (*HT* 1 I 31; dupl. *KUB* IX 31 I 38; cf. B. Schwartz, *JAOS* 58:336 [1938]), *ishiyantes* (e.g. XV 11 II 6), nom.-acc. pl. neut. *ishiyanta* (IX 28 IV 2), *ishiyanda* (*KBo* XIV 23, 4; XV 48 II 13; XVII 1 IV 20; cf. Otten – Souček, *Altheth. Ritual* 36); verbal noun *ishiya(u)war* (I 38 Rs. 5 and 7; I 42 II 3), *is-hi-es-sa(r)* (n.), nom.-acc. sg. *ishessa-mitt-a* (*KUB* XXX 10 Vs. 7; *KBo* XXI 22 Rs. 45 *ishessa-ssit*; cf. G. Kellerman, *Tel Aviv* 5:200 [1978]; for dropping of *-r* cf. e.g. *hanessa*[*r*] s.v. *han-* and see s.v. *iyatar*), instr. sg. *ishesnit* (473/t Vs. 14; cf. H. A. Hoffner, *Essays on the Ancient Near East in memory of J. J. Finkelstein* 105 [1977]), *ishesnant-* (c.), nom. pl. *ishisnantes* (473/t Vs. 11 SA]G.DU-*ann-a ishisnantes appanzi* 'the bindings clasp the head'); iter. *ishiski-*, 1 sg. pres. act. *ishiskimi* (*KUB* IX 27+ VII 8 I 19; *KBo* XVI 24+25 I 51 *nu-s*]*mas ke* ᴰUTU-*ŠI kue ishiūl ishiskimi* 'the obligations which I the king am placing on you'), 3 pl. pres. act. *ishiskan*[*zi* (XVII 36 III 5; cf. Neu, *Altheth.* 123), 3 pl. pres. midd. in *KUB* XXV 17 I 5 UR.MAH.HI.A *kuedani pidi ishiskanta* 'to the spot where the lions are bound ...' (cf. Neu, *Interpretation* 74). Cf. Kronasser, *Etym.* 1:486, 302, 289.

ishima(n)-, *ishiman(a)-*, *ishimen(a)-*, *ishamin(a)-* (c.) 'string, line, cord, rope, strap' (*ishimanas* = Akk. *eblu* in *KBo* I 45 Vs. 1), nom. sg. ᴷᵁŠ*ishimās* (XVII 15 Rs. 11 1 ᴷᵁŠ*ishimās INA*

ishiya-, ishai-

SAG.DU-*ŠU nēanza* 'one [leather] strap [is] placed around [the cow's] head'; cf. V. Haas – M. Wäfler, *Ugarit-Forschungen* 8:82 [1976]; Neu, *Altheth.* 73), acc. sg. *ishimanan* (XX 40 V 9), *i]shimenan* (988/u, 7), *ishaminan* (*KUB* XVII 27 II 31–32 *n-an ishaminan* GIM-*an anda taruppeskit* 'he folded it up like a rope'; cf. ibid. 34 and Götze, *KlF* 222), instr. sg. *ishimanit* (*KBo* XVII 60 Vs. 3), *ishimanda* (*KUB* XVII 28 I 31), *ishimanta* (XVII 5, 15; cf. Laroche, *RHA* 23:67 [1965]), abl. sg. *ishimanaz* (XXXVI 55 II 16), nom. pl. ᴷᵁˢ*ishimānes* (*KBo* XVII 15 Rs. 10 [OHitt.]). For the declension, cf. e.g. nom. sg. *haras*, gen. sg. *haranas*, nom. pl. *hāranis*; that the word is basically an -*n*- stem is proved by the instr. sg. *ishimant/da* (cf. *KUB* XII 21, 11 *istamanta*, XIII 4 III 47 *wedanda*; see e.g. Ehelolf, *IF* 43:316–7 [1926]; Friedrich, *HE* 57–8, 45). Possible deriv. adj. *ishammenas*[*si*- 'rope-related, line-shaped, funiform, restiform' (VIII 75 I 49), cf. ibid. 56 the gloss-wedged (Luwoid) form *ashaimmattanassis* (but contrast Luw. *hishiya*- 'bind'). Cf. Kronasser, *Etym.* 1:182, 195–7, 228; Laroche, *RHA* 9:20 (1948); Souček, *Arch. Or.* 27:8, 10, 380 (1959); Oettinger, *Gedenkschrift für H. Kronasser* 165–8 (1982).

ishiyani- (c.) '(body-)hair', nom. pl. *ishiyanius* (*KUB* XIII 19, 5), *is-hi-e-ni-us* (XIII 4 III 62). Cf. Ehelolf, *KlF* 150–1; Sturtevant, *JAOS* 54:364, 386 (1934); Kronasser, *Etym.* 1:222.

ishiyal- (n.) 'bond, band, belt', nom.-acc. sg. (also pl.?) neut. *ishiyal* (*KUB* VII 53 I 13; *KBo* III 34 I 20 TÚG-*ZUNU* ᵀᵁᴳ*ishial-semett-a kuit natta esha*[*s*]*kanta* 'how come their garment[s] and their belt[s] [are] not bloodied?'), abl. sg. *ishiyalaz* (e.g. *VBoT* 120 III 2–3 *ishiyantan-ma-an-kan ishiyalaz arha lāwen* 'we freed him who was bound from the bond'; cf. Haas – Thiel, *Rituale* 144). Especially 'head-band', = ᵀᵁᴳBAR.SI, cf. *KUB* IX 15 III 2–3 *nu-smas* SAG.DU.MEŠ *IŠTU* ᵀᵁᴳBAR.SI BABBAR *anda ishiyanzi* 'they wrap their heads with a white band'. Cf. Goetze, *Tunnawi* 4, 49–50, *Sommer Corolla* 50, 61–2; Kronasser, *Etym.* 1:323.

ishiul- (n.) 'binding; obligation, injunction; statute; treaty', nom.-acc. sg. (also pl.) neut. *is-hi-ú-ul* (e.g. XIV 12 IV 29–31 *nu-kan* ... [*ish*]*iūl istarni-summi ishiyat* '[he] concluded a treaty between them'; cf. Güterbock, *JCS* 10:98 [1956]; *KUB* XIX 29

IV 9 *ŠA ABI-ŠU-ya-wa-za ishiūl IDI* 'he knew his father's injunction'; cf. Götze, *AM* 18; VI 44 IV 23 *ishiūll-a ēs[du* 'let [it] be [your] injunction'; cf. Friedrich, *Staatsverträge* 1:138; XIX 49 I 60–61 *nu-tta] zilatiya kī ishiūl ēsdu* 'let this in the future be your treaty'; cf. Friedrich, *Staatsverträge* 2:10), gen sg. *is-hi-ú-la-as* (e.g. XIX 49 IV 52; XXI 1 II 8; cf. Kühne – Otten, *Šaušgamuwa* 24–5, on *ishiulas tuppi* 'treaty-tablet'), *ishi]ullas* (XXI 5 II 15; cf. Friedrich, *Staatsverträge* 2:18, 58), nom.-acc. pl. neut. *is-hi-ú-li*HI.A (XXXII 133 I 4). Perhaps borrowed in OAssyr. *ishiul(l)um* (Kültepe) 'wage-agreement' (cf. e.g. Landsberger, *Arch. Or.* 18.1–2:342 [1950]; N. van Brock, *RHA* 20:114 [1962]; Kronasser, *Etym.* 1:138). Cf. Kronasser, *Etym.* 1:325; V. Korošec, *Hethitische Staatsverträge* 21–35 (1931).

ishiulahh- 'bind by treaty; enjoin, instruct', 3 pl. pres. act. *ishiul(l)ahhanzi* (e.g. *KBo* II 2 IV 35 *asi* INIM SUM-*annas kissan ishiulahhanzi* 'the aforementioned matter of giving they enjoin thus'; *KUB* V 3 I 9, 34, etc.; cf. Götze, *AM* 249–50), 1 sg. pret. act. in *KBo* IV 4 III 68 *nu-za* ᴰUTU-*ŠI* KARAŠ.HI.A *ishiullahhun* 'I, my majesty, enjoined the armies' (cf. Götze, *AM* 132); partic. in *KUB* XIII 35 I 31 *apedani-ya memini ishiulahhanza* 'instructed in this matter'. Cf. Kronasser, *Etym.* 1:428.

ishuz(z)i- (c.) 'band, belt, girdle', nom. sg. *ishuzis* (*KBo* XII 126 I 18; cf. Jakob-Rost, *Ritual der Malli* 22), acc. sg. *ishuzzin* (e.g. *KUB* II 6 IV 6 *nu-za ishuzzin* KÙ.BABBAR ... *dāi* 'he takes a silver belt'), gen. sg. (?) *ishuzziass-a* (*KBo* XVI 78 IV 11), *ishuzziyas* (VI 26 II 19–20 [= *Code* 2:75] *ishuzziyass-a ŪL kuiski epzi* 'and none will seize by the belt', lit. '[what is] of the belt'). *ishuzziya-* 'to gird', 3 sg. pres. act. *ishuzziyaizzi* (*Bo* 2839 III 27–28 *ishuzzin-a-za-kan ishuzziyaizzi* 'girds himself with a belt'; cf. Haas, *Nerik* 260), 3 sg. imp. act. *ishuziddu* (*KBo* XII 126 I 19); partic. *ishuzziyant-* (e.g. *KUB* IX 28 I 16 SÍG ZA.GÌN *ishuzziyanza* '[she is] girt with blue wool'; *HT* 1 I 32 IŠTU GÍR-*ya-ssan kuyēs ishuzziyantes* 'those girt with sword'; *Bo* 2721 II 6 TAHAPŠI *ishuzziyan harzi* 'he has girded himself with a t.'; cf. Goetze, *Sommer Corolla* 48, 58). Cf. J. Holt, *Bi. Or.* 15:149 (1958); Kronasser, *Etym.* 1:241. For an alternative postulation of a verbal noun *ishuzzi(y)assa(r)* see Neu, *Festschrift für G. Neumann* 208–9 (1982).

Luw. 3 pl. pres. act. *hishiyanti* (*KUB* IX 31 II 24; cf. B. Schwartz, *JAOS* 58:340 [1938]), matching Hitt. partic. nom. pl. c. *ishiyantis* (IX 31 I 38; ibid. 336). Cf. Otten, *LTU* 16, *Bestimmung* 44–5; *Dict. louv.* 46. Also Hier. *hishimin* (1 pl.?; cf. Meriggi, *Manuale* 1:61, 64; Laroche, *HH* 22).

The *i*- in *ish*- is either phonetically or orthographically prothetic (cf. e.g. Kronasser, *Etym.* 1:48). Cf. IE *seE_2- 'bind' (*IEW* 891–2; Ved. *ásāt* 'he bound', *sā́tum* 'to bind', RV *ava-sātár-* 'unbinder'), suffixed *$séE_2$-*y*- (Avest. *hāy-* 'bind'), *sE_2-é*/*óy*- (Ved. *sayatvám* 'binding', RV *setár-* 'binder', *sétu-* 'bond', Lat. *saeta* 'coarse hair, bristle', ON *seiðr* 'line, rope; magic', *seil* 'cord, rope, fetter', Lith. *siẽti* 'bind', *saĩtas* 'band, string'), *sE_2-*y*- (Ved. *syáti* 'bind'), *sE_2-ī̆*- (Ved. *sitá-* 'bound' [unless from *sE_2-tó*-], Gk. *ἱμά̄ς* 'strap', Avest. *hinu-* 'bond, fetter', OE *sinu* 'sinew'; Skt. *sīmán-* 'parting of the hair; boundary', ON *sīmi*, OE *sīma* 'string, band, bond'). Speculations on further root extensions and cognates in Puhvel, *Lg.* 35:649–50 (1959) = *Analecta Indoeuropaea* 59–60 (1981), *LIEV* 39; cf. Cowgill, *Lg.* 39:256 (1963). See also s.v. *ishamai-*.

3 sg. *ishiyazzi* matches Ved. *syáti*; *ishāi* < *sE_2óye* (cf. RV perf. *sişāya*); Luw. 3 pl. *hishiyanti* shows an intensive reduplication characteristic of Luwian verbs (cf. e.g. *pipissa-*, *wiwidai-*; cf. *Dict. louv.* 143), repeating the second consonant of an initial cluster with *s*- (cf. Skt. *tíşţhati*); *ishima(n)*- < *sE_2ī̆-me*/*on*- (cf. Skt. *sīmán-*); for *ishiyani-*, cf. Lat. *saeta* 'bristly hair' (cf. Oettinger, *MSS* 35:101 [1976]); in *ishuzzi-* the non-suffixed zero-grade *sE_2*- > *ish*- may appear before the suffix *-uzzi-*, unless it be "reductional" for *ishi-uzzi-*.

Of the many discussions of this etymology, cf. e.g. Kuryłowicz, *Symbolae grammaticae in honorem Ioannis Rozwadowski* 101 (1927), *Études* 74; P. Kretschmer, *KlF* 10; Sturtevant, *Comp. Gr.*[1] 246–7; Couvreur, *Hett.* 197–8; Pedersen, *Hitt.* 114–5; Zgusta, *Arch. Or.* 19:453 (1951); Lehmann, *PIEP* 26; E. Risch, *Sommer Corolla* 194; Čop, *Die Sprache* 6:5–6 (1960); Kammenhuber, *KZ* 77:52–3 (1961); Mayrhofer, *IF* 70:248 (1965); G. Jucquois, *Orbis* 16:173–5 (1967).

Sturtevant's connection (*IHL* 51, *Comp. Gr.*[2] 51) of *ishai-* with Avest. *yāsta-*, Gk. *ζωστός*, Lith. *júostas* 'girt', etc. (*IEW*

513), involving an "Indo-Hittite" metathesis of laryngeal and accepted by Lehmann, *PIEP* 77, and E. Polomé, *RBPhH* 30:468 (1952), is unlikely.

Ivanov's suggestion (*Obščeindoevropejskaja* 89–90) that *ishiul* may be analyzed *ishiu-l* and compared with RV+ *syū́man-* 'band, thong, suture', *sū́tra-* 'thread', Gk. ὑμήν, etc., is improbable, since the suffix *-ul* is productive in Hittite (cf. Kronasser, *Etym.* 1:325–6) and there is no evidence of any Hittite verbal derivative of IE *sīw-, syū-* (*IEW* 915–6); for possible nominal cognates, see s.v. *suwel-* and *sum(m)anza(n)-*.

Cf. *sesha-*; *iyasha-*; *ishamai-*; *ishanittarātar*; *ishawar*; *ishunawar*.

ishunawar (n.) 'sinew, bowstring' (^UZU^SA?), nom.-acc. sg. *ishunauwar* (*KBo* X 37 II 32–33 *nu-ssi ishunauwar siyauwar pesten nu-ssi suhmilin* ... 'give him bowshot [lit. 'bowstring-shooting'; cf. *arkuwar tiyauwar* 'plea-presentation'], [give] him arrow'), *ishunāu* (secondary stem patterned on oblique cases, if correct in *KUB* VII 58 I 11 *is-hu-na-a-us-mi-it* GI-*za* 'their bowstring [and] arrow'), gen. sg. or pl. *ishunauwas* (571/u, 8 *ishunauwas* GI[G-*an* 'illness of sinew[s]'), *ishūnauwas* (*Bo* 2351 IV 5; 125/r II 7; cf. Otten, *MDOG* 93:76 [1962]; *KUB* IX 4 I 25), *ishunas* (IX 34 II 25; perhaps "compressed" or erroneous spelling), dat.-loc. sg. *is-hu-na-u-i* (XXV 37 II 8), *is-]hu-na-ú* (*Bo* 2139 + *KUB* IX 4 I 6; cf. *ZA* 71:130 [1981]). Deriv. noun (with "animate" *-nt-* extension) *ishunauwant-* (c.) 'sinew', nom. sg. in IX 4 I 25 *ishunauwanza ishūnauwas* GIG-*an* 'sinew (will take away) illness of sinew'. Cf. Laroche, *OLZ* 57:30–1 (1962), *BSL* 57.1:28 (1962). Alp (*Anatolia* 2:21–4 [1957]) wrongly posited 'abdomen, trunk'. Kronasser (*Etym.* 1:251, 260, 429, *WZKM* 62:312 [1969]) persisted in translating by 'upper arm'.

ishunawar follows the declension pattern of the great mass of neuters in *-war* (Kronasser, *Etym.* 1:297–308) but has no truck with the verb *ishuna(hh)-* or *iskuna(hh)-* (q.v.; wrongly Kronasser, *Etym.* 1:302). Laroche (*OLZ* 57:31 [1962]) first suggested a connection with IE 'sinew' seen in Ved. *snā́van-*, Avest. *snāvarə*, Toch. B *ṣñaura*, Arm. *neard*, Gk. νευρά, Lat. *nervus*.

ishunawar   ishuwa(i)-

Perhaps *ishunawar* < **ishnawar* (with *u* anaptyxis in cluster
before labial *w*) < IE **sH₁nówr̥* (as conceivably in Vedic and
Avestan under "Brugmann's law" [*ā* < **o*], as an alternative to
**sH₁néwr̥* or **sH₁newr*-). IE **snēw*- (*IEW* 977) as an extension
of **snē*- (*IEW* 973; Skt. *snā́yu*- 'sinew', Lat. *neō* 'spin', etc.)
must give way to **sH₁new*-, or possibly **snew*- if **snawar* < IE
**snówr̥* was "contaminated" with forms of *ishiya*- 'bind' (q.v.;
ish- < **sE₂*-), e.g. *ishuzzi*- 'band' (*IEW* 891; cf. OE *sinu* 'sinew',
Skt. *syáti* 'bind', etc.); such folk-etymological interference
would then also account for the *u* of *ishunawar*. Gusmani's
assumption (*KZ* 86:266 [1972]) of "laryngeal metathesis" in
/ishnau/ < **snoH-w*- is improbable. Cf. Oettinger, *MSS*
35:93–7 (1976); Puhvel, *Bi. Or.* 38:351 (1981). L. Isebaert (*KZ*
96:59–60 [1982/3]) wrongly compared Skt. *sā́nu*- : Gk. νῶτον
'back'.

    Cf. *istagga*-.

ishuwa(i)- 'shed, throw, scatter, pour', *arha ishuwa(i)*- 'throw
away, dump, discard, jettison', 1 sg. pres. act. *ishuwahhi* (*KUB*
XV 11 II 8–9 [*nu*] ANA DINGIR-*LIM* ᴰᵁᴳ*harsiyalli* INA ᵁᴿᵁKÙ.
.BABBAR-*ti* Ù INA ᵁᴿᵁ*Hakmis ishuwahhi* 'to the(e,) goddess, I
shall pour into a pithos at Hattusas and Hakmis'; cf. P.
Cornil – R. Lebrun, *Orientalia Lovaniensia Periodica* 3:49
[1972]; A. Archi, *Ugarit-Forschungen* 5:16 [1973]; IX 25 +
XXVII 67 I 3 [bis]), *ishuhhi* (e.g. XXXI 84 III 62–63 NUMUN-*wa*-
-*mu pai nu-war-at-za-kan ammel* A.ŠÀ-*ni-mi* [*an*]*da aniyami
namma-wa ishuēssar ishuhhi* 'give me seed[grain], and I shall
plant it in my field, and further scatter[-sow] it copiously' [figura
etymologica, see sub verbal noun *ishuessar* below; cf. Laroche,
RA 43:73 [1949]; von Schuler, *Dienstanweisungen* 49, 57), 3 sg.
pres. act. *ishuwai* (e.g. *KBo* II 9 IV 5 EGIR-*ŠÚ-ma-kan memal* ANA
TÚL *anda ishuwai* 'thereafter he throws groats into the well';
KUB XXIX 1 IV 18–19 *nu hurpastanus arha* ŪL *ishuwai* '[the tree]
does not shed its leaves'; cf. B. Schwartz, *Orientalia* N.S. 16:38
[1947]; XXIV 9 II 19–20 *pūrut ser ishuwai nu istalakzi* 'she
pours on clay and smoothes [it]'; cf. Jakob-Rost, *Ritual der
Malli* 34), *ishuwāi* (e.g. *KBo* V 2 II 19–20 *memall-a arha ishuwāi*

'pours away groats'; cf. ibid. 20 *ser suhhai* 'pours on'; *IBoT* II 39 Rs. 26 and 27 *ser ishuwāi; KBo* XXIII 10 IV 22 *ser ishuwāi;* ibid. 18 *hūmanta ishuwāi* 'pours all things'; cf. Otten, *Materialien* 38), *is-hu-u-wa-i* (e.g. *KUB* II 7 I 12 *t-as-kan* íD-*i anda ishūwai* 'he throws them [viz. ibid. 4 *passilus* 'pebbles'] into the river'; cf. S. Košak, *Ling.* 16:62 [1976]; XLIV 61 Rs. 10–11 *petesni-ma-ka*[*n* ...] *ser anda ishūwai* 'but into the hole he pours in above'; cf. Burde, *Medizinische Texte* 20; VII 54 III 19–21 EGIR-*anda-ma-kan* GIŠBAN *huittiyanzi nu-kan* GI.Ú.TAG.GA *ti-yanzi* GI.Ú.TAG.GA.HI.A-*ma piran katta ishūwai* 'afterwards they stretch the bow and place the arrow, and it sheds forth arrows'), *is-hu-u-wa-a-i* (e.g. XLIV 63 II 19 *n-at-kan kattanta ishūwāi* 'pours it underneath'; cf. Burde, *Medizinische Texte* 30; XXXVI 89 Vs. 9 NINDA.KUR₄.RA-*kan* KAŠ GEŠTIN NÍG.GIG *tepauwaza hattesni* GAM-*anda ishūwāi* 'thick bread, beer, wine, liver in small amounts he pours down into the hole'; cf. Haas, *Nerik* 142; *KBo* XIX 128 I 14–16 *purpurus* GA.KIN.AG GIŠ*INBI.HI. .A* NINDA-*ya* ŠAPAL LUGAL *ishūwāi* 'one scatters lumps [of] cheese, fruits, and bread under the king'; cf. Otten, *Festritual* 2, 25, and X 24 IV 26–28 *nu* LÚ GIŠPA *paizzi* NINDA*purpurus* LUGAL-*i kattan suhhai* 'the staff-man goes and scatters bread-lumps under the king'; XXI 17, 14–15 *anda lāhui* [...*i*]*shūwāi* 'pours in [a liquid] ... pours'; cf. Burde, *Medizinische Texte* 36; *KUB* XXVII 29 I 12–14 *n-at-kan dampūpi* UKÙ-*si* TÚG*seknus ishūwāi auszi-ma-at* ÚL *kuiski n-at-kan* íD-*i anda ishūwāi* 'then she throws a cloak on the bumpkin; but nobody sees it, and he [?] throws it into the river'; cf. Haas – Thiel, *Rituale* 134–6), *is-hu-ú-a-i* (dupl. *KBo* XXIII 23 Vs. 59 [*n-at-kan*] íD-*i pidai n-at* íD-*i* EGIR-*an* [*ish*]*uuai* 'takes it to the river and throws it back of the river'), *is-hu-i* (II 3 II 31–32 SÍG ZA.GÌN-[*y*]*a-kan pessiyazi karsann-a-kan anda ishui* 'she tosses [away] the blue wool and throws the cut [portion] in[to the doughbowl]'), *is-hu-u-wa-a-iz-zi* (*HT* 5, 6 -*kan* IZI-*i ishūwāizzi* 'throws into the fire'), 1 pl. pres. act. *is-h*[*u-wa*]-*wa-a-ni* (*KUB* XXXII 117 Rs. 10 + *KBo* XIX 156 Vs. 18; cf. Neu, *Altheth.* 222), 3 pl. pres. act. *ishuwanzi* (e.g. *KUB* XV 34 IV 45 *kattan ishuwanzi*; cf. Haas – Wilhelm, *Riten* 206; *IBoT* III 148 III 9 GAM-*anda ishuwanzi*; cf. Haas – Wilhelm, *Riten* 222; *KUB* XXIX 1 III 21 *mān-kan samanus-ma*

ishuwa(i)-

ishuwanzi 'but when they pour the foundations'; cf. B.
Schwartz, *Orientalia* N.S. 16:34 [1947], and the synonymous
Akk. *uššē nadū*), *is-hu-u-wa-an-zi* (e.g. *KBo* IV 1 Vs. 2 [*n-*]*asta
mahhan samanus ishūwanzi*; cf. Witzel, *Heth. KU* 76; *HT* 1 IV 9
]*weteni anda* MUN *ishūwanzi* 'they pour salt into the water'; *KBo*
XXI 34 II 33 ᴳᴵˢ*INBI.HI.A-ya-kan* ᴳᴵˢ*irhuuiti kattan ishūwanzi*
'and fruits they pour down into the basket'; cf. Lebrun,
Hethitica II 120; *KUB* XIII 4 IV 22–24 *sumel-ma-as-kan
halkius hūmandus arha danzi n-as-kan* DINGIR.MEŠ-*as* KISLAH.
.MEŠ-*as anda ishūwanzi* 'they will take away all your grains and
pour them into the granaries of the gods'; cf. Sturtevant, *JAOS*
54:392 [1934]; VII 24 Vs. 6 GIM-*an zenas* DÙ-*ri* ᴰᵁᴳ*harsiyali-kan
ishūwanzi* 'when fall comes, they pour into the pithos'; cf. A.
Archi, *Ugarit-Forschungen* 5:23 [1973]; XXV 44 II 29–32 *nu*
SAHAR.HI.A-*us sarā danzi n-as arha ishūwanzi kuedani-ma-as pidi
ishūwanzi n-at* ŪL *kuitki tuqqāri* 'they take up the cremains and
dump them; but on what spot they dump them, that is of no
account'), *ishūwānzi* (e.g. VII 49, 3 -]*asta* SAHAR.HI.A-*us parā
ishūwānzi*; XV 31 III 52 *kattan ishūwānzi*, with dupl. XV 32 IV
11 *i*]*shuwanzi*; cf. Haas – Wilhelm, *Riten* 164–5), *ishuwānzi*
(*KBo* XV 34 II 11–12 *n-as dammili-ya p*[*edi*] *pedanzi n-as arha
ishuwānzi* 'they take them to another place and throw them
away'), 1 sg. pret. act. *ishuhhun* (VIII 70, 6 *INBU-ya ishuhhun*
'and fruit I poured'; dupl. *KUB* XV 34 II 44 *ish*]*uhhun*; cf.
Haas – Wilhelm, *Riten* 194), *is-hu-u-uh-hu-un* (XVII 10 III 7 ŠA
ᴰ*Kamrusepa* UDU.NITA.HI.A-*ŠU ishūhhun* 'I have thrown the
rams of K.', viz. into the 'sieve of a thousand holes' [ibid. 6]; cf.
Laroche, *RHA* 23:94 [1965]), 3 sg. pret. act. *ishuwais* (*KUB*
XXXIV 26 Rs. 10–11 = *KBo* XIV 3 IV 35–36 *n-an arha
ishuwais* [...] ᴸᵁ́KÚR *sāruw*[*a...*] *ishuwais* 'jettisoned them ... the
enemy jettisoned the booty'; cf. Güterbock, *JCS* 10:76 [1956];
KUB XLIX 60 II 11 *nu pat*]*tar arha ishuwais* 'he discarded the
dish'), *ishuwas* (2030/c + 1703/c + Vs. 3b–4b [OHitt.] ᴰUTU-*us-
-wa-as* ᵁᴿᵁ*Lihzini wetet nu-war-us-za-kan ishuwas samānus* 'the
sun-god, he built for himself at L.; for himself he poured them,
the foundations'; cf. ibid. 1–2 *mān-asta sāmānus suhhanzi*
'when they pour the foundations'; Kammenhuber, *RHA* 20:2
[1962]), *is-hu-u-wa-as* (XXXIII 53, 13; cf. Laroche, *RHA*

23:141 [1965]), 3 sg. pret. midd. *ishuwaittat* (*KBo* VIII 96 Vs. 1 *ishu*]*waitta*[*t*, ibid. 2 *i*]*shuwaitt*[*at*), 3 pl. pret. act. *ishuwāir* (*KUB* XXIX 54 IV 5 and 11; cf. Kammenhuber, *Hippologia* 228; XXVI 84 II 9 *n-an-kan arha ishuwāir* 'and they discarded it'), *is-hu-u-wa-a-ir* (dupl. *KBo* XIV 1 II 12–14 *nu-kan* ABU-YA [... *arha*] *ishūwauw*[*an dāis n-an-kan arha*] *ishūwā*[*ir* 'my father began discarding ... and they discarded it'; cf. Güterbock, *JCS* 10:64 [1956]), 3 sg. imp. act. *is-hu-wa-a-ú* (*KUB* XXXIII 93 + III 24 'let him scatter [gods down from heaven like birds]'; cf. Güterbock, *JCS* 5:152 [1951]); partic. *ishuwant-*, nom. sg. c. *ishuwanza* (e.g. *KBo* XXIII 10 IV 20 *nu-kan* 7 ^{NA_4}*passilas anda ishuwanza* 'seven pebbles [are] thrown in'; cf. Otten, *Materialien* 38), nom.-acc. sg. neut. *ishuwan* (e.g. *KUB* I 13 III 13–14 *nu-smas kez* ŠÀ.GAL *ishuwan kez-ma-as arranza halkis ishuwan* 'on one side feed is poured for them, but on the other washed barley is poured for them'; cf. Kammenhuber, *Hippologia* 64), *ishuwān* (e.g. *KBo* V 2 I 27–28 and 28–29 MUN ŪL *ishuwān* 'salt not added'; *KUB* XV 34 I 10; cf. Haas – Wilhelm, *Riten* 182), *is-hu-u-wa-an* (e.g. *KBo* V 1 II 23 *zíz ishūwan* 'spelt [is] poured'; ibid. 35 ^{GIS}*INBI.HI.A ishūwan* 'fruits [are] poured'; cf. Sommer – Ehelolf, *Pāpanikri* 6*, 8*; *KUB* XII 1 IV 22 NA$_4$ *arha ishūwan* 'stone[work] discarded'; cf. S. Košak, *Ling.* 18:102 [1978]), *is-hu-u-wa-a-an* (e.g. *HT* 5, 7 MUN *ishūwān*; *KUB* XLII 11 II 14 and 15 *anda ishūwān*; cf. P. Cornil – R. Lebrun, *Orientalia Lovaniensia Periodica* 6–7:101 [1975–6]), nom. pl. c. *ishuwantes* (e.g. *KBo* XV 10 I 2–4 *nu-ssan kedani* 7 EME *isnas ishuwān kedani-ya-ssan* 7 EME *isnas ishuwantes* 'into one [is] thrown seven tongues of dough, and into the other [are] thrown seven tongues of dough'; cf. Szabó, *Entsühnungsritual* 12), *is-hu-u-wa-an-te-es* (e.g. *KUB* XXXVIII 12 III 10–11 *arha-at ishūwantes esir* 'they [viz. the old icons] had been discarded'; cf. M. Darga, *RHA* 27:7 [1969]; *KBo* II 6 I 11–12 *katta ishūwantes*; *KUB* IX 28 I 13 *anda* KÙ.BABBAR TUR 7 NA$_4$.HI.A TUR *ishūwantes* 'thrown in [are] a small [piece of] silver [and] seven small stones'); verbal noun *ishuwawar* (n.), gen. sg. *is-hu-wa-wa-as* (*Bo* 2351 IV 12–13 GAM-*an ishuwawas* GAM-*an ishūwanzi* 'what is to be thrown down they throw down'; cf. Ehelolf, *ZA* 43:191 [1936]), *is-hu-wa-u-wa-as* (*KUB* XII 2 II 6 EZEN *zēni ishuwauwas*

ishuwa(i)-

'feast of [leaf-]shedding [?] in the fall'; misspelled ibid. IV 2
is-hu-u-wa-u-hu-u-wa-as [!]), *is-hu-u-wa-u-wa-as* (X 92 VI 13
kat]*tan ishūwauwas ishūwanzi*); supine *is-hu-u-wa-u-wa-an* (*KBo*
XIV 1 II 13, quoted sub 3 pl. pret. act. *ishūwāir* above); verbal
noun *ishuessar* (n.) '(out)pouring, heap', nom.-acc. sg. neut.
ishuēssar (*KUB* XXXI 84 III 63, quoted sub 1 sg. pres. act.
above, in the figura etymologica *ishuēssar ishuhhi* 'pour a heap',
i.e. 'scatter copiously'), *is-hu-u-e-es-sar* (119/w Rs. 5–6 *ammel*
A.ŠÀ A.GÀR-*as anda* [...] [... *ish*]*uwēssar ishūwa*[- 'in my field
[and] meadow ... scatter copiously'; cf. Otten, *Sprachliche
Stellung* 10), dat.-loc. sg. *ishuesni* 'in a heap, copiously' (*KBo*
XVI 60 Rs. 5 [SA]L.SUHUR.LÀL.HI.A *ishuesni* 30 ... 'hierodules in
a bunch, thirty'; cf. Werner, *Gerichtsprotokolle* 48; *KUB* XIV 1
Vs. 7–8 *nu-tta* ^{GIŠ}GIGIR.HI.A [...] ŠE.HI.A NUMUN.HI.A *ishuesni*
pi[*es*]*kit* KAŠ GEŠTIN.HI.A-*ya-tta* BULÙG BAPPIR.HI.A *IMZA* [GA.
.KIN.AG.HI.]A *ishuesni pis*[*kit*] 'he gave you chariots ... [and]
seedgrains in a heap, and he gave you beer [and] wine, malt
[and] barm, rennet [and] cheeses in a heap'; cf. Götze, *Madd.* 2,
62–4), instr. sg. *ishuēsnit* 'heapwise, copiously' (XIII 2 III
36–38 *nu-ssi-ssan ishuēsnit* NUMUN.HI.A-*it* GUD UDU IGI.HI.A-*wa*
harak namma-an-kan IŠTU GA.KIN.AG *IMZI* SÍG.HI.A *asnut* 'see to
his needs copiously with seed[grain], cattle, sheep; also keep
him happy with cheese, rennet, wool'; cf. von Schuler, *Dienstanweisungen* 48, 57); iter. *ishueski-, ishuiski-, ishuwaiski-,* 3 sg.
pres. act. *ishueskizzi* (XXIX 40 IV 22; cf. Kammenhuber,
Hippologia 188), *is-hu-u-wa-is-ki-iz-zi* (X 72 II 24; *KBo* X 47c,
26; context s.v. *akkus*[*s*]*a*), 3 pl. pres. act. *is-hu-is-kán-zi* (*KUB* I
1 IV 73 ^{DUG}*harsiyali-ya-kan ishuiskanzi* 'and they are pouring
[into?] jar[s]'; cf. Götze, *Hattusilis* 38); iterative-"durative"
ishuwan(n)a-, 1 sg. pres. act. *ishuwannahhi* (e.g. VII 5 II 29–30
memallass-a damāi ishuwannahhi 'of groats I pour another
[portion]'; XII 44 III 17 *ishuwannah*[*hi*), 3 pl. pres. act. in XII
58 III 15–16 *n-an* ÍD-*i* [*ishuwa*]*nanzi* 'they throw it into the river'
(?; cf. Goetze, *Tunnawi* 16, who read [*ishun*]*nanzi*).

    ishuwa(i)- is close in meaning to *suhha-* (q.v.; used interchan-
geably in e.g. *KUB* VI 46 IV 54 *ser ishū*[*wai*] and dupl. VI 45 IV
54 *ser suhhai*) but distinct from *lah(h)u(wai)-* 'pour (liquids)',
although some overlap occurs with e.g. wine and salt and with

reference to the emptying of vessels; it is also distinct from *pessiya-* 'throw, toss' and *ispar-* 'spread'.

ishuwa(i)- is plausibly a denominative verb from a noun **ishu(wa)-* matching either Gk. ἰός (< **ἰσϝός*) or Skt. *işu-*, Avest. *išu-* 'arrow' (note *KUB* VII 54 III 21 GI.Ú.TAG.GA.HI.A- -*ma piran katta ishūwai* 'sheds forth arrows'); cf. Skt. *işyati*, *işnä́ti* 'impel', and perhaps Gk. ἰνάω 'empty out, purge', IE **E₁ey-s-(A₁-)* (the laryngeal is present in Ved. *iş-ṇ-á́ti*, *işitá-*). The original paradigm *ishuwaizzi* (cf. *HT* 5, 6 *ishūwāizzi*) : *ishuwanzi* has been analogically revamped to *ishuwai* : *ishuwanzi* under *-hi* conjugation influence (co-occurrence of e.g. *pittaizzi* and *piddāi* beside *piddanzi*). Cf. Kretschmer, *KlF* 10; Sturtevant, *Lg.* 4:160 (1928), *TAPA* 60:28 (1929), *Lg.* 6:151–2 (1930); Couvreur, *Hett.* 222; Hendriksen, *Untersuchungen* 30, 36.

The attempt by Kuryłowicz (*Symbolae grammaticae in honorem Ioannis Rozwadowski* 102 [1927]) to combine both *ishuwa-* and *suhha-* (via "laryngeal metathesis") with Skt. *suváti* 'set in motion' proved abortive (for Skt. *suváti* see rather s.v. *suwai-*); yet efforts have persisted to join etymologically *ishuwa-* and *suhha-* (e.g. Oettinger, *Stammbildung* 503). Schmitt-Brandt's (*Entwicklung* 67) hesitant adduction of IE **seu-* 'press, squeeze' (Skt. *sunóti*), even combining Gk. ὕει 'it rains' and Hitt. *sishau-* 'sweat', is best forgotten.

isiya(hh)- 'announce, betoken, reveal'; *(appa) isiyahh-* 'disclose, expose, denounce, inform on, "finger"'; *isiya-* is attested only in verbal noun *isiyatar* (n.) in *KUB* XVIII 61, 7 *kuit isiyatar* SIxSÁ-*at* 'what revelation had been established'; 3 sg. pres. act. *i-si-ya-ah-hi* (*HT* 20, 4; *KUB* XLIII 77 Vs. 14; ibid. 15 *isiyah[hi*), 3 sg. pres. midd. *isiyahtari* (XIII 9 + XL 62 III 17–18 *appizziyann-a uttar isiyahtari* 'and afterwards the matter is revealed'; cf. von Schuler, *Festschrift J. Friedrich* 448 [1959]; *KBo* XXVII 16 Rs. 8–9 *a[ppi]zziann-a uttar isiyahtari*; cf. Otten, *in Florilegium Anatolicum* 275 [1979]; XV 11 IV 8 IŠTU M]UŠEN.HI.A *isiyahtari* 'is revealed by birds'; cf. Kümmel, *Ersatzrituale* 70; dupl. *KUB* XLI 24 Rs. 4 *isiyahtari*), 2 sg. pret.

isiya(hh)-

act. *isiyahta* (619/u, 3–5]*kuit* IZKIM-*ahhuwar* [...] *zik* ᴰUTU AN
EN-*YA* [... HUL]-*lu isiyahta* 'which omen-giving [...] thou, sun-
god of heaven, my lord [...] hast betokened evil'; cf. Kümmel,
Ersatzrituale 18), 3 sg. pret. act. *isiahhis* (*KUB* XXXVI 104 Vs.
11 [OHitt.] and dupl. *KBo* III 34 I 13 [later copy] *s-an* LÚ
ᵁᴿᵁ*Huntarā isiahhis* 'a man from H. informed on him'; cf.
Kümmel, *Ersatzrituale* 162), *isiyahta* (e.g. *KUB* XIV 4 IV
25–26 *eni-wa kuit* ᴰUTU-*us sakiyahta* [*ŠA* SAL.LUGAL-*war-at*
isiy]*ahta ŪL-wa ŠA* LUGAL-*pat isiyahta* 'the omen which the sun-
god gave betokened [something] for the queen, it did not
betoken [anything] for the king'; V 9 Vs. 6 DINGIR-*LUM eni*
kuitki isiyahta 'has the deity in any way denounced this?';
ibid. 12–14 GUD-*wa-kan* UKÙ-*si ser watkut* 1 GUD-*ma-wa-kan*
ᴳᴵˢ*hurki ser watkut mān* DINGIR-*LUM kī-pat isiyahta nu*
ᴹᵁˢᴱᴺ*HURRI* NU.SIG₅-*du* 'a bovine leaped at a man, but one
bovine leaped on a wheel; if the deity has denounced this, let
the oracular bird be unfavorable!'; cf. ibid. 17–18 GUD.HI.A-*wa*
kuēs wasteskir nu-war-as-kan ŪL kuennir DINGIR-*LUM eni kuitki*
sanahta 'the bovines who did abomination, they did not kill
them; has the deity avenged that in any way?'; cf. G. F. Del
Monte, *AION* 35:339 [1975]; XVI 34 I 9–10 DINGIR-*LUM asi*
marsastarin isiyahta 'the deity has exposed this fraud'; ibid. 16
DINGIR-*LUM asi marsastarrin isiyahta*; cf. Del Monte, *AION* 35:
330, 346 [1975]; V 11 I 27, 30, 44; ibid. IV 50; V 24 II 18; VI 31
IV 12), *i-si-ah-ta* (XXIV 5 Vs. 9 [*zik-wa* ᴰ*SIN* EN-*YA kuit*
IZKI]M-*ahta nu-wa mān ammel* HUL-*lu isiahta* 'as for the fact that
you, moon-god my lord, have given an omen, if you have
betokened evil for me ...'; cf. Kümmel, *Ersatzrituale* 8; ibid. Rs.
13–14 ᴰ*SIN* EN-*YA isiahta-wa* (sic, pro correct dupl. XXXVI 94
Rs. 9 IZKIM-*ahta-wa*) *kuit nu-wa mān ammel* HUL-*lu isiahta*; cf.
Kümmel, *Ersatzrituale* 12; V 22, 19–22 *asi kuis halwassis* ANA
IR-*TI ŠA* ᴰUT[U-*ŠI*] ... *kuitki isiahta nu-wa* MUŠEN.HI.A SIxSÁ-*andu*
nu MUŠEN.HI.A [...] *namma-smas-at eseskir iparwassiss-a* IZKIM-
-*aht*[*a* ...] *ŠA* ᴰUTU-*ŠI-pat ŠA* NÍ.TE-*ŠU kuinki piddulian isiyah*[*ta*
'as for this oracular bird who at his majesty's request ...
revealed something, let the birds confirm it! And the birds ...
then did it for them, and the northwesterly one [?] gave a sign
...; it revealed some anguish of his majesty's being'), 3 sg. pret.

midd. *isiyahtat* (XVI 31 III 4–5 *kī-kan* GIM-*an* ŠA ᴰUTU
ᵁᴿᵁTÚL-[*na*] ŠÀ Ù-*TI isiyahtat* 'as this was revealed by the sun-
goddess of Arinna in a dream'), 3 pl. pret. act. *i-si-ya-ah-hi-ir*
(V 20 I 3), *i-si-ya-ah-ir* (V 22, 33); verbal noun *i-si-ya-ah-hu-u-*
-wa-ar (V 11 I 57), gen. sg. *isiyahhuwas* (XXXVI 127 Vs. 13–15
KU]R ᵁᴿᵁ*Hatti idālu takkiszi nassu* [KUR ᵁᴿᵁ*Mit*]*ttanni* [...
¹*Sun*]*assuras-an istamassi n-at-kan* [...] [...] *āppa isiyahhu*[*was*
'[if someone] plots evil against Hatti or Mitanni, [and you,] S.,
hear of him ... it is [your duty] to inform [on him]', lit. 'it is [for
you a matter] of informing'; cf. Neu, *Interpretation* 75–6), dat.-
loc. sg. *isiyahhuwanni* (VI 4 II 10 ᴰ∪ ᵁᴿᵁ*Neriqqa kuit isiyah-*
huwanni ser SIxSÁ-*at* 'because the storm-god of Nerik had been
singled out for purposes of revelation'); iter. *isi(y)ahhiski-*,
isiahheski-, *iseahhiski-*, 1 sg. pres. act. *isiyahhiskimi* (XIV 1 Rs.
45–46 *nu-wa-mu mā*[*n kururas*] *memian kuis* [*memai u*]*g-a-wa-*
-kan ANA ᴰUTU-*ŠI* Ū[*L kuitki sannaskimi namma-war-at*] *āppa*
isiyahhiskimi 'if someone says a word to me about hostility, I
shall not hide anything from his majesty, I shall moreover fully
disclose it'; cf. Götze, *Madd.* 30), 2 sg. pres. act. *i-si-ah-hi-is-ki-*
-si (XLVIII 123 I 16), *i-si-ah-hi-es-ki-si* (V 22, 52; cf. ibid. 51
i-si-ah-hi-es-ki[-), 3 pl. pres. act. *i-se-ah-hi-is-kán-zi* (*IBoT* I 33,
2–4 *kinun-ma-za namma kuit* IZKIM.HI.A H[UL].HI.A *kikkistari* ŠA
SAG.DU ᴰUTU-*ŠI* HUL *iseahhiskanzi* 'now what further evil
omens occur, for the head of my majesty do they betoken evil?';
cf. Laroche, *RA* 52:152 [1958]).

isiyahhiskattalla- (c.) 'denouncer, informer', nom. sg. *i-si-ya-*
-ah-hi-is-kat-tal-la-as (*KUB* XIV 4 III 14 and 16 ANA SAL.LUGAL
isiyahhiskattallas 'informer against the queen'), *i-si-ya-ah-hi-es-*
-kat-tal-la-as (*KBo* I 30 I 12–13, matching ibid. [Akk.] *ša ina*
nirti māu 'who is full of assassination'; cf. Güterbock, *MSL*
12:214–5 [1969]).

The transliterations *i-si-ah-*, *i-se-ah-* are used here rather
than *i-si-ih-*, *i-se-eh-*; but the latter are also possible, and
instead of a "glideless' spelling *i-si-ah-* one might alternatively
have expected *i-si-a-ah-*; *isihhis, isihta, isihheski-, isehhiski-* may
thus have formal reality.

The base-meaning 'seek (out), track down', posited by
Friedrich (*ZA* 37:197–9 [1927]), led to the tie-in with Skt. *iṣ-*,

isiya(hh)-

OCS *iskati* 'seek' (*IEW* 16) by Kuryłowicz (*Actes du Premier Congrès international de linguistes* 113 [1928], *Études* 75), which has enjoyed moderate assent (cf. Couvreur, *Hett.* 298; O. Szemerényi, *Glotta* 38:232–8 [1960], but also *Mélanges ... offerts à P. Chantraine* 246 [1972]; Oettinger, *Stammbildung* 457) but is effectively eliminated by the more precise semantics established by Kümmel (*Ersatzrituale* 18–9). The central sense is clearly 'announce' and in the mediopassive 'be revealed' (the latter similar in meaning to *istuwa-* 'be[come] manifest' [q.v.]).

The spelling is a notably uniform *i-si-*, where the constant *-s-* indicates [z] or [ž] or [dᶻ] which in Hittite is the outcome of **d(h)y* (cf. *asiwant-, sakui-, sehur* [s.v.]) and quite probably likewise of **g(h)y* (cf. Greek ζ and σσ/ττ). Thus a connection may be made with the Indo-Iranian root **adh-* seen in Skt. *ā́ha* (2 sg. *ā́ttha*) 'spoke', Avest. *āδa* 'spoke', OPers. *azdā* 'announcement' (< **adh-tā*), which O. Szemerényi (*Die Sprache* 12:206 [1966]) also tried abortively (as **edh-tu-* under "Bartholomae's law") on Hitt. *istuwa-*. An **edhyo-* 'announcement' would have yielded Hitt. **esa-* or **isa-*, whence a denominative verb *isiya(hh)-* 'make announcement' (cf. e.g. *lahhiyai-* 'go to war' from *lahha-* 'campaign', and *kururiya[hh]-* 'make war'). An *o*-grade parallel might be seen in Gk. ὄσσα '(divine or oracular) voice' from **odhyA_2*, usually reconstructed as **wokʷyA_2* but without firm digammatic evidence (Attic ὄττα like μέλιττα); with the Hittite ornithomantic usages one might compare ὄρνιθος ... ὄσσαν (Apollonius Rhodius, *Argonautica* 1:1087).

Yet the very absence of spellings with *e-* militates against **edh-*. It may therefore be advisable to postulate rather an **ēĝyo- > *isa-*, cognate with Gk. ἠ̂ 'he said', ἄνωγα 'bid', Lat. *aiō* 'say (yes), affirm' < **E₁ĝyō* (*IEW* 290–1), *adagium* 'proverb', *prōdigium* 'prophetic sign, portent'; except for the vowel grade, Hitt. **isa-* would be identical with Lat. *Aius* (*Locūtius*), the divine Voice who warned the Romans about the impending Gaulish invasion. The semantically related verb IZKIM-*ah(h)-* =*sakiyah(h)-* 'give an omen' (cf. Lat. *sāgus* 'presaging, prophetic') shows the historically more expectable treatment of *g+y* after heavy syllable under "Sievers's law"; but quite

412

plausibly the allophonic system of /y/ was morphophonemically disrupted in derivation layers, as conversely in Lat. *adagium* beside *Aius* after light syllable (*sakiyahh-* is a factitive formation with *-ahh-* from *sagai-* [gen. *sakiyas*] 'omen', whereas *isiya*[*hh*]- is a thematic denominative with suffix *-y-* from **isa-* < **ēĝyo-*).

Cf. *izziya-*.

iskalla(i)- 'slit, slash, split, crack, tear, rip, mangle', spelled *is-kal-*, 3 sg. pres. act. *iskallai* (*KBo* VI 4 I 38–39 *takku* ÌR-*an nasma* GEME-*an* GEŠTUG-*an kuiski iskallai* 'if someone slashes the ear of a male or female slave'), *is-gal-la-i* (ibid. 37 *takku* LÚ *ELLUM* GEŠTUG-*an kuiski isgallai* 'if someone slashes the ear of a free man'; cf. Friedrich, *Heth. Ges.* 52), *iskallāi* (*Bo* 2981 III 6), *is-kal-la-i-iz-zi* (*KUB* XII 58 II 16–17 *namma* TÚG.GÚ.É.A GE₆-*TI kue wassan harzi n-at-si-san* SAL^ŠU.GI *ser katta iskallayizzi* 'then what black shirt he has put on, it on him the old woman slits from top to bottom'; cf. Goetze, *Tunnawi* 14), 3 sg. pres. midd. *iskallari* (*KBo* VI 3 I 39 [= *Code* 1:16 [OHitt.] 'slashes', parallel to VI 4 I 39 above), *iskallāri* (dupl. VI 5 I 18; VI 3 I 37 [= *Code* 1:15, OHitt.], parallel to VI 4 I 37 above; dupl. VI 5 I 16), 3 pl. pres. act. *iskallanzi* (e.g. *KUB* XXX 19 I 43–44 + XXX 22, 8–9 ^GIŠ*tarsen-ma arha iskallanzi n-an-san hassī tianzi* 'but the tray they split in two and put it in the fireplace'; cf. Otten, *Totenrituale* 34), 1 sg. pret. act. *iskallahhun* (XIII 35 IV 24–25 *mān-ma-wa* ^GIŠPISAN *iskallahhun nasma-wa* ^NA₄KIŠIB *duwarnahhun nasma-wa-za dahhun kuitki* 'but if I have ripped the box or broken the seal or taken something for myself'; similarly ibid. 30–31; cf. Werner, *Gerichtsprotokolle* 12), 3 sg. pret. midd. *iskallatta* (*KBo* VIII 37 Vs. 9 and dupl. *KUB* XXIII 7 II 2, in fragmentary context; cf. Güterbock, *JCS* 10:99 [1956]), 2 sg. imp. act. *iskalli* (2030/c + 1703/c + Vs. 16b [OHitt.]), 3 sg. imp. act. *is-kal-la-ú* (XXX 36 II 9–10 *arha iskallau* 'let him split [wood]'), 3 pl. imp. act. *is-kal-la-an-du* (156/v, 7); partic. *iskallant-*, nom. sg. c. *iskallanza* (V 7 Rs. 6–8 3 *BIB*[*RU*] *IŠTU* NA₄ *arha ishūwan harkanzi* 1 *BIBR*[*U*] *arha iskallanza* 'three rhyta of stone they have thrown away, one rhyton [is] badly cracked'), nom. pl. c. *iskallantis* (ibid. Vs. 28–29 *iskallantis-wa-kan antuhses* ŠÀ É DINGIR-*LIM iyantat* 'slashed people came inside the shrine'), *is-kal-la-an-te-es* (ibid. 36 *-kan kukursantes iskallantes antuhses iyantat* 'mutilated [and] slashed people came'); inf. *iskalliyawanzi* (615/f I 13); iter. *iskalliski-, isgalleski-*, 3 sg. pres. act. *iskalliskizzi* (*KBo* III 21 I 6), 3 pl. pres. act. *iskalliskanzi* (*KUB* XXXIX 15 I 9–10 *nu* ^TÚG*kaparin* ZA.GÌN *udanz*[*i n*]*-an* ANA ALAM *piran arha iskalliskanzi n-an arha pessieskanzi* 'they bring a blue tunic [?] and before the picture tear it apart thoroughly and throw it away'; cf. Otten, *Totenrituale* 82), 2 sg. imp. act. *is-gal-li-es-ki* (IX 19, 6).

^TÚG*iskallessar*, ^TÚG*iskallissar* (n.), properly verbal noun 'slitting', hence 'slit dress', nom.-acc. sg. ^TÚG*is-kal-li-es-sar* (e.g. *KUB* XII 8 I 18; XIII 14 Vs. 10 [= *Code* 2:82]), ^TÚG*is-kal-li-is--sar* (dupl. *KBo* VI 26 II 50), *i*]*s-ga-al-li(s)-es-sar* (XVIII 187, 5). Cf. Hrozný, *SH* 71, *Code hittite* 139 (1922). For formation cf. ^TÚG*kuressar* 'headdress' (vel sim.), lit. 'cutting' (from *kuer-*).

In an inspired hunch already Hrozný (*SH* 71) tentatively connected ^TÚG*iskallissar* with IE **(s)kel-* 'split' (*IEW* 923–7), and Benveniste followed suit for the verb (*BSL* 33:139 [1932]), comparing Gk. σκάλλω 'hoe', Arm. *çelum* 'split', Middle Irish *sceilim* 'slice', ON *skilja* 'separate', Lith. *skélti* 'split'. In subsequent literature the only important addition was Frisk's adduction of ^GIŠ*kalmi-* (q.v.) as 'fire-log' (*Indogerm. 27 = Kl. Schr.* 57). Besides Arm. *çelum* (which exceptionally presupposes **sk̑-*), *skalim* 'split, be splintered' has also been compared (e.g. G. Kapancjan, *Chetto-Armeniaca* 127 [1933], *Istoriko-lingvističeskie raboty* 1:385 [1956]; T. Schultheiss, *KZ* 77:222, 225 [1961]). *iskalla-*, like Lith. *skélti* and *skìlti*, may point to **skel-H_2-* or **skl̥-H_2-* (cf. Oettinger, *MSS* 34:126–7 [1976]).

Relevance of the theonym *Iskalli* (paredros or epithet of ^D*Ursui*; cf. Laroche, *Recherches* 52, 63) is uncertain (might be rather *Isk-alli-*); thus A. H. Sayce's tie-in with Gk. γάλλοι 'eunuch priests of Cybele' as a Phrygian cognate (*Classical review* 42:161–3 [1928]) was highly speculative (by itself a Phrygian γάλλος might be cognate with Gk. κόλος 'docked, cropped, stunted', with some kind of voice confusion in borrowing [cf. Gk. κυβερνᾶν > Lat. *gubernā-*], ultimately from *[s]kel-* like Gk. σκῶλος 'pointed stake' or σκάλμη · μάχαιρα Θρᾳκία).

isgapuzzi-   (n.), nom.-acc. sg. hapax in a list of cult objects (*KUB* XII 8 I 16 1 *isgapuzzi,* besides ibid. 14 and 15 1 *tapulli* ZABAR 'one bronze cutter', ibid. 17 1 *warpuzi* ZABAR 'one bronze bathing-utensil', ibid. 18 1 ᵀᚢᴳ*iskallessar* 'one slit dress').

Instrument noun in *-uzzi-* (cf. e.g. *warpuzi-, ispanduzzi-*) from a verbal root *isgap-* (cf. Laroche, *JKF* 1:181 [1950]). It is conceivable that such a root should be accepted as spelled (3 sg. pres. act. *is-ga-a-pí*) in *KUB* X 63 I 26 *n-asta* ᴰ*Āpin ser* IŠTU NINDA KUR₄.RA *isgāpi,* rather than correcting *is-ga-a-pí* into *is-ta-a-pí* (assuming erroneous omission of the final vertical wedge of *ta* [or its haplography next to the initial vertical wedge of *a*], as in *a-ku-ga-al-* [see s.v. *akutalla-*]) and translating 'he stops up the pit with thick bread' (cf. e.g. XXXII 137 II 27 *nu-kan hattessar istāpi* 'he plugs the hole', and M. Vieyra, *RA* 51:88, 101 [1957]). Thereby a tie-in with the widespread IE **skep-* or **skebh-* (*IEW* 930–3) becomes possible, seen in Gk. σκάπτω 'dig, delve', Lat. *scabō,* OHG *scaban* 'scrape, grate', and we might translate 'he digs (or: scoops) over the pit' (using bread-fill). *isgapuzzi-* would then be the tool for such activity (cf. *kuruzzi-* 'cutter' from *kuer-* 'cut'), reminiscent of Lat. *scapula* 'scoop, shovel' (> 'shoulderblade'), *scāpus* 'stick, shaft', Gk. σκαπάνη 'shovel', σκηπάνη, σκῆπτ(ρ)ον 'stick, staff'; perhaps *isgapuzzi-* was (inter alia) the ritual utensil for filling in and smoothing over sacrificial pits, even as the rather heavy, knife-like *tapulli-* (q.v.) may have been a tool used to 'dig' or 'open' the same (cf. e.g. *KUB* XXVII 34 I 19 GÍR ZABAR TUR *dāi nu apez pedā*[*i* 'he takes a small bronze knife and with it he digs'; *KBo* X 45 III 22 ᴰ*Āpi* GÍR-*it ginuzzi* 'he opens up a pit with a knife').

Alternatively, a root *isgap-* can be compared with Ved. *skabh-* 'make firm, support', *skambhá-* 'pillar', besides *stabh-, stambha-* of similar meaning (q.v. s.v. *istap*[*p*]-); in this case Hitt. *istāpi : isgāpi* would match the Indic pair closely, and *isgapuzzi-* might resemble *istappulli-* 'cover, lid, stopper' in

isgapuzzi-   iskar-, iskar(r)a-, iskar(r)iya-

meaning and function. For such rhyming roots cf. IE **ster-* and **sper-* s.v. *ispar(r)-*.

iskar-, iskar(r)a-, iskar(r)iya-   'sting, prick, stab, pierce, skewer; stick, (af)fix, fasten, attach, set, post; (intransitive) stick, hew, cleave, cling (to)', 1 sg. pres. act. *is-kar-hi* (*KUB* XXXI 1 + *KBo* III 16 II 7 *ispannit iskarhi* 'I shall stab with a spit'; cf. Güterbock, *ZA* 44:52 [1938]), *is-ka-a-ar-hi* (*KBo* XVII 96 I 13–14 *nu-smas kattan* NA₄.HI.A *iskārhi* 'I stick stones beneath them [viz. clay-images of deities]'), 3 sg. pres. act. *iskāri* (XVII 13 + XXV 68 Rs. II; cf. Neu, *Altheth.* 144), *is-ka-ri* (XII 126 I 8 [*nu* AL]AM IM *arahzanda iskari* 'she sticks the clay figures all around'), *is-ga-a-ri* (dupl. XI 12 I 9 ALAM.HI.A *arahzanda isgāri*; dupl. *IBoT* II 123 I 9 *a*]*rahzanda isgār*[*i*; dupl. *KUB* XLI 2 I 4 *isg*]*āri*; cf. Jakob-Rost, *Ritual der Malli* 20; XII 58 II 29–30 *namma-ssi* GÌR.MEŠ *kattan* ᴰᵁᴳ[*hū*]*puwaiya isgāri* 'then beneath his feet she sticks the pot'; cf. Goetze, *Tunnawi* 14; *KBo* III 8 II 5–6 + *KUB* VII 1 II 40 *nu-kan anda* UZU *husu-y*[*a*] *isgāri* 'and in addition he also skewers raw meat'; cf. Kronasser, *Die Sprache* 7:150 [1961]), *is-qa-a-ri* (*VBoT* 24 I 45–46 [*kezz-iy*]*a* 7 ᴰᵁᴳGAL *isqāri* [*kezz-iy*]*a* 7 ᴰᵁᴳGAL *isqāri* 'on one side she sets seven goblets, and on the other side she sets seven goblets'; cf. Sturtevant, *TAPA* 58:8 [1927]; *KBo* XV 10 + XX 42 I 38 ALAM.HI.A [...] *isqāri*; ibid. III 28 *i*]*sgāri*; cf. Szabó, *Entsühnungsritual* 18, 38), *is-ga-ra-a-i* (*Bo* 2813 III 18 *ar*]*ahzanda isgarāi*; cf. Götze, *KlF* 409), *i*]*s-ga-ra-iz-zi* (*KUB* XLIX 94 III 14), 3 pl. pres. act. *is-ka-ra-an-zi* (XXXI 71 IV 26–27 ᴳᴵˢBANŠUR DINGIR-*wa kuwapi iskaranzi* 'where they set the table of the deity'; cf. Werner, *Festschrift H. Otten* 328 [1973]; *KBo* XVI 49 I 8–10 UDU.HI.A-*us* ᴸᵁ˙ᴹᴱˢMUHALDIM *appanz*[*i*] *t-us edi lūlias arhi* LUGAL-*i* [...] *iskaranzi* 'the cooks seize the sheep and post them on the far edge of the pond [in some relation to] the king'), *isgaranzi* (e.g. II 3 III 11 [*is*]*tarna-ma-kan* 7 ᴺᴬ⁴*huwasi isgaranzi* 'in between they set seven stone pillars'; cf. Hrozný, *Heth. KB* 82; L. Rost, *MIO* 1:362 [1953]; IV 9 I 22 NINDA *saramma isgaranzi* '[they] skewer palace-bread'; ibid. 23–24 ᴸᵁ˙ᴹᴱˢMUHALDIM-*ma-ssan* ᵁᶻᵁYÀ *zeyanta* NINDA *saramnas ser* *arha isgaranzi* 'the cooks cook meat-fat [and] skewer it on top of the palace-bread'; XV 9 IV 14; cf. Kümmel, *Ersatzrituale* 66), 3 sg. pret. act. *is-qa-ar-ri-it* (*KUB* XXXI 1 + *KBo* III 16 II 13 *ispannit isqarrit* 'stabbed with a spit'), 3 pl. pret. act. *is-ga-ri-ir* (*KBo* XXI 22 Vs. 6; cf. G. Kellerman, *Tel Aviv* 5:199 [1978]), *is-qa-ri-ir* (XV 10 II 1–2 *nu* ALAM.HI.A [... *p*]*edumen n-us dametani* ᴺᴬ⁴*p*[*ir*]*uni kattan isqarir* 'we brought the statues, and they fastened them down to another rock'; cf. Szabó, *Entsüh-nungsritual* 20); partic. *iskarant-*, nom. sg. c. *isgaranza* (*KUB* XV 5 IV 17 *IŠTU* ᴺᴬ⁴NUNUZ *isgaranza* 'set with beads'), acc. sg. c. *isgarandan* (*KBo* XVII 1 III 28 *isgarandan ūk kuin harmi* 'the attached which I hold'; cf. Otten – Souček, *Altheth. Ritual* 32), nom.-acc. sg. neut. *iskarān, isgarān* (e.g. *IBoT* I 36 II 60–62 *ŠA LIM ṢERI-ma kuis* ERÍN.MEŠ-*az nu taksulān tapusa isgarān harzi* GÙB-*las* GÙB-*laz iskarān harzi* [...] ZAG-*s-a* ZAG-*az iskarān harzi* 'but a soldier of the field-legion takes part [in the procession and] hews to one flank; one on the left cleaves to the left, and one on the right cleaves to the right'; cf. Houwink Ten Cate, *Symbolae ... Böhl ...* 206 [1973]; *KUB* XLII 78 II 11–12 1-*EN* AŠ.ME ᴺᴬ⁴ZA.GÌN *arahzanda* [...] NUNUZ GUŠKIN NA₄ *isgarān* 'one sun-disk, lapis lazuli all around ... set with beads, gold, [and] stone[s]'; ibid. 14 EGIR-*an isgarān* 'studded in back'; cf. Sommer, *ZA* 46:30 [1940]; S. Košak, *Ling.* 18:112 [1978]; XLII 11 I 8 *isgarān* 'set, studded'; cf. P. Cornil – R. Lebrun, *Orientalia Lovaniensia Periodica* 6–7:101 [1975–6]), nom. pl. c. *is-ka-ra--an-te-es* (XXXI 117 Vs. 4 [+ XXXV 93 Vs. 9]; cf. Neu, *Altheth.* 223), *is-ga-ra-an-te-es* (e.g. *Bo* 6594 I 10 EGIR-*ŠU isgarantes* 'hewing to [a position] behind her'; cf. Neu, *Altheth.* 99; *KBo* XXV 31 II 10; cf. Neu, *Altheth.* 79; XXV 42 1.Kol. 7; cf. Neu, *Altheth.* 81; X 27 V 15 *piran-set isgarantes* 'sticking to [a position] in front of him'; *KUB* XX 38 Vs. 10–11 SAL.MEŠ LUGAL-*i menahhan*[*da* ...] [*i*]*sgarantes* 'women cleaving to [a position] facing the king'; XXV 14 I 13 EGIR *isgarantes* '[sun-disks] studded in back'; cf. V. Haas – M. Wäfler, *Istanbuler Mitteilungen* 23–24:24 [1973–4]; XVII 25 I 11 *isgarante*[*s*), nom.-acc. pl. neut. *isgaranta* (e.g. *KBo* XI 45 IV 9–10 *nu* ᴳᴵˢPA *kue isgaranta* 'what [meats] are stuck on the staff'; cf. Haas, *Nerik* 234; *KUB* XI 23 V 5–7 DUMU É.GAL ᴳᴵˢŠUKUR *ANA* DUMU

iskar-, iskar(r)a-, iskar(r)iya-

LUGAL *pāi* DUMU É.GAL *ANA* ^D*Zittahari* SAG.DU-*az* NINDA.ERÍN.
.MEŠ *isgaranta-ya ser arha dāi* 'a page gives a spear to the
prince, and the page removes the army loaves which are stuck
on the [spear]head [as an offering] to Z.'; cf. A. M. Jasink
Ticchioni, *Studi classici e orientali* 27:159 [1977], with wrong
translation; XXIX 4 I 8 and 16 EGIR-*an isgaranta* '[objects]
studded in back' [with gemstones]; cf. Kronasser, *Umsiedelung*
6, 41; *KBo* XVII 1 I 19 *isgaranta dāi* 'takes what is attached'),
isgaranda (dupl. XVII 3 I 14; cf. Otten – Souček, *Altheth.
Ritual* 20); verbal noun *isgaratar* (n.) 'stabbing, sting', only in
the expression DINGIR.MEŠ-*as isgaratar* describing a "station" in
ophio- or ichthyomantic tanks used for MUŠ ('snake', i.e.
probably eel) divination, probably a symbolic 'sting (i.e. wrath,
vengeance) of the gods', nom. sg. *isgaratar* (*IBoT* I 33, lines 41,
55, 74), gen. sg. or dat.-loc. pl. *isgaranas* (ibid. 28), abl. sg.
isgaranaza (ibid. 23, 76; cf. Laroche, *RA* 52:152–4, 161 [1958]);
iter. *iskarreski-, iskariski-, isgareski-, isgariski-*, 3 sg. pres. act.
is-ga-ri-es-ki-iz-zi (*IBoT* III 98, 12 ^{NA₄}*kunnan isgareskizzi*
'attaches a bead'), *is-kar-is-ki-iz-zi* (ibid. 13 *apāt iskariskizzi*),
is-kar-ri-es-ki-iz-zi (ibid. 14 *apadd-a iskarreski*[*zzi*), *is-ga-ri-is-
-ki-iz-zi* (*KUB* XXXIII 98 I 9–10 *nu-za* ^D*Kumarbis* ZI-*ni kattan
hattatar* ^{NA₄}NUNUZ *mān isgariskizzi* 'K. sticks wisdom onto his
mind like a bead'; cf. Güterbock, *JCS* 5:146 [1951]), 2 sg. imp.
act. *isgariski* (XXVI 9 + 1256/1969 I 13–14 ^{LÚ.MEŠ}EN.NU.UN [...
i]*sgariski* 'post the watchmen'; cf. Otten, *Orientalia* N.S.
52:134–6 [1983]); iterative-"durative" *iskarranniya-*, 3 pl. imp.
act. *is-kar-ra-an-ni-an-du* (*KBo* VIII 35 II 21 GI.HI.A-*KUNU-ma-
-kan āppa* [*n*]*āu nu sumenzan-pat kir-semet iskarrannian*[*du*] 'he
shall deflect your arrows, and they shall be piercing your own
hearts'; cf. Oettinger, *Eide* 79).

The meaning 'sting, prick' is clearly basic and hence etymologically crucial; in *KUB* XXXI 1 + *KBo* III 16 II 7 and 13
(quoted above sub 1 sg. pres. *iskarhi* and 3 sg. pret. *isqarrit*)
iskar- is used of a spit (*ispatar*), next to *kuer-* 'cut' with some
knife-like tool, as a means of drawing blood.

The connection with IE **(s)ker-* 'cut' (*IEW* 938–47) was
made already by Hrozný, *Heth. KB* 82; besides the general
meaning (OHG *sceran* 'cut', OIr. *scaraim* 'sever', Lith. *skìrti*

418

'separate'), a nuance of tapered sharpness is found in e.g. ON *skera* 'cut, prick', and in OE *scear*, OHG *scar* '(plow)share'; noteworthy is the simultaneous absence of the "moveable" *s*- in Hitt. *kars*- and *kartai*- 'cut' (q.v.; cf. Gk. κείρω 'cut, shear', κουρά < *κορσά 'haircut, shorn locks'; Skt. *kṛt-* 'cut'). The meaning 'stick' is a secondary development, in Hittite and Germanic alike; for the intransitive sense 'cling to' the English glosses 'stick, hew, cleave' offer equally apposite semantic parallels.

Čop's comparison of *iskar-* with Gk. σκηρίπτω 'prop, plant' (*Indogermanica minora* 41–2) is unenlightening and improbable.

Cf. *iskaruh-*.

iskaruh-, iskarih-   (n.), a metal container used in libation (e.g. of iron in *KBo* XVII 74 I 14, of gold in XVII 75 IV 22, of silver and gold in 39/n, 5), employed especially to 'lift', i.e. retrieve (*ser ep*[*p*]-) or 'take in', i.e. collect (*anda ep*[*p*]-) the previously poured libamen, nom.-acc. sg. *iskāruh* (e.g. *KUB* XXVIII 104 IV 10–12 ANA ^LÚSANGA GAL-*ri pāi iskāruh dāi ta-sse-ssan* [*lā*]*hui* '[the cupbearer] gives a cup to the priest; he places an i., and he pours into it'), *isqaruh* (e.g. XI 18 IV 30 *isqaruh* NU.GÁL 'there is no i.' [while the king ibid. 29 toasts deities]), *isgaruh* (e.g. XXX 41 VI 17–18 and 21–22 ᴰU *ekuzi isgaruh* RIKU '[the king] drinks to the storm-god, the i. [is] empty'), *is-ka-ri-u-uh* (1008/c I 4), *iskārih* (*KBo* XVII 74 I 15–16 LUGAL-*i iskāri*[*h*] [*ep*]*zi* 'takes the i. from the king'; cf. Neu, *Gewitterritual* 12, 37; *KUB* XXVIII 104 V 15 *iskārih dāi*), *isqārih* (39/n, 5), dat.-loc. sg. *isqaruhi* (e.g. *KBo* XI 28 II 9, 20, 35, III 17, 35, 45, IV 5, 38 *isqaruhi-kan lāhūwan* 'there [is] pouring into the i.'; ibid. IV 16 *isqaruhi-kan lāhuwan*; dupl. *KUB* XX 26 I 4 [to *KBo* XI 28 III 45] *isqaru-kan lahūwan* [sic]; cf. Lebrun, *Samuha* 152–6), *isqaruh* (e.g. *KUB* II 3 I 29 *isqaruh* RIGA *anda epzi* 'collects in an empty i.'), instr. sg. *iskaruhit* (e.g. *KBo* XVII 75 IV 22 *iskaruhit* GUŠKIN ^GIŠAB-*ya piran sipanti* 'libates out the window with a golden i.'; cf. ibid. 29–30 *ispanduit* KÙ.BABBAR [...] *sipanti*), *isqaruhit* (e.g. *KUB* XXV 6 III 14–15 *isqaruhit* 1-*šu anda epzi* 'collects once with the i.'; dupl. XX 28 III 14), *isgaruhit* (e.g. ibid. 3–4; *KBo* X 25 I

20–21 *isgaruhit* GUŠKIN *RIKUTI ser epzi* '[the cupbearer] collects with an empty golden i.' [viz. that which the king has libated into a *huppar* 'στάμνος' ibid. 17–18]; *KUB* XXX 41 V 4–5 *isgaruhit sannapilit 2-ŠU ser epzi* 'retrieves twice with an empty i.'; ibid. 15–16 *isgaruhit sannapilit anda epzi*; ibid. VI 30 *isgaruhit* GEŠTIN *2-ŠU ser epzi* 'recovers wine twice with an i.'), *isgaruhida* (*IBoT* III 23 III 9–10 *piran isgaruhida sipanti*), *iskaruh* (e.g. *KBo* XX 61 III 46–47 DUMU É.GAL-*kan* GIŠ*luttiyaz arha iskaruh* GUŠKIN *sipanti* 'the page libates out the window with a golden i.'). Cf. Goetze, *Arch. Or.* 17.1:292–3 (1949); Kammenhuber, *MHT* 7, Nr. 5, 352–7 (1976).

The sum total of external characteristics (the unique stem-final *-h*, the variation *-uh-*, *-ih-*, the imperfect paradigmatic integration [occasional reluctance to inflect in dat.-loc. and instr.]) points to a technical loanword from another language, most plausibly Hattic (thus E. Hovdhaugen, *Norsk Tidsskrift for Sprogvidenskap* 25:121 [1971]). The root-connection with *iskar-* 'stick; sting' (q.v.), first suggested by Güterbock (*ZA* 44:61 [1938]) and occasionally repeated (e.g. Kammenhuber, *HOAKS* 286; Čop, *Indogermanica minora* 41, 51; Oettinger, *Stammbildung* 416, 547; V. Georgiev, *Linguistique balkanique* 23.3:10–11 [1980]) as implying a pointed vessel 'stuck' into something to hold it upright (cf. e.g. Kronasser, *Etym.* 1:329) has nothing but homophony in its favor, and derivation remains opaque: the adduction of deverbative Skt. *tanúḥ* (very hesitantly by Pedersen, *Hitt.* 186, who favored loanword origin) and the more sanguine comparison with Skt. *camúḥ* (a vessel, from *cámati* 'sip') by H. Eichner (*MSS* 31:89 [1973]) founder on the likelihood that Vedic *-úḥ* (like *-íḥ* in e.g. *vṛkíḥ*) contains $-A_2$ which disappears in Hittite (same as in thematic nom.-acc. pl. neut. $-a < -eA_2$); even if it were $-A_1$ (as in factitive *newahh-* : Lat. *novā-*), the outcome should be *-hh-* in oblique cases. Kronasser's postulation of hybrid IE root and foreign suffix (loc. cit. and *VLFH* 131) is not helpful.

iski(ya)- 'smear, daub, salve, oil, anoint' (YÀ), 1 sg. pres. act. *iskimi* (*KUB* XXIX 55 I 13–14 *namma* IŠTU YÀ UDU ANŠU.KUR.R[A.HI.A

...] *tepu iskimi* 'I also smear the horses a little with sheepfat'; cf. Kammenhuber, *Hippologia* 150), *isgāmi* (*KBo* III 8 II 19–20 [*n-an* EME-ŠU IŠTU YÀ.NU]N *isgāmi* 'I smear his tongue with butter'; cf. Kronasser, *Die Sprache* 7:155 [1961]), *isgahhi* (*KUB* VII 1 I 40 *n-an tuikkus isgahhi* 'I salve his limbs'; cf. Kronasser, ibid. 144), 3 sg. pres. act. *iskizzi* (e.g. *KBo* XIX 139 II 8–9 *mahhan-ma* [EN SISKU]R [*war*]*pūwaz uizzi nu-za iskizzi* 'when the sacrificer comes from bathing he anoints himself'; cf. Haas –Thiel, *Rituale* 268; ibid. III 8 *mān-za* EN SISKUR.SISKUR--ma iskizzi*; XVI 24 + 25 I 66 [*n-an*] ANA LUGAL-*TIM iskizzi* 'anoints him to kingship'; cf. A. M. Rizzi Mellini, *Studia mediterranea P. Meriggi dicata* 524 [1979]; V 1 III 5–6 *namma--an* YÀ DÙG.GA-*it iskizzi* 'then he anoints [the lamb] with good oil'; cf. Sommer – Ehelolf, *Pāpanikri* 12*; *KUB* XXX 19 IV 5 *n-at IŠTU* YÀ DÙG.GA *iskizzi*), *iskiyazi* (e.g. dupl. XXXIX 8 IV 3; cf. Otten, *Totenrituale* 44; *VBoT* 120 III 17 *mān-za* EN SISKUR--ma iskiyazi*; cf. Haas – Thiel, *Rituale* 146), *iskiyaizzi* (*KUB* IX 31 II 36 *n-at IŠTU* YÀ DÙG.GA *iskiyaizzi*, with dupl. *HT* 1 II 11 *iskizzi*; *HT* 1 I 38 *n-an ēshanta iskiyaizzi* 'he daubs it with blood'; cf. B. Schwartz, *JAOS* 58:338 [1938]), 3 sg. pres. midd. *is-kat-ta-ri* (*IBoT* III 148 I 67 and 68; cf. Haas – Wilhelm, *Riten* 216), 3 pl. pres. act. *is-kán-zi* (e.g. *KUB* XXXVI 90 Vs. 15–18 *lukkatta-as-kan* UD.KAM-*ti* [1]*Duthaliyan tuedas assiyantas pedas* URU*Hakmis* URU*Nerik* AŠŠUM LÚSANGA-*UTTIM iskanzi* 'tomorrow they will anoint D. to priesthood in thy favorite places, H. [and] N.'; cf. Haas, *Nerik* 176–8; XXV 14 I 16 *arranzi iskanzi* 'they wash [and] anoint'; cf. V. Haas – M. Wäfler, *Istanbuler Mitteilungen* 23–24:24 [1973–4]; XLII 98 I 7–8]*warpanzi namma-as* GÌR.MEŠ-*ŠUN*[*U*...] [... *d*]*āgan danzi n-as iskanzi* 'they bathe, and then they ... their feet ... on the ground they take, and anoint them'; *KBo* XXIII 1 I 44 and III 34 BIBRI.HI.A-*ya iskanzi* 'they oil rhyta'; cf. Lebrun, *Hethitica III* 142, 146; XXI 34 I 22 and 47 EGIR-*ŠU*-ma YÀ DÙG.GA *iskanzi* 'but afterwards they smear good oil'; cf. Lebrun, *Hethitica II* 117–8; *KUB* I 13 III 8–9 INA UD.5.KAM-*ma IŠTU* YÀ.NUN IN.NU.DA-*as iwar iskanzi* 'but on the fifth day they smear profusely with good oil'; cf. Kammenhuber, *Hippologia* 64, 59; XXIX 51 I 3 *n-us iskanzi* 'they smear them'; cf. Kammenhuber, *Hippologia* 200; XXIX 40 II 7 *n-us*

iski(ya)-

IŠTU YÀ UDU *iskanzi* 'they smear them with sheepfat'; cf.
Kammenhuber, *Hippologia* 178), *iskiyanzi* (e.g. XXIX 45 I 2
n-us IŠTU] YÀ [UDU] *iskiyanzi*; cf. Kammenhuber, *Hippologia*
170; *KBo* XXI 42 I 8 *n-an arranzi iskiyanzi* 'they wash [and]
anoint her' [viz. the icon of the goddess Isharas]; *KUB* XXIV
5 + IX 13 Vs. 19 *nu* ᴸᵁŠU.DIB *IŠTU* YÀ DÙG.GA LUGAL-*UTTI*
iskiyanzi 'they anoint the captive with the good oil of kingship';
cf. Kümmel, *Ersatzrituale* 10), *iskianzi* (e.g. *KBo* XII 98 Rs. 5),
YÀ-*anzi* (e.g. *KUB* XVII 35 II 18), 3 sg. pret. act. *iskit* (XXXIII
88 Rs. 10 YÀ DÙG.G]A-*ma-za sanizzit iskit* 'she anointed herself
with good oil'; cf. Siegelová, *Appu-Hedammu* 54; IX 34 III 34
karsikarsi-ya-za iskit 'anointed himself with clear fat' [?]), 3 pl.
pret. act. *is-ki-ir* (XXIX 54 IV 18; cf. Kammenhuber, *Hippologia* 228), 2 sg. imp. act. *iski* (*KBo* III 23 Vs. 4 *namma-as iski*
'then anoint them!'; cf. A. Archi, in *Florilegium Anatolicum* 41
[1979]), 3 sg. imp. act. *iskiddu* (III 8 II 32–33 *n-an-kan* EME-*ŠU*
sartāiddu ÚR-*us-ma-an IŠTU* YÀ.NUN *iskiddu* 'let her daub his
tongue, and let her salve his limbs with butter'; cf. Kronasser,
Die Sprache 7:155 [1961]; *KUB* XVII 10 II 22–23 *kāsa* ᴳᴵˢ*līti*
kitta nu ŠA ᴰ*Telipinu* [...] *iskiddu* 'lo, [the oily] 1.-plant is lying
here; let it oil the ... of T.'; cf. Laroche, *RHA* 23:93 [1965]), 3
pl. imp. act. *iskiyandu* (XXXVI 12 III 4 *nu ŠA* ᴳᵁᴰ*Serisu*
SI.HI.A-*ar iskiyandu* 'let them anoint Serisu's horns'; cf. Güterbock, *JCS* 6:14 [1952]); partic. *isk(iy)ant-*, nom. sg. c. *is-kánᵃⁿ-
-za* (*KBo* XXI 41+*KUB* XXIX 7 Rs. 58–59 *kāsa-ma-as* YÀ
DÙG.GA LÀL-*ya* EGIR-*anda lāhun nu-smas urkes* EGIR-*an IŠTU* YÀ
DÙG.GA LÀL-*ya iskanza* 'lo, I have poured good oil and honey
behind, and the trail in their wake is smeared with good oil and
honey'; cf. Lebrun, *Samuha* 124), nom.-acc. sg. or pl. neut.
iskiyan (e.g. *KUB* IX 31 III 4–5 ᴳᴵˢGIGIR-*ya-wa-ta-kkan IŠTU*
ᵁᶻᵁYÀ UDU *iskiyan ēsdu* 'let your chariot be oiled with sheep-
fat'; similarly dupl. *HT* 1 II 38–39; *KBo* XXI 22 Rs. 41–43
*nu-wa wattaru māhhan iyan kunnanit-at wedan arzilit-at hanis-
san* AN.BAR-*at iskiyan* 'how [is] the well made? It [is] built with
copper [?], it [is] plastered with ?, it [is] "smeared" with iron';
iskiya- is here a technical term of metal-working, similar in
meaning to AN.BAR-*it sanh-* 'flush with iron' in *KUB* XXIX 1 III
40), nom. pl. c. *is-kán-ti-is* (XXXIX 15 IV 1–2 *urkis-tis-wa-tta*

YÀ[-*it*] *iskantis asan*[*du*] 'your tracks shall be smeared with oil'; cf. ibid. 6 LÀL 'honey'; Otten, *Totenrituale* 82); verbal noun *iskiyauwar* (n.) in *IBoT* II 120 Rs. 3 YÀ *allassias iskiya*[*uwar* 'unction with oil of the queenship'; iter. *iskiski-*, *iskeski-*, 2 sg. pres. act. *iskiskisi* (*KUB* XXVI 25 II 5–6 *iskiskisi ke-ya-ta-kkan* MAMIT.HI.A Q[*ATAMMA* ...] *katta iskiyan ēsdu* '[as] you keep anointing [yourself], let these oaths likewise be smeared on you'), 3 sg. pres. act. *iskīskizzi* (*KBo* III 40a, 13 *nu-za iskīskizzi* 'keeps anointing himself'), *iskeskizzi* (*KUB* XLIV 61 Rs. 24–27 *n-as mān passaris n-an* [...] [...] *ŪL passaris n-an hapurin* EGIR-*pa damaszi* [...] [...] *iskizzi namma-an hapurin parā huittiy*[*azi* ...] [... SI]G₅-*ri n-an* I[*ŠT*]*U* A.BAR-*pat iskeskizzi* 'if he [is] circumcised [?], ... him ...; [if he is] not circumcised [?], he forces back his foreskin, salves ..., and then draws his foreskin forward ...; [until he] gets well, he keeps salving it with lead'; cf. Burde, *Medizinische Texte* 20).

iski(ya)- (determined already by Hrozný, *MDOG* 56:35 [1915], *SH* 12, 62) is similar in meaning to *sartai-* 'daub' but different from *sah-* which means rather 'plug, stop up' (cf. *KBo* III 8 II 29–33 EM]E-*ŠU sahdu* ... *n-an-kan* EME-*ŠU sartāiddu* ÚR-*us-ma-an* ... *iskiddu* 'let her plug his tongue ... daub his tongue ... salve his limbs'). In addition to practical smearing for grooming and medical purposes it also denotes ritual anointing, including priestly and regal consecration.

Oettinger's suggested analysis *is-ske-* (*Stammbildung* 327) is formally acceptable (cf. e.g. *duskizzi*, *duskiyazi*, *dusgai* 'is glad' from *tus-ske-*, cognate with Skt. *túṣyati* 'is glad'), but his further adduction of Ved. *iṣ-* 'refreshment, strength', esp. 'liquid refreshment', with appeal to a meaning 'squirt, pour vigorously' as a specialization of 'impel' in *iṣyati*, *iṣṇáti* (prefigured by Kronasser, *Studies presented to J. Whatmough* 125 [1957]), is quite problematic semantically, despite the reference to blood-smearing under 3 sg. pres. act. *iskiyaizzi* above ('blood squirts forth' is expressed rather by *ēshar siyari*, q.v. s.v. *sai-*, *siya-*). V. Georgiev's additional comparison with Gk. *ἰάομαι* 'heal' (i.e. *ῑᾱ-*; *Linguistique balkanique* 22.2:14 [1979], 23.3:10 [1980]) is equally questionable: an *isā-yo-* ('practise invigoration' > 'heal') might be cognate with Skt. *iṣṇáti*, but *iski(ya)-* has a very specific base-meaning (like Skt. *añj-*, Lat. *unguō*, Gk. ἀλείφω or χρίω, Goth. *salbōn*) and is therefore best kept isolated; the root of Skt. *iṣ-* is probably present rather in *ishuwa(i)-* (q.v.). Perhaps **is-ske-* or **ish-ske-* shows the weak grade of a root **yes-(A₁-)* 'salve', seen as **isā-* (< **is-éA₁-*) in Gk. ῑ̈ᾱ-, ῐ̈ᾱ-, which latter would then mean originally 'salve' (distinct from ἀκέομαι 'cure, mend', ἄκος 'cure, remedy'; cf. the Homeric ἰητροὶ πολυφάρμακοι ... ἕλκε᾽ ἀκειόμενοι 'healers laden with balms ... mending wounds' [*Iliad* 16:28–29], ἕλκος δ᾽ ἰητὴρ ἐπιμάσσεται ἠδ᾽ ἐπιθήσει φάρμαχ᾽ 'a healer will probe the wound and apply medicaments' [*Iliad* 4:190–1]; ἰητρὸς γὰρ ἀνὴρ ... ἰούς τ᾽ἐκτάμνειν ἐπί τ᾽ἤπια φάρμακα πάσσειν 'a medical man ... when it comes to excising arrows and spreading on soothing drugs' [*Iliad* 11:514–5]). ῑ̈ᾱ-, ῑ̈η- is etymologically separate from ἰαίνω 'soothe, warm, heal' (q.v. s.v. *iyawa-*); the initial shows metrical lengthening spreading from tribrach-elimination in forms like **ἰάετο* (>ῑ̈ᾶτ᾽ in *Iliad* 12:2).

Cf. *isharisk(i)-*.

iskis- (n.) 'back, backside, rear' (*KBo* I 42 II 24 *iskīsa*=Akk. *kutallu*; cf. *MSL* 13:135 [1971]), perhaps also 'ridge' (cf. *KUB* II 1 II 15 ᴴᵁᴿ·ˢᴬᴳ*Iskisas*; Laroche, *RHA* 19:78–9 [1961]; H. A. Hoffner, *RHA* 25:60 [1967]; A. Archi, *SMEA* 16:108 [1975]), nom.-acc. sg. *iskis* (XXXVI 110 Rs. 9–10 *nu-za-pa udniyanza hūmanza iski(s)-smet anda* ᵁᴿᵁ*Hattusa lagan hardu* 'every land shall bend its back to Hattusas'; cf. Forrer, *Meissner AOS* 31; Starke, *ZA* 69:82 [1979]; Neu, *Altheth.* 227; XLIII 53 I 6 *iski(s)-set-a iskisi dākki* 'his back matches the back'; ibid. 23 *iski(s)-set-asta iskisi* GAL-*li* 'his back [is] big [in relation] to the [other's] back'; cf. Sommer, *HAB* 219; Haas, *Orientalia* N.S. 40:415–6 [1971]; XXIX 1 III 18–19 *mān* ᴸᵁNAGAR ᴳᴵˢ*iskis-san--as* ᴳᴵˢ*isparuzzi karsūwanzi paizzi* 'when the carpenter goes to cut the ridgepole and the rafters'; cf. B. Schwartz, *Orientalia* N.S. 16:34 [1947]; *IBoT* III 113 Rs. 3), gen. sg. (or dat.-loc. pl.?) *iskisas* (e.g. *KUB* X 27 I 17–18 *n-at ... ANA* DINGIR-*LIM iskisas* EGIR-*an* [*dāi* '[he] places it in back of the deity'; cf. von Brandenstein, *Orientalia* N.S. 8:70 [1939]; M. Vieyra, *RA* 51:85

[1957]; V 1 IV 49; cf. Ünal, *Hatt.* 2:84; IX 34 III 10 = IX 4 II 26), dat.-loc. sg. *iskisi* (e.g. II 3 II 26; *KBo* XXI 22 Rs. 46; cf. G. Kellerman, *Tel Aviv* 5:200 [1978]), *iskisa* (e.g. V 1 II 18 *iskisa-smas* 'in their rear'; cf. Sommer – Ehelolf, *Pāpanikri* 6*; *IBoT* III 148 III 44 *iskisa* EGIR-*an* 'behind the back'; cf. Haas – Wilhelm, *Riten* 224; *KUB* XVII 28 III 26–29 3 GUD-MAH *kuēs-san* ANA GUD.ÁB *iskisa nāwi pāntes* 18 UDU.ŠIR *kuis-san* ANA UDU.SÍG + SAL *iskisa nāwi pāntes* 'three bulls who have not yet mounted a cow, eighteen rams who have not yet mounted a ewe'; cf. Riemschneider, *MIO* 6:377 [1958]; XVI 8 Vs. 6; XVIII 11 Rs. 6; XXI 38 Vs. 45; XXV 37 I 8 and II 17, 23; cf. *Dict. louv.* 172; *KBo* IV 14 III 74), instr. sg. *iskisitti* (XII 33 III 8 *n-an iskisitti* IṢBAT 'seized him by the back'), abl. sg. *iskisaz(a)* (e.g. XII 126 I 14 *iskisaz karpan* 'lifted by the back'; cf. Jakob-Rost, *Ritual der Malli* 22; *KUB* XXXIII 114 IV 13–14 *nu-ssi-kan* UZU*iskisaza* [...] *markir* 'from his back they cut up'; cf. ibid. 9, and XXXIII 112 IV 14 UZU*ishisaza*; cf. Güterbock, *Kumarbi* *8–*9; Meriggi, *Athenaeum* N.S. 31:144–6 [1953]; Laroche, *RHA* 26:35–6 [1968]; Alp, *Anatolia* 2:29 [1957]; XIV 16 II 14 'from the rear'; cf. Götze, *AM* 42; XV 39 II 26 'from behind'; cf. L. Rost, *MIO* 1:358 [1953], III 12; *KUB* II 5 V 4–5 *iskisaz* EGIR-*pa iyattāri* '[he] retreats backwards'; XXIV 13 III 13 *n-as-si* EGIR-*an namma* UZU*iskisaz hūwāi* 'she then runs behind his back'; cf. Goetze, *Tunnawi* 72; Haas – Thiel, *Rituale* 106), also *iskisānza* (XXX 45 II 18), unless denom. derivative in -*ant*- (nom. sg.; cf. Laroche, *BSL* 57.1:37 [1962], *CTH* 160), nom.-acc. pl. *iskisa* or *iskīsa* (e.g. XIII 29, 8 *iskisa naistin* 'turn your back!'; XX 38 Vs. 15–16 *mēne-smit* LUGAL-*i ne*[-...] *iskīsa* LUGAL-*i na*[- 'turn their [?] face to the king ... turn their [?] back to the king'). Cf. Kronasser, *Etym.* 1:189, 340; Laroche, *RHA* 28:30 (1971).

Judging from the sexual term *iskisa pai-*, the anatomical meaning of *iskis-* is more precisely 'the small of the back, the lumbar region'. Cf. Gk. ἰσχίον 'hip-joint, hip(s), haunches', Hes. ἴσχι · ὀσφύς 'lower part of back, loins'. Further connections are uncertain, but the accord of the Hittite and the otherwise obscure Greek terms is striking. Cf. also F. Ribezzo, *Rivista indo-greco-italica* 4:130 (1920); Juret, *Vocabulaire* 51; Čop, *Ling.* 8:170–2 (1966–8); Neu, *IF* 74:240 (1969).

iskissana- (n.), wooden item of household goods or furniture, nom.-acc. pl. ^GIŠ*is-ki-is-sa-na(-as-si-it)* (*KBo* VI 26 II 5 [= *Code* 2:71], preceded by ^GIŠIG-*ŠU* 'her door' and followed by ^GIŠ*hŭppulli-ssit* [q.v. s.v.]), ^GIŠ*is-ki-is-ta-ni(-se-it)* (dupl. VI 13 I 16, with erasure strokes covering *ta*).

Connection with *iskis-* 'back' (q.v.), as **iskis-na-* 'dorsalis' (vel sim.), and translation as 'bed' (Hrozný, *Code hittite* 133 [1922]) or 'headrest' (cf. Friedrich, *Heth. Ges.* 111) or 'backpack' (H. Eichner, *Die Sprache* 21:163 [1975]) is sheer conjecture. Cf. Kronasser, *Etym.* 1:183.

iskit(t)ahh- 'signal (to), single out', 3 sg. pres. act. *is-kit₉-ta-ah-hi* (*KUB* X 1 I 11 GAL *MEŠEDI iskittahhi* 'the chief of the guard signals'), *is-ki-da-a-ah-hi* (*IBoT* I 36 III 63–64 *nu* 1 ^LÚ*MEŠEDI IŠTU* ^GIŠ[ŠU]KUR *ANA* ^LÚ.MEŠ*MEŠEDUTIM ANA* DUMU.MEŠ É.GAL-*ya iskidāhhi* 'one guard with a spear signals to the men of the guard and to the pages'; cf. Jakob-Rost, *MIO* 11:196 [1966]), *is-ki-ta-ah-hi* (*KBo* XXI 85 I 31 [...] ^DEN.ZU-*as* NINDA.KUR.RA. .HI.A-*i* ^GIŠŠUKUR-*it iskitah*[*hi*] 'singles out with the spear the thick loaves of the moon-god'). Cf. Alp, *Beamtennamen* 14.

The meaning is similar to IZKIM-*ah(h)-* = *sakiyah(h)-* 'give a sign'; but while the latter has ominous connotations (cf. Lat. *sāgus* 'presaging'), *iskittahh-* denotes mundane signalling and may be a denominative factive verb from **iskit(t)a-*, which bears comparison with Lith. *skaistùs, skaidrùs* 'clear, bright' or OHG *ge-schide*, Lat. *scītus* 'clever, shrewd', *scītum* 'determination, decree' (with *iskittahh-* cf. Lat. *scītā-* 'try to determine, inquire', like *newahh-* : Lat. *novā-* 'make new').

iskuna(hh)-, ishuna(hh)- 'stain; stigmatize, denounce; degrade, disgrace, demote', 3 pl. pres. act. *ishunānzi* (*KBo* VI 26 II 19 [= *Code* 2:75] *Ù* DUMU.MEŠ *ishunānzi* 'and they degrade the children' [of a marital misalliance by a free woman]; dupl. *KUB* XXIX 29 Rs. 3 misspelled *u*]*shunan*[*zi*), 3 sg. pret. act. *iskunahhis* (I 16 III 41–42 *huhhas-mis* [*Laba*]*rnan* DUMU-*san* ^URU*Sanahuitti iskunahhis* 'my grandfather demoted his son Labarnas to

Sanahuittas'; cf. Sommer, *HAB* 12–4, 164), 1 pl. pret. act. *ishunahhuwen* (XXIII 13 Vs. 3–4 *anzās-ma-wa-za IŠTU* ^{GIŠ}TUKUL [*ŪL tarahta* ...] ... *nu-wa-ssi wasdazza* [with gloss-wedges] *ishunahhuwen* 'he has not vanquished us with arms, ... and we have stigmatized his depredations'; cf. Sommer, *AU* 314); partic. *iskunant-*, nom.-acc. pl. neut. *iskunanta* (*KBo* IV 2 I 44–45 *kās-wa* GIM-*an hās* GAD.HI.A *iskunanta parkunuzzi* 'as this soap cleanses stained cloths'; cf. Kronasser, *Die Sprache* 8:91 [1962]); iter. *iskuneski-*, 3 pl. pres. act. *iskuneskanzi* (XII 19 I 6; cf. Neu, *Altheth.* 231). Cf. Kronasser, *Etym.* 1:480–1; Oettinger, *MSS* 35:93–4 (1976). For earlier proposed meanings see Sommer, *AU* 317 (*ishunahh-* 'defy'; so still Kronasser, *Etym.* 1:429); Sommer, *HAB* 164 (*iskunahh-* 'make a mark, designate'; so also Kronasser, *Etym.* 1:430; Oettinger, *MSS* 35:100 [1976], *Stammbildung* 156–7; S. R. Bin-Nun, *The Tawananna in the Hittite kingdom* 67–8 [1975]); Alp, *Anatolia* 2:23 (1957; *ishuna*[*i*]- related to *ishuwa*[*i*]- 'shed, throw'); Laroche, *OLZ* 57:30 (1962; *ishuna*[*i*]- 'draw [a bow]'; cf. s.v. *ishunawar*).

The phonetic variation *isk-* : *ish-* is matched by e.g. *iskis(a)-* (q.v.) besides *KUB* XXXIII 112 IV 4 ^{UZU}*ishisaza*. The plausible cognate of *iskuna-* is Gk. αἰσχύνω 'make ugly, disfigure, dishonor', αἰσχύνη 'shame, dishonor' (cf. *Aἰσχύλος*), ᾰἶσχος 'shame, disgrace', αἰσχρός 'ugly, deformed, dishonoring, shameful'. Gk. αἰσχ- has no plausible etymology (only a tortured comparison with Goth. *aiwiski* 'shame' via *aygh^w sk-*; *IEW* 14), and a Gk.-Hitt. isolexeme *ays-gh-* (with Hitt. *i* < *ai*; cf. s.v. *asara-, esara-*) is a welcome common denominator with a putative proto-meaning 'make ugly, stain'. *iskuna-* is probably a denominative factitive verb with *-na-* suffix from a *u*-stem base, like e.g. *sunna-* 'fill' from *su-* 'full', thus comparable to Gk. αἰσχύνω (< *αἰσχύνιω) from *αἰσχύς 'ugly' (supplanted by αἰσχρός); cf. e.g. ταχύνω from ταχύς (τάχος like ᾰἶσχος). *iskunahh-* is a further deverbative derivative with *-ah(h)-* suffix, like e.g. *kururiyah(h)-* 'wage war' besides *kururiya-* 'be hostile' (cf. Gk. ἰσχανάω besides ἰσχάνω).

As an alternative to this uniform interpretation one might detach *iskunahh-* (in *KUB* I 16 III 41–42 quoted above) and translate 'my grandfather proclaimed his son L. (as his successor) at S.' (leading to rebellion by rival sons and factions), rather than taking L. as being rusticated by his father to S. for being ringleader of the rebels; but unlike Sommer (*HAB* 164 'designated') one should then keep apart *iskunant-* used of clothes ('stained, ugly', not 'marked, spotty') and connect *iskunahh-* with Lith. *áiškus, iškùs* 'clear, obvious' (see s.v. *asara-, esara-* 'white, bright', and cf. Lat. *dē-clārā-*); for semantics, cf. also *n-an-kan istarna tekkussami* 'I designate him' (q.v. s.v. *istarna*).

Oettinger (*Stammbildung* 156–8) reconstructed nasal infix verbs $*sH_1unéH_1$- (from an unclear $*sH_1$-ew-H_1-) for *ishuna(hh)-* 'treat shabbily', and $*skunéH_1$- from $*skew$-H_1- for *iskuna(hh)-* 'designate, make spotty', the latter allegedly cognate with Vedic *skauti, skunắti, skunóti* 'poke, rake, tear, mangle', sometimes used technically (*ā-skunóti*) of ear-slashing or perforation of domestic animals for marking purposes. The latter specialized sense is a weak reed on which to hang an already Indo-European meaning 'to mark'; in this case its reapplication from cattle to royal offspring would most likely have been negative ('brand, denounce' rather than 'designate').

H. Eichner (*Die Sprache* 25:205–6 [1979]) allowed *ishunahh-* < *iskunahh-* ("regressive assimilation") and advocated the same tie-in with Vedic *sku-*, postulating an improbable semantic range 'to mark' > 'designate; brand, demean, degrade; set limits for, put in one's place, defy; stain'.

Cf. Puhvel, *IF* 83:138:43 (1978) = *Analecta Indoeuropaea* 373–8; 417–8 (1981), *Bi. Or.* 38:350–2 (1981), *Gedenkschrift für H. Kronasser* 181–2 (1982).

ismanala-, ismanali-   (c.) 'equerry, groom', nom. pl. ^{LÚ.MEŠ}*ismanalis* (*KUB* IX 1 III 18), Cf. Laroche, *RHA* 13:82 (1955); Kronasser, *Etym.* 1:172, 212, 249.

For etymology, cf. s.v. *ismeri-*.

ismeri-   (n.) 'bridle, rein', nom.-acc. sg. ^{KUŠ}*ismeri* (*FHG* 16 II 3; Laroche, *RA* 46:46 [1952]).

LÚ *ismeriyas* 'man of the bridle, coachman, charioteer' (= *KUB* I 1 I 12 ŠA KUŠ.KA.TAB.ANŠU; cf. Götze, *Hattusilis* 6), gen. (?) in *KUB* XXIII 11 II 35 LÚ.MEŠ] *ismeriyas* BELU.HI.A-*us* URUKÙ.BABBAR-*si uwatenun* 'I brought chiefs of charioteers to Hattusas' (cf. R. Ranoszek, *Rocznik Orientalistyczny* 9:56–7 [1934]; Carruba, *SMEA* 18:160 [1977]); cf. ibid. III 5 LÚ.MEŠ *ismeriyas* EN.MEŠ-*us* and XXIII 12 III 6 LÚ.MEŠ *ismeri*[. For the corresponding Hieroglyphic logogram depicting 'reins', see Laroche, *HH* 150.

ismeriyant- 'bridled', dat.-loc. sg. in XXXVIII 1 II 8 ANA *awiti* GUŠKIN-*kan ismeriyanti* 'on a bridled golden *awiti*' (q.v.). Cf. von Brandenstein, *Heth. Götter* 14; L. Rost, *MIO* 8:180 (1961).

Cf. Laroche, *RHA* 13:81–3 (1955); Güterbock, *Oriens* 10:351 (1957).

Etymology uncertain. Laroche (loc. cit.) postulated a heteroclitic **ismer/n-* reflected in Hitt. *ismeri-* and *ismanala-* (q.v.) on the one hand, and Gk. ἱμονιά 'well-rope' (**ismon-*), ἱμάντ- 'strap' (or ἱμάντ-; **ismn̥-*) on the other; but the plausible alternative reconstruction of the Greek words (including ἱμάω 'draw water by rope') as reflecting **sīm(o)n-*, **sīmā-* (from a widespread IE root meaning 'bind') renders this explanation implausible (cf. s.v. *ishiya-*; also Kammenhuber, *KZ* 77:52–3 [1961]; H. Wittmann, *Die Sprache* 19:40–1 [1973]). According to Kammenhuber (ibid.) the initial *i-* in *ismeri-* is etymological (rather than graphic), but there is no proof.

Čop (*Ling.* 2:37–9 [1956]) rejected Laroche, separated *ismanala-*, and adduced Gk. μέρμῑς 'cord, rope', (σ)μήρινθος 'line, string', μηρύομαι 'furl', Hes. σμήριγγες· πλεκταί, σειραί '(twisted) ropes', σμηρία· κισσός 'ivy' (cf. *IEW* 733). He postulated a PGk. **smēri-* identical with Hitt. *ismeri-*. The IE attachments remain unclear: is **s-* "movable" or part of the root? If the latter, **smer-* could still be in heteroclisis with **smen-* or **smn̥-* in *ismanala-*.

ispai-, ispiya- 'get full, be filled, be sat(iat)ed, be saturated' (with food, rarely with drink; cf. the near-synonyms *has*[*s*]*ik*[*k*]-, less restrictive but used with drink when juxtaposed to *ispai-*, and *ni*[*n*]*k-*, exclusively with drink), 2 sg. pres. act. *ispāisi* (*Bo* 6180, 5), 3 sg. pres. act. *ispāi* (*Bo* 4491, 4–5 *Ū*]*L hasekzi* [... *n-*]*as-za ŪL ispāi* 'is not satiated ..., and he is not filled'; *KUB* XXXIII 11 II 11; cf. ibid. 12 *ninga* [3 sg. pres.]; Laroche, *RHA* 23:108 [1965]), 3 pl. pres. act. *ispiyanzi* (*KBo* III 5 I 28 *wetenit ispiyanzi* '[the horses] satiate themselves with water'; cf. Kammenhuber, *Hippologia* 82, with incorrect transitive translation 'they saturate'), 3 pl. pret. act. *is-pí-i-e-ir* (*KUB* XVII 10 I 19–20 *eter n-e ŪL ispiyer ekuyer-ma n-e-za ŪL hassikkir* 'they ate but they were not filled, and they drank but they were not satiated'; XXXIII 24 II 13; XXXIII 19 III 8; cf. Laroche, *RHA* 23:90, 116, 123 [1965]), *is-pí-ir* (XXXIII 32 III 5; cf. Laroche, *RHA* 23:127 [1965]), 2 sg. imp. act. *ispāi* (*KBo* IV 6 Vs. 8–9 *nu-za zik* DINGIR-*LUM* ... ᵁᶻᵁYÀ *et nu-za ispāi* 'thou, deity, eat the fat ... and be filled!'; cf. Tischler, *Gebet* 12), *ispiya* (*KUB* XX 92 VI 8–9 *ezza-zza nu-za ispiya eku-ma nu-za nik* 'eat and get full, drink and get your fill!'), 2 pl. imp. act. *is-pí-it-tin* (XXXIII 62 III 10–11 *sumes ezzastin nu-za ispittin ekuten-ma nu-za nikten* 'eat and be sated, drink and be filled!'), *is-pí-is-te-en* (XII 17, 6–7 *ezza*]*tten nu-za ispisten* [... *ekutt*]*en nu-za nikten*), 3 pl. imp. act. *ispiyandu* (XV 34 I 48–49 *ad*[*and*]*u akuwandu n-at-za ispiyandu ninkandu* 'let them eat and drink, and let them be sated and filled'; cf. Haas – Wilhelm, *Riten* 186); partic. *ispiyant-*, nom. sg. c. *ispiyanza* (*IBoT* III 148 III 10–11 *ispiyanza ninkanza ēs* 'be sated and filled!'; cf. Haas – Wilhelm, *Riten* 222), nom. pl. c. *ispiyantes* (ibid. 6 *ispiyantes asandu*; *KUB* XV 34 III 42 *ispiyantes ninkant*[*es*] *asandu*; cf. Haas – Wilhelm, *Riten* 198; IX 31 III 2–3 and dupl. *HT* 1 II 36–38 *nu-wa kī* ŠÀ.GAL.HI.A *ezzandu nu-war-at ispiyantes asandu* 'let [the horses] eat this fodder and be sated'; *KBo* XI 1 Rs. 20 *ispiyantes-ma-nnas* ANA ME QAZĪ *mahhan* 'as we [are] having our fill of cold water'; cf. Houwink Ten Cate – Josephson, *RHA* 25:110 [1967]; for the construction cf. [with infinitive] *uwanna hassik-* 'satiate oneself looking, see one's fill' [s.v. *au(s)-*]); verbal noun *ispiyatar* (n.) 'satiety', nom.-acc. *ispiyatarr-a* (*KUB* XVII 10 I 11; XXXIII 24 II 16).

ispiyanu- 'satiate, saturate', verbal noun *ispiyanumar* (n.) in

KBo XI 1 Rs. 21 *n-at* DUMU.LÚ.ULÙ.LU *ispiyanumar ēsdu* 'may it be saturation for mankind'.

ispān (n.) 'satiation' (?), nom.-acc. sg. *ispān* (*KBo* VIII 42 Vs. 6), gen. sg. *ispānas* (*KUB* XXXVI 44 I 12 *ispānas* NINDA.KUR₄ .RA.ḪI.AUZU.UTÚL.ḪI.A 'loaves [and] meat-stews of satiation' [?]). Cf. Oettinger, *Stammbildung* 467–8.

The semantic distinction of 'sate (with food)' vs. 'fill (with drink)' is found also in e.g. Hebrew and Egyptian (cf. Ehelolf, *KlF* 141; Friedrich, *Indogermanisches Jahrbuch* 13:377 [1929]); cf. Latin *quom tu satura atque ebria eris* 'when you have had enough to eat and drink' (Terence, *Hecyra* 5.2.3), matching Hitt. *ispiyanza ninkanza ēs* (quoted above).

ispai- is convincingly connected since Sturtevant, *Lg.* 4:2 (1928), *Comp. Gr.*[1] 247, *Lg.* 14:72 (1938), with IE *$speE_1$-(y-)* 'be sated', seen in e.g. Skt. *sphāyate* 'grow fat', OE *spōwan* 'thrive', *spēd* 'prosperity, success, dispatch, speed', OCS *spěti* 'be successful', Lat. *spēs* 'hope', *pro-sperus* 'favorable' (cf. *IEW* 983). A full belly has remained an archetypal image of prosperity (wrongly Pedersen, *Hitt.* 113–4 who reversed the semantics to a basic 'thrive'). *ispāi* < *$spōye$* < *$spoE_1ye$* (stative perfect), with 3 pl. *ispiyanzi* < *spE_1y-ónti*. For further morphological speculations see e.g. Puhvel, *LIEV* 55, *Evidence for laryngeals* 91–2 [1965] = *Analecta Indoeuropaea* 137–8 [1981]; Schmitt-Brandt, *Entwicklung* 66, 74; H. Eichner, in *Flexion und Wortbildung* 86 (1975); Oettinger, *Stammbildung* 461, 466–7.

ispant- (c.) 'night' (GE₆[.KAM]; *MUŠU*), nom. sg. *ispanza* (*KUB* XXV 44 II 25 *mahhan-ma ispanza kisari* 'but when night comes'; *Bo* 2372 III 30 ᴰ*Ispanza*; cf. the deity ᴰ*Ispanzasepa-*, nom. sg. ᴰ*Ispanzasepas* [*KUB* XX 24 III 2; XLIII 30 III 8, besides ibid. 5 *annas Tagānzipas* 'Terra Mater'; cf. Neu, *Altheth.* 77], which may reflect either *ispant-sepa-* [determinative compound] or *ispants + sepas* [fused spelling of appositional 'Night, the Daimon'], hardly a "genitival" *ispants[-sepa]-*; cf. e.g. *Āsga- -sepa-* s.v. *aska-*; Kammenhuber, *KZ* 77:185–6 [1961]; Kronasser, *Etym.* 1:185, who compared *siwanz-anna-* [q.v. s.v. *siu-*]), GE₆-*anza* (e.g. *KBo* III 5 III 73 *mahhan-ma* GE₆-*anza kisari*; cf.

ispant-

Kammenhuber, *Hippologia* 98; perhaps also adverbially as an embedded sentence formula [cf. *lammar* 'this very hour, right away', *nekuz mehur* 'in the evening', *kariwariwar* 'at daybreak', *siwaz* = UD-*az* 'in daytime'], e.g. *KUB* I 11 IV 45 GE₆-*anza* 'at night' [Kammenhuber, *Hippologia* 124; alternatively abl. sg. in -*anza*, cf. GE₆-*az* below and UD-*az*, UD.KAM-*anza*]), *MUŠU* (I 13 IV 43 *mahhan-ma 5 MUŠU ki*[*sari*] 'but when the fifth night comes'; cf. Kammenhuber, *Hippologia* 72), acc. sg. *ispantan* (X 81, 10–11 ᴰUD.SIG₅ *ispantann-a ekuzi* 'toasts the Good Day and the Night'; *Bo* 207, 12 ᴰUD.SIG₅ *ispantann-a*; also incorrect nom. sg. in *KBo* IV 13+ *KUB* X 82 VI 34 DINGIR.MEŠ MUL *ispanza* ᴰ*Hasmaiūn* '[the king toasts] ... the star-gods, the Night, [the deity] H.'; cf. ibid. 37 EME-*as h*[*and*]*anza* instead of correct EME-*an handantan*; cf. Bossert, *Königssiegel* 35, 51), *ispandan* (e.g. *KBo* V 8 III 21 *nu ispandan hūmandan iyahhat* 'I marched the whole night'; cf. Götze, *AM* 158; *KUB* XXIX 55 I 1–3 *mān lukkatta nu nūwa ispandan appizziyas hāliyas naui anku haruwanāizzi* 'when dawn comes but does not yet quite light up the night of the last watch'; cf. Kammenhuber, *Hippologia* 150; *KBo* XXIV 6 Vs. 7 *i*]*spandan laknuwa*[*nzi* 'they pass the night' [lit. 'knock down the night'; cf. English 'kill time']), GE₆-*an* (e.g. dupl. XXIV 5 Vs. 13 *nu* GE₆-*an laknuwanzi*; *KUB* XXXIX 7 III 53 *nu kuitman* GE₆-*an lak*[*nuwanzi* 'while they pass the night'; dupl. XXXIX 8 III 14 *nu kuitman isp*]*andan luk*[*kanuwanzi* [lit. 'light up the night', i.e. burn the midnight oil]; cf. Otten, *Totenrituale* 44; *Bo* 2562 IV 22 GE₆-*an dapian luqqanuwanzi* 'they light up the whole night'; also incorrectly nom. sg. in *KUB* XLVI 27 Vs. 22 GE₆-*za luqqanuwanzi*; I 13 IV 31 and 40 GE₆-*an hūmandan* 'the whole night'; cf. Kammenhuber, *Hippologia* 72), gen. sg. GE₆-*andas* (IV 47 Rs. 29 3 *hāliyas* GE₆-*andas* 'for the three watches of the night'), dat.-loc. sg. *ispanti* (e.g. *KBo* XIX 128 VI 30–31 LUGAL SAL.LUGAL *appiyanzi ta hatkanzi ispanti* 'king [and] queen are done; they close down for the night'; cf. Otten, *Festritual* 16; *KUB* XX 18 VI 11 *ta hatkanzi ispanti*; XXX 10 Rs. 18 *ispanti-mu-ssan sasti-mi sānezzis teshas natta epzi* 'at night in my bed sweet sleep does not take [hold of] me'; *KBo* XVII 6 III 12, XVII 1 III 29, XVII 4 III 14 'at night'; cf. Otten – Souček,

432

Altheth. Ritual 32–4; XXII 5 Vs. 5; XXIII 1 I 57; cf. Lebrun, *Hethitica III* 143), *ispandi* (III 22 Vs. 6 and 18, Rs. 47 'at night'; cf. Neu, *Anitta-Text* 10–12), GE₆.KAM-*anti* (*KUB* XXXV 145 Rs. 3–4 [*kedani* M]U.KAM-*ti kedani* ITU.KAM-*mi kedani* UD.[KAM--*ti*] [*ked*]*ani* GE₆.KAM-*anti lamnī haltatti* 'he will call in this year, in this month, on this day, in this night, at [this] hour'), GE₆-*anti* (*KBo* III 5 I 49 1-*edani* GE₆-*anti* 'in one night'; cf. Kammenhuber, *Hippologia* 84), GE₆-*ti* (e.g. ibid. 79 1-*edani* GE₆-*ti*; ibid. III 66 GE₆-*ti-ma* GE₆-*ti* 'night by night' [epanadiplosis]), GE₆ (ibid. 67 1-*edani* GE₆), *MUŠI* (e.g. ibid. I 32 *INA MUŠI MUŠI-ya* 'and night by night'; ibid. II 55 1-*edani MUŠI*; ibid. I 33 *INA* 5 *MUŠI* 'in the fifth night'; ibid. 31 *INA* 8 *MUŠI* 'for eight nights'; cf. Kammenhuber, *Hippologia* 267–72), abl. sg. *ispantaz* (e.g. *KUB* VII 1 II 18 *n-at ispantaz sarā suhha pedai* 'takes it at night up to the roof'; cf. Kronasser, *Die Sprache* 7:149 [1961]; *KBo* IV 2 I 21; cf. Kronasser, *Die Sprache* 8:90 [1962]; *KUB* XXIII 11 II 22; cf. R. Ranoszek, *Rocznik Orientalistyczny* 9:55 [1934]; Carruba, *SMEA* 18:158 [1977]), *ispandaz* (Maşat 75/13 Vs. 6–8 ᴸᵁKÚR--*wa pangarit ispandaz kuwapi* 6 M[*E* ᴸᵁKÚR] *kuwapi-ma* 6 ME ᴸᵁKÚR *ia*[*ttari*] 'the enemy is on the march in force at night, six hundred in one place, six hundred in another'; cf. Alp, *Belleten* 44:45 [1980]; *KBo* XVII 105 II 15–16 *tug-a hāssan mahhan* [UD-*a*]*z* DUMU.LÚ.ULÙ.LU *anda hūlaliskizzi ispandaz-ma-t⟨ta⟩ anda* DINGIR.MEŠ *hūlāleskanzi* 'as mortal man surrounds thee by day, o hearth, the gods surround thee by night'; cf. A. Archi, *SMEA* 16:86 [1975]; *KUB* XIX 37 III 11–12 *nu t*]*uzzius* UD-*az kāriskinun* [*isp*]*andaz-ma iyahhat* 'in daytime I had my troops take cover, but at night I marched'; cf. Götze, *AM* 172–4), *is-pa-an-da-za* (e.g. ibid. 17–18 HUR.SAG-*an ispandaza istar*[*na arha iya*]*hhat* 'at night I marched along through the mountain[s]'; XXXI 115, 16; cf. A. Archi, in *Florilegium Anatolicum* 42 [1979]), GE₆-*antaz* (*KBo* IV 2 I 37; cf. Kronasser, *Die Sprache* 8:91 [1962], GE₆-*andaz* (*KUB* IV 47 Vs. 3), GE₆-*az* (VIII 38 + XLIV 63 III 17–18 *n-an-si-kan nassu* UD-*az nasma-si-kan* GE₆-*az anda tarneskizzi ŪL kuitki tuqqāri* 'he instils it [viz. eye-drops] into him [i.e. his eyes] either by day or by night, it makes no difference'; cf. Burde, *Medizinische Texte* 30; I 11 III 9 and *KBo* III 2 Vs. 38 'by night'; cf. Kammenhuber, *Hippologia* 115,

140), GE₆-*za* (V 6 II 2; cf. ibid. I 22 *ispandaza*; Güterbock, *JCS* 10:91–2 [1956]), acc. pl. *ispantius* (sic IV 4 III 31 *nu-za* UD.KAM.HI.A *ispantius iyanun* 'I made days nights' [i.e. marched around the clock]; cf. Götze, *AM* 126; possibly from a Luwoid **ispanti-*, cf. e.g. Luw. *apparanti-* 'the future' [q.v. s.v. *appasiwatt-*]), GE₆.HI.A-*us* (*KUB* XXXVI 75 III 7–8 *pittuli*[*ya*]*s piran* UD.HI.A-*us* GE₆.HI.[A-*us*] *laknus*[*ki*]*mi* 'from anxiety I keep killing time around the clock' [lit. 'knocking down days and nights']), *MUŠU* (*KBo* III 5 I 32 and 61 8 *MUŠU* 'eight nights'; cf. Kammenhuber, *Hippologia* 82, 84).

ispant- is clearly the basic term for 'night', the straight antonym of *siwat-* 'day', the animate noun capable of divinization, having relegated the rival *nekut-* to the juxtapositional petrifact *nekuz mehur* 'eventide, evening', also 'nighttime' more generally (cf. *KUB* IV 47 Vs. 11 *nu nekuz mehur kuitman-kan* ᴰUTU-*us nāwi ūpzi* 'in nighttime, while the sun is not yet rising', besides ibid. 3 GE₆-*andaz* 'at night'; wrongly J. Schindler, *KZ* 81:294 [1967]). Unlike Vedic, where *nákt-* (along with the innovational *rā́trī* or *rāmī́-*) fills the centerfield and the night-goddess slot alike at the expense of *kṣáp-*, the Hittite distribution is reminiscent of Iranian, where Avestan *upa-naxtar-* 'bordering on night' is an isolated form (not unlike the synonymous Vedic *api-śarvará-* from the rare *śárvarī* 'night'), and the common term (from Avestan *xšap-* to Persian *šab* 'night') is cognate with Vedic *kṣáp-*.

ispant- (identified as 'night' by Sommer, *Heth. II* 30) has been combined with *kṣap-* since Götze – Pedersen, *MS* 60, with elaborations by Goetze, *Lg.* 27:475 (1951), 30:357 (1954), who postulated **ksep-* (Skt. *kṣáp-*), **ksep(e)r-* (Avest. *xšapar-* 'night', perhaps Gk. ἑσπέρα, Lat. *ve-sper* 'evening'), **ksep(e)n-* (Avest. *xšafn-* 'night'), **ks(e)pont-* (Hitt. *ispant-* < **[k]spant-*). Further discussions by E. P. Hamp (*JKF* 2:257–9 [1965], *Revue des études arméniennes* N.S. 3:13–5 [1966]) tried to cement the relevance of such possible peripheral cognates as Lat. *vesper*, Arm. *gišer* 'night', Welsh *ucher* 'evening', OCS *večerŭ* 'evening', arriving finally at an embedded sentence formula **weiks ksper* 'the time (is) night', matching Hitt. *nekuz mehur* (*Papers from the Sixth Regional Meeting, Chicago Linguistic Society*, 482–3

[1970]; a somewhat different tack by J. Schindler, *Die Sprache* 15:166–7 [1969], produced a prefixal compound **we-kʷsp--ero-*).

For *ispant-*, the main issue concerns the age, type, and composition of the suffix. Rather than comparing primarily (with e.g. Goetze, *Lg.* 27:475 [1951], or Kammenhuber, *HOAKS* 294) the set of *gim(ant)-* 'winter', *zena(nt)-* 'fall', *hamesha(nt)-* 'spring/summer', *wit(ant)-* 'year', where the derivative with *-(a)nt-* coexists with an attested base-form, *ispant-* merits formal collocation with the semantically closer *nekut-* 'evening', *lukat-* 'morning', and *siwat-* 'day'. In the absence of an unsuffixed parallel, *ispant-* is not marked in any way (e.g. as animate or divinized), and there is no reason to postulate a secondary transformation of an **ispat-* into *ispant-* (as suggested by Kronasser, *Etym.* 1:259). Perhaps *ispant-* reflects an original **ksepon-* (gen. **kspnós*; cf. *tekan* < **dheĝhom*, gen. *taknas* < **dhĝhnós*) besides Avest. *xšapan-*, *xšafn-*, with the weak grade extended to **kspn̥t-* (> *ispant-*) on the pattern of **nekʷt-* (> *nekut-*), **lewkot-* (> *lukat-*; cf. Goth. *liuhaþ* 'light'), and **dyewot-* (> *siwat-*; cf. Ved. *dyút-* 'brightness'). Alternatively it is possible to speculate that *ispant-* < **kspon-t-* is built on the locative **kspon* (cf. *dagan* < **dhĝhom*) of an old *r/n*-stem seen in Avest. *xšapar-/xšapan-*, resembling Skt. *heman-tá-* 'winter' (cf. Gk. χίμαρος : χειμών, or Gk. ἔαρ : Skt. *vasan-tá-* 'spring'; Mayrhofer, *IF* 70:247–8 [1965]), thus tying in with Hitt. *gimant-* after all (if *giman-t-* rather than **gim-ant-*). Cf. also Oettinger, *Festschrift für G. Neumann* 239–40 (1982).

There is little plausibility in a comparison of *ispant-* with Goth. *spediza* 'later', OHG *spāti* 'late' (E. Forrer apud S. Feist, *Vgl. Wb. der gotischen Sprache* 444 [1939]); the Germanic words mean literally 'getting along' (cf. English *speed*).

ispatalu in the Cappadocian tablets, allegedly 'night quarters', has been interpreted as a Hittite **ispantalli-* (vel sim.) borrowed into local Old Assyrian (cf. e.g. N. van Brock, *RHA* 20:128–9 [1962]); but the meaning is uncertain, and the relevance doubtful (cf. Kronasser, *Die Sprache* 5:61 [1959], *Etym.* 1:138–9).

ispant- 'pour (a libation), libate, sacrifice' (BAL), rare, mostly Old
Hittite spelling for usual *sip(p)ant-* or *sip(p)and-* (q.v. for
overall treatment), 1 sg. pres. act. *is-pa-an-tah-hé* (*KBo* XVII 3
IV 1 *ispantah]he* and dupl. XVII 1 IV 5 *ispant[ahhe)*, *is-pa-an-*
-tah-hi (XVII 3 IV 6 and dupl. XVII 1 IV 10; XVII 1 III 14 and
dupl. XVII 6 III 6 GEŠTIN-*an ispantahhi* 'I pour wine'; cf.
Otten – Souček, *Altheth. Ritual* 36, 30, 97), 3 sg. pres. act.
is-pa-an-ti (XI 45 IV 20–21 DUMU LUGAL ... [...] *ispan[ti]*), 3 pl.
pres. act. *is-pa-an-ta-an-zi* (XVII 15 Rs. 18 *ispantanzi-ma na[tta*
'but they do not libate'; cf. V. Haas – M. Wäfler, *Ugarit-*
Forschungen 8:86 [1976]); iter. *ispanza(s)ki-* (beside normal
sip(p)anzaki-, both /spantski-/), 3 sg. pres. act. *is-pa-an-za-ki-zi*
(XX 34 Rs. 6), *is-pa-an-za-as-ki-i[z-zi* (XX 37 Vs. 3; cf. Neu,
Altheth. 140).

   ispantuwa- (c.) 'libation-vessel', nom. sg. BAL-*u-wa-as* (*KUB*
XXXVIII 1 I 31 1 BAL-*uwas* AN.BAR 'one libation-vessel of
iron'), acc. sg. *ispantuwan* (*Bo* 181 II 13–16 LUGAL-*i ispantuwan*
KÙ.BABBAR [*p]āi* LUGAL-*us* ... *lāhūwa[i]* 'gives a silver libation-
vessel to the king, the king ... pours'; cf. Otten, *ZA* 53:176
[1959]; Alp, *Belleten* 31:535–6 [1967]; *KUB* XXXII 98, 4; 133/u
Rs. 9), *ispanduwan* (*KBo* XVII 75 I 59–60 *ispanduwan* KÙ.
.BABBAR GEŠTIN *udai nu* ^{GIŠ}BANŠUR-*i* [*pira]n* 3-*šu sipanti* 'brings
a silver libation-vessel with wine and libates before the table
three times'), instr. sg. *ispanduit* (ibid. IV 8–10 *IŠTU BIBRI*
GUŠKIN [...] *ispanduit* KÙ.BABBAR [*sipa]nti* 'from a gold rhyton
[...] libates with a silver libation-vessel'; ibid. 29–30 *ispanduit*
KÙ.BABBAR [...] *sipanti*; ibid. III 13 *ispanduit* KÙ[.BABBAR]), abl.
sg. *ispanduwaz* (*KUB* VII 60 III 8–11 *nu-kan* URU-*LIM* ^{LÚ}KÚR
nassu tapisanit GEŠTIN *nasma* ^{DUG}*ispanduwaz IŠTU* GEŠTIN *sip-*
panti 'he libates with wine to the enemy city either with a wine-
jug or from a libation-vessel'; cf. Haas – Wilhelm, *Riten* 236;
1526/u I 17; *KBo* XV 33 II 30–31 *nu* ^{DUG}*ispanduwa[z* ^{DUG}*is]nū-*
ras piran ^DIM ^{URU}*Kuliuisn[a]* ^D*Halkinn-a mān* KAŠ-[*it*] *mān*
GEŠTIN-*it sipanti* 'from a libation-vessel before the dough-bowls
he libates the storm-god of K. and the grain-god either with
beer or with wine'), *ispanduaz* (ibid. III 31–33 *nu* ^{LÚ}EN É-*TIM*
ishanī EGIR-*anda PANI ZAG.GAR.RA* [^DI]M ^{URU}*Kuliuisna* ^{DUG}*ispan-*
duaz 3-*šu sipanti* 'the housemaster behind the blood facing the

altar libates the storm-god of K. three times from a libation-vessel'), nom. pl. *ispanduwas* (XXI 1 II 5 30 ^{DUG}*ispanduwas* TUR 'thirty small libation-vessels').

ispantuwa- originates in the gen. sg. of the verbal noun *sippanduar* (*KBo* I 42 IV 44; *MSL* 13:141 [1971]) or BAL-*u-wa--ar* (*KUB* III 95, 9; *MSL* 3:79 [1955]), thus DUG *ispantuwas* 'vessel of libation' > $^{(DUG)}$*ispantuwas* (nom. sg.; cf. *KBo* IV 13 III 33 1 UDU *sipanduwas* 1 MÁŠ.GAL 'one sheep of consecration [= sacrificial sheep], one he-goat'). Cf. Carruba, *Beschwörungsritual* 23; Neu, *Anitta-Text* 116, *Gedenkschrift für H. Kronasser* 139 (1982).

ispantuz(z)i- (n.) 'libation-vessel, libation, libate, libamen', nom.-acc. sg. or pl. ^{DUG}*ispantuzzi* (e.g. *KUB* XVII 21 II 16–17 NINDA *harsaus* ^{DUG}*ispantuzzi-ya kuez arha piddāir* 'whence they have brought off breadloaves [and] libation-vessels'; ibid. IV 10 NINDA KUR$_4$.RA ^{DUG}*ispantuzzi* GUD.HI.A UDU.HI.A 'breadloaves, libation-vessels, cattle, sheep'; cf. von Schuler, *Die Kaškäer* 156, 160, XXX 41 II 24), *ispantuzzi* (e.g. *KBo* XXV 112 II 8–9 NINDA *harsa-smas* ... *ispantuzzi-a-smas*; cf. Neu, *Altheth.* 191; *KUB* XXXIII 103 II 5 NINDA.KUR$_4$.R]A-*ya-sma⟨s⟩ ispantuzzi namma* ŪL *kuiski sipanti* 'breadloaves [and] libations nobody will offer you any more'; cf. Laroche, *RHA* 26:49 [1968]; Siegelová, *Appu-Hedammu* 46; II 13 IV 9–11 ^{LÚ}SÌLA.ŠU.DU$_8$.A *ispantuzzi* GIBIL GEŠTIN-*as dāi nu* ... *sipanti* 'the cupbearer takes fresh libamen of wine and ... libates'), ^{DUG}*ispantuzi* (*KBo* XVII 74 I 26–27 [OHitt.] ^{DUG}*ispantuzi* [...] *sipanti*; cf. Neu, *Gewitterritual* 12, 38; *KUB* XXIV 3 III 42 and XXX 13, 2; cf. Gurney, *Hittite Prayers* 36, 26), *ispatuzi* (V 1 I 38 GIG GAL NINDA.KUR$_4$.RA *ispatuzi parnass-a* SIG$_5$ ME-*as* 'the great ailment took breadloaves, libations, and the weal of the house'; cf. Ünal, *Hatt.* 2:38), *ispanduzzi* (e.g. I 16 III 50–51 *nu* NINDA.KUR$_4$.RA.HI.A-*ŠU ispanduzzi-sme[t]* [...] ... *sarā artaru* 'let their breadloaves [and] their libations ... stand ready'; cf. Sommer, *HAB* 14; XXXIII 121 II 7 *nu-za namma* ^{I}*Kessis* DINGIR.MEŠ-*us* NINDA *harsit ispanduzzi* ŪL *kappuizzi* 'K. no longer furnishes the gods libations along with breadloaves'; cf. Friedrich, *ZA* 49:234 [1950]), *ispanduzi* (e.g. *KBo* VI 26 I 29–30 [= *Code* 2:64] *nassu* NINDA *harsin nasma* ^{GIŠ}GEŠTIN *ispanduzi kinuzi* 'he breaks open

either a breadloaf or a wine-jar'; *KUB* XXV 31 Vs. 14–15
^{DUJG}*palhi ispanduzi karuuili* ^{LÚ}GUDÚ *dāi* EGIR-*pa-ma* [...] [*is*]*pan-
duzi nemus* [c. for n.!] ^{LÚ}ZABAR.DIB *pāi* 'the anointed one
deposits in a cauldron old libamen, and in return ... the goblet-
holder gives fresh libamina'), *ispanduzita* (XXXII 124 I 12
NINDA.KUR₄.RA *ispanduzita*, with Hurroid ending; cf. e.g. *aduplita* s.v. *adupli-*, and von Schuler, *Die Kaškäer* 154, 165), acc.
sg. *ispantuz*[*zin*] (XIV 14 Rs. 27), ^{DUG}*ispanduzzi*[*n*] (ibid. 23; cf.
Götze, *KlF* 174), gen. sg. *ispantuzzias* (e.g. *KBo* IV 9 I 16–17 2
huppar KÙ.BABBAR *ispantuzzias* GEŠTIN-*it sūwantes* [c. for n.]
'two silver jars filled with wine of libation'), *ispanduzias* (XX
99 + XXI 52 II 14 *ispanduzias piran dāi* 'places before the
libate'), dat.-loc. sg. ^{DUG}*ispantuzzi* (*KUB* XIII 4 III 58–59
n-asta DINGIR.MEŠ-*as* NINDA *harsi* ^{DUG}*ispantuzzi nahsarattan
mekki tiyan ha*[*rtin*] 'for the breadloaf [and] libation-vessel of
the gods keep your respect very much in place'; cf. Sturtevant,
JAOS 54:386 [1934]), *ispanduzzi* (XXXIII 121 II 12–13 DINGIR.
.MEŠ-*es-kan* ¹*Kessiya ispanduzzi ser kartimmiyauwantes* 'the
gods [were] angry at K. because of the libation'), *ispantuzziya*
(XIV 14 Rs. 29 *ispantuzziya ser*), ^{DUG}*ispantuziya* (X 11 V 6
[*A*]*NA PANI* ^{DUG}*ispantuziya* 'facing the libation-vessel'), instr. sg.
ispanduzzit (XXIV 2 Vs. 12 *nu-tta kāsa mukiskimi* NINDA *harsit*
^{DUG}*ispanduzzit* 'lo, I am entreating you with breadloaf [and]
libation'), *ispa*]*nduzit* (dupl. XXIV 1 I 14; cf. Gurney, *Hittite
Prayers* 16), abl. sg. *ispantuzziaz* (X 11 V 8–11 *n-asta* GAL
DUMU.MEŠ É.GAL *ispantuzziaz* GEŠTIN-*an sarā ... hāni* 'the chief
page draws up wine from the libation-vessel'), *ispanduzziaz*
(XIII 4 I 64–65 *kuis-wa-kan tuēl* DINGIR-*LIM-az* NINDA *harsiyaz*
[^{DUG}*i*]*sp*[*a*]*nduzziaz dās* 'whoever has taken from thy breadloaf
[or] libation-vessel, o god'; for the case-attraction in DINGIR-
-*LIM-az* cf. e.g. *tuetaza memiyanaz* for *tuel memiyanaz* 'at thy
behest' in VIII 48 I 12), gen. pl. ^{DUG}*ispantuzziyas* (XVII 21 II
8–9 *sumenzan nepisas* DINGIR.MEŠ-*as kue* KUR.KUR.HI.A NINDA
harsayas ^{DUG}*ispantuzziyas argamanass-a ēsta* 'your lands, gods
of heaven, which were [purveyors] of breadloaves, libation-
vessels, and tribute'). Instrument noun in -*uzzi*-, cf. e.g. s.v.
isgapuzzi-.

ispantuzziyala- (c.) 'libation-bearer', nom. pl. *ispantuzziy*]*alēs*

(*KUB* XIV 11 III 42), *ispantuzzialius* (sic dupl. XIV 8 Rs. 18–19 *nu-kan keus kuyēs* LÚ.MEŠ NINDA.KUR₄.RA-*us* ᴸᵁ·ᴹᴱˢ*ispantuzziyalius tēpawēs āssantes n-at-m[u le akk]anzi* 'the few bread- and libation-bearers who [are] remaining, they shall not die on me'; cf. Götze, *KlF* 214), *ispantuzziyalas* (XIV 14 Rs. 26 ᴸᵁ·ᴹᴱˢ*ispantuzziyalass-a tepawēs*; cf. Götze, *KlF* 174), *ispantuzzilas* (XIV 8 Rs. 39 *nu-kan* ŠA DINGIR.MEŠ *kuyēs* LÚ.MEŠ NINDA.KUR₄.RA ᴸᵁ·ᴹᴱˢ*ispantuzzilass-a [āss]antes n-at le namma akkanzi* 'what bread- and libation-bearers of the gods [are] remaining, let them not also die'), ᴸᵁ·]ᴹᴱˢ*ispatuzzielass-a* (dupl. XIV 11 IV 9). Denominative agent noun, cf. e.g. ᴸᵁ*harsiyala-* = LÚ NINDA.KUR₄.RA, from (NINDA) *harsi-* 'thick bread, bread-loaf', *asusala-* (s.v. *asusa-*), *auriyala-* (s.v. *auri-*), besides *asusatalla-*, *auriyatalla-*; *ispantuzziyala-* is to Gk. σπονδηφόρος what e.g. *irhuitalla-* 'basket-bearer' (q.v. s.v. *erhui-*) is to καλαθηφόρος.

ispantuz(z)i(y)assar (n.), *ispantuz(z)i(y)assara-* (c.) 'libation-vessel', acc. sg. c. (?) *is-pa-a]n-tu-zi-as-sa-ra-an* (*KUB* XLIII 30 II 21), nom.-acc. sg. or pl. *is-pa-an-tu-uz-zi-ya-as-sar* (XLIII 28 II 8 and III 6; cf. Neu, *Altheth.* 154–5), *ispantuzziassar* (*KBo* XX 88 IV 10–11 *ispantuzziassar* KÙ.BABBAR-*as* [...] SAL.LUGAL-*ri pāi* SAL.LUGAL-*s-a sipanti* 'gives a silver libation-vessel to the queen, and the queen libates'; *VBoT* 113, 6 *isp]antuzziassar* KÙ.BABBAR; *KUB* X 23 IV 12 *ispa]ntuzziassar* GUŠKIN 'libation-vessel of gold'; *KBo* XXV 147 Rs. 3; cf. Neu, *Altheth.* 232; *KUB* II 13 IV 17–19 ᴸᵁSÌLA.ŠU.DU₈.A *ispantuzziassar* GEŠTIN-*as dāi n-asta ... sipanti* 'the cupbearer takes a libation-vessel with wine, and he libates'; ibid. 23 *ispantuzziassar* GEŠTIN), *isp]antuziyassar* (*KBo* XVII 74 III 2 [OHitt.]), *ispantuziassar* (e.g. XVII 43 I 8 *ispantuziassar* KÙ.BABBAR *dāi*, with dupl. XVII 18 II 9; cf. Neu, *Altheth.* 104, 100; *KUB* XLIII 30 II 8 and 12 *ispantuziassar* LUGAL-*i parā epzi* 'proffers a libation-vessel to the king'; ibid. 20 *i]spantuziassar dāi*; cf. Neu, *Altheth.* 77), *ispantuzzisar* (*KBo* IV 9 II 51–52 UGULA ᴸᵁ·ᴹᴱˢMU-HALDIM *ispantuzzisar* GEŠTIN LUGAL-*i parā epzi* 'the chef de cuisine proffers a libation-vessel with wine to the king'), *ispantuzisar* (XI 50 I 24 *ispantuzisar* KÙ.BABBAR), *is-pa-tu-uz-zi--es-sar* (*KUB* XX 87 I 10–12 *ù* ᴸᵁGUDÚ *ispatuzzessar* ŠA

DINGIR-*LIM ANA* ^{LÚ}SANGA *pāi* ^{LÚ}SANGA-*s-a* GUD.MAH *sipanti* 'and the anointed one gives the god's libation-vessel to the priest, and the priest consecrates the bull'), ^{DUG}*ispanduzziyassar* (VII 8 II 11–12 NINDA *harsawus memal* ^{DUG}*ispanduzziyassar* 'breadloaves, groats, libation-vessels'), *ispanduziassar* (*KBo* XVII 74 II 7 [OHitt.] UGULA ^{LÚ.MEŠ}MUHALDIM GEŠTIN-*as ispanduziassar* G[E₆ LUGAL-*i par*]*ā epzi* 'the chef de cuisine proffers a black libation-vessel with wine to the king'; ibid. IV 37–38]*ispanduziassar* GE₆ ŠA GEŠTIN *dāi kuttas piran* [*siuni* 1]-*is sipanti* 'takes a black libation-vessel with wine; before the wall he libates once to the deity'), instr. sg. *is-pa-an-du-uz-zi-ya-as-sa--ri-it* (*KUB* XXV 36 V 5–8 ^{LÚ}*GUDÚ ANA* ^DZA.BA₄.BA₄ *sipanduwa*[*n*] 3-*ŠU QATAMMA irhāizzi* LÚ ^DIM-*as ispanduzziyassarit sarā* 3-*ŠU QATAMMA sunnai* 'the anointed one likewise finishes libating three times to the war-god; the man of the storm-god likewise fills up three times with the libation-vessel'; for supine not formed from iterative and used for infinitive cf. *ishahru iyauwan* 'to shed tears' [s.v. *ishahru-*], beside normal *ēshar sipanduwanzi irhāizzi* 'finishes offering up the blood' [s.v. *arha-*]), *is-pa-an-tu-uz-zi-as-sar-i*[*t*] (ibid. VI 30), acc. pl. *is-pa--an-tu-zi-as-sa-ru-us* (XLIII 30 II 6–7 ^{LÚ.M|EŠ}MUHALDIM *ispantuziassarus* ... [...] *pedanzi* 'the cooks carry the libation-vessels'; cf. Neu, *Altheth.* 77).

ispantuzziyassar, ispatuzzessar as a derivative of *ispantuzzi-* resembles e.g. *alalessar* 'meadow' from *alel-* 'flower, bloom', or **kuttessar* (BÀD-*essar*) 'walling' from *kutt-* 'wall' (for the form of the suffix cf. Kronasser, *Etym.* 1:288). Curiously no heteroclitic oblique cases are found; instead there is evidence of occasional *a*-stem thematization already in Old Hittite (acc. g. c. [?] *ispantuziassaran*, acc. pl. c. *ispantuziassarus*), with instr. sg. *ispanduzziyassarit* resembling dat.-loc. sg. ^{NA₄}*kuttassari* (*KUB* XXVI 92, 11) from **kuttassar* (perhaps Luwoid, cf. Hier. CHISEL *kutasara/i-* 'wall[s]').

Despite the tendency to declare *ispantuwa-, ispantuzzi-,* and *ispantuzziyassar* semantically identical (e.g. Alp, *Belleten* 31:540 [1967]; M. Popko, *Kultobjekte in der hethitischen Religion* 91 [1978]) there are significant differences: *ispantuwa-* and *ispantuzziyassar* are often qualified as to their material (iron, silver, gold) and are clearly primarily terms for containers; *ispantuzzi-*, on the other hand, shades metonymically into the libational contents as well (or even primarily), as a result of which it is frequently collocated with NINDA *harsi-* in a combined formula for the bread-and-wine offerings to the deity.

For etymology (Gk. σπένδω 'libate', Lat. *spondeō* 'pledge, promise') see further s.v. *sip(p)ant-*, likewise for the question why the finite verb has regularized an unusual spelling variant for /sp-/, whereas noun derivatives consistently keep the normal *is-pa-*.

Because of clear derivational links to the verb *ispant-* there is no likelihood in G. B. Jahukyan's comparison of *ispandu(zzi)-* with Arm. *pʿund* 'vessel', ON *spann* 'pail, bucket', OCS *spǫdŭ* 'peck', Lat. *sponda* 'couch, sofa', IE **(s)pondh-* (*Hayerenə ev hndevropakan hin lezunerə* 139 [1970]).

ispar(r)-, isparriya-   'spread, strew, scatter, stretch, shatter, fell; fly(?)', 1 sg. pres. act. *is-pa-ar-hi* (*KUB* XII 44 II 30 *parasdun isparhi* 'I strew plant-shoots'), *is-pár-ah-hi* (VII 57 I 6–8 ᴰIM-*as-wa* ᵁᴿᵁ*Lihzinan* [...] [IGI.HI.A-*wa*] *katta huwappahhi nu--wa-ssan paimi* [...] [...]*hūmanni isparahhi* ˢᴬᴸ·ᴹᴱˢˢU.GI *isparnumi* 'I, the storm-god, shall fling L. face down, and I shall go [...] ... shatter [it and] make the sorceresses scatter'), 2 sg. pres. act. *is-pár-ra-at-ti* (XXI 27 III 29–30 GÌR.MEŠ-*it isparratti* 'you shatter with your feet'), 3 sg. pres. act. *is-pa-ri* (*KBo* IV 2 II 53; cf. Kronasser, *Die Sprache* 8:93 [1962]), *is-pa-a-ri* (e.g. *KUB* XX 46 III 6–8 *ilanas piran happurriyan ispāri* 'spreads h. before the staircase'; *KBo* X 45 II 19–20 *n-us* GÍR.MEŠ-*as* DÙ-*zi n-us* KI-*an ispāri nu-ssan kūs* DINGIR.MEŠ *asasi* 'he makes [the idols] in dagger-form, spreads them on the ground, and sets up these deities'; cf. Otten, *ZA* 54:112 [1961]), *is-pár-ri-iz-zi* (*KUB* XIV 1 Rs. 91 *aliyas-wa* ŪL *wāi* ŪL-*ma-wa wāki* ŪL-*ma-wa isparrizzi* 'the a.[-bird] does not coo, does not bite, does not spread [viz. its wings, = 'fly'?]'; cf. Götze, *Madd.* 38, 143–4, and see the end of this entry), *is-pár-ri-ya-az-zi* (VII 60 II 8–10 *namma* 1 TÚG BABBAR 1 TÚG SA₅ 1 TÚG ZA.GÌN [*dā*]*i n-as* ANA DINGIR.MEŠ ᴸᵁ́KÚR KASKAL.MEŠ *kattan isparriyazzi* 'she also takes a white cloth, a red cloth, [and] a blue cloth, and spreads them as paths for the enemy gods'; cf. Haas – Wilhelm, *Riten* 234), 3 pl. pres. act. *is-pa-ra-an-zi* (e.g. XXX 29 Vs. 4–5 [1]-EN ᴷᵁˢ*sarpassis-a--ka[n]* ᴳᴵˢ*kuppisnas istarna [t]agān isparanzi* 'one cushion between the stools on the ground they spread'; *VAT* 7448 III 3–5 *nu* IŠTU É ᴸᵁGUDÚ KASKAL-*an menahhanda* IŠTU TÚG *isparanzi* ᴺᴵᴺᴰᴬ*purpurus-si kattan ishūwanzi* 'out of the house of the anointed one they lay a cloth-spread on the road and pour bread-lumps down upon it'; *VBoT* 24 II 31–33 ŠA ᴳᴵˢHASHUR. .KUR.RA ᴳᴵˢ*lahhurnuzi isparanzi ser-a-ssan* 3 NINDA.KUR₄.RA *parsiandus tianzi* 'they spread foliage of mountain-apple and on it they place three broken breadloaves'; cf. Sturtevant, *TAPA* 58:10 [1927]; *KBo* XXV 31 III 10 [OHitt.] *isparanzi*), *is-pár-ra--an-zi* (frequent, e.g. dupl. [later copy] XX 32 II 3; cf. Neu, *Altheth.* 80, 83; *KUB* IX 31 IV 17 *nu* ᴳᴵˢ*lahhurnuzzi isparranzi*, with dupl. *HT* 1 IV 22 *nu lahhurnuzzi isparanzi*; *KUB* IX 31 III 62–63 *nu* ᴳᴵˢ*lahhurnuzi kattan isparranzi*; dupl. XLI 17 III 11 *nu* ᴳᴵˢ*lahhurnuzi katta isparran[zi*; dupl. IX 32 Vs. 38 *nu* ᴳᴵˢ*lahhurnuzzi kattan isparranzi*; ibid. Rs. 27 *nu* ᴳᴵˢ*lahhurnuzzi dagān isparranzi* 'they spread foliage on the ground'; *IBoT* III 148 I 31–32 ⁽ᴳᴵ⁾ˢNÁ-*ma-kan parā udanzi n-at* ᴳᴵˢZA.LAM.GAR-*as* É.ŠÀ-*ni isparranzi* 'they bring forth the bed and spread it in the interior of the tent'; cf. Haas – Wilhelm, *Riten* 212; *ABoT* 34, 6 and 16 ᴳᴵˢNÁ *isparranzi*; *KUB* X 92 VI 14–15 *kuitman-ma-kan* ᴰUTU-*us nūwa sarā nu* ᴳᴵˢ*nathita isparranzi* 'but while the sun is still up they spread the couch[es]'; XLIV 1 Rs. 20 ŠÀ É.ŠÀ-*kan* ᴳᴵˢNÁ-*hi na[mulli is]parranzi* 'inside the inner chamber they cover the couch with a bedspread'; VII 8 III 14–15 *nu-ssi* ᴳᴵˢNÁ *namma--ssi* ᴳᴵˢBANŠUR *piran katta isparranzi* 'furthermore they spread a bed for him in front of the table'; ibid. 18–19 *nu-ssi ape-ya kattan isparranzi* 'those [viz. garments] too they spread for him'; *KBo* XXI 10, 12 KUŠ.GUD *isparranzi* 'they spread a cowhide'; cf. Oettinger, *Eide* 16; *KUB* XXIX 45 I 14]*kattan isparranzi* 'they spread out'; cf. Kammenhuber, *Hippologia* 172; *KBo* XV 9 III 7 *ser isparranzi*; cf. Kümmel, *Ersatzrituale* 64), 1 sg. pret. act. *is-pár-hu-un* (*KUB* XV 34 I 40–42 *kāsa-smas* KASKAL.MEŠ ᵀᵁᴳ*kusisiyas* ᵀᵁᴳ*kuresnit isparhun nu-smas-as* BA. .BA.ZA YÀ DÙG.GA *isparhun nu-ssan apiya iyaddumat* 'lo, for you

I have spread paths with a swath of gown-fabric, for you I have
spread paste [and] good oil, now go there!'; cf. Haas – Wilhelm,
Riten 186), *is-pár-ra-ah-hu-un* (VII 60 II 26–27 KASKAL.MEŠ-*ya*-
-*wa-smas* IŠTU TÚG BABBAR ... *kattan isparrahhun* 'paths I have
spread for you with a white cloth'; XVII 27 III 11–12 -]*as-kan*
ser allapahhun n-at anda [GÌR-*i*]*t isparrahhun* 'I have spat on [...]
and in addition shattered it with my foot'), 3 pl. pret. act.
is-pár-ri-ir XXXIII 114 IV 12; cf. Laroche, *RHA* 26:36 [1968]),
2 sg. imp. midd. *is-pár-hu-ut* (XXIII 77 I 4), 2 pl. imp. act.
is-pí-ir-te-en (sic *KBo* XXI 14 Vs. 8), 3 pl. imp. act. *is-pár-ra-an*-
-*du* (VI 34 III 24–29 *n*[*u* ...] *parā epzi n-an* IGI.HI.A-*wa katt*[*a*
huwapp]*āi n-an* GÌR-*it isparranzi nu-sma*[*s ki*]*san tezzi kuis-wa*-
-*kan kūs* NIŠ [DINGIR-*LIM*] *sarrizzi nu uwandu apel* URU-*a*[*n*
DINGIR.M]EŠ ᵁᴿᵁ*Hatti QATAMMA* GÌR-*it isparrandu n-*[*at da*]*n*-
natta URU-*yassessar iyandu* 'he takes [the figurine] and flings it
face down, and they shatter it with their feet, and he says as
follows: "he who breaks these oaths, let the gods of Hatti come
and likewise shatter his city with their feet and make it a
desolate townsite"'; cf. Oettinger, *Eide* 12); partic. *isparrant*-,
nom. sg. c. *is-pár-ra-an-za* (e.g. XVII 61 Vs. 17 *ekza isparranza*
'the net [is] spread'; cf. H. Berman, *JAOS* 92:466 [1972]; *KUB*
XVII 31 I 24 *MAYALU-ma-ssi sastas* É.ŠÀ-*ni isparranz*[*a* 'bedding
[is] spread for him in the inner bedchamber'; cf. Kümmel,
Ersatzrituale 62; ibid. 4 *MAYA*]*LU isparranza*; *KBo* XV 2 IV 1–2
sast[*a*- ...] ... [ᵀᵁᴳ*MAYALU*] *isparranza* 'bed ... bedding [is]
spread', cf. Kümmel, *Ersatzrituale* 60), nom.-acc. sg. neut.
isparran (*KUB* IX 28 I 15 *ispāta* KÙ.BABBAR TUR *isparran harzi*
'she holds a small silver spit outstretched'), nom.-acc. pl. neut.
isparranda (*KBo* XV 2 I 10–11, amended from dupl. *KUB* XVII
14 IV 3–4, [1-*NUTUM* ᴳᴵˢNÁ] IŠTU ᵀᵁᴳ*MAYALI isparran*[*da* 'one
bed covered with a bedspread'; cf. Kümmel, *Ersatzrituale* 56),
dat.-abl. pl. *isparrandas* (XXX 15+XXXIX 11 Vs. 48–49
[ᴳᴵˢNÁ.ME]š *isparranzi nu-kan hastai* IŠTU ᴳᴵˢŠÚ.A *arha d*[*anzi*]
[*n-a*]*t-san* ᴳᴵˢNÁ-*as isparrandas tianzi* 'they spread the bed, take
the bones from the chair, and place them on the spread bed'; cf.
Otten, *Totenrituale* 68); verbal noun *is-pár-ri-ya-u-wa-ar* (*KBo* I
42 V 4 DAG = [Akk.] *meštū* [from *šeṭū* 'spread']= *isparri-*
yauwar; ibid. 5 DAG=[Akk.] *meltū*=KI.MIN-*pat* 'ditto'; cf.

ispar(r)-, isparriya-

Götze, *Madd.* 144, 70; Güterbock, *MSL* 13:142 [1971]); inf.
is-pár-ru-um-ma-an-zi (*IBoT* II 131 I 23); iter. *ispareski-*, 3 sg.
pres. act. *is-pa-ri-es-ki-iz-zi* (*KUB* VII 5 II 19 *n-[at] ispandaz
katta ispareskizzi* 'he will spread it [viz. the garment] out at
night'; iterative-"durative" *isparanna-*, 3 sg. pres. act. *is-pa-ra-
-an-na-i* (*Bo* 404 IV 5).

isparnu- 'spread, spray, scatter', 1 sg. pres. act. *is-pár-nu-mi*
(see above sub 1 sg. pres. act. *isparahhi*), 3 sg. pres. act.
is-pár-nu-zi (*KBo* XX 10+XXV 59 I 11–12 and II 8–9 *ta*
LUGAL-*un suppiyahhi watar 3-šU isparnuzi* 'he purifies the king,
sprays water three times'; cf. Neu, *Altheth.* 131–2; *KUB*
XLVIII 76 I 2–3 *nu ektan [ispar]nuzi* 'spreads the net'; cf.
Oettinger, *Eide* 6), *is-pár-nu-uz-zi* (1144/v, 4), 3 pl. pres. act.
isparnuwanzi (473/t Vs. 13–15 GIM-*an ektan ispar]nuwanzi nu*
ARNABU *ektet [appanzi]* 'even as they spread the net and catch
the hare with the net ...'), 1 sg. pret. act. *is-pár-nu-nu-un* (XLI
19 Rs. 9), 3 sg. pret. act. *is-pár-nu-ut* (XIX 9 IV 12; cf.
Riemschneider, *JCS* 16:115 [1962]); iter. *isparnuski-*, 3 sg. pres.
act. *i]s-pár-nu-us-ki-iz-zi* (XII 29 I 5).

ispar(r)uzzi- (n.) 'rafter' (vel sim.), nom.-acc. sg. or pl.
GIŠ*is-pa-ru-uz-zi* (*KUB* XXIX 1 III 18–19 *mān* LÚNAGAR
GIŠ*iskis-san-as* GIŠ*isparuzzi karsūwanzi paizzi* 'when the carpenter goes to cut the ridgepole and the rafters'; cf. B. Schwartz,
Orientalia N.S. 16:34 [1947]; Goetze, *ANET* 358), GIŠ*is-pár-ru-
-uz-zi* (*KUB* XL 55+1236/u, 16 GIŠ]*isparuzzi* 4 *sēk[an* 'the
rafter[s] four spans' [viz. in length]; cf. Kühne, *ZA* 62:255–6
[1972], who compared Germanic **spar[r]an-* 'spar, rafter').
Literally 'stretcher' (instrument noun in *-uzzi-* like e.g. *ispan-
tuzzi-*; cf. e.g. s.v. *isgapuzzi-*).

Luwoid *par(r)iya-* 'spread' (herbal medicine in the eyes), 3
sg. pres. act. *pa-ar-ri-it-ti*, with gloss wedges (*KUB* XXII 61 I 19
ŠÀ IGI.HI.A *apāt parritti* '[the medicine man] spreads that in my
eyes'), 3 pl. pres. act. *pa-ar-ri-en-zi*, with gloss wedges (ibid. 6 ŠÀ
IGI.HI.A *parrienzi*), 3 sg. pret. act. *pár-ri-ya-i[t* (XXXV 111 II 2;
cf. Otten, *LTU* 101); verbal adj. *pariyawant-*, nom. sg. c.
pa-ri-ya-u-wa-an-za (XXII 61 I 14 ú *pariyauwanza kuit* 'the
herb[al medicine] which has been spread'). The initial of *parritti*
is related to Hittite proper *isparrizzi* (quoted above) like e.g.

444

Luw. *tummant-* is to Hitt. *istaman(a)-* 'ear'. This medical usage is distinct from Hitt. *iski(ya)-*'salve' (q.v.) and from *anda tarna-* 'instil' (viz. eye-drops; e.g. XLIV 63 III 18; cf. Burde, *Medizinische Texte* 30). Cf. Čop, *Ling.* 7:119 (1965).

ispāri goes back to **spóre(y)* (cf. Bechtel, *Hittite Verbs* 17), *isparriya-* (if ancient) may come from **spr̥-yó-*, and *isparnu-* can reflect **spr̥-néw-*. The outcomes of **sper-(H-)* have in Hittite supplanted those of the rhyme-word **ster-(H-)* 'strew, spread' (Skt. *str̥ṇóti*, Avest. *stərənaoiti*, Gk. στόρνῡμι, Lat. *sternō*, OIr. *sernaid*, Goth. *straujan*), which typically yielded words for 'bedding' (Skt. *prastará-* 'cushioning', Avest. *stairiš-* 'bed', Gk. στρῶμα 'bedding', Lat. *strāmen* 'litter, bedding', OIr. *cossair* < **kom-stari-* 'bed', OE *strēaw* 'straw'); thus ^{GIŠ}NÁ *ispar-* matches Gk. λέχος στορέσαι or Lat. *lectum sternere* (cf. Myc. *re-ke-to-ro-te-ri-jo* = λεχεστρωτήριον, Lat. *lectisternium*). For a possible relic see s.v. *istarna*. IE **sper-(H-)* must have been richer in semantic shadings, not merely 'spread, strew, scatter' (cf. Gk. σπείρω 'scatter, sow', σποράς 'scattered', Arm. *sp'ŕem* 'scatter', *p'arat* 'scattered', OE *sprǣdan* [< **spr-éy-d-*] 'spread', OHG *spriu* [German *spreu*] 'chaff') but also 'spray' (cf. Hitt. *isparnuzi* quoted above [beside usual *hurnai-* 'spray', *pappars-* 'sprinkle'], OHG *sprīzan* 'spray') and 'stretch (out), extend' (cf. Hitt. *ispāta ... isparran* 'spit outstretched' quoted above, *ispar[r]uzzi-* 'rafter' cognate with Engl. *spar* and *spear*, Lat. *sparus* 'hunting-spear'). From 'stretch, extend' as applied to body extremities developed another set of nuanced meanings attached to discrete stems, thus Rig-Vedic *sphuráti* 'dart, bound' or 'kick' (e.g. *RV* 1.84.8 *kadā́ mártam arādhásaṁ padā́ kṣúmpam iva sphurat* 'when will he kick the stingy mortal like a mushroom with his foot?'; cf. *apa-sphúra-* 'spurning'), later Skt. 'twitch, quiver', as in Gk. (ἀ)σπαίρω 'jerk, be convulsive' (beside σφυρόν 'ankle'); in other languages the verbal sense is 'kick' (Lith. *spìrti*) leading over to 'spurn' (OE *spurnan* 'kick, spurn'; Lat. *spernō* 'spurn', *asper* 'harsh' < **apo-speros* 'spurning'; perhaps Arm. *spaŕnam* 'threaten'), besides nominalizations such as OIr. *seir* 'heel' (< **speret-*), OE *spor* 'spoor, footstep, track'. GÌR.MEŠ-*it isparratti*, GÌR-*it isparrahhun*, GÌR-*it isparrandu* (quoted above) resembles Vedic *padā́ sphurá-*, but

ispar(r)-, isparriya-

unlike other languages Hittite has not reserved this special
sense for a separate stem; rather Hittite shows overall nuances
of *sper-(H-)* parallel to what e.g. Latin has for *ster-(H-)*:
not only *membra ... stratus* 'with limbs outstretched' (Horace,
Odes 1.1.21–22), but also *moenia ... stravit* 'demolished the
walls' (Ovid, *Metamorphoses* 12:549–550), *sternit ... Troiam*
'lays low Troy' (Vergil, *Aeneid* 2:603), and *strāgēs* 'overthrow';
similarly GÌR-*it isparra-* may be simply an extended meaning in
the same way as English *shatter* is a variant of *scatter* (both
from OE *sceaterian*, cognate with Gk. σκίδνημι 'scatter'); cf.
GIŠ*eyanan isparr*[*a-* 'fell an *eya*-tree' (117/r, 4). Thus 'shatter
with the foot' may well be strictly secondary; it is not even used
in Kumarbi's rantings against the gods (*KUB* XXXIII 93 + III
21–25 *nu-wa*[*r-an iz*]*zan* GIM-*an arha pussaiddu ...* GÌR-*it anda
pasihaiddu ... arha zahreskiddu, ...* GAM *... ishuwāu ... arha
duwarneskiddu* 'let him pound him like chaff, crush (him) with
the foot (like an ant), snap (him off like a reed), scatter down
(all the gods from heaven like birds), break (them like empty
vessels)'.

The separation of the two roots *sper-* (despite suspicions of
ultimate identity, e.g. *IEW* 993) has played the devil with the
etymologizing of *ispar-*. Sturtevant (starting *Lg.* 4:2–3 [1928])
compared Gk. σπείρω exclusively (separating Skt. *sphuráti*;
also *Comp. Gr.*[1] 130, *Lg.* 14:72 [1938], *Comp. Gr.*[2] 45); thus
also e.g. Bechtel, *Hittite Verbs* 17; T. Milewski, *L'indo-hittite et
l'indo-européen* 43 (1936); Kronasser, *VLFH* 30; A. Bernabé P.,
Revista española de lingüística 3:433 (1973). Benveniste (*BSL*
33:139 [1932]) opted for Skt. *sphuráti* as the comparandum and
rejected Gk. σπείρω (thus also Couvreur, *Hett.* 198). In a
mediating vein, W. Petersen (*Arch. Or.* 9:204–5 [1937]) suggested that both roots *sper-* (whatever their ultimate PIE
relationship) had coalesced in Hittite.

Already Götze (*Madd.* 144) compared the two meanings of
ispar- to those of e.g. Akk. *sapānu* ('cover over' and 'throw
down'), and Kronasser (*Etym.* 1:446) adduced Lat. *sternere*
'scatter' and 'lay low, destroy'. Yet attempts to split the
inventory have persisted: C. Watkins (in *Flexion und Wortbildung* 377 [1975]) tried to distinguish *ispar-* 'spread' from

446

isparra- 'tread on', comparing the first to σπείρω (IE **sper-*)
and the second to *sphuráti* (IE **sperH-*); but despite admission
of exceptions, the inventory simply overwhelms attempts at
separation (cf. e.g. above *is-pár-ra-ah-hu-un* 'I have spread' or
'I have shattered'). Oettinger (*Eide* 45, *Stammbildung* 266–71)
came out strongly but wholly unconvincingly for a base-
meaning 'tread, ram' in *isparra-* (thus comparing Skt. *sphuráti*),
explaining 'spread' from a rural habit of spreading straw and
the like with the feet; but he, too, had to admit exceptions,
tying in *isparnu-* as 'spray' with Gk. σπείρω instead.

A further cognate may be found in *partāuwar* 'wing' (q.v.);
cf. Skt. *parṇá-* (n.) 'pinion, wing, feather', OCS *pero* 'feather',
pariti 'fly', Lith. *sparñas* 'wing', and the bird-names Lat. *parra*,
Umbr. *parfa(m)* (< **sparsā*), Goth. *sparwa* 'sparrow', Hes.
σπαράσιον, Toch. A *ṣpār*. Cf. above 3 sg. pres. *isparrizzi*
'spreads (its wings?)'; possibly *isparrizzi* = OCS *paritŭ* 'flies'
(*pittai-* having shifted in the direction of 'run, flee'; *partāuwar*
= *pittar* 'wing')?
Cf. *ispart(iya)-*.

ispart(iya)-, isparz(a)-   'escape, get away, slip away', *sarā ispart-*
'leap up, emerge, accede, come of age', 3 sg. pres. act.
is-pár-ti-i-e-iz-zi (*KBo* XI 14 II 20–21 ᴺᴬ⁴ARÀ-*za-kan* GIM-*an*
kappis ispartiyezzi EN.SISKUR-*kan* ᴰ*Ākni* KAxU-*za QATAMMA*
ispartiddu 'even as a small grindstone slips away, may the
sacrificer likewise escape from the jaws of Akni'), *is-pár-za-i*
(*KUB* VI 7 IV 4; XL 33 Vs. 20), *is-pár-za-a-i* (*KBo* XII 38 II 2;
cf. Güterbock, *JNES* 26:76 [1967]), *is-pár-za-zi* (e.g. XVI 47
Vs. 10–11 *n-us-kan mān kuemi mān-us arnumi mān-mu-kan
arha-ma kuiski isparzazi* 'whether I slay them, or deport them,
if someone escapes from me …'; cf. Otten, *Istanbuler Mitteilungen* 17:56 [1967]; *KUB* XXXI 66 II 6–7 *nu-wa-za mān* [LUGAL-
-u]*s* DINGIR-*LIM-is kisari sarā ku*[*is-kan*] *kuis* LUGAL-*us isparzazi*
'when the king becomes a god, whoever shall accede as king
…'; cf. Houwink Ten Cate, *Anatol. Stud. Güterbock* 130; I 1 IV
87–88 *sarā isparzazi* 'accedes [to the kingship]' or 'comes of
age'; cf. Götze, *Hattusilis* 40; Goetze, *Kizzuwatna* 23–4 [1940];

XXIII 1 II 43 *sarā isparzazi*; cf. Kühne – Otten, *Šaušgamuwa* 10; *KBo* VII 20 II 6 *n]asma* INIM BAL UGU *isparzazi* 'or word of insurrection emerges'; V 9 II 14–16 *nu-kan mān* INA KUR ᵁᴿᵁ*Hatti [idalus] kuiski memiyas sarā isparzazi* 'if in Hatti some bad report emerges'; cf. Friedrich, *Staatsverträge* 1:16; V 13 II 26–27 *namma-kan mān* IŠTU KUR ᵁᴿᵁ*Hatti kuiski idalus memiyas* ŠA BAL *sara isparzazi* 'further if from Hatti some bad word of insurrection emerges'; cf. Friedrich, *Staatsverträge* 1:124), *is-pár-za-az-zi* (the similar passage V 4 Vs. 10; cf. Friedrich, *Staatsverträge* 1:52; IV 3 III 3–4 *[nasma-ka]n* IŠTU KUR ᵁᴿᵁ*Hatti-ya kuiski* AWAT ᴸᵁ́KÚR *sa[rā] isparzazzi nu* ᴸᵁ́KÚR *kuiski* ANA ᴰUTU-ŠI *arāi* 'or from Hatti some word of hostility emerges, and some enemy rises against my majesty'; dupl. IV 7 III 30; cf. Friedrich, *Staatsverträge* 1:132; similarly V 4 Vs. 18; cf. Friedrich, *Staatsverträge* 1:54), *is-pa-ar-zi-zi* (*KUB* IV 72 Rs. 4–5 *nassu-ma-sta* LÚ-*as hatgauwaz petaz isparzizi* 'or the man will escape from a tight spot'), *is-pár-za-iz-zi* (112/u, 6), 1 sg. pret. act. *is-pár-za-ah-hu-un* (XXV 21 III 13–16 GIM-*an-ma--kan ūk* ᴵ*Tu[thaliyas] sarā isparzahhu[n nu-mu]* ᴵ*Hattusi--DINGIR-LIM-is* LUGAL [GAL *sarā dās*] 'but when I, T., came of age, Hattusilis the great king took me up'; cf. von Schuler, *Die Kaškäer* 186), 2 sg. pret. act. *is-pár-za-as-ta* (XIX 49 I 5–6 *man-ta-kkan kue[nnir nu zik] isparzasta* 'they would have killed you, but you escaped'; cf. Friedrich, *Staatsverträge* 2:4), 3 sg. pret. act. *is-pár-za-as* (XXIII 93 III 15 *sarā-pat isparzas*), *is-pár-za-as-ta* (e.g. XXIII 72 Rs. 17 *piran arha isparzas[ta* 'got away'; XIV 1 Vs. 57 1-*is isparzasta* 'alone escaped'; cf. Götze, *Madd.* 14; *KBo* XXII 2 Rs. 8 ᴵ*Hāppis-a isparzasta* 'H. escaped', with dupl. III 38 Rs. 24 ᴵ*Happis[s-a] isparzasta*; cf. Otten, *Altheth. Erzählung* 12; III 60 III 4 [OHitt.] 'escaped'; cf. Güterbock, *ZA* 44:106 [1938]; V 8 III 31–32 *nu-mu-kan* ᴵ*Pittaggatallis-pat* 1-*as isparzasta* 'P. alone escaped from me'; cf. Götze, *AM* 158; III 4 II 77 -*k]an* 1-*as* SAG.DU-*as isparzasta* 'escaped as the only person'; cf. Götze, *AM* 64; II 5 III 37 ᴵ*Aparrus-ma-kan isparzasta* 'but A. got away'; cf. Götze, *AM* 188; *KUB* XIX 37 III 20 *nu-kan* ᴸᵁ́KÚR ᵁᴿᵁ*Timmuhalas* ŪL *isparzasta* 'the enemy from T. did not escape'; ibid. 22–23 *nu-mu-kan hantezzi palsi kuit* ᵁᴿᵁ*Timmuhalas* IŠTU NAM.RA.HI.A

GUD UDU *isparzasta* 'because the first time around T. had escaped from me with deportees, cattle, and sheep'; cf. Götze, *AM* 174; XXXIII 108 II 7 *sarā isparzasta* '[Ištar] leaped up' [from bed]; cf. Friedrich, *JKF* 2:148 [1952]; Laroche, *RHA* 26:72 [1968]; *KBo* VI 28 Vs. 16–17 [*ma*]*hhan-ma* ABA ABI-YA [I]*Su*[*ppiluliuma* LUGAL GA]L UR.SAG *sarā isparzasta* [*nu-*]*za-kan* ANA ᴳᴵˢŠÚ.A LUGAL-*UTTI esa*[*t* 'but when my grandfather S., great king, hero, came of age and seated himself on the throne of kingship'), 3 pl. pret. act. *is-pár-te-ir* (*KUB* XXIII 72+1684/u Vs. 43 ŠA ᴰUTU-*ŠI-ya* ANA ᴳᴵˢTUKUL *kuyēs piran arha isparter* 'those who escaped from my majesty's weapons'; cf. H. A. Hoffner, *JCS* 28:61 [1976]; H. Otten – C. Rüster, *ZA* 67:54 [1977]; XIX 37 III 25 *kappūwantes-pat-mu-kan antuhses isparter* 'few people escaped from me'; cf. Götze, *AM* 174; XIV 1 Vs. 52 *kappū*[*wantes-pa*]*t antuhses isparter*; cf. Götze, *Madd.* 12; *KBo* II 5 IV 5–6 [*nu-m*]*u-kan* URU.DIDLI.HI.A BÀD *kuit* ŠA KUR ᵁᴿᵁ*Kalāsma* [ANA] ᴸᵁKÚR *isparter* 'because the fortress cities of K. had gone over from me to the enemy'; cf. Götze, *AM* 190; III 4 I 55; cf. Götze, *AM* 30), *is-pár-zi-ir* (*KUB* I 6 II 8 *2-ēl isparzir* '[they] jointly escaped'; cf. Götze, *Hattusilis* 16), 3 sg. imp. act. *is-pár-ti-id-du* (*KBo* XI 14 II 21, quoted above sub 3 sg. pres. act. *is-pár-ti-i-e-iz-zi*), *is-pár-za-as-du* (XII 126 I 21 *nu-*]*smas-kan* ᴳᴵˢKAK-*az isparzasdu* 'let him escape from your peg'; cf. Jakob-Rost, *Ritual der Malli* 22); partic. *isparzant-*, nom.-acc. sg. neut. *is-pár-za-an* (VI 28 Vs. 14–15 ᵁᴿᵁ*Hat*]*tusass-a* URU-*as arha warnuwanza ēsta nu-kan* [*akkan-*]*tas* ᴱ*hesti-ya isparzan ēsta* 'the city of H. had been burned down, and [only] the mausoleum of the dead had escaped'; cf. Goetze, *Kizzuwatna* 22 [1940]).

The basic stem is *ispart-*, i.e. /spard-/; the variant *isparz-* originates at juncture-points with endings beginning in -*t*- (*isparzazi* /spartˢtˢi/, *isparzasta* /spartˢt/, *isparzasdu* /spartˢtu/); forms like *isparzai*, *isparzas* are of this secondary kind; cf. the similar phenomena with e.g. *hat-* and *ed-* (s.v.).

Hrozný (*Heth. KB* 234–5) compared *ispart-* with Lith. *spárdyti* 'kick' (and Gk. σπαίρω, Skt. *sphuráti*, Avest. *sparaiti*, which latter belong etymologically most closely with Lith. *spìrti* 'kick' and Hitt. *ispar*[*r*]-, q.v.); further matches involve Arm.

sprdem 'slip away, escape' (G. Kapancjan, *Chetto-Armeniaca* 48 [1931–3]; T. Schultheiss, *KZ* 77:222 [1961]; G. B. J̌ahukyan, *Hayerenə ev hndevropakan hin lezunerə* 139 [1970]), Skt. *spŕdh-* 'contention; competitor, rival', *spárdhate* 'contend, compete, rival', Gk. σπυρθίζειν 'kick up', Goth. *spaúrds*, OE *spyrd* 'track, race(course)' (E. Forrer apud S. Feist, *Vgl. Wb. der gotischen Sprache* 444 [1939]; J. Knobloch, *Kratylos* 4:41 [1959]; H. Eichner, in *Flexion und Wortbildung* 84 [1975]). The base-meaning clearly has to do with stretching, straining, or racing ('outrace' > 'escape'), being thus essentially an extension of **sper-* in the same special sense (q.v. s.v. *ispar[r]-*). A parallel extension to **sper-dh-*, **sper-ĝh-*, is seen in e.g. Skt. *spŗháyati* 'be eager', Gk. σπέρχομαι 'rush', OE *springan* 'leap', causative *sprengan* 'make jump, spring, sprinkle, spray'.

ispatar   (n.) 'spit, skewer', nom.-acc. sg. or pl. *ispatar* (e.g. *KUB* XLII 78 II 6 16 *ispatar* GUŠKIN 'sixteen golden spits'; cf. S. Košak, *Ling.* 18:112 [1978]), ᵁᴿᵁᴰᵁ*ispātar* (e.g. VII 1 II 3–5 *nu-kan kuidani karātis atantes nu-za* ᵁᴿᵁᴰᵁ*ispātar dāi n-us hassaz* EGIR-*pa ispannit* 1-EN-*as* ⟨1-⟩EN-*as daskizzi n-us azzikizzi* 'by whom entrails [are] eaten, he takes a spit and takes them from the fireplace with the spit one by one and eats them'; cf. Kronasser, *Die Sprache* 7:149 [1961]), *ispāta* (IX 28 I 15 *ispāta* KÙ.BABBAR TUR *isparran harzi* 'she holds a small silver spit outstretched'; cf. H. Eichner, *Die Sprache* 21:157 [1975]; for lack of *-r* see s.v. *iyatar*), gen. sg. *ispannas* (IX 35 III 7; cf. Kümmel, *Ersatzrituale* 129), instr. sg. *ispannit* (VII 1 II 4, quoted above; *KUB* XXXI 1 + *KBo* III 16 II 7 *ispannit iskarhi* 'I shall stab with a spit'; ibid. 13 *ispannit isqarrit* 'he stabbed with a spit'), abl. sg. *ispannaza* (*KUB* XXIV 13 II 31; cf. Haas – Thiel, *Rituale* 106).

The comparison with Gk. σπάθη 'blade, spatula', OE *spada* 'spade' (*n*-stem, cf. German *spaten*), initiated by Kammenhuber (*MIO* 3:354–5 [1955], *Sommer Corolla* 105), is formally appealing (heteroclitic **spₑ̄₁dh-ŗ* : **spₑ̄₁dh-n-*, the latter surviving in WGmc. **spadan*), but semantically the nearest parallels are dental extensions of the root form **speE₁-y-* (*IEW* 980–2) such as OE *spitu* 'spit' or Lith. *spitnà, spitulẽ* 'buckle-pin'; *ispatar* (oblique stem *ispann-*) should reflect *$sp\acute{E}_1t\rlap{.}r$ (rather than *$sp\acute{E}_1dh\rlap{.}r$) because *-*tn*- normally yields -*nn*- but -*dn*- does not (cf. Puhvel, *KZ* 86:112 [1972] = *Analecta Indoeuropaea* 221 [1981]).

istagga(i)-   (c.) 'bowstring', nom. sg. ˢᴵᴳ*istaggas* (*KUB* XXVII 67 II 10), acc. sg. ˢᴵᴳ *istaggan* (ibid. II 24 ˢᴵᴳ*istaggann-a* QATAMMA *iyazi* 'and she treats the bowstring in the same manner'; cf. I 24), ˢᴵᴳ*istaggain* (ibid. III 29), dat.-loc. sg. ˢᴵᴳ*istaggai* (e.g. ibid. I 34; *IBoT* II 122, 5).

IE *stāko-? Cf. the neuter nouns ON *stag*, OE *stæg* 'cable, hawser' (*IEW* 1011). See Neumann, *KZ* 77:79 (1961); Gusmani, *Lessico* 69. A possible (Luwoid?) cognate might be borrowed in Hes. ἀσταγανά · ἱμάς (cf. Furnée, *Erscheinungen* 377).

Cf. *ishunawar*.

istalk(iya)-   '(make) level, flatten', 3 sg. pres. act. *is-tal-ak-zi* (*KUB* XXIV 9 II 19–20 *pūrut ser ishuwai nu istalakzi* 'she throws on loam and levels [it]'; cf. Jakob-Rost, *Ritual der Malli* 34), *is-tal-ga-iz-zi* (*KBo* IV 2 I 39–41 *nu hassan* ᴳᴵˢ*karassaniyas dāi n-an-kan pūwati n-an-kan istalgaizzi n-an purpuran* 1-EN DÙ-*anzi* '[s]he takes flakes of soapwort, pounds them, flattens them, and they make them into a lump'; cf. Kronasser, *Die Sprache* 8:91, 104 [1962]), 3 sg. pres. midd. *is-tal-ki-ya-at-ta-ri* (*KUB* IV 3 Vs. 9–10 *nu* A.ŠÀ-*as-tis hallanniyattari istalkiyattari* 'your field will be laid waste [and] levelled'; cf. Laroche, *Ugaritica* 5:781 [1968]); partic. *istalgant-*, nom.-acc. sg. neut. *is-tal-ga-an* (XXXI 86 II 16–17 *purut tiyauwanzi* ... [...] [*namma-a*]*t istalgan ēsdu* 'to put loam ... let it also be levelled'; dupl. XXXI 89, 6; cf. von Schuler, *Dienstanweisungen* 43); iter. *istalkiski-*, 3 pl. imp. act. *is-tal-ki-is-kán*[-*du* (XXXI 100 Rs. 13). Cf. Goetze, *JCS* 1:317 (1947).

Laroche (*Noms* 314, 335, *Athenaeum* N.S. 47:176 [1969]) compared the Kaneshite man's name ᴵ*Is-ta-al-ki-a-an* at Kül-tepe, literally 'flattened, flat-nosed', comparing French *Camus*.

istalk(iya)-   istamahura-   istamas(s)-, isdammas(s)-

Neumann (*Untersuchungen* 94–5) saw in *istalk-* the source of Gk. στλεγγίς, στελγίς, στλαγγίς, στλέγγος (and further variants) 'scraper' (for oil removal from skin); cf. Furnée, *Erscheinungen* 331, 351, 377; Frisk, *GEW* 2:799–800.

**stel-g-* is related to OCS *stĭlati* 'spread', Lat. *lātus* < **stlāto-* 'wide' (*IEW* 1018–9); cf. the similar *-g-* suffix with **ster(H)-* in Lat. *strāgēs* 'overthrow' beside *strātus* 'scattered'. Cf. J. Duchesne-Guillemin, *TPS* 1946:88–9; Kronasser, *Studies presented to J. Whatmough* 122 (1957).

istamahura-   (c.) 'earring', co-occurring in texts with *HUPPI* '(metal) ring' (q.v. s.v. *asusa-*), acc. pl. *istamahurus* (*KUB* XII 1 IV 37–38 4 *TABAL HUPPI* GUŠKIN LÚ ŠÀ-*BA* [...] ... 2 *istamahurus* GUŠKIN 'four pairs of men's gold rings, among them ... two gold earrings'; XLII 69 Vs. 16–17]*istamahurus* GUŠKIN ... [...] *HUPPI* GUŠKIN; cf. S. Košak, *Ling.* 18:103, 115 [1978]), *isdammahurus* (*KBo* XVIII 192 Rs. 6). Cf. Alp, *Belleten* 12:324 (1948); Kümmel, *Ersatzrituale* 124.

Compound of *istaman(a)-* 'ear' and **hura-* (Kronasser, *Etym.* 1:165) of unclear affinity with *ehurati-* '(ear-)plug' (q.v.) and the opaque verb *hurai-* (q.v.). Cf. H. A. Hoffner, *RHA* 21:38 (1963), *Orientalia* N.S. 35:388–9 (1966); H. Eichner, *MSS* 31:87–8 (1973). Van Windekens (*Essays in historical linguistics in memory of J. A. Kerns* 338–9 [1981]) proposed for **hura-* a comparison with Gk. ἀείρω 'couple, suspend, lift' (**A₁wer-*), in the sense of 'pendant'.

istamas(s)-, isdammas(s)-   'hear, listen (to), obey; hear (of), hear (about); perceive' (GEŠTUG; *ŠEMŪ*), 1 sg. pres. act. *is-ta-ma-as-mi* (e.g. *KUB* XIV 3 II 15 *memian ŪL istamasmi* 'I do not hear the word'; cf. Sommer, *AU* 6; XIV 1 Vs. 24 [*ūk*]-*a-wa-kan ku*[*ru*]*ras memian kuez* KUR-*yaz arha ista*[*mas*]*mi* 'out of what land I hear word of hostility'; cf. Götze, *Madd.* 6; *KBo* III 3 IV 10–11 *nu-za kuis kuit arkuwar* DÙ-*zi n-at* ᴰUTU-*ŠI istamasmi* 'what plea each makes, I the king shall hear it'; cf. Hrozný, *Heth. KB* 152), *is-dam-ma-as-mi* (dupl. *KUB* XIX 44 IV 11]ᴰUTU-*ŠI isdamma-*

452

[*smi*]; XXVI 1 IV 39 ᴰUTU-*ŠI-ma-at isdammasmi* 'but I the king hear it'; cf. von Schuler, *Dienstanweisungen* 16), 2 sg. pres. act. *is-ta-ma-as-si* (XXXVI 127 Vs. 14 ¹*Sun*]*assuras-an istamassi* 'you, S., hear of him'; *KBo* VII 28 Vs. 7, 8, 9, 10 *zig-an le istamassi* 'do not listen to him (or: her)'; cf. Friedrich, *Rivista degli studi orientali* 32:218 [1957]; *KUB* VIII 83, 10–11 *takku* IZBU GEŠTUG.HI.A-*ŠU kappān*[*da* ...-]*anza* ŪL *istamasan uttar is*[*tam*]*assi* 'if the ears of an aborted fetus [are] small ..., you will hear something unheard of'; cf. Riemschneider, *Geburts-omina* 57), *is-ta-ma-as-ti* (e.g. *KBo* V 13 III 16–17 *zik mān memian piran parā istamasti* 'if you hear of the matter before-hand'; similarly ibid. 22–23; cf. Friedrich, *Staatsverträge* 1:126; V 3 I 27 *nasma-kan mān* ᴰUTU-*ŠI kuedani anda idālu istamasti* 'or if you hear in someone evil against my majesty'; ibid. II 29–30 *nasma-at zik-ma zikila istamasti* 'or you hear it yourself'; cf. Friedrich, *Staatsverträge* 2:108, 116; V 4 Vs. 11 *zig*]-*an istamasti* 'you hear it'; ibid. Rs. 44 *zig-a istamasti*; cf. Friedrich, *Staatsverträge* 1:52, 66; *KUB* XLVIII 119 Vs. 15]DINGIR-*LUM* EN-*YA istamasti* 'you, god my lord, hear'; cf. G. F. Del Monte, *Oriens Antiquus* 17:180 [1978]; *IBoT* III 148 IV 37]*apel* UKÙ-*as le istama*[*st*]*i* '... of this man you shall not hear'; cf. Haas – Wilhelm, *Riten* 230; *KBo* XII 96 I 13 [*nu* DINGI]R-*LAM le kuēlqa istamasti* 'you, god, do not hear anything!'; cf. Rosenkranz, *Orientalia* N.S. 33:239 [1964]; perhaps archaic construction with genitive, as with IE **k̂lew-* [Hom. κλῦθί μευ]; *KUB* VI 41 III 26), *is-ta-ma-as-zi* (dupl. *KBo* V 13 III 7 *zig-an mān piran parā istamaszi*; cf. Friedrich, *Staatsverträge* 1:126; V 9 II 17 *zik-ma*[-*an*] *istamaszi*; cf. Friedrich, *Staatsverträge* 1:16), *is-ta--ma-zi* (*KUB* XIX 26 I 24–25 *zi*[*k-ma-an*] *istamazi*; cf. Goetze, *Kizzuwatna* 14 [1940]), 3 sg. pres. act. *istamaszi* (e.g. XII 62 Rs. 8–9 *taswanza auszi le duddumiyanza-ma istamaszi le ikniyanza piddai le* 'no way shall a blind [man] see, [or] a deaf [man] hear, [or] a lame [person] run!'; cf. Ehelolf, *KlF* 393–4; H. A. Hoffner, *JCS* 29:151 [1977]; XIV 16 Vs. 18 LÚ ᵁᴿᵁ*Assur-ma-za--kan mahhan pāriyan istamaszi* 'but as the Assyrian hears beyond [i.e. by transference, indirectly]'; cf. Götze, *AM* 28; XXI 37 Vs. 45; cf. Ünal, *Hatt.* 2:124; XL 15 + XXVI 24 + 583/u II 8; cf. H. Otten – C. Rüster, *ZA* 68:270 [1978]), *is-dam-ma-as-*

istamas(s)-, isdammas(s)-

-*zi* (e.g. XXVI 12 III 17 *nu-wa-mu* ŪL *isdammaszi* 'he does not hear me'; cf. von Schuler, *Dienstanweisungen* 26; XXVI 1 IV′8 [*ku*]*inki* HUL-*lun memian isdammaszi* 'hears some bad word'; cf. von Schuler, *Dienstanweisungen* 15; *KBo* VI 34 I 20–22 *nu* ᴸᵁ*ar*[*as*] ᴸᵁ*aran le auszi kāss-a le* [*kūn*] *isdammaszi* 'one shall not see the other, nor shall this one hear the other'; cf. Oettinger, *Eide* 6), 3 sg. pres. midd. *isdammastari* (*KUB* XXI 29 III 30–32 *mān-ma-kan* ŠÀ URU-*LIM* LÚ ᵁᴿᵁ*Gasga kuiski sesz*[*i n-*]*a*[*s*] *isdammastari* ŠÀ É *KILI*[...] *pessiyanzi* 'but if in town some Gasga-man sleeps and he is heard of, they throw him in jail'), 1 pl. pres. act. *is-ta-ma-as-su-wa-ni* (*KBo* XVI 50 Vs. 11 *wes-a istamassuwani* 'but we hear [of it]'; cf. Otten, *RHA* 18:121 [1960]), 2 pl. pres. act. *istamasteni* (*Bo* 2490 III 10 GEŠTUG-*it istamasteni le* 'with the ear you shall not hear'; cf. Ehelolf, *KlF* 396), *istamastani* (*KUB* XV 34 II 34 *nu mān* 1-*ŠU* ŪL *istamastani* 'if you do not hear the first time'; cf. Haas – Wilhelm, *Riten* 192; *KBo* III 23 IV 15 [OHitt.] *kuit i*[*st*]*amastani*; cf. A. Archi, in *Florilegium Anatolicum* 41 [1979]), *is-dam-ma-as-te-ni* (*KUB* XXVI 1 III 49 and 56), 3 pl. pres. act. *istamassanzi* (e.g. *KBo* V 6 III 5–6 LÚ.MEŠ KUR ᵁᴿᵁ*Mizra-ma mahhan* ŠA KUR ᵁᴿᵁ*Amka* GUL-*ahhuwar istamassanzi n-at nahsariyanzi* 'but when the people of Egypt heard [historical present] of the attack on Amka, they were afraid'; cf. Güterbock, *JCS* 10:94 [1956]; XVII 22 II 10–11 [*k*]*uit* DINGIR.MEŠ-*es istamassa*[*nzi* ...] [*i*]*sta-mastu* 'what the gods hear, let him hear'; cf. Neu, *Altheth.* 207), *is-dam-ma-as-sa-an-zi* (*KUB* XXVI 1 IV 34), *is-dam-ma-as-sa-zi* (XXXVI 89 Rs. 38; cf. Haas, *Nerik* 154), 1 sg. pret. act. *istamassun* (e.g. XXXI 66 IV 17 GIM-*an-ma-an istamassun* 'but when I heard it'; cf. Houwink Ten Cate, *Anatol. Stud. Güterbock* 131 [1974]; *KBo* III 4 II 71 [*mahhan-ma* ᴰUTU-*ŠI ist*]*amassun* 'but when I the king heard'; cf. Götze, *AM* 64; *KUB* XXIII 101 II 10; *VBoT* 1, 25; cf. L. Rost, *MIO* 4:335 [1956]), *AŠME* (e.g. *KBo* V 8 III 11 *nu* GIM-*an* ᴰUTU-*ŠI enissan AŠME* 'when I the king thus heard'; cf. Götze, *AM* 156; *KUB* XXI 14, 6 *kū*]*n memian AŠME* 'I heard this word'; cf. Ünal, *Hatt.* 2:113), *AŠMI* (XIV 3 II 12–13 *mān-wa* ... *memian AŠMI* 'I would have heard the word'; cf. Sommer, *AU* 6), 3 sg. pret. act. *istamasta* (e.g. *KBo* III 4 I 27 *nu-mu* ᴰUTU ᵁᴿᵁ*Arinna memian istamasta* 'the sun-goddess of

Arinna heard my word'; cf. Götze, *AM* 22; VI 29 II 18; cf. Götze, *Hattusilis* 49), *is-dam-ma-as-ta* (e.g. XIX 112, 16 ᴰ]ɪŠᴛᴀʀ-*in isdammasta* 'heard I.'; cf. Siegelová, *Appu-Hedammu* 44; *KUB* XIX 55 Vs. 16; cf. Sommer, *AU* 198), ɪŠᴍᴇ (e.g. XXXIII 122 II 6 *udd]ār* ɪŠᴍᴇ, besides dupl. XXXIII 116 III 3 *ist]amasta*; cf. Siegelová, *Appu-Hedammu* 50; XXXIII 121 II 6 and 8 *parā* ᴀɴᴀ ᴅᴀᴍ-*ŠU-pat* ɪŠᴍᴇ 'he had ears only for his wife'; cf. Friedrich, *ZA* 49:234 [1950]; XIV 1 Vs. 61 *mahhan* ɪŠᴍᴇ 'when [he] heard'; cf. Götze, *Madd.* 16), 2 pl. pret. act. *is-ta-ma-as-tin* (XIV 4 III 2), *is-dam-ma-as-tin* (XXVI 1 III 51), 3 pl. pret. act. *is-ta-ma-as-sir* (e.g. XXII 70 Vs. 69 *kāsa-wa* ᴀQʙɪ *nu-wa-mu* ūʟ *istamassir* 'lo, I spoke but they did not listen to me'; cf. Ünal, *Orakeltext* 76; *KBo* III 4 I 6–7 *mahhan-ma* ᴋᴜʀ.ᴋᴜʀ.ᴍᴇŠ ᴸᵁᴋúʀ ᴵ*Arnuandan* ŠᴇŠ-ʏᴀ *irman istamassir* 'but when the enemy lands heard of my brother A.'s illness' [partititive apposition]; cf. Götze, *AM* 14; V 3 I 6–7 *nu-tta ... hūmantes ... arha istamassir* 'all have heard of you'; cf. Friedrich, *Staatsverträge* 2:106; V 13 I 9 *nu mahhan* ʟú.ᴍᴇŠ ᵁᴿᵁ*Māla enessan istamassir* 'when the men of M. heard thus'; cf. Friedrich, *Staatsverträge* 1:112), *is-dam-ma-as-si-ir* (*KBo* XVI 36 + *KUB* XXXI 20 + *Bo* 5768 II 9–11 *n-an-kan* ɢɪᴍ-*an* ᴸᵁᴋúʀ.[ᴍᴇŠ *h]ūmantes menahhanda isdammassir* 'when all the enemies heard of him [coming] to face [them]'; cf. Alp, *Belleten* 41:644 [1977]), *is-dam-ma-as-sir* (*KUB* XIX 23 Rs. 13–14 ɢɪᴍ-*an-ma* Šᴀ ᴰᴜᴛᴜ-*Šɪ* ᴛɪ-*tar isdammassir* 'but when they heard that the king was alive' [lit. of his majesty's life]; ibid. 15 *kinun-ma* ɢɪᴍ-*an* Šᴀ ᴇɴ-ʏᴀ *hargan isdammassir* 'but now that they have heard of my lord's perdition'; cf. S. Heinhold-Krahmer, *Arzawa* 313 [1977]), 2 sg. imp. act. *is-ta-ma-as* (e.g. *KBo* VII 28 Vs. 12–13 ɢᴇŠᴛᴜɢ.ʜɪ.ᴀ-*KA lāk nu āssu uttar* [*i]stamas* 'bend your ears and hear a good word!'; *KUB* XXXVI 89 Vs. 25 *nu-war-an is*[*t]amas* 'listen to him!'; cf. Haas, *Nerik* 144; XVII 4, 13), *is-dam-ma-as* (XXIV 5 Vs. 8 *nu-mu* ᴰ*SIN* ᴇɴ-ʏᴀ *isdammas* 'hear me, moon-god my lord!'; cf. Kümmel, *Ersatzrituale* 8), 3 sg. imp. act. *is-ta-ma-as-tu* (*KBo* XVII 22 II 11 [see sub 3 pl. pres. *istamassanzi* above]), *is-ta-ma-as-du* (XI 1 Vs. 13 and 19; cf. *RHA* 25:106 [1967]; *KUB* I 1 I 6 *n-at* ᴅᴜᴍᴜ.ɴᴀᴍ.ʟú.ᴜʟù.ʟᴜ-*as istamasdu* 'let

mankind hear it'; cf. Götze, *Hattusilis* 6), 2 pl. imp. act.
is-ta-ma-as-te-en (IV 1 II 6; cf. von Schuler, *Die Kaškäer* 170),
is-ta-ma-as-ti-n(i-ya-at) (VI 45 I 28 'and hear it!', beside dupl.
VI 46 I 29 *us-ta-ma-as-ti-ya-at* [sic]), *is-ta-ma-as-tin* (VI 45 I
26–27 *nu-mu ke arkuwarri*HI.A *istamastin* 'hear these my pleadings!', beside dupl. VI 46 I 28 *is-ta-as-tin* [sic]; XV 34 II 34–36
nu mān 1-ŠU ŪL *istamastani* [*nu* 2]-ŠU-*ma ista*[*mastin n*]*u mān*
2-ŠU-*ma* ŪL *istamastani nu* 3-ŠU 4-ŠU [5-ŠU 6-Š] U 7-ŠU *istamastin*
'if you do not hear the first time, hear the second time, and if
you do not hear the second time, hear the third, fourth, fifth,
sixth, seventh time!'; cf. Haas – Wilhelm, *Riten* 192; *KBo* XXII
6 I 11 *istamastin-mu* 'hear me'; cf. Güterbock, *MDOG* 101:19
[1969]), GEŠTUG-*tin* (XII 128, 6 *nu-kku karustin nu* GEŠTUG-*tin*
'be silent and listen!'), 3 pl. pret. act. *istamassandu* (*KUB* XIV 3
I 60–61 [*kue*] AWATE.MEŠ *memahhi nu-war-at* ÌR.MEŠ ŠEŠ-YA-*ya*
[*ist*]*amassandu* 'the words which I speak, let the subjects of my
brother also hear them!'; cf. Sommer, *AU* 4; VI 45 I 36, beside
VI 46 I 39 *i-is-ta-ma-as-sa-du* [sic]); partic. *istamas(s)ant-*,
isdammassant-, acc. sg. c. *istamassantan* (*KBo* XI 72 III 30
is]*tamassantan* GEŠTUG-*an* 'a listening ear'), nom.-acc. sg. neut.
istamassan (e.g. V 8 I 23–24 *nu-mu istamassan kuit harkir*
'because they had heard of me'; cf. Götze, *AM* 148), *istamasan*
(*KUB* VIII 83, 11 ŪL *istamasan uttar* 'something unheard of'
[see sub 2 sg. pres. *istamassi* above] and cf. e.g. *KBo* XII 62 Rs.
14–15 *apinissuwanda* [Ū]L *sakkanta* ŪL *uwanda uddār* 'such
things [are] unknown and unseen [= unheard of]'), *is-dam-ma-*
-as-sa-an (XVI 8 II 32–33 *nu-m*[*u*] [URU*G*]*asgas kuit isdammas-*
san harta 'because the Gasga-town had heard of me'; cf.
Kammenhuber, *Orientalia* N.S. 39:548 [1970]); verbal noun
istamassuwar, isdammas(s)uwar (n.) 'hearing, perception; attention, obedience', nom.-acc. sg. *istamassuwar* (*KUB* XV 34 II
10 and 25 'obedience'; cf. Haas – Wilhelm, *Riten* 190–2;
XXXVI 35 IV 16; cf. Laroche, *RHA* 26:30 [1968]; *FHG* 4, 4
istamassuw[*ar*; cf. Haas – Wilhelm, *Riten* 240), *is-ta-ma-as-su-*
-u-wa-ar (*KBo* I 45 I 5, matching ibid. Akk. *utekku* 'pay heed';
cf. *MSL* 3:59 [1955]), *is-dam-ma-as-su-wa-ar* (I 42 III 52,
matching ibid. Akk. *šimū* 'hear'; cf. Güterbock, *MSL* 13:139
[1971]), *is-dam-ma-su-wa-ar* (*VBoT* 132 II 11 IGI.HI.A-*as*

456

kuiski isdammasuwar 'some perception of the eyes', besides dupl. *KUB* XLI 21 I 10 IGI.HI.A-*as kuiski istam*[*assuwar*; cf. Haas – Thiel, *Rituale* 280, 276, and the normal IGI.HI.A-*as uwatar* 'eyesight' [s.v. *au*[*s*]-]), GEŠTUG-*ar* (*KBo* I 53, 8, matching ibid. Akk. [*še*]*mū* 'hear'; cf. *MSL* 3:87 [1955]); inf. *istamassuwanzi* (*KUB* VI 45 I 31–32 *n-at* DINGIR.MEŠ EN.MEŠ *istamassuwanzi parā tarnistin* 'gods my lords, consign them [viz. my words] to hearing!'); iter. *istamaski-, isdammaski-*, 2 sg. pres. act. *istamaskisi* (XXVI 90 IV 1–3 INIM ŠA KUR *Mizri-ya kuit* GIM[-*an*] *istamaskisi n-at-mu iya*[-...] *hatreski* 'when you also hear some matter concerning Egypt, ... write it to me'; cf. P. Cornil – R. Lebrun, *Orientalia Lovaniensia Periodica* 6–7:88 [1975–6]; *KBo* V 12 III 6; cf. Friedrich, *Staatsverträge* 2:122), 2 or 3 sg. pres. midd. *ist*]*amaskitta* (*KUB* XXXIII 120 III 33, with dupl. XXXVI 1, 10 *istamaszitta* [sic]; cf. Laroche, *RHA* 26:45 [1968]), 2 pl. pres. act. *is-ta-ma-as-kat-te-ni* (*KBo* V 3 IV 18–19 *sumēs-a-mu mān ŪL istamaskatteni* 'but if you do not listen to me'; cf. Friedrich, *Staatsverträge* 2:132), 3 pl. pres. act. *is-dam-ma-as-kán-zi* (*KUB* XXXVI 88 Vs. 10), 3 sg. pret. act. *is-ta-ma-as-ki-it* and 3 pl. pret. act. *is-ta-ma-as-kir* (I 16 II 12 *uddār istamaski*[*t*]; cf. Sommer, *HAB* 3; XIV 3 I 62–64 *n-an* ANA AWATE.MEŠ *kuedas harkun* [*n-a*]*t* ¹*Atpass-a istamaskit* ¹*Awayanass-a* [*is*]*tamaskir* 'the [reproachful] words to which I treated [lit. held] him, A. and A. also kept hearing them'; cf. Sommer, *AU* 4; the construction is the full-blown equivalent of such ellipses as *RV* 4.50.10 *Índraś ca sómaṁ pibataṁ Bṛhaspate* 'drink Soma, I. and B.!', instead of **Bṛhaspate sómaṁ piba Índraś ca pibatam*; cf. Puhvel, *American journal of philology* 98:400 [1977] = *Analecta Indoeuropaea* 383 [1981]), 2 sg. imp. act. *is-ta-ma-as-ki* (e.g. XXXIII 68 II 4–5 *nu* GEŠTUG-*an lagān harak nu-tta kuit* LUGAL [SAL.LUGAL] *memiskanzi n-us istamaski* 'hold your ear bent! What king [and] queen are saying to you, listen to them!'; cf. Laroche, *RHA* 23:128 [1965]), 3 sg. imp. act. *istamaskiddu* (XXXIII 120 I 3; cf. Güterbock, *Kumarbi* *1), 2 pl. imp. act. *is-ta-ma-as-ki-tin* (*HT* 7 Reverse 5; cf. Houwink Ten Cate, *Anatol. Stud. Güterbock* 131 [1974]), 3 pl. imp. act. *is-ta-ma-as-kán-du* (e.g. *KBo* IV 10 Vs. 51 *nu uskandu istamaskandu-ya* 'let them see and hear'; *KUB* XXXIII 120 I 2,

istamas(s)-, isdammas(s)-

4, 5, 7; XIV 3 I 34; cf. Sommer, *AU* 4; XXI 1 III 83; cf. Friedrich, *Staatsverträge* 2:76).

istaman(a)-, istamina-, istamasna- (?) (c.; also n.) 'ear' (GEŠTUG; *UZNU*), nom. sg. c. *is-ta-mi-na-as* (*KBo* I 51 Vs. 16 and 17), acc. sg. c. *is-ta-ma-na-an* (*KUB* XXIV 1 I 15–17 [with dupl. XXIV 2 Vs. 13–14] *nu-tta kuit memiskimi nu-mu* DINGIR-*LUM istamanan lagān harak n-at ist*[*am*]*aski* 'what I say to you, o god, hold your ear bent to me and hear it'; cf. Gurney, *Hittite Prayers* 16; *KBo* VI 3 I 37 [= *Code* 1:15] *takku* LÚ.ULÙ.LU-*as* ELLAM *istamanassan* [< *istamanan-san*] *kuiski iskallāri* 'if someone slashes the ear of a free man'; dupl. VI 4 I 37 and VI 5 I 16 GEŠTUG-*an*; cf. VI 3 I 39 [= *Code* 1:16] and dupl. VI 5 I 18 GEŠTUG-*assan*), nom.-acc. sg. neut. *istaman* (*KUB* XIV 13 I 18–20 *nu-smas arwā*[*nun*] *kuedani memiyani nu-mu istamas*-[(*s*)*mit*] [< *istaman-smit*] [*par*]*ā epten nu-mu istamas*[*tin*] 'in what matter I have prostrated myself before you, proffer your ear and hear me!'), GEŠTUG-*an* (VIII 83, 4 ZAG-*an* GEŠTUG-*an* NU.GÁL 'there is no right ear'; cf. Riemschneider, *Geburtsomina* 57), GEŠTUG (*KBo* XIII 34 IV 14–15 and 26 ZAG-*an* GEŠTUG-*ŠU* 'his right ear'; ibid. 21 GÙB-*lan* GEŠTUG-*ŠU* 'his left ear'; cf. Riemschneider, *Geburtsomina* 28, 35–6), gen. sg. *istamanas* (*Bo* 2139 + *KUB* IX 4 I 4–5 UZU*istamanas-kan* UZU*istamasni* 'ear to ear'; cf. *ZA* 71:130 [1981]), dat.-loc. sg. *istamasni* (sic just quoted; par. IX 34 II 24 UZUGEŠTUG-*ni*), *is-dam-ma-ni-e(s-si)* (*KBo* X 45 II 26 *isdammane-ssi-ya-an asuses* ... I[*NA* G]ÙB *asiskanzi* 'and at her ear they install rings on the left'; cf. Otten, *ZA* 54:122 [1961]), instr. sg. *is-ta-ma-an-ta* (XX 93, 4; *KUB* XII 21, 10–11 *nu kuit* IGI-*it uskisi kuitt-aya istamanta ista*[*masti* 'because you see with your eye[s], and because you hear with your ear[s]'), *is-ta-mi-ni-it* (XXXIII 120 II 33; cf. Laroche, *RHA* 26:43 [1968]), GEŠTUG-*it* (*Bo* 2490 III 8–10 *nu-wa-smas* IGI.HI.A-[*wa dasuwandas*] *dattin* GEŠTUG.HI.A-*ma-wa-smas dud-dumiyandas ta*[*ttin*] GEŠTUG-*it istamasteni le* IGI-*it-ma-wa*['take the eyes of a blind man, and take the ears of a deaf man; with the ear you shall not hear, and with the eye ...'; cf. Ehelolf, *KlF* 396), nom. pl. c. *is-ta-ma-ni-es* (*KBo* XIII 31 II 10–11 *takku sakias* 2 SAG.D[U-*ŠU*] 4 *istamanes* 8 G[ÌR.HI.A-*ŠU* 2 KUN-*ŠU* 'if of a prodigy two heads, four ears, eight feet, two tails ...'; cf.

458

Riemschneider, *Geburtsomina* 76), acc. pl. c. *is-ta-ma-nu-us* (*Bo* 3640 III 7–8 *sākuwa taswa*[*hhanzi*] *istamanuss-a kukkuraskanzi* 'they blind the eyes and mutilate the ears'; cf. Ehelolf, *KlF* 397), *is-ta-a-ma-nu-us* (*KBo* VI 3 IV 43 [= *Code* 1:95] ìR-*s-a* KAxKAK-*-ŠU istāmanus*[*-sus kukkuriskizzi* 'he mutilates the slave's nose [and] ears'), UZNĀ (ibid. 56 [= *Code* 1:99] ŠA ìR KAxKAK-*ŠU* UZNĀ-*ŠU kukkuraskanzi* 'they mutilate the slave's nose [and] ears'; dupl. VI 2 IV 57 UZNĀ-*ŠU*).

D*Istamanassas* (*KUB* XX 24 IV 31; *Bo* 2372 III 28), deity of hearing (i.e. who 'lends an ear', cf. *istamanan lagān hark-*, *istaman parā ep-* above), matches Akk. *Tašmetu* (hurrianized *Tasmisu*) and parallels D*Sakuwassas* from *sakuwa* 'eyes' (ibid. 27; *KUB* XX 24 IV 22). Cf. Laroche, *Recherches* 70, 61; Otten, *JCS* 4:124–5 (1950); Kammenhuber, *HOAKS* 273.

Luw. *tummant-* 'ear' (n.?), nom.-acc. sg. (?) *tum-ma-a-an* (*KUB* XXXV 4 II 5; cf. Otten, *LTU* 10; XXXV 43 II 9 *tu-um-ma-an-te-it-ta*, besides ibid. 8 *tawassati* from *taui-* 'eye'; cf. Otten, *LTU* 42). *tumma(n)tai-* or *tum(m)anti(ya)*-'hear', 3 pl. imp. midd. [*tu*]*-u-ma-an-ti-in-ta-*[*ru*] possible in *KBo* XXII 254 Rs. 10–12 *tappasassin*[*zi*] [*tiyamm*]*assi*[*nz*]*i kuinzi* DINGIR. .MEŠ-*inz*[*i*] [*t*]*ūmantinta*[*ru*] 'may the gods who [are] celestial and terrestrial hear [it]' (cf. H. A. Hoffner, *Bi. Or.* 33:337 [1976]); partic. nom. sg. c. *tu-u-um-ma-a-ta-i-im-mi-is* (*KUB* XXXV 34, 4; cf. Otten, *LTU* 55). Cf. also the following words with gloss-wedges in Hittite context: *du-um-ma-an-te-ya-as* (nom. sg. c. XVII 20 II 10, in a listing of deified abstractions; cf. Bossert, *MIO* 4:202 [1956]), *du-um-ma-an-ti-ya-an* (acc. sg. c. *KUB* XV 35+*KBo* II 9 I 21, in a recitation of "blessings", matching *KUB* XV 34 II 10 *istamassuwar* 'obedience' in parallel context; cf. Sommer, *ZA* 33:98 [1921]; Bossert, *MIO* 4:206 [1956]); in similar context without gloss-wedges there is *tu-u-ma-an-ti-ya-as* (XVII 10 IV 33; cf. Laroche, *RHA* 23:98 [1965]), *tu-um-ma-an-ti-ya-an* (XXIV 1 III 10; cf. Gurney, *Hittite Prayers* 22), *tu-u-ma-an-ti-ya-an* (XV 31 I 57), *tu-u-um--ma-an-ti*[*-ya-an* (dupl. XV 32 I 59; cf. Haas – Wilhelm, *Riten* 154); *du-ma-an-ti-ya-la-as* (acc. pl. c. in *KUB* XLIV 4+*KBo* XIII 241 Rs. 15 *nu-kan* ANA DUMU.NITA *dumantiyalas anda iyandu* 'let them treat on the inside the ears of the baby boy'

istamas(s)-, isdammas(s)-

[instrument noun like e.g. *ariyala-* 'raiser, hanger', *appala-* 'trap', *ardala-* 'saw'; cf. e.g. RV *śrótram* 'ear']). For the phonetics of *istaman(a)-* : *tumman-* cf. the relationship of the Luwoid *par(r)iya-* to Hitt. *ispar(r)-, isparriya-* (s.v.).

Hier. EAR + *TU* + *MI-*, 3 pl. pret. EAR + *TU* + *MI-ti-i-ta* (< **tuma[n]tiyanta*); partic. nom. sg. c. EAR + *TU* + *MI-ma-ti-mi-i-sa*, EAR + *TU* + *MI-ti-mi-sa₄*, EAR + *TU-mi-sà* (i.e. *tumatimis*; cf. Luw. *tūmmātayimmis* above). Cf. J. D. Hawkins, *Anatolian studies* 25:151–2 (1975), *KZ* 92:115 (1978).

IE **ḱlew-* 'hear' and **ōws-* 'ear' have been supplanted in Anatolian by derivatives of a root **stem-*. Such a verbal stem must have denoted sensory activities or experiences on a somewhat indeterminate scale, for even in Hittite, in spite of preemption of the central semantic slots 'hear' and 'ear', there is occasional IGI.HI.A-*as istamassuwar* rather than IGI.HI.A-*as uwatar* for 'eyesight'; thus 'perception' might be a more comprehensive original gloss. A separate specialization is seen in Hitt. *istanh-* 'taste' (q.v.), thus showing the root to be **stem-H₁-*; *istamas-* reflects **stemH₁-s-* (cf. e.g. Hitt. *sanh-* vs. *damas-*) with a suffix *-s-*, an extension which also characterizes the supplanted **ḱlew-* in several branches (e.g. Skt. *śróṣati* 'heed, obey', OHG *hlosēn* 'listen to, obey', OCS *slyšati* 'hear', Toch. A *klyoṣ-* 'hear'; cf. Ivanov, *Obščeindoevropejskaja* 167–8). A neuter noun **stémH₁-n̥* or **stómH₁-n̥* is seen in Hitt. *istaman-* and Luw. *tummant-* 'ear' (replacing **ōws-* 'ear'), appears also in Gk. στόμα(τ-) 'mouth' (στόμαχος 'throat, gullet'), Avest. *staman-* 'maw', Welsh *safn* 'maxilla' (replacing cognates of Hitt. *a[y]is-*; cf. Lat. *ōs* later supplanted by *bucca*), and underlies Germanic **stemnō* 'voice' (OHG *stimma*; cf. the Hittite thematization to *istamana-, istamina-*). These words for 'ear', 'mouth', and 'voice' were brought together already by Sturtevant, *Lg.* 4:123 (1928); for the semantic variation 'ear' : 'sound' cf. e.g. Ved. *śrótram* 'ear' : Avest. *sraoϑram*, OHG *hliodar* 'singing, song'; for 'mouth' : 'taste' cf. Hitt. *istanh-* 'taste' : Gk. στομώδης 'tasty'. Perhaps OE *stincan* 'smell' (otherwise obscure) should also be adduced, adding a further, olfactory semantic component to **stem-H₁-*. A verbal base-meaning 'perceive with the senses' alone suffices as a commor

460

denominator, and all noun formations are strictly secondary, even the most basic one, *stémH₁n̥* or *stómH₁n̥*, which must have meant roughly 'percept(ion)', thence '(organ of) hearing, sound, taste'.

Thus the worry whether 'ear' and 'mouth' are close enough semantically to share the same etymon (e.g. Kronasser, *VLFH* 222; C. Wennerberg, *Die Sprache* 18:30–1 [1972]) seems largely unnecessary, as do attempts to find a binary proto-meaning 'fissure, aperture' (A. Braun, *ARIV* 95.2:379–80 [1936]; C. Wennerberg, *Die Sprache* 18:30–1 [1972], who adduced IE *tem-* 'cut'). There is equally little merit in attempts to attribute primacy to the noun *istaman-* (cf. Tischler, *Glossar* 426) or to an **istama-* extracted from *istamahura-* (q.v.; cf. e.g. C. Wennerberg, *Die Sprache* 18:30–1 [1972]) and to account for *istamas-* denominatively (e.g. Kronasser, *Etym.* 1:182, 399) or in other secondary fashion (e.g. H. Eichner, in *Flexion und Wortbildung* 83 [1975], saw in *istamas-* a back-formation from a syncopational iter. *istamaski-* < **istamaniski-* from a hypothetical **istamaniya-*; Oettinger, *Stammbildung* 195–6, posited a denominal abstract **istamassar* < **istaman-sar*, reanalyzed as **istamass-ar* and spawning a denominative verb *istamas[s]-*). Excessive concern about finding some odd origin for the -*s*- of *istamas-*, whether "aoristic" (Čop, *Ling.* 6:53 [1964], 7:114–5 [1965]) or simply "later addition" (Frisk, *Kl. Schr.* 79–80), is likewise out of order.

Early attempts at comparison included Gk. αἰσθάνομαι 'perceive' (Hrozný, *SH* 77) and Germanic *stam(m)a-, stum(m)-a-* 'mute' (Marstrander, *Caractère* 132). V. Machek's matching of *istamas-* with Gk. ἐπίσταμαι 'understand' (*Lingua Posnaniensis* 7:82–4 [1959]) was abortive, as were assorted stabs at non-IE connection: e.g. Akk. *istami* 'hears' from *šemū* (Hrozný, *SH* 77); Egypt. *śḏm* 'hear' (E. Forrer, *JAOS* 207:243 [1930]).

istanana-   (c.) 'altar' (ZAG.GAR.RA), nom. sg. *is-ta-na-na-as* (*KBo* I 42 IV 20 ᴳᴵˢ*istananas*, matching ibid. 21 ᴳᴵˢZAG.GAR.RA-*as*; cf. Güterbock, *MSL* 13:140 [1971]; *KBo* VIII 74+ III 17 *ist[an]a-nas kitta* 'an altar has been placed'; cf. Neu, *Altheth.* 223), acc.

sg. *istananan* (e.g. *KUB* XXIV 9+*JCS* 24:37 [1971] III 11–12
nu-ssi É-*ZU* *ista*[*nana*]*n* GUN[N]I *QADU* DAM[-*ZU*] LÚ*MUDI-ŠU*
DUMU.MEŠ-*ŠU* Q[*ATAMMA*] *parkunuddu* 'let it likewise purify his
house, altar, hearth along with wife, husband, children!'),
ZAG.GAR.RA-*an* (dupl. XLI 1 III 19 GIŠZAG.GAR.RA-*a*[*n*; *IBoT*
III 100+*HT* 71, 3 ZAG.GAR.RA-*an* GURUN-*it* *unuwan*[*zi* 'they
deck the altar with fruit'), ZAG.GAR.RA (e.g. *KUB* X 91 II 16
ZAG.GAR.RA *IŠTU* GIŠ*ĀRTI* *unūwaizzi* 'decks the altar with a
branch'), dat.-loc. sg. *istanani* (frequent, e.g. XV 42 III 19 *n-at*
istanani EGIR-*pa pessizzi* 'throws it back on the altar'; *KBo* XIX
128 II 29–30 *n-at-san istanani* ANA DINGIR-*LIM* EGIR-*pa dāi* 'he
puts it back on the altar for the gods'; cf. Otten, *Festritual* 6;
XXIII 1 I 52 *n-as-san istanani* EGIR-*pa tian*[*zi* 'they put them
back on the altar'; cf. Lebrun, *Hethitica III* 143; *KUB* LI 79 Vs.
16 EGIR-*pa istanani*; cf. Lebrun, *Samuha* 178; XX 45 IV 14–15
and 22–23 *nu-ssan* DUM[U.LUGAL] *istanani* 3 *AŠRA dāi* 'the prince
puts [it in] three places on the altar'; ibid. 18 and 26 *istanani*
piran; cf. A. M. Jasink Ticchioni, *Studi classici e orientali*
27:153–4 [1977]; *KBo* XIX 128 II 12–14 EGIR-*anda-ma kedas*
ANA DINGIR.MEŠ *kuedaniya* KAŠ *istanani piran* 1-*ŠU sippanti* 'but
afterwards he libates to these gods once each with beer before
the altar'; *KUB* X 15 IV 13 *ta istanani piran* 3-*ŠU sipanti*, besides
ibid. 4 LUGAL-*us* ZAG.GAR.RA-*ni* 3-*ŠU dāi* 'the king puts on the
altar three times'; cf. A. Archi, *SMEA* 1:93 [1966]), *istanāni*
(e.g. *KBo* XV 33 III 13 LÚ.MEŠMUHALDIM-*ma-as istanāni hukanzi*
'the cooks slaughter on the altar'; *KUB* XV 32 I 43–45
kinun-a-wa EGIR-*pa uwattin sumenzan ŠA* EN SISKUR.SISKUR É-*ri*
istanāni GIŠŠÚ.A-*kitti kedani* SISKUR.SISKUR-*ni* 'and now come
back to the house of your offerant, to the altar [and] throne, for
this sacrifice!'; cf. Haas – Wilhelm, *Riten* 152; *KBo* XV 33 II 13
and 41 *istanāni piran*; *KBo* XXI 34+*IBoT* I 7 III 15; cf.
Lebrun, *Hethitica II* 122; *IBoT* II 80 I 12 *istanāni* GÙB-*laz* 'to
the left of the altar', besides ibid. 7 ZAG.GAR.RA-*ni* ZAG-*az* 'to
the right of the altar'), *istananni* (*KUB* XXV 33 I 7–8 *istananni*
GIŠ*eyani sarā hūkan*[*zi* 'on the altar above the *eya*-tree they
slaughter'), abl. sg. in e.g. *KBo* XXIII 49 IV 5–6 *i*]*sdananaz* LÚ
D*IM-as* GIŠ*eyan* [...-]*anzi* 'from the altar they ... the *eya*-tree of
the man of the storm-god', nom. pl. *is-ta-na-ni-is* (*KUB* XVII

10 IV 22 *istananis* DINGIR.MEŠ-*nas handantati* GUNNI *kalmin tarnas* 'the altars were set aright for the gods, the fireplace let go of the log'; cf. Laroche, *RHA* 23:97 [1965]). For further attestations, and discussion of realia, cf. M. Popko, *Kultobjekte in der hethitischen Religion* 66–71 (1978).

A relationship to IE **stā-* 'stand' is probable (cf. *istantai-, tiya-, tittanu-*, s.v.), with noun suffix *-no-* as in Skt. *sthānam*, Lith. *stónas*, OCS *stanŭ* 'a stand' (*IEW* 1008); however, the form *istanana-* with no tendency to haplology must represent a rederivation from a lost nasal stem matching Arm. *stanam*, Lat. *-stinā-*, OCS *stanǫ* (*IEW* 1005).

ista(n)h- 'taste, try (food or drink)', 2 pl. pres. act. *is-tu͗ ͟ te-e-ni* (*KUB* XLI 8 III 31 *li-ma* ᴳᴵˢER[IN *wars*]*ulan istahtēni* 'do not taste the aroma of cedar!'), *istahteni* (dupl. *KBo* X 45 III 40; cf. Otten, *ZA* 54:130 [1961]), 3 pl. pres. act. *is-tah-ha-an-zi* (*KUB* XXXIII 89 + XXXVI 21, 14; cf. Laroche, *RHA* 26:69 [1968]), 3 sg. pret. act. *is-tah-ta* (XXXIII 84, 6 *wars*]*ulan* KAŠ *istahta* 'tasted a drop of beer'; cf. Friedrich, *Arch. Or.* 17.1:234 [1949]; Siegelová, *Appu-Hedammu* 58; *KBo* III 38 Vs. 4–5 ᴰUTU-*us memal issa-ssa su*[*hhas* NINDA.K]UR₄.R[A ...] *s-an istahta* 'the sun-god poured porridge into her mouth, bread ... she tasted it'; cf. Otten, *Altheth. Erzählung* 8); iter. 3 sg. pres. act. *is-ta-ah-hi-es-ki-iz-zi* (701/z, 8), 3 sg. pret. act. *is-ta-an-hi-is-ki-it* (*KBo* VIII 41, 12). Cf. Kronasser, *Etym.* 1:423.

istahatal(l)i- (c.) 'taster', nom. sg. ˢᴬᴸ*is-ta-ha-ta-al-li-is* (*KBo* XVII 102 Rs. 17; XVII 103 Rs. 7), dat. sg. ANA ˢᴬᴸ*istahatali* (ibid. 17). Cf. *kupiyatalli-* 'plotter' (Luwoid *-i-* stem).

istanh- has the same configurations as verbs like *sanh-, tarh-*, pointing to an IE laryngeal root suffix, thus perhaps **stem-H₁-* (with *m* > Hittite *ŋ* before "guttural" *h*). *istanh-* is then related to *istamas(s)-* 'hear' (q.v. for further etymological discussion). Cf. also Puhvel, *California studies in classical antiquity* 6:229–30 (1973) = *Analecta Indoeuropaea* 261 (1981).

H.A. Hoffner (*RHA* 21:36 [1963]) implausibly adduced English *stink* and an alleged IE **stēg-* or **stāg-*, with reference to possible meaning fluctuations between sense-words (taste : smell; see further s.v. *istamas-*); but the assumption of regular *h* from a guttural stop scuttles such a try.

Ivanov's (*Obščeindoevropejskaja* 85) attempted comparison with Cretan Doric στανύω 'set, place' or Arm. *stanam* 'procure' is wide of the mark semantically (allegedly 'take to oneself').

istantai-   'stay put, linger, tarry, be late, take one's time, temporize, procrastinate', 3 sg. pres. act *istantāizzi* (*KBo* XXV 139 + *KUB* XXXV 164 Rs. 8; cf. Neu, *Altheth.* 226), 1 sg. pret. act. *istantanun* (*KBo* V 8 I 18 *mahhan-ma istantanun* 'but when I stayed put' [as opposed to ibid. 15 *man iyanniyanun* 'I would have marched along'; cf. Götze, *AM* 148), 3 sg. pret. act. *istantait* (e.g. ibid. II 9–11 *nu kuitman* KUR.KUR.MEŠ ᵁᴿᵁ*Hurri zahhiskit n-as istantait* EGIR-*az-ma* ᵁᴿᵁ*Gasgaz kūruri*HI.A *mekki niniktat* 'while he was fighting the Hurrian countries he took his time, but in his rear from Gasga-town the enemy greatly levied war'; cf. Götze, *AM* 152; *KUB* XIX 9 I 20 *nu-kan* ABI ABI-YA ⁱ*Suppiluliumas* INA KUR ᵁᴿᵁ*Amurri anda istantait* 'my grandfather S. lingered in the interior of A.'; *KBo* IV 14 II 67 *IŠTU* MU.KAM.HI.A GÍD.DA *arha-ma-kan istantait* 'for long years [the enemy] has temporized'; cf. R. Stefanini, *ANLR* 20:43 [1965]; *KUB* XII 31 Vs. 16; cf. Götze – Pedersen, *MS* 6), *istandāit* (*KBo* III 4 I 17 *n-as-kan asanduli anda istandāit* 'he lingered in garrison'; cf. Götze, *AM* 20), *istatāit* (*KUB* XXII 70 Vs. 44 *kuit* INA É.GAL-*LIM sarā istatāit* 'because [she] has been holed up in the palace'; similarly ibid. Rs. 4 and 6; cf. Ünal, *Orakeltext* 66, 82); partic. *istantant-* 'delayed, postponed; outdated, obsolete, superannuated', nom. sg. c. *istantanza* (XXI 2 I 9; dupl. XXI 5 I 6 *nu memiyas kuit istan[tanza* 'because the issue was outdated'; cf. Friedrich, *Staatsverträge* 2:50, 86), nom-acc. sg. neut. *istantan* (V 7 Vs. 22–23 *nu-kan* DINGIR-*LIM--ya kuit istantan sipānter* [misspelled *si-pa-a-pa-an-te-ir*] *nu-za* DINGIR-*LUM apadda kuitki ser* TUKU.TUKU-*uwanza* 'that they libated to the deity in dilatory fashion, is the deity somehow on that account angered?'); verbal noun *is-ta-an-ta-u-ar* (*KBo* I 42 II 48, matching ibid. Akk. *uhhuru* 'hold back'; cf. Güterbock, *MSL* 13:136 [1971]); causative *istantanu-* 'put off, delay', 2 sg. pres. act. *istantanusi* (*KUB* XLVIII 122 I 3), 1 sg. pret. act.

istantanunun (XXII 67, 6); iter. 2 pl. pres. act. *is-ta-an-ta-nu-us-
-kat-te-ni* (*KUB* XIII 4 IV 7 *mān*[*-ma*]*-at istantanuskatteni* 'if
you keep putting it off'; ibid. 37 *n-at le istantanuskatteni* 'do
not put it off!'; cf. Sturtevant, *JAOS* 54:390, 394 [1934]).

istantai- is derived denominatively from a noun **istant-
< *stA₂-ṇt-* (root **stā-* 'stand'; cf. *istanana-, tiya-, tittanu-,*
s.v.), identical in kind with OE and ON *stund* 'while' (cf. 'while
away the time', German *stunden* 'grant a delay, afford a
respite'; see Götze – Pedersen, *MS* 52, Couvreur, *Hett.* 199).
For the derivation, cf. e.g. *hantai-* from *hant-,* or *handantai-*
from the participle *handant-.* Cf. also Kronasser, *Etym.* 1:481,
and Oettinger, *Stammbildung* 367, who implausibly assumed a
participle **istant-* (matching Lat. *stans,* or from **stA₂ént-;* the
living verbal outcome of the root **stā-* in Hittite is seen in *tiya-,
tittanu-,* and *ista-* appears only in nominal petrifacts).

The direct comparison of **istant-* with Goth. *standan* 'stand'
(Marstrander, *Caractère* 132; Hrozný, *Heth. KB* 169; Sturte-
vant, *Lg.* 4:3 [1928], and down to e.g. P. Fronzaroli, *Atti La
Colombaria* 22:155 [1958], and Tischler, *Glossar* 428) founders
on the infixed character of the Germanic present stem (cf.
Goth. pret. *stōþ*). Kammenhuber, *KZ* 77:62–3 (1961), was
especially wrong in taking *istandai-* as a primary verb like
Goth. *standan,* while denying the presence of **stā-* in *tiya-.*

istanu-, astanu- (c.) 'sun, sun-god(dess), solar deity; majesty'
(ᴰUTU; ŠAMŠU), nom. sg. ᴰUTU(*-us*) (profuse, e.g. *KUB* XVII 1
II 14 *n*[*u* GIM-*an l*]*ukkatta* ᴰUTU-*us-kan kalmaraz uit* 'when it
dawned and the sun came from the mountain'; cf. Friedrich,
ZA 49:238 [1950]; VII 1 II 23–24 *kattera-ma-at dankuwaz
taknāz taknas* ᴰUTU-*us hukkiskiddu* 'but from the dark earth
below let the solar deity of the earth conjure it'; cf. Kronasser,
Die Sprache 7:149 [1961]; stereotyped ᴰUTU-*ŠI*(*-mi-*) = ŠAMŠI =
istanu- + *-mi-* 'my majesty', i.e. 'I the king'; cf. e.g. Sommer,
HAB 27, 72), acc. sg. ᴰUTU(*-un*) (frequent, e.g. VII 1 I 3 *nu-ssi
inanas* ᴰUTU-*un kissan sipantahhi* 'on his behalf I sacrifice to the
solar deity of sickness as follows'), ᴰUTU-*AM* (e.g. II 5 VI 6),
ᴰ*Istanun* (XXV 1 II 42, besides dupl. II 5 I 12 ᴰUTU), ᴰ*Istanu*

(sic *IBoT* I 29 Vs. 63, beside ibid. ^{D}*Tārun*), ^{D}*As-ta-nu-un* (*KBo*
XXI 85 I 12 ANA [sic] ^{D}*Astanun*, beside ibid. 13 ^{D}*Tappīnūn*; cf.
Laroche, *RHA* 31:84–5 [1973]), ^{D}*As-ta-nu-ú-un* (2641/c Rs. 8
^{D}*Astanūn* ^{D}*Tappīnū*[*n*]), voc. sg. ^{D}UTU-*ú-i* (*KUB* XLI 23 II 18
siunan ^{D}UTU-*ui* 'o gods' sun!'), ^{D}UTU-*e* (e.g. XXXI 127 I 1
^{D}UTU-*e isha-mi* 'sun-god, my lord'), ^{D}UTU-*i* (e.g. XXX 10 Rs. 10
^{D}UTU-*i ishā-mi*; VII 1 I 6, 7–8, 15 *inanas* ^{D}UTU-*i* 'solar deity of
sickness'), ^{D}UTU-*us* (e.g. VI 45 III 14 *sarā-kan uwasi nepisas*
^{D}UTU-*us arunaz* 'up you come, sun of heaven, from the sea'; *HT*
1 I 54 *ser katta nepisas* ^{D}UTU-*us* 'sun of heaven above and
below'), gen. sg. ^{D}UTU-*was* (e.g. XXX 42 I 16), ^{D}UTU-*as* (e.g.
ibid. 15; cf. Laroche, *CTH* 162; XXXVI 90 Vs. 9–10 ṢET
^{D}UTU-*as* ŠÚ.A ^{D}UTU-*as* 'sunrise [and] sunset', i.e. 'east [and]
west'; cf. Haas, *Nerik* 176), dat.-loc. sg. ^{D}UTU-*i* (frequent, e.g.
VII 1 I 4–5 *hantezzi-kan* UD-*ti* ^{UDU}*iyantan inanas* ^{D}UTU-*i*
sipantahhi 'on the first day I sacrifice a sheep to the sun-god of
sickness'; XXXVI 89 Rs. 13 ^{D}UTU-*i* DINGIR-*LIM-an* 'toward the
sun of the gods', i.e. 'eastward'; cf. Haas, *Nerik* 152, and see
s.v. *ipat*[*t*]*arma*[*yan*]), abl. sg. ^{D}UTU-*az* (*KBo* III 22, 11–12
[OHitt.] ^{D}UTU-*az utnē* [*kuit k*]*uit-pat arais* 'whatever land under
the sun [?] made an uprising'; for this much-disputed passage
cf. Neu, *Anitta-Text* 10–1, 62–3, who read ^{D}UTU-*az* as *^{D}Siunaz
'with the help of the god Sius', or Starke, *Funktionen* 94–7, who
postulated 'on the sunny side' = 'in the south'; id., *ZA* 69:50–54
[1979], subsequently preferred 'wherever the sun shines' =
'everywhere').

Istanu- is a hittitization of Hattic *Estan-*, *Astan-* (cf. e.g.
Es-ta-a-an matching Hittite ^{D}UTU-*us* in the bilingual 412/b +
Vs. 3 and 6; Kammenhuber, *RHA* 20:2–3, 5–8 [1962]), as was
initially shown by Laroche (*JCS* 1:198 [1947], *Recherches* 25);
the base-meaning is probably 'day' (cf. *KUB* XXVIII 80 I 8
[Hattic] *li-is-ta-a-an* '[his?] days'). This autochthonous word
has supplanted the old IE *l/n-* stem for 'sun' (Ved. *súar*, Avest.
hvarə, Goth. *saúil* and *sunnō*, etc.); a relic might survive in
^{D}UTU-*liya* ^{URU}*Lusna* (*KUB* XVII 19, 9; cf. Laroche, *CTH* 183),
perhaps *Saweliya-* (vel sim.) comparable to Hom. ἠέ-
λιος < *sāweliyos* (Lusna matches classical Lystra in Lycaonia
south of Iconium). In view of Luw. *Tiwat-* (nom. sg. ^{D}UTU-*az* in

IX 31 II 30) and Pal. *Tiyat-* (nom. sg. *Ti-ya-az*) as names of the sun-god (matching Hitt. *siwatt-* 'day', q.v. s.v. *siu-*) there is merit in Neu's attempt (*Anitta-Text* 116–31) to interpret OHitt. ^{D}*Si-i-us* (*KBo* III 22, 47) as an older underlay of ^{D}UTU-*us* (despite the criticism of Starke, *ZA* 69:47–65 [1979]). In view of the etymon IE **dyēws* 'daylight, bright sky', ^{D}UTU-*az* (III 22, 11, discussed above) might still mean 'under the sun', i.e. 'anywhere, anytime' (cf. for formation e.g. *ispantaz* 'at night', and for meaning Lat. *sub Iove* 'out in the open', *diū*[*s*] 'in daytime', Ved. *dyúbhis* 'for a long time'). But the main conclusion would be that in Anatolian a derivative of **dey--(H₂-)(w-)* 'be bright, shine' had come to denote 'sun' in addition to 'day' and 'god' (perhaps under Hattic influence, where *estan* meant both 'day' and 'sun'), unlike Greek and Latin where the sky-god was merged with the thunder-god (Ζεύς, δῖος; *Iov-*, *diēs*, *deus*), and Vedic where *Dyaus* atrophied into a deus otiosus (besides also meaning 'day', distinct from *devá-* 'god'). The borrowed stem *Istanu-* may reflect Hattic antecedents (cf. 659/1969, 3 *e*]*s-ta-nu-ú*) or show the influence of ^{D}*Siu-*. One reason for the supersession of ^{D}*Siu-* by ^{D}*Istanu-* could be that ^{D}*Siu-* was a sun-god, whereas much of the native Anatolian solar pantheon, such as ^{D}UTU ^{URU}*Arinna*, was female (cf. e.g. Laroche, *Recherches* 105–7); perhaps there existed a one-time contrast of *nepisas* ^{D}*Sius* (= ^{D}UTU AN) and *taknas* ^{D}*Istanus* (the Hattic solar deity being called *kattah* 'queen' in *KUB* XXVIII 75 II 22; cf. Laroche, *JCS* 1:197–8 [1947]).

There is also the town name ^{URU}*Istanuwa* (e.g. *KUB* XXX 42 I 2 and IV 14; Laroche, *CTH* 161–3); this Sun City (Heliopolis, Mehrabad) had its own dialect (XLI 15 Vs. 5 *me*]*miskizzi* ^{URU}*istanum*[*nili* 'says in Istanuwan'), was also known as ^{URU}*Astanuwa*, and worshipped the solar deity in tandem with the storm-god (*KBo* IV 11, 38–39 [EGIR]-*šú* ^{D}U ^{URU}*Astanuwa* BAL-*ti* KI.MIN [EG]IR-*šú* ^{D}UTU ^{URU}*Istanuwa ekuzi-pat* 'afterwards he likewise libates to the storm-god of Astanuwa; afterwards he drinks to the solar deity of Istanuwa'; cf. ibid. 1–3 and *Dict. louv.* 163–4; *KUB* XXV 37 IV 39]*ŠA* ^{D}U ^{URU}*Istanuwa* ^{D}UTU-*i*); perhaps this common Anatolian collocation of the thunder-god with the solar deity finds an echo in Agamemnon's

"Trojan oath" invoking jointly Idaean Zeus and Helios πανόπτης (*Iliad* 3:275–6 Ζεῦ πάτερ, Ἴδηϑεν μεδέων, κύδιστε μέγιστε, Ἡέλιός ϑ᾽, ὅς πάντ᾽ ἐφορᾷς καὶ πάντ᾽ ἐπακούεις); cf. *auriyas* ᴰUTU 'solar deity of watch' (s.v. *auri-*).

ᴰ*Izzistanu* (e.g. *KUB* II 15 VI 2; XXX 23 III 12; cf. Otten, *Totenrituale* 76–7) may be composed of a Hurrian first element (see e.g. Haas – Wilhelm, *Riten* 108–9) and *Istanu-*. Laroche (*Recherches* 26, 106) equated ᴰUD.SIG₅ 'Good Day'.

istanza(n)-   (c.) 'soul, spirit, mind, will' (frequently ZI; rarely [*NAPIŠ*]-*TUM*); pl. also 'living things, live chattels, persons, people' (*NAPŠATU*; for meaning cf. e.g. Russian *dúši* 'souls' = 'persons'); *kuedani* ZI-*as iya-* 'do someone's soul's (desire)', *kuelqa* ZI-*ni iya-* 'humor' (lit. 'do for someone's soul'); nom. sg. *is-ta-an-za-as-mi-is* (*KUB* XXX 10 Rs. 14–15 *nu-mu pittuliyai piran istanzas-mis tamatta pedi zappiskizzi* 'from anxiety my spirit keeps dripping over and over [lit. 'in another place']' [rather than *warsiyazzi* 'runs smoothly', in terms of the humoral soul-concept of the Hittites]), *is-ta-an-za-si-is* (XXXIII 5 III 6 *garaz-sis istanzas-(s)is* [or: *istanza-sis*?] 'his innards [and] his soul', i.e. '[his] innermost soul' [hendiadys]; cf. Laroche, *RHA* 23:102 [1965]), *is-ta-an-za-as-me-it* (XLI 23 II 24 [OHitt.] *istanzas-(s)met* [or: *istanza-smet*?] *karazz[a-(s)mess-a* 'their innermost soul', with gender error in *-(s)met*, as ibid. 21, vs. correct 23 and 19 [see below]; cf. Otten, *Altheth. Erzählung* 27–8), *is-ta-an-za-na-as-mi-is* (ibid. 23 *istanzanas-(s)mis karazza-[s]mess-a*), *is-ta-za-na-as-mi-is* (ibid. 19 *istazanas--(s)mis karaz-(s)miss-a*), *is-ta-za-na-as-mi-it* (sic ibid. 21 *istazanas-(s)mit karazza-(s)miss-a*; cf. Ehelolf, *ZA* 43:176 [1936]), ZI-*as* (e.g. XXIV 7 II 53–54 ᴰUTU-*us-kan* AN-*za* GAM *au[sta]* [A]NA GUD ZI-*as parā watk[u]t* 'the sun-god saw down from heaven; to the cow [his] mind sprang forth' [denoting sexual arousal; cf. e.g. Gk. μήδεα 'mental deliberations; genitals']; Friedrich, *ZA* 49:224 [1950]), ZI-*anza* (e.g. XXXIII 98 + XXXVI 8 I 16–17 *katta-kan kuit harzi nu-kan* [...] ZI-*anza parā watkut* 'what she has below, [on this Kumarbi's] mind sprang forward'; cf. Güterbock, *JCS* 5:146–8 [1951]; XIII 3 III 26 *nu*

LUGAL-*as* ZI-*anza ishizzita* 'the king's [= my] animus got the better of me [and I got angry]'), ZI-*za* (e.g. ibid. II 14 LUGAL-*was* ZI-*za ishizziyazi*; cf. Friedrich, *Meissner AOS* 46–7), acc. sg. *istanzanan* (XLI 23 II 15 SILÁ-*as istanzanan dā* 'take the soul of the lamb!'; I 16 III 26–27 [OHitt.] *kinun instanzanaman* [< *istanzanan-man*] ŪL *kuiski dās* '[until] now nobody has taken [i.e. accepted] my will'; cf. Sommer, *HAB* 12), ZI-*an* (e.g. XIII 4 I 26 *n-as* ZI-*an arha lānza* 'he [is] relaxed in spirit'), ZI-*TUM* (e.g. ibid. 34 *mān-ma-asta* ZI-*TUM* DINGIR-LI[*M kui*]*s* TUKU.TUKU--*yanuzi* 'but if someone angers the spirit of a deity'; cf. Sturtevant, *JAOS* 54:366 [1934]), gen. sg. *istanzanas* (e.g. XXX 10 Vs. 8–9 [*nu-mu-za*] *ammel* DINGIR-*YA* [1]*Kantuzilin tuggas-tas istanzanas-tas* ÌR-*KA halzait* 'you, my god, have summoned me, K., as servant of your body [and] your soul'; *KBo* XXI 22 Vs. 14–15 *nu-za kuit Labarnas* LUGAL-*us istanzanas-sas* [ŠÀ-*as-s*]*as ilāliskizzi* 'what L. the king desires in his innermost soul'; cf. ibid. 16 [*nu-za kui*]*t* [SAL]*Tawa*[*n*]*annas* SAL.LUGAL ŠA ZI-ŠU ŠA ZI-ŠU [sic, for ŠÀ-ŠU] *ilaliskizi* 'what T. the queen …'; cf. G. Kellerman, *Tel Aviv* 5:199 [1978]), ZI-*as* (e.g. *KUB* VII 60 III 13–14 *nu-mu* … ZI-*a*[*s*] *iyadu* 'may [he] do my soul's [desire]'; XVI 43 Vs. 10 ZI-*as kisat* 'soul's [desire] was done'), dat.-loc. sg. ZI-*ni* (profuse, e.g. *akkantas* ZI-*ni* 'to the soul of the dead'; cf. Otten, *Totenrituale* 146 et passim; XIII 4 II 63–64 *n-asta* UKÙ-*as* ZI-*ni le-pat iyatteni* 'do not humor the man!'), instr. sg. *istanzanit* (XVII 10 II 21 *istanzanit* ŠÀ-*it* … *āssu harak* 'keep goodness in your innermost soul!'; cf. Laroche, *RHA* 23:93 [1965]; XXXIII 5 III 9 *ista*]*nzanit*; cf. Laroche, *RHA* 23:102 [1965]; XVII 21 I 6 *nu sumes-pat* DINGIR.MEŠ DINGIR.MEŠ-*as istanz*[*an*]*it sekteni* 'you, gods, know with your divine spirit'; cf. von Schuler, *Die Kaškäer* 152), ZI-*nit* (e.g. XXXI 71 III 18–19 *sakuwassarit* ZI-*nit* 'with loyal spirit'; cf. Ünal, *Orakeltext* 123), ZI-*it* (e.g. *KBo* V 3 III 39–40 *n-at zik tuel* ZI-*it le epsi* 'do not [even] conceive it with your mind!' or [possibly] 'do not willfully undertake it!'; cf. Friedrich, *Staatsverträge* 2:126; *KUB* XIV 1 Vs. 41, Rs. 19 and 34 'willfully'; cf. Götze, *Madd.* 10, 24, 28), abl. sg. *istanzanaz* (XXXIII 120 II 2; cf. Laroche, *RHA* 26:41 [1968]), ZI-*az* (e.g. *KBo* III 3 III 11–12 *nu-smas sumel* ZI-*az arha daskatteni* 'you take [them] away of your own volition'), ZI-*za* (*KUB* XXXI 99 Vs. 6 ZI-*za le essa*[*tteni* 'don't act willfully!'), ZI-*azza* (XIII 4 II 45 *mān-at-za* ZI-*azza-ma happiraizzi* 'but if he sells it as he pleases'), acc. pl. *istanzanas* (*KBo* III 21 II 4–5 *n-asta utneyas istanzanas appanna kisri-tti dais* 'he placed the souls [= people] of the lands in your hand for taking'; cf. ibid. 10–11 *nu* KUR-*yas arūwauar* DINGIR.MEŠ *tuk iwārwāir* 'the proskynesis of the lands [i.e. of their people] have the gods conferred upon thee'), *is-ta-za-na-as-me-es* (XVIII 151 Rs. 14 *ita*[*lu i*]*stazanas-(s)mes tas* 'evil took hold of their souls'; cf. Ünal – Kammenhuber, *KZ* 88:164 [1974], with wrong interpretation [dat. pl.]), NAPŠADU (*KUB* XIII 8 Vs. 15–16 ŠA É.NA₄-*ya-za* A.ŠÀ ᴳᴵˢTIR ᴳᴵˢSAR.SAR ᴳᴵˢSAR.GEŠTIN NAPŠADU-*ya le kuiski wāsi* 'nobody shall buy the mausoleum's field, wood, orchard, vineyard, and live chattels'; cf. Otten, *Totenrituale* 106, 124; *KBo* V 7 Vs. 11 NAPŠADU 'persons', matching ibid. Rs. 13 SAG.DU 'persons' [lit. 'heads']; cf. Riemschneider, *MIO* 6:345, 348 [1958]), NAPŠATE.MEŠ (*KUB* XXXVI 117, 12).

ᴰ*Istanzassas* (*KUB* XX 24 IV 17), ᴰ*Istanzassis* (*Bo* 2372 III 27–29 ᴰ*Istanzassis* ᴰ*Sakuwassas* ᴰ*Hantassas* ᴰ*Istamanassas* ᴰ*Kissarassas* ᴰ*Ginuwassas*, listing deities [or deifications] of soul, eye, forehead, ear, hand, and knee). Cf. Laroche, *Recherches* 70; Otten, *JCS* 4:125 (1950).

The basic declension pattern of *istanza(n)*- resembles that of *alanza(n)*- (q.v.), thus nom. sg. *istanzas*, gen. sg. *istanzanas*; nom. sg. *ista(n)zanas*, confined to *KUB* XLI 23 II 19, 21, 23 (besides ibid. 24 *istanzas*), is secondary (cf. *alkistanas* beside *alkistas*, *ishimanas* beside *ishimās* [s.v. *ishiya*-]). The frequent nom. sg. ZI-*(an)za* of the imperial period is neither *istanzan* + -*s* (Kammenhuber, *ZA* 56:208 [1964], *HOAKS* 289) nor **istan-s* (Oettinger, *KZ* 94:58–9 [1980]), but rather the result of an analogical interaction of the developing paradigms of e.g. *sum(m)anza(n)*- (original **suman*+*s*) and *lahhanza(n)*- with *alanza(n)*- and *istanza(n)*-: nom. sg. *summanza* (analogical *summanzās*), *lahhanza*, vs. *alanzas*, *istanzas* (analogical *alanza*, *istanza*), acc. *summanz(an)an*, *lahhanz(an)us*, *alanz(an)an*, *istanzanan*; the common feature is the spread of *n*-declension in the oblique cases, which has reverberated on the nominatives.

470

istanza- is descended from an IE *s(t)ent-to-*, paralleling Lat. *sensus* 'feeling' < **sent-tu-*, OHG *sin(n)* 'sense, mind' < **sent-no-*, Lith. *sintĕti* 'think' (*IEW* 908). The aberrant initial cluster *st-* vs. **s-* has a match in *istark-* (q.v.) vs. Lith. *sir̃gti* 'be ill', *sèrga*, OIr. *serg*, Toch. A *särk* 'illness', and seems to parallel both the **sw-* : **s-* variation (IE **s[w]ek̂s* 'six') and the problem of Hittite *z-* vs. **s-* in the rest of Indo-European (cf. e.g. s.v. *sakkar*); the Greek π(τ)όλις problem (vs. Lith. *pilìs*) is also comparable.

No other proposed etymology merits serious consideration: Lat. *statua, statura* (Goetze, *Mélanges ... Pedersen* 491 [1937]); Gk. σϑένω 'be strong' (Pedersen, *Hitt.* 44); Ved. *tanúḥ* 'body, self' (Juret, *Vocabulaire* 52); Slavic **(j)istŭ* 'self' (V. Machek, *Die Sprache* 4:74–5 [1958]); IE **stA₂ént-* 'standing' (Oettinger, *Stammbildung* 548); IE **pstén* 'female breast, tit, nipple' (*IEW* 990; proposed by H. Eichner, *MSS* 31:98 [1973], endorsed by Oettinger, *KZ* 94:59 [1980]).

istap(p)- 'shut, (en)close, catch, bar, block(ade), besiege, plug (up), stop up, dam', 1 sg. pres. act. *is-ta-a-ap-hé* (*KBo* XVII 3 IV 32–33 *istappulli-set-a suliyas [t]a istāphe* 'its lid is of lead, and I close [it]'; dupl. XVII 1 IV 37 *su]liyas ta istāphe*; cf. Otten – Souček, *Altheth. Ritual* 38), *is-tap-mi* (Yozgat; cf. T. G. Pinches, *Annals of archaeology and anthropology* 3, Plate XXVI, Text II, line 12 [1910]), 3 sg. pres. act. *is-tap-pí* (e.g. *KUB* XL 102 VI 14 *ser istappi* 'plugs up'; XII 16 II 14 *IŠTU* NINDA ERÍN.MEŠ *istappi* 'plugs with army bread'; *KBo* XIX 129 Vs. 31 *IŠ]TU* NINDA *āan istappi* 'plugs with hotcake'; VI 26 I 7–8 [= *Code* 2:58] É.IN.N[U.DA] *istappi* 'he shuts the straw-house'; dupl. *KUB* XIII 15 Rs. 5 É.IN.NU.DA *istappi*), *is-ta-a-pí* (e.g. dupl. XXIX 30 II 17 É.IN.N[U.DA *i]stāpi*; XXIII 137 II 27 *nu-kan hattessar istāpi* 'he closes the hole'; cf. M. Vieyra, *RA* 51:101 [1957], and *isgāpi* s.v. *isgapuzzi-*, which may be erroneous for *istāpi*; *KBo* V 11 IV 14 *nu* LÚÚ.HÚB GIŠAB.HI.A *anda istāpi* 'the deaf man shuts the windows'; ibid. 16 GIŠKUN₅ *anda istāpi* 'bars the staircase'; cf. *KUB* XXXI 89 II 3–4 GIŠ*ilana[s*

istap(p)-

SAG.DU.MEŠ] BÀD.HI.A-*as* ^{GIŠ}AB.HI.A-*us* ^{GIŠ}IG-*antes hattalwant*[*es*
'[let] heads of staircases [and] windows of fortifications [be]
shuttered [and] bolted'), *istapi* (464/w, 6 *istap*[*i*]), *isdapi* (dupl.
IX 22 II 33), *isdāpi* (ibid. 43 *ser-ma-an-kan isdāpi*, besides dupl.
Bo 4876, 4 *istappi*), 3 pl. pres. act. *is-tap-pa-an-zi* (*KBo* XXI 34
I 60–61 *n-an-kan mahhan parnas anda arnuanzi nu* ^{GIŠ}IG *istappanzi* 'when they bring her into the house they shut the door';
cf. Otten, *Baghdader Mitteilungen* 7:139 [1974]; Lebrun, *Hethitica II* 119; IV 2 I 7–8 *n-an-kan* ANA ^{DUG}LIŠ.GAL YÀ [*katt*]*a tianzi
serr-a-sse-ssan* ^{DUG}LIŠ.GAL YÀ *istappanzi* 'they deposit it in a
bowl of oil and plug up the bowl of oil'; cf. Kronasser, *Die
Sprache* 8:90 [1962]), *is-tab-ba-an-zi* (*IBoT* II 23, 4), 3 pl. pres.
midd. *is-tap-pa-an-da-ri* (*ABoT* 60 Vs. 16–18 *mān-wa kūn*
BÀD-*an wedanzi nu-wa-smas* KASKAL.HI.A *ŪL* EGIR-*pa hiswandari
anzas-ma-war-at-kan istappandari* 'if they build this fortress,
the roads will not lie open for you, and they will be closed to
us'; cf. Laroche, *RHA* 18:82 [1960]; Neu, *Interpretation* 77), 3
sg. pret. act. *is-tap-pa-as* (*KBo* III 6 III 56–57 *n-an-kan* INA
^{URU}*Samuha* ŠAH GIM-*an hūmma* [with gloss-wedges] EGIR-*pa
istappas* 'she shut him up at S. like a pig in a sty'; dupl. *KUB* I 8
IV 12]*hūmma* EGIR-*pa istappas*; cf. Götze, *Hattusilis*
32; XXXIII 106 III 37–38 *nu-kan nepis suppa* É.MEŠ DINGIR.MEŠ
^D*Hebaddunn-a anda istappas* 'he laid siege to heaven, the holy
shrines, and Hebat'; cf. Güterbock, *JCS* 6:44 [1952]), *is-tap-ta*
(*KBo* VI 29 II 33–35 *apūn-ma-kan* ^D*IŠTAR* ^{URU}*Samuha* GAŠAN-*YA
*KU₆-*un* GIM-*an hūpalaza* [with gloss-wedges] EGIR-*pa istapta
n-an ishiyat n-an-mu parā pesta* 'My Lady Ištar of Samuha
caught him like a fish with a net, bound him, and handed him
over to me'; cf. Götze, *Hattusilis* 50, and III 21 II 15–16
liliwanza-ma-ssan ikza-tes KUR-*e katta huppan harzi* 'your swift
net holds the land ensnared'), 2 sg. imp. act. *istāpi* (*KUB*
XXXIII 62 III 6 É-*ri-ya* ^{GIŠ}IG *istāpi* 'in the house close the
door!'), 3 sg. imp. act. *istāpu* (XXVIII 82 I 23 *n-at-kan istāpu*
'and let him close it [viz. the lid]'), *is-tab-du* (IX 31 II 38
idalu-kan parā istabdu āssuw-a-kan anda kuragdu 'let [the door]
shut out evil and keep in good'; dupl. *HT* 1 II 12 HÉ-*lu-kan sarā
istabdu* ...; cf. ibid. 35–36 ^{GIŠ}IG-*ann-a hatki* 'closes the door'; B.
Schwartz, *JAOS* 58:342 [1938]), 3 pl. imp. act. *is-tap-pa-an-du*

472

(*KUB* XIII 2 I 7 *nu* URU.DIDLI.HI.A *anda istappandu* 'they shall shut in the towns[people]'; cf. von Schuler, *Dienstanweisungen* 41); partic. *istappant-*, nom. sg. c. *is-tap-pa-an-za* (*IBoT* III 148 III 50–52 *n-as-kan* KAxU-*is kizza* IŠTU KÙ.BABBAR GUŠKIN NINDA.KUR₄.RA-*ya istappanza ēsdu* 'let his mouth be plugged [partitive apposition] with this silver, gold, and thick bread'; cf. Haas – Wilhelm, *Riten* 226; *KUB* VII 54 III 25–27 *nu-wa-ta--kkan* KUŠMÁ.URU.URU₆ *istappanza ēsdu* GIŠBAN-*ma-wa-ta-kkan arha tarnān ēsdu* 'may your quiver be shut, may your bow be unstrung'; thus *istappulli-* [q.v. infra] = Gk. πῶμα 'lid' [φαρ-έτρης 'of quiver': *Iliad* 4:116, *Odyssey* 9:314]), nom.-acc. sg. neut. *is-tap-pa-an* (I 6 II 9 *istappan ēsta* '[the land] had been under siege'; cf. Götze, *Hattusilis* 16; XXIX 4 III 32 *anda istappan* '[the container is] closed'; cf. Kronasser, *Umsiedelung* 24; *KBo* V 1 II 39–40 *n-at* IŠTU LÀL *sūwan ser-ma-at-kan* IŠTU GIŠMA *istappan* 'they [viz. the containers] [are] filled with honey and plugged with figs'; similarly ibid. 41; cf. Sommer – Ehelolf, *Pāpanikri* 8*), nom. pl. c. *is-tap-pa-an-te-es* (III 6 II 24–25 URU.DIDLI.HI.A-*ma kuyēs* ŠA KUR URU*Hatti istappantes eser nu-kan* GUL-*heskir* 'the towns of Hatti which had been block-aded, they struck out'; dupl. *KUB* I 1 II 42 *istappantes*[; cf. Götze, *Hattusilis* 18; L 6 III 17; cf. A. Archi, *SMEA* 22:26 [1980]), nom.-acc. pl. neut. *istappanta* (*KBo* XVII 65 Rs. 10 *anda-ya-at karū istappanta* 'it [viz. the house] has already been shut'; as noun 'covereds, covered footwear, boots', VIII 95 Vs. 10 KUJŠE.SIR *istappanta*; XXVI 34 IV 10 *istappanda* matching ibid. Akk. *šahupatum* 'boot'; cf. Otten, *Vokabular* 41); verbal noun *istappessar* (n.), nom.-acc. *is-tap-pí-es-sar* and abl. sg. *is-tap-pí-es-na-az* (*KBo* XXI 4 + *KUB* XXIX 7 Rs. 48–49 EGIR-ŠU-*ma-ssan* ... *istappessar ienzi istappesnaz-ma-kan* PA₅-*an* [...-]*yan* INA ÍD-*kan anda ienz*[*i* 'but afterwards they make a dam ..., and from the dam they make an outlet into the river'), gen. sg. *is-tap-pí-es-na-as* (ibid. 51–52 *n-asta* GIŠMÁ *istappesnas* PA₅-*as istappes*[*naz*] *parā* ÍD-*kan pedai* 'the outlet of the dam carries the boat forth from the dam into the river'; cf. Lebrun, *Samuha* 124; *KUB* XXXVIII 3 III 11 *istappesnas* SAL.LUGAL-*as* 'queen of enclosure' [?]; cf. von Brandenstein, *Heth. Götter* 20).

istappinu- 'shut, close', 3 pl. pret. act. *is-tap-pí-nu-ir* (*KUB*

VIII 52, 6 *parā-ta-za istappinui*[*r* 'they shut you out'; cf. Friedrich, *ZA* 39:14 [1930]).

istappulli- (n.) 'cover, lid, plug, stopper', nom.-acc. sg. *is-tap-pu-ul-li* (see sub 1 sg. pres. act. *istāphe* above), instr. sg. *is-tap-pu-ul-li-it* (*KUB* XLIV 56 Rs. 13; cf. Haas, *Orientalia* N.S. 45:200 [1976]), nom.-acc. pl. *istappulli* (XXXIII 8 III 7–8 *dankuwāi taknī* AN.BAR-*as* ^{DUG}*palhis kianda istappulli-smit* A. .BÁR-*as* 'in the dark earth lie iron cauldrons; their lids are of lead'; XXIII 66 II 10; par. XVII 10 IV 15 *istappulli-smet*; cf. Laroche, *RHA* 23:103–4, 130, 97 [1965]), *istappuli* (dupl. XXXIII 3, 7 *i*]*stappuli-sme*[*t*); denom. *istappulliya-* 'use as stopper', partic. nom. sg. c. *istappullianza* (*KBo* XI 14 I 8 NINDA. .KUR₄.RA ZÍZ TUR *istappullianza* 'small wheatloaf used as stopper'), acc. sg. c. *istappulliyantan* (ibid. IV 12–13 NINDA. .KUR₄.RA [... *istap*]*pulliyantan*; cf. H. A. Hoffner, *Alimenta Hethaeorum* 165, 194 [1974]). For suffix -*ulli*- cf. Kronasser, *Etym.* 1:213.

The frequent gemination of -*pp*- as the marked spelling variant points to **p* and thus **step*-, e.g. *istāphe* < **stópA₁ey*. The obvious etymon is the root (*IEW* 1011–3) appearing with occlusive-variation as **step*- (Lith. *stẽpas* 'apoplexy', *stapìnti* 'have an erection', OCS *stǫpiti* 'tread [firmly]', *stopa* 'footstep'), **steb*- (Gk. στέμβω 'kick around, abuse', OE *steppan* 'step, tread', pret. *stōp, stempan* 'stamp, stomp'), **stebh*- (Gk. στέφω 'put around, entwine', ἀστεμφής 'firm', Skt. *stabh*- 'make firm, support', *stambha*- 'post, pillar', *vi-ṣṭáp*- 'top, surface' [beside *skabh*- 'make firm, support', *skambhá*- 'pillar', q.v. s.v. *isga-puzzi*-], ON *stefja* 'curb, restrain', OE *stæf* 'staff', *stefn* 'stem', Lith. *stãbas* 'post', *staṁbas* 'stump'). It is conceivable that both variants **step*- and **steb(h)*- are represented in the Hittite paradigm, or even that a dominant **steb(h)*- has partly lost out to a secondary /step-/ created through unvoicing in forms like **stób(h)-A₁ey*. The noun *istappulli*- has seeming parallels in e.g. Gk. σταφύλη 'plummet', OE *stapol* 'post, pillar' (> 'staple'). Cf. also Oettinger, *Stammbildung* 419–20.

A connection with Skt. *stabh*- was first suggested by Benveniste, *BSL* 33:139 (1932). The (rival) tie-in with the Sanskrit causative *sthāpáyati* 'make to stand, stop, arrest' (from *sthā*-

'stand'), championed by Sturtevant (*Lg.* 4:3–4 [1928], 6:156 [1930], *Comp. Gr.*[1] 76, *Lg.* 14:72 [1938], *Comp. Gr.*[2] 60), which others have echoed (e.g. T. Milewski, *L'indo-hittite et l'indo-européen* 49 [1936]) or rejected (e.g. Couvreur, *Hett.* 199–200), may ultimately also be correct in that *sthāpáyati* can represent a **stopéyeti* secondarily associated with the root *sthā-* (cf. OLith. *stapýti*[*s*] 'stand still', ON *stefja* 'curb, restrain').

istark(iya)-, istarak(k)-, istarakkiya-   '(turn) ail(ing), become sick; ail, afflict' (GIG; impersonal subject, or 'illness', or a deity; occasional impersonal construction with agent in abl.; patient in acc.), 3 sg. pres. act. *istarakzi* (e.g. *KUB* I 1 I 44 *mān-mu istarakzi kuwapi* 'if it ever ail me'; cf. Götze, *Hattusilis* 10; V 6 I 45–46 *mān-wa* DINGIR-*LUM* UKÙ-*si menahhanda* TUKU.TUKU-*anza istarakzi-war-an* 'if a god [is] angry at a man and ails him'; VIII 36 II 12 *m*]*ān antuhsan* SAG.DU-*ŠU istara*[*kzi* 'if it ails a man in the head', with partitive apposition; cf. Burde, *Medizinische Texte* 38; Laroche, *CTH* 188), *istarzi* (VIII 38 + XLIV 63 III 8–9 *mān antuhsan* IGI.HI.A-*š*[*U* ...] *apinessan istarzi* 'if it ails a man thus in the eyes'; cf. Burde, *Medizinische Texte* 30), *istarkiyazzi* (*KBo* V 4 Rs. 38 *istarkiyazzi kuinki* 'it ails someone'; cf. Friedrich, *Staatsverträge* 1:66), *istarakkiyazi* (XXI 21 III 4; cf. Burde, *Medizinische Texte* 36), GIG-*zi* (e.g. *KUB* XVII 12 III 16 *nu* GIG-*zi kuin antuhsan* 'the man whom it ails'; *KBo* IV 14 II 57 LUGAL-*un* GIG-*zi* 'it ails the king'; cf. R. Stefanini, *ANLR* 20:42 [1965]; ibid. III 13 LUGAL-*i kuitki nakkēszi nassu* LUGAL GIG-*zi* 'something becomes heavy for the king, or ails the king'; *KUB* XIX 5 Vs. 5]*istarakzi* GIG-*zi-ma-mu* HUL-*lu* GIG-*as-mu* [... *t*]*amassan harzi* 'ails ..., but it ails me, illness has badly beset me'; XXX 26 I 1–2 *mān* UKÙ-*an* ᴰ*Isharaz* GIG-*zi* 'if it ails a man from the goddess I.'; cf. Otten, *Totenrituale* 100; Neu, *Interpretation* 74–5), 3 sg. pret. act. *istarkit* (XIX 23 Rs. 12 EN-*YA-pat kuwapi* ᵁᴿᵁ*Ankuwa istarkit* 'when my lord was ailing at A.'; cf. S. Heinhold-Krahmer, *Arzawa* 313 [1977]), *istarkiat* (*KBo* IV 6 Vs. 24–25 *tuēl* GEME-*TUM istarkiat n-an* GIG-*anza tamastat* 'your servant has become sick, illness has beset her'; cf. Tischler, *Gebet* 14), *istarakta* (*KUB* XIV 15 II 6 *n-an idalus* GIG-*as istarakta* 'a

bad illness afflicted him'; cf. Götze, *AM* 48; XIII 35 III 5
istarakta-wa-mu 'it ailed me'; cf. Werner, *Gerichtsprotokolle* 8;
XXII 70 Vs. 1; cf. Ünal, *Orakeltext* 54), *istarakkit* (*KBo* V 9 I
14–15 *tuk-ma istarakkit nu irmalliyattat* 'it ailed you, illness
afflicted you'; cf. Friedrich, *Staatsverträge* 1:10), *istarakkiyat*
(*KUB* XIV 16 III 41; cf. Götze, *AM* 60), 3 sg. pret. midd.
istarakkiyattat (XIV 15 II 13 *nu-war-an* [*idalus* GIG-*as*] *istarakki-*
yattat 'a bad illness afflicted him'; cf. Götze, *AM* 48; Neu,
Interpretation 77); iter. *istarkiski-* (VIII 36 III 20 *istarkiski*[*zzi*;
cf. Burde, *Medizinische Texte* 40; Laroche, *CTH* 189).

istarni(n)k- 'make ail, afflict', 2 sg. pres. act. *istarniksi* (*KBo*
III 28 II 16 *le nepisi* DINGIR.AŠ.AŠ *istarniksi* 'in heaven do not
afflict the gods'; cf. Laroche, *Festschrift H. Otten* 187 [1973]), 3
sg. pres. act. *istarnikzi* (*Code* 1:10 *takku* LÚ.ULÙ.LU-*an kuiski*
hūnikzi t-an istarnikzi 'if anyone beats up a man and makes him
ailing'), 3 sg. pret. midd. *istarniktat* (III 34 II 39 [OHitt.] 'he
turned ailing'; cf. Neu, *Interpretation* 78), 1 pl. pret. act.
istarninkuen (III 45 Vs. 4 *n*]*episi* DINGIR.MEŠ *istarninkuen* 'in
heaven we have afflicted the gods'), 2 sg. imp. act. *istarnik* (III 28
II 16 *taknā-ma menus istarnik* 'but on earth afflict counte-
nances!'; cf. Laroche, *Festschrift H. Otten* 187 [1973]). For
the causative type (like *har*[*a*]*k-* : *harni*[*n*]*k-*) cf. Kronasser,
Etym. 1:435–7.

istarningai- (c.) 'ailment, affliction', nom. sg. *istarningais*
(*KUB* XXIX 1 I 46–47 ᴰUTU-*was istarningais* 'ailment of the
sun'; cf. B. Schwartz, *Orientalia* N.S. 16:28 [1947]), acc. sg.
istarningain (ibid. II 32 *kās kās istarningain* EGIR-*pa dās* 'so-and-
-so has taken away the ailment'), *is-tar-ni-ka-i-in* (*KBo* XVIII
151 Vs. 5 and 12; cf. Ünal – Kammenhuber, *KZ* 88:164 [1974]).

The meaning 'afflict' seems historically anterior, just as with
Engl. *ail* < OE *eglan* 'cause pain'; for the trend to intransitiviza-
tion see s.v. *arai-*. The impersonal construction recalls that of
Lat. *me piget* 'it chagrins me'. The occasional agent construc-
tion with ablative (UKÙ-*an* ᴰ*Isharaz* GIG-*zi*) resembles Old
Latin *hominem fulminibus occisit* 'it kills a man by bolts',
Russian *otcá dérevom ubílo* 'it killed the father by a tree' (cf.
Sommer, *OLZ* 42:681–2 [1939]; E. Schwyzer, *Rheinisches
Museum* 76:433–9 [1927]); by the same token the *-nt-* deriva-

tives of neuter nouns (predominantly nom. sg., serving as subjects of transitive verbs) are in origin agental ablatives in *-a(n)z(a)* (cf. abl. *luttanza* 'from the window', *nepisanza* 'from heaven', *hassannanza* 'from the family'), secondarily reinterpreted from paradigmatic to derivational status (collected by Laroche, *BSL* 57:1.23–43 [1962]); hence e.g. *KUB* XXX 34 IV 7–8 *nu ēshananza linkiyaza* ^É*halinduwa* É DINGIR.MEŠ *le epzi* means originally literally 'may it not seize the temples of the palace by blood(shed) (and) perjury'.

istark- is most plausibly cognate with Lith. *sergù, sir̃gti* 'be ill', *sèrga*, OCS *sraga*, Toch. A *särk*, Toch. B *sark*, OIr. *serg* 'illness' (cf. Puhvel, *LIEV* 25; Ivanov, *Obščeindoevropejskaja* 65); the initial cluster *st-* vs. **s-* is matched by *istanza-* vs. Lat. *sensus*, OHG *sin(n)*, Lith. *sintĕti* and is thus part of a pattern (resembling **sw-* vs. *s-*; see further s.v. *istanza[n]-*); actually OIr. *serg* can also reflect **sterg-*.

A second possibility involves Gk. στραγγάλη 'cord, noose', Lat. *stringō* (< **strengō*) 'draw tight' (thus Sturtevant, *Lg.* 4:5–6 [1928]); by including OE *stearc* 'stiff', *strec* 'firm', OHG *strang* 'cord', *strengi* 'stiff' (cf. Frisk, *GEW* 2:805), an IE **stér-g-*, **str-ég-* with nasal infix can be postulated. That the notion of tightness, constriction, and smothering may inhere in *istark-* is shown by the nosopoeic onslaughts of the demoness Wisuriyanza (cf. *wesuriya-* 'strangle'; Carruba, *Beschwörungsritual* 49–52). Semantic evolvement in bonam partem ('smother with love') might also explain Gk. στέργω 'be devoted, love' (to which Oettinger, *Stammbildung* 197, actually compared *istark-*).

Other suggested connections for *istark-* have been Gk. στρεύγομαι 'be exhausted, suffer pain' (J. Duchesne-Guillemin, *TPS* 1946:82); Goth. *ga-staúrknan* 'dry up', OE *stearc* 'stiff' (Goetze, *Lg.* 30:403 [1954]); Lat. *stercus* 'filth', Welsh *trwnc* 'urine' (Duchesne-Guillemin, *TPS* 146:82; similarly Puhvel, *LIEV* 25, in the sense of 'pollute'); Lat. *sternō* 'scatter, lay low' (Kronasser, *Studies presented to Joshua Whatmough* 122 [1957]); Ved. *tṛṇáh-, tṛṁhá-* 'crush' (besides *stṛhant-* 'damaging' with *s*-mobile; H. Eichner, *Gedenkschrift für H. Kronasser* 16–21 [1982]).

Cf. *arma(n)-, inan-*.

istarna, istarni, always spelled **is-tar-**, 'between, mutually, in the midst, among(st), within, internally' (ŠÀ; e.g. *KUB* I 1 I 7 DINGIR.MEŠ-*as-kan istarna* beside ibid. IV 88 ŠÀ DINGIR.MEŠ 'among the gods'; cf. Götze, *Hattusilis* 6, 40), *istarna iya-* (or: *pai-*) 'go among; go by, pass (of time)', *istarna tiya-* 'step between; intervene, intercede', *istarna tekkussa(nu)-* 'single out (within a group), designate', *istarna arha* 'away from amongst; right through', *istarna pedi* 'at mid-point, centrally', *istarna siwatti* 'at mid-day', e.g.: *KUB* XXX 29 Vs. 4 ^GIŠ*kuppisnas istarna* 'between the stools'; *KBo* II 3 III 10–11 [*nu pa*]*hhur* ZAG-*az* GÙB-*lazz-iya* BIL-*an*[*zi*] [*is*]*tarna-ma-kan* 7 ^NA₄*huwasi isgaranzi* 'they light a fire to the right and left, and in between they set seven stone pillars'; cf. L. Rost, *MIO* 1:362 [1953]; III 1 II 50 *kuis* ŠEŠ.MEŠ-*n-a* NIN.MEŠ-*n-a istarna idālu iyazi* 'who does evil among brothers and sisters'; XXV 112 III 11 DINGIR.MEŠ- -*nan-a istarna,* ibid. II 12 and 19 DINGIR.MEŠ-*nas-a istarna* 'among the gods' (cf. Neu, *Altheth.* 191–2); *KUB* VIII 41 passim DINGIR.MEŠ-*nas-a istarna* and XXXI 143 passim DINGIR.MEŠ- -*nan-a istarna,* matching Hattic *hawashawipi* (e.g. XXVIII 75 III 6, 9, 13, 17, 22, 27; cf. Laroche, *JCS* 1:187–96 [1947]); XXIV 3 I 30–32 *nu-tta-kkan* ŠUM-*an lamnas istarna nakkī* DINGIR-*LIM- -yatar-ma-ta-kkan* DINGIR.MEŠ-*as istarna nakkī namma-za-kan* DINGIR.MEŠ-*as istarna zik-pat* ^D UTU ^URU*Arinna nakkis* 'your name [is] important among names, and your godhead [is] important among the gods; furthermore among the gods you above all [are] important, sun-goddess of Arinna'; dupl. XXIV 1 II 21 [*nu-tta- -kkan* ŠUM]-*an* ŠUM.HI.A-*as istarnas* [sic] *nakkī*; XXIV 3 I 45 and 49 (cf. Gurney, *Hittite Prayers* 20–4); XXIV 8 I 10–11 KUR-*e-kan istarna apās happinanza* 'within the land he [is] wealthy' (cf. Siegelová, *Appu-Hedammu* 4); *KBo* XXII 102 I 8 *mān* ŠÀ-ŠU *istarn*[*a* 'if within his heart' or 'if his heart within' (cf. Burde, *Medizinische Texte* 47); *KUB* XV 34 II 20–24 *istarna- -kan āssiyauwar ... piskattin* 'within, grant love ...!' (cf. Haas – Wilhelm, *Riten* 190); *KBo* XIX 70, 17 *nu-za-kan istarna* SIG₅- -*antes ēsten* 'be well internally!' (cf. S. Heinhold-Krahmer, *Arzawa* 296 [1977]).

KUB XXIII 101 II 18 *istarni-ma-w*[*ar*]-*an-wa-nnas-kan* SIG₅-*antes* '(let) us (be) mutually dear'; *istarni-smi* 'among (or:

between) them (or: you, us), mutually', spelled *is-tar-ni-is-mi* (*KBo* III 60 II 2–3 *kuis istarni-smi antuwahhis ak*[*i*] *s-an-ap azzikanzi* 'what person dies among them, him they eat'; *KUB* XI 34 I 50), *is-tar-ni-su-um-me* (XXVI 81 I 7 *istarni-summe āssi*[*y-antes* 'mutually dear'; ibid. IV 9 *istarni-summe-as-kan*[; XXVI 43 Vs. 19 *kūs-ma-kan* URU.HI.A *istarni-su*[*mme* 'but these towns mutually ...'; dupl. *KBo* XXII 58 Vs. 9 -]*su-um-me*; cf. Imparati, *RHA* 32:26, 54 [1974]), *is-tar-ni-sum-mi* (*KUB* XXXIII 120 III 4; cf. Güterbock, *Kumarbi* *4; *KBo* XIV 12 IV 29–31 *nu-kan* [*ish*]*iūl istarni-summi ishiyat* '[he] concluded a treaty between them'; ibid. 32, 36, 39 *istarni-summi āssiyantes* 'mutually dear'; ibid. 37–38 *kinun-a-wa-nnas-kan kī-ya istarni-su*[*mmi*] [*kis*]*at* 'even though now this has taken place between us'; cf. Güterbock, *JCS* 10:98 [1956]; XXXI 66 II 9–11 *kī-wa-smas ishiūl iyanun* GIM-*an-ma-nnas-kan* HUL-*uwa* AWATE.MEŠ *istarni-summi wehtat* 'I have made you this injunction; but whereas bad words have been bandied between us ...'; cf. Houwink Ten Cate, *Anatol. Stud. Güterbock* 130).

KUB XLIV 61 Vs. 6 UD.KAM-*ma-kan istarna iyattari* 'but a day goes by' (cf. Burde, *Medizinische Texte* 18); *KBo* XXII 2 Vs. 6 *mān* MU.HI.A *istarna pāir* 'as the years passed' (cf. Otten, *Altheth. Erzählung* 6, 23–4); V 1 I 57 *n-asta apās* UD-*az istarna paizzi* 'that day goes by'; ibid. IV 34 UD-*az-ma-kan istarna paizzi* 'the day goes by' (cf. Sommer – Ehelolf, *Pāpanikri* 4*, 12*, 42–3); IV 14 III 4 [*nu-k*]*an mēhur istarna paizzi* 'time passes' (cf. Stefanini, *ANLR* 20:44 [1965]); *KUB* XVII 12 II 18–19 *n-asta mahhan nassu* UD.2.KAM *nasma* UD.3.KAM *istarna paizzi* 'when either two or three days go by'; XXVII 1 I 1 [*nu*]-*kan mān* MU.HI.A *istarna pantes* 'if years [have] gone by'; similarly ibid. 8–9 and 20 (cf. Lebrun, *Samuha* 75). Cf., without *istarna*, e.g. XXIX 4 I 54 *nu apās* UD.KAM-*as paizzi* 'that day goes by' (cf. Kronasser, *Umsiedelung* 12); *KBo* IV 2 III 45 *mahhan-ma uer* MU.HI.A-*us* EGIR-*anda pāir* 'but as the years came and went by' (cf. Götze – Pedersen, *MS* 4); III 20 I 3 *mān* 1 ME.KAM MU.KAM *pait* 'as a hundred years had gone by' (cf. Güterbock, *ZA* 44:50 [1938]). The literal sense occurs in e.g. *VBoT* 24 III 11 *namma* ANA UDU.HI.A *istarna paimi* 'then I go among the sheep'.

KBo III 3 III 27–28 *mān* DINU-*ma kuitki nu-smas-kan* LÚSANGA

istarna, istarni

ANA DI.HI.A *istarna tieskiddu* 'but if (there is) some court
proceeding, the priest shall intercede for you in legal matters' (cf.
Hrozný, *Heth. KB* 150). The literal rendering applies to *KUB* I
13 III 12–13 ANA GIŠ-*ru-ma istarna tianzi* 'they step between
wood(en troughs?)' (cf. Kammenhuber, *Hippologia* 64).

KBo V 3 I 10 *n-an-kan istarna tekkussami* 'I designate him';
ibid. 4–5 *nu-tta-kkan* ᵁᴿᵁ*Hattusi* ANA LÚ.MEŠ ᵁᴿᵁ*Hayasa-ya
istarna tekkussanunun* 'at Hattusas I have singled you out
amongst the men of Hayasa' (cf. Friedrich, *Staatsverträge*
2:106).

istarna arha 'right through', e.g. *KUB* XVII 28 IV 47 UKÙ-*an*
MÁŠ.GAL UR.TUR ŠAH.TUR *istarna arha kuranzi* 'they cut in two a
man, a he-goat, a puppy, and a piglet' (cf. O. Masson, *RHR*
137:5 [1950]); *KBo* V 4 Rs. 47 *nasma-kan* ᴸᵁKÚR-*ma tuel* KUR-KA
istarna arha iyattari 'or an enemy marches right through your
country' (cf. Friedrich, *Staatsverträge* 1:68); *KUB* XXXI 127 +
I 58–59 4 *halhaltūmari ukturi istarna arha iyattari* 'you traverse
the four firm corners'; *KUB* XXIII 1 IV 17 KUR-KA-*as-kan
istarna arha le paizzi* 'he shall not cross your country' (cf.
Kühne – Otten, *Šaušgamuwa* 16). The literal meaning 'away
from between (amongst, within)', like Akk. *ištu libbi*, is seen in
e.g. VII 31 I 20 *nu-mu-kan* GIDIM-*as istarna arha* [...] '[free] me
from amongst the dead!' (cf. Kümmel, *Ersatzrituale* 62); *KUB*
XV 35 + *KBo* II 9 I 16 *nu-smas-kan istarna arha ehu* 'come away
from their midst!' (cf. Sommer, *ZA* 33:98 [1921]); *KUB* V 1 I
48–49, II 57 HUL-*uwaz-as-kan* GIG GAL-*ya istarna arha uit* 'it
came away from between evil and great ailment', i.e. a rock and
a hard place; similarly ibid. IV 75 (cf. Ünal, *Hatt.* 2:40, 60, 88).

istarna pedi 'at mid-point, centrally', e.g. *KBo* XIX 128 III
17–18 GUNNI *istarna pedi* 'in the midst of the hearth' (cf. Otten,
Festritual 8); *istarna pidi*, e.g. *KBo* IV 1 Vs. 4 and dupl. II 2 I 2;
KUB XX 59 V 20 and VI 4–5, 19; *VBoT* 24 I 12; *KBo* IV 2 I 33;
ibid. 27 *is-tar-na pi-e-ti* (cf. Kronasser, *Die Sprache* 8:90–1
[1962]). For the construction cf. e.g. *tamatta pedi* 'in another
place' beside *damēdani pidi* (s.v. *ta*[*n*]), or *apiya* UD-*ti* 'on that
day' beside *apedani lamnī* 'at that hour' (s.v. *apa-*).

UD.HI.A-*ti istarna pidi*, lit. 'on the day at mid-point' (*KUB* VII
5 II 22) equals ibid. 26 *istarna* UD.HI.A-*ti* 'at mid-day' (both

480

preceded by *karūwariwar* 'at daybreak' and followed by *nekuz mehur* 'at nightfall'; XXVII 29 II 14 *istarni* UD.KAM-*ti* has adjectival congruence (dat.-loc. sg. of *istarniya*-, q.v. infra; cf. Haas – Thiel, *Rituale* 142), in the manner of Lat. *in medias res* 'into the middle of things' (cf. e.g. ZAG-*ni* [GIŠ]*asari* 'at the right of the door' [s.v. *arasa*-]). The same transition is seen between *KUB* IX 31 I 32 [*A*]NA [DUG]KA.[GAG.N]AG *istarna* and dupl. *HT* 1 I 25 ANA [DUG]KA.GAG.NAG *istarni* 1 [GI]A.DA.GUR *tarnai* 'into the center of the goblet he lets drop a spoon'.

istarniya- 'middle, central', nom. sg. c. *istarniyas* (*KUB* XVII 10 IV 9–12 *parnanz-at tarnau istarniyas-at annasnanza tarnau* [GIŠ]*luttanz-at tarnau wawarkima istarniyas-at hilas tarnau* KÁ. .GAL-*at tarnau hilamnanz-at tarnau* KASKAL.LUGAL-*at tarnau* 'may the house let them go, may the central pillar [?] let them go, may the window let them go, to the gate-socket [?] may the central courtyard let them go, may the gate let them go, may the gateway let them go, may the royal road let them go'; cf. Laroche, *RHA* 23:97 [1965]), acc. sg. c. *istarniyan* (XXXIII 62 II 5), nom.-acc. sg. neut. *istarniya* (XXIX 52 IV 2 and XXIX 46 + 53 I 18 *istarniya hāli* 'the middle watch'; cf. Kammenhuber, *Hippologia* 192, 196), dat.-loc. sg. *istarni* (quoted above), *istarniya* (*KBo* XIII 58 III 16–17 *istarniya-ya-kan hāli*; *KUB* VII 2 I 24–25 *nu-za* EN SISKUR.SISKUR É-*ri istarniya esari* 'the offerant seats himself in the center of the house'), dat.-loc. pl. *istarniyas* (*KBo* V 11 IV 18 *istarniyas* KÁ.GAL 'to the center gate'). For formation cf. e.g. *anturiya*- (s.v. *andurza*).

istarnarhana (KUB IX 3 I 9 *šUM-šU istarnarhana šUM-šU istarna*[; cf. A. M. Jasink Ticchioni, *Studi classici e orientali* 27:161 [1977]); for an interpretation see below.

istarna was connected by Hrozný (*SH* 96) with Lat. *sternere* 'spread', OHG *stirna* 'forehead', OCS *strana* 'area', thus IE **ster-H_2*- 'spread'; Sturtevant (*Lg.* 4:5 [1928]) specifically added Gk. στέρνον 'breast', comparing ŠÀ and Akk. *libbu* 'heart' and 'middle', and affirming nominal origin. An underlying noun **sterno*- 'spread, space, extent' was postulated by T. Milewski, *L'indo-hittite et l'indo-européen* 14 (1936), and by Laroche, *RHA* 28:38–9 (1970), *istarna* and *istarni*(-) thus being petrifacts of dat.-loc. (or "directive") origin. While on the one hand stressing semantic parallels such as OCS *srĕda* 'middle' : *srŭdĭce* 'heart', Kronasser (*VLFH* 38, 221) also weighed the homophonous similarity of Hurr. *istani-* 'middle'. Yet further constructional parallels (such as Hurr. *istani-wwas-a*, Akk. *ina libbi-ni*, Hitt. *-nnas istarni-summi* 'in our midst') are merely that, and may not even be close, for *istarna* vs. *istarni-summi* resembles above all *katta* vs. *katti-mmi* (q.v.; cf. Starke, *Funktionen* 188–91) and is thus at best only remotely a noun phrase. Laroche's (*RHA* 28:38–9 [1970]) postulation of "double directives" in *istarna arha* as 'à l'espace vers le bord', implying a double reference to interiority and separation similar to Lat. *inter* (cf. Benveniste, *Noms d'agent et noms d'action en indo-européen* 120–1 [1948]), errs in assuming the still-palpable existence of a noun *istarna-*. The semantics of 'expanse' > 'breast' (specifically Gk. στέρνον) > 'center, middle, interior' are also less than satisfactory.

Instead *istarna* and Lat. *inter* show close similarities in construction, meaning, and usage: *istarni-smi* vs. *inter se* 'mutually'; *istarna iya-* 'pass (away)' vs. *interire* 'perish'; *istarna tiya-* 'intercede' vs. *intervenire*; *istarna tekkussa(nu)-* 'single out, put on the spot' vs. *interdicere* 'interfere with, forbid'; *istarna arha kuer-* 'cut in two' vs. Lat. *intersecāre* 'cut asunder' + *resecāre* 'cut off'; *istarna siwatti* 'at mid-day' vs. *interdiu(s)* 'in daytime'. Parallel to *istarna iya-* 'pass (away)' one might also have expected **istarna iya-* 'do away with, make disappear, spend (time)' (like Ved. *antár dhā-* and Lat. *interficere*; cf. Puhvel, *Analecta Indoeuropaea* 409–10 [1981]).

Perhaps the etymology of *istarna* should be sought in a similar direction. *istar-* can represent **ens-ter* parallel to Lat. *inter*, with the same variation as in Gk. ἐν-, εἰς- or ἐκ-, ἐξ-; *-na* is obscure (cf. Lat. *internus*?) but may be replicated over again in the combination *istarn(a)-arha-na* (see above). *istarna* would thus be cognate with *anda* '(with)in' (q.v.), being sometimes employed very much in the same sense (cf. Friedrich, *ZA* 35:141 [1924], and Lat. *intus*); its specific usages, however, like those of Lat. *inter*, spring from the suffix **-ter* which singles out the marked member of a binary pair ('separately within').

Carruba (*SMEA* 12:87 [1970], *Partikeln* 75) tried to derive the particle *-(a)sta* (q.v.) from *istarna* /starn/. Neumann (*Un-*

tersuchungen 96) saw in Hes. στέρνιξ· ἐντεριώνη 'inmost part, pith' a borrowing from Hitt. *istarn-* (sic) 'middle, midst'.
Cf. *hilistarni-*.

isdusduski-,   *KBo* XXIII 90 I 7 *du]sgaraz isdusdus*[-; dupl. *KUB* XL 23, 12 [*dusgaraz isd]usdusk*[*i-*; dupl. *Bo* 3158 I 13 *dusgaraza isdu*[-; *KBo* XXII 126 Vs. 2–3 *uk]tūriyas halugas isdusdu*[-...] [...]LUGAL *andan uktūri dusgara*[-.

The verb appears in a possible figura etymologica with *dusgaratt-* 'joy', perhaps as a reduplicated transitive counterpart 'gladden' to *duski-* < **tus-ske-* 'be glad', cognate with Skt. *túṣyati*. Since *duski-* is an old formation (of the type **pṛ́k̂ske-* > Skt. *pṛccháti*, Lat. *poscit*) rather than a "living" iterative, an analysis **tus-tuske-* rather than **stu-stu-(ske-)* seems indicated (wrongly Kühne, *ZA* 62:251–2 [1972]; H. Eichner, *Die Sprache* 27:65 [1981]); the "prothetic" *s-* may be merely anticipatory, in the sense that **tustuski-*, unlike *duski-*, was reinterpreted as a true iterative **tustu-ski-* and had "full" reduplication "restored".

istuwa-   'be(come) manifest, be exposed, get out (in the open)', 3 sg. pres. midd. *isduwari* (e.g. *KUB* XXX 10 Rs. 19 *nu-mu-ssan ser assul natta isduwari* 'over me [divine] favor is not manifest'; similarly XXX 11 Rs. 17), *istuwāri* (XIII 3 III 7–8 EGIR-*pizziya--ma-at istuwāri* 'but it subsequently gets out'; ibid. 18–19 *appiziyan-ma-at istuwāri*; cf. Friedrich, *Meissner AOS* 47), *isduwāri* (XIII 4 III 82 [*ta]kk[u] sannāi* EGIR-*zian-ma-at isduwāri* 'if he conceals it, but it subsequently gets out'; ibid. IV 21 *apzian-ma-as isduwāri*; ibid. 30–31 EGIR-*zian-ma-as isduwāri* ... *mān-ma-as* ŪL-*ma isduwāri*; similarly ibid. 46–47, 66–68, dupl. XIII 17 IV 8–9), *is-du-u-wa-ri* (ibid. 25, misspelled *is-̈-u-wa-hu*; cf. Sturtevant, *JAOS* 54:388–96 [1934]), 3 sg. pret. midd. *isduwati* (XXIII 11 III 7–8 *n-as-mu* DINGIR.MEŠ *parā piyer nu-smas-(s)ta uttar arha isduwati n-us-kan haspir* ᴵ*Kukkulinn-a--kan kuinnir* 'the gods handed them over to me, and the plot was exposed on them, and they destroyed them, and they slew K.'; cf. R. Ranoszek, *Rocznik Orientalistyczny* 9:58 [1934]; *KBo* XIX 84, 9 *a]rha isduwati*), *isduwāti* (III 1 II 11 [OHitt.] *mān-us-kan*

¹*Huzziyas kuenta nu uttar isduwāti* 'H. would have killed them, but word [of the plot] got out'; *KUB* XIV 4 I 3 *i]sduwāti*).

Luwoid *dusdumi-* (c.) 'evidence, manifest, voucher', nom. sg. *dusdumis* (*KUB* XIII 35 I 4–6 [*nu*] UNUTUM *kuit kuedani pieskit n-at ŪL siyaeskit nu-ssi dusdumis* (with gloss-wedges) ŪL *ēsta lalamies-si* (with gloss-wedges) ŪL *ēsta* 'what object he had given to whom, that he had never documented; he had neither voucher nor receipt'; *dusdumassi-* 'evidentiary', nom.-acc. pl. neut. *dusdumassa* (ibid. 15–16 ANŠU.KUR.RA-*wa* ANŠU.GÌR.NUN.NA *kui*[*n h*]*arkun nu-wa-mu* ᴳᴵˢL[*EU*] *dusdumassa* [with gloss-wedges] *siyan ēsta* 'as for the horse and mule that I had, there were wooden voucher-tablets as documentation'; cf. Werner, *Gerichtsprotokolle* 4); there is also VII 56 III 10 *dusduma* (without gloss-wedges) in fragmentary context. *dusdumi-* is probably from a Luwian reduplicated verb **du-sdum(a)*- matching Hitt. *(i)sduwa-* (cf. Luw. *hishiya-* : Hitt. *ishiya-*). Cf. Carruba, *Oriens Antiquus* 9:85 (1970).

Sturtevant (*Lg.* 4:4–5 [1928], 6:31 [1930]) compared *istuwa-* with Gk. στεῦται in e.g. στεῦται γάρ τι ἔπος ἐρέειν '(he) looks as if he will say some word' (*Iliad* 3:83). Construed with a participle στεῦται means 'is manifest (doing something)', i.e. 'plainly does' (*Odyssey* 11:584 στεῦτο δὲ διψάων, πιέειν δ᾽ οὐκ εἶχεν ἐλέσθαι 'he was plainly thirsting but could not get to drink'), antonymical to the same construction with λανθάνω 'escape notice' (λάθε βιώσας); it is found also in expressions such as στεῦτο γὰρ εὐχόμενος νικησέμεν 'he openly boasted that he would be victorious' (*Iliad* 2:597) and στεῦτ᾽ ἀγορεύων Τρωσὶ μαχήσεσθαι 'he openly stated that he would fight the Trojans' (*Iliad* 5:832–3). From a reduction of such seemingly semi-pleonastic constructions rose the usage of στεῦται alone with the infinitive in the secondary sense 'claim, declare, promise, threaten', being thus a product of epic formula consolidation. The tertium comparationis, Indo-Iranian *stu-* 'praise, celebrate', offers RV 3 sg. pres. midd. *stáve* 'is celebrated' which as nonthematic not only closely matches στεῦται or στεῦτο (: Avest. *staota* vs. RV *stáve*, like e.g. κεῖται : Avest. *saēta* vs. RV *śáye*; cf. J. Narten, in *Pratidānam* 18–9 [1968]) but in thematic guise (RV also *stávate*) can be closely paired with Hitt. *istuwari* (cf. C. Watkins,

Indogermanische Grammatik III/1, 115–6; H. Eichner, in *Flexion und Wortbildung* 99 [1975]; Oettinger, *MSS* 34:112 [1976]). It is conceivable that the original meaning of I.-Ir. *stu-* is likewise a medial-intransitive 'be(come) manifest', and that e.g. RV 10.22.2 *ihá śrutá Índro asmé adyá stáve* 'here Indra (is) heard of, by *us* to-day he is celebrated' means originally '*here* Indra (is) heard of, to *us* to-day he is manifest', i.e. *we* nowadays fully appreciate Indra's renown (cf. the preceding verse, *kúha śrutá Índraḥ kásminn adyá jáne mitró ná śrūyate* 'where [is] Indra heard of, in what people to-day like a friend is he heard of?'). The development of a productive transitive paradigm of *stu-* in the sense of 'praise, celebrate' may have occurred in early Indo-Iranian hymnic-poetic diction via elliptic formula-reduction similar to the Homeric one described above. In a medial-intransitive Indo-Iranian construct *(śru-+) stu-* 'be (heard of and) manifest' *śru-* was incapable of secondary activization into 'celebrate' due to the pre-existent transitive meaning 'hear'; but *stu-*, denoting in statival fashion visual and by extension cognitive celebrity (cf. IE *weyd-* 'see' > 'know'), first acquired de facto diathetic passivity in contexts such as *RV* 6.26.7 *tváyā yát stávante … vīrás* ('that through you heroes have visibility' > 'that by you heroes are celebrated'); from there the way was clear to an active paradigm (RV *stoṣi* 'thou praisest' [vs. *stavase nas* 'thou art celebrated by us'], *staut*; Avest. *staoiti*; new post-RV middle *stuté* patterned on the active). Thus the media tantum Hitt. *istuwa-* and Gk. στευ- may be more archaic than Indic and Iranian *stu-*; IE *stew-* would be in origin intransitive-stative rather than a verbum dicendi (J. Wackernagel's "feierliche öffentliche Kundgebung" [*Sprachliche Untersuchungen zu Homer* 202]), and e.g. RV *stutí-* 'hymn of praise' denotes originally 'celebrity' (> 'celebration'), vs. *śrúti-* 'auditory lore'. Cf. Puhvel, *AJPh* 104:218–21 (1983).

O. Szemerényi (*Die Sprache* 12:206 [1966]) implausibly connected *istuwa-* with OPers. *azdā* 'announcement' (< *adh-tā* under "Bartholomae's law", thus *isdu-* < *edh-tu-*); a Hittite cognate of the Indo-Iranian root *adh-* may instead be present in *isiya(hh)-* 'announce, reveal' (q.v.).

Cf. *suppesduant-, suppistuwara-*.

isuwan- (n.) 'residue, sediment, refuse, scraps, waste, remains', nom.-acc. sg. *i-su-wa-an* (*KBo* VI 26 I 22–27 [= *Code* 2:63] *takku suppala-sset kuēlqa sieuniahta t-at parkunuzi n-at arha pennāi isuwanalli-ma-kan isuwan dāi ari-ssi-ma-at ŪL tezzi* ^{LÚ}*arass-a ŪL sakki suppala-sset pennāi n-at aki sarnikzil* 'if someone's cattle suffer demonic possession, and he cleanses them and drives them off, but dumps the refuse on a scrap-heap without telling his fellow [shepherd], so that the fellow unwittingly drives his cattle [there], and they die, restitution [is in order]'), instr. sg. *isuwanit* (I 45 Vs. 3 *isuwanit wātar* 'water with sediment' matching ibid. Akk. *lihmu* [cf. *luhummū* 'thick liquid, wet dirt, mire']; cf. *MSL* 3:59 [1955]).

Denom. *isuwanai-*, partic. nom. sg. c. *isuwananza* (*KBo* II 4 III 27–28 and IV 5 1 NINDA KUR₄.RA BA.BA.ZA ŠÀ-*ir isuwananza* 'bread-mash internally sedimental' [from fermentational liquefaction?], vs. ibid. III 25 1 NINDA KUR₄.RA BA.BA.ZA *IŠTU* A *sunnianza* 'water-logged bread-mash', *isunanza* (ibid. II 23 1 NINDA KUR₄.RA BA.BA.ZA ŠÀ-*ir isunanza*; XXIII 95 Vs. 11 ŠÀ-*i*]*r isunanza*), *isuwanza* (sic *Bo* 3481 IV 14 1 NINDA KUR₄.RA BA.BA.ZA ŠÀ-*ni isuwanza*, vs. ibid. 12 1 NINDA KUR₄.RA BA.BA.ZA *IŠTU* A *sunnanza*; cf. Haas, *Nerik* 296).

(i)suwanalli- (n.) 'scrap-heap, refuse dump, midden', dat.-loc. sg. *isuwanalli* (*KBo* VI 26 I 24, quoted above), *suwanalli* (dupl. VI 18 IV 3). For formation cf. Kronasser, *Etym.* 1:212.

For the many past attempts at interpretation see e.g. Friedrich, *Heth. Ges.* 109–10; Imparati, *Leggi ittite* 288–92; Tischler, *Glossar* 439–40; most cogent are the discussions by Güterbock, *JCS* 15:70–1 (1961), and Meriggi, *WZKM* 58:99–100 (1962). The dim view taken by the law of careless or willful disposal of potentially lethal ritual waste-material is patent from *Code* 1:44 (*KBo* VI 3 II 55–56 *takku antuhsan kuiski parkunuzzi kuptarr-a uktūrias* [*pedāi*] *takku-at* A.ŠÀ-*ni nasma parni kuelga pedai alwanzatar* [DI.KUD LUGAL] 'if someone cleanses a person, he also takes the refuse to the incinerator; if he dumps it on someone's field or house[-lot], [this amounts to] sorcery [and is subject to] the king's judgment').

isuwan- is semantically somewhat akin to *mudan-* (n.) 'rinsed dirt, refuse, offal' (q.v. s.v. *mutai-*) which was given as food to dogs and pigs. The fluctuation *(i)suwanalli-* and the etymology are opaque; a connection with *suwai-* 'fill; (midd.) be filled, swell' (e.g. Josephson, *Sentence particles* 286) is not obvious.

idalu- 'bad, evil' (HUL, rarely HÉ; *KBo* I 30 I 16 *idalus* matches Akk. *masku*, just as ibid. 15 the near-synonymous *huwappas* [q.v.] is glossed by Akk. *limnu*; cf. Güterbock, *MSL* 12:214–5 [1969]), nom. sg. c. *idalus* (e.g. *KUB* XIV 15 II 6 *n-an idalus* GIG-*as istarakta* 'a bad illness afflicted him'; cf. Götze, *AM* 48; *KBo* V 13 II 26–27 *kuiski idalus memiyas* ŠA BAL 'some bad word of insurrection'; cf. Friedrich, *Staatsverträge* 1:124), *idālus* (e.g. V 4 Vs. 10 *idālus memia*[*s* Š]*A* BAL; cf. Friedrich, *Staatsverträge* 1:52; ibid. Rs. 10 [*nu* 1-*as* 1-*ed*]*ani menahhanda le idālus* 'one [shall] not [be] evil against the other'; XXXI 86, 2–3 ᴸᴶᵁHUL-*as* [ŠEŠ-*as* ...] *idālus* 'Brother Bad ... evil'; cf. Siegelová, *Appu-Hedammu* 10, 14, 23), HUL-*lus* (e.g. *KUB* XLIV 4 + *KBo* XIII 241 Rs. 28 HUL-*lus* EME-*as* 'evil tongue'), acc. sg. c. *idalun* (e.g. *KUB* XII 58 II 14 *idalun* EME-*an*; cf. Goetze, *Tunnawi* 14), *idālun* (e.g. *KBo* V 3 II 40–41 *idālun antuhsan* 'evil person'; cf. Friedrich, *Staatsverträge* 2:118; XXI 8 III 16 *idālun* EME-*an*), HUL-*un* (e.g. dupl. *KUB* XXIV 10 III 25 HUL-*un* EME[-*an*; cf. Jakob-Rost, *Ritual der Malli* 46), HUL-*lun* (e.g. *KUB* V 13 III 22 *mānn-a* HUL-*lun memian kuinki* ŠA BAL *piran parā istamasti* 'and if you hear in advance some bad word of insurrection'; cf. Friedrich, *Staatsverträge* 1:128), nom.-acc. sg. (also pl.) neut. *idalu* (e.g. XXIV 9 II 11–13 *nassu-wa-an* AN[*A PANI* DINGIR.MEŠ] *kuiski idalu iet nasma-an* ANA PANI DUMU.LÚ.ULÙ.LU[.MEŠ *kuiski*] HUL-*lu iet* 'whether before the gods someone has treated him badly, or before men someone has treated him badly'; cf. Gk. κακὰ ποιεῖν τινα; Jakob-Rost, *Ritual der Malli* 32; *KUB* XXIV 9 II 36 + *KBo* XII 127 II 3 *kī idalu zik ep* 'this evil take thou!', besides dupl. *KUB* XXIV 11 II 15–16 HUL-*lu* [*zik*] *ep*; IX 31 II 38 *idalu-kan parā istabdu āssuw-a-kan anda kuragdu* 'let [the door] shut out evil and keep in good', besides dupl. *HT* 1 II 12 HÉ-*lu-kan sarā istabdu* ...; cf. B. Schwartz, *JAOS* 58:342 [1938]), *italu* (*KBo* XVIII 151 Rs. 19 *italu-wa bayit* 'the bad is gone'; cf.

idalu-

Ünal – Kammenhuber, *KZ* 88:164 [1974]), *idālu* (e.g. *KUB* VII
41 Vs. 18 *idālu papratar* 'evil defilement'; I 16 III 23 *apās idālu iet*
'she has done evil'; cf. Sommer, *HAB* 12; ibid. II 16 LUGAL-*s-an*
idālu k[uitki iyanun 'have I, the king, treated him badly in any
way?', matching ibid. I 16 [Akk.] LUGAL *lemuttam mimma epuš*;
cf. Sommer, *HAB* 4–5; XXXIII 68 II 11–12 *zig-a* ᴰU *idālu uddār*
arha pessiya nu-za āssu uddār dā 'but you, storm-god, throw
away evil words and take unto yourself good words!'; *KBo* XVII
90 II 14 *idālu-ya-kan uddār*; XV 10 I 18 *idālu kue* 'the evil things
which'; ibid. II 15 and III 57 *idālu uddār-set* 'her evil words'; cf.
Szabó, *Entsühnungsritual* 14, 22, 44; *KUB* XXI 5 III 6 *eni]-wa*
idālu kisaru 'let this evil take place!'), HUL-*lu* (e.g. dupl. XXI 1 II
80 *eni-wa* HUL-*lu* DÙ-*ru*; cf. Friedrich, *Staatsverträge* 2:64; XXIV
9 II 32 *kī* HUL-*lu alwanzata* 'this evil sorcery'), HUL (e.g. XXIV 10
III 26 HUL UH₄-*tar* 'evil sorcery'; cf. Jakob-Rost, *Ritual der Malli*
46), dat.-loc. sg. *i-da-la-u-i* (e.g. XIX 54, 19; cf. Friedrich,
Staatsverträge 1:142), *i-da-a-la-u-i* (e.g. XV 32 I 52–53 *nu-wa-*
-kan apedani idālaui antuhsi awan arha uwattin 'come away from
that evil person'; cf. Haas – Wilhelm, *Riten* 152), *i-da-a-la-u-*
-e (e.g. *KBo* II 3 II 36; cf. L. Rost, *MIO* 1:360 [1953]),
i-da-a-la-a-u-i (e.g. V 4 Rs. 45 *nu-ssan idālāui imma parā uskisi*
'you condone evil'; cf. Friedrich, *Staatsverträge* 1:66), HUL-*la-u-*
-i (e.g. *KUB* XXI 1 III 49–50 *nu-kan* HUL-*laui [p]arā uskisi*),
HUL-*u-e* (dupl. XXI 5 III 66 *nu-kan* HUL-*ue parā usgisi*; cf.
Friedrich, *Staatsverträge* 2:74), *i-ta-lu-i* (*KBo* XVIII 151 Rs. 6),
abl. sg. *idalauwaz* (e.g. *KUB* XII 58 III 7 *idalauwaz paprannaz* 'by
means of evil pollution'; cf. ibid. 3–4 and 8–9 *idalu papratar*;
Goetze, *Tunnawi* 16), *idālauwaz* (e.g. XV 34 II 5 *idālauwaz*
papran[naz]; cf. Haas – Wilhelm, *Riten* 190), *idalauwanza*
(XXXI 127 III 43), HUL-*uwaz* (e.g. V 1 I 48 and II 57; cf. Ünal,
Hatt. 2:40, 60), *idālaz* (sic XV 42 II 9 *idālaz uddānaz*), nom. pl. c.
i-da-la-u-e-s(a-an) (VII 53 II 18–19 *idalawes-an kuyēs antuhsis*
paprahhis⟨k⟩ir 'what evil persons were polluting him'; cf.
Goetze, *Tunnawi* 12), *i-da-la-u-e-es* (e.g. XXIV 9 II 23 *alwanzata*
idalawēs teshus 'sorcery [and] bad dreams'; cf. Jakob-Rost,
Ritual der Malli 34), *i-da-a-la-u-e-es* (e.g. *KBo* XV 10 I 13, 15, 23,
27, 33 *idālawēs* 'evil [tongues]'; cf. Szabó, *Entsühnungsritual*
14–8), HUL-*u-e-es* (e.g. *KUB* IX 34 III 45 HUL-*wēs siwannies* 'evil

gods'), *idālauwanzi* (Luwoid *KUB* XXIX 7 + *KBo* XXI 41 Rs. 38 *idālauwanzi-ya* NIŠ DINGIR-*LIM* 'evil perjuries'; cf. Lebrun, *Samuha* 123), acc. pl. c. *idalamus* (e.g. *KUB* VII 53 III 17 *idalamus zashimus* 'bad dreams'; cf. Goetze, *Tunnawi* 20; XXIV 9 II 42 *i-da-la-mu-s*[*a*; cf. Jakob-Rost, *Ritual der Malli* 38), *idālamus* (e.g. XLIV 56 Rs. 12 *idālamus* EME-*us*; ibid. 16 *idālamus* EME.HI.[A; cf. ibid. 14 *i-da-a-la-u-wa-as-sa* [dat.-loc. pl.?]; *KBo* XV 10 I 30–31 *idālamus alwanzinnus* EME.HI.A 'evil, sorcerous tongues'; ibid. II 12 *idālamus* EME.HI.A; cf. Szabó, *Entsühnungsritual* 16, 22), *idālamūs* (ibid. III 54 [*idā*]*lamūs-a* EME.HI.A; *KUB* VIII 67 IV 14 *idā*]*lamūs harziyalus* NE.ZA.ZA.HI.A 'bad snails [and] frogs'; cf. Siegelová, *Appu-Hedammu* 40), HUL-*mus* (IX 34 I 28 HUL-*mus* Ù.MEŠ-*us* 'bad dreams'), *idalus* (*IBoT* III 102 + *Bo* 3436 I 6 *idalus* M[UŠ]EN.HI.A-*us* 'bad birds'; cf. H. Otten – C. Rüster, *ZA* 68:157 [1978]), HUL-*lus* (par. *KUB* IX 34 IV 6 HUL-*lus* MUŠEN.HI.A-*us*), nom.-acc. pl. neut. *idālawa* (XII 44 III 6–8 *idālus-wa-ssan antūwahza idālus* EME-*as idālawa* IGI.HI.A-*wa* 'evil person, evil tongue, evil eye[s]'; cf. G. F. Del Monte, *Oriens Antiquus* 12:122 [1973]), *idalauwa* (e.g. *KBo* V 9 III 21 *idalauwa* INIM.MEŠ 'evil words'; cf. Friedrich, *Staatsverträge* 1:20), *idālauwa* (e.g. ibid. II 46 *idālauwa* A WA TE.MEŠ 'evil words'; XVII 105 III 6 *idālauwa hatuga kue uddār* 'words that [are] evil [and] fearsome', besides ibid. 7 *āssauwa mīyauwa* 'good [and] mild'; II 3 III 43 *idālauwa uddā*[*r*], besides par. *KUB* XXXII 115 + IV 20 and *KBo* XXIV 1 I 19 *idālu uddār* [cf. sub nom.-acc. sg. neut. *idālu* above]; cf. Hrozný, *Heth. KB* 86; L. Rost, *MIO* 1:364 [1953]), dat.-loc. pl. *idālauwas* (e.g. *KUB* XXIV 3 II 55–56 *n-asta l*[*e*] *āssawēs idālauwas anda harkanzi* 'let not the good perish among the evil'; cf. Gurney, *Hittite Prayers* 30), HUL-*uwas* (e.g. IX 34 III 44 HUL-*uwas* DINGIR.MEŠ-*as*).

idalawant- (c.) 'bad(ness), evil', serving in place of *idalu-* (n.) as animate subject with transitive verbs (cf. *assuwant-* s.v. *ass-*), nom. sg. *idālawanza* XXXIII 121 II 17 *i*]*dālawanza* GIG-*anza* 'bad illness'; cf. Friedrich, *ZA* 49:234 [1950]), *i-da-a-la-u-wa-an-za* (*KBo* XVII 62 + 63 IV 10 *idālauwanza uddananza* 'evil thing'), HUL-*u-an-za* (e.g. *KUB* XVI 41 III 16; cf. Ünal, *Hatt.* 2:112; XVI 29 Vs. 2), HUL-*uwanza* (e.g. XVIII 11 Vs. 8), HUL-*lūwanza* (L 71 Vs. 16).

idalawatar, idaluwatar. idalutar (n.) 'badness, evil disposition, malice', nom.-acc. sg. *i-da-lu-wa-tar* (*KUB* XXIV 14 I 25), *i-da]-lu-tar* (XXXIII 93 IV 12, besides dupl. XXXIII 92 III 4 HUL-*tar*; cf. Güterbock, *JCS* 5:22 [1951]), dat.-loc. sg. *i-da-la-u--an-ni* (e.g. *KBo* III 3 II 22, besides ibid. 16 HUL-*anni*; cf. Hrozný, *Heth. KB* 144), *i-da-la-wa-an-ni* (*KUB* VI 41 IV 18), *idālawanni* (dupl. *KBo* V 13 IV 10; cf. Friedrich, *Staatsverträge* 1:134), *idalauwani* (*KUB* XXXIII 103 II 10 *z]ik* ᴰ*Kumarbis* DUMU.LÚ. .ULÙ.LU-*UTTI idalauwani sanhis[kisi]* 'you, K., afflict mankind in malice'; cf. Laroche, *RHA* 26:49 [1968]; Siegelová, *Appu--Hedammu* 46), *idalauwanni* (e.g. XIV 4 II 12; *KBo* V 12 III 14; cf. Friedrich, *Staatsverträge* 2:122; *KUB* XXI 5 III 53, besides dupl. XXI 1 III 18 HUL-*la-u-wa-an-ni* and ibid. 34 HUL-*la-wa-ah-zi* [sic]; cf. Friedrich, *Staatsverträge* 2:70, 72; III 119 Vs. 8, besides dupl. XXI 49 Vs. 6 HUL-*u-an-ni*; cf. Friedrich, *Staatsverträge* 1:6; HUL-*u-an-ni* also e.g. VI 41 I 35; cf. Friedrich, *Staatsverträge* 2:110), *i-da-a-la-u-an-ni* (e.g. XIII 4 II 69; cf. Sturtevant, *JAOS* 54:378 [1934]), *idālauwanni* (XXIV 4 + XXX 12 Vs. 19 *nu* KUR ᵁᴿᵁ*Hatti idālauwanni sanhiskanzi* 'they afflict Hatti in malice'; cf. Gurney, *Hittite Prayers* 28), *idalāuwanni* (*KUB* XIX 67 + 1513/u I 16–17 *nu-ssi-kan idalāuwanni* EGIR-*an* ŪL [*namma*] *maushahat* 'I no longer fell into malice with regard to him'; cf. Neu, *Interpretation* 114–5).

idalawahh- 'treat badly, maltreat' (thus synonymous with *idalu iya-*, rather than a factitival 'make bad'), 1 sg. pres. act. *i-da-la-u-wa-ah-mi* (e.g. *KBo* V 3 IV 31–32 *mān sumes-ma kuwatqa idālu iyatteni nu-smas* ᴰUTU-*ŠI-ya idalauwahmi* 'but if you act badly somehow, I the king shall also treat you badly'; cf. Friedrich, *Staatsverträge* 2:134), 2 sg. pres. act. *idalawahti* (e.g. *KUB* VI 41 IV 12–14 *n-an-zan* SIG₅-*in ēssa idalawahti-ma-an le kuitki mān-an idalawahti-ma kuitki* ... 'treat it well, and do not maltreat it in any way; but if you maltreat it ...'; cf. Friedrich, *Staatsverträge* 1:134), *idalawatti* (sic dupl. *KBo* V 13 IV 5–6 *mān-an idalawatti-ma kuitki*), *idalauwahti* (dupl. IV 3 III 16 *ida]lauwahti-ma-as le kui[tki*), *idalāuwahti* and *idālāuwahti* (V 4 Vs. 26–27 *n-an* SIG₅-*in ēssa idalāuwahti-m[a-an le kuitki] mān-an idālāuwahti-ma kuitki* ...; cf. Friedrich, *Staatsverträge* 1:56), 3 sg. pres. act. *idalawahzi* (*KUB* VI 41 IV 20–21 and dupl. *KBo* V

13 IV 12–13 *nasma-wa-tta idalawahzi kuitki* 'or he maltreats you in any way'; cf. Friedrich, *Staatsverträge* 1:134), HUL-*ahzi* (dupl. IV 3 III 24), HUL-*lauwahzi* (*KUB* XXI 1 III 20), HUL-*wahzi* (dupl. XXI 5 III 35; cf. Friedrich, *Staatsverträge* 2:70), 3 pl. pres. act. *i-da-a-la-u-ah-ha-an-zi* (XIII 4 I 29–30 *n-an-kan nassu kunanzi nasma-kan* KAxKAK-*ŠU* IGI.HI.A-*ŠU* GEŠTUG.HI.A-*ŠU idalauahhanzi* 'they either kill him or they maltreat his nose, his eyes, and his ears'; cf. Sturtevant, *JAOS* 54:366 [1934]), 1 sg. pret. act. *idalawahhun* (*KUB* VI 41 II 34, with dupl. *KBo* IV 3 I 41 HUL-*ahhun*; cf. Friedrich, *Staatsverträge* 1:118), *idālawahhun* (V 13 I 23 *tuk ... ŪL kuitki idālawahhun* 'I have not maltreated you in any way'; cf. Friedrich, *Staatsverträge* 1:114), *idalauwahhun* (dupl. IV 3 I 12, with dupl. IV 7 II 1 HUL-*u*[-]), *i-da-a-la-u-ah-hu--un* (*KUB* XXI 19 III 6), HUL-*ahhun* (e.g. VI 41 I 36; cf. Friedrich, *Staatsverträge* 1:110), 3 sg. pret. act. *idalawahta* (*KBo* XIV 3 III 14 *nu* KUR-*e mekki idalawahta* '[he] had treated the land very badly'; cf. Güterbock, *JCS* 10:67 [1956]; *KUB* XIV 4 III 21 DAM-*YA* SAL.LUGAL *idalawahta kuitki* 'has my wife maltreated the queen in any way?'), 1 pl. pret. act. *i-da-la-u-wa-ah-hu-u-en* (ibid. I 6).

idalawes- 'become bad, go bad, become evil, have a falling out, become alienated', 2 sg. pres. act. *i-da-la-u-e-es-ti* (*KBo* IV 3 IV 32; cf. Friedrich, *Staatsverträge* 1:146), HUL-*u-e-es-ti* (*KUB* XL 39 III 5; cf. S. Heinhold-Krahmer, *Arzawa* 294 [1977]), 3 sg. pres. act. *idalawēszi* (e.g. *KBo* IV 3 IV 23; V 4 Vs. 5), *idalāwēszi* (ibid. Rs. 3 *nu* 1-*as* 1-*edani le idalāwēszi* 'one shall not become evil towards the other'; ibid. 5 [*nu* 1-*as* 1-*e*]*dani menahhanda le idalāwēszi*; cf. Friedrich, *Staatsverträge* 1:60), *idālawēszi* (VI 4 IV 1–2 [= *Code* 1:44] *mān* É-*ri-ya kuitki idālawēszi* 'if something turns bad in the house'), [HUL]-*u-e-es-zi* (*KUB* XL 39 III 6), 2 pl. pres. act. *idalāwēsteni* (*KBo* V 4 Rs. 17), *idālāwēstēni* (ibid. 21), 3 pl. pres. act. *idalawēssanzi* (IV 3 IV 34), *idalāwēssanzi* (V 4 Rs. 8), *idālawēssanzi* (VI 3 II 18–19 [= *Code* 1:31] *appizziann-at-kan nassu idālawēssanzi nasma-at-kan harpantari nu-za* É-*ir taksan sarranzi* '[if] afterwards they become estranged or separate and split up the household'; VI 6 I 13 [= *Code* 1:53] *mān-i-za idālawēssanzi ta-za* É-*ZUNU sarranzi* 'if their relationship goes sour and they divide their holdings'), *idalawesanz*[*i* (dupl. VI 9,

10), *idālauiss[anzi* (dupl. *KUB* XIII 11 Vs. 2), *it[a-* (dupl. *KBo* VI
2 III 7), 3 sg. pret. act. *i-da-la-u-e-es-ta* (IV 8 II 18 *kinun-a apel*
TI-*tar idalawēsta* 'has now her life become bad?'), *i-da-la-ú-e-*
-es-ta (*KUB* XXXVI 25 IV 2 *nu-ssi-kan* ZI-*za anda idalawēsta* 'his
spirits fell'; cf. Laroche, *RHA* 26:73 [1968]), HUL-*u-es-ta*
(XXXVI 35 I 25 *nu-ssi-kan* ZI-*za anda* HUL-*ues[ta* 'she became
depressed'; cf. Otten, MIO 1:126 [1953]). HUL-*u-e-es-ta* (XXXVI
31, 6; cf. Laroche, *RHA* 26:46 [1968]), 3 pl. pret. act. HUL-*(m)es-*
-sir (XXI 17 I 4 HUL-*essir-ma-at kedani memiyani* 'they had a
falling out in the following matter'; cf. Ünal, *Hatt.* 2:18); iter.
idalaweski-, 3 sg. pres. act. HUL-*eskizzi* (*KBo* I 30 Vs. 14; cf. *MSL*
12:215 [1969]).

Luw. *adduwal-* (n.) 'evil', nom.-acc. sg. neut. *ādduwāl* (*KUB*
XXXV 88 II 1 *ādduwāl āannī[ti* 'does evil'; cf. Otten, *LTU* 86),
adduwal-za-pa-tta (XXXV 54 III 22; cf. Otten, *LTU* 61),
attu[w]al-za (ibid. II 38), nom.-acc. pl. neut. *ādduwala* (XXXV
39 III 25–26 *kuis-tar malhassassanzan* EN-*ya ādduwala ānniti*
'whoever does evil to the offerant'; cf. Otten, *LTU* 40).

Luw. *adduwali-* 'evil', nom. sg. c. *adduwalis* (e.g. XXXV 21
Vs. 26 and Rs. 21 *adduwalis* EME-*is* 'evil tongue'; cf. Otten,
LTU 29–30; ibid. Rs. 23 *adduwalis* ITU.KAM-*as* 'bad month';
XXXV 28 I 3 *ad]duwalis issaris* 'evil hand'; cf. Otten,
LTU 34), *ādduwālis* (e.g. XXXV 49 IV 4 *ādduwālis īssaris*; cf.
Otten, *LTU* 51), acc. sg. c. *adduwalin* (e.g. XXXV 45 III 17
adduwalin EME-*in*; cf. Otten, *LTU* 47), *attuwalin* (XXXV 43
II 18; cf. Otten, *LTU* 43), instr. sg. or pl. *adduwalati* (e.g.
XXXV 21 Rs. 32 *a]dduwalati* EM[E-*ti ad]duwalati īss[arati* 'with
evil tongue [and] evil hand'; cf. Otten, *LTU* 30), *ādduwalati* (e.g.
XXXV 48 III 6 *ādduwalati* ŠU.MEŠ-*ti* 'with evil hands', cf. Otten,
LTU 50).

Luw. *adduwalahit-* 'malice', corresponding to Hitt. *idalawa-*
tar, dat. sg. *attuwalahiti* (IX 31 II 26; cf. Otten, *LTU* 16).

Hier. *atuwati-*, *atuwari-* 'bad', BAD-*tisatar-*, BAD-*hita-* 'badness, evil'. Cf. Meriggi, *HHG* 44; Laroche, *HH* 194–5; J. D.
Hawkins, *Anatolian studies* 20:88–9 (1970). For the phonetics,
cf. Umbr. *famerias* < **famedias* beside Lat. *familias*.

Of very doubtful affinity is Lyd. *ɟitala-*, *ɟitolla-*, allegedly
'evil' (Gusmani, *Lyd. Wb.* 90–1), where Oettinger (*KZ* 92:85

[1978]) saw a kind of reduplicates (*ded[w]ala-) of a PAnat. *ed-(w)a-l-.

A PAnat. proto-form *edwal was cogently postulated by Laroche (*RHA* 23:41–2 [1965]) on the basis of Luw. *adduwal* besides the adjectivizations seen in Luw. *adduwali-* and in Hitt. *idalu-*; the latter, from *edwal-u-*, parallels *innar-u- from PAnat. *enar (q.v. s.v. *innar-*). *edwal reflects an IE *edwl̥ in probable heteroclitic relationship to *edwn̥-, *edun- seen variously in Arm. *erkn* '(birth)pangs', OIr. *idain* '(birth)pangs', Gk. ὀδύναι 'pain, pangs, distress' (cf. J. Schindler, *KZ* 89:53–65 [1975]); *edwl̥ : *edwn- resembles in declension the *l* : *n* stem IE *sāwel-, *s(u)wél- : *swen-, *sun- 'sun' (*IEW* 881) and is in origin a petrified verbal noun of the root *ed- 'eat', thus literally 'an eating (away), consumption, ill, pain' (for the semantics cf. e.g. *garātes adantes* 'innards are consumed' denoting acute enteric distress [s.v. *alpant-*], or Lat. *edax* 'gnawing, destructive'). The initial vocalism of Gk. ὀδύνη matches that of ὀδοντ- 'tooth' from the same root; a different action noun *edwr̥ : *edwn- is seen in Gk. εἶδαρ 'food' and Luw. *aduna* 'to eat' (cf. also Oettinger, *Stammbildung* 540).

Implausible earlier comparisons include Lat. *odium* 'hate' (first coyly in Hrozný, *SH* 5, down to Laroche, *RHA* 23:42 [1965]; for *odium* cf. rather s.v. *hatuk-*), OE *īdal*, OHG *ītal* 'idle' (Sturtevant, *Lg.* 6:25 [1930]; V. Pisani, *Rivista indo-greco-italica* 16:90 [1932], down to *Paideia* 7:323 [1952]; G. Bonfante, *BSL* 69.1:69–71 [1974]), Gk. ἀΐδηλος 'fierce, destructive' (W. Petersen, *Arch. Or.* 9:205 [1937], down to O. Szemerényi, *Gnomon* 43:651 [1971]; for ἀΐδηλος cf. rather s.v. *awiti-*), Gk. αἴσυλος 'criminal' (Čop, *Ling.* 1:59–66 [1955], 7:108 [1965]), Gk. δειλός 'wretched', δεινός 'fearsome' (Carruba, *Scritti in onore di G. Bonfante* 132, 141 [1976]), Etruscan *iϑal, eϑl*, allegedly 'bad' (E. Vetter, *Zu den lydischen Inschriften* 60–1 [1959]; often repeated by V. I. Georgiev, e.g. *Linguistique balkanique* 5.1:40 [1962], 14.1:38 [1970], 16.2:17 [1973], 23.3:12 [1980]).

itar (n.) 'way', nom.-acc. sg. *i-tar* (*KUB* XLI 8 I 20–22 *kāsa* DUMU.LÚ.ULÙ.LU *uwanun* GIM *an* ᴰMAH-*as itar wappui daskizzi* Ù

itar   ittaranni-

DUMU.LÚ.ULÙ.LU *wappus karuuilias* DINGIR.MEŠ *kallessuwanzi
uwanun* 'lo, I, mortal man, am come; even as the mother goddess
is wont to take the way to the riverbank, even so I, mortal man,
am come to the banks to invoke the ancient gods'; cf. Otten, *ZA*
54:120 [1961]). Cf. E. Forrer, *RHA* 1:146 (1931); Kammenhuber, *MIO* 2:65 (1954).

The meaning is contextually relatively secure, with *itar da-*
paralleling KASKAL-*an ep(p)-* 'take the road' (q.v. sub *eppun* s.v.
ep[p]-; perhaps a loan translation from Akk. *urha* [or: *harrāna,
girra*] *ṣabātu* 'take the road'; cf. Friedrich, *ZA* 39:46 [1930];
Kronasser, *Etym.* 1:281) and KASKAL-*an iya-* 'make (one's) way'
(q.v. sub *iyat* s.v. *iya-*). The obvious comparison with Lat. *iter*
'way' (gen. *itineris*), Toch. A *ytār* (< *itōr*) 'way' (e.g. Benveniste, *Origines* 10, 104; Kammenhuber, *MIO* 3:352 [1955],
Sommer Corolla 100; van Windekens, *Le tokharien* 610) points
to an ancient heteroclitic derivative from *i-* 'go', antedating the
productive spread of Hittite verbal nouns in *-atar* but sharing
with the latter the non-geminate spelling of /-t-/; in any case
failure to geminate is in itself merely a scriptio facilior and does
not necessarily indicate voice (cf. Puhvel, in *Hethitisch und
Indogermanisch* 211 [1979]). Thus *itar* is not a part of the nonfinite verbal paradigm of Hitt. *i-* but rather a significant radical
isogloss with Tocharian and Italic. Other formations with *-tar*
are *galaktar, kallistar,* and *iyatar* (q.v. s.v.; *iya-tar* from *iya-*
'go').

ittaranni-   (c.) 'runner, messenger' (^{LÚ}KAŠ₄.E), acc. sg. in *KUB* XXIII
77 Rs. 68 [*mān-ma* M]*AHAR* ^DUTU-*ŠI* ^{LÚ}*ittaranni uiskitteni* 'but if
you send a messenger before my majesty' (cf. ibid. 65 [*mān*]
^DUTU-*ŠI-ma* ^{LÚ}KAŠ₄.E *INA* KUR ^{URU}*Kasga pīyami* 'but if I, my
majesty, send a messenger to Gasga-land'; cf. von Schuler, *RHA*
19:21-2 [1961], *Die Kaškäer* 129), gen. pl. *ŠA* ^{LÚ.MEŠ}*itt*[*aranni*
(XXXI 102 IV 2). Cf. Kronasser, *Etym.* 1:221.

Undeclined Hurrian agent noun in *-anni-,* from Hurr. *idd-* 'go'
(vs. *un-* 'come'), synonymous with *izuri* 'runner' (cf. Laroche,
RHA 34:128 [1976]). There is no relationship to Hitt. *i-* 'go' or
itar 'way'.

iduri- (c.), a type of bread or cake, nom. sg. *iduris* (e.g. *KBo* XV 37 I 8 1 ^NINDA^*iduris* ZÍD.DA 'one i.-loaf of meal'; X 34 I 6 1 NINDA *IMZU iduris* 'one sour-dough i.-loaf'; *KUB* XXXII 128 II 16 1 ^NINDA^*iduris*), acc. sg. *idurin* (*KBo* XIV 27 Rs. 15 and XXIII 83, 14–17 1 ^NINDA^*idurin*; *KUB* XI 31 I 19–20 ^NINDA^*idurinn-a parsiyazzi* 'he breaks up an i.-loaf'; XII 15 VI 6–7 1 ^NINDA^*idurinn-a* ... *parsiya*), *i-du-ri-en* (*KBo* XXIII 15 II 4 and XXIII 83, 11 1 ^NINDA^*i-du-ri-en-na*), dat.-loc. sg. (?) ^NINDA^*iduriya*[(XXI 40 Rs. 6), uncertain sg. case 1 ^NINDA^*ituri*[(XXI 28 II 37), nom. or acc. pl. *i-du-ri-es* (IX 118 Vs. 2 18 ^NINDA^*i-du-ri-es*), *i-du-ri-e-es* (XXIII 83, 6 2 ^NINDA^*i-du-ri-e-es*), *iduris* (e.g. *KUB* XXXII 128 II 21–24 *nu ŠA* MÁŠ.GAL *ēs*[*har*] ^UZU^YÀ.UDU-*ya ANA* 1 *UPNU* BA.BA.[ZA] *menahhanda immiyanzi n-as* 2 ^NINDA^*iduris ienzi* 'the blood of the goat and sheep-fat they mix with a handful of bread-mash and make them into two i.-loaves'; cf. A. M. Dinçol, *RHA* 27:29 [1969]; *KBo* XV 37 I 45–46 2 ^NINDA^*iduris* ZÍD.DA; VIII 89 Vs. 8 3 ^NINDA^*iduris*; cf. Haas – Wilhelm, *Riten* 264; V 1 II 18 7 ^NINDA^*iduris kitta* 'seven i.-loaves are set'; cf. Sommer – Ehelolf, *Pāpanikri* 6*), *idurius* (*KUB* XX 98 III 4 2 *idurius*; *KBo* XXIII 83, 5 and XXIV 59 IV 6 2 ^NINDA^*idurius*).

Etymology obscure. According to Neumann (*Untersuchungen* 84–5) Gk. ἴτριον, a kind of cake, is a syncopated loanword from Anatolian.

iuka- (n.) 'yoke' (ŠUDUN), nom.-acc. sg. (and pl. ?) *i-ú-kán* (*KBo* XII 22 I 11 *nu-mu*]-*ssan kī iukan ishaiste*[*n* 'you have bound this yoke on me'; dupl. *KUB* XXXI 4 + *KBo* III 41 Vs. 7 *kī iukan*; cf. Otten, *ZA* 55:158 [1962]), *i-ú-ga-an* (dupl. *KBo* XIII 78 Vs. 7 *ke iugan*; XVII 65 Rs. 52–53 *ANA* GÚ-*šu-ma-ssi-s*[*san ser*] *iugan* [... *dāi*] 'but on her neck he places a yoke'; *KUB* VII 11 Vs. 2 3 ^GIŠ^*iugan* 'three yokes', besides ibid. 7 ^GIŠ^GIGIR-*TI*= *NARKABTI* '[war-]chariot', thus a [Lat.] *trīga*, or perhaps *quadrīga* employing three yoke-devices to harness four horses, schematically ———; VII 8 II 7–8 *nu-ssi* GEME-*KA maniyah n-as-za* ^GIŠ^*iugan kisari*, besides [more correct gen. sg.?] ibid. III 6 ^GIŠ^ŠU.DUN-*as kisāri* 'assign your maid to him [viz. the impotence-sufferer] and he shall become [of] the yoke', i.e. [capable of] coupling [cf.

iuka- iuga-

Shakespeare's 'making the beast with two backs']), dat.-loc. sg.
i-ú-ki (XIII 5 II 20–22 [emended from XIII 6 II 4–5] *nu ap]ūn*
GUD *nassu arha ezzatteni* [*nasma-an-zan-kan*] *hāli anda tarnatteni*
nasma-an-zan-kan iuki [GAM-*an dāitt*]*eni* '[if] you either eat that
ox or let it into the corral or put it under the yoke'; cf. Sturtevant,
JAOS 54:372 [1934]).

iuka- was first identified as 'yoke' by Götze, *IF* 42:327–8
(1924), who also launched the since discredited idea of a
loanword from Indo-Aryan (Skt. *yugám*); *iuka-* is not a
hippological terminus technicus of Mitannian provenance; the
dossier indicates literal reference to the harnessing of oxen and
horses alike and also symbolic and figurative application to
human beings. *iukan* or *iugan* (with constant single spelling of
the intervocalic stop) is from the IE *o*-stem neuter noun **yugóm*
'yoke' and matches Skt. *yugám*, Gk. ζυγόν, Lat. *iugum*, Goth.
juk; cf. Lith. *jùngas* 'yoke', OCS *igo* 'yoke', Toch. A *yokäm* 'gate,
door' (IEW 508–9); such is also the preponderant opinion of
past scholarship (cf. e.g. Mayrhofer, *KEWA* 3:19; Tischler,
Glossar 448–9, with references). The absence of Hittite verbal
reflexes of IE **yew(g)-* 'join, combine' is noteworthy (supplanted by *ishiya-* 'bind' and *taks-* 'join'?) but matched by Slavic
where *igo* is isolated; for the related *iuga-* 'yearling' see the
following entry.

iuga- 'yearling', co-occurring with *tāiuga-* 'two-year-old' (q.v. s.v.
ta[*n*]) in *Code* 1:57–58 (besides parallel MU.1 'one-*year*[-old]'
and MU.2 'two-*year*[-old]' in *Code* 1:60–61, 63, 67), nom. sg. c.
i-ú-ga-as (*KBo* VI 3 III 26–27 *takku* GUD.MAH *kuiski tayazzi*
takku GUD *sauitisza ŪL* GUD.M[AH] *takku* GUD *iugas ŪL* GUD.
.MAH-*as takku* GUD *tāiugas apas* GUD.M[AH 'if someone steals a
breeding bull — if [it is] a suckling calf [it is] not a breeding bull;
if [it is] a yearling bullock [it is] not a breeding bull; if [it is] a
two-year-old bull, that [is] a breeding bull'; dupl. VI 6 I 34–35
GUD *i-ú-ga-as* ... GUD *da-a-i-ga-as*; VI 3 III 30–31 *takku*
ANŠU.KUR.RA.MAH *kuiski dayezzi takku sauitisza ŪL* ANŠU.KUR.
.RA.MAH *takku iugas ŪL* ANŠU.KUR.RA.MAH [*tak*]*ku tāugas apas*
ANŠU.KUR.RA.MAH 'if someone steals a stud stallion — if [it is] a

496

suckling foal [it is] not a stud; if [it is] a yearling [it is] not a stud; if [it is] a two-year-old, that [is] a stud'; dupl. VI 6 I 41–42 *i-ú-ga-as* ... *da-a-i-ú-ga-as*), gen. sg. *i-ú-ga-as* (VI 26 II 40–41 [= *Code* 2:80] ŠA 1 ANŠU.KUR.RA NITÁ *iugas* 10 GÍN KÙ.BABBAR *ŠIM-ŠU* ŠA 1 ANŠU.KUR.RA.SAL.AL.LAL *iugas* 15 GÍN KÙ.BABBAR *ŠIM-ŠU* 'the price of a yearling stallion [is] ten shekels silver; the price of a yearling breeding mare is fifteen shekels silver'), acc. pl. c. *i-ú-ga-as* (e.g. VI 3 III 28–29 5 *tāiugas* [...] 5 GUD *iugas* 5 GUD *sāuitisza pāi* 'he gives five two-year-old [bulls], five yearling bullocks, five suckling bull-calves'; dupl. VI 6 I 36–37 5 GUD *dāiuga*[-...] 5 GUD *iugas*; VI 3 III 32–33 5 ANŠU.KUR.RA.HI.A *tāiugas* 5 ANŠU.KUR.RA *iugas* 5 ANŠU.KUR.RA *sāuitiusza pāi*; dupl. VI 6 I 44 5 ANŠU.KUR.RA *dāiugas* 5 ANŠU.KUR.RA *iu*[-...]; cf. e.g. par. VI 3 III 38 2 GUD MU.2 3 GUD MU.1 2 GUD *sauitisza pāi*).

iugassa- 'yearling', gen. pl. *i-ú-ga-as-sa-as* (*KBo* VI 26 III 16 [= *Code* 2:86] ŠA 2 GUD *iugassas* UZU-*ŠUNU kuis wāsi* 'he who buys the meat of two yearling cattle', *i-ú-ga-as-sa-an* (ibid. II 31–32 [= *Code* 2:78] 1 GUD APIN.LAL 1 GUD ÁB *iugassa*[*n*] 5 [?] GÍN KÙ.BABBAR *ŠIM-ŠU* 'the price of a yearling plow-ox [and] cow [is] five [?] shekels silver'; dupl. *KUB* XXIX 29 Rs. 12]*i-ú-ga-as--sa-a*[*n*]).

The sequence 'suckling' : 'yearling' : 'two-year-old' resembles the classification of stolen domestic animals in the Frankish *Lex Salica*: *si quis porcellum lactantem furaverit ... si quis porcellum anniculum furaverit ... si quis porcum bimum furaverit* (matching OHG *sōhwersō sūganti farah forstilit ... sōhwersō farah iārīgaz forstilit ... sōhwersō zuiiarī suīn forstilit*) 'if someone steals a suckling pig, ... a yearling pig, ... a two-year-old swine' (cf. Friedrich, *JCS* 1:292–3 [1947]).

iuga- and *tāiuga-* are seemingly adjectives; but the sole ending -*as* (even in "acc. pl. c.") points to adjectivization of qualitative genitives of a noun *iuga-* and a compound *tā-iuga-* < **dwoyo-yugo-* (thus GUD *tāiugas* is literally 'a bull of second *iuga-*', much as e.g. *tān pedas* DUMU-*RU* 'a second-string son' is basically 'a son of second place'; cf. Puhvel, *KZ* 92:99–100 [1978] = *Analecta Indoeuropaea* 390–1 [1981]). This *iuga-* is most plausibly identical with *iuka-*, *iuga-* 'yoke' (q.v.) in a qualified sense relating to the yoking age of domestic draft animals, and its morphological (as opposed to syntactic) adjectivization is seen in *iugassa-*, comparable to *witassa-* 'year-related' (from *witt-* 'year'; cf. e.g. Kronasser, *Etym.* 1:189); *iugassa-* thus means 'pertaining to (first) yoking' and is derived from *iuga-* much as e.g. Lat. *anniculus* 'year-old' is from *annus* or Gk. ἔτειος, ἐνιαύσιος 'year-old' are from ἔτος, ἐνιαυτός (in the barnyard sphere cf. esp. Lat. *vitulus* 'bull-calf', Gk. ἔταλον 'yearling', Skt. *vatsá-* 'calf', all cognate with Hitt. *witt-* 'year'). *tāiuga-* signifies 'of second yoking', i.e. embarking on the second season of useful working life, in practice 'two-year-old' (cf. *KBo* VI 26 II 31–32 quoted above, where a yearling plow-ox rates five shekels, less than a full-grown plow-ox [ibid. 30; 12 shekels according to dupl. *KUB* XXIX 22 III 7]). **tāiuga-* (n.) 'second yoking' was a compound like e.g. **tāsiwatt-* 'second day' (*KUB* XXXII 123 III 5 *tā* UD-*ti* following *hantezzi* UD-*ti* 'on the first day'), secondarily adjectivized through use as a qualitative genitive; the adjectival *iugassa-* gained a competitor *iuga-* through similar adjectivization of the gen. sg. *iugas* (thus *tāiuga-* is not in origin a possessive compound adjective like Gk. διετής or Lat. *bīmus*, as wrongly suggested by e.g. Kronasser, *VLFH* 44, and Kammenhuber, *KZ* 77:193, 199 [1961]).

Alternatively Hitt. *iuga-* might be reconstructed as **yewgo-* 'yoking', thus paralleling Skt. *yóga-*, besides *iuka-* 'yoke' matching Skt. *yugám* (cf. W. M. Austin – H. L. Smith, Jr., *Lg.* 13:104–6 [1937]), but the general absence of **yewg-* in Hittite (see s.v. *iuka-*) makes this alternation improbable, and there is further no likelihood in adducing *s*-stems (Gk. ζεῦγος, Lat. *iūgera*) to explain *iugassa-*. The whole question of a wide-ranging time-sense in *iuga-* was implausible elaborated with reference to Skt. *yugám* 'age, generation, era', Lat. *iūgis* 'perpetual', by Austin and Smith (*Lg.* 13:104–6 [1937]; a first hint in Götze, *IF* 42:328 [1924]) who saw a semantic progression of time-spans from ON *eykt* < **jaukiþō* 'work-day' (lit. 'yoke-time', besides *eykr* < **yewgis* 'draft animal') to Hitt. *iuga-* 'of one year' to Skt. and Lat. 'long period', even drawing in solar mythology (yoking of sun-steeds) for support. Benveniste (*Hitt.* 78–80) admitted also a possible borrowing of Indo-Aryan **yuga-* as 'time-span' and its questionable Hittite adjec-

498

tivization as 'year-old' in the alleged manner of Lat. *anniculus* 'year-old' or *vetus* 'old' (cf. further Tischler, *Glossar* 450–1). The very fact that Hitt. *iuga-* refers specifically to draft animals makes it likely that only inner-Hittite references to yoking stages are involved, rather than any more general time-designation. No cognate is afforded by Lith. *dveigỹs* 'two-year-old' (used of cattle), which was compared with *tāiuga-* by Götze – Pedersen, *MS* 68, because the correct segmentation *dvei-gỹs* (cf. *ketvérgis* 'four-year-old') points rather to a suffix *-gi-* (cf. Benveniste, *Hitt.* 78–9).

Implausible connection of *iuga-* with the root of Goth. *juggs* 'young', *ajukduþs* 'eternity' (Skt. *yúvan-* : *ā́yu-*, etc.) has been tried from Hrozný (*SH* 93) to Čop (*Ling.* 5:24–5 [1964], 9:44 [1969]). O. Szemerényi (*Studia mediterranea P. Meriggi dicata* 622–5 [1979]) saw in Skt. *yuga-* 'age' a cognate of Goth. *ajuk--duþs* and extravagantly analyzed Hitt. *tāyuga-* as **day-uga-*, the last segment being **-ut-gho-* (with zero grade of **wet-*'year'); the simplex *iuga-* as **i-uga-* he connected with Gk. *ιός* 'one'.

iwar 'in the manner of, after the fashion of, like, as':

Construed as a postposition with genitive, e.g.: *KUB* XIII 3 II 29–III 2 *kuis-wa papratar iyazi nu-wa* LUGAL-*i harran wātar pāi nu-wa-kan apel* ZI-*an* DINGIR.MEŠ *uwitenas iwar arha lāh-huwatin* 'whoever commits defilement and gives spoiled water to the king, pour away his soul like water, o gods!' (cf. Friedrich, *Meissner AOS* 47); *KBo* VI 34 III 7–9 *n-an* LÚIGI.NU.GÁ[L-*as*] *iwar da*[*suwahha*]*ndu šA* LÚÚ.HÚB-*ma-an iwar* [*duddu-miy*]*andu* 'they shall blind him like a blind man, and make him deaf like a deaf man' (cf. Oettinger, *Eide* 12); *KUB* XXXI 69 Vs. 5–6 *tuel-za waspan* LÚ-*as iwar wassiy*[*asi*] [SAL-*s*]*a-za iwar wassiyasi* 'you put on your clothing like a man, and you put [it] on like a woman' (cf. ibid. 9 SAL-*nili* 'in female fashion' and *Bo* 1966, 13 LÚ-*nili* 'in male fashion'; Otten, *Puduhepa* 13 [1975]); XXI 17 III 7–8 URU*Hattusas iwar* É.MEŠ DINGIR.MEŠ *ser iyanun* 'in the Hittite manner I have erected temples' (cf. Ünal, *Hatt.* 2:24); V 6 II 55 and III 6 URUKÙ.BABBAR-*as iwar* 'in Hittite fashion'; ibid. II 62 URUKÙ. BABBAR-*sas-a-kan iwar* (cf. Sommer,

AU 282); *KBo* III 4 III 73 ŪL ŠA ᵁᴿᵁ*Gasga iwar taparta* '(he) did not rule in Gasga-fashion'; ibid. 75–76 ŠA LUGAL-*UTTI iwar taparta* 'he ruled in the manner of royalty' (cf. Götze, *AM* 88–90); *KUB* VII 60 III 7–8 *nu-za* LUGAL-*us* LUGAL-*weznas iwar wassiyazi* 'the king dresses in regal style' (cf. Haas – Wilhelm, *Riten* 236); *KBo* V 4 Rs. 15 [*n-an*] ᴰUTU-*ŠI* ᴸᵁ́KÚR-*as iwar zahhiskimi* 'I, the king, fight him like an enemy' (cf. Friedrich, *Staatsverträge* 1:62); *KUB* XIV 1 Rs. 93 *nu-wa ū[g]g-a* ŠAH-*as iwar uiyami* 'I shall squeal like a pig' (cf. Götze, *Madd.* 38); XXIII 1 II 15 *š*[*A*] ¹*Masturi iwar le iyasi* 'do not act like M.!'; similarly ibid. 30 (cf. Kühne – Otten, *Šaušgamuwa* 10); *KBo* III 1 II 52–53 (OHitt.) ¹*Zuruwas* ¹*Dānuwas* ¹*Tahurwailiyas* ¹*Taruhsuss-a iwar* 'in the manner of Z., T., T., and T.'; *KUB* XVII 21 I 12 *anzel iwar* 'like we (did)' (cf. von Schuler, *Die Kaškäer* 152); I 13 I 57 and III 9, *KBo* III 5 I 11 and 68, II 26 IN.NU.DA-*as iwar* 'like straw', i.e. 'amply, profusely' (cf. Kammenhuber, *Hippologia* 58–9, 64, 78, 86, 88).

Less commonly *iwar* is a conjunction following a noun, e.g.: *KUB* XXVII 29 II 17–19 *uddar-ma-k*[*an*] *kue* KAxU-*az parā iyattari n-at* LÀL-*it iwar sanizzi ēsdu* 'but the words which issue from the mouth shall be sweet as honey'; cf. Haas – Thiel, *Rituale* 142; XXIV 7 II 5 [*nu-z*]*a* LÚ.MEŠ *huelpi* GA.RAŠˢᴬᴿ *iwar arha kari*[*pta* 'has devoured men like fresh leek' (cf. A. Archi, *Oriens Antiquus* 16:307 [1977]); XXXVI 37 + XXXI 118 II 10 MUŠEN-*is iwar* 'like a bird' (cf. Laroche, *RHA* 26:27 [1968]).

iwar as a conjunction can also be followed by a noun, e.g.: *KUB* VIII 48 I 15–16 *iwar* ᴸᵁ́*TAPPI-ŠU* 'like (i.e. as if you were) their comrade' (cf. Laroche, *RHA* 26:18 [1968]); V 1 I 43 *iwar* ¹*Manini* 'like M.' (cf. Ünal, *Hatt.* 2:38); ibid. III 87 ŪL DÙ-*mi iwar* ¹*Temeti* 'I shall not do like T.'; ibid. 90 *iwar* ¹*Temetti-pat* DÙ-*anzi* 'they will do like T.'; ibid. 93 *iwar* ¹*Temetti* (cf. Ünal, *Hatt.* 2:78–80).

The postpositional usage clearly antedates the conjunctional one; the transition was effected by attraction to conjunctions such as *mān* 'as, like', seen in contexts of the type *KUB* XII 65 + XXVI 71 III 21 [*w*]*arsulas* GIM-*an* 'like a drop' (nom. sg. c. + *mān*) besides dupl. *KBo* XXVI 73, 4 [*wa*]*r*[*su*]*l*[*as*] *iwar* (gen. sg. + *iwar*; cf. Siegelová, *Appu-Hedammu* 52).

Thât *iwar* may be a nominal petrifact was sensed already by Hrozný (*SH* 183), who suggested an action noun in *-war* from the root *i-* 'go'. Sommer (*Heth. II* 11–22) determined the true meaning of *iwar*, warned prophylactically against a facile identification with Skt. *iva* 'like, as' plus "adverbial *-r*" (which did not keep J. Przyluski, *RHA* 2:225–6 [1934], 3:15–7 [1934], from embracing *iva*; thus, too, Mayrhofer, *KEWA* 1:93, and B. Joseph, *KZ* 95:95 [1981]; adverbial *-r* was advocated by Benveniste, *Origines* 89), assumed a nominal proto-sense 'giving' > 'compensation, equivalence' (because of Akk. *šar]āku* 'make a gift' glossing *i-wa-ar[* in *KBo* I 38 Rs. 9, besides ibid. 8 *šir[igdu* 'gift' for *iwaru-* 'gift, dowry' [q.v. s.v.]), and compared the form and usage of Lat. (gen. +) *instar* 'like' (for which see further Puhvel, *Glotta* 37:290–2 [1958] = *Analecta Indoeuropaea* 45–7 [1981], who posited a reconstruction **en-stA$_2$r* resembling German *ein-stand* 'equivalence, tie [in a vote or game]'). The analysis *i-war* 'a going' was asserted again by Friedrich (*ZA* 36:48 [1925]) with reference to German *wegen* 'on account of', and has been subsequently entertained by Sommer (*AU* 256), Kammenhuber (*MIO* 2:65 [1954]), Kronasser (*VLFH* 155, *Etym.* 1:298), and Carruba (*Beschwörungsritual* 16, who distinguished *i-war* 'a going' from *i-war-u-* 'a gift' containing the root of *p-ai-*, *p-iya-* 'give' [see s.v. *iwaru-*], whereas J. J. S. Weitenberg, *Anatolica* 4:167 [1971–2], still grouped *iwar* with *iwaru-*, following Sommer's original hunch [as had Couvreur, *Heth.* 158]).

A derivation of *iwar* from *i-* 'go' is not probable; no verbal noun formation from *i-* is otherwise found except the petrifact *itar* 'way' (q.v.; *i-tar* beside the equally fossilized *iya-tar* 'growth' from *iya-* 'go'). More likely is Gusmani's tie-in with the root *iya-* 'do, make' (*IF* 68:294 [1963]); the verbal noun *iya(u)war* is well attested, and one need not postulate a fossile, *iwar* being a "frozen" reduction form of *iyawar* (cf. e.g. OHitt. *īzzi* for *iyazi*). The basic sense of gen. + *iwar* is '(in) somebody's (manner of) doing', and a figura etymologica can still be sensed in the expression 'so-and-so's *iwar iya-*' 'do someone's doing', i.e. 'act in the manner of somebody'. For the productive construction cf. Lat. *instar* (*instar montis* 'like a mountain'

[Vergil, *Aeneid* 2:15]; *aequoris instar* 'like the surface of the sea' [Ovid, *Metamorphoses* 4:135]) and Gk. δέμας (δέμας πυρὸς 'like fire' [*Iliad* 11:596, 17:366]).

G. Kapancjan (*Chetto-Armeniaca* 84–5 [1931–3]) inconclusively compared Arm. *ibr(u)* 'in the manner of, like', further adducing Georgian *ebr(i)* 'like' (thus also J. van Ginneken, *Zbornik u čast A. Belića* 282 [1937]; V. Polák, *Studia linguistica* 4:102 [1950]).

iwaru-   (n.) 'gift, inheritance-grant, dowry' (*KBo* I 38 Rs. 8 *i-wa-ru* matching Akk. *šir*]*igdu*, i.e. *šeriqtu* 'gift'; ibid. 9 *i-wa-ar*[- corresponding to Akk. *šar*]*āku* 'give, make a gift'), nom.-acc. sg. *iwaru* and *iwāru* (*KBo* VI 4 IV 21 *takku* URU-*ri* A.ŠÀ.ḪI.A-*an sahhann-a iwaru kuiski harzi* 'if in a town someone holds field and fief as an inheritance-grant'; par. VI 3 II 59 [= *Code* 1:46; dupl. VI 2 II 38 *takku* URU-*ri* A.ŠÀ.ḪI.A-*an iwāru kuiski harzi*; dupl. VI 5 IV 24 *takku* URU-*ri sahhanas* A.ŠÀ.ḪI.A *iwa*[- 'if in a town [someone holds] fief-field[s] as an inheritance-grant'; ibid. II 4–6 [= *Code* 1:27] *takku* LÚ-*as* DAM-*ŠU dāi n-an* [ANA É-*ŠU*] *pehutezzi iwaru-ssi*[*t-az*] *anda pedai* 'if a man takes his wife and brings her to his house, he brings along her dowry'; dupl. VI 3 II 1 *i-wa-ru-us-se-it-az*; ibid. 2 *i-wa-ru-se-ta-az*; dupl. *KUB* XXVI 56 II 7 *iwāru-az anda peda*[; VI 5 II 9 *iwaru-sit* LÚ-*as Ū*[*L dāi*] 'the man does not take her dowry'; dupl. VI 3 II 4 *iwaru-sset* LÚ-*as natta* [*dāi*]), gen. sg. *i-wa-ru-as* (VI 2 II 41 [OHitt.] *iwaruas ishās* A.ŠÀ 'the field of the grantor'), *i-wa-ru- -wa-as* (dupl. VI 3 II 62 *iw*]*aruwas ishās* A.ŠÀ.ḪI.A; par. VI 4 IV 25 *iwaruwas* EN-*as* A.ŠÀ).

iwarwai- 'make a gift, bestow, confer', 3 pl. pret. act. *i-wa-a-ar-wa-a-i-ir* (*KBo* III 21 II 10–11 *nu* KUR-*yas arūwauar* DINGIR.MEŠ *tuk iwārwāir* 'the proskynesis of the lands have the gods conferred upon thee'); verbal noun *iwar*[*wauwar* (vel sim.) in I 38 Rs. 9 (quoted above; cf. Kronasser, *Etym.*1:307).

iwarwalli-, nom. pl. c. *i-wa-ar-wa-al-li-i-e*[-*es* (*KBo* V 7 Vs. 25 4 SAG.DU *iwarwalliyēs* 'four *iwaru*-related persons'; cf. Riemschneider, *MIO* 6:345 [1958]); for the suffix cf. e.g. *arkammanalli-*

'tributary' from *arkamma(n)-* 'tribute' (Kronasser, *Etym.* 1:211–2).

Even as *šeriqtu* means 'dowry' in the Code of Hammurabi, *iwaru-* as a technical legal term seems to denote possessions which a grantor (*iwaruwas ishās*; cf. *hannesnas ishās* 'litigator', *ēshanas ishās* 'claimant in a murder-case') bequeathed or at least consigned *ante diem*, either as an advance on inheritance upon a daughter's marriage (thus 'dowry') or as real property for an heir's use (with deferred transfer of title). Because entailed holdings could legally change hands only through inheritance, *iwaru-* may also have involved real estate deals disguised under fictitious adoption practices.

iwaru- has no plausible truck (other than chance homophony) with *iwar* 'in the manner of, like' (q.v.); attempts at a connection from Sommer (*Heth. II* 11–22) down to the survey by J. J. S. Weitenberg (*Anatolica* 4:165–7 [1971–2]) have been unconvincing. Sommer himself (*Hethiter und Hethitisch* 43 [1947]) later found *iwaru-* to be "foreign", and E. Speiser (*JAOS* 55:436 [1935]) first compared Hurr. *ewuru* '(appointed as opposed to natural) heir' at Nuzi and saw similarities between *iwaru-* practices and the Nuzi system of land tenure (cf. Nuzi Akk. *ewuru* 'heir', *ewurutu* 'right to inherit', *ewurumma epēšu* 'inherit'; *CAD* E 415); Kammenhuber's objection (*Gedenkschrift für W. Brandenstein* 255 [1968]) that Old Hittite attestation of *iwaru-* precludes a borrowing from Hurrian is not binding, for the term may well have travelled on a wider and earlier "culture word" orbit (hence also the phonetic discrepancies between *iwaru-* and *ewuru*).

Attempts at inner-Hittite and Indo-European derivation are brittle. A postulated adjectival or nominal **iwar-u-* (cf. Carruba, *Beschwörungsritual* 16; H. Mittelberger, *Kratylos* 12: 156–7 [1967]; J. J. S. Weitenberg, *Anatolica* 4:165–7 [1971–2]) may have parallels in e.g. **innar-u-* (s.v. *innar-*), *idal-u-* (s.v.), **eshar-u-* (s.v. *eshar*), **ishassar-u-* (s.v. *isha-*); Carruba's (*Beschwörungsritual* 16) suggested verbal noun **iwar* from **ai-*, **iya-*, besides compounded *p-ai-, p-iya-* 'give', would have to be a reduction form for the **iyawar* inferrable from *piyawar* (s.v. *pai-, piya-*), even as *iwar* 'in the manner of, like' (q.v.) may stand for *iya(u)war* from *iya-* 'do, make' (cf. the similar land-grant term *pi[y]ett-*, *pitt-* from *pai-*, *piya-*, s.v. and Puhvel, in *Hethitisch und Indogermanisch* 213–4 [1979] = *Analecta Indoeuropaea* 360–1 [1981]).

G. Jucquois (*Orbis* 16:169–73 [1967]) implausibly reconstructed an **iwer-* with zero grade of IE **yewo-* 'grain, corn' (*IEW* 572), assuming that fiefs entailed grain-growing fields (**yewo-* is present[rather in Hitt. *e[u]wa[n]-*, q.v.).

izziya-, hapax 3 sg. pres. midd. *izziattari* (*VBoT* 133 Vs. 7 [*mā*]*n* GIDIM *kuedani izziattari* 'if a ghost appears [?] to somebody').

Most plausible is a variant of *isiya-* 'announce, reveal' (q.v.), thus referring to what an apparition does. *isiya-* : *izziya-* would join other *s* : *z* variations (*sakkar* : *zakkar*, *samankurwant-* : *zamankur*; cf. also s.v. *ezzan*), but the probable origin **dy* or **gy* of the *-s-* in *isiya-* points to [z] or [ž] or [dᶻ] at variance with the [tˢ] value of *z(z)*; still an alternative, irregular voiceless outcome [tˢ] besides [dᶻ] cannot be ruled out, in the same way as $\tau(\tau)$ and $\delta(\delta)$ both appear instead of ζ in some dialectal forms of Greek as the outcome of **dy* or **gy* (e.g. Cretan Doric $T(\tau)\eta\nu\alpha$ for $Z\tilde{\eta}\nu\alpha$).

yaya-, intransitive *-hi* conjugation verb, 3 sg. pres. act. *ya-ya-a-i* or *ya-ya-i*, either coordinated with *katta tarnai* in following clause or itself following it asyndetically: *KUB* XLIV 61 Vs. 9 *namma yayāi katta-ya-an-za-kan tarnai* 'he ? and lets him (viz. the patient) down' (viz. at the end of a treatment); ibid. 16 *nu yayāi katta-ya-an-za-k[an* (cf. Burde, *Medizinische Texte* 18); *KBo* XXI 76, 7]*ŪL tarnāi yayai* 'does not let [and] ?'; ibid. 13]*-kan katta tarnai yaya[-* (cf. Burde, *Medizinische Texte* 24). Unclear in meaning, let alone etymology.

yaspu- (c.) 'jasper' (*YAŠPU*), acc. sg. in *KUB* XV 5 I 4–5 ᴺᴬ⁴*y]aspun halissiyanzi* 'they overlay jasper' (cf. ibid. 4 ᴺᴬ⁴*YAŠPU*). Culture word: beside Akk. *(y)ašpu*, cf. Hebr. *yašpē*, Gk. ἴαδπις.